Routledge Companion to Sport and Exercise Psychology

Written by an international team of expert contributors, this unique global and authoritative survey explores in full but accessible detail the basic constructs and concepts of modern sport and exercise psychology and their practical application.

The book consists of 62 chapters, written by 155 contributors, deriving from 24 countries across the world. The chapters are arranged in nine cohesive parts:

- sport and exercise participants
- the influence of environments on sport and exercise
- motor skills
- performance enhancement
- building and leading teams
- career, life skills and character development
- health and well-being enhancement
- clinical issues in sport psychology
- professional development and practice.

Each chapter contains chapter summaries and objectives, learning aids, questions, exercises and references for further reading.

Its comprehensive scale and global reach make this volume an essential companion for students, instructors and researchers in sport science, sport and exercise psychology, psychology, and physical education. It will also prove invaluable for coaches and health education practitioners.

Athanasios G. Papaioannou is Professor of Sport Psychology at the University of Thessaly, Greece. He is vice president of the ISSP and the editor-in-chief of the *International Journal of Sport and Exercise Psychology*. Professor Papaioannou has co-authored five books and more than 100 articles, and has been the scientific coordinator of national and European projects aiming to promote physical activity and healthy lifestyles.

Dieter Hackfort is Professor of Sport and Exercise Psychology and also currently serves as Head of the Department for Sport Science, both at the University FAF Munich, Germany. His research has been published in 25 books and edited volumes, and in more than 150 contributions in national and international journals. His main research interests are in performance enhancement management, and assessment and training of mental capacities based on the development of an action-theory perspective for human sciences. Professor Hackfort served 11 years (from 1996 to 2006) as a co-editor-in-chief of the *International Journal of Sport and Exercise Psychology* and was president of the ISSP from 2005 to 2009.

International Perspectives on Key Issues in Sport and Exercise Psychology
Series Editors: Athanasios Papaiouannou & Dieter Hackfort

International Perspectives on Key Issues in Sport and Exercise Psychology is a series of edited books published in partnership with the International Society of Sport Psychology. Each title reflects cutting edge research in the psychological study of high level sport, written by key researchers and leading figures in the field of sports psychology.

Books in this series:

Athletes' Careers across Cultures
Edited by Natalia B. Stambulova & Tatiana V. Ryba

Routledge Companion to Sport and Exercise Psychology
Global Perspectives and Fundamental Concepts
Edited by Athanasios Papaioannou and Dieter Hackfort

The Psychology of Sub-Culture in Sport and Physical Activity
Critical Perspectives
Edited by Robert J. Schinke and Kerry R. McGannon

Routledge Companion to Sport and Exercise Psychology

Global perspectives and fundamental concepts

EDITED BY

ATHANASIOS G. PAPAIOANNOU
AND DIETER HACKFORT

Routledge
Taylor & Francis Group

LONDON AND NEW YORK

First published in paperback 2016
by Routledge
2 Park Square, Milton Park, Abingdon, Oxon OX14 4RN

First published 2014
by Routledge
27 Church Road, Hove, East Sussex BN3 2FA

and by Routledge
711 Third Avenue, New York, NY 10017

Routledge is an imprint of the Taylor & Francis Group, an informa business

British Library Cataloguing in Publication Data
A catalogue record for this book is available from the British Library

Library of Congress Cataloging in Publication Data
Routledge companion to sport and exercise psychology : global perspectives and fundamental
concepts / edited by Athanasios G. Papaioannou, Dieter Hackfort.
pages cm. -- (International perspectives on key issues in sport and exercise psychology)
Includes bibliographical references and index.
ISBN 978-1-84872-128-9 (hardback)
1. Sports--Psychological aspects. 2. Exercise--Psychological aspects. I. Papaioannou,
Athanasios G. II.
Hackfort, Dieter.
GV706.4.R675 2014
796.01'9--dc23
2013026406

ISBN: 978-1-84872-128-9 (hbk)
ISBN: 978-0-415-73032-7 (pbk)
ISBN: 978-1-315-88019-8 (ebk)

Typeset in Milo Serif OT
by Saxon Graphics Ltd, Derby

MIX
Paper from
responsible sources
FSC® C013604

Printed and bound by CPI Group (UK) Ltd, Croydon, CR0 4YY

Contents

CONTENTS

CONTENTS

Contributors

Bruce Abernethy, University of Queensland, Australia

Jayashree Acharya, Lakshmibai National University of Physical Education, India

David I. Anderson, San Francisco State University, United States

Mark W. Aoyagi, University of Denver, United States

Paul R. Appleton, University of Birmingham, United Kingdom

Fabienne d'Arripe-Longueville, University of Nice Sophia-Antipolis, France

Susan H. Backhouse, Leeds Metropolitan University, United Kingdom

Patrick H.F. Baillie, Alberta Health Services and Calgary Police Service, Canada

Mark R. Beauchamp, University of British Columbia, Canada

Maurizio Bertollo, University of Chieti-Pescara, Italy

Tirata Bhasavanija, Ramkhamheang University, Thailand

Stuart J.H. Biddle, Loughborough University, United Kingdom

Bettina Bläsing, Bielefeld University, Germany

Boris Blumenstein, Wingate Institute, Israel

Francesca Borgo, Department of Psychology, University of Trieste, Italy

Brenda Light Bredemeier, University of Missouri – St. Louis, United States

Mark W. Bruner, Nipissing University, Canada

Joanne Butt, Sheffield Hallam University, United Kingdom

Chris Carr, St Vincent Sport Performance Center, United States

Sam Carr, University of Bath, United Kingdom

Jennifer Carter, The Center for Balanced Living, United States

Yu-Kai Chang, Graduate Institute of Athletics and Coaching Science, National Taiwan Sport University, Taiwan

Nikos L.D. Chatzisarantis, School of Psychology and Speech Pathology, Curtin University, Australia

Packianathan Chelladurai, School of Physical Activity and Educational Services, Ohio State University, United States

David B. Coppel, University of Washington Medical School, United States

Jean Côté, Queen's University, Canada

J. Gualberto Cremades, Barry University, United States

Henry (Hap) Davis IV, Swimming Canada, Canada

Joaquín Dosil, University of Vigo, Spain

Joan L. Duda, University of Birmingham, United Kingdom

Panteleimon Ekkekakis, Iowa State University, United States

Kai Essig, Bielefeld University, Germany

Jennifer L. Etnier, Department of Kinesiology, University of North Carolina at Greensboro, United States

M. Blair Evans, Wilfrid Laurier University, Canada

Mark A. Eys, Wilfrid Laurier University, Canada

Deborah L. Feltz, Michigan State University, United States

Tamar Flash, The Weizmann Institute of Science, Israel

Kenneth R. Fox, University of Bristol, United Kingdom

Chris J. Gee, University of Toronto, Canada

Lael Gershgoren, Florida State University, United States

Burt Giges, Springfield College, United States

Diane L. Gill, University of North Carolina at Greensboro, United States

Scott Goldman, University of Arizona, United States

Trish Gorely, University of Stirling, United Kingdom

Daniel Gould, Michigan State University, United States

Christy Greenleaf, University of Wisconsin, Milwaukee, United States

Melanie Gregg, University of Winnipeg, Canada

Dieter Hackfort, Universität der Bundeswehr Munich, Germany

Martin S. Hagger, Curtin University, Australia

Howard K. Hall, York St John University, United Kingdom

Thomas Hammond, Deakin University, Australia

David J. Hancock, University of Michigan, United States

Juri Hanin, Research Institute for Olympic Sport (KIHU), Finland

Sheldon Hanton, Cardiff Metropolitan University, United Kingdom

Sarah J. Hardcastle, University of Brighton, United Kingdom

James Hardy, Bangor University, United Kingdom

Antonis Hatzigeorgiadis, University of Thessaly, Greece

Andrew P. Hill, University of Leeds, United Kingdom

Thelma S. Horn, Miami University, United States

Charmayne Hughes, Bielefeld University, Germany

Ernest Tsung-Min Hung, National Taiwan Normal University, Taiwan

Christopher Janelle, University of Florida, United States

Urban Johnson, Halmstad University, Sweden

Gareth E. Jowett, York St John University, United Kingdom

Sophia Jowett, Loughborough University, United Kingdom

Sviatlana Kamarova, Nanyang Technological University, Singapore

Masato Kawabata, Nanyang Technological University, Singapore

Jens Kleinert, German Sport University Cologne, Germany

Dirk Koester, Bielefeld University, Germany

Vikki Krane, Bowling Green State University, United States

Elsa Kristiansen, Norwegian School of Sport Sciences, Norway

Charalampos Krommidas, University of Thessaly, Greece

Alexander T. Latinjak, Universitat de Girona, Spain

Trisha Leahy, The Hong Kong Sports Institute, Hong Kong

Ronnie Lidor, Wingate Institute, Israel

Magnus Lindwall, University of Gothenburg, Sweden

Gill Lines, University of Brighton, United Kingdom

Taru Lintunen, University of Jyväskylä, Finland

Chris Lonsdale, University of Western Sydney, Australia

Ross Lorimer, University of Abertay Dundee, United Kingdom

Todd M. Loughead, University of Windsor, Canada

Clare MacMahon, Swinburne University, Australia

Rouhollah Maher, Victoria University, Australia

Clifford J. Mallett, University of Queensland, Australia

Daryl Marchant, Victoria University, Australia

Matthew P. Martens, University of Missouri, United States

Jeffrey J. Martin, Wayne State University, United States

Jessica L. Martin, University at Albany, United States

Egil W. Martinsen, University of Oslo, Norway

Lauren Mawn, Bangor University, United Kingdom

Jonathan Maycock, Bielefeld University, Germany

Paul McCarthy, Glasgow Caledonian University, United Kingdom

Stephen D. Mellalieu, Swansea University, United Kingdom

Antoinette M. Minniti, American Psychological Association, United States

Ioannis Morres, School of Health Sciences, Queen's Medical Centre, University of Nottingham, United Kingdom and University of Thessaly, Greece

Tony Morris, Victoria University, Australia

Katie L. Morton, University of Cambridge, United Kingdom

Swarup Mukherjee, Nanyang Technological University, Singapore

Krista J. Munroe-Chandler, University of Windsor, Canada

Nikos Ntoumanis, University of Birmingham, United Kingdom and Curtin University, Australia

Erman Öncü, Karadeniz Technical University, Turkey

Iris Orbach, Wingate Institute, Israel

Athanasios G. Papaioannou, University of Thessaly, Greece

Yvan Paquet, Université de la Réunion, France

Trent A. Petrie, University of North Texas, United States

Artur Poczwardowski, University of Denver, United States

Leslie Podlog, University of Utah, United States

Luke R. Potwarka, University of Waterloo, Canada

Maria Psychountaki, National and Kapodistrian University of Athens, Greece

Eleanor Quested, University of Birmingham, United Kingdom

Joohyun Rhee, Texas A&M University, United States

Daniel Rhind, Brunel University, United Kingdom

Santiago Rivera, Centro Excelentia, Spain

Glyn C. Roberts, Norwegian School of Sport Science, Norway

Tatiana V. Ryba, University of Southern Denmark, Odense, Denmark

Amanda M. Rymal, California State University East Bay, United States

Dietmar Samulski†, Centro de Exceléncia, Brazil

Thomas Schack, Bielefeld University, Germany

Malte Schilling, Bielefeld University, Germany

Hiroshi Sekiya, Hiroshima University, Japan

Jamie L. Shapiro, University of Denver, United States

David Light Shields, St. Louis Community College – Meramec, United States

Adam Shunk, St Vincent Sport Performance Center, United States

Gangyan Si, Hong Kong Sports Institute of Education, Hong Kong SAR

Alan L. Smith, Michigan State University, United States

Marit Sørensen, Norwegian School of Sport Sciences, Norway

Natalia Stambulova, Halmstad University, Sweden

Afroditi Stathi, University of Bath, United Kingdom

Traci Statler, California State University – Fullerton, United States

Nektarios A. Stavrou, National and Kapodistrian University of Athens, Greece

Diane M. Ste-Marie, University of Ottawa, Canada

Bernd Strauss, University of Muenster, Germany

John P. Sullivan, University of Rhode Island, United States

Philip Sullivan, Brock University, Canada

Benjamin D. Sylvester, University of British Columbia, Canada

Caroline Symons, Institute of Sport, Exercise and Active Living, Victoria University, Australia

Koji Takenaka, Waseda University, Japan

Adrian H. Taylor, Plymouth University Peninsula Schools of Medicine and Dentistry, United Kingdom

Gershon Tenenbaum, Florida State University, United States

Yannis Theodorakis, University of Thessaly, Greece

Robert J. Vallerand, McGill University, Canada

Michael Van Bussel, Fanshawe College, Canada

Judy L. Van Raalte, Springfield College, United States

Jérémie Verner-Filion, Université du Québec à Montréal, Canada

Francesca Vitali, University of Verona, Italy

Symeon P. Vlachopoulos, Aristotle University of Thessaloniki, Greece

Jin Wang, College of Education, Zhejiang University, China

Daniel A. Weigand, Northwest Christian University, United States

Robert Weinberg, Miami University, United States

Laurel Whalen, Wayne State University, United States

A. Justine Wilson, University of British Columbia, Canada

David L. Wright, Texas A&M University, United States

Paul Wylleman, Vrije Universiteit Brussel, Belgium

Leonard D. Zaichkowsky, Boston University, United States

Nikos Zourbanos, University of Thessaly, Greece

Introduction

ATHANASIOS G. PAPAIOANNOU, UNIVERSITY OF THESSALY, GREECE
DIETER HACKFORT, UNIVERSITY FAF MUNICH, GERMANY

We have had great interest in and support for this book project from the very beginning. The very moment we introduced the concept to the International Society of Sport Psychology (ISSP), immediately there was considerable enthusiasm for such a huge project; ISSP council members were convinced that this undertaking really would fit with the mission of the organization to support and provide a global approach and international perspective on sport and exercise psychology issues. Of course, questions emerged on how to handle such a large body of work and how to coordinate experts from around the world to ensure a global perspective, not only across the issues raised in this book but also with regard to the various themes dealt with in the individual chapters. It was always our aim to encourage and manage international and cross-cultural cooperation as much as possible, and to bring together outstanding researchers and scholars with international reputations in their fields of specialization to realize this book. Now, after three years of intensive and extensive work on the project we are thrilled that 144 colleagues from 24 countries were able to work together to realize this book's mission.

The title of this book, *Routledge Companion to Sport and Exercise Psychology: Global Perspectives and Fundamental Concepts*, is both a message of the key purpose and mission of the project as well as a strong signal for the identification of the publisher with this opus. In complementing the official journal of the ISSP (*International Journal of Sport and Exercise Psychology*) and the series on *International Perspectives on Key Issues in Sport and Exercise Psychology*, to which this volume is but one contribution, we see the realization of the ISSP's vision to disseminate knowledge and skills from outstanding experts in sport and exercise psychology around the world.

The ISSP was founded in Rome in 1965 by a group of enthusiasts from medicine, psychology, and pedagogy who were strongly interested in sports. The initiative was led by the Italian psychiatrist, Dr. Ferrucio Antonelli. At the time, it was commonly understood that sport psychology centered on issues of exercise and performance. During the following five decades various disciplinary relations, especially in the scope of sports sciences and special areas of research led to differentiations and modifications in the labels used to describe sport psychology (see Morris, Hackfort, & Lidor, 2003). In the twenty-first century the expansion of health-oriented contributions led to the inclusion of "sport and exercise" to the discipline. A recent and strong tendency towards the development of performance psychology may yet put an additional emphasis on the integration of sport, exercise, and performance psychology. However, the wide range of issues represented in this volume provide a clear picture of key topics, concepts, and the most up-to-date knowledge in the field at the intersection of sport science and psychology.

Considering perspectives from around the world and approaches characterized by various cultural, methodological and theoretical backgrounds not only enlarges the scope of knowledge but also enriches the body of relevant issues. As a result, on one hand, we must accept differentiation and integration in order to further develop our discipline, and on the other hand it is necessary to reflect on fundamental relations in and the scientific network of the discipline. Figure i provides an illustration of this idea.

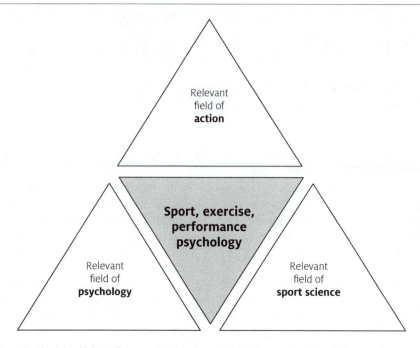

Figure i Constitutional relations for sport, exercise, and performance psychology.

Although sport psychology (the original denomination of the discipline) is a relatively young branch in the scientific network there are already global (ISSP), continental (AASP, ASPASP, ASSP, FEPSAC, SOSUPE), regional and national societies to represent the discipline, as well as the many other journals that have a slightly different focus (research or oriented around applied theory). Sport and exercise psychology is represented in societies for psychology as well as sport science. These are strong indicators for the fast development and significant reputation of the discipline in the relevant fields of science and application. The first laboratory for experimental psychology was founded in 1879 in Leipzig (Germany) by Wilhelm Wundt and one of his assistant researchers, Robert Werner Schulte, who established the first sport psychology laboratory in Berlin (Germany) in 1920. At about the same time, scholars opened sport psychology laboratories in other countries, for example in the US Coleman Griffith opened a laboratory at the University of Illinois in 1925. And even before this, in 1913, Pierre de Coubertin, the

founder of the modern Olympic Games, had organized the First International Congress on the Psychology and Physiology of Sport, and at the time it was the first conference of its kind. During the 1960s, the discipline was developed in Europe and in the US by university professorships, and with the foundation of the ISSP in 1965. Since then, sport, exercise, and performance psychology has developed into a prominent research domain, a scientific discipline taught in academic institutes worldwide and a widespread field of application.

Sport psychology might be a relatively new research discipline but concepts and practices of sport psychology have existed in various cultures for centuries. Scholars have started providing evidence about concepts and applications of sport psychology in Ancient Greece, India and China (e.g., Acharya, 2011; Zervas, 2001; Zhang, 2013), which today are at the center of psychological research, for example, the fundamental philosophical or meta-theoretical concepts of eudaimonia in Ancient Greece and mindfulness in the Buddhist tradition. In the years to come we might learn more about the conceptualization of these and other constructs and the related implications for human physicality and movement in past civilizations. Traditions related to the maximization of motor performance and the promotion of health and psychological well-being through movement can be found across various cultures, and each of these traditions has deep roots in the historical evolution of each culture. Nevertheless, on an individual level, we still know too little about traditions and practices in cultures other than our own. Despite the vast progress in technology and transport and the impressive development of sport psychology research in many countries, we have yet to develop the collective knowledge that we need in the globalization era. We have only just begun to explore cultural variations, not only into traditions and practices relevant to psychological preparation for sport contests, but also into the definition of the very concepts which are at the core of sport psychology research and practice, like the diverse meaning of psychological well-being and happiness across cultures (e.g., Fowers, 2012; Joshanloo, 2012; Lu, Gilmour & Kao, 2001). Hence, on a global level we have still to develop a collective understanding of the variety of pathways across cultures that lead to different end states, such as the different conceptualizations of psychological well-being of international athletes and exercise participants.

Therefore, a central aim of the ISSP is to develop projects like the present book in the series on *International Perspectives on Key Issues in Sport and Exercise Psychology*, bringing together authors from different countries to delineate the existing state of the art of sport and exercise psychology and to facilitate the process of communication among researchers and practitioners across the world. This enables scholars not only to extend international dialogue and research and synthesize diverse perspectives but also to develop new scientific approaches fueled by the richness of cultural diversity. Thus, for this book, we encouraged authors to collaborate with scholars in different institutions and countries. Although this was occasionally challenging, collaborations were accomplished for the large part of this book. We see an essential benefit of this collaboration at a symbolic level. The contribution of 144 authors from 24 countries to the present collective volume elevates the image of the collective international effort for the promotion of sport and exercise psychology across the world, but it is not to downplay the kudos due to individuals and their countries for their unique contribution to the development of sport psychology. We are more than grateful to all outstanding scholars who accepted our invitation to contribute to this book.

THE STRUCTURE OF THIS BOOK

This book is an introduction to sport and exercise psychology. Its main aim is to help readers understand the challenges, the fundamental concepts and how to apply the theory of modern sport and exercise psychology. Each chapter focuses on "what is important to know" and "how to do it". Although each chapter has been written by experts with an impressive record of research and contribution to theory development on their topic, each contributor has presented research and theories concisely and coherently.

This book consists of nine parts, shown schematically in Figure ii. This figure illustrates how sport and exercise psychology consultants interact with individuals and teams, and how social factors influence the behaviour of participants in sport and exercise settings. The major goal of sport and exercise psychology consultants is to help participants to achieve optimal outcomes in sport and exercise settings. These outcomes include motor skill learning and performance enhancement, promotion of exercise, health and psychological well-being, and coping with clinical issues in sports, but they are also related to the wider life of participants, such as developing character and social skills that enable them to have successful lives and careers. Thus, sport and exercise psychology consultants need to have knowledge about participants and teams, the social environment, how to achieve the required outcomes and, indeed, how to develop themselves as professionals. Accordingly, each of the shapes in Figure ii corresponds to a particular part of the book, and in each shape are the topics connected with the message conveyed in that part of the book.

The chapters of the first part focus on the most important characteristics and needs of individuals in sport and physical activity settings that should be taken into consideration by practitioners, parents and consultants who wish to offer them appropriate experiences. These ten chapters were managed by Athanasios Papaioannou (Greece) and Cliff Mallett (Australia). In the first chapter, Thelma S. Horn and Joanne Butt address age-related characteristics and needs, explaining how physical, motor and psychological development occurs from early childhood to late adolescence and how sport and physical activity experiences can be developmentally appropriate for participants. Based on this knowledge, Jean Côté , David J. Hancock and Bruce Abernethy move one step further to provide important information about how talent development in sport can be realized through developmentally-appropriate activities led by coaches and various types of parents' support.

Talent and psychological attributes such as self-esteem determine achievement and adherence in sport and physical activity settings. Coaches and physical education teachers know that most psychological attributes are nurtured, yet they often classify participants according to these features. Of course, it is more fruitful to focus on the exact socio-psychological processes that shape individuals' attributes. Extensive information about environmental influences in shaping

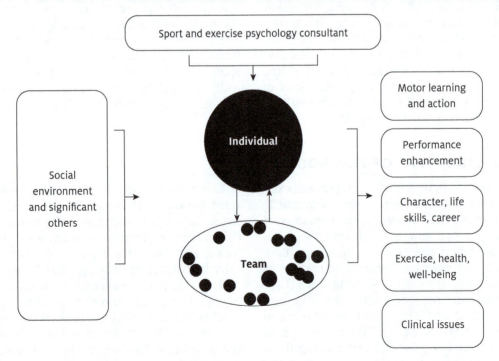

Figure ii Schematic representation of the structure of this book.

character is provided in later parts of this book. However, the first part includes our current knowledge about how some important psychological attributes of the person are constructed. In their chapter, Kenneth Fox and Magnus Lindwall unfold why self-esteem is an indicator of positive health and why it determines participation, performance and positive experiences in sport and exercise, how it is constructed and how significant others can help individuals to build high self-esteem. The role of perceptions of competence in participation and performance in sport is addressed by Glyn Roberts and Athanasios Papaioannou, who explicate how socialization might influence individuals to endorse different definitions of competence that result to divergent types of achievement-related behaviour, emotions and cognitions in sport. Sport motivation is also the topic of Nikos Ntoumanis and Clifford Mallett who explain how coaching might support or thwart sport participants' psychological needs and subsequent motivation. Juri Hanin and Panteleimon Ekkekakis elaborate the concept of emotion by separating it into its various dimensions and types and explaining not only how these influence performance and adherence in sport and exercise but also why they are inherently connected with the notions of psychological well-being and ill-being.

The last four chapters of Part I focus on individuals who are often considered as not "typical" participants in sports. These chapters address the needs, the psychological processes and the challenges that these individuals face when they participate and perform in sports. Jeff Martin, Francesca Vitali, and Laurel Whalen remind us that individuals with disabilities derive many physiological and psychological benefits from participation in sport but face a multitude of personal, social and environmental barriers unique to their condition. This chapter offers several recommendations stemming from sport psychology research that will be of great help to those who wish to support individuals with disabilities to

participate and improve their performance in sport and physical activity settings. Vikki Krane and Caroline Symons present the social barriers for participation and performance in sport for transgender, transsexual and intersex people and provide instructions for these individuals to construct inclusive sport environments. Diane Gill and Tatiana Ryba explain why sport and exercise psychologists should develop cultural competence to address the needs of athletes from different cultures and help practitioners, athletes and exercise participants to become aware of biases and stereotypes, reduce discriminations and develop skills to interact effectively with individuals across cultures. Finally, Howard Hall, Gareth Jowett, and Andrew Hill illustrate how perfectionism is construed within the framework of major theories of personality, and argue that while perfectionism might induce achievement striving, it may also lead to emotional distress.

Part 2 covers the social environmental influences on participants' sport and physical activity experiences. The six chapters included in this part were managed by Athanasios Papaioannou (Greece) and Sophia Jowett (UK). The first three chapters focus on athletes' relationships with significant others and the effects of these relationships on sport involvement. In their chapter, Ross Lorimer and Sophia Jowett provide an overview of the conceptualization of the coach–athlete relationship and the factors contributing to those successful relationships. They offer recommendations for the development of harmonious relationships between coaches and athletes. Sam Carr and Daniel Weigand move the discussion to the parent–athlete relationships and provide guidance for those aiming to strengthen the attachment bond in families and create a positive parental climate for children in relation to their involvement in sport. Alan Smith and Fabienne d'Arripe-Longueville explain how friendships and good peer relationships contribute to learning and motivation in sport and provide implications for coaches that enable them to promote positive peer relationships in sport and physical activity. The next three chapters of the second part address the effects of audiences and media on athletes' and sport officials' experiences. Bernd Strauss and Clare MacMahon explain how audience might affect sport performance and review findings of studies focusing on the home advantage effects. In a second chapter, Strauss and MacMahon illustrate how the crowd and other aspects of competitions such as positioning of officials, reputation of the athletes, order that the athletes compete and color that athletes wear affect officials' judgment and decision making. Finally, Elsa Kristiansen and Gill Lines explain how media affects young individuals' sport-related attitudes and stereotypes and how elite athletes cope with media stress and they provide instructions that might help athletes to develop an adaptive relationship with journalists.

In Part 3, managed by Thomas Schack (Germany) and Hiroshi Sekiya (Japan), essential issues are covered as well as the most up-to-date approaches on the functions of motor action and understanding and promoting motor skills by outstanding experts in the field. Kai Essig, Dirk Koester, Francesca Borgo, and Christopher Janelle emphasize the role of attention from a neurocognitive perspective and refer to various sport situations that are in different ways reliant on attentional width and direction for effective information processing. They report on research in which processes have been deeply investigated by eye-tracking methods and highlight attentional problems and strategies for how to handle them. In the following chapter on modeling and feedback David Anderson, Amanda Rymal, and Diane Ste-Marie highlight two of the most common variables used by instructors to facilitate motor skill learning. They explain the range of factors known to mediate the effectiveness of these two most relevant variables for instructors. David Wright, Hiroshi Sekiya, and Joohyun Rhee elaborate on the organization of practice and Thomas Schack, Bettina Bläsing,

Charmayne Hughes, Tamar Flash, and Malte Schilling extend and specify this issue by elements and construction of motor control. The center of attention is given to the connections between basic elements and sensory inputs, and how internal models account for the various processes of action planning and execution.

Part 4, managed by Dieter Hackfort (Germany), Gershon Tenenbaum (Israel and United States), and Tony Morris (Australia) focuses on enhancing performance and encompasses 12 chapters, each covering a different issue. Joaquin Dosil, Gualberto Cremades, and Santiago Rivera deal with psychological skill training and the focus in this chapter is on implementing psychological skills to enhance performance, establishing effective goals, using relaxation techniques, practicing imagery, reflecting on mental processes, and positive self-talk. Robert Weinberg and Joanne Butt look at goal-setting and sport performance. Their specific aim is to provide guidelines on how to develop and implement a goal-setting program with sports teams and individuals. Tirata Bhasavanija and Tony Morris take on mental techniques which are predominantly used in elite sports like imagery. They explain how imagery can be used for a diverse range of purposes, including learning and practice of skills, preview and review of performance, problem solving, developing psychological variables, supporting injury rehabilitation, and facilitating recovery from heavy training. Antonis Hatzigeorgiadis, Nikos Zourbanos, Alexander Latinjak, and Yannis Theodorakis discuss self-talk and positive thinking. The authors take the reader from definitions and conceptualization to taxonomies, tools for the assessment, factors which shape and influence athletes' self-talk up to guidelines for implementing effective self-talk interventions. Jayashree Acharya and Tony Morris look at techniques for "psyching up" and "psyching down". These terms refer to techniques that are used to increase arousal (psych up) or decrease arousal (psych down). Psyching up techniques (e.g., breathing techniques) include use of arousing words and phrases, behaving in physically arousing ways, and imagining arousing situations in sport, arousing behavior of teammates, as well as stimulating music played before or during performance. Psyching down techniques include bodily relaxation techniques (muscle/somatic), mental relaxation techniques, and other techniques that are based on psychological processes used to manage thoughts and feelings. Boris Blumenstein, Tsung-Min Hung, and Iris Orbach cover self-regulation and biofeedback. This chapter provides the main knowledge about biofeedback, the development of biofeedback and biofeedback training, and two biofeedback training models. In this part of the book, key concepts are also discussed. Deborah Feltz and Erman Öncü look at self-confidence and self-efficacy. They look at the theory of self-efficacy in sport, including sources of self-efficacy information and consequences of high and low self-efficacy beliefs are presented, and methods to enhance beliefs of self-efficacy are described. Sheldon Hanton and Stephen Mellalieu discuss coping with stress and anxiety and provide an outline which enables the reader to understand the stress process and the major strategies deployed for successful coping with stress and anxiety. Daryl Marchant, Rouhollah Maher, and Jin Wang deal with the phenomenon of "choking," focusing on a better understanding of the phenomenon and reports on strategies to reduce the likelihood of choking or beneficial solutions for athletes that experience choking repeatedly. Gershon Tenenbaum and Lael Gershgoren take on individual and group decision making. In this chapter the reader is introduced to the basic perceptual-cognitive processes which determine the act of decision making, cognitive components underlying the decision-making process, such as visual attention, selective attention, working and long-term memory, mental representations, and knowledge base and structure. Ronnie Lidor, Dieter Hackfort,

and Thomas Schack tackle performance routines. The authors explain how routines contribute to achievement and they provide empirical evidence stressing the benefits that athletes can gain by the consistent use of routines, and they also give a number of examples of routines that can be used by athletes. In the final chapter of Part 4, Gangyan Si, Traci Statler, and Dietmar Samulski (this was Dietmar's final contribution during his very intensive and busy life in and for sport psychology to his beloved professional field) report on their experiences in different countries and settings on the preparation of elite athletes for major competitions. All of these chapters refer to theoretical aspects, research and empirical evidence as well as to the application of psychological strategies and mental techniques. They provide a broad scope of insight from various backgrounds, cultural settings, and approaches.

Mark Eys (Canada) and Packianathan Chelladurai (US) managed the six chapters of Part 5, which is devoted to team issues. Although each chapter focuses on a different topic, all of them address the question of how a coach or a physical education teacher can become an effective leader who can maximize teams' performance and individuals' outcomes and well-being in sport and physical activity settings. Blair Evans, Mark Eys, Mark Bruner, and Jens Kleinert overview the processes that unite groups' members and the resulting benefits in sport and exercise settings. They portray team building strategies that were used in interventions to promote group cohesion. Michael Van Bussel and Melanie Gregg provide a definition of norms in the prevailing sport culture and their impact on teams. They explain how norms and rules are formed and changed and how they are used to sustain discipline and, interestingly, positive discipline in sport. Based on achievement goal theory and self-determination theory, Joan Duda, Athanasios Papaioannou, Paul Appleton, Eleanor Quested and Charalampos Krommidas define motivational climate in sport, overview its determinants and consequences and provide evidence-based instructions to coaches and physical education teachers concerning the creation of a positive motivational climate in teams and physical education classes. Philip Sullivan, Sophia Jowett, and Daniel Rhind analyze the communication process in teams and the factors that influence this process and they offer strategies for effective communication between coaches and athletes and between peers. Katie Morton, Benjamin Sylvester, Justine Wilson, Chris Lonsdale, and Mark Beauchamp portray profiles of coaches who exhibit transformational leadership by inspiring, motivating, and encouraging athletes. They provide an overview of the positive outcomes of this important type of leadership on athletes, exercise participants and physical education students and provide instructions for coaches and physical education teachers that might help them to become transformational leaders. Todd Loughead, Lauren Mawn, James Hardy and Krista Munroe-Chandler move the discussion to what makes athletes leaders in their teams. They overview theory, research and practices in sport about how athlete leadership is developed by portraying the various challenges and particularities of sport regarding the selection and training of captains and they analyse the important role of coach mentoring for athlete leadership development.

Part 6 is devoted to the careers and lives of athletes and other individuals that participate in physical activity. Athletes, physical education students and exercise participants have their own personal life which is affected by their sport and physical activity experiences. If they perceive that their participation in sport and physical activity helps them to deal effectively with their challenges in life they will be better adjusted in sport too. Coaches, physical education teachers and policy makers need to know how to offer meaningful sport and physical activity experiences to athletes and students and help them to develop the character and skills that are required to cope

effectively with challenges of everyday life and to participate in life in an adaptive manner for themselves and others. Brenda Bredemeier (US) and Athanasios Papaioannou (Greece) edited this part, which is composed of five chapters. Natalia Stambulova and Paul Wylleman describe the variety of challenges and experiences during different stages of athletes' careers, what we know about determinants of long and successful athletic careers and post-sport careers, and they offer advice that might help athletes to cope effectively with the various challenges during different stages of their career and eventually achieve long and successful careers in sport and life. To achieve the latter, an athlete needs to develop the social and emotional skills that are described by Taru Lintunen and Daniel Gould. These authors also illustrate how to develop sport and physical education programs to effectively teach social emotional skills. Beyond skills one needs to develop character useful to the individual and others, argue Brenda Bredemeier and David Shields. Importantly, these authors provide guidelines for the development of moral and positive characters in sports. An important attribute of a positive character is the ability to control anger and the elimination of aggressive behavior using the skills and strategies which Chris Gee and Luke Potwarka describe. These authors also provide recommendations to make sports less violent. Finally, Robert Vallerand, Jérémie Verner-Filion, and Yvan Paquet explain that to have a successful athletic career and a happy life one needs to be harmoniously but not obsessively passionate in sport. These authors describe the social-psychological processes leading to harmonious or obsessive passion and the resulting emotional, cognitive and behavioral outcomes in sport and life, and they provide implications for the development of harmonious passion in sport and physical activity settings.

Part 7 focuses on the psychology of physical activity, exercise and health. Athanasios Papaioannou (Greece) and Nikos Chatzisarantis

(Australia) invited authors to develop chapters describing the benefits of physical activity on mental health, the challenges that people face to be physically active, the determinants of regular exercise and interventions to promote physical activity. Panteleimon Ekkekakis and Susan Backhouse review the effects of physical activity on pleasant and unpleasant emotions and moods and provide recommendations for exercise professionals to optimize the affective responses to physical activity. Yu-Kai Chang and Jennifer Etnier illustrate the effects of physical activity on various types of cognitions across different populations. Stuart Biddle and Trish Gorely summarize evidence on the health detriments of long periods of sitting, delineate factors associated with high levels of sedentary behaviour and offer ideas to reduce sedentary behavior. Swarup Mukherjee outlines the health benefits of exercise and physical activity and the basic concepts and principles of the process of designing a regimen of physical activity aiming at improving overall health. Nikos Chatzisarantis, Martin Hagger, Masato Kawabata and Sviatlana Kamarova summarize the main theories of health behavior and they explain how they can be used to design effective interventions for physical activity promotion. These theories have been used in the interventions described in the following chapters of this part. Sarah Hardcastle and Adrian Taylor recapitulate the principles and strategies used in counseling to promote physical activity and they focus especially on motivational interviewing which is an effective method particularly with individuals who have not been regular exercisers in the past. Koji Takenaka and Leonard Zaichkowsky recount how they applied theory-based interventions to organization settings and communities in Japan and Canada to promote physical and social activity and community-based sport. Finally, Ioannis Morres, Afroditi Stathi, Egil Martinsen and Marit Sørensen outline the positive effects of exercise programs on treatment of depression in adult patients with major depressive disor-

ders, and they provide recommendations for the structure of exercise programs and the provision of exercise consultancy to increase the motivation and participation of these individuals in exercise.

In Part 8 Trisha Leahy (Hong Kong and UK) managed four chapters addressing clinical issues in sport. Trent A. Petrie and Christy Greenleaf delineate types of eating disorders and the associated signs and symptoms and corresponding diagnostic methods. The authors describe the sport environment and the body image of athletes across various sports in relation to increased risks for developing athletes' eating disorders, and they offer instructions for sport-governing bodies, sport administrators and coaches aiming to prevent and treat eating disorders and establish a "body-healthy" sport environment. Trisha Leahy reminds us why all sport psychologists and coaches should be trained to adopt a definition of sexual abuse that minimizes this hideous but often obscure phenomenon in sport. Leahy also illustrates the traumatic impact of sexual abuse and athletes' disruptions across several life domains, and she summarizes the principles that specialists adopt to treat sexual abuse and the phases of therapeutic interventions. Matthew Martens and Jessica Martin demonstrate the prevalence of alcohol and performance enhancing drug use of athletes and exercise participants across various countries where relevant research has been conducted. They also explain how to diagnose these problems and how interventions such as motivational interviewing (see also Chapter 49 by Sarah Hardcastle and Adrian Taylor for another use of this method), relapse prevention, contingency management and the 12-step programs can be used to prevent and treat substance abuse problems in sport and physical activity settings. Urban Johnson and Leslie Podlog overview theory and research on the psychosocial antecedents to athletic injury and to athletes' return to sport following injury, and they explain how sport psychologists can intervene to prevent injury and to help injured athletes during the rehabilitation process.

The final part, Part 9, is designed to cover fundamental or superior issues in sport and exercise psychology professional development, education, application, and practice. Editors Antoinette Minniti (UK) and Judy Van Raalte (US) managed seven chapters in this area. Artur Poczwardowski, Mark Aoyogi, Jamie Shapiro, and Judy Van Raalte provide information relevant for the development of a professional philosophy and sport psychology consultation. Burt Giges and Paul McCarthy discuss how sport psychology practitioners can identify and understand athletes' psychological needs, and help them with needs that have not been fulfilled. Maria Psychountaki, Nektarios Stavrou, Symeon P. Vlachopoulos, Judy Van Raalte and Antoinette Minniti focus on assessment and diagnosis and the quantitative methods to optimize athletes' and exercise participants' physical performance in particular. Henry (Hap) Davis IV, John P. Sullivan, Chris Carr, David B. Coppel, Adam Shunk, Jennifer Carter, Scott Goldman, Thomas Hammond, and Patrick Baillie emphasize issues in the diagnosis of psychopathology among athletes. Thomas Schack, Maurizio Bertollo, Dirk Koester, Jonathan Maycock, and Kai Essig then provide an overview of technological advancements in sport psychology and introduce various most updated methods used in neurocognitive-oriented research. Antoinette Minniti and Judy Van Raalte identify professional training, supervision, and continuing education as central issues and they present an overview of essential features related to this sector of growing importance. In the concluding chapter of this book, by Dieter Hackfort and Gershon Tenenbaum, ethical issues are addressed. The authors provide resources, describe ethical and moral standards, demonstrate consequences in terms of risk assessment for ethical decision making, and offer guidance related to ethical considerations in applied and empirical work in the field of sport and exercise.

CONCLUSION

The impressive amount of knowledge brought together by the outstanding authors in this book covers almost all major concepts that have been examined and applied in the scientific discipline of sport and exercise psychology. This book is designed to provide an introduction for anyone studying this discipline but it will also be useful for coaches, physical education teachers, fitness instructors or prospective professionals in sports and physical activity work settings. All chapters include a vast array of strategies, examples of interventions, and detailed implications for practitioners. The information has been written in such a way that makes this book easy to read, even by individuals who are not experts in sport and physical activity. For those who want to further develop their knowledge in sport and exercise psychology, the authors provide further readings that focus on more advanced information on each topic. The comprehensive coverage of all concepts makes each chapter essential reading for sport and exercise psychology modules. Once again we would like to express our gratitude to all authors for their excellent cooperation in this project and the unique contribution to the development of this book. The *Routledge Companion to Sport and Exercise Psychology: Global Perspectives and Fundamental Concepts* is destined to assist our international colleagues in their efforts to provide high quality education to the next generation of sport and exercise psychologists, sports scientists, and other professionals in sport and physical activity settings all over the world.

REFERENCES

Acharya, J. (2011). Journey of Sport Psychology from Ancient Times to its Relevance in Present Day Sport: An Indian Perspective. *Proceedings of 6th Taipei ASPASP International congress on Sport Psychology.*

Fowers, B.J. (2012). An Aristotelian framework for the Human Good. *Journal of Theoretical and Philosophical Psychology, 32*(1), 10–23.

Joshanloo, M. (2012). A comparison of Western and Islamic conceptions of happiness. *Journal of Happiness Studies.*

Lu, L., Gilmour, R. & Kao, S.F. (2001). Cultural values and happiness: An East-West dialogue. *The Journal of Social Psychology, 14*(4), 477–493.

Morris, T., Hackfort, D. & Lidor, R. (2003). From pope to hope: The first twenty years of ISSP. *International Journal of Sport and Exercise Psychology, 1* (2), 119–138.

Zervas, Y. (2001). Positive thoughts and sport performance: Ancient thinking sheds light on contemporary questions. In A. Papaioannou, Y. Theodorakis & M. Goudas (Eds.), *Proceedings of the 10th World Congress of Sport Psychology* (pp.214–217).

Zhang, K. (2013). Chinese culture and athletes' medal training. *Proceedings of the 13th World Congress of Sport Psychology, Beijing.*

Part One

Understanding participants in sport and exercise contexts

EDITED BY ATHANASIOS G. PAPAIOANNOU AND CLIFFORD J. MALLETT

Chapter 1

Developmental perspectives on sport and physical activity participation

THELMA S. HORN AND JOANNE BUTT

SUMMARY

The purpose of this chapter is to provide a developmentally-based perspective on youth participation in sport and physical activity contexts. The first part of this chapter contains an overview of the changes that occur over childhood and adolescent years in three domains (physical, motoric, and psychosocial). Within each of these sections, developmental progressions are summarized, and recommendations are provided for practitioners. The second part of this chapter summarizes the research on stages of sport participation and provides recommendations for constructing developmentally-appropriate sport and physical activity experiences. The primary perspective on which this chapter is structured is that the degree to which sport and physical activity programs can exert positive effects on children and adolescents depends on the extent to which such programs are consistent with the research and theory on developmental processes.

INTRODUCTION

Meet Charles Brown. He has spent the last ten years coaching hockey teams at the young adult club level (athletes ranging in age from 19 to 24 years old) and has enjoyed much success (e.g., he developed a number of athletes who now compete at the international level, received numerous coach-of-the year awards, and won several championships). However, Charles has decided to "retire" from the adult sport world and has taken a position as coach of an elite club hockey team at the 12-year-old level. He was specifically hired in this role because of the success he achieved at the older club. However, halfway into the new season with the 11 and 12-year-old athletes, Charles has noted, "this is like learning to coach all over again!" In explaining his frustration, Charles further remarks that: "I can't just coach the way I did when I was working with young adults. I know hockey...I know how to win...I know how to develop players' skills...but I guess I just don't know yet how to work with 11 and 12 year olds!" We (the authors) sympathize with Charles. We have been there, and we know that working with younger athletes is very different than working with older athletes. In this chapter, we explain how and why the age/developmental stage of the children/ adolescents with whom adults work is such an important thing to consider.

OBJECTIVES

After reading this chapter, individuals should be able to:

1 Describe the developmental stages on the road to physical, motoric, and psychosocial maturation.
2 Provide recommendations for physical activity practitioners who work with children of varying ages.
3 Describe the stages from initial entry and through the later stages of participation in sport.
4 Identify the characteristics of "developmentally-appropriate" sport and physical activity learning environments.

DEVELOPMENTAL PERSPECTIVES ON SPORT AND PHYSICAL ACTIVITY PARTICIPATION

Participation by children and adolescents in organized youth sport and physical activity programs has been identified as a valued commodity by national and world health organizations (cf., Mountjoy, Andersen, Armstrong, Biddle, Boreham, Bedenbeck, et al., 2012) due to its potential positive effects on children's physical and psychosocial health. Correspondingly, organized sport participation has been linked to the acquisition of important life-skills (e.g., Gould & Carson, 2008). However, some researchers (e.g., Fraser-Thomas & Côté, 2009) have identified possible negative effects of sport participation on the health and well-being of children and adolescents.

Whether or not any particular sport or physical activity program will exert positive, negative, or even zero effects on children and adolescents is likely due to the quality of the program itself. Effective programs are those that are developed to maximize the growth and development of individual children and are based on developmentally-appropriate structures.

The purpose of this chapter is to provide a developmentally-based perspective on youth participation in sport and physical activity contexts and use this research base to establish recommendations for practitioners. This chapter begins with an overview of the stages through which children progress in the physical, motoric, and psychosocial domains. In the second part, the research and theory concerning the stages through which children progress in the competitive sport environment are summarized, again for the purpose of providing recommendations for practitioners on the construction of developmentally-appropriate youth sport programs.

DEVELOPMENTAL AGES AND STAGES: AN OVERVIEW

A significant amount of physical growth and maturation occurs over the infancy, child-hood, and adolescent years (Malina, Bouchard, & Bar-Or, 2004; Payne & Isaacs, 2011). Consider, for example, that the average full-term baby is approximately 20 inches (50.8 cm) at birth but may grow to reach an adult height of 70 inches (5' 10" or 177.8 cm) by 18 years of age. This growth in total height does not occur at a consistent rate. Rather, there are periods of rapid and slow growth, and different parts of the body may grow at different times. A general summary of the growth patterns is provided in Table 1.1.

As Table 1.1 shows, during the first (prenatal) period physical growth and maturation is very fast (one of the three fastest growth periods), with the primary growth occurring in the head and upper body. Thus, a newborn infant's head and trunk typically comprise about 85% of total body length with the legs being relatively shorter and less developed. The second developmental time period occurs during infancy (birth to 2 years) and represents the second of three fastest growth periods. Again, growth and development are particularly evident in regard to the upper body. As a consequence, a two-year-old child can still appear top-heavy, with a relatively longer head and trunk and comparatively shorter legs.

Table 1.1 *Overview of general physical growth and maturation patterns*

Growth stage	Approximate age range	Growth patterns
Prenatal	Conception to birth	• Very fast growth • Head and trunk grow faster than legs (sitting height at birth comprises about 85% of total body height)
Infancy	Birth to 2 years	• Very fast growth (especially in early months of infancy) • Head and trunk still growing and developing comparatively fast
Early childhood	2 to 6 years	• Slower growth rate • Lower legs grow faster than head and trunk (sitting height at 6 years comprises about 55% of total body height) • Relative loss of fat and increase in muscle and bone
Middle childhood	6 to 10 years	• Slower growth rate but some children exhibit a mid-growth spurt between 6.5 and 8.5 years
Late childhood through early adolescence	10 to 15 years	• Very fast growth rate • Sexual maturation begins • Body shape and composition changes
Middle to late adolescence	15 to 20 years	• Slower growth rate • Continuation of sexual maturation • Continuation of body shape and composition changes

Note: Average boy reaches full physical maturation (end of skeletal growth and completion of sexual maturation) by 20 years of age, and average girl reaches that point by 18 years. For further information on the physical growth and development process, see Malina et al. (2004) and Payne and Isaacs (2011).

The third (2 to 6 years) and fourth (6 to 10 years) growth periods are characterized by slower but very steady growth rates. Furthermore, especially from 2 to 6 years, the legs grow faster than the trunk, and bone and muscle mass generally increase more than does fat. Thus, by the age of 6 years, body length (height) is more evenly divided between the upper and lower body areas, and the increased growth and development of the muscular and skeletal systems provide the six-year-old with more motor and physical skill attributes.

The fifth growth period (late childhood to mid-adolescence) constitutes the last of the three fastest growth times. For girls, the age range from 10 to 13 years represents a time of very fast growth, particularly in regard to height as they may grow eight to nine inches (20.3 to 22.9 cm) in height and gain 30–35 pounds (13.6 to 15.9 kg) in body weight. Typically, such growth begins in the feet and hands and then proceeds to the legs and finally the trunk. Boys go through this same pattern of pre-adolescent growth spurt, but it occurs a bit later (12 to 15 years) and may be somewhat more intense (gain in height of 9 to 12 inches, 22.9 to 30.5 cm, combined with a gain in weight of 35 to 45 pounds, 15.9 to 20.4 kg). Sexual maturation also begins, and some changes in body shape and body composition are evident as well.

The sixth and final growth period occurs during the mid- to late-adolescent years (15 to 20 years). Smaller changes in height, body composition, shape, and sexual maturation are observed.

The information contained in the previous paragraphs and in Table 1.1 provides a description of the growth and development of the average child (i.e., progressions are based on compilation of data from large samples of children). In reality, there is considerable interindividual variability in regard to both the velocity (tempo) and the rate at which children progress through these timelines (Malina et al., 2004; Payne & Isaacs, 2011). First, in the

third period of rapid growth, while many children may exhibit a relatively consistent pattern of growth across the entire three-year period, there are others who go through extreme growth patterns in a more abbreviated timeline. That is, a boy who is 14 years of age may grow eight to nine inches (20.3 to 22.9 cm) over just a few months. Similarly, sometimes a very rapid growth that occurs in the feet (e.g., a boy moving from size six feet to size ten feet in just a few months time) and which precedes growth in the legs and trunk can cause that child to be somewhat motorically awkward (possibly causing a temporary disruption in coordination, balance, and agility).

Another important thing to know is that there is variability between children in the rate at which they go through the stages depicted in Table 1.1 (Malina et al., 2004; Payne & Isaacs, 2011). Early maturing children are those who go through the growth and development patterns at an earlier chronological age than average. Thus, an early maturing girl may go through a big spurt in height between the ages of 8 to 11 (rather than the more typical 10 to 13 years) and also proceed through the next stage at a faster pace, thus reaching full adult height, shape, and composition as well as full sexual maturation by the age of 14 to 15 years (rather than the 18 years evidenced for the average maturer). In contrast, a late maturing girl would be comparably delayed. Her big growth spurt in height may occur between 12 to 15 years, and she would not reach full physical maturation until 19 to 20 years. Similar contrasting patterns are observed among boys.

Since most youth sport programs are set up on the basis of chronological age, it can be obvious that children on the same chronologically-aged team may differ considerably in where they are in the growth and maturation process. Table 1.2 provides comparative profiles of early, average, and late maturing boys and girls (see also, Branta, 1989).

As is evident from these charts, one child (particularly the early maturing one) could possibly look like a "star" athlete at the early

Table 1.2 *Comparative profiles of six children differing in rate of biological maturation*

Boys	Chronological age	Andre Average	Edward Early	Luiz Late
	12 years	4' 10" (147.3 cm) 118 pounds (53.5 kg)	5' 7" (170.2 cm) 153 pounds (69.4 kg)	4' 8" (142.2 cm) 98 pounds (44.5 kg)
	15 years	5' 7" (170.2 cm) 153 pounds (69.4 kg)	5' 9" (175.3 cm) 177 pounds (80.3 kg)	4' 10" (147.3 cm) 121 pounds (54.9 kg)
	18 years	5' 9" (175.3 cm) 177 pounds (80.3 kg)	5' 10" (177.8 cm) 185 pounds (83.9 kg)	5' 7" (170.2 cm) 153 pounds (69.4 kg)
	21 years	5' 10" (177.8 cm) 185 pounds (83.9 kg)	5' 10" (177.8 cm) 190 pounds (86.2 kg)	5' 10" (177.8 cm) 180 pounds (81.6 kg)
Girls	Chronological age	Anabelle Average	Emily Early	Linda Late
	10 years	4' 11" (149.9 cm) 107 pounds (48.5 kg)	5' 7" (170.2 cm) 137 pounds (62.1 kg)	4' 9" (144.8 cm) 97 pounds (44.0 kg)
	13 years	5' 7" (170.2 cm) 137 pounds (62.1 kg)	5' 9" (175.3 cm) 153 pounds (69.4 kg)	5' 0" (152.4 cm) 108 pounds (49.0 kg)
	16 years	5' 9½ " (176.5 cm) 153 pounds (69.4 kg)	5' 10" (177.8 cm) 160 pounds (72.6 kg)	5' 8" (172.7 cm) 138 pounds (62.6 kg)
	19 years	5' 10" (177.8 cm) 160 pounds (72.6 kg)	5' 10" (177.8 cm) 165 pounds (74.8 kg)	5' 10" (177.8 cm) 150 pounds (68.0 kg)

Note: Profiles adapted from similar examples provided by Branta (1989).

adolescent age because he/she is taller, more muscular, and generally more biologically mature than her/his peers. For example, on an all-girls 13-year-old basketball team, Emily Early is only a year away from full physical maturation. Thus, she is already 5' 9" (175.3 cm) and has the bone and muscle structure of someone who is 15 to 16 years old. In contrast, Linda Late is only 5' (152.4 cm) tall and still has the body composition and shape of a pre-adolescent. For boys, as well, Edward Early at age 15 would certainly look like a "superstar" due to his more biologically mature body (5' 9"/175.3 cm) that includes broader shoulders and more defined muscle mass. In comparison, Andre Average at the age of 15 years has just completed a big growth spurt in terms of height (5' 7"/170.2 cm), but has yet to fully develop in terms of body composition and shape. Thus, he may still be relatively linear in body shape with less muscle mass than Edward Early. Even more at a disadvantage is Luiz Late who, at 15 years of age, is still in the early stages of the pre-adolescent growth spurt and thus may look gangly (extra large feet but shorter height and no significant bone/muscle mass).

This variability in rate of maturation is an important factor to consider in sport and physical activity contexts for several reasons. First, it is clear that adults should be cautious about forming expectations or judgments of children's ultimate athletic potential before they are fully mature (see further discussion on this topic by Horn, Lox, & Labrador, 2010). Second, it is important to know that children who are significantly ahead (early maturers) or behind (late maturers) their chronologically-aged peers may differ from their average maturing peers in psychosocial well-being. Research studies have shown that early maturing boys tend to have higher self-esteem and enjoy a higher social status while late maturing boys may be less advantaged psychosocially (e.g., Fairclough & Ridgers, 2010). In contrast, it is the early maturing girls (beginning in the early adolescent years) who may tend to have lower self-esteem, a more dissatisfied body image, and higher levels of social physique anxiety (cf., Negriff & Susman, 2011). Such gender differences are likely due to factors in the sociocultural environment (e.g., media, coaches, parents) that affect boys and

girls in different ways (cf., Horn, Lox, & Labrador, 2010).

Finally, adults should be aware that pre- or early-adolescent children on competitive youth sport teams may be encouraged to specialize in one sport based on their current body size, shape, and composition. So, early maturing children may appear to be most suited for sports that emphasize height, power, and strength (e.g., football, basketball) while later maturing children might be pushed into other sports (e.g., long-distance running, gymnastics). However, once the differing maturation rates even out (mid- to late adolescence), early sport specializers (those who chose, or were pushed into, just one sport from an early age) may end up in a sport activity for which they are no longer well suited.

Similarly, pre-adolescent children on competitive youth sport teams may also be

Figure 1.1 Children's sport performance and proficiency may be affected by where they are in the physical growth process.

assigned to playing positions based on their current body size, shape, and composition. In sports where height is an important factor (e.g., basketball, volleyball), the early maturing (and probably taller) children would tend to be assigned to playing positions such as post/center (basketball) and hitter/blocker (volleyball). In contrast, the average and late maturers would be assigned to guard (basketball) and libero/backrow (volleyball) positions. Although this practice may most benefit the success of the team at that chronological age level, it can result in a situation where each child only learns the skills for one position (a practice known as position specialization). However, as these children advance in the sport development process, their relative sizes and physiques change. The problem, then, becomes that some children/adolescents have not developed the skills for the position that they could/should now play.

RECOMMENDATIONS FOR COACHES, PARENTS, AND OTHER PRACTITIONERS

1   Understand the general physical growth patterns that children go through so that they remain aware of where each child is in the biological growth and development process.

2   Use caution in "cutting" children from competitive sport programs as those who are cut may tend to be the later maturers in their chronological age group. Therefore, if possible, youth sport programs should provide opportunities for all children to participate, perhaps with late maturers placed at more developmentally-based levels until they catch up to their average and early-maturing peers in body size, composition, and maturation.

3   Discourage the practice of specialization in only one sport or physical activity until the mid-adolescent years.

4   Ensure that all children on youth sport teams are taught the skills for all positions as it is not always possible to anticipate the position they may be best suited for by the end of the physical growth and maturation process (mid-to-late adolescence).

MOTOR SKILL DEVELOPMENT

Just as there is a pattern as to how children exhibit physical growth and development from birth through adolescence, there is also a pattern as to how children acquire (or can acquire) development of motor skills and proficiencies (Payne & Isaacs, 2011). This pattern can be divided into three major levels. At the first level (infancy years from birth to 2 years), the child acquires selected reflexes (e.g., searching, rooting, sucking), postural control skills (e.g., rolling over, sitting upright, standing upright), grasping and manipulative skills (e.g., reaching for, grabbing, and manipulating objects), and basic locomotor skills (e.g., creeping, crawling, walking). At the second level (early through late childhood from ages 2 to 10 years), children should acquire the mature pattern for a number of fundamental locomotor (e.g., running, jumping, leaping, hopping) and manipulative (e.g., overhand throwing, catching, kicking) skills. Most typically, children proceed through a series of stages in their acquisition of each of these skills. These skills are labeled as "fundamental" motor skills because they ultimately will serve as building blocks for children's/adolescents' acquisition of more sport-specific skills. For example, once a child has acquired the most mature stage in the fundamental motor skill of the overhand throw, then that child's tennis coach can use that basic pattern to teach that child a tennis serve and a smash. Similarly, the baseball or softball coach can use the basic overhand throwing pattern to teach a child to throw or pitch (overhand), and the volleyball coach uses the basic overhand throwing pattern to teach children to hit and serve in his sport. At this second level of motor development, children should also acquire some basic fine-motor skills (e.g., eye-hand coordination, eye-foot coordination, balance), as well as body control skills (e.g., stopping, starting, accelerating), and information-processing and decision-making skills (e.g., scanning full visual field and selecting task-relevant cues, speed of simple and choice reaction time).

At the third and final level of the motor skill development process, children, adolescents (and adults) move on to acquire sport-specific or activity-specific skills of their choice. Thus, as noted earlier, individuals who are at this third level use the previously acquired fundamental motor patterns to develop skills and abilities that are specific to a range of sport and physical activities.

The important issue to consider here is that all children (with certain exceptions) should acquire some degree of proficiency at the skills in the first two levels. Although all (or most) children do acquire the motor skills at the first level of development, not all children acquire proficiency in the motor skills identified at level 2. Those who don't may be more limited at older ages (adolescent and adult years) in regard to their choice of sport or physical activity participation.

Figure 1.2 Participation in specialized sport activities requires prior mastery of basic fundamental motor and body control skills.

RECOMMENDATIONS FOR COACHES, PARENTS, AND PRACTITIONERS

1 Provide sufficient physical play experiences for children in the infancy years so that they are able to acquire the designated motor/physical skills.

2 The primary focus during the childhood years (ages 2 to 10) should be on the development of the fundamental locomotor and manipulative skills. Although children can (and certainly may want to) participate in sport- or activity-specific programs (e.g., soccer, baseball, martial arts, swimming, dance), the emphasis in these programs should still be focused on development of all of the fundamental skills.

3 Children should likely not specialize in one sport or physical activity prior to the mid-adolescent years as they might be apt to develop only the fundamental motor skills (at level 2) that are important to their particular specialized sport or activity. They may not, then, develop relevant other motor skills at this level that they will want or need later (as adolescents and adults) as they expand their sport and physical activity repertoire for competitive, leisure, social, or fitness reasons.

PSYCHOSOCIAL DEVELOPMENT

A number of theories have been developed in the psychosocial and cognitive literatures to describe how children grow and develop over infancy, childhood, and adolescent years. Two of these theories may be particularly applicable to the youth sport setting. This includes the theories related to self-concept/self-esteem (e.g., Harter, 1999) and those that center on the development of the concept of ability (e.g., Nicholls, 1989).

The more recent theories of self-concept/self-esteem (cf., Horn, 2004) are built on the notion that children's and adolescents' self-esteem or self-worth is based on their perceptions of competence in multiple domains (e.g., academic, social, physical). Theoretically, then, if children's/adolescents' participation in physical activity or sport can enhance their perceptions of physical competence (i.e., encourage them to believe that they are capable or competent in their sport or physical activity) and/or their perceptions of their physical appearance (i.e., help them to feel satisfied with their bodies), then their overall self-concept/self-esteem can also be positively enhanced. The problem may be that not all children/adolescents experience enhanced perceptions of physical competence and/or

physical appearance through their participation in sport/physical activity (e.g., Gould & Carson, 2008; Fraser-Thomas & Côté, 2009). To understand such differential experiences, we need to understand how children of different ages evaluate or judge their physical competence. The research in this area suggests the following developmental sequences (cf., Horn, 2004).

Young children (ages 4 to 7 years) tend to evaluate or judge how good they are in any domain or task based on three things: (1) the feedback they get from significant adults (usually those who are nurturing); (2) simple task accomplishment (completion of a task); and (3) personal effort. Thus, a six-year-old child might say, for example, "I'm really strong because I can lift this big bowling ball" or "I'm really strong because my teacher tells me I'm strong", or "I'm really strong because I tried really hard to lift this bowling ball and then I did!" Children at these younger ages, then, do not really differentiate between ability and effort, and also do not take task difficulty into consideration in their judgment of their competence (e.g., maybe the big bowling ball is not really that heavy and/or maybe everyone their age can lift that ball) (Nicholls, 1989).

As children progress to the next developmental level (ages 7 to 12 years), their judgments or evaluations of their competence at physical tasks become more complicated (i.e., they use more sources of information), but remain very concrete. Thus, children within this age range primarily use such sources as: (a) peer comparison; (b) evaluative feedback (from parents, peers, coaches); and (c) performance outcomes (winning/losing). In particular, the use of peer comparison tends to increase across this age range. Thus, by the time that children reach 12 years of age, it often is one of their primary sources of information. In addition, this peer comparison process is based primarily on comparison to "near" peers (i.e., those peers that the child knows and can directly compare her or himself to on a regular basis) (cf., Horn, 2004).

It's important to note here that children at this developmental age/stage *can* use other sources of information to judge their competence (e.g., skill mastery, learning) but because the peer comparison process may be so obvious and concrete, it becomes the most relevant way. While the use of the peer comparison process may prove effective for some children/adolescents (i.e., those who are the "superstars" in their age group will clearly develop high perceptions of physical or sport competence), their classmates or teammates who do not fare well in the peer comparison process (e.g., the child who scores at the bottom end of his class on physical fitness tests) are certainly at risk for developing low perceptions of physical competence. If, however, significant adults within the sport/physical activity environment encourage and assist their young charges to use other ways to evaluate/judge their competence (e.g., keep a chart in a visible space that highlights the improvement of each child in the physical fitness tests rather than the comparison of children's scores on the tests), then all children's/adolescents' perceptions of competence can be enhanced.

As children move into the adolescent years (13 through 18 years), the sources of information they use to evaluate or judge their physical competence expands to include: (a) peer comparison; (b) evaluative feedback (coaches, peers, parents, spectators, media); (c) competitive outcomes (win/loss and game performance statistics); (d) achievement of self-set goals (e.g., skill mastery); (e) speed/ease of learning (e.g., how quickly/slowly they can learn a new sport or skill); (f) internal information (e.g., perceived effort, self-regulated learning, pre/post competitive event feelings, sport enjoyment, perceived skill knowledge and decision-making abilities) (cf., Horn, 2004).

Adolescents' use of some sources may also change. In regard to peer comparison, for example, adolescents now have the ability to compare themselves not only to known or "near" peers (e.g., teammates, classmates, opponents) but also to unknown or "extended" peers (e.g., others of the same age or developmental level but from such other broader context as national/international). This extension of the peer group can certainly result in changes in the adolescent's perception of sport/physical competence. For example, a hockey athlete who has always been the best player in her/his age group (school, league) may now start comparing her/himself to a broader peer group (all individuals in her/his state/region or country). Thus, the athlete's perception of competence could actually decline somewhat.

Additionally, while athletes' use of evaluative feedback from a variety of others (e.g., parents, peers, coaches) continues, there is also some evidence that the value of these different sources can change. Specifically, parents' feedback may decline in importance, while that from spectators, peers, and especially coaches may increase. Interestingly, older adolescents do appear to use speed/ease of learning as a source of competence information. But, they are now able to differentiate between effort and ability. Thus, if it takes a long time to learn a particular skill, then an individual athlete may perceive that he/she has less ability at that skill/task (Nicholls, 1989).

By the end of adolescence, it may be important that individuals learn to use a variety of sources to evaluate their competence at any particular task, activity, or sport. That is, for older adolescents or adults to continue participation in a physical activity, they need to be able to use not just one source of information (e.g., peer comparison or win/loss record) but also be able to evaluate their competence using additional/other sources (e.g., skill improvement, enjoyment of the activity, achievement of self-set goals). That way, if they lose an important game/match or fail to make a very select team, they can still perceive competence using these other sources of information. Similarly, an older woman who begins participation in competitive running (e.g., triathlons, marathons) can enjoy high perceptions of competence if she evaluates her ability in this activity by using self-comparison sources (e.g., "Am I getting better with continued training?") rather than just performance outcomes (e.g., "Did I win my age-group race?").

RECOMMENDATIONS FOR COACHES, PARENTS, AND PRACTITIONERS

1 Provide younger children (ages 4 to 7 years) with high frequencies of positive feedback and multiple opportunities for simple task accomplishment (e.g., "Can you throw this ball to that wall that is all the way over there?") as opposed to structuring tasks that contain a more outcome-oriented standard (e.g., "You need to knock down all ten pins.").

2 Incorporate the opportunity for children (especially between the ages of 7 through 12) to obtain a wide variety of mastery experiences (e.g., tasks that they cannot initially do but are able to achieve with effort) (e.g., learning to jump rope/hopscotch/serve overhand). Once the child exerts that effort over a period of trials/days/weeks/months and succeeds in mastering the task, provide the child with positive feedback for task outcome but also, and more importantly, for their mastery efforts.

3 Decrease the importance of peer comparison (e.g., "How many push-ups did you do today compared to your classmates?") for children and adolescents (ages 7 through adolescence) and increase the use of self-comparison techniques to evaluate personal competence (e.g., "How many push-ups were you able to do three weeks ago and compare that to how many you did today?").

4 Encourage older adolescents (ages 14 through 18 years) to use multiple sources of information to determine how good they are.

5 As a coach, try to find ways to show each adolescent athlete the value of the specific role that they play in relation to team success (e.g., "It may not be whether you are our leading scorer, but whether you do the things that only you can do for our team.") (see, also, discussion on the facilitation of group/team cohesion in Chapter 33 of this volume).

6 Establish a positive, encouraging, and autonomy-supportive socio-emotional environment (see more specific detail in Chapters 4, 35 and 38 in this volume) as this type of motivational climate has consistently been linked to positive psychosocial growth in children, adolescents, and young adults.

In general, then, the developmentally-based information presented in the previous sections clearly shows that children and adolescents do differ significantly from one developmental stage to the next. Adults should use this information to structure sport and physical activity programs that are appropriate for children and adolescents at each maturational stage. In the next section of this chapter, some recommendations regarding this process are provided.

Figure 1.3 Children's sport enjoyment will be enhanced with the use of developmentally-appropriate learning activities.

CREATING DEVELOPMENTALLY-APPROPRIATE YOUTH SPORT AND PHYSICAL ACTIVITY ENVIRONMENTS

Identifying the characteristics of developmentally-appropriate sport and physical activity environments would appear to be a daunting task. However, this process was made easier with the publication of the Developmental Model of Sport Participation (DMSP) (Côté, Baker, & Abernethy, 2007) (see further discussion of this model and its relationship to talent development in Chapter 42 of this volume). The origins of this model began with a 1999 study by Côté which resulted in the identification of three stages of sports participation, spanning from early childhood through late adolescence. These stages were identified as the sampling (ages 6–13), the specializing (ages 13–15), and the investment years (ages 15–20). Subsequent additional support for Côté's DMSP

has been documented in various athletic talent development studies (e.g., Strachan, Côté, & Deakin, 2009).

Within this DMSP model, the sampling years are characterized by participation for enjoyment and by sampling from a variety of sport-related activities. Children at this stage should be introduced to organized activities (sports and games) in the form of what Côté and colleagues (Côté, 1999; Côté & Hay, 2002) termed deliberate play activities. The primary aim of these activities is to increase motivation and enjoyment. While activities tend to be structured, they do not include significant involvement from adults. Parents, however, should support the emphasis on play (rather than focusing solely on practice) and offer encouragement and support to their child. Coaches should provide children with opportunities to develop fundamental motor skills while also promoting positive motivations and beliefs about sports participation.

During the specializing years, athletes invest significantly more time and effort in practicing the specific skills for their preferred sport(s) as training and competition become more important. Despite the shift toward a more structured training regime, enjoyment should still remain central to athletes' experiences, thus maintaining a balance between deliberate play and practice. Given the focus at this stage on the development of specific sports skills, there may be a need for a more specialized and expert coach.

The transition into the investment years typically occurs around age 15. For those athletes that successfully transition, the focus switches to achieving an elite level of perfor-mance, primarily in one selected sport. During this career stage, athletes invest considerable time and effort in the development of skills and strategies for competition through deliberate practice. It is important that practitioners are aware of the many sacrifices (e.g., personal, extra-curricular activities) that athletes will likely make at this stage of their careers to concentrate on training and competitions.

From an applied perspective, the question still remains – how can practitioners (e.g., coaches, parents) meet the needs of young athletes at various stages of their participation in sport? Based on the research conducted by Côté and his colleagues (Côté, 1999; Côté & Hay, 2002), some guidelines can be identified. Due to the extensive developmental changes that occur between the ages of 6 and 15 (see first section of this chapter), the practical implications provided in the next sections focus on the sampling and specializing years of participation.

RECOMMENDATIONS FOR CREATING AN EFFECTIVE ENVIRONMENT: THE SAMPLING YEARS

As noted earlier, enjoyment and intrinsic motivation should constitute the foci of the sampling years. Indeed, a lack of enjoyment experienced in the latter stages of these years is one reason why children may decrease their participation and/or dropout altogether. To maximize children's enjoyment, adults should create a positive and encouraging environment (cf., Gilbert, 2006).

1 Significant adults should provide ample learning opportunities for children at this stage to develop a wide range of skills. Such an environment will enable all children to demonstrate mastery-based competence and thus develop high perceptions of ability.

2 Coaches should design their play and practice activities in ways that promote excitement and challenge so as to maximize children's levels of enjoyment.

3 Coaches will need to continuously modify task difficulty and provide quality verbal feedback (i.e., technical learning cues combined with positive reinforcement) to children of varying abilities so that all children can experience continued success throughout their years within this stage.

4 For children at this level, enjoyment is very much dependent on the presence of strong peer relationships. Thus, coaches should create a mastery-oriented climate (i.e., emphasize self-improvements) as opposed to using peer-rivalry in order to motivate young athletes' practice efforts.

5 Children's sources of enjoyment appear to change across the sampling years (cf., McCarthy & Jones, 2007). In particular, as children get older, they enjoy competitive experiences. Thus, coaches should provide competitive opportunities and skill-based challenges during deliberate play activities.

However, the emphasis during these tasks should still remain on the individual athlete's mastery rather than on performance outcomes or the peer comparison process.

6 Placing less emphasis on outcome (i.e., winning) does not need to occur at the expense of competitive play and practice. Rather, coaches can and should provide aspiring young athletes with opportunities to be competitive because a competitive mentality is an important psychological characteristic that athletes will need as they successfully transition into the investment years (Mills, Butt, Maynard, & Harwood, 2012).

7 Developing fundamental motor skills through deliberate practice activities remains central to the sampling years of participation. It is possible that children who spend appropriate time engaging in deliberate play activities will spend less time in deliberate practice during the specializing years (cf., Côté, 1999; Côté & Hay, 2002). With this in mind, parents and coaches should avoid the temptation to push children into sport specialization at younger ages.

8 Both parents and coaches should adhere to the notion that intrinsic reasons are the primary focus for participation at this stage. Parents, in particular, should adopt an appropriate perspective on their child's sporting involvement, provide social support, and also encourage ownership (cf., Gould, Lauer, Rolo, Jannes, & Pennisi, 2008).

RECOMMENDATIONS FOR CREATING AN EFFECTIVE ENVIRONMENT: THE SPECIALIZING YEARS

As outlined earlier, following the transition into the specializing years of participation, athletes will begin to invest a great deal of time and effort into practicing their preferred sport(s). Accordingly, training and competition become increasingly structured, and there is a more pronounced focus on the development of sport-specific skills.

1 Coaches should avoid creating an environment that focuses solely on intense levels of training because this can lead to decreases in athletes' intrinsic motivation, and corresponding increases in burnout (cf., Goodger & Kenttä, 2012).

2 Coaches should maintain a balance between deliberate play and deliberate practice activities, as it is still important for athletes at this stage to be exposed to successful mastery experiences in order to maintain or increase their levels of confidence. This can be accomplished through the use of individual and team performance goals (i.e., goals in relation to one's own previous performance).

3 Coaches and parents should teach and encourage athletes to view "making mistakes" as being part of the learning and development process. This attitude will enhance athletes' persistence in learning and developing their skills.

4 Creating friendly-rivalry through challenging and competitive practices is linked to the development of mental toughness. Thus, coaches should encourage athletes to "use" each other in practice to push themselves to improve their skills.

5 Athletes develop their own self-confidence as well as confidence in their coaches during these specializing years (Cote & Hay, 2002). To maximize this process, coaches can implement practices that provide athletes with accomplishments and also acknowledge their achievements. Coaches can also provide athletes with opportunities to "model" confident athletes (e.g., through observing video film or other teammates).

6 Coaches should provide opportunities for athletes to be involved in some decision

making to help empower them to take ownership of their sport development. Specifically, setting up practices that involve active learning (e.g., questioning methods) and problem solving type drills can be implemented. In addition, it may be important for coaches to use strategies to help athletes become aware of their performance (e.g., analysing performance combined with coach–athlete dialogue) through engaging in self-reflection and problem solving drill-based activities.

To conclude, this section of the chapter has revealed that young athletes' journey through the developmental stages of sport participation is a complex and multidimensional process that takes place over a sustained period of time, and is influenced by a range of individual and environmental factors. To assist practitioners who work with these children (e.g., coaches, parents, sport psychology consultants), some practical implications were identified in order for such adults to provide developmentally-appropriate learning environments.

LEARNING AIDS

1 Describe the range of body sizes and shapes a coach might see in a coeducational sport team comprised of children who are all chronologically 12 to 13 years old.

These children are in the late childhood to early adolescent age range. This is a time of rapid growth where many body size, shape, and composition changes occur. Due to variability between children in rate of maturation, the early maturing athletes may already be displaying a more mature body size and shape (i.e., being much closer to their full adult size and shape) while their late maturing peers are still exhibiting a more linear and child-like physique with many maturational changes still to come. Thus, coaches at this age level will likely see a full range of maturational levels within their team.

2 Compare a 12-year-old child's use of near peer comparison to evaluate her or his sport competence with the older adolescent's use of both near and far peer comparison.

"Near" peers are defined as peers that the child knows and can directly compare herself or himself to on a regular basis (e.g., friends, teammates, classmates). As children move into adolescence (13 through 18 years) the sources of information they use to evaluate their physical competence expands and they have the ability to compare themselves not only to "near" peers but also to unknown or "extended" peers (e.g., others of the same age or developmental level but from broader contexts, such as national/international). Due to the extension of the peer group, during these years, adolescents' perceived sport/physical competence might decline because they may now start comparing themselves to a broader peer group (all individuals in their state/ region or country).

3 Identify the three stages of sports participation that are included in Côté's Developmental Model of Sport Participation (DMSP) and explain the key characteristics that define and distinguish each of these stages.

The sampling years are characterized by participation for enjoyment and participation in a variety of sport-related activities. Children are introduced to organized activities (in the form of deliberate play activities) and while activities tend to be structured, they do not include a great deal of involvement from adults.

In the specializing years, athletes invest significantly more time and effort in practicing their preferred sports. Training becomes more important and there is a focus on developing sport-specific skills.

During the investment years, the focus switches to achieving an elite level of performance. Athletes will likely select one sport and invest a great deal of time and effort in the development of skills and strategies for competition through deliberate practice.

REVIEW QUESTIONS

1   A recommendation that was consistently identified in this chapter was that children should probably not specialize in one sport during the childhood and even into the early adolescent years. Provide a rationale for this recommendation using the information from the following three sections/parts of this chapter: (a) physical growth; (b) motor development; (c) stages of participation.

2   Given that children of the same chronological age may vary from each other in their rate of maturation, explain why parents of young athletes who are in the 12–15 year age range should encourage them to use sources other than peer comparison to evaluate how good they are at a sport.

3   You are the coach of a team of young athletes who are in the sampling years. Describe the type of climate you should create. How would this type of climate differ from that which you might create if your young athletes were in the specializing years?

EXERCISES

1   Interview project

Assignment goal: To provide students with an opportunity to see how children of varying ages or stages use different sources of information to evaluate their physical competence.

Assignment description: Students should interview six children, two from each of the following age periods: (a) 4 to 7 years; (b) 8 to 12 years; and (c) 13 to 18 years. Begin the interview by identifying a physical or sport task that each child thinks she or he is really good at. For the younger children, this might be a fundamental motor skill (e.g., running, hopping, throwing) while for older children it might be a more sport-specific skill (e.g., batting in baseball/softball; shooting in basketball; playing defense in volleyball). Once each child has identified such a physical or sport task, ask the child a series of questions to determine how she or he has made that competence judgment. Specifically, the goal of each interview is to determine what sources of information each child uses to evaluate her or his competence at that physical activity or sport task. Follow up this series of questions with a similar set of questions to determine how each child arrives at the conclusion that he or she is not good at a physical activity or sport. When all interviews are completed, write a paper summarizing your results. Discuss not only possible age/stage differences in the sources of information children use but also possible differences between children at the same age level (i.e., two eight year olds may use different sources of information). You might also want to address why some children use different sources to evaluate high and low competence. Why do you think such differences might occur?

2 Case study

Assignment goal: To provide students with an opportunity to understand how an athlete has developed his/her talents to become successful.

Assignment description: Students will be required to conduct a case study by finding an experienced athlete (collegiate or professional athlete) to interview. Using retrospective recall, the interview will focus on the athlete's developmentally-based sport experiences and how he/she progressed through the stages of sport participation. For the interview, students should consider obtaining information about the following important points: (a) the age at which this athlete began to focus on specializing in his/her sport; (b) the factors that influenced the athlete's decision to select and continue participation in his/her chosen sport; (c) the role of significant others (e.g., parents, coaches, teammates); and (d) positive and negative factors influencing transitions into higher levels of participation. At the end of the interview task, students will write a written report on the developmentally-based experiences of the athlete.

3 Development of a model youth sport program

Assignment goal: To provide students with experience in designing a developmentally-appropriate model of sports participation for children and youth that have been selected to participate in a youth sports development academy.

Assignment description: Students should work in small groups to develop an applied model of sports participation. Each group can select a sport of their choice for this assignment. The role for students in each group is to develop, present, and promote their model to the academy performance development manager (i.e., role-playing scenario) and persuade him/her that their model should be adopted because it will be more effective in developing athletic talent. The participants in the academy are aged between 6 and 15 years. In completing this assignment, students should consider some of the following important points: (a) the characteristics of the environment and its appropriateness for participants of varying ages; (b) the role of coaches and parents; and (c) the development of key physical and mental skills.

 ADDITIONAL READING

Horn, T.S. & Harris, A. (2002). Perceived competence in young athletes: Research findings and recommendations for coaches and parents. In F.L. Smoll & R.E. Smith (Eds.), *Children and youth in sport: A biopsychosocial perspective* (2nd ed.) (pp. 435–464). Dubuque, IA: Kendall/Hunt.

Horn, T.S. & Horn, J.L. (2007). Family influences on children's sport and physical activity participation, behavior, and psychosocial responses. In G. Tenenbaum & R.C. Eklund (Eds.), *Handbook of sport psychology* (3rd ed.) (pp. 685–711). NY: John Wiley & Sons.

Malina, R.M. (2008). Biocultural factors in developing physical activity levels. In A.L. Smith & S.J.H. Biddle (Eds.), *Youth physical activity and inactivity* (pp. 141–166). Champaign, IL: Human Kinetics.

Smith, A.L. & Biddle, S.J.H. (2008). (Eds.), *Youth physical activity and inactivity*. Champaign, IL: Human Kinetics.

Weiss, M.R. (Ed.) (2004). *Developmental sport and exercise psychology*. Morgantown, WV: Fitness Information Technology.

Weiss, M.R., Kipp, L.E. & Bolter, N.D. (2012). Training for life: Optimizing positive youth development through sport and physical activity. In S.M. Murphy (Ed.), *Handbook of sport and performance psychology* (pp. 448–475). London, UK: Oxford University Press.

REFERENCES

Branta, C. (1989). Young athletes: Midgets and giants at the same age. *Motor development Academy Newsletter*.

Côté, J. (1999). The influence of the family in the development of talent in sport. *The Sport Psychologist, 13*, 395–417.

Côté, J., Baker, J. & Abernethy, B. (2007). Practice and play in the development of sport expertise. In G. Tenenbaum & R. Eklund (Eds.), *Handbook of sport psychology* (3rd ed.) (pp. 184–202). Hoboken, NJ: Wiley.

Côté, J. & Hay, J. (2002). Children's involvement in sport: A developmental perspective. In J. Silva & D. Stevens (Eds.), *Psychological foundations of sport* (pp. 484–502). Boston, MA: Merrill.

Fairclough, S.J. & Ridgers, N.D. (2010). Relationships between maturity status, physical activity, and physical self-perceptions in primary school children. *Journal of Sports Science, 28*, 1–9.

Fraser-Thomas, J. & Côté, J. (2009). Understanding adolescents' positive and negative developmental experiences in sport. *The Sport Psychologist, 23*, 3–23.

Gilbert, W. (2006). Introduction to Special Issue: Coach education. *The Sport Psychologist, 20*, 123–125.

Goodger, K. & Kenttä, G. (2012). Professional practice issues in athlete burnout. In S. Hanton & S. Mellalieu (Eds.), *Professional practice in sport psychology: A review* (pp.133–164). London: Routledge.

Gould, D. & Carson, S. (2008). Life skills development through sport: Current status and future directions. *International Review of Sport and Exercise Psychology, 1*, 58–78.

Gould, D., Lauer, L., Rolo, C., Jannes, C. & Pennisi, N. (2008). The role of parents in tennis success: Focus group interviews with junior coaches. *The Sport Psychologist, 22*, 18–37.

Harter, S. (1999). *The construction of the self: A developmental perspective*. NY: Guilford Press.

Horn, T.S. (2004). Developmental perspectives on self-perceptions in children and adolescents. In M.R. Weiss (Ed.), *Developmental sport and exercise psychology* (pp. 101–143). Morgantown, WV: Fitness Information Technology.

Horn, T.S., Lox, C. & Labrador, F. (2010). The self-fulfilling prophecy theory: When coaches' expectations become reality. In J.M. Williams (Ed.), *Applied sport psychology: Personal growth to peak performance* (6th ed.) (pp. 81–105). Boston: McGraw-Hill.

Malina, R.M., Bouchard, C. & Bar-Or, O. (2004). *Growth, maturation, and physical activity*. (2nd ed.). Champaign, IL: Human Kinetics.

McCarthy, P. & Jones, M.V. (2007). A qualitative study of sport enjoyment in the sampling years. *The Sport Psychologist, 21*, 400–416.

Mills, A., Butt, J., Maynard, I. & Harwood, C. (2012). Identifying factors perceived to influence the development of elite youth football academy players. *Journal of Sport Sciences, 25*, 1593–1604.

Mountjoy, M., Andersen, L.B., Armstrong, N., Biddle, S., Boreham, C., Bedenbeck, H.P.B. et al (2012). International Olympic Committee consensus statement on the health and fitness of young people through physical activity and sport. *British Journal of Sports Medicine, 45*, 839–848.

Negriff, S. & Susman, E.J. (2011). Pubertal timing, depression, and externalizing problems: A framework, review, and examination of gender differences. *Journal of Research on Adolescence, 21*, 717–746.

Nicholls, J. (1989). *The competitive ethos and democratic education.* Cambridge, MA: Harvard University Press.

Payne, V.G. & Isaacs, L.D. (2011). *Human motor development: A lifespan approach* (8th ed.). NY: McGraw-Hill.

Strachan, L., Cote, J. & Deakin, J. (2009). "Specializers" versus "samplers" in youth sport: Comparing experiences and outcomes. *The Sport Psychologist, 23,* 77-92.

Chapter 2

Nurturing talent in youth sport[1]

JEAN CÔTÉ, DAVID J. HANCOCK AND BRUCE ABERNETHY

SUMMARY

In this chapter, we outline key variables regarding nurturing talent in youth sport. To begin, we present four types of developmental activities that youth engage in, which are important for athletes' development: Deliberate practice, play practice, spontaneous practice, and deliberate play. The role of the coach is also paramount for developing talent in youth athletes, and we provide a definition of an effective coach that is broken down into three components: coach knowledge, coach contexts, and athlete outcomes. Furthermore, we identify key coaching principles that should be implemented depending on the athletes' developmental stage. Finally, we examine the role of parents for developing talent. Parents offer several types of support for their children including emotional, informational, tangible support and companionship. We discuss how parents can fulfill these roles and also offer suggestions for how parents can support their children based on the type of youth sport in which they are engaged.

INTRODUCTION

Achieving elite performance in sport is a feat that is highly acclaimed and can be financially rewarding in today's society and in most countries in the world. Athletes that have the commitment, opportunities, and chance to make it to the top of their sports are highly celebrated and recognized public figures. Achieving Olympic or professional levels of performance in sport has several appealing outcomes; however, the long-term personal and social resources associated with talent development in sport are considerable and are often overlooked when examining only the pinnacle accomplishments of expert athletes.

Talent development in sport is a long-term journey that begins in childhood and has important transition points during adolescence and adulthood. Adults who lead youth sport often generate conflicting messages regarding early talent development that are incongruent with healthy youth development and long-term sport participation. For instance, there is a long history of adult-led youth sports that are based on a talent identification model, in which adults use a rigid skill-based approach to evaluate talent and weed out the less skilled children. This approach implements early selection of "talented" children, which involves an increase in the amount of resources allotted to a special group of athletes, and entails a training schedule that may be inconsistent with a child's motivation to participate in sports. There are a number of problems with these traditional methods of talent identification when applied to children (Vaeyens, Gullich, Warr, & Philippaerts, 2009). For example, characteristics that distinguish success in an adult athlete (i.e., size or speed) may not become apparent until later adolescence. At the same time, there is no guarantee that a young athlete who possesses a desired attribute will possess that attribute as an adult athlete. Additionally, there is the major concern that youth begin maturing at different times and rates; late maturing athletes could be summarily dismissed through traditional early talent identification methods. Finally, there are a number of negative consequences associated with intensive training and rigid skill-based models of children's sport, such as increased level of injuries, burnout, and dropout (Côté, 2009).

The application of a talent selection approach to youth sport programs, such as the one described above, may be effective for the development of talent in sports with large bases of participants in which children could be substituted with other individuals if they do not perform according to standards set by adults. This approach to talent development during childhood rarely considers the well-being and retention rate of children in sport.

Considering that talent in sport is difficult to assess during childhood, an alternative approach is to engage children and create a positive environment in which all children have an equal opportunity to develop their talent. Such a developmental perspective to talent requires input from personal (e.g., motivation, effort, and concentration) and social (e.g., coaches, parents, and equipment) variables over a long period of time for its realization. This chapter presents and discusses the different developmental activities that affect youth involvement in sport and the long-term acquisition of skills by focusing on a talent development approach. Different aspects of talent development in sport will be presented, including the effect of different developmental activities and the influence of coaches and parents.

 ## OBJECTIVES

The four objectives of this chapter are to:

1   Define the developmental activities of practice and play, and their long-term impact on participation and talent development in sport.
2   Understand the concepts of diversity (participating in several sports) and intensity (frequency and number of hours participating in one sport) as variables that affect talent development in sport.
3   Define the role of the coach at different stages of an athlete's development in sport.
4   Define the supporting roles of parents at different stages of athletes' development in sport.

DEVELOPMENTAL ACTIVITIES

Several authors have analyzed and discussed the type of activities that have the most significant impact on talent development in sport.

Côté, Erickson, and Abernethy (2013) recently reviewed this literature and suggested a taxonomy of activities that could be generally categorized as either practice or play. The fundamental difference between practice and play resides in the goal that the activity aims to achieve in a specific sporting situation. The goal of practice activities is to improve performance, whereas the goal of play activities is to have fun. The various practice and play activities that constitute sport fulfills different needs in youth and ultimately affects their current and future sport involvement. The intrinsically-motivating and self-directed nature of primarily play-oriented activities contrasts with the outcome-oriented and often adult-driven nature of mainly practice-oriented activities.

Côté et al. (2013) suggested that the developmental activities of youth in sport can be separated by two axes; first, the social structure of the activity and second, the personal value the activity provides to the participants. The first axis shows the amount of instruction and input that is vested by supervising adult(s) (i.e., the coach) versus the participating youth. At one end of this axis there are sport activities where adults have minimal roles in providing instructions, as in play activities. At the other end of the axis there are sport activities in which adults set the direction and provide instruction in a structured environment, such as the structured practices of organized sport. A second axis relates to the personal values associated with an activity, varying from extrinsic to intrinsic values. Extrinsic values describe activities that are performed with the goal of improving skills or performance (e.g., practice), while intrinsic values symbolize activities that are done for inherent enjoyment (e.g., play). When combined, these two axes form a matrix in which the prototype activities of youth sport can be located and a distinct learning context emerges. Accordingly, the prototype activities of deliberate practice (Ericsson, Krampe, & Tesch-Römer, 1993), play practice (Griffin & Butler, 2005; Launder, 2001), spontaneous practice (Livingstone 2002), and deliberate play (Côté, 1999; Côté, Baker, & Abernethy, 2007) result from the intersection of these two axes. Each of these prototype activities are defined below.

Activities led by adults to improve performance:

- **Deliberate practice**: According to Ericsson and colleagues (1993), engagement in deliberate practice requires effort, generates no immediate rewards, and is motivated by the goal of improving performance rather than its inherent enjoyment. The typical type of deliberate practice in youth sport includes coaches setting up drills that are aimed at improving specific skills in their young athletes. For example, a tennis coach provides instruction and technical feedback to an athlete who purposefully tries to improve her serve during a practice.

Activities led by adults to have fun:

- **Play practice**: Launder (2001) used the term 'play practice' to describe a generic type of activity in sport that is led by adults to emphasize fun and games in a practice environment. An important aspect of play practice activities is to keep youth motivated by designing activities that are enjoyable and represent the typical games that are played by youth. For instance, a coach may design an adapted game in a volleyball practice where all players have to hit underhand shots.

Activities led by youth to improve performance:

- **Spontaneous practice**: Livingstone (2002) suggested that learning that occurs outside of the curriculum of formal institutions or programs is considered an important form of education. An activity that describes this type of learning in sport could be labeled as 'spontaneous practice'. Spontaneous practice in sport is structured by youth in their free time with the goal of improving aspects of their sport skills (e.g., extrinsic value). However, in spontaneous practice, youth do not follow an adult-specified curriculum nor do they

Figure 2.1 Different dimensions of play and practice.

necessarily work on the most important skills to improve their performance. Spontaneous practice is not systematically or pedagogically planned; rather, it originates sporadically in certain situations, which are coordinated and led by the youth themselves. An example of spontaneous practice is when two athletes use their free time to practice their jump shots in basketball without supervision or direction from an adult.

Activities led by youth to have fun:

- **Deliberate play**: Côté and colleagues (Côté, 1999; Côté et al., 2007) defined deliberate play as an intrinsically-motivating activity, that provides immediate gratification, and one that is specifically designed to maximize enjoyment. Deliberate play activities, such as street basketball or soccer, are regu-

lated by rules adapted from standardized sport rules and are set up and monitored by the youth in the activity. An example of this activity is when youth get together in a yard or a public park to play soccer.

Deliberate practice, play practice, spontaneous practice, and deliberate play, and organized competition do not constitute a complete and exhaustive list of all the activities of youth sport. However, these activities are a representation of the typical characteristics of different types of involvement of youth in sport. It has been repeatedly shown that it is important to include each activity in youth sport programs as they contribute to long-term participation in sport and talent development. The developmental activities presented in this section play an important role in youth learning of new sport skills and in motivating young people to stay involved in sport.

DIVERSITY AND INTENSITY IN YOUTH SPORT

Côté and colleagues' Developmental Model of Sport Participation (DMSP; Côté et al., 2007) described two different introductory paths toward elite participation in sport which

account for youths' psychosocial, physical, and talent development. In the first path of the DMSP, children aged 6 to 12 engage in sampling, which consists of participation in a wide variety of sports that involve high levels of youth-led activities. Children who wish to engage in sport for recreational purposes will continue from the sampling years into the recreational years (ages 13+). However, youth interested in elite development will continue into the specializing years (ages 13 to 15) and then into the investment years (ages 16+). The specializing and investment years are characterized by a gradual shift of involvement from diversified sporting activities to a more intense involvement in one organized sport.

The second path of the DMSP consists of an early specialization pathway that begins at approximately age 6. Early specialization involves an intense involvement in one sport that includes mostly developmental activities that are aimed at improving performance in one sport (e.g., deliberate practice).

When considering the dichotomy of sampling and early specialization, it is apparent that both approaches can lead to talent development under optimal conditions. However, the nurturing of talent through the diversification of sports without an intense focus on one sport during childhood can have more positive outcomes and less negative consequences for all children involved in sport. For instance, although an early specialization trajectory can lead to elite performance in sport, it has also been shown to result in a reduction in physical health (i.e., overuse injuries) and enjoyment (Law, Côté, & Ericsson, 2007). Côté and Abernethy (2012) reviewed and discussed the available developmental data on sport participants and highlighted significant costs associated with an early specialization trajectory in sport. The costs of intensity over diversity in sport during childhood can be summarized under three major themes: 1) burnout and dropout; 2) recreational participation; and 3) personal development.

Burnout and dropout: Studies of burnout and dropout athletes indicate that sport programs which focus on early specialization during childhood have more psychological and physical costs than childhood sport programs that focus on involvement in a variety of sports (i.e., early sampling).

Recreational participation: Early specializers have limited exposure to different sports during childhood and this has been shown to reduce their ability and choice to get involved in sport at a recreational level later on in their lives.

Personal development: Youth sport programs provide a platform for positive youth development, and if structured appropriately, they can have direct effects on a youth's development and productivity. The literature suggests that children who sample a variety of sports are exposed to unique socialization experiences that better shape development. Because of its focus on performance outcomes for a select number of children, early specialization programs do not have the same capacity for promoting positive youth development through sport.

Because of the limited number of hours available in a given year for school, sport, and other leisure activities, young people often have to make choices in sport between diversity and intensity. A diversity choice (i.e., early sampling) involves participation in multiple sports on a yearly basis, while an intensity choice (i.e., early specialization) involves a focus on one sport year-round. It is essential that youth and adults understand and appreciate the positive influence of sampling and the costs associated with early specialization in one sport during childhood, prior to making a choice between pursuing diversity versus intensity in youth sport.

COACHING FOR TALENT DEVELOPMENT

Coaches are a central resource for talent development programs in sport. They play an important role in terms of developing athletes' sport skills as well as the personal and social competencies needed to compete at high levels of performance. Côté and Gilbert (2009) recently proposed an integrative definition of coaching effectiveness that focuses on coaches' knowledge, the different contexts in which coaches typically work, and on athlete outcomes. Based on a thorough review of coaching, teaching, athlete development, and positive psychology literature, the definition of coach effectiveness is:

The consistent application of integrated professional, interpersonal, and intrapersonal knowledge to improve athletes' competence, confidence, connection, and character in specific coaching contexts.

Coach knowledge extends beyond the commonly examined area of professional knowledge (sport-specific knowledge), to include also interpersonal (connection with others) and intrapersonal (openness to continued learning and self-reflection) forms of knowledge. Coaching contexts refer to the varied sport settings in which coaching can take place, such as coaching children or coaching adults. The final component of the integrative definition is athlete outcomes, which are defined as the 4Cs (competence, confidence, connection, and character). While the nature of the knowledge required by coaches of different sporting contexts is highly variable, the 4Cs remain stable as the ultimate indicator of athlete outcomes and coaching effectiveness. Vierimaa, Côté, Erickson, and Gilbert (2012) defined the 4Cs as sport specific constructs that serve as a metric of coaching effectiveness.

Competence: Competence is conceptualized as a high level of achievement, performance, or athletic ability. More specifically, sport competence can be broken down into general dimensions, such as: 1) technical skills; 2) tactical skills; and 3) physical skills. Coaches' ability to develop sport competence in their athletes is the most obvious knowledge components of the coaching effectiveness coaching.

Confidence: The athletes' long-term sport experiences should lead to significant and enduring changes in sport confidence. Therefore "trait sport confidence" as opposed to "state sport confidence" should be the best indicator of coaching effectiveness. Using published definitions of sport confidence, Vierimaa et al. (2012) defined sport confidence in the context of coaching as the ability for coaches to instill in their athletes, the belief that they possess the capacity to be successful in the sport that they practice.

Connection: Sport is a social phenomenon that involves interactions with other individuals. Connection is an outcome that indicates the quality of the relationships that athletes develop with other individuals in their sport environment. In order to promote connection, coaches need to engage their athletes in meaningful and positive relationships with their peers and the adults (e.g., coaches and parents) who are also involved in the sport environment.

Character: Character is defined in terms of moral development and sportspersonship behaviors. Specifically, character in sport is generally typified by the engagement in prosocial behaviors and avoidance of antisocial behaviors. 'Prosocial behaviors' are voluntary actions intending to help or benefit others; for example, helping an injured opponent. Antisocial behaviors, on the other hand, are voluntary actions intending to harm or disadvantage others, such as deliberately injuring an opponent. It is important for coaches who are involved in nurturing talent in young athletes to promote the development of character.

The 4Cs provide a concise yet comprehensive framework with which to measure performance (competence) and psychosocial outcomes (confidence, connection, and character) in long-term talent development programs for athletes. Together, these four constructs represent a holistic approach to talent development that incorporates traditional goals of youth sport programs (e.g., skill development and performance) with an added emphasis on positive psychosocial development. Because the road to talent development in sport involves distinct stages and learning contexts, coaches must be aware of the overriding sport context in which they work. In other words, coaches must recognize how the needs of their athletes change across the different talent development phases, from childhood to adulthood.

According to the definition of coaching effectiveness described in this section, coaches in different contexts will require a different mix of professional, interpersonal, and intrapersonal knowledge, in order to develop an athlete's competence, confidence, connection, and character. For example, developing 10-year-old basketball players' 4Cs will require different coaching expertise, than the development of 4Cs in professional basketball players. Based on an extensive review of athlete development literature, Côté and Gilbert (2009) suggested different profiles of coaching objectives for four different types of coaching contexts: 1) participation coach for children; 2) performance coach for young adolescents; 3) performance coach for older adolescents and adults; and 4) participation coach for adolescents and adults. The first three contexts are relevant to coaching athletes who are on a talent development pathway. Keeping with the terminology used in this chapter, we can re-conceptualize the first three of coach contexts as: 1) coach for children; 2) coach for young adolescents who choose to specialize in a sport; and 3) coach for older adolescents and adults who choose to invest in a sport. The different types of knowledge required by coaches at different phases of an athlete's development of talent in sport were adapted from Côté and Gilbert, and are reproduced below.

Coach for children:

1   Adopt an inclusive selection policy as opposed to an exclusive performance-based selection policy.

2   Organize a mastery-oriented motivational climate.
3   Set up safe opportunities for athletes to have fun and engage playfully in low-organization games.
4   Teach and assess the development of fundamental movements by focusing on the child first.
5   Promote the social aspect of sport and sampling.

Coach for young adolescents who choose to specialize in a sport:

1   Organize the sport experience to promote a focus on one sport.
2   Teach the "rules of competition".
3   Offer opportunities for fun with increasingly greater demands for deliberate practice.
4   Teach and assess physical, technical, perceptual, and mental skills in a safe environment.
5   Present positive growth opportunities through sport (i.e., civic engagement, responsibility).

Coach for older adolescents and adults who choose to invest in a sport:

1   Set up a training regime grounded in deliberate practice.
2   Allow athletes the appropriate amount of mental and physical rest.
3   Prepare athletes for consistent high-level competitive performance.
4   Teach and assess physical, technical, and tactical skills in a safe environment.
5   Provide opportunities for athletes to prepare for "life after sport".

The different profiles of coaches presented above illustrate the unique knowledge of each coaching context that is necessary to nurture talent development in sport, which require the integration of the 4Cs in talent development sport programs. Coaches that focus on developing talent will require a high level of professional, interpersonal, and intrapersonal knowledge. However, there will be variation between each context due to the nature of the knowledge required to develop an athlete's competence, confidence, connection, and character.

PARENTS

In a large study of talented teenagers, Csikszentmihalyi, Rathunde, and Whalen (1993) suggested that "a home environment in which one is secure enough to feel cheerful and energetic, and challenged enough to become more goal-directed, increases teenagers' chances of progressively refining their talents" (p. 175). It is essential to recognize that the family is a social group that may appear in diverse forms; families appear in various settings, have a unique set of experiences, and are in constant development. Different types of families include parents and their biological or adopted children, single parent families, and extended families. These properties that define families, underline the distinctiveness of family groups that may be involved in sport. Independent of how a family is constituted, young athletes require a form of support from individuals within the family unit in order to realize their full potential in sport. Because sport literature has mostly studied parents as the provider of support for youth development in sport, the literature on parents will be described below. That being said, it is important to note that other individuals within a family unit can potentially provide the psychological and social support necessary for youth to develop and maintain an identity, self-esteem, and motivation for sport participation and performance.

Hellstedt (1987) suggested that parents' involvement in their children's sport participation can be conceptualized on a continuum from under-involved, to moderately-involved, to over-involved. He proposed that moderately-involved parents provide more positive conditions to an athlete's talent development than over- and under-involved parents. Therefore, on this continuum, parental involvement could range from being perceived as insufficient to overwhelming for athletes, which provokes negative outcomes. Hellstedt's (1987) description of parental involvement provides a generic understanding of the amount of involvement that leads to continued participation in sport; however, the question regarding the optimal amount of parental support necessary for talent development in sport has been underexplored and deserves more consideration. The literature on parental support, which will be discussed next, extends this view by identifying the nature of the support associated with young athletes' motivation and talent development.

PARENTAL SUPPORT

Parents' psychosocial support is an essential element in the development of youth self-esteem, competence, and achievement. Côté and Hay (2002) suggested four categories of psychological needs for young athletes: 1) emotional support; 2) informational support; 3) tangible support; and 4) companionship. Emotional support is provided through parents' comforting gestures during times of stress and anxiety. When parents give their child positive feedback on his or her ability or express belief in their child's capabilities, this enhances the child's belief that he or she is cared for. These supportive efforts and gestures can enhance a child's sense of competence and confidence (Cutrona & Russell, 1990). Informational support refers to parents' provision of advice or guidance in situations of uncertainty. For example, parents can provide general information on how to choose a suitable sport program and when to begin specializing in one sport.

Tangible support refers to the concrete assistance provided to children in order to sustain their participation in sport. Examples of tangible support include providing the financial assistance or the time commitment necessary for lessons, equipment, and travel associated with sport participation. Overall, tangible support is required for participation in most sport programs, and the lack of tangible support can certainly become a constraint to a child's sport participation and talent development. Companionship, or "network support", reflects informal relationships that enable an individual to engage in various forms of social and recreational activities (Cutrona & Russell, 1990). Parents can be involved in various kinds of companionship related to their child's participation in sport. For instance, parents can develop special relationships with their children through sports by attending professional or amateur sporting events with their child, collecting sports cards for their child, getting involved in deliberate play with their child, or simply by spending time travelling to and from practices with their child (Côté, 1999).

Fraser-Thomas, Strachan, and Jeffery-Tosoni (2013) recently reviewed the literature on parental influence and talent development and suggested a series of behaviors that emerge from various studies as being critical elements of parental support. They recommended that independent of an athlete's stage of talent development, parents of youth should create task-oriented climates at home that are supportive of youth autonomy. Furthermore, instead of creating or supporting unreasonable performance objectives for their child-athlete, parents should model life skills and positive sport participation. In terms of age-specific behaviors, Fraser-Thomas et al. emphasized the following behaviors:

Parents of children in sport (approximately ages 6–12):

1 Engage in **play** activities with child.
2 Provide opportunities to sample different sports.
3 Provide positive and encouraging feedback.
4 Avoid giving constant technical instruction.

Parents of adolescents who choose to specialize and invest in a sport (approximately ages 13–18):

1 Increase provision of tangible support.
2 Discuss career transitions and choices regarding intensity of training.
3 Provide feedback regarding youth attitude and effort in sport.
4 Avoid overemphasizing outcomes (e.g., winning).

Parents have a critical role in nurturing talent development in sport during childhood and adolescence. It is important to acknowledge the dynamic role parents play, which begins as a leadership role during childhood, and transitions to a guiding role during adolescence. Parents assume a leadership role during childhood by initially getting their children interested in sport by allowing them to sample a wide range of enjoyable sporting activities. When youth start to invest more seriously in one sport during adolescence, parents become guiding and supporting figures that help youth make the right decisions about the intensity of their involvement. During the stressful adolescent period of talent development in sport, parents' primary role is to foster an optimal learning environment rather than creating new demands or pressure.

LEARNING AIDS

1 Define deliberate practice.

   Deliberate practice is effortful, generates no immediate rewards, and is motivated by the goal of improving performance rather than inherent enjoyment.

2 Explain the difference between talent identification and talent development.

   For talent identification, adults evaluate skill-based performance and select "talented" children to become part of elite programs. Conversely, the primary purpose of talent development is to help children enjoy sport while learning skills and promote a sporting environment that focuses on the development of the person in sport.

3 Describe the relationship between diversity and intensity in sport.

   Typically, as diversity of sports decreases (e.g., going from playing four sports to two sports), the intensity of commitment to the remaining sports increases.

4 Discuss the stages of the Developmental Model of Sport Participation (DMSP).

   The sampling years (age 6 to 12) are characterized by diversity and involvement in various sports, low amounts of deliberate practice, and high amounts of deliberate play. The specializing years (age 13 to 15) involve a narrowing of sporting activities and equal amounts of deliberate practice and deliberate play. The investment years (age 16+) see a focus on one sport and a drastic increase in deliberate practice with low amounts of deliberate play.

5 Identify the three main knowledge components of the coaching effectiveness definition.
   Professional knowledge, interpersonal knowledge, and intrapersonal knowledge. These knowledge bases combine to impact athletes' competence, confidence, connection, and character in sport.

REVIEW QUESTIONS

1 What are the four main types of developmental activities? Describe and provide an example for each activity.

2 What are the pros and cons of early specialization in sport? Which sports typically have athletes who specialize at an early age?

3 In your own words, what is the definition of coaching effectiveness? Provide a unique example of each component of the definition.

4 What types of parental support have been identified in this chapter? Describe and provide an example for each type of support.

EXERCISES

1 Read a biography of a famous athlete. When reading, think about the types of coaching and parental support that the athlete received.

2 Interview a friend regarding their sport experiences. Specifically, ask about the developmental activities that they engaged in (e.g., play versus practice), as well as the sport stream they entered (e.g., sampling versus specializing).

3 Go to a local youth sporting event and sit in the stands with the parents. Record the types of support the parents offer the athletes. Do you think parents are mostly positive or negative with their support?

4 Visit the following web address:

http://www.athleticmanagement.com/2012/02/28/timeless_lessons/index.php. Based on this article, explain how John Wooden met the criteria of an effective coach.

NOTE

1 Authors' note: Preparation of this chapter was supported by Social Sciences and Humanities Research Council of Canada (SSHRC) standard research grant (#410-2011-0472).

ADDITIONAL READING

Bloom, B.S. (1985). *Developing talent in young people.* New York, NY: Ballantine.

Côté, J. & Lidor, R. (2013). *Conditions of children's talent development in sport.* Morgantown, WV: Fitness Information Technology.

Farrow, D., Baker, J. & MacMahon, C. (2013). *Developing elite sport performance: Lessons from theory and practice* (2nd ed.), New York, NY: Routledge.

REFERENCES

Côté, J. (1999). The influence of the family in the development of talent in sport. *The Sport Psychologist, 13,* 395–417.

Côté, J. (2009). The road to continued sport participation and excellence. In E. Tsung-Min Hung, R. Lidor & D. Hackfort (Eds.), *Psychology of sport excellence* (pp.97–104). Morgantown, WV: Fitness Information Technology.

Côté, J. & Abernethy, B. (2012). A developmental approach to sport expertise. In S. Murphy (Ed.), *The Oxford handbook of sport and performance psychology* (pp.435–447). New York, NY: Oxford University Press.

Côté, J., Baker, J. & Abernethy, B. (2007). Practice and play in the development of sport expertise. In G. Tenenbaum & R. Eklund (Eds.), *Handbook of sport psychology* (3rd ed.), (pp.184–202). Hoboken, NJ: Wiley.

Côté, J., Erickson, K. & Abernethy, B. (2013). Practice and play in sport development. In J. Côté & R. Lidor (Eds.), *Condition of children's talent development in sport* (pp.9–20). Morgantown, WV: Fitness Information Technology.

Côté, J. & Gilbert, W. (2009). An integrative definition of coaching effectiveness and expertise. *International Journal of Sports Science and Coaching, 4*, 307–323.

Côté, J. & Hay, J. (2002). Family influences on youth sport participation and performance. In J.M. Silva & D. Stevens (Eds.), *Psychological foundations of sport* (pp.503–519). Boston, MA: Allyn and Bacon.

Csikszentmihalyi, M., Rathunde, K. & Whalen, S. (1993). *Talented teenagers: The roots of success and failure.* New York, NY: Cambridge.

Cutrona, C.E. & Russell, D.W. (1990). Type of social support and specific stress: Toward a theory of optimal matching. In B.R. Sarason, I.G. Sarason & G.R. Pierce (Eds.), *Social support: An interactional view* (pp.319–366). New York, NY: J. Wiley & Sons.

Ericsson, K.A., Krampe, R.T. & Tesch-Römer, C. (1993). The role of deliberate practice in the acquisition of expert performance. *Psychological Review, 100*, 363–406.

Fraser-Thomas, J., Strachan, L. & Jeffery-Tosoni, S. (2013). Family influence on children's involvement in sport. In J. Côté & R. Lidor (Eds.), *Condition of children's talent development in sport* (pp.179–196). Morgantown, WV: Fitness Information Technology.

Griffin, L.L. & Butler, J.I. (2005). *Teaching games for understanding: Theory, research, and practice.* Champaign, IL: Human Kinetics.

Hellstedt, J.C. (1987). The coach/parent/athlete relationship. *The Sport Psychologist, 1*, 151–160.

Launder, A.G. (2001). *Play practice: The games approach to teaching and coaching sports.* Champaign, IL: Human Kinetics.

Law, M.P., Côté, J. & Ericsson, K.A. (2007). Characteristics of expert development in rhythmic gymnastics: A retrospective study. *International Journal of Sport and Exercise Psychology, 5*, 82–103.

Livingstone, D.W. (2002). Mapping the iceberg. Retrieved from http://www.nall.ca/res/54David Livingstone.pdf

Vaeyens, R., Gullich, A., Warr, C.R. & Philippaerts, R. (2009). Talent identification and promotion programmes of Olympic athletes. *Journal of Sports Sciences, 27*, 1367–1380.

Vierimaa, M., Erickson, K., Côté, J. & Gilbert, W. (2012). Positive youth development: A measurement framework for sport. *International Journal of Sports Science and Coaching, 7*, 601–614.

Chapter 3

Self-esteem and self-perceptions in sport and exercise

KENNETH R. FOX AND MAGNUS LINDWALL

SUMMARY

Experiencing self-esteem is one of the most important of psychological needs. It is associated with good mental health, how well we cope with the stresses and strains we face, and has an important influence on our choice of and persistence in behaviours. Our level of self-esteem is determined by the way we see ourselves, or our self-perceptions in the many aspects of life in which we are involved. Those aspects closest to us are the most salient, such as family and friendships, and how we look and how we perform at school or work. This complex of experiences is used to form an overall impression of worth or esteem that carries powerful emotions such as pride and shame. Because we enjoy feeling good about ourselves, we tend to make the most of those aspects of life which provide success and achievement and avoid negative experiences. Sport and exercise involvement is very public and can have strong positive or negative effects on self-perceptions and self-esteem. If coaches, teachers and health professionals are to get the best out of people in terms of their achievement and psychological well-being, it is critical that they understand the whole person and how experiences they help to create affect an individual's self-perceptions and self-esteem. This chapter presents examples from exercise participation and sport performance settings to help leaders develop effective strategies for fostering positive self-perceptions and self-esteem.

INTRODUCTION

Think of times when you were growing up or even more recently as an adult when you might have felt embarrassed, incompetent, unwanted, downhearted, or a hopeless failure. These expe- riences can seriously challenge your self- esteem. It may not have knocked all the stuffing out of you but it certainly made you feel low for a while. Several knocks like this in succession could have a more permanent effect on your feelings and subsequent decisions. The most common response, and the one that seems very sensible at the time, is to avoid from that point on the situation that caused the bad feeling. At school, if you felt useless in sport or physical education, because you could not run fast, throw or kick a ball, or jump as high as others, then it is understandable that you don't look forward to PE lessons. You are likely to drop them as soon as you are allowed, especially if you are made to feel inadequate by an unsympathetic teacher or teasing friends. Similarly, if you feel unattractive or overweight, particularly if you have been told so by people who are important to you, then it might not be surprising that you lack confidence in front of others and tend to shy away from participation. Of course there can be a very positive side to playing sports and exercise. Performing well, being recognized as a good player, being part of a team, improving your fitness or losing weight through hard work can make you feel great and want more and more. These are examples from sport and exercise of how experiences in aspects of our lives can determine our self-perceptions, and how these in turn shape our choices, persistence and performances in different behaviours. These can have both short- and long-term consequences for our self-esteem.

What we think about our *physical* selves, or our bodies in terms of what they look like and how well they work to perform skills and activities, seems to be particularly important. Psychologists have suggested that the physical self functions as the *public* self. Our body is what we display and what people see. It provides the way we present ourselves to others in terms of our prowess, status, personality and sexuality. This has a powerful effect on how one is viewed by others as a person, particularly in the early phases of acquaintance. This in turn can have an important influence on our lives and reflect how we see and value ourselves.

Compared to some behaviours and pastimes such as reading or playing computer games, sport and exercise inherently draw attention to the physical self. They usually take place in the presence of several other people whether they are co-participants or spectators. Our appearance and physical performance are therefore open to public evaluation, making the experience even more salient. Doing well and looking good can make us feel elated and confident, while a poor showing makes us feel incompetent or inadequate in the eyes of others. It is therefore very important for effective sport and exercise leadership to have a good understanding of the way participants react in terms of self-perceptions to their sport and exercise experiences. As sport and exercise professionals, we are usually in a position of power and are often well-regarded so we have a particular responsibility to help our clients develop positive views of their abilities and self-esteem. This in turn will stimulate their motivation, they will try harder, and it will help them to perform and participate to their full potential. This chapter is written to help sport and exercises coaches and teachers achieve this.

 ## OBJECTIVES

The overall aim of this chapter therefore is to help future sport coaches, physical education teachers, and exercise specialists to understand more about the psychology of self so that their practice can be more effective. Specifically by the end of the chapter you should be better equipped to:

1   Understand the meaning of self-esteem and how it is shaped by our feelings about ourselves in different aspects of our lives.
2   Understand how self-esteem affects our attitudes, choices, persistence and performances in sport and exercise.

3 Understand how coaching and teaching decisions can have positive or negative influences on self-esteem and self-perceptions.

4 Develop a style of coaching that promotes involvement in sports and exercise, improves performance and develops self-esteem.

UNDERSTANDING THE SELF

In addition to social and developmental psychology, the self has been the subject of research and debate in disciplines as diverse as sociology, philosophy, theology and even politics. As a result, there are volumes of literature and many different terms are used when discussing this topic, making its study seem complex and confusing.

What is self-concept? If asked to describe yourself, you are likely to mention the roles you hold in life such as being a daughter, student, or athlete, or personal characteristics such as the way you look and how you do things. This self description is often termed *self-concept* and does not necessarily carry any judgment about self. It is just a way of explaining what you see about yourself in terms of your characteristics and who you are.

What is self-esteem? Self-esteem is more critical in that it carries a value judgment. It is interpreted as overall (global) feelings of worth, respect and value for self, and summarized by the degree to which an individual feels they are a good or an 'OK' person. It is a fairly stable construct but powerful and consistent experiences can change self-esteem over time. It is important because it affects our emotions in a deep way helping us feel pride, satisfaction, and optimism when it is high, or sadness, shame and hopelessness when it is low. Each individual to some extent is free to use whatever criteria he/she wishes to determine the degree of 'OK-ness' so the sources vary according to what he or she values. However, the society or culture in which we live and the way we were brought up also set these values for us. Criteria will also vary across the lifespan as our expectations change, with older adults thinking somewhat differently to teenagers about how they would

like to see themselves. Looking slim, fit and attractive and being a high achiever in work or a pursuit such as sport are very powerful and pervasive criteria that hold high status in western societies. Being well brought up suggests that virtues such as honesty, empathy, being unselfish, or a good team player might be important. However, it is also possible that less virtuous characteristics might provide esteem in some subcultures. For example, being the most violent leader in a youth gang or the dirtiest player in the team can also bring esteem in circles that value those characteristics. In that sense, feeling good about the self does not necessarily mean moral goodness. It is derived from what is valued by the person and his/her subculture. Therefore to understand how self-perceptions drive an individual's motivation, we also have to establish what they consider important to them, or their value systems.

What are self-perceptions? This is a general term that usually refers to descriptions or appraisals in specific roles or life settings. Sometimes they reflect identities such as "I am an exerciser" and often provide assessments of competence such as "I am really good at sport", "I am one of the worst spellers in class", or "I am no good with girls because I feel shy". As we develop through childhood and adolescence we become more complex and sophisticated in our self-knowledge, and the life domains where we are able to make self-judgments become more numerous and differentiated. For example, by mid-adolescence we might have unique perceptions of our performance in each school subject and our social competence with same-sex as well as opposite-sex friends. Our views of ourselves in the physical domain includes perceptions of sport competence, physical strength, fitness, and appearance and each of these will be split into perceptions of performance in different kinds of sports, or even different skills in single sports, or different aspects of appearance.

These ratings of competence or adequacy are often gathered to formulate estimates of self-esteem. It appears that these can be organized in a hierarchical way so that very specific competence ratings that are frequently repeated and consistent feed up to more general levels of perceptions and eventually may influence self-

esteem (see Figure 3.1). Very specific self-perceptions such as "I can run a mile in less than seven minutes" tie in with Bandura's (1986) self-efficacy theory and so are often termed "efficacy statements" or "expectancies". Repeated success at this level is thought to improve higher, more global levels of self-perceptions. For example, consistent improvements with performance in the football team or success with a weight loss and exercise plan might improve feelings about the physical self and eventually generalize to higher self-esteem.

OTHER IMPORTANT SELF CONSTRUCTS

The hierarchical organization of the self depicted in Figure 3.1 provides a useful framework for viewing the diverse elements of the

self complex. Over the years, many important elements have received special attention by researchers. For example, because of Western

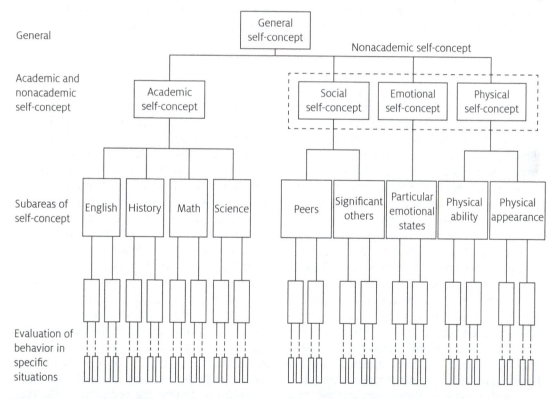

Figure 3.1 Levels of specificity of self-perceptions within the physical domain.

Source Shavelson, R. J., Hubner, J. J., & Stanton, G. C. (1976). Self-concept: Validation of construct interpretations. *Review of Educational Research*, 46, 407–411. Copyright is the American Educational Research Association.

society's emphasis on "looking good", *body image* – and its influence on mental health and behaviours such as eating and exercise – has been widely investigated. Body image has been defined as the internal representation (picture) of our outer appearance (Thompson, Heinberg, Altabe, & Tantleff-Dunn, 1999), or one's body-related self-perceptions and self-attitudes, including thoughts, beliefs, feelings, and behaviour (Cash, 2004). Another concept closely related to body image and the physical self is *social physique anxiety*, which has been described as "a subtype of social anxiety that occurs as a result of the prospect or interpersonal evaluation involving one's physique" (Hart, Leary, & Rejeski, 1989, p. 96). Individuals with high social physique anxiety are more likely to avoid situations in which they are forced to reveal their body (for example, at the gym, on beaches, or in swimming facilities) to others and face a potential evaluation of others.

SELF-MANAGEMENT STRATEGIES

Establishing and maintaining self-esteem is a complex process. The self is nurtured by an innate drive to explore and develop while simultaneously establishing a coherent base from which to operate. Thus, stability across time and consistency across situations in patterns of behaviour and emotional reactions provide the sense of identity and predictability that ties the self together. This is important in order to make lasting relationships and rational decisions because consistency allows people to understand us or get to know us and thus relate to us more effectively. This consistency of identity in turn nurtures the necessary roots for individuals to seek out challenges that facilitate personal learning and growth. The self is left with a delicate balancing act of establishing a solid and recognizable core or identity while retaining sufficient flexibility to accept the challenges of individual development and not stifle opportunities for personal improvement. If I know who I am and I am reasonably happy with myself, then I have the confidence to take on challenges and I am receptive to changing aspects of myself. Those people who have not developed their core fully tend to be defensive of their selves and more conservative in their behavioural choices. They cannot afford to allow themselves to be challenged, as they are more fearful of failure. These processes become transparent during major transitional periods across the lifespan such as adolescence and retirement. They are all too evident in sport where players who lack confidence can be too conservative in their play and avoid taking risks because of a fear of failure. "Let someone else shoot" might be the order of the day. Coaches can help by learning whether this lack of confidence is an issue of low-perceived competence at performing the skill or a more generalized lack of esteem. The former requires specific practices while the latter needs some empathy and sensitivity and perhaps some coaching about how to deal with failure and disassociate it from worth as a person. Behaviours that reflect low self-esteem are feature in Table 3.1.

Human nature is designed for survival and this includes looking after psychological well-being. There is good evidence to show that we are programmed to think positively in order to make the best of what happens in our lives. This function can be conceived as a *self-director* who may operate both consciously and subconsciously to manage behaviours and mentally process what happens to the self in a way that maximizes good feelings. The self-director, which is analogous to a company director, determines where to invest time and energy in serving this mission. This involves making choices, commitment and persistence in relevant tasks to produce positive balance sheets, and deployment of public relation strategies to present the company in the best possible light. There is evidence of several strategies that are used with regard to self-esteem and the physical self. Examples are:

Table 3.1 *Recognizing low self-esteem and confidence in sport*

Although there are some obvious signs of low confidence such as shyness and slowness to step up to the line, there are also some more hidden signs:

- There is a need for a great deal of positive and consistent praise and feedback, especially following a failure or a negative comment.
- There may be a tendency to criticise the performance of other players in order to boost their own standing.
- There is a tendency to be fearful of taking risks but some will also choose high-risk strategies because the expectation is that failure is inevitable and not their fault.
- There may be a tendency for some to accept the blame for all failure and feel depressed. However, others may always try to place blame elsewhere because they are not strong enough to take responsibility for failure.
- They may find it difficult to feel part of the team because they do not feel they are worthy contributors.
- They may avoid putting in maximum effort. The classic phrase "don't let them see me sweat" comes into play here and arises because it is only possible to judge a player's true potential when he/she is stretched to full capacity. These players give the impression they don't really care but in reality are hiding a lack of confidence.

- Customizing the self complex by attaching importance to those aspects or domains of life that yield success and minimizing the importance of those which provide feelings of inadequacy or low competence. This latter process has been termed *discounting* (Harter, 1999). Many adolescent girls, for example, discount the importance of feeling that they are not very good at sports and are apathetic about taking part. However, some areas that carry a high cultural currency may be too overpowering to allow an individual to discount it. Attractiveness is one such area that is troublesome to discount for females, and increasingly for young males.
- Using *self-presentation strategies* to convince others that the self is doing well (Leary, 1995). Such external relations strategies could include accentuating the positive dimensions of the self while concealing the troublesome aspects that leave the self vulnerable to negative evaluation. This extends to choices of behaviours. For example, people will tend to gravitate to settings where they feel they will look good and perform well. This might explain why health clubs tend to attract people who are already reasonably fit and slim.

- *Self-serving bias* is evident in the interpretation of incoming information. Negative information is more likely to be ignored and forgotten while successes are embellished. The self is more likely to ascribe failure to external sources such as luck or an opponent who was too tough while success is attributed to personal ability and effort. Individuals therefore tend to view themselves in a rather optimistic light. They tend to believe they have greater control over events in their environment than they actually have, they tend to accept more than their fare share of successes and sometimes do not fully accept their part in failures, and they tend to view the future in a "rosier" light than might be justified.

Intuitively it might be seen that having these positive illusions might be bad for the individual. However, what is interesting is that positive illusions seem to be related to positive health, both mentally and physically (Taylor et al., 2003). On the whole, they are therefore seen as healthy mental strategies and should be expected and encouraged rather than stifled. Of course there is potential for the self to overplay these self-serving cards. Excessive reliance produces delusions of grandeur, over-confidence, boastfulness and a loss of touch with reality that can result in impairment to further learning and social relationships. Not understanding or accepting the true reasons for success and failure will impair learning for the future. Moreover, discounting certain behaviours such as physical activity that are integrally linked with physical health will impair motivation which is counterproductive to health promotion. In summary, self-serving strategies promote optimism, motivation, confidence and well-being but in excess are dangerous because they can impede learning and progress.

DEVELOPMENT OF SELF-PERCEPTIONS

The concepts described so far apply to maturing adolescents and adults. Children are different because they have not fully developed the cognitive capacity to accurately assess the self and understand how it functions in performance and social interactions (Harter, 1999). Very young children aged between six and around nine years old have very simple views of their self and are quite unrealistic and optimistic in their views of how they rank in comparison to others in school work and physical skills. They have naturally positive views on life and believe that strong performances are simply a result of trying hard. "Jimmy won the race because he tried hardest". They rarely have the capacity to understand abstractions such as health or to be stimulated by distant rewards such as improving fitness. They are highly motivated by the "here and now" so that activity, for example, has to be seen as fun. As children develop, they begin to understand the concept of ability and that it contributes – alongside effort – to level of performance. They realize that other children do not have to try quite so hard to win because they have natural ability. This is important because around ages 10 to 12 years, children become more accurate in their assessment of their own ability levels. If they start to believe that they have low competence, even when they try as hard as they can, and it does not yield success, then they start to look for alternative activities. In severe cases "learned helplessness" can set in where engagement is completely withdrawn. Table 3.2 illustrates this concept in the setting of a fitness test in physical education. Strategies to help such children stay involved are presented later.

Table 3.2 *An example of learned helplessness in fitness testing*

Learned helplessness: No matter how hard I try it does not seem to make a difference
Antony is an overweight 12 year old asked to perform the aerobic fitness shuttle run test in physical education class with all his class mates.

Outcomes:

- Scores low even though he tries hard
- Highly public exposure of his poor performance
- Makes him feel that he could never be like the others
- Convinces him that exercise is to be avoided at all costs

- Starts to use defensive strategies
  - Absence
  - Disruption
  - Never show effort
  - Attach low importance – what's the point in it?
- Avoids similar activities for the rest of his life

Also, children tend to differ in how they view and evaluate things like intelligence and achievement (Dweck, 2000). For example, some view achievement in sport as a fixed thing that you either have or you don't have. Others, instead, view sport achievement as something more dynamic and malleable, something that can be changed and worked on, primarily through effort and commitment. These two different mindsets will also have a large impact on how children and youths behave in the context of sport and exercise. For example, it will influence how they interpret success and failure, and how they are motivated to improve or try out new tasks. A person with the fixed mindset will more often choose the easy way, rather than going for challenging tasks, and making sure of success and avoidance of failure in order to maintain a positive self-esteem. To the contrary, a person with the malleable mindset is more likely to seek out and enjoy challenges as this will probably increase their learning, which is one of the key motivational aspects for them, rather than to constantly win and beat others. In other words, they are less likely to be afraid of failing.

HOW TO HELP PEOPLE EXPERIENCE POSITIVE SELF-ESTEEM AND SELF-PERCEPTIONS

Psychologists have also been drawing upon self-determination theory (SDT) as a framework for building strategies for promoting self-esteem (see Chapter 5). According to this theory, the individual (the self-director) is constantly engaged in a process of integrating appropriate input from the environment into identity (Deci & Ryan, 1985, 2000). In order for the self to develop, flourish and function well, it helps if the individual feels that three fundamental psychological needs are satisfied. These are competence, autonomy or self-determination, and relatedness (for more information on these needs, see Chapter 5). Settings and experiences in sport and exercise can either promote the satisfaction of these basic psychological needs, or hinder and thwart them. Therefore, for coaches and teachers in sport and exercise, an important step in the promotion of positive self-esteem and self-perceptions is to establish relationships, communications style, and challenges that help the individual experience competence, autonomy, and relatedness. This sounds simple enough, but how is it achieved?

BUILDING COMPETENCE

Building perceptions of competence in all people can be difficult as in reality there is a whole spectrum of ability levels for each particular skill. Those interested in helping a whole range of people become active have to work particularly hard as often those least competent are in most need of assistance. It is also not so straightforward for elite performers. Even true objective achievements such as winning a competition may not be enough to make some of them feel competent. The sport and exercise world is full of individuals who, according to league tables and outcomes from competitions, should be viewed as very competent, but who may not see themselves that way. There may be several reasons for this, but often it is caused by over-reliance on social comparison with others. This is fraught with dangers. For example, the young player who is seen as a brilliant young talent at local level is likely to eventually be selected into a group of elite players, all of whom may be more proficient. A high competence rating when compared to local players becomes a low competence rating in the newly acquired group. This "big fish, little pond" phenomena (Marsh and Parker, 1984) is well documented and often happens when youngsters move from junior to senior school. Similarly, if Sue has lost ten kilos over six months through great efforts in the gym but resets her aspirations for becoming similarly slimmer and fitter like those around her, she may not experience the enhanced sense of competence that should come from her obvious success. Social comparisons cause particular problems for the physical educator who is faced with a class of children with a wide range of physical abilities. The challenge becomes how to keep all these children equally challenged, interested and feeling positive about the physical abilities? Clearly, not all children can be *excellent* in terms of sports skills by its very definition.

The world of sport and exercise is full of opportunity to make comparisons with others in terms of appearance and skill level. It is difficult to avoid and we have a natural tendency to seek out how we rank against others in a whole range of personal attributes. However, it is dangerous to rely on this as the main source of competence information. This is because the ability of others is beyond our control. The strongest strategy for the coach or teacher is therefore to encourage people from an early age to focus on personal progress and improvement (see Table 3.3). This self-referencing approach, which is often called a mastery or task orientation, has been widely studied in sport under the framework of achievement orientation theory (see Chapter 4). Ego orientation features a reliance on favourable comparisons against others as the main source of competence. Task orientation, on the other hand, focuses on skill or fitness improvement and task mastery and is the only means by which all people, regardless of actual ability level can experience success. However, it also provides a critical back-up strategy and realistic marker for elite sport performers to interpret win and loss in competition. Feeling that you have played really well but have lost is probably more valuable for self-esteem than winning when playing poorly. An important job for coaches therefore is to create activities and tasks that challenge the individuals skills and abilities in an optimal way while at the same time downplaying the natural tendency to worry about comparisons, rankings and league tables. See Table 3.3 and the case studies in Table 3.4 for some ideas. Working with goal-setting, the coach can help the individual to identify realistic goals. At this point, setting up a plan for how to reach these goals is critical. A general recommendation is to start off gently, in particular with beginners, and make steady progress at each stage or level of difficulty so that individuals have a chance to gradually build confidence in their own ability to succeed. Success breeds further motivation and success.

BUILDING AUTONOMY

If individuals feel controlled, or that they do not have a part to play in their own progress, or that someone else is the master of their actions, the chances that they will feel autonomous are slim. As coaches and teachers, our own sense of reward often comes from seeing the success of those we work with. There is a danger that we will start to believe and operate in a way that convinces our athletes that *we* are the reason for their success. In order to avoid depriving them of a sense of self-determination or autonomy it is important that they are engaged in decisions and choices about their training and progress and that they are allowed to take full credit for successes and failures. In this sense, the coach is best advised to adopt a position of a facilitator and take more of an advisory rather than dictatorial or prescriptive role. Sometimes coaches have to work hard to convince athletes of their full role in outcomes as they may be accustomed to many years of being told what to do. Something like: "You were successful because YOU put in all that effort to training last month. YOU did it. I just advised you on what I thought would lead to that success but YOU did it", might reflect the kind of response needed. This situation can also apply to physical education. PE teachers should consider the percentage of time that they adopt the role of "instructor" and whether or not dominant role of their communication is command style. Although, the practicalities of managing a class of 30 youngsters will always require respect for the teacher as leader, there may be opportunities for youngsters to provide input into choice of activities, designs of exercise circuits, ways of scoring games, and goal setting. For the coach and teacher to provide an environment that fosters autonomy, it is therefore important to express selflessness, respect and empathy in their daily interactions with those they are working with. As a result, there should be a greater chance for growth, improvement, motivation, and commitment.

Table 3.3 *Strategies for helping build confidence and self-esteem*

It is essential to recognize when low self-esteem players need help. Leaders will be more effective if they understand and empathize with their players. Sometimes this does not come naturally to coaches but the following might help:

- For low self-esteem players, provide three times more positive feedback than you think they need.
- Make sure any critique is aimed at their performance and not at them as individuals and always offer a feasible strategy for them to improve.
- Avoid personal stable descriptors such as "You always get that wrong" and provide strategies that lead to solutions.
- Convince them that failures are inevitable, they happen to everyone, and are a vital part of learning. Encourage them to expect failure as a source of important information about how to improve. Rebranding failure as a "good guy" can reduce anxieties and provide licence to take more risks.
- Help build a sense of patience so that improvement is steady but consistent through small incremental goal-setting.

Table 3.4 *Examples in practice*

CASE STUDY 1: MOTIVATING YOUNG KIDS

Billy loves his football. His brother, who is four years older, was selected as a youth player for the town's professional club so Billy was excited when his friend Kyle suggested they join up with a local Saturday morning under 11s squad. For the first three games, although Kyle got to play as a striker, Billy sat on the bench as sub. Although he was disappointed, his big chance came in the second half of a friendly game when his team were winning 2-0 and he was called on. Unfortunately, the other team quickly drew back to 2-2. Although Billy knew that one of the goals was probably his fault, he thought he had played fairly well for a first attempt, the coach decided he was at least partly at fault and decided to sub him back to the bench. Billy felt humiliated and useless and the action of the coach turned some of the other players against him as his team went on to lose 3-2. Billy felt he had let everyone down and that he was no longer liked by his friends. He never turned up for another football team again, even though he became much quicker and more skilful as he matured.

Lessons to the coach:

- Don't sacrifice the self-esteem of young kids for the sake of winning the game
- Explain your actions to players so they develop understanding
- Give players help with how to improve and how to deal with failure

Lessons for Billy:

- Don't give up because you are not the finished product – keep practicing
- Football is not the only important thing in your life
- Find a better coach

Table 3.4 *(continued)*

CASE STUDY 2: WORKING WITH AN ELITE ATHLETE FEARFUL OF FAILURE

Sara is 16 years old and a very talented tennis player. She is the highest ranked player of her age in her country and also ranked top three internationally. As far as she can remember, everybody around her, her parents and coaches, have told her that she has a natural talent for tennis and that she will go all the way to the top. She always won against kids of her own age, and never really had to put any effort to succeed when playing tennis. Come to think of it, she never really experienced any real failure, when playing tennis.

During the last year, however, her coach and parents have decided that it is time to let her take on some tougher opponents, some older girls. However, Sara starts to lose many of her matches. What's more alarming though is the way she loses and her behaviour. She makes many unprovoked errors and plays way below her usual standards. Normally, she is intense and aggressive in her play, but now she looks either mentally absent or bored. To her coach, it actually looks like she doesn't care. When confronted with this, Sara gets angry and replies that she doesn't feel like trying. She has also mentioned a couple of times that she thinks about quitting tennis, and that it's just not fun anymore.

Her coach discusses the issue with a colleague who is a sport psychologist and asks for her advice. They decide they will talk to Sara together. In the first conversations, about why she thinks she is not performing well, Sara is passive and doesn't provide any real answers. However, when they ask her what she thinks about winning and losing, success and failure in general, what those words mean to her, she explains that "Winning is for winners, and I've always been a winner. I still could win if I really wanted to, but I don't feel like it. I'm really good at tennis, I've always been, and if I don't win, its not fun anymore."

A clear pattern emerges. Sara builds a large proportion of her general self-esteem on her tennis performance. Also, for her, performing *is* winning, beating others, even when she does not play well, nothing else. Social comparison with others is the major driving force of her behaviour. She feels good in general when she wins, particularly when she is sure of winning and doesn't have to try for it, when she feels superior. However, when she met opponents that were as good as her, a sudden fear of losing has entered her mind and this terrifies her. Her response is not to try at all, at least then she has an excuse if she is losing.

The sport psychologist and coach have several meetings with Sara, where they talk about how losing and failure are obstacles that all great athletes have to deal with. The sport psychologist suggests to Sara that failure is necessary for learning and improving rather than a statement of low ability. They also discuss the problem of constantly comparing against others and the value of comparing progress with yourself. Together, they set up a goal-setting plan for Sara, focusing primarily on details of her own game and specific behaviour on court that she has more control over, no matter who she plays. Also, one specific goal, that always is highlighted and evaluated is for Sara to always, in every game, try hard, no matter whether she is winning or losing.

After a bumpy start, Sara gradually gets more into focusing on herself, rather than the opponent. Her coach notices that she now really tries hard, even against better players. After having lost a tough game against a player four years older and with a higher ranking, she says to her coach: "Too bad I lost, good game though, I really enjoyed the challenge out there. After tight matches like this, I really feel that I improve as a tennis-player." She has managed to turn her debilitating fear of failure into an asset and advantage. More importantly, her self-esteem is not dependent on the result of the game but on a broader self-respect arising from her courage and convictions. Maybe this can be applied to other things outside of sport.

Lessons to the coach:

- Performance is not all about winning
- Emphasize effort and hard work, "Hard work beats talent when talent doesn't work hard"
- Meeting challenges and failure (losing) are important steps in developing and building a healthy self-esteem
- Comparing with oneself is often more relevant than comparing with others

CASE STUDY 3: BUILDING EXERCISE CONFIDENCE IN OVERWEIGHT WOMEN

Overweight and obese women were signed up to a commercial slimming club. Many chose that particular organization because they wanted to avoid exercise as a way of losing weight. However, the slimming organization had been persuaded, largely because of government pressures, that they should be motivating their members to be more active. They hired a consultant to work with them to develop a programme that would be feasible and acceptable to their class leaders and members. The consultant recognized that the members would have very little recent exercise experience, that their past experiences were often unpleasant, that they knew little about how to exercise safely and effectively, they had very low confidence and perceived competence and negative attitudes. In addition, they had been taught and come to believe that exercise was not effective for weight loss and so had very low value or sense of importance for it. The consultant also realized that because of the burden of weight, more vigorous activity was best avoided. A gradual, softly-softly approach, based on existing behaviour theory and evidence, was required that would build confidence through the successful achievement of goals. These goals were behavioural in nature so the slimming organization set up a recognition system for reaching various targets based on achieving number of sessions per week for at least 15 minutes on each occasion. Intensity of exercise was not emphasized in the early stages. The programme was accompanied by materials aimed at persuading members of the important mental and physical health benefits of exercise. All of this was packaged by the organization in a style that appealed to their clientele.

Evaluations indicate that the class leaders are improving in their willingness and confidence in delivery of the exercise component, and believe that more and more members are taking the materials on board and becoming committed exercisers. Many members report that the exercise has done wonders for their confidence and esteem.

Lessons for the members and consultants:

- Sometimes those things you are most scared of can bring the most gain
- Be patient and make slow but steady progress
- Listen to the experts

Lessons for the organization:

- The customer is not always right – it is possible to change minds and behaviours with the right strategies and materials
- Experts can make successful partners

Lessons for the consultant:

- Commercial partners can access far greater numbers than can be achieved through academia
- Commercial organizations are the experts in marketing materials to their customers

BUILDING RELATEDNESS

A consistent finding in research is that a key reason for participation in physical activity is to experience social benefits. People enjoy playing and exercising with others and feeling part of a team or group. For children and young people, playing sport can be a very important way of developing friendships. Settings that foster feelings of social acceptance, being valued and feeling significant in some way to others may assist in promoting self-esteem. Therefore, an important challenge for coaches and teachers is to create fertile ground for such feelings. From a broader perspective, creating opportunities for individuals to make meaningful connections with others, thereby feeling that they are part of something bigger than themselves, that they belong to a movement or group, is beneficial for feelings of relatedness. This may include the use of small-group activities where the value of cooperation is naturally built into the reward structure. Working together to solve common problems, and learning to depend on others, helps individuals connect to others and build foundations for development of relatedness. A key prerequisite for the development of feelings of relatedness is that the individual experiences trust and respect towards their coach, teacher or parent, and their team-mates. Therefore, regular meetings, one to one, where the coach uses an active listening or discussion approach to understand the athlete's/student's perspective, provides an effective base for the long-term development of social relatedness.

CONCLUSION

We believe that understanding how experiences in sport and exercise affect how children, athletes, adult exercisers see themselves, particularly their physical self is crucial to effective coaching, teaching and leadership. It provides real insight into how each individual feels so that coaches can be more empathetic. This in turn will help build fruitful relationships on the basis of mutual respect. It will also help the leader to understand the decision making and motivation of those they work with, which in turn can maximize motivation and performance. Self-esteem and self-perception theory are at the heart of many motivational theories that you will read about in this book. We encourage you to read more and explore how you can design your coaching and teaching for best effect.

LEARNING AIDS

1   Define the terms self-concept, self-esteem and self-perceptions.

    Self-concept is the individual as known to the individual. It is a self-description using whatever characteristics seem important to the person and might refer to abilities, aspects of appearance, behavioural habits, personality traits or values.

    Self-esteem is an overall rating of self-worth. It is important because it carries emotions so that high ratings result in pride and self-confidence whereas low ratings bring shame and feelings of hopelessness.

    Self-perceptions are any thoughts that you have about aspects of yourself as a person.

2   Provide an example of how self-esteem can be influenced by evaluation in different domains in life, such as sport.

    An 11 year old wants to play football for the team and tries really hard at practices. However, she does not get picked to play in the team. Her coach tells her that she will never be good enough but is welcome to carry on practicing. This reinforces to the young girl that she has little ability and no matter how hard she works at it she will never be good enough. Her perceived competence in football is low and if she considers her success at football to be important enough, it may negatively affect her overall self-esteem.

3   Provide examples of how the way coaches and teachers communicate can have positive or negative influences on self-esteem and self-perceptions.

[Examples should arise out of personal experiences or those of a friend.] *For instance, when a coach merely shows disappointment or anger at a poor performance such as a missed shot or tackle, the end result is likely to be a loss of confidence and raised anxiety in the player. If, alternatively, the coach emphasizes how to learn from the mistake, it provides a basis for improvement. The player can see that it was something that can be corrected and is not a statement of permanently poor ability or uselessness. There is hope and there is a way. Self-perceptions will bounce back.*

4   Describe the strategies that coaches can use to help individuals experience positive self-esteem and self-perceptions.

[Examples feature in Table 3.3 but try to produce two or three of your own.]

REVIEW QUESTIONS

1   What are self-concept, self-esteem and self-perceptions?

2   What are body image and social physique anxiety?

3   How is ability or competence related to self-esteem and self-perceptions?

4   What kind of behaviours reflect low self-esteem?

5   What kind of strategies are used to maintain a positive self-concept?

6   What is learned helplessness and how does it play out in a physical education context?

7   What roles do competence, autonomy, and relatedness play for the development of a positive self-esteem?

EXERCISE

Read the three cases provided in Table 3.4. In groups of four, discuss your past experiences in sport or exercise. Provide examples of how a coach or teacher has created a situation that has had a) a positive effect, and b) a negative effect on self-perceptions and self-esteem that might have had a long-term effect on your motivation or behaviour. Write these up as two extra case studies to add to the class resource.

ADDITIONAL READING

Fox, K.R. (2010). The physical self and physical literacy. In M. Whitehead (Ed.), *Physical literacy* (pp. 71–82). London: Routledge.

Fox, K.R. (2009). How to help your children become more active. In M. Ganzalez-Gross (Ed.), *Active healthy living* (pp. 52–67). Brussels: Coca Cola Europe.

Fox, K.R. & Wilson, P. (2008). Self-perceptual systems and physical activity. In T. Horn (Ed.) *Advances in sport psychology*. 3rd Ed (pp. 49–64). Champaign, IL: Human Kinetics

Fox, K.R. (1998). Self-esteem and confidence in the young player. *Insight: The FA Coaches Association Journal*, 1(2), 35–36.

 ## REFERENCES

Bandura, A. (1986). Social foundations of thought and action: A social cognitive theory. Englewood Cliffs, NJ: Prentice Hall.

Cash, T.F. (2004). Body image: Past, present, and future. *Body image, 1*, 1–5.

Deci, E.L. & Ryan, R.M. (1985). *Intrinsic motivation and self determination in human behavior.* New York: Plenum Press.

Deci, E.L. & Ryan, R.M. (2000). The "what" and "why" of goal pursuits: Human needs and the Self-Determination of Behavior. *Psychological Inquiry, 11*, 227–268.

Dweck, C.S. (2000). *Self theories: Their role in motivation, personality, and development.* Philadelphia: Psychology Press.

Hart, E.A., Leary, M.R. & Rejeski, W.J. (1989). The measurement of social physique anxiety. *Journal of Sport and Exercise Psychology, 11*, 94–104.

Harter, S. (1999). *The construction of the self: A developmental perspective.* New York: Guilford Press.

Leary, M.R. (1995). *Self-presentation: Impression management and interpersonal behavior.* Milwauke, WI: Brown & Benchmark.

Marsh, H.W. & Parker, J.W. (1984). Determinants of student self-concept: Is it better to be a relatively large fish in a small pond even if you don't learn to swim as well? *Journal of Personality and Social Psychology, 47*, 213–231.

Taylor, S.E., Lerner, J.S., Sherman, D.K., Sage, R.M. & McDowell, N.K. (2003). Are self-enhancing cognitions associated with healthy or unhealthy biological profiles? *Journal of Personality and Social Psychology, 85*(4), 605–615.

Thompson, J.K., Heinberg, L.J., Altabe, M. & Tantleff-Dunn, S. (1999). *Exacting beauty: Theory, assessment, and treatment of body image disturbance.* Washington, DC: American Psychological Association.

Chapter 4

Achievement motivation in sport settings

GLYN C. ROBERTS AND ATHANASIOS G. PAPAIOANNOU

SUMMARY

In this chapter we explain motivation in achievement settings like sport and physical education (PE) classes and what energizes, directs and regulates athletes' behavior in the social context of sport. We focus on the achievement goals pursued by individuals in sport or PE classes, explaining how they are developed and how different goal adoption regulates behavior. We describe sport environments where coaches or PE teachers adopt different definitions of success and emphasize different achievement goals. Importantly, we portray how athletes' goal involvement stems from the interaction of individual and contextual differences in the definition of success and goal adoption. Finally, we summarize the evidence concerning the effects of different goal adoption on athletes' and PE students' cognitions, emotions, performance, persistence, social behavior and well-being in sport and in PE.

INTRODUCTION

What is motivation? If we take our cues from everyday life, then it may be arousal, such as the "motivational" tirades of coaches in the locker room, some believe it is a measure of confidence, a winning attitude, or it is a personal entity that may, or may not, be genetically endowed. However, the contemporary understanding of motivation is that it is a process through which we become energized to achieve a valued outcome, and the arguments of researchers tend to revolve around the process of how motivation is energized.

Some theories place particular emphasis on the energization of needs, whether the needs are for power, autonomy and/or competence, and so on. Other theories focus on the activation of motivation from socialization to value the demonstration of competence or autonomy, a learned perspective. This book includes chapters that embrace both schools of thought. Which approach is preferable? Well, that is why researchers conduct their research, to improve their theories and to find out if there is one unifying theory of motivation. At the present time, we have advocates of each school of thought. This chapter treats motivation as a social-cognitive phenomenon. To understand the main implications from research based on theories that evolved throughout the years, we start this chapter with a brief history of the evolution of the Achievement Motivation concept.

 OBJECTIVES

After reading this chapter, readers will:

1   Know the fundamental concepts of achievement motivation theories that have been investigated in sport.
2   Understand the links among different personal theories of achievement, definitions of success and definitions of competence in achievement settings.
3   Understand how different definitions of success and competence are developed and how they emerge as dispositional differences in sport.
4   Understand how different definitions of competence formulate different achievement goals and how the latter energize, direct and regulate behavior in sport.
5   Understand the concept of motivational climate and how task-involving and ego-involving climates are constructed by coaches or PE teachers.
6   Predict relatively accurately the achievement goal pursuits of athletes or PE students when different achievement goals are emphasized or de-emphasized by coaches or PE teachers.
7   Predict quite accurately the motivational outcomes and social behavior of athletes or PE students when task-involving or ego-involving goals are pursued in sport or in PE classes.

Figure 4.1 Determinants of achievement motivation.

FROM THE NEED FOR ACHIEVEMENT TO SOCIAL-COGNITIVE APPROACHES OF ACHIEVEMENT MOTIVATION

Initially Achievement Motivation was conceptualized as the need to overcome obstacles and succeed (Murray, 1938). To measure the need for achievement, Murray developed the Thematic Apperception Test (TAT). In this test individuals respond to pictures and write stories which are then analysed to measure one's motive for achievement. The TAT was later improved by McClelland (1961) and Atkinson (1964), who proposed the theory of need for achievement as it is shown in Table 4.1. Accordingly, individuals who have a high need for achievement are likely to approach success when the probabilities are about 50% (e.g., when playing against someone who has equal abilities) and they ascribe high value to success. These individuals pursue the experience of positive emotions that are elicited after success, such as pride. On the other hand, individuals with a low need for achievement, in similar situations, try to avoid failure and the negative emotions that follow.

This theory established that achievement motivation is determined by expectations and value of accomplishment. Accordingly, we know today that athletes are highly motivated when they try to achieve something that they find valuable which is also challenging to them. For an athlete, a challenging task is not the easy one but neither the very difficult one, it is the task which is relatively difficult for them to carry out in particular. Hence, task challenge should be adapted to the needs of each particular person. Moreover, tasks should be also meaningful to athletes, exercise participants or physical education students.

Weiner (1972) proposed an entirely cognitive approach to explain achievement motivation. Weiner and Kukla (1971) found that individuals with a high need for achievement were more likely to ascribe their success to their abilities and effort than individuals with a low need for achievement. These authors proposed that in comparison to people with a low need for achievement, individuals with a high need for achievement:

- are more likely to approach achievement situations because they attribute success to themselves and hence they feel pride;
- persist with tasks for longer when they experience failures because they ascribe failure to lack of effort but not to lack of ability;
- prefer more challenging tasks because that way they will get better information about their abilities than if they select easy or very difficult tasks.

Based on Weiner's (1972) model, Roberts and Pascuzzi (1979) found that 45% of athletes' attribution of success and failure can be ascribed to four causes: ability, effort, task difficulty, and luck. These can be classified in the two dimensions which are shown in Table 4.2.

Later, Weiner (1985) suggested that the possibly thousands of causes of success or failure can be ascribed to the three dimensions of Table 4.3. According to this model, attributions of causes of success and failure fall in the dimension of:

1 Stability, affect expectations. An athlete ascribing his loss to unstable causes (e.g., hostile referee) is more likely to sustain high expectations to win the same opponent in the future than if he ascribes his loss to stable causes, such as the superior talent of the opponent.

2 Locus, affect self-esteem. An athlete ascribing success to internal causes, like her talent, reinforces her self-esteem; a swimmer who ascribes her failure to win to external causes, such as swimming in the wrong lane of the pool, is less likely to harm her self-esteem.

3 Controllability, affect emotions. For example, an athlete will feel guilt if he ascribes failure to lack of effort (controllable cause) but he will feel ashamed if he ascribes it to lack of talent.

Table 4.1 *Need for achievement theory*

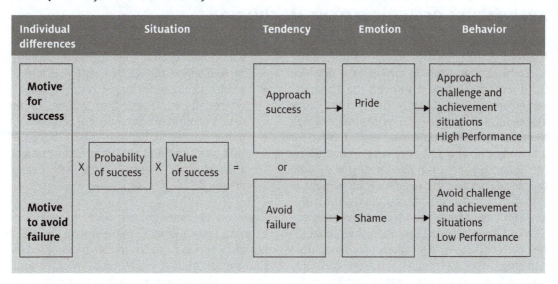

Table 4.2 *Two-dimensional attribution theory*

Stability dimension	Causality dimension	
	Internal	External
Stable	Ability	Task difficulty
Unstable	Effort	Luck

Table 4.3 *Weiner's three-dimensional typology of attributions*

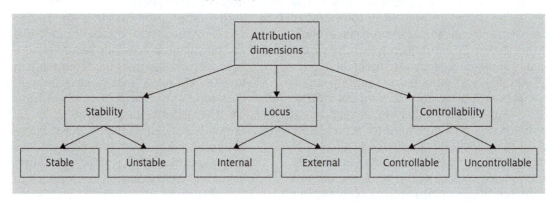

On one hand, coaches can cause athletes, particularly those who lack experience, to ascribe their bad outcomes to relatively unstable causes, such as incorrect strategy, lack of appropriate training, bad luck, etc. On the other hand, they can help them to sustain high self-esteem by ascribing their success to stable causes, such as their talent. However, it is also important to teach athletes that talent is something that is developed through hard work. This is covered more extensively in the latest approaches of achievement motivation presented below.

A SOCIAL COGNITIVE PERSPECTIVE OF ACHIEVEMENT MOTIVATION

The most important assumption of the social-cognitive approach is that humans are active in the environment and initiate motivated behavior through subjective interpretation of the achievement context. And one of the most popular of the social-cognitive theories is achievement goal theory (see Roberts, 2012). In fact, it has been stated by some that researchers' and practitioners' interest in achievement goal theory over the past 30 years has been a watershed in our understanding sport achievement behavior that has triggered a penetrating wave of research into the interpersonal and environmental influences on athlete sport behavior. Thus, the social-cognitive approach has been and remains an important theory in understanding sport achievement behavior.

To understand motivation, the social-cognitive approach argues we need to understand the psychological constructs that *energize*, *direct*, and *regulate* achievement behavior: Why do people do what they do? Achievement goal theory assumes that the individual is an intentional, goal-directed organism and that achievement goals govern achievement beliefs and guide subsequent decision making and behavior in sport achievement contexts. It is the function and meaning of the achievement behavior to the individual that must be taken into account. Individuals give meaning to their achievement behavior through the goals they adopt. It is these goals that reflect the purposes of achievement striving. Once adopted, the achievement goal determines the integrated pattern of beliefs that energize approach and avoid strategies, the differing engagement levels, and the differing responses to achievement outcomes. Thus, an individual's investment of personal resources such as effort, talent, and time in an activity is dependent on the achievement goal of the individual.

The overall goal is assumed to be the desire to develop and demonstrate competence and to avoid demonstrating incompetence. Achievement goal theory assumes that we learn what goals to value, and in our society demonstrating competence is clearly valued. We learn this through our socialization process from our parents, our teachers and coaches, and our peers. When we are young and developing, we are constantly barraged with the value of demonstrating competence. Thus, the demonstration and/or development of competence is the energizing construct of the motivational processes of achievement goal theory. But competence has more than one meaning. It is argued that two conceptions of ability (at least) manifest themselves in achievement contexts. One is ability, which is defined as being more competent than others, specifically our peers in the sport context. We term this as an "other referenced" definition of competence, and a person decides he or she is doing well if he/she is doing better than others. In the research literature this is defined as *ego-involved* ability, or performance. An important aspect of achievement goal theory is how one defines success, so a performance oriented person feels successful when demonstrating superiority and beating others. The second definition of ability is demonstrating competence to oneself, a focus on learning and developing competence over time. We term this as a "self referenced" definition of competence, and a person decides he/she is doing well when he/she is doing better than he/she did earlier. In the research literature this is defined as *task* *involved* ability, or mastery. A mastery oriented person feels successful when they are doing well and exerting effort.

BEING MASTERY OR PERFORMANCE ORIENTED

The extant data shows that children under age 12 are typically mastery oriented and do not differentiate luck, effort, and task difficulty from ability (Nicholls, 1989). Children associate ability with learning through effort, so the more effort a child makes, the more learning (and ability) he/she will achieve. However, by age of 12 children are able to differentiate luck, task difficulty, and effort from ability (Nicholls & Miller, 1983, 1985). This means that children begin to see ability as capacity and that the demonstration of competence involves outperforming others. In other words, they are able to appreciate both orientations. In terms of effort, high ability is inferred when outperforming others and expending equal or less effort or performing equal to others while expending less effort. Therefore for children, when children turn 12 years old it is an important watershed in their cognitive appraisals; they are able to distinguish ability from effort, which they do not when they are younger.

Therefore, by age 12 (or thereabouts) children are able to appreciate both orientations, and the one they employ then becomes a matter of the socialization experiences they are exposed to. For example, when parents use the other referenced criteria of success and failure to evaluate their children and give feedback, then their children are likely to become performance oriented and wish to demonstrate their competence by being better than their peers. In other words, children learn to be mastery or performance oriented after 12 years of age, and this cognitive style stays with them unless it is changed or modified by teachers, coaches, and/or peers.

An individual will approach a task or activity with goals of action reflecting their personal perceptions and beliefs about the form of ability they wish to demonstrate. These perceptions and beliefs form a *personal theory of achievement* of the activity that reflects the individual's perception of how things work in achievement situations. The adopted personal theory of achievement affects one's beliefs about how to achieve success and avoid failure at the activity. Therefore, based on their personal theory of achievement, people will differ in which of the criteria of success and failure they use.

The two conceptions of ability become the source of the criteria by which individuals assess success and failure (Nicholls, 1989). The goal of action is to meet the criteria by which success and failure are assessed. In achievement goal theory, when individuals are motivated to perform because they want to beat other people, then they are defined as being in a state of ego-involved motivation. The goal of action for an ego-involved individual is to demonstrate ability relative to others, or to outperform others, making ability other-referenced. Success is realized when the performance of others is exceeded, especially when expending less effort than others when individuals are motivated to perform because they want to beat other people, then they are defined as being in a state of ego-involved motivation. When individuals are motivated to perform because they want to demonstrate mastery of the task then they are defined as being in a state of *task involved* motivation. When task involved, the goal of action is to develop mastery, improvement, or learning and the demonstration of ability is self-referenced. Success is realized when mastery or improvement has been attained.

THE IMPORTANCE OF THE STATE OF INVOLVEMENT

As we stated above, the overall goal of action in achievement goal theory is assumed to be the desire to develop and demonstrate competence and/or to avoid demonstrating incompetence. Thus, individuals have the goal of demonstrating competence as they conceive it. When task involved, then perceived ability becomes less relevant as the individual is trying to demonstrate or develop mastery at the task rather than demonstrate normative ability. As the individual is trying to demonstrate mastery or improvement, the achievement behaviors will be adaptive, as research has demonstrated that the individual is more likely to persist in the face of failure, to exert effort, select challenging tasks, and be intrinsically interested in the task.

On the other hand, when ego is involved, the individual is trying to demonstrate normative ability, or avoid demonstrating inability, and comparing his/her ability with comparative others becomes important. If the individual is ego involved and perceives him or herself as high in ability, then that person is likely to approach the task and engage in adaptive achievement behaviors. These are the people who seek competitive contests and want to demonstrate superiority. When perceived ability is high, demonstrating high normative ability is likely, therefore the individual is motivated to persist and demonstrate their competence to pertinent others. If one can demonstrate ability with little effort, then this is evidence of even higher ability. Thus, the ego-involved person is inclined to use the least amount of effort to realize the goal of action. If the perception of ability is low, then the individual will realize that ability is not likely to be demonstrated, and he/she is likely to manifest maladaptive achievement behaviors because he/she wishes to avoid demonstrating incompetence. Maladaptive behaviors are those where the individual avoids the task, avoids challenge, reduces persistence in the face of difficulty, exerts little effort, and, in sport, drops out if achievement of desired goals appears difficult. These are the people who avoid competitive contests as their lack of competence is likely to be exposed. While the participant may view these avoidance behaviors as adaptive, because a lack of ability is disguised by these behaviors, they are considered maladaptive in terms of achievement behavior.

The reason the state of involvement is important is because a key tenet of achievement goal theory is that the states of involvement are mutually exclusive: One is either ego or task involved, even though this notion has been questioned in light of parallel processing models of information processing. However, the theory is quite explicit: One's state of motivational involvement may be seen to range on a continuum from task to ego involvement. The goal state is very dynamic, and can change from moment to moment as information is processed (Gernigon, d'Arrippe-Longueville, Delignieres, & Ninnot, 2004). An athlete may begin a task with strong task involved motivation, but contextual events may make the athlete wish to demonstrate superiority to others, and the athlete becomes ego involved in the task. For example, one might be brought out of a state of task involvement by a coach publicly highlighting a mistake, or a competitor or fan making a derogatory comment about one's competence. Similarly, an athlete may begin a competitive event with a strong ego involved state of involvement, but as the event unfolds, the athlete may realize they will win easily (or lose emphatically) and therefore begins to work on mastery criteria instead and become task involved. Thus goal states are dynamic and ebb and flow depending on the perception of the athlete of what it takes to be successful in that particular context.

GOAL ORIENTATIONS

How does one get into a state of ego or task involvement? One way is through one's personal theory of what it takes to achieve success in the context. Some individuals are predisposed to act in an ego or task involved manner; these predispositions are called achievement goal orientations. Individual differences in the disposition to be ego or task involved may be the result of socialization through task or ego-involving contexts either in the home or experiences in significant achievement contexts (e.g., classrooms, physical activities).

This is where it is important not to confuse goal orientations with "traits" or needs. Rather, they are cognitive schemas that are dynamic and subject to change as information pertaining to one's performance on the task is processed. But the orientations do have some stability over time too and are assumed to be relatively enduring. Thus, being mastery or performance oriented refers to the inclination of the individual to be task or ego involved respectively, in an achievement task.

The most important attribute of achievement goal orientations is that they are orthogonal. That is, mastery and performance goal orientations are independent, which means that one can be high or low in each or have both orientations at the same time. Based on developmental research with children, it is possible for an individual to be high or low in both mastery and performance goal orientation, or high in one and low in the other. This orthogonality has been supported in the sport and exercise literature (Duda, & Whitehead, 1998).

The implications of the orthogonality of goal orientations are quite profound, and make the theory quite unique. The research evidence suggests that individuals with both high mastery *and* high performance goal orientation, as well as the high mastery and low performance goal orientations have the most adaptive motivational profiles (Duda & Hall, 2001). As one would expect, when an individual is high in performance and low in mastery orientation, (especially when coupled with low perception of competence) it is generally maladaptive. However, we find that high performance orientation when coupled with high (or moderate) mastery orientation is not maladaptive. Therefore, rather than focusing on whether an individual is mastery or performance goal oriented, it is important to consider the simultaneous combination of mastery and performance goal orientation.

It is interesting that elite athletes are likely to be high in mastery and performance goal orientations. However, the athletes most at risk are the high performance and low mastery oriented. These are the people most likely to exhibit maladaptive motivation, drop out or even be most likely to burn out when they believe they cannot demonstrate competence. The low mastery and performance goal people are the least motivated, and may not even commit to achievement tasks. The important issue in the present discussion is that the orthogonality of the goal orientations has been demonstrated quite conclusively, and the orthogonality of the goals is an important determinant of motivated behavior. The avenue of research related to achievement goals in the context of physical activity has demonstrated that individual differences in goal orientation are associated with different motivational processes and different achievement behaviors.

THE MOTIVATIONAL CLIMATE

One of the most powerful aspects of achievement goal theory is that it incorporates not only the individual difference variables of mastery and performance goal orientations, but also the situational determinants of task and ego involvement. The situation plays a central role in the motivation process. Research within achievement goal theory has examined how the structure of the environment can make it more or less likely that an individual will become task or ego involved in an achievement environment. The premise of this line of research is that the individual perceives the degree to which task and ego criteria are salient within the context. The individual assesses what criteria of success and failure are extant, and the behaviors necessary to achieve success and/or avoid failure. When mastery criteria are clearly evident, then the situation is seen as task involving. When performance criteria are clearly evident, then the situation is seen as ego involving.

The premise of the research from a situational perspective is that the nature of an individual's experiences and how he/she interprets these experiences influence the degree to which a mastery and/or performance climate is perceived as salient. A performance climate is created when the criteria of success and failure are other referenced and ego involving, and the athlete perceives that the demonstration of normative ability is valued by the significant others in the context; teachers, coaches, parents. A mastery climate is created when the criteria of success and failure are self-referenced and task involving, and the athlete perceives that the demonstration of mastery and learning are valued. The athlete (or any other participant) simply assesses the criteria of success and failure the coach, teacher or parent has set for that situation, and does his/her best to match the criteria. In a situation where mastery criteria are assessed, then an individual is assumed to adopt adaptive achievement strategies such as working hard, seeking challenging tasks, and persisting in the face of difficulty. Certainly, the extant research supports that assumption. In a situation where performance criteria are assessed, then an individual is assumed to adopt maladap-

tive achievement strategies such as giving up in the face of failure, working hard only when succeeding, seeking tasks that are easily accomplished, and even dropping out. Again, the extant research supports that assumption. However, sometimes ego-involved individuals also adopt adaptive achievement strategies. When these people are ego-involved people with high perceptions of ability, then they enjoy demonstrating superiority to others. As long as the perception of high ability lasts, these people seek challenging tasks and revel in demonstrating their ability. But as soon as the perception of ability wavers, or the perception of ability becomes low for some reason, then these people are likely to adopt maladaptive achievement strategies.

The extant literature in physical education and sport suggest that the creation of a mastery motivational climate is likely to be important in optimizing positive responses (i.e., well-being, sportsmanship, persistence, task perseverance, adaptive achievement strategies) and attenuating negative responses (i.e., overtraining, self-handicapping). The research is quite clear: Perceptions of a mastery motivational climate are associated with more adaptive motivational and affective response patterns than perceptions of a performance climate in the context of sport and physical education.

An important aspect to recognize is that dispositional goal orientations and perceptions of the climate are two dimensions of motivation that interact to affect behavior. And the powerful and parsimonious aspect of achievement goal theory is that both the individual dispositions and the perception of the motivational climate are encompassed by the theory. However, it is true that research to date primarily deals with dispositional goal orientations and perceptions of the motivational climate as separate constructs in isolation to each other. But researchers are more inclined these days to use an interactionist approach that looks to investigate both variables at the same time (Papaioannou, Marsh & Theodorakis, 2004). This promises to provide a more complete understanding of achievement behaviors in the sport and physical education experience in the future. It is suggested that dispositional goal orientations should be seen as an individual variable that will determine the probability of adopting a certain goal of action, i.e., task or ego state of goal involvement, and a particular behavior pattern in achievement contexts. Perceptions of the motivational climate, however, are suggested to act as moderators of the influence of the individual variables. When the situational criteria are vague or weak, an individual's dispositional goal orientation should hold sway. However, in situations where the situational criteria of success and failure are very strong, then these perceptions of the climate may override an individual's dispositional goal orientation and be a stronger predictor of behavioral, cognitive and affective outcomes. This is very true for children and young adolescents, who have yet to firm up their personal theories of achievement and may be more susceptible to the influence of situational variables than older adolescents and adults.

The result of the limited research that has examined both individual and situational variables has shown that taking into account both of these variables enhances our understanding of the sport context. The limited evidence to date also provides support that situational variables may moderate the influence of goal orientations.

MOTIVATIONAL IMPLICATIONS OF BEING TASK OR EGO INVOLVED

The majority of research in achievement goal theory has focused on the antecedents and consequences of being ego or task involved and has looked at goal orientations and the motivational climate in isolation. As stated above, the most important facet of achievement goal theory is that the individual difference variables (self-schemas, personal theory of achievement, valence, dispositions, goal orientations) and the situational variables (motivational climate, emergent schemas) are part of the same theory and are conceptually compatible. The individual difference variables and the situational variables are both determinants of goal involvement. The kernel of the theory is that it is the state of goal involvement that energizes achievement striving. Thus it is rather artificial to look at goals and climate independently (which is what we have done previously). The essential issue is that it is the state of involvement that drives the achievement striving, therefore it is more conceptually coherent to look at the effect of being task and ego involved, however one gets there! We have already alluded to the difficulty of measuring task and ego involvement in situ, therefore we shall be consistent with the vast majority of the literature and assume that when individuals score high on ego orientation and/or are subjected to a performance climate, then they are more likely to be ego involved. Similarly, when individuals score high in task orientation and/or are subjected to a mastery climate, then they are more likely to be task involved. It makes conceptual sense, therefore, to look at the literature in terms of state of involvement rather than artificially breaking the literature down into orientation and climate, the means to goal involvement. It may be statistically and empirically accurate to relate goal orientations and/or climate to the cognitive, affective, and behavioral variables that we typically study, but it is not strictly conceptually accurate. Accordingly, we shall briefly summarize the findings from research on achievement goal orientations and the motivational climate together, rather than separately as has been the case in reviews in the past.

- **Beliefs about success**. Task-involving goals have been linked with the belief that success stems from high effort, which is beneficial for athletes' motivation, learning and performance, particularly at the early stages of athletic careers (e.g., Van-Yperen & Duda, 1999). High ego-oriented athletes do not place high value on effort but rather on ability (Biddle, Wang, Kavussanu & Spray, 2003), which has no motivational benefits and is detrimental for those who already are unsure about their competence.

- **Purpose of sport**. Achievement strivings of high ego-oriented individuals reflect their beliefs that through success in sport and physical education one might become a competitive person and achieve high social status in life (e.g., Duda, 1989; Papaioannou & MacDonald, 1993). The achievement goal schema of high task-oriented persons incorporates beliefs that through participation and success in sport and physical education one might learn to value improvement, hard work, cooperation and a physically active lifestyle and advance social responsibility and good citizenship (Biddle et al., 2003).

- **Affect and intrinsic motivation**. Task-involvement helps athletes and physical education students to focus on their own mastery, become absorbed by the activity and experience intrinsic motivation and positive affect (e.g., Ntoumanis & Biddle, 1999). Ego-involvement undermines self-determination during training and learning and blocks experiences of intrinsic motivation and positive affect.

- **Self-regulation and achievement strategies**. Task-involving goals facilitate the activation of locomotion, a self-regulation strategy which is concerned with movement from state to state and with committing the psychological resources that initiate or maintain goal-related movement (Papaioannou, Simou et al., 2009). Task-involved individuals adopt adaptive metacognitive and achievement strategies, such as deep-processing strategies that enable them to develop competence

(e.g., Lochbaum & Roberts, 1993; Thill & Brunel, 1995). Ego-involving goals facilitate the activation of assessment self-regulation function and comparisons between oneself and others. Ego-involved individuals adopt the most efficient strategy that enable them to achieve momentary maximum performance at the particular task and sustain self-worth, but these strategies are typically described as "surface" or "superficial"; the easy way to achieve a temporary outcome does not facilitate competence improvement.

- **Effort and performance**. While task-involvement is beneficial for both high and low perceived competence athletes to exert maximum effort in challenging tasks and maximize their performance, ego-involvement is beneficial to performance only for high perceived ability individuals (e.g., Sarrazin, Roberts et al., 2002).

- **Burnout**. Ego-involved athletes are at risk of exhibiting symptoms of burnout, particularly when they also have low perceptions of ability (e.g., Lemyre, Hall & Roberts, 2008).

- **Peer relationships**. Task-involvement facilitates collaboration between peers and mutual support but ego-involvement is linked to egocentric thinking, the perception of others as opponents and interpersonal conflict (e.g., Smith, Balaguer & Duda, 2006).

- **Moral functioning and aggression**. Compared to task-involved athletes, high ego-involved athletes are more likely to adopt any means leading to success, exhibit aggressiveness, lower sportspersonship values and immoral behavior (e.g., Sage & Kavussanu, 2007).

- **Well-being**. The socially supportive climate in task-involving teams facilitates subjective well-being but situations promoting ego-involvement have been found to be associated with ill-being (e.g., Reinboth & Duda, 2004).

OTHER APPROACHES TO ACHIEVEMENT GOALS

Here, we presented achievement goals theory as it was conceived by Nicholls (1989) and has been extensively studied in sport (Roberts, 2012; Duda & Hall, 2001). Another conceptualization of achievement goals was made by Dweck (1986) who suggested that people adopt different theories of ability. Those who believe that ability is stable and not amenable to change are likely to adopt performance goals trying to demonstrate their competence to others. When they fail to exhibit high competence they exhibit the helpless pattern: attribution of failure to lack of ability, negative effect, low expectations for future success, avoidance of subsequent challenge and decreased persistence and performance. Those who believe that ability is malleable and amenable to change are more likely to adopt learning goals to try to develop their competence. For such individuals, mistakes are considered part of learning and failures as temporary occasions and opportunities to take feedback in order to develop further their ability. Thus, coaches and parents should teach young athletes that talent is developed through training and hard work because this facilitates mastery goal adoption, positive affect and expectancies, increased persistence and high achievement.

A third conceptualization of achievement goals is the one offered by Elliot and colleagues who suggested that performance goals (Elliot & Church, 1997) or both mastery and performance goals (Elliot & McGregor, 2001) can be split into approach and avoidance goals. Existing research in sport based on this model implies that the adoption of mastery approach goals is the most adaptive achievement pattern, performance approach goals can be both adaptive and maladaptive (e.g., elicit negative affect), while avoidance goals are maladaptive (Papaioannou, Zourbanos, Krommidas & Ampatzoglou, 2012). Further discussion about the underlying conceptual differences between Elliot's and Nicholls models can be found in Duda and Hall (2001), Roberts, Treasure and Conroy (2007), Roberts (2012) and Papaioannou et al. (2012).

CONCLUSION

Parents, coaches, physical education teachers and others who interfere with children's development are advised to create task-involving climates in sport, home, school and if possible in other socialization settings, such as peer contexts where youngsters interact with their friends for social reasons. Usually the advice for the creation of mastery or task-involving environments are based on the recommendations of Epstein (1989) which were later adopted by Ames (1992) to suggest how to create a task-involving environment and how to avoid an ego-involving environment. These authors suggested there are six basic dimensions of any motivational climate, which can be briefly described with the anagram TARGET (see Table 4.4).

Extensive discussion about these structures and various examples are offered in other chapters of this book (e.g., adaptive motivational climate, Chapter 35; family structures, Chapter 12). In addition, various sport psychology strategies which are described in the chapters, such as goal setting, self-talk, imagery and self-regulation, are appropriate to assist athletes to stay focused on task accomplishment and facilitate task-involvement and personal improvement. Readers are advised to read these chapters for applications in sport which aim to promote task-involving goals.

An implication to be remembered from this chapter is that the philosophy of coaches or PE teachers determines the motivational climate of their teams or classes. A grassroots coach who puts priority on the development of young athletes instead of prioritizing immediate outcomes is more likely to create a task-

Table 4.4 *The TARGET dimensions for task-involving and ego-involving climates*

	Mastery or Task-involving Climate	Performance or Ego-involving Climate
Task	Meaningful, diverse, personally challenging and cooperative tasks	Competitive tasks emphasizing normative outcomes
Authority	The athlete or student participates in decision making	The coach or the PE teacher makes all decisions
Recognition	Based on high effort, progress and task accomplishment	Based on normative performance and normative ability
Grouping	Often changes, mixed ability	Relatively stable and based on normative ability
Evaluation	Personal criteria of evaluation, mistakes are considered as part of learning, low performance is used to provide feedback for improvement	Normative criteria of evaluation, mistakes are considered as indication of low ability, low performance is considered failure
Time	Flexible time for learning and task completion based on athletes' or students' needs	Inflexible time, everyone should accomplish a task within a specific time

involving climate because he can include all athletes in his plans and offer all players the joy of participation in competitions; he can offer the necessary time to all athletes to help them to master a task and apply recently learned techniques in contests, remain confident and not anxious to win, which helps him to provide more constructive feedback to his players; and he can offers choices and opportunities for innovations to his athletes, etc. On the other hand, a coach who prioritizes immediate outcomes is more likely to select the best athletes for competitions, to stay focused on the performance of the best and pay less attention on all athletes' progress, to use more nega-tive comments when an athlete's performance is below his expectations, to limit the opportunities of athletes' initiatives because they pose higher risk for a good outcome, etc. These different approaches in coaching are linked with coaches' different definitions of success. To the first coach described here success is the development of the athlete while to the second coach success is the exhibition of high coaching ability that leads to high performance. In conclusion, how coaches and athletes define success depends on their philosophy about coaching, sport and life, which determine the long-term and short-terms achievement goals that are pursued in sport.

LEARNING AIDS

1 What is achievement motivation?

Individuals' efforts to meet realistic goals, receive feedback and experience a sense of accomplishment. Athletes who are motivated by achievement try to pursue challenging goals, to receive feedback from performance evaluations, and they try to accomplish challenging goals in order to feel satisfaction from accomplishment.

2 What is the substantial difference between achievement goals and other intentional concepts?

The meaning of achievement in goal pursuit! Athletes give meaning to their achievement behavior through the goals they adopt which reflect the purposes of achievement striving. In sport an important purpose is the achievement of success and the demonstration of athletic competence. Other intentional concepts, such as goal setting (Locke & Latham, 1990) or mastery/performance approach and avoidance goals (Elliot & Murayama, 2008) do not incorporate the meaning of achievement in goal construction.

3 Why is it important not to confuse goal orientations with "traits" or needs?

Because goal orientations are developed and mutate through socialization and are subject to change as achievement-related information is processed. However, they have some stability over time because they are cognitive schemas incorporating goal for achievement and reason for goal striving. Athletes have a reason to exhibit relative consistency in their behavior by pursuing task-involving or ego-involving goals across situations. This reason for relative cross-situational consistency in achievement goal pursuit is connected with the meaning of achievement and the definition of success.

4 What is the meaning of achievement for high task or high ego-oriented athletes?

The meaning of achievement reflects wider belief systems and purposes in life. Achievement is a social construct, thus the meaning of achievement is always determined by one's answer to the question "who benefits from success?" For ego-oriented athletes, success primarily serves the one who achieves it; when successful, one indicates that he or she is superior to others. By establishing superiority relative to others one benefits from all the extrinsic rewards which are associated with social status. For a task-oriented athlete one's success serves both the person and the teammates or the team as a whole. For task-oriented individuals success has benefits both for the person and the others or the wider society.

5 Why do different definitions of competence reflect different definitions of success?

For cognitively mature individuals, such as athletes older than 10 to 12 years of age, one's tendency to focus more often on self-referenced (task-involved) or other-referenced (ego-involved) criteria to judge competence is the outcome of socialization process. Several caretakers, such as parents, teach young athletes that sport is a meritocratic context and, therefore, the athlete who deserves more benefits and rewards from successful outcomes should be the one who establishes that she or he has higher abilities than others. However, the one who fails does not deserve equal benefits. This conceptualization of success, which is defined in normative terms, that is, being better than others, leads individuals to focus on comparisons between themselves and the others and to value normative conception of ability. Other caretakers, though, who are very interested in the holistic development of the athletes and their psychological well-being teach athletes that achievement and high ability matters if it is the outcome of maximum effort. High task-oriented individuals also learn that everybody gains from one's success particularly within the team. Even an opponent's high performance is well received because it is seen as a high standard to achieve and not as another's failure. High task-oriented athletes are aspired by high achievement, like a spectacular athletic performance, but what primarily matters is the performance itself and the effort that leads to success. This approach helps athletes to remain unconcerned about failure which minimizes their cognitive and emotional load and helps them to focus on task mastery, task-involvement, and competence improvement.

6   In which climates do athletes' goal orientations prevail?

When the coach or the physical education (PE) teacher does not emphasize any particular achievement goal then athletes' goals prevail and determine the climate of the team or the class. For example, in the laissez-faire approach of a PE teacher who consistently abstains from direction or interference during children's play and gaming activities, children set their own goals which are usually competitive and therefore an ego-involving climate is created by children's behaviors. Of course, coaches and PE teachers do not need to interfere when athletes or students pursue clearly defined, personally challenging goals because these situations are task-involving; for example, when students try to improve their technique or performance using task-specific or personal criteria to judge their improvement respectively.

REVIEW QUESTIONS

1   Summarize the central tenets of early achievement motivation theories including attribution theory and their implications for coaches.

2   For task- and ego-involving goals respectively, explain how success is defined, how effort and ability are perceived, what satisfies athletes, what athletes try to achieve.

3   Explain the socialization process affecting the development of task and ego orientation.

4   Summarize the consequences of achievement goals on athletes' cognitions, self-regulation, affect and behaviors.

EXERCISES

1   Read the learning aids and then find ten other articles that describe the association of achievement goals with beliefs about success in sport or in PE and beliefs or perceptions of the purposes of sport or PE, or life purposes. Describe why these associations emerged. Based on these findings please prepare some implications for coaches or PE teachers regarding the philosophy that they should establish in

their teams or classes in order to promote task-involving goals and climates. Please also prepare some questions that you might use in a workshop involving coaches or PE teachers where you will discuss their coaching or teaching philosophy.

2 Find ten articles describing association of athletes' or PE students' self-regulation strategies (achievement, or cognitive/metacognitive, or coping strategies) with achievement goals in sport or PE classes. Then describe these strategies, the findings and explain why these associations were found. Based on these findings please offer suggestions to coaches or PE teachers concerning the strategies that they should use in order to promote task-involving goals and climates.

3 Find ten articles describing association of athletes' achievement goals with social behavior, including moral behavior, aggression, peer relationships etc. Then describe these findings in your own words, explain why these findings emerged and make a 15-minute presentation for parents explaining what achievement goals are, and why task-involving goals are more preferable than ego-involving goals in order to promote appropriate social behavior.

ADDITIONAL READING

Duda, J.L. & Hall, H. (2001). Achievement goal theory in sport: Recent extensions and future directions. In R.N. Singer, H.A. Hausenblas, C. Janelle (Eds.), *Handbook of sport psychology* (pp.417–443). NY: Wiley.

Roberts, G.C., Treasure, D.C. & Conroy, D.E. (2007). Understanding the dynamics of motivation in sport and physical activity: An achievement goal interpretation. In G. Tenenbaum & R.E. Eklund (Eds.), *Handbook of sport psychology* (3rd ed., pp.3–30). Hoboken, NJ: Wiley.

Roberts, G.C. (2012). Motivation in sport and exercise from an achievement goal theory perspective: After 30 years, where are we? In G.C. Roberts & D.C. Treasure (Eds.), *Advances in motivation in sport and exercise* (pp.5–58). Champaign, IL: Human Kinetics.

Papaioannou, A.G, Zourbanos, N., Krommidas, H., Ampatzoglou, G. (2012). The place of achievement goals in the social context of sport: A comparison of Nicholls' and Elliot's models. In G. Roberts & D. Treasure (Eds.), *Advances in motivation in sport and exercise* Vol. 3 (pp.59–90). Champaign, IL: Human Kinetics.

REFERENCES

Ames, C. (1992). Structures, goals, and student motivation. *Journal of Educational Psychology, 84*, 261–271.

Atkinson, J. (1964). *An introduction to motivation.* Princeton, NJ: Van Nostrand.

Biddle, S., Wang, C.K.J., Kavussanu, M. & Spray, C. (2003). Correlates of achievement goal orientations in physical activity: A systematic review of research. *European Journal of Sport Science, 3*(5), 1–20.

Duda, J.L. (1989). Relationship between task and ego orientation and the perceived purpose of sport among high school athletes. *Journal of Sport & Exercise Psychology, 11*(3), 318–335.

Duda, J.L. & Hall, H. (2001). Achievement goal theory in sport: Recent extensions and future directions. In R.N. Singer, H.A. Hausenblas & C. Janelle (Eds.), *Handbook of sport psychology* (pp.417–443). NY: Wiley.

Duda, J.L. & Whitehead, J. (1998). Measurement of goal perspectives in the physical domain. In J.L. Duda (Ed.), *Advances in sport and exercise psychology measurement* (pp.21–48). Morgantown, W. Va.: Fitness Information Technology.

Dweck, C. (1986). Motivational processes affecting learning. *American Psychologist, 41(10)*, 1040–1048.

Elliot, A.J. & Church, M.A. (1997). A hierarchical model of approach and avoidance achievement motivation. *Journal of Personality and Social Psychology, 72*, 218–232.

Elliot, A.J. & McGregor, H.A. (2001). A 2×2 achievement goal framework. *Journal of Personality and Social Psychology, 80*, 501–519.

Elliot, A.J. & Murayama, K. (2008). On the measurement of achievement goals: Critique, illustration, and application. *Journal of Educational Psychology, 100(3)*, 613–628.

Epstein, J.L. (1989). Family structures and student motivation: A developmental perspective. In C. Ames & R. Ames (Eds.), Vol. 3, *Research on Motivation in Education: Goals and cognitions*, (pp.259–295). San Diego, CA: Academic Press.

Gernigon, C., d'Arripe-Longueville, F., Delignières, D. & Ninot, G. (2004). A dynamical systems perspective on goal involvement states in sport. *Journal of Sport & Exercise Psychology, 26(4)*, 572–596.

Lemyre, P.-N., Hall, H.K. & Roberts, G.C. (2008). A social cognitive approach to burnout in elite athletes. *Scandinavian Journal of Medicine & Science in Sports, 18(2)*, 221–234.

Lochbaum, M.R. & Roberts, G.C. (1993). Goal orientations and perceptions of the sport experience. *Journal of Sport & Exercise Psychology, Vol 15(2)*, 160–171.

McClelland, D. (1961). *The achieving society*. New York: Free Press.

Murray, H. (1938). *Explorations in personality*. New York: Oxford University Press.

Nicholls, J.G. (1989). *The competitive ethos and democratic education*. Cambridge: Harvard University Press.

Nicholls, J.G. & Miller, A. (1983). The differentiation of the concepts of difficulty and ability. *Child Development, 54*, 951–959.

Nicholls, J.G. & Miller, A. (1985). Differentiation of the concepts of luck and skill. *Developmental Psychology, 21*, 76–82.

Ntoumanis, N. & Biddle, S.J.H. (1999). A review of motivational climate in physical activity. *Journal of Sport Sciences, 17(8)*, 643–665.

Papaioannou, A. & Macdonald, A. (1993). Goal perspectives and purposes of physical education as perceived by Greek adolescents. *Physical Education Review, 16*, 41–48.

Papaioannou, A., Marsh, H. & Theodorakis, Y. (2004). A multilevel approach to motivational climate in physical education and sport settings: An individual or group level construct? *Journal of Sport & Exercise Psychology, 26*, 90–118.

Papaioannou, A., Simou, T., Kosmidou, E., Milosis, D. & Tsigilis, N.G. (2009). Goal orientations at the global level of generality and in physical education: Their association with self-regulation, affect, beliefs and behaviours. *Psychology of Sport & Exercise, 10*, 466–480.

Papaioannou, A., Zourbanos, N., Kromidas, H. & Ampatzoglou, G. (2012). The place of achievement goals in the social context of sport: A comparison of Nicholls' and Elliot's models. In G. Roberts & D. Treasure (Eds.), *Motivation in sport and exercise* Vol. 3 (pp.59–90). Champaign, IL: Human Kinetics.

Reinboth, M. & Duda, J.L. (2004). The motivational climate, perceived ability, and athletes' psychological and physical well-being. *The Sport Psychologist, 18*, 237–251.

Roberts, G.C. (2012). Motivation in sport and exercise from an achievement goal theory perspective: After 30 years, where are we? In G.C. Roberts & D.C. Treasure (Eds.), *Advances in motivation in sport and exercise* (pp.5–58). Champaign, IL: Human Kinetics.

Roberts, G.C. & Pascuzzi, D. (1979). Causal attributions in sport: Some theoretical implications. *Journal of Sport Psychology, 1*, 203–211.

Roberts, G.C., Treasure, D.C. & Conroy, D.E. (2007). Understanding the dynamics of motivation in sport and physical activity: An achievement goal interpretation. In G. Tenenbaum & R.E. Eklund (Eds.), *Handbook of sport psychology* (3rd ed., pp.3–30). Hoboken, NJ: Wiley.

Sage L. & Kavussanu, M. (2007). The effects of goal involvement on moral behavior in an experimentally manipulated competitive setting. *Journal of Sport and Exercise Psychology, 29 (2)*, 190–207.

Sarrazin, P., Roberts, G.C., Cury, F., Biddle, S. & Famose, J.P. (2002). Exerted effort and performance in climbing among boys: The influence of achievement goals, perceived ability, and task difficulty. *Research Quarterly for Exercise and Sport, 73(4)*, 425–436.

Smith, A.L., Balaguer, I. & Duda, J.L. (2006). Goal orientation profile differences on perceived motivational climate, perceived peer relationships, and motivation-related responses of youth athletes. *Journal of Sports Sciences, 24(12),*1315–1327.

Thill, E.E. & Brunel, P. (1995). Ego-involvement and task-involvement: Related conceptions of ability, effort, and learning strategies among soccer players. *International Journal of Sport Psychology, 26(1),* 81–97.

Van-Yperen, N.W. & Duda, J.L. (1999). Goal orientations, beliefs about success, and performance improvement among young elite Dutch soccer players. *Scandinavian Journal of Medicine & Science in Sports 9(6),* 358–364.

Weiner, B. (1972). *Theories of motivation: From mechanism to cognition.* Chicago: Rand McNally.

Weiner, B. (1979). A theory of motivation for some classroom experiences. *Journal of Educational Psychology, 71,* 3–25.

Weiner, B. (1985). An attributional theory of achievement motivation and emotion. *Psychological Review, 92,* 548–573.

Weiner, B. & Kukla, A. (1971). An attributional analysis of achievement motivation. *Journal of Personality and Social Psychology, 15,* 1–20.

Chapter 5

Motivation in sport

A self-determination theory perspective

NIKOS NTOUMANIS AND CLIFFORD J. MALLETT

SUMMARY

Self-determination theory (SDT) has been widely applied to the study of motivation in sport settings. In this chapter, we present an overview of some of the constructs proposed by this theory; namely, coaches interpersonal styles, athletes' psychological needs, and motivational regulations. We also explain how coaching behaviors either support or undermine athletes' needs and subsequent motivation, and how the latter result in different levels of engagement, performance, and psychological well-being. Practical suggestions based on this theory are presented for enhancing adaptive athlete motivation. Lastly, potential challenges and solutions for implementing self-determination theory-based instruction and coaching are discussed.

INTRODUCTION

Let us consider a youth basketball match where coaches from both teams encourage their players to work hard and win the game. Consider how coaches might go about encouraging their players to work harder. For example, one male team coach might speak to his players and advise them that if they do not hold the opposition to less than six points in the next quarter they will be required to perform "suicide runs" (repetitive sprints up and down the court). He also uses another strategy to encourage them to shoot accurately: At half time he advises that those play-ers who shoot accurately will be rewarded with free tickets to a professional match. The coach uses these two strategies thinking he is motivating his players to work harder. In other words, the intentions of the coach are quite honorable because he believes that these strategies will increase player motivation. Unfortunately, he is unaware of the potential adverse consequences of these strategies on the players' motivation and subsequent engagement. The key question to ask here is: *How might those strategies not foster positive player engagement?*

Motivating athletes is considered an important aspect of coaching practice. Coaches typically encourage athletes to work hard to achieve success and use specific strategies to "motivate" their athletes because they believe that motivated athletes are more likely to succeed. In an attempt to understand how coaches positively or negatively influence athletes' motivation we might consider some related key questions: *How do coaches attempt to get the best from their athletes? How might research inform coaches about appropriate coaching practices that promote adaptive player engagement?* In this chapter, the theoretical framework of self-determination theory (Deci & Ryan, 1985) will be used to inform adaptive coaching practices that lead to promoting motivationally adaptive player engagement.

 OBJECTIVES

After reading this chapter, you should be able to:

1   Explain the types of motivation and psychological needs proposed by SDT.
2   Identify two major interpersonal styles of coaches, as described by SDT.
3   Provide recommendations for promoting self-determined motivation and need satisfaction in athletes.
4   Identify barriers and solutions for implementing SDT-based coaching.

PROMOTING MOTIVATIONAL COACHING ENVIRONMENTS: AN OVERVIEW

It is widely acknowledged by athletes, coaches, sport psychologists, and the wider sport community that motivation is a key determinant of success and failure in sport. Often, a coach's emphasis is solely on increasing the *quantity* of motivation, the assumption being that higher motivation will lead to better performance. However, motivation research (e.g., Vansteenkiste, Sierens, Soenens, Luyckx, & Wills, 2009) has shown that the *quality* of motivation also matters in that higher levels of motivation might not result in desirable outcomes if the quality of motivation is poor (i.e., if the reasons underlying engagement in particular actions are problematic). Unlike other theoretical frameworks of motivation, self-determination theory (Deci & Ryan, 2000) makes the distinction between quality and quantity of motivation.

This chapter will provide a brief overview of the major constructs proposed by this theory and will explain how these constructs have been operationalized in the context of sport. This chapter will also illustrate how coaches can promote adaptive types of motivation for sport participation, optimal performance, and psychological well-being. Lastly, problems and solutions in implementing SDT-based coaching will be discussed. Although in this chapter we focus on sport, the concepts and intervention suggestions we present are to a large extent applicable to any organized exercise contexts (e.g., aerobics classes) in which fitness instructors aim to maximize their clients' motivation to engage in and adhere to an exercise regime.

PSYCHOLOGICAL NEEDS AND MOTIVATIONAL REGULATIONS

According to Deci and Ryan (2000), SDT is a theory of human motivation and personality.

In a nutshell, the theory argues that individuals have a natural tendency for personal growth and development. This tendency necessitates that the social context facilitates the satisfaction of three basic psychological needs. When these needs are satisfied, individuals will experience higher quality of motivation, psychological well-being, and will engage in adaptive behaviors (e.g., increased behavioral investment).

The three psychological needs identified by the theory are those for autonomy, competence, and relatedness. Autonomy refers to desire to feel ownership over one's behavior. Competence refers to the need to feel effective and achieve valued outcomes. Relatedness is the desire to feel accepted and meaningfully connected with others (Deci & Ryan, 2000). For example, in the context of sport, athletes will experience autonomy-need satisfaction when they are positively engaged in their training and personal development plans; competence-need satisfaction when they are given sufficient opportunities and guidance to achieve success; and relatedness-need satisfaction when they feel accepted and valued by their coach and teammates. Deci and Ryan argue that although these three needs might vary in strength from person to person, they are innate, universal, and essential for optimal human development.

A large volume of research evidence exists to show that the satisfaction of one or more of the psychological needs proposed by SDT can be an important predictor of a number of indices of behavioral investment and psychological well-being/ill-being, such as sport engagement, vitality, self-esteem, and physical health (e.g., Hodge, Lonsdale, & Jackson, 2009). Such findings make theoretical sense. When athletes feel in control of their behavior (autonomy), experience success (competence), and feel accepted and valued by their coach and teammates (relatedness), they will display active engagement and persistence in various activities in training and competition, and will report more positive physical and psychological health states. In contrast, when athletes feel that their psychological needs are frustrated,

that is, when they perceive lack of choice or opportunities for personal input, frequent failure in mastery attempts, and feelings of rejection and isolation, they are more likely to report feelings of burnout and negative emotional states (Bartholomew, Ntoumanis, Ryan, Bosch, & Thøgersen-Ntoumani, 2011).

The satisfaction of the three psychological needs is also expected to lead to higher quality of motivation (i.e., more self-determined; Deci & Ryan, 2000). SDT distinguishes three types of motivation with varying degrees of self-determination: intrinsic motivation, extrinsic motivation and amotivation (see Figure 5.1). Intrinsic motivation represents the highest degree of self-determined motivation. In sport, athletes with high intrinsic motivation freely engage in activities they find interesting and enjoyable, and which offer an opportunity for learning and personal development.

Extrinsic motivation is evident when individuals perform an activity because they value its associated outcomes (e.g., public praise, extrinsic rewards) more than the activity itself. There are four types of extrinsic motivation. These are, in decreasing order of self-determination, integrated regulation, identified regulation, introjected regulation and external regulation. Integrated regulation is evident when behaviors are performed because they are fully assimilated within one's self system. For example, integrated regulation is evident when athletes perceive their sport engagement as part of who they are. Individuals with high identified regulation perform activities out of choice but without necessarily enjoying them. For example, some young athletes may participate in sport because they value the importance of sport engagement for their health and performance goals. Both integrated and identified regulations are associated with a personal endorsement of one's sport participation, and thus are high in self-determination. Introjected regulation describes extrinsically motivated behaviors that are performed out of feelings of guilt/shame or in the pursuit of contingent self-worth. For example, some

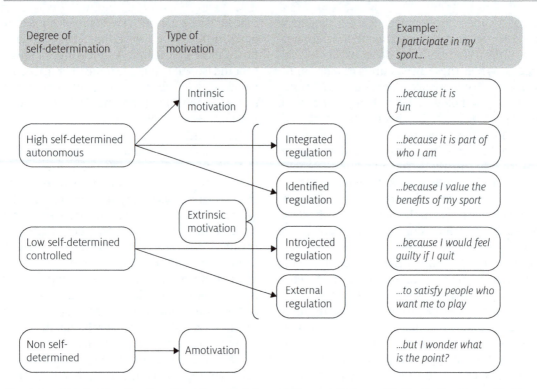

Figure 5.1 Types of motivation along the self-determination continuum with illustrative examples from sport taken from Lonsdale, Hodge, and Rose (2008).

young athletes may participate in sport because they do not wish to let their parents down. Lastly, external regulation refers to behaviors carried out in order to attain tangible rewards (e.g., trophies), social approval, or to avoid punishment. Both introjected and external regulations are associated with low levels of self-determination.

Amotivation represents the absence of intrinsic and extrinsic motivation. It is evident when athletes lack the intention and willingness to engage in sport. It often results from feelings of incompetence and uncontrollability and is frequently linked to decisions to drop out of sport (e.g., Pelletier, Fortier, Vallerand, & Brière, 2002).

The extensive evidence in the sport literature on the application of SDT in sport demonstrates that autonomous/self-determined forms of regulation (intrinsic motivation, integrated and identified regulations), compared to controlled forms of regulation (introjected and external regulations) and amotivation, result in more adaptive outcomes such as higher effort, persistence, performance, and various indices of psychological well-being (cf., Vallerand, 2007; see Figure 5.2). High autonomous types of extrinsic motivation (i.e., integrated and identified regulations) in sport are important given that some behaviors might not be inherently enjoyable (e.g., repetitive drills during training), but could have high instrumental value. Introjected regulation can sometimes lead to persistence, but this is relatively short-lived (Pelletier et al., 2002). Tangible rewards are very frequently used in sport (e.g., athletic scholarships) but evidence suggests that when they are used to motivate athletes they result in athletes being motivated by external regulation (Bartholomew, Ntoumanis, & Thøgersen-Ntoumani, 2009).

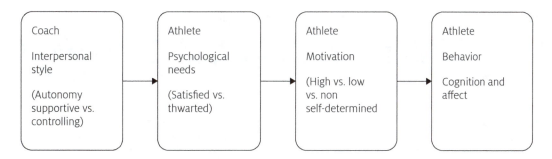

Figure 5.2 A self-determination theory-based motivational sequence adapted from Vallerand (1997).

A coach plays a major role in shaping the psychological experiences his/her athletes derive from their sport participation (Mageau & Vallerand, 2003). Many coach behaviors have a positive influence on athletes' psychological need satisfaction, autonomous motivation, performance, and psychological well-being.

However, maladaptive coaching behaviors are not uncommon. The following section discusses two interpersonal styles that have very different consequences for the quality of athletes' engagement in sport and their psychological well-being.

COACH INTERPERSONAL STYLES

In an effort to understand the underlying motivational mechanisms associated with the use of different coaching behaviors, SDT-based research in sport has primarily focused on the contrast between an autonomy-supportive and a controlling coach interpersonal style (although coaches can adopt both styles to varying degrees). Short descriptions of these contrasting interpersonal styles are presented in Table 5.1.

Despite the label, autonomy-supportive behaviors are theorized and have often been shown in research to predict the satisfaction of not only autonomy, but all three basic psychological needs, as well as autonomous motivation (Mageau & Vallerand, 2003; Reeve, 2009). It is important to clarify that an autonomy-

supportive coaching style does not encourage an athlete to break off ties and become independent of his/her coach. An autonomy-supportive coach offers emotional support, advice and guidance within specific constraints with the aim of helping athletes develop responsibility and take ownership of their actions. In contrast to autonomy support, a controlling coach interpersonal style can actively undermine the three psychological needs and result in controlled forms of motivation, and perhaps over time lead to amotivation. Controlling behaviors have been theorized and empirically shown to predict the thwarting of the three psychological needs and low or non-self-determined motivation (Bartholomew et al., 2011; Mageau & Vallerand, 2003).

PROMOTING NEED SATISFACTION AND AUTONOMOUS MOTIVATION IN SPORT

A number of suggestions have been offered (and tested) in the SDT literature with regard to the promotion of need satisfaction and autonomous motivation. These suggestions center

on the development of a coach autonomy support style and the reduction of controlling behaviors. One of the central dimensions of autonomy support is the provision of choice of

Table 5.1 *Autonomy-supportive and controlling interpersonal style*

Autonomy-supportive	Controlling
An autonomy-supportive coach:	A controlling coach:
<ul><li>Encourages athlete initiative</li><li>Allows athlete participation in decision making</li><li>Offers choices that are relevant to athletes' goals and values</li><li>Provides a rationale for task-engagement</li><li>Acknowledges negative feelings associated with task-engagement</li><li>Is non-judgmental</li><li>Attempts to understand athletes' perspective before offering suggestions (Mageau & Vallerand, 2003).</li></ul>	<ul><li>Behaves in a coercive, pressuring, and authoritarian way in order to impose a preconceived way of thinking and behaving upon their athletes</li><li>Uses excessive monitoring and surveillance</li><li>Marginalizes athletes' input and views</li><li>Attempts to influence aspects of the athletes' lives that are not directly relevant to their sport participation</li><li>Uses intimidating behaviors (e.g., yelling, physical punishment)</li><li>Uses guilt-inducing statements</li><li>Withdraws attention, positive regard and support when athletes are not compliant with his/her instructions and expectations (Bartholomew et al., 2009).</li></ul>

Figure 5.3 Rugby.

activities. Choices offered by the coach should set specific rules and boundaries, be meaningful to the athletes, and meet the athletes' basic psychological needs. For example, a coach should: a) offer his/her basketball players a choice of drills that will help the development of a particular skill (e.g., defense) that is relevant to the athletes' goals and interests; b) ensure that the offered choices are not too numerous or complex for the players; and c) minimize the potential of subsequent intra-team disputes. In addition to choice, meaningful rationales should be offered, particularly for uninteresting or repetitive behaviors. For instance, a young soccer player will more fully internalize the importance of performing flexibility exercises if his/her coach can clearly demonstrate the direct benefits of agility for soccer performance. Rationales are also useful to explain the purpose of existing restrictions and rules (e.g., why certain types of food should be avoided). Understanding the underlying reasons for the selected activities will foster positive engagement. Moreover, athletes are more likely to be self-determined when they are offered explanations that are clear, truthful, and meaningful, as opposed to when they are treated by their coach with an "it's my way or the highway" attitude (Mageau & Vallerand, 2003). Furthermore, athletes should be encouraged to provide some input in strategies and tactics. In this way, coaches will demonstrate that they value athletes' opinions and encourage initiative and problem solving (Vallerand, 2007).

Coaches should also be empathetic and acknowledge the difficulties, negative feelings, or objections that their athletes might have in relation to particular tasks, goals, or rules. For example, they should be empathetic to their athletes' complaints that certain activities in training are unexciting. Expressions of dissatisfaction by athletes should not be discouraged as allowing them gives athletes the message that their voices are heard and respected, and makes it more likely they will develop a sense of being valued. Further, such objections can result in better rationales being provided or in structural changes (e.g., more choices) that could address criticisms.

Coaches should also provide feedback that is constructive, detailed, informative in terms of competence development (e.g., "your awareness of your opponents' movements off the ball has really improved because you are now able to..."), and positive where appropriate. Further, coaches should take time to listen first and then respond to athletes' ideas and goals, be patient with their progress, try to develop an understanding of how their athletes think and feel about certain things, and give them sufficient time and encouragement to take initiatives and develop independently (Mageau & Vallerand, 2003; Reeve, 2009). In terms of goal setting, athletes should be encouraged to set and strive for goals that are congruent with their values and interests. To facilitate competence need satisfaction in particular, training regimes should provide optimally challenging opportunities that are matched with athletes' current and varying levels of skill development. Further, in terms of facilitating relatedness need satisfaction, team building exercises, and one-to-one meetings to discuss both individual and team goals should be scheduled. When required, such meetings should also aim to help athletes fully internalize and volitionally engage in team goals and activities that serve the "greater good", sometimes at the expense of individual goals. In brief, a coach who makes an athlete feel valued, appreciated, and respected will facilitate feelings of relatedness in that athlete.

As stated earlier, the facilitation of psychological-need satisfaction and autonomous motivation requires the reduction of controlling coach behaviors. To this end, a coach should not use language that is verbally abusive, that threatens, humiliates or forces (e.g., via fear or guilt inducement statements such as "don't let me down") athletes to accept rules, limits or activities. Coaches should also avoid monopolizing conversations, discouraging questions or alternative opinions from

Figure 5.4 Football.

their athletes, issuing deadlines, directives and commands, asking controlling questions (e.g., "can you do this the way I want it?"), using praising as a contingent reward (e.g., "you did exactly what I asked you to do"), telling athletes how they ought to feel, offering only predetermined goals and choices, and using over-intrusive behaviors to influence their athletes' lives outside sport (Bartholomew et al., 2009; Reeve, 2009).

POTENTIAL CHALLENGES IN TRANSLATING THEORY TO PRACTICE

Research examining challenges and barriers in the translation of self-determination theory to practice when implementing coaching practices such as those discussed in the previous section is scarce. One exception is an autobiographical case study reported by Mallett (2005) in which he described his own coaching practice as autonomy-supportive. He stated that his general personal orientation was inclined towards autonomy rather than control, which influenced how he coached. Although Mallett reported that his autonomy-supportive coaching developed over many years, he felt that the adoption of an autonomy-supportive pedagogical approach to coaching was somewhat unproblematic. However, for many coaches or educators shifting from a controlling to an autonomy-supportive instructional approach can be complex and challenging (Reeve, 2009). How might a coach shift from controlling to more autonomy-supportive coaching practices? What are the potential barriers to shifting towards an autonomy-supportive approach?

Mageau and Vallerand (2003) proposed that three key factors influence coaches' interpersonal style: their personal orientation, the coaching context, and their perception of athletes' behavior and motivation. These factors probably operate interdependently, so understanding the shift from a controlling to an autonomy-supportive instructional approach should include a consideration of all these individual and social factors.

A coach's personal orientation is influenced by his/her general causality orientation and beliefs about how to motivate athletes (Deci & Ryan, 1985). Socialization factors are likely to shape coaches' personal orientation to be more controlling than autonomy-supportive. Coaches' behaviors, for example, may often reflect parenting styles characteristic of the 1950s and 1960s, in which children's and athletes' compliant behaviors were shaped by reward and punishment. This controlling orientation is unsurprising since coaches typically report that they coach the way they were coached (Lyle, 2002). Coaches are also likely to be socialized into believing that controlling behaviors will increase athletes' motivation, especially in the short term (Reeve, 2009). However, most coaches are probably unaware of the medium to long-term adverse consequences of such controlling behaviors (e.g., amotivation, attrition, psychological ill-being). The shift towards an autonomy-

Figure 5.5 Beep test.

supportive orientation to coaching requires the coach to endorse such a shift (Mageau & Vallerand, 2003). This shift may present some challenges to the coach; for example, the implementation of an autonomy-supportive coaching approach might be difficult for the coach because it takes him/her out of his/her "comfort zone". Several coaches have reported significant challenges in becoming more autonomy-supportive, especially if their personal orientation is controlling. Socialization factors combined with years of coaching with a dominant controlling interpersonal style require the coach to change many implicitly learned coaching behaviors and beliefs about how to motivate others, which understandably demand sufficient time, patience, reflection, and practice.

With regard to the coaching context, the second variable discussed by Mageau and Vallerand (2003) to influence coaches' interpersonal style, several factors are likely to be influential. In elaborating upon these factors, the work by Reeve (2009) on teachers' challenges to be autonomy-supportive, considered alongside a program of coach motivation research by Mallett and colleagues (e.g., Ahlberg, Mallett, & Tinning, 2008), can be very informative. First, in the sporting context, coaches typically exercise a controlling interpersonal style because they are the dominant actor in the coach–athlete relationship. Controlling interpersonal styles are characteristic of those with inherent dominance in differential power relations. In the coach–athlete relationship, the coach is assumed to possess greater knowledge and experience, and thus superior social status. Second, external pressures from parents, club officials, and spectators on coaches to produce winning

Figure 5.6 Tennis.

performances are likely to, consciously or unconsciously, result in coaches transferring those controlling pressures into how they interact with their athletes. Third, the culture of sport supports the use of controlling coaching behaviors. A general perception in coaching is that coaches who use controlling, rather than autonomy-supportive behaviors, are more competent. It is not uncommon to observe controlling coaching behaviors in televised professional sports, which might send a message to viewing coaches and athletes that this approach is the norm. An associated reason is that controlling behaviors also seem to send a message that the coach has a structured coaching practice, which is deemed to be conducive to superior performances. In contrast, an autonomy-supportive approach might send the message that the coach is *laissez-faire* in their approach and perhaps lazy. One example might be the coach's use of questioning to enable players to have some input and to think critically about what strategies to use in what situation. In this example, the players might think that the coach does not know what to do if he/she is asking players questions; coaches usually tell players what to do! Another example might be coaches who provide limited direct input, rather than regularly yelling instructions to players, which might also be perceived as an indication of low coach competence. To some extent these situations reflect players' frames of reference for what is "good" coaching practice; to coach differently might be perceived as inferior coaching.

Anecdotally, sometimes athletes do not want to be in control and prefer their coaches to take that responsibility. In other words, some athletes report that they are happy to be told what to do and when. Perhaps these athletes have been shaped to be passive learners due to socialization experiences or they have impersonal/control orientations, which are the result of need thwarting (Deci & Ryan, 2000). It is also likely that these athletes actually report a preference for a structured coach-

ing environment, where the coach establishes clear expectations, goals and boundaries. However, a structured environment can be autonomy-supportive or controlling, depending on the communication style used by the coach. For example, a coach who pressurizes athletes to meet certain goals and standards is a controlling one, whereas a coach who supports athletes' efforts toward meeting these goals is autonomy-supportive (Reeve, 2009). It is unlikely that many athletes would flourish under a coaching environment where they are shouted at, are put under surveillance, and their opinion/input is never welcome. If coaches are to become more autonomy-supportive, it is also necessary to teach athletes how to deal with increased autonomy (Pelletier, Fortier, Vallerand, & Brière, 2002). For example, coaches might guide athletes in thinking about some options for a particular play in basketball. Part of the discussion with the athletes might consider what the benefits and costs of alternative strategies are before deciding a course of action. Coaches can gradually scaffold these opportunities (in both frequency and complexity) into training and competition contexts.

The third factor considered to influence coach behaviors is the coach's perception of the behavior and motivation of the athlete (Mageau & Vallerand, 2003). Coaches respond to the behaviors of athletes; for example, some athletes are less cooperative than others and in attempting to "motivate" those less cooperative athletes, coaches typically resort to the use of controlling behaviors. Unfortunately, these controlling behaviors will actually undermine self-determined forms of motivation reinforcing further coaches' perceptions about athlete motivation and the need for adopting a controlling interpersonal style (Pelletier & Vallerand, 1996).

There is a significant quantum of research supporting an autonomy-supportive approach to coaching. Autonomy-supportive behaviors could be adopted gradually and tried over time (e.g., choices that athletes might prefer during

Figure 5.7 Netball team.

a training session) so that they are refined to meet athletes' needs. In guiding the shift towards an autonomy-supportive approach to coaching, coaches should become more aware of how they communicate with their athletes (e.g., via videoing and reviewing their sessions or seeking feedback from athletes and other coaches). Questions that could be asked to these coaches include:

- What are the most common controlling behaviors you use? What is the frequency of those behaviors?

- What are the most common autonomy-supportive behaviors you employ? What is the frequency of those behaviors?

- What do you think might be the short-, medium-, and long-term consequences of any controlling behaviors?

- Are you interested in changing any controlling behaviors? If so, which ones and how?

- How is your interpersonal style contributing to your athletes' psychological need satisfaction – autonomy, competence, and relatedness?

CONCLUSION

In conclusion, an SDT approach to coaching has much potential in terms of increasing athlete motivation, however, there are some personal, situational and cultural factors that can act as barriers in promoting autonomy-supportive coaching. Such factors should be identified and tackled when developing SDT-based training programs in order to maximize the efficiency of SDT-based training and coaching.

LEARNING AIDS

1   Explain what is meant by *quality* of motivation.

Many people think that it is important to increase the amount of motivation so that athletes will perform better. Essentially, more motivation is assumed to lead to superior outcomes (e.g., effort, performance). However, the quality of motivation is more important than how much motivation one has. Within SDT, higher quality of motivation (i.e., more autonomous) has been found to lead to positive outcomes such as persistence, performance, and psychological well-being. In contrast, lower quality forms of motivation (controlled motivation and amotivation) are related to negative outcomes such as psychological ill-being and attrition from sport.

2   Describe an autonomy-supportive approach to coaching.

Coaches who consider the degree to which they are positively influencing players' perceptions of choice, competence, and a sense of belonging are considered to have an autonomy-supportive orientation to coaching. In practice, autonomy supportive coaches provide athletes with some choices in what they do in training and competition; they ask questions and listen to what athletes think; they allow athletes some independence and opportunities for showing initiative and problem solving; and they provide informational feedback that guides athletes towards mastering their skills.

3   Identify the three universal psychological human needs advanced by SDT.

Research has supported the key role of three universal psychological needs – autonomy, competence, and relatedness. Satisfaction of these needs fosters optimal human functioning and growth. Autonomy is associated with the perception of choice and personal endorsement in what one does. For example, athletes want to have choice in the design of their training. Also, athletes want to feel good about themselves, especially in activities in which they choose to engage. Experiencing success in sport (e.g., personal improvement in one's skill level) fosters such perceptions of competence. The third psychological need is that of relatedness. People like to belong to groups – for example, athletes need to feel accepted and valued by their teammates.

4   Discuss how punishments undermine autonomous motivation and psychological needs.

In general, athletes try to do the best they can in sporting contexts; that is, they do not plan to make mistakes. Nevertheless, when athletes do make mistakes it is common for some coaches to use punishment as a means to shape the desired behavior – that is, to avoid the repeat of the same or similar mistakes in the future. Unfortunately, use of punishment has the potential to undermine autonomous motivation by thwarting psychological need satisfaction – autonomy, competence, and relatedness. The avoidance of punishment becomes controlling and can undermine an athlete's autonomy. Punishments (or threat thereof) can also invoke a fear of failure. In other words, athletes become fearful or worried they will make a mistake, which can become a self-fulfilling prophecy that over time has the potential to reduce an athlete's perception of competence. Feeling incompetent and worrying about making mistakes can lead to athletes feeling less valued and perhaps not belonging because they perceive they are letting the team down.

NIKOS NTOUMANIS AND CLIFFORD J. MALLETT

REVIEW QUESTIONS

1. Compare and contrast autonomy-supportive and controlling interpersonal styles in coaching.

2. In your own words, explain the difference between autonomous and controlled motivation. Include examples to illustrate your understanding of these different forms of motivation.

3. Explain how the SDT constructs reviewed in this chapter can explain variations in athletes' behaviors (e.g., persistence) and psychological well-being.

4. You have been hired as the new coach of a youth soccer team. One of your first observations is that the players on the team have very diverse reasons for playing soccer. Levels of competence vary substantially within the team, some players seem to have very dominant roles, and the relationships among the players are fragmented. Describe how you will aim to increase levels of autonomous motivation and psychological need satisfaction within this team.

5. Identify some of the barriers in implementing an autonomy-supportive interpersonal style.

6. Describe how your (current/past) coach typically behaves. List those behaviors under two headings – controlled and autonomous interpersonal styles. Review those two lists and decide whether you might characterize your coach as either mostly autonomous or mostly controlling. Justify your decision.

EXERCISES

1. Think about why you play your sport and list these reasons. Classify each of those reasons under six headings representing the six motivational regulations.

2. Interview a coach about how they try to foster their athletes' motivation. How do their views align or not align with the key tenets of self-determination theory? Some questions for the interview might include:

   a. How do you foster players' motivation for sport?

   b. How do you support your athletes' autonomy, competence and relatedness?

   c. Do those same strategies work for all athletes? Describe how you might use different strategies for different athletes. Justify your decisions.

3. Interview an athlete coached by the coach chosen for Exercise 2 and ask them:

   a. Why do they play their sport?

   b. How does their coach support or undermine their motivation to play sport?

   c. In what ways does their coach: (i) provide the athlete with some choices; (ii) make them feel competent; and (iii) make them feel valued?

4. Do the coach and the athlete have similar views as to what coaching behaviors are most adaptive and least adaptive? Video a coach in a training session (with their permission). If you are a coach, video your own coaching for one training session. When reviewing the video, label all coaching behaviors as either

80

controlling or autonomous. Describe the overall coaching interpersonal style in that session using examples to support your conclusions.

5   Describe three controlling behaviors used by the coach in that session. How might you change these behaviors to be more autonomy-supportive? Give specific examples and explanations.

ADDITIONAL READING

Amorose, A. (2007). Coaching effectiveness: Exploring the relationship between coaching behavior and self-determined motivation. In M.S. Hagger and N.L.D. Chatzisarantis (Eds.), *Intrinsic motivation and self-determination in exercise and sport* (pp.209–228). Champaign, IL: Human Kinetics.

Deci, E.L. & Ryan, R.M. (2002). *Handbook of self-determination research*. Rochester, NY: University of Rochester Press.

Gagné, M., Ryan, R.M. & Bargmann, K. (2003). Autonomy support and need satisfaction in the motivation and well-being of gymnasts. *Journal of Applied Sport Psychology, 15,* 372–390.

Ntoumanis, N. (2012). A self-determination theory perspective on motivation in sport and physical education: Current trends and possible future research directions. In G.C. Roberts and D.C. Treasure (Eds.). *Motivation in sport and exercise:* *Vol. 3* (pp.91–128). Champaign, IL: Human Kinetics.

Reeve, J. & Jang, H. (2006). What teachers say and do to support students' autonomy during a learning activity. *Journal of Educational Psychology, 98,* 209–218.

Smith, A., Ntoumanis, N., Duda, J.L. & Vansteenkiste, M. (2011). Goal striving, coping, and well-being in sport: A prospective investigation of the self-concordance model. *Journal of Sport and Exercise Psychology, 33,* 124–145.

Treasure, D.C., Lemyre, P.N., Kuczka, K.K. & Standage, M. (2007). Motivation in elite-level sport: A Self-Determination perspective. In M.S. Hagger and N.L.D. Chatzisarantis (Eds.), *Intrinsic motivation and self-determination in exercise and sport* (pp.153–166). Champaign, IL: Human Kinetics.

REFERENCES

Ahlberg, M., Mallett, C.J. & Tinning, R. (2008). Developing autonomy-supportive coaching behaviors: An action research approach to coach development. *International Journal of Coaching Science, 2,* 3–22.

Bartholomew, K., Ntoumanis, N., Ryan, R., Bosch, J. & Thøgersen-Ntoumani, C. (2011). Self-determination theory and diminished functioning: The role of interpersonal control and psychological need thwarting. *Personality and Social Psychology Bulletin, 37,* 1459–1473.

Bartholomew, K., Ntoumanis, N. & Thøgersen-Ntoumani, C. (2009). A review of controlling motivational strategies from a Self-determination theory perspective: Implications for sports coaches. *International Review of Sport and Exercise Psychology, 2,* 215–233.

Deci, E.L. & Ryan, R.M. (1985). *Intrinsic motivation and self-determination in human behavior.* New York: Plenum.

Deci, E. L. & Ryan, R.M. (2000). The "what" and "why" of Goal Pursuits: Human needs and the self-determination of behavior. *Psychological Inquiry, 11,* 227–268.

Hodge, K., Lonsdale, C. & Jackson, S.A. (2009). Athlete engagement in elite sport: An exploratory investigation of antecedents and consequences. *The Sport Psychologist, 23,* 186–202.

Lonsdale, C., Hodge, K. & Rose, E.A. (2008). The Behavioral Regulation in Sport Questionnaire (BRSQ): Instrument development and initial validity evidence. *Journal of Sport and Exercise Psychology, 30,* 323–355.

Lyle, J. (2002). *Sports coaching concepts: A framework for coaches' behaviour.* London: Routledge.

Mageau, G.A. & Vallerand, R.J. (2003). The coach–athlete relationship: A motivational model. *Journal of Sports Sciences, 21,* 883–904.

Mallett, C.J. (2005). Self-determination theory: A case study of evidence-based coaching. *The Sport Psychologist, 19,* 417–429.

Pelletier, L.G., Fortier, M.S., Vallerand, R.J. & Brière, N.M. (2001). Associations among perceived autonomy support, forms of self-regulation, and persistence: A prospective study. *Motivation and Emotion, 25,* 279–306.

Pelletier, L.G. & Vallerand, R.J. (1996). Supervisors' beliefs and subordinates' intrinsic motivation: A behavioral confirmation analysis. *Journal of Personality and Social Psychology, 71,* 331–340.

Reeve, J. (2009). Why teachers adopt a controlling motivating style toward students and how they can become more autonomy supportive. *Educational Psychologist, 44,* 159–175.

Vallerand, R.J. (2007). A hierarchical model of intrinsic and extrinsic motivation for sport and physical activity. In M.S. Hagger and N.L.D. Chatzisarantis (Eds.), *Intrinsic motivation and self-determination in exercise and sport* (pp.255–280). Champaign, IL: Human Kinetics.

Vansteenkiste, M., Sierens, E., Soenens, B., Luyckx, K. & Lens, W. (2009). Motivational profiles from a self-determination perspective: The quality of motivation matters. *Journal of Educational Psychology, 101,* 671–688.

Chapter 6

Emotions in sport and exercise settings

JURI HANIN AND PANTELEIMON EKKEKAKIS

SUMMARY

Emotions are a fundamental component of the experience of sport and exercise and have a powerful influence on how individuals perform and behave in these contexts. From the perspective of sport psychology, this chapter reviews performance-related emotions experienced by athletes and how these emotions impact athletic performance and are affected by performance processes and performance outcomes. The defining characteristics of emotional experiences affecting athletic performance and those affected by performance are described. How emotional experiences can be used in the optimization of athletic performance is also explained. From the perspective of exercise psychology, this review examines the types of emotional experiences likely to be elicited by exercise participation and the effects that these may have on exercise behavior and adherence. Recommendations for monitoring and enhancing emotional experiences in the context of exercise are also provided.

INTRODUCTION

Sport and exercise participation generate emotions, which are often intense. Although this was not always the case, these emotions are now increasingly recognized as essential components of the sport and exercise experience. Importantly, emotions are not only affected by sport and exercise; they exert powerful influences on how athletes perform in competition and how everyone behaves in the context of exercise. The goal of this chapter is to provide an overview of this prolific and fascinating literature.

Athletes' self-descriptions of competition-related emotions

Sport psychology aims to help athletes maximize their performance with the ultimate goal of achieving and maintaining consistent excellence. The two quotes below suggest that it is important for athletes to understand performance-related emotional *experiences*. The notion of "negative" and "positive" anxiety is also highlighted.

Consider this quote, by a highly skilled female bowler under competitive stress:

1 "... I have to *stop trying too much* in competitions.
2 For instance, my emotional *state* in the Championship was totally *wrong.*
3 At first, I was *confident and carefree.*
4 But then I began to feel *fearful & nervous.*
5 Then I *listened* too much to *other* people's *opinions.*
6 I just *hoped to perform* well but I *didn't do anything* to avoid mistakes.
7 The situation was *out of control* and my *confidence crumbled* completely.
8 I felt *lost* and was even thinking about *giving up.*
9 Finally, I became *over-aroused* and I *tried too much.*
10 *Anxiety got me* and I *couldn't get rid of these feelings...*"

This quote illustrates the dysfunctional impact of elevated anxiety, "forcing" the athlete to try too much (1) and lose control and her ability to cope (5–8, 10). The dynamics of emotional state and the distractive role of excessive communication with other people (5) are also described (3, 4). The athlete recalls her inability to avoid mistakes (5, 6), feeling over-aroused, trying too much, and losing self-confidence (9, 10).

Now consider this quote, illustrating "positive" anxiety in an elite female shooter:

1 "... *Nervousness* is *my best friend* when I shoot...
2 It would be a *disaster* for my shooting if I felt *calm and not nervous.*
3 When I'm *nervous* with the air rifle, it is *positive nervousness* because,
4 *If something goes wrong, I am so confident* that...

5 I will *know how to cope* with the situation.
6 I *know all technical things* that would *help or hinder* me.
7 It is not so with the *small-bore rifle,*
8 I still feel *helpless and pretty lost* there.
9 *I don't know what to do!*"

This second quote shows anxiety that is optimal and helpful for athletic performance. This elite shooter has learned not only to tolerate elevated anxiety but to use it constructively to her advantage. In competition, she feels nervous and at the same time confident that she can deal with potential problems (4–6). The athlete is also aware that feeling calm and not nervous would spoil her performance (2–4, 5). Her high anxiety is "positive" and optimal for shooting with the air rifle (5–7). However, she does not know how to deal with potential problems, feels lost (8, 9), and experiences "negative" anxiety in shooting with the small-bore rifle.

In the following sections, we examine several aspects of athletes' emotional experiences in competitive sport. For instance, are negatively toned emotions always harmful for athletic performance? What is the difference between "sufficient" and "excessive" nervousness? How should you deal with current anxiety? Are positively toned emotions always helpful for athletic performance? How do you identify emotions that are helpful and harmful for athletic performance? How do you predict athletic performance based on emotions? Moreover, we explain why exercise scientists and practitioners should take into consideration individuals' emotions and how to monitor and assess them. Recommendations for exercise professionals on how to promote positive emotions through physical activity are offered in Chapter 44, Physical activity and feeling good.

OBJECTIVES

After reading this chapter you will be able to:

1 Define emotions as a category of *experience*.
2 Describe *form*, *content*, *intensity*, *context*, and *time* dimensions of emotions.
3 Use the in/out of zone notion in the prediction of emotions' impact on performance.
4 Carry out emotion-centered and action-centered profiling.
5 Describe the differences between *core affect*, *emotion*, and *mood*.
6 Use the *circumplex* model to track changes in affect during a session of physical activity.

CATEGORIZING EMOTION AS EXPERIENCE

Emotion is usually defined as an organized psychophysiological *reaction* to ongoing *person-environment* (P-E) relationships. This definition, however, captures only one aspect of the P-E interaction – the person's response to the environment. According to Lev Vygotsky (1926/1984), to study something as an *indivisible unity*, it is necessary to find a construct that appropriately captures the characteristics of both interacting elements. In psychology, *experience* is such a construct; it is appropriate for the study of P-E interactions because it reflects a person's attitude toward different aspects of the environment and the meaning of the environment for the person. Every experience has a biosocial orientation: it is always someone's experience of something and is best represented as a unit of consciousness. Thus in the analysis of a difficult situation, the focus should be not so much on the situation or on the person per se but on *how this situation is experienced by this person*. In other words, emotional experience is an indivisible component of human functioning that reflects the dynamics of past, ongoing, or anticipated P-E interactions. From this perspective, emotion research in sport should describe, predict, and explain an athlete's optimal and dysfunctional experiences accompanying successful and poor performances and well-being (or ill-being).

State-like and trait-like emotional experiences: In sport, there are two interrelated types of directly observable performance-related experiences: *state-like* experiences or emotional states as a component of situational, multimodal, and dynamic manifestations of total human functioning (see first quote above, lines 3, 4, 6, 8; second quote above, line 8) and *trait-like* experiences as relatively stable emotion patterns (emotionality, dispositions, attitudes). For instance, when athletes feel nervous prior to competition, this is triggered by a specific meaning of this particular situation and characterizes their situational emotional state. On the other hand, feeling nervous can be a typical (repeated) experience of the athletes across several competitions. Therefore, trait competitive anxiety would indicate how often the athlete usually experiences elevated anxiety and feels nervous and tense prior to or during several competitions.

Emotion as meta-experience: Emotions are experienced not only directly as an emotional state but also on a reflective level (first quote, line 2; second quote, lines 1–3, 6). These are *meta-experiences* (feelings about feeling) or *reflected* experiences that include awareness, attitudes, preferences for or rejections of emotions. Meta-experiences capture how an athlete feels about his or her past, present, or anticipated (upcoming) emotional experiences and the perceived effects of these emotional experiences on performance and/or general well-being. An athlete's meta-experience is an attitude toward experiencing a high level of anxiety and awareness of its helpful or harmful effects on performance. Meta-experiences can also be situational (state-like) or generalized (trait-like), as a summary of repeated experiences across successful and unsuccessful performances (first quote, line 1). Usually, meta-experiences are formed when athletes spontaneously or deliberately reflect on the conditions leading to successful and unsuccessful performances. Meta-experiences determine an athlete's choice of self-regulation strategies and are often a target of successful interventions.

Research in sport psychology for several decades focused mainly on situational emotional states, such as competitive anxiety, and relatively stable emotion patterns (e.g., trait anxiety). In contrast, meta-experiences were often only implied in the assessment of emotional effects on performance. Meta-experience adds a special meaning and quality to perceived situational state, which is interpreted as helpful or harmful. Evidently, it is easier for athletes to use constructively elevated anxiety if they have a positive attitude and expectation of its helpful effects.

To identify meta-experiences, the athletes are asked to reflect on how they feel about the specific state (anxiety, anger, etc.) and what the impact of this state on performance would be (helpful or harmful). Emotion regulation usually involves reframing an athlete's attitudes toward specific performance situations and related emotional experiences (first quote, lines 2, 8; second quote, lines 7–9). Reflecting on past and current successful and unsuccessful performances and accompanying emotional experiences would be the other approach to the identification of meta-experiences.

DESCRIBING PERFORMANCE-RELATED EXPERIENCES

The five basic dimensions for the multilevel and systematic description of emotional experience include *form, content, intensity, time,* and *context* (Hanin, 2000).

Form dimension: The situational psychobiosocial (PBS) state comprises eight modalities, some of which are emotional and some are not. They are (sample descriptors in parentheses): *cognitive* (alert, focused, confused, distracted), *affective/emotional* (worried, nervous, happy, angry, joyful, fearful), *motivational* (motivated, willing, desirous, interested), *volitional* (determined, brave, daring, persistent), *bodily* (tired, jittery, restless, sweaty, painless, breathless), *motor-behavioral* (sluggish, relaxed, sharp), *operational* (smooth, effortless, easy, clumsy actions), and *communicative* (connected, related, in touch).

To assess emotions, researchers have often included in standardized scales items representing both emotional and non-emotional modalities. Such items as "motivated," "energetic," "charged up," or "determined" would probably not be considered "pure" emotions by emotion theorists. Likewise, idiosyncratic labels generated by the athletes themselves to describe their emotional experiences also often include both emotional and non-emotional descriptors. Thus, although it is important for researchers to distinguish between the emotional and non-emotional modalities of a PBS state, from the applied standpoint, including both emotional and non-emotional experiences in a holistic description of the performance-related state would be appropriate, especially in individually oriented interventions.

Categorizing emotion content: Two approaches to assessing emotions include the *dimensional* approach and the *discrete-emotions* approach (more on this later in this chapter). The dimensional approach assumes that experience can be described along basic dimensions, such as pleasure-displeasure (otherwise referred to as *valence* or *hedonic tone*), quiescence-activation, tension-relaxation, and energy-tiredness. The discrete-emotions approach considers emotions as distinct entities, focusing on their unique relational meaning and qualitative content (anxiety, anger, joy, etc.).

Although different theorists have proposed different lists of discrete emotions, most would agree that the list should include both negatively toned (e.g., anger, anxiety, sadness) and positively toned emotions (e.g., relief, happiness/joy, pride). It is also crucial from the applied viewpoint to identify the most *important* emotions and their impact upon performance (see athletes' quotes above). In sport, the most important emotions are usually personally relevant (idiosyncratic), task-specific, and functionally helpful or harmful.

In the Individual Zones of Optimal Functioning (IZOF) model (Hanin, 1997, 2000, 2007), emotion content is conceptualized within the framework of two factors: *hedonic tone* (pleasure-displeasure or valence) and functional *impact on performance* (success-failure). Idiosyncratic emotion labels generated by athletes are classified into one of four global emotion categories: pleasant and functionally optimal emotions (P+), unpleasant and functionally optimal emotions (N+), pleasant and dysfunctional emotions (P–), and unpleasant and dysfunctional (N–) emotions. These four categories provide a sufficiently broad and robust structure for generating a pool of individually relevant and task-specific emotions experienced by athletes.

Research shows that 80–85% of self-generated emotion labels are not included in the various standardized emotion scales. Scales that consist of researcher-generated items do not assess most of the personally meaningful emotional content in the athletes' own performance-related idiosyncratic subjective experiences. To overcome this problem, practitioners wishing to conduct emotion-centered profiling can use the Emotional State Profile (ESP-40), which is capable of measuring interactive effects of different emotions across the four categories (see Table 6.1).

Table 6.1 *Emotional State Profile (ESP-40)*

The ESP-40 helps to describe *how* you think *you feel* in different performance situations. There are no right or wrong responses! Make sure you:

- Consider how you actually feel (or felt).
- Work across the page.
- Number the words in each row.
- Give 4 to the word that best describes how you feel.
- Give 3 to the next best, then 2, and then 1 to the least.
- Make sure each row has a 4, 3, 2, and 1 (no duplicates).
- Go with your first reaction.

[_] Tired	[_] Tense	[_] Energetic	[_] Easy-going
[_] Sluggish	[_] Dissatisfied	[_] Confident	[_] Tranquil
[_] Reluctant	[_] Furious	[_] Charged	[_] Satisfied
[_] Doubtful	[_] Attacking	[_] Willing	[_] Joyful
[_] Sad	[_] Intense	[_] Motivated	[_] Happy
[_] Unhappy	[_] Angry	[_] Purposeful	[_] Pleased
[_] Upset	[_] Irritated	[_] Certain	[_] Comfortable
[_] Distressed	[_] Nervous	[_] Cheerful	[_] Calm
[_] Fearful	[_] Annoyed	[_] Enthusiastic	[_] Content
[_] Worried	[_] Restless	[_] Alert	[_] Relaxed
[_____]	[_____]	[_____]	[_____]
N–	N+	P+	P–

I felt this way because ....
In what way was this helpful (or harmful) for me? ....

It is important to recognize that the total impact of emotions on performance and well-being depends on optimal and dysfunctional interactions of emotions. These interaction patterns are specific for individual success (N– < N+ < P+ > P–), failure or underperformance (N– > N+ > P+ < P–), well-being (N– < N+ < P+ < P–), and ill-being (N– > N+ > P+ > P–). Although the content of idiosyncratic emotion descriptors may be different for different athletes, emotion intensities and interaction patterns are the same.

Identifying optimal emotion intensity: The optimal or dysfunctional impact of emotions on athletic performance depends not only on their content but also on their intensity. By observing performance-related emotions, it is possible to estimate their optimal and dysfunctional intensity. Research shows that about 65% of athletes perform well if, for instance, their pre-competition anxiety level is either high or low but not moderate. The "in/out of zone" notion describes anxiety-performance relationships at the intra-individual level and suggests that an optimal intensity of anxiety (which can be high, moderate, or low) produces beneficial effects on individual performance. Athletes perform up to their potential if their actual anxiety is within their individually optimal zones of

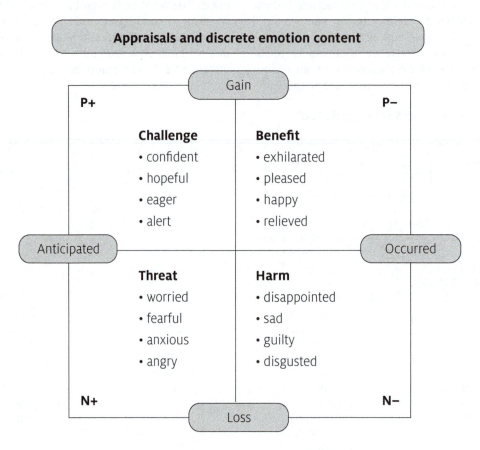

* Modified from Folkman & Lazarus, 1985

Figure 6.1 Discrete emotion content: Gain-loss appraisals in pre- and post-performance situations.

intensity. If the athlete's actual anxiety state is out of her optimal zone (either higher or lower), she is likely to perform below her potential (first quote, lines 4, 6, 9–10).

From a common sense perspective, the intensity of unpleasant emotional states should be reduced or minimized to enhance subjective well-being. However, in high-achievement sport, individually optimal intensity of anxiety can be high, moderate, or low for different athletes. In other words, current anxiety in athletes should be increased, reduced, or maintained to match their individually optimal level. The direction of emotion regulation should be estimated for each athlete by contrasting individually optimal intensity zones and actual level of intensity (i.e., applying the "in/out of zone" principle). This individualized coping aims both to help an athlete enter (or re-enter) the optimal intensity zone and to stay away from the dysfunctional zones by keeping the intensity of performance-impairing emotions at a lower level. Finally, in multi-event sports, such as gymnastics, decathlon, or shooting, the athlete may have different optimal anxiety zones for different events (second quote, lines 7–9).

The in/out of zone concept in the prediction of performance: The in/out of the zone concept is used in the assessment, prediction, and optimization of individual performance. Initially applied to precompetition anxiety, this concept assumes that each athlete has an individually optimal intensity level (high, moderate, or low) and a range or zone of optimal anxiety. Successful performance, particularly in short-duration tasks, occurs when precompetition anxiety is near or within these individually optimal zones. When precompetition anxiety falls outside the zones (higher or lower), the quality of individual performance deteriorates. Therefore, the in/out of the zone concept serves as an individualized criterion and a guiding principle in the description and prediction of anxiety-performance relationships.

The extended in/out of the zone concept is used to describe separate and joint effects of both positive and negative emotions. Specifically, the individual zone of optimal intensity is identified for each functionally optimal emotion based on multiple assessments of successful performances by each athlete. Similarly, the individual zones of dysfunctional intensity are identified for each dysfunctional emotion based on multiple assessments of poor performances by each athlete. There are zones of optimal function in some emotions (P+N+), within which the probability of successful performance is the highest. Likewise, there are also dysfunctional zones in other emotions (P–N–), within which the probability of poor performance is the highest. Optimal and dysfunctional intensity levels can be low, moderate, or high and can vary for the same and different emotions across different athletes. The total effect of positive and negative emotions on performance is determined by the interaction of optimal and dysfunctional effects. Although functionally optimal emotions are important predictors of successful performance, they alone may not be sufficient unless the potentially detrimental effect of dysfunctional emotions is also taken into consideration. The notion of a zone, therefore, as applied to a wide range of positive and negative emotions, seems appropriate since both optimal and dysfunctional interaction effects are considered jointly.

Figure 6.2 shows a visual representation of the interaction effects of two optimal emotion profiles with the predominance of either "challenge" (P+) or "threat" (N+) appraisals. Two dysfunctional emotion profiles are characterized by the predominance of either "dejection" and "harm" (N–) or "benefit" and "complacency" (P–) in response to a previous performance. These intensity interaction profiles are typical for predicting individual success or failure, although the emotion content in different athletes can be idiosyncratic and, therefore, different.

Recalling previous successful and poor performances and the accompanying emotional experiences is the first step in creating individualized profiles. These then need to be validated across multiple actual competitions.

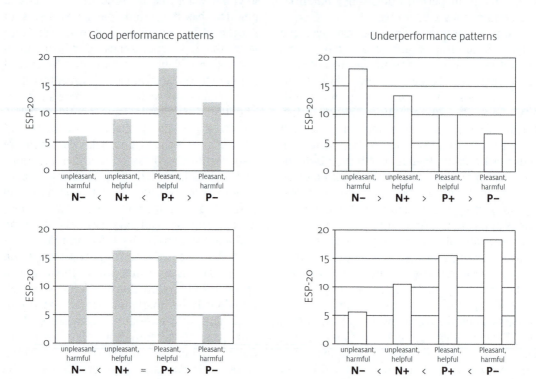

Figure 6.2 Emotion interactive profiles in successful and unsuccessful competitions.

Temporal patterns of emotions: The Time dimension includes *topological* (phases, cycles, sequencing, periodicity) and *metric* (duration, frequency) characteristics of emotional experiences. Short-term dynamics involve changes in emotion content and intensity across three stages of athletic performance, namely pre-event preparation, task execution, and post-event evaluation. In pre- and mid-event situations, the *anticipatory* pleasant (P+ challenge) and unpleasant (N+ threat) emotions are usually optimal for athletic performance. A focus on *outcome* pleasant (P– complacency) and unpleasant (N– dejection) emotions are harmful and dysfunctional (see Figure 6.2). In post-performance situations, outcome emotions are optimal unless they carry over excessive complacency or disappointment to

upcoming competitions or to non-competition contexts. Similarly, high intensity of emotions prior to and during performance can be beneficial for some athletes but detrimental in post-performance situations, if it disturbs recovery. There is a special need to cope with positively toned emotions: pre-event complacency (P–) is usually detrimental, whereas elevated challenge emotions (P+) in post-performance situations may sometimes deplete available resources and slow down recovery.

Context dimension: The Context dimension is an environmental characteristic reflecting the impact of situational, interpersonal, intra-group, and organizational factors on the intensity and content of emotional experiences. Typically, the situational impact is manifested in emotional experiences triggered in practices and competitions by the athletes' anticipated or real interactions with significant others (partners, coaches, teammates).

Research has examined several contexts, including successful and unsuccessful competitions of varying levels of significance (local, national, international), and different practice sessions. Additionally, a number of difficult situations or performance episodes may have special meaning for athletes and teams (weather conditions, competition sites, good and bad memories of past performances).

These situations may also include qualifications, performance in the finals, play-offs, competing against a "weaker" opponent, and performing after repeated successes or a series of slumps. Stress caused by the negative feedback from the coach may sometimes be helpful in dealing with excessive complacency prior to or during important games. The criterion for evaluating the effectiveness of emotional regulation would then be a change in the content and intensity of the emotional state that is optimal for athletic performance.

PERFORMANCE MEASURES

Specific emotional experiences in sport are closely connected to performance. Emotions affect performance and are affected by performance. However, research typically has not considered the process of performance (task execution), since assessments are limited to performance outcomes. Recently, some promising attempts to assess the action process using *"action-centered profiling"* (Hanin, 2010; Hanin & Hanina, 2009) were undertaken.

Assessment of performance outcomes: Performance assessment in sport is often problematic because the existing performance measures focus mainly on performance *outcomes* (objective-subjective, normative, or self-referenced). Understanding emotion-performance relationships is practically impossible without the individual-oriented assessment of the *task execution* or performance *process (action)*. Current practice in the assessment of performance is based mainly on inter-individual and group-oriented measures. However, absolute or "raw" performance (outcome) scores are misleading because transitory factors may affect the outcome and the use of absolute values limits meaningful comparisons across athletic events.

Each athlete's performance can be quantified in relative, self-referenced terms (e.g., a percentage of one's own personal best or one's average capability over recent performances as an intra-individually based measure), and a

criterion-referenced method (e.g., relative to a qualifying standard). Incorporating the concept of individual differences in emotion-performance relationships involves intra-individual measures that capture idiosyncratic aspects in both emotional experiences (emotion-centered profiling) and the in-task execution process (action-centered profiling).

Performance profiling: One of the first attempts to assess the factors affecting the performance process was performance profiling, proposed by Butler (1992). Performance profiling quantifies the *qualities* important for success in the selected sport and/or the *characteristics* of top performers in this sport. The ideal performance characteristics (physical, technical, psychological) are then contrasted with the athlete's current levels to identify the appropriate direction for future development. One of the advantages of performance profiling was an individualized approach to athletes' and coaches' perceptions. The practical utility of performance profiling was tested empirically, particularly in facilitating coach–athlete communication. However, performance as a movement sequence of interconnected actions was not assessed.

Action-centered profiling: To address these concerns, action-centered profiling as a supplement to and extension of IZOF-based emotion profiling was proposed. The validity and practical utility of this approach were examined in multiple case-studies in athletics (jumping, throwing, and running), swimming, diving, car racing, shooting, volleyball, and soccer (Hanin, 2010; Hanin & Hanina, 2009). The main focus in action-centered profiling is on the assessment of a *task execution* or *performance process* as a subjectively perceived movement sequence (or an "action chain") performed in competition. Action-centered profiling is part of the psycho-pedagogical program (termed Identification-Control-Correction or ICC program) that deals with performance difficulties in top-level athletes. The ICC program includes identification of individually optimal performance, control and monitoring of performance process in practices and competitions, and correction of habitual performance errors. Action-centered profiling provides a practical tool for dealing with inconsistencies in athletic performance. In the sections that follow, a brief overview of the assessment procedures employed in the ICC program is provided. The entire approach is described in more detail elsewhere (Hanin & Hanina, 2009).

Identification of individually optimal performance: Action-centered profiling includes several steps for the analysis of the athlete's performance history and the present situation.

1 Using her own words, the athlete describes the entire action as a movement sequence ("chain") of interconnected components.
2 The athlete describes an ideal execution of each component in the movement sequence based on past experience.
3 The athlete selects three to five best and three to five poorest actions and evaluates the quality of execution of each component on a scale ranging from 0 (none) to 10 (maximal possible).
4 The core component(s) positively affecting the outcomes of task execution are then identified by contrasting good and bad performance scores.

5 A list of effective pre-performance foci (mindsets and thoughts) in successful and unsuccessful actions is generated.
6 The optimal effort intensity and its dynamics in successful and unsuccessful performances are identified by comparing the differences between effort level at the beginning and by the end of movement.

A complete action profile created with the above analysis includes four parts: (1) optimal focus in training and competitions; (2) athlete-generated action sequence (a chain) with the description of its optimal execution; (3) effort intensity dynamics in action (from the beginning until the end of action); and (4) action outcomes (qualitative and quantitative). Athletes retrospectively recall (usually assisted by videos) their successful and unsuccessful performances. Optimal execution of each component in the chain is then identified with the accompanying subjective experiences.

Emotion-centered and action-centered profiling can be used to examine emotion-performance relationships as interactions between emotion and action. For instance, it has been found that optimization of action triggers functionally optimal emotions, whereas dysfunctional emotions reflect disrupted performance processes. Therefore, emotion-centered and action-centered profiling should be included in the assessment program as a part of coping in high-achievement sport.

The proposed emotion-centered and action-centered profiling offers an individualized approach to the analysis of emotion-performance relationships. Emotion profiling is individualized by using within-individual assessments and employing idiosyncratic emotion descriptors. Action-centered profiling with idiosyncratic process measures also aims to assess intra-individually the action process at the situational level. Both forms of individualized emotion and action profiling aim to achieve a better understanding of emotion-performance relationships.

EMOTIONS IN EXERCISE PSYCHOLOGY

Exercise psychology deals with people who are not necessarily young, athletic, physically fit, or perfectly healthy. Its objective is the promotion of physical activity and exercise behavior, with the ultimate goal of improving and maintaining fitness and health among people of all ages.

Exercise psychologists have been trying to understand exercise and physical activity behavior primarily by studying cognitions (thoughts, interpretations, evaluations) relevant to exercise. In cognitive theories, for example, it is assumed that someone would be more likely to start an exercise program and stick with it in the long run if she believes that she is capable of carrying out the exercise (can find the time, has the stamina, etc), expects that she will get the anticipated benefits out of it (e.g., will lose 10 kg or lower systolic blood pressure by 15 mmHg), is convinced that exercise is something she truly wants to do rather than something that is imposed by someone else, and has seen signs that important people around her would approve of her exercise efforts, encourage her, and support her. Accordingly, most standard interventions designed to promote physical activity and exercise behavior target such cognitions (i.e., improve self-efficacy, create a positive attitude, cultivate a sense of perceived autonomy, and offer sources of social support).

These thoughts do, to some extent, explain why some people exercise and others do not. However, all this emphasis on how one *thinks* about exercise may cause someone to overlook the important issue of how one *feels* about exercise or in response to exercise. With a little introspection, one quickly realizes that emotional constructs are actually a major part of the exercise and physical activity experience. An obese person begins an exercise program *desiring* to lose weight, may feel *embarrassed* exercising in front of mirrors and other exercisers who seem leaner or in better shape, is *disappointed* that the rate of weight loss is not as rapid as originally hoped, but feels *proud* to be able to walk continuously for 30 minutes without being out of breath. An elderly cardiac rehabilitation patient feels too *tired* to exercise, is *afraid* of having another heart attack while cycling, but soon realizes that exercise results in a boost of *energy* and *invigoration*.

WHY ARE EMOTION-RELATED CONSTRUCTS OF INTEREST TO EXERCISE PSYCHOLOGY?

Emotional responses to exercise and physical activity are of considerable interest to both scientists and practitioners because they seem to have at least three important functions (see Figure 6.3). First, these responses are of interest as outcomes of exercise participation (i.e., as *dependent* variables, in research terminology). Since the early days of exercise psychology, research demonstrated the ability of exercise and physical activity to improve how people feel, both acutely (after a single session) and chronically (after an exercise program lasting for several weeks or months). For example, when asked, many exercisers say that they work out to regulate their mood and manage their tension and stress. Accordingly, a large research literature has developed dealing with the effects of exercise on *mental health* (see Chapter 44).

Second, these emotional responses are also interesting because of the effects they have on subsequent exercise behavior (i.e., as *independent* variables, in research terminology). For example, if a particular type of exercise makes you feel better (e.g., more *energetic* or more *proud*), you cannot wait to do it again. On the contrary, if a particular type of exercise makes you feel worse (e.g., leaves you *exhausted* or

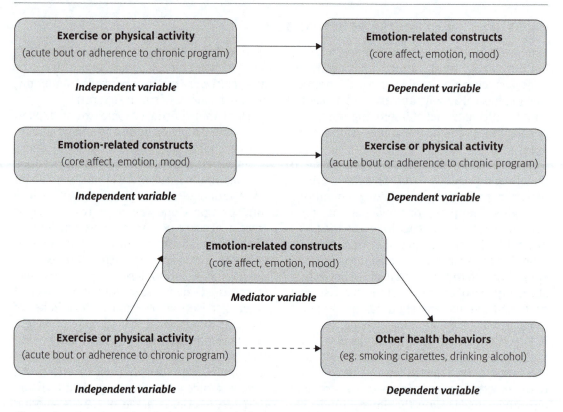

Figure 6.3 Emotion-related constructs, including core affect, emotion, and mood, (a) are influenced by exercise or physical activity, (b) influence exercise or physical activity, and (c) are the reason behind some of the effects of exercise or physical activity on other health-related behaviors.

makes you feel *embarrassed* or *disappointed*), you try to avoid it. So, researchers and practitioners try to find ways to make exercise as pleasant as possible, for as many participants as possible, in an effort to improve exercise adherence and reduce dropout.

Third, these responses may be the reasons behind some other beneficial effects of exercise (i.e., *mediating* variables, in research terminology). For example, exercise reduces cravings for cigarettes, alcohol, or drugs of abuse. These are substances people use to regulate transient disturbances in their mood (e.g., tension, worry), despite the negative long-term effects they may have on health. A strong possibility for why exercise reduces cravings is that it helps people maintain a more positive, relaxed mood, so there is no need to resort to an external substance to regulate one's mood.

TYPES OF EMOTIONAL CONSTRUCTS

In everyday language, we use the term "emotion" in a generic sense, as if the whole category of "emotion" was unitary or undifferentiated. However, to facilitate the scientific study of emotional constructs in the context of exercise, scientists must be very precise about the phenomena they investigate. So, it became necessary to differentiate between different types of phenomena that are generally classified under the rubric of "emotion" (see Figure 6.4).

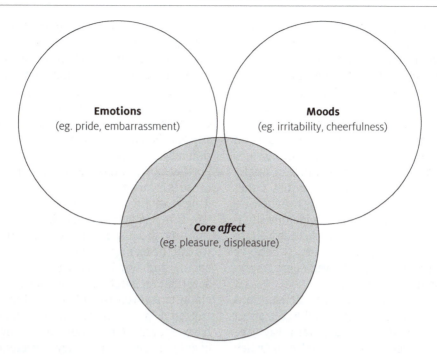

Figure 6.4 In addition to occurring independently, core affect is also a component of emotions and moods (it is what makes emotions and moods "feel" a certain way). However, emotions and moods also have additional components, including cognitive appraisals, physiological responses, and action tendencies.

Consider this. Imagine that a stranger approaches you and, without any provocation, punches you in the chest. What is the first thing you would feel, within the first few milliseconds? A sudden *pain*, a very distinct, inherently *unpleasant* sensation that we experience when our body suffers some type of injury. This type of pain did not require you to think about what happened ("Why did this person hit me?") or the possible future consequences ("I hope I will be OK"). It was an immediate, uncontrollable, automatic response, yet it evoked an unmistakably unpleasant feeling. In scientific terminology, we call this type of raw pleasant or unpleasant feeling that does not require any prior cognitive processing "core affect." Examples of core affect include feeling *pleasure* versus *displeasure*, *energy* versus *tiredness*, or *tension* versus *calmness*.

Now, what will you feel next, possibly just a second later, once you have had a chance to realize what happened? Most likely, you will feel an outburst of *anger* toward this stranger. Qualitatively, this is a very different response from the initial displeasure of *pain*. By comparison, anger is a considerably more complex reaction. This is because in the less than a second that passed, a very important process took place: cognitive appraisal. The physical stimulus underwent recognition ("I was just punched in the chest") and was attributed to a causal agent ("It was this stranger who punched me"). More importantly, the stimulus was placed in context ("This was an unprovoked attack") and its meaning for your physical and social well-being was analysed ("This person violated my rights and threatened my physical safety and social standing"). In scientific terminology, we call these complex types of reactions that require some prior cognitive processing *emotions* or *prototypical emotional episodes*.

Notice that it is not necessary for the cognitive appraisal process to be conscious; oftentimes, these thoughts happen so fast that you only experience their outcome (the emotion, in this case *anger*) but you have no conscious awareness of the process that led to that outcome (the *appraisal*). Nevertheless, theorists believe that it is impossible to have an emotional reaction like anger unless the steps just described (recognition, attribution, analysis, and interpretation) take place first. Other examples of emotions include *fear* (when we appraise that we are facing a dangerous situation), *sadness* (when we appraise that we face an irrevocable loss), and *pride* (when we appraise that we have achieved some important but hard-to-reach goal).

It is important to recognize that emotions include core affect. In fact, it is the core affect that makes emotions *feel* a certain way (e.g., *pleasure* when feeling *proud*, *displeasure* when feeling *embarrassed*). However, in the case of emotion, the core affect does not appear isolated but rather as one element in a broad array of components that together make up the emotion. Specifically, besides the cognitive appraisal and the core affect, emotions also include such components as physiological reactions (e.g., activation of the sympathetic branch of the autonomic nervous system) and action tendencies (e.g., return the punch in retaliation).

Next, imagine waking up the morning after the unfortunate incident with the stranger. It is possible that you will wake up feeling irritable and tense, without any immediately apparent reason. You may tend to speak abruptly to those around you and your threshold for becoming upset and picking a fight may be lowered. Clearly, this psychological state is different from an emotion in several respects. Compared to an emotional episode, the intensity of this type of feeling is lower but its duration may be longer (hours instead of minutes). Furthermore, although in an emotion the cause is clear and the emotion follows the eliciting stimulus instantaneously, in a situation like this it may not be obvious why you feel this way; you just do. In scientific terminology, we call the feelings that just seem to be "there," ebbing and flowing rather than following a specific precipitating event, *moods*. Theorists claim that, even though a mood may not be triggered by a specific stimulus, moods still have a cause (are about something) and a cognitive basis. The key difference with emotions, however, is what is being appraised in each case. In the case of emotions, the appraisal is about something specific (e.g., an unprovoked assault), whereas in the case of a mood the appraisal may be about something much less specific ("What have I done with my life?"), something very distant ("What if my infant child grows up to be a criminal?") or about one's life in general ("My life is a failure"). Examples of moods include feeling *cheerful* or *upbeat*, *grouchy* or *agitated*. As was the case with emotions, core affect is also a component of moods; it is what makes moods feel the way they do, pleasant or unpleasant.

CORE AFFECT, EMOTIONS, AND MOODS IN THE CONTEXT OF EXERCISE AND PHYSICAL ACTIVITY

In the context of exercise and physical activity, we may encounter any one or all of these types of responses: *core affect*, *emotions*, and *moods*. Let us consider some examples. Imagine running outdoors on a hot and humid day and pushing your body to its limit. A sense of exhaustion overpowers you. Your body feels dehydrated, tired, drained of energy. This is a raw, immediate physical sensation, the emergence of which did not require a cognitive appraisal. For the most part, this feeling is unlikely to be suppressed even if you try to control it through cognition (e.g., by telling yourself "I can do it, I can do it"). So, this would qualify as a *core affective* response to exercise. Of course, one may also experience pleasant core affective responses to exercise. In fact, extensive research has shown that feelings of energy, invigoration, exhilaration, and revitalization are among the strongest responses reported after bouts of exercise, at least among people who are healthy and fit (see Chapter 44).

As another example, imagine being self-conscious about the appearance of your body and having a constant tendency to think that others look at you and judge how you look in a negative way. Now picture walking into a gymnasium, with mirrors on the walls and full of young, athletic, seemingly super-fit people in tight clothing. Immediately, there is a rush of negative thoughts and worries about how you look and the critical comments all these people may make about you. You think that all the eyes are on you and everyone is talking about you. An overwhelming feeling of *anxiety* overtakes you; you feel terrible, your palms begin to sweat, your stomach tightens, your heart races, and all you can think about is getting as far away as possible. This is clearly an *emotional* reaction since it arose in response to a very specific situation, following a cognitive appraisal of threat, and it included, besides *core affect* (feeling terrible), other components, such as physiological changes and the desire to get away. On the other hand, of course, people may also experience positive emotional responses to exercise. A good example is the emotion of *pride*, which follows the cognitive appraisal of having accomplished something

challenging and, at the same time, of high personal significance, such as finishing your first 10-kilometer run or walking for 30 minutes without having to stop.

Now imagine going through a very difficult period in your life (e.g., not being able to find a job or being deeply dissatisfied with your current job). You think you have tried everything and have run out of options. There is an overwhelming sense of uncertainty and insecurity about the future. You feel disappointed and sad. In a word, you are depressed. Depression is a disturbance of mood. A characteristic of depression is that it is typically accompanied by the absence of any desire to move, especially going outdoors and socializing. So, while one feels depressed, participation in physical activity is generally reduced. If the person was a regular exerciser before, a period of depressed mood would increase the chances of non-adherence (missing scheduled exercise sessions) or dropout. On the other hand, mustering the courage to exercise can result in much-improved mood and, in turn, a more positive outlook on life.

As these examples illustrate, exercise and physical activity are intricately linked to core affect, emotion, and mood. Simply put, how one feels has a dramatic impact on his or her level of exercise and physical activity and, conversely, engaging in exercise or physical activity can have a dramatic impact on how one feels. So, if we want to understand the psychology of exercise, we must include affect, emotion, and mood as essential components.

MONITORING CORE AFFECT, EMOTION, AND MOOD: ADVICE FOR THE EXERCISE PROFESSIONAL

The common goal of all exercise professionals is to instill in their clients a permanent (ideally, lifelong) exercise or physical activity habit. Obviously, all the health benefits of exercise and physical activity can vanish rather quickly once the person discontinues the activity. So, even being successful in achieving some short-term benefits (e.g., a reduction in body weight) is actually inconsequential if the person reverts to a sedentary lifestyle and the benefits evaporate (e.g., the weight is regained).

With this in mind, it seems reasonable to suggest that exercise professionals should adopt a new, broader view of their mission, with their primary objective being the promotion of exercise and physical activity as a permanent ingredient of people's lives. At the core of this mission is the concept of motivation. Put a little differently, an exercise professional should be, above all else, a motivator. Part of that mission is, therefore, the monitoring and enhancement of all variables known to influence the motivation for exercise and physical activity.

As explained here, affect, emotion, and mood should be considered key motivational variables and should, therefore, be monitored with appropriate self-report measures (which are available in the scientific literature). The goal of monitoring these variables is to detect problems and undertake appropriate interventions to address them (such as changes in a client's exercise mode, frequency, intensity, duration, or setting). Which of the three constructs one should monitor will depend on the particular circumstances (i.e., the characteristics of the client, the exercise, and the social and physical environment). For example, if a particular client is mainly concerned about negative social evaluation within a gymnasium environment, then it would be most appropriate to monitor the emotion of social anxiety. If a client suffers from depression, and this negative mood influences his or her physical activity and other health-related behaviors (e.g., eating or substance abuse), then it would make sense to monitor fluctuations in symptoms of depressive mood. However, in most cases, since core affect is a broader construct than emotion and mood, the consistent monitoring of core affect within exercise settings can prove very informative.

How can one measure core affect? This is a challenging question because there seem to be so many different types of affective feelings and so many different words used to describe how people feel. Scientists have addressed this issue by examining the inter-correlations among words that are used to describe affective states. What they have determined is that these words are not entirely independent of

one another. In fact, they seem to be related in some systematic ways. Specifically, most of the similarities and differences among words used to describe affective states can be accounted for by just two basic dimensions. Essentially, this means that one can get a pretty good idea about how one feels by just asking two key questions: (a) "Is what you are feeling a pleasant or an unpleasant state?" and (b) "Does what you are feeling involve a high level or a low level of perceived activation (or 'arousal')?" In the scientific literature, this two-dimensional model of core affect is known as the affect circumplex (Ekkekakis, 2008; Ekkekakis & Petruzzello, 2002). The first dimension is known as "affective valence" and ranges from pleasant states (*happy*, *glad*) to unpleasant states (*sorry, sad*). The other dimension is known as "perceived activation" and ranges from "high" states (*intense, worked-up*) to "low" states (*quiet, still*). According to the circumplex model, any affective state is essentially a composite of some degree of valence and activation.

Together, valence and activation can be thought of as the two axes of a map of core affect (with affective valence as the horizontal axis and perceived activation as the vertical axis). A person's position and trajectory of change over time (e.g., from before, to during, to after a bout of exercise) can then be plotted on this map (see Figure 6.5). A convenient method of monitoring valence and activation changes in response to exercise is by administering two easy-to-use rating scales: the Feeling Scale (FS) to measure valence, and the Felt Arousal Scale (FAS) to measure activation (see Figure 6.6). The developers of the FS recommend giving respondents the following instructions:

While participating in exercise, it is common to experience changes in mood. Some individuals find exercise pleasurable, whereas others find it to be unpleasurable. Additionally, feeling may fluctuate across time. That is, one might feel good and bad a number of times during exercise. Scientists have developed this scale to measure such responses.

The developers of the FAS recommended the following instructions:

Estimate here how aroused you actually feel. Do this by circling the appropriate number. By "arousal" here is meant how "worked-up" you feel. You might experience high arousal in one of a variety of ways, for example as excitement or anxiety or anger. Low arousal might also be experienced by you in one of a number of different ways, for example as relaxation or boredom or calmness.

If an exerciser remains within the pleasant half of the model (e.g., experiences pleasant high-activation states, such an excitement, during exercise and pleasant low-activation states, such as relaxation, after exercise), the

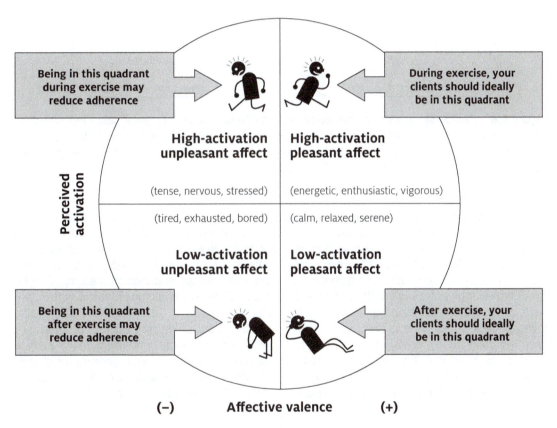

Figure 6.5 According to the circumplex model, core affect is defined by two main dimensions: affective valence (which ranges from pleasure to displeasure) and perceived activation (which ranges from low to high). The combination of these two dimensions yields four varieties of core affect, as shown in the Figure. A central part of the mission of any exercise professional is to promote motivation for lifelong exercise or physical activity. To accomplish this goal, it is important to consistently monitor how clients feel during and after exercise and to make appropriate modifications to the exercise routine to ensure that they derive positive affective experiences.

Feeling Scale (FS)		Felt Arousal Scale (FAS)	
+5	Very good	6	High arousal
+4			
+3	Good	5	
+2			
+1	Fairly good	4	
0	Neutral		
−1	Fairly bad	3	
−2			
−3	Bad	2	
−4			
−5	Very bad	1	Low arousal
Source: Hardy & Rejeski, 1989		Source: Svebak & Murgatroyd, 1985	

Figure 6.6 Affective valence can be measured with the Feeling Scale (FS), while perceived activation can be measured with the Felt Arousal Scale (FAS). Because the FS and the FAS are both single-item measures, they can be administered multiple times during and after exercise without disrupting the activity or placing unnecessary burden on the exercisers.

overall exercise experience will likely register in memory as a positive one and act as an incentive for the person to repeat the activity in the future. On the other hand, if the exerciser moves to the unpleasant half of the model (e.g., experiences unpleasant high-activation states, such as tension, during exercise or unpleasant low-activation states, such as exhaustion, after exercise), then the experience may register in memory as a negative one, with undesirable motivational implications. People are more likely to repeat activities they found pleasant but tend to avoid activities they found unpleasant. Detecting that a client experiences reductions in pleasure or moves into the negative part of the circumplex model should alert the exercise professional that changes need to be made. These could include modifying the dose characteristics of the exercise (frequency, intensity, duration, progression), promoting a sense of autonomy, providing more diverse exercise options to avoid monotony, or changing the social environment of the exercise to eliminate sources of social anxiety.

CONCLUSION

It is important for athletes, coaches, and consultants to understand the function of emotion experiences and their impact on athletic performance and exercise participation. Emotional experiences are multidimensional core components of psychobiosocial (PBS) states that may enhance athletic performance and well-being. Emotion- and action-centered profiling are used for monitoring and enhancing emotional experiences in high achievement sport and exercise settings. The emotion- and action-centered profiling offers an individualized approach to the analysis and enhancement of emotion-performance relationships. The individualized emotion profiling employs idiosyncratic personally relevant emotion and action descriptors and focuses on within-individual assessments at the situational level. There are specific types of emotional experiences likely to be elicited by exercise participation. These should be monitored systematically and used as a guide in tailoring the exercise to the individual. Ensuring that exercise is experienced as pleasant can optimize the benefits for mental health and enhance motivation for continued participation.

LEARNING AIDS

1   Explain how emotion experiences can be categorized.

Usually emotion can be categorized as a situational (state-like) experience. It can also be construed as a relatively stable, repeated (trait-like) pattern of experience. Finally, emotions can be conceptualized as meta-experiences or attitudes and knowledge about situational and stable emotion patterns.

2   Describe how situational emotional experiences are related to other modalities of psychobiosocial (PBS) state.

Emotional experiences are just one modality of PBS state. Other modalities include cognitive, motivational, volitional, bodily, kinesthetic, operational, and communicative forms of functioning.

3   Identify four global emotion content categories based on the two-factor distinction: valence (pleasure-displeasure) and function (helpful-harmful).

There are pleasant-helpful (P+), unpleasant-helpful (N+), pleasant-harmful (P–), and unpleasant-harmful (N–). P+ and N+ are anticipatory and optimal emotions prior to successful performance; whereas N– and P– are emotional responses to occurred events and thus harmful for the forthcoming performance.

4   Explain how to predict athletic performance based on the interaction effects of optimal and dysfunctional emotions.

The "in-out of zone" concept assumes that high probability of successful performance can be anticipated if the current emotional state is close to or in the optimal intensity zone and outside the dysfunctional intensity zone. The highest probability of underperformance is expected when the pre-event emotional state is outside previously established optimal intensity zones and in the dysfunctional intensity zones.

5   Explain how the interactive effects of emotions can either enhance or impair athletic emotions.

Enhancing interactive effects of emotions are observed when emotions P+ and N+ are predominant in the personal emotion profile as measured by the ESP-40 scale. At the same time, dysfunctional emotions (N– and P–) should be of minimal intensity. Impairing interactive effects of emotions are anticipated when the dysfunctional emotions (N– and P–) are predominant, along with minimal intensity of optimal emotions (P+ and N+).

6 Discuss the benefits and limitations of action-centered profiling.

The main benefit of action-centered profiling is in the assessment of task execution with emphasis on individually optimal performance. Action-centered profiling also provides a practical tool for dealing with inconsistencies in athletic performance. It also offers an individualized approach to the analysis of emotion-performance relationships by assessing intra-individually the action process at the situational level. One of the advantages and also limitations of the action-centered profiling is that it has been used mainly with expert performers (national and international level athletes). Additionally, so far, it has been used mainly in individual sports of relatively short duration. Additional research is needed to examine the specifics and potential utility of action-centered profiling in long-duration and team sports.

7 What is the role of emotion-related constructs (i.e., core affect, emotion, mood) in the exercise experience?

These constructs could be: (a) independent variables, influencing exercise behavior (e.g., enhance or reduce motivation for future participation and adherence); (b) dependent variables or outcomes of exercise participation (e.g., reduced anxiety or improved vigor); and (c) mediator variables, underlying the effects of exercise on other outcomes, such as smoking cessation.

8 Define the concepts of core affect, emotion, and mood.

Core affect is a very basic form of valenced (pleasant or unpleasant) feeling. It is a central component of emotions and mood but it also exists independently of emotions and moods and is always accessible to consciousness. Thus, the experience of core affect does not require a prior cognitive appraisal. An emotion is a subjective response to a stimulus that comprises multiple coordinated components (i.e., core affect, cognitive appraisal, physiological changes, expression, and behavioral action). For an emotion to be elicited, a specific precipitating stimulus (e.g., a social exchange) must be cognitively appraised as being potentially consequential for the goals and the present or future well-being of the individual. Moods are typically less intense but longer lasting than emotions. Furthermore, unlike emotions, moods may be delayed, as opposed to instantaneous, reactions to a precipitating stimulus. Importantly, in the case of mood, the precipitating stimulus may be diffuse or unspecific (e.g., "my life" or "my future").

REVIEW QUESTIONS

1 Explain how negatively toned situational emotions can be harmful and helpful for athletic performance.

2 Explain how positively toned situational emotions can be helpful and harmful for athletic performance.

3 Discuss the role of emotional meta-experiences in athletic performance.

4 Discuss five basic dimensions for the systematic description of emotional experiences as a component of the psychobiosocial (PBS) state.

5   Analyze interactive effects of optimal and dysfunctional emotions on performance.

6   Discuss the six steps of action-centered profiling to identify individually optimal performance.

7   What are the dimensions of core affect according to the circumplex model?

8   To facilitate motivation for future participation, in which quadrant of circumplex space should an exerciser be during exercise? After exercise?

EXERCISES

1   Develop your own individualized emotion profile (for a tutorial, see Hanin, 2000, Appendix, pp. 301–316).

2   Interpret your IZOF-emotion profiles (optimal and dysfunctional).

3   Use the Feeling Scale and Felt Arousal Scale to assess, plot, and compare your core affective response to two or more different exercise bouts (e.g., different intensities or different social environments).

ADDITIONAL READING

Ekkekakis, P. (2013). *The measurement of affect, mood, and emotion: A guide for health-behavioral research*. New York: Cambridge University Press.

Ekkekakis, P. (2012). Affect, mood, and emotion. In G. Tenenbaum, R.C. Eklund & A. Kamata (Eds.), *Measurement in sport and exercise psychology* (pp.321–332). Champaign, IL: Human Kinetics.

Hanin, Y.L. (2003, February). Performance related emotional states in sport: A qualitative analysis. *Forum Qualitative Sozialforschung / Forum: Qualitative Social Research* [On-line Journal], 4 (1). At: http://www.qualitative-research.net/fqs-texte/1-03/1-03hanin-e.htmU

Hardy, C.J. & Rejeski, W.J. (1989). Not what, but how one feels: The measurement of affect during exercise. *Journal of Sport and Exercise Psychology*, *11*, 304–317.

Harmison, R.J. (2006). Peak performance in sport: Identifying ideal performance states and developing athlete's psychological skills. *Professional Psychology: Research and Practice*, *37*, 233–243.

Nieuwenhuys, A., Hanin, Y. & Bakker, F. (2008). Performance related experiences and coping during races: A case of an elite sailor. *Psychology of Sport and Exercise*, *9*, 61–76.

Raglin J. & Hanin, Y. (2000) Competitive anxiety and athletic performance. In Y.L. Hanin (Ed.). *Emotions in sport* (pp.93–112). Champaign, IL: Human Kinetics.

Robazza, C. (2006). Emotion in sport: An IZOF perspective. In S. Hanton & S.D. Mellalieu (Eds.), *Literature reviews in sport psychology*. Hauppage, NY: Nova Science.

Robazza, C., Bortoli, L. & Hanin, Y. (2006). Perceived effects of emotion intensity on athletic performance: A contingency-based individualized approach. *Research Quarterly for Exercise and Sport*, *77*, 372–385.

Svebak, S. & Murgatroyd, S. (1985). Metamotivational dominance: A multimethod validation of reversal theory constructs. *Journal of Personality and Social Psychology*, *48*, 107–116.

Woodcock, C., Cumming, J., Duda, J.L. & Sharp, L-A. (2012). Working within an Individual Zone of Optimal Functioning (IZOF) framework: Consultant practice and athlete reflections on refining emotion regulation skills. *Psychology of Sport and Exercise*, *13*, 291–302.

REFERENCES

Ekkekakis, P. (2008). Affect circumplex redux: The discussion on its utility as a measurement framework in exercise psychology continues. *International Review of Sport and Exercise Psychology, 1*, 139–159.

Ekkekakis, P. & Petruzzello, S.J. (2002). Analysis of the affect measurement conundrum in exercise psychology: IV. A conceptual case for the affect circumplex. *Psychology of Sport and Exercise, 3*, 35–63.

Hanin, Y.L. (1997). Emotions and Athletic Performance: Individual Zones of Optimal Functioning Model. *European Yearbook of Sport Psychology, 1*, pp.29–72.

Hanin, Y.L. (Ed.). (2000). *Emotions in sport.* Champaign, IL: Human Kinetics.

Hanin, Y. (2007). Emotions in Sport: Current issues and perspectives. In G. Tenenbaum & R.C. Eklund (Eds.), *Handbook of sport psychology* (3rd ed., pp.31–58). Hoboken, NJ: John Wiley & Sons.

Hanin, J. & Hanina, M. (2009). Optimization of performance in top-level athletes: An action-focused coping. With the Commentaries. *International Journal of Sport Sciences & Coaching, 4*, 47–91.

Vygotsky, L.S. (1926/1984). *Sobranie sochinenii,* [A six-volume collection of works], v. 4 Child Psychology. Moscow, USSR: Pedagogika.

Chapter 7

Individuals with disabilities

JEFFREY J. MARTIN, FRANCESCA VITALI AND LAUREL WHALEN

SUMMARY

Although many people with disabilities are sedentary, physical activity (PA) involvement results in a host of benefits for those that are physically active. In addition to common reasons (e.g., lack of time) noted for low PA levels, people with disabilities also face a variety of individual (e.g., pain), social (e.g., fewer workout friends) and environmental (e.g., no curb cuts) barriers unique to their disability condition. Youth sport opportunities are similar to the limited PA participation opportunities for adults, but the benefits children derive from sport span psychological (e.g., enhanced efficacy), social (e.g., stronger friendships) and physiological areas. Finally, elite level athletes (e.g., Paralympians) have to deal with many sport related challenges and disability derived challenges that can undermine optimal training and performance. However, strong mental skills (e.g., imagery), sport specific psychological factors (e.g., sport efficacy) and personality traits (e.g., tough-mindedness) and mood states (e.g., vigor) are associated with superior performance suggesting important roles for sport psychologists.

INTRODUCTION

The purpose of this chapter is to review the knowledge base on individuals with physical disabilities engaging in physical activity (PA)[1]. The present chapter examines three streams of knowledge with an emphasis on the first two areas. First, we report on the low levels of PA involvement by individuals with disabilities. We then aim to help families, caregivers, and teachers understand the plethora of benefits and barriers associated with PA. In the second section we highlight important psychosocial considerations in youth disability sport in order to illustrate how valuable sport experiences can be in promoting a high quality life for youth with disabilities. Our recommendations here are geared to mostly parents, coaches, and teachers. A discussion of the psychological dynamics of elite sport, such as the mental preparation of Paralympians, is examined last. The goal of our final section, albeit brief, is to help coaches, support staff, and sport psychologists appreciate how mental skills help elite athletes, and the unique challenges they face. To facilitate reader engagement we next present a case study.

CASE STUDY

On a nice day in fall, the physical education class heads outside to the football field, which is covered with artificial turf. Molly, a student, is from an upper Social Economic Status (SES) family and therefore can afford a modern lightweight sport wheelchair. She can wheel pretty well on the turf (not as well as on pavement though) because she plays lots of wheelchair basketball and has a strong upper body. Another student, Van, from a lower SES family, can only afford a heavy traditional wheelchair that is hard to wheel. Because Van does far less physical activity (compared to Molly) he is not as strong. Therefore, he has more difficulty wheeling on the artificial turf. Van's friend Shay, an able-bodied boy, grabs (without asking) Van's wheelchair handlebars in order to wheel him across the artificial turf and Van reluctantly accepts Shay's help, but is clearly upset with Shay and with himself. Drew, a good and athletic friend of Molly's, asks her if she would like to be pushed fast (and waits for an affirmative answer), around the pavement covered edges of the field to get to the playing area on the other side quickly so they can start playing. Molly enthusiastically and gratefully yells "Lets go, time is wasting!"

 OBJECTIVES

After reading this chapter you will be able to:

1 Discuss the most common barriers that make it difficult for people with disabilities to obtain adequate physical activity.
2 Recognize the value of and the role of inclusion in encouraging physical activity and sport participation for children with disabilities.
3 Discuss the psychosocial benefits for youth with disabilities from engaging in sports.
4 Report on how mental skills help athletes with disabilities perform optimally.
5 Discuss the unique challenges that athletes with disabilities face when playing sports.

PHYSICAL ACTIVITY PARTICIPATION

Physical activity engagement

Individuals with disabilities often have higher rates of obesity and being overweight compared to non-disabled individuals, which could be partially addressed through increased PA at a population level. At present, a clear pattern of limited PA for most people with disabilities exists throughout the world (Martin, 2012). Low PA levels have been documented in North America, Europe, Asia, and Africa. Limited PA is evident irrespective of the age group, or setting (e.g., physical education, recess, lifestyle PA). With the exception of hearing impaired individuals, the findings of low PA span all disability types such as spinal cord injury, cerebral palsy, spina bifida, amputees, visual impairments, developmental disabilities, or mixed disability groups (Martin, 2012). Findings of low PA are also consistent regardless of the assessment method (e.g., pedometers vs. self report) (Martin, 2012). People who are older, who have severe disabilities, and are from low SES categories tend to be most at risk for low PA engagement.

A strong rationale for the importance of PA is the many benefits stemming from being physically active. Researchers have documented improvements in fitness across home, community and research settings. Because people with disabilities often have associated secondary conditions (e.g., diabetes, pressure sores), PA is particularly important as a way to prevent or attenuate secondary conditions. In the following sections we note some of the major psychosocial benefits and barriers of PA participation to impress upon the reader how important, yet difficult, it is for individuals with disabilities to be physically active.

Physical activity benefits

Increases in strength and fitness often result in enhanced perceptions of current and future competence. Martin (2012) noted that both social influence (e.g., adult feedback) and mastery experiences jointly influence competence perceptions. Adults experience competence-enhancing benefits from diverse physical activities ranging from horseback riding to wheelchair basketball. For example, participants in therapeutic horse riding programs have experienced significant increases in both physical self-efficacy and behavioral confidence. For individuals such as instructors, teachers, and coaches it is important to create a mastery climate by providing specific and encouraging feedback that acknowledges effort, learning, and self-improvement. Feedback grounded in social comparison processes should be avoided.

Greater feelings of independence from PA involvement are also frequently noted by individuals with disabilities. Hence, PA leaders should ask if help is needed before unilaterally providing it. People with disabilities typically know their limitations and are used to asking for help when it is needed. Providing help that is not needed or unasked for is not useful and can undermine the development of competence and independence. On the other hand, some children appreciate help if it means that they can play more.

In addition to competence and social benefits, engaging in PA is simply enjoyable and such experiences are valuable for quality of life reasons. In addition to the momentary value of increased positive affect, PA can also help in mood management when individuals do not have good days. For example, adults with spinal cord injury (SCI) have reported increased positive affect and decreased negative affect after exercising irrespective of whether participants had positive or negative life events that day. There was also some preliminary evidence that individuals with neurotic tendencies may benefit the most from the mood enhancing benefits of PA.

Caregivers and aids of people with disabilities should view PA involvement as a potential vehicle for mood management and encourage the individuals they work with to be active. A host of researchers have reported that many participants in their research studies enjoy PA and in particular individuals with SCI have often noted that weight training is enjoyable. Clearly, people with disabilities can engage in weight training programs provided the equipment is accessible. Weight training should not be dismissed as an option for someone simply because they might be in a wheelchair or missing a limb. In brief, PA can be enjoyed by people with disabilities and can provide many psychosocial and physiological benefits.

In summary, PA engagement results in a plethora of benefits. The individuals participating and supporting (e.g., teachers, peers) people with disabilities can clearly enhance the PA experience. However, PA doesn't automatically confer social benefits upon participants and instances where people with disabilities are ignored, marginalized, or teased can act as barriers to future participation. Hence, barriers to PA are also important to understand.

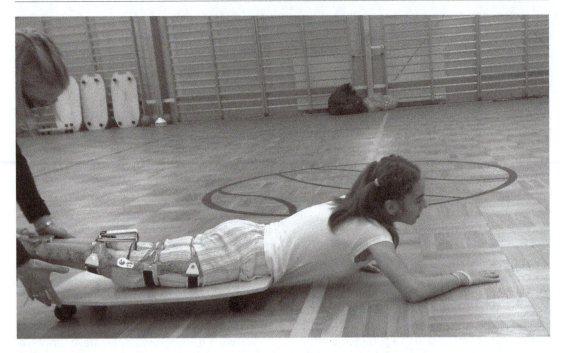

Figure 7.1 Adapted physical education student.

Barriers

"Sometimes, but I really don't know. I don't know if they like me or want me here or not. I can't tell" (Devine, 2004, p. 153).

"I felt like everyone treated me like a baby then, like they had to take care of me and I was already 21 years old" (Devine, 2004, p. 152).

The above two quotes indicate that the PA atmosphere in which individuals with disabilities find themselves may not be particularly inviting. Hence, such atmospheres may contribute to a reluctance on the part of individuals with disabilities to engage in social settings that promote PA. The non-welcoming atmospheres in which individuals with disabilities often face become barriers to their PA participation.

Relative to individuals without disabilities, pain, fatigue, tight joints, and discomfort are major barriers to PA. People with disabilities are also more likely to cite disease, poor health, and secondary injuries as barriers to PA. Clearly, family members and caregivers must recognize that individuals with disabilities may be unwilling to engage in PA because of the discomfort. Like many people, individuals with disabilities may not know where to exercise or how to start and maintain an exercise program. Limited time and money (e.g., expensive gym or club memberships) may also impede efforts to be physically active.

Barriers that are more social in nature are also common. Parents of children with disabilities are often fearful for their offspring's mental health as a result of teasing and their physical health if they engaged in activities perceived as dangerous (e.g., wall climbing for a visually impaired person). Such parents are urged to take appropriate safe guards to insure their children's well-being but to also consider that many children with disabilities participate in PA safely. The injury rates for adapted PA programs, with a few exceptions, are no greater than the injury rates of children without disabilities who are physically active. Parents often criticize community recreation personnel and physical education teachers as limiting to their children's PA because of a lack of knowledge of various disability conditions and how to adapt activities.

PE teachers have also acknowledged that they lack adequate professional preparation. Clearly, physical education teacher certification programs would benefit adapted PE teachers if they were able to offer more classwork and student teacher experiences related to disability and adapted sport and PA programming. PE teachers should refrain from allowing their students with disabilities to miss PE because of unnecessary and blanket medical excuses from doctors. Caregivers of adults in residential care homes with Cerebral Palsy (CP) have, in large numbers (i.e., over 50%) reported that they did not believe exercise was of value for their residents and 33% indicated exercise would not help their CP. Clearly clinicians and teachers in educational and medical programs that train such caregivers need to correct erroneous information and provide accurate guidelines for PA. Legal guardians for children and adults living in group care homes need to be advocates for their wards to insure that they are not denied the same opportunities for leisure, recreation, and PA that non-disabled people receive.

The environment also restricts PA. People with disabilities often note that there are very few places to be active and rarely are the locations convenient. Even programs designed for individuals with disabilities may be limited as some wheelchair basketball leagues ban motorized wheelchairs. Built environment barriers, such as a lack of a curb cut, or crosswalks without auditory signals, can prevent individuals with disabilities from even crossing the street. Ramps that are designed to facilitate access are often built too steep, thereby preventing use by many (Martin, 2012).

Some barriers are subtle. For example, although wheelchairs help people with disabilities move, individuals with SCI view their wheelchair as the number one barrier to PA (Chaves,

Boninger, Cooper, Fitzgerald, Gray, & Cooper, 2005). Ironically, participants rated their wheelchairs as bigger barriers to PA than their disability. Chaves et al. (2005) indicated that most suppliers and clinicians have limited training in prescribing wheelchairs. Finally, many SCI individuals find traditional manual wheelchairs uncomfortable, too wide and heavy, and as a result find them difficult to move. Many people with disabilities, in lower SES groups, cannot afford lightweight modern wheelchairs.

Rimmer and colleagues (Rimmer, Riley, Wang, & Rauworth, 2005) have examined the accessibility of health clubs and found that many (>50%) did not have curb cuts for easy access or clear paths to lockers. Most weight rooms did not have enough room for an individual to transfer from a wheelchair to exercise equipment. Rimmer et al. concluded that people with mobility disabilities and visual impairments would "have difficulty accessing various areas of fitness facilities and health clubs" (p. 2022). Rimmer et al.'s research has also been supported by other similar research efforts. These barriers are not just prevalent in the gym; poorly-lit walking paths and wooded walking trails with exposed tree roots can also be barriers to PA.

In summary, PA barriers can be grounded in individual level considerations such as the nature of a person's disability, and individual's social networks. The built environment can also constrain PA such as when curb cuts, trails, and ramps are missing or not well constructed or maintained. As the quotes introducing this section suggest, able-bodied participants in recreation programs should strive to interact with individuals with disabilities in ways that are similar to how they might interact with other able-bodied participants. It is also appropriate for leaders of such programs to anticipate that individuals with disabilities may feel more uncomfortable than individuals without disabilities. Hence, making extra efforts to prevent individuals with disabilities from feeling isolated are appropriate while avoiding the conveyance of any messages of pity or condescension.

YOUTH SPORT PARTICIPATION

In the last few decades the disability inclusion movement has resulted in increased sporting opportunities and achievements for young people with disabilities. Unfortunately, children with disabilities still have limited opportunities to participate in formal and informal sport compared with peers without disabilities. Sport is important because, in general, youth with disabilities are at greater risk for mental health disorders such as depression, anxiety, stress, frustration, lack of motivation, and social withdrawal compared to children without disabilities. Youth with congenital disabilities tend to report higher trait anxiety, lower mastery, and psychological well-being compared to youth with acquired disabilities. Moreover, disability significantly influences PA levels, perceived participation barriers, and perceived fitness relative to peers without disabilities. Sport can address many of these conditions and feelings.

Barriers

The relatively low number of youth with disabilities who take part in sports can be attributed to several reasons. For instance, some authors highlight the role of architectural barriers and a lack of access to appropriate sporting aids (e.g., wheelchairs). In contrast, others focus on macro explanations, such as weak policies and a lack of best practices promoting sport participation for youth with disabilities. Still other scholars explain reduced participation levels as a function of the discriminating attitudes and negative perceptions of disability embedded in society.

This last explanation supports the idea that one of the reasons why many people with disabilities do not become involved in sports is a result of their own self-perceptions. These self-perceptions are developed in childhood through numerous interactions with able-bodied individuals. Unfortunately, these experiences sometimes result in youth with disabilities developing

low self-confidence in their abilities and negative body-image perceptions.

People's reactions to youth with disabilities are not always positive or neutral and can lead to an undermining of their psycho-emotional well-being. Societal attitudes towards disability have often prevented youth with disabilities from gaining access to sport and physical activities. Also, because of this, children with disabilities often find their social interactions and social networks are limited (Martin, 2002). Hence, they have higher rates of loneliness and fewer friends. Due to disability-related and societal barriers, young people with disabilities often experience difficulties mastering tasks and attaining success. Moreover, youth with disabilities tend to be less encouraged by significant adults to lead active lives and as a

Figure 7.2 Boccia ball player.

Figure 7.3 Wheelchair roadracers.

consequence of sedentary lifestyles they experience a greater risk for health problems compared with peers without disabilities.

People with disabilities have multidimensional identities mediated by the multiple roles, expectancies, aspirations, and perceptions that each person incorporates into the self. As a result, negative perceptions and views about their exercise and sport competencies may be internalized by youth with disabilities. Indeed, external social barriers not only place limits on what children with disabilities can do, but also they restrict and shape their internal "inner worlds". To counter this harmful internalization, children with disabilities need opportunities and experiences to develop confidence in their motor and social abilities. Adults volunteering in sport programs for youth with disabilities should clearly allow time for both skill development and social interaction and promote social cohesion through cooperative and team-building activities.

While understanding why a relatively low number of youth with disabilities take part in sport is important, equally important is creating more opportunities for participation in PA. Childhood is a critical learning period and a lack of sport and PA opportunities and experiences can compromise a future active lifestyle and the attendant benefits. In brief, sport is a context that may assist youngsters in the development of qualities and self-perceptions (e.g., enhanced physical self-concept) not always promoted in other societal domains (Martin, 1999; Martin & Smith 2002).

Benefits and self-perceptions

Sport and physical activity are possible sites for empowering children with disabilities for several reasons. First, as a result of sport, youth with disabilities can derive increased social support, improved friendships, enhanced enjoyment and empowerment, improved perceptions

111

of physical competence and self-efficacy, decreased depression, and an overall increased quality of life. Second, physically active youth with disabilities can increase strength, bone mineral density, vital capacity, and mobility abilities. Third, an active lifestyle for youth with disabilities not only prevents or reduces the risk for health, mental, physical, and functioning problems, but also can decrease the susceptibility to secondary health conditions.

Although there are numerous psychosocial benefits to sport participation, we next focus on three self-perceptions with strong research support: physical competence, self-efficacy, and self-concept. Children with poor motor skills often have lower perceptions of their physical and athletic competence compared to children with better motor skills. Further, among children with movement difficulties, those with the poorer gross motor skills have lower perceived athletic ability compared to children with stronger gross motor skills. Adequate physical competence perceptions are important because they are often strong predictors of global self-worth among children with motor coordination difficulties. Conversely, children with both an adequate sense of competence in their physical abilities and internal control report pleasure in sport, have low anxiety, demonstrate an increase in motivation to participate in sport and PA, and report enhanced sport commitment.

Sport is a primary socializing environment for teaching children with disabilities interpersonal skills and physical competencies that cut across many spheres of life. As a result, the negative effects of low physical and self-competence perceptions often extend beyond the athletic domain. For instance, sport and PA can develop perceptions of independence and control over non-sport life activities and promote empowerment and self-actualization. Conversely, a lack of sport and PA involvement can reduce the already limited opportunities children with disabilities have to gain peer acceptance. In turn, this can deter children from participating in sport and PA

and result in further adverse psychosocial consequences, such as loneliness and depression. Indeed, sport and PA can be a normalizing experience for children with physical disabilities because they provide settings in which social networks of peers are enhanced, which in turn facilitates healthy social identity perceptions.

With positive self-perceptions and strong self-efficacy, a person does not feel threatened by risk or adversity and is able to see challenges as possibilities rather than obstacles (Martin, 2012). Researchers have examined a rehabilitation therapy service climbing program and its influence on the self-perceptions of children with special needs. By the end of the program children with successful climbing experiences showed enhanced efficacy expectations in specific physical and social tasks associated with climbing.

Researchers have also emphasized the importance of self-concept perceptions in sport. Physical self-concept is considered a significant mediating variable that encourages positive outcomes, such as exercise behavior and health-related physical fitness. Significant increases in the physical self-concept of youth with disabilities tends to be due to motor skill development. The type of sport social environment (i.e., integrated, segregated, alternated, and unified) highly influences sport participation outcomes. Some researchers have demonstrated how significant improvements in the physical self-concept of youth with intellectual disabilities is best obtained in segregated and unified sport settings, as opposed to integrated and alternated ones.

Young people with disabilities who experience movement difficulties are generally expected to have lower physical self-perceptions, leading to a reduction in movement confidence and increased risk of avoidance of or withdrawal from mastery attempts in PA and sport settings. Youth who doubt their physical ability tend to show lower participation motivation. Hence, it is important that youth with disabilities have positive physical

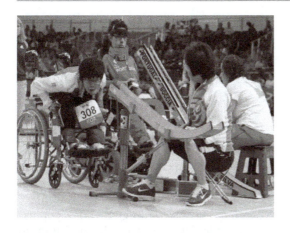

Figure 7.4 Boccia ball player with ramp.

self-concepts because feeling competent enough to participate in sport fosters motivation. Participation in interscholastic adapted sports helps children with disabilities realize not only that the prevailing stereotypes about disability are inaccurate representations of their abilities or potentials, but that participation in adapted sports affords them the opportunity to redefine their physical abilities, enhancing perceptions of their physical self.

Inclusion

Inclusion of children with disabilities is a challenge for coaches and physical education teachers. Inclusion requires adaptations in planning, implementation, and evaluation and tends to be a demanding challenge. The social experiences of children in integrated physical education classes are influenced by the teachers, the social nature of the activities, individual's cultural backgrounds, and the students themselves. In recent years, there has been an increase in the amount of research on inclusion of children with disabilities in general physical education. A recent review of inclusion in physical education identified some important considerations. First, social support for children with disabilities helps them have positive experiences and manage the negative effects that inclusion might have on classmates without disabilities. Second, inclusion of children with disabilities does not inherently have to diminish the experiences of children without disabilities. Third, attitudes and intentions of classmates without disabilities play a critical role in the successful inclusion of students with disabilities. Fourth, students with disabilities typically have similar academic learning time when compared to peers without disabilities, but there are occasions where it is limited.

Two disappointing findings have also been highlighted. First, often the social interactions between students with disabilities and peers without disabilities are limited, which restricts social learning opportunities for all students. Second, physical education teachers often have negative feelings toward inclusion which are grounded in their perceptions of inadequate training and a lack of experience and knowledge on how to successfully include students with disabilities.

Recently, achievement goal theory has been used to examine disability sport and adapted physical education with a focus on the motivational climate. Changing the motivational climate, rather than trying to change individual goal orientations, is thought to be a promising approach. The motivational climate most often endorsed is a mastery climate. Teachers and coaches play a critical role promoting a mastery-involving motivational climate. A mastery climate is developed when teachers put their primary emphasis on the autonomy and individuality of the child, as well as on effort, learning, and improvement, thus enhancing pleasant states. Researchers have assessed an inclusive mastery climate intervention for motor skills development for elementary school children with and without disabilities. Both participants with and without disabilities demonstrated significant improvements in their locomotor and object control skills and similar positive patterns of improvement over time.

Family

Family has long been recognized as an important socialization agency in which children develop sporting tastes and interests. In recent years the literature focusing on sport, family, and disability has considerably developed. Given the potential psychosocial and developmental benefits of sport participation for children with disabilities, it seems important to examine how parents both encourage and discourage sport involvement.

In a recent exploratory study, Fitzgerald and Kirk (2009) focused attention on the intersections of sport, family, and disability and found that sport is a significant context where children's identities are developed. Scholars suggest that family is no longer a significant arena in the lives of youth with disabilities and instead other spheres, such as peers, are seen as more influential social spaces. However, Fitzgerald and Kirk (2009) have underlined how family remains a significant arena, profoundly influencing the construction of identities for children with disabilities. Scientists have also

Figure 7.5 Paralympic shooter.

started to document the relational benefits experienced by families that have children with disabilities who are active and found that such involvement enhances family quality of life. The child with a disability, siblings, parents, and the family as a whole, benefit. For instance, both adaptive skiing or horseback riding experiences have been found to enhance family quality of their life and to contribute to active participants gaining from skiing and horseback riding. Swimming, outdoor skill training programs, outdoor adventure programs, and bike riding, are also popular family activities that have been found to strengthen and deepen family relationships. In particular, the longer duration programs (e.g., outdoor adventure) with in-house instructors have been found to have the added benefit of helping parents overcome and eliminate the typical barriers they might face without non-family assistance. Orienteering, golf, and archery are also activities that children with disabilities have reported to contribute to a feeling of family togetherness and cohesion. Finally, activities designed specifically for individuals with disabilities, such as Challenge Baseball, brings parents together and provides parents with access to other parents who share the challenges and joys of raising children with disabilities. For instance, one mother stated:

> You get to be around other families that also share some of the stressful situations that go along with managing children with special needs. It makes that family feel very welcome in the sense that they can live a normal life; they can participate in normal activities (Castañeda, & Sherrill, 1999, p. 383).

In summary, opportunities to participate in youth sport are not as plentiful for children with disabilities compared to children without disabilities. However, the benefits children can derive from being involved in sport are numerous and encompass enhanced self-perceptions and stronger connections with both peers and family members.

ELITE SPORT PARTICIPATION

"I haven't just been out here training for the last month on the gold coast, I've been training hard for four years: it's the mentally toughest athlete that will win gold, and I know I'm the mentally toughest." (Simon Jackson, Paralympic Gold Medalist)

Like most athletes, elite athletes with disabilities benefit from developing and employing mental skills (Martin & Wheeler, 2011). With the increased focus and importance being placed on the Paralympic Games many elite athletes with disabilities are starting to think about the importance of mental skills in sport and how to develop mental skills such as imagery and other coping skills. Many researchers have substantiated the value of feeling confident, developing optimal mood states, and employing psychological skills in PA. Researchers examining elite amputee soccer players, Paralympic wheelchair basketball players, national level wheelchair road racers, and international level swimmers have all supported the value of mental skills. Well-developed mental skills help athletes manage and cope with stress. While some stress among athletes with disabilities reflects common sport sources of worry (e.g., lack of fitness) other sources are unique to disability sport (e.g., wheelchair or prosthetic concerns) and disability (e.g., pressure sores). A stressor unique to novice SCI athletes is worrying about involuntary urination while playing as the fast nature of wheelchair rugby often precludes a convenient bathroom break to drain urine bags.

Unlike most able-bodied athletes, athletes with disabilities are functionally classified, which means they are graded based on their abilities to perform physical tests. Classification is used so that athletes only compete against other athletes with a similar range of functional ability as a result of the severity or type of disability. Being classified can potentially be stressful because athletes may fear being reclassified at a different level than that which they have normally been rated. If reclassified at a more functional level, athletes may end up competing against athletes who can perform better than their previous competitors, who were at a lower level. Having to compete against more functional athletes could reduce confidence and increase anxiety at a critical time (e.g., 24 hours before competition).

Similar to individuals with disabilities who engage in leisure time PA, athletes with disabilities also have to, at times, endure pain in training and competition. Sport related muscle pain (SRMP) also tends to go up as training volume increases and SRMP can interrupt training anywhere from one to four weeks. In general, athletes with disabilities lose more training time due to injury relative to athletes without disabilities, for example, shoulder injuries are common among wheelchair athletes.

Many athletes may have not had much previous coaching or lack high quality coaching. For example, elite Kenyan Paralympic athletes traditionally have no coaches or the coaches they do have access to are inadequately trained. Common training errors reported in the literature includes overtraining, training inconsistently, training in non-sport-specific ways, failing to taper for major competitions, and failing to rest after major competitive efforts. Clearly, coaches and sport psychologists should be alert that their athletes do not make similar miscalculations in their training. Similarly, helping them prepare for classification and to cope with the results of classification are important.

CONCLUSION

In summary, most athletes are affected by the events and conditions of their sport world. Athletes with disabilities have to deal with many common sport-related challenges and unique challenges. These unique conditions and challenges can pose as barriers to superior sport performance, but athletes, supported by coaches, teammates, and sport psychologists, can develop mental skills to be psychologically prepared for all the challenges they might face, especially in major competitions such as the Paralympics.

LEARNING AIDS

1   Identify the three major benefits of sport participation for children with disabilities.

Psychological (e.g., increased confidence), social (e.g., new friends), and physiological (e.g., increased endurance).

2   Identify an individual, social and environmental barrier to engaging in PA for adults with disabilities.

Individual barrier: pain. Social barrier: Health care workers who do not support PA. Environmental barrier: Wheelchair ramps that are too steep.

3   Name two unique challenges elite athletes face in sport that athletes without disabilities do not face.

Two unique challenges that elite athletes face are lack of quality coaching and stress from the classification process.

4   Why might an offer of help by an able-bodied child be interpreted by one child as helpful and another child as insulting?

One child may see the help as a way to play more whereas another child may perceive the offer of help as a suggestion that he/she lacks ability.

REVIEW QUESTIONS

1   How might inclusion in physical education and sport influence sport participation for children with disabilities? Specifically, what behaviors might able-bodied children demonstrate that could enhance or reduce children with disabilities perceived competence?

2   Why does a mastery climate in physical educational and sport settings tend to positively accommodate all students and young athletes with disabilities? What "standard" of success does a mastery climate promote that is helpful to all students and young athletes?

3   What psychological preparation might a sport psychologist suggest to an athlete who has to undergo a classification test? Be specific in reporting what psychological technique (e.g., imagery, self-talk, deep breathing) might be useful in reducing a specific detrimental emotion.

EXERCISES

1   Find and watch a disability sport competition (e.g. wheelchair basketball) and write a report that compares behaviors you observe to research reported on in the text that confirms or disconfirms what you witnessed. For example, do you see able-bodied children helping, ignoring, or teasing children with disabilities?

2   Plan a focus group inviting from 6 to 12 children with physical disabilities to participate with the aim of discussing physical and sport experiences of participants from one specific setting (e.g., youth sport team, physical education, recess) and related potential benefits and drawbacks.

3   Watch the movie, *Murderball* and note all of the sport challenges the athletes face during wheelchair rugby and how they manage those challenges.

NOTE

1   Deaf individuals often consider themselves to have a different mode of communication and do not see themselves as having a disability.

ADDITIONAL READING

Castañeda, L. & Sherrill, C. (1999). Family participation in challenger baseball: Critical theory perspectives. *Adapted Physical Activity Quarterly, 16*, 372-388.

Shapiro, D. & Martin, J.J. (2010b). Athletic identity, affect, and peer relations in youth athletes with physical disabilities. *Disability and Health Journal, 3*, 79-85.

Wilson, P.M., Mack, D.E., Bengoechea, E.G., Bin, X., Cheung, S. & Sylvester, B.D. (2010). Understanding the basis of sport friendships in adapted sport athletes: Does fulfilling basic psychological needs matter? In B.D. Geranto (Ed), *Sport Psychology* (Chapter 4): Nova Science Publishers.

REFERENCES

Chaves, E.S., Boninger, M.L., Cooper, R., Fitzgerald, S.G., Gray, D.B. & Cooper, R.A. (2005). Assessing the influence of wheelchair technology on perception of participation in spinal cord injury. *Archives of Physical Medicine and Rehabilitation, 85*, 1854-1858.

Devine, M.A. (2004). Being a "doer" instead of a "viewer": The role of inclusive leisure contexts in determining social acceptance for people with disabilities. *Journal of Leisure Research, 36*, 137-159.

Fitzgerald, H. & Kirk, D. (2009). Identity Work: young disabled people, family and sport. *Leisure Studies 28*, 469-488.

Martin, J.J. (1999). A personal development model of sport psychology for athletes with disabilities. *Journal of Applied Sport Psychology, 11*, 181-193.

Martin, J.J. (2012). Exercise psychology for people with disabilities. In E. Acevedo, *Oxford Handbook of Exercise Psychology.* (pp.337-358). New York, NY: Oxford University Press.

Martin, J.J. & Smith, K. (2002). Friendship quality in youth disability sport: Perceptions of a best friend. *Adapted Physical Activity Quarterly, 19*, 472–482.

Martin, J.J. & Wheeler, G. (2011). Psychology. In Y. Vanlandewijck, & W. Thompson. *The Paralympic Athlete.* (pp.116–136). London, England: International Olympic Committee.

Rimmer, J.H., Riley, B., Wang, E. & Rauworth, A. (2005). Accessibility of health clubs for people with mobility disabilities and visual impairments. *American Journal of Public Health, 95*, 2022–2028.

Chapter 8

Gender and sexual orientation

VIKKI KRANE AND CAROLINE SYMONS

SUMMARY

Most mainstream sport is grounded in Western assumptions about sex, gender, and sexuality. These assumptions often are very narrow and lead to different expectations about how females and males should act in sport. The gender binary, or belief that sex, gender, and sexuality are dichotomous (either/or) concepts, leads to gender segregation in sport. Such a framework can lead to environments that are unfriendly or even hostile towards lesbian, gay, bisexual, transgender, and intersex athletes. In this chapter we will explore how common assumptions about sex and gender can lead to inequities; the nature and impact of heterosexism, heteronormativity, homonegativism, and trans prejudice; and strategies to promote safe and inclusive sport climates.

INTRODUCTION

Syd is an 18-year-old athlete who plays tennis. Throughout childhood, Syd struggled with identifying as female or male. Although considered a girl and treated as a girl, Syd did not feel comfortable doing "girl things" and often would rather compete with and spend time with the boys. Over time, Syd began dressing more like the boys and wore very short hair. After identifying as transgender at age 17, Syd requested that friends, family, and teammates refer to him with male pronouns. His family was very supportive, yet most members of the tennis club would not change their pronouns or language and continued referring to Syd as a girl. As Syd was an excep-tional athlete, many girls felt Syd should not be on their team. They often called Syd names like "lezzie," "fag," and "queer" and would not socialize with Syd. The girls did not want Syd to be in their locker room and often screamed when Syd entered it. The parents at the tennis club did not believe Syd should be allowed to compete with the girls and complained to the coaches. Eventually, Syd dreaded being around the members of this club, became sullen, and wanted to quit tennis.

Syd's situation exemplifies how sport often is dependent upon traditional Western expec-tations surrounding gender and how challenges to this system are met with homonegative responses. Most modern sports have separate categories for men and women, boys and girls. This separatism is based on the deep-seated notion that men are naturally better than women at sport. It also is based on the assumption that males and females have a recognizable and distinct chromosomal, hormonal, physiological and anatomical make up (i.e., sex), and corresponding culturally shaped gender (i.e., masculinity and femininity) and gender expression (i.e., the display of gender through dress, movement, speech and action). The most celebrated sportspeople are highly masculine, heterosexual men who dominate play. Outstanding sportswomen usually have to affirm their femininity, heterosexuality, and sometimes their chromosomal, anatomical and hormonal sex to receive unproblematic acceptance and due recognition within the media and sports world. All this also reveals how sex, gender, and sexual orientation become intermixed, which is the foundation for heteronor-mativity (i.e., the presumption that feminine females and masculine males are heterosexual whereas masculine females and feminine males are assumed to be gay or lesbian).

In fact, mainstream sport is based largely on dualistic and oppositional notions of sex, gender, and sexuality, notions that do not correspond with the variability of these vital aspects of human identity, biology, and culture throughout the world. This chapter provides an overview of the human variability of sex, gender, and sexuality. It also documents the consequences of not fitting in with the dualistic sex/gender foundations of mainstream sport, including the nature and impacts of homonegativism, trans prejudice, and heterosexism. We also provide strategies to promote the safety and inclusion of lesbian, gay, bisexual, and transgender (LGBT) oriented and/or identifying athletes, and the well-being of the sport environment more broadly.

OBJECTIVES

After reading this chapter, students should be able to:

1 Articulate what are sex, gender, gender identity, sexual orientation, and the gender binary.
2 Understand how the gender binary functions in sport.
3 Distinguish among transgender, transsexual, and intersex people.
4 Define and differentiate among heterosexism, homonegativism, and trans prejudice.
5 Recognize how heterosexism, heteronormativity, homonegativism, and trans prejudice function in sport.
6 Describe strategies to create inclusive sport climates.

THE VARIABILITY OF SEX/GENDER/SEXUALITY

Stereotypes abound regarding sportswomen and sportsmen. It is assumed that males are "built for sport," they innately like to be athletes, and they are better at it than females. Males are expected to be bigger, stronger, and faster than females. Boys who are not athletic and girls who excel at sport often are teased and harassed by peers. The common epithet, "you throw like a girl" shows just how ingrained these beliefs are – because girls are not expected to be good at sport, it is an insult to be considered a girl in sport – even when we know many girls are better athletes than some boys. This belief in superior male performance abilities has formed the foundation for separating females and males into different sport divisions, even at young ages when girls and boys are very similar physically. When considering all the differences between female and male adult bodies, there is arbitrariness to this expected physical advantage for males. There are as many variations in the physical capacities within one sex as there are between sexes. For example, heart size, lung capacity, muscle mass, height, and body fat vary significantly within females or within males. These differences traverse rather than parallel the divisions of male and female. There are a variety of determinants of athletic performance such as skill and fitness level; psychological aptitude and preparation; and access to specialized sports facilities, equipment, and other resources that muddy this notion of male superiority in sport. At the elite level of sport, where very small physical performance differences matter, top male athletes in events emphasizing strength, stamina and speed, do have physiological advantages that are attributed primarily to the effects of significantly greater levels of testosterone during adolescence and early adulthood.

Within sport as well as sport and exercise science, the terms sex and gender often are conflated or used interchangeably. However, they have distinct definitions: *Sex* refers to the physical body, including the anatomical, hormonal, chromosomal, and physiological composition of bodies. *Gender* is socially and culturally constructed and refers to behaviours, social roles, and attitudes. There are specific mannerisms that are socially expected and rewarded for females and different mannerisms for males. Conventional views require females to be feminine while males are to be masculine. How individual athletes convey their gender through, for example, outward behaviours, attire, hair style, comportment, and attitude is their *gender expression*, which may or may not correspond with social expectations whereas *gender identity* is one's internal sense of being female, male, transgender, or something else.

Gender is socially and culturally constructed because demeanour and behaviour is governed by social expectations and does not reflect innate distinctions between female and male.

For example, there is no physiological reason that girls should like pink and play with dolls or why boys should like blue and play with toy trucks. Yet, there are many rewards for adhering to these dominant prescriptions that are popularly portrayed in the media and consumer culture of many Western nations. Individuals do not have to conform to these social expectations, but at an early age boys and girls learn there are negative consequences of not doing so. These social expectations also are culturally bound. That is, within different cultures social customs may differ. For example, women have been excluded from some Olympic or national sporting teams due to strong cultural prescriptions governing women's attire and physicality in this highly public event.

To comprehend how limited understandings of sex, gender, and sexuality have influenced sport, it is helpful to examine the history of "sex testing" or "gender verification." During the 1960s sex testing of female athletes was introduced at the Olympics and other international sports events (Sullivan, 2011). The purpose of these tests was to ensure that male athletes were not impersonating women and infiltrating women's sport events (putting "real" female athletes at a disadvantage); yet the impact of this pursuit was much more wide-ranging. The first sex tests involved naked female athletes parading in front of a panel of male doctors. This was replaced by chromosomal testing and women who possessed an XX passed their gender verification; women with any chromosomal variation were considered as male. Most of these tests had a relatively high error rate or detected "abnormalities" that did not provide a sport advantage. This resulted in athletes "failing" their sex test and being disqualified from competition. Often these disqualified athletes had lived their whole lives, physically (outward sex), socially (feminine gender expression) and psychologically (identifying strongly) as women, but were classified as genetically male (XY). One condition uncovered in these tests was Androgen Insensitivity Syndrome (AIS), which involved unresponsiveness to testosterone, an impediment to performance (Skirstad, 2000). AIS is one of numerous sex-based variations that do not fit neatly into the two "naturally" based sexes. Athletes with atypical chromosomes, ambiguous sex characteristics or a combination of male and female sex characteristics are *intersex*.

US decathlete, Dr. Tom Waddell came sixth in the Mexico Olympics at the age of 30. As a young man, he had excelled at sports and fully engaged in the aggressiveness of the football field and the "jock" culture of the locker room. These hyper-masculine pursuits were Waddell's closet, his way of performing and appearing heterosexual, his avenue to popularity, friendships, achievement and success. Waddell essentially "did" heterosexuality through these sports. In this way sexual identity is not what you are but what you do, a performance that may not involve sex at all! Waddell waited until his athletic career was over before he came out as gay. He became a leader in the gay community of San Francisco during the late 1970s and 1980s and founded the international Gay Games there in 1982. The Gay Games has become the largest Lesbian, Gay, Bisexual, Transgender, Intersex and Queer (LGBTIQ) event in the world, engaging from 10,000–15,000 participants from all continents of the world, in 32 sports and a large cultural and human rights program. Read Waddell's biography *The Gay Olympian* (Waddell & Schaap, 1996) and Symons (2010) *The Gay Games: A history*, for more details.

In traditional Western societies, gender often is conflated with sex, and both are considered naturally determined and relatively unchangeable. This perception hinges on the perceived *gender binary* in which only two categories are recognized and they are explained as opposites of one another; to be male and masculine is not to be female and feminine. In other words, male and masculine (with the qualities of strength, assertiveness, independence and stoicism) are oppositional to female and feminine (characterized by emotionalism, weakness, gentleness, nurturance and gracefulness). It is expected that all athletes will fall neatly into one of these two categories. When they do not, sexual orientation often is called into question, further conflating sex, gender, and sexuality. When males are not perceived as appropriately masculine or females are not appropriately feminine, they often face homonegative bias in sport. These norms form the foundation of many sport settings, from youth and community sport to elite levels.

However, sociological and anthropological research demonstrates significant cultural variability of gender and sexuality. In a number of indigenous societies third genders and complex variations across sex, gender, and sexuality lines exist. There are the *berdache* of

Figure 8.1 Canal Pride Parade celebrating the Gay Games, Amsterdam 1998. © Ann P. Meredith.

the North American Indian, the Indonesian *waria,* the *kathoey* of Thailand, the Philippines *bayot*, the Moroccan *hasas*, the Luban *kitesha* in parts of the Congo and the *mati* of Suriname for instance (Herdt, 1994; Wekker 1999). Multiple genders were evident in Native American tribal societies within North America such as women-men (males who had taken on some or all of the social roles of women) and "two-spirited" Native Americans. In Tahiti and Hawaii, men who adopt the gender characteristics, mannerisms, dress, and social and work roles (gender expression) attributed to women are known as *mahu*, in Somoa they are known as *fa'afafine* (literally "in the fashion of a woman") and in Tonga *fafafefine*. Polynesian women who live as liminal men also exit, but in significantly fewer numbers (Besnier, 1994). This sex/gender variability differs markedly from dualistic Western conceptualizations. What is important to recognize is that sex and gender are more complex than often considered and there is need to think about sex and gender more broadly than is evident in conventional sport.

Gender liminality does not automatically align with same-sex relations or identity in the Pacific Island cultures. Same-sex relations are viewed "as an optional consequence of gender liminality, rather than its determiner, prerequisite or primary attribute" (Besnier 1994, p. 300). This is quite different from Western notions of gay and lesbian identity, where *sexual orientation* (a person's enduring sexual and/or romantic attraction towards another person) is the significant definer. In Western societies, *transgender* refers to individuals whose gender identity does not match their gender assigned at birth and/or their physical sex. *Transsexuals* are individuals who have begun or plan to begin hormone therapy to change their body chemistry to align their physicality with their gender identity. Some, but not all, transsexual people will undergo components of, or complete, sex reassignment surgery. The latter involves hormone therapy and permanent surgical changes to genitalia

and/or breasts, to resemble the desired gender. Transgender people experience a period of transitioning in which they begin to identify and live with a different gender expression. Hormone therapy often begins during this time and results in changes to the internal body chemistry. Indigenous transgender or third gender traditions are not based on this medical understanding of transgender. Transsexual and some transgender people want to identify completely as the gender they live and take on the corresponding conventional gender expressions of this gender identity (masculine male or feminine female). However, *genderqueer* individuals have flexible or fluid gender and may not identify as male or female. All of these "trans" people challenge sport to extend how we conceptualize sex and gender as well as how to be inclusive of people with non-conventional sex and gender identities.

Many misunderstandings about trans athletes lead to discriminatory actions towards them. As their outward appearance may not align with their anatomy and physiology, much confusion may result. As sport psychologists, coaches, and athletes recognize the variations among sex, gender, and gender identity, and understand the process of transitioning, not only can bias decrease, but safe spaces for trans people in sport can be supported. A common prejudice against trans athletes, especially male-to-female trans, is that they have an unfair advantage benefitting their sport performance (Lucas-Carr & Krane, 2011). When someone on a female team looks too much like a male, often it is assumed that that person should not remain on the female team. However, some trans athletes may have a male gender identity, yet their body still is female. If they have not begun hormone therapy to change their body chemistry, then the only difference between these athletes and others on the team is outward appearance. Challenges to their team membership then is parallel to prejudice due to ethnicity; based solely on what one looks like.

As trans athletes undergo hormone therapy, changes occur in their bodies leading to increased characteristics of the sex to which they are becoming (Reeser, 2005). For example, female-bodied athletes who take testosterone will gain muscle mass, facial hair, and other secondary sex characteristics of males. Male-bodied athletes who take oestrogen will lose muscle mass and bone density, and gain body fat. After one year of continuous hormone therapy, trans bodies have the physiology consistent with their new hormone make-up. Consistently, medical research supports that male-to-female trans athletes have hormones and muscle mass consistent with non-trans females and female-to-male athletes have bodies similar in physiology to non-trans males (Ljungqvist, & Genel, 2005). When policies about trans athletes are in place, they often allow the athlete to compete in the sex/gender category consistent with body make-up, as long as they have not begun hormone therapy. Once trans athletes have been on hormones for one or more years, existing sport policies typically allow them to compete in the sex/gender category consistent with their gender identity and current body chemistry. Some policies, such as the Stockholm Consensus of the International Olympic Committee, mandate that to compete in the sex category different from which one was born, the athlete must undergo sex-reassignment surgery (SRS) (Sullivan, 2011). The procedures encompassing SRS are complex and often entail multiple surgeries (e.g., top/breast surgery and bottom/genital surgery). There may be complications or lengthy rehabilitations with these surgeries, which seriously impair an elite athlete's ability to train. Perhaps more important, changes to athletes' breast/chest and genitalia have no effect upon sport performance; from an athletic perspective they only change the athlete's physical appearance. Monitoring hormonal changes and levels in trans athletes, while intrusive, is consistent with the emphasis on maintaining a level playing field for all athletes. Mandating that athletes endure major surgery to be athletically eligible is unwarranted.

Today, trans athletes are participating in community, school, and elite levels of sport. Their involvement is challenging sport administrators to reconsider fundamental assumptions about sex, gender, and athletic bodies. While difficult issues are being raised, it is imperative that sport psychologists be familiar with the controversy and truth surrounding these athletes (Lucas-Carr & Krane, 2011). Sport psychology consultants are in a position to confer with coaches and administrators, they can educate athletes and their parents, and most importantly, they can work to reduce trans prejudice and discrimination against any athletes whose gendered appearance and behaviours are called into question, including but not limited to trans athletes.

HOMONEGATIVISM AND TRANS PREJUDICE IN SPORT

Sexual identity refers to a person's sense of identity based on emotional and sexual attractions (*sexual orientation*), and membership in a community of others who share this orientation (APA, 2008). Sexual orientation within Western societies usually is considered in terms of heterosexual (attraction to "opposite" sex/gender), gay/lesbian (attraction to same-sex/gender), and bisexual (attraction to both men and women). It often is discussed as the defining feature of a person, like sex or age. This is incomplete as sexual orientation concerns intimate personal relationships with others involving "deeply felt needs for love, attachment, intimacy...mutual support and ongoing commitment" (APA, 2008, p. 1). It is relational and social as well as individual. People with sex/gender/sexuality characteristics outside the dominant, normalized, and naturalized parameters of heterosexuality and conventional gender identity and expression often face marginalization, discrimination,

Figure 8.2 Charlotte Avery and Sabra Williams celebrate their gold medal win in the pair figure skating. Gay Games New York, 1994. © Ann P. Meredith.

and even violence. In her 2011 landmark speech calling for the recognition of lesbian, gay, bisexual, and transgender (LGBT) rights as human rights at the United Nations in Geneva, US Secretary of State, Hillary Clinton spoke of the work:

> ...left to do to protect one group of people whose human rights are denied in too many parts of the world today...They (LGBT) are arrested, beaten, terrorized, even executed. Many are treated with contempt and violence by their fellow citizens while authorities empowered to protect them look the other way or, too often, even join in the abuse. They are denied opportunities to work and learn, driven from their homes and countries, and forced to suppress or deny who they are to protect themselves from harm.

LGBT discrimination takes many forms including verbal harassment, violence, and exclusion; and inequity in employment, housing, health care, and education, and relationship/

family recognition. Further, *heterosexism* and *heteronormativity* form the basis of many social institutions. Both of these terms refer to institutionalized and ideological belief systems that assume heterosexuality is normal whereas other sexual orientations and identities are rendered deviant. Heterosexism specifically refers to discriminatory attitudes that disregard people who are not heterosexual. Heteronormativity reflects an ever-present cultural bias in favour of heterosexuality and the omission of other forms of sexuality. Heteronormativity is hegemonic; that is, the privileging of heterosexuality is so common and pervasive, it seems normal and alternative sexualities are unnoticed.

In sport, these types of prejudices also are present. In intolerant sport environments there are two dominant norms: silence and homonegativism. *Silence* refers to the lack of any mention that there may be athletes or coaches who are not heterosexual. While seemingly innocuous, such a climate, which can also be described as heterosexist, promotes the message that sport is not accepting of LGBT people. Within these climates, LGBT athletes face a "don't ask, don't tell" atmosphere in which they feel compelled to hide their non-conforming sexual orientation or gender identity. More than simply not talking about their sexual orientation or gender identity, LGBT athletes in these settings may feel compelled to act in ways to present a socially acceptable image. This may include not being seen in public with a romantic partner, not talking about mundane things such as with whom they spent time over the weekend, and generally acting in gender stereotypical manners. In this type of environment, athletes may not feel personally insulted, yet they also will not feel it is safe to reveal their sexual orientation or gender identity.

Homonegative sport environments include overtly bigoted actions such as negative comments or jokes about LGBT people, blatant hostility towards athletes perceived as LGBT, and even violence towards athletes perceived as LGBT. When this hostility is based on gender

Figure 8.3 Participants at the Gay Games in Cologne, 2010. © Bridie. Victorian Equal Opportunity and Human Rights Commission (VEOHRC).

identity and aimed at trans people, it is referred to as *trans prejudice* or *transnegativism*. While homonegativism is aimed at sexual orientation, it often is levelled at athletes with non-conforming gender expression. As early as youth sport, boys who act or appear feminine often are labelled gay and face homonegative bullying. Girls who appear too masculine or who are highly skilled athletes are marked as lesbian and may be bullied by peers. Brackenridge, Rivers, Gough and Llewellyn (2006) found that such labelling and bullying of young people acted to drive down participation in sport generally.

Unfortunately, research supports that homonegative and transnegative sport settings are common worldwide. For example, Shang and Gill (2011, 2012) found that Taiwanese LGBT athletes perceived their sport and physical activity climates as hostile, and Iida and colleagues (2010) found that sexual minority participants in Japan described homonegative climates in which LGBT athletes were ignored and/or ridiculed because of their sexuality and gender expression. A comprehensive study in Australia (Symons, Sbaraglia, Hillier, & Mitchell, 2010) also revealed hostile sport climates for LGBT athletes. Comprehensive reviews of research on homonegativism in sport in the United Kingdom (Brackenridge, Alldred, Jarvis, Maddocks, & Rivers, 2008), Canada (Demers, 2006), and Europe (Baks & Malecek, 2004) report similar findings.

In heterosexist, homonegative, and transnegative sport environments, athletes commonly hear offensive remarks and feel pressure to be feminine (females) or masculine (males). Athletes who face homonegativism and transnegativism often remain closeted (i.e., hide their sexual or gender identity) and are fearful that their sexual orientation or gender identity will be discovered as it is perceived that this may lead to personal attacks. Discrimination has been particularly pronounced in sports which highlight and reinforce sex and gender difference and promote and celebrate a dominant, conventional, and even hyper-masculinity/femininity (e.g., rugby or American football). Examples abound of elite male athletes calling opponents or referees derogatory names such as "faggots" or making homonegative comments on Twitter. Gareth Thomas, an openly gay male on the Crusaders Rugby League team was confronted with homonegative taunting by a group of spectators. Coaches of elite women's teams openly reject lesbian players. Regrettably, there are many, many similar examples across all levels of sport. These incidents reinforce the necessity that sport psychologists recognize how misunderstandings or stereotypes about sex, gender, and sexuality can affect sport participants.

This homonegative and transnegative prejudice and discrimination can have social and personal consequences, including negative stereotyping and negative impacts on health and well-being (especially mental health).

Figure 8.4 Rainbow socks worn at Fair go, Sport! family day, Melbourne 2011. © Bridie. VEOHRC.

Athletes who face overt homonegativism are likely to experience a decline in self-confidence and self-esteem, high levels of stress, an increase in depressive symptoms, and generally lower psychological well-being (Krane, Surface, & Alexander, 2005). These experiences also can negatively impact sport performance. High levels of stress can impede skilled execution, harassment can lead to lower motivation, and some athletes may leave a particular team or drop out of sport altogether. If the homo- or transnegativism becomes intolerable, some athletes may attempt suicide (cf. Russell, Ryan, Toomey, Diaz, & Sanchez, 2011). Homo- and transnegativism also have a significant impact on the team atmosphere. There may be divisions among team members, and athletes who are not the target of prejudice may find the climate unacceptable. Yet, due to their fear of becoming a target, they may not confront or challenge negative behaviours

which can lead to feeling guilty as well as other negative emotions.

People of all ages and sporting abilities participate in sport for reasons of enjoyment, the promotion of health and fitness, connecting with others and community making, as well as gaining a sense of achievement and performing at a high standard. Non-inclusive, unsafe, and discriminatory sporting environments are antithetical to these essential benefits of sport. Over the past decade there have been some major attitudinal changes occurring in many Western countries marking greater acceptance of LGBT people and a noticeable reduction in homonegativism. Several national and international sport organizations are promoting anti-homonegativism campaigns such as Red Card Homophobia in European football, the You Can Play campaign spearheaded by the National Hockey League in North America, and the French Rugby League

Federation who signed the Charter Against Homophobia in Sport presented by the French Ministry of Sport. These are just a few of the growing number of similar programs at all levels of sport.

FAIR GO, SPORT!

Fair go, sport! is a ground breaking social inclusion project in Australian sport, funded by the Australian Sports commission, to promote safety and inclusion for LGBT people involved in field hockey. It seeks to increase awareness of sexual and gender diversity and to develop a model that other sports and governing bodies can emulate. Beginning with four clubs, the program developed initiatives to engage and educate all participants within hockey including players, coaches, officials, administrators, managers, board members, and spectators at all levels of the sport. They also developed resources, tools, and strategies to enable inclusive sport climates; including approaches for initiating positive conversations, raising awareness, teaching proactive leadership, updating policies and codes of conduct, revising promotional materials, and implementing effective inclusion strategies. Fair go, sport! also helps sport clubs respond to homo- and transnegative issues and discrimination. The successful social inclusion strategies and lessons from Fair go, sport! are currently being shared with other sports organizations across Australia. Go to: http://www.humanrightscommission.vic.gov.au/index.php/fair-go-sport-home

---

There are many advantages to developing LGBT inclusive sport and welcoming climates. On inclusive sport teams the strengths and contributions of all members will be recognized and all members will be valued for the contributions they bring to the team. When athletes feel the need to conceal LGBT identities, stress and distraction can interfere with their focus on performance. Removing this source of stress and distraction ultimately can lead to better overall team performances. As Krane (2008) suggested, creating and maintaining team norms of inclusiveness will lead to healthy and productive sport conditions. For example, norms of supporting and accepting all team members can lead to increased commitment to the team, negative stereotypes being refuted, opportunities to learn from one another about a wide range of social identities, and a primary focus on achieving team goals. Additionally, team members also can become role models of acceptance for their peers. Another way of thinking about LGBT teammates is to consider their resilience. Some LGBT athletes have faced bullying or much discrimination, yet they have persevered and developed into skilled athletes. These individuals have learned to cope with adversity and thrived in the face of many barriers. This should be the type of athlete who is supported and celebrated.

CREATING INCLUSIVE TEAM AND SPORT ENVIRONMENTS

Developing new team norms or organizational expectations can be challenging, yet also can lead to many constructive consequences. Eliminating prejudice and inequity should be a primary concern of sport leaders, and especially sport psychologists who have the opportunity to directly condemn inappropriate actions and reinforce respectful and just behaviours. As such, sport psychologists can have an essential role in changing team and organizational climates. Further, we consider it an ethical responsibility of sport

Figure 8.5 The water polo competition at the Gay Games in Cologne, 2010. © kind-des-olymp. Federation of Gay Games.

psychologists to ensure that all sportspeople participate in safe and just environments.

Policy development can be an initial step for sport organizations seeking to improve their climate for LGBT participants. While policy that prohibits discrimination may not change people's attitudes, it can lay the foundation for initial behaviour change. These policies should include procedures for managing discrimination-based complaints as well as disciplinary action for those who breach anti-discrimination policy. Other policies in the organization (e.g., team selection policies, volunteer and staff recruitment policies, and membership policies that define partners and families) may also need to be reviewed to ensure they are LGBT inclusive. Policies are a first step in enabling change. Sport psychologists can assist sport organizations that decide to develop and implement new policies that make LGBT discrimination unacceptable.

Using a consultative approach to policy development, sport psychologists can guide sport leaders during policy development. This process may need to begin with educating members of the sport organization about homonegativism, heterosexism, and trans prejudice as well as increasing their awareness of the benefits of LGBT inclusion and the negative consequences of discrimination and harassment on individuals and teams. Sport psychologists can work with all organization and team members to help them understand and support policy implementation.

When advocating for more inclusive sport environments, educating coaches, athletes, parents, and other sport personnel may be needed. Sport psychologists can have a central role in educating constituent groups. Development of informational handouts, in readily understandable language, can be helpful. Sport psychologists can set out ground rules to

Figure 8.6 Fair go, Sport! project participants join the Melbourne Pride March, 2011. © Bernie. VEOHRC.

ensure safe and respectful settings when leading group discussions. The discussion may flow more easily if the sport psychologist expresses the goals of the session, emphasizes the benefits of becoming more inclusive, and then progresses into a well-developed plan clearly delineating expectations of the specific group (e.g., athletes, parents, coaches). When introducing topics that are likely to be new to the participants, such as issues concerning transgender athletes, providing opportunities for questions and providing factual (rather than value-laden) responses will assist in gaining understanding and acceptance. In some cases, it may be helpful to allow participants to submit questions in writing, anonymously. Sport psychologists can emphasize that in a compassionate and successful sport setting, all teammates are championed and discrimination aimed at LGBT athletes is indefensible; supporting diverse teammates is part of being a team player (Griffin & Carroll, 2010; Lucas-Carr & Krane, 2011).

A primary goal of educational sessions can be to create solidarity among coaches and administrators to fight heterosexism, homonegativism, and trans prejudice and to support LGBT athletes. There is a steadily increasing number of programs, internationally, that sport groups can adopt and implement. For example, Opening Doors and Joining In (http://www.thefa.com/TheFA/WhatWeDo/Equality/Homophobia) is an action plan to reduce anti-LGBT sentiment through education, visibility, partnership, recognition, reporting and monitoring. Coaches can encourage teams to be proactive and take a stand in one of the many programs available to athletes. Examples include Football v Homophobia in the UK (http://www.football-vhomophobia.com/http://www.thefa.com/football-rules-governance/equality/football-v-homophobia), It Gets Better campaign in the US (http://www.itgetsbetter.org/), become an Athlete Ally (US) (http://www.athleteally.com/), br{ache the silence (US) (http://www.freedomsounds.org/), Step Up! Speak Out! Canadian ally campaign (http://www.stepup-speakout.ca/e/), or take the Captains Challenge at You Can Play (www.youcanplayproject.

org). All of these programs encourage respectful behaviour toward LGBT athletes, encourage speaking out in support of LGBT people, and allow athletes to take a stand for inclusion in sport.

Implementing these types of programs is most likely to be successful if athlete leaders take a lead role in the process. Players look up to team captains, senior, and admired teammates; these athlete leaders model ideal behaviours, those that allow them to excel and be respected (Krane, 2008). In turn, other team members follow their lead and take on their characteristics. When athlete leaders are compassionate and encouraging toward LGBT teammates or support anti-negativity campaigns, it is likely that others will act similarly. Sport psychologists can introduce and educate team members about these types of programs and entrust team leaders with the responsibility of gaining the support of the rest of the team. One step, for example, could be for the athlete leaders to be the first team members to become an Athlete Ally (http://www.athleteally.com/) or they can take the Captains Challenge (www.youcanplayproject.org) as mentioned above. Additionally, supportive organizational leadership is essential to ensuring the team or sport culture is LGBT inclusive. Sport psychologists and other leaders (e.g., coaches, club and association presidents/managers) also can model inclusive attitudes and behaviour, clearly communicate their expectations of acceptance of all athletes, become role models of acceptance, and set the tone for the team. Accordingly, these leaders also need to communicate their disapproval of homonegative language and actions and follow through with organization reprimands.

Another avenue to creating a more inclusive and welcoming sport setting is to change the language and/or break the silence surrounding LGBT sport participants. The language used by people in sport creates the climate. It is common in sport to use sexist, homonegative, or trans prejudiced language; this practice is so common that many athletes perceive it as not being about LGBT people, rather it is just a common put down. However, sexist, homonegative, or trans prejudiced language is hurtful and creates a climate marginalizing LGBTs. Sport psychologists can intervene when biased language is used and explain why such language is unacceptable. Have team members consider that it is very likely that someone on the team knows someone who is LGBT or may be LGBT and to act respectfully. Specific to trans athletes, sport psychologists should use the names and pronouns associated with an athlete's gender identity and gender expression and educate all coaches and athletes to do the same.

Not only can sport psychologists, and other team leaders, denounce improper comments, they should also model using inclusive language and avoid inferring or assuming that all members of a team are heterosexual or normatively male or female. Rather than asking male athletes, for example, if they have a girlfriend, ask if they are dating anyone. Such a simple change in wording opens up a whole

Figure 8.7 Straight–gay ally organization working to promote equality, respect and safety for LGBT athletes: http://youcanplayproject.org

different conversation. In the first instance, a gay male athlete may simply say no. In the second, he may talk about a person he is dating (with or without revealing the gender of that person). Further, same-sex partners of team and club members can be overtly welcomed to team activities. Sport psychologists also can encourage coaches to recognize that some athletes may have same-sex parents or guardians, who are crucial to the well-being and on-going sports involvement of their child.

When issues related to LGBT athletes come up in everyday conversation, they become normalized. That is, it does not seem strange or awkward to talk about them. Sport psychologists can mention current news about LGBT issues when they appear in the media. For example, when well-known athletes come out as LGBT or there is a discriminatory incident, the door is opened to educate team members. In casual conversation, athletes may feel comfortable asking questions; these conversations further promote and support an inclusive team climate. Sport psychologists also can address sensational stories or inaccurate information about LGBT athletes or issues presented in the media. For example, there is much misinformation surrounding transgender athletes in the media. Informally countering stereotypical or misleading facts sets a positive tone for subsequent discussion. If a sport psychologist is not prepared to address these issues spontaneously, she or he can simply state, "let me look into this" and then report back at the next meeting. In this manner, athletes still receive the message that it is natural and acceptable to discuss trans, or LGBT, issues and the sport psychologist continues the dialogue and reduces the stigma surrounding these topics. Another approach to sensational or incorrect media about LGBT athletes is to help athletes reframe this issue. For example, when prejudice or bias is presented, sport psychologists can acknowledge the challenges that LGBT athletes face and reframe the discussion to emphasize their strength and courage; help athletes realize that coping with adversity is a form of being mentally tough.

Sport psychologists can take the lead in helping teams and organizations become more inclusive regarding gender and sexuality. They can educate athletes, coaches, administrators, and parents about the relevant issues. With coaches, sport psychologists can highlight the benefits of creating inclusive and welcoming sport climates: It will benefit team cohesion, communication, and even performance. Being inclusive also will provide important life lessons for all team members who have the opportunity to interact with diverse individuals, support their teammates, and are freed from prejudices of all sorts in sport. LGBT will particularly benefit as they can simply focus on becoming a skilled athlete.

LEARNING AIDS

1   Explain why homonegativism and transnegativism can interfere with athletic performance.

Athletes facing prejudice may have decreased performance because of a loss of motivation (no longer liking their team), increased anxiety (due to fear of negative comments if a mistake is made), distraction (concerned about social climate and not performance cues). These effects can occur in LGBT as well as non-LGBT athletes. It also can interfere with team cohesion.

2   Why is it important to recognize the sex/gender binary in sport?

Binary beliefs about sex and gender often lead to biased expectations where female athletes are expected to be less skilled than male athletes. The binary also forms the foundation for a lack of recognition of transgender and intersex athletes as well as the prejudice against transgender and intersex athletes.

3   Why is it important that coaches and administrators recognize and stop homonegativism and transnegativism?

Leaders in sport set the tone for a team. If coaches correct athletes who use homo- or trans- negative language, teammates will learn that it is unacceptable. Setting team rules about homonegativism and transnegativism opens space for conversation as well as sets team expectations for inclusion.

REVIEW QUESTIONS

1   Distinguish among sex, gender, gender identity, gender expression, sexuality, and sexual orientation.

2   Outline how the sex/gender binary functions in sport.

3   Define and give examples of heterosexism. How does it differ from homonegativism?

4   Discuss how these forms of discrimination affect sport environments.

5   Distinguish among transgender, transsexual, and intersex people.

6   Explain the main impacts of heterosexism, homonegativism, and trans prejudice on LGBT athletes.

7   Describe five strategies to reduce homonegativism in sport.

8   Describe five strategies to reduce trans prejudice in sport.

EXERCISES

1   Provide a brief overview of the international Gay Games. What are they, when, where and why are they staged? Review one Gay Games since 1994 and summarize how these Games have been inclusive of the diverse LGBT communities (locally and globally). Refer to Symons (2012, pp. 1–3, 10–12 and Chapters 6–8), or Hargreaves (2000, pp. 129–173) to assist with your response to this question.

2   Gus Johnson played field hockey in Australia at a state representative level. Gus discusses the ways that being gay has had a significant impact on his sporting experience. View his YouTube clip: http://www. youtube.com/watch?v=AnK1qOMG5dI. Summarize his story and the main points Gus makes about the impact of homonegativity and heterosexism in sport. What did you learn from this video? Search for media articles on Gus and use the *Come Out to Play* report (Symons, Sbaraglia, Hillier and Mitchell, 2010: especially 6–12, 39–51) to contextualize your response to this question.

3   Review the website of one of the LGBT ally or anti-LGBT discrimination in sport programs. Read about their program and consider how it could be adopted by a sport group you are familiar with. Summarize the main strategies of the program that could be adopted by this sport group. Assume that you were actually going to implement the program: who would you talk with to get the program started, what barriers or·challenges might you run into, and how might you overcome these challenges?

4   Develop a plan to allow transgender youth to participate in football (soccer). Develop the rationale for why the plan/policy is necessary. What difficulties might you anticipate in implementing your plan? What would be the benefits of your plan?

5   Seek out and examine policies regarding Olympic athletes who are transgender, transsexual, or intersex (available at the International Olympic Committee website). Summarize the policies. Then consider who is best served by the policy and who is excluded by the policy. What changes might you suggest to the policy?

ADDITIONAL READING

Griffin, P. & Carroll, H.J. (2010). *On the team: Equal opportunity for transgender student athletes*. Retrieved from: http://www.nclrights.org/site/DocServer/TransgenderStudentAthleteReport.pdf?docID=7901

Kauer, K.J. & Krane, V. (2010). Inclusive excellence: Embracing diverse sexual and gender identities in sport. In S.J. Hanrahan & M.B. Andersen (Eds.), *Routledge handbook of applied sport psychology: A comprehensive guide for students and practitioners* (pp.764–779). NY: Routledge.

Sullivan, C.F. (2011). Gender verification and gender policies in elite sport: Eligibility and "fair play." *Journal of Sport and Social Issues, 35*, 400–419.

Symons, C. (2010). *The Gay Games: A history*. London: Routledge.

REFERENCES

American Psychological Association (APA) (2008). *Answers to your questions: For better understanding of sexual orientation and homosexuality*. Washington DC. Retrieved from: www.apa.org/topics/sorientation.pdf

Baks, B. & Malecek, S. (2004). *Synopsis on homophobia and discrimination on sexual orientation in sport*. Retrieved from European Gay and Lesbian Sport Foundation website: http://www.gaysport.info/eglsf/publications/EGLSF_synopsis_on_homophobia_2003pr.pdf

Besnier, N. (1994). Polynesian gender liminality through time and space. In G. Herdt (Ed.), *Third sex, third gender: Beyond sexual dimorphism in culture and history* (pp.285–329). New York: Zone Books.

Brackenridge, C., Alldred, P., Jarvis, A., Maddocks, K. & Rivers, I. (2008). *A review of sexual orientation in sport*. Sportscotland Research Report no. 114. Retrieved from: http://www.sportscotland.org.uk/ChannelNavigation/Resources/TopicNavigation/Collections/Research/A+literature+review+of+sexual+orientation+in+sport.htm

Brackenridge, C., Rivers, I., Gough, B. & Llewellyn, K. (2006). Driving down participation. Homophobic bullying as a deterrent to doing sport. In C.C. Aitchison (Ed.), *Sport and Gender identities: Masculinities, femininities and sexualities* (pp.122–139). London: Routledge.

Clinton, H. (2011). Remarks in recognition of International Human Rights Day, Palaisde Nations, Geneva, Switzerland, December 6, 2011. Retrieved from: http://www.state.gov/secretary/rm/2011/12/178368.htm

Demers, G. (2006). Homophobia in sport – Fact of life, taboo subject. *Canadian Journal of Women in Coaching Online, 6*(2). Retrieved from: http://23361.vws.magma.ca/WOMEN/e/journal/apr2006/pg1.htm

Griffin, P. & Carroll, H.J. (2010). *On the team: Equal opportunity for transgender student athletes.* Retrieved from: http://www.nclrights.org/site/DocServer/TransgenderStudentAthleteReport.pdf?docID=7901

Hargreaves, J. (2000). *Heroines of sport: The politics of difference and identity.* New York: Routledge.

Herdt, G. (Ed.) (1994). *Third sex, third gender: Beyond sexual dimorphism in culture and history* (pp.63–72). New York: Zone Books.

Iida, T., Kazama, T., Raita, K., Yoshikawa, Y., Fujiyama, S., Fujiwaya, N., Matsuda, K., Sano, N. & Itani, S. (2010). *A Study Concerning the Sense of Exclusion and Freedom that Sexual Minority People Experience in Sport in Japan.* Unpublished report.

Krane, V. (2008). Gendered social dynamics in sport. In M. Beauchamp & M. Eys (Eds.), *Group dynamics advances in sport and exercise psychology: Contemporary themes* (pp.159–176). New York: Routledge.

Krane, V., Surface, H. & Alexander, L. (2005). Health implications of heterosexism and homo-negativism for girls and women in sport. In L. Ransdall & L. Petlichkoff (Eds.), *Ensuring the health of active and athletic girls and women* (pp.327–346). Reston, VA: National Association for Girls and Women in Sport.

Ljungqvist, A. & Genel, M. (2005). Essay transsexual athletes – when is competition fair? *Lancet, 366,* S42–S43.

Lucas-Carr, C.B. & Krane, V. (2011). What is the *T* in LGBT? Supporting transgender athletes via sport psychology. *The Sport Psychologist, 4,* 532–548.

Reeser, J.C. (2005). Gender identity and sport: Is the playing field level? *British Journal of Sports Medicine, 39,* 695–699.

Russell, S.T., Ryan, C., Toomey, R.B., Diaz, R.M. & Sanchez, J. (2011). Lesbian, gay, bisexual, and transgender adolescent school victimization: Implications for young adult health and adjustment. *Journal of School Health, 81*(5), 223–230.

Shang, Y-T. & Gill, D.L. (2011). *Lesbian and non-lesbian athletes' perception of sport climate in Taiwan.* Paper presented at the North American Society for the Sociology of Sport Conference, Minneapolis, MN, USA.

Shang, Y-T. & Gill, D. L. (2012). Athletes' perceptions of the sport climate for athletes with non-conventional gender expressions and sexual orientations in Taiwan. *Journal for the Study of Sports and Athletes in Education, 6,* 67–82.

Skirstad, B. (2000). Gender verification in competitive sport: Turning from research to action. In T. Tannsjo & C. Tamurrini (Eds.), *Values in sport: Elitism, nationalism, gender equality and the scientific manufacture of winners* (pp.117–121). London: E & FN Spon.

Sullivan, C.F. (2011). Gender verification and gender policies in elite sport: Eligibility and "fair play." *Journal of Sport and Social Issues, 35,* 400–419.

Symons, C. (2010). *The Gay Games: A history.* London: Routledge.

Symons, C., Sbaraglia, M., Hillier, L. & Mitchell, A. (2010). *Come Out To Play. The sports experience of Lesbian, Gay, Bisexual and Transgender (LGBT) people in Victoria,* Institute of Sport, Exercise and Active Living, Victoria University, Melbourne, Australia. Available at: http:/apo.org.au/research/come-out-to-play

Wekker, G. (1999). "What's identity got to do with it?" Rethinking identity in the light of Mati Work in Suriname. In E. Blackwood & S. Wieringa (Eds.), *Female Desires: Same-sex relations and transgender practices across culture* (pp.119–138). New York: Columbia University Press.

Chapter 9

Cultural diversity

DIANE L. GILL AND TATIANA V. RYBA

SUMMARY

Cultural diversity characterizes sport and exercise, and influences all participants. Culturally competent sport and exercise psychology professionals cannot simply treat everyone the same. However, we cannot go to the other extreme and assume that all members of any cultural group are alike and should be treated the same way. Culture is dynamic and best understood within a framework that recognizes multiple, intersecting identities and identifications, power relations, and action for social justice. Sport and exercise psychology has barely begun to address cultural diversity in research and professional practice. As cultural sport and exercise psychology gains a greater presence in our scholarship and educational programs, we will increase awareness and deepen understanding of cultural diversity and move to cultural competence in sport and exercise psychology.

INTRODUCTION

How many goodly creatures are there here! How beauteous mankind is! O brave new world that has such people in it! From William Shakespeare's *The Tempest, V, 1, 182*

As was clear in Shakespeare's time, long before the internet, planes, trains and automobiles, and when most people communicated only through face-to-face conversation, the world has a wondrous diversity of people. We do not need to search the world for evidence of such diversity (even through the internet); we can find it in our own community sport and physical activity programs. For example, imagine that you are working with a youth recreational

sport program in a community like mine (Diane L. Gill). My community is quite racially and ethnically diverse, with families of all socio-economic levels that speak nearly 100 different primary languages in their homes. How might culture come into play and affect you and the participants in a youth program? Do you think the participants in the program would be representative of this particular American community? Would you expect different behaviors or would you behave differently if you were working with children who were recent immigrants from a non-western culture? Would it matter if the parents were refugees fleeing a hostile environment or business professionals in an international company? Would it matter if the child was a boy in a t-shirt or a girl wearing a hijab?

Culture is real and powerful and embedded in society. Although cultural diversity is indeed beauteous, culture may constrain behavior and opportunity. Attention to cultural diversity is vital to our scholarship and essential to professional practice in sport and exercise psychology. If you try to treat everyone the same, you will have difficulty – one size does not fit all. Take up the challenge to be alert to cultural diversity, strive for a deeper understanding of its complexities, and incorporate that understanding into sport and exercise psychology. Most of all, keep reminding yourself that *one size does not fit all.*

OBJECTIVES

After reading this chapter you will be able to:

1 Define culture (in your own words).
2 Describe cultural diversity in sport, exercise and physical activity.
3 Understand how power or privilege relates to cultural diversity.
4 Understand how cultural stereotypes and biases affect behavior and relationships.
5 Describe cultural competence and its components.
6 Identify ways to enhance your own cultural competence, and ways to enhance cultural competence within sport and exercise psychology programs and institutions.

UNDERSTANDING CULTURAL DIVERSITY

This chapter begins with basic concepts and reviews related scholarship to help you expand and deepen your understanding of cultural diversity. We emphasize applications and suggestions for promoting cultural competence in sport and exercise psychology. In line with our emphasis on diversity and inclusion, we interpret sport and exercise broadly to include play, games, dance, exercise for training or optimal health, and all levels and forms of sport. We hope this chapter will help you develop an understanding of cultural diversity that leads to action – specifically, action to promote safe, inclusive physical activity for all, and to strive for cultural competence in sport and exercise psychology.

CULTURAL DIVERSITY BASICS

Cultural diversity is often overlooked in sport and exercise psychology, but the larger field of psychology, and particularly the American Psychological Association (APA), has developed a scholarly base and resources on multicultural psychology that we will draw on to help clarify terms and provide a guiding framework. To start, multicultural psychology may be defined as the *"systematic study of behavior, cognition and affect in many cultures"* (Mio, Barker-Hackett & Tumambing, 2006, p. 3). The study of behavior, cognition and affect (emotion) is psychology, and thus, this chapter focuses on sport and exercise psychology in many cultures.

Culture, however, is complex and not easily defined. We adopt a broad definition of culture as: *shared values, beliefs and practices of an identifiable group of people.* Culture is often equated with race and ethnicity, but culture is not limited to race and ethnicity. For example, language, spirituality or occupation might also identify culture.

Before continuing with the basics, a note on *race* and *ethnicity* is warranted. Race and ethnicity are often connected or used interchangeably, but race and ethnicity are not the same. We often associate race with biological markers such as facial features and particular skin color, and we tend to associate ethnicity with cultural traditions of a nation or geographic region. Hazel Markus (2008), who is widely recognized for her cultural psychology scholarship, has offered a unified theory of race and ethnicity that helps to clarify the issues. As Markus and many other scholars have noted, race is not a clear, biologically-determined category, as often assumed. Both race and ethnicity are dynamic, historically derived and institutionalized ideas and practices. That is, race and ethnicity are not objective, identifying characteristics, but the meanings that we associate with the characteristics. We also tend to categorize characteristics as oppositional binaries (e.g., white/black, good/bad, smart/stupid, fast/slow, etc.), which gives more power to one part of the binary category than the other. Culture affects people, but people make up culture. This means that culture is constituted and also contested along the axes of race, gender, and so on.

Markus further suggested that race and ethnicity differ in that race is more often imposed, associated with differential value and power between groups, whereas ethnicity is more often a claimed identity associated with a sense of belonging and pride. The U.S. and many western countries have a long history of discrimination on the basis of race and even today we find more subtle indicants of racial discrimination. For example, white people are over-represented in positions of power, such as political leaders, business leaders and athletic administrators. Cultural differences based on ethnicity may also involve discrimination, but power and privilege are particularly associated with race relations, which like gender relations stem from the hierarchically perceived "naturally" existing categories.

Cultural diversity highlights the "many" cultures in the above definition of multicultural psychology. Culture encompasses many different identifying characteristics; people are culturally diverse in many ways. And, each individual has many different cultural identities.

Cultural competence refers to the ability to work with people of different cultures. Cultural competence is a key professional competency for sport and exercise psychology, as it is for anyone interacting with people of many cultures.

THEMES FOR CULTURAL SPORT AND EXERCISE PSYCHOLOGY

To help develop a deeper understanding of cultural diversity and move toward cultural competence in sport and exercise psychology, we offer three themes to keep in mind. First, remember that we all have multiple, intersecting cultural identities. Furthermore, those identities vary across individuals, time and contexts. For example, two young women may both identify as black, Christian women athletes. One may very strongly identify as a Christian athlete, whereas the other more strongly identifies as a black woman. Moreover, the salience of those identities may vary

across contexts, such as with family, teammates or in school.

Second, remember that culture and cultural relationships involve power and privilege. To understand culture, we must consider who makes the rules and who is left out. In many societies, and particularly in sport, white, European men have privilege and hold positions of power.

Finally, a deeper understanding of culture and recognition of power relations leads to action for social justice. Culturally competent professionals develop their own multicultural competencies and also advocate for cultural competence in our programs and institutions.

Keep these themes in mind as you read this chapter and continue to develop your understanding of cultural diversity in sport and exercise psychology. The first step is to understand your own cultural identity and how that affects your behavior and relationships. To help you get started, try Exercise 1 at the end of this chapter, which asks you to list as many as you can of your own cultural identities and identify three that are the most salient/influential to you. You could extend the exercise further and come back to it again. If so, you may find that you want to revise the list, or that different identities are more salient than others. Returning to the exercise and re-thinking your own identity can help you understand the complexities of culture.

Now let's look at power relations as we continue the exercise. When considering culture, we must also consider relationships. Many, perhaps most, cultural relationships involve power. That is, relationships involve privilege and oppression. *Privilege* refers to social status, power or institutionalized advantage gained by virtue of valued social identities. *Oppression* refers to discrimination or systematic denial of resources to members of groups who are identified as different, inferior or less deserving than others. Given that most people have many cultural identities, most people have some identities that confer privilege, and other identities that lead to oppression. For example, if you are white, male, heterosexual, educated (college student or graduate), or able-bodied, you have privilege in that identity. You are more likely to see people who look like you in popular media and in positions of power, and you are more likely to see yourself in those roles. It is difficult to recognize our own privilege, but it is easier for those in an oppressed group to see privilege of others.

Consider the following example from the second author's research. In this example a North American student in a Finnish university wrote in her reflective journal of cultural adaptation:

> One thing I have to say that I am actually glad about is that I'm not a minority here. I have dual-colored hair with black/brown hair underneath, blue eyes and a Scandinavian look. I fit in here. I don't look any different. If I did, I would probably feel like an outcast all the time. Instead, people talk to me in Finnish all the time. I get mistaken for a Finnish person every day! I love it. I don't think I could ever go to a country where I was the minority. The other day in the cafeteria line, the cafeteria lady told me the price in Finnish. The girl after me in line was Asian and she automatically spoke English to her. I just don't like being under the radar. I like to be different, but on my own terms, not because others can identify me as different.

Developing your ability to recognize power relations and see privilege in sport and exercise is a key to developing cultural competence. To help, you might first think about a time when you felt "different" or left out; perhaps you were the only girl or only person of your ethnic group at a program, or the only one who didn't know the answer or couldn't do the skill. If you have been injured and needed to use crutches or a wheelchair, you may have experienced some of the oppression that people with disabilities face. Even if you have more privilege in your cultural relations (and most readers do), recognizing power and privilege is a big step toward cultural competence. Try to identity power relations in your cultural relations in Exercise 2, which asks you to list ways that your cultural identity gives you power or privilege and ways that you are oppressed or excluded because of your cultural identity. If you are like most people, you can identify ways that you are privileged and also ways that you are oppressed. We hope this exercise not only helps you recognize your own multiple, intersecting identities, but also helps you think about how culture affects all your behaviors and relationships. As you understand your own cultural identity, and identify power relations, you may better see how cultural relations operate for other people in sport and exercise. That recognition and understanding may well prompt action to emphasize social justice and advocacy in your continuing sport and exercise psychology study and practice.

Action and advocacy, the third theme of our multicultural framework reflects what some have called cultural praxis. Ryba (2009, p. 35) explained that cultural praxis is an active and reflexive process of linking theory, lived culture, and social action in research and practice. That is, your understanding of culture is realized in all your actions and relationships. Such "action" and incorporating cultural understanding in practice reflects cultural competence. How might sport and exercise professionals move into action and cultural competence? Often professionals try to adopt a "colorblind" or culture-blind approach, and purposely ignore race, ethnicity, gender, etc. so that they "treat everyone the same." Such a culture-blind approach may seem to be desirable and "fair" to all. However, a culture-blind approach is a one-size-fits-all approach. Moreover, the one size is always the "size" of the privileged culture and fails to reflect an understanding and awareness of cultural diversity. Try Exercise 3 to help understand why culturally-blind might not be culturally-informed and might not reflect cultural competence.

By adopting the cultural sport and exercise psychology framework of this chapter, you can advance your understanding of cultural diversity, and develop cultural competence for professional practice – but that's no easy task. As well as recognizing multiple, intersecting cultural identities, attending to power relations and acting for social justice, sport and exercise psychologists also must retain concern for the individual. The importance of individualizing professional practice is often emphasized in sport and exercise psychology, and rightfully so. In calling for cultural competence, we are also arguing for contextualizing professional practice, and specifically for recognizing cultural diversity as part of the context. The ability to simultaneously recognize and consider both the individual and the cultural context is the essence of cultural competence in sport and exercise psychology. For example, a student-athlete's family traditions and cultural values may have just as much influence on her adjustment to college as the pressures for athletic performance.

CULTURAL DIVERSITY IN SPORT AND EXERCISE: PARTICIPATION AND POWER

Even casual observations suggest that sport and exercise participants are culturally diverse. However, in line with our multicultural framework, to understand cultural diversity and move toward cultural competence, we must go deeper to consider power and privilege. Noted multicultural psychology scholar Derald Wing Sue (2004) illustrated the power differential in U.S. society in noting that while white males make up just 33% of the U.S. population, they hold the large majority of power positions in government and business, and of special interest here, *99% of the athletic team owners.* Several scholars within the emerging *cultural sport psychology* movement have made similar arguments. Butryn (2002), in particular, has helped illuminate "white privilege" and its ubiquitous, but often unrecognized, influence in sport and exercise psychology.

Cultural diversity in athletics: Several easily-accessed reports provide data that highlight power relations and white privilege in sport and exercise settings, at least within the U.S.. Richard Lapchick's annual *Racial and*

Gender Report Cards (available at: http://www.tidesport.org/) clearly show racial and gender inequities in U.S. sport, with little progress. In the 2010 report card, (Lapchick, 2011) whites were 62.5% and African-Americans were 24.9% of all male college athletes; white women were 77.2% and African-Americans were 11.6% of the female athletes. Thus, African-Americans are slightly over-represented compared to their population percentage in U.S. college sports, but other cultural minorities are clearly under-represented with Latino/a athletes at about 4% and Asian American and Native American athletes at very low percentages.

When we consider power relations in U.S. college sport, cultural diversity drops dramatically. The Racial and Gender Report Card indicated that whites hold approximately 90% of the head coaching positions in U.S. college athletics, and administration remains solidly white male. About 90% of Division I athletics directors are white and only 8.3% are women. Before 1972, when Title IX was enacted barring sex discrimination in education, over 90% of U.S. women's college athletic teams were coached by women and had a woman athletic director. Vivian Acosta and Linda Carpenter have documented the decline in the number of women coaches since then. Their most recent 2012 update (Acosta & Carpenter, 2012; available at: http://www.acostacarpenter.org) indicates that while participation of female athletes has increased, the percentage of female coaches remains low and under 50% of coaches of women's teams. The proportion of female athletic directors, head athletic trainers, and sports information directors is even lower and far below male numbers.

Although international data are lacking, the under-representation of women coaches at the elite level is likely a global trend. The United States Olympic Committee's (USOC) website indicated that only 8 of 40 (20%) head coaches of women's teams were women in the 2008 Summer Olympics in Beijing, and Norman (2010) reported that only 9 of 43 (20.9%) coaches at the senior national teams of both men and women's major sports in the UK were women. The limited data available also suggest even fewer women coaches at the youth level than at the collegiate and elite levels.

The 2012 London Olympics showcased an increasing number of women athletes, and also demonstrated themes of multiple intersecting cultural identities and power relations. The U.S. sent more female than male athletes to the London Olympics, but women were vastly under-represented in several delegations with three Muslim countries (Saudi Arabia, Qatar, and Brunei) each sending their first woman to the Olympics after several years of all male teams. As some commentators have noted, Muslim women have been competing for some time, with or without more traditional Muslim clothing, which illustrates the intersection of cultural identities. Gender roles and behaviors across cultures; appropriate behaviors and attire for women are different in the U.S. and Saudi Arabia, and even vary among Muslim cultures. The Turkish women who won gold and silver in the 1500-meter race in London may not be immediately identified as Muslim and they come from very different cultural traditions than the Saudi women, further highlighting intersecting identities. Power relations are also evident in the recent 2012 Olympics. Although we see more women athletes and athletes from varied cultural backgrounds, coaching positions are heavily dominated by men, and Olympic officials are not as diverse as the athletes. Clearly, elite sport is culturally elite.

Cultural diversity in exercise and physical activity: Perhaps exercise and physical activity are more diverse than elite sport – or perhaps not. Think about the fitness centers or activity programs in your community. Who do you see there? Do the participants reflect the cultural diversity of the community? U.S. census data and public health reports indicate that physical activity is limited by gender, race, class, and especially by physical attributes. Physical activity decreases across the adult lifespan, with men more active than women, racial/ethnic minorities less active across all ages. The Centers for Disease Control (CDC) tracks physical activity as well as other health statistics, and the CDC website (http://www.cdc.gov/) provides data on those trends as well as helpful information.

CULTURAL DIVERSITY IN SPORT AND EXERCISE PSYCHOLOGY

Despite the diversity of participants, clear power imbalances in opportunities and need for cultural competence, sport and exercise psychology has generally ignored cultural diversity in research, professional practice, and educational programs. Duda and Allison (1990) first identified the lack of research on race and ethnicity, reporting that less than 4% of the published papers considered race and ethnicity, and most of those were simple sample descriptions. Ram, Starek and Johnson (2004) updated that report by reviewing articles in sport and exercise psychology research journals between 1987 and 2000 for both race/ethnicity and sexual orientation content. They confirmed the persistent void in the scholarly literature, finding that only 20% of the articles made reference to race/ethnicity and 1.2% to sexual orientation. More important, those few articles provided few insights to advance our understanding. Ram et al. concluded that there is no systematic attempt to include the experiences of marginalized groups.

Kamphoff and colleagues (Kamphoff, Gill, Araki & Hammond, 2010) surveyed the Association for Applied Sport Psychology (AASP) conference programs from the first conference in 1986 to 2007 and found little attention had been paid to multicultural issues. Only about 10% of all abstracts addressed cultural diversity issues, and most of those were simple comparisons of gender differences with few analyses that extend beyond group differences. Almost no abstracts addressed race, ethnicity, sexual orientation, social class, physical disabilities or any other cultural diversity issue. AASP program content extends beyond the research to professional issues, but the review of program abstracts suggests the continuing neglect of cultural diversity in sport and exercise psychology.

Recently, as part of a graduate seminar, the first author (Gill) and several graduate students conducted an informal survey of recent issues of our major sport and exercise psychology journals. Specifically, they reviewed the last two years (2010–2012) of *Journal of Sport & Exercise Psychology* (JSEP), *The Sport Psychologist* (TSP), *Journal of Applied Sport Psychology* (JASP), as well as the European journal *Psychology of Sport and Exercise* (PSE) and the *International Journal of Sport & Exercise Psychology* (IJSEP), looking for articles addressing cultural diversity. Almost no articles explicitly address cultural diversity. Authors do come from several different countries, but almost all are in North America and Europe, even in the international journal. The published and informal reviews demonstrate a continuing neglect of cultural diversity in sport and exercise psychology. Check for yourself in Exercise 4.

To expand our worldview, sport and exercise psychology must expand the research on cultural diversity. To get started, we can draw from related multicultural psychology scholarship.

RESEARCH ON STEREOTYPES AND BIAS

Much psychology research on culture focuses on stereotypes and their effects. *Stereotypes* are generalizations about a group or its members based on a particular characteristic. We have a lot of stereotypes that can affect participation and behavior in sport and exercise, and many are based on culture. For example, do you have any stereotypes about long distance runners or weight lifters? If you have ever been a student-athlete, have you been in a classroom with an instructor that seemed to have some stereotypes about athletes? Did that affect your behavior or reactions in the class? Stereotypes are important because they affect our thoughts, feelings and behavior. Much of the power and privilege associated with cultural relations is grounded in stereotypes. In this section, we will highlight racial stereotypes and weight bias, which are prevalent and relevant in sport and exercise psychology.

Claude Steele's (1997) extensive research on stereotypes and *stereotype threat* – the fear that one will confirm a negative stereotype – shows the power of stereotypes to affect performance. That research, largely in academic settings, indicates that the most devastating effects are on those minority group members who have abilities and are motivated to succeed. For example, assume that you are a student-athlete striving for good grades to get into medical school. However, you know that one of your instructors thinks all athletes care only about athletics and lack intelligence and motivation for academic work. The instructor has a negative stereotype (lack intelligence), you have the capability and want to do well, but you are aware of that stereotype. That's stereotype threat, and that awareness may create anxiety and interfere with your performance. On the positive side, research also suggests that even simple manipulations that take away the stereotype threat (e.g., telling students the test is not related to race or gender) can help. Beilock and McConnell (2004) reviewed the related sport and exercise

psychology literature, concluding that negative stereotypes are common in sport and lead to performance decrements.

The prevalence of negative stereotypes for racial and ethnic minorities, particularly Black athletes, is well-documented (see Gill, 2007 for references). Clearly, stereotype threat is a relevant issue for sport and exercise psychology. Ruth Hall (2001), who is particularly eloquent on intersections of gender, race and class, began a discussion of women of color in sport with the following commentary:

> ...Race and gender are firecrackers that ignite America's social conscience, rattle the cages that bind us – cages that block our passage to equality. It's a double whammy for African American female athletes since we aren't the dominant norm – we're not white. Race and racism loom large and throw a level playing field off-kilter. Many of us don't fit the Anglo mold. We stretch the parameters of gender roles by our presence, our physical appearance, and sometimes unorthodox style. We aren't "feminine" they say. Commentators describe figure skaters Debbie Thomas and Surya Bonaly and the tennis star Venus Williams as "athletic," "muscular" meaning not feminine. We create dissonance with our skin color, body type, and facial features. We are the other... (Hall, 2001, pp. 386–387)

Although Hall's quote is over ten years old, the stereotype issues are still relevant, and illustrate intersections of gender and culture.

PHYSICALITY STEREOTYPES AND WEIGHT BIAS

Sport and exercise psychology professionals deal with physical activities, and thus, physical abilities and characteristics are prominent. Moreover, people are privileged and excluded based on physical abilities, skills, size, fitness, and appearance – collectively referred to as physicality. Physical skill, strength and fitness

are key sources of restrictions and stereotyping. Physical appearance influences outcomes in subjectively judged sports such as gymnastics or figure skating – and perhaps in some not so subjectively judged. Physical size is a clear source of social stigma and oppression, and increasing public attention on obesity has created a negative culture for overweight and obese persons. Elite sport implies physically elite. Indeed, exclusion on the basis of physicality is nearly universal in sport and exercise, and this exclusion is a public health and social justice issue.

Rimmer (2005) notes that people with physical disabilities are one of the most inactive segments of the population; he further argues that rather than physical barriers, organizational policies, discrimination and social attitudes are the real barriers. Like many scholars in disability studies, Semerjian (2010) focuses on culture in her work on disability in sport and exercise psychology. She illustrates the power of stereotypes, but also takes a critical cultural perspective and highlights the larger cultural context as well as the intersections of race, gender and class with physicality.

Many studies (e.g., Puhl & Heuer, 2011) document clear and consistent stigmatization of obese individuals in employment, education and health care. And, several studies indicate that sport and physical activity professionals hold negative stereotypes and biases. Greenleaf and Weiller (2005) found that physical education teachers held anti-fat bias and strong personal weight control beliefs

(obese individuals are responsible for their obesity), and Chambliss, Finley and Blair (2004) found a strong anti-fat bias among exercise science students. Similarly, Robertson and Vohora (2008) found evidence of a strong anti-fat bias among fitness professionals and regular exercisers in England. Negative stereotypes about obese people are so prevalent that we may not realize our biases. That is, we may have implicit biases even if we do not explicitly state or recognize those biases. However, implicit biases are powerful and influence behaviors. A great deal of research has been done on implicit biases and their effects (see Project Implicit website at Harvard University: https://implicit.harvard.edu/implicit/) and you can check your own implicit biases in the Exercise. Implicit biases are particularly likely with weight and size given the media coverage. Research confirms that obese individuals are targets for teasing, more likely to engage in unhealthy eating behaviors, and less likely to engage in physical activity (Puhl & Wharton, 2007; Storch, Milsom, DeBranganza, Lewin, Geffken & Silverstein, 2007). Check the Yale Rudd Center website (http://yaleruddcenter. org/) for resources and information on weight bias in health and educational settings.

CULTURAL SPORT (AND EXERCISE) PSYCHOLOGY

Although the reviews cited in earlier sections show a lack of attention to culture and cultural diversity of sport and exercise psychology, a few dedicated scholars have been highlighting culture and developing *cultural sport (and exercise) psychology* over the last ten years. Fisher, Butryn and Roper (2003) advocated cultural studies as a promising perspective for sport psychology, and Ryba and Wright (2005) similarly called for a cultural studies model. Within a cultural studies framework, culture is ordinary and embedded in everyday meanings and practices. For example, most women's exercise and health promotion advertisements contain images of a thin and toned body implying that being thin means being healthy and beautiful.

Is it surprising that most women at some point in their lives participate in various weight loss practices? Today, girls as young as six years of age become concerned with their weight and start dieting! Because culture offers us a set of ready-made and often common-sense "pre-understandings" of our experiences, it is crucial to gain insights into constitutive dynamics between the individual psyche and the socio-cultural context. By understanding complex interactions of power and socio-cultural difference occurring in sporting contexts, we can increase the possibilities for positive change in sport and exercise.

Those authors and several colleagues have continued working for a greater cultural presence in sport and exercise psychology. The publication of Schinke and Hanrahan's (2009) edited text, *Cultural sport psychology*, might be considered a mark that cultural sport and exercise psychology is a recognized area. Ryba, Schinke and Tenenbaum's (2010) edited volume, *The cultural turn in sport psychology*, moves to a more critical cultural studies approach and challenges readers to examine culture in all areas of sport and exercise psychology. Responding to that challenge, the edited collection of Stambulova and Ryba (2013a), *Athletes' careers across cultures*, examines athletic careers as a socially and culturally constituted context in which the development of athletes occurs. Critiquing the cultural universalism operating in sport psychology, the authors show how cultural assumptions ingrained in everyday practices of social institutions, such as national sport organizations, enable athletes to develop certain skills while restricting the development of others. For example, how do you understand talent? Is it something we are born with or develop in the course of athletic practice? What are the implications of thinking about talent as innate or acquired? In Scandinavian countries, which largely view talent as a nurtured and acquired asset, athletes from early age are encouraged to work hard. In contrast, in Brazil, talent is considered to be mostly innate. As a consequence, calling an athlete a hard worker is similar to saying that the athlete has no talent (Stambulova & Ryba 2013b).

The concept of constituted culture may also contribute to our enhanced understandings why some nations excel in particular sports. For example, Girginov and Sandanski (2004) studied the success of Eastern European elite gymnastics. Reflecting on experiences of Bulgarian coaches invited to work in Britain, the authors concluded:

To be a successful athlete one has to employ the best methods and practices available. These methods, however, were not a simple body of knowledge that could be taken from the shelf, learned and reproduced. Rather they were deeply rooted in and represented local cultural practices, rituals, traditions, norms and attitudes (p. 820).

A growing movement in cultural sport psychology highlights the dynamics of cultural diversity within the discipline of sport and exercise psychology. Recently, two of our journals have devoted special issues to cultural sport and exercise psychology. The *International Journal of Sport and Exercise Psychology* special issue (Ryba & Schinke, 2009) highlighted the dominance of the western worldview in our research and practice, which usually results in comparing the cultural other with white, male, heterosexual and usually North American subjectivity. By doing so, sport psychology implies that white male's way of knowing is the norm, perpetuating the already unequal power relations in sport and exercise. Ryba and Schinke emphasized *cultural praxis*, which refers to an active and reflexive process of blending theory, lived culture, and social action in professional settings, as the key feature of cultural sport psychology. As a practical example of cultural praxis, consider the many new programs and campaigns aimed at reducing racism or homophobia in sport, such as FIFA's *Say No To Racism* or the *Pride House* in London. The *Journal of Clinical Sport Psychology* special issue (Schinke & Moore, 2011) on culturally informed sport psychology called for understanding, respect and integration of culture in professional practice, and included both theoretical articles and contributions on culturally informed direct service provision.

The continuing work of these scholars gives culture and cultural diversity a greater presence in sport and exercise psychology. Cultural sport and exercise psychology fits with the framework of this chapter, and brings a cultural studies perspective to our research and professional practice. Cultural sport and exercise psychology calls for awareness of (and a critical look at) our own cultural identity, and continuing study and reflection to gain a deeper understanding of culture within sport and exercise psychology. Also, in line with the third theme, cultural sport psychol-ogy calls for action with an emphasis on cultural praxis. That brings us to the topic of cultural competence.

CULTURAL COMPETENCE IN SPORT AND EXERCISE PSYCHOLOGY

Cultural competence takes cultural diversity directly into action and to professional prac-tice. Culturally competent professionals act to empower participants, challenge restrictions and advocate for social justice. Cultural competence is required in psychology and health professions, providing models for sport and exercise psychology. Cultural competence includes both understanding and action, and is needed at both the individual and organiza-tional level. That is, sport and exercise psychol-ogy professionals not only continue to develop their own cultural competence, but also work to ensure that their educational programs, professional practices and organizations are welcoming and inclusive of cultural diversity. For example, as an individual you might seek out a workshop on consultation with interna-tional athletes or find out as much as you can about a particular client's cultural background and experiences. At the same time, you might advocate for the inclusion of cultural compe-tence in professional standards. Psychology has resources and actively promotes multicul-tural competence, which may be described as: *the ability to work effectively with individuals who are of a different culture.* Stanley Sue (2006), one of the leading scholars in multicultural psychology, developed a widely-used model and continues to provide guidance on cultural competence for psychology professionals. Most multicultural psychology resources adopt a model of cultural competence with three key components: 1) *awareness* of one's own cultural values and biases; 2) *understand-ing* of other worldviews; and 3) development of culturally appropriate *skills*. The American Psychological Association (APA) followed that model in the APA (2003) Multicultural Guide-lines, which call on psychologists to develop and apply knowledge and awareness of cultural

diversity, and to promote culturally informed organizational policies and practices.

Sport and exercise psychology can also look to the AASP Ethical Guidelines, Principle D (Respect for People's Rights and Dignity), which clearly calls for cultural competence,

> ...AASP members are aware of cultural, indi-vidual, and role differences, including those due to age, gender, race, ethnicity, national origin, religion, sexual orientation, disabil-ity, language, and socioeconomic status. AASP members try to eliminate the effect on their work of biases based on those factors, and they do not knowingly partici-pate in or condone unfair discriminatory practices (AASP, 2006; available at: http:// www.aaasponoline.org).

William Parham (2005), a leader in APA's multi-cultural efforts as well as an active sport psychology professional, offers the following three guiding premises:

- *Context is everything.* First, context is key when providing services to diverse indi-viduals (and all sport and exercise psychol-ogy professionals work with diverse individuals); history, economics, family and social context are all relevant.
- *Culture, race and ethnicity as separate indi-ces do little to inform us.* Parham reminds us that cultural groups are not homoge-nous, and every individual has a unique mix of cultural identities.
- *Use paradigms reflecting differing world-views.* People from culturally diverse back-grounds may have developed sources of resiliency and strength in dealing with power relations. The typical U.S. world-view emphasizes independence, competi-

tiveness and individual striving. Emphasis on connectedness rather than separation, deference to higher power, mind-body interrelatedness rather than control, and a sense of "spirit-driven energy" may be more prominent in another's worldview.

More recently, Parham (2011) offered further helpful guides to enhance cultural competence in sport and exercise psychology. Parham's vision of a more culturally informed sport and exercise psychology rests on the following guiding premises: a) the explanatory power of the scientific method relative to culture, race, and ethnicity is limited; b) culture, race and ethnicity, gender, age and other elements of personal identification are operative in every social and research-based interpersonal interaction; c) the quality of the relationship represents a foundational ingredient in interpersonal interactions; d) sport psychology has not moved along in advancing a cultural agenda; e) context is very important; and f) culture, race and ethnicity as separate indices do little to inform us about within- and across-group variability. Parham proposes a model that considers the immediate and historical cultural context of both parties in the communication, to move forward. Overall, Parham calls for "more of thee and less of me" in research and practice. That is, professionals are listening as much (or more than) talking while engaging in culturally-informed interactions. Parham's premises highlight multiple, intersecting cultural identities and emphasize dynamic interactions and relationships. To understand and communicate effectively you must ask questions and listen more than you offer advice and directions.

Cultural competence as a continuing process: Most sources view cultural competence as a developmental process. Cross, Bazron, Dennis, and Isaacs (1999), describe a continuum of cultural competence moving from the lowest level of cultural destructiveness to the highest level of cultural proficiency:

- *Cultural destructiveness* – characterized by policies, actions and beliefs that are damaging to cultures.
- *Cultural incapacity* – not intending to be culturally destructive, but lack ability to respond effectively to diverse people (e.g., bias in hiring practices, lowered expectations).
- *Cultural blindness* – philosophy of being unbiased and that all people are the same (e.g., encouraging assimilation, blaming individuals for not "fitting in").
- *Cultural pre-competence* – desire but no clear plan to achieve cultural competence.
- *Cultural competence* – respect and recognition for diversity, genuine understanding of cultural differences (e.g., seek training and knowledge to prevent biases from affecting work, collaboration with diverse communities, willingness to make adaptations, continued training and commitment to work effectively with diverse groups).
- *Cultural proficiency* – culture held in high esteem and it is understood to be an integral part of who we are (e.g., conducting research to add to knowledge base, disseminating information on proven practices and interventions, engaging in advocacy with diverse groups that support the culturally competent system).

The Cross et al. (1999) model and APA multicultural guidelines reflect similar themes. That is, professionals recognize and value cultural diversity, continually seek to develop their multicultural knowledge and skills, translate those understandings into practice, and extend their efforts to advocacy by promoting organizational change and social justice. Remember that cultural competence is a process; continual vigilance and effort is needed to maintain and enhance your cultural competence. As with any physical skill, the adage "use it or lose it" holds. You must continue to practice and train to reach and maintain excellence.

Psychology and most of the health professions are far ahead of sport and exercise psychology in recognizing the essential role of cultural competence, and, most health education programs address cultural competence in their curricula (Luquis, Perez & Young, 2006). Unfortunately, that is not yet the case for sport and exercise psychology. We can look to psychology and health for models and resources; as cultural sport and exercise psychology gains a greater presence in our scholarship and educational programs, cultural competence will be the rule.

LEARNING AIDS

1   Define culture.

   Shared values, beliefs and practices of an identifiable group of people.

2   Define cultural competence.

   The ability to work effectively with individuals who are of a different culture.

3   Explain the role of power and privilege in cultural relations.

   Cultural relationships involve power. One (dominant) cultural group may have privilege, *which refers to social status, power or institutionalized advantage gained by virtue of valued socio-cultural identities, while other cultural groups are oppressed or discriminated against.*

4   Describe the status of cultural diversity in sport and exercise psychology scholarship.

   Reviews of the major journals and conference abstracts reveal very few articles or submissions that address cultural diversity.

REVIEW QUESTIONS

1   Identify and briefly explain the three themes in the multicultural framework for this chapter.

2   Explain privilege in cultural relations. Give a specific example of "white privilege" in sport and exercise.

3   Define stereotype threat, and explain how stereotype threat might operate in sport and exercise.

4   Describe the stereotypes and biases related to obesity, and explain how weight bias might affect participants and professionals in physical activity programs.

5   Define cultural competence and identify the three general areas of multicultural competencies.

6   Give two specific things a sport and exercise psychology professional could do to move up to a higher level of cultural competence. Describe how sport psychology professionals might promote cultural competence and social justice at the organizational level.

EXERCISES

1. Identify your own multiple cultural identities: List as many as you can of your own cultural identities (racial and ethnic identity, gender, social class, sexuality, spirituality/religion, physicality, etc.). Go beyond the typical cultural categories. For example, you might identify as an athlete or student. You should have a long list. Next, try to mark three aspects of your cultural identity that are especially salient or influential for you (that won't be easy, as different identities are more or less salient in different situations).

2. Power and privilege in cultural relationships: Think about your cultural identities, as in the previous exercise. First, list two ways that your cultural identity gives you power or privilege. Then, list two ways that you are oppressed or excluded because of your cultural identity. This is more difficult than the previous exercise. We often don't recognize our own privilege. It may be easier to recognize ways that you are oppressed. For example, you might think about a time when you were the only *one* (girl, person of your ethnic group, one who couldn't do the skill, etc.); you may have felt excluded.

3. Treating everyone the same – culture-blind or culturally-informed? As a professional, you want to be fair and provide opportunities for all of your students or clients. Should you ignore culture and treat everyone the same? How might that be problematic? How might treating everyone the same be unfair to participants? How might considering (rather than ignoring) culture help you better understand and work with participants?

4. Cultural diversity in sport and exercise psychology research: Select one of the sport and exercise psychology journals, such as *IJSEP* or *JASP*. Review the articles published over the last two years and try to identify any articles that address any aspect of cultural diversity. We hope you will find more than previous reviews have found, and that some articles will provide directions for improving cultural competence in sport and exercise psychology.

5. Stereotypes in sport and exercise: Think about how stereotypes might affect you or the participants in the following cases: a) you are watching a youth baseball team with many boys, but only two girls on the team; b) you are running a training program for an upcoming marathon race, and three older adults (over age 60) join the many 20–30 year olds in the program; and c) your new client at the fitness center is clearly obese. What are your first reactions to the girls? to the older adults? to the obese client? Do your reactions reflect stereotypes? How do you react to the other participants (or did you forget about them)? How might stereotypes affect behaviors and relationships? How might reactions based on stereotypes be limiting to participants? How could you avoid those limiting or discriminatory reactions?

6. Working with culturally diverse clients: Assume that you are a sport and exercise psychology professional. You begin working with a client from a culture about which you have limited knowledge. What could you do to increase your understanding and work more effectively with this client? List three ways you can learn more about the client's culture. How might this greater understanding affect your relationship with the client?

7. Consider your own cultural competence: How culturally competent are you? Review the continuum of cultural competence and think about your current or possible sport and exercise psychology activities.

Are you culturally proficient or competent? How so? Are any of your activities culturally destructive or incapacitating? How could you move "up" the cultural competence continuum? List two specific things you could do to enhance your cultural competence. Let's move to the organizational level. Where does your school, agency or program fit on this continuum? List two specific things that would help your organization become more culturally competent.

ADDITIONAL READING

Gill, D.L. & Kamphoff, C.S. (2010). Gender and cultural diversity. In J.M. Williams (Ed.), *Applied sport psychology* (6th ed.) (pp.417–439). New York, NY: McGraw Hill.

Ryba, T.V., Schinke, R.J. & Tenenbaum, G. (2010). *The cultural turn in sport psychology.* Morgantown, WV: FIT.

Schinke, R. & Hanrahan, S. (2008). *Cultural sport psychology.* Champaign, IL: Human Kinetics.

Schinke, R. & Moore, Z.E. (2011). Culturally informed sport psychology: Introduction to the special issue. *Journal of Clinical Sport Psychology, 5,* 283–294.

REFERENCES

Acosta, V.R. & Carpenter, L.J. (2012). *Women in intercollegiate sport: A longitudinal, national study thirty-five year update 1977–2012.* Unpublished document. Retrieved from: http://www.acostacarpenter.org/.

American Psychological Association (2003). Guidelines on multicultural education, training, research, practice and organizational change for psychologists. *American Psychologist, 58,* 377–402. (available online at APA PI directorate: www.apa.org/pi)

Beilock, S.L. & McConnell, A.R. (2004). Stereotype threat and sport: Can athletic performance be threatened? *Journal of Sport and Exercise Psychology, 26,* 597–609.

Butryn, T.M. (2002). Critically examining white racial identity and privilege in sport psychology consulting. *The Sport Psychologist, 16,* 316–336.

Chambliss, H.O., Finley, C.E. & Blair, S.N. (2004). Attitudes toward obese individuals among exercise science students. *Medicine and Science in Sports & Exercise, 36,* 468–474.

Cross, T., Bazron, B., Dennis, K. & Isaacs, M. (1999). *Towards a culturally competent system of care.* Washington, D.C. National Institute of Mental Health, Child and Adolescent Service System Program Technical Assistance Center, Georgetown University Child Development Center.

Duda, J.L. & Allison, M.T. (1990). Cross-cultural analysis in exercise and sport psychology: A void in the field. *Journal of Sport & Exercise Psychology, 12,* 114–131.

Fisher, L.A., Butryn, T.M. & Roper, E.A. (2003). Diversifying (and politicizing) sport psychology through cultural studies: A promising perspective. *The Sport Psychologist, 17,* 391–405.

Gill, D.L. (2007). Gender and cultural diversity. In G. Tenenbaum & R.C. Eklund (Eds.), *Handbook of Sport Psychology* (3rd ed.) (pp.823–844). Hoboken, NJ: Wiley.

Girginov, V. & Sandanski, I. (2004). From participants to competitors: The transformation of British gymnastics and the role of the Eastern European model of sport. *International Journal of the History of Sport, 21,* 815–831.

Greenleaf, C. & Weiller, K. (2005). Perceptions of youth obesity among physical educators. *Social Psychology of Education, 8,* 407–423.

Hall, R.L. (2001). Shaking the foundation: Women of color in sport. *The Sport Psychologist, 15,* 386–400.

Kamphoff, C.S., Gill, D.L., Araki, K. & Hammond, C.C. (2010). A Content Analysis of Cultural Diversity in the Association for Applied Sport Psychology's Conference Programs. *Journal of Applied Sport Psychology, 22,* 231–245.

Lapchick, R. (2011). *The 2010 Racial and Gender Report Card.* (retrieved May 2012 from http://www.bus.ucf.edu/sport).

Luquis, R., Perez, M. & Young, K. (2006). Cultural competence development in health education professional preparation programs. *American Journal of Health Education, 37*(4), 233–240.

Markus, H.R. (2008). Pride, prejudice, and ambivalence: Toward a unified theory of race and ethnicity. *American Psychologist, 63,* 651–670.

Mio, J.S., Barker-Hackett, L. & Tumambing, J. (2006). *Multicultural psychology: Understanding our diverse communities.* Boston: McGraw-Hill.

Norman, L. (2010). The UK coaching system is failing women coaches. *International Journal of Sports Science and Coaching, 3* (4), 447–467.

Parham, W.D. (2005). Raising the bar: Developing an understanding of athletes from racially, culturally, and ethnically diverse backgrounds. In M.B. Anderson (Ed.), *Sport psychology in practice.* (pp.201–215). Champaign, IL: Human Kinetics.

Parham, W.D. (2011). Research vs. me-search: Thinking more of thee and less of me when working within the context of culture. *Journal of Clinical Sport Psychology, 5,* 311–324.

Puhl, R. & Heuer, C.A. (2001). Obesity stigma: Important considerations for public health. *American Journal of Public Health, 100,* 1019–1028.

Puhl, R.M. & Wharton, C.M. (2007). Weight bias: A primer for the fitness Industry. *ACSM's Health & Fitness Journal, 11*(3), 7–11.

Ram, N., Starek, J. & Johnson, J. (2004). Race, ethnicity, and sexual orientation: Still a void in sport and exercise psychology. *Journal of Sport & Exercise Psychology, 26,* 250–268.

Rimmer, J.H. (2005). The conspicuous absence of people with disabilities in public fitness and recreation facilities: Lack of interest or lack of access? *American Journal of Health Promotion, 19,* 327–329.

Robertson, N. & Vohora, R. (2008). Fitness vs. fatness: Implicit bias towards obesity among fitness professionals and regular exercisers. *Psychology of Sport and Exercise, 9,* 547–557.

Ryba, T.V. (2009). Understanding your role in cultural sport psychology. In R.J. Schinke and S.J. Hanrahan (Eds.) *Cultural sport psychology* (pp.35–44). Champaign, IL: Human Kinetics.

Ryba, T.V. & Schinke, R.J. (2009). Methodology as a ritualized eurocentrism: Introduction to the special issue. *International Journal of Sport and Exercise Psychology, 7,* 263–274.

Ryba, T.V., Schinke, R.J. & Tenenbaum, G. (2010). *The cultural turn in sport psychology.* Morgantown, WV: FIT.

Ryba, T.V. & Wright, H.K. (2005). From mental game to cultural praxis: A cultural studies model's implications for the future of sport psychology. *Quest, 57,* 192–212.

Schinke, R. & Hanrahan, S. (2008). *Cultural sport psychology.* Champaign, IL: Human Kinetics.

Schinke, R. & Moore, Z.E. (2011). Culturally informed sport psychology: Introduction to the special issue. *Journal of Clinical Sport Psychology, 5,* 283–294.

Semerjian, T.Z. (2010). Disability in sport and exercise psychology. In T.V. Ryba, R.J. Schinke & G. Tenenbaum (Eds.). *The cultural turn in sport psychology.* (pp.259–285). Morgantown, WV: FIT.

Stambulova, N.B. & Ryba, T.V. (2013a). *Athletes' careers across cultures.* London: Routledge.

Stambulova, N.B. & Ryba, T.V. (2013b). Setting the bar: Towards cultural praxis of athletes' careers. In N. Stambulova & T.V. Ryba (Eds.). *Athletes' careers across cultures* (pp.235–254). London: Routledge.

Steele, C.M. (1997). A threat in the air: How stereotypes shape intellectual identity and performance. *American Psychologist, 52,* 613–629.

Storch, E.A., Milsom, V.A., DeBranganza, N., Lewis, A.B., Geffken, G.R. & Silverstein, J.H. (2007). Peer victimization, psychosocial adjustment, and physical activity in overweight and at-risk-for-overweight youth. *Journal of Pediatric Psychology, 32*(1), 80–89.

Sue, D.W. (2004). Whiteness and ethnocentric monoculturalism: making the "invisible" visible. *American Psychologist, 59,* 761–769.

Sue, S. (2006). Cultural competency: From philosophy to research and practice. *Journal of Community Psychology, 34,* 237–245.

Chapter 10

Perfectionism

The role of personality in shaping an athlete's sporting experience

HOWARD K. HALL, GARETH E. JOWETT AND ANDREW P. HILL

SUMMARY

This chapter explains how the personality characteristic of perfectionism influences the thoughts, feelings and actions of sport participants. It first describes what is meant by the term personality, and it illustrates why perfectionism should be considered to be a multi-dimensional personality characteristic rather than a narrow pattern of achievement behavior epitomized by striving to reach exceptionally high standards. It then outlines how different approaches to personality account for the development and maintenance of perfectionism. It presents an argument that demonstrates why perfectionism is not an adaptive attribute, and it explains why, because of its debilitating features, it is not a characteristic that should be actively encouraged by sport coaches or a quality that should be venerated in athletes who exhibit it. The chapter presents evidence from sport research to confirm the debilitating consequences of perfectionism and it concludes by highlighting various strategies that can be employed by athletes and coaches to effectively manage perfectionism in sport.

INTRODUCTION

In the field of sport psychology there are many who believe that aspects of personality contribute significantly to sporting accomplishment, and that athletes who perform at the highest level appear to share some common personality characteristics (Gould & Maynard, 2009). It is also recognized that the influence of personality extends far beyond sport performance and that it plays an important role in determining how individuals will adjust to the sporting environment, shaping the way that participants think, feel and act in sporting contexts (Vealey, 2002). Of course, the question to which almost all coaches and those interested in performance development would like a definitive answer is: "Which personality characteristics will be most influential in contributing to an athlete's sporting success?"

Based upon empirical research (Stoeber, 2011), a systematic review of the literature

(Gotwals, Stoeber, Dunn & Stoll, 2012) and anecdotal evidence collected from coaches and athletes, perfectionism is a personality characteristic that some argue may not only be an important attribute underpinning exceptional sport performance but a hallmark feature of elite athletes (Gould, Dieffenbach & Moffatt, 2002). The implication of this argument for future talent development is that if those responsible for the preparation and guidance of young athletes are able to nurture this aspect of personality, and facilitate sustained perfectionistic striving, they may be able to increase the probability that their athletes will excel.

The recent achievements of world-leading athletes such as Victoria Pendleton, a two-time Olympic cycling gold medalist and a self-declared perfectionist, provide testimony to the claim that perfectionism may have beneficial performance effects. However, one must exercise some caution before concluding that perfectionism is an adaptive personality characteristic that should be nurtured, and recognize that while Victoria Pendleton's perfectionism may have contributed to her considerable athletic success, it has, at times, been found to be a considerable psychological impediment. This is because her harsh self-critical style has not only left her feeling profoundly dissatisfied with the results of her achievement striving, but frequently distressed with the perceived consequences of falling short. For Pendleton, appraising her performance in this unforgiving manner has given rise to repeated bouts of emotional turmoil and an enduring sense of vulnerability, the roots of which lie in perceiving that her efforts are frequently insufficient to meet her own demanding standards and the perceived high expectations of others.

Perfectionism thus seems to be something of a paradox. It appears to energize a pattern of achievement striving that while contributing to favorable performance outcomes, gives rise to a plethora of debilitating processes. These may ultimately diminish the quality of both

motivation and performance and lead to psychological distress (Flett & Hewitt, 2005; Hall, Hill & Appleton, 2012). Clearly, if coaches and others involved in the development of athletes are to make use of this information they must begin to consider a number of important issues. First, it is imperative that they have a precise understanding of what it means when individuals exhibit perfectionism. This will enable them to appreciate the distinctive makeup and broad implications of this specific characteristic. It will also allow them to differentiate between perfectionistic striving, that has its roots in an individual's personality structure, and other forms of intense achievement striving which may involve the pursuit of exceedingly high standards, but have no direct association with an athlete's personality.

Because it is largely the potent energizing features of perfectionism which convince some to label it as a hallmark quality of elite athletes, it is important that coaches consider whether there is robust evidence to support claims that this personality characteristic can sustain adaptive patterns of motivation without eliciting psychologically debilitating consequences. Without such evidence, coaches must reflect on whether deliberately nurturing the development of perfectionism can be morally justified when it is apparent that this personality characteristic is associated with a wide range of psychologically debilitating outcomes. Regardless of whether perfectionism has status as a hallmark quality, it is important for coaches to consider how best to create sporting environments in which perfectionistic athletes can thrive, and reduce the likelihood that debilitating consequences will result from their particular form of intense achievement behavior.

This chapter will help guide thinking on these important issues. In it, we will first explore what is meant by the term "personality", and outline the reasons why perfectionism is best viewed as a personality characteristic rather than as a behavior, which reflects almost any pattern of sustained striving toward exceptionally high goals. We will then briefly examine different conceptual models of personality development and consider how these approaches have explained the development and maintenance of perfectionism. We will then consider what is known about perfectionism in sport and explain why it is considered by many theorists and practitioners to be a fundamentally maladaptive personality characteristic. We will attempt to refute claims that perfectionism can manifest as an adaptive facet of this personality characteristic, and explain why striving for high goals does not in itself constitute perfectionism. Through this approach we will challenge the view that perfectionism is a hallmark quality of elite performers and establish that it is more likely to be the features of adaptive achievement striving, rather than perfectionism that exceptional athletes have in common. Finally, we will consider how best to create optimal environments for sport participation in order to nurture these adaptive features and manage the maladaptive self-appraisal that is characteristic of perfectionism.

 ## OBJECTIVES

After reading this chapter you will be able to:

1 Understand the meaning of the term personality.
2 Define perfectionism and explain what makes it a personality characteristic.
3 Describe how different approaches to personality have explained the concept of perfectionism.
4 Differentiate between perfectionism and adaptive achievement striving.
5 Explain why perfectionism is a fundamentally debilitating personality characteristic and why it cannot be deemed to reflect an adaptive pattern of motivation in sport.
6 Describe how to facilitate striving for excellence and manage the maladaptive features of a perfectionistic personality.

WHAT IS PERSONALITY?

A historical analysis of the sport psychology literature would almost certainly reveal that while personality is an instrumental factor in explaining many aspects of sport and exercise behavior, there is little conclusive evidence that athletes exhibit a particular personality type (Vealey, 2002). One of the underlying reasons that sport researchers have been unable to generate much convincing evidence for this is that there are widely differing views on the meaning of the term personality and the manner in which it should be assessed. In its broadest sense personality simply reflects those internal attributes which render individuals unique. However, more precise definitions have been offered by psychologists such as Child (1968), who suggested that it reflects "the more or less stable, internal factors that make one person's behavior consistent from one time to another, and different from the behavior other people would manifest in similar situations" (p. 83). While countless definitions of personality have been proffered, Peterson (1992) summarized the key attributes which appear to be captured by most definitions. He claimed that personality is not only an internal feature, but an integrated facet of an individual, reflecting who they are and governing how they behave. Personality is thus a psychological construct that is concerned with an individual's thoughts, feelings and actions rather than a material or physical construct reflected by possessions, status or bodily structure. It appears to be made up of a variety of characteristics which collectively provide an individual with a unique psychological signature that influences the manner and the degree to which they are able to adapt to situations which they experience on a daily basis (Davey, 2004).

Although this psychological signature will be exclusive to each individual, a considerable proportion of an individual's personality is derived from factors which may be common to others (Kluckhorn & Murray, 1953). For example, genetic makeup, common environments

and social customs are all shared features that influence the development of personality. However, it is the exclusive manner in which humans process information, express beliefs, convey attitudes, demonstrate motivation and experience learning that renders each and every individual distinct from all others. Thus, if perfectionism represents a personality characteristic rather than a broad term to describe any form of sustained striving toward exceptionally high goals, then the defining qualities which underpin its psychological signature ought to correspond with those attributes proposed by Peterson (1992).

WHAT IS PERFECTIONISM? A PERSONALITY CHARACTERISTIC OR A TERM THAT DESCRIBES ANY FORM OF INTENSE GOAL-STRIVING?

By applying the attributes outlined by Petersen (1992) to accepted definitions of the construct, it can justifiably be argued that perfectionism is best thought of as a personality characteristic. Although it energizes motivation, and leads to the relentless pursuit of exceedingly high standards, it must be regarded as more than an impassioned form of achievement striving. One of the first to recognize this was Burns (1980) who maintained that while perfectionism was characterized by the compulsive and unremitting pursuit of impossible goals, this action was governed by an underlying belief that both successful accomplishment and heightened productivity would bring about enhanced self-worth. Others have also noted that perfectionism incorporates much more than the behavioral act of striving to reach high standards, viewing it as a largely debilitating psychological construct that represents a distinct way of thinking about achievement behavior, which is informed by both irrational beliefs and dysfunctional attitudes (Flett & Hewitt, 2002; Hamachek, 1978).

So what appears to be distinctive about perfectionistic thinking? One notable facet is the instrumental significance that individuals attach to the act of achievement striving. This

means that perfectionists do not pursue exceedingly high goals because accomplishment is imbued with intrinsic value, but because achievement is an effective means through which to gain social acceptance, recognition and establish a sense of personal value. Moreover, perfectionists attach such irrational significance to achievement that success and failure appear to be almost dichotomous, and it is the employment of such stringent criteria which elicits the pursuit of both rigid and inflexible goals (Pacht, 1984).

Unfortunately, when this form of achievement striving is also accompanied by harsh self-criticism, performances that fall short are often met by personal condemnation. The employment of such rigid criteria for accomplishment provides little margin for error, however, and this intensifies concern about making mistakes. As a result, perfectionists become hyper-vigilant about avoiding flaws and so profoundly sensitive to evaluation from others that any perception of failure or criticism has an undermining influence on self-worth. The constant preoccupation with personal deficiencies and the possible impact of failure further contribute to vague doubts about whether personal resources can be found to satisfactorily meet goals, and these doubts impede the ability to determine whether tasks have been satisfactorily completed, leaving the individual in a state of dissonance. In conjunction with the behavioral act of striving to reach exceedingly high personal standards, this distinctive pattern of irrational thought reflects the core qualities of perfectionism, and these particular features collectively encourage individuals to engage in obsessive striving as a self-validation strategy (Frost et al., 1990).

Hall (2013) recently attempted to capture both the complexity of perfectionistic thinking and the motivational process it energizes in a summary definition of perfectionism. He not only specified what perfectionism entailed, but attempted to explain why it underpinned a much more intricate pattern of achievement behavior than the behavioral act of striving to accomplish high standards. Based on the work of leading theorists (Frost et al., 1990; Flett & Hewitt, 2002) Hall suggested that:

> Perfectionism is a multi-dimensional personality characteristic. It encompasses a specific constellation of achievement-related cognition and behavior associated with the compulsive pursuit of flawlessness in contexts that hold personal relevance for the individual. While perfectionism has the potential to bring about positive outcomes, it may also induce maladaptive motivational processes because harsh self-evaluation, or perceived criticism from others follows perceived failure to meet internalized ideal standards. The foundation for this thought process is the belief that self-acceptance is inextricably tied to accomplishment, and it is this belief which fosters an overdependence on personal attainment and impels individuals to strive compulsively (p. 59).

From this description it is easy to see that perfectionism involves much more than the act of intense goal striving, and that its complex make-up depicts the essential qualities of a personality characteristic. It is clearly a psychological rather than a physical construct as it is governed by internal cognitive processes, and it is these processes which give rise to relatively stable behavior patterns that become observable in meaningful achievement contexts. Moreover, because these cognitive processes appear to be firmly integrated into an individual's identity, they not only reflect how individuals will tend to behave, but will often define who they are (Flett & Hewitt, 2002). This means that while perfectionism may appear to have much in common with other personality characteristics such as conscientiousness, the pattern of thinking that underpins perfectionism is distinct because there is always the potential for individuals to experience vulnerability and distress when perceived achievement outcomes are believed to reflect poorly on the self. The complex set of beliefs associated with perfectionism thus results in more than intense goal striving and frequently will give rise to an extreme and potentially adverse form of achievement behavior, which may undermine self-definition.

The belief that perfectionism is dysfunctional is characteristic of the two dominant approaches that have influenced the direction of research on the subject in the last 25 years. The first, put forward by Frost et al. (1990), considers that perfectionism reflects a number of cognitive attitudes such as concern about mistakes, doubts about one's actions and a commitment to high personal standards. It also incorporates two social-cognitive dimensions that represent perceived pressures and expectations from parents. The second approach proposed by Hewitt & Flett (1990) suggests that perfectionism is a characteristic that may manifest along each of three dimensions. Self-oriented perfectionism describes individuals who demand perfection of themselves and who respond with self-criticism when they come up short. Other oriented perfectionism reflects a demand that others must demonstrate perfection, whereas socially prescribed perfectionism denotes a perception that others not only demand perfection, but that they will evaluate achievement striving harshly. Both of these approaches argue that perfectionism is distinct from striving for excellence. They suggest that there is a fundamental difference between aspiring to do one's best and seeking perfection, and it is the pattern of cognition, affect and behavior associated with the quest for flawlessness which becomes dysfunctional, regardless of whether the pattern of achievement striving is the result of personal or perceived social pressure to be perfect (Flett & Hewitt, 2006).

APPROACHES TO PERSONALITY: DIFFERING EXPLANATIONS OF THE DEVELOPMENT AND MAINTENANCE OF PERFECTIONISM

Historically, perfectionism has been regarded as a debilitating personality characteristic because the psychological basis for the achievement striving exhibited by perfectionists was considered to be either abnormal or irrational. Some of the earliest ideas about the nature and development of perfectionism were provided by psychodynamic personality theorists such as Alfred Adler (Ansbacher and Ansbacher, 1956) and Karen Horney (1950). Even Freud (1926/1959) offered a view on perfectionism, considering that it was a symptom of obsessive behavior, in that perfectionistic striving served to appease a harsh and punitive superego (conscience), which demanded superior levels of achievement (Hall & Lindzey, 1978). Psychodynamic theorists purport that individuals' personalities emerge as a consequence of attempts to resolve unconscious emotional conflicts that largely arise in childhood. Adler considered that striving for perfection was innate and gave impetus to people's lives. He believed, however, that this form of striving could manifest in many ways. Those individuals categorized as normal were thought to pursue goals which placed social interest and public welfare above private gain, whereas neurotic individuals were characterized by the pursuit of selfish or egoistic goals involving enhanced self-esteem, increased power or self-aggrandizement. He also believed that individuals were motivated by feelings of inferiority that arose out of a sense of incompletion or imperfection in any life domain, and while he argued that this did not necessarily reflect abnormal behavior, he suggested that when feelings of inferiority were exaggerated to compensate for life events such as overindulgence, rejection, or deprivation of affection in childhood, they would lead to abnormal behavior in the manner individuals strive for perfection.

Another psychodynamic explanation of perfectionism was provided by Horney (1950), who argued that neurotic needs for perfection developed out of a distorted belief that problems with disturbed human relations could be overcome by appearing to be flawless and impregnable. She referred to these needs as "the tyranny of the should" (p. 64), and argued that perfectionistic individuals assign excessive value to the achievement of idealized standards because they believe that successful accomplishment will provide them with a sense of infallibility. She further claimed that striving to meet their ideals encourages individuals to pursue both rigid and excessive standards. Unfortunately, failure to live up to these ideals is an inevitable consequence, which tends to elicit acute self-criticism and emotional distress. This cognitive process derives from the belief that achievement not only has inherent value, but that it should always be possible. Horney recognized that the constant self-deprecation exhibited by perfectionists will lead to a range of debilitating emotional responses, many of which may appear disproportionate to an unassuming observer, but will seem entirely fitting to the individual concerned. Not only does the meaning of successful achievement striving carry elevated personal significance for the perfectionist, but falling short of one's ideals risks undermining identity and has the potential to be psychologically catastrophic.

More recent writing on perfectionism adopts a trait perspective. Trait psychologists assume that an individual's unique psychological signature is a function of the degree to which particular personality traits are exhibited. Traits describe various tendencies for individuals to think and behave in a consistent manner. While it is feasible that individuals possess all known traits to a greater or lesser degree, it is believed that each person will display their own stable combination of traits across both time and context, and that this particular blend will predispose individuals to behave habitually, regardless of the situation in which they find themselves. The exact number of personality traits which, in combination, inform an individual's personality has been the subject of considerable debate for many years. Both Jung (1964) and Eysenck (1991) created models of personality in which they identified three broad traits. In contrast, Cattell (1946) presented evidence for the existence of 16 source traits, one of which he labeled perfectionism. However, critics of Cattell's work such as Costa and McRae (1992), argue that there appear to be no more than five core traits. These include extroversion, neuroticism (emotional stability), openness to experience, agreeableness and conscientiousness. Various dimensions of perfectionism have been found to be associated with conscientiousness and neuroticism (e.g. Hill, McIntyre & Bacharach, 1997). However, while perfectionists may exhibit qualities of conscientiousness such as hard work, organization and perseverance, it is the features of emotional instability such as worry, self-consciousness and vulnerability which consistently give rise to psychological debilitation in perfectionists.

One of the main criticisms of trait psychology is that traits do not always appear to be stable and enduring, and that across situations behavior lacks consistency (Mischel, 1968). This is borne out by research in sport, where perfectionism in athletes has been reported to be a domain-specific phenomenon rather than a characteristic which is exhibited consistently across all realms of life (e.g. McArdle, 2010). Moreover, while some clinical psychologists report that those exhibiting extreme forms of perfectionism appear to exhibit harsh self-critical striving across a wide variety of achievement contexts, this has not been replicated when perfectionism has been investigated by social, educational and sport psychologists. Rather, perfectionistic striving appears to be constrained, and is only exhibited in those achievement contexts which are found to be personally salient, suggesting that the environment may have an important role to play in determining when this form of behavior is evoked.

The importance of the environment in personality development can be seen in the psychological tradition of behaviorism, which emphasizes that personality characteristics are established and sustained as a result of both reward and punishment, and that behavior is shaped by a pattern of contingent reinforcement. Owens and Slade (2008) have argued strongly that the development of perfectionism may be a function of this process. They suggested that when individuals are motivated to strive for exceedingly high standards, and the achievement of positive outcomes reinforces the action, perfectionistic behavior becomes strengthened. However, as individuals may be equally motivated to strive to avoid any negative consequences from failure, the act of perfectionistic striving may become further reinforced when aversive outcomes are avoided.

The idea that perfectionism is only displayed in meaningful contexts is, however, most consistent with an interactionist rather than a behavioral perspective on personality. An interactionist perspective considers that both the environment and internal psychological processes act collectively to influence an individual's behavior. This means that those who exhibit characteristics of perfectionism when playing sport may not inevitably be perfectionistic in other achievement domains. While sport may provide them with the necessary opportunities to establish a meaningful identity, validate self-worth or gain recognition through accomplishment, other environments may not carry the same degree of significance. Consequently, they would not be considered as sufficiently important contexts in which to achieve and thus, they would be unlikely to induce compulsive striving. An interactionist perspective may also explain why perfectionism appears to be neither exclusively adaptive nor universally debilitating. Evidence from social psychology (Flett, Hewitt, Endler & Tassone, 1995) suggests that perfectionism may elicit a pattern of behavior that looks like any other form of adaptive achievement striving when success is perceived. However, when perfectionists begin to experience persistent achievement difficulties or encounter repeated failure, a maladaptive pattern of cognition emerges that brings with it emotional distress and leads to the employment of dysfunctional achievement strategies that accompany compulsive striving.

While many current approaches to the study of personality adopt an interactionist approach, some argue that a phenomenological approach may offer even greater explanatory power. This is because phenomenological approaches not only give credence to individuals' subjective experience of the environment and personal notions about self, but they consider that behavior is a direct consequence of the way individuals ascribe meaning to their world. Vealey (2002) has suggested that phenomenological approaches focus on what people do rather than the qualities they possess, and they attempt to determine the underlying reasons that people give for their behavior in any particular context. This particular feature advances knowledge that can be gained from trait psychology because trait approaches are often poor predictors of behavior, and they don't permit detailed analysis of the underlying reasons behind an individual's thoughts, feelings and actions. A number of contemporary approaches to understanding sport motivation can be considered to reflect phenomenological approaches. For example, in Achievement Goal Theory (AGT) the meaning individuals ascribe to success and failure is considered to be the critical determinant of achievement behavior (see Duda & Hall, 2001). In Self Determination Theory (SDT) the fulfillment of innate personal needs for competence, autonomy (perception of meaningful choice) and relatedness (feeling connected to others) are assumed to be essential for personal growth, integrity and well-being (see Ryan & Deci, 2007).

A phenomenological approach to the study of perfectionism in sport may be seen in research which has utilized the central tenets of both AGT and SDT. AGT has been used to explain the manner in which an individual's achievement goals and the perceived reward structures that emanate from the social environment convey specific meaning to perfectionistic striving. Perhaps the first to note that perfectionism was underpinned by a characteristic pattern of achievement goals was Covington (1992). He used the term "overstriving" to describe individuals who were energized by both extreme approach and avoidance motives, and suggested that it was a desire to establish self-worth that led these individuals to strive incessantly toward ever-greater accomplishments. He noted that while these individuals craved success, they simultaneously experienced thoughts about failure and its aversive consequences, and it was this hybrid combination of goals that energized perfectionistic striving.

Sport researchers have recently confirmed that perfectionistic athletes exhibit similar combinations of achievement goals that give meaning to perfectionistic striving (e.g. Stoeber, Stoll, Pesheck & Otto, 2008). Specifically, perfectionist athletes have been shown to endorse both mastery and performance approach goals which lead them to strive for success, not only to demonstrate ability, but to gain social recognition. However, because they simultaneously endorse performance avoidance goals they also strive relentlessly in order to avoid any demonstration of incompetence. It has been argued that this specific pattern of goals will energize continued motivation under conditions of success because goal satisfaction and social recognition reflect positively on self-worth. However, because perceived success tends to be fleeting, this same pattern of achievement goals will begin to have extremely corrosive effects on motivation when individuals experience difficulty or failure and aversive outcomes undermine perceived self-worth (Hall, Hill & Appleton, 2012).

Perfectionism can also be explained from a phenomenological perspective by the employment of SDT. For perfectionists, the social environment seems to evoke a combination of intrinsic motivation, self-induced pressures to succeed and external pressure to gain reinforcement and social recognition. With this composite profile, the regulation of motivation tends to be relatively low in self-determination and relatively high in perceived external control. This not only governs how achievement information is appraised, but contributes to the thwarting rather than the fulfillment of basic needs for autonomy and competence. Over time, this process will not only have a detrimental effect on the quality of motivation but will impact negatively on psychological well-being. For example, a sense of obligation to strive for perfection will significantly undermine an individual's perception of autonomy, and regularly appraising performance to be discrepant from rigid, inflexible and excessive standards will have a similarly undermining effect on perceived competence. Failing to fulfill what self-determination theorists consider to be basic psychological needs will give rise to further compulsive striving as individuals seek to redress perceived performance discrepancies and fulfill basic psychological needs. However, striving for excessively high standards will precipitate further debilitating patterns of achievement related cognition and behavior when individuals fall short, basic needs become thwarted and failure impacts negatively on self-worth.

From this brief synthesis, it is evident that over the last century a number of approaches to personality have been employed to describe and explain the characteristic of perfectionism. While there may be considerable overlap in the qualities described by each approach, all differ markedly in the assumptions they make about perfectionism and the central processes that sustain its characteristic pattern of cognition and behavior. Although paradigmatic advancements in the study of personality and social psychology have contributed significantly to an enhanced understanding of perfectionism and the psychological mechanisms which appear to underpin it, one dispute that has yet to be adequately resolved is whether perfectionism can ever be considered to reflect a psychologically adaptive characteristic. Several researchers have argued that many perfectionists exhibit an adaptive subtype of the personality characteristic (e.g. Owens & Slade, 2008), and it is this claim which has led some in sport to endorse Owens and Slade's view that "positive perfectionism" ought to be nurtured in aspiring athletes. Others disagree, arguing that while the act of conscientious achievement striving ought to be encouraged, it would be morally questionable to nurture in young athletes a personality characteristic where self-worth is conditional, based predominantly upon the achievement of rigid and illusory standards and where individuals strive compulsively for self-validation (Flett & Hewitt, 2006; Hall et al., 2012).

AN ARGUMENT AGAINST POSITIVE PERFECTIONISM

The possibility for perfectionistic striving to be adaptive appears to be rooted in ideas first put forth by Adler (Ansbacher & Ansbacher, 1956), who believed that this form of achievement behavior would be positive when individuals' innate social interests were motivated by social welfare rather than private gain. The idea that perfectionistic striving for personal gain may also be motivationally adaptive can be traced back to the writings of Hamachek (1968). He proposed that the expression "normal perfectionism" described the motivation of individuals who anticipated pleasure from the pursuit of challenging goals, gained intrinsic satisfaction from personal mastery and acquired self-esteem from their accomplishments. Hamachek's description of this behavior as reflective of perfectionism has, however, been challenged by various scholars on the grounds that what he described does not correspond with accepted definitions of perfectionism where individuals place irrational value on achievement, measure their worth in terms of accomplishment and maintain a rigid commitment to excessive goals in order to avoid criticism (Greenspon, 2000; Hall et al. 2012; Flett & Hewitt, 2006). His critics argue that in the case of "normal perfectionism" Hamachek appears to confuse striving for excellence with perfectionism. Specifically, he fails to recognize that the distinctive psychological signature that characterizes perfectionism requires that individuals exhibit all of the core qualities of the construct and not simply one behavioral quality which, in isolation, appears to denote the conscientious pursuit of high standards.

It must be recognized that when defining perfectionism, its core dimensions cannot be disregarded or disaggregated without fundamentally altering the construct. A baking analogy may help to illustrate why this is the case. If we liken the core dimensions that collectively represent perfectionism to the core ingredients which constitute a cake, we can extrapolate from the baking process to demonstrate how disaggregating the characteristic qualities of perfectionism will significantly alter the meaning attached to the construct. It is generally agreed that a basic cake mix requires a baker to first combine five or six core ingredients. These include, a base (e.g. flour), a sweetener, a binding agent (e.g. eggs), a fat (e.g. butter), a liquid and a leavening agent (e.g. yeast or baking powder). In combination, these ingredients form the basis for a wide variety of cakes, but for any product to be classified as a cake, all of its core components must be incorporated into the mix. If one begins to selectively exclude core ingredients, the resultant product may be significantly altered. By including only a limited number of its core ingredients and omitting others, the result of the cooking process will not be cake, but some other product such as crepes, shortbread, scrambled eggs, custard or meringue. The important point to conclude from this baking analogy is that any decision to represent a construct by selective utilization, or omission, of core components will not only transform its underlying structure but fundamentally change its meaning. It is for this reason that it is both conceptually and methodologically inappropriate for researchers or practitioners to label one particular quality, such as striving to reach excessively high standards, as perfectionism. Nor is it appropriate to consider an individual who strives to reach exceedingly high standards as a perfectionist unless they also exhibit the debilitating qualities that are considered to be core elements of this personality characteristic, for it is only in combination that these dimensions render an individual a perfectionist.

Not all researchers agree with this view, however. Some maintain that because perfectionism is a multidimensional construct it makes sense to be able to differentiate between those dimensions that appear broadly adaptive, reflect perfectionistic striving and lead to positive outcomes, and those which reflect evaluative concerns, and are generally associated with both maladaptive processes and debilitating outcomes (Stoeber, 2011; Gotwals, Stoeber, Stoll & Dunn, 2012). When factor analysis has been employed to group various measures reflecting the core components of perfectionism into two broad dimensions (perfectionistic striving and evaluative concerns), researchers have claimed that this establishes that perfectionism is multifaceted, and therefore it cannot be regarded as a broadly debilitating personality characteristic. Evidence to support this claim comes from the fact that perfectionistic striving is typically associated with benign or occasionally positive motivational processes (Gotwals et al., 2012).

Further evidence has been claimed from the examination of athlete profiles. Findings reveal that those who strive for perfection in the absence of evaluative concerns tend to exhibit generally adaptive patterns of motivation and experience beneficial outcomes. In attempts to further substantiate that perfectionism can take a positive form, some have argued that while there is a strong positive correlation between perfectionistic striving and evaluative concerns, this association may, in fact, mask the magnitude of the positive effects to be derived from perfectionistic striving, and that the genuine consequences are clearly evident when the influence of evaluative concerns is removed (Gotwals et al., 2012). While tests that have employed partial correlations to statistically control for the effects of evaluative concerns provide some support for this argument, the approach has been challenged on the grounds that the strategy may create interpretive problems that bring the revised associations into question. Researchers have, however, made other claims in support of the positive effects of perfectionistic striving (e.g. Gaudreau & Verner-Filion 2012). They suggest that rather than acting together with dysfunctional beliefs and attitudes to produce a psychologically destructive personality characteristic, this particular form

of achievement behavior may provide a buffer against the debilitating effects of evaluative concerns. However, evidence in support of this mechanism remains inconclusive.

Without detailed scrutiny, one should remain skeptical about how perfectionistic striving may interact with other dimensions of the construct, and exercise caution when it is claimed that perfectionism can manifest as a positive, adaptive or healthy characteristic. Greenspon (2000) has argued that there is nothing remotely healthy about feeling compelled to perform perfectly and evaluating yourself as inadequate each time you fall short. It is therefore essential to recognize that while perfectionistic striving may stimulate elevated performance and exhibit a positive association with various adaptive outcomes, this pattern will only be evident when selective dimensions of perfectionism are considered in isolation, in circumstances where perfectionistic striving is disaggregated from the other core dimensions of the construct, or when perceived success moderates the debilitating influence of evaluative concerns. It seems conceptually inappropriate to consider perfectionism to be a multidimensional construct that reflects a broad personality characteristic and then suggest that one particular facet represents a positive version of perfectionism simply because those dimensions representing perfectionistic striving are associated with an array of adaptive correlates. Likewise, it appears to be a similarly questionable strategy to classify individuals who score high on perfectionistic striving and low on evaluative concerns as positive or healthy perfectionists. Individuals with this profile cannot be considered to be exhibiting perfectionism simply because they display heightened achievement striving.

What research evidence points toward is that when athletes strive for excellence and seek personal mastery, their motivation tends to be adaptive because they are not riddled with debilitating evaluative concerns that may undermine motivation, performance or psychological functioning. It is clear, however, that this pattern of cognition and achievement behavior does not correspond with the characteristic qualities of perfectionism, and therefore it is inappropriate to consider athletes who may exhibit it to be perfectionists of any type. The term perfectionism must have a more precise meaning if it is to enable us to better understand the nature of achievement behavior in sport. It must be limited to athletes whose psychological make-up induces compulsive striving for perfection, elicits harsh evaluative concerns and promotes the belief that self-worth is contingent on productivity and sporting accomplishment. There is considerable evidence to suggest that far from being a positive attribute and a hallmark feature of exceptional athletes, when considered in this manner perfectionism is a psychologically debilitating personality characteristic that may impair sporting performance and lead to considerable emotional distress.

PERFECTIONISM IN ATHLETES

Research indicates that the motivation that underpins the distinct pattern of cognition, affect and behavior exhibited by perfectionistic athletes is regulated by a combination of approach and avoidance goals (see Hall 2013; Hall et al., 2012 for a review). While they crave success, it is because of their prevailing fear of failure that perfectionistic athletes report experiencing unremitting pressure to meet their own, or others', exceedingly high standards in their quest to achieve social recognition, acceptance and self-validation. Various studies have demonstrated that perfectionism not only leads athletes to exhibit maladaptive forms of motivation but it also induces considerable disaffection in a domain where achievement is of immense personal significance. It has been shown to contribute to heightened anxiety over performance, depressed affect that stems from unsatisfactory performance appraisal, a sense of anger when goals are thwarted and fluctuating self-worth because success is perceived to be fleeting and one's worth is constantly on the line. Unfortunately, when perfectionistic athletes attempt to cope they tend to employ maladaptive strategies that perpetuate their achievement difficulties. While success may bring some temporary respite, it is because perfectionists' goals are both excessively high and rigid, that constantly coming up short induces chronic disaffection. Over time, this becomes psychologically corrosive and increases the likelihood of athlete burnout. Clearly, when perfectionism is considered to be a multidimensional personality characteristic that incorporates the features of both perfectionistic striving and evaluative concerns, it is difficult to conclude from the growing body of research evidence in sport that this disposition is in any way positive, adaptive or healthy. What cannot be disputed, however, is the fact that perfectionism is something of a paradox. Its energizing qualities will induce achievement striving, which may underpin both exceptional sporting accomplishments and the attainment of positive outcomes, but the downside of perfectionism is that it also creates a way of thinking about success and failure in sport that becomes manifestly debilitating at the point when performance is perceived to be discrepant from desired standards.

MANAGING PERFECTIONISM IN ATHLETES

Psychologists have found that individuals exhibiting perfectionism are often slow to respond to standard therapeutic interventions. This is because meaningful change involves altering the fundamental belief system that underpins the structure of personality. Furthermore, because perfectionists will often attribute successful accomplishment to this personality characteristic, they may demonstrate a reluctance to change their approach to achievement striving, fearing that it will inhibit future accomplishment. They may also be unwilling to accept that compulsive striving, aimed at self-validation, represents an unhealthy commitment to excessively high standards rather than a genuine passion for the activity in question, and so feel no need to change. Despite being difficult to treat, however, perfectionism is commonly managed with cognitive behavioral therapies (CBT). The use of CBT is predicated on the assumption that the underlying cause of perfectionism lies in an individual's distorted beliefs and attitudes, and that this dysfunctional pattern of cognition can be challenged through relatively short interventions that focus on the mechanisms which maintain perfectionistic thinking. However, short-term interventions may not always be effective. This is because it is necessary to change structural beliefs that involve both the need to be perfect and a desire for conditional acceptance. These are at the heart of the personality characteristic, and because they have been embedded and reinforced over time they may require long-term treatment to modify.

While it is recommended that the treatment of perfectionism in athletes is best undertaken by those with an appropriate background in clinical or counseling psychology, there are a number of strategies that a coach may employ to help perfectionistic athletes manage the potentially debilitating consequences of this personality characteristic. The management of perfectionism in athletes may be built into basic psychological skills training. For example, educational programs which enable athletes to employ effective self-talk and cognitive restructuring may help them to understand the difference between perfectionistic striving and striving for excellence.

Similarly, teaching athletes how to set challenging, flexible goals, employ effective strategy development and appraise performance against goals of this type will help to foster striving for excellence rather than perfectionistic striving. Teaching thought-stopping techniques may further help athletes to manage repetitive, intrusive negative thoughts that are common place in perfectionists, especially when performance is perceived to be discrepant from desired standards.

Coaches may also wish to structure the learning and performance environment so that it helps to challenge the value of perfectionistic thinking and facilitate adaptive achievement striving. Because Shafran, Egan and Wade (2010) have argued that the development of perfectionism is largely a consequence of socialization processes, the promotion of a mastery-oriented climate should be considered essential to counteract the debilitating cognition that is a common feature of perfectionism. This is because when adaptive motivational cues are made salient, athletes are encouraged to view achievement in self-referent terms that focuses their striving towards personal growth, mastery and learning. It is equally important for coaches to avoid creating performance-oriented climates. Perfectionistic athletes become particularly vulnerable in these environments as coach rewards and social recognition are reserved for those who demonstrate superior ability, and criticism of mistakes is common. The environment created by coaches may be instrumental in helping perfectionistic athletes challenge notions of contingent self-worth. SDT suggests that when environmental conditions support the fulfillment of basic needs for competence, autonomy and relatedness, adaptive functioning will be promoted and this not only helps develop true self-esteem, but enhanced psychological well-being.

CONCLUSION

Based on the available evidence it is our view that perfectionism is not a hallmark quality of exceptional athletes. It is a broadly debilitating personality characteristic that differs markedly from striving for excellence. Irrational beliefs about achievement encourage individuals to strive compulsively, in the belief that successful accomplishment will bring about recognition and self-worth. The pattern of motivation it engenders may on occasion result in favorable performance outcomes. However, without effective coping strategies to manage dysfunctional cognition, perfectionism cannot provide a foundation for sustained achievement striving as psychological turmoil is an inevitable consequence.

LEARNING AIDS

1   According to Peterson (1992) what are the key attributes of personality?

   An integral part of an individual. It is psychological. Made up of numerous characteristics. It is unique to each individual.

2   Outline the defining qualities of perfectionism.

   It is multidimensional. It involves more than the pursuit of high standards, but an inflexible commitment to flawlessness. It reflects irrational thinking about achievement. It involves harsh self-critical evaluation. Self-worth is tied to accomplishment.

3   Identify some common irrational thoughts of perfectionistic athletes that coaches might challenge.

   Self-worth is contingent upon goal achievement. If I fall short of the standards I'm trying to achieve, it is complete failure. Any performance that is less than perfect will be criticized by others. If I make mistakes, people will think less of me. Anything less than perfect performance is not good enough. I must always excel in things that are important to me. I'm worthless when I fail to reach my goals.

4   Identify five negative outcomes that perfectionistic athletes have been known to experience.

   Anxiety, anger, depressed mood, fluctuating self-esteem, burnout.

REVIEW QUESTIONS

1   Explain what makes perfectionism a personality characteristic.

2   Identify what you consider to be the differences between striving for excellence and perfectionism.

3   Write a sentence that describes the features of the following approaches to personality: A psychodynamic approach; A trait approach; An environmental approach; An interactionist approach; A phenomenological approach.

4   Discuss why perfectionism cannot be thought of as a positive, adaptive, or healthy characteristic.

EXERCISES

1   Describe where you believe the origins of perfectionism might lie, and explain how perfectionism might be sustained in young athletes.

2   Make a list of the long-term costs and benefits of athletic perfectionism.

3   Make a list of the advantages and disadvantages for an athlete in seeking to change their perfectionistic behavior.

4   You have been asked by the welfare officer of a youth sports club to create a plan that will help an athlete to manage debilitating perfectionism. What actions might you suggest for the athlete to help them to manage their perfectionism? What actions might you advise the coach to take to help the athlete to manage their perfectionism? What advice might you provide for the parents to help the athlete to manage their perfectionism?

ADDITIONAL READING

Flett, G.L. & Hewitt, P.L. (2002). *Perfectionism: Theory, research, and treatment.* Washington, DC: American Psychological Association.

Flett, G.L. & Hewitt, P.L. (2005). The perils of perfectionism in sports and exercise. *Current Directions in Psychological Science., 14*, 14–18.

Frost, R.O., Marten, P.A., Lahart, C. & Rosenblate, R. (1990). The dimensions of perfectionism. *Cognitive Therapy and Research, 14*, 449–468.

Hall, H.K., Hill, A.P. & Appleton, P.R. (2012). Perfectionism: A foundation for sporting excellence or an uneasy pathway to purgatory? In G.C. Roberts & D.C. Treasure (Eds.), *Advances in motivation in sport and exercise* (Vol. 3, pp.129–168). Champaign, IL: Human Kinetics.

Hall, H.K., Hill, A.P. & Appleton, P.R. (2013). Perfectionism: Its development and influence on emerging talent in youth. In J. Cote & R. Lidor (Eds.), *Conditions of children's talent development in sport* (pp.117–137). Morgantown, VA: Fitness Information Technology, Inc.

Hewitt, P.L. & Flett, G.L. (1991). Perfectionism in the self and social contexts: Conceptualization, assessment, and association with psychopathology. *Journal of Personality and Social Psychology, 60*, 456–470.

Stoeber, J. (2011). The dual nature of perfectionism in sports: Relationships with emotion. *International Review of Sport and Exercise Psychology, 4*, 128–145.

REFERENCES

Ansbacher, H.L. & Ansbacher, R.R. (Eds.). (1956). *The individual psychology of Alfred Adler.* New York: Basic Books.

Burns, D.D. (1980). The perfectionists script for self-defeat. *Psychology Today, 14* (November), 34–51.

Cattell, R.B. (1946). *Description and measurement of personality.* New York, NY: World Company Books.

Child, I.L. (1968). Personality in culture. In E.F. Borgetta & W.W. Lambert (Eds.), *Handbook of personality theory and research.* Chicago, IL: Rand McNally.

Costa, P.T. & McCrae, R.R. (1992). *NEO PI-R. Professional manual.* Odessa, FL: Psychological Assessment Resources, Inc.

Covington, M.V. (1992). *Making the grade: A self-worth perspective on motivation and school reform:* Cambridge University Press.

Davey, G. (Ed.). (2004). *Complete Psychology*: Hodder & Stoughton.

Duda, J.L. & Hall, H.K. (2001). Achievement goal theory in sport: Recent extensions and future directions. In R.N. Singer, C.M. Janelle & H.A. Hausenblas (Eds.), *Handbook of sport psychology* (Second ed., pp.417–443). New York, NY: Wiley.

Eysenck, H.J. (1991). Dimensions of personality: 16, 5, or 3? Criteria for a taxonomic paradigm. *Personality and Individual Differences* (12), 773–790.

Flett, G.L. & Hewitt, P.L. (2002). Perfectionism and maladjustment: An overview of theoretical, definitional, and treatment issues. In G.L. Flett & P.L. Hewitt (Eds.), *Perfectionism: Theory, research, and treatment.* (pp.5–31). Washington, DC: American Psychological Association.

Flett, G.L. & Hewitt, P.L. (2005). The perils of perfectionism in sports and exercise. *Current Directions in Psychological Science, 14,* 14–18.

Flett, G.L. & Hewitt, P.L. (2006). Positive versus negative perfectionism in psychopathology: A comment on Slade and Owen's dual process model. *Behavior Modification, 30,* 472–495.

Flett, G.L., Hewitt, P.L., Endler, N.S. & Tassone, C. (1995). Perfectionism and components of state and trait anxiety. *Current Psychology, 13,* 326–350.

Freud, S. (1956). *Inhibitions, symptoms and anxiety* (Vol. 20). London: Hogarth Press.

Frost, R.O., Marten, P.A., Lahart, C. & Rosenblate, R. (1990). The dimensions of perfectionism. *Cognitive Therapy and Research, 14,* 449–468.

Gaudreau, P. & Verner-Filion, J. (2012). Dispositional perfectionism and well-being: A test of the 2 x 2 model of perfectionism in the sport domain. *Sport, Exercise and Performance Psychology, 1,* 29–43.

Gotwals, J.K., Stoeber, J., Dunn, J.G.H. & Stoll, O. (2012). Are perfectionistic strivings in sport adaptive? A systematic review of confirmatory, contradictory, and mixed evidence. *Canadian Psychology* (53), 263–279.

Gould, D.R., Dieffenbach, K. & Moffett, A. (2002). Psychological characteristics and their development in Olympic champions. *Journal of Applied Sport Psychology, 14,* 172–204.

Gould, D.R. & Maynard, I. (2009). Psychological preparation for the Olympic games. *Journal of Sports Sciences, 27,* 1393–1408.

Greenspon, T.S. (2000). "Healthy perfectionism" is an oxymoron!: Reflections on the psychology of perfectionism and the sociology of science. *The Journal of Secondary Gifted Education, 11,* 197–208.

Hall, C.S. & Lindzey, G. (1978). *Theories of Personality* (3 edn). New York: John Wiley & Sons.

Hall, H.K. (2013). From adaptive achievement striving to athletic burnout: The debilitating influence of perfectionism. In D. Hackfort & I. Seidelmeier (Eds.), *Bridging gaps in applied sport and exercise psychology* (pp.53–78). FIT Publishers.

Hall, H.K., Hill, A.P. & Appleton, P.R. (2012). Perfectionism: A foundation for sporting excellence or an uneasy pathway to purgatory? In G.C. Roberts & D.C. Treasure (Eds.), *Advances in motivation in sport and exercise* (Vol. 3, pp.129–168). Champaign, IL: Human Kinetics.

Hamachek, D.E. (1978). Psychodynamics of normal and neurotic perfectionism. *Psychology, 15,* 27–33.

Hill, R.W., McIntire, K. & Bacharach, V.R. (1997). Perfectionism and the big five factors. *Journal of Social Behavior and Personality, 12,* 257–270.

Horney, K. (1950). *Neurosis and human growth.* New York: Norton.

Jung, C. (1964). *Man and his symbols.* Garden City, NY: Doubleday.

Kluckhorn, C. & Murray, H. (1953). *Personality in nature, society and culture.* New York: Knopf.

McArdle, S. (2010). Exploring domain-specific perfectionism. *Journal of Personality, 78,* 493–508.

Mischel, W. (1968). *Personality and assessment.* London: Wiley.

Owens, R.G. & Slade, P.D. (2008). So Perfect It's Positively Harmful? Reflections on the Adaptiveness and Maladaptiveness of Positive and Negative Perfectionism. *Behaviour Modification, 32,* 928–397.

Pacht, A.J. (1984). Reflections on perfection. *American Psychologist, 39,* 386–390.

Peterson, C. (1992). *Personality.* New York: Harcourt Brace Jovanich.

Ryan, R.M. & Deci, E.L. (2007). Active human nature: Self-determination theory and the promotion and maintenance of sport, exercise and health. In M.S. Haggar & N.L.D. Chatzisarantis (Eds.), *Intrinsic motivation and self-determination in exercise and sport.* Champaign, IL: Human Kinetics Publishers.

Shafran, R., Egan, S. & Wade, T. (2010). *Overcoming perfectionism: A self-help guide using cognitive behavioural techniques.* London: Robinson.

Stoeber, J. (2011). The dual nature of perfectionism in sports: Relationships with emotion. *International Review of Sport and Exercise Psychology, 4*, 128–145.

Stoeber, J., Stoll, O., Pesheck, E. & Otto, K. (2008). Perfectionism and goal orientations in athletes: Relations with approach and avoidance orientations in mastery and performance goals. *Psychology of Sport and Exercise, 9*, 102–121.

Vealey, R.S. (2002). Personality and sport behavior. In T.S. Horn (Ed.), *Advances in sport psychology* (Vol. 2). Champaign, IL: Human Kinetics Publishers.

Part Two

Understanding the influence of environments on sport and exercise

EDITED BY SOPHIA JOWETT AND ATHANASIOS G. PAPAIOANNOU

Chapter 11

Coaches

ROSS LORIMER AND SOPHIA JOWETT

SUMMARY

In sport, coaches and athletes work closely together and often form long-term, mutually dependent relationships. The manner in which coaches and athletes interact can have a profound impact upon the effectiveness of their training sessions. Their relationship may directly or indirectly influence such factors as personal satisfaction, enjoyment, motivation, and performance. The aim of this chapter is to provide a critical overview of this area with explicit focus on the 3+1Cs conceptual model. This chapter will define the coach–athlete relationship and provide an overview of how this relationship has been conceptualised. Moreover, aspects that may potentially contribute to developing the quality and effectiveness of coach–athlete relationships will be discussed. Finally, practical methods for developing and maintaining a harmonious relationship will be examined.

INTRODUCTION

The phenomenon of the coach–athlete relationship

Relationships are a key ingredient for a fulfilling and successful life. People are surrounded by relationships in diverse domains of life including familial, marital, social, work, school, and sport. A relationship is an association between two or more people and usually involves a level of interdependence with many factors affecting its members and the quality of their interactions. Relationships have the capacity to either promote growth or thwart it. It is important to ensure that the relationships people develop are harmonious and stable. Like other interpersonal relationships, the coach–athlete relationship can be described as the interdependence of a coach and athlete's emotions, actions, and thoughts; the coach and athlete interacting with the main aim to develop skill, tactical awareness, and succeed in their chosen sport. The relationship itself can provide the vehicle for a long journey that aims to transport the athlete and the coach to performance-related development and ultimately to performance success. Moreover, the relationship as a vehicle also aims to make the journey a positive and satisfying experience, and this can only be achieved when the relationship is harmonious; a discordant relationship is more likely to make the journey negative, unfulfilling, and less satisfying.

There are numerous anecdotal examples within competitive sport that highlight the nature and functions of interdependence between coaches and athletes. One such example is coach Sally Pearson and athlete Sharon Hannah (100m Hurdles World Gold in Daegu 2011; Olympic Silver in Beijing, Olympic Gold in London 2012). Their relationship has spanned over a decade and has been character-ised as one of the most effective partnerships in sport due to their shared respect and belief for one another, unshakable commitment to their relationship and the goals they set out to achieve, as well as tireless mutual support and endless hard work. The nature of their interde-pendence has propelled them to extraordinary performance heights while making the process personally rewarding and satisfying.

OBJECTIVES

After reading this chapter readers will be able to:

1   Define the coach–athlete relationship.
2   Outline the conceptual model and measurement of the coach–athlete relationship.
3   Examine what athletes/coaches should look for in an effective relationship.
4   Discuss how coach–athlete relationships are maintained.

A CONCEPTUAL MODEL OF THE COACH–ATHLETE RELATIONSHIP

The coach–athlete relationship has been defined as a social process in which coaches and athletes' feelings, thoughts, and behav-iours are interconnected and interdependent (Jowett, 2005). In order to develop our under-standing of this it has been important to describe and 'capture' this process by develop-ing a conceptual model. This allows both the description of the components involved in the process and the associations between these components, and provides a template for future research, education and best practice. Currently the most prevalent and widely inves-tigated model of the coach–athlete relation-ship is the 3+1Cs model (Jowett, 2007). This model provides an operational definition whereby coaches and athletes' feelings, thoughts, and behaviours can be systemati-cally studied through the constructs of close-ness, commitment, complementarity, and co-orientation.

The construct closeness characterises the perceived affective experience between the coach and the athlete, and represents the emotional element of their relationship. It refers to the coach and athlete feeling emotion-ally close to one another and reflects positive mutual feelings of trust, respect, and interper-sonal liking, as well as emotionally support-ing, caring for, and appreciating one another. Commitment expresses the coach and the athlete's long-term view of the direction of their relationship, their strength of proximity within it, and it also refers to the cognitive aspect of the relationship. It represents the future expectations of the coach and athlete and their intention to maintain the relation-ship over time through good experiences and not so good ones. Complementarity is concerned with a coach and an athlete's actions, the interaction between them during training or competition, and refers to the behavioural element of the coach–athlete rela-tionship. It embodies the type of interaction that the coach and athlete perceive as co-oper-ative and useful.

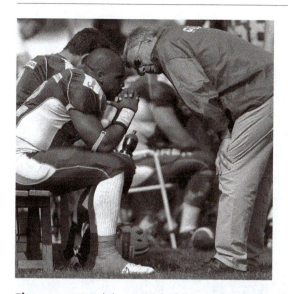

Figure 11.1 Coach has a "quiet" word with player.

Complementarity also reflects two sets of interpersonal behaviours: (a) corresponding behaviours that are affiliative (e.g., both coach and athlete are responsive to each other's effort); and (b) behaviours that are reciprocal and role-based (e.g., coach instructs and athlete executes). Reciprocal and role-based complementarity highlights that on average coaches are likely to be in charge, lead and direct, and athletes are more likely to execute, consider and follow. It is worth noting, however, that this notion doesn't mean that athletes are not in charge, leading, and directing. On the contrary, athletes are in control of their own actions when in training, executing instructions, or leading the proceedings in competition. For complementarity to be maintained the coach needs to be in charge even when the athlete is in command. For example, a coach has suggested that the athlete play as centre forward in the next game, but his athlete doesn't agree with the coach's decision. If the coach dismisses the issue raised by the athlete it would result in non-complementarity (both in control without any positive effect; this is opposite of co-operation). If, however, the coach deals in a way that truly puts him back in a position of leadership through negotiation such as, "How about you play centre forward for the first half and then based on performance we consider changing you to an outside forward position?" then he confidently takes charge and maintains a sense of reciprocally complementary transactions.

The construct of *co-orientation* forms the final part of this model (i.e., +1C) and brings together the other three Cs. It represents the level of understanding and similarity between the coach and the athlete; essentially the concurrence of closeness, commitment, and complementarity; it considers the coach and the athlete's interpersonal perspectives. Co-orientation encapsulates two interpersonal perspectives of the coach and the athlete (Jowett, 2009). The direct-perspective refers to the coach and the athlete's self-perceptions about how they feel, act, and think in regards to their relationship. In contrast, the meta-perspective refers to the coach and athlete's perceptions of how they believe their partners feel, act, and think in regards to the relationship. While the individual perspectives are important in themselves, the combination of the different perspectives allows the examination of co-orientation from a number of dimensions: (a) actual similarity (the congruence of the coach and athlete's direct-perspective); (b) assumed similarity (congruence of an individual's own direct-perspective and meta-perspective); and (c) empathic understanding (congruence of an individual's own direct-perspective and their partner's meta-perspective). These three dimensions describe the degree to which the coach and the athlete are co-oriented in the ways they view and understand the quality of their relationship and each other and thus provide valuable prognostic and diagnostic information to coaches and athletes as well as sport psychology consultants.

While the 3+1Cs model is the most researched relationship model within sport psychology literature other researchers have also developed alternative frameworks, though often similar, perspectives on the coach–athlete relationship (see Jowett & Poczwardowski, 2007). Wylleman's (2000)

Figure 11.2 Coach responds to performance and provides feedback and instructions.

conceptualisation of the coach–athlete relationship was focused on the behaviours that coaches and athletes enact. Accordingly, these interpersonal behaviours are divided into three dimensions: acceptance–rejection, dominance–submission, and social–emotional. The model emphasises the need for the coach and the athlete to be complementary in these dimensions, displaying either reciprocal or correspondent behaviours as appropriate. These ideas significantly overlap with the 3+1Cs model's construct of complementarity and both place an emphasis on the reciprocity/ correspondence of interpersonal behaviours. Another alternative conceptualisation was put forward by Poczwardowski (1997) which suggests that the coach–athlete relationship is based upon recurring patterns of mutual care

between coaches and athletes, the meaning they ascribe to their relationship, and the relationship-specific activities they engage in. The model suggests these exchanges can have both behavioural and cognitive-affective dimensions. In a similar way to Wylleman's model, and the 3+1Cs model, this model places an emphasis on interpersonal behaviours that are complementary. Additionally, it shares a focus with the 3+1Cs model's dimension of closeness by emphasising the affectivity within the relationship through mutual care. Despite there being several alternative models, the 3+1Cs model has attracted a concerted investigative effort and systematic research that has generated a great deal of knowledge and understanding in the area of coach–athlete relationships over the past decade.

ASSESSING THE COACH–ATHLETE RELATIONSHIP

While a definition of the coach–athlete relationship and a conceptual model is important, it is equally important to be able to assess the coach–athlete relationship. This is essential to allow researchers to further knowledge and understanding of coaching and the coach–athlete relationship but also to allow sport psychologists and other practitioners to more easily work with and improve coach–athlete relationships.

Assessment of the coach–athlete relationship can be approached using a variety of methods and from several perspectives. The majority of previous investigations have focused on the perspective of the athlete. While the athlete is the one who actually produces the final performance, and so is arguable an important person in the relationship, this can provide a limited view of the relationship. Instead, investigations must consider both members of the coach–athlete relationship. Additionally, it is important to assess not only how the coach and the athlete view their relationship, but to also consider how each views their partner's perspective. Lorimer and Jowett (2009) have shown that coaches and athletes do not always accurately understand what their coach is thinking and feeling, while Smoll and Smith (1984) showed that athletes' behaviour is most strongly influenced by how they perceive their coach (and not by what actually the coach does in training and competitions). This means it is the reality created within the individuals' mind, their perceptions, that are most influential. It is therefore essential to assess all possible perspectives in order to understand the links between what coaches and athletes think, feel and do, and what they are perceived by each other to think, feel, and do. This then allows us to investigate how reality and inferred perceptions overlap and is in turn related to the success and effectiveness of the coach–athlete relationship.

The majority of sport psychology practitioners and early research investigations have relied on interviews and other qualitative methods such as observation to assess the interaction of coaches and athletes and the coach–athlete relationship. However, in order for research to make generalisations about findings and for practitioners to monitor improvements or other changes in the relationship, it is important to be able to quantify the quality of the coach–athlete relationship. To date only the Coach–Athlete Relationship Questionnaire (CART-Q; Jowett, 2009; Jowett & Ntoumanis, 2004), which assesses the relationship based upon the 3+1Cs model, has seen wide use in both research and practice.

The CART-Q has been widely adopted for a number of reasons. Unlike many psychometric inventories, the CART-Q allows the assessment of a variety of perspectives. The questionnaire comes in four forms: two questionnaires for the coach (example statement: I trust my athlete) and two for the athlete (example statement: I trust my coach). Each pair of questionnaires (for coach and athlete) has a statement to assess the direct-perspective (e.g., I trust my coach/athlete) and a statement that assesses the meta-perspective (e.g., My athlete/coach trusts me). This means researchers and practitioners can pick and choose what they assess according to their own aims. Perhaps they only want to compare how the coach and athlete perceive their relationship (direct-perspective vs. direct-perspective), or perhaps they want to examine how an athlete's perspective is influenced by how they infer their coach's perception of them (athlete direct-perspective vs. meta-perspective). Ideally, they would assess all four perspectives in order to explore the interdependence of both coaches' and athletes' direct- and meta-perspectives via the different dimensions of co-orientation. Another reason the questionnaire has been widely adopted is because it is available in a number of languages including Chinese (Yang & Jowett, 2010), Greek (Jowett & Ntoumanis, 2003) and Dutch (Balduck & Jowett, 2010). This has allowed researchers and practitioners to examine relationships across different cultures without the need to consider the problematic issue of language/culture that can often be an issue with the predominately English-language inventories and questionnaires that dominate modern sport psychology.

FACTORS IN THE DEVELOPMENT OF RELATIONSHIPS THAT WORK

Existing research has looked at identifying factors that lead to effective relationships and what the outcomes of these relationships are (e.g., improved performance). The purpose of this has been to fully describe and understand the coach–athlete relationship with the view to develop interventions to promote and enhance the quality and success of coach–athlete relationships and the coaches and athletes who form them. Coaches and athletes work closely together, have a high degree of interaction, and inevitably increased reliance upon each other. Thus, it would seem to be important that both athletes and coaches know what to look for in order to form an effective relationship and what factors may influence the success of that relationship.

Individual and team sports

Coach–athlete relationships are shaped by the environment in which they unfold. Perhaps the most obvious being the type of sport. Lorimer and Jowett (2009) have found that coaches and athletes demonstrate better empathic understanding (a dimension of the conceptualisation and operationalisation of co-orientation) in individual sports compared to team sports. Coaches in team sports are more likely to interact with a group of athletes as a whole than those involved in individual sports, and interactions with any given individual athlete may be limited. This means that in team sports what the coach is saying/doing may not apply to each member of the team or group but to some or few or the majority. In another study, Rhind and colleagues (2012) found that athletes in individual sports were much closer, committed, and complementary with their coaches than athletes in team sports. They further found that athletes in individual sports were more satisfied than their team sports counterparts. It may be that athletes in team sports experience increased satisfaction if their coaches create a relational environment; an environment that promotes mutual trust, respect, interpersonal liking, a long-term orientation between the coach and the athletes, as well as a sense of co-operation in terms of responsiveness and directiveness.

As a coach in a team sport it is particularly important to make time to get to know each and every one of the athletes on the team, both through formal meetings and informal chats (see Rhind & Jowett, 2011). Athletes need to be aware that coaches working with larger groups will not always be focused on the same things as them nor will they see things in a similar way. It is therefore important to work with a coach that encourages open channels of communication, especially feedback. Athletes should provide feedback that goes beyond simply acknowledging their understanding of technical instruction and movement execution but also include information regarding how they think and feel about the present, past, and future in and outside the domain of sport. Communication, in the form of relationship enhancement strategies as put forward by Rhind and Jowett (2011), is not only likely to enhance the relationship quality but its effects may also transfer to the individual athlete and coach as each may start feeling more satisfied, happier, positive, energetic, and successful.

Level of competition

Another important environmental factor is the level of performance that an athlete trains at and coach instructs at. At a recreational level most athletes participate in a sport because they are intrinsically motivated by the activity (e.g., enjoy being with friends, learning new skills, challenging their abilities), while at higher levels of performance external reasons and goals may become more important (e.g., ranking, winning, trophies, fame). Research has shown that elite coaches and athletes who are closer and more co-orientated increase the likelihood of achieving their shared goals such as performance success (Jowett & Cockerill, 2003) while coaches and athletes who are distant, isolated, and discordant increase the likelihood of failing to achieve performance-related goals (Jowett, 2003, 2009). Additionally, a high performance-level coach–athlete dyad with poor relationship quality is more likely to experience conflict and decline in interaction (Jowett & Meek, 2000a). On the other hand, coach–athlete dyads at the highest level of performance have been found to be both highly interdependent and satisfied with personal treatment, training, instruction, and performance (Jowett & Nezlek, 2011).

This research highlights the importance athletes and coaches attach to their relationship for successful performances. While successful performance is highly prized by both coaches and athletes, it would appear that when athletes are successful both the athlete and the coach are praised and their roles acknowledged, whereas, when athletes are unsuccessful, the coach more often than not receives a large portion of the blame and responsibility. Nonetheless, it is important that coaches and athletes communicate about all aspects that might affect performance as this will help ensure that both the coach and athlete operate as a unit toward performance excellence. Subsequently, an athlete should look for a coach who has good interpersonal skills: (a) the skill to develop a relationship that is respectful and trusting; (b) the skill to make the athlete feel comfortable and relaxed as opposed to feeling uneasy and stressed; (c) the skill to make the athlete feel that he/she is a valued member of the team or squad; (d) the

skill to transfer confidence in the direction employed and practices applied to improve performance; and (e) the skill to aspire a sense of connectedness in terms that "we are in this together". Performance success takes time and thus a coach and an athlete would need to be committed and assured that the relationship formed will serve them well over a period of time where both individuals take responsibility for successes and failures.

Relationship duration

Relationship duration may be linked to the level of performance (see Jowett & Nezlek, 2011) in that it takes a considerable time for an athlete and a coach to progress to the higher levels of performance. It has been suggested that up to ten years of training is required to develop the expertise needed to develop one's talent. Whether an athlete and a coach stay in an athletic relationship for ten years or not is not the issue here. The issue is that coaches and athletes will have to invest time, energy, and effort if they are to enjoy the benefits of an effective relationship. A decline in the relationship quality is often associated with a decline in performance accomplishments (see Jowett & Cockerill, 2003) and thus maintaining the quality of the relationship may be as important as ensuring continuous performance development. In more long-term coach–athlete dyads, co-orientation or a sense of a common ground can decline (Jowett & Clark-Carter, 2006). Co-orientation typically increases during the initial phase of relationships as individuals get to know each other before decreasing in the later phases of the relationship as the coach and athlete fall into habitual behaviours.

Thus, coaches and athletes both need to acknowledge the importance of long-term relationship if the dyad's goal is to progress to higher performance levels. Relationships develop in the mind of its members and in the physical world where dyads interact and their relationship unfolds. It is as important to try

Figure 11.3 Nadal working with his coach.

continuously and consciously to update the information about the people with whom we relate, communicate, and interact. People and relationships change and thus it becomes imperative to remain sensitive to one another's needs, values, opinions, preferences, likes, and dislikes as they are subject to change over time. Athletes and coaches need to ensure a high level of communication because it allows them to continuously update their common ground by sharing their experiences, joys and fears. Relationship strategies proposed by Rhind and Jowett (2011) may help enhance the quality and maintenance of relationships that are effective and successful.

Age

To an extent, competitive level and relationship duration are both associated with the age of athletes. At an early age social development and self-esteem are important factors for those involved in physical activity. Younger individuals are more sensitive to punitive actions of their coach (Smith, Smoll, & Cumming, 2007) and coach behaviours that aim to pressure and control are thought detrimental for athletes' motivation and well-being (Bartholomew, Ntoumanis, & Thogersen-Ntoumani, 2009). As athletes develop, particularly during puberty and beyond it, the need and demands for technical development increases and they are likely to focus more on the instructional feedback and social support of their coach (Chelladurai & Carron, 1983). Athletes become increasingly independent of their parents and more reliant on their coach and the quality of the relationship they start to form (Jowett & Timson-Katchis, 2005). At a later stage, as athletes continue to mature, they may even want to have a bigger part in the coaching process and practice by taking an active role in the decision making, the direction and intensity of their training. Such a balanced mutuality of dependence between the coach and the athlete may arise when athletes develop the knowledge and skill-based "power" that permits them to establish a relationship on equal terms with their coach.

Coaches need to be aware of the differences in athletes' needs depending on their age and stage of development. They need to understand their athletes' specific needs, wants, and aspirations in any given time. Parents are advised to find coaches who are interpersonal rather than impersonal and who thus have the capacity to create an interdependent relationship that can serve as a facilitative and positive learning environment for the developing athlete. A coach that has the young athlete's development and well-being at heart is also the coach that is likely to create an interpersonal environment where the athlete wants and is prepared to work hard and enjoy the process of skill development and participation in sport. Older athletes should look for a coach that has the interpersonal skills that are needed to foster an interdependent relationship. Coaches who are inherently interested, supportive – who care for all individual athletes in the team or squad, provide opportunities for the athletes to express themselves in an environment that is positive, happy, and light-hearted – not only create a clear direction and structure but are also more likely to develop rapport with each individual athlete.

Personality

Personality can play a crucial role in determining the nature of close relationships. Personality describes intrinsic differences in individuals that are thought to influence how they think, feel, and behave. Currently, the most established theory in personality research is the Big Five Factor model that describes personality in terms of five basic traits: extraversion, agreeableness, conscientiousness, emotional stability, and intellect. Jowett, Yang and Lorimer (2012) found that those athletes with high levels of agreeableness viewed their relationships more positively. This is likely because they are more capable of interacting in a pleasant and accommodating manner and this higher level of complementarity allows other areas of the relationship to more easily develop.

Yang and Jowett (2012) have argued that as a coach's main role is to support and instruct their athletes' coaches personality will have a minimum effect on athletes. Their study found that athletes' personality determined how their coaches viewed the relationship quality whereas coaches' personality did not have any effect on how athletes' viewed the coach–athlete relationship. Moreover, one's attachment style (e.g., the type of bonds one develops with others) has also shown to influence one's own perceptions of relationship quality in the coach–athlete dyad, however only athletes' attachment style influence coaches' perceptions of relationship quality (Davis & Jowett, 2013). Athletes and coaches should be aware of how personality is likely to drive their behaviour and influence their interactions and perceptions. Such awareness could help explain their own behaviour relative to others and others' behaviour relative to them. Awareness can further help an athlete and a coach maximise their interactions by acknowledging their shortcomings.

Gender

Another potentially important factor is the gender of the coach and the athlete in the coach–athlete dyad. The relationship quality can be affected by whether it is an opposite-gender relationship or a same-gender

Figure 11.4 A coach displaying frustration and dissatisfaction.

relationship. In friendships it has been shown that female–female relationships are closer than male–male relationships (Unger & Crawford, 1992). Athletes and coaches in same gender relationships seem to be closer, more committed and complementary, perhaps because they can more easily understand each others' perspectives (Jowett & Nezlek, 2012).

Different combinations of coach–athlete gender may also affect empathic understanding, and female athletes with males coaches have been shown to be more responsive than male athletes, or female athletes with a female coach (Lorimer & Jowett, 2010). This may be because of perceived gender roles and the associated power-dynamics and dominance of males (i.e., a female athlete needs to understand their male coach as they will have the least perceived power). Coach–athlete relationships with their greater focus on external performance goals and the inherent power of the coaches' role have different dynamics than friendships and other social relationships. Nonetheless, the key is that

coaches and athletes are on the same page because this allows them to interact more effectively by understanding the reasons behind why they act and interact in the ways they do.

Relationship type

The quality of the coach–athlete relationship can depend on what other relationships the coach and athlete share. In a typical relationship, the coach and the athlete have no other relation to each other outside of the sport. However, in an atypical relationship they already share another bond such as parent–child or husband–wife. Jowett and Meek (2000b) suggest that in an atypical relationship coaches and athletes will have a stronger emotional connection and a greater degree of interdependence than a typical relationship. While this higher level of closeness can be viewed positively there also exists the chance that this over familiarity can lead to the blurring of relationship boundaries and in turn to the decline of its effectiveness.

The risk of distinct roles being fused together is a problematic one (Jowett, Timson-Katchis, & Adams, 2007). Conflict can occur if individuals use their additional relationship roles to influence the coach–athlete relationship, or if the interactions are carried across relationship contexts. An example may be a parent/coach grounding their child/athlete at home for not behaving at a training session. It is important for an athlete that clear boundaries are established so that the roles are kept separate. This is not to say atypical relationships cannot be successful or effective, but instead that in these relationships the coach and athlete need to be aware of how and why their roles change depending on the context in which they operate. Based on the limited research, it would appear that sport roles are preferably kept distinct from other roles.

Culture

Culture and ethnicity has been shown to influence how athletes perceive their coaches and hence the quality of the relationships they form. Cultural background can potentially influence an individual's views of a sport and the purpose and meaning of the coach–athlete relationship. Jowett and Frost (2007) found that footballers working with coaches of different ethnicities reported that they didn't think their coach understood them as well as coaches of the same ethnicity. It was further uncovered that athletes also felt that closeness, commitment, and complementarity would have been heightened if their coaches were of a similar cultural background as them. In another study, Jowett and Ahmad (2012) uncovered that athletes were much more interdependent with local Kuweiti coaches than foreign coaches yet athletes acknowledged that although cultural including religious homogeneity may promote the coach and the athlete bond, coaches' knowledge and expertise may also help these bonds.

It is important to invest time, effort and energy in developing quality relationships regardless of one's background. Communication and getting to know one another could facilitate greatly perceived understanding and similarity. It is important that coaches and athletes maximise their common ground. They need to establish a central focus when interacting and make frequent checks to ensure that they understand what is going on and that both are addressing the same topic and hold the same views. While coaches and athletes of similar cultural background may find it easier to form high quality relationships athletes should not shy away from working with coaches of different backgrounds. Diverse views may aid in the development of the athlete and make the relationship greater than the sum of its parts. Instead, an athlete should seek out a coach who is sensitive to their culture and adaptive to their views and needs.

Coach education and experience

Coaches who have been coaching for longer, have more varied experience, or hold higher level coaching qualifications are more likely to have a closer understanding of their sport, its requirements and demands. It is possible that coaches with coaching qualifications and greater experience may be able to respond better to an athlete's needs and deal with several of the previous issues raised such as differences in competitive level, age, relationship needs, and different cultures. Additionally, athletes may respond better to coaches who they perceive to be more knowledgable and skilled. If this is the case then these coach–athlete relationships would display higher levels of such relational properties as complementary behaviours and co-orientated perspectives. This would in turn lead to the development of a more interdependent relationship.

While athletes may need to be careful of working with coaches who lack the relevant education or experience to meet the requirements of their own athletic development they also need to be aware that a good coach is a coach that keeps up-to-date about the sport and about each one of his/her athletes in the team or squad. Lorimer and Jowett (2010) have shown that some coaches with greater experience may believe that they "have seen it all" and in turn display a limited ability to understand and respond to the individual needs of their athletes. Essentially their greater experience and knowledge can lead to over confidence, causing them to make incorrect assumptions because they do not pay the attention to the on-going, most current available information. Both athletes and coaches need to be aware that knowledge gained from education and past experience may not always be directly transferable without careful consideration of the specifics of the current situation, athlete, and coach–athlete relationship.

MAINTAINING AN EFFECTIVE COACH–ATHLETE RELATIONSHIP

Even if a coach and an athlete form effective relationships there is no guarantee that these relationships will have a substantial duration. While the concept of commitment expresses the coach and the athlete's long-term view of the direction of their relationship and their intention to remain together, this desire for a long-term and stable relationship is not always enough in itself to sustain it. Instead, a great deal of time and effort must be invested in preserving this relationship. One method that can be employed by both coaches and athletes is the use of maintenance strategies. These strategies can be thought of as any action by the coach or athlete that attempts to keep their relationship in a specific state or condition, such as being open about problems or minimising conflict. Coaches and athletes can use a variety of strategies to: (a) prevent the decline of their relationship; (b) further enhance their relationship; and (c) repair and re-establish a relationship that has already experienced decline or conflict. The use of these maintenance strategies is associated with positive outcomes such as satisfaction and success, and it has been suggested that use of maintenance strategies is the primary method via which coaches and athletes within close relationships sustain their relationship quality.

The COMPASS model of relationship maintenance

Rhind and Jowett (2010) have proposed a model of maintenance strategies that can be used by both coaches and athletes to help sustain and improve their relationships. This model encompasses seven strategies that form the acronym COMPASS; Conflict management, Openness, Motivational, Positivity, Assurance, Support and Social Networks. The first strategy, conflict management, reflects co-operation in the discussion of conflict and both the proactive and reactive reactions to unmet expectations. Openness relates to discussion of feelings and individual thoughts and full and honest disclosure. Motivational strategies are about demonstrating your willingness to work with your partner and includes aspects of demonstrating your ability, enjoyment, effort, and attempting to motivate your partner. Positivity is about changing one's behaviour to suit the preferences of your partner and positively dealing with events outside of sport. Advice is defined as giving opinions on problems encountered and providing and receiving feedback in a positive and open way. Support strategies are about demonstrating your commitment and providing both sport-specific and personal support. Finally, social networks relates to spending social time with your coach or athlete, along with team/squad mates, outside of the sport context, away from training and competition.

The use of maintenance strategies can be assessed using the Coach–Athlete Relationship Maintenance Questionnaire (CARM-Q; Rhind & Jowett, 2010) which contains 28 questions that measure the use of the seven relationship maintenance strategies. Although this is more of a tool for researchers or psychologists examining correlates of maintenance strategies such as relationship quality. Instead, coaches and athletes should be aware that the COMPASS model suggests they should actively focus on motivating their partner to work with them and not purely to continue in the sport. The quality of coach–athlete relationship is not static. Coaches' and athletes' thoughts, feelings, and behaviours are constantly changing and interacting. Therefore coaches and athletes must constantly monitor and interact in a way that enhances their relationships if they do not wish to experience enduring conflict or see their relationship decline or break up.

CONCLUSION

There is an obvious need for the development of knowledge in sport psychology regarding the influence of coaches on athletes and how the two form effective and successful partnerships. This highly complex and interdependent process primarily unfolds in training, during periods of practicing the requisite skills and techniques needed to develop sport talent. While the coach–athlete relationship has been placed at the heart of sports training/coaching and cited as being a key ingredient in athletic performance and success, its impact can potentially have ramifications beyond sport.

Recent years have seen researchers developing a growing understanding of the quality and functions of the coach–athlete relationship. Underpinning this has been the definition and conceptualisation of the coach–athlete relationship using the 3+1Cs model and its accompanied psychometric tools. It can capture the interdependent and ever-changing nature of these relationships and provides a vehicle for understanding how coaches and athletes interact to generate individual and joint outcomes such as personal satisfaction and performance accomplishments.

LEARNING AIDS

1   Provide the definition of the coach–athlete relationship.

A social process in which coaches' and athletes' feelings, thoughts, and behaviours are interdependent.

2   Name the three key factors of psychology associated with the constructs of closeness, commitment, and complementarity.

The three constructs are relationship specific dimensions of affect (closeness), cognition (commitment), and behaviour (complementarity).

3   Identify and explain three different dimensions of Co-ORIENTATION.

(1) Direct-perspective: how the coach or athlete views their relationship. (2) Meta-perspective: how the coach or athlete believes their partner views their relationship. (3) Empathic understanding: how accurate the coach or athlete's inference of their partner's perspective is.

4   Name the seven coach–athlete relationship maintenance strategies.

(1) Conflict management, (2) Openness, (3) Motivational, (4) Positivity, (5) Assurance, (6) Support, and (7) Social networks.

REVIEW QUESTIONS

1 Why is the coach–athlete relationship one of the most important relationships in the context of an athlete's sport?

2 Why is it important to consider both the coach and the athlete when considering training and performance?

3 What are the implications of unstable and ineffective coach–athlete relationships on an athlete's performance?

4 How could relationship maintenance strategies be used to promote better coach–athlete relationships?

EXERCISES

1 Observe a coach–athlete relationship over a period of one week and record your thoughts about the quality of the relationship in terms of closeness, commitment, and complementarity. Following your observations, organise to meet the dyad for a short interview and make notes. Are they both affectively close (e.g., is there mutual trust, respect, appreciation)? Is their relationship close enough to last over time? Do they work co-operatively in an environment that is friendly and responsive but also well-structured? Are they co-oriented; does the dyad view the relationship in similar terms? Ensure that any necessary ethical-related procedures are in place to undertake this mini-project. You could also observe more than one relationship in order to discern any differences in the quality of the relationship:

- A relationship that has a long-term and a dyad that has a short-term relationship.

- A relationship that has same gender composition such as male/coach-male/athlete and a dyad that has other gender composition such as male/coach-female/athlete.

- A relationship that has different cultural composition such as a foreign coach–local athlete or one that has similar cultural composition such as local coach–local athlete.

2 Drawing upon your own experiences as either a coach or an athlete, consider how your relationship with your coach/athlete influenced your/their performance. Think on how much you liked, trusted, and respected them, the level of commitment you both had, and how well you worked together. Reflect on how you believe they felt, thought, and acted towards you. How does this relate to closeness, commitment, and complementarity? List the important factors in your relationship. Think about what helped your/their performance and what didn't. Reflect on the ways in which you or your coach's/athlete's behaviour may have damaged your relationship. Was any factor particularly important? Finally, write a list of the things you both did to maintain your relationship. Consider your everyday actions as well as anything special you did in order to promote the quality of your coach–athlete relationship. How does this relate to the COMPASS model? Is there anything you will change or would do differently next time to maintain your relationship?

ADDITIONAL READING

Jowett, S. (2008). Moderator and mediator effects of the association between the quality of the coach–athlete relationship and athletes' physical self-concept. *International Journal of Coaching Science*, 2, 43–62.

Lorimer, R. & Jowett, S. (2012). Empathic understanding and accuracy in the coach–athlete relationship. In J. Denison, W. Gilbert & P. Potrac (Eds.), *Handbook of Sports Coaching*. London: Routledge.

Rhind, D.J.A. & Jowett, S. (2011). Working with coach–athlete relationships: Their quality and maintenance. In S. Mellalieu & S. Hanton (Eds.), *Professional Practice in Sport Psychology: A Review*. London: Routledge.

REFERENCES

Balduck, A.L. & Jowett, S. (2010). An Examination of the Psychometric Properties of the Belgian Coach Version of the Coach–Athlete Relationship Questionnaire (CART-Q). *Scandinavian Journal of Medicine and Science in Sports*, 4, 73–89.

Bartholomew, K.J., Ntoumanis, N. & Thøgersen-Ntoumani, C. (2009). A review of controlling motivational strategies from a self-determination theory perspective: Implications for sports coaches. *International Review of Sport and Exercise Psychology*, 2, 215–233.

Chelladurai, P. & Carron, A.V. (1983). Athletic maturity and preferred leadership. *Journal of Sport Psychology*, 5, 371–380.

Davis, L. & Jowett, S. (2013). An attachment theory perspective in the examination of relational processes associated with coach–athlete dyads. *Journal of Sport and Exercise Psychology*, 35, 156–167.

Jowett, S. (2005). On repairing and enhancing the coach–athlete relationship. In S. Jowett & M. Jones (Eds.), *The psychology of coaching*. Leicester, UK: The British Psychological Society.

Jowett, S. (2007). Interdependence analysis and the 3+1Cs in the coach–athlete relationship. In S. Jowett & D. Lavallee (Eds.), *Social psychology in sport*. Champaign, IL: Human Kinetics.

Jowett, S. (2009). Validating coach–athlete relationship measures with the nomological network. *Measurement in Physical Education and Exercise Science*, 13, 1–18.

Jowett, S. & Ahmad, H. (2012) [Manuscript under review] The quality of the relationship between coaches and gymnasts in kuwait.

Jowett, S. & Clark-Carter, D. (2006). Perceptions of empathic accuracy and assumed similarity in the coach–athlete relationship. *British Journal of Social Psychology*, 45, 617–637.

Jowett, S. & Cockerill, I.M. (2003). Olympic Medallists' perspective of the athlete–coach relationship. *Psychology of Sport and Exercise*, 4: 313–331.

Jowett, S. & Frost, T.C. (2007). Race/Ethnicity in the all male coach–athlete relationship: Black footballers' narratives. *International Journal of Sport and Exercise Psychology*, 3, 255–269.

Jowett, S. & Meek, G.A. (2000a). A case study of a top-level coach–athlete dyad in crisis. *Journal of Sport Sciences*, 18, 51–52.

Jowett, S. & Meek, G.A. (2000b). The coach–athlete relationship in married couples: An exploratory content analysis. *The Sport Psychologist*, 14, 157–175.

Jowett, S. & Nezlek, J. (2011). Relationship interdependence and satisfaction with important outcomes in coach–athlete dyads. *Journal of Social and Personal Relationships*, 29, 287–301.

Jowett, S. & Ntoumanis, N. (2003). The Greek Coach – Athlete Relationship Questionnaire (GrCART – Q): Scale development and validation. *International Journal of Sport Psychology*, 34, 101–124.

Jowett, S. & Ntoumanis, N. (2004). The Coach–Athlete Relationship Questionnaire (CART-Q): development and initial validation. *Scandinavian Journal of Medicine and Science in Sports*, 14: 245–257.

Jowett, S. & Poczwardowski, A. (2007). Understanding the coach–athlete relationship. In S. Jowett & D. Lavallee (Eds.), *Social psychology in sport* (pp.3–14). Champaign, IL: Human Kinetics.

Jowett, S. & Timson-Katchis, M. (2005). Social networks in the sport context: The influence of parents on the coach–athlete relationship. *The Sport Psychologist, 19*, 267–287.

Jowett, S., Timson-Katchis, M. & Adams, R. (2007). Too close for comfort? Dependence in the dual role of parent/coach–child/athlete relationship. *International Journal of Coaching Science, 1*, 59–78.

Jowett, S., Yang, X, & Lorimer, R. (2012). Role of personality, empathy, and satisfaction with instruction within the context of the coach–athlete relationship. *International Journal of Coaching Science, 6*, 3–20.

Lorimer, R. & Jowett, S. (2009). Empathic accuracy in coach–athlete dyads who participate in team and individual sports. *Psychology of Sport and Exercise, 10*, 152–158.

Lorimer, R. & Jowett, S. (2010). Feedback of information in the empathic accuracy of sport coaches. *Psychology of Sport and Exercise, 11*, 12–17.

Poczwardowski, A. (1997). *Athletes and coaches: An exploration of their relationship and its meaning.* Unpublished doctoral dissertation. University of Utah, Salt Lake City.

Rhind, D.J.A. & Jowett, S. (2010). Relationship maintenance strategies in the coach–athlete relationship: The development of the COMPASS Model. *Journal of Applied Sport Psychology, 22*, 106–121.

Rhind, D.J.A. & Jowett, S. (2011). Linking maintenance strategies to the quality of coach–athlete relationships. *International Journal of Sport Psychology, 41*, 55–68.

Rhind, D.J., Jowett, S. & Yang, X.S. (2012). A comparison of athletes' perceptions of the coach–athlete relationship in team and individual sports. *Journal of Sport Behavior, 35*, 433–452.

Smith, R., Smoll, F. & Cumming, S. (2007). Effects of a motivational climate intervention for coaches on young athletes' sport performance anxiety. *Journal of Sport & Exercise Psychology, 29*, 39–59.

Smoll, F. & Smith, R. (1984). Leadership and research in youth sports. In J. Silva & R. Weinberg (Eds.), *Psychological foundations of sport*, Champaign, IL: Human Kinetics.

Unger, R. & Crawford, M. (1992). *Women and gender: A feminist psychology*. Philadelphia: Temple University Press.

Yang, S.X. & Jowett, S. (2010). Validation of the Chinese version of the Coach–Athlete Relationship Questionnaire (CART-Q): Factorial and Concurrent Validity. *International Journal of Coaching Science, 4*, 73–89.

Yang, S. & Jowett, S. (2012). Effects of Big-Five personality traits on the quality of relationship and satisfaction in coach–athlete dyads. *Manuscript under review.*

Wylleman, P. (2000). Interpersonal relationships in sport: Uncharted territory in sport psychology research. *International Journal of Sport Psychology, 31*, 555–572.

Chapter 12

Families

SAM CARR AND DANIEL A. WEIGAND

SUMMARY

Key figures in the history of psychology (e.g., Sigmund Freud, John Bowlby, Harry Harlow, Alfred Kinsey, and Melanie Klein) have consistently recognised the important role that *familial relationships* appear to play in the development of personality and psychological well-being. Nothing is a more significant determinant of the quality of our experiences than the nature of our connections to family. *Familial relationships* can also be an important consideration in sport psychology and sport psychology researchers have numerous frameworks that can help them to investigate and understand this complex area. The purpose of this chapter is to outline the various avenues of discussion linked to familial relations in the context of sport, highlighting key themes and offering practical applications related to them.

INTRODUCTION

In their article Krane et al. (1997) present a case study of Susan, a former elite gymnast who spent the majority of her childhood and adolescence training and competing at an international level. The case study paints a picture of a young girl who quit gymnastics with severe psychological and physical difficulties, including low self-esteem, an eating disorder, and overtraining-induced chronic injury. The authors explored the range of factors that seemingly led to Susan's psychological collapse (and ultimate withdrawal from her sport) and it is clear that her family had a part to play. In one paragraph Susan suggests:

My parents always expected more of me. Always. I was always expected to act a lot older than I was. When I was five, I was

acting like I was eight. When I was eight, I acted like I was twice [as old]. I really had a very high maturity level because they made me that way. My father expected perfection (Krane et al., 1997, p. 60).

The authors also report that:

After Susan's serious neck injury and paralysis, her doctors told the family that she should retire from gymnastics because one wrong move could result in permanent paralysis. Still, her parents allowed her to return to gymnastics (p. 60).

These brief extracts raise interesting questions related to the importance of *familial relationships* in the context of sport. For example, when parents are heavily involved in either "managing" or "coaching" their child in sport, are they at risk of compromising other important aspects of a loving *parent–child bond*? In their pursuit of success for their child, do they adopt a more emotionally distant and objective perception of the child (e.g., as a "source of income" or as "the means to an end") that is incompatible with features of a caring and secure parental bond? If there is a risk of this, how can parents who are involved in their children's sporting endeavours avoid such

pitfalls? How can they ensure that they contribute to the development of positive experiences in sport for their children and that they do not serve simply to create high levels of anxiety, low self-esteem, and unhealthy psychological and physical well-being? These and other important questions arise from consideration of the above case example. However, there is no simple answer to such questions and the role of families in the context of sport psychology is a complex and multifaceted issue.

OBJECTIVES

This chapter has the following objectives:

1 To explore the critical role of the parent–child relationship to involvement in the sport and physical activity.

2 To pay specific attention to the broader issue of parent–child *attachment* and its trickle-down influence on the self in the context of sport.

3 To pay specific attention to the manner in which parental beliefs and values in the context of sport (with particular reference to the *motivational climate*) influence how young athletes experience the context.

4 To examine how the *family systems* in which athletes find themselves situated are likely to influence, and be influenced by, the role of the athlete.

5 To develop understanding of how knowledge of athlete *family systems* can be a valuable consulting tool for sport psychologists.

ATTACHMENT

The influence of parental relationships on a child's development both within and beyond the context of sport can be examined in various ways. In developmental psychology, *attachment* theorists (e.g., Bowlby, 1969/1982) have provided important evidence that it is the nature of parents' caregiving behaviours toward their children (particularly during moments when the child is distressed, in pain, or in need of care) that are particularly important because they help to sculpt the basic parameters around which children begin to *learn* how to relate to others in close bonds. As children develop, *attachment* theory predicts that the experiences of care and support

provided by their key caregivers (typically but not always parents) help them to construct (or not in many cases) a general feeling of security and relational behaviours that will function to protect and guide them in subsequent relationships (Weimer et al., 2004). These systems of cognition, affect, and behaviour reflect what Bowlby termed *internal working models* that are constructed in response to the parental *attachment* experiences that children encounter. These internal working models can be thought of as a *psychological organisation* that serves to guide children's beliefs with respect to important issues such as: (a) the availability of key *attachment* figures as a source of comfort and security (i.e., "How likely is it my parents will be available when I need them emotionally and physically? How likely is it they will be able to comfort me in such situations?"); (b) judgements about their own self-worth and deservedness in *attachment* relations (i.e., "If my parents are available it suggests I am worthy of love and support; If they are not available then perhaps there is something about me that is not worthy of such a connection?"); and (c) how best to deal with distress within the constraints of the *attachment* environment in which they find themselves (i.e., "When I am distressed does it seem worthwhile to seek the support of others? Can others help me?"). When youngsters develop a *secure attachment* style with parents they ultimately develop a positive internal representation of themselves in *attachment* contexts, viewing potential *attachment* figures as psychologically available and responsive and developing a positive sense of their self-worth in *attachment* contexts. However, when they develop an *insecure* style they adopt a negative internal representation, fearing rejection and inconsistent responses from *attachment* figures and adopting a negative sense of self in close relational contexts.

So how might such deep features of the parent–child *attachment* relationship translate to the wider world of sport? One possibility is that the *attachment* styles children construct as a consequence of initial *attachment* bonds with parental caregivers will serve as a sort of psychological *template* for future patterns of cognition, affect, and behaviour in other close relationships in which they partake. This means that the *attachment* styles children form (in their early life and largely outside of sport) with their parents are likely to be part of the internal template they use when they seek to form relationships *outside* of the parental bond. In sport, children and adolescents' experiences (such as motivation, stress and anxiety, decisions to drop out of sport, or feelings of isolation) are closely linked to the *quality of the relationships* they are able to form with peers,

coaches, and teammates (Carr, 2012). *Relationship quality* in this sense can be thought of as the degree to which relationships with peers, coaches, or teammates are perceived to embody key features such as closeness, commitment, self-esteem support, conflict resolution, loyalty, and emotional intimacy (e.g., Jowett & Ntoumanis, 2004; Weiss & Smith, 1999). Being part of such relationships in the context of sport has been shown to serve important functions such as enhancing motivation, protecting individuals from stress and isolation, and supporting the development of self-esteem (see Carr, 2012). However, it is not a given that *all* young people will possess the psychological characteristics it takes to construct such warm and empathic relationships with others in the context of sport.

Sport researchers (Jowett & Wylleman, 2006) have therefore suggested that relationships in sport are also likely to be a reflection of the critical and affectively charged attachment styles young people share with parental caregivers. This is because: (a) young people whose early experiences enable them to develop a secure *attachment* style are more likely to develop internal perceptions of *themselves* (e.g., "I am worthy of being loved") and *others* (e.g., "Others typically *want* to be close to me") that facilitate positive relationships in sport; (b) that young people often relate to others in a manner that closely reflects the *attachment* bond that they share with parents (e.g., an individual whose mother is rejecting and withholds support and affection may come to respond in a similar manner towards their friends); and (c) that young people can internalise complex patterns of emotional regulation (e.g., self-protective distancing strategies that help them to avoid dealing with anticipated rejection or unavailability if they seek proximity) developed in early *attachment* bonds and subsequently reproduce these strategies in their relationships with their peers (see Carr, 2012).

This is precisely what the sporting literature (Carr, 2009; Carr & Fitzpatrick, 2011) is beginning to uncover. For example, it has been identified (Carr, 2009; Carr & Fitzpatrick, 2011) that children who are involved in team sports but exhibit features of an insecure *attachment* style in the context of their parental relationships are less likely to be part of high-quality relationships (relationships where both parties share common interests, are supportive, are loyal and intimate, manage conflict effectively, and have a general positive "tone" to their relationship) with their best friends in sport and more likely to be generally viewed as "difficult to like" by their teammates. Given the enormous importance that the literature has afforded to the development of good quality friendships in sport, it is of significance to understand that parental *attachment* provides a platform from which children will be helped or hindered in constructing these important sporting relationships including friendship, coaching, and other such relationships.

So what is the practical significance of such knowledge? It would be nice if there were a set of "parental recommendations" that are designed to help sporting parents to develop a secure *attachment* bond with their children, helping to ensure that the child develops the emotional and social capabilities that would ultimately benefit their participation and rela-

tionship formation in sporting contexts. However, the formation of a secure *attachment* is an enormously complex part of human development and is dependent upon numerous complexities that range from the existing *attachment* characteristics of parents themselves, the social context within which the parent–child bond takes place, and a plethora of other significant factors. Despite this, the facilitation of change towards a more secure parent–child *attachment* bond is likely to depend heavily upon factors such as awareness and willingness on the part of parents to help foster, develop, and maintain a level of *attachment* security in the bond that they share with their children. Understanding the role of sport-related parent–child interactions in facilitating and/or inhibiting these processes will be an important part of future research developments in this area. Furthermore, to be aware on a much deeper level of the manner in which sporting relationships are likely to be partially dependent upon the early relational tools that were carved out for us through participation in parental *attachment* bonds is also a significant reminder that sporting relationships cannot develop in isolation from the network of key familial relationships in which individuals are intertwined.

MOTIVATIONAL CLIMATE

In the previous section we focused on the idea that parental care and support in a broader sense (i.e., outside of the sport and physical activity domain) might have significant implications for young people's involvement in sport and exercise. Other avenues of research have focused upon a different aspect of parental influence by examining how parental *belief systems* and *values* (and *children's perceptions* of these beliefs and values) within the context of sport and physical activity are linked to children's experiences and involvement. From this perspective, the beliefs that children believe that their parents hold in relation to their children's sport and physical activity involvement

(and to their own) are likely to be linked to children's psychological responses. This idea essentially suggests that parental beliefs in relation to children's sport involvement are "felt" by children and play a role in the development of contextual cognition, affect, and behaviour. Studies have revealed that some parents are a major source of stress, pressure, and attitudinal influence in youth sport (e.g., Brustad, 1993). One popular way of thinking about these issues is the idea that children's perceptions of the *motivational climate* emphasised by their parents in relation to their sport experiences are linked to key psychological responses such as stress, pressure, and thoughts about success.

Based upon the work of Ames (Ames, 1992; Ames & Archer, 1987) the *motivational climate* emphasised by a given parental figure is determined by that parent's own personal goals, the evaluation and reward processes that he/she emphasises, and the way he/she structures tasks. Through the way that they interact with their children in sport, parents are responsible for sending signals that implicitly (and often explicitly) suggest that certain values are more or less important than others. When a *mastery/ task climate* is created, the signals from the parent suggest that their child's success is synonymous with improvement and learning, regardless of normative ability. When a *performance/ego climate* is created, parents are suggesting that their child's success is about the level of ability they demonstrate compared to others and this is achieved when children exhibit superiority in comparison to others. Children can pick up on these cues and their thoughts and emotions may be partially shaped by them. So how exactly do parents tend to create a *motivational climate* that reflects either a mastery or performance-oriented environment? It is helpful to break this down and examine some of the key structural features (Epstein, 1989) of the sporting environment that parents can control in order to convey mastery or performance-oriented signals to children.

TASK OR OBJECTIVES

Parents often (willingly or unwillingly) communicate to children the goals that they would like them to achieve from their sporting endeavours. A parent who predominantly presents children with the idea that their goal is to demonstrate their superiority (i.e., everything is seen as a race or competition; winning is the goal) is creating a *performance climate*. A *mastery climate* is more about constructing the idea that your child's central objective from sport (in your mind) is to develop his or her personal ability and to learn (i.e., personal bests are goals).

AUTHORITY

In a performance climate, children tend to feel "controlled" by the social agent. That is, it feels as though their sporting experiences are dictated by their parent. This might mean they are told by parents what sport to get involved in, or what skills they will practice, for how long, and in what order; they are not involved in the decision-making process (i.e., goals are set for them and parents may even be controlling behaviour, such as giving orders and suggestions to coaches). Such an environment is less sensitive to children's need for autonomy/ control and may involve more controlling feedback from adults as a consequence (e.g., feedback is typically of a more controlling nature: "You must...", "I told you not to do it like that!", "What on Earth did you do that for?"). A *mastery climate* places more authority in the hands of children, enabling them to have a say in how and what they develop (e.g., perhaps setting their own goals or choosing the types of sport they get involved with in the first place). By handing authority over to children they are more likely to learn about themselves and their sport.

RECOGNITION

Recognition and praise from our parents is paramount. A parent who consistently recognises her child (through her use of praise or material rewards) for demonstrating superiority, and punishes them (by withholding praise or verbal and even physical punishments) when they demonstrate lesser ability or make mistakes, is creating a performance climate. Such a climate might also involve parents demanding that their child be selected for the "first team," demanding that their child "wins," or selecting teams for their children to play for who have superior winning records. Conversely, parents who reward their children for making personal progressions, trying hard, learning, or improving (regardless of their normative ability), are creating a *mastery climate*.

EVALUATION

How do parents ultimately judge their children as having succeeded or failed in sport and physical activity? When this evaluation judgement is solely based upon outcomes or winning, a *performance climate* exists. When it is based upon personal improvement, learning, and effort, a mastery climate is evident.

TIMING

If your overall goal is the learning and development of your child, then an environment that is insensitive to the fact that some individuals need to devote more time to developing certain aspects of themselves than others is unhelpful. A *performance climate* tends to involve parents dictating the timing required for children to develop their skills and progress, whereas a *mastery climate* is sensitive to the time various children may require in order to learn and develop fully. In other words, a *mastery climate* allows for children to develop at their own pace, rather than a pace determined by their parents (as evident in a *performance climate*).

When children are exposed to a *mastery climate* from their parents (in accordance with the key features identified above) they have been shown to be more likely to develop intrinsic motivation, to feel good about themselves, to experience a sense of autonomy and relatedness, to enjoy sport, to experience lower levels of anxiety, to be more focused, and to remain involved in sport for longer. A *mastery climate* has been linked to such positive aspects of sport involvement because it is more likely to support children's feelings of competence, autonomy, and relatedness, which are thought to be important to human well-being. A *performance climate* tends to thwart such important psychological needs (White et al., 1998).

FAMILY SYSTEMS

The above sections have focused almost exclusively upon the key influence of *parents* on the development of their children through sport. However, it is also helpful to look beyond this unidirectional parent-to-child influence (although we believe it is an extremely important familial influence) and to think of the *family systems* within which athletes find themselves. Family systems theorists tend to think of the family as a fully interacting social system that functions according to components such as power hierarchies, rules, interactional systems, and subsystems (Hellstedt, 1995). Furthermore, this family system is also subject to developmental transitioning and this means that each of the components mentioned above (power hierarchies, rules, and interactional systems) will be subject to changes as the nature of the family develops. First, think about the different types of *family systems* that surround athletes. Athletes may be part of the following systems:

- Single young people
- Newly married couples
- Parents of very young children
- Parents of adolescent children
- Families with children who are old enough to leave home
- Families with adult children

You have probably noted from the above discussion exercise that being an athlete is inevitably likely to get caught up in the *family systems* and developmental challenges in which individuals are enveloped. For example, what happens when a young, talented athlete is plucked from the family unit, leaving home early to spend most of his or her adolescence overseas in a talent development camp? How does this influence the life of the family they leave behind and how does it influence the athlete not to be part of that normal family transition? How does it influence the family of a talented adolescent swimmer who is required to spend long hours training and travelling, utilising his or her parents' time, money, and emotional resources whilst doing so? How does a young adolescent athlete who is seeking to travel the world in pursuit of her talent development negotiate her relationship with a mother who is reluctant to allow her the physical and emotional independence to do so? What impact could this have on her development?

Table 12.1 *Some examples of the developmental challenges that different* family systems *might face*

Family Stage	Developmental challenges
Single young adult	• Develop an independence from parents in an emotional, economic, and practical sense. • To develop a network of social relationships that help support them. • To forge out a career and a life pathway.
Newly married couple	• Develop a functional relationship with the other in relation to closeness, commitment, need satisfaction, and practical living. • Continue to maintain a self-identity that is supported by the relationship.
Parents of young children	• Make space for the children to be part of the family unit. • Share parenting and other responsibilities to ensure that the needs of the new family are met.
Parents of adolescent children	• Allow gradual transition of independence to adolescent children. • Maintain boundaries within which adolescents are able to develop independence yet remain part of the family system. • Maintain spousal relationship as a stable base. • Continue to develop self-identity.
Parents of children who are leaving home	• Manage the changes that inevitably appear when children finally leave the parental home. • Continue to develop and cultivate self-identity and development. • Refocus the spousal relationship on other goals and needs.
Parents of adult children	• Grow into other roles such as grandparenting. • Prepare for, adjust to, and enjoy retirement.

Clearly, the above examples highlight the critical relationship between athletic identity and family. However, what can sport psychologists and clinicians do in order to gain an insight into how such *family systems* are implicated in their athletes' psychological well-being and performance? Hellstedt (1995) has advocated a clinical interviewing procedure that focuses upon the following issues in relation to the family system:

- *The intensity and sources of stress in the family*: This might include issues such as the level of stress that the family is under; who seems to be experiencing the stress most intensely (e.g., is a particular family member experiencing stress more profoundly?); whether the source of the stress is internal (i.e., it comes from within the family itself, such as the father is having an extramarital affair) or external (e.g., perhaps members of the family are being bullied or abused by outsiders); and the specific nature of the stress (e.g., financial, emotional).

- *The amount of cohesion that the family seems to display*: What kind of cohesion does the family unit portray when they are interviewed? It may be clear that certain members of the family dominate others, speak for others, or do not value the thoughts and feelings of the others. This may provide a strong indicator of the extent to which the family operates as a cohesive unit or not.

- *How well the family can adapt to change*: How well families adapt to the changes that are thrust upon them is an issue that relates to their ability to communicate with each other, solve problems together, and resolve conflict. The issues that families may be required to adapt to could include internal issues such as how they deal with the quest for individuation that adolescent members experience as they mature, or external issues such as the death of a young person's girlfriend or boyfriend.

- *The patterns of interaction and communication within the family*: How does the family interact? What is the nature of the interaction (is it serious, fun, playful, full of conflict)? What roles are played by key family members during typical family interactions? How do the family resolve conflict? Are they close and how do they express their needs for intimacy? These sorts of issues are strong indicators of the patterns of interaction that characterise a family system.

In his *family systems* approach to sport psychology consulting, Hellstedt (1995) suggests that interviews with families can help consultants begin to piece together the picture of specific families in relation to these issues. Then, when the nature of the family is uncovered, consultants are likely to be in a better position to assist the family in moving forward when they encounter issues that relate to the athletic member of the family unit. For example, it may be that a consultant can predict that an adolescent athlete's need to move away from the family home for talent development in another country will be an issue that will place the family under undue stress and that they will likely deal with that stress in a manner that is likely to hinder the psychological well-being of the athlete whilst away from the family. Accordingly, measures (e.g., support provision, education, or communication training) can be put in place to avoid the issue causing undue stress to the family and the welfare of the athlete.

Dealing with *family systems* and the stresses that athletes are likely to encounter as a consequence of dysfunction within the family unit is undoubtedly an issue that may require attention to some of the principles espoused by family systems psychologists (Brown, 2001). To this end, there have been a number of approaches offered by the clinical literature that help families get to grip with such issues. Firstly, there is an approach typically labelled as the *here and now approach* which is essentially designed to facilitate communication in the here and now to stimulate familial change. This approach tends to utilise techniques such as defining problems, clarifying goals, formulating action plans, homework tasks, and psychoeducational methods. Alternatively, *transgenerational* interventions tend to tackle familial issues by identifying and changing *patterns* within extended families that have been passed down through generations and are often the source of key familial difficulties. To this end, interventions may involve the development of genograms (a diagrammatic representation of family relationships across generations) and the inclusion of wider family into the therapeutic intervention process. Finally, *ecosystemic* approaches pay particular attention to the family as it is situated within a range of other systems such as the world of work, education, and sport, focusing specifically upon how the family system is affected by and situated within these interconnected systems. All of these important therapeutic perspectives may be important for consultants to consider when working with athletic families (Brown, 2001).

LEARNING AIDS

1   Numerous parents become involved with their children's sporting experiences in a significant way when they also become their child's coach. Discuss whether you believe it is possible to be a child's coach and still provide your child with the same sense of parental security and caregiving experiences *outside* of sport? Do you believe being the child's coach conflicts with being the child's caregiver (and if so, how). Or do you believe being the child's coach enhances such caregiving roles of the parent?

Especially at elite level in the contemporary world of sport, coaching a child performer may involve a significant focus on producing a high-level performance (elite sport often fosters a performance climate). From this perspective, there is a high chance that children might be viewed by coaches as "athletes" who are required to produce "a performance." Researchers in the area of child show business have argued that in some situations it is hard for parents who are responsible for their children's talent development/performance production/performance outcome to switch out of this mode of perceiving their child when in the familial setting. That is, parenting may be impeded by viewing your child as a "performance."

2   The earlier outline of the parental *motivational climate* is an example of how parents' values are likely to be extended to children's involvement in sport and physical activity. The practical implications seem clear in the sense that there are useful guidelines for helping parents create a mastery climate by manipulating the various structural features identified above (e.g., recognition, evaluation). However, the issue of parental *motivational climate* is far from simple. Discussing the following questions will help you to appreciate this complexity:

   a   Is it possible that a parent can create a strong *mastery climate* for his or her child's experiences in a given sport but a coach creates a contrasting climate (e.g., a strong *performance climate*)? If so, how would this influence the child? Is the child more likely to be influenced by one or the other climate? If so, how would this work? What factors would come into play?

It is possible that children's developmental status may be an important factor here. For example, younger children may spend much more time in the company of their parents than older children (who are more inclined to individuate as they enter adolescence) and may therefore be more susceptible to influence from parental values and beliefs.

b   As a child moves into adolescence, is it likely that the influence of the *motivational climate* from parents will change? If so, can you explain why you believe this to be the case? Who might become more influential if parental influence declines? Can you think of a situation where parental influence might increase as children become adolescents?

As youngsters form an identity outside of the family unit it is likely that they will develop new relationships that help them to do this effectively. As they develop new social bonds such as peers, other adult bonds, and romantic relationships, the influence of parents may become less pronounced. However, there may be some situations where children are thrown into an adolescence that places them in increased proximity to their parents (e.g., a child who spends their entire adolescence being coached by a parent–coach) and inhibits their extra-familial bonding.

c   What might be the link between *attachment* styles (i.e., the secure and insecure styles mentioned in the first section of this chapter) and the *motivational climate*? How might mastery versus performance climates enhance or inhibit the development of *attachment* styles in the context of the parent–child relationship?

If part of a secure attachment is about feeling like we are valued and accepted by a significant other, especially in times of vulnerability, then it makes sense to suggest that an environment (e.g., a performance climate) where we are shown contempt or are not accepted when we make mistakes or fail (and are feeling vulnerable) is unlikely to foster a sense of security.

3   Think for a moment about each of the *family systems* identified earlier and try to identify what you think some of the key developmental tasks or challenges might be for individuals involved in such *family systems*.

An example might be that as part of a newly-married couple, it is necessary for each spouse to adjust to living as part of a partnership, taking the needs of the other into account. [You can compare your suggestions to those provided in Table 12.1. Also begin to think about how being an elite athlete might enhance or impede some of the developmental tasks you list for discussion.]

REVIEW QUESTIONS

1   Describe what is meant by an internal working model of *attachment*.

2   How do securely and insecurely attached individuals have different internal working models of *attachment*?

3   In what ways might these secure and insecure models link to experiences of sport? Give three possible examples.

4   What is the parental *motivational climate*? What are the structural features that help to make up the climate?

5 Outline the main differences between a mastery and performance climate.

6 Describe how mastery and performance climates from parents might influence young people's involvement in sport.

7 What are the different types of *family systems* in which athletes might find themselves?

8 How might being an athlete influence and be influenced by the various *family systems* identified?

EXERCISES

1 Consider a child who has an insecure parental *attachment*. Such children, as we discussed in the earlier sections, adopt a negative internal representation, fearing rejection and inconsistent responses from *attachment* figures and adopting a negative sense of self in close relational contexts.

2 If you were to design a sport-based program designed to assist the relational development of insecurely attached children, what would your program involve? What would be the cornerstones of your program and why? What difficulties or obstacles might your program face?

3 We learned earlier that the *motivational climate* that parents create for their children in sport may have a significant impact on their development. However, how organisers, coaches, and governing bodies get this message across to parents is a question of education. Design a leaflet for parents of children involved in sport of your choice, informing them of the importance of the *motivational climate* they create, and giving them practical guidance on how to create such a climate in the context of your chosen sport.

4 Think about and write down the nature of the family system you are currently involved in (are you a single young adult, part of a young couple, a parent of new children?). Then, write down an honest, personal, and full reflection of the following in your family system:

● Write down the main sources of stress in your family. Are they internal or external?

● How cohesive is your family in terms of working together to solve problems and conflicts? Provide yourself with examples.

● How has your family responded to significant changes that it has been faced with? Again, provide examples.

● What are the typical patterns of interaction in your family? How are things communicated? Who does the communicating? In what style?

Now, having considered the above, try to reflect upon how the key features you have identified in relation to your family system could influence or be influenced by the athletic role of one of the members (i.e., if one of your family members was/is an athlete, how might this relate to the issues you identify above?).

5 Next, try to interview an athlete that you know in relation to their family. Talk about the same features as you reflected upon in task three and then try to understand how the nature of their family system influences and is influenced by their role as an athlete.

REFERENCES

Ames, C. (1992). Classrooms: Goals, structures, and student motivation. *Journal of Educational Psychology*, 84, 261–271.

Ames, C. & Archer, J. (1987). Mothers' beliefs about the role of ability and effort in school learning. *Journal of Educational Psychology*, 79, 409–414.

Bowlby, J. (1969/1982). *Attachment and Loss*, Vol. 1. *Attachment*. New York: Basic Books.

Brown, C. (2001). Clinical cross-training: Compatibility of sport and *family systems* psychology. *Professional Psychology: Research and Practice*, 32, 19–26.

Brustad, R.J. (1993). Who will go out to play? Parental and psychological influences on children's attraction to physical activity. *Journal of Sport and Exercise Psychology*, 14, 59–77.

Carr, S. (2009). Adolescent–parent *attachment* characteristics and quality of youth sport friendship. *Psychology of Sport and Exercise*, 10, 653–661.

Carr, S. (2012). Relationships and sport and performance. In S. Murphy (Ed.), *Oxford handbook of sport and performance psychology* (pp.400–418). Oxford Library of Psychology. NY: Oxford University Press.

Carr, S. & Fitzpatrick, N. (2011). Experiences of dyadic sport friendships as a function of self and partner *attachment* characteristics. *Psychology of Sport and Exercise*, 12, 383–391.

Epstein, J. (1989). Family structures and student motivation: A developmental perspective. In C. Ames & R. Ames (Eds.), *Research on motivation in education* (Vol. 3, pp.259–295). New York: Academic Press.

Hellstedt, J. (1995). Invisible players: A *family systems* model. In S. M. Murphy (Ed.), *Sport psychology interventions*. Champaign, IL: Human Kinetics.

Jowett, S. & Ntoumanis, N. (2004). The coach–athlete relationship questionnaire (CART-Q): Development and initial validation. *Scandinavian Journal of Medicine and Science in Sports*, 14, 245–257.

Jowett, S. & Wylleman, P. (2006). Interpersonal relationships in sport and exercise settings: Crossing the chasm. *Psychology of Sport and Exercise*, 7, 119–123.

Krane, V. Greenlaf, C.A. & Snow, J. (1997). Reaching for gold and the price of glory: A motivational case study of an elite gymnast. *The Sport Psychologist*, 11, 53–71.

Weimer, B.L., Kerns, K.A. & Oldenburg, C.M. (2004). Adolescents' interactions with a best friend: Associations with *attachment* style. *Journal of Experimental Child Psychology*, 88, 102–120.

Weiss, M.R. & Smith, A.L. (1999). Quality of youth sport friendships: Measurement development and validation. *Journal of Sport & Exercise Psychology*, 21, 145–166.

White, S.A., Kavussanu, M. & Guest, S. (1998). Goal orientations and perceptions of the *motivational climate* created by significant others. *European Journal of Physical Education*, 3, 212–228.

Chapter 13

Peer relationships and the youth sport experience

ALAN L. SMITH AND FABIENNE D'ARRIPE-LONGUEVILLE

SUMMARY

The sport environment consists of several important social relationships that can influence the quality of a young athlete's sport experience. Relationships with peers are particularly important because they foster athletic and psychological development within a context where young athletes are among equals. Thus, children can play an active part in shaping the quality of their own sport experience. This development is realized through processes associated with both the broad peer group and specific friendships. In the present chapter we define peer relationships and briefly overview conceptual perspectives on how peers are important to the development of young people. We then address how peers can play a role in both the learning of sport skills and sport motivation. We emphasize how key adults can shape the sport environment to enable formation of positive peer relationships and associated developmental outcomes.

INTRODUCTION

As sport psychologists, we take great interest in the characteristics of individual performers and outcomes of sport involvement. Such characteristics include anxiety proneness, mental resilience, and confidence. We also recognize that the social context of sport contributes to sport outcomes. As parents, coaches, and physical activity professionals, we tend to focus our attention on adult roles in youth sport. We wish to understand how adults like ourselves can construct sport to offer positive experiences for young athletes and limit negative experiences. We less often

attend to young athletes as important social agents themselves, yet fellow teammates and competitors intensively engage with athletes and can shape their experience. Consider two youth football teams one of the authors recently observed. One team was engaged in demanding skill work, with extensive teammate interaction. There was encouragement after mistakes, observable helping/teaching behaviors, and verbal communication about football and topics unrelated. The children clearly enjoyed football and being together. After practice several players stayed to kick goals, see who could punt the ball the farthest, and clown around. The other team was similarly engaged in skill work. However, the players were self-focused and minimally communicative. Frustration was a common reaction to challenges and responsive helping behaviors or encouraging comments from teammates were infrequent. The children exerted strong effort, but in an obligatory fashion, not in a joyful way. After practice most players immediately left the field. There was limited exchange among teammates and the body language of the athletes did not signal satisfaction or enthusiasm. Few stayed to engage in unstructured play. The social dynamics of these teams showcase peer relationships as central to a quality youth sport experience. To foster understanding of peer relationships in sport, we introduce key definitions and concepts below and overview how peers contribute to skill learning and motivation.

OBJECTIVES

After reading this chapter you should be able to:

1   Recognize peers as important social agents in the sport context.
2   Identify key features of peer relationships.
3   Understand how peers are important to learning and motivation.
4   Construct sport settings that promote positive peer relationships and mitigate peer conflict.

PEER RELATIONSHIPS – DEFINITIONS AND CONCEPTUAL PERSPECTIVES

Most research on peers in youth sport focuses on same- or near-age individuals who engage in sport together, be they teammates or competitors within organized settings or co-participants within informal settings (see Smith, 2007). Similarity in skill, experience, or other characteristics could be used to classify peers, but overwhelmingly the similarity cue that researchers use to specify peers is age. This distinguishes peers from significant adults in the sport context, such as coaches and parents. These adults have a degree of control over a young athlete's sport experience, particularly in organized settings. They determine and enforce rules of conduct, oversee practice regimens, hold expectations for time investment and performance, provide resources such as transportation and equipment that are necessary for participation, and so forth. Within informal settings parents set boundaries for where a child can play, determine when a child may be outdoors, and direct children toward and away from certain playmates. This reflects an imbalance of power whereby adults have a great deal of control in framing the sport experiences of young people.

At the same time, young people play an active role in their sport experience, making participation decisions in line with personal goals, exerting their best efforts in activities that attract them, and seeking social and other means of support for their interests (see Coakley, 2009). This occurs in a social context that contains fellow participants of similar age who have relationships characterized by relatively more balanced power. The more balanced nature of these relationships can allow for a sense of personal control within sport, whereby young athletes cultivate friendships, work with one another to master skills, and develop shared goals. In light of young people citing affiliation with peers and social acceptance as primary sport participation motives (see Weiss & Amorose, 2008), peer relationships in sport should be a central consideration when seeking to understand the quality of the youth sport experience.

Conceptual perspectives on human development and motivation have been used to guide research on youth peer relationships in sport (see Smith & McDonough, 2008). A particularly influential perspective on peer relationships stems from Sullivan's (1953) Interpersonal Theory of Psychiatry. This theory overviews the importance of interpersonal relationships to human development from infancy through late adolescence and addresses how early relationships can have implications for adjustment in adulthood. Sullivan proposed that the larger peer group *and* specific dyadic relationships (i.e., friendships) offer unique contributions to human development. From young childhood onward, acceptance by the peer group is important in framing perspectives on, for example, competition and cooperation. Through interactions with the peer group, individuals progressively form an understanding of the self in relation to others. Beginning in middle childhood, young people seek greater interpersonal intimacy and social validation. To fulfill these needs they pursue friendships with same-sex peers. Friendships are relationships that are typically defined as dyadic, close in nature, and mutually acknowledged (Bukowski & Hoza, 1989). Friendships offer the opportunity to form close bonds that further promote developmental growth. Figure 13.1 depicts the timing of peer acceptance and friendship as contributors to child development. The large arrows represent the emergence of peer acceptance from early childhood and friendship from middle childhood as developmentally important social constructs. The small arrows represent the compensatory nature of these constructs, another important feature of Sullivan's theory.

Peer acceptance and friendship can be developmentally protective when there are challenges in one of the relationship systems.

Said another way, if a child is not well accepted by the larger peer group but has a close friendship of good quality, then the friendship can fulfill the developmental functions required for positive development. Support for this social buffering is found in youth sport research (Smith, Ullrich-French, Walker & Hurley, 2006; Ullrich-French & Smith, 2006), suggesting that attention to multiple forms of peer relationships can benefit research and practice. To best understand and promote peer relationships, attention should be paid to both the peer group and specific friendships.

Friendships have a number of features that are exhibited in sport. Weiss, Smith, and Theeboom (1996) conducted an interview study of 8- to 16-year-old summer sport program participants to obtain a descriptive account of the nature and expectations of sport best friendships. Their findings highlighted a breadth of positive friendship dimensions. Best friendships were described by the participants as sources of companionship, enjoyment, self-esteem enhancement, help and guidance, intimacy, and emotional support. Participants also said that best friends engaged in prosocial behavior, were loyal, held similar interests and values, and had attractive personal qualities such as a nice personality or attractive physical appearance. Participants reported that conflict was minimal within their best friendship in sport and that they had the capacity to resolve conflict when it arose. Overall, the findings point to many possible ways to promote positive peer relationships on athletic teams. Providing opportunity for peers to work together when developing athletic skills, teaching athletes to reinforce one another for strong efforts and encourage one another after challenges, and providing opportunity for informal exchanges are strategies that could foster the development of positive peer relationships.

Despite the largely positive nature of sport best friendships reported by the participants, Weiss et al. (1996) also uncovered negative dimensions. Best friendships in sport were not always conflict free and the participants

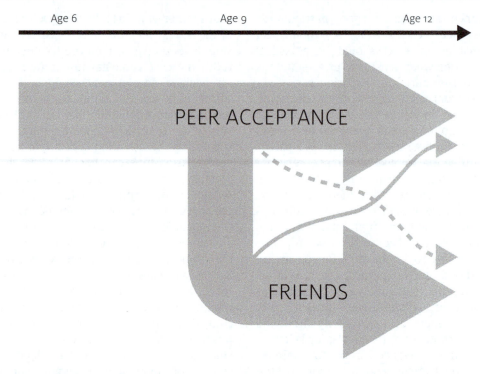

Figure 13.1 Sullivan's (1953) Interpersonal Theory of Psychiatry specifies peer acceptance and friendship as distinct yet related contributors to child development.

reported unattractive personal qualities, betrayal, and inaccessibility as features of these relationships. Accordingly, researchers and practitioners must attend to negative features as well as supportive functions of peer relationships in their work with young athletes. This is corroborated by recent work by Holt, Knight, and Zukiwski (2012), who showed that conflict tied to performance and to relationships is salient among female teammates on successful university teams. The athletes they interviewed shared potentially useful approaches to managing conflict on teams. Specifically, the athletes recommended team building early in the season, addressing conflict immediately, mediation by third parties, and holding deliberately structured team meetings. Holt and colleagues also recommended that personal conflict resolution skills be taught to athletes, as the overwhelming bulk of their respondents indicated a reticence to directly address conflict.

In addition to peer acceptance and friendship, which are the most frequently studied peer constructs by researchers, there are many other peer constructs that should be considered in sport contexts. In an overview of peer research on youth physical activity behavior, Smith and McDonough (2008) categorized peer constructs within: (a) peer group; (b) specific peer; and (c) peer referenced categories. A peer group construct of interest, for example, would be the peer network. The peer network can be defined in terms of relational connections within a sport team, the presence of cliques, or the centrality of particular team members, providing a structural view of a group of peers. With regard to specific peers, one can focus on characteristics of particular peers, the quality of relationships with specific peers, or modeling of thoughts, emotions, or behaviors by viewing others in the sport context. Research on friendship indicates that whether or not one has friends, the characteristics of one's friends, and the closeness or quality of friendships offer unique contributions to the understanding of youth development (Hartup, 1996). Finally, peer referenced constructs are more global in nature, reflecting broader social concerns of young people. For example, social goals like the desire to be admired by others, concerns about how one comes across to others, and perceptions of social expectations (e.g., toward cheating, playing while injured) would fall into this category. As one considers this breadth of peer constructs, it is clear that there are many potential ways to promote peer relationships in sport. In the following sections we provide an overview of the knowledge of the role of peers in fostering skill learning and sport motivation.

PEER-ASSISTED LEARNING

Learning is a fundamental component of the sport experience, especially for children in the beginning stages of their sport careers. Though we consider adults, particularly coaches, as the primary source of instruction during the learning process, there are a variety of ways that young athletes may contribute to one another's physical and psychological skill development. Research on peer-assisted learning (PAL) offers a helpful framework for understanding this important role of peers. PAL is the acquisition of knowledge or skills through the active help and support of status-equal or matched companions (Topping & Ehly, 1998). PAL encompasses various learning methods, including three outlined below: peer modeling, peer tutoring, and cooperative learning. Though the effects of PAL interventions mostly have been studied in academic settings, research has recently emerged that supports the benefits of PAL in sport and physical activity contexts (d'Arripe-Longueville, Gernigon, Huet, Cadopi & Winnykamen, 2002a; d'Arripe-Longueville, Gernigon, Huet, Winnykamen & Cadopi, 2002b).

Peer modeling

Bandura's (1986) social cognitive theory has served as a framework for many studies of modeling, also known as observational learning. Modeling is a process whereby individuals learn through observing and imitating others. The characteristics of the model being observed and imitated can have an influence on the psychological responses and motor performance of observers (see McCullagh, Law & Ste-Marie, 2012). If a learner perceives a model to possess similar characteristics to oneself, this can lead to more focused attention to the model and greater motivation to learn the target behavior. This can benefit the learning process because acquiring a behavior through observation requires attending to relevant features of the behavior, retaining what is observed, and having sufficient motivation and capability to produce the behavior.

One way this has been examined in the educational psychology literature is to consider the effects of peer mastery versus peer coping models on observers. Mastery models demonstrate errorless performance and verbalize confidence, whereas coping models display gradual improvement in performance and progressively more positive and confident statements (Schunk, Hanson & Cox, 1987). The peer coping model would be expected to be perceived by new learners as most similar and, therefore, most effective in fostering learning. Sport studies have shown that both mastery and coping models can facilitate skill learning, with coping models appearing to have a stronger effect on self-concept and emotional outcomes (e.g., Weiss, McCullagh, Smith & Berlant, 1998). Though more work is needed to draw firm conclusions in sport contexts, these findings suggest that: (a) peers can be effectively used as models in teaching sport skills; and (b) coping models might offer value when learning skills that are highly dependent on confidence and emotional control (e.g., tasks with potential to raise fear of injury).

Peer tutoring

In the cognitive development domain, Vygotsky (1934/1962) referred to the *zone of proximal development*, which represents the difference between what a learner can do independently and what potentially can be done with guidance or collaboration. He suggested that learning can occur within the zone of proximal development through asymmetrical relationships, whereby one actor is more knowledgeable and expert than the other. The asymmetry offers scaffolding for the less expert member of the relationship to learn. This is the conceptual basis for using peer tutoring in learning contexts. Peer tutoring is the most widely known peer-assisted learning method. It involves specific role-taking, with one peer assuming the role of tutor and the other being the tutee (Topping & Ehly, 1998). One-to-one peer tutoring, class wide peer tutoring, and reciprocal peer tutoring, in which the students alternate the role of tutor and tutee, are recommended forms of this PAL method. In the educational domain such approaches have shown cognitive and socioemotional benefits for tutors, tutees, or both (Robinson, Schofield & Steers-Wentzell, 2005).

Early peer tutoring studies in physical activity contexts have used Class Wide Peer Tutoring interventions in Physical Education (CWPT-PE), which are based on reciprocal peer tutoring, to help students learn new skills and assess each other (e.g., Johnson & Ward, 2001). Other studies have examined the effects of one-to-one peer tutoring on outcomes for tutors or tutees, as well as how tutor characteristics potentially shape such outcomes. For instance, d'Arripe-Longueville et al. (2002a) examined how the skill level of a peer tutor links to achievement motivation and performance of novice learners in a swimming task. For boys, tutees of skilled tutors showed the best swimming skills, whereas for girls, tutees of both skilled and intermediate tutors showed better skills than a control group. Tutees with skilled tutors had higher confidence that they would improve and received more demonstrations and verbal instructions than tutees in the control group. Other sport-based research has shown motivation and performance benefits to those who serve as peer tutors (Legrain, d'Arripe-Longueville & Gernigon, 2003a) and that tutor training is beneficial to tutoring outcomes (Ensergueix & Lafont, 2011; Legrain, d'Arripe-Longueville & Gernigon, 2003b). Overall, the findings suggest that *both* tutors and tutees receive benefits from a peer tutoring relationship, particularly when the tutors are provided with training.

Cooperative learning

Cooperative learning is a generic term that refers to numerous methods for organizing and conducting instruction. Current psychological research into cooperative learning is informed by two previously autonomous strands of work. The first is neo-Piagetian, conceiving of cognitive development as acquired through the cognitive conflict and challenge afforded by symmetrical dyads (e.g., Doise & Mugny, 1984). Peers may have similar levels of cognitive development, yet different viewpoints that stimulate such challenge. The second strand stems from research conducted in the United States whereby cooperative learning is seen as an interaction mode in small groups to reach a specific goal. Social interdependence theory provides a foundation on which cooperative learning is built (e.g., Johnson & Johnson, 2009).

Although research on cooperative learning in sport and physical activity contexts is scarce, this method is considered a valuable instructional model to promote social, physical and cognitive learning outcomes (Dyson, Griffin & Hastie, 2009). Darnis-Paraboschi, Lafont and Menaut (2005) have reported the positive role of dyadic verbal peer interactions in team sport decision-making tasks. Moreover, d'Arripe-

Longueville et al. (2002b) have reported that cooperation in a physical education context was more frequent in symmetrical dyads and in females than in asymmetrical dyads and in males. This speaks to the importance of careful pairing of youth in sport contexts. Also, when considered alongside findings on peer tutoring, it suggests employing a mix of PAL techniques is important. Asymmetry offers benefits within a trained, tutoring context whereas symmetry shows benefits in cooperative learning settings. More research is required to offer concrete recommendations, but it is evident that consideration of the context and characteristics of the participants is necessary to tailor the best PAL strategy to promote learning outcomes.

How can a sport environment that maximizes the benefits of peer-assisted learning be constructed? First, it is important to take integrative approaches to PAL methods (Ginsburg-Block, Rohrbeck & Fantuzzo, 2006; Topping & Ehly, 1998). There is no dominant PAL method, and the most effective approach at a given time will be determined by characteristics of the athletes and contextual features. For example, cooperation is more likely to arise in symmet-rical conditions and in females, and necessitates athletes possessing skill prerequisites. Peer tutoring is predominant in dyads that are asymmetrical as to skill and/or age. Peer modeling can be effective in symmetric and asymmetric dyads when there are sufficient similarity cues (e.g., gender, playing position) to facilitate attention to the model and motivation. Second, coaches or other professionals can encourage helping behaviors and collaborative peer interactions among athletes. Settings that emphasize mastery, skill improvement, and cooperation are recognized to foster more prosocial behaviors than settings that prioritize winning and normative comparisons to assess who is "best" (Gernigon, d'Arripe-Longueville, Debove & Puvis, 2003; Johnson & Johnson, 2009). Relatedly, because friendship influences positive social interactions and achievement in academics (Newcomb & Bagwell, 1995) as well as motivation in sport (Smith, 2007), affording opportunity for the formation of friendships within sport could positively impact learning. Finally, it is important to prepare and train peers to their role, specifically when implementing peer tutoring programs for new and vulnerable learners.

PEERS AND MOTIVATION

Motivation is a topic of great interest to sport psychologists and practitioners who seek to enhance athlete performance and well-being. Two general approaches to motivation are prevalent in the sport psychology literature (Weiss & Chaumeton, 1992). One approach frames motivation as the direction and intensity of effort (Gill, 1986). Direction pertains to the choices that an individual makes, such as whether to participate in a sport or not, whether to pursue easy or challenging goals, and whom to interact with in the sport setting. Intensity pertains to how much effort is exerted when engaging in a given activity and the degree of persistence when faced with challenges. For example, a tennis athlete may exert considerable effort early in a match, only to give a half-hearted effort after losing a set. Another tennis athlete may continue to exert strong effort in the same situation. The second athlete would be considered to possess greater motivation than the first. This approach specifies motivation as a behaviorally observable outcome and of finite capacity. In seeking to understand peers and athlete motivation, emphasis is placed on how peer relationships predict the choices, effort, and persistence of athletes.

An important motivational outcome of concern to researchers and practitioners is the decision of a young athlete to continue or discontinue participation in a sport. Though many reasons exist for a young athlete to discontinue a sport, including a developmentally-healthy interest in trying different activities, such a decision can reflect a poor quality sport experience, will slow or prevent further skill development in that sport, and closes one avenue of access to social connections. A recent study by Ullrich-French and Smith (2009) examined perceived peer acceptance, perceived friendship quality, and perceived mother–child and father–child relationship quality as predictors of soccer continuation behavior in competitive players, ages 10 to 14 years, one year after collection of relationship measures. The social relationship variables contributed to prediction of continuation behavior after controlling for age and other motivation-related variables (i.e., enjoyment, stress, perceived competence, and self-determined motivation). Athletes with higher perceived friendship quality showed a greater likelihood of playing soccer on their team one year later. However, a significant interaction of social constructs suggested that this would not be true if both perceived peer acceptance and mother–child relationship quality were relatively low. This is consistent with the buffering role of social relationships specified by Sullivan (1953) and showcased in sport-based peer relationships research (Smith et al., 2006; Ullrich-French & Smith, 2006). Moreover, this finding highlights the importance of considering peer relationships within the broader social context when seeking to understand motivational outcomes in sport. Athlete peer relationships co-occur with relationships with coaches, parents, non-sport peers, and so forth.

Motivation can also be framed as an individual difference variable that is reflected in the reasons, goals, and attributions tied to an athlete's sport involvement (see Weiss & Chaumeton, 1992). Sport behavior can be shaped by individual perspectives on achievement, perceptions of the self, and other constructs that are not behaviorally observable yet represent the "motives" that underpin an athlete's sport experience. In seeking to understand the role of peers from this frame of reference, emphasis can be placed on peers as a motive for involvement or as

shaping the achievement climate on a team. Motivation-related constructs such as enjoyment, commitment, self-determination, perceived competence and others become important markers of potential peer influence in sport. Importantly, the outcome-based and individual difference approaches to framing motivation are not mutually exclusive. Motives for sport involvement are expected to both predict and be shaped by behavioral outcomes. Accordingly, adopting either approach to studying peer relationships and motivation can offer much to understanding the youth sport experience.

A variety of studies have been conducted that show a link between peers and important motivation-related constructs in sport. For example, work has shown a positive association between perceived peer acceptance and perceived physical competence in young sport participants (e.g., Weiss & Duncan, 1992; Smith et al., 2006), a core construct in many achievement motivation theories (see Weiss & Amorose, 2008). Beyond perceived competence, recent work has shown associations of peer relationships constructs with maladaptive perfectionism, motivational climate perceptions, autonomy and relatedness perceptions, and intrinsic motivation in young athletes (e.g., Jõesaar, Hein & Hagger, 2011; Ommundsen, Roberts, Lemyre & Miller, 2005; Riley & Smith, 2011). In a study of athletes aged 14 to 18 years, Escartí, Roberts, Cervelló, and Guzmán (1999) found dispositional goal orientation to be closely aligned with perceptions of the criteria of sport success used by sport friends and non-sport friends. For example, greater tendency to conceive of success in sport as achieving mastery, learning, and expending effort (referred to as task orientation) was associated with greater tendency to view friends as adopting the same criteria in judging the athlete's success. Such findings, as well as a proliferation of work exploring motivational climate as shaped by particular social agents (e.g., see Keegan, Harwood, Spray & Lavallee, 2009), have resulted in recent efforts to understand the peer motivational climate in youth sport.

Vazou, Ntoumanis, and Duda (2005) conducted essential foundational research on the peer motivational climate in sport. Through interviews with adolescent athletes they constructed a detailed description of features of the motivational climate as shaped by peers. Ntoumanis and Vazou (2005) built upon this descriptive foundation by conducting multiple studies to create a measure of key features of the peer motivational climate. Improvement, relatedness support, and effort were key features to emerge that are considered *task-involving* within achievement goal perspectives on motivation (see Ames, 1992). That is, peers can encourage one another and cooperate, value and accept one another, and encourage and reinforce effort and persistence, respectively. Other features emerged that are considered *ego-involving* within achievement goal perspectives, namely intra-team competition and ability and intra-team conflict. These features pertain to competitiveness among teammates and measuring worth of teammates based on sport ability and various unsupportive behaviors, respectively. When individuals perceive their team to have a peer climate that is relatively high in task-involving features, they are expected to show relatively adaptive motivational outcomes. Relatively high ego-involving peer climate perceptions are expected to link with less adaptive or maladaptive motivational outcomes. These expectations have been supported in research on young athletes, with peer climate shown to link with motivation-related constructs such as self-perceptions, need satisfaction, enjoyment, anxiety, burnout, intrinsic motivation, commitment, and effort (Jõesaar, Hein & Hagger, 2011, 2012; Ntoumanis, Taylor & Thøgersen-Ntoumani, 2012; Smith, Gustafsson & Hassmén, 2010; Vazou, Ntoumanis & Duda, 2006).

How can a sport environment be constructed so that it promotes an adaptive peer motivational climate? Many recommendations presented earlier in this chapter, designed to foster positive peer relationships, will be helpful. For example, teaching athletes how to encourage one another, directing them to focus this encouragement on effort and skill development, and involving peers in the instructional process as cooperative learners and/or peer tutors can cue young athletes to foster a task-involving peer motivational climate. Improvement, relatedness support, and effort become salient features of sport involvement that are reinforced by key adults and peers alike. Vazou et al. (2006) showed peer motivational climate and coach-created motivational climate constructs to be moderately correlated, suggesting the potential for key adults to institute strategies that ultimately become propagated through the athlete peer network. Team-building activities early in the athletic season, and reinforced throughout the season, offer the opportunity for peers to feel valued, accepted, and that their opinions matter within the group. Such team building should include occasions for informal exchange as well as activities outside of the sport setting (e.g., team meals, team outings). This can further build on perceptions of relatedness support. Finally, by teaching personal conflict management skills and attending to within-team conflicts immediately and equitably, unhealthy competitiveness, a rigid pecking-order based on athlete ability, and intra-team conflict can become less salient features of the peer motivational climate. In combination, these strategies maximize the potential for athletes to have an adaptive, high-quality youth sport experience.

CONCLUSION

Children can play an active part in determining the quality of their own sport experience. As team members and friends, they have the power to impact the learning and motivation of fellow sport participants. By attending to the principles of effective modeling, carefully training peer tutors, encouraging collaborative learning, and nurturing a sport setting that allows a task-involving peer motivational climate to emerge, significant adults such as coaches and parents can leverage peer relationship processes to generate positive sport experiences for young people.

LEARNING AIDS

1 Which social agent (coach, parent, peer) is most important to learning and motivation of young athletes?

A direct answer to this question is not possible. Many studies are designed to assess the "most" important social agent in predicting sport-related outcomes and physical activity behavior in young people. Yet, depending on personal factors (e.g., gender, skill level) and features of the specific sport context (e.g., coaching style, cohesiveness of a team, expected level of parent involvement), the answer will vary. A static answer is improbable because circumstances change, individuals develop, and therefore social agents vacillate in their influence over time. Moreover, it is the combination of relationships an athlete has with others that is likely most salient to outcomes of sport involvement. Regardless of the dominance of a particular adult in a young athlete's experience, for example, athletes train, compete, consult, commiserate, and experience sport with co-participants. There are few if any competitive sport experiences that do not involve peers.

2 How are friendships important to sport experiences of young athletes?

Friendships are important in a number of ways. Many young athletes become involved in sport because they wish to make friends. Friends offer help and support behavior during the learning process and competition, they serve as reliable allies in challenging circumstances such as playing for a difficult coach, they provide validation of worth, and they serve as behavioral models. Friendships can also consist of conflict, jealousy, and other less adaptive relationship features that impede an athlete's development. Therefore, key adults should work to develop sport settings that allow friendship development and that lead to encouraging, supportive interactions among peers.

3 Do peers serve as models of sportspersonship?

Yes. Just as physical skills can be acquired by observing others, so too can behaviors, attitudes, and values that pertain to issues such as cheating and aggression. By observing how teammates and competitors behave, and how they are rewarded and punished, athletes come to understand the written and unwritten expectations of sport involvement. Such behaviors include verbal communications and instructions that illustrate values, direct rule-breaking or prosocial behavior during play, and responses to rule-breaking such as making light of harm that is caused, blaming the victim, and displacing responsibility to others.

4   Explain how peers influence sport motivation of young athletes.

There are a variety of ways that peers can influence sport motivation. One is through behaviors that increase or decrease a young athlete's sense of competence. Motivation theories hold competence perceptions as central to motivational outcomes in achievement contexts like sport. Another is by influencing affective states such as enjoyment, which is linked to adaptive motivation, and anxiety, which can foster maladaptive motivation. Peers also may provide a sense of relatedness that is important to retention of interest and motivation in sport. They also can contribute to a sense of autonomy by, for example, showing pathways to skill improvement and buffering difficulties that stem from controlling relationships with adults in the sport setting. These processes can be influenced by the overarching motivational climate. When peers encourage one another, cooperate, value and accept one another, and reinforce effort, adaptive motivational outcomes are likely. When peers foster within-team competition, unsupportive behaviors can emerge that undermine athlete motivation.

REVIEW QUESTIONS

1   Define peer acceptance and friendship.

2   Identify and describe four dimensions of sport friendship quality.

3   Explain how peers can assist young athletes in learning sport skills.

4   Discuss how peers can shape attitudes about cheating in sport.

5   Discuss how peers can impact the motivation of young athletes.

EXERCISES

1   You have been recently hired by a gymnastics club to work with intermediate gymnasts, mostly ages 10 to 12 years. Though your gymnasts come with a basic skill set, they continue to require significant skill development and you would like to institute a cooperative learning strategy to facilitate athlete progress. Develop a written strategy and set of lesson plans that you will follow over your first three weeks of work with the gymnasts. Address the following matters: how you will pair athletes, how you will train athletes to be effective tutors or collaborative learners, how you will promote positive peer relationships, and how you will assess the effectiveness of your strategy.

2   You are the finalist for a position as head coach of an elite youth football club. The previous coach was released because of concerns about the performance of the team, which you are told can be traced to poor group cohesion. Your technical skills are well regarded, but so were those of the previous coach. The selection committee, therefore, is particularly interested in how you will address the interpersonal climate of the football club. The committee asks that you prepare an extensive response to share at your final interview. What will you communicate to the selection committee? In preparing your response,

develop multiple strategies for enhancing each of the following features of the peer motivational climate: improvement, relatedness support, and effort. Also develop multiple strategies for reducing debilitative intra-team competition and normative comparisons as well as intra-team conflict. Finally, describe how you intend to implement these strategies over your first month working with the club.

ADDITIONAL READING

Smith, A.L. (2003). Peer relationships in physical activity contexts: A road less traveled in youth sport and exercise psychology research. *Psychology of Sport and Exercise, 4*, 25–39.

Ward, P. & Lee, M.A. (2005). Peer-assisted learning in physical education: A review of theory and research. *Journal of Teaching in Physical Education, 24*, 205–225.

Weiss, M.R. & Stuntz, C.P. (2004). A little friendly competition: Peer relationships and psychosocial development in youth sport and physical activity contexts. In M.R. Weiss (Ed.), *Developmental sport and exercise psychology: A lifespan perspective* (pp.165–196). Morgantown, WV: Fitness Information Technology.

REFERENCES

Ames, C. (1992). Classrooms: Goals, structures, and student motivation. *Journal of Educational Psychology, 84*, 261–271.

Arripe-Longueville, F. (d'), Gernigon, C., Huet, M.L., Cadopi, M. & Winnykamen, F. (2002a). Peer tutoring in a physical education setting: Influence of tutor skill level on novice learners' motivation and performance. *Journal of Teaching in Physical Education, 22*, 105–123.

Arripe-Longueville, F. (d'), Gernigon, C., Huet, M.L., Winnykamen, F. & Cadopi, M. (2002b). Peer assisted learning in the physical activity domain: Dyad type and gender differences. *Journal of Sport & Exercise Psychology, 24*, 219–238.

Bandura, A. (1986). *Social foundations of thought and action: A social cognitive theory*. Englewood Cliffs, NJ: Prentice Hall.

Bukowski, W.M. & Hoza, B. (1989). Popularity and friendship: Issues in theory, measurement, and outcome. In T.J. Berndt & G.W. Ladd (Eds.), *Peer relationships in child development* (pp.15–45). New York: Wiley.

Coakley, J. (2009). *Sports in society: Issues and controversies*. New York: McGraw-Hill.

Darnis-Paraboschi, F., Lafont, L. & Menaut, A. (2005). A social-constructivist approach in physical education: Influence of dyadic interactions on tactical choices in an instructional team sport setting. *European Journal of Psychology of Education, 20*, 171–184.

Doise, W. & Mugny, G. (1984). *The social development of the intellect*. New York: Pergamon Press.

Dyson, B., Griffin, L.L., Hastie, P. (2009). Sport education, tactical games and cooperative learning: Theoretical and pedagogical considerations. *Quest, 56*, 226–240.

Ensergueix, P.J. & Lafont, L. (2011). Impact of trained versus spontaneous Reciprocal Peer Tutoring on adolescent students. *Journal of Applied Sport Psychology, 23*, 381–397.

Escartí, A., Roberts, G.C., Cervelló, E.M. & Guzmán, J.F. (1999). Adolescent goal orientations and the perception of criteria of success used by significant others. *International Journal of Sport Psychology, 30*, 309–324.

Gernigon, C., Arripe-Longueville, F. (d'), Debove, V. & Puvis, A. (2003). Situational indexes of achievement motivation, help-seeking, and performance: Influences of the learning context and gender differences. *Research Quarterly for Exercise and Sport, 74*, 473–479.

Gill, D.L. (1986). *Psychological dynamics of sport*. Champaign, IL: Human Kinetics.

Ginsburg-Block, M.D., Rohrbeck, C.A. & Fantuzzo, J.W. (2006). A meta-analytic review of social, self-concept, and behavioral outcomes of Peer-

Assisted-Learning. *Journal of Educational Psychology, 98,* 732–749.

Hartup, W.W. (1996). The company they keep: Friendships and their developmental significance. *Child Development, 67,* 1–13.

Holt, N.L., Knight, C.J. & Zukiwski, P. (2012). Female athletes' perceptions of teammate conflict in sport: Implications for sport psychology consultants. *The Sport Psychologist, 26,* 135–154.

Jõesaar, H., Hein, V. & Hagger, M.S. (2011). Peer influence on young athletes' need satisfaction, intrinsic motivation and persistence in sport: A 12-month prospective study. *Psychology of Sport and Exercise, 12,* 500–508.

Jõesaar, H., Hein, V. & Hagger, M.S. (2012). Youth athletes' perception of autonomy support from the coach, peer motivational climate and intrinsic motivation in sport setting: One-year effects. *Psychology of Sport and Exercise, 13,* 257–262.

Johnson, D.W. & Johnson, R. (2009). An educational psychology success story: Social inter-dependence theory and cooperative learning. *Educational Researcher, 38,* 365–379.

Johnson, M. & Ward, P. (2001). Effects of classwide peer tutoring on correct performance of striking skills in 3rd grade physical education. *Journal of Teaching in Physical Education, 20,* 247–263.

Keegan, R.J., Harwood, C.G., Spray, C.M. & Lavallee, D.E. (2009). A qualitative investigation exploring the motivational climate in early career sports participants: Coach, parent and peer influences on sport motivation. *Psychology of Sport and Exercise, 10,* 361–372.

Legrain, P., Arripe-Longueville, F. (d') & Gernigon, C. (2003a). Peer tutoring in a sport setting: Are there some benefits for tutors? *The Sport Psychologist, 17,* 77–94.

Legrain, P. & Arripe-Longueville, F. (d') & Gernigon, C. (2003b). Influence of trained peer tutoring on tutors' motivation and performance in a French boxing setting. *Journal of Sport Sciences, 21,* 539–550.

McCullagh, P., Law, B. & Ste-Marie, D. (2012). Modeling and performance. In S. Murphy (Ed.). *The Oxford handbook of sport and performance psychology.* Oxford: Oxford Press.

Newcomb, A.F. & Bagwell, C.L. (1995). Children's friendship relations: A meta-analytic review. *Psychological Bulletin, 117,* 306–347.

Ntoumanis, N., Taylor, I.M. & Thøgersen-Ntoumani, C. (2012). A longitudinal examination of coach and peer motivational climates in youth sport: Implications for moral attitudes, well-being, and behavioral investment. *Developmental Psychology, 48,* 213–223.

Ntoumanis, N. & Vazou, S. (2005). Peer motivational climate in youth sport: Measurement development and validation. *Journal of Sport & Exercise Psychology, 27,* 432–455.

Ommundsen, Y., Roberts, G.C., Lemyre, P.-N. & Miller, B.W. (2005). Peer relationships in adolescent competitive soccer: Associations to perceived motivational climate, achievement goals and perfectionism. *Journal of Sports Sciences, 23,* 977–989.

Riley, A. & Smith, A.L. (2011). Perceived coach-athlete and peer relationships of young athletes and self-determined motivation for sport. *International Journal of Sport Psychology, 42,* 115–133.

Robinson, D.R., Schofield, J.W. & Steers-Wentzel, K.L. (2005). Peer and cross-age tutoring in math: Outcomes and their design implications. *Educational Psychology Review, 17,* 327–362.

Schunk, D.H., Hanson, A.R. & Cox, P. (1987). Peer model attributes and children's achievement behaviors. *Journal of Educational Psychology, 79,* 54–61.

Smith, A.L. (2007). Youth peer relationships in sport. In S. Jowett & D. Lavallee (Eds.), *Social psychology in sport* (pp.41–54). Champaign, IL: Human Kinetics.

Smith, A.L., Gustafsson, H. & Hassmén, P. (2010). Peer motivational climate and burnout perceptions of adolescent athletes. *Psychology of Sport and Exercise, 11,* 453–460.

Smith, A.L. & McDonough, M.H. (2008). Peers. In A.L. Smith & S.J.H. Biddle (Eds.), *Youth physical activity and sedentary behavior: Challenges and solutions* (pp.295–320). Champaign, IL: Human Kinetics.

Smith, A.L., Ullrich-French, S., Walker, E., II. & Hurley, K.S. (2006). Peer relationship profiles and motivation in youth sport. *Journal of Sport & Exercise Psychology, 28,* 362–382.

Sullivan, H.S. (1953). *The interpersonal theory of psychiatry.* New York: Norton.

Topping, K. & Ehly, S. (1998). *Peer-assisted learning.* Mahwah, NJ: Lawrence Erlbaum Associates.

Ullrich-French, S. & Smith, A.L. (2006). Perceptions of relationships with parents and peers in youth sport: Independent and combined prediction of motivational outcomes. *Psychology of Sport and Exercise, 7,* 193–214.

Ullrich-French, S. & Smith, A.L. (2009). Social and motivational predictors of continued youth sport participation. *Psychology of Sport and Exercise, 10,* 87–95.

Vazou, S., Ntoumanis, N. & Duda, J.L. (2005). Peer motivational climate in youth sport: A qualitative inquiry. *Psychology of Sport and Exercise, 6,* 497–516.

Vazou, S., Ntoumanis, N. & Duda, J.L. (2006). Predicting young athletes' motivational indices as a function of their perceptions of the coach- and peer-created climate. *Psychology of Sport and Exercise, 7,* 215–233.

Vygotsky, L.S. (1934/1962). *Thought and language.* Cambridge, MA: MIT Press.

Weiss, M.R. & Amorose, A.J. (2008). Motivational orientations and sport behavior. In T.S. Horn (Ed.), *Advances in sport psychology* (3rd ed., pp.115–155). Champaign, IL: Human Kinetics.

Weiss, M.R. & Chaumeton, N. (1992). Motivational orientations in sport. In T.S. Horn (Ed.), *Advances in sport psychology* (pp.61–99). Champaign, IL: Human Kinetics.

Weiss, M.R. & Duncan, S.C. (1992). The relationship between physical competence and peer acceptance in the context of children's sports participation. *Journal of Sport & Exercise Psychology, 14,* 177–191.

Weiss, M.R., McCullagh, P., Smith, A.L. & Berlant, A.R. (1998). Observational learning and the fearful child: Influence of peer models on swimming skill performance and psychological responses. *Research Quarterly for Exercise and Sport, 69,* 380–394.

Weiss, M.R., Smith, A.L. & Theeboom, M. (1996). "That's what friends are for": Children's and teenagers' perceptions of peer relationships in the sport domain. *Journal of Sport & Exercise Psychology, 18,* 347–379.

Chapter 14

Audience influences on athlete performances

BERND STRAUSS AND CLARE MacMAHON

SUMMARY

Professional sports cannot exist without spectators or the audience, not least for economic reasons. Given that the audience is an integral part of sports, an obvious question is whether and how spectators in the audience can influence athletes' performances. To answer this question, it is useful to look at different situations in which spectators are present during athlete performances. For example, a very basic situation can be the mere observation of an athlete by a spectator, or a more complex situation where a stadium is filled with a crowd which supports their team and provides a home advantage. The purpose of this chapter is to present some models and ideas which will provide some insight into audience effects.

INTRODUCTION

In his writing, Polybius, one of the most important ancient Greek writers, mentioned an event which can be seen as one of the first reports of the impact of spectators on motor performance. His story is as follows (see e.g., Guttmann, 1986, p. 17f): On the occasion of the Panhellenic Games, 216 BC, the young and ambitious non-Greek boxer Aristonicus, from Alexandria, challenged the famous Greek boxer Clitomachus. During that time it was common for Greek audiences to support the underdog Aristonicus. At the beginning of the fight – against all expectations – Aristonicus was the superior fighter. He was dominating Clitomachus, who was considered invincible. During a break in the contest, Clitomachus turned to the audience and asked them to

show patriotism: As a Greek audience they should support the Greek boxer. From that point on, the audience cheered for Clitomachus who thereupon defeated Aristonicus.

Thus, since ancient times it has been commonly believed that supportive sport spectators can positively influence the performances of their athletes (e.g., a loud, supportive audience can inflate performance indices e.g., goals scored) of the home team. However, there are several instances which indicate that an audience does not have as large an impact as is supposed. A good example can be found in the Italian Premier Soccer Leagues in the 2006/2007 season. For safety reasons, 20 soccer games had to be played without an audience. If the crowd had a strong impact on performances of the home team, these spectator-less games should result in the home advantage disappearing and result in a performance decline for the home team. However, nothing happened, as concluded by Nils van de Ven (2011), a Dutch psychologist, who presented these data. There was no change at all in the win/loss statistics for games played in an empty stadium. This result also holds when comparing games in an empty stadium to games played by the home team in a stadium fully-packed with spectators.

These two examples of similar findings regardless of the presence or absence of an audience also reflect the wide range of ideas, theories and data that researchers have presented during the last decades while pursuing an understanding of audience effects on sports performance. The social support hypothesis suggests that spectators have a strong impact on the intended outcome of performance because of the encouragement they provide to the home team. On the other hand, supportive spectators can be responsible for a decrease in performance of their team due to the increased pressure athletes feel (the social pressure hypothesis or choking under pressure). A third position says that the influence of spectators in some sports on athletes' performances is very small, if existing at all (the so-called non-influence-hypothesis, Strauss, 2002a and 2002b). We will review each of these in this chapter.

OBJECTIVES

After reading this chapter the reader will be able to:

1 Describe different forms of spectator influence.
2 Describe the idea of social facilitation.
3 Describe different theories of spectator influence.
4 Describe the idea of a home advantage.
5 Explain the role of the audience in the home advantage.

SPECTATOR INFLUENCES

It is a common belief among athletes, coaches, referees, managers, spectators, and journalists that spectators can influence sports performance. Sometimes this belief is related to improvements (e.g. cheering by the home team or a more motivated runner) to deterioration of performance (e.g., by booing or other disruptive spectator behaviour).

Before we go into more detail, it is necessary to differentiate potential kinds of influences. The most basic differentiation is the one between a "trivial kind of influence" and "non-trivial kind of influence". A trivial influence is where the influence is obvious, for example, a spectator running on to the field to stop play or competition or attempting to assault a player. A terrible example of the latter is the on-court assault of famous tennis player Monica Seles in 1993 by a fanatic spectator. A non-trivial kind of influence is harder to account for, and thus needs to be explained and embedded in psychological or sociological theories. This means that the explanation of the influence is not trivial, is probabilistic in nature, and has theoretical and empirical support. In this chapter, we give an overview of this non-trivial influence.

To continue to discuss spectator influences in a general sense, we can go back to 1935 when Dashiell published a list of potential kinds of non-trivial influences exerted by people on performers. Dashiell's list is useful to derive ideas for potential areas to study in this field.

Table 14.1 *Influence of other persons on performers according to Dashiell (1935)*

1   A passive audience
2   Other persons as co-actors, not in competition with the actor
3   Competitors
4   Other persons as evaluators (e.g. referees and judges)
5   Other persons who work together with the actor, e.g. team colleagues
6   Other persons who control information given to the actor (e.g. coaches, trainers who are giving feedback)
7   Prestigious and large audiences

This list reflects a wide range of possible spectator behaviours but numbers 1 to 4, and number 7 are the main relevant topics for this chapter. Dashiell started with passive spectators who are merely present and do not act in any way (1), he then introduced coactive performers as spectators (2) and went on to include competitors as yet another kind of spectator. Interestingly, these differentiations can be found in the social facilitation research.

Social facilitation research has been around for more than 100 years. The term "social facilitation" itself goes back to the seminal work of Allport (1924) and implies "an increase in response merely from the sight or sound of others making the same movement" (Allport, 1924, p. 262). Allport mainly looked at 'coacting' situations, in which other persons are doing exactly the same tasks as the performers (no. 2 in Dashiell's list), such as rowers in a boat or pupils in a classroom. This means, social facilitation research is not restricted in the kind of the tasks, which are considered (e.g. all kinds of cognitive tests or motor tasks).

Strauss (2002a) gives an overview about social facilitation research, in particular with respect to motor tasks. However, the first empirical study using motor tasks was conducted by Norman Triplett (1898). He observed what happened when coacting persons were competing with his participants (no. 3 in Dashiell's list). He started by examining archives containing outcome statistics for the cycle racing season of 1897. These revealed that racing cyclists accompanied by pacemakers were at least 25% faster than those without.

Triplett proposed that this was because the physical presence of another person sharpened the competitive instinct. He tested this preliminary assumption more precisely with an experiment in which school children had to turn a handle as quickly as possible on his specially constructed "competition machine". Some children benefited from the presence of others, others clearly did not.

During the last century many theories have been proposed to explain Triplett's findings and why some athletes benefit from the presence of others and other athletes do not. However, the biologically-oriented model by Robert Zajonc (1965) was a real breakthrough. Zajonc postulated that his model was true for each species. The basic assumption was that the mere presence of a spectator (see no. 1 in Dashiell's list) of the same species would cause a non-specific increase in activation as an innate reaction of the organism, preparing it to respond to any potential unexpected actions by others. This enhanced activation level should increase the probability of the so-called dominant reactions and, in contrast, decrease the probability of subordinate reactions. Zajonc understood dominant reactions as those reactions to a specific stimulus situation that have priority over the others in a person's repertoire of behaviours. In simple or well-learned tasks, the dominant reaction is a correct solution. Therefore, the mere presence of others leads to performance increments of simple tasks. In complex tasks that were not well-learned the dominant reaction tends to be an incorrect execution of the correct motor skill. This means that performance in this situation is influenced negatively by the presence of others. This elegant model had a huge impact on research as it could explain confusing and controversial results within one model. It is notable that already the mere presence of other spectators can lead to significant performance changes.

Many researchers were attracted by Zajonc's model and used it to explain audience effects of merely present spectators in motor performance. In the following years many empirical studies as well as new models have been presented, among them are those which assume that the described social facilitation effects only occur if a human being shows evaluation apprehension, alertness and monitoring or others which present a self presentation process as explanation for the effects (e.g., Strauss, 2002a gives a deeper insight into these models).

In no. 4 in his list, Dashiell noted sport judges who evaluate independently and non-emotionally (e.g., referees, see our other chapter within this textbook) or spectators who provide specific emotional comments (e.g., spectator behaviour, like cheering or booing to support or discourage performers, see no. 4). As far back as 1924, Gates ascertained that spectator encouragement enhanced performance on, among others, a motor task. However, why should supportive behaviour have such positive effects? These effects could also be explained in terms of, for example, learning theory through the principle of positive reinforcement. It could be assumed that supportive spectators may enhance performance through the process of social support and would increase the exertion and motivation of the performers. This should have mainly positive effects on performances in tasks which are mainly dependent on the extent of aerobic and anaerobic parameters like in endurance, speed and strength-related tasks. These kind of tasks can typically be mainly mastered successfully by investing a considerable amount of energy. With respect to Zajonc (1965) these tasks can be viewed as being either simple or well-learned. Participants generally exhibit only quantitative differences in performance, for example, running faster or lifting heavier weights, but not qualitative differences which are typical for coordination tasks like balancing, gymnastics or others (see Strauss, 2002a for more details).

Dashiell's list starts with quiet and passive spectators (no. 1) and ends with a huge crowd in a stadium during a game or event which gives multiple frequently emotional reactions (no. 4) related or not-related to the individual or team performances (no. 7). This seventh type of scenario is highly relevant for this chapter.

The seventh category of prestigious and large audiences is mostly discussed with respect to the obvious home advantage individuals and teams have if they are performing in the presence of a huge, loud, and supportive crowd. The common belief about the strong influence of spectators is often based on anecdotal evidence and that the audience is mainly responsible for that home advantage. However, anecdotal evidence or an unsubstantiated belief is not empirically-based knowledge and we next discuss this in more detail. As the reader will see, we will come back to some issues, which are related to no. 1 (passive audience) and no. 4 (other persons as evaluators such as referees or judges) categories of spectators in Dashiell's list.

THE HOME ADVANTAGE

The home advantage is one of the best-documented phenomena in sport psychology. Generally, it is defined as the higher probability of completing a sport competition successfully under "home" conditions, which means, for example, in "one's own" stadium, or in "one's own" country.

In team sports like basketball, soccer, hockey, and football, the home team is said to have an advantage when they win more than

50% of their home games (see Courneya & Carron, 1992). This measure (number of games won of all games played at home) is called an absolute home advantage. However, there are some other possible measures of the home advantage. For example, the number of points won (e.g. if the winner receives three points, and for a draw both teams get one point); the relative home advantage (percentage of games won, of all decided games); goal differences, or other performance-based measures. In individual sports, other measures may be more appropriate, such as rankings. Regardless of different measures, it can be argued that the home advantage can be empirically found in every team sport, but not in every individual type of sport like racing, tennis, or ice-skating.

The first study on home advantage using archival data was done by Schwartz and Barsky (1977), who examined home advantage in baseball, American football, and other sports. One of their findings was that a key factor in the actual home advantage is the strength of both competitors.

In subsequent years after Schwartz and Barsky's (1977) work, in several seminal papers Bert Carron and Richard Pollard as well as Alan Nevill (e.g. Courneya & Carron, 1992; Nevill & Holder, 1999; Pollard & Pollard, 2005) provided strong empirical evidence for a home advantage around the world and in several team sports. However, they found that the size of the home advantage depends on the region and country and the specific kind of sport: For example, a weak home advantage is found in baseball, meaning that while it is an advantage to play at home, it is not a very strong effect. Higher rates of home advantage occur in American football, ice hockey, basketball and the highest rate is in soccer. However, the home advantage in soccer has significantly decreased over the last 100 years (in soccer they examined the English premier league) whereas in World Series Baseball and NFL American football it has remained constant. Gender is also a factor in the strength of the home advantage. A new study by Pollard and Gomez (2012) shows that the home advantage in the European female Premier Soccer Leagues also exists, but it is much smaller than in the parallel male soccer leagues.

In a summary of published empirical data in a recent meta-analysis, Jamieson (2010) showed that the overall home advantage in men for several team sports like soccer, hockey, basketball and baseball in total is close to 61% (relative home advantage). However, there is a wide range with respect to different sport types, which supports the pattern of the already reported studies by Carron, Pollard or Nevill. For example, in baseball the home advantage is the smallest with 55.6% of home games won. Jamieson further reports rates for American football (57.3%), basketball (62.9%) and for soccer (67.4%). The latter is the highest home advantage score Jamieson found.

EXPLANATIONS FOR THE HOME ADVANTAGE

Numerous explanations for the home advantage can be found in the literature. A conceptual framework for potential reasons for the home advantage such as spectator influence, psychological factors, or favourable home rules (e.g. ice hockey home team has last line change so home team coach can get favourable match ups) has been provided e.g. by Courneya and Carron (1992). They also include travel factors (e.g. length of journey to stadium, travelling through time zones), familiarity with the stadia, and the judgment bias in referees. Meanwhile, it is often discussed that referees' biases could be the most relevant reason for the empirical evidence of home advantage in all team sports. In our chapter on referee decisions (see Chapter 15, The psychology of decision making in sports officials, this text) we present some evidence for this. There could also be psychological explanations. Some correlative surveys have shown that athletes associate different expectations with a home or an away game, and that this results in differences in their motivation. For example, basketball players feel more motivated in home games due to the support of their fans and they report more self-confidence. This self-confidence is assumed to originate from the fact that the location of the game triggers expectations and, in particular, efficacy expectations regarding the impending performance. The idea here is that athletes themselves anticipate an advantage in a home game or a disadvantage in an away game, which then influences the way that they play.

HOME ADVANTAGE AND THE CROWD

Despite previous discussion, the most frequently discussed factor in the home advantage is the spectators. Spectator influence is discussed in terms of the number of spectators, crowd size, density, and concrete spectator behaviour. The idea of most crowd studies is to show empirical evidence for the social support hypothesis. As already pointed out, this assumes that spectator behaviour initiates a process of social support that as a consequence leads to better performance. This is the most popular hypothesis.

One frequent assumption within the social support hypothesis of audience effects is that a greater number of spectators represents an advantage for the home team, and a disadvantage for the away team. The argument is that a large number of spectators generates stronger social support for the home team (e.g. through a greater intensity of supportive behaviour) and, simultaneously, social rejection for the away team. However, many of the archival studies (which use recorded statistics on performance and crowd sizes) found that there are no or only very low correlations between the absolute number of spectators in a stadium and the outcome of the match. This result also holds for the audience density. Using the social support hypothesis, some researchers have argued that a higher density (the total number of spectators divided by the capacity of the stadium) is a better predictor for home advantage, where a fully packed stadium gives more support. However, this has not been shown empirically by many researchers (see Strauss, 2002b for an overview).

Looking at empirical studies directly investigating the influence of overt spectator behaviour (cheering, booing, and aggressive behaviour) on motor performance, or players' behaviour in team sports, one can notice that the number of studies is fairly small. Greer (1983), for example, used observation to study the influence of booing in American basketball teams (the number of fouls, turnovers, and baskets). When booing occurred for at least 15 seconds during a game, the following five minutes were labelled the "booing interval", otherwise it is called the "regular interval". Booing generally followed referees' decisions against the home team, or actions by the away team. Greer showed that neither home nor away teams profited significantly from booing on the performance variables of baskets and turnovers, but that there were changes in the number of fouls. In particular, spectator booing leads to significantly more foul assignments by the referee for the away team. Figure 14.1 shows the extent of this effect.

A similar study has been conducted by Strauss (2002b). However, he focused on the performance effects of supportive behaviour, in this case cheering in American football by using a longitudinal study within different home games. He did not find any influence of the cheering crowd on the performances during the specified intervals. Using an experimental approach Epting et al. (2011) also did not find any positive effect of cheering on performance accuracy in golf (a golf swing task), basketball (a free-throw task) and baseball (a pitching task) in comparison to a silent condition. However, they registered worst performances in the baseball pitching task after jeering only and in the golf task after jeering or cheering (in comparison to the silent

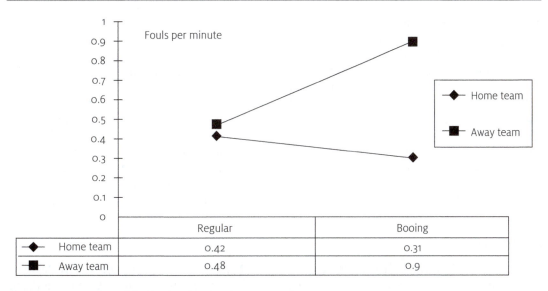

	Regular	Booing
Home team	0.42	0.31
Away team	0.48	0.9

Figure 14.1 Number of fouls after booing (Greer, 1983).

condition). Finally, spectator behaviour (cheering, jeering) didn't influence the number of successful basketball free throws, neither positive nor negative. The latter finding can support Greer's basketball results (1982) that booing does not have an impact on the performance variable (the number of baskets).

To sum up the research: The findings related to the home advantage on all of the social support factors mentioned (crowd size, density, booing and cheering) are rather inconclusive, and, on the whole, these factors alone are unable to explain the stability and robust strength of the home advantage, particularly in team sports. This means that the hypothesis of a non-influence (or at least of a very small influence, smaller than usually assumed) could be true.

Moreover, in particular cases some researchers have found evidence for the opposite to the support hypothesis, that a supportive crowd can have negative performance effects (see e.g. the already reported Epting et al. [2011] results concerning the chosen golf task). Despite a cheering crowd providing social support, performance may decline. However, the results of "choking-under-pressure" research (a deterioration of performances in pressure situations although the athlete is highly motivated) can

explain this result. Choking under pressure research predicts declines in performance when the spectators' anticipation of success results in social pressure.

The idea of crowds inducing choking under pressure came up in the seminal archival study of Baumeister and Steinhilber (1984) who showed that home teams lost their home advantage in the decisive finals of the NBA (basketball) and the World Series baseball finals. Not all of the subsequent studies confirmed these results, but we can assume that most athletes are highly motivated in a situation in which the home audience definitely expects success in a final game at home. This kind of social pressure can lead to unexpected decrements of performance.

In an interesting experimental study, Butler and Baumeister (1998) asked college students to perform difficult mental arithmetic tasks and computer games in front of a purportedly friendly audience, versus a neutral audience, versus an aversive audience, behind a one-way mirror. Results showed that performance was worst when actors believed that they were dealing with a friendly audience. Interestingly, actors felt happier and less stressed in front of this friendly audience, and preferred working on the task in this condition compared to the others. However, they produced poor performance in front of friendly faces. A new interesting study by McEwan, Martin Ginis, and Bray (2012) examines the situation and when choking effects occur. They investigated shootouts in NHL ice hockey. These occur when teams are tied in regulation play. In order to decide the winner, each team is given three one-on-one shots against the goal keeper. If the score is still tied after these shots, the teams are each given one more attempt until one team scores and the other misses, in subsequent 'best of one' rounds. This format creates two types of scenarios for shots. A loss-imminent situation is one in which a goal avoids a loss by creating a tie, but a miss results in a loss, and a win-imminent situation in which a goal by the shooter will lead to a win, and a miss will maintain a tie. The home advantage in shootouts only occurred when a team needed to score to avoid a loss (the loss-imminent situation). Otherwise a home disadvantage was more probable.

CONCLUSION

Keeping in mind Dashiell's list (Table 14.1), we can say that there is an abundance of evidence that these spectator effects exist in general in different fields. However, there is still much to be explored. Questions remain around the direction in which these effects work (positive, negative) and make the problem complex. In any case, research has shown that supportive behaviour does not necessarily lead to performance increments. Often, nothing happens or also decrements can also occur under certain circumstances. Several hypotheses have been put forth, with supportive and unsupportive findings, again indicating that this area of study continues to provide potential for further exploration.

LEARNING AIDS

1 Define trivial and non-trivial spectator effects.

Answer: A trivial spectator effect is obvious. A non-trivial spectator effect needs to be explained and embedded in a psychological or sociological theory. It is only probabilistic in nature, and has theoretical and empirical support.

2 Explain the effects of mere presence of spectators.

The basic assumption is that the mere presence of a spectator causes a non-specific increase in activation as an innate reaction of the organism. This enhanced activation level should increase the probability of the so-called dominant reactions and, in contrast, decrease the probability of subordinate reactions.

3 Define "home advantage" in team sports.

Generally, home advantage is defined as the higher probability of completing a sport competition successfully under "home" conditions, which means, for example, in one's "own" stadium, or in one's "own" country. In team sports the home team is said to have an advantage when they win more than 50% of their home games.

4   Define the non-influence hypothesis, the social pressure hypothesis as well as the support hypothesis of crowd influences.

On one hand, the social support hypothesis suggests that spectators have a strong impact on the intended outcome of performance. On the other hand, supportive spectators can be responsible for a decrease in performance of their team due to the increased pressure athletes feel (the social pressure hypothesis or choking under pressure). The non-influence-hypothesis is that the influence of spectators in some sports on athletes' performances is very small, if existing at all.

5   Define choking under pressure.

This means a deterioration of performances in pressure situations although the athlete is highly motivated. For example, pressure can occur if the athlete can receive a high reward, if the athlete anticipates failure, or in audience pressure situations.

REVIEW QUESTIONS

1   Explain Zajonc's theory in your own words.

2   Describe the variations of home advantage in different sports.

3   Describe Dashiell's list and give examples for each category.

4   Describe the "idea" of Greer's study about booing in team sports.

5   Explain the basic differences between the social pressure and social support hypotheses.

6   List possible reasons why a home advantage can occur.

EXERCISES

1   Create a study to measure supportive and non-supportive spectator behaviour.

2   Interview an athlete about the reasons why he or she feels better performing at home.

3   Collect statistical data from the latest yearbook of your favourite sports and calculate different measures of the home advantage.

4   Read the study by van de Ven and give a short report in your own words.

5   Study the effects of mere presence by your own experience. Ask a friend to perform in different situations and tasks, alone and in front of you. Compare the results.

ADDITIONAL READING

Carron, A.V., Loughhead, T.M. & Bray, S.R. (2005). The home advantage in sport competitions: Courneya and Carron's (1992) conceptual framework a decade later. *Journal of Sports Sciences, 23,* 395–407.

Guerin, B. (1993). *Social facilitation.* Cambridge: Cambridge University Press.

Pollard, R. (2006). Worldwide regional variations in home advantage in association football. *Journal of Sports Sciences, 24,* 231–240.

Schlenker, B.R., Philipps, S.T., Boniecki, K.A. & Schlenker, D.R. (1995a). Championship pressures: Choking or triumphing in one's own territory. *Journal of Personality and Social Psychology, 68,* 632–643.

Strauss, B. (1999). Wenn Fans ihre Mannschaft zur Niederlage klatschen. Lengerich, Germany: Pabst.

REFERENCES

Allport, F.H. (1924). *Social psychology.* New York: Houghton Mifflin.

Baumeister, R.F. & Steinhilber, A. (1984). Paradoxical effects of supportive audiences on performance under pressure: The home field disadvantage in sports championships. *Journal of Personality and Social Psychology, 47,* 85–93.

Butler, J.L. & Baumeister, R.F. (1998). The trouble with friendly faces. Skilled performance with a supportive audience. *Journal of Personality and Social Psychology, 75,* 1213–1230.

Courneya, K.S. & Carron, A.V. (1992). The home advantage in sport competitions: A literature review. *Journal of Sport and Exercise Psychology, 14,* 13–27.

Dashiell, J.F. (1935). Experimental studies of the influence of social situations on the behavior of individual human adults. In C. Murchison (Ed.), *A handbook of social psychology* (pp.1097–1158). Worcester, MA: Clark University Press.

Epting, L.K., Riggs, K.N., Knowles, J.D. & Hanky, J.J. (2011). Cheers vs. jeers: Effects of audience feedback on individual athletic performance. *North American Journal of Psychology, 13*(2), 299–312.

Gates, G.S. (1924). The effects of an audience upon performance. *Journal of Abnormal and Social Psychology, 18,* 334–342.

Greer, D.L. (1983). Spectator booing and the home advantage: A study of social influence in the basketball arena. *Social Psychology Quarterly, 46,* 252–261.

Guttmann, A. (1986). *Sports spectators.* New York: Columbia University Press.

Jamieson, J.P. (2010). The home field advantage in athletics: A meta-analysis. *Journal of Applied Social Psychology, 40,* 1819–1851.

McEwan, D., Martin Ginis, K.A. & Bray, S.R. (2012). 'With the Game on His Stick': The home (dis)advantage in National Hockey League shootouts. *Psychology of Sport and Exercise, 13,* 578–581.

Nevill, A.M. & Holder, R.L. (1999). Home advantage in sport. An overview of studies on the advantage of playing at home. *Sports Medicine, 28,* 221–236.

Pollard, R. & Gomez, M.A. (2012). Comparison of home advantage in men's and women's football leagues in Europe. *European Journal of Sport Sciences, 12,* 1–7.

Pollard, R. & Pollard, G. (2005). Long-term trends in home advantage in professional team sports in North America and England (1876–2003). *Journal of Sports Sciences, 23,* 337–350.

Schwartz, B. & Barsky, S.F. (1977). The home advantage. *Social forces, 55,* 641–661.

Strauss, B. (2002a). Social facilitation in motor tasks: A review of research and theory. *Psychology of Sport and Exercise, 3,* 237–256.

Strauss, B. (2002b). The impact of supportive sports spectators on performance in team sports. *International Journal of Sport Psychology, 33,* 372–390.

Triplett, N. (1898). The dynamogenic factors in pacemaking and competition. *American Journal of Psychology, 9,* 507–533.

Van de Ven, N. (2011) Supporters are not necessary for the home advantage: Evidence from same-stadium derbies and games without an audience, *Journal of Applied Social Psychology, 41,* 2785–2792.

Zajonc, R.B. (1965). Social facilitation. *Science, 149,* 269–274.

Chapter 15

The psychology of decision making in sports officials

CLARE MacMAHON AND BERND STRAUSS

SUMMARY

When we think of sport and sport psychology, we should not think only of the athlete and the coach. We should not only think of the athlete and the coach. A referee, judge, or umpire can have a profound impact on the outcome of a contest. In addition, officiating is a fascinating role through which we can continue to understand the influence of the environment on performance. This chapter reviews sports psychology and the sports official (referee, judge, umpire), considering the official as the performer. It reviews how judgments and decisions are influenced by the environment in a broad sense, where the athlete is part of this contextual influence. For example, it looks at how judgments differ depending on whether they are in the first or second half of a game; the colour competitors wear, and the positioning of the referee. It also examines the influences of reputation, and prior experience, where an influence can be built over time.

INTRODUCTION

The decisions of sports officials can have a profound influence on the outcome of a contest, with the soccer referee, for example, becoming a target for supporters' anger and frustrations. A famous example involves what has been called Argentinean football star Diego Maradona's "hand of God goal". In the 1986 FIFA World Cup, Argentina played England in the quarterfinals. Maradona jumped to contest a high kick against the much taller English goaltender (Peter Shilton), and illegally handballed the ball in to the goal, reaching it with his left fist. The Tunisian referee, Ali Bin

Nasser, did not see the handball, and allowed the goal in the 51st minute. After a second goal by Maradona, scored three minutes later, Argentina won 2-1, and went on to win the World Cup, beating West Germany in the final. Maradona commented later that the goal was scored "a little with the head of Maradona, a little with the hand of God". This goal is often relived, with video and analysis readily available on YouTube, and cited as an incident that has fuelled the rivalry between England and Argentina. Hindsight, and such analyses lead spectators to question the skills of referees ("how could he not have seen it?"). However, the complexity of the demands of officiating, and the social pressures that accompany these demands, create an extremely difficult task, and errors are inevitable.

Excellent calls by officials can also be difficult to celebrate as they often do not stand out, for example, when a potential controversy or problem has been narrowly avoided. In many sports, officials also strive to go unnoticed, knowing they have performed well when this is the case. Kenny Bayless is an example of a boxing referee who is considered one of the best, partly because he is never involved in any controversies, and stops fights at just the right moment. In boxing, as in many sports, referees who "let the fighters fight" or "let the players play" are considered to be doing their job. Despite their "invisibility", there are many examples of excellent and even admired officials, similar to Kenny Bayless. Pierluigi Collina, for example, was named by the International Federation of Football History and Statistics as the best referee of the last 25 years (http://www.iffhs.de, retrieved April 19, 2012). Collina was known for enforcing the rules, often using facial expressions, notable for his bald head and striking blue eyes. He was also known for his ability to understand players (see http://en.rian.ru/sports/20120124/170922 770.html, retrieved April 19, 2012), and was famously "too objective" and thus not bribeable. Putting our finger on exactly what makes these top officials so good can be very difficult, as there are tangible, more measurable (enforcing the rules), but also somewhat intangible (communicating with athletes, timing) skills. In this chapter we will begin to understand the complexities and influences on these skills.

OBJECTIVES

After reading this chapter, you should be able to:

1 Describe the different types of sports officials according to their demands.
2 Describe different factors that have been found to influence officiating judgment.
3 Explain and provide an example of "game management".
4 Describe the influences of conscious and unconscious processing on decision making.
5 Explain the evidence for the role of individual differences in officiating performance.

THE DEMANDS OF SPORTS OFFICIATING

Though often neglected, the role of the sports official is fascinating from a psychological point of view. First of all, though we may classify officials as one "group" within sport, there are many different types of officials. The type of sports official dictates the type of demand that he or she will face, whether emphasizing interaction with athletes, the ability to judge and perceive performance quality, or the need to be physically fit in order to move about the playing field.

If we think about sports officials, it is obvious that there are large differences between different types. For example, a gymnastics judge has a much different role to the soccer referee. In order to help deal with these differences and understand these roles from a psychological point of view, three main loose classifications have been devised (MacMahon & Plessner, 2008). These classifications are based on considering two main factors: the number of cues or athletes that the official is asked to keep track of or monitor, and how much interaction the official has with the athletes. Loosely, these two factors take in to account the perceptual and decision-making demands, as well as the physical, and interpersonal or communication demands.

Using these two factors to classify officials, the first category of official is termed the interactor. A classic example of the interactor is the soccer referee. This official is on the same competition surface as the athletes. In the case of the soccer official, this means that physical training becomes important to be able to move quickly to the most appropriate place and view the action for subsequent decisions. There is also a large amount of communication directly with the athletes in directing the play and enforcing the rules.

A second classification of official is the monitor. Monitors have very low movement and interaction demands, although they may on the other hand have very high perceptual demands and need to keep track of numerous cues or athletes. A perfect example of the monitor is the gymnastics judge, who is stationary while judging, but watching a complex set of cues such as a gymnast's feet, arms, body position, often during extremely fast-moving actions. In this case, perception and cognitive processing are emphasized, with few physical demands.

The final category captures the type of official who has low demands in terms of both the number of cues or athletes being monitored, as well as the movement about the competition space or interaction with athletes. The reactor official is exemplified by the tennis line judge, who is concerned mainly with the landing position of the ball, and will react to this cue with simple communication, and little to no interaction.

JUDGMENT AND DECISION MAKING

Keeping in mind the general demands of different types of officials, the key responsibility we associate with referees, judges and umpires, the responsibility we talk about, criticise and complain about, is judgment and decision making. To understand judgment and decision making in sports officials, it is useful to consider the different types of decisions officials are faced with. In some cases, sports officials are asked to evaluate performances and assign scores or marks, which are compared between competitors to determine the final winner. This is mostly the case for the monitor official, such as the figure-skating judge. In other cases, officials are asked to enforce the rules of a sport to ensure a fair contest, with the points and winners resulting from the actions in this contest. In this second case, characteristic of the interactor official, like the rugby referee, it is useful to further distinguish between two types of rules.

Constituent rules are the written rules of the game or sport. In basketball, the written rules dictate that it is a non-contact sport. In practice, however, the normative or unwritten rule, is that contact is allowed unless it is excessive (when a foul may be called). Some written rules are clear cut and are not changed, or normalized depending on the situation. One example is rules that require perception, but little judgment, such as the offside rule in soccer, which may be applied by the assistant referee, a monitor official. Similarly, context does not have a strong bearing on the rule that a tennis player's foot may not be over the line when serving the ball. (We will see later that, although these rules may be more clear cut, they are still vulnerable to error.) There are also rules that are clear cut because they involve the safety of athletes, and similar to the positioning rules described above, require no interpretation and may not be influenced by context. An example is when a player is deliberately and obviously tripped in soccer, as in the case of an ankle tap from behind, which will always result in a direct free kick. Having mentioned context, let us now examine how it can influence some decisions.

CALIBRATION AND GAME MANAGEMENT

Beyond the fact that context can be used to shift a constituent rule towards a normative rule that becomes "accepted practice", context also plays a part in changing decisions case by case in officiating. In particular, there are two specific effects that have been shown. The first effect is called calibration. When asked to make a judgment, we, as humans often need a reference point. For example, if you are asked to judge how big a given sports ball is, you will find it easier if you first see three other balls. A tennis ball is smaller than a volleyball, medicine ball, and soccer ball. It is bigger, however, than a table tennis ball, a squash ball, or a golf ball. Although we are not aware of it, we subconsciously help ourselves out in making these judgments. To explain, if the process of judging the size of sports balls is more detailed, and you are asked to use a rating scale where "1" is "small" and "5" is "large", then you may start out by rating the tennis ball as a "3". Though you may not be doing this explicitly and consciously, choosing the middle of the scale for the very first item you see gives you the room to move either up or down the scale, depending on what comes next.

What does rating the size of sports balls have to do with officiating? This calibration process, which is used in many judgments such as attractiveness, also happens in officiating. Officials use different reference points depending on things like the standard of play (Unkelbach & Memmert, 2008). Although the rules are the same for the most part, a referee does not officiate an under 12s soccer game the same way she would officiate the finals for a senior women's international tournament. Different aspects of the game may be emphasized and different levels of aggression may be tolerated (MacMahon & Plessner, 2008). This is a case where the level of play may drive the different normative rules that are necessary and applied. To make adaptations, however, the soccer referee cannot simply sit back and watch the players play first to get an accurate idea of the level of play and establish a reference point. But they do calibrate automatically and subconsciously. A study of soccer referees showed that the way that officials call fouls differs in the first and second halves of the game (Unkelbach & Memmert, 2008). Specifically, officials award fewer yellow cards earlier in games. Similar to rating a tennis ball as a "3" on the size scale because it is the first ball encountered, in the first half, referees "get a feel for the game", and avoid extreme decisions (e.g., awarding a yellow card). This means that they will have more flexibility to call more yellow cards later, as they adjust to the game.

A second highly influential effect that is proposed to work in combination with calibration is game management. In contrast to calibration, game management can be a conscious process, where an official uses context to guide judgments and decisions. Game management has been referred to as "the art" or "craft" of officiating. Contingency decisions are an example of decisions that show that game management may be both conscious and unconscious.

Several studies have shown that referees are more likely to award a penalty to one and then the other team, rather than two penalties in a row against the same team (e.g., Plessner & Betsch, 2001). They are also more likely to award a penalty if they have not awarded one in the previous situation in which one could have been awarded. In this way, penalties are balanced out, and previous decisions have an influence on subsequent decisions (decisions are *contingent* on the context and previous decisions, explaining the term contingency decisions).

Game management is seen as "reading the game"; a soft, intangible skill. Officials assess the action taking place, but make use of the context of decisions, and shift from more objective standards to more subjective standards, in the search for *fairness*, and to manage the contest. It is also of course important to note that game management *influences*, but does not *drive* decision making on the part of officials. An example of game management is preventive refereeing, where a rugby referee might tell a player that she is offside, and give the player the opportunity to get in an onside position before a penalty is called and the game is stopped. Similarly, a referee may use game management to prevent the escalation of violence. This conscious process is also highly advantageous over time, as officials inevitably encounter rule changes, such as a change to allow lifting in the line-out in rugby.

PREVIOUS EXPERIENCE (EXPECTATIONS)

When we examine the number of cues or athletes a given sports official must keep track of, as we considered when we discussed the classification of officials, it is clear that some officials have a great deal to process. For example, for the rugby referee, there are 30 players on the field, who are often in close proximity to each other, obstructing a view of the ball, and can move quickly and unexpectedly, and are often also acting deceptively to fool their opponents. Our minds naturally make difficult situations like these easier by taking short cuts, sometimes when we don't even know it. We fill in the blanks with our expectations. This is shown in general psychology with the classic case (see Figure 15.1) where an incomplete letter in one context (between the letters "B" and "T") is read as an "A" (to form the word BAT), and in another (between the letters "S" and "E") as an "H" (to form the word SHE). Sports officials, though they are not often conscious of it, do the same thing, using the context and their expectations to fill in information when they are making difficult assessments.

In gymnastics competitions, the stronger gymnasts are often put at the end of the within-team order. This is because coaches are aware that judges need to calibrate, as we have discussed, with more conservative scoring early, and higher scores and more flexibility preserved for later in the flight. A study of gymnastics judges shows that the order in which a gymnast competes creates an expectation which influences how they are judged (Plessner, 1999). Using video presentation of gymnastics routines, researchers found that when these routines were shown in fifth posi-tion, they were scored higher than when these exact same routines were shown in the first position. It is important to keep in mind that in this study, the first and fifth routines were highly similar. Thus, much like the effects of game management, expectations based on order of presentation were not driving the assessments, but simply used as additional information that influenced assessments. Moreover, this effect was shown for the events that are more perceptually difficult for processing because they are fast moving (vault, pommel horse, high bar). In events where there is more time to process information (rings, floor, parallel bars), these expectations

Figure 15.1 Context influences perception: the middle letter is interpreted as an "H" in one context, and an "A" in another.

were not influential. The slower moving events did not create the same gaps that needed to be filled with the extra information from the order of presentation and expectation that the later athletes would be more skilled.

Similar to the within-team order effect, a study in figure skating showed that reputation creates an expectation that also has an influence on judging (Findlay & Ste-Marie, 2004). In this case, judges who were aware of figure skaters' positive reputations awarded higher scores to these athletes compared to judges who were not familiar with the skaters. This prior experience with an athlete does not necessarily have to be built up over a long period of time, however. Yet another study in gymnastics shows that simply watching a

warm up can build expectations that influence judgments of specific moves (Ste-Marie & Lee, 1991). The study used videos of specific moves to simulate judges passively watching warm up and then judging competition. It showed that watching this warm up had an influence on judgments. When there was a difference between how moves were performed in warm up compared to competition, judging was less accurate. The warm up had a lasting influence by improving competition scores for moves that were performed better at warm up, and decreasing scores for moves that were performed worse at warm up. The warm up performance created an expectation for the quality of the moves, which drove the assessments during competition.

POSITIONING

As we discussed, prior processing and expectation effects seem to arise predominantly in perceptually difficult situations such as assessing a fast-moving pommel horse routine. This emphasizes the importance of the information that is used to make assessments for officiating, and how this information is taken in by the official. Although monitors like gymnastics and figure skating judges are mainly in a fixed position to view the action, interactors, and some reactors (e.g., the assistant referee in soccer) may change their location. Positioning has been shown to be important for all officials, but is arguably more of a challenge for those with greater movement. Indeed, the most notable case in which positioning has been shown to have an influence on perception and subsequent decisions is that of the soccer assistant referee.

A player in soccer is considered to be in an offside position if he or she is nearer to the opponents' goal line than both the ball and the second last defender at the moment the ball is played by a team member. The assistant referee judges offside from the sideline, by positioning him or herself in line with the second last defender (the last defensive player before the

goal keeper). When there is an error in judging offside, it can be either a flag error (calling offside when a player is onside) or a non-flag error (neglecting to call offside).

The nature of the offside rule means that the offside line is constantly changing with the movement of the players and the ball, requiring the assistant referee to also adjust position. A study by Dutch researchers found that Assistant Referees (AR) make errors in judging offside because they are often out of position, frequently too far behind the last defender and offside line (Oudejans et al., 2000). The interesting part of the study is that the researchers were able to predict the type of error (flag error, non-flag error) depending on the area of the field where the action takes place (near versus far from the assistant referee, and inside or outside of the defender; see Figure 15.2). The position of the AR and the players specifically influences the projection of the scene viewed on the eye's retina (the retinal image), with players perceived either erroneously behind or erroneously in front of the offside line when the AR is positioned incorrectly to start with. Assistant referees' decisions thus directly reflect the situations as

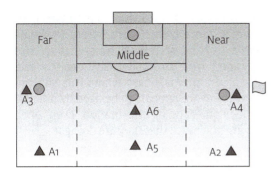
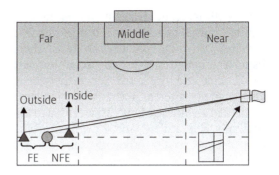

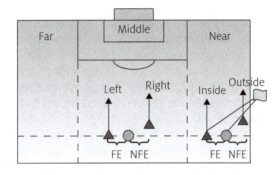

Figure 15.2 Oudejans and colleagues show how the position of the assistant referee on the sideline influences the perception of player positions and offside situations.

Source: Oudejans, R.R.D., Verheijen, R., Bakker, F.C., Gerrits, J.C., Steinbrückner, M., & Beek, P.J. (2000). Errors in judging 'offside' in football: Optical trickery can undermine the assistant referee's view of this ruling. Nature, 404 (6773), 33.

they are projected on their retinas, showing how important correct positioning is. As mentioned, positioning is also important for relatively more stationary officials, and thus we note that similar effects of the viewing position on decisions have been found in gymnastics and baseball. The main message then, is that even experienced officials are influenced in a predictable way by basic perceptual illusions as they can be created by imperfect viewing positions.

The fact that positioning can lead to missing information is also explicitly shown in the use of an extra video referee in some sports. For example, in rugby league and rugby union, when a potential try has been scored, but the ball and players are obstructed, the decision is put to a referee who can use video replay from multiple angles, essentially using a number of positions to gain more information.

COLOURS

We have discussed how expectations of performance can be based on previous experience, knowledge of the athletes, or the structure of competition, which then have an influence on judgments. A more general factor that influences judgments is the colour that competitors wear. This influence draws on cultural interpretations and associations for colour that exist outside of experience with the sport or athletes. In a fascinating study in tae kwon do, referees were shown videos of an athlete in blue competing against an athlete in red. These two athletes were well matched (Hagemann, Strauss & Leißing, 2008). The athlete in red, however, was awarded 13% more points. The researchers tested what would happen if the red athlete was now in blue and vice versa. When the videos were digitally altered, a change to red gear resulted in an increase in points awarded to the originally blue athlete, and a change to blue gear resulted in the originally red athlete's points decreasing. Tae kwon do is a martial art in which the athletes score points for being more active and aggressive; traits that are also associated with the "aggressive" colour red. Once again, this is a case where this subconscious influence appears to be used by officials to fill in the gaps in information, even when they are not aware that they are doing it.

SOCIAL PRESSURES

The home advantage is the benefit that is seen to be enjoyed by the team or athlete who is competing at their home venue. We have learned from the chapter on audience influence (see Chapter 14, this volume) that audiences do not have a strong direct impact on the home advantage. However, some researchers discuss the role of the referee in the home advantage, examining decisions for the home and away teams or athletes. Mainly they argue that either the audience gives cues to the referees (e.g., in the case of a foul) which mostly favour the home team or the audience is responsible for the social pressure, at least in part.

An English study showed a group of referees videos of soccer action for which they were asked to call fouls (Nevill, Balmer & Williams, 2002). When the videos were accompanied by crowd noise, the referees called fewer fouls for the away team, giving the home team the advantage. When they compared this to the actual foul calls in the game from which the videos were taken, this mirrored the on-field referees' behaviours. Similarly, Unkelbach, and Memmert (2010) confirmed this result by investigation of the referees' use of yellow cards. Dohmen (2008) also showed that the home team was given an advantage by the referee by calling more stoppage time when the home team was losing compared to when the home team was winning, suggesting that this gave the home team more opportunity to score. It seems, then, that officials are influenced by crowd noise. The details of this are currently being investigated, however, as a developing area of research.

As well, further study of the home advantage in soccer shows that there are individual differences, with some referees exhibiting more differences in home and away penalties than others. One individual difference that has been shown to have an impact is the ability to cope with social pressure. For some referees a larger crowd led to a stronger home advantage effect than for other referees (Boyko et al., 2007). A second factor is how much experience the referee has. More experienced referees have been found to show less home advantage in their decision-making behaviours (Boyko et al., 2007). The combination of these two factors has a strong link with research on choking and expertise in sport.

Our discussion of the impact of crowd noise highlights that officials, like athletes, have performance demands and must navigate performance barriers. Simply learning a skill does not guarantee its performance. The role of attention becomes quite influential. To explain, when we first learn a skill, we think a great deal about it. For example, when we learn to tie our shoes, we may learn it in a few steps (make one loop, make a second loop, cross them over and pull through). We pay close attention to these steps, completing them very deliberately in order to complete the action of tying our shoes. As we gain experience, we consider tying our shoes to be one action, not separate parts. What's more, we no longer need to pay attention to the action, and can talk to someone at the same time that we tie our shoes, and do it quite quickly. This skill becomes so automated, that if we then try to go

Figure 15.3 Football referee.

Figure 15.4 Basketball referee.

back to thinking about it, and break it down in to its separate parts, we actually now find it difficult. The skill has become automated, and thinking about it too much now interferes with letting it run off on its own.

This process of how a skill that is automated is disrupted when we consciously pay attention to it is what some researchers think is behind the phenomenon of choking. The idea is that, although a basketball player can be an excellent free throw shooter in practice, once that same player is in a high pressure situation in a game, she may now start to think too much about the mechanics of her free throw, and now perform much worse because she is de-automating an otherwise automated skill. Some individuals seem to choke under pressure more than others, however. Some researchers have devised a scale that can be used to indicate whether someone is more or less likely to choke under pressure (Kinrade, Jackson & Ashford, 2010). The scale is called the Reinvestment Scale, with the idea that under pressure individuals "reinvest" their attention and begin to consciously process.

The ideas around automated behaviour, choking, and reinvestment have also been applied to decision making. One important acknowledgment is that some decisions do require conscious processing, whereas others do not. For example, a referee may very automatically process player positions and call a penalty for offside, with little conscious thought. On the other hand, in preparing for the upcoming action, a referee may very consciously decide where to position himself or herself. Both of these types of decisions can be interfered with, however, with the tendency to think about them too much. In order to capture these differences, the Decision Specific Reinvestment Scale (DSRS) measures two factors that help identify individual differences. Decision Reinvestment measures whether someone has a tendency to involve conscious processing in automated decisions, which leads to interference, similar to our discussion above. For those decisions that need more conscious

processing, there can still be interference with too much thinking. This comes about when someone makes a poor decision or an error, and spends time thinking about this past decision. Now, the resources that can be used to make other decisions are taken up by ruminating on these past decisions. You can probably relate to this scenario, even if it's not as an official, but as an athlete. You make a poor decision – maybe you make a poor pass that is intercepted and the other team scores a crucial point. You are now thinking a great deal about this decision error and are thrown off your game for the next while. This tendency to ruminate over poor decisions is called Decision Rumination.

We can easily consider decision reinvestment and decision rumination for referees dealing with crowds. A vocal crowd can make the referee aware that decisions will be scrutinized, and lead to the tendency to think more about otherwise automated decisions in order to make sure they are "right". Similarly, a critical crowd may increase a tendency to think about past decisions, especially errors. Although more research is needed in this area, there is some evidence from a laboratory-based study that referees who score high in the tendency to ruminate about decisions (Decision Rumination) are more susceptible to crowd effects (Poulton, Siu & Masters, 2011).

As discussed, personality factors may in fact have an impact on decision making in officiating. This also underscores our earlier discussion regarding the complexity of officiating, underlining factors such as stress and self-confidence as influential for officials. Acknowledging this complexity again, factors such as motivation gain importance in light of the need for highly demanding training. Performance-related psychological skills training, with tools such as goal setting and imagery are also relevant in the training and performance of officials. We thus highlight that many other sections of this text can be applied to and relevant for the sports official, particularly when considered in combination with the classification of officiating types.

CONCLUSION

In conclusion, the sports official is an important, though often-neglected participant in sport. Though spectators frequently regard officiating as a straightforward task, there is evidence of many factors that influence performance, and complicate the role. Though there are certainly a variety of physical demands in officiating, and other areas of psychology are relevant, we have focused on decision making. We have identified both conscious and unconscious influences on decisions, as well as individual factors. As shown in this chapter, our understanding of officiating and performance is growing, and will continue to grow through the application of sports psychology.

LEARNING AIDS

1   Describe the two dimensions which are considered in classifying types of sports officials.

The amount of movement about the playing surface; amount of interaction with performers.

2   Define game management.

Game management is the use of context and a "feel for the game" in officiating decision making. It considers previous play, time of the game, and the flow and tempo of play.

3   Explain the process of calibration that takes place in officiating.

Soccer research shows that referees give fewer yellow cards in the first half of games. The explanation is that referees are calibrating to the game by "getting a feel" for factors like the level of play and the individual players, and also sometimes using verbal warnings. The number of yellow cards goes up in the second half. Gymnastics research also arguably shows a certain amount of calibration in that seeing a warm up influences assessments of moves that are seen later. Calibration is thus the idea of becoming attuned to the particulars of the competition and performances and is related to expectations.

4   Summarize the way in which expectations can influence officiating decision making.

Officials have been shown to be influenced by a number of factors that show the role of their expectations. Judgments are influenced, for example, by the reputation of the athlete, with higher marks for those with a better reputation (as a good performer). Because gymnastics coaches place their better performers at the end of the within-team order, judges have been shown to assign higher scores for performers who perform later. Their expectation that later performers are better has thus been shown to have an influence on scores. These influences are measurable and evident, however, they have been shown to influence decisions, not change them (e.g., from a decision to call a pitch a ball to calling it a strike). They illustrate that information is often missing when officials make difficult judgments, and that additional information is used, whether officials are aware of this or not, and even when the information used may be unrelated to performance (e.g., the colour a competitor is wearing).

5   Define "decision rumination" and "decision reinvestment".

Decision rumination is reflection on prior decisions; it is "rethinking" and "revisiting" previous decisions. Decision reinvestment is monitoring decision making and trying to understand one's own individual process of decision making.

REVIEW QUESTIONS

1 What are the main factors that are important when thinking about officiating skill that are presented in this chapter?

2 Considering the factors presented here, which would you consider individual differences, and which would you characterize as changeable from situation to situation?

EXERCISES

1 Work out a training programme for two different types of officials (e.g., an interactor and a reactor). Use the material in this chapter to justify the activities and emphases in your programme. Justifications should involve an analysis of the demands of the particular type of official: physical, interaction, rules and the emphases used in activities chosen.

2 Review the demands of the interactor official. Using the other chapters in this book, highlight three chapters that you would direct an interactor official to review as relevant for their role, explaining the particular aspects and why. Do the same for a monitor official. Justifications should show a reflection on demands such as the influence of crowd behaviours and stress, motivation for continued physical training, as examples.

ADDITIONAL READING

American Sport Education Program (Ed.) (2011). *Successful sports officiating* (2nd ed.). Champaign: Human Kinetics.

Bar-Eli, M., Plessner, H. & Raab, M. (2011). *Judgment, decision making and success in sport.* Chichester, UK: Wiley.

Poolton, J.M., Siu, C.M. & Masters, R. (2011). The home advantage gives referees something to ruminate about. *International Journal of Sports Science and Coaching, 6(4)*, 545–552.

Plessner, H. & MacMahon, C. (2013). The sport official in research and practice. In D. Farrow, J. Baker & C. MacMahon (Eds.), *Developing sport expertise: Researchers and coaches put theory into practice* (2nd ed), pp 71–92. London: Routledge.

REFERENCES

Boyko, R.H., Boyko, A.R. & Boyko, M.G. (2007). Referee bias contributes to home advantage in English Premiership football. *Journal of Sport Sciences, 25 (11)*, 1185–1194.

Dohmen, T.J. (2008). The influence of social forces: Evidence from the behavior of football referees. *Economic Inquiry, 46(3)*, 411–424.

Findlay, L.C. & Ste-Marie, D.M. (2004). A reputation bias in figure skating judging. *Journal of Sport and Exercise Psychology, 26*, 154–166.

Hagemann, N., Strauss, B. & Leißing, J. (2008). When the referee sees red. *Psychological Science, 19(8)*, 769–771.

Kinrade, N.P., Jackson, R.C. & Ashford, K.J., (2010). Dispositional Reinvestment and Skill Failure in Cognitive and Motor Tasks, *Psychology of Sport and Exercise, 11*, 312–319.

MacMahon, C. & Plessner, H. (2008). The sports official in research and practice. In D. Farrow, J. Baker & C. MacMahon (Eds.), *Developing elite sports performers: Lessons from theory and practice.* London: Routledge.

Nevill, A.M., Balmer, N.J. & Williams, A.M. (2002). The influence of crowd noise and experience upon refereeing decisions in football. *Psychology of Sport and Exercise, 3,* 261–272.

Oudejans, R.R.D., Verheijen, R., Bakker, F.C., Gerrits, J.C., Steinbrückner, M. & Beek, P.J. (2000). Errors in judging 'offside' in football: Optical trickery can undermine the assistant referee's view of this ruling. *Nature, 404 (6773),* 33.

Plessner, H. (1999). Expectation biases in gymnastics judging. *Journal of Sport and Exercise Psychology, 21,* 131–144.

Plessner, H. & Betsch, T. (2001). Sequential effects in important referee decisions: The case of penalties in soccer. *Journal of Sport and Exercise Psychology, 23,* 254–259.

Ste-Marie, D. & Lee, T.D. (1991). Prior processing effects on gymnastic judging. *Journal of Experimental Psychology: Learning, Memory, and Cognition, 17,* 126–136.

Unkelbach, C. & Memmert, D. (2008). Game management, context effects, and calibration: The case of yellow cards in soccer. *Journal of Sport and Exercise Psychology, 30,* 95–105.

Chapter 16

Media

ELSA KRISTIANSEN AND GILL LINES

SUMMARY

This chapter draws upon sociological and psychological research to consider media influences on the development of sporting attitudes and behaviours. The first part of the chapter introduces the global sport media complex and discusses ways in which media audiences, especially young people, may be influenced by the types of sport and sport stars they watch and read about.

The second part of this chapter elaborates upon how elite athletes cope with both journalists and sports reporting. While the best advice is to be understanding of the journalists' need for stories and inside information, media coverage is perceived as a constant stress factor for athletes, who work hard not to take it personally.

The chapter concludes with review questions for you to reflect upon how sports psychologists can educate young performers about media influences and help elite athletes to cope with media stress.

INTRODUCTION

Norwegian cyclist Kurt Asle Arvesen "almost" won the 17th stage of the 2005 Tour de France, but came second behind another athlete, Savoldelli, from Lance Armstrong's team Discovery Channel. In bike racing, the mixed zone (where athletes and journalists meet) starts when the riders are still in motion. Someone (usually from the team), grabs the bike to help riders to stop forward progress, and then immediately, the riders are surrounded by journalists. Arvesen had no recovery time, and the number of journalists surrounding him was incredible. Many were intrigued by his stoic calmness (and lack of obvious disappointment) at the time. Six years

later in a telephone conversation with Kristiansen about media pressures he reflected on the way fame may easily get to an athlete and underlined that: "It is vital to understand that sport is just something minor in a bigger picture, for me it is about passion of doing my favourite sport and the following lifestyle that I love and am able to live".

This example shows how an elite sport star today can face challenging demands from media reporters. Tears of joy and tears of disappointment have become an important aspect for sports reporters keen to personalise athletes' stories of success and failure in order to draw in audiences. The popularity of bike

Figure 16.1 Newspaper headlines can create different types of stress for elite athletes as well as draw the reader's attention to both positive and negative messages about the sporting performance and behaviour of sport stars.

racing in Norway can be attributed to the results of bikers like Arvesen, Hushovd and Boasson Hagen – in addition to the extensive media coverage of events like Tour de France.

As this suggests, the prolific growth of media sport products has opened up a wealth of opportunities for mass audiences to engage with a range of different global sports, stars and events. The extent to which individuals draw upon their media experiences to inform their attitudes, behaviour and performance in sport should be an important consideration for sports psychologists. Whilst significant others such as parents, teachers and coaches have been the foci of attention there has been relatively little research on the media. Yet the hours people spend watching and reading about sport suggests that the media has the potential to impact on everyone taking part in sport, not just elite athletes.

 OBJECTIVES

After reading this chapter you will be able to:

1 Discuss the role of the media as a significant other to influence sporting participation.
2 Identify how the sport media can shape young people's sport-related attitudes and motivations.
3 Describe how role models and gender stereotypes can impact on individual self-perceptions and sporting identities.
4 Explain media stress, coping strategies and its impact on elite athletes.
5 Discuss the impact of motivational climate on perceptions of media stress.
6 Identify and understand the relationship between sport journalists and elite athletes.

THE EFFECTS OF THE MEDIA ON AN INDIVIDUAL'S PERCEPTIONS AND BEHAVIOURS IN SPORT AND PHYSICAL ACTIVITY

The media sport complex, audiences and effects theory

The media is a prevalent part of everyday life and for many people the use of various media products forms an important leisure time activity. Certainly there has been global concern that media engagement has encouraged a sedentary lifestyle that limits time available for active pursuits. For some, mediated sports viewing exceeds time spent playing sport or taking part in physical activity and some know more about sport through watching televised events than through active participation.

The vast array of media products covering sport provide the audience with a wealth of images and messages about sport, physical activity, health and the body. As Boyle and Haynes (2009) indicate, the media sport complex is driven by a business relationship where sport has the potential to draw in huge audiences, and so the media buys sport events in the market place and promotes those sports, events and stars that it believes will attract the highest viewing figures. This has implications for minority sports, where there is little prospect to get to know more about the sport, and where interested participants may rarely have the occasion to see high-level performance. For instance, some sports such as netball, trampolining and badminton, which feature prominently in English Physical Education programmes, are rarely shown on UK terrestrial television.

In addition to the commercial dimension, the media sport complex affords a cultural context for the transmission of sporting values and ideals. Sport media discourses of sporting prowess, bravery and overcoming adversity, for example, are combined with tales of nation, class, gender and race. Images of the body too are prevalent and the sport media provides discourses about "ideal" athletic bodies. This has the potential to impact on an individual's perception of their own desired body image

and views about their suitability for sport and physical activity.

The production of media sport is a selective process with media professionals determining which sports to prioritise, which events to spectacularise, which stars to promote as celebrity icons and which narratives to amplify. Whilst there are some events that attract huge global audiences such as World Cup football finals and Olympic opening and closing ceremonies (see Billings [2008] for a discussion of viewing figures), local media coverage can be parochial and thus it is important to remember that national audiences can have different mediated experiences of sport. For example, whilst Arvesen may receive high coverage for his cycling exploits in Norway he is likely to receive less coverage in other countries where their national stars and most popular sports are more likely to dominate coverage. In the UK, for instance, male football and its stars generally dominate sports news coverage. Sport media research across the globe (Markula, 2009) also affirms the patriarchal nature of the terrain, where daily coverage given to male sports far exceeds that accorded to women. This may afford girls and women fewer opportunities to watch females in action and may limit female perceptions about the type of sports and physical activity that are acceptable for women to participate in.

Whilst the media has the potential to influence its readers or viewers there has been little sustained research into sport media audiences which has been able to empirically prove "effects" with regard to behavioural or attitudinal change towards sport and physical activity. Billings (2008) offers one attempt to examine media effects when watching an Olympic event but this focuses more on what the audience thought happened at the event rather than how the event actually influenced their sports participation. McQuail (2005) explains that media effects are of central concern when exploring the role of the media in society and discusses the different types of effects, both short and long term for example. Early theoretical approaches saw the media as all-powerful in shaping audience opinions and behaviour and there were attempts to scientifically measure changes but this has lost some credibility in recent years. Gauntlett (2008) provides a useful critique, highlighting a number of weaknesses with this theoretical approach. Clearly, the media works in different ways and individuals respond according to their own social backgrounds, experiences and cultural competencies. It is therefore important in this chapter to remember that the media can impact on individuals in different ways and actual media effects may be difficult to disentangle from the range of other influences exerted on an individual's sporting attitudes and behaviours. Recent trends in audience theory advocate that consideration should be given to how an individual might make use of the media and articulate pleasures and meanings gained from the experience. The following section provides some examples for you to consider.

How can the sport media shape young people's sport-related attitudes and motivations?

Common sense suggests that the sport media can have an impact on individuals. For example, research shows how during televised sports events some young people are encouraged to purchase the clothing of their favourite sports star or team, are motivated to take part in that sport and try to copy skills they admire (Lines, 2007). However, this does not automatically ensue and it is important for sports coaches, teachers and psychologists to consider how they might utilise sport media opportunities to help inform and motivate young people's sports behaviour and performance.

Socialisation is a process through which individuals learn the shared values and norms of a society or group. Tomlinson (2010) identifies the different roles of family and other

Figure 16.2 The televised sports experience in this photograph illustrates the opportunity for team and national identification and the modelling of sports-related behaviours.

institutions, such as the media, in the socialisation process. He also refers to socialisation in sport and clearly there are values and behaviours to be learnt about different sports cultures and groups. Lines (1999) illustrates below three ways in which the media can function as a sport socialising agency.

Firstly, as indicated above, engagement with sport media products can be inspirational. There is often an initial impetus to participate after watching a successful event or performance and young people make comments that suggest watching a successful performer or team play well can motivate them to go out to play that sport (Lines, 2007). The excitement generated by a mega-sporting event, such as the Olympics, can also have this same effect.

However, the impetus is not always sustained and enthusiasm can wane for a number of reasons, such as lack of immediate success, perceived incompetency in relation to elite performers and the absence of self-determination to continue. Individual personality traits may also determine whether an individual can act on the initial motivation and continue to sustain regular participation and enhance performance. Young people's comments (Lines, 2007) suggest that they can quickly become disillusioned at their inability to emulate high-level performance. Therefore, it is important for teachers and coaches to consider how self-confidence in an individual's own ability can be boosted and how the motivation to participate, initially generated through media engagement, can be sustained. These issues are more thoroughly covered in other chapters of this book (e.g., Chapter 2, 3, 4, 36).

Secondly, the media can function as a knowledge provider. In a positive way, engagement with sport media can, for example, provide knowledge about sports skills, tactics; develop aesthetic appreciation and awareness of Olympic ideals. This knowledge can in turn develop certain attitudes towards sport, enhance performance and heighten evaluation and appreciation of movement. However, the media can amplify violent sporting incidents and aggressive behaviour which, if emulated, may negatively impact on performers and spectators. Sports that are amplified by the media gain status and popularity. Thus, on a negative note, some sports, including popular recreational sports, can be marginalised in media coverage limiting the potential knowledge and enthusiasm that might be generated for that sport. Often the sport media experience is not overtly seen as an educational experience by young people who mainly tune in for the excitement of seeing their team or favourites win. Therefore the learning aspect may be undermined in the viewing process unless young people are given guidance in how to make best use of the sporting behaviours they see in order to improve their own performance.

The media too can promote discourses about health and lifestyles by providing public information and messages on topics such as obesity, inactivity risks and eating disorders. The claims made may not always be fully justified or critiqued and may encourage young people to think about their bodies, eating habits and lifestyles in particular ways which may or may not be helpful or realistic. Evans et al. (2008) provides further reading on this.

Thirdly, the media can provide a modelling function – it can promote a sense of belonging and identification towards a team or individual offering sporting role models whose techniques, dress and behaviour can be emulated. Hailed as an inspiration and role model for others, Sir Steven Redgrave, the British Olympic rower who won five gold medals, comments on the difficulty of determining the sources of inspiration in the desire to become a top level performer. However, he does allude to the potential of media sport stars: "To be honest, I can't tell you what inspired me. Not with absolute conviction. I can say that it might have been the Olympians I watched and admired on television when I was growing up…" (Redgrave, 2009, p.1).

Certainly, historically and in public discourses, sport stars have been perceived to have a responsibility as role models. Whilst there is some debate about the concept of the role model (Lines, 2001; Whannel, 2002; Gauntlett, 2008) "…the term continues to have a prominent profile in everyday parlance, a powerful presence in media and cultural industries, and a place in sport policy development" (Tomlinson, 2010, p.394–395).

Certainly, young people suggest that there are sport stars they consider worth looking up to, but they are also realistic and acknowledge that there are flawed sport stars whose behaviour they would not wish to emulate (Lines, 2002). For whilst sport stars are publicly promoted as role models they can, however, display negative sporting behaviour such as, aggressive on-field behaviour, rule breaking and drug taking. This does generate some concern that young aspiring performers may be encouraged to develop less positive sporting attitudes and values as a result of watching and reading about these stars. However, individuals are also influenced by significant others in their sporting lives and their social backgrounds will allow them to make their own readings of appropriate sporting behaviours.

Role models, gender stereotypes and individual self-perceptions and sporting identities

The last section began to consider role models and how the sport media is in a powerful position to promote a range of stars across varied sports and from different social divisions. The portrayal of sport stars has the potential to impact on individual self-perceptions and attitudes about aptitudes for particular sports. This embraces a range of features, such as how boys and girls across different social and cultural groupings (for example, gender, ethnicity, disability, sexuality) are encouraged to develop exercise adherence, how they learn about an athlete's role identity, and how they might perceive their body image in relation to varied forms of physical activity.

One aspect of sport media research highlights the role of the media in generating stereotypical representations of different social groups. Desmarais and Bruce (2010) identify how media language and imagery can contribute to cultural stereotyping in sport and implicate televised sport in the construction of national stereotypes, for example. As Tomlinson (2010, p.444) suggests, "Stereotyping of sports people according to cultural assumptions, physical features, or purported psychological characteristics is harmful, undermining the potential of individuals or groupings to develop sporting potential to the full".

There are several points to consider here. Firstly, the media may provide a limited range of role models from particular social groupings – for example, until recently there has only been marginal coverage of sport for those

with disability. In preparation for the London 2012 Olympics the British media strove to raise the profiles of athletes likely to compete in the Paralympic competition. Yet coverage is variable across countries and an internet broadcast station named ParalympicSportTV (see www.youtube.com/paralympicsporttv/) has been initiated to provide wider global access to images of disability sport. Although it is difficult at this stage to assess the implications of this, one possible outcome could be that such a raised status may provide young people with role models from a wider range of disabilities, taking part in a wider variety of sports. This may act to generate a motivational climate for an individual with disability, enhancing their self-belief that they can access opportunities in sport at all levels. Research by Hargreaves and Hardin (2009) has shown that simply offering more images may not necessarily be as positive as it appears if the framing of the athletes is limiting. Their study provides qualitative data from a group of female wheelchair athletes who discuss their pleasures and issues with sport media consumption. An important topic they raise is that intersections with gender and disability can make a lack of sport media representations a further problematic for females with disability.

Lines (2002) examines in more detail how young people's engagement with sport stars legitimises the bond between masculinity and sport and reveals that knowledge of, and affiliation with, female sport stars is limited. It is already well known that female adherence to long-term exercise and sports participation is more challenging than that for many males. Whilst this is often attributed to natural sex differences, girls engaging in sport experience a range of social contradictions with femininity. Markula (2009) provides a range of international perspectives on ways in which sportswomen are represented and this highlights how the media might be a significant player in accentuating tensions for females as they develop their own athletic identity. Whilst boys are provided with many images applauding masculine values and behaviour in sport, females who challenge the gender order and display overtly aggressive, powerful and muscular attributes may be marginalised, ridiculed, or even questioned about their sexuality. The most highly profiled female sport stars often conform to stereotypical images of heterosexual femininity and are shown in highly sexualised images. This too may have implications for girls' self-perceptions about the "ideal" athletic body shape and contradictions with their own body image. Additionally, media coverage infers that certain sports are "feminine-appropriate" and valued as more acceptable for women. For example, in the UK, female sports such as football, rugby and cricket rarely receive sustained media coverage and this may act to restrict girl's perceptions about, and participation in, competitive team sports. Certainly, there are far fewer female role models profiled in these sports in the British media. Conversely, males may also experience far fewer opportunities to view men performing in more aesthetic-type physical activities. Gender stereotyping by the media may then give males and females different values, beliefs and attitudes about their sporting identities.

Media coverage also provides the opportunity to view sportsmen and women from a range of different racial and ethnic backgrounds and how media professionals choose to represent different groups can be influential in the ways that individuals from these groups might think about themselves in sport. Indeed, as Sterkenburg, Knoppers and De Leeuw (2010, p.820) emphasise "the social power of televised sport is evident in the popularity of male sport stars like Usain Bolt or Thierry Henry, who may serve as role models and a source of empowerment for many black media users". Likewise the high profile of the tennis players Venus and Serena Williams may be motivational and raise perceptions that tennis is an accessible sport for other black girls.

However, Sterkenburg et al. (2010) and Billings (2008) review a number of studies which show racial or ethnic bias in sports reporting and there can be negative connotations when different ethnic groups are either over- or under-represented in particular sports or sporting roles, and when stereotypical explanations are given for sporting success or failure. This type of reporting may serve to make an individual question whether their own ethnicity will limit their competence in a particular sport as media commentary rarely draws upon social implications in athletic achievements.

To summarise so far, the sport media complex draws in vast audiences and without doubt there are a number of roles that the media can play as an individual develops their own values and views about their sporting identity. Whether the media has a moral obligation in the sporting content that it provides or whether the commercial aspect should be the key driver is a key question to be considered. Also, the exact power of the media to influence sporting attitudes and behaviour is still difficult to ascertain and further research with different audience groups is required. Finally, institutions of sport and sports practitioners need to develop strategies to deal with the issues raised so far. Lines (2007) identifies a number of recommendations for Physical Education teachers with regard to how young people can be educated to utilise the media to enhance their performance and also how to perceive the media in a more critical way. For example, children can be asked to reflect upon stereotypical comments or incidents of violent sporting behaviour reported in the media and discuss how this might impact on their own sporting behaviour and how they might adapt their behaviour in order to have positive outcomes on their performance. Similarly, media images portraying different body types could be used in discussion with young people in schools or sports clubs to foster greater awareness and understanding about health, eating disorders and the obesity debate. Elite athletes too could be invited to talk to aspiring young athletes about how they have overcome stereotypes and negative media coverage.

Figure 16.3 Venus Williams illustrated here provides contradictory media messages. On the one hand she can be seen as a role model as she is a highly successful tennis player in a sport with a history of relatively few black champions. Conversely, media coverage has also critiqued and questioned her and her sister's (Serena Williams) more "masculinised" body images and style of play.

ELITE ATHLETES AND THE MEDIA

Since the 1990s, the volume of sport journalism has increased, the previously narrow focus on results has expanded and there has been a growth in tabloid sports journalism reporting on the personal lives of sport stars in addition to their sporting prowess. Elite athletes depend on the media for publicity, but as both athletes and role models they are scrutinised. During Christmas 2009 Tiger Woods hit the headlines, but not because of his amazing golf results. Instead, he had to make several public appearances and apologise to his wife (and probably also sponsors) about his marital infidelity. He had served as a role model for the non-white golfer for years, and had to take a break from sport in order to recover from this public disgrace. No wonder some of the most applauded athletes often perceive the media as a source of strain: As Tiger Woods suddenly experienced, a media superstar may easily be discarded and face more critical questioning.

The impact of media coverage on elite athletes is an understudied topic in sport psychology research. The rest of this chapter will focus on the media as a stressor (i.e., types of stressors that originate from the interaction with journalists or exposure to media reports). Actually, it seems as though the stress originating from the media has the power to affect and exacerbate the entire interplay between competitive, organisational and personal stressors for athletes.

Coping with media coverage

from the literature that investigates media stress, we discern that athletes feel the presence of the journalists as intrusive and that media reports are not always factual (Durand-Bush & Salmela, 2002). So what are the criteria of a "high-quality" sport story? If you ask journalists and athletes this question, you will get completely different answers (Kristiansen & Hanstad, 2012). Athletes are sometimes taken by surprise by the journalists' angle of a sport story and their questioning, and on occasion the angle might be on non-performance issues like the feminine or masculine appearance of female athletes, organisational issues publicly revealed, intense focus on personal issues or simply on fabulous results that may create performance pressure. Elite athletes can take years to learn how to cope with and constantly negotiate issues such as these. Consequently, the media reporting (if extensive) may take away athletes self-confidence and self-worth by questioning them (Gauntlett, 2008). Furthermore, and as Tiger Woods experienced, media coverage might have an impact on family relations and social lives as well. Consequently, elite athletes openly admit that "the media is a hidden stress factor, I think many athletes don't realize how invasive it can be, and how much it might affect you" (Kristiansen, Hanstad, & Roberts, 2011a, p. 449). Naturally, elite athletes who are successful find ways to cope with this stress factor that goes with the job. Coping consists of learned behavioural responses that successfully lower arousal by neutralising or minimising the importance of a threatening condition (Lazarus & Folkman, 1984), for example, getting "upset" when your personal life makes the front page cover of the world's tabloid press. Research into media stress has revealed that athletes use three main strategies to cope with pervasive exposure and negative media reporting: social support, problem-focused thinking and avoidance

coping (Kristiansen et al., 2011a; Kristiansen & Roberts, 2011; Kristiansen, Roberts, & Sisjord, 2011b).

First of all, social support is considered to be a buffer to stress as well as being a coping resource (e.g., Lazarus & Folkman, 1984). Informational support from the coach may be critical (e.g., Kristiansen et al., 2011b), what the coach thinks is evidently more important than the media reporting. Therefore coach support is important in rebuilding of self-confidence if it is fragile after a "failure". Emotional support from family and friends may be vital in this process as well.

Second, avoidance coping is crucial to avoid the media influencing the athletes thinking. Avoidance coping can consist of both behavioural (remove from situation) and cognitive blocking strategies (Krohne, 1993). Some athletes deliberately avoid contact with sport news and evaluations of performance, though, family, friends and the fans want to discuss performance any way. As their "knowledge" of the performance is drawn from media reports, it is not easy to ignore what is reported (Kristiansen & Roberts, 2011). Athletes may therefore need the help from coach, team and family in order to avoid the reports completely.

Media break (i.e., getting time off from the media attention in order to focus on an upcoming event) is a "drastic" type of avoidance coping that concerns more than avoiding the actual reporting, this implies avoiding being questioned as well. Six months before the 2010 Vancouver Olympic Winter Games, one of the Norwegian medal hopes told the Norwegian media that she would not be as available for the press as she had been in previous years. She also added that the media's previous extensive coverage with a focus on underperformance had made it harder for her to get the right focus to compete. Her request of a media break was respected and debated by the journalists, but not as much after she won several gold medals. However, the media's approval is needed to be able to accomplish such a task (Kristiansen et al., 2011a), if not, the media will probably be even more critical and the situation will simply facilitate more stress.

Finally, athletes use several types of problem-focused strategies to cope with perceived negative media exposure. Problem-focused coping strategies embrace a wide array of problem-solving strategies and strategies that are directed inwards (Lazarus & Folkman, 1984), and these types of strategies may be used to manage or alter the media by action on yourself and your relationship to the media. For example, in football, the importance of post-game team debriefing and analysis of the game with the coach in charge is helpful (Kristiansen & Roberts, 2011).

With experience, athletes become better able to cope and they use more problem-focused strategies (Kristiansen et al., 2011a). These strategies were also used concurrently to make coping effective (Nicholls, Holt, & Polman, 2005). As an example, some athletes even admitted the use of strategies to appear colourless or "grey" so the journalists will turn to more colourful personalities in their team (Kristiansen et al., 2011b). This is a combination of avoidance and problem-focused strategies; they meet the media's basic requirements but act in a manner such that they are left alone.

Mastery climate as a team coping strategy

Apparently, the media may act as an environmental stressor that impacts the perceived motivational climate of a team or individual athletes. When journalists constantly question athletes about results and the likelihood of winning, it is perceived as stressful. The media attention may also affect how the coach handles the situation as well. According to Achievement Goal Theory (AGT), even positive media coverage makes the outcome more salient and this in itself is likely to make the upcoming competition more ego involving (read more about AGT in Chapter 4,

this volume). Coaches foster a mastery climate when they focus on learning and self-referenced improvement, emphasise effort in the learning of new skills, and regard mistakes as an aspect of learning. In such a climate, athletes are likely to perceive that success is achieved when effort is displayed and mastery is demonstrated (read about the empowering climate in Chapter 36, this volume). Coaches promote a performance climate when they focus on interpersonal competition, public evaluation of performance, normative feedback, where mistakes are punished, and when reinforcement is tempered by the demonstration of normative competence. Here athletes perceive that success is achieved when superiority is displayed and normative competence demonstrated. From research we know that a performance climate exacerbates the perception of media stress, while a mastery focus in the climate has a buffering effect on media stress (Kristiansen, Halvari, & Roberts, 2012).

How important is the motivational climate when an entire team has to cope with negative media exposure? This was the case in a recent research study when a team reflected back on an unsuccessful season (Kristiansen & Roberts, 2011), and in the following quote one of the football players at the team shared his experiences and insights:

In the beginning, when we lost, the media tried to explain why. When they had done that a few times, they started speculating about the need to buy new players, get a new coach and kind of made up stories about us. And we were only half way through the season... (Experienced footballer in an elite division, Kristiansen & Roberts, 2011, p. 356)

This sort of media framing is probably not meant as a contribution to solve the problems within the team. The coaching staff and the sport organisation may exacerbate or lessen the perception of media stress through the motivational climate that is extant in the athletic environment. As some of the players admitted, when team administrators made public announcements (as they often do in crises) and publicly called for a "change of results", this behaviour increased the pressure on the coach who, in turn, increases the pressure on the players. In this negative spiral the players began to care more about their own futures and began to wonder where they could get a better contract, etc. As a result, team effort might be lost as a result of a more performance-oriented climate when winning becomes so paramount and discussed in the media as well.

What should a coach do in situations like these that often happen in team sport? As an example, Kristiansen and Roberts (2011) were told stories about one highly admired coach. His trick was to use strategies to take the focus away from the team when they lost a game by saying something "stupid" or totally irrelevant to the press. The result was that the media would focus on him instead of the team. By this intentional approach, the coach created a supportive climate for the next game with his team rather than having the players dwell too much over their mistakes (that would not help for an upcoming game). He also protected the players from saying something laughable or absurd, the media "feeds" on the player who speaks without thinking, or makes inflammatory comments, providing the headlines for the next issue. When a performer is angry, tired, and they have just lost an important game/competition, it is too easy to blame someone, and it results in increased stress for the one blamed. It is important for the coach to keep these issues to the locker room. Media exposure may easily elevate competitive stress when an athlete feels that their performance is being scrutinised both from within (coach, owners, team mates) and by outside sources (media and fans). However, when they won important games, the coach discussed above would always step back and let them take the credit. By this action, this coach also protected the self-confidence of players and taught them to trust themselves. He was the supportive "glue" in the team by his constant informational

support whatever happened. In the present context, this coach understood that a task focus was the best focus for the individual players to adopt to overcome a performance slump.

As a final reflection of motivational issues whilst understanding that mastery climate is preferable, in a society evolving towards a strictly performance oriented environment, sponsors or managers may want more "concrete goals" stated publicly. However, choosing a mastery approach is not about not wanting to win, but it is the most efficacious way of taking a long-term dream goal like winning the league. Therefore, focusing on the steps toward achieving that goal should be encouraged by the athletes in a public forum. In comparison, when athletes have publicly stated performance goals, both the media and the sporting public are able to evaluate progress (or lack of progress) and therefore create a performance-oriented motivational climate they have to cope with.

The journalists–athlete relationship

Not only is the ability to cope with the coverage important for elite athletes, but they are also expected to meet with the press after competing. This is often hard after a failure, at a time when the athlete should be refocusing and recuperating, instead of elaborating upon what went wrong (or how they feel after being beaten). The journalists have no ethical problems broadcasting or describing the athletes' emotions, as they consider it a good story both when winning or failing. The journalists argue that they have an obligation to report and inform why some succeeded and others didn't, for them sport at elite level is both circus and entertainment. To write in a boring manner about the athletes and the events is the last thing some journalists want to do. As one respected Norwegian journalist admitted:

It is naive of the athletes to come to interviews and believe that we will ask them about their anaerobic threshold or the

Figure 16.4 During the 2010 Vancouver Olympics Norwegian cross-country skier Petter Northug created a media storm when he refused to talk to the media after a disappointing event and took a media break. A huge debate followed in Norway about what to expect of athletes; today his relationship with the press is more friendly and he has chosen to get help from a media advisor (right in the picture)/ when meeting with the press.

©Nils Maudal/www.drammensbilder.no

training results the past week or what they are planning to do the following one. [...] We are supposed to create an interest for their sport, and we have to entertain our readers. The athletes need to understand this (Kristiansen & Hanstad, 2012, p. 241).

Therefore, journalists prefer stories with a more "appealing" framework like when two athletes make a dispute public. A focus on conflicts within a team or between rivals may, by the help of the media, easily escalate into a "soap opera". In the history of sport there have been various examples of soaps, real or created – or both, as in the case of the 1994 Oslo Olympics involving skaters Nancy Kerrigan and Tonya Harding (Stoloff, 2000). Naturally, from a journalist's point of view, covering such a scoop (or violent drama) may be considered a "high-quality" story.

Seen from the perspective of an athlete, it is these high-quality sport stories that are hardest to cope with. When Kristiansen and Hanstad (2012) confronted a group of journalists with athletes statements about this type of sport reporting, the journalists simply responded that they believe that athletes at an elite level of sport who do not have the ability to cope with tabloid-style news coverage have no right to feel violated by their reporting. In support of such a claim, the teams with the most successful athletes have understood this and developed a personal relationship with the journalists and feed them with stories from their blogs, for example. Personal relationships may be an advantage for both athletes and journalists: Some journalists end up following an athlete's entire career and become part of the "entourage". The athletes start to trust them, and they will be kept informed about progress and thoughts, more than what they publish. Naturally, the framing of the stories may become more positive as a result. The advantage for the journalists is that they easier gain exclusive stories by this relationship, and that they can contact the athletes directly.

CONCLUSION

To sum up, athletes are allowed to be disappointed, but they need to understand that the journalists have a job to do too. To Kristiansen and Hanstad (2012) the journalists claimed that they have a professional relationship in what they report, and the journalists expect the same approach for the athletes. Elite sport is "show business", as one elite football player underlined: "We are in show business; we must give of ourselves to the newspapers. It's our job, people come to see us play and pay for it, and we must never forget that" (Kristiansen et al, 2011b, p. 8). Furthermore, they accept that media contact is necessary because the federations need the publicity and the sponsors need showcasing of products. However, when a team or individual does not deliver or fail to obtain a medal (preferably gold), then the athletes should prepare themselves for a discussion on what is an acceptable performance. Obviously, the athlete's goals and the media's goals for the athlete and the event are not always compatible. In the end, media is something unavoidable for sport superstars. Finding a way to enjoy being in the spotlight without losing what is important to a sports performer is imperative.

LEARNING AIDS

1   Describe two key characteristics of the contemporary sport media complex.

The sport media complex is a business relationship where both sport and the media can benefit from each other commercially. Additionally sport media products provide a cultural context for the transmission of sporting values and ideals.

2   Identify three ways in which the media can act as a sport socialising agency.

The media can act as a motivating tool; it can be a source of knowledge and information about sport and it can provide a modelling function.

3   Define the term "role model".

A role model is seen as someone who is an exemplar with attributes that others might wish to emulate.

4   Describe why avoidance coping may be a good strategy before major competitions.

Avoidance coping may be an advantage with chronic stressors, like the media, for the truly elite athletes. If they continue to take every media reporting personally the media may easily become overwhelming and energy draining for them.

5   Define the importance of the coach when meeting with the media.

The coach should try to lessen the athletes' perception of stress by helping them in the interview situation and keeping the climate mastery oriented.

6   Describe the advantages of a personal relationship between journalists and athletes.

A professional relationship between journalists and athletes that becomes a personal contact may make it easier for the journalists to get their story – and for the athletes to control the content and get a more positive framing in the media.

REVIEW QUESTIONS

1   Why is it difficult to determine precise effects of the media on an individual's sporting attitudes and behaviour?

2   In what ways are different types of role models and media stereotypes influential in creating a motivational climate for young people to take part in sport?

3   How might a sports psychologist work with a young sports performer to counter potential positive and negative influences of the media on their sporting attitudes and behaviour?

4   Athletes may perceive media reporting as negative criticism instead of positive speculation according to the journalists. What type of reporting is considered negative and as a distraction by athletes?

5   How do athletes cope with extensive (and/or negative) media reporting?

6   How might a sports psychologist work with elite athletes to help them cope with media stress?

EXERCISES

1   The media may treat an individual athlete without respect or simply discard them if they fail on the field. One recent example is the footballer Fernando Torres. He was a feared striker before becoming a Chelsea player in early 2010 but the sports reporting of him has changed drastically since then. Study some of the changes of reputation and reporting revealed in the media of him or another athlete of your choice that has had similar experiences. Discuss: a) to what extent an elite athlete might be affected by this type of media coverage; and b) how media coverage of this sport star might influence young people's sporting behaviour and attitudes as a potential role model.

2   Headlines sell! But athletes frequently expressed scepticism towards what they considered as negative headlines. How can journalists overcome athletes' scepticism concerning apparent negative reporting?

3   Select one sport and identify ways in which the media marginalises or stereotypes particular social groupings in this sport. How would you recommend a sports psychologist works with aspiring performers in this sport to counteract any negative issues?

ADDITIONAL READING

Kristiansen, E., Hanstad, D.V. & Roberts, G.C. (2011). Coping with the media at the Vancouver Winter Olympics: "We all make a living out of this". *Journal of Applied Sport Psychology*, 23(4), 443–458.

Lines, G. (2007). The impact of media sport events on the active participation of young people and some implications for PE pedagogy. *Sport, Education and Society*, 12(4), 349–366.

REFERENCES

Billings, A. (2008). *Olympic media. Inside the biggest show on earth*. London: Routledge.

Boyle, R. & Haynes, R. (2009). *Power play*. Harlow: Pearson Educational.

Desmarais, F. & Bruce, T. (2010). The power of stereotypes: Anchoring images through language in live sports broadcasts. *Journal of Language and Social Psychology, 29*, 338–362.

Durand-Bush, N. & Salmela, J. (2002). The development and maintenance of expert athletic performance: perceptions of world and Olympic champions. *Journal of Applied Sport Psychology, 14*(3), 154–171.

Evans, J., Rich, E., Davies, B. & Allwood, R. (2008). Education, disordered eating and obesity discourse: Fat fabrications. London and New York: Routledge.

Gauntlett, D. (2008). *Media, Gender and Identity. An introduction* (2nd edition). London: Routledge.

Hargreaves, J.A. & Hardin, B. (2009). Wheelchair Women athletes' views: Competing against Media Stereotypes. *Disability Studies Quarterly, 29* (2). Available at: www.dsq-sds.org/

Kristiansen, E., Halvari, H. & Roberts, G.C. (2012). Organizational and media stress among professional football players: Testing an Achievement goal theory model. *Scandinavian Journal of Medicine & Science in Sports, 22*, 569–579.

Kristiansen, E. & Hanstad, D.V. (2012). Journalists and Olympic athletes: A Norwegian case study of an ambivalent relationship. *International Journal of Sport Communication, 5*, 231–245.

Kristiansen, E., Hanstad, D.V. & Roberts, G.C. (2011a). Coping with the media at the Vancouver Winter Olympics: "We all make a living out of this". *Journal of Applied Sport Psychology, 23*(4), 443–458.

Kristiansen, E. & Roberts, G. (2011). Media exposure and adaptive coping in elite football. *International Journal of Psychology, 42*, 339–367.

Kristiansen, E., Roberts, G. & Sisjord, M.K. (2011b). Coping with negative media coverage: The experiences of professional football goalkeepers. *International Journal of Sport & Exercise Psychology, 9*(4), 295–307.

Krohne, H.W. (1993). Vigilance and cognitive avoidance as concepts in coping research. In H.W. Krohne (Ed.), *Attention and avoidance: Strategies in coping with aversiveness* (pp.19–50). Seattle, WA: Hogrefe and Huber.

Lazarus, R.S. & Folkman, S. (1984). *Stress, appraisal, and coping*. New York: Springer.

Lines, G. (1999). Setting the Challenge: Creating Partnerships, Young People, PE/Sport and the Media. *British Journal of Physical Education, 2* (2), 7–12.

Lines, G. (2001). Villains, Fools or Heroes? Sports stars as role models for young people. *Leisure Studies, 20*, 285–303.

Lines, G. (2002). The Sports Star in the Media. The gendered construction and youthful consumption of sports personalities. In J. Sugden & A. Tomlinson (Eds.), *Power games. A critical sociology of sport* (pp.196–215). London: Routledge.

Lines, G. (2007). The impact of media sport events on the active participation of young people and some implications for PE pedagogy. *Sport, Education and Society, 12* (4), 349–366.

Markula, P. (Ed.) (2009) *Olympic Women and the Media. International Perspectives*. Basingstoke: Palgrave Macmillan.

McQuail, D. (2005). *Mass Communication Theory: An Introduction*. London: Sage.

Nicholls, A.R., Holt, N.L. & Polman, R.C. (2005). A phenomenological analysis of coping effectiveness in golf. *Sport Psychologist, 19*(2), 111–130.

Redgrave, S. & Mott, S. (2009). *Inspired. Stories of sporting greatness*. London: Headline.

Sterkenburg, J.V., Knoppers, A. & De Leeuw, S. (2010). Race, Ethnicity and Content Analyses of the Sports Media: A critical reflection. *Media, culture and Society, 32*, pp.819–839.

Stoloff, S. (2000). Tonya Harding, Nancy Kerrigan, and the bodily figuration of social class. In S. Birrell & M.G. McDonald, (Eds.), *Reading sport. Critical essays in power and representation* (pp.234–250). Boston: Northeastern University Press.

Tomlinson, A. (2010). *Oxford dictionary of sport studies*. Oxford: Oxford University Press.

Whannel, G. (2002). *Media sport stars: Masculinities and Moralities*. London: Routledge.

Part Three

Promoting motor skills

EDITED BY THOMAS SCHACK AND HIROSHI SEKIYA

Chapter 17

Attention and neurocognition

KAI ESSIG, CHRISTOPHER JANELLE, FRANCESCA BORGO AND DIRK KOESTER

SUMMARY

Attention plays a central role in action and movement control and refers to the processing of relevant and suppression of irrelevant information. Following the theoretical background, we describe spatial and temporal brain bases for attentional control. These provide the neural underpinnings for cognitive aspects of attention such as *"what"* (object identity) and *"where"* (object location) information. The next section describes different forms of attentional focus in the context of various sport situations that are differently reliant on attentional width and direction for effective information processing. These processes have been deeply investigated by eye-tracking methods, often emphasizing visual search. Visual search strategies reflect the temporal focusing and extraction of context relevant information depending on bottom-up and top-down processes. Visual search is often used within the expertise approach. In this approach the gaze patterns of athletes of different skill levels are compared to relative non-experts to determine the cognitive processes underlying optimal and non-optimal (motor) performances. The chapter concludes with aspects of distraction and other attentional problems.

INTRODUCTION

In competitive situations such as a basketball game, attention is a major determinant of success. But how does attentive play increase the likelihood of winning, and is attention a uniform process for different situations? In most play situations, for example, a fastbreak, players have to keep almost the whole playing field in mind. In particular, the positions of their teammates and of the opponents relative to their own position, the distance to the basket, etc. In addition to spatial aspects, timing is also critical. When is the latest moment to pass the ball safely to a teammate when being attacked by an opponent? While concentrating on all of this information, the players have to shield themselves from processing irrelevant information such as the noise created from the crowd outside the field.

In other situations, for example, free throws, requirements for focused play differ dramatically. Here, the position of the other players does not matter. The timing is more relaxed. In a free throw situation, these aspects become irrelevant and should be suppressed in order to focus on relevant aspects, namely, the position of the basket and the perception of the ball. Furthermore, players have to be able to switch quickly between such distinct forms of processing, e.g. when the (last) free throw fails and the game proceeds immediately (Keele & Hawkins, 1982).

OBJECTIVES

After reading this chapter, you should be able to:

1 Illustrate attentive processing with an example from your sport setting.
2 Explain the differences between bottom-up and top-down processing.
3 Explain the different forms of attentional focus.
4 Illustrate what the differences in the attentional gaze patterns of experts and novices tell us about the underlying cognitive processes.
5 Define advanced cue utilization with an example from your sport.

DEFINITION OF ATTENTION

Anecdotally, coaches and athletes often invoke attention-based explanations for their successes and failures. References to attention, particularly the need to remained "focused" is perhaps the most common, albeit ill-defined, attribution in most pre- and post-competition press conferences. Finding a single concise definition for *attention* is challenging if not impossible; the concept of attention is too multifaceted and multidimensional. Attention is typically described as a *concentration* of awareness in which one focuses on particular cues to the exclusion of others. This is consistent with traditional points of view, stemming from the William James (1890) definition over a century ago:

> Everyone knows what attention is. It is taking possession by the mind, in clear and vivid form, of one out of what seems several simultaneously possible objects or trains of thought. Focalization, concentration of consciousness are the essence. It implies withdrawal from some things in order to deal effectively with others.

This definition of attention indicates clearly that humans, because of a limited attentional capacity, have to selectively direct attention to relevant scene objects to understand the whole visual scene through a combination of computationally less demanding, localized visual analysis problems. Helmholtz (1925) was among the first to propose visual attention as an essential perceptual mechanism. He described attention as a small region of space wandering to new things, controlled by conscious and voluntary effort (*"where"* – eye movements to spatial locations); (Duchowski, 2007). There is a relationship between shifts of gaze and locus of attention (a shift of gaze is invariably preceded by a shift in attention; Vickers, 2007). When a shift of attention is accompanied by eye movements we call this *overt attention*. Humans are also able to dissociate their attention from the foveal direction of gaze (*covert attention*). In contrast, James (1890) described attention mainly in terms of the *"what"*, or the identity, meaning or expectation associated with the focus of attention. More recent research showed that peripherally located image features may drive attention in terms of *"where"* to look next, so that we may identify *"what"* detail is present at those locations.

Treisman and Gelade (1980) brought the two concepts ("*what*" and "*where*") together in the *Feature Integration Theory* (FIT) of visual attention. For each fixated object, the stimulus properties are encoded in separate neural pathways which encode simple and useful scene properties, like color, orientation, size and stereo distance into different feature maps (Duchowski, 2007). Attention is the "glue" integrating the separated features in a kind of *master map* of higher brain centres. Yarbus (1967) recorded different scan-patterns when viewing an image under different queries specific to the situation, demonstrating sequential viewing patterns over particular image regions. *Inhibition of Return* (IOR) plays a central role during scene viewing. IOR is a cognitive mechanism which inhibits briefly the return of attention to previously examined stimuli, preventing the visual system from oscillating between regions of interest (Leek, Reppa & Tipper, 2003). These studies show that a coherent picture of the scene is constructed piecemeal by serially viewed *regions of interest*.

Although James' definition broadly encompasses many aspects of attention, purveyors of the various disciplines of psychology continue to apply attentional concepts in quite distinct ways. For example, the classical and enduring view of cognitive psychologists is that attention is a control process that dictates whether information picked up by sensory stores will be transferred to short-term memory (and potentially onward to long-term memory) for response selection and execution. Neuroscientists are concerned with the neural substrates that underlie these processes. Ultimately, however, psychologists are interested in behavior. For sport psychologists, behaviors of interest are those that are related to motor performance and sport achievement. Janelle and colleagues (e.g., Janelle & Hatfield, 2008), among others, have argued that when considering the psychological constructs that are known to affect performance change, it is attentional allocation that is the most critical *proximal* predictor of performance. Simply stated, performers have to pay attention to the right things at the right time to perform effectively. This is not to say that other psychological constructs such as motivation, emotion, and confidence, among others, are not important. They are, but *distally* so. Experts have learned to control their gaze so that they can perceive the optimal information at the right time. Motor performance is affected by both bottom-up factors (stimulus-driven), such as novelty or object shape, and top-down factors, such as anticipations, expectancies, goals, and intentions. An overview about the domain of attention as well as on new perspectives in the cognitive science of attention and action can be found in Abernethy, Maxwell, Masters, Van der Kamp, and Jackson (2007) and Bruya (2010).

NEUROANATOMICAL BASIS OF ATTENTION NETWORK

Rapid advancement of assessment tools and instrumentation in recent years have permitted scientists to more specifically pinpoint the underlying neural mechanisms of attention. This advancement includes localization of attentional function, temporal succession, and connectivity among cortical and subcortical brain structures that are involved with regulating attentional focus (providing a "*window to the mind*").

Importantly, attention is not rooted in *one* specific brain area. Attention is rather supported by a neural network of multiple brain areas. These networks are often investigated using functional magnetic resonance imaging (fMRI; see Method highlight). Within these networks, information is exchanged and adjusted in a number of ways. For vision, information is transmitted to visual brain areas (see Figure 17.1; e.g., Knudsen, 2007). In these areas, information is analysed and then transmitted to higher cognitive centers. This direction of information flow corresponds to bottom-up processing (Buschman & Miller, 2007). In brain

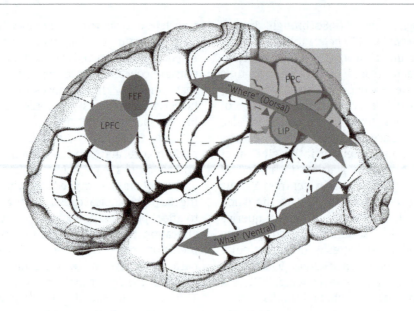

Figure 17.1 Schematic representation of the sideview onto the left hemisphere of a human brain and the neuroanatomical brain systems involved in attention. The encircled areas play a specific role in attention. *"What"* information is processed in the ventral pathway, whereas *"where"* information is processed in the dorsal path (see also text; Ungerleider & Mishkin, 1982; Goodale & Milner, 1992; Buschman & Miller 2007).

areas of higher cognitive functions, the relevance of perceived objects is evaluated. For example, a fast moving object (e.g., a ball shot at a goal) will attract processing resources in the lateral intraparietal area (LIP, part of the posterior parietal cortex, PPC) because it is very salient. The LIP contains a saliency map. The saliency of an object (the ball in our example) could be determined by its high speed which reflects stimulus-driven processing (bottom-up).

Method highlight – (f)MRI

Magnetic resonance imaging (MRI) is based on the physical phenomenon of nuclear spin and can provide a structural image of biological tissue. It basically measures density differences (e.g., between the brain and cerebrospinal fluid) which are used to render an image that resembles a macroscopic photograph-with the advantage that the image can be rendered at any depth of the tissue (brain).

Functional magnetic resonance imaging (fMRI), in contrast, measures changes in blood flow, i.e., increased or decreased oxygen consumption, and the recorded signal is correlated with neurons' local field potentials (Logothetis, Pauls, Augath, Trinath, & Oeltermann, 2001). Thus, the fMRI signal is thought to reflect neuronal calculations (whatever the information of the particular brain area is). The major advantage of fMRI is the high spatial resolution (up to 1mm). The downside is the low temporal resolution (multiple seconds).

Attentive processing also encompasses neural information flow in the opposite direction, i.e., top-down processing. From higher cognitive areas (prefrontal cortex), where expectations are formed, attentive processes are guided by goal-related features (Buschman & Miller, 2007). That is, objects that are critical for the current action goal are put into focus while processing of irrelevant objects is attenuated. Specifically, prefrontal areas (frontal eye field, FEF & lateral prefrontal cortex, LPFC; see Figure 17.1; Shulman & Corbetta, 2002) modulate stimulus processing based on expectations for the given situation (top-down influence; dashed arrows in Figure 17.1). The FEF and LPFC modulate the sensitivity of neural circuits in the LIP. For example, in a soccer game situation, the player in possession of the ball may be looking for a teammate in order to pass the ball. The best teammate cannot be found by his salient sensory features as all players are similarly dressed. The task to find the free player is a *goal* and therefore requires top-down processing. In functional neuroanatomic terms the goal would be generated and maintained in LPFC. This goal representation in LPFC influences the saliency map in the LIP. For example, the goal representation may selectively enhance the saliency of the free player, who then may be selected for processing. The selection is based on goals rather than on stimulus features. The FEF is involved in overt and covert shifts of attention (this pathway involves further anatomical structures in the depth of the brain which are not discussed here further).

For bottom-up processing an important discovery regarding the neuroanatomical underpinnings was the spatial segregation of two processing streams for different content information. Ungerleider & Mishkin (1982; see also Goodale & Milner, 1992) proposed a functional *neuroanatomic* dissociation between a "*what*" (ventral) and a "*where*" (dorsal) pathway (see solid arrows in Figure 17.1). The ventral visual pathway is largely concerned with object recognition ("*what*") whereas the dorsal visual pathway translates spatial information into an internal reference frame for space ("*where*").

While these neuroanatomical networks delineate the structural brain basis for attentional control, their temporal interplay is functionally another critical factor. Fast brain processes are difficult to measure with fMRI, but other techniques, for example electroencephalography (EEG; see Figure 17.2 & Method highlight), recording summed electrical activity at the scalp can provide information on cortical activity with high temporal resolution in the msec range. Methods like EEG permit the investigation of processing precedence of different types of information. For example, spatial location of a relevant object ("*where*" information) is processed with precedence over other features of this object (e.g., color, contour, texture; "*what*" information; Hillyard & Anllo-Vento, 1998). Hence, the presence of an object can be checked in the periphery, but the identification of object details requires further processing, e.g., a fixation in the near neighbourhood of the particular object.

Method highlight – EEG

The **electroencephalogram** (EEG) is the summed electrical potential of the cortex (i.e., outer sheet of the brain) recorded at the scalp. As, by and large, all cognitive functions are supported by the cortex, the EEG reflects the summation of many cognitive processes; from perception, attention, memory, language to movement control.

To measure the brain's specific response to a stimulus, for example, movement initiation in response to an auditory stimulus such as a starter's gun, one can calculate the **event-related potential** (ERP) from the EEG. The ERP is usually calculated as the average of multiple 1 to 2 seconds of EEG signal time-locked to a specific event such as the starter's gun. ERPs have a very high temporal resolution (msec range) with a limited spatial resolution (multiple cm). So-called ERP components, i.e., deflections with a typical polarity, latency and scalp topography, can yield insights into the nature and temporal succession of cognitive processes. For example, the *P300* (a positivity with a average latency of 300 msec after a stimulus) reflects a participant's attentive processing capacity (see Figure 17.2).

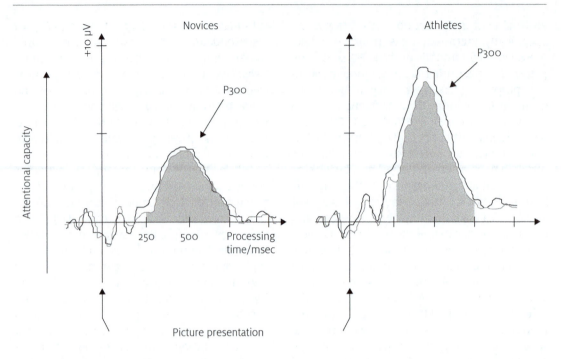

Figure 17.2 ERPs illustrating the temporal unfolding of attentive stimulus evaluation (from Koester, Güldenpenning & Schack, under review). Participants had to categorize pictures of body postures as either showing an approach or a flight phase of the Fosbury-flop. Two pictures were presented in fast succession in either the natural (approach-flight) or reversed order (flight-approach; cf. Güldenpenning, et al., 2011). The latency of the ERP component *P300* suggests that the *evaluation* of body postures needs at least 250 msec and can be performed without the possession of motor skills for the Fosbury-flop. The *P300* amplitude suggests that athletes have increased (attentive) processing capacities for their movement repertoire (high jump) compared with novices (larger overall amplitudes for athletes). Also, athletes but not novices can distinguish the temporal order (modulation of the *P300* amplitude for athletes but not for novices; more positive amplitude for natural than for reversed order).

TYPES OF ATTENTION: WIDTH AND DIRECTION OF ATTENTION

The early work of Robert Nideffer (1976) provided a descriptive account of the dimensions of attentional focus. Nideffer described attention along continuous dimensions of span (broad vs narrow) and direction (internal vs external). The span (or width or breadth) of attentional focus refers to the number (or extent) of environmental or mental factors to which attention is allocated. A broad attentional focus allows simultaneous processing of multiple cues, while a narrow attentional focus involves concentrating only on one or two critical cues. The direction of attentional focus refers to whether concentration is directed externally (to an object or person) or internally (to thoughts or feelings). Using the two dimensions of attention focus creates four combinations that each plays a unique role in sport performance (Table 17.1):

The ability to shift the direction and span of attentional focus in response to different situations is vital for sport performance. Shifts of

Table 17.1 *Attention along continuous dimensions of span (broad vs narrow) and direction (internal vs external)*

Span		Broad	Narrow
Direction	External	Assess a situation: survey the defense to see who is open	Concentrating on only a few external cues (e.g., the hoop in a basketball game)
	Internal	Planning general strategies after getting the play from the coach (e.g., creating plays or game tactics)	Identifying a specific emotional reaction

attentional focus can cut across each of the four quadrants of attentional span and direction, in a matter of moments. In team sports like basketball (see Figure 17.3), for example, a player will often receive a play from the coach on the sideline (typically coded as a number or word, such as "Red 96"). The player must then analyse the play (broad/narrow) in terms of what that play actually is, in basketball terms, as laid out in the playbook. This task is accomplished using a broad internal perspective. Then, using a broad external attentional focus, the player must survey the relative position of her teammates, the defenders, and the ball, to determine which of the multiple alternatives is the most advantageous at that moment.

Figure 17.3 Basketball expertise requires high aptitude across diverse attentional styles.

The individual's focus of attention also affects the effectiveness and efficiency of motor skill learning and performance. Wulf and Lewthwaite (2010) have shown that instructions and feedback that direct the performer's attention to the movement effect on the environment (external focus) facilitate performance and learning compared to either those that direct attention to the movements themselves (internal focus) or to those that lack any attentional focus instructions. External focus not only decreases the necessary physical effort (like, reduced oxygen consumption and reduced force), but it also reduces mental effort (as indicated by improved secondary-task performance) and leads to faster movement execution. The adoption of an external focus promotes the utilization of relatively automatic control processes.

A narrow, external attentional focus may be used, in our basketball example, when the player decides to dribble drive, pass, or shoot the ball. If the shot is missed, the pass deflected, or the ball stolen, the player may direct a narrow internal focus to quickly regulate the negative affect that would likely follow as a consequence of the error. Negative affect is one of many *internal cues* that can serve to distract attention from the critical cues that are necessary for effective performance. *External distractors* are also replete in most sports contexts. As such, sport psychologists have devoted extensive efforts to understanding the conditions under which athletes are likely to be distracted and the means by which training protocols can be developed to minimize potential distraction.

DIVIDED AND SELECTIVE ATTENTION

Divided attention refers to the ability to devote attention to two or more tasks simultaneously. For example, referees in soccer have to follow the player in possession of the ball, keep an eye on (nearby) players from both teams in case of a foul or insult, and be alert to signals from the linesmen. A major research question is whether, and under what conditions, attentional resources can be divided among more than one task given that processing resources are limited. Research suggests that attention can only be divided among tasks if the tasks are of low difficulty or a high level of automatization has already been established (Shiffrin & Schneider, 1977). Clearly, it is often a difficult task for referees to judge under high time pressure whether a foul was committed or whether a goal was scored (cf. research highlight *attentional blink*). Consequently, enduring and repeated practice is necessary to automatize the required tasks to allow for simultaneous processing, i.e., divided attention. Research in this area suggests that elite performers overlearn their psychological skills as they do with their physical skills (Gould, Eklund & Jackson, 1993). While it is certainly critical to understand how attention is divided and how performance may be altered accordingly, attention researchers have largely shifted their efforts to selective attention. This paradigm shift has been largely motivated by the realization that divided attention necessitates refined selective attention skills, because we have to allocate our available attentional resources to several channels of information at the same time as needed (e.g., in dual-task experiments, where participants must perform two tasks at the same time), which may weaken performance.

Research highlight – Attentional Blink: Can you stay totally focused?

In some sports athletes have to stay focused over long periods of time – hours or even days as, for example, during a golf tournament (see Figure 17.5). Of course, athletes must have "mental breaks" for such long durations. For much shorter durations, researchers asked how long the "unbroken" or uninterrupted *attentive* time window is. In the range of seconds, attentional focus itself can be disrupted by attentive processes (e.g., Luck, Vogel, & Shapiro, 1996). That is, in this temporal range attention may not always be continuous.

The phenomenon called *attentional blink* refers to a temporary suppression of visual attention in analogy to an eye blink which prevents the uptake of visual information for a split second. To investigate the attentional blink, a series of events, for example numbers or letters are rapidly shown on a screen and participants have to identify two out of a large number of events. This task can be done easily. However, if the second event occurs between 200 and 600 msec after the first, identification performance for the second event decreased significantly. This decrease in performance is not due to perceptual or motor processes but to the (missing) attentional resources bound by the first event. This effect of attentional disruption in fast scenarios is interesting because it may be related to feint actions in sports. For example, in martial arts double attacks are very common and often are successful. One may wonder whether the success, i.e., the hit of the second attack, could be partly due to temporary reduction of attentional resources as a consequence of (the opponent's) reaction to the first attack.

Selective attention refers to the ability to focus on specific cues and to ignore others. As in virtually all achievement domains, it is desirable to maintain focus on relevant cues and to ignore those that are irrelevant or unimportant to perform sport specific skills. Selective attention has been metaphorically compared to a "searchlight" that focuses on things that have the most behaviorally-relevant importance. In contemporary psychological science, the searchlight and other metaphors have served as the foundation for neuroscientific approaches. For example, Posner (2012) has advocated three fundamental findings in regards to selective attention as a neurophysiological process: (a) the attention network of the brain is anatomically separate from the data processing systems that analyse specific inputs even when attention is oriented somewhere else; (b) attention is carried out by a network of brain areas, and is not the product of a single center; and (c) each area involved in attention carries out a unique function that can be specified in cognitive terms (e.g., orienting to sensory events, determining stimulus saliency for conscious processing, and maintaining an alert state). Selective attention can also be intentional (voluntary) or incidental (involuntary) in nature. For example, sitting at a noisy restaurant, you purposely choose to attend to the conversation at your table (intentional attention). However, when a glass falls off a table at the next table over, you suddenly shift your attention away from the conversation to the breaking glass (incidental attention).

EXPERTISE-BASED GAZE BEHAVIOR

Recent research support the existence of at least two qualitatively distinct modes of attentive processes when viewing scenes: global and local scanning (e.g., Land & Tatler, 2009). Global scanning periods, restricted to the first two seconds of viewing photographic scenes, are associated with large amplitude saccades (see below) and short duration fixations, whereas local scanning periods are associated with smaller amplitude saccades and longer fixations. Thus, fixation duration can be considered as a measure of the effort of information processing: The longer a fixation lasts, the longer it presumably takes to deal with the visual information presented (i.e., higher cognitive load). Several experiments have demonstrated that the eye can in fact be a *window to the mind* (Holmqvist et al., 2011).

An eye tracker records participants' gaze position usually with infra-red cameras mounted on a headset or bicycle helmet. The two most important types of eye movements are fixations and saccades. During a fixation, the eye remains motionless for a period of around 200–300 ms, enabling the processing of the information from the fixated region (Holmqvist, et al., 2011). Visual information is processed mainly during fixations. Because only the fovea allows clear vision, the eye has to be moved so that different parts of the scene can be processed in sequence. These movements are called saccades. Saccades are jerky eye movements between two successive fixations. During saccades the eye is accelerated up to 30–500°/s and the saccade duration ranges from 30–80ms. We are effectively blind during most of the saccade (Holmqvist et al., 2011). The measurement of eye movements provide key visual search parameters such as fixation location (area of interest), search rate (number and duration of fixations and saccades), and temporal search order, all of which are assumed to be indicative of the perceptual strategy used by the performer to extract meaningful information (Williams & Ward, 2007). So-called attention maps are used to calculate the overall attention distribution of several participants (Holmqvist et al., 2011). In an attention map, pixels are encoded by a color gradient. In attention maps typically colors are used to visualize the extent to which image areas are fixated. For example, red means that the area is highly fixated, whereas non-relevant regions are darkened (see Figure 17.4 for a black and white version).

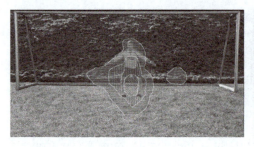

Figure 17.4 Attention Maps (action task) for experts (left) and novices (right) when the goalkeeper is displaced +1.5% to the right relative to the center on the goal line. Experts' attention is mainly focused on the goalkeeper. Novices fixate on the goalkeeper but also the area to the left and right to find the open side, i.e., the area of greater size, for the penalty shot. In the black and white picture diagonal crossed, vertical and horizontal textured areas show intensive, strong and moderate fixated areas, respectively.

VISUAL SEARCH AND ADVANCED CUE UTILIZATION

Although athletes' search behavior is influenced by various factors, such as the nature of the task and the stress level. Furthermore, skilled performers show more effective and efficient visual search behavior than less skilled performers in an attempt to extract the most pertinent information, such as advance visual cues or to identify patterns of play (Williams & Ward, 2007). These skill-based differences are indicative of more refined selective attention processes and enhanced task-specific knowledge structures. In order to investigate visual perception processes, eye-tracking studies have been applied to sport settings since the early 1980s. Tydesley, Bootsma, and Bomhoff (1982) investigated the eye movements of experienced and inexperienced players looking at a right-footed soccer player taking a penalty kick in a static slide presentation. Participants had to anticipate the direction of the penalty kick by pressing one of four response keys representing four alternative shot directions (high/low, left/right). Their results revealed a more structured and consistent gaze behavior for the experienced players: Fixations were restricted to the right side of the body and the shooting leg, while neither the supporting leg nor the left side were scanned. Additionally, the fixation duration for the inexperienced players was 26.6ms longer than for the experienced counterparts, showing that they had more problems picking up the relevant information from the scene. A high proportion of the first fixations (60%) were directed toward the hip, with 30% of first fixations directed toward the legs, feet and ball. In contrast, second fixations appeared more on the shoulder regions. This search strategy reveals that initial information from the lower body followed by the upper body are used to determine the direction and height of the penalty kick (for comparable research in more realistic settings, incl. video projections see Helsen & Pauwels, 1992 and Williams & Ward, 2007).

Vickers (2007) investigated the types of gaze behavior underlying successful and non-successful performances in order to explain the perceptual and cognitive processes that define optimal and non-optimal motor performance. She defined the *quiet eye* as the final fixation or tracking gaze that is located on a specific location or object in the visuo-motor workspace. Elite performer's quiet-eye onset is invariably earlier and longer than that of lower skilled performers, i.e., skilled players see critical information earlier and process the visual information longer than less-skilled athletes. It has been shown in a number of studies that quiet eye training contributes to unusually large increases in performance (Vickers, 2007).

Essig, Siegers, Weigelt, Lex, and Schack (2010) extended the study of Masters, Van der Kamp, and Jackson (2007) to further investigate the influence of conscious and unconscious cues on the penalty situation in soccer. Soccer-experts and novices were shown static images of a goalkeeper displaced relative to the center on the goal line (left vs. centre vs. right) and their gaze positions were recorded. In the action task, participants had to react with a pedal press to the 'open' area of the goal, i.e., the area of greater size. In the following perception task, they were asked to estimate whether the goalkeeper stood at the centre or if he was displaced to the left or right. Additionally, participants rated the confidence in their decisions. Results of the perception task show that both groups could not consciously notice small displacements of the goalkeeper in the *"perception corridor"* between −1.5% to +1.5% from the centre, but decided to kick the ball to the *"open"* side in the action task. Experts were more confident in their decisions than novices and both groups showed lower confidence ratings for displacements within the corridor. Attention distributions show that experts mainly directed their focus on the goalkeeper, whereas novices fixate the goalkeeper but also the area to the left and right to find the open side for the penalty shot. In the action task, participants focused on both the goalkeeper and the side they intend to shoot at (see Figure 17.4).

Differences between the visual search strategy of experts, near-experts and novices were also reported by Raab and Johnson (2007; see also Williams, Janelle & Davids, 2004). They investigated expertise-based differences in search and option-generation strategies in a two-year longitudinal handball study. They found that experts used extensively *spatial* gaze strategies (i.e., they scan only a part of the visual field), whereas near-experts use primarily *functional* gaze strategies (i.e., they scan the whole visual field), which may explain the expertise-based differences in the option-generation task.

A cue signifies a crucial source of perceptual information. When this particular information is occluded, performance may either be impaired or the missing information may be compensated with information that had been excluded from other cues (Williams & Ward, 2007). This usage of several concurrent and overlapping cues may be an important factor for high level performance, and it has been demonstrated in many technical skills, such as controlling a ball in soccer (Williams, Weigelt, Harris & Scott, 2002). It is not clear, however, if performers always use the cue information (maybe they adopt a more *"wait and see"* approach to save costs), or if they decide to not use cue information during actual matches (James, Caudrelier & Murray, 2005). This interplay between costs and benefits associated with the anticipation process merits further consideration (Williams & Ward, 2007).

CONCENTRATION

The term concentration is often used interchangeably with attention. Schmid and Peper (1993) advocated that attention broadly refers to general awareness of environmental or cognitive stimuli, but concentration refers to being able to focus one's attention on the task at hand and thereby not be disturbed or affected by irrelevant external and internal stimuli. Practically speaking, effective concentration skills mandate that one optimizes both selective and divided attention. Moran (2004) further distinguished concentration from attention, advocating that deliberate effort is essential to concentration. In other words, concentration is the act of intentionally directing one's attention to specific, important environmental stimuli or mental processes.

Concentration is of particular interest in sport psychology, and is considered to be composed of four components: (1) focusing on important environmental cues, which is called *selective attention* (and inherently requires divided attention skill); (2) sustaining that focus of attention over a period of time (*vigilance;* cf. research highlight *focus of attention*); (3) having a general awareness of the situation and one's whereabouts (*situation awareness*); and (4) changing and adapting attentional focus when needed (*attentional flexibility*). Sport psychologists would argue that performance is optimized when these four components of attention are effectively regulated. Clearly, however, the attentional demands of different sports vary widely. Successfully developing the components of effective concentration skill is difficult, yet necessary for the attainment of higher skill level in sport. Having the ability to select environmental cues that are relevant to the task occurs as a result of extended exposure to practice and competitive settings, and the development of implicit knowledge and explicit rules that increase the likelihood of knowing how to successfully adapt attentional focus for maximal performance. Perhaps not surprisingly, expert athletes consistently exhibit a wider repertoire of domain-specific knowledge that allows them to select and use appropriate cues.

Research highlight – Focus of attention: Better "looking" inside or outside?

Learning new skills or improving already acquired skills does not happen by itself or automatically. That is, for such learning processes people have to attend to their practice activity. Since we cannot attentively process all available information, the question arises as to what should a learner attend to when practicing a (new) skill? Does it make a difference at all, if one attends to body movements, like joint angles of the knees and elbows (**internal focus** of attention) or to movement effects, like a basketball trajectory (external focus)? Maybe people adopt the best form of attentional focus spontaneously?

Research by Wulf and others (Wulf, 2007; Wulf & Lewthwaite, 2010; Wulf & Prinz, 2001) show that the focus of attention does impact skill learning. Interestingly, an external focus yields learning effects compared to an **internal focus** of attention. That is, it is more beneficial, if one attends to movement effects rather than to the movement execution itself. The theoretical idea behind this phenomenon is that an **internal focus** leads to more controlled (conscious) movement execution. Such controlled processes then interfere with automatic processes of motor control and overall performance decreases. In contrast, an external focus seems to promote automatic movement execution. However, people seem not to adopt an optimal focus of attention by themselves, and in some situations the use of an **internal focus** can be required. Thus, supervision for effective skill acquisition is indicated and practitioners at any level can benefit from educated supervision.

A somewhat different definition of external focus is used by Nideffer (Nideffer, 1976). In his model, two dimensions of attention are recognized: width (broad to narrow) and direction (external to internal). Crossing these two dimensions leads to four attention styles as follows: i) narrow + external: is the focused style which is used whenever a task is actually performed in real time; ii) narrow + internal: is a rehearsal or preparatory-check-list style, and it also applied to systematic and conscious efforts to regulate one's inner state and arousal levels (anticipatory and retrograde control); iii) broad-internal: involves cognitive processes and time frames (long-term, future-oriented) analyzing patterns over time to develop useful streategies or plans for the future; iv) broad-external awareness: requires sensitive attention to the total situation in order to allow for quick and labile responses to dynamic circumstances. All of theses attention styles will be needed across various stages of athletic training and performance according to the demands of their sports.

DISTRACTION AND OTHER ATTENTION PROBLEMS

Some of the most prevalent causes of distracted attention are anxiety, worry, and irrelevant thoughts. Anxiety can cause attentional focus to shift from current performance goals or tasks to possible negative performance results that athletes are trying to avoid. For example, a baseball player may worry about striking out rather than the primary task of making solid contact with the ball. In turn, worries (e.g., performance pressure) manifest in attentional shifts, i.e., to focus attention on the execution of the skill (internal focus) in order to consciously intervene and ensure correctness of execution that predispose the athlete to failure (because internal focus is detrimental to skilled performers). Specific fears (i.e., fear of negative evaluation, self-presentation concerns, injury and financial risk) and general heightened levels of precompetitive anxiety may lead to performance problems and choking (Hill, Matthews, Fleming & Hanton, 2011; Mesagno & Mullane-Grant, 2010).

While there is broad agreement on the basic premise that emotional problems preclude performance problems, and that the primary psychological mechanism driving these performance changes is attentional in nature, specifically how attention acts to alter sport performance remains debatable. Popular contemporary notions of attentional change centre on (1) attentional narrowing; (2) distraction; (3) self-focus/conscious processing; and (4) efficiency-based explanations (Janelle, 2002). *Attentional narrowing* explanations attribute performance alterations to the robust finding that as anxiety and arousal increase, the perceptual field is constricted, eliminating the ability to identify and process relevant cues in the peripheral attentional field. *Distraction*-based explanations suggest performance problems will be encountered when the athlete relates to more cognitive tasks (such as attending and thinking about irrelevant cues) as they compete for limited working memory. However, for highly automated motor tasks, attention is not specifically needed for skill execution, thus

distraction (e.g., counting backwards) has been found not to harm performance. Thus, the breakdown of automacity through skill-focused attention is more relevant for motor tasks as an explanation. The likelihood of distraction occurring is greater as the intensity of the distracting stimulus is increased, or as emotional intensity increases (as is the case in a loud stadium in a big game, for instance).

A third possibility is that the automaticity associated with highly practiced sports skills can be compromised by inappropriately directing attention to internal thoughts or movements themselves (*Explicit Monitoring Hypothesis*; Beilock & Carr, 2001). The hallmark characteristic of expert performance is the rather attention-free means by which movements are executed. Research has clearly indicated, however, that when anxious or confronted with augmented information, individuals are inclined to consciously process aspects of the skill and their performance will most likely suffer. Under pressure, people try and exert more control over the performance of the movement in order to ensure correctness of execution. It is a false sense of control. Conscious processing hypotheses imply a comparative lack of efficiency in movement execution due to greater cognitive input. Applying a dual task strategy, designed to prevent skill focused attention, can prevent choking under pressure. For example, Land and Tenenbaum (2012) examined skilled and novice golfers (see Figure 17.5) on a putting task under high- and low-pressure, while carrying out either a golf-specific (i.e., monitoring club-head ball contact) or an irrelevant letter generation task to prevent skill-focused attention. They found that both secondary tasks prevented choking under pressure and increased movement variability associated with improved performance for skilled players, but not for novices.

Attentional inefficiency has been implicated in other contemporary theories invoked to account for performance changes under stress. One of the main assumptions of *attentional control theory* is that there is a crucial difference between processing efficiency and performance effectiveness, and that anxiety affects the former more than the latter (Eysenck, Derakshan, Santos & Calvo, 2007). Attentional control theory contends that anxiety and worrisome thoughts consume attentional resources. Attention, thereby, is diverted away from the task to process the worrisome thoughts. Under these conditions, the athlete must be willing and able to marshal more attentional resources to compensate for those that are being directed toward dealing with anxiety. By default, an inefficient system results. Under such conditions, the efficiency of the system is compromised as more resources are used to accomplish the same task. If attentional resources are exhausted, not only will performance be less efficient, it will also be less effective. In order to maintain overall performance efficiency, some compensatory effort is required. Conceivably, athletes may make an increased effort to focus processing resources again on task-relevant information or employ additional processing strategies. Widespread empirical evidence, both sport specific and general, are supportive of the basic tenants of attentional control theory. Implications for training and intervention to ameliorate athletes against the impact of anxiety can be derived from the described theories, such as attentional control theory (for exam-

ple, to prevent the athletes from focusing on irrelevant cues) or explicit monitoring theory (for example, the use of secondary tasks to divert attention away from skill execution to prevent choking under pressure).

Figure 17.5 Golf players in a tournament need to focus their attention on the task to prevent choking under pressure.

LEARNING AIDS

1   Define the role of the dorsal path in vision.

Ungerleider and Mishkin (1982) suggested that visual information is not processed unitarily by the brain but segregated according to spatial and content information, i.e., location and object meaning. The two processing streams in the brain are anatomically distinct; there is a ventral (towards the abdomen) and a dorsal stream (towards the back). The dorsal stream handles the location of objects, i.e., "where" information. This information is critical to determine where to look to (gaze control) but also to anticipate where objects will be in the near future, e.g., to anticipate a ball's trajectory.

2 How do various eye tracking measures differ?

Gaze behavior can be divided, i.e., eye movements can be divided into states where the eye remains still over a period of time (fixations) and movements (saccades). During fixations, information from the environment is taken up, processed and the following saccade is programmed. Saccades are the actual alignment to the next point of interest. We are blind during most of the saccade (Holmqvist et al., 2011). Location and duration of fixations can be informative about what is relevant to the athlete and how difficult the fixated object is to process. Saccades show which objects in the environment are of most interest to the athletes' anticipation. Fixations and saccades can also be combined to create the so called scan paths. These scan paths reveal which aspects of a visual scene capture high attention within a certain timespan.

3 What are the spatial and temporal brain bases for attentional control?

While not the whole brain is functionally involved in attentional control, attention is also not supported by one brain area alone. Rather, a network of multiple areas are necessary. Temporal brain aspects of attention refer to the latency of a brain response, how the brain responds (e.g., with synchronization or desynchronization of nerve cell activity) and what type of information is processed earlier (or later). Of particular importance are posterior and prefrontal areas of the cortex; the posterior parietal cortex plays an important role in bottom-up processing whereas the frontal eye field and the lateral prefontal cortex are more important for top-down processing. For the temporal order of brain activity, EEG work shows that location of an attended object ("where") is processed before other object features ("what") are processed.

4 Imagine a marathon runner getting abdominal cramps – which type of attentional focus would the runner switch to?

First the runner uses a narrow-internal focus to feel and concentrate on the muscle tension. His attention is also affected: His concentration becomes narrowed and internally focused. He is distracted by his own thoughts (e.g., worries about his pain) and has trouble concentrating on important information (e.g., positions of the opponents, instructions of the coaches). Depending on the severity of the pain, his thoughts may focus on aspects, such as "can't lose", "what causes the pain?", "may I have to give up?". Depending on his emotional status (both psychologically and physically) he may make further mistakes. Finally, he may apply a broad external focus to check his opponents in order to come to a final conclusion, i.e., to give up or to continue.

5 Summarize the current state of knowledge concerning the mechanisms by which attentional allocation is altered under anxiety and performance pressure.

Attentional allocation can be altered from internal and external distractors. Internal distractors include attending to worries (e.g., performance pressure), fatigue, lack of motivation/concentration, attentional inefficiency, switch from external to internal focus, attentional narrowing, focusing on irrelevant cues, and overanalysing body mechanisms. External distractors include visual factors, such as the audience, and auditory cues (crowd noise) as well as opponent's gamesmanship or deceptive movements.

REVIEW QUESTIONS

1   Discuss the differences between William James' definition of attention and Herman von Helmholtz's definition.

2   How does the mechanism devoted to top-down modulation of spatial information work?

3   Discuss the differences between bottom-up and top-down influences on perception and the possible consequences on motor behavior.

4   Consider the effects of expertise on gaze behavior and cue utilization.

5   Do negative emotions always lead to decreased motor performance or can you also imagine performance benefits due to negative affect?

EXERCISES

1   Identify proper attentional focus in a particular defensive situation of a competitive sport, e.g., for a soccer goalkeeper during the following action sequence: a) defending the goal when an opponent, in possession of the goal, is completely alone approaching the goal; b) during the successful defensive procedure; c) passing the ball to a teammate.

2   Select a training partner and develop a quiet-eye decision-training program (pick your sport). a) List five quite-eye characteristics that are needed to perform well in your sport and name the cognitive/ attentional skills that are most important for each characteristic (e.g., selective attention, focus and concentration, memory); b) design a training program to improve you performance; c) practice this program for 20 minutes each day to develop the optimal focus. Record your results and what quiet-eye characteristics helped you most.

3   Watch a tennis match at any level of proficiency, possibly with a classmate. Make a list of all events (include events that take place in the background). For psychological processes of the players (e.g., anger, joy, motivation, etc.), it may be helpful to converge on a joint interpretation. Subsequently, divide the events into those that are relevant or irrelevant for the players. Then divide the relevant events into those that need to be processed and those that are distracting and should be ignored. Can you find a pattern of types of events that precede the winning or loosing of a point for the players? Do you find events in which a psychological response led to winning or loosing a point?

4   During the last 10 years several neuroimaging techniques have been applied in sport science to monitor physical activity and to improve performance. If you want to investigate the neural basis of movement control, it is not sufficient to employ movement observations or the measurement of reaction times. With the help of some textbooks, think about methods of cognitive neuroscience and how they can be applied to investigate and to improve performance in your sports. Discuss in particular their different properties like spatial and temporal resolution. Which methods are correlational in nature and which interfere with neural activity?

5   Consider a typical sport situation, for example, a football quarterback under time pressure to understand the defense and pick out the correct receiver. Identify the attentional and movement requirements for the different phases. Describe which top-down and bottom-up information are important and where in the brain these information have to be processed (i.e., ventral or dorsal pathway).

6   Imagine you are a coach of a pub team (pick your sport) that always loses games due to concentration and attention deficits at critical times during the game. You want to take the team to the top by optimizing their concentration behavior during the game. Define different game and training situations, drills, exercises, and strategies you can apply to improve the concentration and attention skills of your team members.

ADDITIONAL READING

Itti, L., Rees, G. & Tsotsos, J. (2005). *Neurobiology of attention*. Amsterdam: Elsevier.

Wulf, G. & Prinz, W. (2001). Directing attention to movement effects enhances learning: A review. *Psychonomic Bulletin & Review, 8,* 648–660.

Wulf, G. (2007). *Attention and motor skill learning*. Champaign, IL: Human Kinetics.

REFERENCES

Abernethy, B., Maxwell, J.P., Masters, R.S.W., van der Kamp, J. & Jackson, R.C. (2007). Attentional processes in skill learning and expert performance. In G. Tenenbaum & R.C. Eklund, (Eds.), *Handbook of Sport Psychology* (pp.245–263). Hoboken, NJ: John Wiley & Sons.

Beilock, S.L. & Carr, T.H. (2001). On the fragility of skilled performance: What governs choking under pressure? *Journal of Experimental Psychology: General, 130,* 701–725.

Bruya, B. (2010). *Effortless attention: A new perspective in attention and action*. Cambridge, MA: MIT Press.

Buschman, T.J. & Miller, E.K. (2007). Top-down versus bottom-up control of attention in the prefrontal and posterior parietal cortices, *Science, 315,* 1860–1862.

Duchowski, A. (2007). *Eye tracking methodology. Theory and practice.* Springer Verlag: London.

Essig, K., Siegers, R., Weigelt, M., Lex, H. & Schack, T. (2010). Selection of the 'open' side – An eye-tracking study on the expertise-based influence of conscious and unconscious cues on the penalty situation in soccer. *Conference of the North American Society for the Psychology of Sport and Physical Activity* (NASPSPA), Tucson, Arizona, June 2010, p. 160.

Eysenck, M., Derakshan, N., Santos, R. & Calvo, M. (2007). Anxiety and cognitive performance: Attentional control theory. *Emotion, 7,* 336–353.

Goodale, M.A. & Milner, A.D. (1992) Separate visual pathways for perception and action. *Trends in Neuroscience, 15,* 20–25.

Gould, D., Eklund, R. & Jackson, S. (1993). Coping strategies used by more versus less successful Olympic wrestlers. *Research Quarterly for Exercise and Sport, 64,* 83–93.

Güldenpenning, I., Koester, D., Kunde, W., Weigelt, M. & Schack, T. (2011). Motor expertise modulates the unconscious processing of human body postures. *Experimental Brain Research, 213,* 383–391.

Helmholtz, H. von (1925). *Treatise on physiological optics*, (Vol. III, Translated from the Third German ed.). Rochester, NY: The Optical Society of America.

Helsen, W. & Powels, J.M. (1992). A cognitive approach to visual search in sport. In D. Brogan, A. Gale & K. Carr (Eds.), *Visual search*, Vol. 2, (pp.379–388). London: Taylor & Francis.

Hill, D., Matthews, N., Fleming, N. & Hanton, S. (2011). Alleviation of choking under pressure in elite golf: An action research study. *The Sport Psychologist, 25,* 465–488.

Hillyard, S.A. & Anllo-Vento, L. (1998). Event-related brain potentials in the study of visual selective attention. *Proceedings of the National Academy of Sciences USA, 95,* 781–787.

Holmqvist, K., Nyström, M., Andersson, R., Dewhurst, R., Jarodzka, H. & van de Weijer, J. (2011). *Eye tracking – A comprehensive guide to methods and measures.* New York, NY: Oxford University Press.

James, N., Caudrelier, T. & Murray, S. (2005). The use of anticipation by elite squash players. *Journal of Sports Sciences, 23,* 1249–1250.

James, W. (1890). *The principles of psychology.* New York: H. Holt and Co.

Janelle, C.M. (2002). Anxiety, arousal and visual attention: A mechanistic account of performance variability. *Journal of Sports Sciences, 20,* 237–251.

Janelle, C.M. & Hatfield, B. (2008). Visual attention and brain processes that underlie expert performance: Implications for sport and military psychology. *Military Psychology, 20,* 117–134.

Keele, S.W. & Hawkins, H.L. (1982). Exploration of individual differences relevant to high skill level. *Journal of Motor Behavior, 14,* 3–23.

Knudsen, E.I. (2007). Fundamental components of attention. *The Annual Review of Neuroscience. 30,* 57–78.

Koester, D., Güldenpenning, I. & Schack, T. (under review). Motor expertise modulates the perception of complex human body postures: Electrophysiological evidence.

Land, M.F. & Tatler, B.W. (2009). *Looking and acting – Vision and eye movements in natural behavior.* New York: Oxford University Press.

Land, W. & Tenenbaum, G. (2012). An outcome- and process-oriented examination of a golf-specific secondary task strategy to prevent choking under pressure. *Journal of Applied Sport Psychology, 24,* 303–322.

Leek, E.C., Reppa, I. & Tipper, S.P. (2003). Inhibition of return for objects and locations in static displays. *Perception & Psychophysics, 65,* 388–395.

Masters, R.S.W., van der Kamp, J. & Jackson, R.C. (2007). Imperceptibly off-center goalkeepers influence penalty-kick direction in soccer. *Psychological Science, 18,* 222–223.

Mesagno, C. & Mullane-Grant, T. (2010). A comparison of different pre-performance routines as possible "cocking" interventions. *Journal of Applied Sport Psychology, 22,* 343–360.

Moran, A. (2004). *Sport and exercise psychology: A critical introduction.* London: Routledge.

Nideffer, R. (1976). *The inner athlete.* New York: Thomas Crowell.

Posner, M.I. (2012). Attentional networks and consciousness. *Frontiers in Psychology: Consciousness Research,* 1–4.

Raab, M. & Johnson, J.G. (2007). Expertise-based differences in search and option generation strategies. *Journal of Experimental Psychology: Applied, 13,* 158–170.

Schmid, A. & Peper, E. (1993). Training strategies for concentration. In J.M. Williams (Ed.), *Applied sport psychology: Personal growth to peak performance* (pp.262–273). Mountain View, CA: Mayfield.

Shiffrin, R.M. & Schneider, W. (1977). Controlled and automatic human information processing: II. Perceptual learning, automatic attending, and a general theory. *Psychological Review, 84,* 127–190.

Shulman, G.L. & Corbetta, M. (2002). Control of goal-directed and stimulus-driven attention in the brain. *Nature Reviews: Neuroscience, 3,* 201–215.

Treisman, A. & Gelade, G. (1980). A feature integration theory of attention. *Cognitive Psychology, 12,* 97–136.

Tyldesley, D.A., Bootsma, R.J. & Bomhoff, G.T. (1982). Skill level and eye movement patterns in a sport-orientated reaction time task. In H. Rieder, H. Mechling & K. Reischle (Eds.), *Proceedings of an International Symposium on Motor Behaviour: Contribution to Learning in Sport* (pp.290–329). Cologne: Hofmann.

Ungerleider, L.G. & Mishkin, M. (1982). Two cortical visual systems. In D.J. Ingle, M.A. Goodale & R.J.W. Mansfield (Eds.), *Analysis of Visual Behavior* (pp.549–586). Cambridge, MA: MIT Press.

Vickers, J.N. (2007). *Perception, cognition and decision training: The quiet eye in action.* Champaign, IL: Human Kinetics.

Williams, A.M., Janelle, C.J. & Davids, K. (2004). Constraints on visual behavior in sport. *International Journal of Sport and Exercise Psychology, 2,* 301–318.

Williams, A.M. & Ward, P. (2007). Perceptual-cognitive expertise in sport: Exploring new horizons. In G. Tenenbaum & R.C. Eklund (Eds.), *Handbook of Sport Psychology* (pp.203–223). Hoboken, NJ: John Wiley & Sons.

Williams, A.M., Weigelt, C., Harris, M. & Scott, M.A. (2002). Age-related differences in vision and proprioception in a lower limb interceptive task: The effects of skill level and practice. *Research Quarterly for Exercise and Sport,* 73, 386–395.

Wulf, G. & Lewthwaite, R. (2010). Effortless motor learning? An external focus of attention enhances movement effectiveness and efficiency. In B. Bruya (Ed.), *Effortless Attention: A New Perspective in Attention and Action* (pp.75–101). Cambridge, MA: MIT Press.

Yarbus, A.L. (1967). *Eye movements and vision.* New York, NY: Plenum Press.

Chapter 18

Modeling and feedback

DAVID I. ANDERSON, AMANDA M. RYMAL AND DIANE M. STE-MARIE

SUMMARY

Modeling and feedback are two of the most common variables used by instructors to facilitate motor skill learning. Although the two variables have been studied more extensively than most other variables known to influence learning, our understanding of how to use modeling and feedback effectively is still developing. In the current chapter, we have adapted a recently developed applied framework to highlight the range of factors known to mediate the effectiveness of the two variables. Our analysis represents a synthesis of the current state of knowledge about how modeling and feedback influence the learning process.

INTRODUCTION

An Olympic diver stood perched in the hand-stand position at the edge of the ten-meter diving platform. He was determined to nail his front armstand double somersault tuck on his fifth attempt in the practice session that day, despite the trepidation he had about the dive. He hesitated a little longer in the handstand position, then breathed out and let his body fall forward. Two seconds later, after what seemed like a nearly flawless series of breathtakingly fast flips and subtle body contortions to the spectators at the pool, the diver was deep in the water, amidst a fizz of bubbles. His hands hurt and the top of his shoulders felt like they had been slapped hard. The dive had not gone as planned. He swam slowly to the side of the pool and gazed intently at the large flat screen TV on the pool deck, where a video of

his dive was just about to play. The video confirmed his suspicion about what had gone wrong. His coach gave a knowing look that said "You did it *again*." He nodded in frustration, his mistake was obvious on the video. Two minutes later the diver was back on the 10-meter platform; determined to correct his mistake.

Meanwhile, a small group of young children on the other side of the pool – who were supposed to be watching one of their peers conquer his fear of doing a back dive from the one-meter springboard – were drawn like magnets to the Olympian's dive. Despite the repeated exhortations from their teacher to watch their hapless classmate perform his dive and to listen to her feedback about what he did correctly and incorrectly, the children were mesmerized and awed by the Olympian's ability to do what they had considered to be impossible.

Some variant of the scenario just described plays out in sporting contexts across the globe on a regular basis. The scenario highlights that opportunities for observing others perform skills and to receive feedback on skills we perform are ubiquitous in sport. Those opportunities exist regardless of the sport or skill in question and regardless of the age and exper-

tise of the learner (Figure 18.1). However, the scenario also highlights that the ways in which modeling and feedback are utilized can vary dramatically depending on the characteristics of the learner and the task to be learned. In this chapter, we examine what we know about the roles of modeling and feedback in motor skill learning and we underline the range of factors that must be considered to utilize these variables effectively.

Figure 18.1 Opportunities for observing others perform skills and to receive feedback on skills we perform are ubiquitous in sport.

OBJECTIVES

After reading this chapter you should be able to:

1   Differentiate modeling and augmented feedback.
2   Describe the different types of models and augmented feedback.
3   Explain the general principles that underlie effective practice.
4   Discuss the variables that influence the effectiveness of modeling and augmented feedback.
5   Develop a plan for providing modeling and feedback in a sport setting.

MODELING AND FEEDBACK

Instructors face a dizzying array of choices when they organize practice. There are so many considerations that need to be taken into account that it is often difficult to know where to begin. It is perhaps not surprising then, that much of what occurs during practice is based on tradition rather than a scientific understanding of the variables most likely to help or hinder learning. This situation is particularly apparent in the context of providing augmented information to the learner.

DEFINITIONS

Two broad sources of information are available during the learning and performance of any skill: *task-intrinsic* information and *extrinsic* or *augmented* information. Task intrinsic information refers to the information naturally inherent in the task. Such information specifies the physical context, for example the sights, the sounds, and the smells, one experiences prior to initiating an action, and the resultant sensations one experiences during and after the action. Typically, the learner is able to gauge the success of an action based on task-intrinsic information. Whether the ball went in the hole or the basket, whether the target was knocked over, or whether the opponent was successfully beaten on a particular play can all be determined via task-intrinsic information. Augmented information refers to information that is added to the performance or learning context. It is *not* normally inherent to the context. For example, instructions from a coach, the presentation of a demonstration, or the display of errors identified by a teacher are all sources of augmented information. In this chapter, we focus on how augmented information can be used to facilitate motor skill learning.

Modeling is a form of augmented information that can be provided to learners before, during, and even after they initiate an action. Instructors can choose from many different model types, with a primary decision reflecting whether to observe others or observe the self. Five different model types can be chosen when the decision is to observe another person: *skilled models*, *unskilled models*, *learning models*, *coping models*, and *mastery models*. A *skilled model* demonstrates the to-be-learned skill free of errors whereas an *unskilled model* demonstrates the skill with a certain number of errors. When observing a *learning model*, the learner sees the individual progress from unskilled to skilled execution. In contrast to the unskilled model, the learning model provides evidence of the reduction in errors that occur as skill improves. A *coping model* demonstrates improvements in skill proficiency as well as changes in verbalizations that are initially negative and become increasingly positive as performance improves.

Mastery models, however, immediately begin with a high degree of skill on the task while consistently verbalizing high levels of confidence and ease of performance.

Two techniques are utilized when observing the self as a model; *self-observation* and *self-modeling*. *Self-observation* involves watching the self perform a task at the current skill level with whatever errors characterize performance (e.g., watching a video replay of a practice attempt). *Self-modeling,* on the other hand, eliminates those errors by editing the videos to show only the desired target performance. We will differentiate two types of self-models later in the chapter.

Augmented feedback refers to information that is provided to learners during or after an action. In contrast to most types of modeling, the information is contingent on what the learner does. Augmented feedback provided during an action has been labeled *concurrent augmented feedback* whereas *terminal augmented feedback* is the label used when it is provided after an action. Two further distinctions are commonly made within the augmented feedback family: *knowledge of results* (KR) and *knowledge of performance* (KP).

KR refers to information about the outcome of an action. For example, if a golfer's practice goal was to consistently hit balls 100 yards with a short iron, then KR might consist of the actual distance each ball traveled. Note that KR is often redundant with *task-intrinsic feedback* about the success of an action. KP is typically information about the movement pattern that was used to accomplish the task goal. The golfer might be more interested in improving her weight shift during the swing rather than hitting the golf balls a particular distance. In this case, KP could be provided on the timing or magnitude of the weight shift. KR and KP are often provided together after a practice attempt, although the two sources of feedback can be identical when the goal of the task is to perform a particular movement, such as in diving, gymnastics, and figure skating. KP about the position or movement of a body segment would be identical to KR in these situations because the desired outcome is to produce specific positions and movements of the body segments. Of course, the performer in these situations might also be provided with additional sources of KR, like a score or rating.

EFFECTIVE PRACTICE

Do general principles exist regarding the most effective ways to use modeling and augmented feedback to facilitate skill acquisition? The answer to this question is an unreserved yes, and these principles have been gleaned from theoretical discussions about what constitutes *effective practice*. Nicolai Bernstein (1967) has provided some of the most profound insights into this issue. According to Bernstein, effective practice is a form of "repetition without repetition" (p. 134). Understanding this paradox provides the key to understanding how to maximize learning during practice. For Bernstein, learning is a form of context-dependent problem solving, wherein the goal is to discover and refine solutions to the problems presented by a particular task.

For example, one of the problems for the novice basketball player is to discover the most effective way(s) to get the ball through a relatively small hoop suspended 10 feet above the floor, while ensuring that the rules that govern the sport are not violated. If learning is a form of problem solving then effective practice is practice that encourages the learner to become an effective problem solver. The learner practices solving the problem using means that are refined from one practice attempt to the next. Consequently, the process of solving the problem from attempt to attempt is repeated during practice, whereas the means by which the problem is solved varies as the learner gains deeper insight into the task as well as the resources that are available for coping with the task demands.

Contemporary discussions of Bernstein's ideas on practice stress that practice is best viewed as a search process. The "search" metaphor is useful because it highlights how variables like modeling and feedback can be used to enhance the effectiveness of practice by enabling the search process. Basically, the instructor must determine how to use modeling and feedback to channel the search for appropriate task solutions, without subverting the problem-solving process. This is a delicate balancing act. Giving learners solutions to problems will not enhance their capacity to become independent learners. At the same time, allowing the learner to flounder, particularly during the early stages of skill acquisition, could have an extremely negative effect on the person's desire to persist in learning the task. In the next section, we lay out an applied model that can help the practitioner to achieve the delicate balancing act to which we have just alluded. The framework highlights the range of variables and moderating factors that determine just how much or how little external guidance is needed to learn a task effectively.

AN APPLIED MODEL

Ste-Marie and colleagues (2012) developed an Applied Model to help practitioners use observation to enhance performance and facilitate skill acquisition. Over 100 observation (modeling) articles were coded based on the five "Ws" (why, where, who, what, when) and one "H" (how) structure of journalistic research. The Applied Model's first recommendation is to consider the observer and task characteristics before choosing a type of modeling intervention. These two characteristics emerged as important moderators of the effectiveness of any modeling intervention. The next recommendation is to consider the desired outcome (*why*) and the context in which modeling will be applied (*where*). These two key variables will guide the practitioner's choice of the most appropriate person to observe (*who*), as well as the source of that information (e.g., live vs video model) and potential supplemental information associated with the modeling (*what*). The final step is to determine *when* the model should be observed and *how* the observed information should be delivered. As we will demonstrate in the next section, these questions are just as appropriate when applied to the implementation of augmented feedback as they are to the implementation of modeling. The only difference is the emphasis placed on each of the questions.

Why and where (modeling and feedback)

Cumming et al. (2005) identified three reasons why athletes choose to engage in observation: 1) to learn new skills; 2) to develop or execute game strategies; and 3) to regulate psychological and physiological states. Feedback is used for similar purposes, although the most common uses are to facilitate skill learning and motivate learners to persist in the learning process. We focus on the learning of skills in the current chapter, with occasional reference to the motivational functions of modeling and feedback. Although modeling and feedback can be utilized in many different contexts (e.g., laboratory, competition, rehabilitation, and practice) we focus on the practice context.

Who

Modeling: Many model types can be used to facilitate skill acquisition and deciding which one is best is often overwhelming. Should we observe ourselves or another? Is it better to view a skilled or unskilled model? Coaches and teachers typically assume that a skilled model will benefit learning the most, however, considerable research shows that this is not necessarily the case. Earlier, we defined the different model types: *skilled models, unskilled* models, *learning models*, *coping models*, and *mastery models*. Within these categories, the model can be a peer, matched in gender or age (for example), or a non-peer. Skilled models are often more effective for learning new skills, however, unskilled or learning models can be as effective if the learner also receives the model's KR or KP. A learning model may actually induce more strategy use and problem solving than a skilled model. Peer models may be more effective than non-peer models, though the advantage is minimized if the learner also receives the model's KR or KP. Mastery models, who demonstrate skilled performance and express high beliefs in their ability to perform a skill, appear to be the most effective type of peer model, though coping models can have a greater influence on psychological factors, such as self-efficacy.

Learners also have the opportunity to view themselves learning a skill and this is accomplished by-and-large via video replay (as noted in the diving scenario at the beginning of the chapter). Earlier, we defined two types of self models: *self-observation* and *self-modeling*. Observing the self appears to have a greater effect on learning than observing another person, though task characteristics may influence the extent to which this conclusion holds true. The benefits of *self-observation* are perhaps not surprising given that researchers have continuously emphasized the importance of perceived similarity of the observer to the model; and, of course, the most similar model is a self-model.

Self-modeling techniques can be further divided based on the editing of the performance. The *positive self-review* technique shows the best performance the individual has done thus far. For example, a basketball player may view a highlight video of his best-ever defensive plays (Figure 18.2). The *feedforward* technique requires further editing to allow

Figure 18.2 In the positive self-review technique, a video of a basketball player's best-ever performances can be edited together to create a highlight video that can be viewed before a big game.

learners to view themselves performing a skill that has not yet been achieved in a specific sequence or context. For example, footage from a gymnast's previous performances could be edited together to create an optimal tumbling line. Although the positive self-review and feedforward techniques have not been compared empirically, they both offer exciting possibilities for enhancing skill acquisition.

Feedback: A dearth of research has been conducted on the "who" question relative to provision of augmented feedback. This is probably the case because it is obvious that the learner will always be the target of feedback. Nevertheless, important questions about who should provide the feedback remain unanswered. For example, taking the lead from the modeling literature, we might ask whether it is more beneficial to receive feedback from a peer versus a non-peer, or from a skilled performer versus an unskilled performer. There is considerable scope for research in this area.

What

Modeling: Intra- and inter-limb coordination, specified by the relative motion between the joints and segments, is argued to be one of the most salient movement features that observers pick up when watching a model (Scully & Newell, 1985) (Figure 18.3). Relative motion information can be highlighted through the use of point light displays (PLD); a technique that involves placing light-reflecting markers on certain joints and videotaping the person performing an action. For example, a novice high jumper may watch a PLD demonstration of a skilled high jumper to gain valuable information about the timing between the shoulders, hips, and knees during the Fosbury Flop.

Information about the absolute motion of the distal end of a limb segment can also be picked up and highlighted by a model (i.e., end point displays). Whether highlighting relative motion or the absolute motion of an end point

Figure 18.3 Intra- and inter-limb coordination, specified by the relative motion between the joints and segments, is one of the most salient movement features that observers pick up when watching a model.

is the most effective way to facilitate skill learning seems to depend on task characteristics and most likely on learner characteristics. For example, highlighting relative motion has been shown to benefit the learning of cricket bowling, but the information from a single endpoint display has proved sufficient for learning how to kick a soccer ball. When more joints and segments must be coordinated in the kinematic chain, such as in cricket bowling, endpoint displays may be less effective.

PLDs have also been compared to full body live models and video models to determine what (or how much) information needs to be conveyed to the learner. Constraining the information by using a PLD does not seem to enhance learning any more than providing a full body demonstration. This is good news because PLDs can take considerable time and effort to create. More research is needed, however, to determine whether constraining information in a PLD might be more or less effective for children, whose capacity to process information is limited, or for complete novices, who are often overwhelmed by the amount of information that needs to be processed in the early phase of skill acquisition.

The information highlighted in a demonstration can also be supplemented with other information (e.g., verbal cues) or with activities (e.g., imagery) to increase the learner's attention to what is being modeled and to help create a cognitive blueprint to guide motor reproduction. Both types of supplements have been shown to facilitate learning. Using the high jump example again, a verbal instruction such as "drive your hands forward and up at take off" could be provided while learners observe the model. Alternatively, learners could be asked to visualize themselves performing the jump after they have watched the model. The learner's age and characteristics of the to-be-learned task have an important influence on whether models need to have supplemental information or activities. Younger children benefit more from observation when a verbal component is added, especially when the task has a strategic component (e.g., motor sequencing tasks). Whether information should be added to the model before, during, or after the demonstration remains unresolved. It is important to consider, however, that children may not have the attentional capacity to process concurrent information during the demonstration, in which case the addition of information prior to or after the demonstration would be most beneficial.

Feedback: Unlike modeling, the question of what information should be (or could be) highlighted for the learner has been seriously neglected. This situation likely reflects the preoccupation researchers have had with studying KR, where the question of what to provide augmented feedback on is relatively straightforward – feedback should be provided on whatever criterion defines a successful outcome on the task. Moreover, we know even less about how the feedback we provide needs to change as the learner becomes more skilled at the task. The importance of asking what information is important as feedback for the learner has only recently become apparent as researchers have shifted their attention away from KR and toward KP.

The first question an instructor might ask is whether to provide the learner with KR or KP or both sources of information. The answer to this question can be fairly obvious in many situations. For example, a player practicing basketball free throws doesn't need KR from the coach about whether she made or missed the basket. However, we should not assume that because the athlete can usually determine the outcomes of their practice attempts that KR will typically be redundant in most naturalistic sport settings. It is not always easy to determine when KR will be redundant with task-intrinsic feedback because learners often use KR to confirm their own assessment of success or failure. For example, a golfer may be able to estimate just how far his golf ball landed from the pin, but might also like KR on the precise distance to confirm his estimate. In some situations, KR is absolutely necessary to confirm whether the goal has been achieved, particularly when the goal is to perform a task in a certain amount of time. A swimmer attempting to swim 200 meters with specific split times will want KR from the coach to confirm whether the target split times were achieved. In each of the aforementioned situations, the instructor might choose to provide KR as the only source of augmented feedback to the learner. The decision to focus solely on KR is often made in order to motivate the learner or to encourage the learner to discover their own strategies to solve the problems posed by the task.

The decision to use KP creates many more choices for the instructor. The first problem is to answer the big question posed earlier; what aspect(s) of performance should be emphasized for the learner? Following the discussion on modeling, we might ask whether it is better to provide feedback on relative motion versus absolute motion, however, this question has not been addressed in the literature. Consequently, the instructor's knowledge of the skill becomes critical. The instructor should first perform a task analysis to identify the critical features of the task and then rank those features in terms of their importance; i.e., develop a priority list. Ideally, the features would be ranked in terms of how highly they correlate with success on the task. The critical features can be transformed into *descriptive* or *prescriptive* KP statements once they have been ranked. A *descriptive* KP statement simply describes what just happened. For example, "your back was arched at the top of the handstand." A *prescriptive* KP statement identifies what has happened, but through suggestions about how to make changes on subsequent attempts. For example, "tuck your hips under more and keep your ribs in while holding your handstand." Beginners and young children are likely to profit more from prescriptive KP than descriptive KP because they don't yet understand the underlying causes of their performance errors (Figure 18.4). Conversely, descriptive KP statements may be sufficient for

Figure 18.4 Beginners and young children are likely to profit more from prescriptive KP than descriptive KP because they don't yet understand the underlying causes of their performance errors.

more experienced learners and may also inject a desirable degree of problem solving into the learning process.

Three other questions have been addressed relative to the question of what aspect of performance to feedback to the learner: 1) what level of precision is appropriate?; 2) should augmented feedback focus on errors versus correct performance?; and 3) should augmented feedback be on task features that encourage an external or internal focus of attention? Regarding precision, it is advisable to provide beginners and young children with less precise information and to increase precision as the ability to detect and correct errors improves. Beginners and young children may even profit from qualitative information rather than quantitative information. It may be sufficient, for example, to tell a young javelin thrower that his release angle was too steep whereas a more experienced thrower might benefit from knowing that his release was at 45 degrees rather than 35 degrees.

The question about whether it is better to provide feedback on errors versus correct performance is more difficult to answer. Early research showed that feedback on errors led to better learning than feedback on correct performance. This seems logical if one considers that learning a new skill consists largely of correcting or eliminating errors in performance. However, recent research suggests that providing augmented feedback on correct performance can enhance motivation to learn a task, perhaps benefiting skill acquisition because the learner is more engaged in the learning process or more committed to persisting with practice. Self-efficacy is likely an important moderating variable when deciding whether to provide augmented feedback on errors versus correct performance. Learners who have low self-efficacy might need the motivational benefit that comes from receiving information about correct performance whereas learners with higher self-efficacy might be able to tolerate and profit from information about errors.

The final question about whether augmented feedback should be on features that encourage an external or internal focus of attention is also difficult to answer. Instructions that encourage an external focus of attention on movement effects or outcomes have been shown to facilitate performance and learning. The general explanation for this effect is that focusing internally can disrupt the automatic control processes involved in movement execution that are usually governed by lower levels of the motor control hierarchy. Recent findings suggest that the performance and learning benefits associated with an external focus of attention have implications for the aspects of performance on which to provide feedback. Some evidence suggests that providing feedback on movement effects, such as the trajectory of a ball or the swing path of a club, can facilitate learning relative to providing feedback on movements of the joints and body

segments. The desirability of focusing augmented feedback on external features requires further research, however, before it can be recommended without reservation. This is particularly evident when one considers that skill acquisition often requires the learner to interfere with automatic control processes. Without such interference, it can be difficult to break persistent habits of coordination that impede the discovery of more optimal movement patterns. This finding may explain why some research suggests than an internal focus of attention may be more appropriate for beginners and an external focus more appropriate for skilled performers.

When

Modeling: When is the best time to observe a model? This may seem like a simple question with a simple answer but unfortunately very few studies have investigated whether viewing a model is more effective before, after, or interspersed throughout physical practice. The conclusion so far is that learning is not influenced by *when* the model is introduced to the learner. That said, most researchers have presented models to their learners before and during physical practice. Clearly, more research is needed to confirm whether the timing of a demonstration has any impact on learning.

The other question that can be asked relative to when to observe a model is how frequently should demonstrations be provided to the learner? The limited research on this question suggests that the more times the model is viewed, the better. This assumption has an important caveat attached to it. When learners are given control over the number of times they request to see a model, they request it very *infrequently*, and yet they learn the task as effectively as learners who are shown the model more frequently (e.g., 100%). The self control given to the learner appears to offset the limited number of times the model is seen. Presumably, the learner requests a demonstration when they want to review a specific aspect of the task they don't fully comprehend. Consequently, they may attend to the demonstration in a much more focused manner when they request it than when it is imposed on them. (Note: Ste-Marie and colleagues [2012] place the frequency of viewing in the "how" section of their Applied Model, however, we have included it here to maintain consistency with the feedback literature).

Feedback: When to provide augmented feedback has been studied more extensively than nearly any other variable known to influence motor skill learning. Our understanding of when to provide augmented feedback has been driven by the *guidance hypothesis.* The guidance hypothesis states that augmented feedback scaffolds the learning process by providing the learner with a temporary crutch that will not be available in the performance context. When delivered appropriately, augmented feedback guides the discovery of effective solutions to movement problems and it guides discovery of the critical sources of task-intrinsic feedback that will support performance in the absence of augmented feedback. Learners can, however, develop a dependency on augmented feedback if it is given in a way that discourages the processing of task-intrinsic feedback. Learning suffers when this happens; bringing us back to the importance of the delicate balancing act introduced earlier.

One of the first decisions an instructor makes is whether to present *augmented feedback* (AF) during a practice attempt (*concurrent augmented feedback*; CAF) or after a practice attempt (*terminal augmented feedback*; TAF). An example of how CAF might be presented to a learner is when an athlete returning from an ankle injury is shown a graphic representation of her postural sway while balancing one-legged on a force plate. The same information could be provided to the learner terminally by showing her the graphic representation of postural sway after the practice trial. CAF has been shown to facilitate the rate of perfor-

mance improvement during practice relative to TAF, however, learners are far more likely to become dependent on CAF and suffer a regression in performance when AF is removed.

Removing AF after practice is a common way to determine how much was learned during practice. A test given after practice without the benefit of AF is referred to as a *retention* or *transfer* test. Researchers use retention and transfer tests to separate the temporary changes associated with practice from the relatively permanent changes associated with learning. We call this separation the *performance-learning* distinction. AF is one of many variables known to produce different effects on performance and learning. Much of the attention given to the question of when to provide AF has been motivated by curious disassociations between what happens during practice and on the retention or transfer test. Providing AF concurrently with performance, providing it too quickly after performance, providing it too frequently, or providing it in a way that makes it too easy to use can encourage dependency, such that practice performance is facilitated but learning is degraded. Problem solving and the processing of critical sources of task-intrinsic feedback can be compromised in each of these situations.

A number of scheduling procedures have been developed to decrease the likelihood that learners will become dependent on augmented feedback. These procedures include: reducing the frequency of AF or fading it out over practice, delaying its presentation after a practice trial, delaying AF by a certain number of trials, delaying AF over trials and presenting it in summary form, and providing AF only after the learner exceeds a certain bandwidth of error tolerance. In each of these procedures the learner is forced to work harder to utilize the AF and so must direct more attention to task-intrinsic feedback to improve on the task. Having learners estimate their errors prior to receiving AF is another way to encourage the processing of task-intrinsic feedback and discourage dependence on AF. Finally, similar to what was noted in the modeling section above, allowing learners to decide when they receive AF has proven to be a simple and effective way to facilitate learning. Learners request feedback on surprisingly few trials when given control over its presentation, similar to what has been found in the modeling literature, and they seem to prefer it on what they perceive to be successful practice attempts.

Several variables are known to moderate the effects of different schedules of AF. Learner characteristics and task characteristics are among the best understood of these variables. The key to utilizing AF to promote learning is to provide each learner with a challenge that matches their skill level relative to the complexity of the task. When the learner is young or inexperienced, or the task is complex, AF can be provided more frequently, or in an easier-to-use form to guide the learner toward solving the movement problem. As skill level increases, however, the frequency can be reduced and the AF can be made more difficult to use. The most difficult schedules of AF should be reserved for the most experienced learners or the simplest tasks. Guadagnoli and Lee (2004) have provided an excellent discussion of how to modify challenge levels during practice to promote skill learning.

How

Modeling: How a model is presented to a learner has been characterized in at least two ways: the viewing angle and the viewing speed. These two variables have not been studied extensively and so the conclusions we draw in this section are tentative. The viewing angle can be from an *objective, subjective*, or *looking glass* perspective. For example, an objective view would be represented in a situation where a dance instructor faces her students while demonstrating a new stepping sequence. If the dance instructor turned around and presented her back to the students while demonstrating the stepping sequence she would be providing a subjective viewing angle. If the instructor

mirrors the stepping sequence to her students (e.g., moves her left leg when the learner is supposed to move his right leg), this would be classified as a looking glass viewing angle. The objective and looking glass views are thought to require more cognitive involvement because the learner must flip the information from the modeled behavior to produce the desired movement. More cognitive involvement should facilitate the development of a stronger cognitive representation of the skill and so it should also facilitate learning. In contrast, the subjective view has been shown to lead to faster improvement because it does not require the learner to flip the visual information. The cognitive representation of the skill may be weaker, however, because cognitive involvement is diminished.

We also view models through video demonstrations and so the speed at which the movement is seen can be varied. Researchers have speculated that slow motion viewing benefits skills with high complexity, where relative timing and coordination are important, but may hinder skills where absolute timing or timing variations are required. For example, a young gymnast may benefit from viewing a video in slow motion of another gymnast performing a kip on the uneven bars but get more out of watching a video of a gymnast performing a jump up mount on the balance beam in real time. The focus in the kip is on the coordination among many body segments, whereas the focus on the jump up mount is on the speed with which it has to be executed.

Feedback: Augmented feedback can be presented to the learner either verbally or non-verbally. It is far more common to present feedback verbally than non-verbally, probably because it's so much easier to verbalize to the learner what they are doing correctly or incorrectly. Nevertheless, researchers have devised a number of clever non-verbal ways to present augmented feedback.

Video feedback (equivalent to *self-observation* in the modeling literature) is probably the most common non-verbal method of providing augmented feedback. Despite how common video feedback is in practice settings, it is important not to overwhelm learners, particularly in the beginning stages, because they are unable to differentiate which aspects of performance are important to process and which are irrelevant. In support of this notion, video feedback seems to be most effective when visual or verbal cues are used to underscore which aspects of performance the learner should attend to when watching the video. Although much more research is needed to ascertain what variables moderate the effectiveness of video feedback it is probably safe to say that this form of feedback will be useful for beginners and younger children only if verbal and visual cueing accompanies it, but more useful on its own for highly skilled learners, such as the Olympic diver mentioned at the beginning of the chapter.

A variety of electronic devices have been used to provide augmented feedback to learners and several manufacturers of sports clothing are working on interactive garments that can provide real-time feedback on physiological parameters such as heart rate and respiration in addition to information about movement characteristics. Sports equipment manufacturers have developed devices to provide instantaneous feedback on parameters such as club head velocity and orientation at ball contact in the golf swing. Computers have been used to visually provide kinematic and kinetic feedback on movement patterns and the forces that underlie them and a number of software programs are available to manipulate the presentation of video feedback to a learner; enabling, for example, a video of the learner to be shown next to a video of an expert, a video to be shown at different playback speeds, and a video to be highlighted with text or arrows or various other graphic symbols. Many of these programs are also available as applications on smart phones, providing opportunities to provide non-verbal augmented feedback to learners in virtually any context. A variety of programs also exist to compile, synthesize, and present game or match statistics to an athlete. Again, researchers have not confirmed how effective the presentations of many of these newer forms of feedback are for facilitating skill learning and so more research is needed in this area.

Kinematic and kinetic feedback is often provided to learners in an auditory form. One of the earliest applications was in swimming, where researchers attached force transducers to paddles that were strapped to the swimmers' hands and clipped an accelerometer onto a belt that the swimmers wore around their waists. The outputs from the sensors were converted into an auditory signal that varied in pitch when the force on the paddle or whole body velocity changed. This type of augmented feedback led to clear improvements in swimming performance. Similar devices have been used to provide real-time feedback on joint angles during a movement and in one case researchers used such a device to improve gymnasts' movement form on the pommel horse. The gymnasts received an auditory signal every time their knee joint angle exceeded a certain threshold during their routine. Auditory feedback on the stability of the gun barrel has also been used to improve rifle shooting performance. (See Magill & Anderson, 2012, for many examples of how kinetic and kinematic feedback have been used to enhance the learning of sports skills.)

Unfortunately, there is a shortage of research comparing the effectiveness of presenting augmented feedback in one form versus another. Comparisons across different methodologies are extremely difficult because there are so many different ways to present augmented feedback to the learner and it is nearly impossible to control the information content when feedback is presented in one form versus another. Nevertheless, some general principles can be gleaned from the literature. For example, auditory feedback is a better way to convey temporal information to the learner and visual feedback is a better way to convey spatial information. Beginners and young children are far less likely to profit from non-verbal forms of augmented feedback because these forms often provide information that the beginner simply can't assimilate. Consequently, it is better to save the more sophisticated methods of providing augmented feedback for advanced learners. It is also worth bearing in mind that sometimes the simplest forms of feedback are the most effective. For example, researchers recently showed that providing light touch to a gymnast's thigh had an immediate and dramatic effect on stability in the handstand position.

CONCLUSION

Instructors must choose from a vast selection of alternatives when determining the most effective manner in which to present augmented information to learners. The decision-making process can be simplified and systematized, however, by focusing on the five "Ws" (why, where, who, what, when) and one "H" (how) described in this chapter. Although we still have much to learn about how to use modeling and feedback effectively, the Applied Model we have presented provides an excellent guide for researchers and practitioners by highlighting what we currently know and what we need to know.

LEARNING AIDS

1   Describe the different types of models that can be used to present information to a learner.

A skilled model demonstrates the proper execution of the skill being learned. An unskilled model demonstrates the skill with errors. A learning model progresses from executing the skill with errors to executing the skill without errors. A coping model demonstrates improvement in performance while decreasing the frequency of verbalizations expressing performance difficulty and lack of confidence and increasing verbalizations expressing performance ease and confidence. A mastery model consistently demonstrates proper execution of the skill and consistently expresses confidence and ease of performance. Self-observation involves viewing the self perform a skill at the current skill level; thus, including errors (i.e., basic video replay). Self-modeling attempts to eliminate performance errors by editing the videos to show only the desired target performance (e.g., edited video replay).

2   Differentiate between knowledge of results (KR) and knowledge of performance (KP) and provide examples to show how each is used in a sport context.

KR refers to information about the outcome of an action. Showing a pistol shooter where her shots landed on a target would be an example of KR. KP is typically information about the movement pattern that was used to accomplish the task goal. Showing a rower a graphic representation of the relation between his knee angle and trunk angle during a stroke would be an example of KP.

3   Discuss what implications the idea that practice is a type of repetition without repetition has for the use of modeling and feedback.

Repetition without repetition implies that the learner repeatedly attempts to solve the movement problem using means that are improved from practice attempt to practice attempt. Essentially, the learner searches for better and better ways to solve the problem. Consequently, modeling and feedback should be used to help channel the search process. The practitioner needs to find a balance and provide just the right amount of information. With too much information, the learner can come to rely on the practitioner and ultimately become an ineffective problem solver. With too little information, the learner can lose confidence and motivation to continue learning the task because of limited success.

4 Provide an example of a question one might ask when considering each of the variables in the Applied Model (i.e., why, where, who, what, when, how)

Will modeling and augmented feedback be used to learn new skills or regulate psychological or physiological states (why)? Will modeling and augmented feedback be used during practice or during competition (where)? Is it more appropriate for a skilled or an unskilled performer to model a skill or provide augmented feedback (who)? Should a model or augmented feedback highlight the relative motions among joints and body segments or the absolute motion of the distal end of a limb segment (what)? Should modeling and augmented feedback be provided after every practice attempt (when)? Should modeling and augmented feedback be provided in real time or slow motion (how)?

5 Describe a situation where modeling and augmented feedback might be used together to facilitate skill acquisition.

Modeling and augmented feedback are frequently used together to promote skill acquisition. For example, a golf instructor might demonstrate to a beginner the correct way to execute a pitch shot before the beginner starts to practice. During the practice session, the instructor might provide prescriptive KP statements to the learner. The instructor could supplement the KP statements given during practice with additional demonstrations of the correct way to execute the shot. The instructor should be mindful of the guidance hypothesis when presenting information to the learner.

REVIEW QUESTIONS

1 Describe the difference between task-intrinsic and augmented information.

2 Explain how modeling is different from augmented feedback.

3 Identify the two variables that are important moderators of the effectiveness of any modeling or feedback intervention.

4 Describe the difference between *self-observation* and *self-modeling*.

5 Discuss the difference between descriptive and prescriptive KP statements.

6 Discuss what instructors can do to decrease the likelihood that learners will become dependent on augmented feedback.

EXERCISES

1   Use the information provided in the table; the *moderating variables*, *why*, *where*, and the **outcome** of the intervention are provided for you. Design an observation intervention and a feedback intervention for each scenario. Use the space provided in the table to rationalize why you believe the component you chose was the most appropriate for your intervention.

Moderators	Why	Where	Who	What	How	When	Outcome
Observer and task: Novice 6 year old child; fastball (baseball pitch; child has never pitched a fastball)	Skill Learning (general movement pattern)+ Confidence in throwing fastball	At practice; on baseball diamond actively practicing fastball					Improved performance and confidence in ability to throw fastball
Intermediate level curlers learning curling strategies as measured by accuracy and speed of decisions	Strategy learning in curling	Training; sport club					Improved strategies for curling (accuracy and speed of decisions)

2   For the following scenario, develop an intervention using the five "Ws" and one "H" using both sources of augmented information to optimize skill acquisition (i.e., how could modeling and feedback work together to enhance skill acquisition)? Scenario example: Katie, a 12-year-old novice trampolinist, is attempting to learn a back straight (i.e., straight body back somersault in the air) on the trampoline from three bounces. Her goal is to learn how to keep her legs straight and have an open body position throughout the somersault. Katie has a competition in three months and is working hard in the trampoline club so she can complete the skill in her routine. It might help to draw out a table similar to the applied framework.

ADDITIONAL READING

Bandura, A. (1986). Social Foundations of Thought and Action. Englewood Cliffs, NJ: Prentice-Hall.

Kernodle, M.W. & Carlton, L.G. (1992). Information feedback and the learning of multiple-degree-of-freedom activities. *Journal of Motor Behavior*, 24, 187–196.

McCullagh, P., Law, B. & Ste-Marie, D.M. (2012). Modeling and performance. In. S. Murphy (Ed.), *The Oxford handbook of sport and performance psychology*. pp.250–272. New-York, NY: Oxford University Press.

Salmoni, A.W., Schmidt, R.A. & Walter, C.B. (1984). Knowledge of results and motor learning: A review and reappraisal. *Psychological Bulletin*, 95, 355–386.

Williams, A.M. & Hodges, N.J. (2005). Practice, instruction and skill acquisition in soccer: Challenging tradition. *Journal of Sports Sciences*, 23, 637–650.

Wulf, G., Shea, C. & Lewthwaite, R. (2010). Motor skill learning and performance: A review of influential factors. *Medical Education*, 44, 75–84.

REFERENCES

Bernstein, N.A. (1967). *The co-ordination and regulation of movements.* Oxford: Pergamon.

Cumming, J., Clark, S.E., Ste-Marie, D.M., McCullagh, P. & Hall, C. (2005). The functions of observational learning questionnaire (FOLQ). *Psychology of Sport and Exercise, 6,* 517–537.

Guadagnoli, M.A. & Lee, T.D. (2004). Challenge point: A framework for conceptualizing the effects of various practice conditions in motor learning. *Journal of Motor Behavior, 36,* 212–224.

Magill, R.A. & Anderson, D.I. (2012). The roles and uses of augmented feedback in motor skill acquisition. In N.J. Hodges and A.M. Williams (Eds.), *Skill Acquisition in Sport: Research, Theory and Practice* (2nd ed., pp.3–21). NY: Routledge.

Scully, D. & Newell, K. (1985). Observational learning and the acquisition of motor skills: toward a visual perception perspective. *Journal of Human Movement Studies, 11,* 169–186.

Ste-Marie, D.M., Law, B., Rymal, A.M., O, J., Hall, C. & McCullagh, P. (2012). Observation interventions for motor skill learning and performance: an applied model for the use of observation. *International Review of Sport and Exercise Psychology, 5,* 145–176.

Chapter 19

Organization of practice

DAVID L. WRIGHT, HIROSHI SEKIYA AND JOOHYUN RHEE

SUMMARY

Although there is a saying "practice makes perfect," studies on motor skill learning have found that only extensive exposure to "quality" practice leads to expertise. Therefore, an emphasis should be placed on both the quantity and quality of practice as important aspects of effective motor skill training. This chapter first introduces differentiation of temporary performance effects and more persistent learning effects of practice. Then, from viewpoints of composition and scheduling, we consider how skill acquisition can be facilitated through the use of specificity and variability of practice, dyad training, massed and distributed practice, and incorporating contextual interference into training environments.

INTRODUCTION

The effective use of practice time is a critical consideration for many coaches, teachers, instructors, and clinicians in a broad set of recreational, amateur, and professional settings that have as their goal the improvement in skilled behavior or functional recovery through rehabilitation. For example, consider the high school volleyball coach who, every season, has to deal with a limited allocation of gym time in preparation for the year ahead. Or the soccer coach that has to share field time with the rugby team because they both have seasonal play during the autumn. Practice is also an issue that is relevant to the physical therapist who, due to insurance restrictions, is limited to two hours of interaction every two weeks with a patient recovering from hip surgery. Despite this restriction the therapist is expected, and hopes, to work toward quickly correcting the patient's perturbed gait kinematics in a manner that allows the patient to safely navigate their home environment after they leave the confines of the clinical setting. In each of these situations a core question entertained by the coach is how best to organize bouts of practice or training to maximize the functional capacity of the player or athlete. It is this very question that is the focus of this chapter with the intent being to highlight features of practice organization that can be used to facilitate the design and delivery of practice for successful behavioral outcomes.

OBJECTIVES

After reading this chapter you should be able to:

1 Describe the difference between the performance and learning components of skill acquisition.
2 Discuss some characteristics of deliberate practice.
3 Describe the difference between practice composition and scheduling.
4 Identify examples of practice composition and scheduling.
5 Explain how the identified examples of practice composition and scheduling facilitate motor skill learning.

DIFFERENTIATING PERFORMANCE AND LEARNING

Before delving into specific features of practice that impact learning, one must clearly understand the time frame over which the change in behavior is expected. In the world of athletics, a logical boundary during which a change in behavior would be targeted is commonly driven by the training regime of the athlete. For example, improvements in the serving action of an elite-level tennis player from practice manifest as reduced variability in placement of their topspin serve to the "ad" court, will hopefully remain at least until the next practice period later that day or at practice the following day. Or the young child, who attends gymnastic training twice a week, hopefully returns to the second of these sessions with some residual knowledge of the handstand that they were trying to fine-tune during the previous session. In both cases the focus is on the retention of knowledge that was acquired during practice such that it is readily available for use to guide the production of the practiced skill at a later date. Performance during delayed retention (i.e., performance of the skill on the second of the days indicated in the previous examples) is often used as an index of the extent of learning that has occurred as a result of the previous practice.[1]

However, it should not be overlooked that there are times in which practice can be used to induce a more immediate or rapid change in behavior. Sometimes a change is necessary "right away" without regard for persistence of the skill during later practice episodes. Practice in this case is not being used to influence learning but to temporarily meet a demand that, at present, is unattainable. For example, if an American football coach wants to ensure that an offensive lineman executes a particular blocking scheme during the next set of downs, he may have him "physically practice" while on the sideline, listen to detailed instruction, or review a set of images that depict the desired or erroneous behavior. The goal here is not to enable this athlete to successfully execute the practiced action when the team returns to practice the following week, rather, the intention is to increase the likelihood that this player immediately executes the correct play for the remainder of the current game.

The previous examples highlight the fact that practice has the power to induce relatively transient effects on performance, as in the case of the offensive lineman. However, we must be cautious in assuming the change in performance is indicative of the learning that has taken place as a consequence of practice. Indeed, researchers have described numerous examples of practice manipulations that induce rapid improvement in performance but little learning as indexed by retention or transfer tests (Salmoni, Schmidt & Walters, 1982). The present chapter focuses on identifying practice organizational strategies that support persistent as opposed to transient, short-lived performance changes. To identify the features of practice organization that differentially influenced performance (short-term transient changes) and learning (more permanent change associated with learning), researchers frequently use the transfer paradigm which has both an acquisition and test phase. The *acquisition* component is a period of practice during which the critical manipulation of the "practice" independent variable is made (e.g., massed or distributed practice). In contrast, the *test* phase is a further set of practice trials presented after a sufficient temporal delay (i.e., often 24 hours to mimic "real" training schemes) to assess; (a) "relatively permanent or persistent" capacity to exhibit the newly-acquired behavior using a retention test; or (b) the propensity to exhibit generalizability of the new behavior to a novel demand evaluated with a transfer test (see Endnote 1).

ORGANIZING PRACTICE: HOW MUCH?

Before evaluating the contribution of practice organization for performance and learning of motor skills it is critical to note the importance of practice extent. It goes without saying that achieving expertise is a result of experiencing a lot of practice. To be blunt, there is no shortcut to mastering a skill of interest, the learner must engage in as much practice as possible. Indeed, the significance of practice extent to learning is central to an ongoing, contemporary discussion, couched in terms of a nature–nurture debate, addressing the relative contribution of talent (innate predisposition for exhibiting a high degree of motor skill) and experience (usually resulting from practice) to the attainment of expertise (Ericsson, 2006).

Deliberate practice

It should be noted that expertise is a consequence of *deliberate practice,* which needs to be distinguished from other "recreational" practice or activity. Ericsson (2006) proposed that deliberate practice is designed to constantly challenge the performer to develop an increasingly detailed database of domain-specific knowledge as well as encourage the use of a more complex mental representation that governs the execution of skilled behaviors. Indeed, Ericsson proposes that the learner is better served by not completely automating critical behaviors, a characteristic of many theoretical accounts of skill acquisition. Instead, practice that is deliberate incorporates activities that demand continual self-reflection and evaluation which are cognitively taxing. An early demonstration that a long-term commitment to deliberate practice is associated with superior performance for musicians is depicted in Figure 19.1 from Ericsson, Krampe, and Tesch-Romer (1993). Similar data has since emerged from studies that have examined other sports including field hockey, figure skating, and soccer.

Why is deliberate practice so critical for learning?

For the coach or teacher the take-home message should be clear, investing in more extensive practice is paramount to skill acquisition. This is not the whole story however. Instructors and athletes alike should avoid what Ericsson referred to as "mindless drill" activity. This type of practice is not focused on correcting errors and fails to encourage meta-cognitive or reflective activity that might guide future corrective actions to an imperfect skill. Rather, the coach must strive to use deliberate practice characterized by goal-directed activities (designed by the coach or the performer) that target a current weakness in the skill of interest. It typically involves activities that are presently outside the scope of current capability of the athlete and will likely be

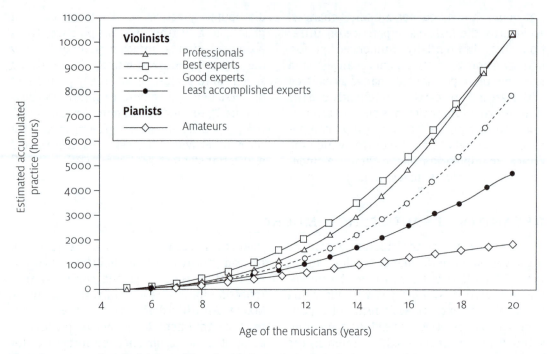

Figure 19.1 Despite all of the musicians in this figure being relatively accomplished, it is clear to see that an investment in a greater number of hours of solitary (deliberate) practice is associated with greater recognition (professional or best-expert). Taken from Ericsson, K.A., Krampe, R.T. & Tesch-Romer, C. (1993). The role of deliberate practice in the acquisition of expert performance. *Psychological Review*, 100, 363–406.

characterized by considerable performance error during any particular period of practice. This is counter to the goal of many "real-world" learning environments in which "successful practice" is sought via the use of detailed instruction, feedback, or through the use of external devices that guide the performer to execute the required behavior (e.g., PlaneFinder™ in golf, see Figure 19.2).

The "big-picture" goal of deliberate practice is to encourage and continually improve the learner's capacity to plan, control, modify, and continually evaluate their performance. This is expected to be associated with significant mental and/or physical effort (cf. autom-

atized behaviors when arrested development has occurred), a large degree of concentration, and in some cases a reduction in the amount of fun associated with practice. So, more practice – deliberate practice – should be the first prerogative of the coach and athlete when learning is concerned. This being the case, the next goal is to consider how one can manipulate the practice environment to ensure features of deliberate practice are present during training. The next sections identify a few approaches to organizing practice, which have undergone considerable research scrutiny, that might fit the bill.

Figure 19.2 The PlaneFinder™ claims to facilitate a golfer's ability to assess what they are doing right and wrong when trying to execute the swing with the correct trajectory.

ORGANIZING PRACTICE: COMPOSITION

Some years ago, Shea, Shebilske, and Worchel (1997, p. 234) proposed that organizing practice should consider two interrelated components referred to as composition and scheduling. *Practice composition* addressed the specific nature of the skill that is practiced. In an experimental setting a question focused on composition would be characterized by the individual being exposed to different forms of practice or engaging in practice activities that were fundamentally unique from one another. Common examples would include, but are not limited to, experiments comparing the effectiveness of practice variability vs. specificity, observation vs. physical practice, and/or whole vs. part practice. In contrast, *practice scheduling* focuses on questions related to how a set of skilled activities influence ongoing performance and retention when presented in: (a) different orders (e.g., inducing greater contextual interference by arranging practice in a random or interleaved schedule as opposed to a blocked or fixed schedule); and (b) across different time periods (e.g., including greater rest in practice through more distributed training rather than massed training). In essence, in the case of scheduling, individuals in all experimental conditions are eventually exposed to exactly the same amount and type of activity but the presentation of the activities, in either order or time, is arranged differently for each learner. The next sections review experimental evidence addressing practice procedures that fall within the purview of practice composition and scheduling that also incorporate some of the core features of deliberate practice. We begin with an examination of two practice composition manipulations – *practice variability* and *dyad training*.

COMPOSITION: SPECIFICITY AND VARIABILITY OF PRACTICE

Most coaches are familiar with the specificity of training principle that is used to guide the organization of strength training plan. This principle suggests that exercises are selected such that they target a particular muscle group of interest and the intended adaptation. In the case of motor learning, a similar approach is referred to as specificity of practice. In this case, the coach targets a skill that needs to improve (i.e., free throw shooting) and then organizes either part or all of a practice bout that is tailored "specifically" to facilitate this skill (e.g., 100 free throw shots from the free-throw line). One question that has been considered in recent years is if specificity of practice is indeed the optimum way to organize motor skill repetitions during training to enhance learning.

The potential effectiveness of practice variability for learning was broached by Richard Schmidt (1975) in his schema theory of motor skill acquisition. This account included the prediction that practice variability as opposed to specificity would support transfer. This was important because Schmidt envisioned motor learning as a form of "rule learning" and practice variability is critical to developing rules. In an applied setting one might envision a golf instructor, supervising a "driving" practice, requiring his client to change the club being used as opposed to hitting thirty "drivers." According to schema theory, frequent changes in club use, during practice, is more likely to develop the capacity to navigate the diverse "driving" demands the golfer might face during a round of golf. Golf, like many sports, seems to place a heavy premium on movement adaptability which, according to Schmidt, is achieved through experiencing practice variability.

A much more intriguing question is if practice variability could also enhance acquisition of an isolated specific skill, such as the free-throw skill noted earlier, as opposed to a more general capacity to execute a "shooting" skill (i.e., range of set shots that would include the free throw). Shea and Kohl (1990) made the astonishing claim that practice of the target task (i.e., shooting free throws) in conjunction with related variations actually supports the development of a richer memory for the target task reflected not only in superior transfer but also retention. Across two experiments participants performed a sub-maximal force production task in one of three practice compositions. In the first, called the specific condition, the performers only practiced a target response, to exert a 175N force, executed every 16 s. A second and third experimental condition, referred to as specific-variable and specific-specific respectively, involved performing additional trials of a force production task that were either 25–50N above or below the criterion task force of 175N or more attempts at the criterion force of 175N. Retention of the criterion task was evaluated 24 hours later.

Experiencing practice variability supported superior performance both for the first trial of the test (in some situations in sport the performer only gets one opportunity to "perform") and for the first block of test trials. Interestingly, just adding more repetitions of the target force during the 16 s interval, as was the case in the specific-specific condition, actually led to the poorest test performance. Squeezing in too many repetitions within the 16 s was detrimental to learning. We will return to this issue later when discussing practice distribution. For now, these data argue that practice of task variations that are related to a target skill can contribute to the acquisition of the target response.

In subsequent work Shea and Kohl (1991) went a step further and asked if the type of variability introduced while practicing a target task influences the resultant learning. In this work participants again executed repetitions of a sub-maximal force (150N) combined with: (a) no additional practice; (b) more practice of the target response; (c) intervening practice of related tasks (150N $\pm$ 25 or 50N); or (d) intervening practice of an unrelated tracking task (see Figure 19.3a). Figure 19.3b shows that during the test trials administered 24 hours later, the smallest error (i.e., best performance) was displayed by the participants exposed to variability that was related to the target response. Practice of an unrelated task provided a much smaller benefit to retention.

How does experiencing practice variability support learning?

A prominent explanation for the benefit of practice variability for skill learning is the encoding variability account. This position argues that a comparison of task-specific information with other related knowledge has the potential to enrich the details of the task being learned, making it stand out from alternative options when selecting an appropriate response is necessary. Alternatively, it has been argued that identifying relationships with other associated responses affords the opportunity to increase the likelihood of successful retrieval as the performer can reconstruct the requisite knowledge from other associated information when needed. Thus, more retrieval "routes" become available as a result of practice variability.

In summary, coaches and instructors of motor skills should be careful in assuming that specificity of practice is the most effective method to develop all motor skills. While there is relatively limited evidence supporting substantial gains for the retention of a target task from practice variability, in situations in which the performer is required to generalize a learned motor skill to novel performance conditions or exhibit a range of movement flexibility, introducing variability into the practice environment seems especially productive. The good news is that recently there has been a renewed interest in the specificity-variability of practice issue. For example, there is a growing body of knowledge targeting "especial skills" which is the emergence of a highly specific exemplar task (e.g., the free throw), that results from specific practice, but exists within a very general performance capability (e.g., set shots) that is facilitated by variable practice (Keetch, Schmidt, Lee & Young, 2005). Another proposal that is getting some attention contends that "variability" is not a unitary construct. Rather variability is present from multiple sources when learning a motor skill (e.g., variability in intent or goal, variability in motor output) and understanding how to best use each sources of variability will be important for acceleration in learning (Ranganathan & Newell, 2013).

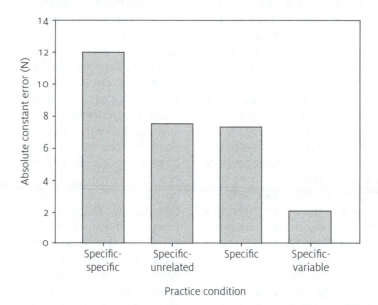

Practice condition	Training		Test
Specific	T T T T T		TTT
Specific + specific	TTTTTTTTTTTTTTTTTTTTTTT		TTT
Specific + variable	T A B C T A B C T A B C T A B C T		TTT
Specific + unrelated	T 123 T 123 T 123 T 123 T		TTT

Figure 19.3a, 19.3b Top panel (Figure 19.3a) displays the practice conditions used by Shea and Kohl (1991) to examine specificity (specific and specific+specific groups) and variability (specific+variable and specific+unrelated). Letters and numbers represent repetition of tasks (T is target task). The bottom panel (Figure 19.3b) indicates that error is lower as a result of related variability (i.e., specific-variable). Information adapted from Shea & Kohl (1991).

DYAD TRAINING

When thinking about learning motor skills most people first think about how to use physical practice. Yet, as is stated in other chapters in this book, other forms of non-physical practice can effectively contribute to the acquisition of complex motor skills. There is ample evidence that both observation and imagery can influence the planning and execution of behaviors encountered in many sports. A unique practice composition protocol termed *dyad training* takes advantage of combining physical practice and observation. It was first examined in the context of a video game called Space Fortress which was an experimental game that included many components, both perceptual and motor, that had to be considered and acted upon to achieve success. Some considered this game to mimic the dynamic environment in which pilots operate when flying complex aircraft used in the military. Many of the demands that made Space Fortress "complicated" are present in a variety of sporting situations: demanding quick decisions, establishing priorities, allocating attention, and executing complex motor responses. It turns out that a protocol called *active interlocked modeling* (AIM), in which two individuals performed Space Fortress together but distributed the task load between them, was an effective means of successfully performing in the video game. In essence, learning occurred despite the fact an individual performed only part of the overall skill but in the context of the entire skill being executed.

The early accounts as to why this form of dyad training worked focused on the role played by observation in the context of also having the opportunity to engage some physical experience with the skill of interest. As a result of this work other investigators directly evaluated the effectiveness of combining trials of physical practice and observation. Shea, Wulf, and Whitacre (1999) had individuals practice a balance task on their own or as a dyad. The dyad protocol involved either: (a) alternating between physical practice and observation every trial; or (b) one individual of the pair observing a string of trials performed by their partner on the balance task before roles were switched. The results revealed that practicing within a dyad format initially suppressed performance but eventually led to significantly superior performance during delayed tests administered the

next day when the dyad involved alternating between physical practice and observation every trial. This suggested that it was not the observation or physical practice per se that was critical, rather it was the manner in which these formats interacted that was most powerful when experienced in close temporal proximity.

Shea, Wright, Wulf, and Whitacre (2000) demonstrated that dyad training is also effective in supporting the development of flexible skilled behaviors. They had individuals practice a two-hand coordination task, again a common feature of many sport activities, using just physical practice alone or as part of a dyad that involved the alternation of physical practice and observation. Learning in this case was assessed both in terms of retention (reproducing the two-hand coordination task) and transfer (capacity to effectively generalize to a variation of the original two-hand coordination task). While the dyad participants displayed equivalent retention performance to the physical practice alone condition, transfer performance was significantly better following dyad training than for the physical practice group.

These findings are remarkable when you consider a dyad will experience approximately 50% less physical practice than the physical practice alone counterparts yet adequately supports both retention and transfer. Creating a practice environment that is so efficient (i.e., training two for the price of one or training an individual at half the cost) is rare in most skill acquisition domains and is of course particularly attractive to instructors of all type of skills. Moreover, the potential importance of this practice protocol when athletes are carrying an injury or are fatigued would be very appealing to most instructors.

HOW DOES COMBINING OBSERVATION AND PHYSICAL PRACTICE USING DYAD TRAINING SUPPORT LEARNING?

There have been a number of proposals that have been offered to explain why dyad training is successful. One proposal highlights the

social interaction between the partners in the dyad that is absent when training alone. This can take the form of competition and or cooperation that might both benefit learning (McNevin, Wulf & Carlson, 2000). The introduction of competition, for example, might be seen as introducing an effective challenge to the learner to pursue predetermined goals which is a prominent characteristic of deliberate practice described by Ericsson (2006). An additional source of social facilitation that may result from dyad training is an increased sense of accountability. That is, when performing in a pair, each participant is, in a sense, contributing to another athlete's ability to learn the task. Further increasing accountability by requiring the participants of dyads to share the strategies used in a previous trial may induce even greater cognitive investment that can be useful for learning.

Shea and colleagues (2000) viewed the effectiveness of dyads a little differently. They proposed this training format allowed participants to quickly identify strategies or techniques used by a partner that was unsuccessful. This allowed them to quickly eliminate these approaches from the potential pool of solutions that needed to be tried by the current observer on subsequent physical practice trials. Likewise, promising strategies could be immediately sampled during the next opportunity. Alternatively, observing offers an opportunity to engage task planning that might otherwise not be entertained during physical practice because of the concomitant motor demands associated with physically performing the task. That is, executing the task may require the learner's full attention early in practice. Having the chance to observe on some trials may give the learner the opportunity to extract important information that would be missed if only physically practicing.

ORGANIZING PRACTICE: SCHEDULING

Recall that *practice scheduling* is focused primarily on how the instructor can present the same set of activities in either different orders or across different time periods to maximize ongoing performance and more importantly induce a persistent capacity for reproducing the skilled behavior. In the following sections we review two practice scheduling manipulations – *distribution of practice* and *contextual interference* – that have been the focus of considerable research efforts in recent years.

SCHEDULING: DISTRIBUTION OF PRACTICE

Consider for a moment that you are a high-school volleyball coach that has just received word from the athletic director that, due to renovations to your gymnasium, you will share an alternative gym space with the other sports in your school for the upcoming season. As a result you will be allotted 10 hours per week for your team to practice. The instructor must now dissect the available time allotted into: (a) the number of sessions; and (b) the time per session that will maximize learning. The importance of how to successfully distribute practice does not stop here. During any one session the instructor is again faced with how to best organize the activities during each session (e.g., number of trials or repetitions) to optimize each specific bout of practice with the athlete. In general, practice distributions that have a relatively larger rest interval between practice (e.g., either between a practice session or between repetitions) is referred to as *distributed practice* whereas a practice distribution involving a relatively shorter rest interval between practice events (e.g., between a practice session or between repetitions) is referred to as *massed practice*. Let's take a look at a couple of ways this issue has been addressed experimentally.

Distribution of sessions and days: Spacing macrostructure

Pyle, as early as 1913, demonstrated that for a fixed amount of practice time, providing the learner more sessions of shorter duration compared to fewer session that lasted longer, was more effective in improving verbal learning and simple mathematic skills. A more elaborate version of Pyle's work addressing motor skill learning was conducted by Baddeley and Longman in 1978. In this study British postal workers were administered 60 hours of training in a new method for sorting mail. The challenge for the researchers was how to best schedule 60 hours of training in terms of: (a) the time spent during each session of practice; and (b) the number of sessions that would be used each day. This is similar to the situation faced by football coaches in spring practices when they organize two-a-days or soccer coaches organizing preseason practice. Baddeley and Longman used four combinations of these two factors displayed in Figure 19.4a. As you can see in Figure 19.4b, receiving one session a day of only one hour, the most distributed practice condition, led to faster acquisition of the motor skill and to superior retention that was assessed as long as nine months later! The most massed condition, which consisted of two practices a day of two hours, resulted in the slowest acquisition of the sorting skill. While the latter condition finished the 60 hours sooner (i.e., 15 days), spacing the practice out over 60 days was ultimately more effective when the goal is long-term retention or persistence of knowledge (see Lee & Wishart, 2005, for an alternative perspective on these data regarding training efficiency).

More recently, Shea, Lai, Black and Park (2000) examined a similar question to Baddeley and Longman using a gross motor skill that involved dynamic balance, an important feature for many athletic endeavors. Participants tried to keep their balance for 90 s on a stabilometer followed by 90 s of rest. Some individuals' practice stretched over two days with each day involving seven 90 s trials. Alternatively, other participants had two sessions of seven trials during one day with a 20-min rest interval between sessions. Thus, practice distribution in this experiment consisted of merely lengthening the temporal interval between the last trial in Session 1 from 20 minutes to 24 hours! Retention test trials were administered 24 hours after practice was completed. While there was little performance difference in Session 1, practice spread across two days resulted in superior performance during the second set of seven trials as well as during the retention test. In a follow-up study Shea and colleagues revealed the same finding when examining the impact of distributing the same amount of practice over three days rather than one for a task requiring greater manual dexterity, a key-pressing task, than the balance task used in the previous work. Similar findings were reported by Dail and Christina (2004) for novice golfers.

Taken together, the early laboratory work of Baddeley and Longman (1978) as well as Shea and colleagues, in conjunction with translation of these efforts to the golfer's putting green, suggest that some attention to organizing practice over more rather than fewer sessions is important for learning. Importantly, this impact seems rather robust given the benefit exists for a range of tasks (e.g., gross vs. fine motor) as well as across a wide range of temporal distribution schemes.

Distribution of trials within a session: Spacing microstructure

An additional feature of practice distribution pertains to how one should organize the activities contained in any single session (e.g., how trials of the sorting task were executed within each hour in the Baddeley and Longman study). In essence the instructor must decide to squeeze as many repetitions into a session as possible (i.e., massed practice) or be willing to spread out repetitions as would be the case in a more distributed practice regime. This

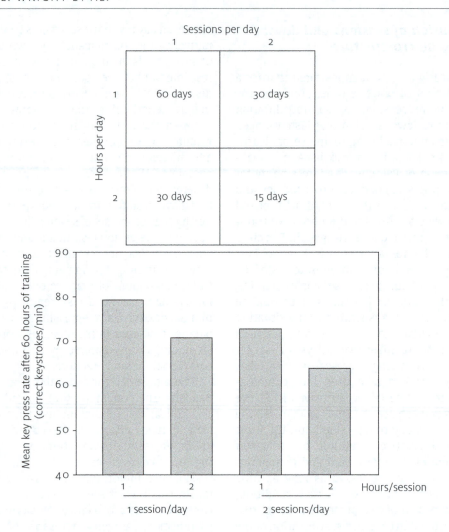

Figure 19.4a, 19.4b Top panel (Figure 19.4a) displays the distribution of 60 hrs of training used by Baddeley and Longman (1978). The most distributed schedule of the 60 hrs of training (1 hr once per day) resulted in the best performance (i.e., highest number of key presses/min) at the end of training (Figure 19.4b).

issue revolves around determining the appropriate inter-repetition interval. An early example of experimental work that targeted this problem was reported by Bourne and Archer (1956). In this study participants practiced a 30-s pursuit rotor tracking task for 21 trials with inter-trial intervals of 0, 15, 30, 45 or 60 s. The 0-s inter-trial interval was of course the most massed practice condition whereas the 60-s inter-trial interval was the most distrib-

uted situation. Although the performance for each inter-trial interval condition improved with practice, differences among conditions grew larger as a function of increasing inter-trial intervals, such that at the end of training, the 60-s inter-trial interval condition yielded the highest performance with the 0-s inter-trial interval group performing relatively poorly. Unfortunately, the tests trials were administered only five minutes after practice was completed, thus making an assessment of the resultant learning difficult. Nonetheless, the longer the inter-trial interval that facilitated acquisition also supported superior short-term retention.

Since there are other examples of findings similar to those of Bourne and Archer it is tempting to conclude that larger inter-trial intervals would be the best choice for instructors striving to optimize the return from practice. However, as was the case with this previous work, most of the early efforts to examine the importance of the length of the inter-trial interval failed to evaluate long-term capacity. Reviews of this literature (Lee & Genovese, 1988; Donovan & Radosevich, 1999) highlight the importance of the type of task being acquired when determining how the coach contemplates the ideal inter-trial interval. Specifically, continuous tasks – those that have an arbitrarily-defined beginning and end as well as usually being significantly longer in duration (e.g., swimming) – benefit from distributed rather than massed practice for both performance and learning.

The most suitable inter-trial interval for discrete skill learning, a skill most frequently characterized by having a clearly defined start and end as well as being relatively short in duration from start to finish (e.g., golf swing), has received far less experimental scrutiny. According to Lee and Genovese the sparse experimental data available appears to suggest massing practice can aid both acquisition and test performance of a discrete skill (Lee & Genovese, 1989). It is worth returning for a moment to the work of Shea and Kohl (1991, see Figure 19.3), discussed earlier, in which specific practice (a more distributed grouping of trials) was compared to more massed practice conditions (i.e., smaller inter-trial intervals) that were composed of more practice of the target task (i.e., specific-specific) or variations of the target task (i.e., specific-variable). Some observations are noteworthy from this study. First, the force production task used in this work certainly fits the definition of a discrete skill.

Second, making practice more massed (i.e., smaller inter-trial interval) by inserting more repetitions of the same force production task within a fixed time interval led to poorer retention of this skill compared to the more distributed condition. Finally, creating a more massed practice condition, by inserting variations of the target force, was more effective than the most distributed practice condition. Thus, using very small interval inter-trial intervals or massed practice, can be productive for learning as long as what is repeated induces a full complement of information processing during the repetition.

Why does spacing facilitate learning?

For the most part, distributed practice, either between sessions of practice or within a session, supports ongoing performance and learning. Why is this the case? The first, and probably most obvious explanation, is that spacing sessions or practice and/or repetitions may reduce fatigue – not just physical but also cognitive fatigue. A second possibility focuses on a potential negative consequence of massing practice – the encouragement of deficient processing. A deficient processing account proposes that repetitions experienced closer in time demand less rehearsal or attention with each trial. This is exactly what Ericsson argued should be avoided if learning is the goal. A third explanation targets a positive facet of distributing practice and falls under the rubric of encoding variability, and account previously highlighted in the variability and specificity section. Advocates of this position suggest that when a repetition occurs across a larger time span the potential to encode the knowledge a little differently from when the same task was encountered in the preceding encounter. In essence, task-specific knowledge is coded in a slightly altered context which potentially provides a larger array of contextual cues that can be used to aid later recall. This would also be a reason why the massed practice condition that incorporated practice variability in the work of Shea and Kohl actually provided an avenue for learning. Finally, a theoretical position offered specifically to account for the spacing of practice sessions focuses on the facilitation of consolidation, a fundamental memory process that converts labile memories into a stable form. Research in neuroscience has shown that learners given sufficient time (e.g., 4–6 hours) exhibit greater resistance to interference from practice with related information presumably because the original learning was exposed to adequate consolidation.

CONTEXTUAL INTERFERENCE: ORGANIZING PRACTICE VARIABILITY

You will recall earlier that exposure to practice variability, a practice composition manipulation, can enhance retention as well as the learner's capacity to exhibit generalization. The issue of practice variability is further scrutinized under the rubric of the *contextual interference* effect. Assume for a moment that all learners can be exposed to the same extent of practice variability, the next issue for the instructor is, can the variability be scheduled in a particular way to garner a greater return? Let's consider the following example to look a little closer at this issue. A tennis coach intends to teach a beginning class the forehand and backhand drives including both cross-court and down the line shots. One practice schedule that could be adopted by the coach, called blocked practice, involves executing a predetermined number of trials (or maybe time) focused on one of the skills (e.g., forehand, cross-court) before introducing practice of the next variation (e.g., backhand, down the line). This continues until the intended number of trials or repetitions with each variation of the tennis ground strokes has been experienced by the students. This practice format involves a relatively small degree of contextual interference because each tennis stroke is executed in a very similar practice context. Alternatively, a random practice schedule could be used by the coach that entails unsystematic presentation of all four variations within each practice session. In this case a relatively high level of contextual interference is created because the requisite skill changes from trial to trial. The beauty of this manipulation is that the extent of variability can be equated (either in terms of number of trials or time) during a bout of practice thus affording the opportunity to independently assess the contribution of contextual interference to transient changes in performance and long-term learning.

To cut to the chase, there is a sizeable body of literature that has developed over the past 20 years that has demonstrated that blocked practice typically leads to faster improvements in immediate performance but significantly poorer retention. Random practice is also particularly effective in inducing a superior capability for generalization to novel task demands. Moreover, the advantage of random practice is most clearly evident when tests are conducted within a random format which mimics a great many sports domains (e.g., tennis serves or shots, hitting in baseball, etc). These findings were all evident in the original demonstration of the contextual interference effects over 30 years ago by Shea & Morgan (1979). Individuals were administered a total of 54 trials of practice in either a blocked or random format for three separate arm-movement tasks that had unique spatial demands. Test trials were provided after both 10 minutes and 10 days in either a blocked or random format. Initial training clearly revealed an advantage for blocked practice but after only a ten-minute delay individuals trained in a random as opposed to blocked format exhibited superior test performance which persisted for 10 days. This was especially true in the tests that were conducted in a random test environment. This basic profile has now been replicated in numerous applied settings such as baseball, basketball, tennis, and volleyball to name just a few.

How does more interference enhance learning?

A great deal of experimental effort has been exerted over the last 20 years to try to understand why random practice provides the impetus for more successful learning than its block practice counterpart. Two main theoretical accounts have emerged, namely the forgetting-reconstruction, and the elaborative processing positions (see Wright et al., 2004 for comparison of these theoretical positions). The first of these, proposed by Lee and Magill (1985), places special importance on the additional retrieval practice and other unspecified reconstructive processes that occur in random but not blocked practice. Lee and Magill argued that trial-to-trial repetition of the same task during blocked practice reduces the likelihood that information specific to that task is forgotten at the beginning of each subsequent repetition of the task. In this case, little reconstructive activity in terms of movement planning is necessary because the requisite information remains in working memory. On the other hand, during random practice, the learner must deal with intervening responses assumed to cause forgetting of task-specific information. This then demands more extensive response planning is engaged during each repetition of a task.

Shea and Zimny (1983) focus on the organization and richness of knowledge contained in long-term memory from random and blocked practice. This occurs as a result of using two qualitatively different forms of information processing during practice. Intra-task processing consists of task analyses that exclude reference to information directly related to the other tasks being acquired or other knowledge in memory. Inter-task processing serves to highlight the similarities and differences between the tasks being acquired by between-task analyses or evaluation of new information with old knowledge. Shea and Zimny suggest that random practice is well designed to encourage the latter processing mode that is assumed to contribute to a far richer knowledge network that can support accurate task reproduction during delayed tests. This occurs because inter-task processing requires information about multiple tasks is present together in working memory, which frequently occurs during random practice.

An earlier section of this chapter highlighted the importance of using variability to develop an athlete's capacity to exhibit performance flexibility or adaptability. This section, addressing contextual interference, suggests that each coach must further consider scheduling the variability in a random manner to maximize the learning benefit. Explanations as to why this type of practice organization appears to support long-term retention is congruent with core facets of deliberate practice. That is, random practice appears to continue to challenge the performer throughout a bout of practice, requiring that each repetition is independently handled in terms of planning and execution in a manner that contributes to updating the performer's current task-specific knowledge base.

DELIBERATE PRACTICE REVISITED: THE TAKE-HOME MESSAGE ABOUT ORGANIZING PRACTICE

Practice might be considered the single most important tool available to the coach to directly impact the success of their athletes and teams. Very few people would argue with the basic tenet that increasing practice exposure will be accompanied by a positive impact of long-term performance capacity. This is congruent with the basic rule of thumb that is proposed in a recent bestselling book[2] that claimed that the engagement of 10,000 hours or 10 years of practice was associated with the accomplishment of "expertise." The reader must be careful however not to infer from this "rules of thumb" that merely entertaining this amount of practice is in itself sufficient to exhibit an expert-level of performance. More specifically it is the accumulation of many hours of *deliberate practice*, a form of practice that is intensely focused, goal-oriented, challenging for the learner, and accompanied by constant self-reflection: that is the true "golden ticket" to expertise.

In this chapter a number of ways to organize practice were reviewed in terms of their potential for supporting long-term retention or learning, including increasing practice variability and spacing of practice trials, ensuring sufficient contextual interference, and pairing learners in dyads. Each of these practice arrangements is uniquely implemented on the field or in the gymnasium. However, the common thread running through each method is a heightened challenge placed on the learner throughout training such that they are encouraged to constantly improve the planning, control, and execution of the skill being learned, a crucial requirement of deliberate practice as described by Ericsson (2006). Indeed, there is evidence that some of the practice procedures discussed (e.g., high contextual interference condition such as random practice) are characterized by relatively greater attention demands and concentration, another crucial component of deliberate practice.

On the flip side, some practice organizations, proposed herein to enhance learning, have also been viewed as more motivating or fun. For example, it has been argued that one benefit of practice variability, at least for children is that it fosters intrinsic motivation. This is counter to the interpretation of deliberate practice as not being "fun" by skilled violinist and ice hockey players. Furthermore, there is evidence of sophisticated meta-cognitive clarity of individuals exposed to high variability or contextual interference (Simon & Bjork, 2001), another feature at the heart of the deliberate practice position, yet a lack of conscious awareness of the benefits of greater spacing of practice for postal workers assigned to a training condition involving greater spacing of practice has also been reported (Baddeley & Longman, 1978). Clearly, there is much work to be done to fully understanding how specific practice organization can capture the essential ingredients presumed to define deliberate practice. In the meantime, the practice composition and scheduling protocols discussed here can act as a springboard for coaches and athletes alike to reconsider the effectiveness of some of the commonly-adopted practices, assumed to support learning in sport today.

LEARNING AIDS

1 Define alternative ways in which a program of training can include greater practice distribution. Explain why using greater distribution would help your athlete.

A practice organization that involves fewer sessions, each of greater duration is termed massed practice; this has been classically distinguished from distributed practice that would entail more frequent number of sessions that are of shorter duration. With respect to each individual practice session, the term "massed practice" is used when inter-repetition intervals are shorter, whereas "distributed practice" is associated with relatively longer inter-repetition intervals. Research has generally shown that distributed practice, in comparison to massed practice, leads to better performance in acquisition and retention of motor skills.

2   Can contextual interference be used to learn any type of motor skill across the entire period of learning?

Contextual interference (CI) effects have been found not only for simple tasks designed to be used in the laboratory but also for more complex sport skills. However, the benefits of more contextual interference has been reported to be greater for laboratory tasks than for sport skills. Guadagnoli and Lee (2004) proposed a challenge point framework to explain the interaction between the influence of skill characteristics, learner characteristics, and characteristics of practice schedules on the resultant learning benefits. According to this framework, the interaction of task characteristics (e.g., skill complexity) and learner characteristics (e.g., expertise) should dictate the appropriate level of CI created in practice. Relatively low levels of CI are predicted to facilitate learning when unskilled learners practice complex skills, whereas higher levels of CI are needed to facilitate learning for skilled learners practicing simple skills. Although this framework provides a useful beginner's guide for implementing practice features discussed in this chapter, a significant amount of experimental effort is still needed to fully understand the complex dynamics that exist between the learner, the task, and the learning environment.

3   Can composition and scheduling practice manipulations be combined to maximize learning?

Most of the experimental work that has been conducted and presented herein focuses on isolating the specific influence of a feature of composition or scheduling that might enhance motor skill learning. It should not be ignored however, that in the "real world" the coach is afforded the luxury of trying to combine practice features that might expedite acquisition or stabilize memories for motor skills that have been well learned. The use of practice variability to enhance the use of massed practice was one example that was mentioned in this chapter. We also noted the literature that is developing on "especial" skills which involve a unique way of thinking about combining specificity and variability of practice. No matter what combination of composition and scheduling methods the coach chooses to combine, the overarching guiding principle should be the inclusion of characteristics of deliberate practice that were introduced in the first part of the chapter in each and every practice.

 ## REVIEW QUESTIONS

1   Explain how distribution of practice can be examined across sessions and for an individual practice session.

2   Explain why high contextual interference facilitates learning.

3   Describe how dyad training captures characteristics of deliberate practice.

4   Describe the relationship between variability of practice and contextual interference.

EXERCISE

1 Choose a sport in which you participate as a learner or coach/teacher, and describe how you might organize practice sessions for one month. You must specify the outcomes (i.e., changes in behavior) that you anticipate as a result of the practice. Describe how the specific features of your practice plan (i.e., across session, within session) will instigate specific characteristics of deliberate practice described by Ericsson (2006). Explain how you have modified features of your practice plan to accommodate unique learner (e.g., skill level, disability) and/or skill (e.g., task complexity) components.

NOTES

1 In many studies the focus of some long-term behavioral change is not only effectively recalling the action i.e., the serve to the "ad" court that was the focus of the previous practice bout but also enhancing the performer's capacity to generalize this behavior to related but less-practiced actions. Extending the previous example, the instructor would welcome some transfer of the topspin serve improvement noted from shots hit to the "ad" court to facilitate execution of the same serve to the "deuce" court. Practice manipulations that improve both retention and transfer of skills would be important to instructors and coaches.

2 See *Outliers* by Malcolm Gladwell (Penguin, 2009).

ADDITIONAL READING

Magill, R.A. (2010). *Motor Learning and Control: Concepts and Applications* (9th ed.). NY: McGraw-Hill.

Schmidt, R.A & Lee, T.D. (2011). *Motor Control and Learning: A Behavioral Emphasis* (5th ed.). IL: Human Kinetics.

REFERENCES

Baddeley, A.D. & Longman, D.J.A. (1978). The influence of length and frequency of training session on the rate of learning to type. *Ergonomics, 21*(8), 627–635.

Bourne, L.E. & Archer, E.J. (1956). Time continuously on target as a function of distribution of practice. *Journal of Experimental Psychology, 51*(1), 25–33.

Dail, T.K. & Christina, R.A. (2004). Distribution of practice and metacognition in learning and long-term retention of a discrete motor task. *Research Quarterly for Exercise and Sport, 75*(2), 148–155.

Donovan, J.J. & Radosevich, D.J. (1999). A meta-analytic review of the distribution of practice effect: Now you see it, now you don't. *Journal of Applied Psychology, 84*(5), 795–805.

Ericsson, K.A. (2006). The influence of experience and deliberate practice on the development of superior expert performance. In K.A. Ericsson, N. Charness, P.J. Feltovich & R.R. Hoffman (Eds.), *Cambridge Handbook of Expertise and Expert Performance* (pp.685–705). Cambridge University Press. New York, NY.

Ericsson, K.A., Krampe, R.T. & Tesch-Romer, C. (1993). The role of deliberate practice in the acquisition of expert performance. *Psychological Review, 100*, 363–406.

Guadagnoli, M.A. & Lee, T.D. (2004). Challenge point: A framework for conceptualizing the effects of various practice conditions in motor learning. *Journal of Motor Behavior, 36*(2), 212–224.

Keetch, K.M., Schimdt, R.A., Lee, T.D. & Young, D.E. (2005). Especial skills: Their emergence with massive amounts of practice. *Journal of Experimental Psychology: Human Perception and Performance, 31*(5), 970–978.

Lee, T.D. & Genovese, E.D. (1988). Distribution of practice in motor skill acquisition: Different effects for discrete and continuous tasks. *Research Quarterly for Exercise and Sport, 59*(4), 277–287.

Lee, T.D. & Genovese, E.D. (1989). Distribution of practice in motor skill acquisition: Learning and performance effects reconsidered. *Research Quarterly for Exercise and Sport, 60*(1), 59–65.

Lee, T.D. & Magill, R.A. (1985). Can forgetting facilitate skill acquisition? In D. Goodman, R.B. Wilberg & I.M. Franks (Eds.), *Differing Perspectives in Motor Learning, Memory, and Control* (pp.3–22). Amsterdam: North-Holland.

Lee, T.D. & Wishart, L.R. (2005). Motor learning conundrums (and possible solutions). *Quest, 57*(1), 67–78.

McNevin, N.H., Wulf, G. & Carlson, C. (2000). Effects of attentional focus, self-control, and dyad training on motor learning: Implications for physical rehabilitation. *Physical Therapy, 80*(4), 373–385.

Pyle, W.H. (1913). Economical learning. *Journal of Educational Psychology, 4*(3), 148–158.

Ranganathan, R. & Newell, K.M. (2013). Changing up the routine: Intervention-induced variability in motor learning. *Exercise & Sport Sciences Reviews, 41*(1), 64–70.

Salmoni, A.W., Schmidt, R.A & Walter, C.B. (1982). Knowledge of results and motor learning: A review and critical reappraisal. *Psychological Bulletin, 95*(3), 355–386.

Schmidt, R.A. (1975). A schema theory of discrete motor skill learning. *Psychological Review, 82,* 225–260.

Shea, C.H. & Kohl, R.M. (1990). Specificity and variability of practice. *Research Quarterly for Exercise and Sport, 61*(2), 169–177.

Shea, C.H. & Kohl, R.M. (1991). Composition of practice: Influence on the retention of motor skills. *Research Quarterly for Exercise and Sport, 62*(2), 187–195.

Shea, C.H., Lai, Q., Black, C. & Park, J. (2000). Spacing practice sessions across days benefits the learning of motor skills. *Human Movement Science, 19,* 737–760.

Shea, C.H., Shebilske, W. & Worchel, S. (1993). *Motor Learning and Control.* Englewood Cliffs, NJ: Prentice Hall.

Shea, C.H., Wulf, G. & Whitacre, C. (1999). Enhancing training efficiency and effectiveness through the use of dyad training. *Journal of Motor Behavior, 31*(2), 119–125.

Shea, C.H., Wright, D.L., Wulf, G. & Whitacre, C. (2000). Physical and observational practice afford unique learning opportunities. *Journal of Motor Behavior, 32*(1), 27–36.

Shea, J.B. & Morgan, R.L. (1979). Contextual interference effects on the acquisition, retention, and transfer of a motor skill. *Journal of Experimental Psychology: Human Learning and Memory, 5*(2), 179–187.

Shea, J.B. & Zimny, S.T. (1983). Context effects in memory and learning movement information. In R.A. Magill (Ed.), *Memory and Control of Action* (pp.145–366). Amsterdam: North-Holland.

Simon, D.A. & Bjork, R.A. (2001). Metacognition in motor learning. *Journal of Experimental Psychology: Learning, Memory, and Cognition, 27,* 907–912.

Wright, D.L., Brueckner, S., Black, C.B., Magnuson, C.E. & Immink, M.A. (2004). Long-term motor programming improvements occur via concatenation of movement sequences during random but not during blocked practice. *Journal of Motor Behavior, 36:* 39–50.

Chapter 20

Elements and construction of motor control

THOMAS SCHACK, BETTINA BLÄSING, CHARMAYNE HUGHES, TAMAR FLASH AND MALTE SCHILLING

SUMMARY

Athletes of all sports must be able to process and integrate sensory information from various sources (e.g., the environment, their own body, produced action effects), in order for skilled motor performance to occur. In this chapter, we introduce the basic elements and building blocks of motor control, the connections between these basic elements and sensory inputs, and how internal models account for the various processes of action planning and execution. Most importantly, we want to emphasize how these components work together and contribute to motor control. Secondly, we show how modeling approaches and theoretical considerations on control frameworks help to understand the interaction of these components and their contributions to motor performance and motor control. For this purpose, we introduce an integrative model that illustrates the hierarchical nature of cognitive motor control. Based on this model we present consequences for applied work and the usage of different coaching methods.

INTRODUCTION

Motor planning and motor control are central topics in sports; almost all of our daily activities require that we plan, execute, and control our movements in a skillful manner. Indeed, via our motor actions we are able to interact with the environment and with each other. As in sporting contexts, our movements are purposeful and aim at achieving particular action goals. These goal-directed actions require that we integrate information about the current context from the environment via sensory inputs, and consider background knowledge in our motor plans. Furthermore, it has been argued that the central function of our brain appears to be to serve motor control (e.g., Bernstein, 1967). For example, we do not acquire memories to remember, but to learn relations and causation about the temporal unfolding of events and movements. This in turn allows us to produce movements that are adaptable and suitable by anticipating possible consequences of an action and adapting to it before performing the action. This of course reduces the probability that we do not accomplish our intended goal, or injure ourselves while performing the movement.

Before discussing the elements and construction of motor performance in more detail, we first illustrate a practical example of motor problems in a sporting context. While studying golf performance at a local golf club last year, we observed the following phenomenon. One of the golf students, who we shall call Marty, struggled to skillfully execute the basic elements of the golf putt when he started taking golf lessons. During his lessons, he learned the proper golf stance, the correct way to grasp the golf club, and how to swing the golf club in such a way that the club contacts the ball properly at the end of the swing. Despite his lessons, the ball would roll either too close or too far from the hole, and did not have the anticipated distance or spin required for a successful putt. Quite expectedly, Marty was frustrated by the fact that he was unable to achieve the planned action goal based on his motor actions.

Frustration due to suboptimal motor performance is not limited to Marty's experience. Many of us may remember similar learning experiences in activities such as dancing, guitar playing, soccer playing, or even when holding a tray while working as a waitress. It is amazing to see how beginners struggle with so many details (or elements) of a motor action, and how difficult it is to simultaneously control these different aspects and elements of motor performance in a goal-directed and effect-oriented manner.

The good news is that dedicated practice in a given task leads to improvements in motor performance. Marty, for example, has taken golf lessons for just over a year, and they have greatly improved his golf game. His stance is more stable, he grasps the club with a better grip, which in turn leads to a more appropriate ball contact. Furthermore, Marty is able to better control the movements of his body, and the effect of the golf putt is much better than one year before. Because he has mastered the basics of the golf putt, he is now able to focus on details such as arm control, clubface position, etc. Taken together, once the fundamental aspects of the movement are mastered, it is possible to build up subsequent levels and work on more specific details of motor control. In this chapter, we describe the elements and principles of the motor system that enable us to control movements such as striking the tennis ball at the right time, or coordinating steps and arm movements in dancing. These principles form the basis of motor performance and skill learning in all sporting contexts.

 OBJECTIVES

After reading this chapter you should be able to:

1 Define the *basic elements* of motor control.

2 Understand and discuss the *principles of integration* of these elements into the motor system.

3 Describe the levels and the architecture of the whole motor system.

4 Know consequences of an architectural understanding of motor control for applied work.

5 Apply the defined architectural understanding of motor control and related training techniques to improve the motor performance of athletes.

BUILDING BLOCKS AND ARCHITECTURE OF MOTOR CONTROL

In this chapter, we present a functional model of the motor system that highlights the interplay between movement goals, motor representations, and perceptual feedback. Using research from related fields, we illustrate how this hierarchical model is composed of interdependent levels, of which goal-directedness is the highest level of action organization. In the following sections, we outline the model in a bottom-up manner, focusing first on the basic building blocks of motor action, followed by the basic principles of integration. We then move on to the topic of motor architectures, explaining how motor actions are organized at a higher (cognitive) level. Finally, we illustrate how the described theoretical foundations can be applied to complex motor actions in sports.

COMPONENTS OF MOTOR CONTROL

Research from multiple disciplines has demonstrated that motor actions are based on modular structures, comprised of individual building blocks or motor primitives that are organized in a hierarchical way. The basic structure of motor actions affords a highly flexible and versatile system that allows for adaptation on different levels of the central nervous system, and at different time scales. Various fields of studies have approached the issue of modularity from disparate perspectives.

In the field of motor control, Schmidt's generalized motor program (GMP) (Schmidt, 1975) theory has been one of the most prevalent theories explaining how we control coordinated movement. The GMP theory is based on feedback based models (Adams, 1971) and adopts the concept of schema, making it more adaptable and thereby a more realistic explanation of motor learning, especially in sporting contexts. In general, motor programs describe the temporal structure of motor action, and are understood as being rather invariant partial motor actions. In contrast, Schmidt describes GMPs as templates that serve as abstract plans for basic movements. GMPs can be adapted to individual situations by modifying variant and invariant parameters. Parameters such as absolute timing, absolute force and building blocks (individual muscle actions) within the GMP can vary (variant parameters). In contrast, the sequence, relative timing and relative force of these building blocks remain invariant.

Schmidt uses the term schemata (recall schema, recognition schema) to explain how movements can be learned on the basis of GMPs. Support for schematic organization comes from research investigating the underlying neuronal structures of movement. According to these studies, the basic definition describes organization principles in action and perception that are based on neuronal structures, but include functional levels of behavior and cognition, up to and including language (e.g., Arbib, Conklin, & Hill, 1987). According to Arbib's theory, motor schemata and perceptual schemata interact in complex ways, but are coordinated by control programs which generate and control action performance on a higher level.

More recently, event segmentation theory (Zacks, Speer, Swallow, Braver, & Reynolds, 2007) has provided an interesting approach to studying modularity in action perception and memory, showing that the way in which a person spontaneously segments an observed action determines the understanding and later memorizing of this action (e.g., Zacks, Kumar, Abrams & Mehta, 2009). The latter approach can be well applied to sporting contexts. When watching a basketball match, we spontaneously segment the observed stream of movements performed by the different athletes into meaningful actions. Our understanding of the scenario is based on the way we segment what we see, the number of segmentation points, the choice of cues etc. Naturally, the quality of our understanding is strongly influenced by our own experience and (in this case, basketball) expertise.

The presented theoretical and empirical approaches to studying the modularity of (human) motor action illustrate the significance of the concept of basic building blocks for understanding everyday activities as well as complex movements in sports. Despite of their slightly different perspectives, these works demonstrate that the nature of these building blocks is fundamentally linked to the performance as well as the perception of actions. Before we turn to the question of how such building blocks are integrated and hierarchically organized, we present two approaches to studying the basic components of motor action in more detail.

Motor primitives

Within the scientific discussion about biological and cognitive principles of motor control the term motor primitive has been created and used in the last 15 years to address basic elements and building blocks of the motor system. For instance Flash and colleagues (e.g., Flash & Hochner, 2005) have taken advantage of the existence of motor invariants and templates at the level of trajectory planning in order to identify and characterize motor primitives. Their research has shown that human subjects tend to resort to stereotypical movements when performing movement tasks, such as pointing to a target or grasping for an object. These movement invariants include invariance in hand path and velocity profiles during reaching movements (Flash & Hogan, 1985; Flash & Hochner, 2005), and are thought to result from underlying control structures known as motion primitives. Early support for the existence of motion primitives was found at the kinematic level. In a study examining trajectory modification during unimanual point-to-point move-

ments (Flash & Henis, 1991) the principle of superposition was derived. Authors demonstrated in their study that when subjects are instructed to change motor plans, it is possible to model the resultant movements by a superposition of submovements. This gives arguments for a parallel planning of movement elements. The aim of such a research perspective is the simulation and reconstruction of a movement based on the superposition of different submovements.

Evidence for the existence of motor primitives also comes from studies investigating the temporal order of actions. In their learning-based approach, Giese et al. (2009) addressed temporal primitives in the sense of particular sub-movements in longer movement sequences. The main task in analysis is a segmentation of natural action sequences in temporal segments with a functional meaning in the whole action (for instance movement phases, like "run up" and "jump" in a volleyball attack hit). Therefore the movement trajectories were characterized by a set of robust trajectory features (e.g. zeros of the velocity in individual degrees of freedom). Temporal primitives have been investigated, for instance, in the context of complex action sequences, such as forms in martial arts (Mezger, Ilg & Giese, 2005). These and other approaches, like the definition of movement primitives at a level of muscle synergies (d'Avella, Portone, Fernandez, & Lacquaniti, 2006) are important steps to understand and discuss basic building blocks of movement organization and their interaction in the motor control system.

Cognitive building blocks of action

Perceptual-cognitive approaches propose that motor actions are formed by representations of target objects, movement characteristics, movement goals, and the anticipation of potential disturbances. Movements can be understood as a serial and functional order of goal related body postures (Rosenbaum, Meulenbroek, Vaughan, & Jansen, 2001) and their transitional states. The link between movements and perceptual effects is bi-directional and based on information that is typically stored in a hierarchical fashion in long-term memory. Complex movements can be conceptualized as a network of sensorimotor information. The better the order formation in memory, the more easily information can be accessed and retrieved. This leads to increased motor execution performance, which reduces the amount of attention and concentration required for successful performance. The nodes within this network contain functional subunits or building blocks that relate to motor actions and associated perceptual (including related semantic) content. These building blocks can be understood as representational units in memory that are functionally connected to perceptual events; or as functional units for the control of actions, linking goals to perceptual effects of movements.

Research in complex actions in sports (e.g., Schack & Hackfort, 2007; Schack & Mechsner, 2006), dance, rehabilitation, and manual action have demonstrated that Basic Action Concepts (BACs) are fundamental building blocks at the cognitive level of representation. BACs are based on the chunking of body postures related to common functions in the realization of action goals, and are conceptualized as representational units in long-term memory that are functionally connected to perceptual events. The idea that actions are represented in functional terms as a combination of action execution and the intended or observed effect is well established in cognitive psychology (Hommel, Müsseler, Aschersleben, & Prinz 2001; Koch, Keller, & Prinz, 2004) and has received growing acceptance in the fields of motor control and sport psychology.

BASIC PRINCIPLES OF INTEGRATION

In the last section we have described the elements (building blocks) of motor actions. In this section, we go a step further in explaining the construction of motor action, and discuss the basic principles of sensorimotor integration. These principles exemplify how movement primitives are integrated and organized in a goal directed manner.

Synergies in motor action

There is strong evidence that the human motor system simplifies movement control by organizing the multiple degrees of freedom (DOF) (defined by muscles and joints) into functional groups, or synergies. There are, for example, a total of 27 DOF in the human hand that need to be controlled during prehensile movements. In contrast to controlling each DOF separately, a modular organization based on synergies substantially simplifies the control of adaptive hand postures and dexterous manual actions.

The concept of synergies as solution to the DOF problem was first addressed by Bernstein (1967), who defined synergies as high-level control of kinematic parameters. Since its first exposition by Bernstein, the definition of synergy has extended to include patterns of muscle activation, joint angles, or grasping forces (e.g., Gabbiccini, Bicchi, Prattichizzo & Malvezzi 2011), and can be observed at the postural level (shared patterns of postural variations over time), the kinematic level (spatiotemporal patterns in the joint angular velocity profiles), and in dynamic synergies (stable correlations between joint torques) (Vinjamuri, Sun, Chang, Lee, Sclabassi & Mao, 2010). Bicchi, Gabbiccini and Santello (2011) defined postural synergies as patterns of most frequent use, or enabling constraints, and emphasized the interaction of motor and sensory synergies.

The concept of postural synergies has been applied to the control of robotic hands using low-dimensional sets of basic postures, and taking advantage of the compliant nature of many modern robot hands (e.g., Bicchi et al., 2011; Vinjamuri et al., 2010). Although the majority of studies have involved reaching and grasping movements (e.g., Santello, Flanders & Soechting, 1998), synergies have also been described for haptic object exploration (Thakur, Bastian, & Hsiao, 2008), piano playing (Furuya, Flanders, & Soechting, 2011), arm movements involved in reaching and catching (D'Avella et al., 2006; Bockemühl, Troje & Dürr, 2010), and cyclic body movements (Freitas, Duarte & Latash, 2006).

Synergies on the muscular level are typically recorded via electromyography (EMG). These studies have shown that muscle activation patterns are highly correlated with kinematic synergies extracted from simultaneously recorded joint angle data (Weiss & Flanders, 2007). Evidence for synergies underlying manual actions has also been provided by physiological studies, showing that complex finger movements closely resembling synergies in voluntary hand movements can be elicited via transcranial magnet stimulation (TMS) of the motor cortex (Gentner & Classen, 2006).

Sequential effects in motor action: Motor hysteresis

Numerous experiments have revealed that our current actions are influenced by our preceding actions (e.g., Rosenbaum & Jorgensen, 1992; Weigelt, Rosenbaum, Hülshorst & Schack, 2009; Schuetz, Weigelt, Odekerken, Klein-Soetebier, & Schack, 2011). An early observation of such sequential effects in reaching and grasping was reported by Rosenbaum and Jorgensen (1992). In that study, participants reached for a dowel horizontally supported on a stand, and placed either the left end or right end of the dowel against a target (located at one of 14 targets arranged vertically on a bookshelf). The authors demonstrated that grasp selection (overhand vs. underhand) was influenced by the type of grasp used in the previous

trial, so that participants persisted in using an underhand grasp in the descending target condition and an overhand grasp in the ascending target condition. This sequential effect finding is also known by the term motor hysteresis (Kelso, Buchanan & Murata, 1994), which describes the phenomenon that any system (organic or inorganic) exhibits path-dependence of its output signal. Motor hysteresis is consistent with the idea that the motor system evolved to economize resources, and assumes that making minimal successive changes to each motor act is less cognitively demanding than generating an entirely new plan for every motor act. From this perspective, perseveration from trial to trial is a computationally efficient motor strategy, and allows for resources (e.g., attention) to be allocated for other demands.

Goal-directed motor planning

Motor actions are intentional events, and are always performed so that the actor can successfully accomplish a specific action goal. In other words, motor actions are context-specific, goal-directed, and provide an action-regulating function to the elements involved in the system (e.g., motor primitives, synergies, etc). For example, we might use a different grip posture to grasp a spoon depending on whether we wish to place the spoon on the table or use it for eating.

One example of goal-directed motor planning is the end-state comfort effect (ESC) (Rosenbaum, Marchak, Barnes, Vaughan, Slotta, & Jorgensen, 1990), where individuals are willing to transiently adopt uncomfortable initial limb positions as long as this leads to a comfortable position at the end of the movement. This sensitivity toward comfortable end postures has been taken as evidence that final body postures are represented in memory, and that these postures are specified before movements are initiated (Rosenbaum et al., 2001). More importantly, the ESC effect clearly demonstrates that movements are planned, controlled, and executed with respect to anticipated final positions.

There is ample evidence that reaching, grasping, and object manipulation are actively controlled processes influenced by the properties and affordances of the to-be-grasped object, and the intended goal of a task (Gibson, 1977; Marteniuk, Mackenzie, Jeannerod, Athenes, Dugas, 1987; Santello & Soechting 1998). Furthermore, the physical and task-related properties of objects are intricately interlinked, and their relationship has been investigated by several authors (e.g., Cohen & Rosenbaum, 2004; El-Khoury & Sahbani 2010; Herbort & Butz 2010). For example, Cohen and Rosenbaum (2004) found that the height at which an object is grasped is strongly influenced by future task demands (e.g., the height of the target position where the object is to be placed).

Development of goal-directed motor planning (End-State-Comfort)

Rosenbaum et al. (1990) showed that people choose different initial grips when reaching for a horizontally suspended rod, depending on which end of the rod they planned to fit into a target. Through this manipulation of object end-orientation, Rosenbaum found that participants avoided completing their movements with awkward end postures (i.e., holding the rod with the thumb pointing down). Rather, they were more likely to grasp the rod with an initially uncomfortable grip (i.e., holding the rod with that same underhand grip). Using the same bar transport task, Weigelt and Schack (2010) showed that the ESC effect develops gradually with the sensory-motor maturation of children. Specifically, a step-wise pattern was revealed, in which 18% of the 3-year olds, 45% of the 4-year olds, and 67% of the 5-year olds used an underhand grip, when this resulted in holding the bar in a comfortable final posture. Building on this work, Stöckel, Hughes & Schack (2012) investigated anticipatory motor planning and the development of cognitive representations of body postures in children aged 7, 8, and 9 years. Overall, 9-year old children were more likely to plan their movements to end in comfortable postures, and showed more distinct representational structures of certain body postures, compared to the 7- and 8-year old children. Additionally, the sensitivity toward comfortable end-states was related to the mental representation of certain grasp postures.

MOTOR ARCHITECTURES

When looking at motor control from a systems perspective, a crucial aspect is that of the underlying architecture. Two questions arise from this perspective: First, which action should be performed in a given situation? And second, how should one perform that action? So far, we have concentrated on the second question, focusing on the modular organization of motor actions, on the building blocks and motor primitives, and the question of how these elements are integrated into functional synergies by basic control mechanisms. Nonetheless, when looking at the big picture, we must consider the higher level aspects of single action controllers and their acquisition. Actions – unlike simple reflex pathways – are usually not restricted to single actuators, such as individual joints or muscles. Rather, actions comprise the coordinated integration of various actuators into a functional context. Therefore, actions are quite complex and require the coordination of all involved movements on different levels and scales. Furthermore, complex actions are not simply triggered by a single sensory signal, but depend on a multitude of sensory inputs from different modalities, several of which are redundant (e.g., the position of the hand is estimated by proprioceptive information reflecting joint positions, somatosensory information from the skin, tendons, and muscles, as well as visual and acoustic information; Makin, Holmes & Ehrsson, 2008). Therefore, actions are not only goal-directed, they also depend on the current state of the body in a given situation.

The relation between the current state and the action context is part of the action representation, which is captured in an internal model. This internal model is defined as a representation of functional relations on a sensorimotor level. It reflects how movements of individual body parts relate to each other and integrates redundant multisensory information. Motor control is assumed to be based on such internal models. For example, when we grasp an object, an internal model translates the position information of the target object, and provides a temporal sequence of muscle activations moving the hand towards the target position. Internal models, therefore, can be considered important parts of the motor system's architecture.

The function of an internal model is not always completely tied to single actions, but to the represented relations involved in different kinds of actions. While there are multiple forms of different internal models, the two most discussed ones are inverse and forward models (see Wolpert & Gharahmani, 2000). Inverse and forward models directly address the two questions asked in the beginning of this section, namely which action should be performed in a given situation, and how should that action be performed? Generally speaking, inverse models provide an action impulse for a given goal, and specify how to perform the specific action. In contrast, forward models predict the consequences associated with the execution of an action impulse, and can be used to evaluate the outcome of an action with respect to the given goal, and thereby to decide the relevant action in the given context.

Key functions for internal models at a sensorimotor level

1　Models subserving target control (Inverse Models): Many limb movements are visually guided and are target oriented. This presupposes the ability to interpret the perceived target position as a configuration of the limb, which has to be transformed into single joint movements in order to move the hand to the desired position. An inverse model has to take into account the structure of the limb (i.e., joint and segment characteristics) and how the limb relates to the environment while performing the intended movement.

2　Predictive models: When internal models are not restricted to capturing correlations between pieces of information at a given point in time, they become more significant. In this case, they can represent temporal relationships, and thus reflect the unfolding of events and actions. In this way, they are predictive. For a given current state and a selected behavior, the internal model describes the development of the behavior over time. As sensory feedback is restricted by the delays of neuronal pathways, predictive models can provide an informed guess for the sensory feedback, which is immediately available. Fast ballistic movements, like catching a ball, are only possible on the basis of such predictive models.

3　Integration of sensory information: The central nervous system comprises many redundant sensory systems. Having multiple sensors that provide similar information allows the system to exploit this redundancy and cancel out noise. This presupposes that the relation between the different sensory systems is known. In this way, it is possible to overcome measurement errors.

Lately, an increasingly coherent picture has emerged regarding how internal representations on a sensorimotor level are related to goal-directed motor control. First, internal models capture functional and temporal relations in service for motor control tasks. Second, the same internal models can be recruited by different tasks (e.g., visual perception of an observed action involves mapping it onto one's own internal body representation, whereas the same internal model can be used for planning an action and evaluating the predicted outcome). This perspective is supported by recent research on the organization of the central nervous system. Parts of the brain originally assumed to exclusively serve motor control have been found to be involved in perception, higher planning processes, and even language (Rizzolatti & Sinigaglia, 2010).

Evidence that brain areas involved in motor control are also active during action observation comes from the finding that individual cells exist that code for the performance and perception of individual actions. The first studies in this field were conducted using single cell recordings of individual neurons in special premotor areas of the monkey brain (Gallese, Fadiga, Fogassi, & Rizzolatti, 1996). Later studies showed that these cells were tuned not only to specific movement characteristics (e.g., hand movement trajectories), but to a higher level notion of actions (e.g., conforming goals such as grasping for food; see Rizzolatti & Craighero, 2004). Subsequently, studies have employed neuroimaging techniques (e.g., functional Magnetic Resonance Imaging, fMRI) to identify brain areas with corresponding response characteristics. This emerging line of research showed that perception is tightly coupled to action, and is highly influenced by our expectations of what to perceive (e.g., Calvo-Merino, Glaser, Grèzes, Passingham, & Haggard, 2005). When we perceive an object in an action context (e.g., a tennis ball in the hand of a person holding a racket), the context situation determines the way in which we perceive the object. Our understanding is not only driven by current percepts, but even more by our experience. Actions determine how a situation develops over time, and thus are central to our understanding of perception-action coupling. We also tend to predict the movements of others based on our own motor experience and sensorimotor representations acquired in similar situations. For example, we can predict the movements of the tennis player based on our own motor experience of having played tennis ourselves, but also based on our visual experience of having observed such actions (e.g., even if we have never played tennis, we are able to see when a ball is too far from the player to be hit). Taken together, sensorimotor representations are complex and flexible in nature, and thus are key features not only in motor control, but also in perception and cognition. The representation of the own body is a basic one on which further representations (e.g., of movements, the environment, and context situations) are built up. In this way, internal models are highly interrelated and interconnected.

Having discussed sensorimotor representations, we now move towards more cognitive representations, taking a bottom-up perspective. From an evolutionary and learning perspective, conscious cognitive functions can be assumed to emerge from more elementary functions. Whereas elementary functions (e.g., reflexes) are influenced directly by stimulus constellations, mental control functions are guided intentionally. From this point of view, building blocks on the level of cognitive representations have to integrate and organize "lower-level" building blocks (see also Perrig & Hofer, 1989; Viviani, 1986). Within such a hierarchical system or architecture, learning can be conceptualized as a process of developing and modifying the mediating cognitive-perceptual structures in motor memory.

As we know from actions in everyday life or from complex movements in sports, certain aspects of our motor actions are prospectively

---

Simulation models of motor control

One way of accessing the hypothetical structure of motor control is through modeling approaches. In contrast to experiments in which scientists try to uncover the underlying and organizing mechanisms by observing behavioral responses, computational modeling techniques start from such mechanisms and, through simulation, generate the resulting response. In this way, computational models provide a cycle for refining hypothetical mechanisms and the organization of the motor control system. A computational model can be used to test derived mechanisms, refute, or refine them. In a next step, a good model can be used to generate new, interesting, and decisive research questions, which again guide future experiments.

In movement science, computational models are commonly used to provide frameworks of how the central nervous system relates sensory signals and motor commands. An essential aspect of most computational models is their predictive nature (e.g., Dean & Cruse, 2003; Kalveram, 2004; Wolpert, Ghahramani, & Jordan, 1995). From a more general perspective, computational models are important tools for simulating different stages of action implementation and action control (Dean & Cruse, 2003). It is important to distinguish between mechanism and methods of computation (e.g., artificial neuronal networks) and the simulated model (e.g., information processing in biological neuronal networks in the brain). Computational models (e.g., artificial neural networks) are used in the fields of movement science, biocybernetics and robotics (see Bläsing, 2006; Schack & Ritter, 2009; Pfeifer & Bongard, 2006) to investigate mechanisms of motor control and to implement the empirical results on technical platforms such as different types of robots.

---

controlled, while others are goal directed and anticipative. Automatization of actions occurs in the context of special stimuli (e.g., catching an object if it is thrown close to our body). The difference between anticipated and actual effects is clearly distinguishable in sporting contexts in which an athlete repeatedly produces an error in a specific part of the movement sequence. Athletes and coaches often devote too much time trying to de-automatize flawed movement elements. Therefore, it is useful to think about different levels of movement organization in more general terms. The idea that movement control is hierarchically organized has been approached from different perspectives. One perspective focuses on a hierarchy of differing levels of representation (see, e.g., Keele, 1986; Perrig & Hofer, 1989; Jeannerod, 2004; Rosenbaum, 1987; Saltzman, 1979), while another perspective focused more strongly on the aspect of a

hierarchical execution regulation (Keele, Cohen, & Ivry, 1990; Marken, 2002). In recent years a third perspective has emerged that proposes that the functional construction of motor actions can be based on a reciprocal assignment of performance-oriented regulation levels and representational levels (Table 20.1; see also Maycock, Dornbusch, Elbrechter, Haschke, Schack, & Ritter, 2010; Schack & Ritter, 2009). These levels can be differentiated according to their central tasks into regulation and representation levels; each level is assumed to be functionally autonomous.

The lowest level of sensorimotor control (I) is based on movement primitives and is directly linked to the environment. In contrast to the highest level of mental control (IV), which is induced intentionally and is relevant for anticipation, the level of sensorimotor control is induced perceptually, built on functional units composed of perceptual effect representations, afferent feedback, and effectors. The essential invariant (set value) of such functional units is the representation of the movement effect within the framework of the action. The system is broadly autonomous, and automatisms emerge when this level of sensorimotor control possesses sufficient correction mechanisms to ensure the stable attainment of the intended effect.

The need for a level of sensorimotor representation (II) is apparent in this context and is discussed in the context of internal models (see page 313). It can be assumed that the modality-specific information representing the effects of the particular movement is stored on the level of sensorimotor representation. Subsequently, relevant modalities change as a function of the level of expertise in the learning process and as a function of the task context. For instance, when we first learn to perform a golf putt, we use visual information to monitor body posture and movement timing. In later stages of the learning process, proprioceptive information gains increased meaning, and we no longer need to consciously monitor aspects related to body position and timing.

The level of mental representation (III) predominantly forms a cognitive workbench for the level of mental control (IV), and has already been sketched for voluntary movement regulation and the coding of the anticipated outcome of a movement. Level III is organized conceptually, and is responsible for transforming anticipated action outcomes into movement programs that sufficiently bring about desired outcomes. Because an action is a structure subdivided into details (Bernstein, 1967), action organization has to possess a working model of this structure. Therefore, mental representations of movement structures (see Chapter 22) are located within level III. Basic action concepts (BACs) have been identified as major representation units for such mental representation in motor control. Their characteristic set of features arise from the perceptive and functional properties of action effects (i.e., they tie together functional and sensory features). These functional features are derived from action goals, which links BACs to level IV. Furthermore, BACs integrate sensory features of partial actions (e.g., through chunking). As a result, they also refer to the perceptual effects of movements, which connects BACs to motor processes at lower levels.

CONSEQUENCES FOR APPLIED WORK

When taking an applied perspective in sport, the theoretical concept of motor action construction (see Table 20.1) is fundamental to both the development of suitable diagnosis procedures and the selection of appropriate training methods. It becomes plausible to define relevant systems of motor action more precisely. In applied work, it is exceptionally important to understand that such different systems play a part in motor performance. A frequently observed practical problem is that athletes are able to perform a certain movement optimally in practice, but fail to do so in competitive settings. Such situations can lead to phenomena like choking under pressure in athletes (DeCaro, Thomas, Albert & Beilock, 2011), or stage fright in dancers or other artistic performers (see Tenenbaum, Hatfield, Eklund, Land, Calmeiro, Razon, & Schack, 2009). If the movement structure is accessible under less stressful circumstances (e.g., in practice situations and training), it can be concluded that it is optimally represented in the athlete's memory, and that the problem is rather linked to deficits of mental control. We have developed specific methods for a reliable diagnosis of how a movement is represented (Güldenpenning, Koester, Kunde, Weigelt & Schack, 2011; Schack, 2004; Schack & Ritter, 2009), enabling both researchers and practitioners (i.e., coaches) to control the goal-directedness of psychological training. Problems which may, for instance, be based on flawed emotion regulation or motivation are likely to result from deficits in mental control and can be ascribed to the level of mental control (see Figure 20.1).

Psychological training procedures which intervene at this level, particularly those targeting attention control, optimization of self-talk, and stress and anxiety control (see Figure 20.1), aim to improve basic regulation (Schack & Hackfort, 2007). In contrast, training procedures that aim to optimize process regulation (i.e., optimal technical execution of a movement) ought to be allocated to the level of mental representations and lower levels responsible for sensorimotor processes and automatization. For this purpose, specific mental training based on motor imagery can provide a valuable contribution to the overall training effect and can be specifically beneficial during extremely physically exhausting training periods, or for athletes recovering from injury.

Table 20.1 *Levels of motor action (modified from Schack, 2004; Schack & Ritter, 2009)*

Code	Level	Main function	Subfunction	Tools
IV	Mental control	Regulation	Volitional initiation control strategies	Symbols; strategies
III	Mental representation	Representation	Effect-oriented adjustment	Basic action concepts
II	Sensorimotor representation	Representation	Spatial-temporal adjustment	Perceptual representation Internal models
I	Sensorimotor control	Regulation	Automatization	Motor primitives basic reflexes

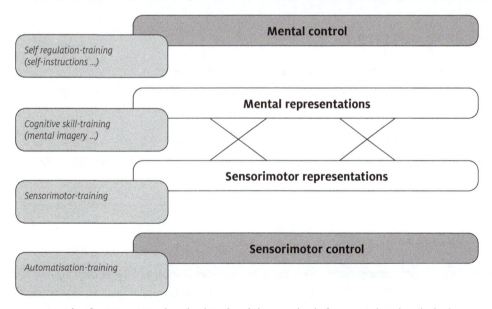

Figure 20.1 Levels of motor control and related training methods for mental and technical preparation (modified from Schack & Hackfort, 2007).

LEARNING AIDS

1   What are motor primitives?

Motor primitives are invariant elements in motor control structures. We differentiate between kinematic and temporal invariants (primitives).

2   Describe the difference between an inverse model and a forward model.

An inverse model provides an action impulse for a given goal, and specifies how to perform the specific action, whereas a forward model predicts the consequences associated with the execution of an action impulse, evaluates the outcome of an action with respect to the given goal, and selects the most relevant action required to achieve that goal.

3   Define the term motor hysteresis, and provide an explanation for this phenomenon.

Motor hysteresis can be defined as sequential effect in systems exhibiting path-dependence of their output signal, by making minimal successive changes to a motor action, rather than generating an entirely new plan for every motor action. Plan recall is thought to be a more computationally efficient motor planning strategy that allows allocating resources for other cognitive demands.

4   How do action and perception influence our goal-directed movements?

Action and perception are bi-directionally linked. Our actions are influenced by our prior motor experience in a similar context, as well as the sensorimotor experiences (e.g., sight, sound, and touch) associated with such events.

REVIEW QUESTIONS

1   Explain the differences between children and adults in goal-directed motor planning.

2   Identify the performance-oriented regulation, and representational levels of motor actions.

3   Define the term *synergy* and explain its role in the control of action.

4   Identify the main functions of internal models at the sensorimotor level.

5   Identify the variant and invariant parameters associated with the theory of generalized motor programs (GMP).

EXERCISES

1   Describe your own motor performance in two different types of sport and define particular performance problems. Discuss the functional background of these problems (primitives, levels) and derive consequences for training procedures based on the architecture model (see Figure 20.1).

2   Select an action within a sport (i.e., the tennis serve). Make a list of physical behaviors that expert tennis players exhibit when executing this action. Make a list of physical behaviors that novice tennis players exhibit. What differences exist between novices and experts? What mistakes are novices making in contrast to experts? Identify the level of sensorimotor control, which is most likely responsible for each error, and suggest how the novice can improve his or her motor performance.

ADDITIONAL READING

Bläsing, B. (2010). The dancer's memory: Expertise and cognitive structures in dance. In B. Bläsing, M. Puttke & T. Schack (Eds.), *The Neurocognition of Dance.* (pp.75–98). London, UK: Psychology Press.

Knuf, L., Aschersleben, G. & Prinz, W. (2001). An analysis of ideomotor action. *Journal of Experimental Psychology: General, 130,* 779–798.

Prinz, W. (1997). Perception and action planning. *European Journal of Cognitive Psychology, 9,* 129–154.

Ritter, H., Steil, J.J., Noelker, C., Roethling, F. & McGuire, P. (2003). Neural architectures for robotic intelligence. *Reviews in the Neurosciences, 14 (1–2),* 121–143.

Rizzolatti, G., Craighero, L. (2004). The mirror neuron system. *Annual Review of Neuroscience, 27,* 169–192.

REFERENCES

Adams, J.A. (1971). A closed-loop theory of motor learning. *Journal of Motor Behavior, 3,* 111–150.

Arbib, M., Conklin, E. & Hill, J. (1987). *From schema theory to language.* New York: Oxford University Press.

Bernstein, N.A. (1967). *The Co-ordination and Regulation of Movements.* Pergamon Press Ltd.

Bicchi, A., Gabiccini, M., Santello, M. (2011). Modelling natural and artificial hands with synergies. *Philosophical Transactions of the Royal Society B, 366,* 3153–3161.

Bläsing, B. (2006). Crossing large gaps: A simulation study of stick insect behavior. *Adaptive Behavior, 14(3),* 265–285.

Bockemühl, T., Troje, N.F. & Dürr, V. (2010). Inter-joint coupling and joint angle synergies of human catching movements. *Human Movement Science, 29 (1),* 73–93.

Calvo-Merino, B., Glaser, D.E., Grèzes, J., Passingham, R.E. & Haggard, P. (2005). Action observation and acquired motor skills: an fMRI study with expert dancers. *Cerebral Cortex, 15(8),* 1243–1249.

Cohen, R.G. & Rosenbaum, D.A. (2004). Where grasps are made reveals how grasps are planned: generation and recall of motor plans. *Experimental Brain Research, 157,* 486–495.

D'Avella, A., Portone, A., Fernandez, L. & Lacquaniti, F. (2006). Control of fast-reaching movements by muscle synergy combinations. *The Journal of Neuroscience, 26 (30),* 7791–7810.

Dean, J. & Cruse, H. (2003). Motor Pattern Generation. In A. Michael (Ed.), *Handbook for Brain Theory and Neural Network.* Cambridge MA: MIT Press Bradford Book.

DeCaro, M.S., Thomas, R.D., Albert, N.B. & Beilock, S.L. (2011). Choking Under Pressure: Multiple Routes to Skill Failure. *Journal of Experimental Psychology: General, 140 (3),* 390–406.

El-Khoury, S. & Sahbani, A. (2010). A new strategy combining empirical and analytical approaches for grasping unknown 3D objects. *Robotics and Autonomous Systems, 58,* 497–507.

Flash, T. & Henis, E. (1991). Arm trajectory modifications during reaching towards visual targets. *Journal of Cognitive Neuroscience, 3,* 220–230.

Flash, T. & Hochner, B. (2005). Motor primitives in vertebrates and invertebrates. *Current Opinion in Neurobiology, 15,* 1–7.

Flash, T. & Hogan, N. (1985). The coordination of arm movements: an experimentally confirmed mathematical model. *The Journal of Neuroscience, 5*, 1688–1703.

Freitas, S.M.S.F., Duarte, M. & Latash, M.L. (2006). Two kinematic synergies in voluntary whole-body movements during standing. *Journal of Neurophysiology, 95*, 636–645.

Furuya, S., Flanders, M. & Soechting, J.F. (2011). Hand kinematics of piano playing. *Journal of Neurophysiology, 106 (6)*, 2849–2864.

Gabiccini, M., Bicchi, A., Prattichizzo, D. & Malvezzi, M. (2011). On the role of hand synergies in the optimal choice of grasping forces. *Autonomous Robots, 31*, 235–252.

Gallese, V., Fadiga, L., Fogassi, L. & Rizzolatti, G. (1996). Action recognition in the premotor cortex. *Brain, 119*, 593–609.

Gentner, R. & Classen, J. (2006). Modular organization of finger movements by the human central nervous system. *Neuron, 52*, 731–742.

Gibson, J.J. (1977). The Theory of Affordances. In R. Shaw & J. Bransford (Eds.). *Perceiving, Acting, and Knowing: Toward an Ecological Psychology.* Hillsdale, NJ: Lawrence Erlbaum, 67–82.

Giese, M.A., Mukovskiy, A., Park A., Omlor, L. & Slotine J.J.E. (2009) Real-Time Synthesis of Body Movements Based on Learned Primitives. In D. Cremers, B. Rosenhahn & A.L. Yuille (Eds), *'Statistical and Geometrical Approaches to Visual Motion Analysis', Lecture Notes in Computer Science,* 5604 (pp.107–127). Springer Verlag.

Güldenpenning, I., Koester, D., Kunde, W., Weigelt, M. & Schack, T. (2011). Motor expertise modulates the unconscious processing of human body postures. *Experimental Brain Research, 213*, 383–391.

Herbort, O. & Butz, M.V. (2010). Planning and control of hand orientation in grasping movements. *Experimental Brain Research, 202*, 867–878.

Hommel, B., Müsseler, J., Aschersleben, G. & Prinz, W. (2001). The Theory of Event Coding (TEC): A framework for perception and action planning. *Behavioral and Brain Sciences, 24 (5)*, 849–878.

Jeannerod, M. (2004). Actions from within. *International Journal of Sport and Exercise Psychology, 2 (4)*, 376–402.

Kalveram, D.T. (2004). The inverse problem in cognitive, perceptual and proprioceptive control of sensorimotor behavior. *International Journal of Sport and Exercise Psychology, 2 (3)*, 255–273.

Keele, S.W. (1986). Motor control. In L. Kaufmann, J. Thomas & K.R. Boff (Eds.), *Handbook of perception and performance.* New York: Wiley.

Keele, S.W., Cohen, A. & Ivry, R. (1990). Motor programs. In M. Jeannerod (Ed.). *Attention and performance XIII: Motor representation and control* (pp.77–110). Hillsdale, NJ: Erlbaum.

Kelso, J.A.S., Buchanan, J.J. & Murata, T. (1994). Multifunctionality and switching in the coordination dynamics of reaching and grasping. *Human Movement Science, 13*, 63–94.

Koch, I., Keller, P. & Prinz, W. (2004). The ideomotor approach to action control: Implications for skilled performance. *International Journal of Sport and Exercise Psychology 2*, 362–375.

Makin, T.R., Holmes, N.P. & Ehrsson, H.H. (2008). On the other hand: Dummy hands and peripersonal space. *Behavioural Brain Research 191 (1)*, 1–10.

Marken, R.S. (2002). The hierarchical behaviour of perception. In R.S. Marken (Ed.). *More mind readings: Methods and models in the study of purpose* (pp.84–116). Chapel Hill, NC: New View Publications.

Marteniuk, R.G., Mackenzie, C.L., Jeannerod, M., Athenes, S. & Dugas, C. (1987) Constraints on human arm movement trajectories. *Canadian Journal of Psychology, 41(3)*, 365–378.

Maycock, J., Dornbusch, D., Elbrechter, C., Haschke, R., Schack, T. & Ritter, H. (2010). Approaching manual intelligence. *KI – Künstliche Intelligenz, Issue Cognition for Technical Systems*, 1–8.

Mezger, J., Ilg, W. & Giese, M. (2005). Trajectory synthesis by hierarchical spatio-temporal correspondence: comparison of different methods. *APGV*: 25–32.

Perrig, W.J. & Hofer, D. (1989). Sensory and conceptual representations in memory: Motor images that cannot be imaged. *Psychological Research, 51*, 201–207.

Pfeifer, R. & Bongard, J. (2006). *How the body shapes the way we think: a new view of intelligence.* Cambridge, Mass.: MIT Press.

Rizzolatti, G. & Craighero, L. (2004). The mirror neuron system. *Annual Review of Neuroscience, 27*, 169–192.

Rizzolatti, G. & Sinigaglia, C. (2010). The functional role of the parieto-frontal mirror circuit: Interpretations and misinterpretations. *Nature Reviews Neuroscience, 11(4)*, 264–274.

Rosenbaum, D.A. (1987). Successive approximations to a model of human motor programming. *Psychology of Learning and Motivation, 21*, 153–182.

Rosenbaum, D.A. & Jorgensen, M.J. (1992). Planning macroscopic aspects of manual control. *Human Movement Science, 11*, 61–69.

Rosenbaum, D.A., Marchak, F., Barnes, H.J., Vaughan, J., Slotta, J.D. & Jorgensen, M.J. (1990). Constraints for action selection: overhand versus underhand grips. In M. Jeannerod (Ed.). *Attention and performance XIII: Motor representation and control* (pp.211–265). Hillsdale, NJ: Erlbaum.

Rosenbaum, D.A., Meulenbroek, R.G.J., Vaughan, J. & Jansen, C. (2001). Posture-based motion planning: Applications to grasping. *Psychological Review, 10*, 709–734.

Saltzman, E. (1979). Levels of sensorimotor representation. *Journal of Mathematical Psychology, 20*, 91–163.

Santello, M., Flanders, M. & Soechting, J.F. (1998). Postural hand synergies for tool use. *The Journal of Neuroscience, 18*, 10105–10115.

Santello, M. & Soechting, J.F. (1998). Gradual molding of the hand to object contours. *Journal of Neurophysiology, 79*, 1307–1320.

Schack, T. (2004). The cognitive architecture of complex movement. *International Journal of Sport and Exercise Psychology, 2*, 403–438.

Schack, T. & Hackfort, D. (2007). An action theory approach to applied sport psychology. In G. Tenenbaum & R.C. Eklund (Eds.), *Handbook of Sport Psychology* (3rd ed.; pp.332–351). Hoboken, NJ: Wiley.

Schack, T. & Mechsner, F. (2006). Representation of motor skills in human long-term memory. *Neuroscience Letters, 391*, 77–81.

Schack, T. & Ritter, H. (2009). The cognitive nature of action-functional links between cognitive psychology, movement science and robotics. *Progress in Brain Research, 174*, 231–252.

Schmidt, R.A. (1975). A schema theory of discrete motor skill learning. *Psychological Review, 82*, 225–260.

Schuetz, C., Weigelt, M., Odekerken, D., Klein-Soetebier T. & Schack, T. (2011). Motor control strategies in a continuous task space. *Motor Control 15*, 321–341.

Stöckel, T., Hughes, C.M.L. & Schack, T. (2011). Representation of grasp postures and anticipatory motor planning in children. *Psychological Research, 76*(6), 768–776.

Tenenbaum, G., Hatfield, B.D., Eklund, R.C., Land, W.M., Calmeiro, L., Razon, S. & Schack, T. (2009). A conceptual framework for studying emotions-cognitions-performance linkage under conditions that vary in perceived pressure. *Progress in Brain Research, 174*, 159–178.

Thakur, P.H., Bastian, A.J. & Hsiao, S.S. (2008). Multidigit movement synergies of the human hand in an unconstrained haptic exploration task. *The Journal of Neuroscience, 28*, 1271–1281.

Vinjamuri, R., Sun, M., Chang, C.C., Lee, H.N., Sclabassi, R.J. & Mao, Z.H. (2010). Temporal postural synergies of the hand in rapid grasping tasks. *IEEE Transactions on Information Technology in Biomedicine, 14*(4), 986–994.

Viviani, P. (1986). Do units of motor action really exist? *Experimental Brain Research, 15*, 201–215.

Weigelt, M., Rosenbaum, D.A., Hülshorst, S. & Schack, T. (2009). Moving and memorizing: Motor planning modulates the recency effect in serial and free recall. *Acta Psychologica, 132*, 68–79.

Weigelt, M. & Schack, T. (2010). The development of end-state comfortplanning in preschool children. *Experimental Psychology, 57*, 476–482.

Weiss, E.J. & Flanders, M. (2007). Muscular and postural synergies of the human hand. *Journal of Neurophysiology, 92*, 523–535.

Wolpert, D.M., Ghahramani, Z. & Jordan, M.I. (1995). An internal model for sensorimotor integration. *Science, 269*, 1880–1882.

Wolpert, D.M. & Ghahramani, Z. (2000). Computational principles of movement neuroscience. *Nature Neuroscience, 3*, 1212–1217.

Zacks, J.M., Kumar, S., Abrams, R.A. & Mehta, R. (2009). Using movement and intentions to understand human activity. *Cognition, 112*, 201–216.

Zacks, J.M., Speer, N.K., Swallow, K.M., Braver, T.S. & Reynolds, J.R. (2007). Event perception: A mind/brain perspective. *Psychological Bulletin, 133*, 273–293.

Part Four

Enhancing performance

EDITED BY DIETER HACKFORT, GERSHON TENENBAUM AND TONY MORRIS

Chapter 21

Psychological skills training and programs

JOAQUÍN DOSIL, J. GUALBERTO CREMADES, SANTIAGO RIVERA

SUMMARY

Psychological Skills Training is implemented in athletes and/or teams to enhance their overall performance. When implementing this training, a sport psychologist may work with an athlete who needs to enhance psychological aspects related to sport performance, or if the athlete has a clinical problem and will then need to be referred to a clinical psychologist. In this chapter, the focus is on implementing psychological skills to enhance performance. Establishing effective goals, using relaxation techniques, practicing imagery, reflecting on mental processes, and having a positive self-talk are appropriate psychological techniques. There are two types of programs: the Psychological Skills Training Program (PSTP) which allows athletes to learn psychological strategies that can be applied in practice sessions or competitions, and the Applied Psychology Program to Practice Sessions (APPPS) which aims at optimizing practice sessions, so the psychologist focuses on enhancing these sessions through psychological strategies. Clinical, field, or online intervention are three types of programs the sport psychologist must implement depending on the athlete's or team's needs.

INTRODUCTION

In this chapter, psychological skills training programs and techniques will be described. The chapter will begin with a brief summary on the state of applied sport psychology and subsequently, three fundamental questions will be answered:

- What psychological skills should athletes be trained in?
- How should psychological skills be trained?

- Where should psychological skills training occur?

The first question seeks to enhance our understanding of the main psychological skills that should be developed to improve an athlete's performance as well as how to develop some of the psychological techniques most often used in the sport psychology field. Sport psychologists should be able to handle these psychological skills with ease, in order to use them at specific times during the season with athletes and to be able to advise coaches in their application.

The second question responds to the key factors that must be taken into account in how psychological skills are being implemented within the Programs of Assessment and Psychological Intervention (PAPI) (Dosil, 2008), the Psychological Skills Training Program (PSTP) and the Applied Psychology Program to Practice Sessions (APPPS).

The third question presents the different ways one can deliver sport psychology services as well as the implications of each one in the process of performance enhancement.

OBJECTIVES

After reading this chapter you will:

1   Understand the intervention models used in applied sport psychology.
2   Distinguish between the main psychological skills that should be developed and the intervention techniques athletes must use to enhance performance.
3   Know how to apply psychological skills training programs.
4   Identify which are the psychological intervention types that are usually implemented in the sports field.

STATE OF APPLIED SPORT PSYCHOLOGY

Psychological skills training in the sports arena is based on the implementation of mental strategies that aim to enhance the athlete's or team's performance. With this in mind, the aim is not only to reduce their "mental weaknesses" but also to enhance their skills and develop their talent.

However, over time, general psychology has been linked to an intervention model based on problem solving, primarily focusing on negative aspects and contributing to the adoption of a pessimistic understanding of human nature (Seligman, 2002).

This could be explained by several reasons (Friedrickson, 1998): first, the natural tendency to study phenomena that threatens human well-being has led to the focus on those emotions that help us cope with a dangerous or pressing situation. Therefore, it is easier to define the desired adaptive direction of change if one is seeking to restore normality (Aspinwall & Staudinger, 2003) (e.g., demanding an urgent intervention to decrease pre-competition anxiety before a final match). Second, there is a tendency to neglect what is normal and to pay more attention to what is abnormal, when experiencing a state of well-being as a given; then, everything that contributes to jeopardize that well-being is the focus of interest and study (e.g., the unusual decline in the performance of an elite athlete). Third, the fact that there are fewer words to describe positive emotional states rather than negative has a tremendous impact in our perception of such states (i.e., positive) making them more difficult to distinguish, and in turn, these negative states become automatic since these emotions are part of our inner core (e.g., this translates into the difficulty that many athletes find to self-assess their performance objectively). Fourth, there are differences in the expression of emotions, as the negative ones have specific facial features that facilitate their universal recognition (e.g., it is easy to recognize an angry athlete; however, it is not always easy to recognize a relaxed one).

From a holistic perspective, the most complete and advanced intervention strategy would be one that integrates relative aspects of health and well-being (e.g., collective emotions that result after winning a match) along with other usual elements. These elements focus on the deficit (e.g., lack of attentional focus during clutch points in a match) from the evaluation process and through all phases of the intervention (Hervás, Sánchez, & Vásquez, 2008).

Similar to what has been happening in the field of general psychology, sport psychology has also been associated with an intervention model that is based on problem solving, in which the psychologist deals with athletes that experience "clinical problems" (which may or may not be related to sport), by implementing techniques that stem from the clinical psychology field. This approach has created controversy in the psychology field as well as in the sports arena. In the psychology field there is some confusion about whether these treatments can be placed within sport psychology or within clinical psychology. Likewise, in the sports field, this is an old subject matter that prompts many athletes to associate a sport psychologist with problem-solving scenarios. This fact greatly narrows the field of intervention.

It is important to understand that when an athlete seeks a psychologist because he or she has a clinical problem (e.g., feeling sad because he or she is going through divorce and believes that it is impacting his or her athletic performance), the service delivered may be well performed by a clinical psychologist without any training in sport sciences, since working with an athlete becomes of lesser importance. When there is a problem that is directly linked to athletic performance (e.g., being overly anxious before competition or choking), either a clinical psychologist or a sport psychologist may indeed work along with the athlete, even though a sport psychologist specialist with knowledge and experience in the specific domain should be recommended. Finally, when an athlete seeks a professional to enhance psychological aspects related to sport performance, there is no doubt that the appropriate professional is the psychologist who specializes in sport, as the clinical limitations in these cases are obvious.

Many clinical psychologists have been trained in sport sciences, which allows them to face any situation and are able to work through the problems as well as indicate to the athlete the potential that the field of psychology has to offer when linked to performance enhancement (the virtues of psychology to enhance performance is usually "unknown" by most people in the sport context). In addition, a sport psychologist without clinical training will have to refer specific cases that, due to their nature, are more suitable to treatment in the clinical setting. Professionals in the field of sport psychology (Andersen, Denson, Brewer, & Van Raalte, 1994; Schack, Moncier III, & Taylor, 2007) have indicated several considerations that must be taken into account when a sport psychologist has doubts about whether to refer a case to a clinical professional. Although sport psychologists do not have to be competent to work with clinical disorders, they should be able to evaluate such disorders and know when to refer the client to a clinical professional (Frank, Gardner & Moore, 2006).

WHAT PSYCHOLOGICAL SKILLS SHOULD ATHLETES BE TRAINED IN?

The difference between athletes with similar physical, technical, and tactical abilities is in the psychological component. So far there has not been a massive influx of psychologists to the sports arena; thus, there are not many athletes who are psychologically trained. It is appreciated that the majority of the best athletes have learned "techniques" by themselves to problem solve different situations, which have provided them with an edge over their rivals. Other athletes have sought their own strategies to enhance their performance, but have not been successful in their endeavor. It is this aspect that sport psychology must emphasize as a science that provides strategies for the athlete to achieve a peak performance.

If all the athletes were to include psychological skills training in their schedule for the season, the quality of those that would succeed in reaching the elite would be far greater.

The study of psychological characteristics in successful athletes has been covered in recent years (see Table 21.1). The ability to cope with problems has been considered one of the most important characteristics, leading to the conclusion that to achieve the highest level of performance it is necessary to use different strategies to problem solve the difficulties that arise throughout the season (Dosil, 2008).

Table 21.1 *Studies including psychological characteristics in successful athletes*

Author(s)/Year	Characteristics in successful athletes
Van den Auweele, De Cuyper, Van Mele & Rzewinicki (1993)	– High self-confidence – Pre and post-competition low anxiety levels – Techniques to regulate anxiety – Attentional focus in specific tasks and movements – Ability to cope with unexpected/poor executions – Positive self-talk
Gould, Eklund & Jackson (1992) Gould, Dieffenbach & Moffett (2002)	– Positive self-instructions – Ability to focus and block out distractions – Mental toughness/resiliency – Have a more comprehensive mental training – Ability to cope with and control anxiety – Confidence – Sport intelligence – Competitiveness – Hard-work ethic – Ability to set and achieve goals – Coachability – High levels of dispositional hope – Optimism – Adaptive perfectionism
Anshel (2003)	– Risk taking – Sensation seekers – Competitiveness – Self-confidence – Attentional style – Expectations of success – Mental toughness – Ability to regulate stress levels
Orlick (2008)	– Focus – Commitment – Confidence – Positive images – Mental readiness – Distraction control – Ongoing learning

Intervention techniques in sport psychology

Techniques are the "tools" that the psychologist uses to work with athletes; thus, mastering psychological skills through the use of such techniques is essential when attempting to assess or intervene in the sport context. Likewise, athletes, coaches, referees, and managers should know these techniques too in order to better understand how sport psychologists work with athletes and to provide them with opportunities to practice on their own.

All athletes and coaches have acquired, throughout their lives, different strategies to cope with difficulties that arise in practice and competition, so the psychologist's role sometimes will simply be perfecting such strategies; however, other times, the psychologist will help the athlete to change them (if they are inadequate) or teach the athlete new strategies to modify their behavior in specific situations. The goal of behavior modification in athletes is "to promote change through psychological intervention techniques to improve individuals' behavior. In this way, individuals develop their potential and opportunities available in their surroundings, optimize their environment, and adopt attitudes, values, and behaviors useful for adapting to what cannot be changed" (Cruzado, Labrador, & Muñoz, 1993, p. 31).

Psychological intervention techniques best suited for implementation in the sport context must be distinguished according to the desired objective. If the athlete has a specific issue, some techniques will work better than others. Similarly, if one is seeking to enhance the athlete's psychological skills, some techniques are more suitable, since they can be applied to a wider spectrum of situations in sport.

In summary, what one seeks to attain by improving psychological skills is what is called "flow," which is defined as a "state in which the individual is so involved in an activity that nothing seems to matter" (Csikszentmihalyi, 1990, p. 4). In sport, a state of optimal performance is considered when an athlete experiences a maximum control over himself and the competition (Jackson, 2000; Jackson & Csikszentmihalyi, 1999). Peak performance and flow is one of the goals of using techniques to improve skills.

The skills that athletes display may be the result of individual or guided learning (Dosil, 2008). There are several authors that have pointed out the most appropriate techniques to be able to reach an optimal condition for competition, under the justification that these techniques are the foundation to develop psychological aspects in the athlete. Porter (2003) indicates that to reach a peak mental performance during training sessions and competitions is necessary to master five techniques:

1 Establishing effective goals.
2 Relaxation techniques.
3 Visualization or imagery practice.
4 Recording thoughts.
5 Affirmation statements or positive self-talk.

In a similar topic, Hardy, Jones and Gould (1996) and Vealey (2007) propose five basic techniques that athletes must learn: goal setting, relaxation skills, visualization/mental rehearsal, self-talk/positive thoughts, and biofeedback techniques. In the following section, we provide only a brief comment on each one of these techniques as they will be developed in depth in other chapters.

In addition to the techniques mentioned above, interpersonal skills may also be added, which are often taken for granted in the sports arena (LaVoi, 2007) even though it has been shown that interpersonal skills training enhances performance (Freeman, Rees, & Hardy, 2009).

Goal setting

The literature on goal-setting is extensive and it has been applied to laboratory, field, and real-world settings using numerous tasks (Roberts &

Kristiansen, 2012). It is one of the most widely used techniques in sport psychology (Dosil, 2008), and it is considered essential when enhancing performance (Hardy, Jones, & Gould, 1996). "Setting a goal" is to identify what one wants to achieve or carry out, what one will attempt to attain, as well as the motive for which one will carry out a behavior and will persist in it. Its usefulness in the field of sport and physical activity is unquestionable, since it is the main determinant of the athlete's motivation.

Burton, Naylor, and Holliday (2001) reviewed the benefits of this technique in 56 sport psychology articles and found, in 44 of those articles, that there was an improvement in sports performance with its use. However, other researchers, such as Locke and Latham (1990 and 2002), indicate that such technique produces greater effects in organizational rather than sport contexts. One way or another, setting goals when planning for the season as well as before, during, and after practice and competition is considered essential to regulate motivation and positively influence other performance-related factors: attentional focus, anxiety/stress, self-confidence or team cohesion (Dosil, 2008). Roberts and Kristiansen (2012) suggest that setting specific and challenging goals is a key factor that differentiates performance from individuals who set no goals or who are simply told to do their best.

Relaxation

Relaxation is one of the techniques most often used in general psychology as well as sport psychology, so most individuals are aware of its use and associate relaxation with the sport psychologist's work. Its usefulness is unquestionable but its abuse may cause more harm than good. The psychologist must use it at appropriate times and once the athlete's basic psychological needs have been addressed first (or when it is considered that the use of this technique is a priority to solve a problem).

The pursued objective with the use of relaxation is to facilitate the athlete or individual in the sport context with a strategy (it is also very useful when working with coaches, managers, or referees). This strategy allows self-regulation of arousal levels (Dosil, 2008), management of physical energy (Vealey, 2007), or similarly, it is an instrument that can be used to decrease anxiety or stress levels. The technique, as indicated, should be used with caution, since its impact can be positive or negative (some activation facilitates performance, while being too relaxed may be detrimental). Similarly, relaxation practice is well suited for specific times during the season: it aids in the recovery process during the physical overload stage, it helps to lower activation levels (in between competitions) when there are many competitions, it reduces pain when the athlete suffers an injury or improves sleep patterns before a competition.

Hardy, Jones, and Gould (1996) suggest that relaxation techniques are frequently used in peak performance, as the ability to regulate arousal is one of the traits in the best athletes. However, Moran (2004) argued that such technique is only suitable in specific sports and with a specific type of athlete.

There are several relaxation procedures such as autogenic training and progressive relaxation, and the psychologist must help the athlete to use the one that is most appropriate and that adapts to the circumstances (situations) in which one can implement it.

Imagery

Visualization or imagery is one of the most widely-used techniques in the sports arena and one of the best documented in sport psychology. It is considered one of the key strategies that a psychologist must implement in the intervention stage when working with athletes (Perry & Morris, 1995) and its importance has been established in different studies (Holmes & Collin, 2002; Hardy, Jones, & Gould, 1996; Morris, Spittle, & Watt, 2005). Its main functions include: motor control, enhancing motivation, changing arousal and affect, problem solving and understanding, confidence and self-efficacy, prevention and recovery of injuries, as well as artistic functions (Murphy, Nordin, & Cumming, 2008).

There are many elite athletes that have reported the use of imagery before taking on a training session or a competition, with the idea of "living" the situation before it becomes a reality and thus, ensuring a successful performance (e.g., Tiger Woods, Michael Jordan, André Agassi, etc.). Some athletes use it in unstructured manner and intuitively, while others implement it with structure and specific purposes. However, this technique should be applied under the supervision of a sport psychologist and at the right time since it can become harmful and even hinder the athlete's optimal performance. In addition, different methods should be implemented to assess an athlete's imagery ability such as the Movement Imagery Questionnaire (MIQ-R; Hall & Martin, 1997) which relies on a self-report from the individual or the electroencephalogram (Cremades and Pease, 2007) which provides brain wave activity mapping during imagery performance.

Self-talk

One feature that successful athletes display is the capacity to control thoughts that arise during training sessions and competitions. In recent years, cognitive techniques have found a privileged position in research and application, turning into one of the most often used strategies among sport psychologists (Dosil, 2008).

The difficulty of thought control during an activity and the complexity of channeling one's self-talk correctly is an asset. In the majority of modalities, the athlete competes in physical conditions (e.g., elevated heart rate) where such control is more complicated, because thoughts come and go at high speed (like flashes). However, most athletes do not realize the power of thought.

Self-talk is the key to achieve cognitive control (Zinsser, Bunker, & Williams, 2001). In general, many athletes and individuals are not aware of the internal dialogue that happens throughout the day (possibly due to the speed in which it arises and the abstract/invisible nature of our thoughts). During training sessions and competitions, self-talk is fundamental since it is the means by which an athlete or individual is able to control their thoughts. There is empirical evidence suggesting that the use of positive messages during an activity causes athletes to increase their performance, while the use of negative messages hinders performance (Van Raalte, Brewer, Rivera, & Petitpas, 1994).

Biofeedback

Biofeedback can be defined as the use of instruments to detect and amplify internal physiological processes, in order to make this information available to the athlete. This information is ordinarily out of reach and limits the belief in the work that can be accomplished by a psychologist. Thus, one can understand that "feedback" is information, and "biofeedback" is information on the status of a biological process. Any technique that facilitates information about one's physiological activities and that allows these activities to be controlled can be considered a procedure or process of biofeedback. Moss and Wilson (2012) mentioned the main general procedures used to facilitate optimal performance: surface electromyography, electrodermal biofeedback, thermal biofeedback, respiratory training, heart rate and heart rate variability biofeedback.

Several researchers have documented the multiple benefits of implementing biofeedback techniques in the sport and exercise science field (Ekkekakis & Petruzzello, 2002; Tenenbaum, Corbett, & Kitsantas, 2002). Among these benefits, two are considered to be more significant for the purpose of this chapter: the application of biofeedback as a tool that serves to demonstrate the influence of mind over body and a method to train the psychological component. In turn, this will help the athlete to improve performance and to enhance his/her self-regulation skills.

A specific type of biofeedback is called "neurofeedback". This term is used as a more modern term for electroencephalography (EEG) biofeedback, taking into consideration that EEG is the variable to work with, and providing an addition to the peripheral biofeedback applications (Othmer & Othmer, 2012).

Hammond (2007) considers that sport psychologists will find that neurofeedback is cutting-edge technology that holds potential for improving concentration and attention, lowering anxiety and disruptive mental chatter, as well as assisting in the rehabilitation from concussions and mild head injuries.

Communication skills

Communication skills are fundamental in any aspect of life, which is why it is an area that requires training in sport. In addition, athletes utilize communication strategies in their environment that contribute to the creation of an appropriate atmosphere to focus on performance. Communication skills training has focused on coaches (Weinberg & Gould, 2011), parents (Gimeno, 2003), teams (Stuntza & Garwood, 2012), or even managers and referees (Dosil, 2008).

First, the athlete will be assessed through observation and video recordings to determine his interactions with others in the field (e.g., coach, teammates). Once the athlete has been observed, he will then be interviewed and his/her verbal communication and emotional expressions (e.g., voice tone and pitch, hand movement, facial gestures) will be assessed. Based on his/her communication skills, the sport psychologist will work on a specific technique(s). Two common methods being used in the sport psychology field are assertiveness and empathy training.

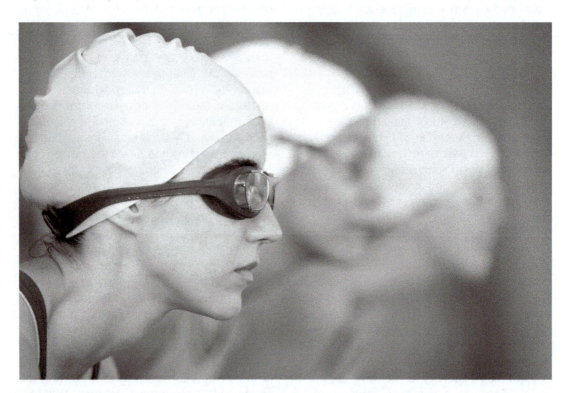

Figure 21.1 Studies including psychological characteristics in successful athletes.

HOW SHOULD TRAINING FOR PSYCHOLOGICAL SKILLS BE IMPLEMENTED?

The type of psychological skills training to be implemented with an athlete or team will depend on several factors. Among them, the team or athlete's time availability and financial budget are fundamental. Dosil (2008) identifies two types of psychological skills training programs: Psychological Skills Training Program (PSTP) and Applied Psychology Program to Practice Sessions (APPPS).

Psychological Skills Training Program (PSTP)

PSTP is a program aimed at learning psychological strategies that can be applied in practice sessions or competitions. It is implemented parallel to physical training programs, it requires a high degree of involvement by the athlete, and it is often recommended to athletes/teams that have exclusive dedication to the sport (e.g., members of a peak performance training center).

To use this program, the athlete must become involved in psychological training in a similar way that he would be involved in physical training. The lack of knowledge of what one can actually achieve with this type of preparation results in the fact that very few athletes have engaged in psychological skills training. Thus, it is considered a training that still must be exploited and which will be a differentiating factor in the competition of the future.

Balaguer and Castillo (1994) identify two phases within PSTP: general and specific. The former refers to the development of basic psychological skills through techniques, which are necessary for any subsequent applied work: relaxation, positive self-talk, self-activation, visualization, and concentration. The latter consists of transferring the learned skills to specific situations within the sport context, with the aim that the athlete finds the practical value of such skills.

In this type of mental training program, athletes have a difficult time transferring the skills from the first phase to the second. The role of the psychologist is fundamental for the athlete to achieve the appropriate motivation and confidence levels. Petitpas, Giges, and Danish (1999) indicate that PSTP effectiveness tends to be dependent on the relationship that is established between the athlete and the sport psychologist. The estimated PSTP duration is three to six months, with an applied sequence of three to five sessions per week lasting 15 to 30 minutes to learn each one of the techniques.

It is appropriate to begin with a plan when there is no competition, preferably in the preseason or during rest periods of physical training. It is common to find this type of program in centers where everything revolves around sport and athletes have the opportunity to work with a psychologist on a weekly basis. In this regard, Vernacchia (2003) indicates that psychological skills training is the best way to ensure a peak performance state.

This type of psychological skills training has proven to be efficient in 75–80% of cases (Vealey, 1994; Weinberg & Comar, 1994), which confirms that its development is conducive to improving the performance and well-being of the athlete/team. However, the degree of involvement this training requires is considered a burden, which is reflected in the number of athletes who do not participate because they believe the cost/benefit ratio is inadequate.

Applied Psychology Program to Practice Sessions (APPPS)

APPPS is a program aimed at optimizing practice sessions, so the psychologist focuses on enhancing these sessions through psychological strategies. This type of program justifies that psychology must be integrated into the physical, technical, and tactical training which is considered the fundamental basis for performance enhancement (Vealey, 2007). In contrast to PSTP, the psychologist focuses on what happens during practice sessions and determines how to collaborate to optimize them. The cost for the athlete is minimal and the benefits are immediate, so motivation and confidence usually increase with mental training.

APPPS would be the recommended program to implement since athletes and coaches perceive a greater involvement by the sport psychologist, being an authentic specialist in such modality (Dosil, 2006). The role of the psychologist consists of providing specific strategies for each situation, with the aim of solving potential conflicts and optimize performance. These strategies are facilitated with information provided by athletes and coaches from each modality, as well as observations and data collection instruments (Fifer, Henschen, Gould, & Ravizza, 2008).

The main objective for a psychologist who is focused on the application of psychological strategies during practice sessions is to achieve adherence, since this is the key to improve physical, technical, tactical, and psychological aspects. To achieve this, the psychologist must look after the environment that surrounds the athlete (Gould, Dieffenbach, & Moffett, 2002), as well as establishing the aspects that motivate the athlete to stay in the sport and give everything to reach success.

Once this objective is achieved, each modality and each athlete will have specific needs the psychologist must cover. In general, one can follow Balague's instructions (1997) which suggest that motivation, tolerance to fatigue,

perseverance, and concentration are characteristics the sport psychologist must reinforce during practice sessions in order to achieve quality. Motivation is the engine of practice; it is what makes the athlete sacrifice himself day by day to accomplish an objective. Tolerance to fatigue is fundamental when one practices a modality that requires many hours of training. Fatigue may be physical and/or mental, and it is advisable to have it under control during periods of training (Dosil, 2006).

Likewise, perseverance is important, without it major goals become unattainable. Persevering athletes tend to have faith in themselves and work extremely hard to achieve their planned goals. It is a feature that can be seen in almost all those who have achieved success in a given modality (e.g., staying after practice to work on a specific movement that needs improvement). What makes a great athlete is the desire to excel, to break down barriers, and to not set limits. Finally, concentration is essential during practice. In this regard, practice sessions should enable the athlete to rehearse the ability to concentrate on the task, as well as to control the aspects on which one should focus on: connect-disconnect from certain topics when appropriate (e.g., leaving family problems "outside" the stadium).

In short, with APPPS the psychologist takes into account all the psychological variables that may impact the athlete's performance and well-being, adapting intervention strategies to each modality and to each athlete (e.g., some will need to be motivated, others to improve their capacity for suffering, others to reduce anxiety prior to specific practice sessions, etc.).

WHERE SHOULD PSYCHOLOGICAL SKILLS TRAINING OCCUR?

The place where psychological skills training should be implemented varies from case to case. It is important to start from the principle that the sport psychologist should be the one that adapts to the athlete's or club's needs. Thus, we describe three intervention types

that are usually implemented in the sports field, knowing that in some cases the ideal will be a field intervention, and, in other cases, office or online work. Being able to understand and to implement these three intervention types (even simultaneously) allows sport psychologists to optimize psychological services to athletes and clubs. Dosil (2006) provides a more thorough description of these types of interventions:

Clinical intervention

This is the classic option in sport psychology. It stems from clinical psychology and involves carrying out psychological training in the team or club office or in a clinical psychology practice. Although the office can be used to assess and treat athletes, important contextual information is easily lost. Any myths surrounding clinical psychological work should be dispelled, especially when many athletes still struggle with the idea of going to a sport psychology office with the intention of improving performance rather than solving problems, which continues to be the most frequent reason for their visits (e.g., lack of motivation to train, lack of consistency, being overly negative, becoming nervous, etc.). In the office, whilst priority should be given to athletes' problems, it is also an exceptional opportunity to inform them of the possibilities psychological training has to improve their performance and well-being.

Field intervention

Involves going into the sports environment to perform psychological assessments of coaches and athletes. The principal objective of this form of psychological training is to integrate psychologists into the teams with which they are collaborating, operating in their natural setting and providing them with strategies that can be adapted to their day-to-day situations. It is advisable to use a field intervention in those sports where a successful clinical assessment is more difficult. On occasions, problems may arise when sport psychologists have no suitable place to meet with athletes (like an office), and to some extent, lose the confidentiality this setting would provide. This has certain repercussions in the training of some strategies which require time to be learned and an adequate location in which to work on them correctly (e.g., relaxation or visualization).

Online intervention

Is one of the lesser-developed methods in psychology and scarcely employed in sport psychology. Nevertheless, various studies have demonstrated its use to be just as effective as the more traditional forms of guidance, if not more so (Zirri & Perna, 2002). It may become one of the professional possibilities of the future since it offers certain advantages over the aforementioned approaches (e.g., confidentiality, anonymity for those athletes who wish to remain unknown, speed of response/treatment, etc.). This form of guidance has limited requests but it is becoming more popular among athletes. However, on some occasions, psychologists need to consult with athletes in person. In addition, it is extremely effective to guide coaches (by way of "psychological advice"), give simple action guidelines to some athletes, or work using records, making it a tool of undoubted value in current day sport psychology.

CONCLUSION

Throughout the chapter, answers have been given to three key questions concerning the training of psychological skills in the sport context: what, how and where psychological skills training should be practiced. The skill one practices should not present major changes, but the form of the training and place it is undertaken do. Skills training programs that have been implemented with positive results have been proposed in recent years, but the area where major changes lie ahead is the place training is implemented and how these services are provided.

In the future, cyberspace will acquire greater prominence thanks to new technologies (smartphones and tablets). These technologies are going to drastically influence the application of psychological training programs. The Internet is already allowing virtual interventions and the development of applications for devices which will facilitate evaluation and online training for athletes without the need for the psychologist's physical presence. However, one must pay special attention to this phenomenon because it brings both advantages and disadvantages. Timely intervention in any place and at any time is an important aid, but the "virtual relationship" can affect other aspects necessary in the communication, all of them related to non-verbal communication.

LEARNING AIDS

1   What is psychological skills training?

Psychological skills training is based on the implementation of mental strategies that aim to enhance the athlete's or team's performance. The aim is to reduce "mental weaknesses" as well as to enhance their skills and talent.

2   When should athletes work with a clinical psychologist or a sport psychologist?

When an athlete seeks a psychologist because he or she has a clinical problem (e.g., feeling sad because he or she is going through divorce and believes that it is impacting his or her athletic performance), the service delivered may be well performed by a clinical psychologist without any training in sport sciences, since working with an athlete becomes of lesser importance.

When there is a problem that is directly linked to athletic performance (e.g., being overly anxious before competition and choke), either a clinical psychologist or a sport psychologist may well work along with the athlete, even though a sport psychologist specialist with knowledge and experience in the specific domain should be recommended.

3   Mention five intervention techniques athletes must use to reach a peak performance.

- *Establishing effective goals.*
- *Relaxation techniques.*
- *Visualization or imagery practice.*
- *Recording thoughts.*
- *Affirmation statements or positive self-talk.*

4   What is goal setting?

Setting a goal is to identify what one wants to achieve or carry out, what one will attempt to attain, as well as the motive for which one will carry out a behavior and will persist in it. Ultimately, goal setting is about how objectives are achieved.

5   What is relaxation?

The objective of relaxation is to facilitate the athlete with a strategy that allows self-regulating arousal levels, managing physical energy, or as an instrument that can be applied when anxiety increases or when one feels "stressed out".

6   What are biofeedback and neurofeedback?

Biofeedback and neurofeedback can be defined as the use of instruments to detect and amplify internal physiological processes, in order to make this information available to the athlete. This information is ordinarily inaccessible and limits the belief in the work that can be accomplished by a psychologist.

7   Describe three intervention types that are usually implemented in sport psychology.

- *Clinical intervention: This stems from clinical psychology and involves carrying out psychological training in the office or a psychology practice. Although the clinic can be used to assess and treat athletes, important contextual information is easily lost.*

- *Field intervention: This involves going into the sports environment to perform psychological assessments of coaches and athletes. The objective of this form of psychological training is to integrate psychologists into the teams with which they are collaborating, operating in their natural setting and providing them with strategies which adapt to their day-to-day situations.*

- *Online intervention: Is one of the lesser-developed methods in psychology and scarcely employed in sport psychology. However, it may become one of the professional possibilities of the future since it offers certain advantages over the aforementioned approaches (e.g., confidentiality, anonymity for those athletes who wish to remain unknown, speed of response/treatment, etc.).*

REVIEW QUESTIONS

1   Analyse an athlete's motives for carrying out a psychological skills training program.

2   Discuss the differences between clinical psychology and sport psychology.

3   Explain the motives for which athletes are not involved in psychological skills training programs.

4   Choose several psychological skills used by athletes beginning with the most critical skill in successful performance. Justify your response.

5   Discuss the differences between PSTP and APPPS.

6   Analyse the positive and negative aspects of online interventions and new technologies for psychological skills training.

7   Describe two types of psychological skills training programs.

EXERCISES

1   You have been hired by a sports club in the community and have been tasked with the objective of improving athletes' psychological skills. Develop a program that includes the contents you would work on, how you would apply them and where you would work on these skills. As a starting point, take into account the situation and the actual sports club needs by interviewing a few club members. Try to carry out a real interview, but if this is not possible, you can do a role-play instead.

2   Carry out a review of ten applications for mobile devices that relate to psychological skills training and explain the benefits of each one of them.

3   Think about an application for mobile devices that may not exist but would be useful in your profession. Use imagination and be creative.

ADDITIONAL READING

Andersen, M. (2000). *Doing sport psychology.* Champaign, IL: Human Kinetics.

Dosil, J. (2006). *The sport psychology handbook: A Guide for sport specific performance enhancement.* Chichester, UK: Wiley.

Hanrahan, S.J. & Andersen, M.B. (2010). *Routledge handbook of applied sport psychology: A comprehensive guide for students and practitioners.* New York, NY: Routledge.

REFERENCES

Andersen, M.B., Denson, E.L., Brewer, B.W. & Van Raalte, J.L. (1994). Disorders of personality and mood in athletes: Recognition and referral. *Journal of Applied Sport Psychology, 6,* (2), 168–184.

Anshel, M.H. (2003). *Sport psychology: from theory to practice.* San Francisco: Benjamin Cummings.

Aspinwall, L.G. & Staudinger, U.M. (2003). A psychology of human strengths: Some central issues in an emerging field. In L.G. Aspinwall, & U.M. Staudinger (Eds.), *A psychology of human strengths: Fundamental questions and future directions for a positive psychology* (pp.9–22). Washington, DC: American Psychological Association.

Balaguer, I. & Castillo, I. (1994). Entrenamiento psicológico en el deporte. In I. Balaguer (Ed.), *Entrenamiento psicológico en el deporte.* Valencia: Albatros.

Burton, D., Naylor, S. & Holliday, B. (2001). Goal setting in sport: Investigating the goal effectiveness paradox. In R.N. Singer, H.A. Hausenblas & C.M. Janelle (Eds.), *Handbook of sport psychology* (2nd. ed., pp.497–528). New York, NY: Wiley.

Cremades, J.G. & Pease, D.G. (2007). Concurrent validity and reliability of lower and upper alpha activities as measures of visual and kinesthetic imagery ability. *International Journal of Sport and Exercise Psychology, 5* (2), 187–202.

Cruzado, J.A., Labrador, F.J. & Muñoz, M. (1994). Introducción a la modificación y terapia de conducta. In F.J. Labrador & M. Muñoz (Eds.), *Manual de técnicas de modificación y terapia de conducta.* (pp.31–46). Madrid: Pirámide.

Csikszentmihalyi, M. (1990). *Flow: the psychology of optimal experience.* New York, NY: Harper & Row.

Dosil, J. (2006). Applied sport psychology: A new perspective. In J. Dosil (Ed.), *The sport psychology handbook: A guide for sport specific performance enhancement* (pp.3–18). Chichester, UK: Wiley.

Dosil, J. (2008). *Psicología del la actividad física y del deporte* (2nd ed.). Madrid: McGraw Hill.

Ekkekakis, P. & Petruzzello, S.J. (2002). Biofeedback in exercise psychology. In D. Blumenstein, M. Bar-Eli & G. Tenenbaum (Eds.), *Brain and body in sport and exercise: Biofeedback applications in performance enhancement* (pp.77–100). West Sussex, UK: Wiley.

Fifer, A., Henschen, K., Gould, D. & Ravizza, K. (2008). What works when working with athletes. *The Sport Psychologist, 22,* 356–377.

Frank, L., Gardner, Z. & Moore, E. (2006). *Clinical sport psychology.* Champaign, Il: Human Kinetics.

Freeman, P., Rees, T. & Hardy, L. (2009). An intervention to increase social support and improve performance. *Journal of Applied Sport Psychology, 21* (2), 186–200.

Friedrickson, B. (1998). What good are positive emotions? *Review of General Psychology, 2,* 300–319.

Gimeno, F. (2003). Descripción y evaluación preliminar de un programa de habilidades sociales y de solución de problemas con padres y entrenadores en el deporte infantil y juvenil. *Revista de Psicología del Deporte, 12,* (1), 67–79.

Gould, D., Eklund, R.C. & Jackson, S.A. (1992). 1988 US Olympic wrestling excellence: Mental preparation, precompetitive cognition and affect, *The Sport Psychologist, 6,* 358–382.

Gould, D., Dieffenbach, K. & Moffett, A. (2002). Psychological talent and their development in Olympic champions. *Journal of Applied Sport Psychology, 14,* (3), 172–204.

Hall, C. & Martin, K. (1997). Measuring movement imagery abilities: A revision of the Movement Imagery Questionnaire. *Journal of Mental Imagery, 21* (1&2), 143–154.

Hammond, C. (2007). Neurofeedback for the enhancement of athletic performance and physical balance. *The Journal of the American Board of Sport Psychology 1,* 1–9.

Hardy, L., Jones, J.G. & Gould, D. (1996). *Understanding psychological preparation for sport: Theory and practice of elite performers.* Chichester, UK: Wiley.

Hervás, G., Sánchez, A. & Vázquez, C. (2008). Intervenciones psicológicas para la promoción del bienestar. In Hervás, G. & Vásquez, C. (Eds.), *Psicología positiva aplicada* (pp.41–74), Bilbao: Desclée de Brower.

Holmes, P. & Collin, D. (2002). Functional equivalence solutions for problems with motor imaginary. In I. Cockerill (Ed.), *Solutions in sport psychology* (pp.120–140). London, UK: Thomson.

Jackson, S.A. (2000). Joy, fun and flow state in sport. In Y.L. Hanin (Ed.), *Emotions in sport* (pp.135–156). Champaign, Il: Human Kinetics.

Jackson, S.A. & Csikszentmihalyi, M. (1999). *Flow in sport.* Champaign, Il: Human Kinetics.

LaVoi, N.M. (2007). Interpersonal communication and conflict in the coach–athlete relationship. In S. Jowett & D. Lavallee (Eds.), *Social psychology in sport* (pp.29–40). Champaign, IL: Human Kinetics.

Locke, E.A. & Latham, G.P. (1990). *A theory of good setting and task performance.* Englewood Cliffs, NJ: Prentice-Hall.

Locke, E.A. & Latham, G.P. (2002). Building a practically useful theory of goal setting and task motivation. *American Psychologist, 57,* 705–717.

Moran, A.P. (2004). *Sport and exercise psychology: A critical introduction.* London: Routledge.

Morris, T., Spittle, M. & Watt, A.P. (2005). *Imagery in sport.* Champaign, IL: Human Kinetics.

Moss, D. & Wilson, V. (2012). The use of general biofeedback in the pursuit of optimal performance. In W.A. Edmonds & G. Tenenbaum (Eds.), *Case studies in applied psychophysiology: Neurofeedback and biofeedback treatments for advances in human performance.* Chichester, UK: John Wiley & Sons, Ltd.

Murphy, S., Nordin, S. & Cumming, J. (2008). Imaginary in sport, exercise and dance. In T. Horn (Ed.), *Advances in sport psychology* (pp. 297–324). Champaign, IL: Human Kinetics.

Orlick, T. (2008). *In pursuit of excellence* (4th ed.), Champaign, IL: Human Kinetics.

Othmer, S. & Othmer, S.F. (2012). Performance enhancement applications of neurofeedback. In W.A Edmonds & G. Tenenbaum (Eds.), *Case studies in applied psychophysiology: Neurofeedback and biofeedback treatments for advances in human performance* (pp.17–30) Chichester: John Wiley & Sons, Ltd.

Perry, C. & Morris, T. (2005). Mental imagery in sport. In T. Morris & J. Summers (Eds.), *Sport psychology: Theory, applications and issues* (2nd ed.) (pp. 344–387). Brisbane, AU: Wiley.

Petitpas, A.J., Giges, B. & Danish, S.J. (1999). The sport psychologist-athlete relationship: Implications for training. *The Sport Psychologist, 13* (3), 344–357.

Porter, K. (2003). *The mental athlete.* Champaign, IL: Human Kinetics.

Roberts, G. & Kristiansen, E. (2012). Goal setting to enhance motivation in sport. In G. Roberts & D. Treasure (Eds.), *Advances in motivation in sport and exercise* (3rd ed.) (pp. 207–228). Champaign, IL: Human Kinetics.

Schack, T., Moncier III, J. & Taylor, R. (2007). Sport psychology: A clinician's perspective. In G. Tenenbaum & R. Eklund (Eds.), *Handbook of sport psychology* (3rd ed.) (pp.310–331). Hoboken, NJ: Wiley.

Seligman, M.E.P. (2002). *Authentic happiness: Using the new positive Psychology to realize your potential for lasting fulfillment*. New York, NY: Free Press.

Stuntza, C.P. & Garwood, K.E. (2012). Enhancing social goal involvement through cooperative instructions. *Journal of Applied Sport Psychology, 24* (3), 260–274.

Tenenbaum, G., Corbett, M. & Kitsantas, A. (2002). Biofeedback: Applications and methodological concerns. In B. Blumenstein, M. Bar-Eli & G. Tenenbaum (Eds.), *Biofeedback applications in performance enhancement: Brain and body in sport and exercise* (pp.101–122). New York, NY: Wiley.

Van den Auweele, Y., De Cuyper, B., Van Mele, V. & Rzewinicki, R. (1993). Elite performance and personality: From description and prediction to diagnosis and intervention. In R.N. Singer, M. Murphy & L.K. Tennant (Eds.), *Handbook of research on sport psychology*. New York: Macmillan.

Van Raalte, J.L., Brewer, B.W., Rivera, P.M. & Petitpas, A.J. (1994). The relationship between observable self-talk and competitive junior tennis players'

match performances. *Journal of Sport and Exercise Psychology, 16*, 400–415.

Vealey, R.S. (1994). Current status and prominent issues in sport psychology interventions. *Medicine and Science in Sport and Exercise*, 495–502.

Vealey, R.S. (2007). Mental skills training in sport. In G. Tenenbaum & R. Eklund (Eds.), *Handbook of sport psychology* (3rd ed.) (pp.287–309). Hoboken, NJ: Wiley.

Vernacchia, R.A. (2003). Working with individual team sports: The psychology of track and field. In R. Lindor & K.P. Henschen (Eds.), *The psychology of team sports*. Morgantown, WV: FIT.

Weinberg, R. & Gould, D. (2011) *Foundations of Sport and exercise psychology* (5th ed.). Champaign, IL: Human Kinetics.

Weinberg, R. & Comar, W. (1994). The effectiveness of psychological interventions in competitive sport. *Sport Medicine Journal, 18*, 406–418.

Zinsser, N., Bunker, L.K. & Williams, J.M. (2001). Cognitive techniques for improving performance and building confidence. In J.M. Williams (Ed.), *Applied sport psychology: Personal growth to peak performance* (4th ed.) (pp. 284–311). Mountain View, CA: Mayfield.

Zirri, S.J. & Perna, F.M. (2002). Integrating web pages and e-mail into sport psychology consultations. *The Sport Psychologist, 16* (4), 416–431.

Chapter 22

Goal-setting and sport performance

Research findings and practical applications

ROBERT WEINBERG AND JOANNE BUTT

SUMMARY

The purpose of this chapter is to provide insight into effective goal-setting with the specific aim of providing guidelines on how to develop and implement a goal-setting program with sports teams and individuals. Guidelines are provided to facilitate understanding on how to identify goals, the importance of setting different types of goals (i.e., outcome, performance, process), and also which type of goals to prioritize in different situations (e.g., competition vs. training). The current research on goal-setting in sport and exercise domains to illustrate why goals are important is also reviewed. From an applied perspective, a case study is provided to demonstrate the principles needed for effective goal-setting, and how these principles can be used in developing and implementing a goal-setting program.

INTRODUCTION

Coaches and athletes have long been using goal-setting as a mental strategy to enhance sport performance. It is considered one of the most popular strategies for increasing motivation, confidence, and task-focus in athletes. Specifically, setting goals can help athletes prioritize what is most important to them in their sport and subsequently guide daily practices by knowing what to work on. The two quotes below; the first one from an athlete, and the second one from a coach, demonstrate the important roles that goals can have on an athlete's drive to be successful, and also that setting goals can provide focus and direction.

"The coach must have goals. The team must have goals. Each individual tennis player must have goals – real, vivid, living goals. Goals keep everyone on target. Goals commit me to the work, time, pain and whatever else is part of the price of achieving success" (Weinberg, 2002, p. 34).

"The purpose for me is to make sure that I stay on-line and stay on track. I don't want to just muddle around, I want to have something to work for and toward" (Weinberg, Butt, Knight, & Peritt, 2001, p. 391).

OBJECTIVES

After reading this chapter the reader should be able to:

1 Describe the three different types of goals.
2 Understand how goals work to influence performance.
3 Understand the principles of goal-setting.
4 Apply goal-setting principles to competitive sports situations.

GOAL-SETTING: RESEARCH TO PRACTICE

It is common for athletes to know what they want in sport (e.g., winning a tournament, be selected for try-outs), but it is most important that they learn how to set the right type of goals, and develop appropriate plans and strategies that can help them work towards achieving the goals set. This chapter begins by defining the different types of goals, followed by providing an overview of the empirical evidence on goal-setting specific to sport and exercise settings. The final part of this chapter includes a case study demonstrating the principles of effective goal-setting, and outlines the three phases involved in designing a program to achieve them.

DEFINING GOALS

In the scientific literature, a goal is considered to be objective in nature and centers on achieving a specific standard of proficiency. The most commonly accepted definition of a goal was put forward by Locke, Shaw, Saari and Latham (1981) who defined a goal as attaining a specific level of proficiency in a task, usually within a specified time limit. A swimmer who sets a goal to decrease his/her finish time by two seconds is setting an objective and specific goal. Athletes can also set subjective goals, such as wanting to have more fun this season than the last one. Setting both subjective and objective type goals is considered important; however, objective goals are easier to quantify than subjective goals. That is, by quantifying goals in an objective manner we can monitor our progress, and know when we have reached them. In the sport and exercise literature, three types of goals are predominantly discussed: *outcome*, *performance* and *process* goals. *Outcome goals* typically focus on the end result or outcome of an event or competition, such as winning and losing. Examples of an outcome goal might include, winning a league championship, beating an opponent on points/scores, achieving a specific ranking, or achieving a 12–6 record for a season. The key point to remember about setting outcome goals is that we are seldom in control of whether or not we achieve them. Consequently, achieving an outcome goal, to a large degree, depends on the performance of others (i.e., the opposition). Athletes who focus solely on outcome goals can become anxious and often distracted during competitions because they are more concerned with the end result rather than focusing on the task at hand.

Performance goals, on the other hand, help athletes focus to improve their own performance. That is, when athletes set these types of goals they are making comparisons to their own previous performances rather than opponents. Examples of a performance goal include improving one's first serve percentage in tennis from 50% to 60%, increasing one's batting average compared to last season, and sprinting a personal best time. Performance goals are considered to be more controllable because athletes do not need to rely on others' performances to achieve them. Accordingly, setting performance goals can increase athletes' intrinsic motivation and levels of self-confidence.

Process goals focus on how an athlete performs a specific skill (i.e., the actions a player must focus on to execute a performance). Examples of process goals include, a volleyball player perfecting his/her service toss, or a rugby kicker focusing on foot placement in relation to the ball. Due to the nature of process goals, they tend to be used mostly in training sessions, because this is where athletes practice refining specific skills. However, it is not uncommon for athletes to switch to a more process-oriented thinking during pressure moments in competition, to help them focus on the execution of performing a skill well rather than the outcome. Setting each type of goal can improve sports performance, and it is recommended that athletes learn to prioritize their goals because it is likely that different types of goals might be more effective for different situations (e.g., competition vs. training). Indeed, research

with elite athletes indicates that setting these three types of goals in combination is linked to better performance (Filby, Maynard, & Graydon, 1999). It is important to note that performance and outcome goals are important to athletes but, for every outcome goal, there should be several performance and process goals set that provide the *stepping-stone pathway* to achieving that outcome.

Key points

There are three different types of goals.

- Outcome goals focus on the end result or outcome of an event or competition such as winning and losing.
- Performance goals help athletes focus on improving their own performance.
- Process goals focus on how an athlete performs a specific skill.
- For every outcome goal, there should be several performance and process goals set that provide the stepping-stone pathway to achieving that outcome.

WHY DO GOALS WORK? RESEARCH IN ORGANIZATIONAL AND SPORTS SETTINGS

According to research conducted by Locke and his colleagues (Locke et al., 1981; Locke & Latham, 1990), goal-setting is effective because an individual's *conscious goals* while trying to perform a task, in turn, actually regulate task performance. Goals are formed by using internal comparisons and standards to evaluate performance; thus, it is thought that athletes can achieve a higher performance level if *specific and hard goals* are set. Generally, it is thought that *goals direct attention and action* and help athletes focus on what they need to do in both the short term and the long term. Research supports that setting specific and hard goals produce better perfor-

mance than easy goals, "do your best" goals, or no goals at all.

Research on goal-setting has been conducted in industrial and organizational settings for over 45 years (cf., Locke & Latham, 2002). A central principle of Locke's initial goal-setting theory was that *specific, difficult, challenging goals* lead to higher levels of task performance than setting *easy goals, no goals or "do your best" goals*. This aspect of the theory has received most attention over the years, and has been tested extensively. For example, in a large-scale review of 201 studies conducted by Locke and Latham (1990), 91% provided support for Locke's initial hypothesis. The studies that were reviewed consisted of over 40,000 participants and involved approximately 90 different tasks across laboratory and field settings, and thus, demonstrate the robustness of the findings. A second important aspect of Locke's goal-setting theory relates to goal difficulty and performance. That is, according to Locke, there is a linear relationship between the degree of goal difficulty and performance, with the exception of when participants reach the limits of their ability at high goal difficulty levels, which results in performance leveling off. Overall, there has been extensive support for harder goals producing higher levels of task performance than easy goals in the industrial setting.

It is important for practitioners to understand how and why goal-setting influences performance. One of the common explanations put forward is known as the *mechanistic perspective*. Specifically, in explaining the effectiveness of goals on enhancing performance, Locke et al. (1981) contended that goals influence performance in four ways. That is, goals are thought to influence performance by helping athletes to direct their attention to the task at hand, and therefore, helping them to focus on the relevant cues involved in executing the appropriate skills. In addition to directing attention, goals can also increase effort and persistence because, through systematic monitoring of the goals, feedback can be obtained on one's progress. Finally, goals can influence performance in helping athletes to develop relevant learning strategies. Specifically, when athletes set goals, strategies negotiated by the athlete and his/her coach can be put in place to help them achieve these goals. Support for the mechanistic view in explaining the effectiveness of goals on enhancing sports performance has been found in studies conducted by Weinberg and his colleagues (e.g., Weinberg, Burton, Yukelson, & Weigand, 1993; Weinberg, Stitcher, & Richardson, 1994; Weinberg, Butt, Knight, & Perritt, 2001). For example, in a study conducted with collegiate athletes, it was reported that setting goals to focus attention on the task at hand was the most important reason for setting goals (Weinberg et al., 1993). To illustrate the role of feedback on one's progress, Weinberg et al. (1994) conducted a season-long study on collegiate lacrosse players. Specifically, results revealed that athletes setting both short- and long-term goals demonstrated consistently higher levels of offensive and defensive measures of performance throughout the season compared to the group of athletes who did not set goals.

Key points

- Setting specific, difficult, challenging goals leads to higher levels of task performance than setting easy goals, no goals or "do your best" goals.
- The mechanistic view explains why goals influence performance in three ways:
  - Helping athletes to *direct their attention* to the task at hand.
  - *Increase effort* and *persistence*.
  - Help athletes to *develop relevant learning strategies*.

Due to the evidence found for the motivational and performance-enhancing effects of goal-setting in the organizational setting, it was later adopted in sport, although it was not systematically researched in sport and exercise settings until the 1980s. Empirical support for goal-setting as a tool to enhance sport and exercise performance was illustrated in a meta-analysis (Kyllo & Landers, 1995), which comprised 36 studies. After this first large-scale study was conducted, research on goal-setting continued to grow, with further reviews reporting an increasing number of references to goal-setting research in sport and exercise settings (cf., Burton & Weiss, 2008; Naylor & Holliday, 2001). Collectively, results from this research indicated a moderate to strong relationship between goal-setting and performance (i.e., 80% effectiveness rate). In support of these findings, Olympic athletes perceived goal-setting to be one of the most often used psychological interventions, and leading sport psychology consultants have also reported goal-setting to be effective when working with Olympic athletes (e.g., Burton, Pickering, Weinberg, Yukelson, & Weigand, 2010). It is important to note that a number of factors, such as personality, degree of commitment, incentives, and an athlete's ability to achieve the goal influence effective goal-setting. It is with these mediating factors in mind that Locke (1968) argued against a simple causative relationship between goals and behavior.

The next part of this chapter introduces effective goal-setting, and how to design a goal-setting program. While the principles of goal-setting enable our practice from an applied perspective, it is important to consider some of the research and empirical data that the principles are based on, and therefore, underpin some of the principles that are presented below. As mentioned earlier, it is well documented that goal-setting has a positive impact on sports performance (e.g., Filby et al., 1999; Weinberg et al., 2010). One of the key principles involved in helping goals to be positively related to performance is *goal specificity* and *goal difficulty*. In particular, setting specific goals that are *challenging but realistic* tends to result in improved performance more so than setting *subjective* or *"do your best"* type goals (Mento, Steel, & Karren, 1987). A study involving elite and non-elite boxers utilizing performance profiling (Butler & Hardy, 1992) to help with setting specific goals at an appropri-

ate level of challenge, has supported these principles of goal-setting (e.g., O'Brien, Mellalieu, & Hanton, 2009). It is clear that setting specific goals can encourage athletes to focus on the task at hand. Similarly, research has revealed that both short- and long-term goals are needed to maintain motivation and performance (e.g., Kane, Baltes, & Moss, 2001). While athletes and exercisers can readily identify and set outcome goals that tend to be long term, it is the short-term goals that help them focus on smaller improvements, while providing continuous feedback if monitored frequently. Research also supports the suggestion that goals should be recorded and written down (O'Brien et al., 2009). Despite the research findings, qualitative research reports from athletes and coaches indicate that this does not always occur in the systematic way that should increase goal effectiveness (e.g., Weinberg et al., 2001). Finally, setting both *practice and competition goals* is another key principle involved in goal-setting (Weinberg et al., 2001). In particular, setting practice goals has received support from research findings involving coaches and athletes. For example, Côté, Salmela, and Russell (1995) observed expert coaches, and found that one of the things these coaches did consistently was set goals in practice to keep athletes focused and motivated. Similarly, Orlick and Partington (1988) reported that setting practice goals was a critical factor that differentiated successful and unsuccessful Olympic athletes.

PRINCIPLES OF GOAL-SETTING

Although we know that goal-setting can enhance performance and personal growth in sport and exercise environments, it is misleading to think, however, that all types of goals are equally effective in achieving these ends. For example, according to achievement goal theory, mastery (improving against yourself) and outcome (comparing to others) goal orientations lead to different goal-setting practices and effectiveness. Similarly, different situa-

tions, such as setting up a mastery or outcome environment, would also elicit different levels of goal effectiveness. In essence, it is important to emphasize the distinction between the "science" and the "art" of setting goals. Specifically, researchers can provide practitioners with the science of goal-setting, which leads to the development of certain principles. But situational constraints and individual differences always play a role; thus, coaches need to know their teams and individual athletes well to maximize goal-setting effectiveness. The effectiveness of any motivational technique, therefore, is dependent on the interaction of the individuals and the situation in which the individuals are placed. The goal-setting principles stated below should be viewed within this context.

Set specific and measurable goals

Athletes often hear coaches and teachers tell participants simply to "go out and do your best." With "do your best" goals, however, athletes/exercisers never fail because they can always say that they did their best. Although this "do your best" type of instruction can be motivating, it is not as powerful in enhancing motivation and performance as encouraging participants to go out and achieve a specific goal. In fact, it has been consistently shown that specific and *measurable goals* produce significantly better performance than "do your best" goals. One of the reasons that goals need to be specific is that they also need to be measurable so that performers know they are making progress towards achieving them. For example, telling a basketball player to improve her foul shooting percentage would not be as helpful as telling her that you want her to improve her percentage from 70% to 80% by extending her elbow on the follow through. This gives the player a specific goal to shoot for and a way to measure if she achieved the goal.

Set realistic but challenging/ moderately difficult goals

When setting goals, a consistent principle to follow is that they should be challenging and realistic. Goals that are too easy do not present a challenge to individuals, which lead to becoming complacent and exerting less than maximum effort. Conversely, if goals are too difficult, individuals will have a tendency to lose motivation and possibly give up when they fall short of their goal. But how does one determine if a goal is realistic and challenging? Here is where the art of coaching becomes important, as coaches need to know each individual athlete in order to determine the appropriate challenge for that athlete.

A good rule of thumb to keep in mind is to set more immediate goals no more than 5% above current performance over the past couple of weeks. However, in many sports (e.g., swimming, skiing, track) even a 1% increase in performance can be a significant improvement and mean the difference between winning and losing. Thus, the secret is to find a balance between setting oneself up for failure (goals too difficult) and allowing for easy success (goals too easy). In this middle ground reside challenging, realistic, moderately difficult, attainable goals.

Set short-term and long-term goals

Coaches and athletes are always told to set both short-term and long-term goals. But why are both of these types of goals necessary? Coaches typically set outcome-oriented and long-term goals such as winning their league championship, and athletes might set individual long-term goals such as winning a medal at the Olympics. These long-term goals are very important for success as they provide coaches and athletes with a direction and destination, and can sometimes act as dream goals. In essence, they keep the focus on where one wishes to eventually go. As some athletes would say, "keep your eye on the prize."

Research has also revealed that both short- and long-term goals are needed to maintain motivation and performance over time (Weinberg et al., 2001). *Short-term goals* are important because they help individuals focus on small improvements and also provide continuous feedback concerning progress toward the long-term goal. This feedback can serve a motivational function and allow adjustment of goals either upward or downward, depending on the situation. A *long-term goal* may seem out of reach; but breaking it up into manageable short-term goals can make the seemingly impossible become possible. A good way to envision the interaction of short-term and long-term goals is to think of a staircase with the long-term goal at the top, the present level of performance at the bottom, and a sequence of progressively linked short-term goals connecting the top and bottom of the stairs.

Set goals for practice and competition

Many societies seem to be focused on winning in sport competition, and thus setting goals generally focuses solely or predominantly on competition goals. However, for most sports, daily practices encompass much more time commitment than competitions. This is especially the case in sports such as gymnastics, swimming, figure skating, and track and field where there usually are only a few important meets; the rest of the time is spent on practice, practice, and more practice. This is not to say that competition goals aren't important (although they should focus more on performance and process); rather setting a *practice goal* is a good way to keep an athlete motivated and focused during long, arduous and often repetitive practice sessions. Some typical practice goals could include getting to practice on time, giving teammates positive reinforcement and encouragement, displaying leadership behaviors, and achieving certain performance standards for specific drills. Research with high school and college coaches (Weinberg et al., 2001, 2002) has confirmed that coaches feel it is important to set goals both in practice and in competition. But let's not totally forget competition goals. The important point is not to focus on winning; rather focus more on doing the things that will help you win (which are usually more in the form of process goals). The process goals in practice should help athletes learn their skills so well that they become automatic in competition. This is the ticket for peak performance in competition.

Develop plans to reach goals

In Locke's (1968) seminal work, he proposed that one of the mechanisms underlying the effectiveness of goals in enhancing performance is the development of relevant learning strategies. Unfortunately, this aspect of goal-setting is often neglected as coaches often seem to believe that simply having goals will improve performance. However, strategies need to be specific (as noted above), and should involve definite numbers (e.g., how much, how many, how often). Therefore, when setting goals, one should always ask the question, "What do I need to do to reach my goals?" For example, what would a baseball player do to increase his batting average from .250 to .300? A golfer reducing her average score from 78 to 74? Or a basketball player increasing his foul shooting percentage from 70% to 80%? Setting more specific process goals would help achieve the performance goals that were set. Using the baseball example, the player might decide to change his stance and move further back in the batter's box to get a better look at the ball. He may change his routine while in the on-deck circle and employ some imagery before he gets up to bat. Or she may decide he needs to lift more weights to build up his upper body strength.

Set individual and team goals

Coaches often think that setting *individual goals* would undermine the greater *team goal*. However, there is a place for individual goals within a team sport, as long as the individual goals do not conflict with team goals (Weinberg et al., 2000). If athletes meet their individual goals, then this should theoretically help ensure success as a team. In fact, researchers have found that team goals enhance performance as effectively as individual goals if they foster individual goal-setting (Locke & Latham, 1990). For example, setting a goal to improve one's shooting percentage from 45% to 55% should enhance the team's goal of winning the championship. However, increasing one's individual goal from averaging 10 points per game to 15 points per game may undermine the team goal of winning a championship because the player may simply take more shots to get the 15 points. Thus, sport psychology consultants should be cautious when athletes set individual goals, making sure they contribute to overall team goals.

Re-evaluate goals

Goal-setting should be a starting place and not an ending place. Many coaches and athletes make the mistake of setting goals and never going back to them to see how they are progressing toward those goals. However, goals should be re-evaluated periodically based on current performance versus the original goal that was set and potentially made easier or more difficult. For example, if a baseball player set a goal to bat .300 and was hitting only .220 at midseason, then he should probably readjust his goal to be more realistic, such as hitting .275 by the end of the season.

However, if he was hitting .340 at midseason, he might increase his goal to .325 as that now would seem very realistic. The point is that one's goal can be altered based on the current situation (maybe the player got injured or simply got off to a very slow or fast start). By periodically revisiting (and then potentially adjusting) the goal, it always remains realistic but challenging as noted above. This should help keep athletes optimally motivated as they strive to meet their goal.

Some common problems identified with goal-setting

- Convincing athletes, coaches and exerciser to set goals.
- Setting too many goals too soon.
- Failing to monitor goals and re-evaluate goals regularly.
- Setting only outcome goals without setting performance and process goals.
- Failing to set specific and measurable goals.

GOAL-SETTING: A CASE STUDY

There have been many articles written both inside and outside of sport detailing the principles of goal-setting. In talking with coaches, many understand the principles, but few actually implement a full-blown goal-setting program as opposed to simply setting some individual and/or team goals. To try to alleviate this problem, a case study of a basketball coach and his team is presented which employs many of the principles involved in setting goals, as well as highlighting obstacles to setting up and implementing a goal-setting intervention.

Preparation and planning phase

Coach Elliot Stone was taking over a collegiate school basketball program that had experienced nine consecutive losing seasons and finished in last place in their division eight of nine years. He wanted to change the culture of losing so that the players would have more positive attitudes as well as specific offensive, defensive, and fitness goals. Thus, one of the first things he did was to talk to his assistant coach (who was returning from last year), and his two co-captains. Based on their experiences the past couple of seasons, Coach Stone had them assess both individual and team needs, and he personally looked at game statistics to help round out his needs assessment. The captains and assistant coach identified several specific skill areas such as rebounding, turnovers, and shot selection. But Coach Stone was careful to include other needs besides performance improvements, such as enjoyment, supporting/encouraging teammates, mental preparation, and intrinsic motivation.

Such needs then formed the basis on which specific goals would be set.

Once the needs were determined, Coach Stone planned on specific strategies to help achieve the goals set for the coming season. For example, Coach Stone found that the team percentage for three-point field goals was a dismal 20% and thus he dedicated 15 minutes every practice to work on these shots including specific technical changes. In addition, he felt the team was too negative last year so he insisted on encouraging positive statements among teammates.

The biggest reason that the other coaches didn't always follow-through with their goal-setting programs is perceived lack of time. Coach Stone knew this (as it happened to him before), and he was determined to overcome this obstacle. Therefore, he instructed his assistant coach and co-captains to meet weekly to discuss how the goal-setting program was going and report to him any changes that needed to be made to ensure that the players were setting their goals and working hard to reach their goals. Finally, Coach Stone has come to understand that goals cannot be set in a vacuum. Specifically, athletes' potential commitment and opportunities for practice must be assessed before goals can be set. For example, it does no good to set goals to be completed outside of practice (e.g., mental preparation) if the athletes are not committed or disciplined enough to work on these goals on their own.

Education and acquisition phase

A formal meeting and a series of brief, less formal, meetings were scheduled before practice and classes began. During these meetings, Coach Stone provided the players with examples of effective and ineffective goals, along with basic information about different types of goals (e.g., outcome, performance, and process). Although most athletes had set goals, they generally had not set them in a way that maximizes their effectiveness. The principles noted above were typed out and handed to all players so that they could get a better understanding of the different types of goals and the most effective ways to set goals. These were then discussed by the coaching staff and players, and specific examples were provided to the players resulting in a better understanding of how to set goals effectively.

Because the players were getting so much goal-setting information, Coach Stone felt they needed time to process this information, and should not be expected to be able to list their specific goals immediately. Rather, players should think about setting goals in specific areas, as well as implementation strategies. This provided them with an opportunity to think about different options instead of having to come up with goals and strategies on the spot. Thus, based on the input from the assistant coach and the co-captains, Coach Stone asked players to be ready for the next meeting by setting three personal goals (using the goal-setting principles), and three team goals in the areas of field goal percentage, turnovers committed, and rebounds per game. He knew that setting too many goals could be ineffective, so he asked his players to only focus on a few specific goals. In fact, depending on the player and past experience with goal-setting, Coach Stone asked each player to only focus on one goal and achieve that before moving on to another goal. Besides these performance goals, Coach Stone wanted each player to have a strategy (process goal) outlining how to reach each performance goal. For example, if one's individual goal was to improve his rebounds from four to seven per game, he might practice proper "boxing out" technique and coaches could rate him on a 1-10-scale regarding how effective he was in boxing out during practice.

After the initial meeting, Coach Stone scheduled a second meeting where team goals were discussed and decided upon by the coach and team. To do this, each player's team goals for the three areas noted by Coach Stone were placed on the blackboard and were then discussed. In this way players had input into the final goals and thus would be more committed to, and invested in, actually working hard to achieve these goals. After this discussion, a vote was taken on each team goal and Coach Stone recorded the different strategies needed to reach each of these team goals. For example, a half-hour of practice three days a week was targeted to proper shooting technique making sure players followed through on their shots (to improve field goal percentage).

In addition to the team meetings, Coach Stone and his assistant coach met individually with all players to discuss, set, and record their specific goals. This was done in a way in which players felt that they "owned" their goals but the coaches were critical in helping players decide on realistic goals. Thus if a player shot 35% from the field last year and set a goal to shoot 55% this year, the coach suggested that this would be extremely difficult to accomplish. He suggested and encouraged the player to set a more realistic goal, such as increasing his shooting percentage to 45%. But eventually it was up to the player to agree to the specific goal. All goals were then written down and displayed in a prominent place (e.g., taped on lockers or on the locker-room wall) so that these goals would be seen by all teammates every day. He even taped the goals to the wall outside the gymnasium so that all students could see. This increased goal commitment as players generally did not want to let their teammates down (or their friends) and worked hard to reach their goals. Finally, the coaches worked with players to help provide them with very specific strategies to reach their goals, as this often was the reason goals were not achieved.

Goal follow-up and evaluation phase

Probably the stage that is most neglected is the evaluation stage, as coaches become so busy with other things (e.g., schedules, paperwork, reports) they just don't make the time to evaluate the goals that were set. Coach Stone knew that most coaches don't really follow through

to evaluate the effectiveness of their goal-setting program. It was enough that they set it up; but evaluating it and staying on top of players regarding their goals often just seemed too onerous. Coach Stone did not want to fall into this scenario. Therefore, he streamlined the evaluation process by having managers record and post practice and game statistics related to players' goals, and then coaches provided feedback on players' progress.

In addition, Coach Stone knew it was important that goals be re-evaluated, as conditions can change throughout the year owing to a variety of circumstances. For example, academic pressures in the form of tests and papers were a critical part of being a successful student, and could interfere with reaching their basketball specific goals. Specifically, if a player had a goal to practice field goal shooting an extra hour per day, but they had several papers and exams during this week, then they might not be able to achieve their practice goal. With this situation, players met with coaches on a bi-weekly basis to discuss their academic schedules in relation to time spent on their basketball goals.

Furthermore, Coach Stone, or his assistant coach, set up goal evaluation meetings once a month with each player. These meetings were short (15 minutes maximum) to minimize his or his assistant's precious time. At this time, the player's progress toward his goals was evaluated, and then goals could be revised upwards or downwards. For example, if a basketball player had a goal of improving his rebounding from four to eight per game, but at mid-season he averaged three rebounds per game because of a knee injury that slowed him down the first half of the season, the goal was modified from averaging eight per game to six per game. The key point is that Coach Stone and his staff were going to keep goals to the fore of player's minds and continually assess and record their progress toward reaching the goals. In this way, each player was held responsible for his individual goals. In addition, Coach Stone, or the assistant coach, held a brief (30 minutes) meeting with the team once every two weeks to review how players meet their team goals. Goals were also potentially altered if appropriate. At all points these goals were recorded, and as noted above, kept in places the individuals and/or team would see them on a daily basis.

LEARNING AIDS

1   Define the three different types of goals.

Outcome goals typically focus on the end result or outcome of an event or competition, such as winning and losing. Performance goals focus on improving your own performance as opposed to beating an opponent. Process goals focus on how an athlete performs (i.e., the actions a player must focus on to execute a performance).

2   Discuss the drawbacks of setting outcome goals.

Outcome goals can be problematic since they depend in part on the performance of others. Since athletes can't control what others do, outcome goals tend to be (at least in part) out of their control.

3   Summarize the mechanistic approach to why setting goals work.

Goals are thought to influence performance by helping athletes to direct their attention to the task at hand, and therefore, helping them to focus on the relevant cues involved in executing the appropriate skills. In addition to directing attention, goals can also increase effort and persistence because, through systematic monitoring of the goals, feedback can be obtained on one's progress. Finally, goals can influence performance in helping athletes to develop relevant learning strategies. Specifically, when athletes set goals, strategies negotiated by the athlete and his/her coach can be put in place to help them achieve these goals.

4   Explain why setting "do your best" type of goals is not as effective as setting objective goals.

"Do your best" goals are not specific enough since athletes really do not know if they did their best. However, setting a specific goal such as running a mile in five minutes, can give athletes clarity in terms of what they are trying to achieve.

5   Discuss the relationship between team and individual goals.

There is a place for both team and individual goals in a team sport as long as the individual goals are consistent with team goals. In essence, if a basketball team's goal is to get more rebounds than their opponents each game, then setting an individual goal for number of rebounds would seem to be consistent with the team goal. However, one has to be careful that helping to achieve the rebound goal does not negatively affect the goal of winning. For example, a player might leave his opponent open for an outside shot to position himself for a rebound if the shot is missed. In this case the player might get more rebounds but at the expense of having the player he is guarding get more points.

REVIEW QUESTIONS

1   Discuss three psychological factors that can be affected (positively or negatively) by the setting of goals.

2   Discuss the research on industrial/sport/exercise settings and how these research findings have influenced the effectiveness of goal-setting in applied settings.

EXERCISES

1   Overcoming problems with goal-setting: For the following common problems with goal-setting listed below discuss how you would overcome each of these.

   (a)   Failing to set specific goals

   (b)   Failing to set performance and process goals

   (c)   Failing to adjust goals

2   Analysing your goals: Identify five goals that you have set for yourself in sport or exercise, and rate if these goals match the principles provided below.

   (a)   Specific

   (b)   Measurable

   (c)   Realistic

   (d)   Short-term

   (e)   Long-term

   (f)   Practice

   (g)   Competition

   (h)   Plans to reach the goals

3   Goal-setting plan: Assume you are coaching a collegiate basketball team. Based on the three phases of goal-setting describe in detail what you would do to enhance the effectiveness during each phase.

4   Principles of goal-setting: Choose three of the principles of goal-setting that you think are most important to enhancing performance and explain why.

ADDITIONAL READING

Burton, D., Weinberg, R. & Yukelson, D. (1998). The goal effectiveness paradox in sport: Examining the goal practices of collegiate athletes. *The Sport Psychologist, 12,* 404–418.

Kingston, K. & Hardy, L. (1997). Effects of different types of goals on processes that support performance. *The Sport Psychologist, 11,* 277–289.

Weinberg, R. (2010). Making goals effective: A primer for coaches. *Journal of Sport Psychology in Action, 1,* 57–65.

Weinberg, R. & Butt, J. (2011). Goal-setting practices. In T. Morris & P. Terry (Eds.), *The New Sport & Exercise Psychology Companion* (pp.213–226). Morgantown WV: Fitness Information Technology.

REFERENCES

Burton, D. & Weiss, M. (2008). The fundamental goal concept: The path to process and performance success. In T. Horn (Ed.), *Advances in Sport Psychology* (3rd ed., pp.339–375). Champaign IL: Human Kinetics.

Burton, D., Naylor, S. & Holliday, B. (2001). Goal-setting in sport: Investigating the goal effectiveness paradigm. In R. Singer, H. Hausenblas, & C. Janelle. (Eds.), *Handbook of Sport Psychology* (2nd ed., pp. 497–528). Wiley, New York.

Burton, D., Pickering, M., Weinberg, R., Yukelson, D. & Weigand, D. (2010). The competitive goal effectiveness paradox revisited: Examining the goal practices of prospective Olympic athletes. *Journal of Applied Sport Psychology, 22,* 72–86.

Butler, R. & Hardy, L. (1992). The performance profile: Theory and application. *The Sport Psychologist, 6,* 253–264.

Côté, J., Salmela, J.H. & Russell, S. (1995). The knowledge of high-performance gymnastic coaches: Methodological framework and competition and training considerations. *The Sport Psychologist, 9(1),* 65–95.

Filby, W., Maynard, I. & Graydon, J. (1999). The effect of multiple goal strategies on performance outcomes in training and competition. *Journal of Applied Sport Psychology, 11,* 230–246.

Kane, T., Baltes, T. & Moss M. (2001). Causes and consequences of free set goals: An investigation of athletic self-regulation. *Journal of Sport and Exercise Psychology, 23,* 55–75.

Kyllo, L.B. & Landers, D.M. (1995). Goal-setting in sport and exercise: A research synthesis to resolve the controversy. *Journal of Sport & Exercise, 17,* 117–137.

Locke, E.A. (1968). Toward a theory of task motivation incentives. *Organizational Behavior And Human Performance, 3,* 157–189.

Lock, E.A. & Latham, G.P. (1990). *A theory of goal-setting and task performance.* Prentice-Hall, Englewood Cliffs, NJ.

Locke, E. & Latham, G. (2002). Building a practically useful theory of goal setting and task motivation: A 35 year Odyssey. *American Psychologist, 57,* 705–717.

Locke, E.A., Shaw, K., Saari, L. & Latham, G. (1981). Goal-setting and task performance. *Psychological Bulletin, 1,* 125–152.

Mento, A.J., Steel, R.P. & Karren, R.J. (1987). A meta-analytical study of the effects of goal-setting on task performance: 1966–1984. *Organizational Behavior & Human Decision Processes, 39,* 52–83.

O'Brien, M., Mellalieu, S. & Hanton, S. (2009). Goal-setting effects in elite and non-elite boxers. *Journal of Applied Sport Psychology, 21,* 293–306.

Orlick, T. & Partington, J. (1988). Mental links to excellence. *The Sport Psychologist, 2(2),* 105–130.

Weinberg, R. (2002). *Tennis: Winning the mental game.* Oxford, OH: H.O. Zimman, Inc.

Weinberg, R., Burton, D., Yukelson, D. & Weigand, D. (1993). Goal-setting in competitive sport: An exploratory investigation of practices of collegiate athletes. *The Sport Psychologist, 7,* 275–289.

Weinberg, R., Butt, J. & Knight, B. (2001). High School coaches' perceptions of the process of goal-setting. *The Sport Psychologist, 15,* 20–47.

Weinberg, R., Butt, J., Knight, B. & Perritt, N. (2001). Collegiate coaches' perceptions of their goal-setting practices: A qualitative investigation. *Journal of Applied Sport Psychology, 13,* 374–398.

Weinberg, R., Stitcher, T. & Richardson, P. (1994). Effects of a seasonal goal-setting program on lacrosse performance. *The Sport Psychologist, 8,* 166–175.

Chapter 23

Imagery

TIRATA BHASAVANIJA AND TONY MORRIS

SUMMARY

Imagery is one of the most widely practiced performance enhancement techniques in sport. It involves the creation of experiences in the mind that can affect behavior, thoughts, and emotions. A number of theories have been developed to explain how imagery works. These include psychoneuromuscular theory, symbolic learning theory, bioinformational theory, and triple code theory. Imagery measures help to identify the types of imagery athletes use, as well as their imagery strengths and weaknesses. Based on this information, psychologists develop imagery training to suit individual athletes. Measurement of imagery also provides a means of monitoring progress of imagery use. Understanding how imagery works is being extended by study of brain processes when athletes imagine sports performance. Imagery has been extensively studied in relation to sport, which has aided in understanding the factors that influence its effective operation. Imagery can be used for a diverse range of purposes, including learning and practice of skills, preview and review of performance, problem-solving, developing psychological variables, supporting injury rehabilitation, and facilitating recovery from heavy training. A number of models have been developed to guide the delivery of imagery training in sport. There is still much to be learned about the way that imagery works, yet psychologists already apply imagery with great effect to assist athletes to achieve their goals.

INTRODUCTION

Imagery is a ubiquitous cognitive process. Everyone imagines experiences in all aspects of life from considering what to cook for dinner to preparing for an important job interview. Athletes imagine their sport in many ways, including specific elements, such as how to execute a particular shot or move, as well as the broadest aspects, such as how they will win Olympic gold and stand atop the five-ring podium. Imagery often occurs spontaneously, without the conscious control of the imaginer. A substantial proportion of this imagery is negative. Sport psychology researchers have found that this can lead to performance decrements (Morris, Spittle, Watt, & Gaskin, 2005). Tennis players imagine double faulting on service at critical moments; then they do it. Golfers imagine hooking their drive into the trees or water; then it happens. Sport psychologists have long been aware of the potential of imagery to enhance or detract from performance. They aim to help athletes to control their imagery to avoid the disastrous consequences of negative images and maximize positive outcomes of imagery. Researchers in sport psychology aim to understand how imagery works, so that practitioners have the best information to apply imagery interventions effectively (Morris, Spittle, & Watt, 2005).

 ## OBJECTIVES

After reading this chapter you should be able to:

1 Understand the conceptual background and definition of imagery.
2 Identify techniques of imagery and how they work.
3 Describe how imagery can be used for different purposes.
4 Explain the application of imagery to assist athletes to achieve their goals.
5 Discuss the measurement of imagery for monitoring progress of imagery use.

DEFINITION AND CONCEPTUALIZATION OF IMAGERY

Because it is an ephemeral mental process, imagery has been defined in many ways (see Morris et al., 2005 for a detailed discussion). Imagery has also been used and confused with a number of other concepts. These include mental practice, mental rehearsal, and visualization. Mental practice and mental rehearsal are both broader than imagery in one way, namely that one can mentally practice thoughts that are not images, such as when a telephone number or a song lyric are repeated in the head. On the other hand, the terms practice and rehearsal seem to be narrower than imagery because they refer specifically to a learning function, whereas imagery can be used for many purposes that do not involve learning. Visualization is a popular term in the non-scientific literature, but psychologists who study imagery criticize it because of the pre-eminent position it gives to the visual sensory modality (Munroe-Chandler & Morris, 2011). Many psychologists propose that imagery is most effective when all the sensory modalities are involved, as they would be in the actual experience (Morris et al., 2005).

A definition of imagery that has stood the test of time was proposed by Richardson (1969), who described imagery as "quasi-perceptual experiences of which we are self-consciously aware and which exist for us in the absence of those stimulus conditions that are known to produce their genuine sensory or perceptual counterparts" (pp. 2–3). Thus, imagery is an experience and because the imager is self-consciously aware of what they imagine; imagery is distinguishable from dreams. Also, imagery is usually under the volitional control of the imager, although there are occasions when people imagine circumstances they would choose not to think about. In sport, this includes athletes' common reports that they imagine performance errors, such as missing a putt, serving a double fault, or missing a penalty shot at goal. Richardson's definition does not seem to be inclusive enough, focusing on perceptions, while not mentioning sensory or emotional experience. Morris et al. defined imagery in sport as:

the creation or re-creation of an experience generated from memorial information, involving quasi-sensorial, quasi-perceptual, and quasi-affective characteristics, that is under the volitional control of the imager, and which may occur in the absence of the real stimulus antecedents normally associated with the actual experience (p. 19).

In addition to presenting definitions, researchers have proposed models that aim to conceptualize imagery. Paivio (1985) proposed a popular model that became the foundation for a unique measure, the Sport Imagery Questionnaire (see Measures section of this chapter), as well as many research projects. Paivio argued that imagery has cognitive and motivation uses, and these uses can be specific or general. Thus, cognitive specific imagery focuses on the execution of specific skills, such as a shot or a pass, whereas cognitive general imagery is concerned with the execution of strategies like a set move in basketball or football. Motivational specific imagery focuses on goal-oriented responses, whereas motivational general imagery is concerned with broader aspects of motivation, like arousal and goal achievement. Other models, described in Munroe-Chandler and Morris (2011) include the Applied Model of Imagery Use in Sport, which consists of four sequential components: aspects of the sport situation, the type of imagery, imagery ability, and the outcome of imagery; the Levels of Imagery model, which includes three levels: understanding the nature of imagery, using imagery to achieve performance goals, and the meaning of the image to the athlete; and the PETT-LEP model, which is described in the applied section of this chapter. Imagery is such a wide-ranging mental process that it is difficult for one definition or conceptual model to encapsulate all that it represents, but each contribution appears to add insight to the understanding of this fascinating process.

THEORIES OF IMAGERY

Psychologists have proposed answers to the question "how does imagery work?" for many years. Thus, there are many theories, but none has been supported to a sufficient extent to be considered the "correct" explanation. Here we can only describe some of the major theories, especially those that appear to have direct relevance for sport (for a more extensive discussion and references see Morris et al., 2005, Chapter 3). In psychoneuromuscular theory, Jacobson (1930) proposed that just as action is triggered by messages sent from the brain down efferent nerve pathways to muscles and feedback about muscle action returns to the brain along afferent nerves, imagery sends messages around the same nerve pathways, but the level of innervation is much weaker, so action does not take place. Research that monitored imagery, for example, measuring muscle electrical activity (EMG) in the biceps during imagery of a biceps curl, did show low-level innervation, provided some support for this theory. It was pointed out, however, that this could be a bi-product of imagery with no performance outcome because there was no measurement of physical performance (see Morris et al., 2005). Sackett (1935) put forward symbolic learning theory, proposing that imagery does not facilitate learning of motor aspects of skills, but enhances cognitive or symbolic aspects of motor tasks, such as the sequence of movements in a gymnastics floor routine, as opposed to technical production of somersaults, rolls, and twisting movements. Research has supported the contention that imagery enhances cognitive skills more than movements (see Morris et al., 2005). This benefit of imagery would mean that more attentional capacity is freed up to focus on skill production. A problem with symbolic learning theory is that research does show improvements of motor skills through imagery rehearsal, which is difficult for Sackett's theory to explain. Also, motor tasks might be much more difficult to learn than simple sequences, so it might just be that they take longer to show improvements through imagery and most imagery studies have relatively short duration. Although Jacobson's and Sackett's propositions still carry weight, support has also been shown for more recent alternatives. Probably the most favored theory of imagery related to sport is Lang's bioinformational theory. Lang (1977, 1979) proposed that behavior is based on two kinds of mental representation. Stimulus propositions represent the stimulus characteristics related to an action, whereas response propositions represent aspects of the response. Lang argued that imagery of stimulus propositions facilitates behavior, imagery of response propositions has a greater effect, and imagery of both is most powerful. Although research is limited, what does exist is supportive of the role of propositions, especially response propositions (see Munroe-Chandler & Morris, 2011). One more theory of imagery that has gained traction in sport imagery research and practice

is triple code theory (Ahsen, 1984). Ahsen proposed three components of imagery. First, is the image (I) itself, which is a centrally generated representation that possesses all the attributes of an actual sensation. Second, is the somatic response (S), which recognizes that imagery is associated with physiological changes in the body. Third is the meaning (M) of the image. What an image means to different athletes depends on their unique previous experiences. There has been little empirical examination of triple code theory in sport. Munroe-Chandler and Morris (2011) noted that none of these theories accounts for all five types of imagery developed from Paivio's (1985) model of imagery use in the Sport Imagery Questionnaire. Later in this chapter we discuss some aspects of the neurophysiological research that is developing in relation to the study of how imagery works. This might be a route to a more complete theory of imagery, but it lies in the future.

MEASUREMENT OF IMAGERY

Imagery is a cognitive process, so it cannot be observed directly. As discussed later in this chapter, developments in neurophysiology could lead to measures of imagery based on brain activity (electroencephalographs or EEGs) in the future. To date, however, the way in which psychologists have measured imagery is by asking people to report on their own experience of imaginal processes. Two aspects of imagery have been measured, imagery use or function and imagery ability.

Imagery use

Hall, Mack, Paivio, and Hausenblas (1998) developed a measure of imagery use based on Paivio's model which categorized imagery based on two dichotomies. As noted previously, Paivio proposed that imagery could be cognitive or motivational and it could be specific or general, producing four uses, namely cognitive specific, cognitive general,

motivational specific, and motivational general imagery. Hall et al. developed the Sport Imagery Questionnaire (SIQ) to measure these four uses of imagery. In their initial validation of the SIQ, exploratory factor analysis revealed five factors, not the four expected. Examination of the items in each factor by Hall et al. indicated that motivational general imagery split into two factors, one that related to arousal (motivational general – arousal) and another associated with mastery (motivational general – mastery). This 5-factor structure was replicated in further validation.

Researchers have examined the relationship of the 5-factor SIQ with a range of psychological variables and it has consistently been shown that greater use of certain types of imagery relates to variables like anxiety, motivation, and flow, as well as to performance. This has implications for the design of imagery interventions, which have been shown to be particularly effective when instructions or scripts for imagery focus on the most pertinent types of imagery use, based on correlations between the five types of imagery use and key aspects of the target variable. For example, in contexts as different as tennis and dance, where we correlated the SIQ sub-scales with the nine dimensions of flow state, we found that cognitive specific and motivational general – mastery imagery had the strongest influence on flow. In intervention studies where we gave instructions that emphasized those aspects of imagery, tennis players and dancers showed noteworthy increases in flow state (e.g., Koehn, Jeong, Morris, & Watt, 2005). At a theoretical level, there has been some debate about whether what the SIQ measures is more precisely termed imagery use or imagery function (see Munroe-Chandler & Morris, 2011). In practice, it seems that measuring imagery use on the SIQ is a strategy that can be used both to match the imagery rehearsed with the aims of imagery interventions and to ensure that athletes use the most effective imagery processes.

Imagery ability

Originating early in the 20th century, the self-report measurement of imagery ability has a much longer history than the assessment of imagery use (for a more extensive description of the measures listed here see Morris et al., 2005, Chapter 4). Morris et al. (2005) described Betts' (1909) questionnaire, measuring imagery ability across all the sense modalities, based on vividness, Gordon's (1949) scale, which focused on the ability to control images, and Marks' (1970) questionnaire, which narrowed down to the measurement to vividness of visual imagery.

More relevant to the current account are scales developed to measure imagery for movement or sport. These include the Movement Imagery Questionnaire (MIQ; Hall, Pongrac, & Buckolz, 1995), the Vividness of Movement Imagery Questionnaire (VMIQ; Isaac, Marks, & Russell, 1986), the Sport Imagery Ability Measure (SIAM; Watt, Morris, & Andersen, 2004), and the Sport Imagery Ability Questionnaire (SIAQ; Williams & Cumming, 2011).

MIQ: The MIQ comprises nine basic movements like standing on one leg and patting the top of the head. Participants physically perform each movement twice. On one occasion they then imagine the movement visually and on the other occasion they imagine what the movement felt like (kinesthetic imagery). For each sensory modality for each movement, participants rate each imagery experience. Visual and kinesthetic scores are derived by summing the nine ratings for that type of imagery. One strength of the MIQ is its use of immediate physical experience as the basis for performing imagery. An issue raised is the substantial length of time it takes to perform and imagine nine movement sequences twice. Another concern is that although the MIQ provides a sound test of imagery for basic movements, it has questionable ecological validity for complex sports. Hall and Martin (1997) revised the MIQ, reducing the number of movements to four, so the MIQ-2 takes less time than the MIQ to administer.

VMIQ: The VMIQ includes 12 movement-related experiences, which respondents rate for vividness of visual imagery from an internal perspective and imagining watching somebody else, as well as rating kinesthetic imagery. Again, the items are meaningful for movement, but less so for sports. In addition, it has been argued that imagining somebody else performing tasks is not what is meant by external perspective imagery, which involves imagining oneself from an external perspective, as if watching a video. In the VMIQ-R, Roberts, Callow, Hardy, Markland, and Bringer (2008) revised the VMIQ, changing the instructions for external perspective imagery to imagining oneself performing the movements. The VMIQ-R was shown to have good reliability and validity.

SIAM: The SIAM is based on a measure called the Sport Imagery Questionnaire (SIQ), but different to the Hall et al. (1998) imagery use measure. This SIQ was developed by Martens to measure imagery ability in applied work with athletes and popularized in Vealey in several versions of her seminal book chapter on imagery in sport (see Vealey & Greenleaf, 2006), but neither validated the SIQ. Based on the format of Martens' SIQ, the SIAM presents descriptions of four generic scenes from sport. Respondents imagine each scene and rate their imagery on six sense modalities (visual, auditory, kinesthetic, tactile, gustatory, olfactory), five imagery dimensions (vividness, controllability, speed, duration, ease) and the emotion associated with imagery. The 12 ratings for each scene are made by placing a cross (×) on 100mm visual analogue scales (VAS). Strengths of the SIAM include the experience of imagery immediately before rating it, use of ecologically valid sport scenes, the breadth of its 12 sub-scales, and the sensitivity of the 101-point VAS scale (0–100). A concern with the SIAM is the length of time it takes to administer, typically 20–30 minutes, which is not popular with busy athletes.

SIAQ: The SIAQ includes four sub-scales that measure the ease of imagining sports skills. Thus, it focuses on the aspect of imagery ability related to the ease of generating images. The original version of the SIAQ included four sub-scales, but this was extended to five sub-scales. These measure skill, strategy, goal, affect, and mastery imagery ability. Reliability and validity of the SIAQ were established in the original sequence of four studies, including concurrent validity in relation to the MIQ-3, a new version of the Movement Imagery

Questionnaire. An important observation that emerged from the validation studies on the SIAQ was the importance of separately assessing imagery ability for different content.

Measurement of imagery is important. In all research it is critical to ensure that participants have moderate to high imagery ability, at least in the modalities key to the imagery training to be delivered, or else a finding of no effect of imagery training could be accounted for by poor imagery ability as well as an ineffective intervention. Thus, an imagery measure should be used for screening potential participants. In much imagery research, it is of interest to determine whether imagery training affects imagery ability, so a measure should be used at pre-test and post-test. In applied work, it is also important to screen athletes for imagery ability and use because it would be a waste of time to have athletes perform many sessions of imagery training if they are not then able to apply the imagery effectively due to low imagery ability. In that case a different kind of imagery training should be recommended to develop imagery ability. To maximize the impact of imagery in applied work, imagery training scripts or instructions should focus on imagery strengths determined from initial screening. As noted elsewhere in this chapter, imagery has the potential to produce highly positive outcomes in terms of performance and psychological variables, as long as the imagery training is delivered in an appropriate way. One of the most important steps in ensuring this is to measure imagery ability and use.

IMAGERY AND THE BRAIN

Study of the brain is appealing for researchers and practitioners who are interested to understand how imagery works so that it can be applied effectively in sport. One reason is that imagery is a mental process that is not directly observable. This means that much of the research and anecdotal information on the basis of which researchers draw conclusions

from their studies and practicing psychologists apply imagery in sport depends on inference. If imagery is used in a particular way and performance improves, it is inferred that the imagery technique is responsible. The truth is that we don't know, but by minimizing alternative explanations psychologists increase their confidence that imagery accounts for the change in performance. Cognitive processes are associated with changes in brain activity, an observable, physical process. Thus, it is proposed, if brain activity is consistently observed when a certain type of imagery process occurs, this produces observable evidence of the functioning of imagery. This is an extension to movement and sport of a major thrust in neuroscience.

The term *movement* and sport is used here advisedly. This is because technical problems have limited the examination of brain activity during sport. Monitoring of the brain involves the measurement of minute levels of electrical activity using EEGs, when processes occur in some of the millions of neurons that make up the brain. Much of the brain is active to some degree most of the time. Thus, the minute levels of electrical activity of interest, the "signals", must be detected against a background of all sorts of other activity, called "noise". It is like trying to hear a quiet friend talking to you across a room at a party when noisy music is playing and people are shouting at each other. Physical activity also generates electrical activity and the level of this electrical activity is many times larger than the brain signals. Continuing the party analogy, this would be like somebody turning the music up really high, so nobody could hear anybody else talk! For this reason, over many years, EEG research has been conducted with participants keeping very still. Even then, small eye movements and heart activity create electrical signals that swamp EEGs. Much work has been invested in finding ways to screen or clean EEGs to be able to monitor them in this noisy environment. As advances have occurred it has been possible to start examining small movements.

Of course, imagery does not involve movement, so it is possible to monitor brain activity during imagery. This permits different kinds of imagery to be studied, but to interpret imagery in the context of movement and sport, researchers need to monitor EEGs during movement and compare them to EEGs during imagery of the same movement. One reason for doing this is that a popular proposition is that, in the brain, imagery is functionally equivalent to movement, that is, proponents of this proposition claim that the same or similar brain activity occurs during imagery as occurs during actual movement, but the final signal to activate the movement does not occur.

In recent years, there have been significant advances in the technology of brain monitoring. Some of these relate to the way in which EEG signals are screened and cleaned. Because there is greater regularity to much of the background noise than the signal, it is possible to recognize much of the noise and filter it out. In addition, rapid advances in data processing have meant that much larger amounts of information can be collected and processed in a very short time, so very small signals can be identified by their multiple recurrence. In this context, a small number of researchers, who have particular interest in movement, imagery, and brain function have begun to produce noteworthy research. In particular researchers whose interest is motor imagery, such as Guillot and Collet, have developed this field substantially. This work can be perceived as one step removed from sport imagery, but Guillot and Collet (2010) have proposed a model to link brain activity, motor imagery, and imagery in sport. For further examination of this approach the text edited by Guillot and Collet (2010) is highly recommended. The next decade seems likely to see major breakthrough research and application of this work.

Another recent development that has potential for application in sport is the discovery of "mirror neurons" (Pineda, 2010). First discovered in monkeys, then in the human brain, mirror neurons are so-called because they are activated during observation and copying of movement, but not during the creation of original movement. It has been demonstrated that mirror neurons are also activated during imagery of movement (Pineda, 2010). Because of their association with movement observation and imitation, mirror neurons appear to have great potential to study the use of imagery for the purposes of learning and performance in sport.

On a more applied note, one approach that is based on monitoring EEGs has already been applied in sport, namely neurofeedback. The basic principle underlying neurofeedback is that monitoring the brain during performance can lead to the identification of patterns of brain activity that are consistently associated with optimal performance. Athletes can be trained to create those brain patterns by providing them with feedback that signals when they are producing the desired brain activity. This is simply a neural version of biofeedback in which the electrical signals come from the heart, the muscles, or other biological processes. Research conducted in the 1980s and 1990s in sports like shooting and archery, where movement is minimal, provided support for the application of neurofeedback in sport (Landers, Petruzzello, Salazar, Crews, Kubitz, Gannon et al., 1991).

USES OF IMAGERY IN SPORT

Because imagery is a creative thought process, one can imagine anything that comes to mind. Thus, the only limit to what athletes can imagine is the athletes' own thoughts, plus stimulation from coach and sport psychologist. Research suggests that imagery must be based in reality to affect behavior. A club athlete will not win Olympic gold just by imagining it. Here, we briefly describe some of the ways in which athletes have used imagery that have been supported by qualitative or quantitative research.

Promoting learning and performance

The most common use of imagery in sport is to help athletes learn new skills or to maximize their performance of existing skills. Crucial to this use of imagery is an accurate example of the skill that can be used as a model for the imagery, that is, athletes must imagine the correct skill for actual performance to be enhanced. Using a self-modeling video is a powerful way to do this. Athletes film themselves performing the skill as well as they can and then imagine performing it immediately after watching the video. For performance development, where athletes might not yet have the skill level to do this, they can watch other athletes performing the skill. Athletes who are similar to them, but a little more skilled will usually be more appropriate models than those who are much more skilled. Highly-skilled athletes can use the self-modeling approach to help them maintain and reinforce the skills. This is often useful when they cannot do physical practice, such as when travelling or injured.

Preview and review

To prepare for performance, athletes often find imagery preview useful. This is most common in closed skills, where a predetermined movement sequence is to be performed, such as a springboard dive or a gymnastics floor exercise routine. Physical preview is often not possible in constrained competition environments, so imagery can be used to "run" the movement sequence in the mind in the build up to performing it. For this to be successful, athletes must have good control of their imagery through substantial practice away from competition to ensure their imagery reflects best performance. In review, the mental run through occurs soon after performance. When athletes perform successfully, the imagery review helps to consolidate their performance in memory, so they can run it in future not only to enhance their skills, but also to build confidence by experiencing effective task performance. When athletes perform badly, it is not advisable to perform an imagery review right away as this can negatively affect emotions. Instead, it might be best to do this

24 hours or more after the event, when emotions are less raw and a more objective review can be done to identify what went wrong. Imagery can then be used to correct the errors and reinforce best performance.

Problem-solving

When something does go wrong during performance, the source of the problem might not be immediately obvious. In this case, review of performance using imagery can help athletes to identify where they made the mistake and act as a tool in the diagnosis of the reason for the error. The ability to run the imagery in "slow motion" can often help, with "fast forward" in imagery being used to skip the parts that are not problematic. As with the use of video, athletes can often use their imagery to "zoom in" on a technical aspect of their performance that might be at fault. Once a problem is identified the focus should shift to remedial action, which could involve both physical and imagery practice of the correct technique. If the problem is strategic, again imagery rehearsal of the correct strategy can increase the probability that athletes will perform as they intend in future.

Modifying psychological states

Research in sport psychology has identified many examples of psychological factors that can interfere with performance. Anxiety has been the most widely studied psychological variable that can disrupt performance. In extreme cases this can lead to "choking". Other common psychological issues include attentional problems, low motivation, and low confidence. Psychological states that negatively affect performance can be addressed using imagery. In the content of the imagery, athletes target management of the problematic psychological state in demanding circumstances, leading to effective performance. For example, athletes can imagine feeling calm and in control at the climax of a crucial match to address issues related to anxiety or they can imagine being totally focused on their performance in contexts that often cause distraction.

Facilitating rehabilitation from injury and recovery from intense exercise

A range of issues relate to effective rehabilitation from injury. These include coping with pain from the injured region of the body, managing stress associated with the pain, belief in the rehabilitation process, reducing frustration at being unable to train and compete, and performing the behaviors required to facilitate rehabilitation. Imagery programs can be devised that address each of these issues separately or together. For example, imagining a large, brightly-colored ball represents the pain and then shrinking the ball and fading the color to a pale grey can help reduce the pain. Imagining successfully executing the rehabilitation exercises can build confidence that they can be done and motivate athletes to follow their prescribed rehabilitation. It is also possible to facilitate the physical rehabilitation process by imagining the area of the calf where a muscle is torn, and seeing and feeling warm, fresh blood flowing in to repair the damage. A similar process can be used to facilitate recovery from heavy training, where blood is imagined to be infusing and cleansing the tired and aching muscles.

It is important to emphasize that in all these examples of uses of imagery a good understanding of the issue is essential to ensure that the imagery developed is technically correct. Thus, when developing sports skills, advice from expert coaches will ensure that the correct technique is included in the imagery. Similarly, in the creation of an imagery program to build confidence and motivation for rehabilitation, medical or physiotherapy experts should advise on the accurate depiction of the rehabilitation exercises needed by that athlete with that injury. The effective delivery of imagery depends on a range of factors that are discussed next.

APPLYING IMAGERY IN SPORT

Examining factors that influence the efficacy of imagery training programs is one of the most popular areas of research on imagery in sport. Sport psychologists have proposed models to guide the application of imagery based on that research. So many personal and contextual variables have been shown to influence imagery efficacy that it is only possible to summarize some of the main ones here. Before considering specific factors, we discuss some of the most popular models.

Models of imagery application in sport

A variety of models have been proposed for the application of imagery in the sport context. An early model was VisuoMotor Behavior Rehearsal (VMBR; Suinn, 1976). Suinn proposed that the first stage of imagery training should be progressive muscle relaxation. Once athletes are able to relax then they undertake imagery. A model that has stimulated considerable research during the last decade is Holmes and Collins' (2001) PETTLEP model. Holmes and Collins proposed that there are seven key factors that need to be considered in the design of customized imagery training. These are the physical (P), the environment (E), the task (T), the timing (T), learning issues (L), emotion (E) and perspectives (P). Studies that have developed imagery training based on PETTLEP have produced support for this approach. Morris et al. (2005) proposed a broader imagery training program model (ITP). Morris et al. suggested that six components should be considered, each covering key factors, namely personal prerequisites, environmental factors, the content, rehearsal routines, enhancement techniques, and evaluation. Morris et al. argued that each component relates to aspects of the literature that are diverse and changing as research is developed. Thus, imagery program designers should examine the latest literature related to these components and apply them to the characteristics relevant to their context. For example, with reference to the personal prerequisites, practitioners should consider the latest research on age, gender, skill level, experience and so on. Thus, there is considerable advice about how to develop imagery-training programs based on research to date (see Morris et al., 2005, Chapter 8).

Factors that influence the application of imagery in sport

Among the large and diverse array of studies of imagery in sport, there is evidence of the influence of many factors on the effective application of imagery. Often, however, the quantum of studies on a specific factor is insufficient to be considered persuasive that a clear effect has been demonstrated. Efforts to draw conclusions are hampered by contradictory findings. Here we consider just a selection of those factors that have been more widely investigated.

Perhaps the most obvious issue to address is whether imagery should be positive or negative. Munroe-Chandler and Morris (2011) reported some research that has identified a "paradoxical effect" of negative imagery, that is, imagining poor performance led to improvements in actual performance. Nonetheless, the balance of research indicates that when athletes imagine negative performance their actual performance declines and when they imagine performing well their performance outcomes are enhanced.

A factor that has been examined for some time is the type of task to which imagery is applied. In their seminal meta-analysis, Feltz and Landers (1983) claimed the evidence at that time suggested that imagery is more effective in cognitive tasks or tasks with large cognitive components than motor tasks. Another aspect of tasks that has been examined is environmental variability. Closed skills, such as shooting or diving, take place in stable environments, whereas the environment is constantly changing in open skills like soccer or tennis. Recent research suggests that closed-skill performers use specific imagery functions more than open-skill athletes (Munroe-Chandler & Morris, 2011).

A question that has raised considerable interest is whether skill level is related to imagery use. Evidence suggests that highly-skilled athletes use imagery more than beginners, which might relate to their greater capability to imagine skills, especially their correct execution (Munroe-Chandler & Morris, 2011). This is consistent with findings that highly-skilled athletes' performance shows greater benefit from using imagery. Nonetheless, it has been proposed that beginners might benefit from imagery that is designed to take into account their developmental stage.

Imagery function, based on the SIQ (Hall et al., 1998) is another factor that has been examined in relation to the effect of imagery on performance outcomes. Although cognitive specific (CS) imagery would intuitively be expected to be useful for the enhancement of sports skills, perhaps more support has been forthcoming for the benefit of motivational general – mastery (MG-M) imagery in that context (Munroe-Chandler & Morris, 2011). It is possible that a mediator of any link between MG-M imagery and performance is self-efficacy. Researchers have demonstrated a link between MG-M imagery and self-efficacy. Similarly, there is substantial evidence of a positive association between self-efficacy and performance. Imagining mastery of the skill seems to increase confidence and performance. A combination of MG-M and CS imagery, which has been shown to be beneficial to tennis players (Koehn et al., 2005) could be an effective approach in which specific skills are imagined along with more general mastery.

Imagery perspective is another factor that has attracted attention from researchers. Internal perspective imagery is experienced from athletes' own perspective, that is, it is what they hear, see, and feel when they perform, whereas during external imagery athletes experience their own performance from outside their body. The visual aspect of this can be from many angles: in front, behind, to either side, or even above or below. Researchers still debate whether internal or external imagery produces greater performance benefits. It seems likely that each perspective has benefits in different contexts, which are yet to be fully understood (Morris & Spittle, 2012). It is recommended that practitioners consider imagery perspective because all imagery must adopt a perspective. If athletes were to use a less appropriate perspective, performance could suffer. Research indicates that even skilled athletes often choose perspective on the basis of personal preference, rather than what is most likely to enhance performance (Morris & Spittle, 2012).

To summarize this section, many variables affect the benefits of imagery for performance. While research has given hints about the influence of variables like positive or negative imagery, skill level, type of task, imagery function, and imagery perspective, it must be stressed that recommendations can only be indicative here, because research outcomes remain equivocal.

Frequency, duration, and intensity of imagery training

Although there is a large research literature on aspects of the application of imagery in sport, there has been little systematic examination of one of the questions that research students often ask first, namely how much imagery is enough? This is actually a complex question to address. Within an imagery session there will be a number of repetitions of the imagery. This will differ greatly depending on the activity. For example, a pistol shot or golf putt takes a few seconds to imagine, although imagining the preparatory activities could extend this, whereas a gymnastics floor routine could take five minutes to perform once. An individual imagery session can vary in duration. Studies have examined sessions as short as one minute and as long as one hour. Most research and applied imagery programs lie somewhere between these extremes, but there is limited study of this issue. Further, the duration of the session cannot be studied without taking into account the number of repetitions in it. A 10-minute imagery session with 10 repetitions of a basketball free-throw shot is quite different to 10 minutes with 30 repetitions. In discrete skills at least, the number of repetitions completed in unit time (duration) can be considered the intensity of the imagery session.

Added to this is the frequency of imagery training sessions, usually described as number of sessions per week. Again, the number of repetitions per session and the duration of each session affect frequency. For example, three sessions per week of 15-minute imagery sessions with four repetitions per minute of golf putting (180 repetitions per week) is very different to three 5-minute sessions with two repetitions per minute (30 repetitions per week), although both examples involve three sessions per week. Thus, research that examines one of these variables without controlling the others is not very meaningful. Nonetheless, studies that have been done typically have found that little additional benefit is gained by increasing sessions much above three per week. How many weeks an imagery program should continue is a question that simply compounds the problems of the previous questions. Studies of imagery and applied imagery programs have lasted for just a week or continued for a whole season. In practice, regular evaluation of progress for individual athletes is advisable because of the number of confounding personal, structural, and contextual factors (Morris et al., 2005).

Delivery of imagery training

A wide range of issues pertain to the delivery of imagery training (Morris, 2010), so only those considered most pertinent are addressed here. Circumstances often dictate what is prac-

tical in terms of the modality of imagery program delivery. For example, although delivery using advanced technology might be considered to be an effective option, such technology might not be available or practical. Presenting imagery on video, so that it includes self-modeling of correct skills as the basis for imagery rehearsal of those skills has been shown to be beneficial for many athletes. While athletes might make the effort to visit a location where they can use a DVD player and monitor during a research project, adherence is not usually maintained over the longer term in practice. Perhaps some athletes would be in a position to use a DVD player and monitor at home, some might not. On the other hand, audio CDs might not be as attractive as video, leading to low adherence again. We recently examined the use of mobile technology in the form of an iPod touch. We found that adherence was higher for the iPod touch than for players who had to come to a fixed computer system. The iPod touch users also improved performance significantly more than those using the fixed system. Mobile technology has practical advantages, but presently it is an expensive option.

Whatever delivery system is chosen a critical element of the delivery of imagery training programs is the specific content of the "script", that is, the instructions given to athletes for how to actually do imagery and what to imagine. There is little research on this crucial matter. In fact, many studies gloss over the details of their scripts and there is limited information about how to construct a script. In several projects we have conducted, preliminary work measuring imagery functions with the SIQ and key variables of interest then correlating imagery functions with those variables has provided some relevant information. For example, in studies of flow we correlated the five imagery functions of the SIQ with the nine flow dimensions of the Flow State Scale-2 and identified correlations between cognitive specific and motivational general – mastery functions and flow dimensions of challenge-skills balance, clear goals, total concentration, and sense of control. Script content was then written for the specific sports context that referred to these combinations of imagery functions and flow dimensions. Of course, this only addresses one aspect of the script. In general, scripts need to be written in language that is meaningful to the athletes who will use them. Also, the PETTLEP model has been the basis for scripts used in a number of studies where imagery use was successful. This includes inclusion of Lang's stimulus and response propositions. Beyond this, at present, writing imagery scripts might be classified more in the realm of art than science. It is another area for research attention and one that requires a systematic as well as a sound methodological approach.

CONCLUSION

Imagery is widely used in sport, sometimes unintentionally and with negative consequences. Sport psychologists train athletes to use imagery to enhance their performance, manage the demands of sport competition, and cope with injury. They base their application on the best evidence available from research, which continues to increase understanding of exactly how imagery enhances the sport experience. Nonetheless there is much research still to do on central issues related to the effective application of imagery. In the meantime, practitioners should study the literature carefully, so they ensure they adopt only proven imagery techniques in their work with athletes.

LEARNING AIDS

1 How does imagery differ from mental practice?

Mental practice refers to any mental process used for the purpose of practice. It can include the use of images, but it can also include language, such as when actors learn their lines or when people remember phone numbers. Imagery involves the generation of experiences that mimic those processed through the senses. Imagery can be generated in relation to an infinite variety of experiences, many not associated with practice, such as reliving a pleasant emotional experience or managing pain.

2 Name and exemplify the four imagery functions identified by Paivio.

Cognitive specific imagery is exemplified by imagining the production of a key skill in sport, cognitive general imagery is exemplified by imagining the execution of a strategy planned for the upcoming game, motivational specific imagery is exemplified by imagining the achievement of a key goal in a match, and motivational general imagery is exemplified by imagining mastery in one's chosen sport.

3 Name the sensory modalities and dimensions measured by the Sport Imagery Ability Measure (SIAM).

The sensory modalities measured by SIAM are visual, auditory, kinesthetic, tactile, olfactory (smell), and gustatory (taste). The dimensions are vividness, control, ease, speed, and duration of imagery. The SIAM also measures emotion experienced during imagery.

4 Name the seven elements of the PETTLEP model that should be considered in devising imagery programs.

PETTLEP is an acronym for Physical, Environment, Task, Timing, Learning issues, Emotion, and Perspectives. These have all been shown to be important to consider when devising imagery-training programs. Research continues on the details of their optimal use.

5 How does internal imagery differ from external imagery?

Internal perspective imagery is imagery from the perspective of the performer. The athlete experiences what they would see, hear, feel, smell, and taste if they were actually performing. External perspective imagery is imagery from the perspective of an observer. The athlete experiences what they would see, hear, feel, smell, and taste if they were observing themselves from outside their body. There is an infinite number of external perspectives, some of which are not possible in reality.

REVIEW QUESTIONS

1 What are the key elements of a definition of mental imagery?

2 Why is it important to measure imagery in sport?

3 Why are mirror neurons important to our understanding of imagery processes related to sport?

4 What are the five uses of imagery in sport? Give examples.

5 What are the seven elements of the PETTLEP model?

6 Why does it matter whether athletes have positive imagery experiences?

7 Do elite athletes benefit more from using imagery than novices?

8 How can the five functions of imagery, measured by the SIQ be used to help develop optimal imagery scripts?

9 How does research address the question of whether internal perspective imagery is superior to external perspective imagery?

10 How do you think that portable devices like iPods can enhance imagery training?

EXERCISES

1 Write a 300-word imagery script for a 25 year-old elite basketball player to enhance her free throw shooting performance, using all seven elements of the PETTLEP model. Annotate the script to indicate how and where you use each PETTLEP component.

2 Draft a 300-word imagery script to help a tournament golfer to stop hooking his drives, by using only positive imagery of performance and outcomes. Annotate.

3 Develop a 400-word imagery script for a 15 year-old high-board diver, using internal perspective imagery in the first half and external perspective imagery in the second half. Annotate.

4 Generate a 400-word imagery script to enhance performance and confidence of a soccer player for taking penalties based on cognitive specific and motivational general – mastery imagery. Annotate.

5 Produce a 300-word imagery script for a wheelchair Paralympic sprinter to increase their power in the first 10 meters of the race by emphasizing motivational general – arousal imagery. Annotate.

ADDITIONAL READING

Guillot, A. & Collet, C. (Eds.) (2010). *The Neurophysiological Foundations of Mental and Motor Imagery.* Oxford: Oxford University Press.

Morris, T. (2010). Imagery. In S.J. Hanrahan & M.B. Andersen (Eds.) *Handbook of Applied Sport Psychology* (pp.481–490). London: Routledge.

Morris, T., Spittle, M. & Watt, A.P. (2005). *Imagery in Sport.* Champaign, IL: Human Kinetics.

Munroe-Chandler, K. & Morris, T. (2011). Imagery. In T. Morris & P. Terry (Eds.) *New Sport and Exercise Psychology Companion* (pp.275–308). Morgantown, WV: Fitness Information Technology.

REFERENCES

Ahsen, A. (1984). ISM: The triple code model for imagery and psychophysiology. *Journal of Mental Imagery, 8,* 15–42.

Feltz, D.L. & Landers, D.M. (1983). The effect of mental practice on motor skill learning and performance: A meta-analysis. *Journal of Sport Psychology, 2,* 211–220.

Guillot, A. & Collet, C. (Eds.) (2010). *The Neurophysiological Foundations of Mental and Motor Imagery.* Oxford: Oxford University Press.

Hall, C.R., Mack, D.E., Paivio, A. & Hausenblas, H.A. (1998). Imagery use by athletes: Development of the Sport Imagery Questionnaire. *International Journal of Sport Psychology, 29,* 73–89.

Hall, C.R. & Martin, K.A. (1997). Measuring movement imagery abilities: A revision of the Movement Imagery Questionnaire. *Journal of Mental Imagery, 21,* 143–154.

Hall, C.R., Pongrac, J. & Buckolz, E. (1985). The measurement of imagery ability. *Human Movement Science, 4,* 107–118.

Holmes, P.S. & Collins, D.J. (2001). The PETTLEP approach to motor imagery: A functional equivalence model for sport psychologists. *Journal of Applied Sport Psychology, 13,* 60–83.

Isaac, A.R., Marks, D.F. & Russell, D.G. (1986). An instrument for assessing imagery of movement: The Vividness of Movement Imagery Questionnaire (VMIQ). *Journal of Mental Imagery, 10,* 23–30.

Jacobson, E. (1930). Electrical measurements of neuromuscular states during mental activities: Part I. Imagination of movement involving skeletal muscle. *American Journal of Physiology, 91,* 567–606.

Koehn, S., Jeong, Eun Hee, Morris, T. & Watt, A.P. (2005). Measuring Imagery Use for the Development of Imagery Interventions in Sport and Dance. In T. Morris, L. Ievleva, S. Gordon, S. Hanrahan, G. Kolt, P. Terry & P. Tremayne (Eds.). *Promoting Performance and Health: Proceedings of the XIth ISSP World Congress of Sport Psychology.* Sydney, Australia: ISSP.

Landers, D.M., Petruzzello, S.J., Salazar, W., Crews, D.J., Kubitz, K.A., Gannon, T.L. & Han, M. (1991). The influence of electrocortical biofeedback on performance in pre-elite archers. *Medicine & Science in Sports & Exercise, 23,* 123–129.

Lang, P.J. (1977). Imagery in therapy: An information processing analysis of fear. *Behavior Therapy, 8,* 862–886.

Lang, P.J. (1979). A bio-informational theory of emotional imagery. *Psychophysiology, 17,* 495–512.

Morris, T. (2010). Imagery. In S.J. Hanrahan & M.B. Andersen (Eds.) *Handbook of Applied Sport Psychology* (pp. 481–490). London: Routledge.

Morris, T. & Spittle, M. (2012). A default hypothesis of the development of internal and external imagery perspectives, *Journal of Mental Imagery*, *36*, 1–30.

Morris, T., Spittle, M. & Watt, A.P. (2005). *Imagery in Sport*. Champaign, IL: Human Kinetics.

Morris, T., Spittle, M. & Watt, A.P. & Gaskin, G. (2005). Imagery research. In T. Morris, M. Spittle & A.P. Watt (Eds.), *Imagery in Sport*. Champaign, IL: Human Kinetics.

Munroe-Chandler, K. & Morris, T. (2011). Imagery. In T. Morris & P. Terry (Eds.) *New Sport and Exercise Psychology Companion* (pp. 275–308). Morgantown, WV: Fitness Information Technology.

Paivio, A. (1985). Cognitive and motivational functions of imagery in human performance. *Canadian Journal of Applied Sport Sciences, 10*, 22–28.

Pineda, J.A. (Ed.) (2010). *Mirror Neuron Systems*. New York: Humana Press.

Richardson, A. (1969). *Mental imagery*. New York: Springer.

Roberts, R., Callow, N., Hardy, L., Markland, D. & Bringer, J. (2008). Movement imagery ability: Development and assessment of a revised version of the Vividness of Movement Imagery Questionnaire. *Journal of Sport & Exercise Psychology, 30*, 200–221.

Sackett, R.S. (1934). The influences of symbolic rehearsal upon the retention of a maze habit. *Journal of General Psychology, 10*, 376–395.

Suinn, R.M. (1976). Visuo motor behavior rehearsal for adaptive behavior. In J. Krumboltz & C. Thoresen (Eds.), *Counseling methods* (pp.360–366). New York: Holt Rinehart & Winston.

Vealey, R.S. & Greenleaf, C.A. (2006). Seeing is believing: Understanding and using imagery in sport. In J.M. Williams (Ed.), *Applied Sport Psychology: Personal Growth to Peak Performance* (pp.306–348). New York, NY: McGraw-Hill.

Watt, A.P., Morris, T. & Andersen, M.B. (2004). Issues of reliability and factor structure of sport imagery ability measures. *Journal of Mental Imagery, 28*, 112–125.

Williams, S.E. & Cumming, J. (2011). Measuring athlete imagery ability: The Sport Imagery ability Questionnaire. *Journal of Sport & Exercise Psychology, 33*, 416–440.

Chapter 24

Self-talk

ANTONIS HATZIGEORGIADIS, NIKOS ZOURBANOS, ALEXANDER T. LATINJAK AND YANNIS THEODORAKIS

SUMMARY

The purpose of this chapter is to provide an understanding of the self-talk phenomenon and the links between thought and action. First, definitions, conceptualizations and the different taxonomies of self-talk are introduced. Issues regarding the assessment of self-talk and descriptions of athletes' self-talk are then presented. Subsequently, the factors that shape and influence athletes' self-talk are briefly identified, and the relationships between self-talk and sport performance are revealed. The mechanisms that may explain how self-talk affects performance are then discussed. Finally, the importance of developing self-talk strategies is argued and guidelines for implementing effective self-talk interventions are offered.

INTRODUCTION

What better way to 'convince' you of the power of self-talk than through a selection of quotes; famous quotes, quotes from famous athletes, or simply quotes from ordinary athletes who have made super achievements.

The power of human thought

The power of human thoughts is perfectly demonstrated in these quotes from two famous leaders:

> We are what we think.
>
> (Buddha)

> Whether you think you can or think you can't, you are right.
>
> (Henry Ford)

Totally prepared

A perfect state of mind before competing is described by the thoughts of two athletes who have achieved Olympic glory:

> My thoughts before a big race are usually pretty simple. I tell myself: Get out of the blocks, run your race, stay relaxed. If you run your race, you'll win...channel your energy. Focus.
>
> (Carl Lewis, Track & Field, Olympic Gold medalist)

> When standing on the blocks, I just said to myself: OK, I'm going to do a 200 butterfly, and I've done a million 200 butterflies in my life. I have been training for this and I know exactly what I need to do.
>
> (Misty Hyman, Swimmer, Olympic Gold medalist, on the gold medal race)

Keeping a positive perspective

A humorous, yet excellent example of keeping a positive perspective through rational thinking is presented by another Olympic Gold medalist:

> There is water in every lane, so it is OK.
> (Ian Thorpe, Swimmer, Olympic Gold medalist, on being in Lane 5 for a final, rather than his usual Lane 4 where the best qualifying time goes)

Focusing where it matters

Finally, an ideal setting for focusing where it matters is provided in our last quote:

> I was not thinking of what would happen if I score; I was not thinking of what would happen if I miss. I only thought where I am going to send the ball.
> (Vassilis Tsiartas, Football player, European Champion, just before taking a crucial penalty kick)

There are countless displays of athletes reporting on the power of self-talk. The most convincing is probably that of world and Olympic champion and serial world record breaker in pole vault Helena Isinbayeva, going through her self-pole-talk routine before every single jump she attempts.

The mind is the ultimate tool and self-talk one of its most powerful assets.

 OBJECTIVES

After reading this chapter you should be able to:

1 Describe the concept of self-talk and its dimensions.
2 Know how athletes' self-talk is assessed.
3 Identify the major research questions for the study of self-talk.
4 Recognize the factors that influence and shape athletes' self-talk.
5 Understand how athletes' self-talk influences their performance.
6 Identify the basic principles for developing effective self-talk interventions.

WHAT IS SELF-TALK?

Self-talk refers to what people say to themselves. Several terms have been used to describe this phenomenon, such as automatic thoughts, internal dialogue, inner conversation, and self-statements. The term self-talk has prevailed in the sport psychology literature. Athletes talk to themselves a lot, if not all of the time, when training or competing. They talk about things that have happened, as a reflection or evaluation of events and action (e.g., 'that was great', 'so stupid'), things that are happening, to provide direction and drive, or express affect and cognitions (e.g., 'steady', 'let's go now', 'can't concentrate', 'I'm fed-up'), or things that will happen, in an anticipative manner ('I'm going to win this trophy', 'this will hurt'). It is a normal thing to happen, and it can happen either silently or aloud, inherently or strategically. In simple words, self-talk refers to all the things individuals say to themselves, to stimulate and reinforce, direct and evaluate events and actions.

To further describe and facilitate the understanding of self-talk various taxonomies can be made.

With regard to its generation, self-talk can be described as inherent or strategic. Inherent self-talk refers to thoughts that individuals experience intrinsically, also referred to as automatic self-talk, because these are the things we say to ourselves which are not planned or prepared. In contrast, strategic self-talk refers to the instrumental use of cues or phrases that are planned or used in a systematic way as a mental self-regulatory strategy.

Sometimes athletes express themselves by muttering or they might express themselves loudly, compelling others to observe or listen; but the majority of things athletes say to themselves are not heard. With regard to its *form of expression*, self-talk can be described as internal and external. Internal refers to self-talk athletes have within their head, also termed silent self-talk; whereas external refers to self-talk that is audible, which is also termed vocalized, or out-loud self-talk.

With regard to its *content*, self-talk can be characterized as positive (e.g., 'great shot'), or negative (e.g., 'this sucks'), but also as neutral (e.g., 'I'd love a shower'), solely depending on the wording that is used. Furthermore, depending on the content self-talk can be described as instructional or motivational. Instructional self-talk refers to cues aiming to provide direction for action (e.g., 'smooth' or 'attack her backhand'), whereas motivational self-talk refers to cues aiming to increase drive or confidence (e.g., 'I can do that', 'come on now'). Considering the content in combination with the generation of self-talk, it could be argued that inherent self-talk is mostly positive or negative; whereas strategic self-talk is mostly instructional or motivational.

It is very important at that point to stress that the content should be differentiated from the *outcome*. It is generally endorsed that negative self-talk is associated with negative outcomes and performance, whereas positive self-talk is associated with positive outcomes and performance. Nonetheless, this is not always the case. Thus, positive self-talk can have a negative effect and negative self-talk can have a positive effect. For example, a tennis player thinking 'I'm gonna win this set', which is a positive thought, when leading five-two in games, may lose focus, which is a negative outcome, and subsequently lose the set. Respectively, a player thinking 'I'm gonna lose this set', which is a negative thought, when behind five-two in games, may increase efforts as a reaction or to counterattack, which is a positive outcome, and may subsequently win the set. Thus, the content of self-talk should be viewed as a separate dimension from the outcome of self-talk. With regard to the *outcome*, as described in the previous example, self-talk can be regarded as facilitating – when having desirable effects and enhancing performance – or debilitating when having detrimental effects and hurts performance (Hardy, 2006).

Self-talk is...

... what people say to themselves either silently or aloud, inherently or strategically, to stimulate, direct, react and evaluate events and actions.

Research questions

The study of self-talk in sport has a relatively long history but until recently has not been systematic. The research interest centers around three fundamental questions: description, antecedents, and effects of self-talk with particular emphasis on performance. Descriptive research aims to portray the content of self-talk and to explore individual differences. Research on the antecedents attempts to identify the factors that shape and determine athletes' self-talk. Finally, research on the effects of self-talk has dominated the self-talk literature. This research has focused on the relationship between self-talk and performance. Given the interest of athletes and coaches for performance enhancement, sport psychologists have directed their attention to the quest of factors that influence performance; thus most of the self-talk literature in sport is performance related. A complementary research line with regard to the effects of self-talk concerns the mechanisms through which self-talk influences performance; in simple words, these are mostly non-performance outcomes that may explain why self-talk influences performance and what the changes are that occur and are responsible for these effects (e.g., effects on attention and motivation).

The study of self-talk has only recently flourished in sport. Given the priority of researchers to the relationship between self-talk and performance, research on the antecedents and the mechanisms is still at the early stages. Overall, two research approaches have been used: (a) an experimental approach, which corresponds to what was earlier described as strategic self-talk, i.e., the use of self-talk as a mental strategy, within which researchers have implemented interventions to investigate the effects of self-talk strategies on performance; and (b) a field approach, which involves mostly, but not exclusively, inherent self-talk, within which researchers try to identify the content and the correlates of self-talk either as the antecedents or consequences. What we have learned from the self-talk research thus far will be presented in the following sections.

Assessment

Assessing athletes' self-talk is not an easy task, especially so when we are interested in what their self-talk is during training or competition. As self-talk is something that cannot be assessed objectively, or by any means not involving the individual, assessment is based on self-reports. Among the various methods of assessing human self-talk, retrospective self-reports through the use of questionnaires is the most popular in sport.

Based on the two aforementioned approaches of self-talk, different types of questionnaires have been developed: (a) questionnaires aiming primarily at assessing the content of athletes' inherent self-talk; and (b) questionnaires developed to assess primarily the use (or strategic use) of self-talk. With regard to the *content*, but also the structure and the frequency of athletes' self-talk Zourbanos, Hatzigeorgiadis, Chroni, Theodorakis, and Papaioannou (2009) developed the Automatic Self-Talk Questionnaire for Sport. The process of the development supported the multidimensional nature of athletes' self-talk. The final instrument comprises eight distinct dimensions. Four of them have been clustered as positive and include self-talk described as psych-up (e.g., 'let's go') confidence (e.g., 'I can make it'), anxiety control (e.g., 'calm down'), and instruction (e.g., 'concentrate'); whereas four of them have been clustered as negative and include self-talk described as worry (e.g., 'I'm going to lose'), disengagement (e.g., 'I want to stop'), somatic fatigue (e.g., 'I'm tired'), and irrelevant thoughts (e.g., 'what I'm doing later?').

With regard to the *use* of self-talk several instruments exist in the literature. The Self-Talk Use Questionnaire (Hardy, Hall, & Hardy, 2005) explores four descriptive dimensions of self-talk: where, when, what, and why athletes use self-talk. The Self-Talk Questionnaire (Zervas, Stavrou, & Psychountaki, 2007) assesses the motivational and instructional function of self-talk; and finally, the Functions of Self-Talk Questionnaire (Theodorakis, Hatzigeorgiadis, & Chroni, 2008) identifies five likely mechanisms through which self-talk facilitates performance namely: self-talk can serve to enhance concentration, boost confidence, regulate effort, control cognitive and affective reactions, and trigger automatic responses.

From a different methodological perspective, Van Raalte, Brewer, Rivera, and Petitpas (1994) developed the Self-Talk and Gestures Rating Scale, an instrument to assess observable self-talk based on a rating system that assesses three broad self-talk dimensions, positive (e.g., 'keep it up'), negative (e.g., 'that was a terrible shot'), and instruction (e.g., 'hit through the ball').

Describing athletes' self-talk

As already mentioned, athletes have an abundance of self-talk when training or competing. Descriptive studies based on self-reports suggest that athletes report more frequent self-talk during training, and prior to and during competition; most of this self-talk is internal and involves mostly short phrases rather than full sentences; self-talk is equally used in the first and second person; and finally, athletes have more positive compared to negative self-talk (e.g., Hardy, Gammage & Hall, 2001; Zourbanos et al., 2009); nonetheless, results from observational studies showed more negative compared to positive self-talk (e.g., Van Raalte et al., 1994). Several hypotheses can be made for this inconsistency. One is that athletes keep positive self-talk internal, but express negative self-talk more externally; another is that athletes under-report negative and over-report positive self-talk; a final hypothesis is that as the assessment of self-talk happens mostly retrospectively athletes may selectively remember or forget what their self-talk was. Most of athletes' positive self-talk involves psyching-up (such as, 'let's go', 'come on'), in an attempt to get in a state of readiness, increase confidence and maximize effort; whereas most athletes' negative self-talk involves worries about not performing well or lacking ability (such as, 'I'm not going to achieve my goal', or 'I'm not good enough'). However, factors such as gender, sport type, competition level (Hardy et al., 2005), and cultural origin (Peters & Williams, 2006) may influence the frequency and the content of athletes' self-talk.

FACTORS INFLUENCING ATHLETES' SELF-TALK

What people think about is particularly sensitive to individual, situational and social-environmental factors. Similarly, athletes' personal attributes, the circumstances of a specific situation and the progress of goal-directed behavior, and finally the stimuli arising from the surroundings and significant others can make an important difference to what athletes say to themselves. Research on the antecedents of self-talk is limited; nevertheless it has provided valuable evidence for the identification of factors that shape athletes' self-talk.

Personal attributes

Among the potential personal factors that influence self-talk, motivational orientations have received notable attention. Achievement goal theory has dominated sport motivation research for a long time. Yet, only a few studies have examined relationships between achievement goals and self-talk (e.g., Harwood, Cumming, & Fletcher, 2004; Hatzigeorgiadis & Biddle, 2002). Task orientation has been negatively related to negative self-talk and positively related to positive self-talk. Results for ego orientation have not been consistent, suggesting that other factors, such as perceived competence or task orientation, may interact with ego orientation in predicting athletes' self-talk. Thus, athletes aiming to improve their own skills and using self-referenced criteria tend to talk to themselves more positively compared to those aiming at outperforming others and using comparative criteria. Moreover, athletes with higher ego orientation are more vulnerable to impulses to disengage from a sport activity when they perceive they cannot avoid defeat.

Situational circumstances

Research on the situational factors affecting self-talk has examined pre-competition anxiety and the progress of performance (e.g., Hatzigeorgiadis & Biddle, 2008; Van Raalte, Cornelius, Hatten, & Brewer, 2000). Regarding anxiety, pre-competition anxiety intensity, and in particular cognitive anxiety, has been positively related to negative self-talk, and mostly performance worries, during competition. Furthermore, perceived direction of anxiety has been also found related to negative self-talk, with athletes perceiving their anxiety levels as debilitative, reporting more negative self-talk than athletes perceiving their anxiety levels as facilitating.

Regarding the progress of performance, it has been found in runners that identifying discrepancies between the goals athletes sought and actual performance generated negative self-talk. In other words, when things go wrong, or when athletes understand that they are not in a position to attain the goal they have set, they tend to experience negative self-talk. Game circumstances are also related to athletes' self-talk. Negative self-talk has been found to follow lost points of fault serving in tennis; nonetheless, in certain instances positive, instructional and motivational, self-talk has been observed after losing points to provide encouragement.

Social environmental factors

The 'human' environment surrounding the sporting experience has also a critical role in shaping athletes' self-talk. The most important individual for athletes in sport is the coach. The coach is also the most important individual in creating the climate in which sport takes place. Thus, the behaviors adopted by the coach and the way information is communicated can have a significant influence on athletes' self-talk (Zourbanos, Hatzigeorgiadis, Tsiakaras, Chroni, & Theodorakis, 2010). Supportive coaching behavior (i.e., coaches being comprehensive and providing athletes choices and options) is positively related to positive self-talk and negatively related to negative self-talk; and in contrast, negative behaviors characterized by tension and nerves are related to athletes' negative self-talk. Moreover, the way the coach behaves, the motivational climate that is promoted through the coach's practices is also important. A learning motivational climate, a climate focusing on mastering skills and personal improvement is linked to athletes experiencing more positive and less negative self-talk. In contrast, a climate that focuses on outperforming others and highlights a winning-at-all-costs attitude has been linked to negative self-talk. Finally, there is also evidence that manners, body language and actual vocalized self-talk of opponents may have an effect on self-talk; usually fostering negative self-talk.

Why is it important to study the factors that influence athletes' self-talk?

It is important to study the factors that influence athletes' self-talk because it will allow us to identify ways to intervene, where this is possible, and modify such factors for the promotion of self-talk that facilitates performance.

Which of these antecedent factors should be prioritized?

The antecedent factors that should be prioritized are those for which intervention is possible and can have a direct effect on athletes' self-talk, such as leadership factors and coaching behavior, motivational climate and pursued goals.

Methodological note!

Most of the findings on self-talk antecedents are correlational. The lack of experimental research, suitable to claim causal relationships, makes the interpretation of the findings tentative, in particular for the situational and the environmental factors.

SELF-TALK AND PERFORMANCE

The most interesting question in terms of competitive sport is the relationship between self-talk and performance: it is a reciprocal relationship. On one hand, how athletes perform influences what they say to themselves, and in turn what athletes say to themselves may influence their performance. When training and probably even more when competing, the quality of performance and the progress athletes make towards attaining their goals determines to a large extend their self-talk. When performing well, athletes are more likely to have more positive (e.g., self-affirmative; 'nice [shot]', 'let's go') and less negative (e.g., self-deprecatory; 'you're stupid', 'not good enough') self-talk; and in contrast, when performing poorly athletes are more likely to have more negative (e.g., self-blame; 'another mistake', 'can't take it anymore') and less positive (e.g., self-praising; 'doing well', 'keep going') self-talk.

On the other hand, talking positively to oneself may increase confidence and provide appropriate focus, which can result in improved performance; whereas when having negative self-talk athletes may feel disheartened and helpless, and subsequently reduce efforts or abandon the pursuit of goals. Still, these relationships are not straightforward. Athletes doing well may be distracted and have interfering, not task-related thoughts such as celebrations and follow-up interviews; and in contrast, athletes not doing well may use task-relevant self-statements in an attempt to improve their concentration and maximize their efforts to reach their goal. For these reasons evidence from field correlational studies have provided, in certain instances, inconsistent results regarding the relationships between athletes' self-talk and performance (Hatzigeorgiadis & Biddle, 2001; Van Raalte et al., 1994). Similarly, talking positively to oneself may introduce overconfidence or displace attention, thus having detrimental performance effects, and having negative self-statements may have motivating or rebooting effects thus facilitating performance. What can be concluded from these field studies is that self-talk and performance are related, but this relationship may be regulated by other personal and situational factors.

> ### Self-talk and performance
>
> Performance influences self-talk; self-talk influences performance.

Self-talk strategies

The links between cognition and behavior, or thought and action, led sport psychologists to the development of self-regulation strategies. In other words, practitioners aimed to develop strategies to regulate athletes' self-talk in order to improve performance. Self-talk strategies involve the use of cue words or small phrases with the aim of enhancing performance through the activation of appropriate responses. The rationale behind the use of self-talk strategies is that athletes provide appropriate instructions or directions for action to themselves and subsequently execute the correct or appropriate action by simply following the self-instruction they have used.

Interventions involving the use of self-talk strategies have dominated the sport psychology literature because, obviously, performance enhancement is the ultimate goal for athletes and coaches. A wide range of studies with different characteristics has been carried out (e.g., Landin & Hebert, 1999; Mallet & Hanrahan, 1997; Theodorakis, Weinberg, Natsis, Douma, & Kazakas, 2000). In terms of samples, self-talk interventions have been tested in school and university students, young and adult, beginner and experienced athletes. In terms of tasks, a variety of fine (e.g., dart throwing) and gross (e.g., cycling), basic motor (e.g., sit-ups) and sport specific (e.g., golf-putting) tasks have been employed. With regard to the type of self-talk, various cues have been used mostly in the form of technical instruction (e.g. 'steady head') and motivational (e.g., 'you can do it') self-talk. Finally, with regard to the characteristics of the intervention, studies have been carried out using from cross sectional to short (three to five sessions) and more extensive (eight to 12 weeks) training interventions. Overall, contrary to the inconsistent field correlational evidence, the results of experimental-intervention studies have supported the effectiveness of appropriate self-talk on performance, and thus the value of self-talk strategies.

A meta-analysis of studies on the effectiveness of self-talk interventions in enhancing performance (Hatzigeorgiadis, Zourbanos, Galanis, & Theodorakis, 2011) has provided more robust evidence for the value of self-talk strategies. Overall, it was found that self-talk interventions have a moderate effect on sport task performance (effect size = .48). Furthermore, a number of factors which regulate the effectiveness of self-talk were identified. It was reported that the effectiveness of self-talk varied depending on factors pertaining to the characteristics of the task, the type of self-talk used, and the intervention that was implemented. In particular, it was revealed that self-talk was more effective: (a) when participants practiced self-talk over some sessions, rather than just using it without practicing it; (b) for relatively fine tasks, such as precision and accuracy tasks (e.g., passing and shooting accuracy or tennis forehand), compared to relatively gross tasks such as power and endurance tasks (e.g., cycling or jumping performance); for novel tasks and tasks in the learning stage compared to well learned tasks.

Self-talk strategies...WORK!

How self-talk facilitates performance

Considering the findings regarding the facilitating effects of self-talk strategies on sport performance, it becomes particularly interesting to explore the functions of self-talk, that is the mechanisms through which self-talk benefits performance. This will allow us to develop the most appropriate strategies, according to individual needs. Research on the mechanisms that explain the effects of self-talk on performance is new, relatively restricted, and mostly based on athletes' reports and perceptions. Such reports emphasize the attentional and motivating function of self-talk. Athletes who have participated in self-talk interventions have reported that the use of self-talk cues helped them to improve concentration and focus attention, increase confidence, and regulate mood; furthermore, it seems that the attentional function of self-talk is the most pertinent, at least in the early task-learning stages. Experimental evidence has provided support for some of the hypothesized mechanisms identified by the Functions of Self-Talk Questionnaire. In particular, it has been shown that instructional and motivational self-talk reduce interfering thoughts, that instructional focus can shift the focus of attention and change thought content, and that motivational self-talk increases self-efficacy and confidence, and reduces cognitive anxiety (e.g., Hatzigeorgiadis, Zourbanos, Mpoumpaki, & Theodorakis, 2009; Latinjak, Torregrosa, & Renom, 2011; Wadey & Hanton, 2008).

Why is it important to study the functions of self-talk?

Because knowledge of how self-talk works will allow the development of effective interventions targeted towards individual needs.

> **Methodological note!**
>
> Several functions of self-talk have received empirical support; however, none of the studies have fully tested the mediational effects of self-talk. Thus it remains a hypothesis to be tested that these are actually the mechanisms explaining why self-talk is effective. Nevertheless, accepting that self-talk has attentional and motivational effects, and considering that attention and motivation are important determinants of performance, these hypotheses seem quite strong.

FROM THEORY TO PRACTICE: DEVELOPMENT AND APPLICATION OF SELF-TALK STRATEGIES

The implementation of effective self-talk interventions can be routed on the guidelines stemming from three questions related to the application of self-talk strategies: (a) for what purposes shall we use self-talk; (b) what sort of self-talk shall we use; and (c) how can we develop effective self-talk interventions? These questions will be now addressed.

For what purposes shall we use self-talk?

The basic goals of self-talk strategies are to facilitate learning and enhance performance. Facilitating learning involves acquiring new skills, correcting mistakes, and improving technique. Enhancing performance may involve being in a state of readiness, choosing and applying effective tactics, regulating cognition and emotion, handling stressful situations or coping with adverse and unexpected events. Furthermore, self-talk can also help to develop psychological skills and enable athletes to perform according to their potential. Towards the attainment of these goals self-talk can be used as follows: as an instructional strategy to improve concentration, focusing and directing attention and to give feedback; as a motivational strategy to increase effort, persistence, and commitment; and as a self-regulatory strategy to increase self-belief, self-esteem and self-control.

What sort of self-talk shall we use?

Different self-talk cues may be more or less suitable for different purposes; the effectiveness of self-talk is based on the activation of appropriate functions. The activation of the different functions does not happen independently from one another. Several functions operate simultaneously to produce the desired results. Nonetheless, some functions are more critical for the specific goal we aim for, and these should be targeted through the use of self-talk.

Instructional self-talk is more suitable for attentional purposes such as focusing attention, improving concentration, and directing attention; whereas motivational self-talk is more suitable for purposes such as increasing confidence, improving readiness, and regulating drive. In addition, a number of parameters can be considered for deciding what are the appropriate self-talk cues to use: task characteristics, learning stage and experience, and the setting/circumstances are factors that should be considered in relation to the functions the different self-talk cues may serve; what has been termed as the matching hypothesis.

Matching task motor demands to self-talk type

Instructional and motivational cues may serve different functions. Instructional cues can be more effective in helping athletes to improve concentration, direct attention, and focus on technical aspects of a movement. Motivational cues can be more effective in psyching-up, increasing drive, and maximizing physical effort. Considering that for fine tasks attention can be a more crucial factor for performance, whereas for gross tasks, drive and physical effort can be more crucial, instructional self-talk should work better for fine tasks and motivational self-talk should work better for gross tasks.

Matching learning stage with self-talk type

At the early stages of learning, the use of explicit cues in the form of instructional self-talk can improve concentration, and help them identify and shift attention to the task-relevant stimuli, thus facilitating the learning process. At more advanced performance stages athletes may benefit more from motivational cue words that refer to psychological and physical activation, the building of confidence and increasing readiness for performance. Thus, instructional self-talk should be more effective for novel tasks, or tasks at the early stages of learning, whereas motivational self-talk should be more effective for well-learned tasks, or tasks at the automatic stage of performance. Accordingly, *matching athletes' experience with self-talk type*, beginner athletes are more likely to benefit more from instructional cues, whereas more experienced and highly-skilled athletes should benefit more from motivational cues. Expert performance can even be harmed by the use of self-talk, in particular instructional, causing the ironic effect. When a skill is well learned and performed automatically with little effort and without conscious monitoring, instructional self-talk would provide explicit rules that can be detrimental for performance causing what has been termed *paralysis by analysis*.

Matching the setting to type of self-talk

Finally, *matching the setting to type of self-talk*, motivational self-talk seems more appropriate for the competitive circumstances, whereas instructional self-talk should be mostly used in training. As instructional self-talk can be more effective for learning, correcting mistakes, or improving aspects of performance, it seems more appropriate for the practice phase; in contrast, as motivational self-talk can be more effective for increasing readiness and psyching-up, it seems more appropriate for the performance phase.

How can we develop effective self-talk interventions?

Regarding this final question, several steps should be considered. Some of the important steps are presented below, along with examples of a swimmer's self-talk intervention plan, to help the understanding of these steps. To begin with, athletes must identify what they want to achieve with the use of self-talk in a given situation, and organize their action towards the goal (e.g., need to improve (a) reaction time for the start, (b) left arm recovery, and (c) leg input for the finish). Once the athletes' needs are identified, and the specific purposes have been targeted, the matching principles should be considered to select the best possible type of self-talk (e.g., a readiness cue for 'a', an instructional cue for 'b', and a motivational cue for 'c'). Then, a list of cue words that could be tested has to be developed. With regard to the cue words, they have to be brief – either one word or a short phrase – and logically associated to both the task and the central idea of the desired goal (e.g., for 'a', go / explode / time; for 'b', high / elbow / reach; for 'c', power legs / give it all / strong). These cues should be extensively practiced. In training, the cues have to be used systematically (e.g., 'a' for all starting drills; 'b' for the warming-up sets; 'c' for the lactate tolerance sets). Not only is self-talk more effective when trained previously, athletes also perceive the technique as less difficult and more effective after repeated applications. Once the athletes have practiced with the list of cue words they should be able to identify those self-talk cues that are most effective for the goal they want to achieve. The cues should be then organized for the development of complete self-talk plans, possibly comprising several combinations of cues to match different situations ('time' for the starting blocks, and 'power legs' off the last two turns). Finally, those plans should be applied and practiced until the application of self-talk is perfected.

When not to use self-talk

One should be careful for making reasonable use of self-talk, rather than overuse, because it is possible that talking through and overanalysing an action, disrupts and subsequently harms performance; this was earlier identified in this chapter as the ironic effect. This could be especially true for instructional self-talk, since instructional cue words often are very similar to explicit rules, which can be detri-

mental for the performance settings. In particular, the use of instructional self-talk could be potentially harmful when used for a well mastered skill, at the automated stages of performance, in high levels athletes, or in a competitive setting because it may interrupt the flow of performance.

How can we implement effective self-talk (ST) interventions?

ST-IMPACT
- **I**dentify what you want to achieve
- **M**atch self-talk to needs
- **P**ractice different cues with consistency
- **A**scertain which cues work best for you
- **C**reate specific self-talk plans
- **T**rain self-talk plans to perfection

CONCLUSION: BEYOND SPORT

Within the physical activity context, the use of self-talk strategies has been mostly applied in sport, less so in physical education, and almost not at all in exercise settings. Nonetheless, the application of self-talk can help not only for the wider context of physical activity, including exercise, but also for the accomplishment of goals and objectives in other life contexts such as health behaviors or educational learning. The *sport experience* can provide the guidelines for the development of effective self-talk plans towards all directions.

LEARNING AIDS

1 Describe the difference between inherent and strategic self-talk.

   Inherent self-talk refers to all self-addressed statements athletes have, which are neither planned nor prepared; whereas strategic self-talk refers to the intentional use of self-talk cues for self-regulatory purposes.

2 Define positive and negative self-talk.

   Positive and negative self-talk are primarily differentiated based on the content. Positive self-talk refers to statements related to regulating effort, building confidence, and providing instruction; whereas negative self-talk refers to statements related to worries, fatigue, and disengaging thoughts.

3   Identify the factors that influence athletes' self-talk.

Athletes' self-talk can be influenced by their personal attributes, such as their motivational orientations, situational factors, such as anxiety and the progress of the competition, and finally by stimuli arising from the sport environment, such as the behavior of the coach.

4   Discuss the relationship between self-talk and performance.

Self-talk influences performance and performance influences self-talk. Typically, positive and negative self-talk are respectively related to good and poor performance, and vice versa. However, sometimes it is possible that positive self-talk is detrimental to performance due to over-analysis, or overconfidence, and negative self-talk may have motivating effects thus facilitating performance.

5   Explain how self-talk strategies facilitate performance.

The use of self-talk strategies can serve to improve concentration and focus attention, increase confidence, maximize effort, regulate cognitive and affective reactions, and trigger automatic skill performance.

6   Discuss the circumstances where athletes should use instructional and motivational self-talk strategies.

Instructional self-talk is mostly helpful for beginners, for the early stages of learning, when improving or mastering a skill, and in particular for tasks, characterized by accuracy and precision and tasks requiring attention. Motivational self-talk is mostly helpful at the performing stage of a skill, in competition, and for experienced athletes, in particular for tasks requiring strength and endurance.

REVIEW QUESTIONS

1   Discuss the research questions that have been investigated in the self-talk literature and the methodological approaches that have been used to address them.

2   For an individual sport of your choice, describe, based on the factors that influence self-talk, what you would do as a coach to foster positive/facilitating self-talk for your athletes.

3   For a sport of your choice, describe for what specific to that sport purposes you could use self-talk strategies.

4   Identify the factors that regulate (moderators) the facilitating effects of self-talk strategies on performance and discuss the potential applications.

5   Based on ST-IMPACT, design self-talk interventions to improve:

   (a)   Performance of a new and a well learned skill in tennis (or another sport of your liking).

   (b)   Free-throw percentages (or a similar task in another sport) to a beginner and an experienced basketball player.

   (c)   Performance for the two events of a biathlon athlete (biathlon includes cross-country skiing and rifle shooting).

For each of the above, describe alternative self-talk plans and a training schedule explaining how the intervention will be implemented.

EXERCISES

1   Interview an athlete immediately after the conclusion of a competition with regard to his/her self-talk. Write a report of the interview material, and try to link the information with the material of this chapter (content, antecedents, effects).

2   Try to learn a new skill, practicing with the help of a self-talk strategy.

   (a) Choose a task.

   (b) Decide how you are going to evaluate learning improvement.

   (c) Design and implement a self-talk training plan for one week.

   (d) Evaluate your progress and write a report of your experience.

ADDITIONAL READING

Hardy, J. (2006). Speaking clearly: A critical review of the self-talk literature. *Psychology of Sport and Exercise, 7*, 81–97.

Hatzigeorgiadis, A., Zourbanos, N., Galanis, E. & Theodorakis, Y. (2011). Self-talk and sports performance: A meta-analysis. *Perspectives on Psychological Science, 6*, 348–356.

Theodorakis, Y., Hatzigeorgiadis, A. & Zourbanos, N. (2012). Cognitions: Self-talk and performance. In S. Murphy: *Oxford Handbook of Sport and Performance Psychology. Part Two: Individual Psychological Processes in Performance*, (pp.191–212). New York: Oxford University Press.

REFERENCES

Hardy, J., Gammage, K. & Hall, C.R. (2001). A description of athlete self-talk. *The Sport Psychologist, 15*, 306–318.

Hardy, J., Hall, C.R. & Hardy, L. (2005). Quantifying athlete self-talk. *Journal of Sports Sciences, 23*, 905–917.

Harwood, C.C., Cumming, J.J. & Fletcher, D.D. (2004). Motivational profiles and psychological skills use within elite youth sport. *Journal of Applied Sport Psychology, 16*, 318–332.

Hatzigeorgiadis, A. & Biddle, S.J.H. (2001). Athletes' perceptions of how cognitive interference during competition influences concentration and effort. *Anxiety, Stress and Coping, 14*, 411–429.

Hatzigeorgiadis, A. & Biddle, S.J.H. (2002). Cognitive interference during competition among athletes with different goal orientation profiles. *Journal of Sports Sciences, 20*, 707–715.

Hatzigeorgiadis, A. & Biddle, S.J.H. (2008). Negative thoughts during sport performance:

Relationships with pre-competition anxiety and goal-performance discrepancies. *Journal of Sport Behavior, 31*, 237–253.

Hatzigeorgiadis, A., Zourbanos, N., Galanis, E. & Theodorakis, Y. (2011). Self-talk and sports performance: A meta-analysis. *Perspectives on Psychological Science, 6*, 348–356.

Hatzigeorgiadis, A., Zourbanos, N., Mpoumpaki, S. & Theodorakis, Y. (2009). Mechanisms underlying the self-talk-performance relationship: The effects of motivational self-talk on self-confidence and anxiety. *Psychology of Sport and Exercise, 10*, 185–202.

Landin, D. & Hebert, E.P. (1999). The influence of self-talk on the performance of skilled female tennis players. *Journal of Applied Sport Psychology, 11*, 263–282.

Latinjak, A., Torregrosa, M. & Renom, J. (2011). Studying the effects of self talk on thought contents with male adult tennis players. *Perceptual and Motor Skills, 111*, 249–260.

Mallett, C.J. & Hanrahan, S.J. (1997). Race modeling: An effective cognitive strategy for the 100 m sprinter? *The Sport Psychologist, 11*, 72–85.

Peters, H. & Williams, J. (2006). Moving cultural background to the foreground: An investigation of self-talk, performance, and persistence following feedback. *Journal of Applied Sport Psychology, 18*, 240–253.

Theodorakis, Y., Hatzigeorgiadis, A. & Chroni, S. (2008). The Functions of Self-Talk Questionnaire: Investigating how self-talk strategies operate. *Measurement in Physical Education and Exercise Science, 12*, 10–30.

Theodorakis, Y., Weinberg, R., Natsis, P., Douma, I. & Kazakas, P. (2000). The effects of motivational versus instructional self-talk on improving motor performance. *The Sport Psychologist, 14*, 253–272.

Van Raalte, J.L., Brewer, B.W., Rivera, P.M. & Petitpas, A.J. (1994). The relationship between observable self-talk and competitive junior tennis players' performances. *Journal of Sport and Exercise Psychology, 16*, 400–415.

Van Raalte, J.L., Cornelius, A.E., Hatten, S.J. & Brewer, B.W. (2000). The antecedents and consequences of self-talk in competitive tennis. *Journal of Sport & Exercise Psychology, 22*, 345–356.

Wadey, R. & Hanton, S. (2008). Basic psychological skills usage and competitive anxiety responses: Perceived underlying mechanisms. *Research Quarterly for Exercise and Sport, 79*, 363–373.

Zervas, Y., Stavrou, N.A. & Psychountaki, M. (2007). Development and validation of the Self-Talk Questionnaire (S-TQ) for Sports. *Journal of Applied Sport Psychology, 19*, 142–159.

Zourbanos, N., Hatzigeorgiadis, A., Chroni, S., Theodorakis, Y. & Papaioannou, A. (2009). Automatic Self-Talk Questionnaire for Sports (ASTQS): Development and preliminary validity of a measure identifying the structure of athletes' self-talk. *The Sport Psychologist, 23*, 233–251.

Zourbanos, N., Hatzigeorgiadis, A., Tsiakaras, N., Chroni, S. & Theodorakis, Y. (2010). A multi-method examination of the relationship between coaching behavior and athletes' inherent self-talk. *Journal of Sport and Exercise Psychology, 32*, 764–785.

Chapter 25

Psyching up and psyching down

JAYASHREE ACHARYA AND TONY MORRIS

SUMMARY

In this chapter we consider psyching up and psyching down in sport. These terms refer to techniques that are used to increase arousal (psych up) or decrease arousal (psych down). We introduce the topic by explaining the central role of arousal in sport. Then we consider the relationship of arousal to performance, noting that although precise effects have not been determined, we now consider that there is an inverted-U relationship when cognitive state anxiety is low, but that this breaks down as cognitive state anxiety increases. Arousal is also related to enjoyment, but again the relationship is complex. In some circumstances some people find high arousal pleasant, but for others it is unpleasant. Our conclusion for these two relationships is that it is important to manage arousal level to optimize performance and motivation. To do this it is necessary to measure arousal. We explain that this has not been a simple task. We discuss physiological, self-report, and behavioral measures. We then move onto the main topic, the discussion of techniques to increase (psych up) and decrease (psych down) arousal. Psyching up techniques are divided into personal and environmental categories. Personal techniques are those where athletes address their own physical and psychological processes. These include breathing techniques, use of arousing words and phrases, behaving in physically arousing ways, and imagining arousing situations in sport. Environmental techniques originate outside the individual. They include arousing behavior of teammates, as well as stimulating music played before or during performance. Psyching down techniques include bodily relaxation techniques (muscle/somatic) that aim to calm the mind by relaxing the body, mental relaxation techniques that focus on calming the mind, so that physical arousal reduction follows, and other techniques that are based on psychological processes used to manage thoughts and feelings. Throughout the chapter we make two important points. First, all these techniques involve learning skills and that is a process like the learning of sports skills that requires substantial practice. Second, arousal control is a complex process. A trained psychologist should be involved to monitor and advise athletes. Even then psyching up and psyching down are still part science, part art, and part trial and error.

INTRODUCTION

Competitive sport is inherently stressful at all levels. Although some of us can get very "wound up" about a seaside mini-golf game with a friend, generally as the skill level increases, so do the amount of training and the intensity of competition. At the highest levels in some sports, athletes can gain incredible financial rewards or global immortality. As the importance of performing well increases, both due to objective circumstances and in the minds of athletes, whose identities become inextricably entwined with their sport performance, stress can become a major obstacle to success. The athletes who manage highly stressful situations best are usually the winners of those crucial competitions. Thus, research and applied work in sport psychology have long focused on the question of how to manage high levels of stress, associated with the subjective experience of high anxiety and the physiological reaction of high levels of arousal (Hanton, Neil, & Mellalieu, 2011).

In some sports the need to be calm and relaxed to perform well is paramount. Performing well in fine motor skills like pistol shooting and archery requires low levels of arousal. On the other hand, there are sports in which high arousal levels are beneficial or even essential (Weinberg, 2010). Weightlifters must summon extreme levels of physical effort to lift weights that are often much heavier than their own body. Sprinters on the track, in the pool, or at the cycling velodrome must unleash 10, 20, or 30 seconds of explosive power. In many sports, such as team ball games and racquet sports, athletes experience occasions when their arousal level is lower than it needs to be for optimal performance. They feel a little lethargic, lack motivation and can't "get themselves going". Athletes in this state also seek ways to increase arousal level. The scientifically tested or superstitious techniques athletes use to increase their arousal levels for maximal effort have been called "psyching up" in sport. Whether this is a scientifically meaningful term is debatable, but it is now part of the language of sport. To match it, ways to reduce arousal levels can be termed "psyching down".

In this chapter we will consider the scientific view of psyching up and psyching down that has been examined in research by sport psychologists and has been applied in sport by the practitioners in this field. The focus of this chapter is the applied techniques for managing arousal levels, both to increase and to decrease arousal. Before discussing these, we must take a little time to clarify what we mean by level of arousal, why it is important, and how we can measure it.

OBJECTIVES

After reading this chapter you should be able to:

1 Understand the concept, terms and purpose of psyching up and psyching down.
2 Identify the central role of arousal in sports and its relationship to performance.
3 Describe techniques to increase and decrease arousal.
4 Discuss physiological, self-report, and behavioral measures of arousal.
5 Discuss why a trained psychologist should be involved to monitor and advise athletes in using psyching up and psyching down techniques.

ROLE OF AROUSAL IN SPORT

Arousal is a physiological process that is determined in the brain, communicated via the nervous system, and objectively measurable in terms of a range of physiological indicators. Some of these indicators are more central within the body, such as heart rate and brain activity itself, whereas others are peripheral, including skin conductance, peripheral temperature, and muscle tension. Individuals subjectively experience signs of arousal level, such as pounding heart, sweaty palms, tight muscles, or shortness of breath. In sport, level of arousal can affect performance in ways that typically depend on the characteristics of the sport, but also vary to some extent on the basis of the context and the individual. In addition, arousal affects enjoyment of sport. This is important because enjoyment is closely related to intrinsic motivation, the drive to do an activity for its own sake. When intrinsic motivation in sport is low (low enjoyment is a major cause) athletes drop out or reduce effort.

AROUSAL AND PERFORMANCE

Arousal level can be thought of as the activity level of the nervous system. A long-standing proposition about how arousal affects performance is the Yerkes-Dodson law (1908), which predicts an inverted U-shaped function between arousal and performance. This means that as arousal increases from a low level, such as feeling drowsy or sluggish, to a moderate level performance increases, but as arousal continues to increase from feeling alert to being very excited or agitated, performance declines again. Alternatives include Individual Zones of Optimal Functioning (IZOF), Reversal Theory and Catastrophe Theory (these are discussed in Chapter 28). Currently, Catastrophe theory, which combines the principle enshrined in the inverted-U hypothesis with acknowledgement that when a person is very worried the smoothly increasing, then decreasing inverted-U breaks down. It is recognized that some people perform best with low arousal, some with a medium amount, and others with a higher level of arousal. The nature of the activity also affects the level of arousal that is associated with best performance. Weightlifters and sprinters must explode with power meaning that high arousal levels are essential, whereas shooters and archers must be totally calm as they shoot. Optimal arousal for sports like tennis, gymnastics, and football fall somewhere between these extremes. Because a great deal of research and endless anecdotal reports from athletes and coaches indicate that sports performers need to be at their optimal arousal level to perform well, psychologists have identified a range of techniques that athletes can use to psych up (increase arousal) or psych down (decrease arousal) to help them perform at their best.

AROUSAL AND ENJOYMENT

People have different responses related to arousal. Enjoyment of arousal also varies between people. Some people seek stimulation, whereas others avoid it. Arousal can easily be a pleasurable state where individuals "feel more alive" and experience positive stimulation from the physiological effects of being aroused. People who seek arousal are often known as "sensation seekers" (Zuckerman, 1979). On the other hand, arousal can be uncomfortable. When athletes are aroused they have less control over their actions. Many athletes have a high need for a sense of control and the "letting go" that arousal can involve makes them avoid many forms of stimulation and consequent arousal. Whether a particular level of arousal is experienced as pleasurable or uncomfortable, thus, depends on characteristics of each individual, as well as their perception of the context. The same people who seek high arousal in extreme sports are likely to experience a similar level of arousal as unpleasant during an academic examination that is critical to their future. An important aspect of the experience of arousal during sport competition as enjoyable or unpleasant is the implication this can have for continued participation. Enjoyment is closely associated with intrinsic motivation, the motivation to perform an activity for its own sake. Researchers have shown that intrinsic motivation is a key factor in long-term sports participation. Thus, athletes who experience arousal as enjoyable are likely to seek more opportunities to participate, whereas those who find their arousal level before and during performance to be unpleasant have a tendency to drop out. For the vast majority of athletes, who do not get rewards from sport, such as wealth and fame, it is important to ensure that they enjoy their involvement to motivate continued participation. This is another reason why it is necessary to understand psyching up and psyching down techniques that aid in the management of arousal levels.

MEASURING AROUSAL

There are a number of ways to assess level of arousal. These include direct, objective measures of the physiological processes that constitute arousal (physiological indicators), reports from individuals about their subjective experience (self-report measures), and observations of athletes' behavior that indicate arousal level (behavioral signals).

Physiological indicators

Because arousal is a process that involves most tissues and organs in the body, there are many ways to measure the level of operation of those body parts. Some of these are complex and sensitive. They require expensive equipment and can be invasive. Research and experience have shown that, for practical purposes, a number of relatively simple, non-invasive methods are indicative. Heart rate (HR) is a widely used indicator of arousal level. It is measured in beats of the heart per minute. HR can be monitored by electrodes placed on the chest over the heart that transmit the heart rate to a recording device, usually a computer. Higher levels of arousal are indicated by faster HR and bands of HR can be used to indicate appropriate arousal levels for different sports and purposes. Another very common measure is skin conductance or Galvanic skin response (GSR). As arousal increases sweat is secreted, which increases the salt on the surface of the skin, producing higher levels of electrical activity, which is usually measured by an electrode placed on the finger. Peripheral temperature changes as level of arousal increases. Unlike the other indicators, as arousal increases, temperature decreases. Thinking about the association between warmth and relaxation (how a warm environment makes people drowsy) is an easy way to remember this. PT can be monitored in the skin using a thermal detector. For easy practical use there are commercially available systems that monitor HR, GSR, and PT, as well as other indicators of arousal level, with one device that has a "sleeve" for each finger containing a different monitoring device. All signals are fed back to a computer and managed by software for different purposes.

A problem with the use of physiological indicators as measures of level of arousal is that various indicators often present different information. This is primarily because different systems within the body operate in different ways and at various speeds, so not all physiological indicators will reflect a change triggered by the brain at the same time. Further, research that used physiological and self-report measures of level of arousal together quickly showed that level of agreement between the physiological and psychological indicators was low, except at extreme levels of arousal (e.g., Martens, Burton, Vealey, Bump, & Smith, 1990). One reason for this is that people are not always sensitive to their ongoing bodily processes. Another problem is that subjective perceptions are affected by psychological processes that can change interpretation of bodily sensations. At the same time, physiological indicators only indicate *level* of arousal; they don't identify the *meaning* of that arousal level. Thus, for example, a high level of arousal could reflect debilitating anxiety or high excitement. In many sports, the use of physiological indicators is not very helpful as a monitor of arousal level; even now that wireless technology and miniaturization mean that athletes, even in vigorous contact sports, can wear monitors during matches. This is because the change in arousal level related to the physical exertion of the game is much larger than the changes related to psychological factors, so the psychological impact is swamped by the physical causes of arousal.

Self-report measures

Paper and pencil, self-report measures represent a common way of assessing psychological variables. They provide insights into a range of thoughts and feelings that are difficult for observers to appreciate. It must be recognized that questionnaires are limited by the questions that are included in them. In addition, various psychological processes can influence responses. In psychology and sport psychology there are many measures of anxiety, activation, or arousal, so only those most commonly used in sport will be mentioned here.

The Competitive Sport Anxiety Inventory-2 (CSAI-2; Martens et al., 1990) is by far the most widely used measure. The CSAI-2 is based on the conceptualization of two components of state anxiety, cognitive anxiety and somatic anxiety,

and a third sub-scale that measures self-confidence. Cognitive anxiety relates to the worrying thoughts that people experience, whereas somatic anxiety is concerned with the bodily symptoms associated with anxiety. Thus, it is easy to think of somatic anxiety as being an indicator of level of arousal. Somatic anxiety is, however, a self-report of athletes' subjective perception of bodily symptoms, which is influenced by various psychological factors. For example, if athletes think reporting high somatic anxiety in some contexts might negatively affect their status because it will be reported to coaches, they might report lower levels of somatic anxiety than they actually experience to protect their position. Some researchers have shown that athletes can also unconsciously repress their feelings of anxiety when they are tested close to matches because they believe that if they are anxious their performance will suffer. It is also possible for the effects of physical exertion to be interpreted as somatic anxiety, inflating the self-report, or such exertion can obscure somatic anxiety that is actually moderate to high. Thus, it is important to use measures like the CSAI-2 somatic anxiety subscale with caution, recognizing that scores are an indication of self-perceived bodily reactions, not a direct measure of level of arousal.

Another approach to the self-report measurement of arousal is through adjective checklists. These involve a range of adjectives that describe arousal or activation states. The most popular of these is the Thayer Activation-Deactivation Adjective Checklist (ADACL), which is described in a short form by Thayer (1986). This includes 20 adjectives that describe arousal-related states, for example, energetic, calm, tired, tense, scored on a 4-point scale. These adjectives reflect four states, namely tension (high preparatory activation) and calmness (low preparatory activation), energy (general activation) and tiredness (general deactivation). Some researchers and practitioners have employed single-item self-report measures, which simply ask people how they feel and ask for a response on a dimension from very calm/relaxed/tired to very tense/excited/energetic. Combinations of self-report measures with physiological measures can be used to gain the sensitivity of objective physiological indicators along with the subjective interpretation of self-report measures. In his extensive study of mood and affect, Thayer noted that while individual physiological indicators did not correlate highly with each other or with self-report measures, a combined score from a range of physiological measures did correlate significantly with self-reported arousal level.

Behavioral signals

The behavioral approach to the measurement of arousal is based on the recognition that people produce certain kinds of observable behaviors when they are aroused. These include physical signs, such as flushing (reddening, particularly of the face and neck), pallor, and sweating, and behaviors, including fidgeting, talking excessively, silence, hand tapping, and shaking. Care must be taken in basing assessments of level of arousal on behavioral indicators alone because many have explanations unrelated to arousal level. For example, people flush when they are hot and they become silent when they are thinking intently. It can also be difficult to observe less extreme versions of these behaviors in real time so video recording is useful, but not always practical. In any event, it is safer to use behavioral indicators in combination with physiological or self-report indicators, rather than relying on them alone.

PSYCHING UP

Psyching up is a term that originated in sport, but is now defined in the Oxford dictionary. It refers to techniques that lead to an increase in level of arousal, which usually results in higher levels of energy that enhance effort and motivation. Most techniques are personal, that is, they involve behaviors conducted by athletes to increase their arousal, when they believe it is too low for optimal performance. In addition, there are some techniques that are presented by the environment. In this section, we examine a range of common personal techniques and two common environmental techniques.

Personal techniques

The source of personal techniques is the individual. Thus, they are behaviors that athletes undertake with the intention to increase their arousal level. There are many personal psyching up techniques. The most commonly used approaches are described here.

Rapid breathing: Breathing is an often practiced, but seldom-mastered art. In the course of a normal day (24hrs) we take over 20,000 breaths. With more physical activity, such as walking to work, taking the stairs, and going to the gym, this figure could be as high as 30,000. Even top athletes can fail to breathe optimally and specific training of the breathing muscles can improve the performance of highly trained athletes. Athletes who understand how they should breathe during training and performance can improve control over their emotions, which saves energy and has the potential to enhance performance.

When people are anxious or highly aroused, their breathing becomes rapid and shallow. At extreme levels, people often characterize fear in terms of feeling they cannot breathe. Because rapid, shallow breathing is associated with high arousal, one way to increase level of arousal is to intentionally take many short breaths. This should not be a prolonged exercise because that could lead to arousal becoming too high. It is also likely to deplete oxygen in the body, and oxygen is an important fuel for performance. Rapid breathing should not be an ad hoc activity. It should be practiced away from competition to develop the skill, so it can be effectively applied before or during competition as needed.

Arousing words and thoughts: Just as words, such as adjectives, can be used to measure level of arousal, they can also be used to increase arousal. Words like "energetic", "lively", "dynamic", or "explosive" are understood by most people. Individual athletes might also have personal associations with particular words that do not have an arousal-related meaning to others. One popular kind of word in sport is animal names. The characteristics of certain animals can signify the corresponding behavior for an athlete. For example, cheetahs are renowned for their speed, bears for their strength, lions and tigers for aggression. Athletes can be encouraged to choose a word and then put it into a short phrase that associates the characteristic with them. "I am explosive" might be a term that will help a sprinter to generate the level of arousal needed to explode off the starting blocks and quickly achieve full speed, whereas "I feel like a bear" might be a useful statement for a front row forward in rugby. Some athletes might feel comfortable repeating their arousing word or phrase out loud a number of times in preparation for performance, after practicing it during training. For more reserved athletes the arousing term might be repeated as a thought, rather than out loud (see Weinberg, 2010).

Psyched up behavior: When athletes feel like their arousal, energy, or motivation is lower than required for the task they are performing, they can start to behave in ways that mimic being highly aroused. This might mean just walking tall or with a swagger, it could involve running on the spot or jumping up and down. Tennis players could slap the racket head, basketball players could bounce the ball hard and repeatedly, and some sports performers actually slap themselves on the thigh, the bottom, the chest, or even the face in increase arousal. This kind of psyching up behavior is often called getting "pumped up". It involves athletes behaving in a psyched-up manner in an effort to make themselves feel more aroused. It can also involve shouting at oneself or other loud verbal behavior. A risk with this kind of behavior is that it is unacceptable in the culture or even the rules of various sports. Players using this kind of approach must be careful not to go too far. With the exception of some of the milder forms of psyching up behavior, such as jumping or running on the spot, it seems that getting too pumped up is not worth the risks for performance, as well as fines or even disqualification, when there are so many alternatives that can be practiced and used in a controlled way (see Weinberg, 2010).

Stimulating imagery: As noted in the chapter on imagery in this book, imagining behavior or emotions can have potent effects. This also applies to the manipulation of arousal level (Weinberg, 2010). To increase level of arousal, athletes can imagine themselves in highly arousing situations. In sports where it is important to have a high level of arousal from the start, shortly before a match begins imagining being in the midst of competition against the impending opposition can help athletes to run onto the field with their arousal tuned to the level that will allow them to start the match with full intensity. An alternative that might be preferred in some contexts is for athletes to imagine their own physiological processes becoming prepared for the performance needed. This might be more suitable for athletes, such as weightlifters, who must feel and produce maximal power, but with only a few seconds to deliver it. Imagining the heart pumping vigorously and the oxygen-rich blood rushing to those muscles that must produce that supernormal effort, feeling the muscles infused and bursting with power, should be an effective approach for such performers.

Environmental techniques

The source of environmental techniques is outside individuals in the things that happen as part of the competition context in different sports. It is sometimes possible for athletes to control aspects of their environment to help increase their level of arousal prior to or during competition. On other occasions, environmental factors impinge on athletes whether they find them helpful or not. Here we refer to two factors than sometimes occur as a part of the pre-competition or competition environment, but which athletes can manipulate if they plan ahead.

Stimulating teammates: When teammates are energizing themselves for performance, their behavior can influence other athletes. In sports like football and rugby it is common for there to be a lot of noise in pre-game changing rooms as athletes shout at teammates and themselves to increase their level of arousal. Some athletes are known to indulge in physical psyching up behaviors. They can bounce off the walls or body check each other to prepare themselves to be highly aroused when they run out onto the pitch for the start of the game. Just being in that kind of environment can be very arousing for some athletes, such as introverts, who do not need a great deal of external stimulation to become aroused. Athletes, like extroverts, who do need more external stimulation to achieve high levels of arousal, can get involved in those activities, asking teammates to shout at them or to physically contact them to help them psych up. An interesting custom in this context is the immediately pre-game, on-pitch Hakka performed by New Zealand rugby union and rugby league teams, which has its origins in warriors' preparation for battle. A combination of loud chanting, aggressive movements, and grotesque facial contortions by the whole team in unison acts to psych up the players and is also intended to psych *out* their opposition.

Arousing music: Athletes have long used music to stimulate arousal. During the last 20 years, psychologists have studied the role of music in sport (Terry & Karageorghis, 2011). This research has shown that certain music does increase levels of arousal, whereas other music is experienced to be relaxing. Research-

ers have shown that arousing music can enhance effort and lead to increases in the performance of power, speed, and endurance tasks. The effects of music on arousal are more complex than this, however. The particular pieces of music that arouse athletes depend on past experiences of those athletes, so a piece that some athletes find psyches them up in a useful way could lead to a negative experience for another athlete because of a past association of failure with that music. Further, it has been found in practice that excerpts of music that an athlete finds arousing for a period of time lose their potency with frequent repetition. Psychologists can advise athletes about how and when to use music beneficially, but the athletes must be involved in choosing the pieces of music and determining when their effect wanes, so they need to be replaced.

To summarize the psyching up section, there is a great diversity of ways in which athletes can increase their arousal to produce great effort, speed, power, or endurance in sport. Because the processes underlying different techniques vary, it is important for psychologists to understand how each technique works in order to apply them optimally with athletes. All individuals are different, so understanding each athlete is also a prerequisite for the effective use of psyching up techniques. Further, in all cases, psychologists should monitor the impact of use of techniques designed to increase arousal level. They should employ a range of methods to do this including objective tests and measures, where possible, self-report from athletes, and their own observation of athlete behavior. Determining the most effective techniques for each athlete and ensuring they continue to be effective involves that combination of science, art, and trial and error that require the special training of a psychologist.

PSYCHING DOWN TECHNIQUES

Psyching down as a term has not entered the language in the same way as psyching up, perhaps because it is easy just to say "relax-

ing". We use psyching down here, first, to contrast its purpose with that of psyching up and, second, to emphasize that it is largely a psychological process that is best managed by psychologists. A wide variety of techniques have also been developed to help individuals psych down. Because of the wide range of situations that cause anxiety or panic in everyday life, psychologists and other health practitioners have devised many psych down techniques that have been applied in sports contexts. A number of psyching down techniques involve relaxation. Some of these have been called muscle-to-mind techniques because they involve doing something physical, typically to the muscles to reduce arousal level. Psychologists also call these somatic (bodily) techniques. Other relaxation techniques have a mental focus, making the assumption that a calm mind will promote a relaxed body. These are called mind-to-muscle or cognitive techniques. Other psyching down techniques are not directly designed to induce relaxation, but they can help to reduce arousal level.

Somatic or muscle-to-mind relaxation techniques

Breathing: People often use slow, deep breathing as a way to reduce level of arousal, that is, to help them relax. Just as rapid, shallow breathing characterizes excitement or anxiety, slow, deep breathing is readily associated with relaxation. Just watch people who are sleeping, the extreme relaxation end of the arousal continuum, and see how few breaths sleepers take. Breathing techniques mostly originate in Eastern spiritual or meditational practices, but a variety of simplified methods have been devised in the West, often based on counting. A long count on inhalation, followed by a short count for exhalation, e.g., 5:2, is common, whereas a shorter inhalation and longer exhalation, e.g., 2:4, can be used. Long inhalation and exhalation, e.g., 4:4, is probably the most favored approach to train somebody to relax. Yoga breathing, being one of the foundations of the slow deep breathing techniques, is similar to this approach.

Yoga *breathing* is also called *Pranayama* (*prana* and *yama*) in Sanskrit, meaning the control (*yama*) of a healthy way of life through breathing (*prana*). *Pranayama* consists of modifications of the breathing process brought about deliberately and consciously. In *Pranayama* the act of breathing has four distinct stages. They are: (i) inhalation (*Puraka*), which in yoga is a continuous process, evenly controlled; (ii) a pause in breathing, called *Kumbhaka*, retaining the air in the inflated lungs; (iii) exhalation (*Rechaka*), which again should be a smooth and continuous process, a letting go from the inflation of the lungs, the expansion of the thoracic cage, and the pressing down of the diaphragm; (iv) a pause in breathing again, this time on emptying the lungs. This is an effortless breath suspension, at the end of which a slow smooth inflow of air through the nostrils commences, and stage (i) is repeated to start the cycle again.

Progressive relaxation: Modern progressive relaxation techniques are all variations of those outlined by Jacobson (1929). Jacobson's progressive relaxation (PMR) procedure requires that individuals lie on their backs. The room should be fairly quiet and arms and legs should not be crossed, to avoid unnecessary stimulation. While the goal of any progressive relaxation program is to relax the entire body in a matter of minutes, in the beginning, it is essential that individuals practice the technique for at least one hour every day. Once the relaxation procedure is well learned, relaxation can be achieved in a few minutes. Jacobson's method calls for individuals to tense a muscle group before relaxing it. Jacobson warned that only the first few minutes of any relaxation session should be devoted to muscle tensing. The remaining time should be focused on gaining complete relaxation. For a muscle to be considered relaxed, it must be completely free of any contractions and must be limp and motionless. Jacobson argued that tensing the muscles during the early stages of training is important because many people have habitually tense muscles, so the best way to show them what relaxation feels like is to contrast it with tension.

Thus, the PMR program can be divided into two parts. Part one is a conditioning program. The aim of this program is to enable people to recognize tension in the main muscle groups. In the second part, relaxation is deliberately induced. Jacobson's full progressive relaxation procedure involves systematically tensing and relaxing specific muscle groups in a predetermined order. Often this starts at the head and moves down the body to the feet. Alternatively, it can start at the feet and move up to the head. Because muscle groups that are close to each other are addressed in this kind of sequence, as individuals practice, relaxing one muscle group acts as a trigger to relax the next in the sequence, and this triggers the next. A well-developed relaxation training program requires a great deal of practice in the beginning, but if it is practiced in a sequence of juxtaposed muscle groups, the time it takes to relax is reduced by this kind of domino conditioning effect (see also Weinberg, 2010).

Cognitive or mind-to-muscle relaxation techniques

Relaxation response: Relaxation and ease of mind can be helpful in almost any undertaking, but in sports it is important that athletes are not so relaxed that they stop caring whether or not they win the contest. Thus, when psyching down athletes should aim to be calm, but alert. The relaxation response is a term that Benson (1976) developed to refer to a version of transcendental meditation "routinized" to make it more accessible and mainstream and disassociate it from negative interpretations. The relaxation response requires two essential components: (i) a mental device; and (ii) a passive attitude. Benson proposed the following steps for inducing the Relaxation response:

1   Pick a focus word, sound, phrase, prayer, or muscular activity.
2   Sit in a comfortable position.
3   Close your eyes.
4   Relax your muscles, progressing from your feet to your calves, thighs, abdomen, shoulders, head and neck.
5   Breathe slowly and naturally, and as you do, say your focus word, sound, phrase, or prayer silently to yourself as you exhale.
6   Assume a passive attitude. Don't worry about how you're doing. When other thoughts come to mind, simply say to yourself "Oh well," and gently return to your repetition.
7   Continue for 10 to 20 minutes.
8   Do not stand immediately. Continue sitting quietly for a minute or so, allowing other thoughts to return. Then open your eyes and sit for another minute before rising.
9   Practice the technique once or twice daily. Good times to do so are before breakfast and before dinner.

As just described, the relaxation response is a very passive approach to psyching down. It takes a lot of disciplined practice to gain effects. For some time, the subjective experience is just sitting doing nothing. Athletes are mostly active people. They make things happen by doing. Thus, many athletes might not have the discipline to continue practicing the relaxation response until they experience the calm awareness that is the goal. For those athletes who are suited to it, the relaxation response will be a rewarding way to relax away from competition that can be transferred to pre-competition contexts once learned (see Weinberg, 2010).

Autogenic training: Autogenic training involves using the mind to tell the body to relax. Different exercises and self-statements have been suggested to bring about the relaxation response using autogenic training. The originators of autogenic training, Schultz and Luthe (1969) proposed six stages each associated with self-statements. Thus, the meditator says or thinks: (i) my right arm is warm and heavy; (ii) both my arms are warm and heavy;

395

(iii) both my legs are warm and heavy; (iv) it breathes me (breathing is automatic, not controlled); (v) my solar plexus is warm; (vi) my forehead is cool. Although somewhat unusual, these are the kinds of phenomenal experiences reported to Schultz by his hypnosis clients. Autogenic training is a mind to muscle technique that involves long, slow training in its original format where the self-statements accumulate over time. Each step should be practiced two to three times a day for around two weeks. It is only after at least 12 weeks that the level of relaxation is achieved to allow self-statements about other physical and mental characteristics to be introduced. In our research and applied work, we have found that athletes respond well to an abbreviated form of autogenic training in which all the self-statements are introduced in one session, then practiced regularly. For psyching down purposes, autogenic training is not particularly suitable for immediate pre-competition use, but regular practice should produce a general feeling of greater calmness and self-suggestions can focus on controlling pre-match emotions (see Weinberg, 2010).

Meditation: Meditation, as a form of relaxation, is tied directly to the concepts of selective attention. In practicing meditation, individuals attempt to uncritically focus their attention on a single thought, sound, or object. The practice of meditation as a form of relaxation and thought control has its origin in Eastern cultures more than four thousand years ago. The most common mental device used in transcendental meditation is the silent repetition of a mantra. It is clear that the various forms of meditation can reduce anxiety and tension by evoking the relaxation response.

Meditation can, thus, help athletes psych down to achieve the optimal state of mind for peak performance in sport. There are a number of different forms of meditation that can help athletes to relax, some of which have already been mentioned. As well as yoga, transcendental meditation, and Anapanasati meditation, other meditational practices associated with Buddhist traditions are common, including Zen. Athletes need to find meditational techniques that suit them. They should also be careful to understand the goal of the selected technique. Some techniques, including certain forms of yoga, aim to achieve an inner focus that closes attention to the environment, whereas in others, such as Zen, the goal is to be relaxed, but with a heightened sensitivity to the environment. Psychologists can help athletes to choose a technique that suits their temperament and is consistent with their goal in psyching down.

Other psyching down techniques

Thought-stopping: Thought-stopping is associated with self-talk because it is based on acknowledgement that people often have negative thoughts, like self-talk, and these often produce high levels of arousal. This is common in sport, which led psychologists to identify ways to help athletes to stop having negative thoughts. One of the early thought-stopping techniques to be developed involves concentrating on the undesired thought briefly and then using a cue or trigger to stop the thought and clear the mind. Triggers can be verbal, such as "stop" or "park it" or "bin it" or they can be an action, like clicking the fingers or slapping the thigh. This sounds neat and simple, but negative thoughts do not readily disappear. More recent thought-stopping techniques have included the replacement of the unwanted, arousing thought by a pleasant, relaxing one. This takes practice. Psychologists need to identify a pleasant thought for that particular athlete. It could be a personal thought, such as being in a comfortable, relaxing location with loved ones. Alternatively, it could be a sport-related thought, for example, a time when the athlete played exceptionally well or an outcome like winning a major event. Once the positive thought is identified, the athlete practices recognizing negative thoughts, using their trigger, and thinking the positive thought. After substantial practice, the positive thought should become associated with the trigger, so it occurs automatically. Then the technique can be used in and before competition because using the trigger should automatically stimulate the positive thought.

Rationalization: This is a cognitive technique that originates in therapies, including cognitive therapy and rational emotive therapy (Smith, Smoll, & O'Rourke, 2011). These psychological approaches recognize that everybody has irrational thoughts. Athletes are no different to people in general. They experience a range of irrational thoughts. Common ones are "I can't play in this strong wind" and, at a deeper level, "I must be perfect for the coach and the fans to love me". The first is irrational because it implies that other players are not affected by the wind. Using rationalization, an expert psychologist can dispute this, establishing that everybody's performance is affected by the wind. If the athlete working with the psychologist accepts this, tries to understand the wind, and works hard to play as well as they can, then they can have an advantage over those players who continue to think the wind will defeat them. Similarly, through disputation, that is, questioning and arguing against the position that love is contingent on perfection, a psychologist can help the athlete to realize that everybody makes mistakes, and that people admire and respect athletes who work hard and try their best. This change should lead the athlete to focus on performing to the best of their ability, not being knocked off track by the occasional missed shot under pressure. Once again, it is important to appreciate that this technique does require substantial training to deliver, so it should be the responsibility of a psychologist.

Imagery: Imagery is a technique widely used by athletes for diverse purposes. In the imagery chapter in this section of the book, Bhasavanija and Morris discuss how imagery works and how it can be applied. Athletes can use imagery in many ways to help relax the mind and the body. A popular imagery technique to psych down is imagining a favorite place, often somewhere that feels comfortable,

safe, and relaxing. It is common for people to imagine an idealized relaxing scene, that is, not somewhere they actually know. For example, one relaxing type of scene involves lying in soft, lush, green grass, by a stream that presents a calming trickling sound. The sky is deep blue and the sun is warm. Note how the scene involves many sense modalities, including the auditory, tactile, and kinesthetic, as well as the visual sense. This helps to make the imagery more powerful. An alternative is to imagine bodily sensations that are associated with arousal and manage them. For example, athletes can imagine their heart beating quite rapidly and then slow it down in their imagery to become more relaxed. Yet another common alternative is to imagine the kind of context that triggers high arousal, such as a tight score in a crucial match. Imagining performing well and achieving the desired outcome can reduce arousal level for that type of event. With athletes experienced in the use of imagery and known to be good at controlling their imagery, this technique could be used to imagine performing well in the upcoming match. This approach should not be used with novice imagers whose imagery control is not well developed because they could imagine negative outcomes, increasing stress and thus arousal level, rather than psyching down. This kind of imagery can also be used in conjunction with one of the relaxation techniques already described. Athletes can do breathing, PMR, or autogenic exercises to create a relaxed state in which they imagine the competition environment, thus, associating competition with the feeling of relaxation. Imagery is a powerful technique that can be tailored to the specific context, but it should always be guided by an expert because of the potential for negative imagery to intrude on what otherwise should be a relaxing and confidence-building experience.

Self-talk, cognitive-affective stress management training, and biofeedback are techniques that can be used to psych down. They are discussed in Chapters 23, 20, and 26 of this book respectively.

CONCLUSION

The experience of using a range of psyching up and psyching down techniques in practice has demonstrated that these techniques can work. Unfortunately, sport psychologists have not yet discovered the formula that determines when and how much to use these techniques. Thus, for sport psychologists, psyching up and psyching down remain part art as well as part science, and trial-and-error is often involved. What we do know is that individual characteristics and the nature of the sport and its context both affect optimal arousal level. Further, even the same athlete in the same sport context will react differently on different occasions. Sport psychology practitioners will continue to use all their skills, along with the most up-to-date science available, to deliver the best outcomes they can for athletes. The aim must be to help athletes learn to understand themselves because, ultimately, it is each athlete's thoughts and emotions in the critical moment when a match can be won or lost that must be the basis for the decision whether to psych up, psych down, or leave well alone.

LEARNING AIDS

1   How would you distinguish arousal from anxiety?

Arousal is a term that describes a physiological state. It is measured by instruments that monitor the body's electrical and mechanical activity, including heart rate, skin temperature, breathing, and muscle contraction. Anxiety is a subjective experience that is measured by self-report, usually on validated questionnaires. Physiological measures indicate level of arousal, but high arousal can reflect joy or trepidation. High anxiety is a subjectively unpleasant state that is usually associated with high levels of arousal.

2   What is the difference between somatic and cognitive state anxiety?

State anxiety is a transient experience of unpleasant emotion. Cognitive state anxiety refers to the worrying thoughts that occupy athletes' minds, often distracting them, so their performance suffers. Somatic state anxiety refers to the bodily sensations people experience that are interpreted as indicators of arousal level. Strong bodily sensations, such as muscle tension and tremor can negatively affect performance and such experiences can be distractions that affect focus on performance. Physical techniques can often help in the management of somatic anxiety, whereas techniques that address thought processes are required to manage cognitive anxiety.

3   Distinguish between the terms psyching up and psyching down.

Arousal is related to athletic performance. High levels of arousal usually facilitate performance of power, strength, speed, and endurance tasks, such as sprinting and weightlifting, whereas low arousal level is not associated with optimal performance. For fine motor skills, such as shooting and archery, high arousal is usually detrimental to performance and low arousal facilitates performance. To achieve the optimal performance state, power and speed athletes often need to increase arousal. They use a range of techniques in the process of increasing arousal level, which is called psyching up. Fine motor skill sport athletes frequently need to reduce arousal to facilitate performance. The process of reducing arousal is called psyching down.

4   Is breathing a technique that is used to psych up or to psych down?

Different breathing techniques can be used to increase or decrease arousal level. Slow, deep breathing helps calm athletes down and reduce arousal. Rapid, shallow breathing stimulates arousal. Thus breathing of different kinds is both a psyching up and a psyching down technique.

5   How can imagery be used to psych up and to psych down?

Athletes can imagine anything that they can conceive. Much imagery is associated with emotion, so imagining an event that has an emotional connection for an athlete can stimulate that emotion. Thus, an athlete who imagines the greatest moment in their involvement in sport is likely to experience emotions like joy, euphoria, and excitement, which will increase their arousal level. Such imagery plays a psyching up role. Imagining being in a quiet, calm, peaceful place is likely to help athletes to relax, thus, reducing arousal and playing a psyching down role.

REVIEW QUESTIONS

1   What is the relationship between arousal and performance and why is it important?

2   Identify TWO physiological indicators, TWO self-report measures, and TWO behavioral indicators of level of arousal?

3   How would you use breathing to increase athletes' arousal level?

4   What are FIVE words or phrases that commonly increase level of arousal?

5   What might be a risk of using psyched up behavior during competition?

6   What are TWO things you would take into account when considering music to help increase level of arousal?

7   What are TWO muscle-to-mind or somatic techniques to reduce level of arousal?

8   What are TWO mind-to-muscle relaxation techniques?

9   How would you help athletes to stop having negative thoughts that increase their arousal to undesirable levels?

10   How would you use imagery to reduce competition-specific arousal?

EXERCISES

1   From the literature, choose one breathing technique to increase arousal and one to decrease arousal that appeal to you. Perform the psyching up technique twice a day for one week, noting your experience in a log after each session. Then do the same for the psyching down technique. Examine the experiences in the log to gain insights into how you reacted to each technique.

2   Identify FIVE words or terms that reflect energy and power to you. Sit quietly and repeat the terms to yourself for five minutes three times a day for a week. Use them the next time your energy is low and see how you respond.

3   Write a progressive muscle relaxation script for yourself. Justify why you start at the head or the feet. Practice the script every day for a month. Notice how your muscles become relaxed more quickly over time. When could you do the whole session without looking at the script? [Caution: PMR is a popular hypnosis induction technique. It should NOT create an altered state without accompanying suggestion, but just to be sure, always flex your arms and legs a few times and ensure you feel alert when you complete a session.]

4   Draft FOUR self-affirmation statements that you think will help make you feel calm just before competition. State them to yourself three times a day for two weeks. Monitor how you feel when you compete.

5   Identify a recurring worry for you. Use the parking technique described in the thought-stopping section when the concern comes to mind any time for two weeks. Record the experience for the two hours after using parking.

ADDITIONAL READING

Hanin, Y. (2000). *Emotions in sport*. Champaign, IL: Human Kinetics.

Hanton, S., Neil, R. & Mellalieu, S.D. (2011). Competitive anxiety and sporting performance. In T. Morris & P. Terry (Eds.) *The new sport and exercise psychology companion* (pp.89–105). Morgantown, WV: Fitness Information Technology.

Martens, R., Vealey, R.S. & Burton, D. (Eds.) (1990). *Competitive anxiety in sport* (pp.117–213). Champaign, IL: Human Kinetics.

Weinberg, R. (2010). Activation/arousal control. In S.J. Hanrahan & M.B. Andersen (Eds.) *Routledge handbook of applied sport psychology* (pp.471–480). Abingdon, UK: Routledge.

REFERENCES

Benson, H. (1976). *The relaxation response*. New York: Morrow.

Hanton, S., Neil, R. & Mellalieu, S.D. (2011). Competitive anxiety and sporting performance. In T. Morris & P. Terry (Eds.) *The new sport and exercise psychology companion* (pp.89–105). Morgantown, WV: Fitness Information Technology.

Jacobson, E. (1938). *Progressive relaxation*. Chicago, IL: University of Chicago Press.

Martens, R., Burton, D., Vealey, R.S., Bump, L.A. & Smith, D.E. (1990). Development and validation of the Competitive State Anxiety Inventory-2 (CSAI-2). In R. Martens, R. Vealey & D. Burton (Eds.) *Competitive anxiety in sport* (pp.117–213). Champaign, IL: Human Kinetics.

Schultz, J. & Luthe, W. (1969). *Autogenic methods* (vol. 1). New York: Grune & Straton.

Smith, R.E., Smoll, F.L. & O'Rourke, D.J. (2011). Anxiety management. In T. Morris & P. Terry (Eds.) *The new sport and exercise psychology companion* (pp.2–3). Morgantown, WV: Fitness Information Technology.

Terry, P.C. & Karageorghis, C.I. (2011). Music in sport and exercise. In T. Morris & P. Terry (Eds.) *The new sport and exercise psychology companion* (pp.359–380). Morgantown, WV: Fitness Information Technology.

Thayer, R.E. (1986). Activation-Deactivation Adjective Checklist: Current overview and structural analysis. *Psychological Reports, 58,* 607–614.

Weinberg, R. (2010). Activation/arousal control. In S.J. Hanrahan & M.B. Andersen (Eds.) *Routledge handbook of applied sport psychology* (pp.471–480). Abingdon, UK: Routledge.

Yerkes, R.M. & Dodson, J.D. (1908). The relation of strength of stimulus to rapidity of habit formation. *Journal of Comparative and Neurological Psychology, 18,* 459–482.

Zuckerman, M. (1979). *Sensation seeking: Beyond the optimal level of arousal.* New York: L. Erlbaum Associates.

Chapter 26

Self-regulation and biofeedback

BORIS BLUMENSTEIN, TSUNG-MIN HUNG AND IRIS ORBACH

SUMMARY

The goal of this chapter is to describe the current state of biofeedback research in sport and its implications for enhancing athlete performance in different sport disciplines. The chapter provides the main knowledge about biofeedback, includes a brief literature review of the background and development of biofeedback and biofeedback training based on the psychophysiological principle. Also presented are two biofeedback training models, Neurofeedback training and the Wingate Five-Step Approach. Numerous examples from the latest research, as well as practical applications to sport, are discussed and illustrated.

INTRODUCTION

The following anecdotal evidence occurred during an international competition in windsurfing. During one of the first events the athlete, the coach, and the first author waited for the wind for about one hour in the boat at sea. The athlete played with a PC and a portable Biofeedback (BFB) device in the boat, focusing on his concentration and relaxation skills with different BFB games. For example, in these games the athlete used relaxation and concentration skills in order to move the image of a surfer from left to right. According to our experience, the athlete should achieve three jumps with the surfer's image during a one-minute period while experiencing an optimal concentration state. These games demonstrate to the athlete the link between his concentration-relaxation skills and his performance,

help the athlete to transfer this skill into practice, show his current mental possibilities with psychophysiological responses, and demonstrate his current self-regulation level.

After a few minutes, other windsurfers from different countries showed curiosity, approached us and asked for our permission to take part in the games. Most of them could not perform these exercises successfully according to our norms, and realized that good performance requires training. This situation showed our athlete his strength and superiority in mental skills above his competitors. On that day he won in two races and said: "Today I was very fast and confident". This story is an indication of how the mere knowledge of the BFB devices has a positive impact on performance.

Besides the performance benefits, the use of BFB training helped in building good rapport and trust between the consultant, the athlete, and the coach. In addition, most of our mental training was provided at sea, together with the coach and the athlete. This situation had a positive effect on our relationship and the good atmosphere during our cooperation.

(Blumenstein & Orbach, 2012a, pp. 140–142)

OBJECTIVES

After reading this chapter you should be able to:

1   Understand the background and development of biofeedback and biofeedback training.
2   Discuss the main psychophysiological principles interrelations between the physiological and the mental components of behavior (i.e., psychophysiological principle).
3   Describe the latest research in the area of biofeedback.
4   Understand Neurofeedback training.
5   Explain the Wingate Five-Step Approach.
6   Define the Periodization principle of sport training.

SELF-REGULATION AND BIOFEEDBACK IN SPORT AND EXERCISE

One of the major goals in mental preparation in sport is improving self-regulation skills. According to Schwartz (1979), self-regulation is a fundamental component of mental diagnostic and/or intervention activities applied as part of athlete preparation. Self-regulation in sport is the athlete's ability to control emotion, behavior, and desires during training and competitive events. More specifically, self-regulatory processes such as self-talk, self-monitoring, self-evaluation and strategy selection are vital in an athlete's biofeedback training. Hence it follows that biofeedback training is the practice of improving the athlete's self-regulation.

The history of psychophysiological approaches to sport performance is the root of modern biofeedback. The concept of biofeedback was introduced at the end of the 1960s. The first biofeedback applications were limited to clinical medical practices conducted by the researchers Basmajian (1967) and Kamiya (1969). Basmajian (1967), who showed that subjects could learn to control single motor units in their spinal cord. Kamiya (1969) demonstrated that subjects could voluntarily control their brain waves. In 1975, Zaichkowsky proposed the use of biofeedback in sport.

Biofeedback (BFB) is the use of instruments (electronic devices with electrodes and sensors) in order to assess, monitor, and feed psychophysiological information back to a person. Modern technology gives the possibilities to measure rapidly, in real-time, a variety of biological functions, such as: heart rate, muscular activity, blood pressure, skin temperature, sweat gland activity, respiration, and brain wave activity. This information from mind–body activity is monitored and is helpful in learning to regulate the mind and body according to the psychophysiological principle, namely the interrelations between the physiological and the mental and emotional components of behavior. This principle is described below and is presented in Figure 26.1.

Every change in the physiological state is accompanied by an appropriate change in the mental emotional state, conscious or unconscious, and conversely every change in the mental emotional state, conscious or unconscious, is accompanied by an appropriate change in the physiological state.

(Green, Green, & Walters, 1970, p. 9)

It is important to understand that although the terms "biofeedback" and "biofeedback training" are frequently used synonymously, they need to be set apart. *Biofeedback training* is a technique of gaining control of self-regulation which is based on information or feedback received from an athlete's body. After intensive BFB training, the psychological skills become automatic reflexes. The final result is a more stable, optimized, and balanced mind/body interaction in athletic performance.

Competitive stress is usually demonstrated by increased changes in physiological and psychological parameters, such as an increase in EMG, HR, BP, R (see below), and state anxiety, and a decrease in GSR and body/mind regulation, self-confidence, and the ability to relax. The athlete is exposed to BFB training with different BFB modalities, and learns to improve self-monitoring and self-regulation in lab and field settings. As a result, there is an optimized effect on physiological and psychological parameters as can be seen in Figure 26.2. The final result is an improvement in the athlete's self-regulation skills, which leads to performance enhancement under competitive stress.

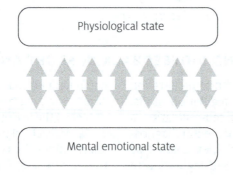

Figure 26.1 Schematic description of the psychophysiological principle.

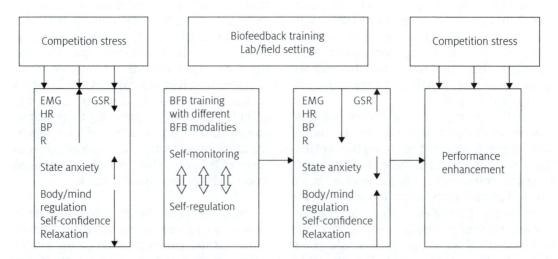

Figure 26.2 Conceptual model for the role of BFB training in sport.

BIOFEEDBACK MODALITIES

Biofeedback training includes the monitoring of different biofeedback modalities:

- *EMG*, electromyography or muscle feedback, is the measurement of muscle tension. EMG usually increases in muscle tension as arousal increases.
- *HR*, cardiovascular or heart rate feedback is the measurement of heart activity by electrocardiography. HR generally increases with increased arousal. The most recent form of HR BFB is heart rate variability (HRV), which is measured by interbeat interval (IBI) – the time between heart beats in msec.
- *EDA*, Electrodermal Activity feedback, is the measurement of electrical properties of the skin. EDA includes measurement of skin resistance (SR, historically known as "galvanic skin response", GSR), skin conductance (SC), and skin potential (SP).

The most used measurement is SC, which increases with higher arousal.

- *BP*, blood pressure feedback, is the measurement of blood pressure. It generally increases with increased arousal.
- *R*, respiration feedback, is the measurement of respiration rate and amplitude. Respiration generally increases with increased arousal.
- *EEG*, electroencephalographic feedback, is the measurement of the brain's electrical activity. EEG frequency increases when shifting from sleep (delta and theta waves) to excitement (beta waves). Recently, EEG feedback has been known as neurofeedback (NF).
- *T*, thermal feedback, often referred to as "temperature", is a measurement of peripheral skin temperature as an index of peripheral blood flow. In the relaxation state temperature increases while during stress temperature decreases ("cold hands").

LITERATURE REVIEW

Early research has examined BFB as a tool for teaching athletes to decrease anxiety and improve performance by reducing muscular tension; for strength training, reducing pain and muscle fatigue; and to increase flexibility (e.g. Blumenstein, 2002). Research has established a significant positive role of BFB training with different modalities on athletic performance in various sports. For example, Zaichkowsky (1983) found a positive effect of EMG BFB training on college age gymnasts' performance. Costa, Bonaccorsi, and Scrimali (1984) found a decrease in precompetitive anxiety in handball with skin conductance (SC) BFB training. Landers and his colleagues (1991) found that EEG BFB training improves athletes' performance in archery and shooting. Blumenstein (1999) and Blumenstein and Bar-Eli (1998) found that SC and EMG BFB training along with relaxation and imagery can reduce precompetitive

stress and improve performance in judo and canoe/kayak. Several studies have suggested that biofeedback training can improve athletes' performance when the training is employed as a component of a larger "package" of mental skill interventions (e.g., Blumenstein, Bar-Eli, & Tenenbaum, 2002; Petruzzello, Landers, & Salazar, 1991). Numerous reviews discussing the efficacy of BFB in sport have been published, for example by Blumenstein (2002), Leonards (2003), Zaichkowsky and Fuchs (1988).

Following is a summary of the effect of biofeedback training on performance, based on the literature review:

- Research findings indicated that psychological parameters, such as stress during training and competition, can be reduced by biofeedback training and thus performance can be enhanced.

- Biofeedback training has shown some promising potential when used as part of a larger intervention package.
- BFB training requires specification of the modalities based on sport disciplines. For example, EMG and GSR BFB are used in combat sport (e.g., judo, wrestling, and fencing); EEG, HR, and respiratory biofeedback training are related to performance in aiming tasks (e.g., archery, shooting, golf).

- There are some *limitations* to be considered in BFB training:
  - The ability "...to transfer the learned response to performance in the real world" (Crews, Lochbaum, & Karoly, 2001, p. 578).
  - Research with BFB training requires special and expensive BFB equipment.

NEUROFEEDBACK TRAINING

BFB training is the single most efficient way to teach, acquire, or enhance self-regulation skills (Zaichkowsky, 2009). Training self-regulation with BFB begins in the laboratory under sterile conditions in which the athlete attempts to self-regulate specific physiological functions. The following are two major training BFB programs: The first, Neurofeedback training, presents BFBT with one modality and the second, the Wingate Five-Step Approach, is a multifaceted BFBT program which includes several BFB modalities as part of a psychological intervention package.

Neurofeedback (NF), or electroencephalographic (EEG) feedback, is one of the BFB modalities and purports to teach individuals the sensation of being in specific cortical activity states and eventually how to activate such states under their own will (Angelakis et al., 2007). NF is characterized by electrode scalp placement and frequencies' categories. The placement of electrodes is designated by capital letters (i.e., F, T, C, P, and O) and numbers. The capital letters correspond to the location of the electrodes on the scalp: Frontal, Temporal, Central, Parietal, and Occipital lobes of the brain. Odd/even numbers indicate the left/right hemisphere side, respectively. For example, F1 represent an electrode that is placed on the Frontal lobe of the left hemisphere site. The frequency ranges are grouped according to bands: Delta (1–4 Hz), theta (4–7 Hz), alpha (8–12 Hz), beta (13–36 Hz), and gamma (36–44 Hz). For example, Alpha activa-

tion indicates on a relaxation state and beta/gamma represents an activation state. During NF training EEG is recorded, and relevant components are extracted and feed back to the individual online by audio, visual, or a combination of the two signals. For example, a vertical bar with the amplitude of a target frequency is displayed to a trainee and a marker is placed at a certain height on the bar to represent the threshold of the NF training. The trainee's task is to either increase or decrease the size of the bar to reach the threshold. Whenever this goal is met, a tone sounds and a symbol appears to indicate a point scored. The aim of the training is to score as many points as possible.

NF sessions typically last for less than an hour, and are usually administered twice or three times per week. The number of sessions needed for treatment varies substantially, ranging from 25–80 sessions, depending on factors such as the condition being treated, the individual's learning success, and the severity of the condition (Lubar, 1991; Sterman, 2000).

NF has been shown to effectively reduce the symptoms of disorders such as ADHD, anxiety, epilepsy, and addictive disorders, while traumatic brain injury (TBI), learning disabilities, depression, and schizophrenia are potential candidates (Monastra, 2003). In addition to these disorders, research has been extended to investigate applications of NF to the nondisordered population for enhancing attention performance (Egner & Gruzelier, 2001; Hanslmayr, Sauseng, Doppelmayr, Schabus, & Klimesch, 2005), cognitive performance (Angelakis et al., 2007), dance performance (Raymond, Sajid, Parkinson, & Gruzelier, 2005), and sport performance (Arns, Kleinnijenhuis, Fallahpour, & Breteler, 2007; Hung & Kao, 2011; Landers et al., 1991; Vernon, 2005; Wang & Hung, 2006).

The rationale for developing NF protocols to enhance sport performance is based on associations. By identifying associations between particular patterns of cortical activity that are considered "optimal" as well as specific states or aspects of behavior, we can train an individual to enhance performance by mirroring the patterns of cortical activity seen during such optimal states. An implicit assumption that underpins current practice is that the training process will lead to changes in EEG, which in turn will produce changes in behavior.

Past studies have found some EEG signatures associated with the attentional process prior to motor execution. These include left temporal alpha power (T3α) (Hatfield, Landers, & Ray, 1984; 1987), central occipital alpha power (Ozα) (Loze, Collins, & Holmes, 2001), alpha coherence between mid-frontal and left temporal areas (Fz-T3α coherence) (Deeny, Hillman, Janelle, & Hatfield, 2003; Wu, Lo, Lin, Shih, & Hung, 2007), and alpha event-related desynchronization (ERD) in central, right central, and mid-frontal areas (Babiloni et al., 2008). Among these EEG indices, T3α is probably the most studied EEG signature in this line

of research. As such, most of the few NF studies in sports have developed NF protocols based on increasing T3α.

EEG/NF training is used in performance on aiming tasks such as shooting, archery, and golf. In a study by Wang and Hung (2006), 20 pre-elite air pistol shooters were assigned to either a NF or a control group. The NF consisted of a total of 16 sessions, 30 minutes per session, targeted at enhancing shooters' T3α in a span of six weeks. The training followed parts of the Wingate Five-Step Approach (simulation and transformation steps; for more details see next section) developed by Blumenstein, Bar-Eli, and Tenenbaum (1997). Individualized levels of T3α were determined before the beginning of NF. Shooters were trained to increase the level of T3α first in a seated position in a quiet environment, and then progressively moved to an aiming position in the shooting range. Both EEG and shooting performance were measured before and after NF training. The results showed that NF was effective in increasing T3α and shooting scores. Taking another example from an aiming task, golf, Figure 26.3 depicts a golfer who underwent NF, first in a seated position with both visual and auditory feedback.

Figure 26.4 demonstrates a golfer who progressed after training with NF in a sitting position, then to an NF training during putting position with only auditory feedback.

In Figure 26.5 data during NF training demonstrates the changes in alpha power when an athlete has effective control over it.

THE WINGATE FIVE-STEP APPROACH

The Wingate Five-Step Approach (W5SA) is a self-regulation approach incorporating BFB training that enables athletes to transfer the psycho-regulative skills performed in the sterile laboratory setting to real training conditions (Blumenstein et al., 2002a). This stepwise approach consists of five steps of training with biofeedback and a self-regulation test (SRT). The SRT is used to examine the athlete's level

of self-regulation at various points before each step in the W5SA (for more detail see Blumenstein, Bar-Eli, & Collins, 2002). The W5SA includes: (1) Introduction, in which the athlete learns fundamental self-regulation techniques such as relaxation, breathing, and imagery adding BFB modalities at the end of the step (e.g., HR, EMG, and GSR). Usually, the athlete begins with the frontalis EMG feedback

Figure 26.3 NF training with golfer (visual and auditory feedback).

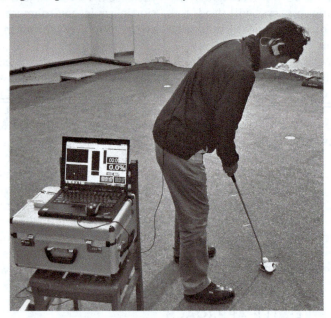

Figure 26.4 NF training with a golfer (auditory feedback).

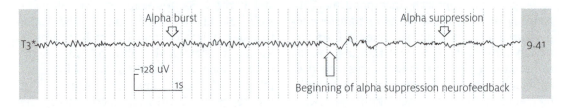

Figure 26.5 The changes in alpha rhythm during NF training.

with three surface electrodes placed on the frontalis muscle (Kondo, Canter, and Bean (1977). Later in this step GSR and HR BFB are used; (2) Identification, in which the focus is on strengthening the most efficient BFB modality relevant to the specific personal psychophysiologic characteristics and to the specific sport discipline. For example, in judo or fencing, sports in which performance involves high levels of tactile and proprioceptive sensitivity and intense emotional involvement, EMG and GSR seem to be the most efficient modalities to measure (Blumenstein, et al., 2002a, b). In contrast, shooting and archery demands from the athlete a stable muscle, breathing, and body position, and therefore EEF (electroencephalography) is more suitable (Landers et al., 1991); (3) Simulation, in which BFB training is accompanied by simulative competitive stress, such as competitive noises, VCR-fragments, and competitive situations. The main aim of using video clips in this step is to bring about a gradual elevation of the simulated stress; (4) Transformation, in which the preceding mental preparation procedure

acquired by the athlete is taken from lab to training conditions by using portable BFB devices. The main purpose of this step is to enable the athlete to enter real future competitions with an improved self-regulation ability; (5) Realization, in which the athlete obtains optimal regulation in competitive conditions. The first three steps take place in a laboratory setting and the last two steps take place under field conditions (see Figure 26.6).

In the next figure an example of BFB training with GSR modality is presented through a mental session in Step 1 (Introduction). The GSR BFB data is taking place while the athlete practices his relaxation skills for 15 minutes. Generally speaking, when the line goes down it indicates the ability of the athlete to relax and when the line goes up it indicates the inability of the athlete to self-regulate his or her mental state. Therefore, the data from Figure 26.7 reveal relatively weak relaxation skills in the first five minutes. In the next seven minutes the athlete is able to self-regulate himself and show effective relaxation skills.

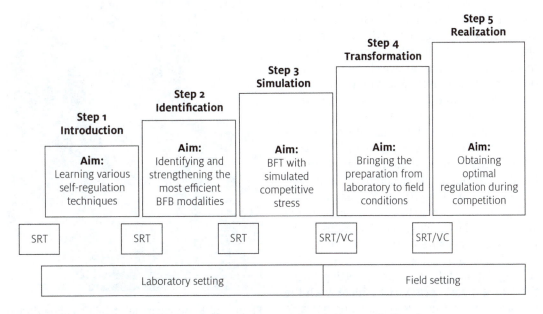

Note: BFT: Biofeedback training; SRT: Self-regulation test; SRT/VC: Self-regulation test with video clips

Figure 26.6 Schematic description of the W5SA for mental training.

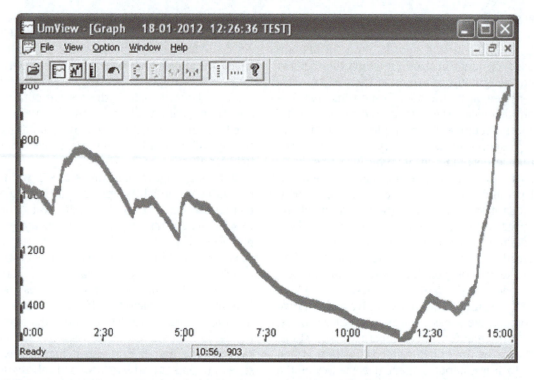

Figure 26.7 Sample GSR BFB data during the Introduction step of the W5SA.

In the following figures video fragments of Steps 2 (Identification) and 3 (Simulation) are demonstrated. In Figure 26.8 the Identification step is presented. The athlete trains with EMG feedback, with three surface electrodes placed on the frontalis muscle, and with HR feedback, which is measured by placing one electrode on the tip of the thumb to measure HR.

In Figure 26.9 the Simulation step is presented. The athlete is practicing self-regulation skills under competitive stress created by VCR fragments and competitive noises. During the training process his reactions are being monitored by EMG and GSR BFB, which are measured by placing two electrodes on the fingertips to measure sweat gland activity.

In Figure 26.10 an athlete is practicing his self-regulation skills in a training setting during the Transformation step. The athlete, with the guidance of the first author, is using portable GSR BFB, which is measured by placing two electrodes on the fingertips to measure sweat

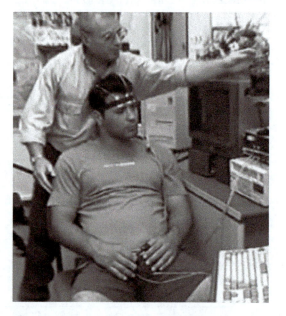

Figure 26.8 An example of BFB training during the Identification step of the W5SA.

Figure 26.9 An example of BFB training during the Simulation step of the W5SA.

gland activity. The feedback is given to the athlete by a color change on the GSR display (e.g., change from red to green indicates relaxation and from green to red indicates excitation). The portable GSR BFB can be used during pauses in the training and competition, such as before and after warm up, between attempts, matches, and fights, and any other periods in which the athlete prepares to perform.

In the last step of the W5SA, the Realization step, the athlete applies the previously acquired mental techniques during competition. Modifications and adjustments to the skills can be recommended to the athlete to optimize his or her readiness to competition. The W5SA is a relatively flexible approach. Once an athlete is exposed to the whole program, it is possible to practice the relevant steps/skills in the next season. In addition, the length of each step can be shorter.

A strong side of the W5SA is the relationship with the athlete's training process. By following the W5SA the athlete is able to transform his or her learned mental skills from the laboratory to the field. For an effective transformation, the demands of training and the specificity of sport should be taken

into account. The Periodization principle of sport training can be used as a framework for this process (e.g., Bompa, 1999; Bompa & Haff, 2009). Periodization is a key subject in training and planning, and consists of three major periods: Preparatory (general and specific), competitive, and transition. In each of these periods the athlete's preparation (i.e., physical, technical, tactical, and psychological) is adjusted, based on the specific goals and demands of training and sport discipline. Only recently has this principle been used in regard to psychological preparation (Balague, 2000; Blumenstein, Lidor, & Tenenbaum, 2007; Blumenstein & Orbach, 2012a; Holliday, Burton, Sun, Hammermeister, Naylor, & Freigang, 2008). Based on our experience, the use of the W5SA can be more effective when used in line with the Periodization principle (Blumenstein, & Orbach, 2012a, b, c; Blumenstein & Weinstein, 2011) (see Figure 26.11).

Figure 26.10 An example of BFB training during the Transformation step of the W5SA.

Training phases				
Preparation		Competition	Transition	
General	Specific			
The Wingate Five-Step Approach (W5SA)				
Introduction Identification (laboratory setting)	Identification Simulation (laboratory setting)	Transformation Realization (field setting)		

Figure 26.11 Training phases and the W5SA.

LEARNING AIDS

1   Explain the psychophysiological principle.

The psychophysiological principle concerns the interrelations between the physiological and the mental and emotional components of behavior.

2   Discuss the differences between biofeedback and biofeedback training.

It is important to understand that although the terms "biofeedback" and "biofeedback training" are frequently used synonymously, they need to be set apart. Biofeedback (BFB) is the use of instruments (electronic devices with electrodes and sensors) in order to assess, monitor, and feed back psychophysiological information to a person. Biofeedback training is a technique of gaining control of self-regulation which is based on information or feedback received from the athlete's body.

3   Identify the biofeedback modalities.

Biofeedback modalities include the following: (1) EMG, muscle feedback, is the measurement of muscle tension by electromyography; (2) HR, cardiovascular or heart rate feedback is the measurement of heart activity by electrocardiography. The most recent form of HR BFB is heart rate variability (HRV), which is measured by interbeat interval (IBI), the time between heart beats in msec; (3) EDA, Electrodermal Activity feedback, is the measurement of electrical properties of the skin. EDA includes measurement of skin resistance (SR, historically known as "galvanic skin response", GSR), skin conductance (SC), and skin potential (SP); (4) BP, blood pressure feedback, is the measurement of blood pressure; (5) R, respiration feedback, is the measurement of respiration rate and amplitude; (6) EEG, electroencephalographic feedback, is the measurement of the brain's electrical activity. Recently, EEG has become known as neurofeedback (NF); (7) T, thermal feedback, often referred to as "temperature", is a measurement of peripheral skin temperature as an index of peripheral blood flow.

4   Describe the conceptual model for the role of BFB training in sport.

Competitive stress is usually demonstrated by increased changes in physiological and psychological parameters, such as an increase in EMG, HR, BP, R, and state anxiety, and a decrease in GSR and body/ mind regulation, self-confidence, and the ability to relax. The athlete is exposed to BFB training with different BFB modalities in order to improve self-monitoring and self-regulation in lab and field setting. As a result, there is an optimized effect on physiological and psychological parameters. The final result is an improvement in the athlete's self-regulation skills, which leads to performance enhancement under competitive stress.

5   Describe the measurement method of NF training.

NF is characterized by electrodes scalp placement and frequencies categories. The placement of electrodes is designated by capital letters (i.e., F, T, C, P, and O) and numbers. The capital letters correspond to the location of the electrodes on the scalp: Frontal, Temporal, Central, Parietal, and Occipital lobes of the brain. Odd/even numbers indicate the left/right hemisphere side, respectively. The frequency ranges are grouped according to bands: Delta (1–4 Hz), theta (4–7 Hz), alpha (8–12 Hz), beta (13–36 Hz), and gamma (36–44 Hz).

6   Summarize the Wingate Five-Step Approach.

The W5SA consists of five steps of training with biofeedback, and a self-regulation test (SRT). The W5SA includes: (1) Introduction, in which the athlete learns fundamental self-regulation techniques, such as relaxation, breathing, and imagery, adding BFB modalities at the end of the step (e.g., HR, EMG, GSR); (2) Identification, in which the focus is on strengthening the most efficient BFB modality relevant to the specific personal psychophysiological characteristics and to the specific sport discipline; (3) Simulation, in which BFB training is accompanied by simulative competitive stress, such as competitive noises, VCR-fragments, and competitive situations; (4) Transformation, in which the preceding mental preparation procedure acquired by the athlete is transformed from lab to training conditions using portable BFB devices; (5) Realization, in which the athlete obtains optimal regulation in competitive conditions. The first three steps take place in a laboratory setting and the last two steps take place under field conditions.

8   Discuss the relationship between the Periodization principle and the W5SA.

The Periodization principle is a key subject in training and planning, and consists of three major periods: Preparatory (general and specific), competitive, and transition. In each of these periods the athlete's preparation (i.e., physical, technical, tactical, and psychological) is adjusted based on the specific goals and demands of training and sport discipline. Only recently this principle has been used in regard to psychological preparation. The use of the W5SA is more effective when it is used in line with the Periodization principle.

REVIEW QUESTIONS

1   Explain the psychophysiological principle and the major difference between biofeedback and biofeedback training.

2   What are the biofeedback modalities and their response to an increase in arousal? Provide examples of BFB modalities suitable to the sport discipline.

3   What is the major goal of the W5SA and each of its steps? What is the connection between the W5SA and the Periodization principle?

EXERCISES

1   Case study: Select an athlete and plan a training protocol according to the W5SA. Consider the sport discipline, Periodization principle, and the appropriate BFB modalities.

2   Imagine you are a sport psychology consultant, specializing in BFB training. How would you present the concept of biofeedback training and the W5SA to athletes at different sport levels and in sport disciplines?

3   Perform muscle relaxation with portable EMG/GSR BFB for 1, 2, 3, and 5 minutes.

4   Perform imagery of a competitive event with portable EMG/GSR BFB (e.g., swim start, combat fight, free-throws in basketball).

ADDITIONAL READING

Blumenstein, B. (2002). Biofeedback applications in sport and exercise: Research findings. In B. Blumenstein, M. Bar-Eli & G. Tenenbaum (Eds.), *Brain and body in sport and exercise: Biofeedback application in performance enhancement* (pp.37–54). Chichester, UK: Wiley.

Blumenstein, B., Bar-Eli, M. & Collins, D. (2002). Biofeedback training in sport. In B. Blumenstein, M. Bar-Eli & G. Tenenbaum (Eds.), *Brain and body in sport and exercise: Biofeedback applications in performance enhancement* (pp.55–76). Chichester, UK: Wiley.

Blumenstein, B. & Orbach, I. (2012a). *Mental practice in sport: 20 case studies.* New York, NY: Nova Science Publishers.

Blumenstein, B. & Orbach, I. (2012b). The road to Olympic medal. In A. Edmonds & G. Tenenbaum (Eds.), *Case studies in applied psychophysiology: Neurofeedback and biofeedback treatments for advances in human performance* (pp.120–133). Chichester, UK: Wiley.

Blumenstein, B. & Orbach, I. (2012c). Biofeedback training at sea. In A. Edmonds & G. Tenenbaum (Eds.), *Case studies in applied psychophysiology: Neurofeedback and biofeedback treatments for advances in human performance* (pp.134–143). Chichester, UK: Wiley.

Blumenstein, B. & Weinstein, I. (2011). Biofeedback training: Enhancing athletic performance. *Biofeedback, 39*(3), 101–104.

Vernon, D. (2005). Can neurofeedback training enhance performance? An evaluation of the evidence with implications for future research. *Applied Psychophysiology and Biofeedback, 30*(4), 347–364.

Wilson, V. & Gunkelman, J. (2001). Neurofeedback in sport. *Biofeedback, 29*(1), 16–18.

Zaichkowsky, L.D. (2009). A case for a new sport psychology: Applied psychophysiology and fMRI neuroscience. In R. Schinke (Ed.), *Contemporary sport psychology* (pp.21–32). New York, NY: Nova Science Publishers.

REFERENCES

Angelakis, E., Stathopoulou, S., Frymiare, J.L., Green, D.L., Lubar, J.F. & Kounios, K. (2007). EEG Neurofeedback: A brief overview and an example of peak alpha frequency training for cognitive enhancement in the elderly. *The Clinical Neuropsychologist, 21,* 110–129.

Arns, M., Kleinnijenhuis, M., Fallahpour, K. & Breteler, R. (2007). Golf performance enhancement and real-life neurofeedback training using personalized event-locked EEG profiles. *Journal of Neurotherapy, 11,* 11–18.

Babiloni, C., Del Percio, C., Iacoboni, M., Infarinato, F., Lizio, R., Marzano, N. & Eusebi, F. (2008). Golf putt outcomes are predicted by sensorimotor cerebral EEG rhythms. *Journal of Physiology, 586,* 131–139.

Balague, G. (2000). Periodization of psychological skills training. *Journal of Science and Medicine in Sport, 3*(3), 230–237.

Basmajian, J.V. (1967). *Muscles alive: Their functions revealed by electromyography.* Baltimore, MD: Williams & Wilkins.

Blumenstein, B. (1999). Mental training with biofeedback in combat sport. In V. Hosek, P. Tilinger & L. Bilek (Eds.). *Proceedings of the Xth European Congress of Sport Psychology, Part I* (pp.119–121). Prague, Czech Republic: Charles University.

Blumenstein, B. (2002). Biofeedback applications in sport and exercise: Research findings. In B. Blumenstein, M. Bar-Eli & G. Tenenbaum (Eds.), *Brain and body in sport and exercise: Biofeedback application in performance enhancement* (pp.37–54). Chichester, UK: Wiley.

Blumenstein, B. & Bar-Eli, M. (1998). Self-regulation training with biofeedback training in elite canoers and kayakers. Special issue. In V. Issurin (Ed.), *Science and practice of canoe/kayak high performance training* (pp.124–132). Elite Sport Department, Wingate Institute, Israel.

Blumenstein, B., Bar-Eli, M. & Collins, D. (2002a). Biofeedback training in sport. In B. Blumenstein, M. Bar-Eli, & G. Tenenbaum (Eds.), *Brain and body in sport and exercise: Biofeedback applications in performance enhancement* (pp.55–76). Chichester, UK: Wiley.

Blumenstein, B., Bar-Eli, M. & Tenenbaum, G. (2002b) (Eds.). *Brain and body in sport and exercise: Biofeedback applications in performance enhancement.* Chichester, UK: Wiley.

Blumenstein, B., Lidor, R. & Tenenbaum, G. (2007). Sport psychology and the theory of sport training: An integrated approach. In B. Blumenstein, R. Lidor & G. Tenenbaum (Eds.), *Psychology of sport training* (pp.8–18). Oxford, UK: Meyer & Meyer Sport.

Blumenstein, B. & Orbach, I. (2012a). *Mental practice in sport: 20 case studies.* New York, NY: Nova Science Publishers.

Blumenstein, B. & Orbach, I. (2012b). The road to Olympic medal. In A. Edmonds & G. Tenenbaum (Eds.), *Case studies in applied psychophysiology: Neurofeedback and biofeedback treatments for advances in human performance* (pp.120–133). Chichester, UK: Wiley.

Blumenstein, B. & Orbach, I. (2012c). Biofeedback training at sea. In A. Edmonds & G. Tenenbaum (Eds.), *Case studies in applied psychophysiology: Neurofeedback and biofeedback treatments for advances in human performance* (pp.134–143). Chichester, UK: Wiley.

Blumenstein, B. & Weinstein, I. (2011). Biofeedback training: Enhancing athletic performance. *Biofeedback, 39*(3), 101–104.

Bompa, T. (1999). *Periodization: Theory and methodology of training* (4th ed.). Champaign, IL: Human Kinetics.

Bompa, T. & Haff, G. (2009). *Periodization: Theory and methodology of training* (5th ed.). Champaign, IL: Human Kinetics.

Costa, A., Bonaccorsi, N. & Scrimali, T. (1984). Biofeedback and control of anxiety preceding athletic competition. *International Journal of Sport Psychology, 15,* 98–109.

Crews, D.J., Lochbaum, M.R. & Karoly, P. (2001). Self-regulation: Concepts, methods, and strategies in sport and exercise. In R. Singer, H. Hausenblas & C. Janelle (Eds.). *Handbook of sport psychology* (pp.566–581) (2nd ed.). New York, NY: Wiley & Sons.

Deeny, S. P., Hillman, C.H., Janelle, C.M. & Hatfield, B.D. (2003). Cortico-cortical communication and superior performance in skilled marksmen: An EEG coherence analysis. *Journal of Sport and Exercise Psychology, 25,* 188–204.

Egner, T. & Gruzelier, J.H. (2001). Learned self-regulation of EEG frequency components affects attention and even-related brain potentials in humans. *Neuroreport, 12,* 4155–4160.

Green, E., Green, A. & Walters, E. (1970). Voluntary control of internal states: Psychological and physiological. *Journal of Transpersonal Psychology, 2,* 1–26.

Hanslmayr, S., Sauseng, P., Doppelmayr, M., Schabus, M. & Klimesch, W. (2005). Increasing individual upper alpha power by neurofeedback improves cognitive performance in human subjects. *Applied Psychophysiology and Biofeedback, 30,* 1–10.

Hatfield, B.D., Landers, D.M. & Ray, W.J. (1984). Cognitive processes during self-paced motor performance: An electroencephalographic profile of skilled marksmen. *Journal of Sport Psychology, 6,* 42–59.

Hatfield, D.B., Landers, D.M. & Ray, W.J. (1987). Cardiovascular-CNS interactions during a self-paced intentional attentive state: Elite marksmanship performance. *Psychophysiology, 24,* 542–549.

Holliday, B., Burton, D., Sun, G., Hammermeister, J., Naylor, S. & Freigang, D. (2008). Building the better mental training mousetrap: Is periodization a more systematic approach to promoting performance excellence? *Journal of Applied Sport Psychology, 20,* 199–219.

Hung, T. & Kao, S. (2011). *Effects of neurofeedback training on competitive mental state and golf putting performance.* Paper presented at the 13th European Congress of Sport Psychology, Madeira, Portugal.

Kamiya, J. (1969). Operant control of the alpha rhythm. In C. Tart (Ed.), *Altered states of consciousness* (pp.507–515). New York, NY: John Wiley & Sons, Inc.

Kondo, C., Canter, J. & Bean, J. (1977) Intersession interval and reductions in frontalis EMG during biofeedback training. *Psychophysiology, 1,* 123–137.

Landers, D.M., Petruzzello, S.J., Salazar, W., Crews, D.L., Kubitz, K.A., Gannon, T.L. & Han, M. (1991). The influence of electrocortical biofeedback on performance in pre-elite archers. *Medicine and Science in Sport and Exercise, 23,* 123–129.

Leonards, J.T. (2003). Sport psychophysiology: The current status of biofeedback with athletes. *Biofeedback, 31,* 20–23.

Loze, G.M., Collins, D. & Holmes, P.S. (2001). Pre-shot EEG alpha-power during expert air-pistol shooting: A comparison of best and worst shots. *Journal of Sport Sciences, 19,* 727–733.

Lubar, J.F. (1991). Discourse on the development of EEG diagnostics and biofeedback for attention-deficit/hyperactivity disorders. *Biofeedback and Self-Regulation, 16,* 201–225.

Monastra, V.J. (2003). Clinical applications of electroencephalographic biofeedback. In M.S. Schwartz & F. Andrasik (Eds.), *Biofeedback: A Practitioner's Guide* (pp.438–463). New York, NY: The Guilford Press.

Petruzzello, S.J., Landers, D.M. & Salazar, W. (1991). Biofeedback and sport/exercise performance: Application and limitations. *Behavior Therapy, 22,* 379–392.

Raymond, J., Sajid, I., Parkinson, L.A. & Gruzelier, J.H. (2005). Biofeedback and dance performance: a preliminary investigation. *Applied Psychophysiology & Biofeedback, 30,* 64–73.

Schwartz, G.E. (1979). Disregulation and systems theory: A biobehavioral framework for biofeedback and behavioral medicine. In N. Birbaumer & H.D. Kimmel (Eds.), *Biofeedback and self-regulation* (pp.19–48). New York: Erlbaum.

Sterman, M.B. (2000). Basic concepts and clinical findings in the treatment of seizure disorders with EEG operant conditioning. *Clinical Electroencephalography, 31,* 45–55.

Vernon, D.J. (2005). Can neurofeedback training enhance performance? An evaluation of the evidence with implications for future research. *Applied Psychophysiology and Biofeedback, 30*(4), 347–364.

Wang, Y. & Hung, T. (2006). *Effects of neurofeedback training on EEG and pistol shooting performance.* Paper presented at the Conference for Chinese Society of Sport Psychology, Wuhan, China.

Wu, C., Lo, L., Lin, J., Shih, H. & Hung, T. (2007). The relationship between basketball free throw performance and EEG coherence. *International Journal of Sport and Exercise Psychology-Chinese Section, 5,* 448–469.

Zaichkowsky, L.D. (1975). Combating stress: What about relaxation and biofeedback? *Mouvement, 1,* 309–312.

Zaichkowsky, L.D. (1983). The use of biofeedback for self-regulation of performance states. In L.E. Unestahl (Ed.). *The mental aspects of gymnastics* (pp.95–105). Orebro, Sweden: Veje.

Zaichkowsky, L.D. (2009). A case for a new sport psychology: Applied psychophysiology and fMRI neuroscience. In R. Schinke (Ed.), *Contemporary sport psychology* (pp.21–32). New York, NY: Nova Science Publishers.

Zaichkowsky, L.D. & Fuchs, C.Z. (1988). Biofeedback applications in exercise and athletic performance. In K.B. Pandolf (Ed.), *Exercise and sports science reviews* (pp.381–421). New York, NY: Macmillan.

Chapter 27

Self-confidence and self-efficacy

DEBORAH L. FELTZ AND ERMAN ÖNCÜ

SUMMARY

Self-efficacy is an important attribute in sport performance. Athletes and coaches call it self-confidence and associate the concept with successful performance. This chapter presents the theory of self-efficacy in sport, including sources of self-efficacy information and consequences of high and low self-efficacy beliefs. Definitions of the terms self-confidence, sport-confidence, and self-efficacy are presented along with self-efficacy measurement methods. The chapter concludes with descriptions of methods to enhance beliefs of self-efficacy, and provides learning aids, review questions, and exercises.

INTRODUCTION

One's self-confidence or self-efficacy beliefs are considered to be one of the most influential psychological variables influencing achievement strivings in sport. For example, in the 2008 European Cup in football, sportswriters suggested that the Turkish team came from behind to beat the Czechs 3-2 in the quarterfinal, in large part, because of the team's strong confidence beliefs in their ability. The Turkish players went into the game having had previous similar success in coming from behind in the match before with Switzerland, and even though the Czechs had what most sports analysts considered the best goalkeeper in the world at the time, Petr Cech, they likely went into the match with a resilient sense of efficacy that carried them through to the end.

Although there are many examples of athletes, teams, and coaches who have attributed their successes to their staying beliefs in their capabilities, it is the amount of research evidence that supports these examples that gives weight to these claims. In the sport and motor performance field, there have been over 200 papers published on self-efficacy (Moritz, Feltz, Fahrback & Mack, 2000). This research has shown that approximately 16% of the variance in athletic performance can be attributed to self-efficacy beliefs—a very meaningful percentage in sport performance.

OBJECTIVES

After reading this chapter you should be able to:

1   Define self-efficacy, self-confidence, and sport confidence.
2   Explain the theory of self-efficacy.
3   Identify sources of efficacy information.
4   Discuss the influences of efficacy beliefs on behavior and sport performance.
5   Explain how to measure self-efficacy beliefs.
6   Identify ways to enhance self-efficacy beliefs.

DEFINING SELF-EFFICACY AND SELF-CONFIDENCE

The terms self-efficacy and self-confidence are used interchangeably in the sport psychology literature to describe *a person's perceived capability to accomplish a certain level of performance* (Bandura, 1977, 1997). This view of self-confidence is different from a global trait view that accounts for overall performance optimism (Feltz, Short & Sullivan, 2008). For instance, one's self-confidence or efficacy belief might be to sink 20 consecutive free throw shots in basketball, to outrun a particular defender in football, or to run 10 kilometers three times per week for the next month. The desired accomplishment might be very specific (e.g., running for the next three minutes at a very fast pace) or more broadly defined (e.g., performing successfully in one's sport this season). The degree of specificity at which self-efficacy beliefs are measured is determined by the context of the performance situation, and the situation to which one wishes to generalize (or predict).

The concept of self-efficacy was first defined by Bandura (1977). About a decade later, Vealey (1986) defined the concept of sport confidence as *the degree of certainty individuals possess about their capability to be successful in sport.*

Sport confidence has been conceptualized into trait-like and state-like components, with the former being associated with more enduring beliefs (e.g., beliefs about performing successfully in one's sport this season), and the latter being associated with specific sport contexts. Whether one uses the term sport confidence or self-efficacy, the concept of interest is the cognitive process by which athletes make judgments about their capabilities to accomplish a particular goal in sport.

Common to both constructs is the treatment of athletes' perceived judgment of efficacy as a cognitive mediator of their motivation and behavior within a goal-striving context. That is, self-efficacy judgments are about what one thinks one can do (e.g., I think I can ski down the most difficult slopes on the mountain), not about what one has (e.g., I have strong legs for skiing) or about one's sense of self-esteem (I value myself as a skier). Thus, both self-efficacy and sport confidence allow for a discussion of how the concepts relate to various motivational processes, including goal setting. This sets self-efficacy concepts apart from other self-concepts that are not set within a goal-striving framework, such as self-esteem.

SELF-EFFICACY THEORY IN SPORT

Bandura's (1977, 1997) theory of self-efficacy was developed within the framework of a larger social cognitive theory. In social cognitive theory, people are viewed as being in charge of their own cognitions and functioning. They can reflect on and appraise their own capabilities, plan future actions, and regulate their behavior. Bandura views self-efficacy belief as a common cognitive mechanism that mediates between sources of people's self-appraisal and their subsequent motivation as well as their thought patterns, emotional reactions, and behavior (see Figure 27.1). Efficacy beliefs are a product of a complex process of self-appraisal that relies on cognitive processing of diverse sources of efficacy information (Bandura, 1997). That is, people take in information from their environment and use it to make evaluations about their capability for a task. Bandura categorized these sources of information as past performance accomplishments, vicarious experiences, verbal persuasion, and physiological states, which we explain in more detail in the next section of the chapter.

Efficacy beliefs, in turn, are hypothesized to influence the challenges people undertake, the effort they expend in the activity, and their perseverance in the face of difficulties. Efficacy judgments are also hypothesized to influence certain thought patterns and emotional reactions, such as pride, shame, happiness, and sadness, which also influence motivation. As Feltz, Short, and Sullivan (2008) note, these motivated behaviors and thought patterns are important contributors to performance in sport. "High-efficacious athletes are not afraid to pursue challenging goals, they cope with pain, and they persevere through setbacks. Athletes with low self-efficacy avoid difficult goals, worry about possible injury, expend less effort, and give up in the face of failure." (p. 5).

Bandura (1977, 1997) has provided some qualifiers to the predictive power of self-efficacy judgments. Self-efficacy beliefs are a major determinant of behavior and performance only when people have sufficient incentives to act on their self-perceptions of efficacy and when they possess the requisite skills. Some people may have the necessary skill and high self-efficacy beliefs, but no incentive to perform. Self-efficacy beliefs exceed actual performance when there is little incentive to perform the activity or when physical or social constraints are imposed on performance. According to Bandura, discrepancies between efficacy beliefs and performance will also occur when tasks or circumstances are

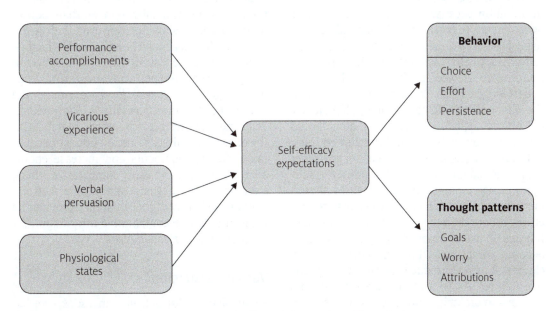

Figure 27.1 Relationship between sources of efficacy information, efficacy judgments, and consequences.

complex or ambiguous, or when one has little information on which to base efficacy judgments. For instance, when one is first learning a skill, there is little experience on which to base an accurate efficacy judgment. Likewise, in tasks that are complex, one may have more difficulty assessing one's capability accurately.

Sources of efficacy information

One may wonder how people form their self-efficacy beliefs. Bandura (1997) theorizes that self-efficacy judgments rely on the cognitive processing of different sources of information. This process involves selecting information from one's environment, interpreting that information, and integrating it to form an efficacy judgment. As mentioned previously, Bandura categorized these sources of information as past performance accomplishments, vicarious experiences, verbal persuasion, and physiological states.

Performance accomplishments

Bandura proposed that one's past performances provide the most dependable source of efficacy information because they are based on one's own mastery experiences. If one has cognitively processed these experiences as successes, self-efficacy beliefs will increase; if these experiences are viewed as failures, self-efficacy beliefs will decrease. Thus, if an athlete thought she was successful in her past few golf matches, her efficacy beliefs for the next match should continue to build; however, if she viewed them as failures where she did not meet her goals, her confidence should wane. Additionally, the self-monitoring or emphasis on successes should provide more encouragement and enhance self-efficacy more than the self-monitoring of one's failures. However, sport participants can also become complacent through success, which can result in performance plateaus or competitive failures. As Feltz et al. (2008) noted, this happens more with proficient athletes than with those who are developing their skills. If

athletes continue to set challenging goals for themselves and maintain positive reactions to substandard performances they are more apt to maintain their efficacy beliefs and motivation to continue achievement striving.

Vicarious experiences

Vicarious sources of efficacy information are based on information gained from observing and comparing oneself to others. If one views one or more other individuals successfully mastering a task, this may provide information that the task is learnable or the challenge is surmountable. For instance, a young diver, who may not have attempted a jackknife dive before, observes another young diver who has mastered the dive and gains efficacy information that he can master this dive, too. People can also generate efficacy beliefs by imagining themselves or others behaving successfully or unsuccessfully in anticipated performances. Imaginal experiences are sometimes viewed as a separate category of information (Maddux, 1995). However, Bandura (1997) refers to this source as cognitive self-modeling and describes it as a form of vicarious influence. These types of information are thought to be generally weaker than performance accomplishments; however, their influence on self-efficacy can be enhanced by factors, such as perceived similarities to the person being observed who performs successfully (e.g., in age, gender, or skill level), or imagining oneself performing successfully. For instance, Feltz and Riessinger (1990) showed that imagining oneself winning against an opponent could raise efficacy judgments and increase endurance performance. In using comparative others, Bandura (1997) suggests that people who are similar or slightly higher in ability provide the most informative comparative information for judging one's own capabilities.

Verbal persuasion

Persuasive information includes verbal persuasion, evaluative feedback, expectations by others, self-talk, and other cognitive strategies. Coaches, teachers, parents, and peers widely use persuasive strategies to influence an athlete's perceptions of efficacy. Self-efficacy beliefs based on persuasive sources are also likely to be weaker than those based on one's accomplishments, according to the theory. Words of encouragement from others are not as strong as one's own experience. However, the strength of the persuasive influence on self-efficacy depends on the prestige, credibility, expertise, and trustworthiness of the persuader. Thus, in sport settings, a trusted coach can have stronger persuasive influence on an athlete's self-efficacy than other individuals. Persuasive influences can also undermine one's confidence more easily than it can enhance it. Bandura (1997) indicates that the debilitating effects of persuasory information are more powerful than the enabling effects. As Feltz et al. (2008) note, it is more difficult for a coach to enhance strong beliefs of self-efficacy by persuasion alone than it is to undo those beliefs. Thus, coaches must be careful in the feedback that they provide regarding their athletes' strengths and weaknesses in order to cultivate a strong sense of efficacy.

Physiological information

Physiological information includes autonomic arousal that is associated with fear and self-doubt or with being psyched-up and ready for performance, as well as perceptions regarding one's fitness, fatigue, and pain. Physiological information influences efficacy beliefs positively or negatively depending on how individuals interpret it. For instance, an athlete could associate his or her level of autonomic arousal with fear and self-doubt or with being "psyched up" and ready for performance. Although physiological information also is considered a weaker form of efficacy information compared to mastery experiences, it has been shown to be more important in sport and physical activity tasks than in non-physical tasks (e.g., Feltz & Riessinger, 1990).

Similarly to physiological information, one's emotional state can be a supplementary source of information in forming efficacy perceptions. Positive affect states, such as happiness, exhilaration, and tranquility, can enhance efficacy judgments, whereas negative affective states, such as sadness, anxiety, and depression, are associated with uncertainties about performing a certain task (Bandura, 1997).

Unique sources of sport confidence

Vealey and her colleagues extended the sources of information beyond self-efficacy theory to identify the most salient sources of confidence for athletes based on the unique sociocultural aspects of sport competition (Vealey, Hayashi, Garner-Holman & Giacobbi, 1998). They developed the Sources of Sport Confidence Questionnaire (SSCQ) to measure nine sources of confidence information specific to the sport setting. Most of the sport confidence sources of information overlap with Bandura's categories. However, those that are unique to the sport context include physical self-presentation, coaches' leadership, environmental comfort, and situational favorableness. Physical Self-Presentation pertains to athletes' perceptions of their physical selves (e.g., "feel good about my weight"). Coaches' Leadership is a source of confidence based on the athlete's belief in the coaches' skills in decision making and leadership skills (e.g., "believe in my coach's abilities"). Environmental Comfort is based on feeling comfortable in a competitive environment such as a particular field, gymnasium, or pool where competition will occur (e.g., "perform in environment I like"). Situational Favorableness involves gaining confidence by feeling that the breaks of the situation are going in one's favor (e.g., "get breaks from the officials"). Thus, if athletes feel good about their physical selves, believe in their coaches' abilities, feel comfortable in their competitive environment, and think the competitive situation is in their favor, they should have higher confidence in their ability to achieve success.

People use multiple sources of information to make judgments of their confidence to perform a task, although some sources are more influential than others. In the athletic realm, past performance accomplishments and mastery experiences have been shown to be the strongest source of efficacy information for judging one's capability (Feltz et al., 2008). Vealey et al. (1998) found that high school and collegiate athletes gained most of their confidence in their sport from mastery and demonstration of ability (similar to performance accomplishments), physical and mental preparedness (similar to physiological and emotional states), social support (similar to verbal persuasion), and physical self-presentation factors. How various sources of information are weighted and processed to make judgments by individuals is still unknown, but various strategies and interventions based on one or more sources of efficacy information, can alter self-efficacy beliefs.

Influences of efficacy beliefs on behavior and sport performance

As described within self-efficacy theory, the consequences of people's efficacy judgments determine their motivation, as reflected in the challenges they undertake, the effort they expend on those challenges, and their perseverance in the face of difficulties. Their efficacy judgments also may influence their success or failure images, worries, goal intentions, and causal attributions.

Challenges undertaken

According to Bandura (1997), people will choose to undertake physical challenges and set goals that they believe they can master and will avoid those that they think exceed their capabilities. Research in sport supports this hypothesis (Feltz et al., 2008). In addition, people set goals based on their perceived self-efficacy. Those with higher levels of self-efficacy will choose more challenging goals than those with lower levels of efficacy beliefs.

Effort and perseverance

One's efficacy beliefs also influence the degree of effort one expends to reach one's goals and perseverance in the face of challenges and obstacles. In athletic performance, effort and perseverance are strongly associated with high performance results, especially in training and endurance activities (Feltz et al., 2008).

Thought patterns and emotional reactions

According to self-efficacy theory, perceived self-efficacy influences stress and anxiety through one's beliefs about personal control of actions, thoughts, and affect (Bandura, 1997). Athletes with high self-efficacy focus on the challenge and what they need to do to accomplish their goal. Athletes with low self-efficacy tend to worry about defeat, possible injury, or the inability to control their stress. These thought patterns lead to anxiety reactions and feelings of nervousness, distress, and tension.

However, the emotional arousal that is involved in performance situations may not always be perceived as debilitative anxiety. Self-efficacy has been shown to influence an athlete's interpretation of emotional arousal. Athletes with higher self-efficacy perceive their emotional arousal as more facilitative than debilitative. They may rate themselves as being nervous about the performance, but consider this high level of nervousness to be helpful to their performance. Athletes with lower levels of self-efficacy are more likely to interpret their emotional arousal as anxiety arousal and a sign of their inability to prevent, control, or cope with the potential difficulties of the competitive situation.

Athlete's efficacy beliefs for coping with competitive pressure and controlling negative thoughts may be more important for alleviating feelings of anxiety than their efficacy beliefs about being a skillful performer. Athletes who have a high sense of confidence in their ability to control anxiety are more able to remain task focused instead of thinking about the pressure at hand. They are also more able to cope with mistakes and failure and not let their performance shortfalls interfere with the performance of the moment.

Performance

One's goal choices, effort, persistence, and thought patterns are important contributors to performance. Additionally, as Bandura (1997) notes, in sport, efficacy beliefs for performance include reading shifting game situations, selecting effective performance strategies, predicting opponents' likely actions, making in-the-moment decisions, utilizing visualization, managing pressure and setback situations, and managing distractions. Thus, the relationship between one's efficacy beliefs for performance and one's actual performance outcome is complex. Nonetheless, research has supported a consistent positive relationship between self-efficacy beliefs and sport performance (Moritz et al., 2000). Based on 45 different studies, Moritz and her colleagues determined that approximately 16% of the variance in athletic performance could be attributed to self-efficacy beliefs. And as Feltz et al. (2008) noted, because of the complex nature of sport performance, efficacy beliefs should not be expected to be the only predictor of performance. If performance measures are used where factors beyond one's control are partially responsible for the performance, such as winning percentage and finish place, then self-efficacy will not be as strong of a predictor of performance as performance is of self-efficacy.

MEASURING SELF-EFFICACY AND SPORT CONFIDENCE

In assessing self-efficacy, most researchers construct their own self-report scales tailored to their specific research question. Typically, a questionnaire is constructed by listing a series of tasks, usually varying in difficulty, stressfulness, or complexity on which respondents rate their certainty that they can execute the task on a 100 point probability. Self-efficacy scales have more predictive value when items are sufficiently difficult and challenging to distinguish difference among respondents. An example of such a scale is illustrated in Figure 27.2. For those interested in measuring the broader domain of sport confidence, Vealey's (1986) Trait Sport Confidence Inventory and State Sport Confidence Inventory should be used. Each inventory consists of 13 items, in which respondents rate their confidence on a nine-point Likert scale.

Self-efficacy beliefs have less predictive power if they are measured far in advance of performance because situational circumstances could change one's beliefs during the interval between efficacy judgments and performance assessment. This problem occurs in self-efficacy research in sport because it is difficult to obtain self-efficacy assessments after a contest has begun. Self-efficacy judgments are typically obtained within a 24-hour period before competition, but changes in beliefs can occur if athletes find themselves ahead or behind where they thought they should be during the contest.

ENHANCING SELF-EFFICACY BELIEFS

Bandura's theory of self-efficacy has very practical implications for athletes and coaches to enhance self-efficacy beliefs for sport performance. Based on the four major sources of self-efficacy information, strategies can be developed to enhance the efficacy beliefs of sport participants. Feltz et al. (2008) provided a review of how to enhance an athlete's sense of

Times:	Rating of certainty		
	Complete uncertainty		Complete certainty
15 seconds	0 ...... 1 ...... 2 ...... 3 ...... 4 ...... 5 ...... 6 ...... 7 ...... 8 ...... 9 10		
30 seconds	0 ...... 1 ...... 2 ...... 3 ...... 4 ...... 5 ...... 6 ...... 7 ...... 8 ...... 9 10		
45 seconds	0 ...... 1 ...... 2 ...... 3 ...... 4 ...... 5 ...... 6 ...... 7 ...... 8 ...... 9 10		
60 seconds	0 ...... 1 ...... 2 ...... 3 ...... 4 ...... 5 ...... 6 ...... 7 ...... 8 ...... 9 10		
1 minute, 15 seconds	0 ...... 1 ...... 2 ...... 3 ...... 4 ...... 5 ...... 6 ...... 7 ...... 8 ...... 9 10		
1 minute, 30 seconds	0 ...... 1 ...... 2 ...... 3 ...... 4 ...... 5 ...... 6 ...... 7 ...... 8 ...... 9 10		
1 minute, 45 seconds	0 ...... 1 ...... 2 ...... 3 ...... 4 ...... 5 ...... 6 ...... 7 ...... 8 ...... 9 10		
2 minutes	0 ...... 1 ...... 2 ...... 3 ...... 4 ...... 5 ...... 6 ...... 7 ...... 8 ...... 9 10		
2 minutes, 15 seconds	0 ...... 1 ...... 2 ...... 3 ...... 4 ...... 5 ...... 6 ...... 7 ...... 8 ...... 9 10		
2 minutes, 30 seconds	0 ...... 1 ...... 2 ...... 3 ...... 4 ...... 5 ...... 6 ...... 7 ...... 8 ...... 9 10		

Figure 27.2 Illustration of efficacy measure for abdominal strength.

self-efficacy. Space does not allow for a detailed presentation of these strategies here, but brief descriptions are provided. The interested reader should consult Feltz et al., Chapter 6, for a more in depth review.

Performance-based techniques

The strongest and most durable source of efficacy information is based on one's performance accomplishments. Thus, the strongest way to enhance self-efficacy beliefs is by facilitating performance improvement and success. Performance-based techniques to enhance self-efficacy include instructional strategies, such as providing a progressive sequence of modified activities for the targeted skill, breaking a difficult skill into parts, providing performance aids, physical guidance, or a combination of these strategies. For example, a coach or instructor could design a series of progressive skills to teach a young gymnast a round off in tumbling, could physically guide a diver through the movements of a dive, or could have a skier learn proper technique on a simulation training device before trying the technique on an actual ski slope. The idea is to build success based on relevant and realistic progressions and to remove physical guidance and performance aids as soon as possible to allow athletes to engage in self-directed mastery. Another performance-based technique uses simulated situations, such as one with built-in distractions that are as realistic as possible, where the athlete can practice a skill while trying to block out the distractions.

Modeling-based techniques

Models can also be a powerful way to enhance self-efficacy beliefs. Observing others when an athlete has had no prior experience with a skill is one way of providing information by which to judge one's own capability. For instance, if an athlete observes another athlete on his football team perform a bicycle kick, he may judge, by comparing his abilities to his teammate, that he can learn this skill too. Similarly, observing another athlete cope with a threatening situation reduces the uncertainty for the observer and, therefore, increases the predictability and preparedness for a similar situation. Feltz et al. (2008) suggest that the athlete model in this situation can describe problems, explain how they were overcome, as well as show that the next stage of the recovery can be reached. Similarity of personal characteristics (e.g., age, race, sex) is important, but similarity of skill sets is the most important factor in modeling. In essence, the similar model instills the sense that "If that athlete can do it, so can I."

Using multiple models can help to increase the effectiveness of modeling on self-efficacy. Bandura (1997) reasoned that the more people that an individual sees succeed at a skill, the stronger the confidence will be that he or she can succeed as well. Additionally, imagery (sometimes referred to as cognitive self-modeling, Bandura, 1997) can help improve skills. To be effective, the imagery should be structured to be slightly beyond what the athlete can do at that time. The imagery should be challenging but attainable.

Persuasion-based techniques

Persuasion strategies are best used in conjunction with performance-based techniques. Persuasion techniques involve effective communication from the coach (or instructor) to the athlete and include performance feedback and rewards. Performance feedback should be provided in a manner that is contingent to performance. Self-persuasion, in the form of self-talk is another technique that is often used among athletes (Vargas-Tonsing, Myers & Feltz, 2004).

In terms of effective communication, persuasive techniques are effective only if the persuader's communication (e.g., "you can win this race") is within realistic bounds. The extent of persuasive influence on one's self-efficacy beliefs also depends on the credibility of the persuader. For instance, if a coach's word has been realistic in the past, the athlete

should feel more confident after hearing the coach's reassurance. But, if a coach has been unrealistic about the athlete's capabilities and the athlete has come up short of expectations, the coach's word will lose credibility.

Performance feedback must be given contingently based on defined performance standards. Coaches or instructors should acknowledge mistakes, but can also focus on positive aspects of performance. Because losing is inevitable in competitive sport at some point, it should be redefined as a learning experience from which an athlete can gain valuable information. When an athlete loses or is unsuccessful, coaches and instructors should acknowledge the loss or failed attempt, and instead of only focusing on the things that went wrong, they should constructively appraise the performance, discuss the positive aspects, and make resolutions for improving performance in the future. In this way, losing and failure are kept in perspective and a negative experience can be tempered with the identification of learning experiences and constructive hindsight.

Athletes also can help persuade themselves through positive self-talk (Feltz et al., 2008). Athletes sometimes engage in negative self-talk or disruptive thinking. They talk themselves out of the possibility of success. Positive self-talk can help athletes correct the faulty beliefs that lead to an impaired sense of self-efficacy. Coaches can help athletes identify their faulty negative beliefs and replace them with positive statements.

Anxiety-reduction techniques

As stated previously, physiological arousal can also provide athletes with efficacy information. If athletes are experiencing a high level of anxiety in a task situation, they may interpret the anxiety as fear of not being able to perform successfully. These feelings of self-doubt can, in turn, increase further feelings of anxiety, resulting in distracted focus, inefficient information processing, muscle tension, and overall performance decrements. Techniques to prevent athletes from interpreting physiological arousal as the fear that they cannot cope successfully with the task at hand include some of the strategies already mentioned, such as self-talk and persuasion. In addition, relaxation techniques, such as deep breathing, controlled breathing, and progressive muscle relaxation, can be used to help athletes regain a sense of control over their physiological arousal levels, which can help them build a sense of coping control (Feltz et al., 2008). Reducing the anxiety levels of athletes helps to change their cognitive appraisal of the situation in a positive direction, resulting in higher efficacy expectations. However, these techniques may be more influential when combined with verbal persuasion that lowering arousal will improve performance.

CONCLUSION

Self-efficacy, the belief in one's own capability to accomplish a certain level of performance, is one of the most influential psychological variables to influence performance in sport. One can gain efficacy information from a number of sources, including past performance accomplishments, observations of others, verbal persuasion, and interpretations of one's physiological arousal. Coaches and instructors can help boost athletes' levels of efficacy expectations through techniques that are based on the sources of efficacy information. These techniques may also help experienced athletes, especially when they reach "performance plateaus" or "performance barriers." These barriers may represent a temporary loss of self-efficacy, and changing their performance beliefs may help them out of their performance slumps.

In addition to improving the performance of athletes, efficacy belief research has been extended to coaches, teams, and sports officials (Feltz et al., 2008). Coaching efficacy is the extent to which coaches believe they have the capacity to affect the learning and performance of their athletes, and is a significant predictor of coaching behavior and athlete and team performance. Team efficacy, a belief by team members in their conjoint capabilities to organize and execute the courses of action to accomplish a given level of team performance, has been shown to be positively related to team performance, especially in sports where team members must coordinate and communicate their actions for team success (Dithurbide & Feltz, 2012). Self-efficacy of sports officials is the extent to which referees believe they have the capacity to perform successfully in their job (Guillén & Feltz, 2011). Although a model of referee efficacy has only recently been developed, there are numerous research possibilities and techniques that could help sports officials to be more confident in their performance. Thus, the concept of self-efficacy can offer valuable insights into people's motivation and performance in all aspects of sport from athletes to coaches to teams, and sport officials.

LEARNING AIDS

1   Define and compare self-confidence and self-efficacy.

The terms self-efficacy and self-confidence are used interchangeably in the sport psychology literature to describe a person's perceived capability to accomplish a certain level of performance (Bandura, 1977, 1997). This view of self-confidence is different from a global trait view that accounts for overall performance optimism (Feltz, Short & Sullivan, 2008).

2   Define sport confidence.

Vealey (1986) defined the concept of sport confidence as the degree of certainty individuals possess about their capability to be successful in sport. Sport confidence has been conceptualized into trait-like and state-like components, with the former being associated with more enduring beliefs (e.g., beliefs about performing successfully in one's sport this season), and the latter being associated with specific sport contexts.

3   Describe two ways to enhance self-efficacy.

One technique to enhance self-efficacy, which is based on performance accomplishments, involves using a series of progressive skills to build success based on relevant and realistic challenges that the participant can master step by step.

A second technique is based on modeling, or observational learning, where the model provides efficacy information by which to judge one's own capability. This is especially helpful to those who have no prior experience with the task. The participant observes another (the model), of similar ability, performing the intended task, thus demonstrating that the participant can learn this skill, too.

4   Describe the importance of self-efficacy to performance in sport.

Efficacy beliefs influence performance in sport through the challenges athletes undertake, the effort they expend in practice and training, and their perseverance in the face of difficulties. Additionally, as Bandura (1997) notes, in sport, efficacy beliefs for performance include reading shifting game situations, selecting effective performance strategies, predicting opponents' likely actions, making in-the-moment decisions, utilizing visualization, managing pressure and setback situations, and managing distractions. Thus, self-efficacy beliefs are important in all aspects of sport performance.

5   Discuss the sources of self-efficacy.

Bandura (1997) describes four major sources of self-efficacy information: past performance accomplishments, vicarious experiences, verbal persuasion, and physiological states. Performance accomplishments are based on one's own mastery experiences, and have been shown to be the most dependable source of information. Vicarious experiences are based on social comparisons to the capability of observed others. Verbal persuasion is based on the persuasive communication by trusted others that the participant is capable of succeeding at the task, but can also include self-persuasion through positive self-talk. Physiological states are sources of information that include autonomic arousal associated with fear and self-doubt or with being psyched-up and ready for performance, as well as one's fitness, fatigue, and pain, for example, in strength and endurance activities. Physiological information is a more important source of efficacy information in sport tasks than in non-physical tasks.

6   Explain how to measure self-efficacy.

In assessing self-efficacy, typically, a questionnaire is constructed by listing a series of tasks, usually varying in difficulty, stressfulness, or complexity on which respondents rate their certainty that they can execute the task on a 100-point probability scale. Self-efficacy judgments are typically obtained within a 24-hour period before competition.

REVIEW QUESTIONS

1   What is self-efficacy? Provide two samples that demonstrate the importance of self-efficacy in sport

2   What are the sources of efficacy information that Bandura categorized?

3   What are the sources of sport-confidence?

4   What is the difference between sport-confidence and self-efficacy?

5   What are the advantages of high self-efficacy for sport performance?

6   How are the performances of athletes affected by low and high self-efficacy levels?

7   What are some ways to enhance self-efficacy in sport?

EXERCISES

1   Think of a skill or activity in which you lacked self-efficacy in performing or learning. Describe why you think you lacked confidence. What could have helped you to build your confidence?

2   Think of a skill or activity in which you had high self-efficacy in performing or learning. Describe why you think you had high confidence. What could have lowered your confidence?

3   Construct a scale to measure self-efficacy on some task with which you are familiar. Then test yourself on your self-efficacy belief for the task. After evaluating your self-efficacy, test your performance on the task. How close were you to your efficacy judgment?

4   Design a series of progressive skills in the sport of your choosing that would build a novice athlete's self-efficacy. Pay attention to relevant and realistic progressions. If physical guidance and performance aids are to be used, show how they are to be removed in a progressive fashion to allow athletes to engage in self-directed mastery.

ADDITIONAL READING

Dithurbide, L. & Feltz, D.L. (2012). Self and collective efficacy. In G. Tenenbaum, R. Eklund & A. Kamata (Eds.), *Handbook of measurement in sport and exercise psychology* (pp.251–263). Champaign, IL: Human Kinetics.

Feltz, D.L., Short, S.E. & Sullivan, P.J. (2008). *Self-efficacy in sport*. Champaign, IL: Human Kinetics.

Gilson, T.A. & Feltz, D.L. (2012). Self-efficacy and motivation in physical activity and sport: Mediating processes and outcomes. In G. Roberts & D. Treasure (Eds.), *Advances in* *motivation in sport and exercise* (3rd ed.) (pp.271–297). Champaign, IL: Human Kinetics.

Short, S. & Rose-Stewart, L. (2008). A review of self-efficacy based interventions. In S.D. Mellalieu & S. Hanton (Eds.), *Advances in sport psychology: A review*. New York, NY: Routledge.

Vealey, R.S. & Chase, M.A. (2008). Self-confidence in sport. In T. Horn (Ed.), *Advances in sport psychology* (3rd ed.). Champaign, IL: Human Kinetics.

REFERENCES

Bandura, A. (1977). Self-efficacy: Toward a unifying theory of behavioral change, *Psychological Review* 84: 191–215.

Bandura, A. (1997). *Self-efficacy: The exercise of control.* New York: Freeman.

Dithurbide, L. & Feltz, D.L. (2012). Self and collective efficacy. In G. Tenenbaum, R. Eklund & A. Kamata (Eds.), *Handbook of measurement in sport and exercise psychology* (pp.251–263). Champaign, IL: Human Kinetics.

Feltz, D.L. & Riessinger, C.A. (1990). Effects on *In vivo* emotive imagery and performance feedback on self-efficacy and muscular endurance. *Journal of Sport and Exercise Psychology, 12*, 132–143.

Feltz, D.L., Short, S.E. & Sullivan, P.J. (2008). *Self-efficacy in sport.* Champaign, IL: Human Kinetics.

Guillén, F. & Feltz, D.L. (2011). A conceptual model of referee efficacy. *Frontiers in Movement Science and Sport Psychology, 2(25)*, 1–5.

Maddux, J.E. (1995). Self-efficacy theory: An introduction. In J.E. Maddux (Ed.), *Self-efficacy, adaptation, and adjustment: Theory, research, and application* (pp.3–33). New York: Plenum Press.

Moritz, S.E., Feltz, D.L., Fahrbach, K. & Mack, D. (2000). The relation of self-efficacy measures to sport performance: A meta-analytic review. *Research Quarterly for Exercise and Sport, 71*, 280–294.

Vargas-Tonsing, T.M., Myers, N.D. & Feltz, D.L. (2004). Coaches' and athletes' perceptions of efficacy-enhancing techniques. *The Sport Psychologist*, 18, 397–414.

Vealey, R.S. (1986). Conceptualization of sport-confidence and competitive orientation: Preliminary investigation and instrument development, *Journal of Sport Psychology* 8: 221–246.

Vealey R.S., Hayashi, S.W., Garner-Holman, M. & Giacobbi, P. (1998). Sources of sport-confidence: Conceptualization and instrument development. *Journal of Sport & Exercise Psychology, 20*, 54–80.

Chapter 28

Coping with stress and anxiety

SHELDON HANTON AND STEPHEN D. MELLALIEU

SUMMARY

This chapter aims to outline the stress process and highlight the major strategies deployed to enable successful coping with stress and anxiety experiences in sport. Specifically, we seek to do the following: define key terms and concepts used within the stress, coping, and anxiety field; describe the demands performers encounter in relation to their involvement in sport and the anxiety and coping responses experienced as a result of these demands; summarize stress management interventions designed to *reduce* intensity of anxiety symptoms encountered and those that seek to *restructure* interpretations of anxiety symptoms from negative to positive (i.e. debilitative to facilitative); and, highlight the key personal and situational factors that sports psychologists need to consider when selecting appropriate interventions for performers to adopt in order to cope with the subjective appraisals and interpretations that underpin the experience of stress and anxiety symptoms.

INTRODUCTION

Lots of hockey fans think that every tough guy loves the fighting part of his job. Nothing could be more wrong. I can't think of anything more intense than to start a fight with a tough guy who loves it...I could be injured, hurting everywhere, it didn't matter. If I had to go, I simply had to...For every moment in the 60 minutes of a game, I had to remain alert and vigilant, ready to go nose to nose with another guy who was probably only in the lineup because his coach figured he was strong enough and mean enough to tangle with me. The state of stress it put me into was sometimes unbearable. Especially on nights when I didn't feel in top shape... those permanent feelings of anxiety and stress, when you add them to the constant fear...That's one of the reasons I've always said that this job is 10 percent muscle, 90 percent mental...And when a fight occurred, even though it almost never lasted more than a minute, I needed a lot more than the five minutes spent in the penalty box to recover from the stress and the massive dose of energy needed for it.

Former Montreal Canadiens ice hockey forward Georges Laraque, 2011

The high potential for the experience of stress in elite sport and the challenges associated with the environments that surround the modern day performer are widely acknowledged. Indeed, the stress, coping, and anxiety literature is one of the most studied and frequently cited topics within applied sport psychology. An integral element within performers' competitive preparation programs includes, therefore, some form of stress management focused on the achievement of an optimal pre-performance mental state and strategies to cope with in-event experiences. This chapter aims to outline the stress process and highlight the major strategies that can be adopted by athletes to enable successful coping with stress and anxiety in sport.

 OBJECTIVES

After reading this chapter you should be able to:

1 Understand key concepts and definitions within the stress, coping, and anxiety field.
2 Identify the common demands sports performers encounter and the anxiety and coping responses following exposure to these demands.
3 Summarize interventions designed to *reduce* the intensity of anxiety symptoms encountered.
4 Describe interventions designed to *restructure* anxiety symptom interpretations from negative to positive.
5 Highlight key considerations when selecting interventions for coping with stress and anxiety.

KEY CONCEPTS AND STRATEGIES FOR INTERVENTION

The stress process

Contemporary approaches in psychology have adopted a functional perspective to studying stressful encounters. Here, the focus is on a 'process' orientation that seeks to understand the individual factors that cause the production of emotion, such as anxiety, and the resultant actions or efforts to manage these experiences (Hackfort & Schwenkmezger, 1989). In sport psychology a common cognitive approach to the stress and coping process is Lazarus' (1991) cognitive motivational relational theory (CMRT). Here, the experience of stress is viewed as one of an ongoing judgment or evaluation (appraisal) of the demands an individual experiences in relation to themselves and their surrounding environment (i.e., the relationship between the person and the environment). One's view of potentially stressful situations (stress appraisals) typically focuses on whether threat, harm/loss, or challenge is likely to be experienced. Individuals evaluate the situation to determine if the demands placed upon them are likely to be stressful (primary appraisals) and whether they possess the necessary resources available for dealing with the stress and the likely outcomes that will ensue (secondary appraisal). Central to CMRT is the notion of transaction and the specific relational meaning construed by an individual operating in a particular environment. Transaction indicates the dynamic relationship that exists between the demands of the environment an individual faces and the resources they possess. Relational meaning is the label for the meaning a person interprets from their relationship with this environment. Based on these views, the individual will then attempt to cope with or manage the situation accordingly. The notion of coping is synonymous, therefore, with constantly changing cognitive, affective, and behavioral efforts to manage the specific internal or external demands present in the environment. The next section outlines some typical demands faced in sport by performers and the responses experienced in relation to these demands.

Demands encountered and responses experienced

The intense physical and psychological demands that performers are placed under in competitive sport emanate from a range of sources relating to competition, organization, and personal factors presented within the environment. Competitive stressors relate to the demands associated primarily and directly with competitive performance, while organization and personal stressors relate to the demands associated primarily and directly with the sports organization and personal life of the individual(s) respectively (Mellalieu, Hanton, & Fletcher, 2006). A range of stressors have been identified in the sport psychology literature, stemming mainly from competition and organization sources. For example, competition stress demands include: the physical preparation of the performer; the standard or level of the opponent; pressures and expectations to perform; team atmosphere; relationship issues with significant others; the nature of the event; and issues regarding self-presentation and social evaluation. Organizational stressors include, for example, factors such as the performer's role in the sport organization; sport relationships and interpersonal demands; athletic career and performance development issues; and, the actual organizational structure and climate of the sport within which the performer is operating.

Psychological responses to these demands are typically associated with the emotional experience of competitive anxiety. Competitive anxiety is viewed as a situation-specific negative emotional response to one's view of competitive stressors, and the general undertaking/ involvement in sporting competition, as threats. This response may include symptoms such as worry, along with a heightened perception of one's physiological state or arousal levels. These two distinct responses represent the cognitive and somatic components of anxiety. Within this multidimensional perspective, cognitive anxiety responses are the thoughts performers' experience in stressful situations such as worries, negative expectations, and apprehensions about performance (i.e., performers' mental responses to stressors). Somatic responses, on the other hand, are the performers' perceptions of their physiological arousal state in stressful environments (i.e., performers' perceived physical response to stressors). Symptoms categorized as somatic anxiety include muscular tension, butterflies in the stomach, increased heart rate, and perspiration. The specific antecedents or causes of competitive anxiety include, for example, perceptions of readiness for peak performance; the performers' attitude toward previous performances; and, their perceptions of environmental conditions and position goal. Research also suggests that differences exist as a function of characteristics related both to the individual (personal) and the environment itself (situational) including gender, the skill level of the individual, and the nature of the sport. For example, female performers' cognitive anxiety experiences have been shown to be predicted by their perceptions of their readiness to perform and the importance of doing well, while males' cognitive anxiety responses have been predicted by their perceptions of their opponents' ability in relation to themselves and their perceived likelihood of winning.

Despite its inherently damaging conations, negative emotions such as anxiety that occur as a consequence of the stress process can actually have beneficial effects for performance (Hackfort, 1991). Under certain conditions anxiety is viewed as a signal that indicates the presence of threat and stimulates action on behalf of the individual. Inherent within this 'action' are the functional effects of

Figure 28.1 The experience of stress in sport is a personal event that is very much unique to an individual. It has a multitude of causes and leads to a wide range of cognitive, emotional and behavioral responses from athletes in an effort to cope effectively and perform successfully.

anxiety upon an individual's attention, planning, motivation, and effort towards managing the demands placed upon them (i.e., the coping processes). The next section considers how performers 'cope' with the stress process, specifically their experiences of competitive anxiety, and how this helps to shape strategies for effective stress management.

STRESS AND COPING IN SPORT

As a consequence of the challenges and emotional experiences associated with sport individuals require the deployment of a range of cognitive, affective and behavioral strategies to cope with and subsequently produce effective and desirable performance (Crocker, Kowalski, & Graham, 1998). Coping strategies fall broadly into two categories. Problem-focused coping involves efforts to alter or manage the stress for the individual. Examples include goal setting, information gathering, problem solving, and time management. Emotion-focused coping reflects coping efforts to regulate the emotional response that emanates from the problem causing the stress (i.e., competitive anxiety symptoms). These may include relaxation strategies or efforts to change the meaning of the situation (Hardy, Jones, & Gould, 1996).

Although the concepts of stress, anxiety, and coping are inexorably linked, the sport psychology literature has traditionally tended to study each topic in isolation, particularly the literature on coping in sport. In sport psychology, strategies relating to the management of the experiences of stress in sport have typically fallen under the 'emotion-focused' coping umbrella. Indeed, a considerable amount of literature has investigated how and why negative emotional responses to the stress process, such as competitive anxiety, occur and how performers are able to successfully manage these experiences to perform effectively (see Thomas, Hanton, & Mellalieu, 2009). Emotion-focused coping efforts to manage stress can be considered into either the reduction or restructure approaches. Essentially, sport psychologists seek to teach performers to deploy cognitive, affective, and behavioral strategies to either 'reduce' the intensity of the competitive anxiety symptoms experienced, or 'restructure' their interpretations of the symptoms from a negative to a positive viewpoint (i.e., debilitative to facilitative). Within the reduction approach, stress management strategies include cognitive and behavioral relaxation and meditation techniques. For symptom restructuring, strategies include mental imagery and cognitive restructuring via self-talk. The following sections describe the content of such interventions in more detail.

Interventions designed to reduce intensity of anxiety symptoms

Interventions that seek to reduce the intensity of competition anxiety symptoms can be classified broadly into mental and physical approaches, and are based on the principle that the treatments should target or *match* the dominant anxiety symptoms that the performer experiences in a stressful encounter. If the anxiety response is predominantly somatic in nature (i.e., the intensity of the physical symptoms is greater than that of the mental symptoms), then the treatment is focused on attempting to reduce somatic symptoms. However, if cognitive anxiety symptoms dominate, a mental approach with less concern for the treatment of any physical anxiety symptoms is encouraged. Using the 'matching' approach sport psychologists select a treatment based on the performers' dominant anxiety responses.

The most common physical strategy used to reduce somatic anxiety symptoms is progressive muscular relaxation (PMR). Here, performers learn the skill of physical relaxation through a series of logical, progressive stages working towards the goal of being able to achieve a relaxed physical state rapidly in response to any stressful situation. The preliminary stage of learning the skill requires individuals to consciously tense and relax different gross muscle groups within the body and focus their attention on the difference between a tense (anxious) state and a relaxed (less anxious) one. Typically, to aid with mastering this process individuals use an audio track that contains instructions to guide them through the muscle groups of their body. Once they are able to attain a suitable state of physical relaxation, the audio track is removed and the performer is asked to simply relax the gross muscle groups (rather than tense *and* relax). Once proficient, performers progress onto the third stage, whereby they focus on some form of cue that acts as an association trigger to help activate the relaxed state. This trigger can adopt several forms. For example, performers may condition the response through the use of self-talk in the form of cue words such as 'relax.' Alternatively, a physical action, such as gripping the ball before preparing a run up to bowl a delivery in cricket, may be appropriate. Finally, an individual may use a trigger conditioned to the exhalation phase of their breathing. The fourth stage of the process seeks to transfer the use of the skill into more realistic settings. Here, performers are taught to avoid tensing the muscles that are not involved in a particular movement and actively relax those that are involved in the activity (during the time prior to movement). Up to this point, performers will have tended to hone their relaxation skills in non-threatening familiar environments that are typically quiet and comfortable. During the penultimate stage of learning the skill, performers work to integrate the technique into naturally occurring semi-stressful environments away from the sporting arena. This process requires performers to take two or three deep breaths focusing on their conditioned trigger during the exhalation phase of breathing to gain an associated level of physical relaxation. Examples of where this technique may be practiced include queuing whilst waiting for public transport, when running late for a social event, or when stuck in traffic while driving. The final stage of the PMR process involves application training whereby the performer practices their technique in increasingly stressful sporting environments. This may initially take the form of a training session, then a practice race or competition, and finally a competitive event or match (see e.g., Ost, 1988; Rotella, 1985).

A common mental relaxation technique used with sports performers is transcendental mediation (TM). With TM the goal for the performer is to learn the skill of cognitive relaxation through a series of steps designed to change their mental state from one of being anxious to one of being calm. Typically, the skill of TM requires performers progress through four stages to a desired outcome where they are able to lower levels of cognitive anxiety in a matter of seconds. In the first stage, performers learn a general meditative technique that focuses on breathing and the use of a mantra. A mantra refers to a word that is repeated to aid concentration in meditation exercises. Individuals are asked to introduce a mantra on each breath out, and once relaxed, count down from 10 to 1 on each exhalation and then upwards from 1 to 7 on each inhalation. An audio track is often provided to aid this process, containing relaxing music and appropriate verbal instructions. In the second stage, a further audio track is provided that contains verbal instruction but no music. The directions ask performers to focus on their mantra, and the counting procedure is subsequently reduced to 5 to 1 on exhalation, and then 1 to 3 on inhalation to shorten the time it takes to achieve mental relaxation. In the next stage, the audio track is removed altogether with performers instructed to discard all counting procedures and concentrate on inha-

lation and repeat their mantra phrase on every exhalation. During this phase, performers are also asked to transfer the skill into more realistic stressful settings (but away from sport) to reduce the mental anxieties experienced in these situations. The final stage, as with PMR, involves integrating this skill into progressively stressful sport environments (see Hanton, Thomas, & Mellalieu, 2009, for further details of the application of the technique to sport environments).

Other mental relaxation techniques to treat cognitive anxiety associated with the reduction approach include using calming mental imagery and autogenic training. Specifically, calming imagery can be used to help reduce cognitive anxiety whereby performers imagine themselves in a relaxing environment such as on a warm beach with the sound of the waves lapping the shore, or lying in a field on a pleasant summer's day. Autogenic training is essentially a form of relaxation training using self-suggestion whereby performers learn to associate a series of verbal cues and visual images with feelings of warmth and cold in different parts of the body. At the same time, performers practice the regulation of a number of physiological activities (e.g., heart rate) in response to these cues and images. Once performers have acquired these skills, they are then able to generate these responses to reduce cognitive anxiety symptoms as desired during stressful sporting encounters.

A number of alternative techniques exist to reduce cognitive anxiety that fall outside the classification of relaxation skills and include the use of the thought control techniques such as thought stopping or positive thought control. With thought stopping, performers are instructed to identify a trigger word such as 'stop' or 'no' to act as a technique to block the negative thoughts. Positive thought control is as an extension to the thought stopping process whereby rather than ending the process with the reciting of a blocking trigger word, performers are instructed to 'replace' the negative thought with a positive one to develop a more positive psychological orientation. Specifically, performers initially identify any negative thoughts experienced, block the thought using a thought stopping trigger word, and then replace the negative thought with a positive thought to create a positive cognitive orientation (see Hanton et al., 2009, for a full description of the technique).

On a final note, the 'matching' approach to coping with stress and anxiety advocates the use of these individual psychological skills as distinct treatment frameworks in line with the performer's dominant anxiety response (mental or physical). However, for certain sports the use of combined mental and physical treatment packages may be advisable to treat the full range of anxiety symptoms performers experience within stressful encounters. Further, situations may arise where reduction of anxiety symptoms may be unsuitable for the arousal and activation demands of the sport in question; the next section, therefore, considers an alternative approach.

Interventions designed to restructure anxiety symptom interpretations from negative to positive

Rather than attempting to alter the level or amount of anxiety symptoms, the restructuring approach suggests that sport psychologists should focus on the performers' appraisals or interpretations of these symptoms. Here, the experience of competitive anxiety is viewed as a natural process in elite sport with cognitive anxiety signifying the importance of the event and stimulating levels of effort needed to perform well, while somatic anxiety signifies physical readiness to perform. An overview of the strategies within the restructuring approach is one that advocates combining various techniques into an integrated framework. These focus on performers first using mental imagery to first recreate anxious thoughts and feelings, then adopting forms of self-talk (cognitive restructuring and rationalization) to challenge these experiences, and finally using

imagery once more to see themselves performing successfully in the stressful situation.

Typically, in a restructuring intervention performers are first asked to recreate symptoms associated with their anxious thoughts and feelings in relation to competition using mental imagery. Here, sport psychologist and performer use imagery scripts and audio tracks to aid the creation of symptoms. For example, the sport psychologist asks the performer to identify stressful situations where the images have been experienced, and then recall their experiences of these symptoms, possibly with the aid of video footage. Here, the performer is encouraged to include as much information as possible in order to recreate a vivid image. Finally, the performer uses the information gleaned to create a series of images that depict the experiencing of the symptoms associated with the stressful situations.

Once performers are able to recreate anxious thoughts and feelings, they are taught to restructure and rationalize symptoms via the use of self-talk and forms of cognitive rational-emotive behavioral therapy (REBT). Use of these skills is based on the notion that performers experience and appraise situations that lead to beliefs that are either rational (i.e., positive interpretation of anxiety symptoms) or irrational (i.e., negative interpretation of anxiety symptoms). Rational beliefs lead to functional (beneficial) consequences for performance, whereas irrational beliefs lead to dysfunctional (harmful) consequences. Performers apply REBT and self-talk skills to question the interpretation of the negative symptoms experienced and turn them around to form a positive interpretation, thereby creating beliefs that lead to functional consequences for performance. Traditionally, performers are taken through three progressive stages that focus on *identifying*, *disputing*, and then *replacing* negative interpretations of anxiety symptoms. First, performers record/describe the negative mental and physical anxiety symptoms they experience. Then, they *identify* that the symptoms are indeed irrational and will have a negative impact upon preparation and performance. This is achieved through guided questioning in relation to the symptoms they experience: 'Is my appraisal based on fact?' 'Does my appraisal help me achieve my sporting goals?' and "Does my appraisal help me to feel positive about my upcoming sport performance?" If the performers answer 'no' to these questions, then they are asked to challenge this initial appraisal and provide examples of how these interpretations can be *disputed*. Performers are then taught to change the appraisal of their anxiety symptoms by questioning whether symptoms experienced such as tension and worry are invariably detrimental to performance. Performers are asked to replace these thoughts with ones that suggest the worries they experience are natural and highlight the personal importance of the event, creating an importance that equates to increased effort and a more focused and concentrated state. Finally, performers are educated to consider that the physical symptoms they are experiencing actually indicate a level of physical preparedness for the task in hand and a readiness to physically perform optimally.

Following the rationalization and restructuring of symptoms mental imagery can be employed as a confidence management strategy to allow individuals to see themselves successfully managing the emotions that accompany participating in competitive sport (e.g., completing a pre-shot routine under stressful conditions). The content of such images fall broadly into two categories: mastery of performance-related plans (e.g., tactical plans/strategies being executed correctly) and specific skills related to the performers' role (e.g., successful shooting skills such as a penalty kick in soccer). Initially, the sport psychologist and performer develop a series of imagery scripts and audio tracks for the performer to use to perfect their imagery skills. For example, if the core of the imagery routine that performers require is to focus on images depicting mastery of certain skills within their sport under stress-

ful conditions, the sport psychologist asks the performer to: (a) record the key skills for their role in their sport, for example, shooting skills as a goal attack in netball; (b) recount recent good performances of these skills, possibly making use of video at this point; and (c) include as much information as possible to recreate a vivid image of the performer's mastery of the skill. The psychologist and performer then use this information to create a series of imagery routines the performer can use to create images depicting mastery of skills while experiencing the symptoms associated with the stressful situation. The input of the performer into this process and the use of their knowledge base of the sport is a key feature in creating individualized imagery routines that have relevance to the performer. After gaining competence at recreating images in non-threatening situations away from the competitive arena, the performer incorporates the use of the skill into progressively increasing stressful environments within their sport (i.e., training, practice matches, main events) to gain full control over the skill in intense, pressurized competitive settings.

A further strategy to assist performers to gain control over themselves, the situation, and the symptoms they experience is goal setting. Specifically, performers maintain a greater degree of control over process goals (demonstration of a certain behavior, skill, or strategy related to a sport task) and performance goals (absolute or self-referenced value e.g., a split time in a 800m race) than outcome goals (competitive outcomes i.e., match result or position in a race). Consequently, when performers maintain greater levels of control over a situation they are more likely to interpret their anxiety symptoms as positive toward performance. Performers working towards developing positive anxiety interpretations should therefore be encouraged to set performance and process goal types. Although perceived controllability over outcome goals can be a concern for a performer, and unrealistic outcome goals can actually create anxiety, the potent motivational properties of outcome goals cannot be ignored. Therefore, performers should set all three types of goals, but place a greater degree of importance on performance and process goals as the competitive event becomes more imminent. Hanton et al. (2009) provide an excellent overview contribution for the reader to learn more about these techniques in further detail.

The key distinction of restructuring interventions over those that solely seek to reduce the level of anxiety experienced is the presence of an appraisal process whereby performers gain control over themselves, the situation, and the symptoms they experience in stressful environments. A range of psychological techniques has been advocated to allow performers to gain control over their anxiety and restructure and interpret symptoms (both mental and physical) as helpful (or positive) for optimal performance. The combination of these various techniques into an integrated framework is advocated in order to create individualized psychological skills programs that are designed to meet the specific needs of the performer. In this respect the following section outlines further considerations for the design of strategies to cope with stress and anxiety in sport.

Key considerations when selecting interventions for coping with stress and anxiety

In seeking to apply intervention strategies with performers, a number of individual difference variables have been identified for consideration in the scientific literature with respect to how performers respond to the demands of competition (Mellalieu et al., 2006). These relate to the characteristics of the client themselves (personal) and the context in which they compete (situational) and include the level or amount of a number of traits associated with self-confidence, resiliency and mental toughness, the type of sport/activity engaged in, the skill level of the performer, and the timing of the intervention strategy.

One of the most consistent findings in the stress and coping literature is that individuals who perceive their intense symptoms associated with the competitive anxiety response as facilitative or helpful to performance also report greater levels of self-confidence than performers who view anxiety symptoms as negative and debilitating. Above all other individual difference variables, therefore, self-confidence may be the most significant factor in discriminating how performers interpret and cope with stressful situations. Specifically, elite performers use self-confidence to buffer debilitating interpretations of competitive anxiety via cognitive confidence management strategies that include mental rehearsal, thought stopping, and positive self-talk. Confidence protection strategies should therefore be developed with performers that seek to build robust appraisals of their enactive mastery or performance accomplishments, as they appear to have the strongest influence upon self-confidence symptoms and protection against negative anxiety interpretations. In conjunction with the use of mental imagery, individual-specific mental skill packages should therefore be developed that incorporate other forms of confidence/efficacy enhancement. These may include forms of verbal persuasion such as positive self-talk or external encouragement from the coach or significant others. Further, the recent literature suggests that a range of factors linked to performance accomplishments, mental and physical preparation, social support and psychological skills, particularly coping strategies and self-awareness techniques, help to develop the breadth (i.e., sources and types) and the strength of the beliefs performers hold about their confidence (see Chapter 29 for further detail on increasing self-confidence and expectations).

A further personal factor for consideration for the practitioner is the traits and psychological skills associated with resiliency and mental toughness. In particular, hardiness, a form of dispositional resilience, has been associated with lower levels of worry and a more facilitative interpretation of the anxiety response in elite performers when compared to their less successful or non-elite counterparts. A possible mechanism for this influence may be the hardy performer's ability to transform their view of the stressful encounter they are experiencing into a more positive fashion, termed transformational coping and aligned to the restructuring approach to stress management outlined in the preceding section. Sport psychologists should seek to identify and develop such behaviors within performers to enhance more resilient coping methods for dealing with stress and anxiety. In relation to how performers appraise or view the demands of competition is their disposition to respond to stress-inducing situations. Two broad categories of individuals exist in this respect: repressors and sensitizers (Byrne, Golightly, & Sheffield, 1965). Repressors seek to avoid anxiety-provoking situations and/or control the situation by downplaying it as harmless or insignificant. In contrast, sensitizers tend to approach threatening situations and react with increased attention. Consequently, sensitizers' threshold for an anxiety-inducing situation is lower and they are more likely to view situations as more threatening and stressful than repressors. Sport psychologists therefore not only need to work to develop skills that promote resiliency and confidence management in performers, but also appreciate the predispositions that may influence the level and experience of existing reactions to stressful encounters in sport.

In relation to the consideration of situational or environmental factors that influence the response to the demands of competition another prominent factor is the type of sport or activity engaged in. Although the relaxation strategies outlined in the earlier sections may be effective in reducing the symptoms associated with competitive anxiety intensity such techniques may not be appropriate for the activation and arousal demands of certain sports. In particular, the reduction of anxiety intensity may decrease the performer's activation state, and subsequent mental and physical

readiness for competition. Indeed, it may not be possible, or even desirable, to reduce such symptoms via these techniques due to the relative high levels of activation states required for task performance. In such circumstances, sport psychologists should attempt to develop strategies with performers that restructure negative interpretations of their competitive anxiety symptoms, rather than reducing symptom intensity *per se*. Further, performers may need to reduce symptom intensity, restructure cognitions, and then reactivate themselves to appropriate levels, particularly if they possess insufficient confidence to protect themselves against negative interpretations of symptoms (for a more detailed discussion on psyching-up strategies see Chapter 25 this volume).

Interestingly, to date, research has indicated that it is the more elite performers who may gain the most out of such an approach. The more advanced psychological skills used within the restructuring approach being better suited to higher-level performers. In contrast, for lower level skilled non-elite performers, programs based on reduction (i.e., relaxation) may be more suitable in the first instance, as these groups of performers consistently report lower self-confidence levels and negative anxiety symptom interpretations when compared to their elite counterparts. Elite performers who view their anxiety symptoms negatively, however, may be better advised to implement cognitive restructuring techniques using psychological skills and strategies to interpret their anxiety as facilitative to performance.

A final social or environmental variable is the time context within which the intervention is administered and the need to consider the amount of time (expressed as a percentage) or frequency with which anxiety symptoms about the competition occupies a performer's mind. The scientific literature indicates performers' intensity and frequency of experiences, and subsequent interpretation of emotional states changes over time in the pre-competition period, and in the lead up to, and during, an event. Detailed assessment of a performer's emotional patterns in the lead up to competition is therefore required to allow implementation of suitable reduction and/or restructuring cognitive intervention strategies to manage not only the intensity but also the frequency and direction, of the performers' thoughts and feelings across times scales beyond that typically associated with the hour before competition.

LEARNING AIDS

1   Explain Lazarus' (1991) cognitive motivational relational theory (CMRT) and its role in the stress process.

Cognitive motivational relational theory (CMRT, Lazarus, 1991) views stress as an ongoing judgment or evaluation (appraisal) of the demands experienced in relation to oneself and one's surrounding environment (person-environment relationship). One's view of potentially stressful situations (stress appraisals) focuses on whether threat, harm/loss, or challenge is likely to be experienced. Individuals evaluate the situation to determine if the demands placed upon them are likely to be stressful (primary appraisals) and whether they possess the necessary resources available in order to deal with the stress and the likely outcomes that will ensue (secondary appraisal). Central to CMRT is the notion of transaction and the relational meaning construed by an individual operating in a particular environment. Transaction indicates the dynamic relationship that exists between the demands of the environment an individual faces and the resources they possess. Relational meaning labels the meaning a person interprets from their relationship with this environment. Based on these views, the individual will then attempt to cope with or manage the situation accordingly.

2   Outline the demands encountered when competing in sport.

The demands that performers encounter in sport emanate from competition, organization, and personal sources. Competitive stressors relate to the demands associated primarily and directly with competitive performance, while organization and personal stressors relate to the demands associated primarily and directly with the sports organization and personal life of the individual(s) respectively. Competition stressors include: physical preparation of the performer; standard or level of the opponent; pressures and expectations to perform; team atmosphere; relationship issues with significant others; nature of the event; issues regarding self-presentation and social evaluation. Organizational stressors include: performer's role in the sport organization; sport relationships and interpersonal demands; athletic career and performance development issues; and, the actual organizational structure and climate of the sport within which the performer is operating.

3   Summarize the typical responses performers experience when competing in sport.

Responses typically associated with the emotional experience of competition relate to cognitive and somatic competitive anxiety. Cognitive anxiety responses are thoughts performers' experience in stressful situations such as worries, negative expectations, and apprehensions about performance (mental responses). Somatic responses are the performers' perceptions of their physiological arousal state in stressful environments (perceived physical responses). Symptoms categorized as somatic anxiety include muscular tension, butterflies in the stomach, increased heart rate, and perspiration.

4 Identify the different types of coping strategies performers use to manage stress in sport.

Coping strategies fall into two categories: Problem-focused coping involves efforts to alter or manage the stress for the individual. Examples include goal setting, information gathering, problem solving, and time management. Emotion-focused coping reflects coping efforts to regulate the emotional response that emanate from the problem causing the stress (i.e., competitive anxiety symptoms). These may include relaxation strategies or efforts to change the meaning of the situation.

5 Summarize the main techniques that psychologists recommend to performers to 'reduce' the intensity of symptoms experienced associated with competing in sport.

Interventions to reduce intensity of competition anxiety symptoms comprise mental and physical approaches, and are based on the 'matching' hypotheses (treatments target or match the dominant anxiety symptoms experienced in stressful encounters). The most common physical strategy to reduce somatic anxiety symptoms is progressive muscular relaxation (PMR). Here, performers learn the skill of physical relaxation through a series of logical, progressive stages and work towards the goal of being able to achieve a relaxed physical state rapidly in response to any stressful situation. The main mental relaxation technique used with sports performers is transcendental mediation (TM). With TM the performer learns the skill of cognitive relaxation through a series of steps designed to change their mental state from one of anxious to one of being calm using a combination of breathing and mantra techniques. Manta is a word that is repeated to aid concentration in meditation exercises. Other mental relaxation techniques to treat cognitive anxiety associated with the reduction approach include calming mental imagery, autogenic training, thought stopping, and positive thought control.

6 Describe a typical 'restructuring' stress management intervention for a performer.

The restructuring approach suggests sport psychologists should focus on the performers' appraisals or interpretations of these symptoms. Here, the experience of competitive anxiety is viewed as a natural process in elite sport with cognitive anxiety, signifying the importance of the event and stimulating levels of effort needed to perform well, while somatic anxiety signifies physical readiness to perform. An overview of the strategies within the restructuring approach is one that advocates combining various techniques into an integrated framework. These techniques focus on performers first using mental imagery to first recreate anxious thoughts and feelings, then adopting forms of self-talk (cognitive restructuring and rationalization) to challenge these experiences, and finally using imagery once more to see themselves performing successfully in the stressful situation. See also Case Study 2.

REVIEW QUESTIONS

1 Discuss the role of appraisal in how a performer experiences and manages the stress associated with competing in sport.

2 Consider how negative emotions such as anxiety that occur as a consequence of the stress process can actually have beneficial effects for performance.

3 Compare the two approaches to dealing with the symptoms associated with demands of competing in sport.

4 How can knowledge of the variables associated with the 'restructuring' approach aid the psychologist in designing interventions for coping with stress and anxiety?

EXERCISES

1 We present two case studies below highlighting approaches to treating competitive anxiety symptoms performers may experience. These case studies discuss Frank, a competitor in the Olympic sport of target rifle shooting, and Katrina, a performer in the Olympic sport of rowing.

Case study 1: Frank

The performer: Frank is a 33 year-old target rifle shooter who has been competing in his event for 11 years at the elite level.

Reason for referral: As a target rifle shooter, Frank had suggested to his coach and psychologist for the team that he was struggling to deal with potentially negative and distracting thoughts when preparing to shoot. In addition, he reported experiencing high levels of physical tension in his shooting arm and shoulder prior to firing. He indicated to the team psychologist that he was feeling anxious prior to his competitions, he felt his performances were below average, and that he did not remember thinking or feeling a similar way when he had performed at his best.

Background: Following this discussion between Frank, the coach, and the psychologist it was agreed Frank would spend some time working with the psychologist to address the issue. The psychologist asked Frank to fill in a series of validated questionnaires to assess the levels of anxiety Frank was experiencing. Frank would also keep a diary of any thoughts and feelings experienced directly before competing in important events. The psychologist sat down in a one-to-one consultation with Frank and discussed these issues. Based on these assessments the psychologist determined that Frank had high levels of both mental and physical anxiety both prior to performance and between shots on the rifle range.

Professional assessment: As relatively low levels of both mental and physical symptoms are required to achieve an appropriate activation state to demonstrate a readiness to perform in target rifle shooting, the psychologist recommended an intervention program that followed the reduction approach to the treatment of competitive anxiety symptoms. As Frank reported his level of negative thoughts (i.e., cognitive anxiety) and negative feelings (i.e., somatic anxiety) were inhibiting his performance, and the evaluation indicated both of these responses were high, the intervention targeted reduction of both physical and mental anxiety symptoms.

Intervention: An intervention program was constructed for Frank that comprised mental and physical skills to reduce the levels of symptoms he was experiencing. A progressive muscle relaxation program was provided to treat his physical anxieties, and a transcendental meditation program was

---

given to help to combat the mental anxieties he reported. Due to Frank reporting his symptoms as distracting both prior to and during competition (i.e., between shots), both programs were designed as full progressive techniques in order for Frank to be able to use them before competing and between shots on the rifle range.

Outcome: Following the successful learning and application of the physical and mental relaxation programs recommended by the psychologist (a process taking approximately a total of 14 weeks), Frank reported he could now control his physical symptoms effectively during competition. However, while he felt the transcendental meditation program was having a degree of success at reducing his mental anxieties, Frank suggested this was a minor distraction to him. The psychologist subsequently recommended the adoption of a calming imagery technique. Following a further five weeks of training and learning this additional skill, Frank reported that he felt comfortable and able to regulate mental anxiety levels experienced before and during shooting performance.

Case study 2: Katrina

The performer: Katrina is a 26 year-old competitive rower. She has competed in her event for five years at the elite level and represented her country at two World Championships and one Olympic Games. Although achieving the qualification time for the Olympic Games at her recent national trials, she felt that her performance and time in this regatta failed to satisfy her, or her coaches', expectations.

Reason for consultancy: As a competitive rower, Katrina had indicated to her national team's psychologist that prior to the recent Olympic trials and, indeed, during the warm up events to the trials, she was having problems dealing with distracting negative thoughts and high levels of muscle tension when in the waiting room preparing to race. Katrina suggested that she was conscious of these mental and physical symptoms prior to the race, indicating they were having a negative impact on pre-race preparation. While such symptoms had been ever-present throughout her career, more recently she felt unable to control their impact on herself and her performance.

Professional assessment: Following this discussion, Katrina and the psychologist agreed to put in place a program of work to alleviate Katrina's concerns. The psychologist asked Katrina to complete a series of validated questionnaires assessing pre-race anxiety levels and whether she viewed experiencing these symptoms as positive or negative toward impending performance. The psychologist included information relating to how Katrina was interpreting her anxiety-related symptoms due to the fact she had talked about a lack of control over how she thought the anxiety symptoms were likely to affect future performance. The psychologist also adopted an individual one-on-one interview with Katrina to seek further understanding of her anxiety responses. After this consultation it was determined that Katrina's levels of pre-event anxiety were high and that she interpreted these symptoms as having a detrimental effect on performance. Given that rowing is an explosive event that requires a high degree of power as well as controlled aggression, the appropriate activation state for Katrina that demonstrates a readiness to perform is one where she experiences a relatively high level of controlled physical and mental symptoms. Consequently, the psychologist recommended an intervention program that adhered to the principles of the restructuring approach.

Suggesting techniques that only sought to reduce Katrina's symptoms may have had a detrimental effect upon performance, due to the fact that she may have become too mentally and physically relaxed for the activation demands of this event.

Intervention program: An intervention program based upon restructuring the interpretation (negative to positive) of both mental and physical anxiety was provided to Katrina. The key focus of this program was to seek to enable Katrina to restructure her anxiety interpretations to one where she viewed her mental symptoms as indicators of the importance of the event and her physical ones as indicators of her physical readiness to perform. The psychologist also provided confidence maintenance techniques (i.e., mental imagery and goal setting) in order to help protect from the effects of potential negative interpretations of anxiety-related symptoms together with any subsequent performance decreasing effects resulting from the anxiety symptoms experienced. Over time, Katrina was tracked through the restructuring program outlined in this chapter. Specifically, the process educated Katrina to view her symptoms as a positive consequence for performance, removing the negative effects of anxiety on her race preparation.

Outcome: After undertaking the intervention program for a ten-week period, the treatment resulted in a reinterpretation of Katrina's anxiety from negative to positive without reducing the level of anxiety symptoms experienced (suggesting that Katrina had obtained a suitable state of activation prior to competition). Furthermore, Katrina reported after the intervention that her physical and mental symptoms now indicated the importance of the event, the amount of effort she was prepared to invest towards it, and how the symptoms could actually improve her performance.

ADDITIONAL READING

Hackfort, D. & Schwenkmetzger, P. (1993). Anxiety. In R.N. Singer, M. Murphy & L.K. Tennant (Eds.), *Handbook of research on sport psychology* (pp.328–364). New York: MacMillan Publishing Company.

Hanton, S., Thomas O. & Mellalieu, S.D. (2009). Management of competitive stress in elite sport. In B. Brewer (Ed.), *International Olympic Committee sport psychology handbook* (pp.30–42). Blackwell Publishing.

Thomas, O., Mellalieu, S.D. & Hanton, S. (2009). Stress management in sport: A critical review and synthesis. In S.D. Mellalieu & S. Hanton (Eds.), *Advances in applied sport psychology: A review* (pp.124–161). Routledge.

REFERENCES

Byrne, D., Golightly, C. & Sheffield, J. (1965). The Repression-Sensitization scale as a measure of adjustment: Relationship with the CPI. *Journal of Consulting Psychology, 29*, 586–589.

Crocker, P.R.E., Kowaloski, K.C. & Graham, T.R. (1998). Measurement of coping strategies in sport. In J. Duda (Ed.), *Advances in sport and exercise psychology* (pp.149–161). Morgantown: Fitness Informational Technology.

Hackfort, D. (1991). Emotion in sport: An action theoretical analysis. In C.D. Spielberger, I.G. Sarason, Z. Kulcsar & G.L. Van Heck (Eds.), *Stress and emotion: Anxiety, anger, and curiosity, Volume 14* (pp.65–73). New York: Hemisphere Publishing Corporation.

Hackfort, D. & Schwenkmezger, P. (1989). Measuring anxiety in sports: Perspectives and problems. In D. Hackfort & C.D. Spielberger (Eds.), *Anxiety in sports: An international perspective* (pp.55–74). New York: Hemisphere.

Hanton, S., Thomas O. & Mellalieu, S.D. (2009). Management of competitive stress in elite sport. In B. Brewer (Ed.), *International Olympic Committee sport psychology handbook* (pp.30–42). Blackwell Publishing.

Hardy, L., Jones, G. & Gould, D. (1996). *Understanding psychological preparation for sport: Theory and practice of elite performers.* Chichester, England: Wiley.

Laraque, G. (2011). *The story of the NHL's unlikeliest tough guy.* Canada: Penguin.

Lazarus, R. (1991). *Emotion and adaptation.* New York: Oxford University Press.

Mellalieu, S.D., Hanton, S. & Fletcher, D. (2006). A competitive anxiety review: Recent directions in sport psychology. In S. Hanton & S.D. Mellalieu (Eds.), *Literature reviews in sport psychology* (pp.1–45). Hauppauge, NY: Nova Science.

Ost, L.G. (1988). Applied relaxation: Description of an effective coping technique. *Scandinavian Journal of Behavior Therapy, 17,* 83–96.

Rotella, R.J. (1985). Strategies for controlling anxiety and arousal. In L.K.N. Bunker, R.J. Rotella & A. Reilly (Eds.), *Sport psychology* (pp.273–287). Michigan: McNaughton and Gunn.

Thomas, O., Mellalieu, S.D. & Hanton, S. (2009). Stress management in sport: A critical review and synthesis. In S.D. Mellalieu & S. Hanton (Eds.), *Advances in applied sport psychology: A review* (pp.124–161). Routledge.

Chapter 29

Perspectives on choking in sport

DARYL MARCHANT, ROUHOLLAH MAHER AND JIN WANG

SUMMARY

Thirty years of systematic and imaginative choking research beginning with Baumeister (1984) through to Land and Tenenbaum (2012) has shone a light onto seemingly every conceivable aspect of choking. Apart from Roy Baumeister, researchers including; Rich Masters, Sian Beilock, Geir Jordet, Chris Mesagno and Denise Hill have been key contributors both in quality and quantity to the now extensive body of peer reviewed choking research. The degree of interest in choking within the sport psychology community is also reflected in the media and the general public where choking remains a conversational chestnut every time a champion athlete fails under pressure or 'defeat is snatched from the jaws of victory' in a major event. While instances of choking provide additional drama, colour and unpredictability to major sporting events, sport psychologists are focussed on more fully understanding the choking phenomenon and providing strategies to reduce the likelihood of choking or beneficial solutions for athletes that experience choking repeatedly. Given that from a research resource perspective the topic of choking in sport rarely attracts funding, we believe sport psychology researchers have collectively made substantial steps in understanding what causes choking and are now substantiating useful evidence-based interventions.

INTRODUCTION

When elite athletes choke it represents a classic psychological conundrum. How can the performance of highly trained professional athletes deteriorate so rapidly, often just when victory seems almost assured? There seems little reason to doubt that high profile athletes who are touted as chokers in the media represent a minute proportion of athletes across the full spectrum of sports that have choked in

their careers. Aside from sport, there are a number of other performance domains (e.g., music, dance, public speaking, acting) where choking occurs. As discussed previously (see Marchant, 2010), rapper Eminem released the song *Lose Yourself* (2002) with the lyrics cleverly describing choking from a stage performer perspective and represents the occurrence of choking in performance domains Although, choking is not a serious threat to physical health and is sometimes treated as trivial or inconsequential, for some performers, such as professional athletes, the consequences can be more serious. Anxiety, distraction, missed opportunities, and frustration seem to prevail when choking is evident. Paradoxically, choking occurs despite high motivation and maximal effort from the performer.

 OBJECTIVES

After reading this chapter you should be able to:

1 Understand how choking in sport can be a serious occupational risk for professional athletes.
2 Define choking in sport and understand the key explanatory theories.
    3Appreciate the diverse range of mechanisms and underlying causes that have been linked with choking.
4 Better understand your own performances and observations in sport of poor performances under pressure.
5 Cite evidence-based treatments that have been shown to decrease susceptibility and/or increase resistance to choking.

PERSONAL REFLECTION

I (first author) vividly recall as a teenager my first (of numerous) experiences with choking in sport. In summary, our sports obsessed gang decided on a 'social' game of doubles tennis. Social sport was an anathema in our group with everything being highly competitive irrespective of the circumstances. On this occasion, I partnered Tony who was the only member of the group with a decent level of tennis expertise. This should have been an easy win, with Tony on my side how could we lose? What followed was an out of body experience (not in a flow kind of way)! I somehow managed to block or undercut a series of routine shots fully into the distant fence. I'm not talking about near misses but wild shots a few of which escaped over the high perimeter fence. The first few miss hit shots produced considerable mirth and astonishment in the group – *what is he doing?* I certainly felt weird, like some evil genie was gripping the racquet and hitting the ball. My initial bemusement was followed by embarrassment. During the game, I responded by conducting an ongoing causal search for an explanation, including an interrogation of Tony who after offering perfectly reasonable suggestions declared emphatically that "you are beyond help." I was then banished to the net and placed in charge of a one metre square piece of court space not technically out of court but practically rendering the game a one vs two affair. This first choking experience evoked a personal and sustained fascination that likely fuelled my professional interest in choking. Furthermore, it contained many of the hallmarks that have subsequently been shown to correlate with choking in sport, such as fear of negative evaluation, self-consciousness, anxiety and ineffective coping.

For professional and semi-professional performers, however, choking may be viewed as a serious career risk that can be accompanied by embarrassment, humiliation and derision depending on the level of media scrutiny. Although there is widespread anecdotal evidence of elite athletes choking for obvious reasons, it is difficult to substantiate the extent of choking in high level sport using traditional research methods. One of the few attempts to actually measure the extent of performance failure under pressure was recently conducted by Wells and Skowronski (2012) who in using archival data convincingly demonstrated that the performance of professional PGA golfers typically deteriorates in the magnitude of approximately .50 shots between the third and final rounds in PGA tournaments. Based on 2007 data, this type of third to final round score decrement equated to the difference between the 19th placed player and the 57th placed player in the tour average score. While Wells and Skowronski provided average data for all PGA tour players in calculating the average performance decrement, clearly the performance decrement for particular players (e.g., the 80–100 percentile of players on final round decrement) would likely fit the definition of choking as being a substantial decrement in performance and, although not reported, would be much greater than .50 shots. Recently, Mesagno and Hill (in press-a) have questioned how researchers have operationally defined choking and contend that researchers have often reported and possibly confused what is actually under performance as choking. Mesagno and Hill (in press-a) are concerned that the current definitions of choking are not explicit regarding the level of performance decrement that is required before using the term choking is justified. Mesagno and Hill (in press-b) and Jackson (in press), therefore, argue for more distinct and multi-level considerations of the magnitude of choking. Apart from the direct and indirect financial losses that result from habitually scoring poorly in the final rounds of tournaments there are knock-on effects in terms of psychological well-being, diminished enjoyment and goal achievement, reduced capacity for automatic entry into subsequent events and loss of prestige in being regarded as a player that does not perform well in pressure circumstances. (For additional evidence of how elite soccer players can struggle to perform under the pressure of executing penalty kicks see Jordet 2009a, 2009b, Jordet & Hartman, 2008 & Jordet, Hartman, & Sigmundstad, 2009.)

FROM BAUMEISTER TO THE PRESENT

An overview of choking research

to describe over 35 years of choking research the analogy of constructing a wall seems apt (sorry in advance if you find the analogy annoying). This analogy is also sometimes used in generic research methods. A sturdy or reliable wall is built on solid foundations (i.e., good theory). Each subsequent brick (e.g., study) builds on the previous brick and contributes to the overall size, strength and aesthetic of the wall. From a multi-dimensional perspective rather than a wall of knowledge, the image of the construct of choking as surrounded by interconnected walls of understanding perhaps works best. In what ways have researchers constructed the bricks in the walls of understanding choking in sport? There are now well over 100 published peer reviewed articles (i.e., bricks) in which choking features in the title. Are the foundations of the walls sound? To what points do the perpendicular walls meet? To what extent is the mortise able to bind the bricks into a unified edifice? Where are the strong points in the walls and where are the weak points or gaps currently? Interestingly, Mesagno and Hill (in press-b) have recently and independently used a brickyard analogy where they question whether choking researchers are adequately distinguishing the metaphorical edifice of knowledge (theory) from piles of bricks. Stated bluntly, after 35 years what do we know about choking? What solutions can we provide for athletes experiencing choking or for coaches working with these athletes? In what ways does current theory or current best practice require tweaking, alteration or a major makeover? This chapter is largely about answering these questions including a conclusion that looks at where we are at now.

Nearly 30 years ago Baumeister (1984), a social psychologist, published what is widely regarded as the first investigation of choking in sport. This seminal paper reported on the results of six related studies and sparked what has remained a hot topic of research, initially by social psychologists and subsequently by sport psychologists. Baumeister defined choking, developed a model of choking and successfully manipulated choking experimentally. The initial definition and findings were sufficiently interesting and equivocal to draw other researchers into choking research. The methods Baumeister and colleagues (e.g., Baumeister & Showers, 1986) used including; pressure manipulations, manipulation checks and measuring independent variables with self-report questionnaires are still widely used in choking research.

Baumeister (1984) simply defined choking as "performance decrements under pressure circumstances" (p. 610). In the ensuing years, researchers have argued for a more expansive definition primarily for the purposes of precision and uniformity of understanding in research. For example, Masters (1992) defined choking as "the failure of normally expert skill under pressure." (p. 344). Although, discussions on the adequacy of definitions are ongoing, two recent definitions are being regularly used in the related literature. Mesagno, Marchant and Morris (2008) defined choking as "a critical deterioration in the execution of habitual processes as a result of an elevation in anxiety under perceived pressure, leading to substandard performance (p. 439)." The Mesagno et al. definition was essentially a refinement on an earlier definition proposed by Wang (2002) who first pointed out that perception of

pressure, the level of performance decrement and habitual processes were necessary components of a choking definition. Wang defined choking as "deterioration in the execution of habitual processes of performance under pressure (p. 140)." Wang further explained that deterioration refers to a clear disruption in the quality of performance characterized by the performer trying too hard. Similar to other definitions, choking only occurs under pressure circumstances. According to this definition, choking reflects the combined problems of both perceptual control and skill execution. Pressure may cause these problems, resulting in an altercation of an athlete's habitual processes of performance. This process is repeated in a cyclical pattern, resulting in choking. Habitual processes of performance refer to performance patterns that performers typically execute. A second definition regularly used in the related literature proposed by Hill, Hanton, Fleming, and Matthews (2009) offers an alternative definition of choking "as a process whereby the individual perceives that their resources are insufficient to meet the demands of the situation, and concludes with a significant drop in performance (p. 206)."

Whichever definition is more representative of choking is possibly semantics, however, the critical elements of perceived pressure, anxiety and inappropriate attention result in a performance substantially below the normal level occurs and constitutes a choke. We intentionally use the term *choke* as is used in common sporting vernacular and strongly recommend that researchers discontinue using the term *choking under pressure* because pressure is a necessary condition for choking to occur, and hence the addendum *under pressure* is a tautology. Stated simply, if there is no perceived pressure, there will be no choke.

EXPLANATORY THEORIES OF CHOKING

Although, theories to explain choking have now been evolved considerably, in this first section, we provide an overview of the two

predominant generic models, namely self-focus and distraction explanations. In proposing the self-focus model (also referred to as explicit monitoring, automatic execution and execution focus in the related literature) to explain choking; Baumeister (1984) drew on a number of researchers. For example, Martens and Landers (1972) who suggested that focusing evaluative attention on the *process* of performance may impair the performance more than focusing attention on the performance *outcome*. In the context of coaching practices where an outcome focus is eschewed in favour of a process focus, the Martens and Landers finding runs counter to conventional wisdom, and hence provides a potential alternative or caveat for particular types of high pressure situations. Numerous examples can be found in the early sport psychology literature where theorists subscribe to the importance of focussing on the performance process. Nideffer and Sagal (1998) recommended that athletes use the 'process focus' while performing to reduce the distraction of an 'outcome focus'. For example, Nideffer and Sagal provided an example of avoiding an outcome focus by suggesting that in competitions swimmers should attend to some technical aspect of their stroke during performance. The subsequent years of research in choking has resulted in sports psychologists being more reticent to subscribe to a unilateral process focus, particularly for choking-susceptible athletes in pressure circumstances. Baumeister described his understanding of the self-focus model; under pressure, a person realizes consciously that it is important to execute the behavior correctly. Consciousness attempts to ensure the correctness of this execution by monitoring the process of performance (e.g., the coordination and precision of muscle movements); but consciousness does not contain the knowledge of these skills, so that it ironically reduces the reliability and success of the performance when it attempts to control it (p. 610).

In further explaining self-focus, Lewis and Linder (1997) emphasized the centrality of self-awareness (S-A) and the potential for competition, audiences, ego-relevance, reward and punishment contingencies to heighten S-A. Beilock and Carr (2001) described *Self-focus* theories as pressure raising self-consciousness and anxiety about performing correctly, that in turn increases the attention to skill processes and their step-by-step control. Attention to execution at this step-by-step level is thought to disrupt well-learned or proceduralized performances. Put another way, Masters (1992) stated that in pressure situations, individuals begin thinking about how they are executing the skill, and attempt to control it with their explicit knowledge of movement mechanics.

Supporters of self-focus theories have explained that increased levels of self-awareness (S-A) result in athletes inwardly focusing attention. Self-focus theories are contingent on stages of learning (Fitts & Posner, 1967). A novice during performance for example, attends to the explicit rule-based aspects of the skill rather than executing the task automatically. According to self-focus theorists, the process of well-learned and automated tasks is implicitly outside working memory and breakdowns in performance result from reinvestment in well-learned skills and conscious processing through working memory (Hill et al., 2010b; Masters & Maxwell, 2008). Explicit Monitoring Hypothesis (EMH; Beilock & Carr, 2001), and in particular, the Consciousness Processing Hypothesis (CPH; Masters, 1992) are the most renowned and cited self-focus theories. The key distinction is that Beilock and Carr in describing EMH state that step-by-step *monitoring* of performance causes the disruption in the execution of skills, whereas when Masters describes CPH he states that conscious *controlling* of the performance is detrimental. The available evidence shows that disrupting conscious control supersedes explicit monitoring as a detrimental performance explanation (Hill et al., 2010b; Jackson, Ashford, & Norsworthy, 2006). Attentional Threshold Hypothesis (ATH; Hardy, Mullen, & Martin, 2001; Mullen, Hardy, & Tattersall, 2005) has been proposed as an alternative hypothesis for CPH to explain performance decrements owing to the combination of anxiety-related cognitions and explicit instructions that exceed the attentional capacity threshold. Correspondingly, anxiety occupies a part of attentional resources normally required for performance. Hence, diminution of attentional resources has a detrimental effect on performance, when both components, anxiety-related cognitions and explicit instructions, are added collectively and individually (Gucciardi & Dimmock, 2008; Mesagno, Marchant & Morris, 2009; Mullen, Hardy, & Tattersall, 2005).

When skilled performers are required to focus on performance suddenly, they normally lack specific information about skill execution, because they are not accustomed to thinking about the specific process while performing. This raises the interesting and seemingly counter-intuitive possibility that as sports people become more increasing skilled and their level of explicit skill execution knowledge increases commensurately they become increasingly vulnerable to performance degradation under stress (Liao & Masters, 2002). Consequently, Beilock and Carr (2001) have pointed out that despite have a large amount of explicit knowledge at their disposal experts develop a type "expertise-induced amnesia" (p. 703) might be considered expertise-induced *inattention* because experts generally do not attend to explicit procedural knowledge when performing skills.

The primary alternative to self-focus models are generically termed distraction models and are founded on the belief that decrements in performance under pressure occur because of interference with task concentration that creates a type of dual task where the performer is switching between task relevant and task-irrelevant cues (Lewis & Linder, 1997). Distraction, by definition, is any stimulus or response requirement irrelevant to the individual's primary task whether it is an external or an internal stimulus (Sanders, Baron & Moore, 1978). In pressure situations individuals may accept too much information during performance, thus reducing their ability to focus on the task at hand. As a consequence, increased arousal leads to narrowing attention, resulting in a conflict between attending to the task at and attending to distracting stimuli (Sanders & Baron, 1975). Furthermore, Sanders et al. proposed that the increased arousal is likely to impair performance on complex tasks, because such tasks require more attention resources. Researchers have tested and reported positively on the relevance of Processing Efficiency Theory (PET; Eysenck & Calvo, 1992), a revised version of distraction theory, whereby athletes sometimes overcome inefficient processing under pressure by applying increased effort (Murray & Janelle, 2003; Wilson, 2008; Wilson, Smith, & Holmes, 2007). Employing effort, however, may not be sufficient or advisable in pressure circumstances, because attentional capacities may be overwhelmed by virtue of high levels of anxiety (Williams, Vickers, & Rodrigues, 2002; Hill et al., 2010b). Recently, PET has been developed and represented as Attentional Control Theory (ACT; Eysenck, Derakshan, Santos, & Calvo, 2007). The interaction of two attentional systems including a stimulus-driven system and a goal-driven system determines attentional selection. It is presumed that anxiety damages the efficiency of the goal-driven system and decreases attentional control through focusing attention on the stimulus-driven system. Applying compensatory strategies, such as increased effort, however, may avoid decrements in performance effectiveness (Moser, Becker, & Moran, 2012; Wilson, 2008).

Beilock and Carr (2001) pointed out that self-focus models and distraction models are based on different mechanisms causing choking and can be viewed as opposite explanations. Comparing and contrasting explanatory models is important, because a therapeutic intervention might emphasize reducing the athlete's distractions and refocusing on task-relevant features while performing. If a self-focus model is used, however, to drive practice, interventions to reduce choking might emphasize attention away from the specific aspects of skills during performance. Despite these differences in underlying mechanisms, Beilock and Carr have demonstrated different instances where both self-focus and distraction explanations are applicable. For example, distraction theory is most applicable when skill execution is reliant on working memory for storage of decision and action-relevant information. Whereas, distraction models may be more applicable for strength and endurance dominant tasks and for novice and medium ability performers who have not fully automated their skills (Wang, 2002). In using a well-designed sequence of interrelated studies Beilock and Carr found that self-focus theories were the primary cause of choking but also cautioned that the most applicable theory is possibly dependent on (a) task complexity, (b) the degree that tasks become proceduralized with practice, and (c) the degree of motor activity and cognitive activity required in tasks. Beilock, Kulp, Holt and Carr (2004) have shown that for non-sensorimotor tasks, such as challenging mental arithmetic problems, distraction theories provide a better explanation of poor performance under pressure. From a sports perspective Jackson, Ashford and Norsworthy (2006) discuss the possibility that process goals relating to strategic features of a task may engage attentional processes that serve metacognitive roles and thereby prevent a step-by step focus on the processes governing skill execution. It is also widely recognised that distraction theories offer a better explanation for poor performance under pressure for novice performers (e.g., Beilock, et al. 2004).

In the last ten years researchers have consistently shown that when experts are performing complex motor tasks they regularly perform better in dual task conditions. That is, because experts can complete tasks at the procedural or autonomous level they actually perform better under pressure when they are mentally loaded with an additional secondary task while performing the primary task (e.g., counting backward from 100 while putting in golf). It is widely believed that the additional secondary task enables non-attention to the mechanics of the primary task that can break under pressure (Beilock & Carr, 2001, 2004; Beilock, Wierenga, & Carr, 2002; Gray, 2004). Conversely, when novices are required to carry out dual tasks under pressure they normally perform worse than in a single task condition because they require their working memory to assist with step-by-step task execution.

MODERATORS ASSOCIATED WITH CHOKING

Self-focus models and distraction models have been used to explain the broad relationship between attention and performance under pressure. There is also considerable accumulated knowledge now available about the specifics of numerous factors that precipitate choking. Self-consciousness as measured through self-report has been shown to predict choking although, contrary to the early work of Baumeister (1984) where low self-conscious individuals were at risk to choking, the prevailing body of sport research has shown that high self-conscious individuals are more susceptible to choking (Dandy, Brewer & Trotman, 2001; Wang, March-ant, & Gibbs, 2004; Wang, Marchant & Morris, 2004). Similarly, high reinvesters (i.e., high propensity for reinvestment in controlled processing) have been shown to be more susceptible to choking (Masters, Polman, & Hammond; 1993; Poolton, Maxwell, & Masters, 2004). It should be noted that the similarity in choking susceptibility with both high self-conscious individuals and high reinvesters is hardly surprising given that over half of the reinvestement scale items (Masters et al., 1993), typically used to measure reinvestment, are drawn directly from the self-consciousness scale (Fenigstein, Scheier, & Buss, 1975) and thus, share considerable variance. In drilling down into why some athletes self-monitor under pressure, Mesagno, Harvey and Janelle (2012) argue that efforts to generate a positive self-image to others helps to minimise social anxiety. Conversely, in situations where people doubt they will be successful, self-presentation concerns increase anxiety because of the possible ramifications for how the unsuccessful self may be viewed by others. For example, Wilson & Eklund (1998) have discussed a number of self-presentation concerns that athletes experience including concerning the inability to handle pressure or incompetency. Drawing on Leary (1992), Mesagno, Harvey, and Janelle (2011) state that people experience more social anxiety particularly if those impressions lead others to devalue, avoid, or reject them. They also argue that being portrayed as unsuccessful under pressure (e.g., choking) can lead to self- and relational devaluation. Also based on a self-presentation model, Mesagno, et al. (2012) demonstrated how a related concept, fear of negative evaluation (FNE), can precipitate choking. Watson and Friend (1969) defined fear of negative evaluation as "apprehension about others' evaluations, distress over their negative evaluations, avoidance of evaluative situations, and the expectations that others would evaluate oneself negatively" (p. 449). Mesagno et al., (2012) used dichotomous groups (i.e., high and low in FNE) to demonstrate that high FNE basketball players performed poorly under pressure (i.e., inference of choking). Self-presentation and FNE as underlying contributors to choking are especially relevant because self-presentation and FNE have been consistently linked with both anxiety and attention (i.e., via self-focus), the two key domains that constitute choking.

Other potential moderators associated with choking include; trait anxiety (Baumeister & Showers, 1986), self-confidence (Baumeister, Hamilton, & Tice, 1985), skill level (Beilock & Carr, 2001), task properties (Beilock & Carr, 2001), stereotypical threat (Chalabaev, Sarrazin, Stone, & Cury, 2008), public status (Jordet, 2009a), dispositional reinvestment (Masters et al., 1993), fear of negative evaluation (Mesagno et al., 2012), audience effects (Wallace, Baumeister, & Vohs, 2005), and coping style (Nicholls, & Polman, 2007, 2008; Wang et al., 2004).

For those that subscribe to the view that sport psychologists should focus on transferring their knowledge and expertise to solve practical problems then choking is a worthy topic. To date, the majority of choking interventions have been designed to test distraction theories and self-focus theories. Yet, most of the research has been theoretically driven rather than practically driven. Possibly researchers, for some years, were reluctant to test evidence-based interventions because, as Baumeister and Showers (1986) suggested, "The development of therapeutic techniques for ameliorating choking must wait until this debate is resolved" (p. 377). The 'debate' referred to here is whether the self-focus model or the distraction model provides the best explanation of choking. As discussed earlier in the chapter, recently there has been considerable research deciphering in which circumstances the self-focus models and distractions models are most applicable and, although theories will continue to be examined, researchers are beginning to focus more intentionally on testing choking interventions and practical solutions (e.g., Gucciardi & Dimmock, 2008; Hill, Hanton, Matthews, & Fleming, 2011; Mesagno et al., 2008, 2009). Consequently, the previous imbalance between the high proportion of theoretically-driven studies and low proportion of intervention-driven studies is being re-balanced.

INTERVENTIONS AND KNOWLEDGE TRANSFER IN CHOKING

Based on choking theories, researchers have employed various interventions to test the efficiency of proposed choking alleviation solutions. For example, Gucciardi and Dimmock (2008) compared the CPH and the ATH theories and found that a focus on explicit technical instruction for novice golfers caused choking, whereas experienced golfers were able to maintain their performance by concentrating on an abstract 'swing thought' (e.g., smooth, tempo) or irrelevant thought (i.e., a color) while executing a putting task under pressure circumstances. Oudejans and Pijpers (2009) investigated the effectiveness of anxiety training on choking with elite basketball and darts players. They found that intentionally practicing the task in pressurised environments is beneficial in reducing performance decrements. A novel approach to reducing choking susceptibility was recently tested by Beckmann, Gröpel, and Ehrlenspiel (2012) who had participants squeeze a soft ball in either their left or right had for 30 seconds prior to executing soccer penalty kicks, taekwondo kicks and badminton serves in three inter-linked studies. The rationale underlying squeezing the ball is linked to evidence that under pressure right hemisphere activity is increased via increased activity of the Broca's region of the brain which is involved in language production. Hemisphere-specific priming (e.g., ball squeezing) can apparently be activated by contralateral movements. That is, squeezing the ball with the left hand will increase activity in the right hemisphere and vice versa. Beckmann et al., state; "It can be argued that this disadvantageous hemispheric asymmetry reflects a regression to the cognitive phase of motor learning, which occurs under pressure and, in turn, produces choking (p. 3)." With all three sport tasks left hand ball squeezing was associated with superior performance when comparing pre-pressure and post-pressure skill execution. The Beckmann et al., study opens a further line of inquiry for sport choking researchers apart from traditional intervention methods (i.e., imagery, routines, and arousal control). We expect researchers will follow-up with further studies to examine other potential hemisphere priming actions. The ball-squeezing task is appealing from a practical perspective because it can easily be built into established routines in many sports

(Beckmann et al). Whether we see golfers walking up the final fairway of a major or tennis players during a break in games squeezing a soft ball in their left hand remains to be seen. Nevertheless, hemisphere activation provides an example of the diverse range of interventions that are being tested to ameliorate or dampen choking effects.

There have been calls for a move away from the predominant experimental approaches toward more qualitative and ecologically valid designs (Gucciardi & Dimmock, 2008; Mesagno et al., 2009). Hence, changing the research paradigm may be necessary to produce a greater weight of evidence especially regarding choking interventions. To date, only a few researchers (Mesagno et al., 2008, 2009; Hill et al., 2010a, 2011) have attempted to combine qualitative and quantitative methods to examine the effectiveness of interventions on CS athletes. Mesagno et al., (2008 & 2009) applied defined selection criteria to sample participants based on three variables consisting of high self-consciousness, high trait anxiety and approach coping style. To examine the efficacy of a pre-performance routine (PPR) for choking alleviation, Mesagno et al., (2008) intervened with elite tenpin bowlers utilising a single subject design and in-depth interviews. The rationale for employing interviews was that participants who evidently choked should be interviewed to provide the textual depth of narrative relating to their choking experience. Mesagno et al. (2008) concluded that PPR intervention had a preventative influence on choking. In the second study, Mesagno et al., (2009) had experienced basketball players listening to specifically selected music that contained lyrics to challenge anxious thinking before the task and subsequently the players were to focus on these lyrics while performing free-throw shots. This second intervention, again with a small number of purposively selected participants was also effective. Interviews were conducted after completion of the experimental manipulation to examine perceptions of choking and cognitions relating to the effects of the interventions. The data derived from these interviews provided detailed knowledge about participants' choking experience not normally achievable through quantitative studies. These studies represented initial attempts to transfer knowledge into practical contexts and a practical technique for alleviating choking through the combination of qualitative and quantitative methods. Hill et al., (2010a) explored the experiences of six elite CS and five CR golfers qualitatively. Moreover, the perceptions of their coaches was also taken into account and thus provided a degree of triangulation. Hill et al., (2010a) found that self-confidence, focus, anxiety management and perceived control were enhanced by applying mental skills in the pre and post-shot routines. These mental skills included cognitive restructuring, imagery, simulated practice and holistic swing thoughts with the result being a reduction in performance decrements under pressure. Hill et al., (2011) also further examined the effectiveness of an evidence-based intervention on choking incorporating a multi-model strategy including process goals, cognitive restructuring, imagery and simulated training with two professional golfers who have frequently been negatively affected by choking. Qualitative evaluations indicated that the interventions were again beneficial.

CONCLUSION

Choking in sport and other performance domains continues to be a topic of considerable discussion both in the popular press and sport psychology related literature. Sport psychologists have defined choking, examined multiple causal factors and developed plausible explanatory theories. Self-focus and distraction models have remained the dominant theoretical explanations, however, the application of these theories is nowadays more sophisticated and nuanced. Choking remains a relatively difficult area to explore experimentally. Even choking-susceptible athletes do not choke on cue and will not necessarily choke under pressure. Furthermore, there are obvious practical and ethical limitations to the degree of pressure that can be induced experimentally. Some researchers have wisely chosen to examine choking-resistant athletes, those that have a high performance pressure threshold. Closely examining the differentiating factors, including both trait and state factors, that characterise the approach of choking-resistant athletes is potentially useful. For example, a better understanding of the key differentiating factors between choking-resistant and choking-susceptible athletes should provide avenues for determining which aspects of successfully dealing with performance pressure are trainable.

In recent years there has been a significant change in research direction with greater attention on knowledge transfer with numerous choking interventions being tested in pseudo or actual competition settings. A new research direction into brain hemisphere priming has recently opened up another direction for researchers seeking to bridge the gap between theory and practice or, in colloquial terms, improve the 'push through' to athletes and coaches. Furthermore, the recent trend toward examining choking qualitatively opens up the possibility for genuine knowledge exchange. That is, rather than the sport psychologist expertly prescribing evidence-based solutions to 'treat' choking in a didactic manner, a more collaborative exchange takes place, where sport psychologists researchers or practitioners seek to understand the full range of approaches that athletes take to better deal with performance pressure. Although sport psychology researchers have produced a range of potentially beneficial choking interventions, we believe there is scope to more fully embrace the hard fought knowledge borne from athletes and artists from years of performing in sport and other high pressure environments.

LEARNING AIDS

1   Explain how the application of self-focus models of choking and distraction models of choking have been used to explain poor performance under pressure for both experts and novices?

Researchers applying self-focus models have consistently shown that, under pressure, choking-susceptible athletes consciously attempt to monitor the execution of performance. As a consequence, the smooth and automatic execution of performance is disrupted. Researchers have also demonstrated that, under pressure, novices can be susceptible to choking when they are distracted either externally (by opponents) or internally (by non-task relevant thoughts) whereas, novices perform better when attending to performance step-by-step.

2   Explain why researchers have found that elite athletes can sometimes perform better under pressure when they are required to carry out a dual tasks (i.e., skill execution and counting backward from 100 simultaneously).

The additional requirements of executing dual tasks takes up 'attentional load' and consequently insufficient available memory is free to become self-focused.

REVIEW QUESTIONS

1   Discuss the difference intervention options that have been shown to reduce choking susceptibility. Which of these options appeals to you and why?

2   Discuss how sport psychologists have defined choking. Which definition do you prefer?

3   Based on your own experiences and reading, discuss the causes of choking.

4   Discuss the potential benefits of studying the specifics of how choking-resistant athletes respond to pressure.

EXERCISES

1   Outline a group of exercises and drills that could be used in everyday training to assist athletes in better managing performance pressure.

2   Design your own experiment to examine choking in sport using the hemisphere priming method. Include a research question, recruitment of participants, ethical issues, measures, methods to collect data and hypothesis.

ADDITIONAL READING

Beckmann, J., Gröpel, P. & Ehrlenspiel, F. (2012). Preventing motor skill failure through hemisphere-specific priming: Cases from choking under pressure. *Journal of Experimental*

Psychology: General. Advance online publication. doi:10.1037/a0029852

Beilock, S.L. (2010). Choke: What the secrets of the brain reveal about getting it right when you have to. New York: Free Press.

Beilock, S.L. & Carr, T.H. (2001). On the fragility of skilled performance: What governs choking under pressure? *Journal of experimental*

psychology: General, 130(4), 701–725. doi: 1100.111037//0096-3445.130.4.701

Gladwell, M. (2000). Performance studies, "the art of failure," The New Yorker, August 21, pp.84–93.

Mesagno, C., Marchant, D. & Morris, T. (2009). Alleviating choking: The sounds of distraction. *Journal of Applied Sport Psychology*, 21, 131–147. doi:10.1080/10413200902795091

REFERENCES

Baumeister, R.F. (1984). Choking under pressure: Self-consciousness and paradoxical effects of incentives on skilful performance. *Journal of Personality and Social Psychology*, 46, 610–620. doi:10.1037/0022-3514.46.3.610

Baumeister, R.F., Hamilton, J.C. & Tice, D.M. (1985). Public versus private expectancy of success: Confidence booster or performance pressure? *Journal of Personality and Social Psychology*, 48(6), 1447–1457. doi:10.1037/0022-3514.48.6.1447

Baumeister, R.F. & Showers, C.J. (1986). A review of paradoxical performance effects – choking under pressure in sports and mental tests. *European Journal of Social Psychology*, 16(4), 361–383. doi:10.1002/ejsp.2420160405

Baumeister, R.F. & Steinhilber, A. (1984). Paradoxical effects of supportive audiences on performance under pressure: The home field disadvantage in sports championships. *Journal of Personality and Social Psychology*; *Journal of Personality and Social Psychology*, 47(1), 85.

Beckmann, J., Gröpel, P. & Ehrlenspiel, F. (2012). Preventing motor skill failure through hemisphere-specific priming: Cases from choking under pressure. *Journal of Experimental Psychology*: General. Advance online publication. doi:10.1037/a0029852

Beilock, S.L. & Carr, T.H. (2001). On the fragility of skilled performance: What governs choking under pressure? *Journal of experimental psychology*: General, 130(4), 701–725. doi: 1100..111037//0096-3445.130.4.701

Beilock, S.L. & Carr, T.H. (2004). From novice to expert performance: Memory, attention, and the control of complex sensori-motor skills. Skill acquisition in sport: Research, theory and practice, 583–616.

Beilock, S.L., Kulp, C., Holt, L. & Carr, T.H. (2004). More on the fragility of performance: Choking under pressure in mathematical problem solving. *Journal of Experimental Psychology-General*, 133(4), 584–599. doi: 10.1037/0096-3445.133.4.584

Beilock, S.L., Wierenga, S.A. & Carr, T.H. (2002). Expertise, attention, and memory in sensorimotor skill execution: Impact of novel task constraints on dual-task performance and episodic memory. *The Quarterly Journal of Experimental Psychology*: Section A, 55(4), 1211–1240. doi:10.1037//1076-898X.8.1.6

Chalabaev, A.S., Sarrazin, P., Stone, P. & Cury, J. (2008). Do achievement goals mediate stereotype threat? An investigation on females' soccer performance. *Journal of Sport and Exercise Psychology*, 30, 143–158.

Dandy, J., Brewer, N. & Trotman, R. (2001). Self-Consciousness and performance decrements within a sporting context. *Journal of Social Psychology*, 141 (1), 150–152.

Eysenck, M.W. & Calvo, M.G. (1992). Anxiety and performance: The processing efficiency theory. *Cognition & Emotion*, 6, 409–434. doi: 10.1080/02699939208409696

Eysenck, M.W., Derakshan, N., Santos, R. & Calvo, M.G. (2007). Anxiety and cognitive performance: Attentional control theory. *Emotion*, 7, 336–353. doi:10.1037/1528-3542.7.2.336

Fenigstein, A., Scheier, M.F. & Buss, A.H. (1975). Public and private self-consciousness: Assessment and theory. *Journal of Consulting and Clinical Psychology*, 43(4), 522–527.

Fitts, P.M. & Posner, M.I. (1967). Human performance. Belmont, CA: Brooks/Cole.

Gray, R. (2004). Attending to the execution of a complex sensorimotor skill: Expertise differences, choking, and slumps. *Journal of Experimental Psychology Applied*, 10(1), 42–54.

Gucciardi, D.F. & Dimmock, J.A. (2008). Choking under pressure in sensorimotor skills: Conscious processing or depleted attentional resources? *Psychology of Sport and Exercise*, 9, 45–59. doi:10.1016/j.psychsport.2006.10.007

Hardy, L., Mullen, R. & Martin, N. (2001). Effect of task-relevant cues and state anxiety on motor performance. *Perceptual and Motor Skills*, 92, 942–946.

Hill, D.M., Hanton, S., Fleming, S. & Matthews, N. (2009). A re-examination of choking in sport. *European Journal of Sport Science*, 9(4), 203–212. doi: 10.1080/17509840903301199

Hill, D.M., Hanton, S., Matthews, N. & Fleming, S. (2010a). A qualitative exploration of choking in elite sport. *Journal of Clinical Sports Psychology*, 4, 221–240.

Hill, D.M., Hanton, S., Matthews, N. & Fleming, S. (2010b). Choking in sport: A review. *International Review of Sport and Exercise Psychology*, 3, 24–39.

Hill, D.M., Hanton, S., Matthews, N. & Fleming, S. (2011). Alleviation of choking under pressure in elite golf: an action research study. *The Sport Psychologist*, 25, 465–488.

Jackson, R.C. (in press). Babies and bathwater: Commentary on Mesagno and Hill's proposed re-definition of 'choking'. *International Journal of Sport Psychology*.

Jackson, R.C., Ashford, K.J. & Norsworthy, G. (2006). Attentional focus, dispositional reinvestment, and skilled motor performance under pressure. *Journal of Sport & Exercise Psychology*, 28, 49–68.

Jordet, G. (2009a). When superstars flop: Public status and "choking under pressure" in international soccer penalty shootouts. Journal of Applied Sport Psychology, 21(2), 125–130.

Jordet, G. (2009b). Why do English players fail in soccer penalty shootouts? A study of team status, self-regulation, and choking under pressure. Journal of Sports Sciences, 27(2), 97–106.

Jordet, G. & Hartman, E. (2008). Avoidance motivation and choking under pressure in soccer penalty shootouts. *Journal of Sport & Exercise Psychology*, 30(4), 450–457.

Jordet, G., Hartman, E. & Sigmundstad, E. (2009). Temporal links to performing under pressure in international soccer penalty shootouts. *Psychology of Sport & Exercise*, 10(6), 621–627.

Land, W. & Tenenbaum, G. (2012). An outcome and process oriented examination of a golf specific secondary task strategy to prevent choking under pressure. *Journal of Applied Sport Psychology*, 24(3), 303–322.

Lewis, B.P. & Linder, D.E. (1997). Thinking about choking? Attentional processes and paradoxical performance. *Personality and Social Psychology Bulletin*, 23, 937–944. doi: 10.1177/0146167297239003

Leary, M.R. (1992). Self-presentational processes in exercise and sport. *Journal of Sport & Exercise Psychology*, 14(4), 339–351.

Liao, C.M. & Masters, R.S.W. (2002). Self-focused attention and performance failure under psychological stress. *Journal of Sport and Exercise Psychology*, 24(3), 289–305.

Marchant, D.B. (2010). Anxiety. In J. Hanrahan & M. L.B. Anderson (1st Ed.), The Routledge handbook of applied sport psychology: A comprehensive guide for students and practitioners (p.265). London: Routledge.

Martens, R. & Landers, D.M. (1972). Evaluation potential as a determinant of coaction effects. *Journal of Experimental Social Psychology*, 8(4), 347–359.

Masters, R.S.W. (1992). Knowledge, knerves and know how: The role of explicit versus implicit knowledge in the breakdown of a complex sporting motor skill under pressure. *British Journal of Psychology*, 83, 343–358. doi:10.1111/j.2044-8295.1992.tb02446.x

Masters, R.S.W. & Maxwell, J.P. (2008). The theory of reinvestment. *International Review of Sport and Exercise Psychology*, 1, 160–183.

Masters, R.S.W., Polman, R.C.J. & Hammond, N.V. (1993). "Reinvestment": A dimension of personality implicated in skill breakdown under pressure. *Personality and Individual Differences*, 14, 655–666. doi: 10.1016/0191-8869(93)90113-H

Mesagno, C., Harvey, J.T. & Janelle, C.M. (2011). Self-presentation origins of choking: Evidence from separate pressure manipulations. *Journal of Sport and Exercise Psychology*, 33(3), 441. Doi:10.1016/j.psychsport.2011.07.007.

Mesagno, C., Harvey, J.T. & Janelle, C.M. (2012). Choking under pressure: The role of fear of negative evaluation. *Psychology of Sport and Exercise*, 13(1), 60–68. doi:org/10.1016/j.psychsport.2011.07.007

Mesagno, C. & Hill, D.M. (in press-a). Definition of choking in sport: Re-conceptualization and debate. *International Journal of Sport Psychology*.

Mesagno, C. & Hill, D.M. (in press-b). Choking under pressure debate: Is there chaos in the brickyard? *International Journal of Sport Psychology*.

Mesagno, C., Marchant, D. & Morris, T. (2008). A pre-performance routine to alleviate choking in "choking-susceptible" athletes. *The Sport Psychologist*, 22, 439–457.

Mesagno, C., Marchant, D. & Morris, T. (2009). Alleviating choking: The sounds of distraction. *Journal of Applied Sport Psychology*, 21, 131–147. doi: 10.1080/10413200902795091

Moser, J.S., Becker, M.W. & Moran, T.P. (2012). Enhanced attentional capture in trait anxiety. *Emotion*. 12(2), 213–216.

Mullen, R., Hardy, L. & Tattersall, A. (2005). The effect of anxiety on motor performance: A test of the conscious processing hypothesis. *Journal of Sport and Exercise Psychology*, 27, 212–225.

Murray, N.P. & Janelle, C.M. (2003). Anxiety and performance: A visual search examination of the processing efficiency theory. *Journal of Sport and Exercise Psychology*, 25, 171–187.

Nicholls, A.R. & Polman, R.C.J. (2007). Coping in sport: A systematic review. *Journal of Sport Sciences*, 25(1), 11–31.

Nicholls, A.R. & Polman, R.C.J. (2008). Think aloud: Acute Stress and coping during golf performances. *Anxiety, Stress, & Coping*, 21, 283–294. doi.org/10.1080/02640410600630654.

Nideffer, R.M. & Sagal, M.S. (1998). Concentration and attention control training. In J. M. Williams (Ed.), Applied sport psychology: Personal growth to peak performance (3rd ed.), Mayfield, Mountain View, CA (1998), pp.296–315.

Oudejans, R.R.D. & Pijpers, J.R. (2009). Training with anxiety has a positive effect on expert perceptual-motor performance under pressure. *Quarterly Journal of Experimental Psychology*, 62, 1631–1647.

Poolton, J., Maxwell, J.O.N. & Masters, R. (2004). Rules for reinvestment perceptual and motor skills, 99(3), 771–774. doi: 10.2466/pms.99.3.771-774

Sanders, G.S. & Baron, R.S. (1975). The motivating effects of distraction on task performance. *Journal of Personality and Social Psychology*; *Journal of Personality and Social Psychology*, 32(6), 956.

Sanders, G.S., Baron, R.S. & Moore, D.L. (1978). Distraction and social comparison as mediators of social facilitation effects. *Journal of Experimental Social Psychology*, 14(3), 291–303.

Wallace, H.M., Baumeister, R.F. & Vohs, K.D. (2005). Audience support and choking under pressure: a home disadvantage? *Journal of Sport Sciences*, 23, 429–438.

Wang, J. (2002). *Developing and testing an integrated model of choking in sport* (Unpublished doctoral dissertation). Victoria University, Melbourne, Australia. Retrieved from http://vuir.vu.edu.au/id/eprint/230.

Wang, J., Marchant, D. & Gibbs, P. (2004). Self-consciousness and trait anxiety as predictors of choking in sport. *Journal of Science & Medicine in Sport*, 7(2), 174–185. doi: 10.1016/S1440-2440(04)80007-0

Wang, J., Marchant, D. & Morris, T. (2004). Coping style and susceptibility to choking. *Journal of Sport Behavior*, 27(1), 75–92.

Watson, D. & Friend, R. (1969). Measurement of social-evaluative anxiety. *Journal of Consulting and Clinical Psychology*, 33(4), 448.

Wells, B. M., & Skowronski, J. J. (2012). Evidence of choking under pressure on the PGA tour. *Basic and Applied Social Psychology*, 34(2), 175–182. doi: 10.1080/01973533.2012.655629

Williams, A.M., Vickers, J. & Rodrigues, S. (2002). The effects of anxiety on visual search, movement kinematics, and performance in table tennis: a test of Eysenck and Calvo's processing efficiency theory. *Journal of Sport & Exercise Psychology*, 24, 438–455.

Wilson, M. (2008). From processing efficiency to attentional control: A mechanistic account of the anxiety-performance relationship. *International Review of Sport and Exercise Psychology*, 1, 184–202.

Wilson, P. & Eklund, R.C. (1998). The relationship between competitive anxiety and self-presentational concerns. *Journal of Sport & Exercise Psychology*; *Journal of Sport & Exercise Psychology*.

Wilson, M., Smith, N.C. & Holmes, P. S. (2007). The role of effort in influencing the effect of anxiety on performance: Testing the conflicting predictions of Processing Efficiency Theory and the Conscious Processing Hypothesis. *British Journal of Psychology*, 98, 411–428. doi: 10.1348/000712606X133047

Chapter 30

Individual and team decision-making

GERSHON TENENBAUM AND LAEL GERSHGOREN

SUMMARY

How do performers make decisions as individuals and within a team? How does the environment affect their perception and cognition? What are the cognitive processes involved in team decision-making? In this chapter the reader is introduced to the basic perceptual-cognitive processes, which determine the act of decision-making. The chapter introduces the cognitive components underlying the decision-making process, such as visual attention, selective attention, working and long-term memory, mental representations, and knowledge base and structure. Briefly presented are affective/emotional variables, which affect the cognitive processes underpinning response selection and action execution. A cognitive perspective leads the section describing team decision-making. Shared mental models are presented as the underlying mechanisms of decision-making within a team framework. The chapter includes recommendations for enhancing individual and team decision-making.

INTRODUCTION

We ask the reader to imagine a basketball player in an offensive situation dribbling the ball, and observing: (a) the positions of his/her teammates; (b) the positions of his/her opponents; and (c) the 24 seconds time clock. What decisions must the player make before acting? Here are some ideas:

1   Where should he/she look (i.e., gaze) in order to better capture the situation?
2   Which are the most important cues he/she should attend to?
3   Based on what he/she sees, what is going to happen next (i.e., anticipation)?

4   Based on this, which decision should he/she make?
5   Which decision should he/she hold in case the first one isn't good?
6   At what time should he/she carry out the decision?

The first decision pertains to visual attention – valuable information must be forwarded to the brain for further elaboration. The second decision pertains to selective attention – only a portion of the environment is important – not all, thus, which is this portion? The third decision pertains to anticipation – the players continuously change position, thus, what happens next? The fourth and fifth decisions pertain to the elaborative process of response selection – based on the information stored in long-term memory (LTM), the current situation is processed for the appropriate solution to be made. The last decision pertains to the timing of carrying out the decision. Thus, the decision-making process consists of serial mental operations, which together are termed the DM process (Tenenbaum, 2003). The more skilled and experienced the performer, the more proficient and efficient the DM process, and the more reliable its operation under environmental pressure.

Decision-making (DM) is a deliberate cognitive operation of selecting a response to a stimulus among other available responses stored in long-term memory (LTM), while interacting with either the external environment or internal needs. DM is in essence a cognitive operation made by an individual or a group, which mediates between the environment and the behavior-performance; thus, it is considered an "adaptive operation" (Tenenbaum, 2003). When decisions are made under extremely constrained temporal conditions they are considered to be coupled within the perceptual and motor system; there is no time for intentional deliberations, so the motor system is "self-organized."

In most cases, however, performers attune their senses (the most dominant sense is vision) to the environment in order to pick-up information valuable for further elaboration (e.g., interaction with knowledge stored in LTM) and DM. One can assume therefore that making a decision entails other operations, such as visual searching for cues via visual attention, anticipating upcoming events based on the current state of events, processing the incoming information by activating stored information in LTM, calling to mind alternative responses/solutions, selecting one for execution (the DM act), and deciding upon its execution. This "cognitive processing" approach works relatively slowly, but becomes automatic after extensive deliberate practice and experience in similar situations (Tenenbaum, 2003). Both systems, the fast self-organized, and the slow-deliberative, are governed and controlled by the neural network containing task-specific information, which is retrievable and ready for processing upon request (Tenenbaum, Hartfield, Eklund, Land, Camielo, Razon, & Schack, 2009). The system that allows extensive and ongoing collaboration between the environment and the neural network in the brain is termed Long-Term-Working-Memory (LTWM). We shall elaborate on it later in this chapter.

 ## OBJECTIVES

After reading this chapter you should be able to:

1 Understand the terms and processes associated with individual DM.
2 Understand the terms and processes associated with team decision-making.
3 Be able to distinguish between decision-making processes made in deferent environments.
4 Apply the concept of DM in real life situations and offer methods to enhance the DM process.
5 Understand the social and affective variables related to the decision-making process.
6 Develop critical thinking about the cognitive processes, which operate under both social and emotional pressures.
7 Conceptualize the models and make sense of their components separately and interactively.
8 Understand the concept of DM within a team setting: How do team members coordinate actions to secure DM and actions.
9 Be familiar with the terms and concepts of team DM and shared/team mental models.

COMMON CONCEPTS OF DECISION-MAKING IN THE BEHAVIORAL AND SOCIAL SCIENCES

DM is a concept that receives much attention in the economic, business, and statistical domains. The person is perceived, according to the prescriptive approach, as outcome driven and goal-oriented. Accordingly, the person makes attempts to maximize his/her effort and information processing toward achieving the designated goal. In the processes, comparisons among alternatives are made against a designated and preferable solution. An application of this approach has been made in gambling behaviors where the product was unknown, thus, necessitated probabilistic estimations related to alternative solutions. Because of its poor ecological validity, prescriptive theoretical normative models showed limited utility in the decision-making process of people.

Since "expected values" are too simplistic for being the mere drive of DM, the cognitive-oriented approach has considered various environmental constraints to study how people make decisions. Cognitive capacity was considered to be the major constraint. De Groot (1965) and Chase and Simon (1973) demonstrated that repeated exposure to and experiences of a given environment allow the performer to make decisions by more clearly recognizing patterns, overcoming the limitations of working memory, and making superior decisions because of their task-specific, perceptual-cognitive capabilities.

Another approach, which accounts for DM behavior, is the naturalistic-descriptive approach (NDA). According to NDA, the DM process consists of both rational and irrational processes, and incorporates personal values, morals, motivation, and emotions. The person defines the problem, seeks alternative solutions and makes choices, which are also affected by their psychological states. Theoretical models, such as image theory, explanation-based theory, recognition-primed DM (RPD), and cue-retrieval of action attempted to account for DM behaviors. Heuristics have been offered within the NDA to account for the underlying mechanisms of DM in the real world. In RPD, Klein (1993) postulated that DM consists of cue identification, situational goals, alternative action generations, and expectations for possible alterations; all affected by experience. The more complex the situation, the more practice needed to efficiently adapt to it. This concept gives credit to the mental representations (i.e., knowledge structure) for guiding, monitoring, and executing the decision process. NDA is therefore a knowledge-driven discourse, which consists of accumulating both declarative and procedural neural circuits necessary for DM in situations that vary in complexity and certainty. The RPD within the NDA is an approach that has influenced the current concepts of DM in the sport and exercise domain.

A MENTAL REPRESENTATION GUIDED CONCEPTUAL MODEL OF DM

DM depends to a large extent on the nature of the sport. In open and dynamic environments, such as soccer, basketball, team handball, rugby, and field hockey, the decision-making takes place "on the run". Players must attend to many events and cues, which change locations, anticipate upcoming events, and make decisions as to the appropriate action and its execution timing. In more stationary and constrained environments, such as shooting, archery, penalty kicks, and foul shooting, attention is directed to the bodily signals (e.g., heart rate, breathing, the target), and the decision pertains to the temporal and spatial features of the action. The decision about the action and execution timing are governed by a control system, which consists of neural networks in the brain. The neural networks constitute a schema; a schema is a neural network that contains information, and is termed mental representation (Tenenbaum et al., 2009). Athletes develop more sophisticated mental representation networks with repeated exposure to the same situations and through deliberate practice (Ericsson, Krampe, & Tesch-Romer, 1993). A more sophisticated structure of the mental representation network allows the performer to feed-forward the information to the information-processing system (i.e., the brain) more efficiently, and then retrieve an appropriate response faster and more proficiently (i.e., make a decision). Indeed, Ericsson and Kintsch (1995) found that when deliberately training the memory, a mental representation structure is further developed, which allows the performer to memorize and retrieve information more accurately, and with much more capacity. Mental representations, which become a structured knowledge in various domains, are task-specific. Extended memory or anticipatory capacity are applicable and useful in the specific task, which was practiced (e.g., handball, chess, basketball, soccer), and their transfer into other tasks is very limited – dependent on the "shared elements" between the original task and the new task. Studies in the last three decades provide extensive evidence to support the notion that deliberate practice and repeated exposure to tasks enhance the structure and functionality of mental representations, which enables expert performers to become superior in perceptual-cognitive skills, such as visual search strategy (Abernethy, 1993; Williams, Davids, & Williams, 1999), anticipation (Abernethy, 1987; Tenenbaum et al., 1996; Tenenbaum, Sar-El, & Bar-Eli, 2000), memory (Chase & Simon, 1973; de Groot, 1965; Tenenbaum, Tehan, Stewart, & Christensen, 1999), and DM (Tenenbaum, 2003). Figure 30.1 presents this concept where mental representations control the perceptual-cognitive processes until a decision is made and sent for execution to either the motor or the cognitive systems. Deliberate practice and

extensive exposure to similar situations make the process automatic, and one that necessitates less deliberate cognitive effort. Automaticity allows the performer to attend to other valuable stimuli in the environment, and shift attention from automatic control to intentional control. The capacity to shift from automatic to intentional control of attention is termed attention flexibility. Attention flexibility allows the performer to make better decisions, and to perform them precisely, on time, and proficiently. One should keep in mind that we use symbolic annotations to describe how the brain interacts with the environment; an interaction that is chemical and electrical in nature, but is exhibited as a behavior in the form of an action.

To summarize this concept, DM in the sport domain constitutes a set of adaptive behaviors that allow the performer to operate efficiently within a competitive environment, which is loaded with emotional, temporal, social, and other demands. The efficiency of the information processing system to make decisions depends on the richness and structure of the knowledge system, i.e., the mental representations network. Encoding information via the perceptual system, delivering it to the higher-level processing system via LTWM, processing and retrieving responses are all a function of how developed and structured the knowledge system is. When the system chokes under pressure, a breakdown in the mental representation network occurs (Tenenbaum et al., 2009), and the perceptual-cognitive-motor linkage is not as functional as it should be.

The perceptual-cognitive concept in the sport domain: Dynamics and underlying mechanisms

Because DM is the last process preceding response/action implementation, it is dependent on several perceptual and cognitive processes. We briefly introduce these processes, as these are essentials for the decision quality.

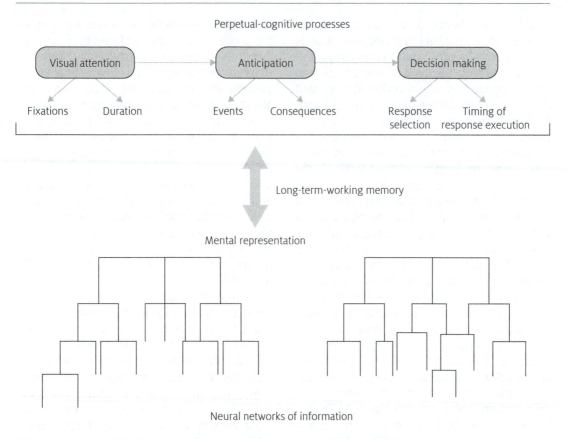

Figure 30.1 Neural representation control of perceptual-cognitive process.

Visual-spatial attention (VSA), priming, and attention flexibility: Visual-spatial attention is a perceptual mechanism that allows the performer to select relevant cues essential for DM from an array of environmental cues. The mechanism works to reduce uncertainty (Prinz, 1977), and provide the information processing system reliable, useful, and relevant information for DM. VSA depends on visual scanning of the environment. This can be done by using a target control strategy where the vision follows a target like a soccer ball. Under this strategy there are many eye-fixations; each for a short duration. In contrast, visual search, which consists of context control, is a strategy where vision is fixated on one location, and all relevant information around this fixation is captured. Under this strategy, there are fewer fixations for longer duration. As one can assume, context control VSA is more efficient as it does not overload working memory, it captures patterns, and is less sensitive to details. It reduces information load delivered to the cognitive system, and simplifies the elaboration between working memory and LTM. Research in various sports, such as basketball (Bard & Fleury, 1976), gymnastics refereeing (Bard, Fleury, Cariere, & Halle, 1980), and cricket (Abernethy & Russell, 1987) showed that expert performers made fewer fixations for longer durations than their non-expert counterparts (see Williams, Davids, & Williams, 1999 for review). Ripoll (1991) also found that expert performers opted for syntactic visual search, where most features in the display can be captured in minimal number of eye-fixations. He further argued that in situations of uncertainty, expert players employ strategies that optimally adapt the sensory-motor system to the extremely high constraints of the situation. A target visual-control strategy is limited in its capacity to allow sufficient time for both detection and response selection to be as efficient as when they were being used in a context control strategy. Studies in sport (see reviews by Tenenbaum & Bar-Eli, 1993a,b, 1995) indicated that accumulation of both declarative knowledge (e.g., facts, rules) and procedural knowledge (e.g., how to solve and act) shifts the VSA from target to context control, which allows for more efficient elaboration with the environment, and results in fewer errors and appropriate DM.

The VSA allows athletes to prime responses faster. When the environment causes the athlete to feel uncertain about the sequence of field events, the search for a response is slower. Experienced and high-level athletes acquire the declarative and procedural knowledge of their respective sport, and prime the essential cues very quickly via VSA; consequently, a response is primed, which then is implemented in the form of an action. The knowledge base and structure accumulating with practice and experience allow the VSA to reduce attention load by gazing toward large areas in the display and avoiding the search for details. The task-specific knowledge base enables the athlete to assign "if X then with what probability Y" propositions. "Probability values" allow the VSA to forward selective information to the cognitive system, which results in effortless and almost automatic DM processing. This efficient process is termed a benefit. When the performer lacks a "probability" type proposition, the perceptual-cognitive system is slower as the VSA search for details and information processing is slower; this slower process is termed a cost, and the cost/benefit ratio is an indicator of the perceptual-cognitive system operational efficiency. In competitive situations, athletes choose the priming option that has the highest utility value, i.e., the option that ensures the best chance of triggering the appropriate response at the proper time.

Cave and Bichot (1999) claimed that visual selection is important for action, but it is not always implemented in the last stages of information processing as evidenced in studies using brain mapping methods of planning and performance areas. However, it has a strong effect on response selection and action. In beginners, the process is serial and perceptually and cognitively demanding, while for experts it is automated with alertness to disturbances.

Perceptual anticipatory mechanisms (PAM): The visual attention system enables the performer to detect the most salient environmental patterns and cues, which enable the anticipation of events in advance. The PAM, when deliberately practiced and experienced, allows a quick and efficient elaboration with the mental representation network of the LTM. Only partial or initial (e.g., short exposure) information is sufficient to trigger a response when one develops expertise since "ready access scenarios" are stored as templates in LTM, and are ready to be accessed. Advanced PAM reduces the response time, which is required under short temporal conditions, and allows selection of a response that provides advantage to the athlete, rather than a response that is selected randomly and is limited in scope and vision.

Mental representations in long term memory: A rich and structured knowledge base secures a smooth and efficient continuous interaction between the perceptual-cognitive and the motor systems even under conditions of heavy cognitive and environmental load. When knowledge base in the form of mental representations is lacking, the internal and external distractors attract most of the performer's attention, resulting in limited capacity to confront the situation, slowing down the information processing relevant to the task, and resulting in a decision, which has high probability to be inappropriate. As early as the middle of the 20th century, DeGroot (1965) and Chase and Simon (1973) showed that extended knowledge in chess enables players to reconstruct structured and logical patterns after five seconds of visual exposure. These could not be repeated when the chess pieces were randomly placed on the board. It then became evident that knowledge base and structure, and visual attention lead players to chunk the patterns on the chessboard, and then use them for retrieval. The more experienced the player, the larger chunks in the form of logical patterns can be stored, and later retrieved, upon demand. Recall studies in dynamic sport have reported similar results (see Tenenbaum, Levi-Kolker, Bar-Eli, & Weinberg, 1994).

About 30–40 years later, Ericsson and Kintsch (1995) proposed the existence of long-term working memory (LTWM) as a mechanism that accounts for unusual task-specific memory, which cannot be generalized to other domains. LTWM overcomes the notion that memory storage capacity is limited and decays immediately after stimulus onset, particularly in expert memory performance where concurrent activity seems to present limited interference. LTWM develops through repeated exposure to stimuli (e.g., domain-specific retrieval structure), which is stored in an accessible and less interference-prone form. Task-specific memory traces can be retrieved rapidly and efficiently based upon fast encoding and storing processes. These memory traces allow the performer to retrieve a quick response and leave one or more as alternate responses. In such a way, DM can be altered "on the run" because LTWM enables flexible changes and quick changes to be made when new information is presented.

French and McPherson (1999) have explored the network of conceptual knowledge required to make tactical decisions and execute them, while engaged in a dynamic open-ended sport environment. They presented mental representations for action profiles, game situation prototypes, competitive scripts, and sport-specific strategies. French and McPherson reported that the knowledge base was hierarchically structured and consisted of macro- and micro-level routes. The micro-level routes managed by working memory enable athletes to attend to the ongoing events in the environment. Advanced visual scanning strategies and anticipation capability allow further processing aimed at retrieving the response, which is best executed at a given time. The macro-level routes refer to game plans and strategies that allow the performer to regulate the sensory system and stay within the designated plan boundaries.

Conceptualization of mental representations has been developed recently, but was presented in detail by Schack (see Chapter 20 in this book). This approach assumes that the motor system responds to intentional cognitive signals, and this process relies on mental regulations stored in LTM as mental representations. Accordingly, each action has a mental representation network in the brain. The neural networks are tied by pathways to information, labeled as emotions, actions, and coping plans. Intentional (goal-) directed motor action assumes that voluntary movements are stored in memory and contain anticipated consequences in the form of neural schema, so they are of extreme relevance to the control of movement production (Tenenbaum et al., 2009). Thus, when an action must be initiated, planned, and executed, the sensory system (mainly the visual system) is guided by the neural schema through long-term working memory (Ericsson & Kintsch, 1995). The control of the visual system allows anticipatory decisions to be made, and consequently actions to be retrieved from long-term memory (LTM). Furthermore, knowledge structures in the form of mental representations not only allow efficient control over decision-making and action, but also allow the perceptual-cognitive motor linkage for anticipated changes to occur once fast changes in the environment necessitate such alteration. When such representations are nonexistent, alternative decision plans and actions are likely to result in failure of the motor system to respond appropriately (see Tenenbaum, 2003 for details). Furthermore, mental representations consist of action plans associated with affective and motivational components, such as self-efficacy. If an appropriate action is retrieved, it may still be interfered with once self-efficacy and emotions are deemed non-optimal.

PERCEIVED STRESS, EMOTIONS, SELF-EFFICACY, AND SELF-REGULATION EFFECTS ON DM

Competitive events are overloaded with social and emotional stress. DM which takes place under such conditions depends largely on how the stressful events are perceived, how confident the performer is that they can cope with the pressure-evoking situation, and how they regulate themselves to get through the situation. We briefly summarize crucial points related to the variables that affect the DM process and outcome.

Anxiety

Both somatic and cognitive anxieties affect attention, which in turn affects DM. Low anxiety directs attention inward ignoring essential cues deemed important for DM. In high anxiety states, attention narrows down so that crucial cues cannot attract attention, and are thus missed. The span of attention is narrower than usual, so the entire perceptual-cognitive processing system may be dysfunctional. The detrimental effect of anxiety on performance is mostly prominent in complex and dynamic environments, which rely on the efficiency of the attention system to locate and forward essential information to the cognitive system (Tenenbaum, 2003). In most cases anxiety is perceived as a debilitative state, which results in a distraction through engagement with interfering thoughts. However, in some events, such as shot-putt, anxiety can be functional and facilitative to generate maximal force output.

Cue utilization theory and attention narrowing under anxiety or a high level of perceived stress indicate that under such conditions the information needed for DM is lacking, thus, the crucial cues do not prime the appropriate response; in many such cases an error occurs in DM and the wrong action is performed. Accordingly, each performer has an "individual zone of optimal functioning" where he/she can attend to the most essential cues, and thus prime the most appropriate response for that specific event (See Hanin, 2000; Kamata, Tenenbaum, & Hanin, 2002). "Being in zone" means to be in a state of sustained alertness (i.e., vigilance), alertness preservation (i.e., concentration) over a given period of time, and provision of a feeling of flow. Under pressure accompanied by negative emotions, the cognitive system is distracted by interfering thoughts, which divert attention and concentration from the task to the internal concerns associated with cognitive state anxiety. This process hurts the beginner performer most. Expert performers must secure their movement automaticity, thus, they should not allow the interfering thoughts divert their attention to the task details. Pressure and anxiety in high-caliber athletes causes them to return to "a step by step" cognitive process, which is detrimental to their performance (see Beilock & Gray, 2007 for extensive review).

To sum up, perception of pressure and feeling of emotions (e.g., anxiety, sadness, disappointment, happiness, pride) affect performance through the mediation of attention. It is the individual's perception of the valence of the emotional state (i.e., degree of pleasure), intensity (e.g., from low to high), and functionally (e.g., debilitative-facilitative), which affects the perceptual-cognitive system and determines the specific resources needed to perform the task. Through practice and experience, each performer establishes a unique affective-emotional zone within which they can activate the cognitive system to operate optimally the perceptual-cognitive system so that an optimal decision is made and executed (see Hanin, 2000).

Self-efficacy

The belief an athlete holds about his/her ability to accomplish a task or a sequence of tasks and meet successfully their goal is termed self-efficacy (Bandura, 1997). Accordingly, when the athlete believes in their resources to make the right decision, the probability to make it right increases. Because of its specific connotation, to increase one's probability of making the right decision, athletes should believe in their ability to regulate their emotions, pay attention to the important internal and environmental cues, analyse them appropriately, and be able to execute the selected response at the right time and space. Research findings have shown that self-efficacy plays a major role in affecting both the cognitive and motor systems (Feltz, Short, & Sullivan, 2008; Tenenbaum et al., 1996).

The role of self-regulation and coping strategies in DM

The competitive sport environment is overloaded with expectations and demands, which evoke emotional reactions. To enable the performer to process the valuable environmental information efficiently, they must be in the optimal state of mind. Self-regulation is the method athletes use, misuse, or avoid using to adopt appropriate coping strategies when performing a task. The use of coping strategies, such as relaxation, imagery, self-talk, and breathing techniques can be seen through their effect on the autonomic nervous system, i.e., measures of EEG, EMG, GSR, HR, HRV, and breathing pattern (see Blumenstein, Bar-Eli, & Tenenbaum, 1997 for extensive review). Additionally, sleep deprivation, certain nutritional ingredients, and physical conditioning status play a role in affecting the information processing system and DM through their influence on affective-emotional-arousal state and attention alertness levels.

Lazarus and Folkman (1984) categorized all coping strategies into two clusters aimed at changing the performer's appraisal of the current situation: problem-focused (e.g., solve a problem, which is seen as an obstacle), and emotion-focused (e.g., regulate the emotional state, which is currently detrimental to performance). Strategies such as denial, distancing, and avoidance, show a motivation to disengage from the interfering stimuli and promote efficient visual attention and information processing; all leading to DM and decision execution.

TEAM DECISION-MAKING: TEAM COORDINATION – HOW DO MEMBERS' DECISIONS BECOME A TEAM PLAY?

Although team decision-making consists of separate decisions made by individual members, this part of the chapter centers on the interaction of the team members while making a decision in a team. Unfortunately, very few studies have studied team decision-making in sport (Eccles, 2010); thus, we rely on research conducted in the military where team members make decisions under pressure.

In individual sports, athletes select a response based on internal and external cues. For example, a rifle shooter determines when to pull the trigger based on internal indicators, such as body position, breathing pattern, and muscle tension, as well as external ones (e.g., sights position, wind). Nevertheless, each rifle shooter's decision is not affected by the decisions made by teammates. In interactive team

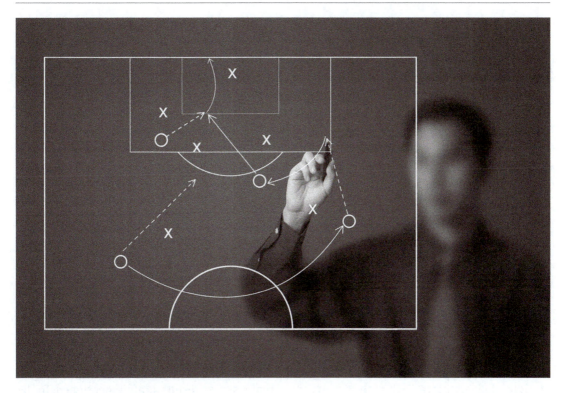

Figure 30.2 Planning possible moves given players' positions: Mapping and storing information for later decision-making and actions.

sports, such as football, soccer, and basketball, the importance of external cues in general, and those transmitted through the visual system in particular, for decision-making is prominent as performance attainment depends on members' ability to interact and coordinate their actions (Eccles & Tenenbaum, 2004; Tenenbaum, 2003).

The importance of coordination to team performance was supported in research conducted almost a century ago. In an unpublished study by Ringelmann in 1913 (cf. Eccles, 2010), subjects performed a tug-of-war task individually and in a group setting. The results revealed that as members were added to the team, additional force was employed, but in a diminishing fashion. In addition, each member's performance gradually declined. Although social loafing was proposed to play a role in these results, Ringelmann largely attributed the results to coordination deficits.

Replicated and comparable studies yielded similar results (see Comrey, 1953; Ingham, Levinger, Graves, & Peckham, 1974). These accumulating findings support the claim that diminution in coordination debilitates performance. Expert teams who coordinate flawlessly, maximize each member's contribution and create a whole that exceeds the sum of its parts (Eccles, 2010; Eccles & Tenenbaum, 2007; Pedersen & Cooke, 2006).

One has to keep in mind that in team sports coordination between team members is not always sufficient as each decision must consider also the opponents and the specific context within which the decision is made (e.g., the ball location, the score, field conditions). In any case, with so many variables to consider while making a decision, being able to coordinate actions within the team is, at least, a very good place to start.

BEING IN SYNCH: DOING THE RIGHT THING AT THE RIGHT TIME IN THE RIGHT PLACE

Coordinated actions

In a conceptual framework of team coordination, Rouse, Cannon-Bowers, and Salas (1992) suggested that in order to be in synch, team members must share knowledge pertaining to "what", "how", and "why" things should be done. The idea of knowing "what" should be done relates to coordinated actions. Eccles (2010) has used a soccer scenario to illustrate the importance of coordinated actions. In his scenario, a striker prepares to execute a heading task predicting the winger will chip the ball (i.e., deliver a high ball). However, as a ground pass arrives, the striker lacks sufficient time to adjust their body to perform a ground kick.

Commonly, more than one option exists to perform the same task (i.e., the "what"). For instance, a chipped ball can be "sliced" straight, delivered in a high arch, or curved towards the striker's head. Therefore, preferably, members will be able to predict their teammates' execution and adjust (i.e., make the right decision) accordingly. Pertaining to developing shared knowledge of "how" actions are about to be carried out, Eccles and Tenenbaum (2004) claimed that "through experience and practice, team members gain knowledge of the habits, preferences, and idiosyncrasies of their fellow members with regard to the operations they are likely to perform for a given task status change, which leads to a refined and shared knowledge of situational probabilities" (p. 552). Briefly stated, by knowing the team members' operation tendencies, athletes can predict upcoming actions more accurately, and consequently make better decisions pertaining to action required by them. The idea of jointly understanding "why" a certain action is chosen over another affords team members to be on the same page by accepting the underlying mechanisms of their teammates' execution.

Such understanding was noted to be vital for team performance (Reimer, Park, & Hintsz, 2006).

Timing

Eccles and colleagues (2004, 2010) expanded the team coordination conceptual framework proposed by Rouse et al. (1992), by incorporating a "when" element. Specifically, in sport, team members must be in synch with their timing to successfully complete a collaborative task. Eccles (2010) continued his soccer-related example to illustrate the importance of action timing to coordination. He noted that chipping the ball too early or too late causes the striker to arrive too late or too early to the ball, respectively. Consequently, a heading performance does not occur. Lack of timing in coordination can be attributed to Ringelmann's (1913) results as aforementioned. In the example of tug-of-war, when maximal force is employed when all members pull simultaneously, each member's deviation affects the total score. In such cases, a coach, or a team member is assigned to set the team's pace. Sports such as rowing and track/swimming relays depend greatly on coordinated timing. In swimming relays, for instance, lack of timing can not only affect the final score, but also easily lead to disqualification if one swimmer dives in too early.

Meeting in space

An additional element of coordination pertains to being in synch on "where" actions are about to take place (Eccles, 2010; Eccles & Tenenbaum, 2004). Staying with the winger-striker coordination example in soccer, Eccles (2010) illustrated the necessity of appropriately predicting what is about to happen in space to decision-making. Thus, facing lack of coordination in space, the striker decides to reach the near post expecting to receive the ball there, while the winger chips the ball to the far post. In such an instance, the striker might not have sufficient time to recover and reach the far post on time to execute the header. In a tug-of-war task as examined by Ringelmann (1913), where members were gradually added, coordination in space can become of great importance when members are crowded around the rope. Then, members have to coordinate their movements to circumvent limitations in range of motion that may lead to decreased force exertion. In sports, such as football, soccer, basketball, and team handball, where each teammate's movement in space opens or closes field spaces for others, coordination in space is vital.

THE ROLE OF COMMUNICATION IN TEAM DM

Communication in a team is used for: (a) motivation augmentation (e.g., encouragement, pep talks); (b) increasing the likelihood of appropriate behaviors, and decreasing the likelihood of undesired ones (i.e., reinforcement and punishment); (c) guiding performance on field through directions and feedback; (d) providing social support; (e) establishing a team framework for a season or a specific game (Yukelson, 2006). It is not surprising, therefore, that communication has been claimed to be crucial for reaching optimal performance (Shaw, 1981). In teams, communication and collaboration have been specifically noted as essential in situations in which diverse skills and knowledge foundations are necessary for producing efficient decision-making (Kellermanns, Floyd, Pearson, & Spencer, 2008). This claim was supported in an experimental study where proactive information sharing was found to be an effective way for making proper decisions under pressure (Yen, Fan, Sun, Hanratty, & Dumer, 2006).

Communication was one of the key constructs proposed by Eccles and Tenenbaum (2004, 2007) as essential to reach high levels of coordination in team sports. In their conceptual framework, Eccles and Tenenbaum (2004) acknowledged the importance of both verbal and nonverbal communication to coordination. However, costs in terms of time and cognitive resources were also noted. Initially, the usefulness of communication in three time frames, prior, during, and after performance, is discussed.

Establishing understanding prior to performing

Communication must be used to establish a framework for achieving team's goals (e.g., rules and operating procedures) (Yukelson, 2006). During practice, communication, in the forms of instructions, directions, and reinforcement, is used by both coaches and teammates to convey information pertaining to expected and preferred behaviors. Closer in time to performance itself, communication may be useful to establish a unified game plan. In a study conducted by Marks, Zaccaro, and Mathieu (2000), teams that received a five-minute briefing prior to a tank war-game simulation mission made significantly more accurate decisions with fewer errors than teams not given this opportunity.

In sport, Lausic, Tenenbaum, Eccles, Jeong, and Johnson (2009) found that communication prior to serving in tennis dyads was doubled in its quantity for teams who won the point in comparison to those who lost it. Furthermore, teams winning the point incorporated significantly more action-related comments than their losing counterparts. In addition to doubles tennis, football and baseball were exemplified as sports in which coaches and players call a play or a pitch prior to its initiation (see Eccles & Tenenbaum, 2004). In many cases, such calls are coded in advance to withhold from the opponents the knowledge of what is about to happen. Therefore, prior to performance, team members transfer overt communication to a covert form developing implicit communication.

Communicating during performance

Stout, Cannon-Bowers, Salas, and Malanovich's (1999) study links from pre-process planning to in-process communication, as well as demonstrates the contribution of communication to performance. Using a simulated helicopter piloting performance task, Stout et al. (1999) revealed that following team planning, team members were better able to deliver the proper information at the right time. Lu and Lajoie (2008) conducted a study pertaining to collaborative decision-making in simulated medical emergencies. Results revealed that the teams who shared more information made better and quicker decisions regarding their patients. Eccles and Tenenbaum (2004) noted that communication during performance provides team members with information pertaining to status changes in the task, or cues, pertaining to upcoming events or actions. Subsequently, team members can base their future actions on the deliberate cognitive process of decision-making instead of relying on their reaction time (Tenenbaum, 2003).

Debriefing performance for future purposes

Communication is often used post performance as part of a learning process aimed at enhancing future performances. Often, team members discuss past performances and coordination breakdowns (Eccles & Tenenbaum, 2007). Then, alternative decisions are proposed and variations of the situation are discussed. For instance, the soccer striker may question the winger's decision to pass a ground ball instead of a chip. Following a discussion of possible options for action, a preferred decision ought to emerge. Next, the discussion may continue to hypothetical situations, such as the defender being two steps behind or to the side. Subsequently, the "old" preferred solution

is being examined while another decision may become salient. Through this kind of communication, team members can better put themselves in their teammates' shoes, and more accurately predict their teammates' course of action. Consequently, the likelihood of making a coordinated decision increases.

The usefulness of post-performance evaluation has been supported in the literature. For example, Rasker, Post, and Schraagen (2000) compared teams who were able to evaluate and discuss their simulated firefighting performance between trials to those who were not. Superior performance was evident for teams in which post-performance evaluation was permitted.

Limitations of relying on communication to enhance decision-making

Despite various benefits of communication for decision-making, several costs must be considered. First, communication demands time and cognitive resources because the message should be encoded appropriately, reach its destination, and be decoded properly. Unfortunately, this process can be easily interrupted (Adler & Rodman, 2002; Eccles & Tenenbaum, 2004, 2007). Examples of interruptions in sport are distance between teammates on the field and fans who are loudly cheering. Under high workload, time and cognitive resources might not be available, making the reliance of decision-making on communication problematic. Indeed, experienced aircrews decreased their reliance on communication under high-pressure conditions (Orasanu, 1993). In addition, Kidd (1961) concluded that team performance deteriorated under high workload because the team leader spent a substantial amount of time coordinating the team's work.

An additional cost relates to information transparency. In sport, when athletes communicate on the pitch to coordinate their actions, this information can also disclose future actions to the opposing team. Hence, although team members may make better decisions, the opponents can use this information to guide and improve their decisions too. Expert teams overcome these shortcomings by: (a) establishing implicit communication (i.e., coded communi-cation which is non-transparent to the opponents; Kanki, Lozito, & Foushee, 1989); and (b) developing shared mental models (SMM; Entin & Serfaty, 1999). The construct SMM is present next.

THE ROLE OF SHARED MENTAL MODELS IN TEAM DM

Defining Shared Mental Models (SMM)

The term shared mental models (SMM) refers to an "organized understanding or mental representation of knowledge that is shared by team members" (Mohammed, Klimoski, & Rentsch, 2000, p. 123). Throughout the literature, synonyms of the concept SMM are collective cognition, team knowledge, shared knowledge, team mental model, and implicit coordination (Cannon-Bowers & Salas, 2001; Eccles & Tenenbaum, 2004). Specifically, SMM was defined by Cannon-Bowers, Salas, and Converse (1993) as "knowledge structure(s) held by each member of a team that enables them to form accurate explanations and expectations for the [team and task], and in turn, to coordinate their actions and adapt their behavior to demands of the task and other team members" (p. 228). Therefore, SMM is a dynamic cognitive process that governs team-related decision-making and affords coordination even when communication is limited or absent.

Theoretical frameworks of SMM

Resnick (1991) noted that the term sharing holds a double meaning of both "having in common" as sharing personal characteristics, and "dividing up" as sharing workload or house assignments. These "communality" and "division" aspects correspond to the teamwork and task-work elements that have been conceptualized to underlie SMM (Cannon-Bowers & Salas, 1998; Klimoski & Mohammed, 1994; McIntyre & Salas, 1995). Taskwork knowledge centers on role-specific performance demands and goals associated with these roles (Mohammed, Ferzandi, & Hamilton, 2010). Taskwork can be represented by the quarterback's ability to aim a pass that reaches its target in time and space (Eccles & Tenenbaum, 2004). Teamwork knowledge relates to interpersonal interaction requirements as well as actions of teammates (Mohammed et al., 2010). Exemplifying teamwork, Eccles and Tenenbaum (2004) claimed that to complete the task successfully, the quarterback relies on guards blocking the defense line, the running back faking receiving the ball, other receivers' movements that deflect the defense from identifying the true target, and the target itself executing the play correctly in time and space. In conclusion, to complete a team play appropriately, team members must be able to interact properly, execute their own task skillfully, but also "to be in their teammates' shoes", understanding what they are about to do.

Enhancing SMM

Team coordination can be developed through pre-, during-, and post-performance process (Eccles & Tenenbaum, 2004; Fiore, Salas, Cuevas, & Bowers, 2003). Thus, it is not surprising that SMM interventions have targeted these processes. Cross training is an example of a SMM enhancement pre-performance training. Cross-training has been defined as "an instructional strategy in which each team member is trained in the duties of his or her teammates" (Volpe, Cannon-Bowers, Salas, & Spector, 1996). Therefore, the aim of cross training is to enhance decision-making by being able "to walk in your teammates' shoes."

Team coordination and adaptation training is an example of in-performance training that centers on transition from explicit coordination (i.e., communication) to implicit coordination (i.e., SMM) under stressful or high workload conditions (Entin & Serfaty, 1999). The idea of this training is to train members under stressful conditions, while restricting communication channels. In sport, a coach may put players under time pressure by increasing the intensity of a drill, leaving them with little to no time to communicate. Guided team reflexivity represents a post-performance SMM development method. According to this method, team members are expected to reflect on their past performances, and identify decision-making related strengths and weaknesses. Viewing films of past performances is a common way to meet this end as plans pertaining to how the observed weaknesses may be addressed ought to emerge (Gurtner, Tschan, Semmer, & Nägele, 2007).

Limitations of SMM

A main shortcoming of the SMM construct in sport is that to date, the unknown exceeds the known. Only several conceptual frameworks (e.g., Eccles & Tenenbaum, 2004, 2007) and research investigations (e.g., Mascarenhas, Collins, & Mortimer, 2005; Webber, Chen, Payne, Marsh, & Zaccaro, 2000) have been published on this topic. Ward and Eccles (2006) claimed that not only were most of the SMM publications not sport-related, but most of the studies used relatively novel tasks that make the findings somewhat questionable when generalizing to expert teams. Despite the necessity of further research to better understand SMM, general agreement regarding its importance to team decision-making, coordination, and performance do exist.

LEARNING AIDS

1 Describe the decision-making (DM) process – from visual-attention to response-selection.

To select a response, the performer relies on the relevant environmental cues by using either target or context control. Attention flexibility allows the performer to anticipate the upcoming events early in the process, and consequently to reduce the dependence on reaction-time. The number of eye fixations and their duration indicate how efficient the perceptual-cognitive process is. Long exposure and deliberate practice change these indicators, and enable deliberate information processing, which after some time becomes automated, and allows an attention shift when necessary. Thus, response-selection and its execution depend largely on perceptual components and strategies preceding it.

2 Relate briefly to the term knowledge-base, and describe how it is related to long-term memory and mental-representations.

Knowledge can be either declarative or procedural. Knowing facts increases the declarative store in long-term memory, but does not secure the use of this knowledge under conditions such as competition and stress-evoking situations. For this aim, procedural knowledge develops through deliberate experiences and practices. The knowledge is accumulated and stored in the form of neurological network, and is viewed symbolically as a hierarchy. The more intense the exposure to the same environment, the more prominent the use of knowledge stored in LTM via the use of long-term-working-memory (LTWM). Knowledge base and structure support the DM process.

3   Why and how do emotions affect perceptual-cognitive skills and motor performance?

Under stressful conditions, such as competition, performers feel pressure that is sometimes interpreted as anxiety, fear, and worry, or sometimes as excitement and enthusiasm. When pressure is perceived positively it is facilitative to performance, but when perceived negatively it is debilitative to performance. Perceived pressure affect the ability to attend to relevant environmental cues (e.g., "narrowing"). When this happens, the entire perceptual-cognitive process is impaired. This is detrimental to DM and its execution.

4   How do team members coordinate their actions and why do coordination errors occur?

Through practice performers develop shared mental models (SMM), which allow them to expect what each other is doing at any time. When SMM are not sufficiently present, verbal communications are needed for team coordination. With practice and experience SMM develop to a degree where verbal communications are not needed to achieve desired team coordination. There are several techniques aimed at increasing SMM and reducing coordination errors.

REVIEW QUESTIONS

1   Name the perceptual-cognitive components that constitute the DM process.

2   Explain the logical sequence of the DM process.

3   Describe the nature of serial, parallel, and automatic information processing and their effect on DM.

4   Elaborate how knowledge base and structure govern the DM process through "priming," attention flexibility, visual search strategies, anticipation, and long-term-working-memory.

5   Name possible macro- and micro-level routes that may enhance DM in basketball, soccer, team handball, volleyball, and rugby.

6   How do anxiety levels affect the DM process?

7   How does attention mediate the link between emotions and actions?

8   Describe how self-efficacy and self-regulation affect the quality of the DM process.

9   What kind of shared mental models must team members have to better coordinate their action and DM process?

10 How do "time" and "space" relate to a team's DM and coordination?

11 Describe how communication affects the team's coordination and DM process.

12 Establish a communication plan to enhance the team's DM process and coordination.

13 Plan a program for enhancing shared mental models and DM process in a team sport of your choice.

EXERCISES

Select a five-minute video clip that shows a competition between two teams. Watch the clip twice. During the first viewing, select one team and observe its players. As you watch, try to attend to each player's decision-making. What decisions are made? Are the decisions-actions well coordinated? Which DM-actions end in errors (the opponent team took control over the ball)? What types of communication are made by the players (verbal and non-verbal)? Which actions were made after each communication exchange? Take a five-minute rest, and watch the same video clip again. However, while observing the clip, write the following:

1   What actions have taken place in the game?

2   How many of them were successful?

3   How many of them were unsuccessful?

4   How many and what kind of verbal and non-verbal communications have been made?

5   How many of them were followed by a successful action?

6   How many of them were followed by an unsuccessful action?

7   What do these observations indicate about the quality of DM and coordination of the team players you have observed?

8   Elaborate your findings briefly and tie them to the DM process and SMM you have learned in this chapter.

ADDITIONAL READING

Adler, R.B. & Rodman, G. (2002). *Understanding human communication* (8th ed.). New York: Oxford University Press.

Eccles, D.W. (2010). The coordination of labour in sports teams. *International Review of Sport and Exercise Psychology, 3*, 154–170.

Eccles, D.W. & Tenenbaum, G. (2004). Why an expert team is more than a team of experts: A social-cognitive conceptualization of team coordination and communication in sport. *Journal of Sport & Exercise Psychology, 26*, 542–560.

Eccles, D.W. & Tenenbaum, G. (2007). A social-cognitive perspective on team functioning in sport. In G. Tenenbaum & R. Eklund, *Handbook of sport psychology* (3rd ed.) (pp.264–283). New York: Wiley.

Gurtner, A., Tschan, F., Semmer, N.K. & Nägele, C. (2007). Getting groups to develop good strategies: Effects of reflexivity interventions on team process, team performance, and shared mental models. *Organizational Behavior and Human Decision Processes, 102*, 127–142.

Tenenbaum, G. (2003). Expert athletes: An integrated approach to decision-making. In J.L. Starkes & K.A. Ericsson (Eds.), *Expert performance in sports* (pp.191–218). Champaign, IL: Human Kinetics.

REFERENCES

Abernethy, B. (1987). Anticipation in sport: A review. *Physical Education Review, 10*, 5–16.

Abernethy, B. (1993). Attention. In R. Singer, M. Murphey, & L. Tennant (Eds.), *Handbook of research in sport psychology* (pp.127–170). New York: Macmillan.

Abernethy, B. & Russel, D.G. (1987). Expert-novice differences in selective attention task. *Journal of Sport and Exercise Psychology, 9*, 326–345.

Adler, R.B. & Rodman, G. (2002). *Understanding human communication* (8th ed.). New York: Oxford University Press.

Bard, C. & Fleury, M. (1976). Analysis of visual search activity during sport problem situation. *Journal of Human Movement Studies, 3*, 214–222.

Bard, C., Fleury, M., Carriere, L. & Halle, M. (1980). Analysis of gymnastics judges' visual search. *Research Quarterly for Exercise and Sport, 51*, 267–273.

Beilock, S.L. & Gray, R. (2007). Why do athletes choke under pressure? In G. Tenenbaum & R.C. Eklund (Eds.), *Handbook of sport psychology* (3rd ed., pp.425–444). New York: Wiley.

Blumenstein, B., Bar-Eli, M. & Tenenbaum, G. (1997). A five-step approach to mental training incorporating biofeedback. *The Sport Psychologist, 11*, 440–453.

Cannon-Bowers, J.A. & Salas, E. (1998). Team performance and training in complex environments: Recent findings from applied research. *Current Directions in Psychological Science, 7*, 83–87.

Cannon-Bowers, J.A. & Salas, E. (2001). Reflections on shared cognition. *Journal of Organizational Behavior, 22*, 195–202.

Cannon-Bowers, J.A., Salas, E. & Converse, S.A. (1993). Shared mental models in expert team decision-making. In N.J. Castellan (Ed.), *Individual and group decision-making* (pp.221–246). Hillsdale, NJ: Lawrence Erlbaum Associates.

Cave, K.R. & Bichot, N.P. (1999). Visuospacial attention: Beyond a spotlight scheme. *Psychonomic Bulletin and Review, 6*, 204–223.

Chase, W.G. & Simon, H.A (1973). Perception in chess. *Cognitive Psychology, 4*, 55–81.

Comrey, A. (1953). Group performance in a manual dexterity task. *Journal of Applied Psychology, 37*, 85–97.

De Groot, A.D. (1965). *Thought and choice in chess.* The Hague: Mouton.

Eccles, D.W. (2010). The coordination of labour in sports teams. *International Review of Sport and Exercise Psychology, 3*, 154–170.

Eccles, D.W. & Tenenbaum, G. (2004). Why an expert team is more than a team of experts: a social-cognitive conceptualization of team coordination and communication in sport. *Journal of Sport & Exercise Psychology, 26*, 542–560.

Eccles, D.W. & Tenenbaum, G. (2007). A social-cognitive perspective on team functioning in sport. In G. Tenenbaum & R. Eklund, *Handbook of sport psychology* (3rd ed.) (pp.264–283). New York: Wiley.

Entin, E.E. & Serfaty, D. (1999). Adaptive team coordination. *Human Factors, 41*, 312–325.

Ericsson, K.A. & Kintsch, W. (1995). Long term working memory. *Psychological Review, 102*, 211–245.

Ericsson, K.A., Krampe, R.T. & Tesch-Romer, C. (1993). The role of deliberate practice in the acquisition of expert performance. *Psychological Review, 100*, 363–406.

Fiore, S.M., Salas, E., Cuevas, H.M. & Bowers, C.A. (2003). Distributed coordination space: Toward a theory of distributed team process and performance. *Theoretical Issues in Ergonomic Science, 4*, 340–364.

Feltz, D.L., Short, S.E. & Sullivan, P.J. (2008). *Self-efficacy in sport.* Champaign, IL, Human Kinetics.

French, K.E. & McPherson, S.L. (1999). Adaptations in response selection processes used during competition with increasing age and expertise. *International Journal of Sport Psychology, 30*, 173–193.

Gurtner, A., Tschan, F., Semmer, N.K. & Nägele, C. (2007). Getting groups to develop good strategies: Effects of reflexivity interventions on team process, team performance, and shared mental models. *Organizational Behavior and Human Decision Processes, 102*, 127–142.

Hanin, Y.L. (2000). *Emotions in sport.* Champaign, IL: Human Kinetics.

Ingham, A.G., Levinger, G., Graves, J. & Peckham, V. (1974). The Ringelmann Effect: Studies of group size and group performance. *Journal of Experimental Social Psychology, 10*, 371–384.

Kamata, A., Tenenbaum. G. & Hanin, Y. (2002). Individual zone of optimal functioning (IZOF): A probabilistic conceptualization. *Journal of Sport and Exercise Psychology, 24*, 189–208.

Kanki, B., Lozito, S. & Foushee, H. (1989). Communication indexes of crew coordination. *Aviation, Space, and Environmental Medicine, 60*, 56–60.

Kellermanns, F.W., Floyd, S.W., Pearson, A.W. & Spencer, B. (2008). The contingent effect of constructive confrontation on the relationship between shared mental models and decision quality. *Journal of Organizational Behavior, 29*, 119–137.

Kidd, J.S. (1961). A comparison of one-, two-, and three-man work units under various conditions of workload. *Journal of Applied Psychology, 45*, 195–200.

Klein, G. (1993). A recognition primed decision (RPD) model of rapid decision-making. In G.A. Klein, J. Orasanu, R. Calderwood & C. Zsambok (Eds.), *Decision-making in action: Models and methods* (pp.138–147). New Jersey: Ablex: Norwood.

Klimoski, R. & Mohammed, S. (1994). Team mental model: Construct or metaphor? *Journal of Management, 20*, 403–437.

Lausic, D., Tenenbaum, G., Eccles, D.W., Jeong, A. & Johnson, T. (2009). Intrateam communication and performance in doubles tennis. *Research Quarterly for Exercise and Sport, 80*, 281–290.

Lazarus, R.S. & Folkman, S. (1984). *Stress, appraisal, and coping*. New York: Springer.

Lu, J. & Lajoie, S.P. (2008). Supporting medical decision-making with argumentation tools. *Contemporary Educational Psychology, 33*, 425–442.

Marks, M.A., Zaccaro, S.J. & Mathieu, J.E. (2000). Performance implications of leader briefings and team-interaction training for team adaptation to novel environments. *Journal of Applied Psychology, 85*, 971–986.

Mascarenhas, D.R.D., Collins, D. & Mortimer, P. (2005). The accuracy, agreement and coherence of decision-making in rugby union officials. *Journal of Sport Behavior, 28*, 253–271.

McIntyre, R.M. & Salas, E. (1995). Measuring and managing for team performance: Emerging principles from complex environments. In R. Guzzo & E. Salas (Eds.), *Team effectiveness and decision-making in organizations* (pp.149–203). San Francisco: Jossey-Bass.

Mohammed, S., Ferzandi, L. & Hamilton, K. (2010). Metaphor no more: A 15 year review of the team mental model construct. *Journal of Management, 36*, 876–910.

Mohammed, S., Klimoski, R. & Rentsch, J.R. (2000). The measurement of team mental models: We have no shared schema. *Organizational Research Methods, 3*, 123–165.

Orasanu, J.M. (1993). Decision-making in the cockpit. In E. Wiener, B. Kanki & R. Helmreich (Eds.), *Cockpit resource management* (pp.137–172). San Diego, CA: Academic Press.

Pedersen, H.K. & Cooke, N.J. (2006). From battle plans to football plays: Extending military team cognition to football. *International Journal of Sport and Exercise Psychology, 4*, 422–446.

Prinz, W. (1997). Perception and action planning. *European Journal of Cognitive Psychology, 9*, 129–154.

Rasker, P.C., Post, W.M. & Schraagen, J.M.C. (2000). Effects of two types of intra-team feedback on developing a shared mental model in command and control teams. *Ergonomics, 43*, 1167–1189.

Reimer, T., Park, E.S. & Hinsz, V.B. (2006). Shared and coordinated cognition in competitive and dynamic task environments: An information-processing perspective for team sports. *International Journal of Sport and Exercise Psychology, 4*, 376–400.

Resnick, L.B. (1991). Shared cognition: Thinking as social practice. In L.B. Resnick, J.M. Levine, & S.D. Teasley (Eds.), *Perspectives on socially shared cognition* (pp.1–20). Washington, DC: American Psychological Association.

Ringelmann, M. (1913). Recherches sur les moeurs anime's: Travail de l'homme [Research on animate sources of power: The work of man]. *Annales de l'Institute National Agronomique, 2e serie-tome XII*, 1–40.

Ripoll, H. (Ed.) (1991). Information processing and decision-making in sport (special issue). *International Journal of Sport Psychology, 3–4*, 187–406.

Rouse, W.B., Cannon-Bowers, J.A. & Salas, E. (1992). The role of mental models in team performance in complex systems. *IEEE Transactions on Systems, Man, & Cybernetics, 22*, 1296–1308.

Shaw, M.E. (1981). *Group dynamic: The psychology of small group behavior* (3rd ed.). New York, NY: Mcgraw-Hill.

Stout, R.J., Cannon-Bowers, J.A., Salas, E. & Milanovich, D.M. (1999). Planning, shared mental models, and coordinated performance: An empirical link is established. *Human Factors, 41*, 61–71.

Tenenbaum, G. (2003). Expert athletes: An integrated approach to decision-making. In J.L. Starkes & K.A. Ericsson (Eds.), *Expert performance in sports* (pp.191–218). Champaign, IL: Human Kinetics.

Tenenbaum, G. & Bar-Eli, M. (1993a). Decision-making in sport: A cognitive perspective. In R. Singer, M. Murphey & L.K. Tennant (Eds.), *Handbook of research in sport psychology* (pp.171–192). New York: Macmillan.

Tenenbaum, G. & Bar-Eli, M. (1993b). Personality and intellectual capabilities in sport in sport psychology. In D. Sakulufske, & M. Zeidner (Eds.), *International handbook on personality and intelligence* (pp.687–710). New York: Plenum.

Tenenbaum, G. & Bar-Eli, M. (1995). Contemporary issues and future directions in exercise and sport psychology. In S.J.H. Biddle (Ed.), *Exercise and Sport Psychology: A European Perspective.* (pp.292–323), Champaign, IL: Human Kinetics.

Tenenbaum, G., Levy-Kolker, N., Bar-Eli, M. & Weinberg, R. (1994). Information recall of younger and older skilled athletes: The role of display complexity, attentional resources, and visual exposure duration. *Journal of Sports Sciences, 12*, 529–534.

Tenenbaum, G., Hatfield, B., Eklund, R.C., Land, W., Camielo, L., Razon, S. & Schack, K.A. (2009). Conceptual framework for studying emotions-cognitions-performance linkage under conditions, which vary in perceived pressure. In M. Raab, J.G. Johnson. & H. Heekeren, (Eds.), *Progress in brain research: Mind and motion – The bidirectional link between thought and action* (pp.159–178), Elsevier Publication.

Tenenbaum, G., Levi-Kolker, N., Sade, S., Lieberman, D. & Lidor, R. (1996). Anticipation and confidence of decisions related to skilled performance. *International Journal of Sport Psychology, 27*, 293–307.

Tenenbaum, G., Sar-El, L. & Bar-Eli, M. (2000). Anticipation of ball location in low and high skill performance: A developmental perspective. *Psychology of Sport and Exercise, 1*, 117–128.

Tenenbaum, G., Tehan, G., Stewart, G. & Christensen, S. (1999). Recalling a floor routine: The effect of skill and age on memory for order. *Applied Cognitive Psychology, 13*, 101–123.

Volpe, C.E., Cannon-Bowers, J.A., Salas, E. & Spector, P.E. (1996). The impact of cross-training on team functioning: An empirical investigation. *Human Factors, 38*, 87–100.

Ward, P. & Eccles, D.W. (2006). A commentary on "team cognition and expert teams: Emerging insights into performance for exceptional teams." *International Journal of Sport and Exercise Psychology, 4*, 463–483.

Webber, S.S., Chen, G., Payne, S.C., Marsh, S.M. & Zaccaro, S.J. (2000). Enhancing team mental model measurement with performance appraisal practices. *Organizational Research Methods, 3*, 307–322.

Williams, A.M., Davids, K. & Williams, J.G. (1999). *Visual perception and action in sport.* Routledge: London.

Yen, J., Fan, X., Sun, S., Hanratty, T. & Dumer, J. (2006). Agents with shared mental models for enhancing team decision-makings. *Decision Support Systems, 41*, 634–653.

Yukelson, D.P. (2006). Communicating effectively. In J.M. Williams (Ed.), *Applied sport psychology: Personal growth to peak performance* (5th ed.) (pp.174–191). New York, NY: McGraw-Hill.

Chapter 31

Performance routines in sport – meaning and practice

RONNIE LIDOR, DIETER HACKFORT AND THOMAS SCHACK

SUMMARY

Athletes typically adopt performance routines in order to feel in control – both physically and psychologically – over what they are doing before, during, and after a sporting act. In order to achieve a high level of proficiency in their sport and to be optimally prepared for participating in competition, athletes should know in advance what they are going to do during their actual performance. In addition, they need to know how to assess their performances in order to benefit from the result of this assessment in future performances. Task-pertinent performance routines can help athletes prepare themselves effectively for the sporting act, and in turn improve their performances. In this chapter we will elaborate upon the contribution of routines to achievement, and provide some empirical evidence stressing the benefits that athletes can gain by the consistent use of routines. We will also provide a number of examples of routines that can be used by athletes.

INTRODUCTION

A search for the meaning of the term routine in the Oxford Dictionary yields the following: "a fixed and regular way of doing things" (*Oxford Advanced Learner's Dictionary*, 1992, p. 1103). Looking at another version of the Oxford Dictionary (*Concise Oxford Dictionary*, 1984) yields the following: "a regular course of procedure, unvarying performance of certain acts" (p. 910). Not surprisingly, in both sources examples from the domain of sport are given to illustrate the meaning of the term routine, such as a set sequence of movements in a dance or some other physical performance.

Indeed, in some sports such as gymnastics, swimming, and track and field, athletes are required to perform fixed sets of movements which have been repeatedly and extensively practiced. One of the main objectives of athletes in these sports is to master these routines in order to achieve the highest level of athletic performance they are capable of.

In this chapter, we examine the use of routines in sport; however, we will not discuss those sets of movements that are performed by the athlete as part of his or her athletic performance (e.g., routines performed by the gymnast in her floor exercise). We will examine the use of performance routines used by athletes before, during, and after the performance – those that are *associated* with his or her actual athletic performance. In other words, this chapter discusses the use of routines aimed at helping the athlete to ready him- or herself for the sporting task, so that the preconditions for a high level of performance will be attained.

Before starting to discuss performance routines in sport, we would like to illustrate the following two cases. These cases can be observed quite often in basketball (Case 1) and volleyball (Case 2), in actual situations in which athletes attempt to prepare themselves for a sporting act.

Case 1: Tom stands on the throwing line and prepares himself for a free-throw shot in basketball. Tom is a 17-year-old shooting guard playing for his high-school basketball team. He is now taking part in a conference game against one of the strongest teams in the conference. One of the players on the opposing team has fouled him. He is standing on the free-throw line, waiting for the referee to hand him the ball. Until the ball is handed to him he imagines himself shooting the ball. He focuses on his breathing to control arousal. He likes to stand on the line and feels good being there. In his mind he sees himself performing the shot smoothly and perfectly, as he has done numerous times before. When the referee hands him the ball, he directs his eyes to the rim of the basket, dribbles the ball three times, takes a deep breath, and makes the shot. He does not have to look at the outcome of the throw; he listens to the noise generated by the ball as it whooshes into the net. The ball is in.

Case 2: Debbie stands in the serving zone and prepares herself to serve the ball in volleyball. Debbie is a 21-year-old volleyball player who plays for her college team. It is her last year in the college. Although she has played for the team for the last four years, she has always had difficulties readying herself for the serv-

ing act. She feels that she is not able to focus appropriately before and during the serve. Sometimes she focuses on the net, and sometimes she focuses on one of the players from the opposing team. Her eyes move from one point to another. She feels that she would be happier if instead someone else from her team were standing in the serving zone and serving the ball. After receiving a signal from the referee, she performs the serve. The serve was easily received by one of the players from the opposing team. She felt that she did not perform well.

What can we learn from Cases 1 and 2? In Case 1, it seems that Tom feels comfortable being at the shooting line. He knows exactly what he needs to do in order to succeed with the shooting task. He knows how to prepare himself for the shooting act, and therefore feels in control over what he has to do to shoot accurately. He even activates a number of physical (e.g., dribbling the ball before releasing the ball) and psychological (e.g., focusing attention and imagery) behaviors that help him to perform well. However, in Case 2 things are different. Debbie does not feel comfortable in her role serving the ball. She is anxious and lacks confidence in her ability to serve the ball successfully. She has to deal with the negative thoughts that are entering her mind. She lacks the ability to be focused before and during the act, and doesn't have any tools available to prepare herself for the anticipated action. It appears that she was not ready – physically or psychologically – to perform the serve.

An attempt is made in this chapter to examine the use of performance routines in sport – routines that can help athletes to improve their preparation for the sporting task, as well as assist them to be in control during the time they perform the sporting task. In some cases these performance routines can help the athlete assess his or her actual performance, so that this feedback can be used to improve their next attempt.

OBJECTIVES

After reading this chapter you should be able to:

1 Define the term routine in sport – pre-performance routines, during-performance routines, and post-performance routines.
2 Outline the main components included in an effective routine – the physical components and the psychological components.
3 Explain why athletes can benefit from the use of task-pertinent routines.
4 List sport tasks, in both individual and team sports, in which routines can be effectively performed.
5 Develop task-pertinent routines based on an analysis of the task to be performed, the environment where the task is performed, and the requirements and preferences of the performer.

PERFORMANCE ROUTINES – CHARACTERISTICS AND KEY FEATURES

A performance routine can be defined as a systematic sequence of physical (motor) and psychological behaviors that are demonstrated before, during, and after the execution of a sporting task (Lidor, 2007; Velentzas, Heinen, Tenenbaum, & Schack, 2010). A performance routine is an integral part of the athlete's repertoire when he or she: (a) is preparing him- or herself for the sporting act (i.e., a pre-performance routine); (b) is executing the sporting act (i.e., a during-performance routine); and (c) is assessing and reacting to the way he or she performed the sporting act and/or the outcome of the act (i.e., a post-performance routine).

Practically speaking, an effective performance routine should include a set of overt physical behaviors demonstrated by the athlete before he or she begins the sporting task. For example, a warm-up session conducted by the athlete before a practice session, a competition, or a game can be considered as a physical component of a routine. It is assumed that the athlete regularly conducts the same warm-up session before he or she begins to perform, and therefore this session becomes a routine for the performer. In another case, a volleyball player bouncing the ball a number of times immediately before serving can also be considered as a physical component of a routine. It is assumed that in this case the volleyball player maintains the

same number of dribbles before each serve of the ball, and therefore the bouncing act is adopted as a routine.

A good routine should also be composed of elements that help the athlete cope with psychological challenges, such as self-talk and imagery procedures, in order to reduce tension and increase self-control over what he or she does before and during execution. In addition, a routine should include psychological elements, such as focusing attention, in order to enable the performer to cope effectively with distractions associated with the performed act – both external (e.g., noise generated by the crowd) and internal (e.g., negative thoughts). For example, some tennis players consistently use a loud breathing technique after they hit the ball as a during-performance routine, in order to stay focused on what they are doing, as well as to control the pace of their during-game movements.

An effective routine should also include elements that can be applied by the athlete at the end of his or her practice/competition/game. For example, a performance routine should help him or her cope with feelings such as disappointment or frustration. Also, routines should help the athlete to reorganize his or her thoughts after the competition/game in order to be ready for the next competitive event.

A number of interesting and different explanations have been offered that aim to clarify the mechanisms that make routines effective. Each explanation provides a different perspective on how routines work. Some of the accounts complement each other, while others are in sharp contrast. These explanations address components such as attention, physiological states, and motor programs, as well as different cognitive components (see Schack et al., 2005; Velentzas et al., 2011). Based on an action theory approach to applied sport psychology (Schack & Hackfort, 2007), we prefer to use the mental calibration model to explain the basic mechanism of routines. The mental calibration model (Schack & Hackfort, 2007; Schack et al., 2005) suggests that most of the problems that arise during competition are likely to be caused by a mental breakdown rather than by physiological difficulties. From such a point of view, actions in sport are intentional events based on mental integration strategies. This means that the basic elements and sequences from which a motor action is built are integrated and organized in order to attain a specific action goal. Being mentally prepared to perform their best is essential for athletes to achieve their competitive goals. All of the athletes' physical preparation would be pointless if they were not also mentally ready. Moreover, the physiological problems that arise are often due to failures in athletes' mental functioning. The best way for athletes to affect physiological functioning is to direct mental skill strategies towards resolving the cause of the physiological deterioration – for example, changing the negative thinking that causes anxiety during competition.

Thus, routines function much like a mental scanning instrument, in that they enable athletes to evaluate competition conditions. For example, bouncing a ball in a volleyball serve routine supplies the server with information about the ball, the floor, and the state of his or her muscles. This information can then be used to calibrate the motor system in order to be optimally prepared for the serve. Routines also enable athletes to adjust and fine-tune their preparations based on those evaluations, in pursuit of a particular competitive goal. This adaptation can involve adjustment to the conditions, opponents, competitive situations, or internal influences that can affect performance. Similar to adjusting a race-car engine to the conditions of the track, air temperature, and weather, performance routines calibrate all competitive components to a mental level that enables the athlete to achieve optimal performance.

All together, an important task of routines is to create a mindset that will initiate optimal mental and physiological preparation in a particular task and environmental condition, and foster the athletes' best performances. Examples of an optimal psycho-physiological calibration and resulting task-oriented mindset include: establishing a performance goal, generating a task-specific mental rehearsal, and identifying mental tools (e.g. self-instruction) to trigger beneficial performance reactions. Such mindsets act as a mental reference structure at different levels of action organization, and support competitive performance as well as appropriate coping with the outcome.

THE USE OF PERFORMANCE ROUTINES – MACRO AND MICRO SPORTING EVENTS

A performance routine – pre-performance, during-performance, or post-performance – can be applied by athletes in what we term macro and micro sporting events. A macro sporting event is the entire event in which the athlete is engaged, such as a practice session, a competition, or a game. All patterns of behavior that are demonstrated by the athlete and are associated with the macro event can be considered as performance routines, as long as the athlete exhibits these patterns of behavior on a regular basis. In essence, what the athlete does on a regular basis throughout: (a) the days/hours/minutes before the event; (b) the actual event; and (c) the days/hours/minutes after the event, can be considered as performance routines. For example, if a soccer player maintains a consistent schedule of events during the day before a game – practices with the team in the morning, watches video clips of the opposing team at the end of the practice with his or her teammates, eats lunch and supper at given hours, and goes to sleep at a fixed time, and follows this schedule in the last day/s before each game during the season, then he or she is already using pre-performance routines. If the soccer player regularly activates performance routines during the game itself (e.g., uses a relaxation procedure in the break between the first and second half of the game) or after the game (e.g., performs a cooling-down procedure), then he or she also adopts a routine behavior during or after the macro sporting event.

Performance routines can also be used in micro sporting events. A micro sporting event is considered to be a specific event within the macro event. For example, a free-throw shot in basketball is a micro event within a basketball game: the shooter should activate task-specific performance routines in order to succeed in this particular task. Task-specific routines can be performed immediately before the shooter performs the free-throw shot (e.g., a number of seconds before the shot), during the actual shooting act, and after he or she completes the shot (if time permits). Other examples of micro sporting events are the 11-m penalty in soccer, the take-off in the 100 meter sprint, and the serve in table-tennis, tennis, and volleyball. In order to achieve a high level of proficiency in these specific tasks, the athlete is required to use routines that reflect: (a) the specific requirements of these tasks; (b) the specific characteristics of the environment in which the task is executed; and (c) the needs and preferences of the shooter. These routines differ from those the athlete uses to prepare him- or herself for the macro event.

For the purposes of this chapter, we will focus on the use of performance routines in micro sporting events. Typically, a micro sporting event, such as the free-throw shot in basketball, the putt in golf, and the long jump in track and field, is characterized as a self-paced event. Self-paced events are those taking place in a relatively stable and predicable environment, where there is adequate time to prepare for their execution (Lidor, 2007). In these, the athlete can activate a plan, a strategy, a protocol, or what we term a performance routine. The main objective of an effective performance routine is to facilitate learning, performance, and achievement. Effective performance routines are usually mastered with a high degree of consistency; they become an integral part of the micro event – the self-paced act – either deliberately or subconsciously, depending on the skill level of the athlete (Lidor & Singer, 2003).

Self-paced events typically can be performed in two ways – either when the performer executes the sporting task only once, as in the case of performing one free-throw shot in basketball (e.g., after the offensive player makes a field shot but is also fouled by one of the players from the opposing team, and therefore is rewarded one more free-throw shot from the line), or when the performer consecutively executes the sporting task a number of times, as in the case of shooting two or three free-throw shots in basketball (e.g., when a player is fouled by one of the players from the opposing team, and therefore is rewarded two or three free-throw shots from the line). In both instances, pre-performance, during-performance, and post-performance routines can be used, as can be seen in Figure 31.1.

When the performer executes the task only once, he or she can use performance routines before the execution and during the execution, and if time permits a post-performance routine can also be implemented (see Figure 31.1, Part A). For example, a basketball player is

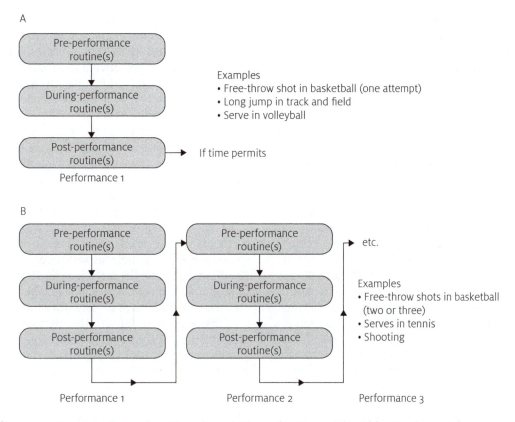

Figure 31.1 Types and use of routines in a single performance (A) and in two (or more) consecutive sporting performances (B).

rewarded with one free-throw shot. After completing the task, either successfully or missing the basket, the player has to continue to play (e.g., play defense), and therefore does not have the time to use a post-performance routine. However, if the performer executes the task a number of times in a row (e.g., the basketball player is rewarded with two or three free-throw shots), then he or she can activate not only pre-performance and during-performance routines, but also post-performance routines (see Figure 31.1, Part B). Furthermore, the performer can use the post-performance routine to reflect upon the outcome of his or her previous attempt (e.g., Performance 1 in Figure 31.1, Part B): if the performer succeeds in his or her first attempt then one type of post-performance routine can be used (e.g., using a psychological cooling-down technique to relax, or adopting a physical pattern of behavior such as making a fist to exhibit satisfaction). However, if the performer fails in his or her first attempt, then another type of post-performance routine can be adopted (e.g., focusing attention). In the case of performing a number of self-paced events, the post-performance routines used after the first performance can be combined with the pre-performance routine used before the second performance in order to strengthen the preparation of the performer for the second performance.

Another characteristic of a self-paced event in sport, regardless of the number of times the task can actually be performed, is that short-duration time intervals of preparation are available to the athletes, according to the rules of the sporting event. For example, according to the rules of the International Basketball

Federation, basketball players are allowed five seconds to prepare themselves for the free-throw shooting act (International Basketball Federation, 2008). According to the Fédération Internationale de Volleyball (2004), volleyball players are allowed to have eight seconds for preparation before serving the ball. These rules state that athletes are required to apply their selected routines within time constraints; all routines should be activated during a specific number of seconds immediately prior to the performance of the sporting task. However, the athletes can, for instance, also use the time while walking to the line, or they can use other parts of the game as elements for their routines.

Interestingly, some evidence has shown that the time available for the athletes to prepare themselves for the self-paced event can be longer than the time officially allocated to them according to the rules of the game. For example, in Lidor and Mayan's (2005) study on volleyball players, it was found that a time interval of 12 seconds was measured between the moment the server knew that he was going to serve the ball until he actually performed the serve (four seconds more than the number allowed for preparation according to the official rules of the game). This additional interval of time could be used by the servers in performing their routine prior to the serving act. In a study on basketball players (Lidor, Arnon, Aloni, Mayan, & Afek, 2012), a time interval of about 23 seconds (18 seconds more than the time officially allowed for preparation) was measured from the moment the players knew that they were going to perform the free-throw shot until the moment they actually released the ball. Presumably, this time could be used for additional preparation for the free-throw acts.

As indicated before, in this chapter we focus on the use of performance routines in micro sporting events, namely in self-paced tasks. The main reason for the selection of self-paced tasks is that in most of the studies that examined the contribution of performance routines to achievement in sport, the participants performed self-paced events (see Lidor, 2007 for a review on the use of performance routines in self-paced tasks). Therefore, our discussion on performance routines in this chapter reflects solid evidence emerging from both laboratory and applied inquiries.

EMPIRICAL SUPPORT FOR THE USE OF ROUTINES

Studies focusing on the use of performance routines in self-paced tasks can be classified into two categories – observational and experimental (Lidor, 2007). In observational studies, the researcher typically observes the physical behaviors of the performer in a natural setting (Thomas, Nelson, & Silverman, 2011). For example, the researcher observes what an elite basketball player does when she prepares herself for the shooting act. In another case, the researcher observes what a weightlifter does before he begins his final lift in the competition – a lift that, if made successfully, can earn him a medal. Based on these observations, the researcher can describe unique patterns of physical behaviors demonstrated by the performer (i.e., a skilled athlete) when he or she prepares him- or herself for the act.

In experimental studies, the researcher can manipulate treatments or conditions that have the potential to improve performance (Thomas et al., 2011). In the area of performance routines, one of the main objectives of the researcher is to examine the effectiveness of task-pertinent routines on performance quality. That is, the aim of the researcher is to compare the results of conditions in which a routine was presented to the participants with those where a routine was not provided to them.

In this section, we describe four studies that focused on different aspects of performance routines in sport: two observational studies (one on swings and putts in golf and one on free-throw shots in basketball), and two experimental studies (both on serving in volleyball).

In one observational study, Crews and Boutcher (1987) analyzed the pre-shot routines of both full-swing and putting strokes among 12 tour players of the Ladies Professional Golf Association (LPGA). We can learn from the observations collected in this study that all golfers were consistent with regard to time and physical patterns of behaviors, such as waggles and glances at the hole. Among the pre-shot routines observed for the full swing were standing behind the ball, setting the club behind the ball with one glance at the target, setting the feet, and then swinging. Among the pre-shot routines that were observed for the putt were standing behind the ball, moving beside the ball, setting the club behind the ball with one glance at the target, setting the feet, and then putting. It was also found in this observational study that the more successful golfers used longer time periods for their full shot and putting routines.

In another observational study, Wrisberg and Pein (1992) looked at the relationships between pre-performance behavior and performance accuracy of free-throw shots performed in real competitive basketball games. They measured the length of the pre-shot interval and the number of free-throw shots made by varsity and intramural basketball players during Division 1 games. From the collected observational data, the researchers calculated means and standard deviations of the pre-shot intervals, in order to determine the average duration and within-player temporal consistency, respectively, of pre-performance accuracy. A negative relationship resulted between the standard deviations of the pre-shot duration and achieving success in the free-throw shots: the more accurate shooters were more consistent than the lower percentage shooters in the amount of time they spent preparing themselves for the shooting event. It was also found in this study that the average time duration a player took before shooting was a matter of personal preference, and that there was no optimal time associated with greater accuracy. Based on these findings,

the researchers recommended that each player should develop a pre-performance routine according to his or her personal preferences. In other words, no one specific routine fits the needs of all players.

These observational studies (Crews & Boutcher, 1987; Wrisberg & Pein, 1992) focused on different aspects of pre-performance routines associated with self-paced tasks such as swinging and putting in golf and shooting free-throw shots in basketball. An attempt was made in these two studies to describe what performers actually do when preparing themselves for the execution of the task. In the following two experimental studies we will learn how researchers attempt to teach pre-performance routines to sport performers, and how they assessed the contribution of these routines to achievement.

In one experimental study (Lidor & Mayan, 2005, Study 2), two types of pre-performance routines were examined in beginning female volleyball players: a motor-emphasized pre-performance routine and a cognitive-emphasized pre-performance routine. In the motor-emphasized routine, learners were asked to: (a) be in a ready position on the serving line; (b) feel the ball with two hands while being in a ready position; (c) dribble the ball with the dominant hand (four or five times); and (d) hold the ball with the nondominant hand and then execute the serve. In the cognitive-emphasized routine, learners were told to: (a) stand in a ready position on the serving line; (b) imagine themselves successfully performing the serving task; (c) focus attention on an external cue related to the task or learning environment; and (d) execute the serve. The motor-emphasized pre-performance routine group and the cognitive-emphasized pre-performance routine group were compared to a group of learners who were not given any pre-performance routine instructions (a control condition). The findings of this study showed that the volleyball learners who were instructed to use the motor-emphasized pre-performance routine were more accurate than both the learners who were instructed to use a cognitive-emphasized pre-performance routine and those who were not provided with pre-performance instructions. The authors of this study suggested that it might be helpful to first teach beginning learners a routine emphasizing the physical readiness of the performer, and only then to add cognitive elements to the learned routine.

In another experimental study (Velentzas, Heinen, & Schack, 2011), the influence of two different routine integration strategies on volleyball float-serve performances and on the structure of players' mental representations was examined. One group of volleyball players was trained to use an imagery routine before serving the ball. The internal (kinesthetic) imagery technique was presented in combina-

tion with a preceding five-minute breath control and relaxation exercise. Another group of players was instructed to use the method of introducing routines, namely the participants were taught specific volleyball serving routines. A third group of players did not receive any pre-performance routine guidelines (a control condition). The researchers measured a number of variables in their study, among them hand and ball velocity, serving accuracy, and players' mental representation of their movements. It was found in this study that the imagery group served significantly more accurately, showed significantly increased ball velocity, and the players' mental representations of their movements were covered more clearly than the other groups of players who participated in this study.

BENEFITS OF PERFORMANCE ROUTINES

Based on the above observational and experimental studies, as well as on other studies examining the contribution of performance routines to achievement in sport (e.g., Cohn, 1990; Schack, Whitmarsh, Pike, & Redden, 2005; Southard & Miracle, 1993; Velentzas et al., 2010), it can be observed that athletes who use performance routines on a regular basis are better prepared for the practice, competition, or game than athletes who do not use these routines. Being prepared to perform their best is essential for athletes so that they can achieve their training and competitive goals. By the use of an effective routine, the athlete can integrate his or her physical and psychological preparations so that optimal preparation can be achieved.

According to Schack and colleagues (2005), adequate physiological activation is presumed to be a basic requirement of competitive performance, and as a result psychological components are also influential contributors to performance. However, most of the problems that exist during actual competitions or games are more likely caused by a psychological breakdown rather than by physiological barriers. For

example, when preparing him- or herself for the serving act in volleyball, a server can have difficulties in organizing his or her thoughts or being focused (see Case 2 at the beginning of this chapter). In another case, a bowler has difficulty planning the trajectory of his or her second bowling attempt, after failing to hit all the pins in the first attempt. In both examples, the performers have to overcome psychological barriers and not physiological ones. However, their psychological state also influences their physiological state. Since they are not focused appropriately (as in the example of the volleyball player) or are not effectively planning their task (as in the example of the bowler), they probably feel nervous or anxious (e.g., their heart rate is elevated and they perspire heavily). One effective way for athletes to influence their physiological state is to direct psychological skill strategies towards resolving the cause of the physiological deterioration (e.g., elevated heart rate or increased perspiration level). For example, the use of attentional strategies or self-talk can assist the athlete in monitoring his or her physical/physiological state before and during the performed act.

The following four benefits illustrate the contribution of a systematic use of performance routines in sport:

- Routines help athletes to be in control of what they are doing before and during the sporting task, particularly the self-paced task. Since the components of the routine – both physical and psychological – have been practiced by the athletes many times in the past, athletes feel familiar with the task and comfortable in executing it.
- Routines help athletes to be focused before and during the execution of the sporting task. It is almost impossible to achieve a high level of proficiency in a self-paced task without being totally focused on the task. Routines can help the performer to block external distractions, such as noise generated by the fans, as well as to minimize internal distractions, such as negative thoughts and reflections.
- Routines help performers develop a plan of action. Since performance routines can be executed immediately before the initiation of both a macro sporting event and a micro sporting event, the athlete can use the routine, and particularly its psychological elements, to perform a last-minute rehearsal of what he or she is going to do. The routine can be used to review the plan of action that the athlete developed for the given task.

- Routines help athletes reduce stress. Since the athlete has practiced his or her routine behaviors numerous times, he or she feels in control, and therefore feels less stress about what is expected of him or her.

The above-mentioned four benefits of performance routines can illustrate to athletes that they can achieve their best by performing self-paced sport skills. However, athletes should be aware of the potential risks associated with the use of task-pertinent performance routines. Among these risks are: (a) lack of time to use all components of the routine; (b) noise generated by the crowd or hostile behavior demonstrated by athletes from the opposite team or by other competitors during the performance of the routine; and (c) relevant information related to the ongoing sport event may be ignored when attention is focused solely on the implementation of the routine (e.g., verbal instructions related to the next defensive position of the team given by the coach are ignored when the basketball player is focused on his or her preparation for the free-throw shot). These risks, if they indeed occur during a competition or a game, can negatively influence the psychological state of the performer; he or she can become anxious and nervous. Therefore, skilled performers should be ready to perform self-paced tasks also under conditions where they are not able to optimally use their performance routines.

TEACHING BEGINNING ATHLETES PERFORMANCE ROUTINES

As indicated before, it is assumed that all skilled athletes who are involved in sports more or less use some kind of performance routine, either taught by the coach/instructor or developed intuitively. For example, in Lidor and Mayan's (2005) study, elite volleyball players reported that the pre-performance routines they had used before serving the ball were ones that they had developed themselves as part of their preparation for the serving act. They stressed that in the early phases of their sport development none of their coaches had taught them how to use a routine before, during, or after the completion of the serve. In essence, they realized that effective preparation for the serving act was essential, and therefore they developed preparatory routines on their own.

However, to effectively use performance routines in sport, and particularly routines associated with the execution of self-paced events, athletes should acquire these routines as early as possible during the process of learning the sport tasks themselves (Lidor, 2007; Lidor & Singer, 2003). If the techniques of the sport skill (e.g., a self-paced skill) are acquired at an early age, then the preparation routines that are performed in combination with these techniques (e.g., dribbling the ball before shooting free-throw shots in basketball or being in a ready position before serving the ball in tennis) should be taught to the athlete in early stages of practice as well.

When working with young athletes, coaches and instructors should consider the athletes' learning and performance capabilities, as well as their expectations (Côté & Fraser-Thomas, 2010). To enhance the strategic behavior of young athletes at an early stage of the learning process, coaches and instructors should be particularly aware of the beginners' information-processing and attentional capabilities. Therefore, coaches can assist young athletes in developing performance routines by introducing the components of the routine – physical and psychological – as part of the technical instructions of the skill, in order to create the essential link between the technique and the routine.

A three-phase model of teaching pre-performance routines to beginning athletes engaged in learning and performance of self-paced events in sport has been proposed by Lidor (see Lidor, 2007, 2010 for a full description of the model). This instructional model is composed of the following phases:

Phase 1 – Preliminary preparatory instructions. The objective of Phase 1 is to expose athletes to the basic components of preparatory routines associated with the self-paced events. The athletes should experience different routines in order to be able to select the most appropriate ones for themselves. In this phase, a dialogue concerning how to use the routines should be conducted between the coach and the athlete. The coach should listen to the athlete's demands and preferences when he or she is practicing different routines. The coach should present various routines to the athlete that can be used when performing self-paced tasks, for example, imagery, self-talk, and focusing attention. Adequate time should be allocated so that the athlete will be able to practice the routine and become familiar with its basic foundations.

Phase 2 – Task-specific preparatory instructions. The objective of Phase 2 is to enable the athlete to adopt a consistent set of routines that best reflects his or her individual needs and preferences. After experiencing different routines in Phase 1, the athletes should establish their own routines. They should feel comfortable with the selected routines and integrate their components with the techniques of the performed self-paced task. For example, in this phase the basketball player should establish a fixed routine composed of physical (e.g., dribbling the ball three times while standing on the shooting line) and psychological (e.g., looking at the front area of the rim before and during the shot) components when performing the free-throw shot. This routine should be smoothly integrated with the techniques of the free-throw shot, such as dribbling the ball (a physical component) when staying in a shooting-ready position (a technique of the shot), or focusing attention on the rim (a psychological component) when moving the ball up to the shooting position (a technique of the shot). In this phase, the athlete should feel confident with the established routine. He or she should believe that this selected routine will enable him or her to reach the highest level of performance.

Phase 3 – Preparatory instructions for the real-life self-paced event. The objective of Phase 3 is to enable the athletes to practice their selected routines in conditions simulating the real-life self-paced events that they may face during actual practices, games, or competitions. Two situational conditions are taken into account in this phase – time constraints and external distractions. As indicated earlier in our chapter, in real-sport situations athletes are given limited time to prepare themselves for the execution of the self-paced event (e.g., five seconds are allotted to the basketball player to prepare him- or herself for the free-throw shot).

Therefore, the selected routines should be performed within the time frame allocated to the athlete according to the rules of the competition/game. In addition, in various self-paced events the athlete is exposed to external distractions generated either by the crowd attending the sporting event or by athletes from the opposing team. In this phase the athlete should practice the routines under simulated conditions reflecting what he or she may face in the actual event. For example, the routine (and the self-paced task itself) should be practiced under noisy conditions (e.g., performing while a tape recorder generates the noise of hostile fans).

DEVELOPING PRE-PERFORMANCE ROUTINES IN SELF-PACED TASKS – A FREE-THROW SHOT IN BASKETBALL AND A STROKE IN GOLF

In order to illustrate how pre-performance routines are developed, we provide an example of a pre-performance routine for the free-throw shot in basketball, and an example of a pre-performance routine for a stroke in golf. The components of the routines are based on the patterns of physical behaviors and psychological techniques used by elite performers.

A free-throw shot in basketball

For the physical components, the player is recommended to:

(a) Get in a position on the free-throw line (e.g., setting the feet and assuming a comfortable position);
(b) Dribble the ball a number of times (e.g., bouncing the ball three to five times);
(c) Hold the ball after completing the dribbling act;
(d) Spin the ball while it is held in his or her hands;
(e) Use breathing control (e.g., inhaling deeply and exhaling slowly while holding the ball in the hands);
(f) Release the ball;
(g) Follow-through (e.g., hands should follow the ball towards the basket).

For the psychological components, the player is recommended to:

(a) Imagine her/himself performing the shot while standing on the shooting line (e.g., imagining the trajectory of the ball to the basket; imagining how the ball goes through the rim; imagining the sound generated by the ball when it goes through the rim and touches the net);
(b) Focus attention on the front area of the rim before and during the shooting act (e.g., directing the eyes at the rim; clearing the mind of any thoughts; relaxing);
(c) Self-talk while holding the ball (e.g., using selected words associated with the shooting task, such as: "be focused," "be relaxed," and "do it");
(d) Evaluate the techniques of the shot and its outcome, if time permits (e.g., after the completion of the first attempt and while preparing for the second attempt). An assessment can be made of the physical aspects of the shot: "Did I release the ball on time?" "Was the arc of the shot at a correct angle?" "Did I follow through?" Also, an assessment can be made of the psychological aspects of the shot: "Was I relaxed?" "Was I confident in my shot?" "Did I focus on the front area of the rim?".

A stroke in golf

For the physical components, while the player stands behind/beside the ball, he or she is recommended to:

(a) Determine the most appropriate distance from the ball;
(b) Select the most comfortable position behind/beside the ball (e.g., setting the feet, the club, and the grip);

(c) Perform a number of practice strokes without hitting the ball (e.g., performing one to three strokes);

(d) Use breathing control (e.g., inhaling deeply and exhaling slowly while holding the ball in the hands);

(e) Hit the ball at a target.

For the psychological components, the player is recommended to:

(a) Focus attention at the target (e.g., directing the eyes at the targeted flag/hole, relaxing, clearing the mind of any thoughts);

(b) Imagine executing the stroke while standing behind/beside the ball (e.g., imagining the trajectory of the ball to the target, imagining how the ball will approach the target, imagining the sound the ball will make when it hits the club, imagining the sound of the ball when it lands on the fairway);

(c) Self-talk while standing behind/beside the ball (e.g., using selected words associated with the stroke: "distance," "be focused," "be relaxed," and "go").

When coaches attempt to apply the principles of the above-mentioned three-phase model, it is recommended that they enable the basketball player or the golfer to practice the various routines, as required in Phase 1. Only after the players have gained some experience with the different routines can they select those routines that fit their individual needs and preferences, and in turn start to develop their own consistent routines (i.e., Phase 2). When a consistent routine is established, the players can be encouraged to activate the established routines in more challenged conditions, such as under distracted conditions or time constraints (i.e., Phase 3).

LEARNING AIDS

1   What are the main components of an effective performance routine?

In order for the athlete to benefit most from an effective performance routine, the routine should be composed of two main components – physical and psychological. Each of these components, as well as the interaction between the two, will result in better preparation for the sporting event as well as improved performance.

2   Why are performance routines effective in self-paced tasks?

Self-paced tasks are those performed in relatively stable and predictable settings. In these settings, the athlete knows in advance what he or she is going to do, and therefore task-pertinent performance routines can be developed and implemented.

3   Should only skilled athletes use performance routines?

No. Every athlete aimed at preparing him- or herself for the sporting event (either macro or micro) should acquire performance routines. It is advised to teach beginning athletes the physical and psychological foundations of performance routines as part of their early training programs.

4   Explain why a during-performance routine can help the athlete perform well.

Various self-paced tasks, such as free-throw shots in basketball or serving in tennis, require an optimal stage for focusing attention. A good during-performance routine can help the performer focus on one specific external cue, and in turn block out any internal or external distractions.

REVIEW QUESTIONS

1 Explain the differences between a macro sporting event and a micro sporting event.

2 Explain the differences between performance routines used in macro sporting events and those used in micro sporting events.

3 Identify the main characteristics of a self-paced task in sport.

4 Discuss the contribution of a pre-performance routine to achievement in self-paced sporting tasks.

5 Explain how beginning athletes can learn a performance routine.

EXERCISES

1 Watch two basketball games at any level (e.g., professional, amateur, or recreational). When you watch the games, you should record what the players of each team are doing when they prepare themselves for free-throw shots. Make a list of all the physical behaviors that the players demonstrated when they prepared themselves for the shooting act. What were the most frequent behaviors exhibited by the players? Did the players maintain a fixed set of behaviors?

2 Watch two professional golfers prepare themselves for the putt/swing. Select 10 putts and 10 swings. Make a list of what they were doing before they hit the ball with the club. Now, pick up a club and a ball and practice those physical behaviors demonstrated by the golfers when they prepared themselves for the putting/swinging acts. Do you think that their behaviors can help you prepare yourself for the strokes? Do you think that it is better for you to modify some of the behaviors that were exhibited by the two professional golfers?

ADDITIONAL READING

Boutcher, S.H. (1990). The role of performance routines in sport. In J.G. Jones & L. Hardy (Eds.), *Stress and performance in sport* (pp.221–245). New York, NY: Wiley.

Lidor, R. (2004). Developing metacognitive behavior in physical education classes: The use of task-pertinent learning strategies. *Physical Education and Sport Pedagogy, 1*, 55–71.

Lidor, R. (2009). Free-throw shots in basketball: Physical and psychological routines. In E. Tsung-Min Hung, R. Lidor & D. Hackfort (Eds.), *Psychology of sport excellence* (pp.53–61). Morgantown, WV: Fitness Information Technology.

Moran, A.P. (1996). *The psychology of concentration in sport performers: A cognitive analysis.* Hove, East Sussex, England: Psychology Press.

REFERENCES

Cohn, P.J. (1990). Preperformance routines in sport: Theoretical support and practical implications. *The Sport Psychologist, 4*, 301–312.

Concise Oxford Dictionary (1984). Oxford, UK: Clarendon Press.

Côté, J. & Fraser-Thomas, J. (2010). Play, practice, and athlete development. In D. Farrow, J. Baker, & C. MacMahon (Eds.), *Developing sport expertise – Researchers and coaches put theory into practice* (pp.17–28). London, UK: Routledge.

Crews, D.J. & Boutcher, S.H. (1987). An exploratory observational behavior analysis of professional golfers during competition. *Journal of Sport Behavior, 9,* 51–58.

Fédération Internationale de Volleyball (2004). *Official volleyball rules.* Seville, Spain: Fédération Internationale de Volleyball.

International Basketball Federation (2008). *FIBA activities.* Retrieved from www.FIBA.com.

Lidor, R. (2007). Preparatory routines in self-paced events: Do they benefit the skilled athletes? Can they help the beginners? In G. Tenenbaum & R.C. Eklund (Eds.), *Handbook of sport psychology* (3rd ed., pp.445–465). New York, NY: Wiley.

Lidor, R. (2010). Pre-performance routines. In S.J. Hanrahan & M.B. Andersen (Eds.), *Routledge handbook of applied sport psychology* (pp.537–546). London, UK: Routledge.

Lidor, R., Arnon, M., Aloni, N., Yitzak, S., Mayan, G. & Afek, A. (2012). Pre-preparatory and preparatory routines in free-throw shots in basketball: Are routines influenced by situational pressure? In R. Schinke (Ed.), *Sport psychology insights* (pp.307–325). New York, NY: Nova Science Publishers.

Lidor, R. & Mayan, Z. (2005). Can beginning learners benefit from preperformance routines when serving in volleyball? *The Sport Psychologist, 19,* 343–363.

Lidor, R. & Singer, R.N. (2003). Pre-performance routines in self-paced tasks: Educational, developmental, and psychological considerations. In R. Lidor & K. Henschen (Eds.), *The psychology of team sports* (pp.69–88). Morgantown, WV: Fitness Information Technology.

Oxford Advanced Learner's Dictionary (1992). Oxford, UK: Oxford University Press.

Schack, T. & Hackfort, D. (2007). An action theory approach to applied sport psychology. In G. Tenenbaum & R.C. Eklund (Eds.), *Handbook of sport psychology* (3rd ed., pp.332–351). New Jersey: Wiley.

Schack, T., Whitmarsh, B., Pike, R. & Redden, C. (2005). Routines. In J. Taylor & G. Wilson (Eds.), *Applying sport psychology – Four perspectives* (pp.137–150). Champaign, IL: Human Kinetics.

Southard, D. & Miracle, A. (1993). Rhythmicity, ritual, and motor performance: A study of free throw shooting in basketball. *Research Quarterly for Exercise and Sport, 3,* 284–290.

Thomas, J.R., Nelson, J.K. & Silverman, S.J. (2011). *Research methods in physical activity* (6th ed.). Champaign, IL: Human Kinetics.

Velentzas, K., Heinen, T. & Schack, T. (2011). Routine integration strategies and their effects on volleyball serve performance and players' movement mental representation. *Journal of Applied Sport Psychology, 23,* 209–222.

Velentzas, K., Heinen, T., Tenenbaum, G. & Schack, T. (2010). Functional mental representation of volleyball routines in German youth female national players. *Journal of Applied Sport Psychology, 22,* 474–485.

Wrisberg, C.A. & Pein, R.L. (1992). The pre-shot interval and free-throw shooting accuracy: An exploratory investigation. *The Sport Psychologist, 6,* 14–23.

Chapter 32

Preparing athletes for major competitions

GANGYAN SI, TRACI STATLER AND DIETMAR SAMULSKI*

SUMMARY

Sport psychology consultants in China, the United States, and Brazil provided comprehensive and systematic service to their national athletes in preparation for the Olympics under their own sport systems and cultures. The Chinese section of this chapter depicts a locally developed mental training model called the "Adversity Coping Framework" for Olympic athletes and describes how a psychology service was blended with indigenous culture. The American section describes how the two different service delivery systems, via the United States Olympic Committee and via independent contractors employed by a sport's National Governing Body, support elite athletes. The Brazilian section introduces the characteristics of mental preparation work for both Olympic and Paralympic athletes and elaborates on the use of psychological routines as an effective way to mentally prepare athletes.

INTRODUCTION

In the 2004 Athens Summer Olympic Games, Matthew Emmons, an American sport shooter in the men's 50 meter rifle competition had a three point lead right before the last shot. Despite such an advantage, he cross-fired his last shot, hit the target of his opponent and astonishingly lost the gold medal. In the 2008 Beijing Summer Olympic Games, he once again had a 3.3 point lead after the first nine shots, but he hit only 4.4 (out of 10) points on the final shot, again losing the gold medal which was almost in his hand.

Jennifer Heil, a Canadian freestyle skier and gold medalist in the 2006 Turin Winter Olympic Games, told us the difficulty she went through in the two years leading up to the 2010 Vancouver Games. Working with sport psychologists regularly, she has learnt how to deal with the tremendous expectation from various parties, control the emotion and channel the focus to the right spot. She said that she could feel "completely ready" and "smiling belly" before the competition, indicating she was calm and confident. She performed well and won a silver medal in the 2010 Games, finally (Barker, 2012). This story, like many others, reminds us that all athletes need excellent psychological skills to perform under great pressure in competitions

* Professor Doctor Dietmar Martin Samulski: Born February 7, 1950—Died December 1 2012.

like the Olympic Games. Nowadays psychological training is frequently embedded in the elite sport training systems around the world, particularly in preparation for the Olympic Games.

This chapter introduces how Olympians from China, the United States and Brazil access specific psychological training aimed at preparing them to perform at their optimal level.

OBJECTIVES

After reading this chapter you should be able to:

1 Understand the specific environments of China, the United States and Brazil with regard to their psychological preparation of Olympic athletes.
2 Comprehend a locally developed, Chinese mental training model referred to as the "Adversity Coping Framework".
3 Understand two different ways sport psychology and mental training services are generally provided to elite American athletes.
4 Learn how to develop a pre-performance routine for athletes.

SPORT PSYCHOLOGY FOR CHINESE OLYMPIC ATHLETES

Chinese sport psychology consultants provided comprehensive and systematic services to Chinese national athletes for the Olympics. As an attempt to extract the core elements from this important service provision, two main aspects are described in this section: (a) a mental training model "Adversity Coping Framework" which is locally developed and widely employed in China will be introduced; and (b) psychology services delivery which is coherent with the local sport culture (i.e., the Whole-Nation system and Chinese traditional culture) will be discussed.

Mental training model for Chinese Olympic athletes

The key issue of Olympic service provision is to implement mental training with top athletes. Sport psychologists employ various mental training models in order to carry out mental training effectively. The Adversity Coping Framework is a mental training program developed in a uniquely Chinese way and widely used by Chinese sport psychology consultants in their Olympic psychological

service. Peak performance is the goal for virtually all athletic training and competitions. Understanding peak performance is crucial to sport psychologists, coaches, and athletes. Si's framework (2006a), motivated by those difficulties encountered by sport psychologists when applying traditional mental training models to help athletes reach peak performance, proposed a new/alternative understanding/definition of peak performance and the transformation of mental training patterns. The main difficulty in traditional programs seems to be the concept of peak performance, which suggests that athletes have perfect performance when they possess an optimal psychological state (as described in a multitude of traditional theories on optimal performance). Some examples of this concept include the Profile of Mood States (POMS) "Iceberg Profile" (Morgan, 1980), optimal levels of anxiety (Martens et al., 1990), individualized zones of optimal functioning (Hanin, 1989), optimal combination of physical arousal and cognitive anxiety (Hardy & Parfitt, 1991), and flow state (Jackson, 1996).

Using these more traditional theories, practitioners seek to find this elusive construct of peak performance by examining the athletes' past experiences, then, by way of mental skills training, attempt to train for, activate, and maintain this "peak" state. Athletes participate in long periods of mental training, but still are often not sure if they will actually be able to reach this "peak" state at the time when they want it. Also, the coaches are typically only minimally involved in this process.

Problems with this traditional mental training model are three-fold: (1) How are these subjective peak states in the athletes determined, especially when some young athletes may not have yet had the chance to experience such peak states in their previous competitions? (2) How can the peak states be activated whenever athletes need them? (3) As conditions change and adversities appear, which can interfere with or destroy peak states, how can those peak states be maintained during competitions?

On the basis of practical experiences and applied research findings (Si & Liu, 2004), Si (2006a) proposed a new definition of peak performance, namely, successful adversity coping in competitions (described as the Adversity Coping Model). The differences between "optimal theory" and "adversity coping" are shown in Table 32.1 (Si, 2006a). According to Si, adversity in competition is normal, and athletes' success in coping with each adverse situation is closely related to their successful performance. In other words, even though athletes may not achieve a "peak" state at the time of the competition, if they can reasonably cope with most or all adversities, effectively overcome their mistakes or compensate for their loss, their performance should still be regarded as successful.

Following this line of reasoning, peak performance can be defined as a dynamic, continuously adjusted process during competition. In this way, the purpose of mental training is not primarily to discover or pursue the mechanism leading to the athletes' optimal performance during competition, but rather to explore the mechanism of adaptation when the athletes are placed under extremely stressful situations.

Based on this new definition, Si (2006a) developed a four-stage adversity coping training framework that includes: (1) Identifying and confirming typical adverse situations. The

Table 32.1 *Differences between "optimal theory" and "adversity coping"*

	Optimal theory	Adversity coping
Concept derivation	Top down	Bottom up
Awareness	Problem is not normal	Problem is normal
Adaptability	Emphasizing an optimal zone	Emphasizing a dynamic adaptation
Operation	Training goal is abstract Unstable replication	Training goal is concrete Stable replication
Evaluation	Subjective evaluation Possible difference between subjective and objective Evaluate feeling or experience	Subjective and objective evaluation Consistency between subjective and objective Evaluate rationality with behavior

typical adversity could be a specific situation, a target competition, or a particular opponent; (2) Seeking appropriate coping methods that contain the single coping strategy or method, integrated coping strategies or methods, and pursuit of the rationality of coping; (3) Conducting individualized training which may include: (a) evaluating the athlete's ability in adversity coping; (b) strengthening the athlete's awareness, learning skills, and habit formation; (c) transforming from training to competition, and (d) implementing the training periodically; and (4) Evaluating training outcomes. This evaluation may include: evaluation of awareness, attitude, application; evaluation of improvement of target behavior; evaluation of rationality; and evaluation of performance.

When compared with traditional mental training programs, Si's program replaces "peak"/optimal states of performance with optimal coping (i.e., awareness and application) of adverse situations. In general, this training model is characterized by: (a) a consistency in both athlete's and coach's subjective and objective evaluations (e.g., the number of times when an athlete is successful in handling adverse situations during competitions, and the outcome of competitions); (b) clear direction and close involvement of the coaches; (c) more tightly integrated on-field support service; and (d) more heuristic meaning.

Over the past few years, Si's framework has been applied with encouraging outcomes in both Hong Kong and mainland China (Han, 2008; Si, 2006b, 2007; Si, Lee, & Liu, 2008). Through adversity coping training, athletes are able to reach their ideal performance state (i.e., peak performance by new definition) and achieve promising results under either favorable or less favorable circumstances. During preparations for the 2008 Beijing Olympics, several sport psychology consultants working with top Chinese athletes either employed or borrowed ideas from this adversity coping model for their practice (Si, Zhang, Zhang, Zhang, Zhao, & Su, 2012).

For the purpose of strengthening athletes' awareness and guiding their behaviors, a 15-item guideline of athletes' adversity coping has been established as follows:

1 Problems are normal, while smoothness is an exception.
2 There is always something happening at the wrong time.
3 You cannot guarantee all necessary factors for success.
4 When a "stupid" method works, it is not "stupid" any more.
5 A pre-determined plan can never be carried out exactly as planned, particularly while confronting a strong rival.
6 Important things are always simple things.
7 Simple things are always hard to do.
8 Right before competition, if you still feel unprepared about something, it probably means that you have prepared too much.
9 If you have considered or analysed your rival in every aspect, remember that the rival has done the same thing to you.
10 Previous success will never appear again in the way you expect.
11 It is more your teammate's mistakes than your rivals' attacks that disturbs your mood.
12 If you know when to "open" and "close" your mind, your rivals will never disturb your mind.
13 It is equal to committing suicide if you try to avoid risks when you are approaching success.
14 Accumulation of tiny negative thoughts will lead to a sudden mental collapse.
15 There is only one rationale that can be adapted to specific situations, there is no general one that can be applied to the entire world.

The Whole-Nation system and Chinese traditional culture

Chinese sport psychology consultants working with athletes for various games and tournaments fall under the big umbrella of the Whole-Nation system, directly related to sport policy

Figure 32.1 Olympic flags.

of the central government of the People's Republic of China (PRC). The Whole-Nation system includes the administrative policies governing and financing elite sport development. Sport psychology services are also organized within those administrative policies and function as a top-down collective service model. Borrowing from a study about the 2008 Beijing Olympics, the service delivery model for Chinese athletes can be explained (Si et al., 2012).

Si and his colleagues (2012) conducted a qualitative study, interviewed 15 sport psychology consultants who had been systematically serving national athletes involved in the 2008 Beijing Olympics. Findings revealed that instead of the bottom-up approach that includes athletes' and coaches' referral and qualification accreditation of consultants like some other countries (Bond, 2002; Halliwell, 1989; Pensgaard, 2008; Vernacchia & Henschen, 2008), sport psychology service in PRC is a top-down process. Since 2005, the General Administration of Sport of China (China Sport Ministry) has asked each of the 20 sport centers (i.e., official administrative centers of each sport), which coordinate all related parties and sport psychology consultants, to take part in Olympic sport psychology projects. It is a service program targeting a common collective goal. Similar to those in other countries, the service process includes initial intervention, implementation and evaluation. However, the Chinese collective service model cause exhibits its significant differences. For example, intervention in this collective service model began, for the most part, as a project-based condition arranged by the administration, where athletes and coaches were expected to cooperate, rather than athletes and coaches taking initiative and requesting a service. Also, during the implementation stage, the service program was collectively and centrally operated, so that some innovative services, once "officially" endorsed, could be put into practice effectively and efficiently (e.g., an Olympic psychology website, psycho-educational movies, and a mobile psycho-clinic minibus). This centralized plan also allowed for regular communication among sport psychology consultants, whereas consultants working in an individual service model could only focus on specific problem solving and relied on their own resources. Lastly, during the evaluation stage, due to a clear collective goal and centralized resources, the service was much more results-oriented and multi-disciplinary within sport science areas, whereas an individual service model could only obtain evaluation on a personal basis. (Si et al., 2012).

Many Chinese scholars (e.g., Li, Li, & Liu, 2010; Si, 2006a, 2008, 2010; Zhang & Zhang, 2010) have advocated for integration between Chinese culture and sport psychology intervention and some have started their exploration in practice. For example, two sport psychology consultants (Si et al., 2012) employed Zen Buddhism, (i.e., Buddhism rooted in Chinese culture) to guide their psychology service provision for the 2008 Beijing Olympics. Another two sport psychology consultants (Si et al., 2012) adopted Chinese traditional elements such as fables, stories and philosophy as a means to deliver messages during their interventions for the top athletes in the 2008 Olympics. Nevertheless, the current condition of such integration does not yet appear to be systematic nor pervasive in the culture. Chinese sport psychology consultants have been acquiring a range of experience from their practices (for a review, see Si, Lee & Lonsdale, 2010), examining theories and exploring ideas and thoughts from Chinese culture such as Confucianism, Taoism, and Buddhism, with the objective of blending these approaches and ultimately putting them into practice (Si et al., 2011).

Working with top Chinese athletes, Chinese sport psychology consultants have been learning from their experiences and blending traditional Chinese culture into their newly-developed service/treatment models, into the Adversity Coping Model in particular. Preparing them for major competitions, the Chinese Whole-Nation system further maximizes the service effectiveness by setting the goals and facilitating the implementation process. Major competitions are held cyclically. Continually reflecting, Chinese sport psychology consultants endeavored to provide professional, individual specific and culturally sounded service to coaches and athletes.

SPORT PSYCHOLOGY SERVICE PROVISION FOR ELITE AMERICAN ATHLETES

This section will describe the varying ways sport psychology and mental training services are often delivered to elite level American athletes, particularly those training to represent the US at World Championships, Olympic, Paralympic and Pan American Games. Two different service delivery scenarios will be described – via the United States Olympic Committee (USOC) and via independent contractors employed by a sport's National Governing Body (NGB). It should be noted that although some combination of these models is most likely for elite level American performers, individually contracted sport psychology are also available.

USOC sport psychology service provision

The United States Olympic Committee: The United States Olympic Committee (USOC) has at its center the mission to support US Olympic and Paralympic athletes in achieving sustained competitive excellence and to preserve the Olympic Ideals (Team USA, n.d.). The USOC, founded in 1894 and headquartered in Colorado, serves as both the National Olympic Committee and National Paralympic Committee for the United States. As such, the USOC is responsible for the training, entering and funding of US teams for the Olympic, Paralympic, Youth Olympic, Pan American and Parapan

American Games, while serving to encourage and promote the Olympic movement throughout the country. In addition to its international Games responsibilities and its work to advance the Olympic movement, the USOC aids America's Olympic and Paralympic athletes through their National Governing Bodies (NGBs), providing financial support and jointly working to develop customized, creative and impactful athlete-support and coaching education programs. Additionally, the US Olympic Training Center facilities (USOTCs) and certified training centers often provide athletes with performance services, including sports medicine, strength and conditioning, psychology, physiology and nutritional assistance, and performance technology. These sport science services are coordinated by a centralized Sport Performance Division (Team USA, n.d.).

Elite performance training centers: The United States Olympic Committee has partnered with elite athlete training centers to allow American athletes the best training venues and facilities for their sport development. The mission of the US Olympic Training Sites are to provide additional resources, services and facilities for athletes and NGBs while creating an elite athlete training environment that positively impacts performance. Three main centers – Colorado Springs, Colorado, Lake Placid, New York and Chula Vista, California – serve as official United States Olympic Training Centers (USOTCs), however, there are a number of additional sport-specific US Olympic and Paralympic designated facilities throughout the country. For many of these locations, athletes chosen by their NGB or sports federation (usually the top 10–15% in the US) are given the option to live and train on-site. In addition to this athlete-in-residence option, NGBs will often send athletes and their coaches to USOTC "camps", where they will reside at the training centers for shorter periods (often a few weeks at a time) to take advantage of the resources and support options these locations offer.

In addition to (or sometimes in lieu of) the opportunities provided by the USOTCs and sport-specific centers, athletes may choose instead to train more regionally or locally, or closer to their sport's NGB headquarters, rather than on location at one of the official USOTCs. When this is the case, the assigned USOC sport psychologist and other sport science staff members will often work with the athletes and coaches remotely, incorporating telephone, email and Skype consultation, as well as maximizing any face-to-face opportunities that arise at competitions or training camps.

Sport psychology service provision within the USOC model

The Sport Performance Division provides support to athletes, coaches and sport NGBs by utilizing experts in a variety of sport sciences, including psychology. The USOC Sport Psychology Professional Team, initiated in 1987, collaborates with the other members of the USOC Sport Performance Division and works with national team coaches and athletes, as well as through the individual sport NGBs, to support Olympic success, with the belief that exceptional mental skills are necessary for exceptional Olympic performances. This work includes consulting with teams and individuals, creating practical educational materials for coaches and athletes, and supporting teams on the road, from training camps to the Olympics.

The full-time sport psychologists employed by the United States Olympic Committee work closely with American athletes, teams and coaches to assist them with the mental and psychological preparation needed to perform at the elite level. The USOC Psychology team consists of highly educated individuals with extensive knowledge and background in sport performance. At present, this staff consists of two women and three men with over 50 years of combined work with Olympic athletes and coaches. Four of these psychologists are based in Colorado Springs at the USOC headquarters, with another located at the Olympic Training Center in Southern California.

Figure 32.2 Olympic rings.

Sport Psychology service provision for the numerous sports within this USOC structure gets disseminated among these five individuals, with each sport psychologist generally responsible for a number of sports, clustered into portfolios. These portfolios generally center around common themes, such as "Winter Sports", "Team Sports", "Combative and Gymnastic Sports", and "Endurance Sports", however, as these categories sometimes overlap, decisions about which psychologist will work with which team can fluctuate. Furthermore, although some sports will technically "fit" into one of these portfolios, the specific sport NGB may choose to hire their own non-USOC service provider, as described later in this section.

Clearly, with the vast geography of the United States, and a philosophy of supporting international competition, the USOC Sport Psychologists spend quite a bit of time traveling and attempting to provide effective service from remote locations. As such, it becomes impera-

tive for these individuals to build and maintain effective relationships with the athletes, coaches and NGB administrators to ensure the highest quality service delivery possible. This requires an effective organizational structure that fosters and facilitates these relationships. At present, the USOC employs a hierarchical administrative model that echoes the organizational structure of many sport NGBs and American university athletic departments. The current USOC Sport Performance model incorporates (1) a Chief of High Performance, who oversees (2) Team Leaders, who in turn supervise (3) High Performance Directors, and then, (4) the actual service providers (e.g. Senior Sport Psychologists).

Sport psychology service provision philosophy

The sport psychologists employed by the USOC (as well as those outside contractors hired directly by the sport NGBs described later in this section) work to bring cutting edge science to athletes and coaches in an applied sense. They have the ability to collaborate with world-class service providers in other sport disciplines to ensure complementary training programs that can promote the highest levels of sport performance.

The actual day-to-day activities of the USOC sport psychologists working with elite American athletes varies, but is guided by the philosophy that exceptional mental skills are needed to succeed at the elite level of sport. To win at the highest level requires mental toughness. Without mental training, athletes often miss opportunities to succeed because although they are physically ready, they are not mentally ready (Sport Psychology Mental Training Manual, 2004). Furthermore, this philosophy posits that mental training isn't easy. "Athletes who do make the effort to train the mind discover that it takes time, effort and persistence, just like physical training. But just like physical training, the rewards can be great" (Sport Psychology Mental Training Manual, 2004, p. 1).

The sport psychologists of the USOC generally introduce a simple model for educating coaches and athletes on the benefits of sport psychology and mental skills training. This is referred to as the "ABC Model" in which a *situation* (A) generates a *reaction* (B) which then leads to a *response* (C).

A (situation) ➜ B (reaction) ➜ C (response)

If the *situation* (i.e., your first time competing for your country at the Olympic Games) causes the *response* (i.e., elevated anxiety and thoughts of self-doubt), are you in control of the *reaction*, or is the *situation* in charge? The USOC sport psychology group emphasizes that what your brain does when placed in a situation produces the response. Your *reaction* is what you say to yourself and what images go through your mind. The *reaction* is the critical element emphasized because your *reaction* is the only thing you can completely control. Sport psychology then is about learning to control your reaction to the situations with

which elite athletes must deal in an effort to generate the most effective response.

A summary of the USOC Sport Psychology Team's "Top Ten" Guiding Principles for Mental Training (see below) addresses these concepts, as well as other foundational beliefs of this group. The full description of these ideas can be found in the USOCs Athlete and Coach Sport Psychology Mental Training Manuals (2004, 2006).

The USOC Sport psychology's "Top Ten" Guiding Principles for Mental Training are:

1   Mental training cannot replace physical training and talent.
2   Physical training and physical ability is not enough to succeed consistently.
3   A strong mind may not win an Olympic medal, but a weak mind will lose one.
4   Coaches frequently don't know what their athletes are thinking.
5   Thoughts impact behavior. Consistency of thinking = consistency of behavior.
6   Coaches often differ in their approach to technical versus mental mistakes.
7   Coaches must be involved in the mental training process.
8   Sometimes it is OK to push athletes to take the time to do mental training.
9   Like any other skill, mental skills need to be measured in order to maximize performance of those skills.
10 Coaches need to think about their own mental skills.

NGBs and individually contracted sport psychology service provision

In the United States, individual sport NGBs have the ability to hire sport science consultants in addition to, to complement, or as a substitution for the USOC. A number of NGBs choose this option (e.g., track and field, swimming, speed skating, skiing, etc.), with each independently determining the philosophy, magnitude and content of service delivery. When this is the case, every effort is made to collaborate with the USOC Sport Psychologist "assigned" to the sport, such that additional support can be provided when needed (for example, at Olympic Games).

Often, when an NGB hires their own dedicated sport psychology consultant, that person (or persons) will work at all stages of the NGBs talent development hierarchy. For example, the team of sport psychology consultants that work with USA Track & Field provide services to youth, junior and elite level national teams, as well as interacting with coaches at each of these levels. Frequently, these individuals also conduct sport-specific psychology workshops, training camps and other educational sessions nationwide, in efforts to educate developing athletes and their coaches about the systematic provision of mental training.

These consultants generally introduce, teach, and reinforce the benefits of mental training, including such skills as energy management, imagery, relaxation, motivation, goal setting, effective communication, confidence and composure. They also work to educate coaches in how to incorporate mental training into existing physical, technical, and tactical workout routines to more seamlessly integrate it into the athlete's repertoire, as well as garner day-to-day coaching reinforcement of these psychological principles.

A number of sport psychology consultants have documented their particular experiences with specific NGBs in the extant literature (i.e., Gordin & Henschen with USA Ski and Snowboard, 2012; Gould with USA Freestyle Skiing, 2001 and wrestling 1993; Vernacchia and Henschen with USA track & field, 2008) and several others have synthesized common issues and experiences they have had consulting with Olympians across NGBs (i.e., Haberl & Petersen, 2006; McCann, 2000, 2008). The purpose of this section was simply to explain the varying pathways for sport psychology and mental skills training at the elite levels of performance in the United States. As there is such variety to how sport psychology services are provided to elite American athletes, their teams and their coaches, an all-encompassing explanation of the specifics of service delivery for these individuals is impossible. Therefore, the interested reader is encouraged to seek those references where more detailed explanations of service provision for particular athletes or teams are provided.

PSYCHOLOGICAL PREPARATION OF BRAZILIAN OLYMPIC AND PARALYMPIC ATHLETES

In the last few years, sport psychology has contributed effectively to a better understanding of how psychological factors influence athletic performance, especially in elite performance demonstrated at Olympic (McCann, 2008; Orlick, 2008; Samulski & Lopes, 2008) and Paralympic Games (Samulski, Noce, & Costa, 2011).

> Successful Olympic performance is a complex, multifaceted, fragile and long-term process that requires extensive planning and implementations. Attention to detail counts, but must also be accompanied by flexibility to deal with numerous unexpected events. (Gould et al., 1998, p. 53).

Gould, Dieffenbach and Moffet (2002) investigated Olympic champions' psychological characteristics and their development. These athletes showed the following characteristics: coping with and controlling anxiety, confidence, sport intelligence, the ability to focus and block out distractions, competitiveness, hard work, ethics, ability to set and achieve goals, coachability, high levels of dispositional hope, optimism, adaptive perfectionism, and mental toughness.

In the next part of the chapter, we present the concept of psychological preparation of Brazilian Olympic athletes, considering the development of psychological characteristics of elite performance.

Psychological preparation of Brazilian Olympic athletes

At the moment, the Brazilian Olympic Committee (COB) does not have a systematic strategy to mentally prepare athletes and teams for the upcoming Olympic Games in London (2012) and Rio de Janeiro (2016). Each Brazilian Sport Federation has its own responsibility to prepare their athletes and teams. For this reason, only some athletes and teams receive systematic psychological support. In some cases, a sport psychologist is invited by the head coach of a national team as an integrated part of the coaching staff.

One outstanding sport in Brazil, which offers continuous psychological service to their athletes and teams, is volleyball. The Brazilian Volleyball Confederation (CBV) has built a National Training Center, in Saquarema, near to Rio de Janeiro. The main objective of the National Training Center is to prepare and train the male and female Brazilian National volleyball teams in an interdisciplinary way for international competitions, including World Championships and Olympic Games. An integrated part of the training center is the department of psychological support. This department is responsible for the psychological preparation of all the indoor and beach volleyball teams.

At the training center, the department of psychological support performs the following actions: mental preparation of all indoor and beach volleyball teams; individualized psychological assistance to athletes with emotional problems; psychological support to the coaches regarding coaching and communication; ongoing meetings with the coaching staff to discuss strategies for interdisciplinary preparation of athletes; group dynamics to develop group cohesion and team spirit; and psychological counseling during International Competitions and Olympic Games upon request of the coach. For example, at the 2008 Beijing Olympics, a sport psychologist, as a member of the coaching staff, accompanied the Women's Volleyball National Team that won the gold medal. This success contributed to a better recognition of sport psychology in Brazil.

This model of interdisciplinary team work at the National Training Center in Rio de Janeiro is a good model for Brazil. Visiting national teams from other countries also train at this center to prepare their athletes for the upcoming Olympic Games.

Some athletes invited specialists in mental coaching to help to prepare them for the 2012 Olympics in London. The objective of mental coaching is not only to improve sports performance but also to develop mental health and quality of life.

Psychological preparation of Brazilian Paralympic athletes

In 2000, the Brazilian Paralympic Committee (CPB) invited a sport psychologist to prepare Brazilian athletes and teams for the 2000 Paralympic Games in Sydney. This sport psychologist was part of the Brazilian delegation and was responsible for coaching and counseling before and during the Olympic Games.

In 2002, the CPB established a National Commission of Evaluation and Scientific Support, and sport psychology was integrated into this committee. The main objective of this committee was the evaluation and scientific monitoring of athletes and teams.

At the last Paralympic Games in Beijing (2008), five experts in sport psychology accompanied the Brazilian delegation and provided psychological support to athletes during the Olympics. Brazil won 16 gold medals and was ranked ninth among the participating nations. The head of this delegation attributed a great part of this success to the psychological support provided to athletes.

In preparation for the 2016 Paralympic Games in Rio de Janeiro, the CPB has developed strategies for psychological evaluation of athletes' performance and for psychological training at the Paralympic training centers. The main objective is the development of mental skills and psychological routines for competition; and coaching the teams at international events such as the Pan-American Games, World Championships and Paralympic Games. In this case, the sport psychologist is part of the coaching staff; realization of training seminars about topics like motivation, leadership, communication, team building, and effective coaching.

A crucial aspect of psychological preparation for the Olympic and Paralympic Games is the development of a psychological routine for competition (PRC) in order to emotionally stabilize the athlete during the competition. These routines depend on the specificity of the sport and the characteristics of personality of each athlete.

Psychological routines for competition

Silva, Metzler, & Lerner (2007, p. 144) define a routine as a "set of task-related behaviors or actions exhibited by an athlete that provides a sense of control, stability and readiness". The authors affirm that routines are established in conjunction with the athlete and are controlled by the athlete. A critical moment to implement psychological routines is in the pre-competitive period, which is operationally defined as the 24-hour interval leading up to competition. A routine will provide much-needed stability during this intense time when the athlete's mental preparation is especially significant.

Studies show that athletes who apply mental preparation routines before or during competition perform better than athletes who do not. The key elements of a psychological routine are: positive attitude, goal setting strategies, regulation of stress and activation levels, imagery and visualization techniques, attention and concentration control and positive self-verbalization statements.

A routine is different from a ritual. According to Samulski (2009, p. 160), "a psychological routine represents a combination of different physiological and psychological techniques with the aim of stabilizing the emotional behavior of athletes and helping them to direct their attention to the stimuli relevant to the task to be carried out". The main characteristic of a ritual consists in the fact that it is based on superstitions, and often the behaviors repeated have no task relation to performance (Silva, Metzler, & Lerner, 2007).

Psychological routines can be developed and applied in group and in individual sports, such as psychological routines for swimming (Table 32.2), and judo (Table 32.3), as presented in the following tables:

As can be seen from Table 32.2, the function of the psychological routine in swimming is to help the athletes to maintain focus on the goal. Athletes report that it is very common to be preoccupied with the opponent's performance or to feel insecure because a superior opponent with a better time is in the same competition. Above all, psychological routines help the athletes to avoid negative thoughts and maintain the focus on the task.

Table 32.3 shows the sequence of behaviors between the combats in judo in order to recover energy, to relax physically and mentally, and to develop a strategy plan for the next combat. The last step of this routine is to develop a high level of concentration at the beginning of the combat. This routine is an integrated part of mental preparation of a Brazilian world champion.

CONCLUSIONS OF BRAZILIAN SPORT PSYCHOLOGY WORK

Most of the Brazilian athletes and coaches gave positive feedback on the psychological support during the Olympic and Paralympic Games. There was excellent cooperation and interaction between the sport psychologist and other members of the medical staff, especially with the physiotherapist regarding the rehabilitation and recovery of injured athletes.

Table 32.2 *Example of psychological pre-competitive routines in swimming (Samulski, 2009). Mental routine duration: BP = basic program: 10 minutes; SP = short program: 5 minutes; FP = flash program: 2 minutes*

Mental routine in 4 phases	BP	SP	FP
1st Phase: deep respiration Objective: optimal arousal level	2′	1′	30″
2nd Phase: visualization of success Objective: winning feeling	4′	2′	30″
3rd Phase: positive self verbalization Objective: positive attitude	2′	1′	15″
4th Phase: visualization of the perfect swimming technique Objective: mental focus	2′	1′	45″
Total time of mental routine	10′	5′	2′

Table 32.3 *Example of psychological routines between the combats in judo (developed for a judo World Champion)*

Main objective	Energy recuperation and mental preparation for the next combat
Sequences of Mental Routines	
First step	Disconnect mentally from the previous combat
Second step	Psychological and physiological recovery; replace energy; rehydration; application of physiotherapeutic techniques; mental relaxation and mental recovery
Third step	Develop a mental strategy plan (MSP) for the next combat
Fourth step	Physical and mental warm up
Fifth step	Total concentration (focus!) at the beginning of the combat

CONCLUSION

Psychological preparation has to be an integrated and long-term preparation process, oriented and supervised by an expert in coaching and counseling. Young athletes in particular need intensive mental preparation and emotional support. Sport psychology is not the only key to sport excellence, but it is one of the most important and crucial elements for success.

LEARNING AIDS

1   Outline the four steps involved in setting up an adversity coping training program for athletes.

   An adversity coping training program may include four steps: (1) identifying and confirming typical adverse situations; (2) seeking appropriate coping methods; (3) conducting individualized training; (4) evaluating training outcomes.

2   Describe the two different ways sport psychology and mental training services can be provided to elite American athletes.

   Elite American athletes can receive sport psychology service delivery either through their sport's National Governing Body (NGB), via independently contracted consultants, or if they are eligible, through the full time sport psychologists employed by the US Olympic Committee.

3   Outline the four steps involved in setting up a psychological routine for a sport.

   A psychological pre-competition routine may have the following steps: (1) creating an optimal arousal level; (2) visualizing a success; (3) having a positive self-talk; (4) concentrating on the target.

REVIEW QUESTIONS

1   Discuss the difference between the two mental training models "Optimal Theory" and "Adversity Coping".

2   Discuss how sport psychologists fit into the framework of the USOC's Sport Performance Division.

3   Discuss the meaning and function of a psychological routine for competition.

EXERCISES

1   Develop an adversity coping training program for an athlete.

2   Describe how an athlete not living on-site at one of the American USOTCs can still receive training in sport psychology and mental skills.

3   Develop a pre-competitive routine in a sport of your choice.

ADDITIONAL READING

Dosil, J. (Ed.) (2005). *The sport psychologist's handbook: A guide for sport-specific performance enhancement.* Chichester: John Wiley & Sons.

Schinke, R. (Ed.) (2010). *Introduction to sport psychology: Training, competition and coping.* New York, NY: Nova Science.

Si, G.Y. & Lee, H.C. (2007). Cross-culture issue. In S. Jowett & D. Lavallee (Eds.), *Social psychology in sport* (pp.279–288). Champaign, IL: Human Kinetics.

REFERENCES

Bond, J.W. (2002). Applied sport psychology: Philosophy, reflections and experience. *International Journal of Sport Psychology, 33*, 19–37.

Gordin, R.D. & Henschen, K.P. (2012). Reflections on the psychological preparation of the USA ski and snowboard team for the Vancouver 2010 Olympic Games. *Journal of Sport Psychology in Action, 3 (2)*, 88–97.

Gould, D. (2001). Sport psychology and the Nagano Olympic Games: The case of the U.S. freestyle ski team. In G. Tenenbaum (Ed.), *The practice of sport psychology* (pp.49–76), Morgantown, WV: Fitness information Technology.

Gould, D., Dieffenbach, K. & Moffet, A. (2002). Psychological characteristics and their development in Olympic champions. *Journal of Applied Sport Psychology, 14*, 172–204.

Gould, D., Greenleaf, C., Guinan, D., Medbery, R., Lauer, L., Chung, Y. & Peterson, K. (1998). Factors influencing Atlanta Olympian performance. *Olympic Coach, 8(4)*, 9–11.

Haberl, P. & Peterson, K. (2006). Olympic-size ethical dilemmas: Issues and challenges for sport psychology consultants on the road and at the Olympic Games. *Ethics & Behavior, 16*, 25–40.

Halliwell, W. (1989). Delivering sport psychology services to the Canadian sailing team at the 1988 Summer Olympic Games. *The Sport Psychologist, 3(4)*, 313–319.

Han, L. (2008). Sport psychologist's working diary on 2007 National Rhythmic Gymnastics Championship. *Chinese Journal of Sports Medicine, 27(4)*, 511–517.

Hanin, Y.L. (1989). Interpersonal and intragroup anxiety in sports. In D. Hackfort & C.D. Spielberger (Eds.), *Anxiety in sports: An international perspective* (pp.19–28). New York: Hemisphere.

Hardy, L. & Parfitt, C.G. (1991). A catastrophe model of anxiety and performance. *British Journal of Psychology, 82*, 162–178.

Jackson, S.A. (1996). Towards a conceptual understanding of the flow state in elite athletes. *Research Quarterly for Exercise and Sport, 67(1)*, 76–90.

Li, S.H., Li, J.C. & Liu, S.H. (2010, November). *Application of Chinese literature on shooters' mental intervention*. Paper presented at the 12th Annual Meeting of China Association of Science and Technology, Fuzhou, China.

Martens, R., Vealey, R.S. & Burton, D. (1995). *Competitive anxiety in sport*. Champaign, IL: Human Kinetics Publishers.

McCann, S.C. (2000). Doing sport psychology at the really big show. In M.B. Andersen (Ed.), *Doing sport psychology* (pp.209–222). Champaign, IL: Human Kinetics.

McCann, S.C. (2008). At the Olympics, everything is a performance issue. *International Journal of Sport & Exercise Psychology, 6*, 267–276.

Morgan, W.P. (1980). Test of Champions: The Iceberg Profile. *Psychology Today. 14(2)*, 92–108.

Orlick, T. (2008). *In pursuit of excellence*. (4th ed.). Champaign, IL: Human Kinetics.

Pensgaard, A.M. (2008). Consulting under pressure: How to help an athlete deal with unexpected distracters during Olympic Games 2006. *International Journal of Sport and Exercise Psychology, 3*, 301–307.

Samulski, D. (2009). *Sports psychology: Concepts and new perspectives* (Portuguese). São Paulo: Manole.

Samulski, D. & Lopes, M. (2008). Counseling Brazilian athletes during the Olympic Games in Athens 2004: Important issues and intervention techniques. *International Journal of Sport and Exercise Psychology, 6*, 277–286.

Samulski, D., Noce, F. & Costa, V. (2011). Mental Preparation. In Y. Vanlandewijck & W. Thompson (Eds.), *The paralympic athlete* (pp.198–213). London: Wiley-Blackwell.

Si, G.Y. (2006a). Pursuing "ideal" or emphasizing "coping": the new definition of "peak performance" and transformation of mental training pattern. *Sport Science (China), 26(10)*, 43–48.

Si, G.Y. (2006b). Sport psychologist's working diary on 48th World Team Table Tennis Championship. *Chinese Journal of Sports Medicine, 25(6)*, 732–736.

Si, G Y. (2007). Sport psychologist's working diary on 19th Asian Tenpin Bowling Championship. *Chinese Journal of Sports Medicine, 26(3)*, 360–363.

Si, G.Y. (2008). Adversity coping of young athletes. *Journal of Tianjin University of Sport, 23(3)*, 185–186.

Si, G.Y., Duan, Y.P., Li, H.Y. & Jiang, X.B. (2011). An exploration into social-cultural meridians of

Chinese athletes' psychological training. *Journal of Clinical Sport Psychology, 5,* 325–338.

Si, G.Y., Zhang, Z.Q., Zhang, C.Q., Zhang, C.H., Zhao, D.L. & Su, N. (2012). Psychological preparation of Chinese athletes for the 2008 Beijing Olympic Games. *China Sport Science and Technology, 4,* 3–20.

Si, G.Y., Lee, H.C. & Liu, J.D. (2008). Intervention and evaluation for changing low frustration tolerance. *Acta Psychologica Sinica. 40(2),* 240–252.

Si, G.Y., Lee, H.C. & Lonsdale, C. (2010). Sport psychology research and its application in China. In M.H. Bond. (Ed.), *The Oxford handbook of Chinese psychology* (pp.641–656). Hong Kong: Oxford University Press.

Si, G.Y. & Liu, H. (2004). A study on sport achievement goals of elite table tennis players. *Journal of Beijing Sport University, 27(5),* 617–621.

Silva, J., Metzler, J. & Lerner, B. (2007). *Training professionals in the practice of sport psychology.* Morgantown: Fitness Information Technology.

Team USA (n.d.) Retrieved from: http://www.teamusa.org

United States Olympic Committee. (2004). *Sport psychology mental training manual.* Colorado Springs, CO.

Vernacchia, R.A. & Henschen, K.P. (2008). The challenge of consulting with track and field athletes at the Olympic Games. *International Journal of Sport and Exercise Psychology, 6,* 254–266.

Zhang, K. & Zhang, L.W. (2010, September). *The "Dao" and "Shu": The enlightenment of Chinese culture to the consultation and mental training for athletes.* Paper presented at the 9th Chinese National Sport and Exercise Psychology Conference. Shanghai, China.

Part Five

Understanding how to build and lead teams

EDITED BY MARK A. EYS AND PACKIANATHAN CHELLADURAI

Chapter 33

Building cohesive groups

M. BLAIR EVANS, MARK A. EYS, MARK W. BRUNER AND JENS KLEINERT

SUMMARY

Groups are a ubiquitous aspect of physical activity settings, and come in a variety of forms including teams and exercise groups. Described as the social bond that unites group members, cohesion receives a great deal of attention because it is important for performance, enjoyment, and adherence. Cohesion is evident in both task and social settings, and is identified according to group members' perceptions of: (a) the closeness and bonding amongst group members; and (b) their own attractions to the group. This chapter summarizes relevant group research, with a specific focus on how leaders can use this knowledge to improve cohesion. Team building approaches are presented as the primary means of improving cohesion within sport and exercise settings. Readers will emerge from this chapter with a clear understanding of cohesion and how group principles can be used to enhance group environments.

INTRODUCTION

It figures. In a World Cup that saw the sport's top individual stars all exit by the quarterfinals – adiós, Lionel Messi; cheerio, Wayne Rooney; adeus, Kaká and Cristiano Ronaldo – Spain had to turn everything into a team affair. That included the decisive goal... Not even Rolex produces movement so coordinated and true (Wahl, 2010, para. 2–4).

The importance of group cohesion cannot be overstated. In the preceding quote, the ability of the Spanish football (soccer) team to execute their game plan in a united and cohesive manner during the 2010 World Cup is presented in contrast to other teams who potentially did not integrate their individual stars as effectively. Furthermore, Spain's ability to successfully combine the efforts of 11 talented players forced other teams to reconsider their strategies and tactics. Most notable was the change in approach taken by the Dutch team in the final game; shifting from elegant to aggressive play to try and disrupt the flow of the Spanish team. The present chapter focuses on the concept of cohesion, summarizes empirical evidence regarding its importance in sport, and briefly highlights team building suggestions designed to increase individuals' perceptions of their group's integration and their own feelings of connectedness to the team.

OBJECTIVES

After reading this chapter you should be able to:

1   Discuss the importance and prevalence of groups in sport and exercise.
2   Describe cohesion, how it is measured, and its related outcomes.
3   Explain the importance of cohesion for efficient group functioning.
4   Integrate cohesion within other existing theoretical frameworks.
5   Discuss team building approaches for developing group cohesion.

PREVALENCE OF GROUPS IN SPORT AND EXERCISE SETTINGS

Groups are vital entities within physical activity settings, as exercise and sport environments provide ample opportunities for individuals to interact with other participants (e.g., teammates). In considering some of the most popular sports in the world – such as soccer, cricket, and volleyball – participants work together as teams, and against other teams. Even in popular sports that do not involve a coordinated group *task* – such as gymnastics, swimming, and golf – individuals frequently contribute to shared objectives (e.g., team scores) and/or interact with important others including training partners, coaches, and physiotherapists.

Overall, groups are such an inherent part of everyday physical activity that 'social settings' are included as a major factor in the World Health Organization's *global recommendations on physical activity and health* (World Health Organization, 2010). In this report, social environments are promoted for physical activity considering how play, sport, and recreation all occur within the context of family and community. The report also included messages from a number of countries (i.e., Canada, Australia, United States, and the Pacific Region) that advise physical activity participants to include their friends and family, engage in exercise classes or sport teams, and use support networks to help keep them involved.

However, not all social collectives have the characteristics required to be a group, nor are all groups created 'equal'. A number of traits are required for a collection of two or more people to be considered a 'group' including: mutual benefit, work on a common task, shared structured social relationships, and members defining themselves as a group (Carron & Eys, 2012). Collectively, the majority of group definitions identify one key group characteristic: interdependence. Interdependence in tasks, fates, and goals is what connects group members together, and generally refers to the degree that individuals rely on one another. More specifically, interdependence is defined as the degree that individual and group-level task performance, goal attainment, and general experiences are contingent on contributions from all group members (Johnson & Johnson, 1989).

There are a number of ways for individuals to be interdependent. *Task* interdependence is largely responsible for our current reliance on classifying sport types into team (e.g., soccer) and individual (e.g., running) categories. Team sports are those where athletes train together and compete in a collective group task, whereas individual sport team members do not work together to achieve a collective group task. Thus, it is often assumed that group processes will have greater influence in team sport because interaction is essential. However, there are a number of alternative ways that team members can be interdependent above and beyond the task. Group members can also be *outcome interdependent* through shared goals or rewards, which form

Figure 33.1 Team sports are highly interdependent environments. Photograph by Mike Whitehouse, WLU Athletics. Reprinted courtesy of Wilfrid Laurier University.

additional connections among group members. For example, a school team of tennis players may compete in events where group members' scores are aggregated and overall titles are awarded to the highest scoring teams. Individual sports may also differ in the degree that group members are required to compete against one another, such as in cross country running events. Furthermore, group members can be interdependent with respect to the allotment of resources (e.g., sharing coaches, training facilities, and equipment) and within training tasks (e.g., working together, travel, training plans). Considering the assortment of ways that group members can rely on one another, it is clear that group processes can have an important influence even when members do not work together specifically on a task. As a result, the prevalence and variety of interactive environments within sport and exercise necessitate the examination of the dynamics underlying groups.

GROUP DYNAMICS IN SPORT AND EXERCISE

'Group dynamics' refers to the "actions, processes, and changes that occur within groups and between groups" (Forsyth, 2010, p. 2) and summaries of the existing literature can be found in texts devoted to this topic in organizational psychology (e.g., Forsyth, 2010) and physical activity (e.g., Beauchamp & Eys, 2007; Carron & Eys, 2012). While it is not the purpose of the present chapter to cover each group dynamics topic in depth (other authors within this section of the book provide excellent information regarding leadership, group climate, and communication), it is worthwhile to highlight a useful conceptual framework

Figure 33.2 Team outcomes are influenced by the structure, processes, and cohesion of the group. Photograph by Mike Whitehouse, WLU Athletics. Reprinted courtesy of Wilfrid Laurier University.

(Carron & Eys, 2012) for the study of sport and exercise groups that underscores its complexity. This conceptual framework emphasizes the need to first consider aspects relating to the physical/psychological attributes of group members as well as the environment in which the group is operating. With respect to the former, for example, it is important to consider the amount, variability, and compatibility of all the requisite skills that members can contribute. In the case of the latter, the organizational needs and even physical location (i.e., playing at home vs. away) are considerations of the group's environment.

These inputs are proposed to influence a number of factors leading to both individual and group outcomes including: the structure of the group (e.g., leadership, role responsibilities, normative expectations, status hierarchies), its processes (e.g., communication, coordination, cooperation), and the degree to which the team is united with respect to task and social objectives (i.e., cohesion). It is important to consider all of the factors pertaining to group involvement in sport and exercise. However, the remainder of the chapter will focus on the concept of cohesion.

GROUP COHESION

Definition and conceptualization of cohesion

Group cohesion is defined as a "dynamic process which is reflected in the tendency for a group to stick together and remain united in the pursuit of its instrumental objectives and/or for the satisfaction of member affective needs" (Carron, Brawley, & Widmeyer, 1998, p. 213). A number of characteristics of cohesion are evident within this definition. First, Carron and colleagues suggested that cohesion is *dynamic*; thus, it can change over the lifespan of a group and is amenable to improvement via intervention.

Second, Carron and colleagues proposed that the concept of cohesion is *multidimensional*. Through their initial work developing a measure of cohesion for sport, Carron, Widmeyer, and Brawley (1985) identified four distinct ways that athletes can perceive cohesion that can be distinguished according to two factors. First, cohesion can be considered with respect to task as well as social aspects of the group. For example, cohesion can be perceived during game performances (task) or between members after games (social). Cohesion is also viewed according to the perceptual orientation, as it is considered both through individuals' perceptions of their own attractions to the group as well as their perceptions regarding the degree of integration of the group as a whole.

In combination, the above distinctions yield four dimensions that are important to consider when examining group cohesion: (a) individual attractions to the group – task (i.e., members' personal attractions to task aspects of the group, ATG-T); (b) individual attractions to the group – social (i.e., members' personal attractions to social aspects of the group, ATG-S); (c) group integration – task (i.e., individuals' perceptions of how united the group is regarding task objectives, GI-T); and (d) group integration – social (i.e., individuals' perceptions of how united the group is regarding social objectives, GI-S).

Measuring cohesion

A number of measures have been developed in the attempt to gauge perceptions of cohesion. Created in conjunction with their conceptual model, Carron et al. (1985) developed what is considered to be the most widely accepted measure of cohesion in a sport environment; the Group Environment Questionnaire (GEQ). The GEQ assesses the four dimensions of cohesion discussed previously (i.e., ATG-T, ATG-S,

GI-T, and GI-S) through an 18-item inventory and the validity and reliability of this tool have been consistently demonstrated with populations for which it was designed (i.e., adult, recreational/competitive, interactive sport teams).

Carron, Brawley, and Widmeyer (2002) were clear that greater consideration needs to be made for using the GEQ as an assessment tool for other populations. As a result, a number of researchers have created measures specific to their population of interest. As examples, Estabrooks and Carron (2000) created a 21-item measure of cohesion (i.e., Physical Activity Group Environment Questionnaire) specific for an adult exercise environment, and Heuzé and Fontayne (2002) developed a questionnaire (i.e., Questionnaire sur l'Ambiance du Groupe; 18 items) that could be used with French-speaking athletes. Finally, two measures have been created for use with younger populations (i.e., youth and children). In the development of the Youth Sport Environment Questionnaire, Eys, Loughead, Bray, and Carron (2009) provided evidence that adolescent athletes (approximately 13–17 years of age) do not distinguish group versus individual level perceptions. As a result, this questionnaire assesses only task and social cohesion. This structure was also used by Martin, Carron, Eys, and Loughead (2012) for their Child Sport Cohesion Questionnaire proposed for use with children approximately 9–12 years of age.

Importance of group cohesion

As stated in the introduction to this chapter, cohesion is an incredibly important consideration within sport. First and foremost, there is strong evidence supporting the link between cohesion and team performance. Carron, Colman, Wheeler, and Stevens (2002) conducted a meta-analysis to summarize the literature pertaining to the cohesion-performance link and found a moderate to large positive relationship. This relationship was found regardless of type of cohesion (i.e., task vs.

social cohesion) or type of sport (interdependent vs. independent sport). Furthermore, there is consistent evidence that perceptions of cohesion are positively related to athletes' intentions to return to their sport team as well as their actual return (e.g., Spink, Wilson, & Odnokon, 2010).

Moving beyond these two major outcomes, there are a myriad of other factors that appear to be related to perceptions of cohesion (see Carron & Eys, 2012 for a summary of specific research studies). These include personal cognitions such as attributions for responsibility and self-handicapping, as well as athletes' emotional states including competitive state anxiety and satisfaction. Furthermore, a number of group-level variables have been positively associated with cohesion in a sport environment including athletes' perceptions of their role (e.g., role clarity), conformity to group normative expectations, and the collective efficacy of the group. While the majority of research has taken a cross-sectional/correlational approach, it can be safely assumed that a more cohesive group will generally yield more positive individual and group perceptions (although disadvantages to highly cohesive groups have been introduced; Hardy, Eys, & Carron, 2005).

The findings summarized above pertain to perceptions of cohesion within a sport environment. However, it is imperative to point out the benefits of cohesion within an exercise setting as well. Two meta-analytic reviews succinctly provide evidence of the benefits in facilitating positive group processes within exercise. First, Carron, Hausenblas, and Mack (1996) found a moderate, positive association between perceptions of task cohesion and adherence behaviors across six studies. Second, Burke, Carron, Eys, Ntoumanis, and Estabrooks (2006) noted that physical activity interventions employing group dynamics strategies (and thus facilitating cohesion) were most effective in eliciting a number of positive outcomes (compared to standard exercise group and individual oriented exercise).

Following on from the findings across physical activity settings (i.e., sport and exercise) that demonstrate the importance of cohesion in relation to other variables, the next two sections of this chapter: (a) link the concept of cohesion within larger explanatory theoretical frameworks and; finally, (b) discuss methods by which positive group processes can be facilitated.

Cohesion from the standpoint of related theories

Interventions (e.g., team building) should be developed on the basis of a theoretical understanding or modeling of how things work. Such theoretical considerations may further explain *why* and *how* cohesion varies and are thus of high practical significance since they provide frameworks for the development of diagnostic and intervention tools. In addition to existing frameworks highlighting inputs/outputs of cohesion (e.g., Carron & Spink, 1993), it may be useful to consider two perspectives of cohesion that afford links with other theories, even if these perspectives are not totally separate. One perspective of cohesion links to theories that explain how and why individuals view *commonality* with other people; for instance, shared attitudes, goals, or any other kind of shared property (e.g., similarity). Theory pertaining to the concept of structural interdependence, discussed earlier in this chapter, would have relevance from this perspective. In addition, Social Identity Theory is proposed as an additional salient theoretical approach to commonality in the subsequent paragraphs. Another perspective of cohesion addresses not only the similar properties of individuals in a group but links to theories that explain *how and why individuals relate* to each other. Finally, Balance Theory can help to understand how similarity/uniformity and interpersonal relations work together with respect to group dynamics.

Cohesion as "something in common". Cohesive entities (e.g., a football team) occur very often with a specific amount of uniformity. In psychological terms, among other things, cohesion is characterized by an explicit or implicit commonality or oneness of psychological attributes or properties. In Social Identity Theory (Tajfel & Turner, 1985) the individual's social identity is described as that part of an individual's self-concept derived from his/her membership in groups. The mechanism by which such a social identity is developed – and by which the extent of similarity with the group is defined – is known as the self-categorization process. Self categorization is mainly a comparison between: (a) perceived prototypical attributes and properties of a given group (i.e., the group prototype); and (b) a person's own attributes and properties. Using Social Identity Theory as a backdrop, cohesion enhancement contains two steps: characterization of a group's prototype and the individual's identification with this prototype in a self-categorization process.

The Optimal Distinctiveness Theory (ODT) by Brewer (1991) adds an interesting and mean-ingful consideration to social identity theory. Brewer stated that two human needs, namely the needs for assimilation and individuation, influence the individual's behavior within a group. Whereas Social Identity Theory addresses the idea of assimilation needs (e.g., belonging), ODT adds the human motivation for being and feeling unique within a group. Hence, from an ODT perspective, strategies toward the enhancement of cohesion should not only find a shared group identity but also attempt to satisfy the group members' needs for individuation; a delicate balance.

Cohesion as "positive interrelations with others". In addition to comparisons of individual attributes and the properties of group members, cohesion can also be considered via the perspective of *interpersonal relations*. More specifically, interaction and communication between group members are subjectively evaluated by the individuals who are involved, which subsequently affects how each group member interprets interpersonal relationships

Figure 33.3 Cohesion is characterized by an explicit or implicit communality or oneness among group members. Photograph by Adam Gagnon, WLU Athletics. Reprinted courtesy of Wilfrid Laurier University.

with other members. Understanding these processes has a foundation in different social psychological theories, which mainly address relation-oriented human needs.

Humans are social and therefore strive for positive relations with others. Different theorists have defined basic, or even innate, needs to explain the human tendency of affiliation, connectedness, and bonding ("need to belong", Baumeister & Leary, 1995; "need for relatedness", Deci & Ryan, 2000). Moreover, Bowlby's attachment theory (for an overview see Hazan & Shaver, 1994) may explain how these needs interrelate with the striving for security, love, and confidence. These theoretical approaches suggest that group members' behaviors, cognitions, and affective responses are strongly connected to the satisfaction of basic and psychologically central needs. Thus, cohesion enhancement can provide group members with the expectation of the satisfaction of needs of belongingness or relatedness in future group communication or interaction.

Cohesion as "the balance of team members' relationships and task motivation". Finally, one theoretical concept provides a framework for the integration of similarity and relationship quality; Balance Theory (Heider, 1958). Heider's approach describes the interpersonal dynamic (in a dyad) as a triangle that includes the two people involved in an interaction (P and O) and any third object or person (X). If all three relations (i.e., the triangle's sides) are congruent with one another, then the interpersonal dynamic is balanced. For example, if a team member (P) and his/her partner (O) pursue the same goal in a cooperative task (X) their relationship (P-O) is positive, assuming the task is defined similarly and/or both partners allocate similar values or competencies to the task (P-X is similar to O-X). Any change in one relation has consequences on the balance of the whole figure. Thus, if one person shifts his/her approach to attaining the goal (or if the relationship between the two individuals

changes) then all three relationships will change to compensate. Balance theory explains the strong interdependence between the team members' roles and task motivation (P-X, O-X) on the one hand, and the affective and rational relationship (P-O) on the other hand. The implications of this theory with respect to developing cohesion is that attempts to foster one side of the triangle (e.g., changes in roles or competencies) may have simultaneous consequences for the other sides of the triangle (e.g., interpersonal relationship) as well as for the whole team dynamic.

Overall, the main point of the above discussion is to encourage greater integration between cohesion and existing theoretical frameworks within sport/exercise psychology as well as the broader social psychological literature. This integration is useful in explaining important links that have been demonstrated in the past (e.g., positive cohesion-performance relationship) in addition to highlighting novel strategies for facilitating positive group perceptions. The following section will discuss current approaches to developing cohesion within sport and exercise groups.

Promoting group cohesion

Given the noted importance of cohesion in sport and exercise settings, it prompts us to ask how we can develop this dynamic group construct. The psychological intervention of team building (TB) has been identified as an effective strategy to build cohesion (Burke et al., 2006; Martin, Carron, Burke, 2009). One of the attractions of TB is the steady accruement of evidence supporting the benefits associated with TB to individuals (e.g., improved confidence, individual satisfaction, exercise adherence) in addition to groups (e.g., enhanced cohesion, performance) in a number of populations including youth, young adults, and the elderly (see Table 33.1 for a summary of benefits).

Table 33.1 *Summary of the benefits of team building*

Outcomes	Example author(s), year
Enhanced cohesion	Bruner & Spink, 2010; Carron & Spink, 1993; Dunn & Holt, 2004; Newin, Bloom, & Loughead, 2008; Pain & Harwood, 2009; Senecal, Loughead, & Bloom, 2008; Spink & Carron, 1993; Watson, Martin Ginis, & Spink, 2004; Yukelson, 1997
Enhanced performance	Pain & Harwood, 2009
Improved confidence	Dunn & Holt, 2004
Builds trust	Pain & Harwood, 2009
Enhanced understanding of self and others	Dunn & Holt, 2004; Pain & Harwood, 2009
Increased individual satisfaction	Carron & Spink, 1993
Increased team satisfaction	Bruner & Spink, 2011
Increased attendance	Bruner & Spink, 2011; Watson, Martin Ginis, & Spink, 2004
Decreased lateness	Spink & Carron, 1993
Fewer drop-outs	Spink & Carron, 1993

Background and definition of TB. With its origins in the organizational development literature (see Shuffler, DiazGranados, & Salas, 2011 for a review), one of the more accepted definitions of TB put forward by Newman (1984) highlights that the central purpose of TB is to build cohesion: a group-based intervention designed to "promote a greater sense of unity and cohesiveness, and to enable the team to function more smoothly and effectively" (Newman, 1984, p. 27). The key role of cohesion within TB was further accentuated in two recent research syntheses of citation practices in TB studies in sport and exercise settings (Bruner, Eys, Beauchamp, & Côté, 2013; Bruner, Eys, McFadden, & Côté, 2009).

TB frameworks and approaches. Within the sport and exercise psychology literature, a number of TB conceptual frameworks and approaches have been developed and implemented based upon four primary approaches in the organizational development literature including the improvement of goal setting, problem solving, interpersonal relationships, and role development (Buller, 1986). Buller also noted that TB approaches rarely exist in 'pure form' in that they often involve elements from the others.

Keeping Buller's comments in mind, TB approaches in sport and exercise settings can be classified based upon two distinguishing characteristics. The first characteristic is the focus of the TB approach guiding the intervention. As highlighted above, some TB studies in sport and exercise settings focus on one of the four predominant TB approaches (e.g., goal-setting; Senecal, Loughead, & Bloom, 2008) while others have considered elements from several approaches in their intervention (e.g., Newin, Bloom, & Loughead, 2008). A second important distinction within TB research in the sport and exercise psychology literature is the implementation strategy used. TB interventions in which the intervention specialist (e.g., sport psychology consultant) works directly with the team or group utilize a *direct* approach (e.g., Yukelson, 1997) while an *indirect* approach refers to situations in which the TB interventionist does not work directly with the team or group; rather, he/she trains the coach or exercise leader to implement the TB strategies with his/her respective team or exercise group (Carron, Spink, & Prapavessis, 1997).

Carron and Spink (1993) developed one of the most established and applied TB conceptual frameworks (Bruner et al. 2013). In this framework, cohesion within a group is viewed as an output that flows from three different categories of group characteristics including the group's environment, structure, and processes. Within each of these three catego-

ries, a number of TB factors have been identified as promoting cohesion in an exercise and sport setting including: (a) *group distinctiveness* and *togetherness* in the group environment category; (b) *role clarity* and *acceptance, leadership, group norms/conformity to standards*, as well as *individual positions* in the group structure category; and (c) *individual sacrifices, goals* and *objectives, cooperation*, as well as *communication and interaction* in the group processes category (Carron & Spink, 1993).

This TB conceptual framework is typically implemented indirectly and in four stages. The first three stages occur at a TB workshop. Stage 1 begins with the coaches or exercise leaders being introduced to the benefits of group cohesion and the TB factors within Carron and Spink's (1993) conceptual framework (e.g., distinctiveness) that are proposed to build cohesion. Stages 2 and 3 involve the coaches and exercise leaders brainstorming and then identifying practical strategies that they could use with their team or exercise club

Figure 33.4 Coaches play a vital role in team building. Photograph by Thomas Kolodziej, WLU Athletics. Reprinted courtesy of Wilfrid Laurier University.

to build cohesion (e.g., introduce a club name). The final stage involves the coaches and exercise leaders delivering the TB strategies that they had developed at the workshop to their team or exercise groups (see Table 33.2 for examples of strategies for each of the TB factors). Carron and Spink's (1993) TB conceptual framework and indirect intervention has been successfully implemented in sport and exercise settings with a number of populations including youth, young adults, and elderly populations (Bruner & Spink, 2010, 2011; Newin et al., 2008; Watson, Martin Ginis, & Spink, 2004).

In addition to Carron and Spink's TB model, there are other effective TB approaches for coaches and exercise leaders to consider implementing such as Personal Disclosure Mutual Sharing (PDMS), which builds trust and communication among its group members (Dunn & Holt, 2004), and Group Goal Setting (Senecal et al., 2008).

Recommendations. Prior to undertaking any TB intervention, it is imperative that coaches and exercise leaders: (1) carefully consider the needs of the team or exercise group; (2) define a priority list of goals; (3) select the best TB approach to build cohesion; and (4) develop strategies to evaluate the TB intervention. Furthermore, a common problem plaguing TB studies has been the lack of evaluation of the TB approaches (Bruner & Spink, 2010). Without proper evaluations (e.g., surveys, interviews) coaches and practitioners will not be able to determine what worked (and what didn't) to enhance future TB interventions.

Table 33.2 *Team building factors and examples based upon Carron and Spink's (1993) model*

Team building factor	Examples
Group environment	
Group distinctiveness	• Develop a group name • Have group music • Encourage group identity by allowing players to identify what makes them unique and distinctive • Develop a group cheer/chant • Buy group clothing (team headbands, hats, t-shirts, socks, track suits, jackets, gym bags) • Get similar hair cut/color • Create group logo, symbol or flag
Group togetherness	• Travel to games and tournaments together as a team (if travelling in separate vehicles, change participants) • Establish a common team area for athletes to meet for snack or meal breaks during tournaments or games • Organize team meals or social outings (e.g., games night, study sessions, potluck) • Train in offseason together • Prohibit cell phones and portable music players during road trips • Warm-up as a big group • Run a team fundraiser (e.g., car wash, 3 on 3 tournament) or event for charity • Make a team meal before a game/match • Arrange a team trip to an away tournament or sporting event • Engage in group counting during stretching

Table 33.2 *(continued)*

Team building factor	Examples
Group Structure	
Role clarity and acceptance	• Make sure that all team members understand how they can contribute to team success • Assign roles to each player for equipment set-up • Schedule individual player meetings with coaches to discuss roles
Leadership	• Rotate/switch participant leaders for warm-up, cool-downs, group meetings, etc. • Establish team captains and assistant captains • Allow each team member to suggest a sport-specific activity or drill for practice • Allow athletes to vote for a captain • Pair senior athletes with rookie teammates
Group norms/Conformity to standards	• Promote a strong work ethic as a group characteristic • Create a team motto • Discuss expectations for behavior on the court/field and in the community • Establish routines (pre-game/game day, on the road) • Develop a constitution or contract • Praise people for hard work • Highlight the importance of preparation and punctuality • Establish consequences for those who do not follow team standards/rules (ideally at start of season)
Individual positions	• Establish a "home" or set formation for warm-up or cool down • All group members to pick their own spot and encourage them to remain in it throughout the year
Group processes	
Individual sacrifices	• In exercise groups, ask regulars to help new people (e.g., fitness friends) • Ask older group members to select young group members to practice with during warm-up (Rotate each practice) • Ask team to miss lunch to go over game tape or strategy • Participate in team practices or games over work, concerts, or other social activities • Accept roles for the good of the team (e.g., scorer vs. grinder)
Goals and objectives	• Ask two or three people for a "team goal of the day" • Set short-term and long-term team goals and revisit them often throughout the season • Make team goals visual (e.g., on chart paper in locker room) • Set individual goals and go over them with the group for feedback and support • Announce a goal at the start of each practice (write it up on the board) • Decide which goal(s) are most important for the team

- Write goals on a stick or ball to keep them visible
- Meet with each player to discuss goals at start, middle, and end of the season
- Establish rewards for achieving team goals

Cooperation

- Add cooperative drills and activities into practices (i.e., see how many times we can complete an activity as a team)
- Participate in a challenging cross-training activity for the team members to work together (e.g., wall climbing, high ropes)
- Allow coach(es) to periodically participate in drills

Communication and interaction

- Encourage peer/partner feedback
- Pair up with different partners for every activity/drill
- Make a group on Facebook

Note. Adapted from Prapavessis, H., Carron, A.V., and Spink, K.S. (1996). Team Building in Sport. *International Journal of Sport Psychology*, 27, p. 275 and Carron, A.V. & Spink, K.S. (1993). Team Building in an Exercise Setting. *The Sport Psychologist*, 7, 13.

LEARNING AIDS

1   If a collection of individuals exhibits interdependence, what does it mean for them?

Interdependence among a group of individuals means that they rely on one another in at least one way (e.g., working together on a task or sharing an outcome) and will influence how each member interacts with one another.

2   Explain why a group exercise leader should develop cohesion in their group.

Perceptions of cohesion in exercise groups are related to a number of positive individual and group outcomes. Most notably, increased perceptions of cohesion are associated with increased adherence (i.e., attendance) to exercise group sessions.

3   What is the purpose of team building?

Team building is typically conducted to foster perceptions of cohesion within group members, under the expectation that the group will feel more united and work better together as a group.

4   Identify the difference between direct and indirect team building approaches.

With a direct team building approach, the practitioner works within the team environment (e.g., directly leads group sessions). Meanwhile, with an indirect approach the practitioner teaches team building concepts and practices to group leaders, who independently implement team building strategies.

REVIEW QUESTIONS

1. Describe the one key trait that distinguishes groups in "team" sport from those in "individual" sport, and discuss whether or not you feel group cohesion will *always* be more important in one sport type, over another.

2. Define cohesion and outline the original four dimensional model proposed by Carron and colleagues (1985).

3. How can other theoretical frameworks, such as social identity theory, inform our understanding of group cohesion?

4. What are five benefits (in addition to increased cohesion) that team building can provide in sport and exercise settings to the team and individual?

EXERCISES

1. Consider one group that you are, or have recently been, a member of in a sport or exercise setting. This could include a high school sport team, a structured exercise group, or an informal group of friends that meet to exercise together. In reference to this group, please:

   (a) Describe the group, and the relationships amongst group members. Specifically consider the ways that group members are/were interdependent on one another.

   (b) Provide two/three examples of aspects of the group that could be changed to promote more interdependence among group members.

   (c) Indicate how it is expected that the group's cohesion levels would change as a result of the new group structure.

2. Cohesion is important for all groups. However, the way in which physical activity researchers think about cohesion may differ from other research areas. Using your library resources, find three journal articles that focus on cohesion within another context (e.g., work, family, etc.). Briefly summarize and contrast what is presented in those articles with the information presented in the current chapter.

3. Imagine that you are a new high school teacher who has been approached by the principal to start an after-school exercise club to promote physical activity. Remembering this chapter, you recall the benefits of enhanced cohesion on an individual's physical activity adherence (e.g., increased attendance, decreased drop-out, lateness) and decide it is important to "team build" with the kids involved in the club. In pairs or small groups, select five team building factors from Carron and Spink's (1993) team building framework that you hope to target to lead to increase cohesion and ultimately improve physical activity adherence among group members. Identify two specific strategies for each of the five TB factors (10 strategies total) that you would use to build cohesion in the club. Upon completion, share the strategies amongst the different groups in the class.

ADDITIONAL READING

Bloom, G.A., Loughead, T.M. & Newin, J. (2008). Team building for youth sport. *Journal of Physical Education, Recreation and Dance, 70*, 44–47.

Bruner, M.W. & Spink, K.S. (2010). Evaluating a team building intervention in a youth exercise setting. *Group Dynamics: Theory, Research, and Practice, 14*, 304–317.

Carron, A.V., Colman, M.M., Wheeler, J. & Stevens, D. (2002). Cohesion and performance in sport: A meta-analysis. *Journal of Sport & Exercise Psychology, 24*, 168–188.

Carron, A.V., Widmeyer, W.N. & Brawley, L.R. (1985). The development of an instrument to assess cohesion in sport teams: The group environment questionnaire. *Journal of Sport Psychology, 7*, 244–266.

Martin, L.J., Carron, A.V. & Burke, S.M. (2009). Team building interventions in sport: A meta-analysis. *Sport & Exercise Psychology Review, 5*, 3–18.

Senecal, J., Loughead, T.M. & Bloom, G. (2008). A season-long team-building intervention: Examining the effect of team goal setting on cohesion. *Journal of Sport & Exercise Psychology, 30*, 186–199.

Tajfel, H. & Turner, J.C. (1985). The social identity theory of intergroup behavior. In S. Worchel & W.G. Austin (Eds.), *Psychology of intergroup relations* (2nd ed., pp.7–24). Chicago: Nelson-Hall.

REFERENCES

Baumeister, R.F. & Leary, M.R. (1995). The need to belong: Desire for interpersonal attachments as a fundamental human motivation. *Psychological Bulletin, 117*, 497–529. doi:10.1037// 0033-2909.117.3.497

Beauchamp, M.R. & Eys, M.A. (2007). *Group dynamics in exercise and sport psychology: Contemporary themes.* Oxford: Routledge.

Brewer, M.B. (1991). The social self: On being the same and different at the same time. *Personality and Social Psychology Bulletin, 17*, 475–482. doi:10.1177/0146167291175001

Bruner, M.W., Eys, M., Beauchamp, M. & Côté, J. (2013). Examining the origins of team building in sport: A citation network and genealogical approach. *Group Dynamics: Theory, Research, and Practice, 17*, 30–42.

Bruner, M.W., Eys, M.A., McFadden, K. & Côté, J. (2009). *A citation path analysis of team building literature in sport and exercise settings.* Paper presented at Societé Canadienne D'Apprentissage Psychomoteur et de Psychologie du Sport, Toronto, Canada.

Bruner, M.W. & Spink, K.S. (2010). Evaluating a team building intervention in a youth exercise setting. *Group Dynamics: Theory, Research, and Practice, 14*, 304-317. doi:10.1037/a0018296

Bruner, M.W. & Spink, K.S. (2011). Effects of team building on exercise adherence and group task satisfaction in a youth activity setting. *Group Dynamics: Theory, Research, and Practice, 15*, 161–172. doi:10.1037/a0021257

Buller, P.F. (1986). The team building-task performance relation: Some conceptual and methodological refinements. *Group & Organization Studies, 11*, 147–168. doi:10.1177/105960118601100303

Burke, S.M., Carron, A.V., Eys, M.A., Ntoumanis, N. & Estabrooks, P.A. (2006). Group versus individual approach? A meta-analysis of the effectiveness of interventions to promote physical activity. *Sport and Exercise Psychology Review, 2*, 19–35.

Carron, A.V., Brawley, L.R. & Widmeyer, W.N. (2002). *The Group Environment Questionnaire: Test manual.* Morgantown, WV: Fitness Information Technology.

Carron, A.V., Colman, M.M., Wheeler, J. & Stevens, D. (2002). Cohesion and performance in sport: A meta-analysis. *Journal of Sport & Exercise Psychology, 24*, 168–188. doi:10.1080/026404102317200828

Carron, A.V. & Eys, M.A. (2012). *Group dynamics in sport* (4th ed.). Morgantown, WV: Fitness Information Technology.

Carron, A.V., Hausenblas, H.A. & Mack, D.E. (1996). Social influence and exercise: A meta-analysis. *Journal of Sport & Exercise Psychology, 18*, 1–16.

Carron, A.V. & Spink, K.S. (1993). Teambuilding in an exercise setting. *The Sport Psychologist, 7*, 8–18.

Carron, A.V., Spink, K.S. & Prapavessis, H. (1997). Team building and cohesiveness in the sport and exercise settings: Use of indirect interventions. *Journal of Applied Sport Psychology, 9*, 61–72. doi:10.1080/10413209708415384

Carron, A.V., Widmeyer, W.N. & Brawley, L.R. (1985). The development of an instrument to assess cohesion in sport teams: The group environment questionnaire. *Journal of Sport & Exercise Psychology, 7,* 244–266.

Deci, E.L. & Ryan, R.M. (2000). The "what" and "why" of goal pursuits: Human needs and the self-determination of behavior. *Psychological Inquiry, 11,* 227–268. doi:10.1207/S15327965PLI1104_01

Dunn, J.G.H. & Holt, N.L. (2004). A qualitative investigation of a personal-disclosure mutual sharing team building activity. *The Sport Psychologist, 18,* 363–380.

Estabrooks, P.A. & Carron, A.V. (2000). The Physical Activity Group Environment Questionnaire: An instrument for the assessment of cohesion in exercise classes. *Group Dynamics: Research, Theory, and Practice, 4,* 230–243. doi:10.1037//1089-2699.4.3.230

Eys, M.A., Loughead, T.M., Bray, S.R. & Carron, A.V. (2009). Development of a cohesion questionnaire for youth: The Youth Sport Environment Questionnaire. *Journal of Sport & Exercise Psychology, 31,* 390–408.

Forsyth, D.R. (2010). *Group dynamics* (5th ed.). Belmont, CA: Wadsworth, Cengage Learning.

Hardy, J., Eys, M.A. & Carron, A.V. (2005). Exploring the potential disadvantages of high team cohesion. *Small Group Research, 36,* 166–187. doi:10.1177/1046496404266715

Hazan, C. & Shaver, P.R. (1994). Attachment as an organizational framework for research on close relationships. *Psychological Inquiry, 5,* 1–22. doi:10.1207/s15327965pli0501_1

Heider, F. (1958). *The psychology of interpersonal relations*. Hillsdale: Erlbaum.

Heuzé, J. & Fontayne, P. (2002). Questionnaire sur l'Ambiance du Groupe: A French-language instrument for measuring group cohesion. *Journal of Sport & Exercise Psychology, 24,* 42–67.

Johnson, D.W. & Johnson, R.T. (1989). *Cooperation and competition: Theory and research*. Edina, MN: Interaction Book Company.

Martin, L.J., Carron, A.V. & Burke, S.M. (2009). Team building interventions in sport: A meta-analysis. *Sport & Exercise Psychology Review, 5,* 3–18.

Martin, L.J., Carron, A.V., Eys, M.A. & Loughead, T. (2012). Development of a cohesion questionnaire for children's sport teams. *Group Dynamics: Theory, Research, and Practice, 16,* 68–79. doi:10.1037/a0024691

Newin, J., Bloom, G.A. & Loughead, T.M. (2008). Youth ice hockey coaches' perceptions of a team building intervention program. *The Sport Psychologist, 22,* 54–72.

Newman, B. (1984). Expediency as benefactor: How team building saves time and gets the job done. *Training and Development Journal, 38,* 26–30.

Pain, M. & Harwood, C. (2009). Team building through mutual sharing and open discussion of team functioning. *The Sport Psychologist, 23,* 523–542.

Prapavessis, H., Carron, A.V. & Spink, K.S. (1996). Team building in sport. *International Journal of Sport Psychology, 27,* 269–285.

Senecal, J., Loughead, T.M. & Bloom, G. (2008). A season-long team-building intervention: Examining the effect of team goal setting on cohesion. *Journal of Sport & Exercise Psychology, 30,* 186–199.

Shuffler, M., DiazGranados, D. & Salas, E. (2011). There's a science for that: Team development interventions in organizations. *Current Directions in Psychological Science, 20,* 365–372. doi: 10.1177/0963721411422054

Spink, K.S. & Carron, A.V. (1993). The effects of team building on the adherence patterns of female exercise participants. *Journal of Sport & Exercise Psychology, 15,* 39–49.

Spink, K.S., Wilson, K.S. & Odnokon, P. (2010). Examining the relationship between cohesion and return to team in elite athletes. *Psychology of Sport and Exercise, 11,* 6–11. doi:10.1016/j.psychsport.2009.06.002

Tajfel, H. & Turner, J.C. (1985). The social identity theory of intergroup behavior. In S. Worchel & W.G. Austin (Eds.), *Psychology of intergroup relations* (2nd ed., pp. 7–24). Chicago: Nelson-Hall.

Wahl, G. (2010, July). The agony and the ecstasy. *Sports Illustrated*. Retrieved from http://sportsillustrated.cnn.com/vault/article/magazine/MAG1172073/2/index.htm

Watson, J., Martin-Ginis, K. & Spink, K. (2004). Team building in an exercise class for the elderly. *Activities, Adaptation & Aging, 28,* 35–47. doi:10.1300/J016v28n03_03

World Health Organization. (2010). *Global recommendations on physical activity and health*. Geneva, Switzerland: WHO press.

Yukelson, D. (1997). Principles of effective team building interventions in sport: A direct services approach at Penn State University. *Journal of Applied Sport Psychology, 9,* 73–96. doi:10.1080/10413209708415385

Chapter 34

Norms, rules, and discipline in sport

MICHAEL VAN BUSSEL AND MELANIE GREGG

SUMMARY

This chapter highlights behavior found within the team environment and factors that influence this behavior. Initially, group norms are defined and given purpose as they relate to sporting culture. Subsequently, the ability to change norms within the group is discussed using practical examples. This chapter continues with an analysis of rule formation and the distinction of discipline and punishment. As leaders of teams or sporting groups, how can we utilize discipline? The discussion of positive discipline incorporates several practical solutions for coaches and sporting leaders. Understanding group norms, the influence of rules, and the correct approach to reinforcing behavior is significant in creating a positive and productive sporting environment for all.

INTRODUCTION

It is quarter past six in the evening and the local girls' club volleyball team has just finished warming up for practice. Ashley, the team's top middle blocker and a rookie player, has just arrived. The coach calls the two team captains over and points out the late arrival. The captains agree, it's important for everyone to arrive on time, ready to go for the six o'clock start of practice. The team begins a hitting drill, and the coach instructs Ashley to hurry and get her kneepads, ankle braces, and court shoes on so she can join in the drill. Ashley swings and hits her first three sets into the belly of the net.

At the end of practice the coach debriefs with the team. After the talk, the captains ask Ashley "what's up, why are you late?" Ashley explains that her dad was late getting home from work so she couldn't get a ride on time for practice. The captains explain that it is important to be on time so that she gets a proper warm-up in so she does not get injured. They also inform her being on time is important so everyone is ready to start the drills and get the most out of the two hours they have together to work as a team. The captains suggest that Ashley could ride her bike, take the bus, or call someone on the team for a ride to practice so she does not have to rely on her dad and his work schedule. Ashley agrees this is a good plan; she admits that she felt really out of it when she first got to practice.

OBJECTIVES

After reading this chapter you should be able to:

1   Understand what norms are and how they impact teams.
2   Conceptualize how norms are formed and changed.
3   Recognize the distinction between discipline and punishment.
4   Comprehend methods in rule creation and enforcement.
5   Realize that all members of the team are essential in the creation of a positive culture.

DEFINING NORMS

Norms are expectations and beliefs to which members of a group are thought to adhere. Norms can be subtle, and we do not always recognize them until they are violated. There are many examples of norms in everyday life. An everyday example of a norm is when someone walks through a door in front of you; the expectation is that they hold it open. We do not really think about this norm until someone walks through the door, does not hold it open, and it closes in your face. Our reaction is typically irritation and disbelief that this norm has been violated.

Norms differ from rules (rules are discussed in more detail later in this chapter) and unofficial norms can serve to complement official rules. In the great cycling race the Tour de France, for example, riders do not take advantage when another rider is slowed by something out of their control; instead, they wait for the rider to rejoin the group (Fink & Smith, 2012). Norms can be conceptualized as operating within a bandwidth in that there is an acceptable range of behaviors that can fit within the norm. As such, norms are some-what flexible and are not formally laid out by the group. In the case of Ashley, the rookie volleyball player in the introduction, she was likely unaware of the norm of arriving on time and warming-up with the team. This norm would not have been stated as a formal rule, and it was not until she violated the norm that her nonconformity was highlighted (illustrating the *unobtrusive* nature of norms). Had Ashley only been a few minutes late and participated in some of the team warm-up, it is unlikely her late arrival would have been an issue at all. The volleyball team members adhere to the norms of team warm-up, arrive on time to practice because they feel a part of the team and experience a sense of *satisfaction*. They do not necessarily adhere to the norm because of fear of sanctions. Note that there was no punishment for Ashley's first violation of the norm, nor were there any overt rewards for her previous conformity to the norm. Consequences for violation of the norm would likely occur, however, if the violations continued or deviated from the acceptable range of behavior.

PURPOSE OF NORMS

Norms serve three purposes (Weinberg & Gould, 2003):

1   Indicate a level of performance toward which group members should strive:

e.g., NHL player Jordan Staal, playing for the Pittsburgh Penguins and leading the NHL in post-season goal scoring, described the expectation of the team as "It's our mentality of playing it one game at a time, just five minutes at a time and keep chipping away" (Kasan, 2012).

2   Outline a pattern of behavior expected from group members:
    e.g., from the opening vignette of this chapter we learn the expectations of the club volley-ball team are that all players arrive on time and complete the team warm-up.

3   Describe a belief of the group:
    e.g., it is common for NHL players to grow "playoff beards" as they believe it will bring good luck to their team. Teams may, however, shave off the beard to change the team's luck following a loss.

Thus, norms function to provide group members with *information*:

> Norms help the individual gain insight into the group; they provide a standard against which a new member can validate his/her opinions, attitudes, and behavior. Norms also ensure that the individuals' opinions,

attitudes, and behavior don't deviate dramatically from other team members' (Carron & Eys, 2012, p. 209).

In the opening vignette the captains brought to the attention of the rookie player that her behavior of arriving late for practice was deviating from the team's norm of being on time and doing the warm-up together.

Norms also provide parameters for *integration* – group members begin to conform to the norms of the group (Carron & Eys, 2012). Those who conform are brought into the group and feel as though they belong; those who resist conforming feel left out and may be removed from the group (e.g., cut from the team) (Carron & Eys, 2012). For example, it is likely that if Ashley continues to resist conforming to the norm of arriving to practice on time, the coach will decrease her playing time, her team mates will become frustrated, and she may not be invited back to the team next season.

TYPES OF NORMS

There are four types of group norms: prescribed, proscribed, permissive, and preference (Mott, 1965). *Prescribed* norms reflect the pattern of behavior considered proper by the group (Mott, 1965). Team members arriving on time for the start of practice and completing the warm-up together are examples of prescribed norms.

Proscribed norms reflect the pattern of behavior considered improper by the group (Mott, 1965). Showing up 15 minutes after the start of practice and not doing a warm-up are behaviors that are contrary to being punctual and working as a team.

Permissive norms reflect behavior allowed but not expected (Mott, 1965). In a 100 metre

sprint, for example, the rule is that any runner who false starts twice is disqualified. A starter may choose to restart a race or claim there was a starting pistol malfunction if the runners were all youth athletes compared to university athletes.

Preference norms reflect the pattern of behavior favoured but not expected (Mott, 1965). A recreational beach volleyball game illustrates preference norms when players admit that they brushed a ball with their finger tips that then lands out of bounds that would otherwise be their point if they had not touched it.

FORMATION OF NORMS

Norms emerge as the result of *interactions* among group members and the *reinforcement* of acceptable behaviors. Observe teenagers at a

shopping mall as a classic example of individuals who are influenced by group norms. It is by interacting with their peers that they learn

Figure 34.1 Involving athletes in norm development creates a connection to the norm and promotes an opportunity for empowerment.

what style of jeans are "in" and what styles are "out". Wearing the *out of style* jeans may result in teasing or not being invited to a party. Wearing the *in style* jeans is reinforced by compliments and/or others copying the style. The same patterns of interaction and reinforcement are seen with the emergence of norms for sport teams. These standards of behavior, or norms, help the group to function efficiently. The result of these interactions and reinforcements is that the range of acceptable behaviors narrows and becomes more specific (Colman & Carron, 2001).

Prapavessis & Carron (1997) defined *conformity* as individual behavior that is influenced by others' behavior. The individual will behave in ways that are different to the ways they would behave if the group was not exerting pressure. An example of conformity was highlighted during the Vancouver riots following the loss of the Vancouver Canucks in the final game of the 2011 Stanley Cup National Hockey League playoffs. Hundreds of people reported acting with the crowd and behaving uncharacteristically. It is unlikely any of these hockey fans acting alone would have looted stores or set fire to police cars. Yet being caught up in the moment and encouraged by the crowd led to these appalling behaviors.

Compliance and acceptance are two types of conformity (Carron & Eys, 2012). *Compliance* occurs when an individual goes along with group behavior but in truth does not agree with the conduct (Carron & Eys, 2012). In contrast, *acceptance* occurs when the individual behaves in the way expected by the group and believes in what they are doing (Carron & Eys, 2012). During the 2012 season, the New Orleans Saints of the National Football League were sanctioned because of the use of a bounty system; the system paid players for hits that injured opponents. Though some of the players may have embraced this behavior (acceptance), it is likely many engaged in the bounty system because they were instructed by influential members of the team (compliance) while not necessarily believing in it. Coaches and other team leaders influence the conformity of the team to norms. Norms that are *accepted* by the group members are more resistant to change (Carron & Eys, 2012). To gain acceptance of positive norms, athletes should be informed of the rationale behind the norm and benefits of conforming to the norm. In addition, acceptance is fostered when athletes have a say in the development of the norm and feel some ownership for it.

FACTORS INFLUENCING CONFORMITY

Conformity to norms is influenced by personal and situational factors. Research has examined a range of personal factors in relation to conformity to social and performance norms (i.e., Prapavessis & Carron, 1997). However, personal status and the related idiosyncrasy credit (i.e., the collection of positive impressions of an individual that allows that individual to behave outside the expectations of the group without negative repercussions) have demonstrated the most consistent relationships to norm conformity (Hollander, 1958). Higher status individuals are generally identified as those team members who are leaders or are the most able athletes. These high-status individuals are most influential in developing team norms and regulating adherence of the group to the norms (Weinberg & Gould, 2003). Due to their high-status and long-term conformity to the team norms they are given an idiosyncrasy credit (Hollander, 1958). Because they are viewed favourably by the group they have some flexibility in their conformity to the norm. In other words, high-status individuals can deviate from the group's norms more than low-status team members. We can see from the opening scene of this chapter that Ashley was given limited latitude in her conformity to the norm. This is to be expected as Ashley is a rookie – a first-year player – with the team. Any norm violations at this early stage must be checked so that they do not progress or influence others. Had one of the team captains arrived late for practice and missed the team warm-up it is unlikely the other captain would have made an issue of it, and the coach likely would have given it cursory attention.

Numerous situational factors have also been identified as influencing norm conformity such as, group size and leadership. The influence of group size affects conformity in two ways (Bond, 2005). The first way is that the more individuals conforming to a norm results in increased conformity (Widmeyer, Brawley & Carron, 1990). Similarly, when the number of individuals resisting the norm increases, there is increased resistance. The group becomes less effective as the number resisting the norm increases (Carron, 1980). Conformity is also related to group cohesion (Widmeyer, Brawley & Carron, 1985). As cohesion increases norm conformity increases, and as conformity increases cohesion is further increased, thusly the relationship between cohesion and conformity to group norms is reciprocal (Prapavessis & Carron, 1997).

Clarity of the team norm further influences conformity (Bond, 2005). When a team norm is clear (e.g., arrive at the scheduled start time for practice) it is easy for team members to conform to the norm. When there is ambiguity in the norm – it could be interpreted in various ways – it is more challenging to consistently conform to it. An example of an ambiguous norm is that all players should put in their best effort during training. Some players may interpret this as having to push themselves to give 100% effort, others as 80% so they save themselves for the game the next day, still others may see it as being the amount of effort they feel like expending that day.

Leadership is the second situational factor that impacts conformity (Shaw, 1981). Democratic leadership engages a number of individuals in decision making, empowering individuals throughout the process. This environment of empowerment creates buy-in and ultimately produces positive pressure from the group members for others to conform to established norms. When power is dispersed, more team members can influence their team mates to conform. Keeping in mind both the personal and situational factors that influence conformity to group norms, coaches and team captains/leaders should realize they have a key responsibility in setting and ensuring conformity to positive norms and modifying or eliminating inappropriate norms.

CHANGING NORMS

Inappropriate norms are sometimes established in the team environment. This is unfortunate as norms are resistant to change (Carron & Eys, 2012). An example of an inappropriate norm would be an athlete talking during a practice when receiving instructions from a coach. This behavior is inappropriate as the athlete is distracted from the instruction given, she/he may miss critical points, and the talking distracts others around them and the coach. Inappropriate norms can gradually be changed through methods such as: (a) communication (discussed in more detail in the next few paragraphs); (b) having influential, high status team members (e.g., team captain) model appropriate normative behaviors; (c) having the team set collaborative goals that highlight how appropriate norms will contribute to goal achievement; and (d) creating a code of conduct for the team (see Exercise 2 near the end of this chapter).

As described by Penrod (1986), effective communicators have high status and, as discussed earlier in the chapter, high status individuals have more influence in the formation of and conformity to group norms. Effective communicators are also more likely to use rhetorical questions. Rhetorical questions help individuals feel they made some contribution to the decision and that they have an investment in the group norms (Penrod, 1986).

What the communicator says, or the nature of the communication, is also important. There are several factors related to the nature of the communication that affect group norms (Penrod, 1986). Watch a scene from a sports movie of your choice, take note of the nature of the communication of a coach or team leader who is attempting to change a group norm. For example, in the movie *Coach Carter* several of these techniques are used in an attempt to change the norm that basketball players do not have to study or attend class in order to get a passing grade.

Another factor in communication is the listener, the individual receiving the communication. There are numerous factors that influence how receptive the listener is to the communication (Turman, 2003). As hinted with the use of rhetorical questions, encouraging a perception of choice is essential (Penrod, 1986). As with the stubborn toddler who refuses to eat vegetables, when asked "You can choose, do you want carrots or peas?" they may be more likely to select one and feel they have control over their food choices.

DEVELOPING RULES

The development of rules for a team is a continuous process that involves evaluation, consultation, and re-evaluation. Some coaches may establish the rules themselves or may involve the participants in the process. Involving the athletes in the rule creation process not only creates an opportunity for empowerment but also "buy-in" regarding the rules they have created. Creating this type of "buy-in" culture also assists in enforcement of rules, as the athletes themselves may (depending on the level of maturity) become self-regulating. Setting out on the journey of rule creation, an evaluation of individual and team values must be made. Reflected in these values are issues that are considered important both operationally and ethically to the team. Once these values have been established the formalization of rules can begin. The following are guidelines for formalization of rules:

- Rules should be based on respect for all parties;
- Keep the list of rules brief;
- Rules must be specific, this legitimizes their existence;
- There should be sound justification for the creation of rules;
- Prescribe, rather than proscribe, in the creation of rules;
- Each rule should have a consequence, with single or multiple points of action if rules are contravened;
- Rules and consequences should be written and provided to the players. (Martens, 2004)

Other criteria must also be considered during the rule creation process: (1) Is the rule necessary? (2) Is the rule enforceable? and (3) Is the rule fair? (Jones, Wells, Peters & Johnson, 1993). If coaches and players can answer these questions in the affirmative, then the formalization of rules should be considered a productive team activity.

Once rules are in place it is essential that coaches or organizational leaders enforce

Figure 34.2 Consistent enforcement of rules is critical to their success.

these rules in a consistent manner. Any inconsistency in enforcement can seriously undermine the credibility of the coach. As Martens (2004) stated, "enforcing rules inconsistently is worse than not having rules at all" (p. 154).

Moreover, it is important for leaders to model this prescribed behavior to their athletes by abiding by the rules that have been established. Enforcement of team rules is a process in promoting and maintaining discipline within the group.

DISCIPLINE

When one thinks of the word discipline, more often than not, it has a negative connotation. Images of running sprints after misbehaving or sitting out a portion of the game because individuals were late for practice are often related to this negative view. Is this a fair analysis of discipline or are there other ways to think about this concept in light of leading teams? To answer this question, first a distinction should be made between discipline and punishment. *Punishment* is the institution of a penalty for a transgression or offense, used to shape subsequent behavior (e.g., running sprints or not starting a game). Indeed, punishment is a negative way to cultivate a willingness for prescribed conduct. This is quite different from the definition of discipline. *Discipline* should be viewed as a "state of mind that produces a readiness for willing, intelligent and appropriate conduct" (Tozer, 1997, p. 233). This view of discipline seeks a holistic view of self and self-awareness in light of norms established by the group, organization, or the society in which the individual resides. As Jones et al. (1993) described it:

> Discipline can be defined as the attempt to set limitations and modify behavior. In athletics these limitations take many forms – the rules of the game, the authority of the officials, and the request and demands of the coach for training behavior and performance. (p. 18)

Discipline is also considered an important part of learning and acquiring the ability to be successful as an individual or as a team. As Lynch (2001) highlighted, "discipline is a learning process that helps athletes to develop drive, self-control, character, and skill" (p. 119). Indeed, leaders must consider the ability of their athletes to adapt, learn, and develop into value-added members of the team. The development of discipline can be looked at in three ways:

1. **Imposed discipline** is akin to the militaristic approach to training utilized by armed forces across the globe (Tozer, 1997). Discipline is imposed on recruits so they understand prescribed standards of behavior, are responsive to hierarchy, and have appropriate responses to demanding situations that are characterized by high stress. This type of discipline involves an authoritarian approach to both training and leadership. Once recruits have overcome challenges and gain satisfaction from reaching these goals, they ultimately foster their own self-discipline (Tozer, 1997).

2. **Self-discipline** entails the adherence to an inherent set of standards that regulate conduct and behavior (Tozer, 1997). This strong internal control may require setting aside personal wants and needs in order to achieve larger goals of the group or organization. Incorporated into self-discipline are elements of mental self control and an awareness of the external environment, including the needs of others. The evolution of self-discipline "varies from person to person and its level depends on the number of factors, including the influences on people in early life" (Tozer, 1997, p. 234).

3. **Collective discipline** is the assembled self-discipline of the membership of a team or group (Tozer, 1997). The team members must sacrifice personal interest in order for the group to be successful. Positive outcomes of collective discipline range from the promotion of stability of performance and the ability to deal with stressful situations (Tozer, 1997). It is imperative for team leaders to recognize the importance and power of collective discipline for the overall effectiveness of the group. Leaders who fail to identify the need for a strong culture of self-discipline do so at their own peril.

Whether it be collective, imposed or self-discipline, two factors are key to the evolution of discipline within individuals and the team. The first factor, self-control, is an essential element in maintaining strong constitution and sound discipline (Tozer, 1997). The ability to focus one's thoughts in order to deal with stress, fatigue, and uncomfortable situations is the cornerstone to sustaining a disciplined approach (Tozer, 1997). For example, team training camps are notorious for promoting the three aforementioned elements of stress, fatigue, and uncomfortable situations. The stress of making the team, the fatigue of multiple practices a day, and the uncomfortable situation of learning new systems or playing a new position may be compounded with moving to a new city or starting a new academic program. Athletes who are prepared to face these challenges, and have the ability to adapt to unforeseen obstacles, will recognize the most success during training camp.

The second factor, sense of duty, highlights a link between the individual and the organization, its membership, and its constituents (Tozer, 1997). As Tozer (1997) explains, "nothing would be accomplished in any crisis by a person without a sense of duty. This sense is instilled through our discipline because through it we are taught to do what is right as a matter of course, and to know that it is wrong not to do so" (p. 236). This sense of duty also reflects an attitude of self-sacrifice, a means of connection to a collective, and a longing for belonging to a group with a similar philosophy. Numerous examples can be found of group members sacrificing themselves, in body and mind, because they feel this sense of duty to the team. In the formation of discipline it is important for leaders to base this sense of duty on elements of fairness, consistency, and trust. The connection between self-sacrifice and sense of duty is inherent in the trusting relationships established between leaders and participants. An inability for leaders to trust participants (and vice-versa) will most definitely destroy discipline, both collectively and individually.

How can leaders impact the development and maintenance of discipline? There are several actions that team leaders should include in their repertoire of discipline. The first action begins with the leader modelling appropriate behavior (Lynch, 2001). Modelling of behavior ties back to the elements of consistency previously discussed. What kind of message does it send to athletes if a coach has rules about being on time yet he/she is late for practices or meetings? Another example could be the coach's use of negative language in high-pressure situations. If athletes are supposed to maintain their poise in these situations then why should the coach not maintain her composure? A "practice what you preach" mentality goes a long way to strengthen the messages being sent to constituents and further legitimizing future messages.

The second action is to ritualize discipline through consistent daily practice (Lynch, 2001). Implementing daily practice or pre-game rituals allows athletes to activate body and mind and produces a much more focused participant. This focus becomes part of the athlete's daily routine and part of his/her discipline. Rituals may also become player led. The promotion of player awards after the game, instituted by players, allows the athletes to be active participants in the building of team culture and motivation of the group. Rituals also extend beyond daily routines, to weekly practice structure or seasonal events that include opportunities for team building and player recognition outside the game or practice.

The third action is that leaders should strive to make discipline fun (Lynch, 2001). This concept might seem like an oxymoron to some. How can something that may involve punishment be fun? Sport leaders should recognize that athletes will be willing to work harder if there is fun and enjoyment in what they are doing. As Lynch (2001) explains, "coaches who have disciplined teams realize that athletes will be more receptive to hard work if there is some fun involved: they will go the extra mile if they enjoy what they do" (p. 132). Promoting fun does not mean having a laissez-faire attitude toward leadership. Instituting fun into your training regimen involves creative work, knowledge, and skill (Lynch, 2001). Creative work requires organizing sessions that incorporate elements of enjoyment and a positive competitive spirit. The knowledge comes from finding or designing workouts or drills that are fun for athletes. Finally, the skill is based on the ability of the coach to empower her/his athletes to provide feedback about what they enjoy and what they would like to see within their team, and ultimately using this feedback to create a positive team environment where athletes grow, thrive, and enjoy being participants.

The final action is to reinforce discipline when positive results occur (Lynch, 2001). In many instances a coach will only stop a session when a technique is incorrect or if something has gone wrong. While error correction is important, recognition of positive behavior is equally important. Recognizing positive behavior by letting your athletes know that it has not gone unnoticed, or providing encouragement when they have completed a new and complex task has a positive impact on reinforcing discipline.

Figure 34.3 Open communication is an important element in developing discipline.

Ultimately, the fostering of discipline entails numerous decisions and adjustments depending on each unique individual and situational needs. At the same time there are certain key factors such as respect, trust, and communication that are essential building blocks for both collective and self-discipline. As a coach there are several affirmations that should be considered in the development and maintenance of discipline:

- The coach creates an environment of mutual respect, communication, acceptance, trust, and compassion. Without this, athletes will resist and resent discipline.
- The coach embraces patience, capable of using the element of time to great advantage. Timing is the essence of great play.
- The coach is focused on discipline, capable of creating athletes who enjoy an ordered approach to discovering their greatness. (Lynch, 2001, p. 135)

Understanding the complex nature and the importance of discipline is essential for leaders in order to provide a positive and productive environment for all.

POSITIVE DISCIPLINE

The term *positive discipline* was popularized in North America by Dr. Jane Nelsen (Nelsen, 1981). This term was derived from the work of Alfred Adler and Rudolf Dreikurs (Nelson, 2006; Dreikurs & Cassel, 1972; Dreikurs, 1968). Nelsen outlined three main approaches regarding interaction and discipline. The first approach is strictness, which is characterized by excessive control. Strictness entails "order without freedom" where individuals have no choice (Nelsen, 2006, p. 8). The second approach is permissiveness which has no limits on behavior. Permissiveness engenders "freedom without order" where individuals can do anything they want (Nelsen, 2006, p, 8). The third approach, positive discipline, involves kindness and firmness at the same time. Positive discipline involves "freedom with order" highlighting the fact that individuals have choice within limits that shows respect for all (Nelsen, 2006, p. 8). An example of positive discipline is defined by Nelsen (2006):

Together we will decide on the rules for our mutual benefit. We will also decide together on solutions that will be helpful to all concerned when we have problems. When I must use my judgement without your input, I will use firmness with kindness, dignity and respect. (p. 8)

In light of the previous discussion of discipline in this chapter, positive discipline involves many factors that are linked to productive, collective and self-discipline.

The concept of positive discipline has also been adapted into physical education and sport settings for many years. Papaioannou (1998) examined the individual differences in goal orientation in relation to reasons for being disciplined in the physical education classroom. This study utilized Self-Determination Theory (SDT) to rationalize elements such as "students' reasons for discipline" and "teachers' strategies for sustaining discipline" (Papaioannou, 1998). Utilizing a broad framework such as Self-Determination Theory (SDT) allows researchers to define elements of intrinsic and extrinsic motivation and their impact on social development (Deci & Ryan, 2002). This theory also addresses the internalization of rules by individuals that may lead to responsible behavior which is the objective of positive discipline. Self-Determination Theory is discussed at length in Chapter 5 of this volume and is also addressed in relation to Achievement Goal Theory in Chapter 4 and motivational climate in Chapter 35.

Papaioannou (1998) revealed that for students, "the perception of an environment emphasizing personal improvement seems to promote discipline in the lesson" (p. 437). This relates directly to the premise of positive discipline which emphasizes "freedom with order" (Nelsen, 2006). As students are allowed to make decisions regarding their personal improvement they become more engaged and hence more disciplined in their activity. For instructors, this concept is equally important as "the perception of teaching strategies promoting student determined reasons for behaving well were strong positive predictors of discipline reported by students" (Papaioannou, 1998, p. 437). Strategies such as involving athletes in the creation of team goals and rules, and their increased belief in these elements, promotes an environment of empowerment and may in fact foster conformity of these goals and rules much more strongly than the group itself (Carron & Eys, 2012). Conversely, Papaioannou (1998) also revealed that an authoritative approach had a negative impact where "the teacher tries to impose the rules and makes [the students] feel ashamed when they misbehave." (p. 437).

If coaches choose to engage in this style of authoritative leadership for an extended period they may see a lack of discipline occur and, in fact, they may lose the group they are trying to lead.

Other research that is closely linked with positive discipline in physical activity is the work of Hellison (1995) that examines *Teaching Responsibility*. Recent additions to this book highlighted several awareness or developmental levels. These levels included a progression from *respect*, to *effort*, to *self-direction* to finally to *caring and helping* (Hellison, 2011). Again, the internalization of appropriate altruistic values such as caring and helping reflect the responsibility apparent in positive discipline. Positive discipline was also adapted to coaching and managing player behavior (Martens, 2004). In this adaptation, positive discipline also included elements of instruction, training, and correcting (Martens, 2004). Instruction involves the teaching of both sport and life skills. Training provides an opportunity to rehearse these skills utilizing realistic scenarios. Finally, correcting is facilitated by the coach to address errors in skill or behavior. As Martens (2004) stated, "positive discipline is about understanding that discipline is more than just correcting behavior; it is about teaching behavior too" (p. 143). This approach is seen as productive because it seeks a common ground of mutual respect between coach and athlete; "coaches who use positive discipline inspire excitement, enthusiasm, and positive motivation" (Martens, 2004, p. 145). Indeed, positive discipline is a subtle balance that provides boundaries while allowing athletes to grow and explore their environment.

LEARNING AIDS

1   What are norms and what implications do they have for groups?

Group norms are patterns of social behavior that reflect group values and beliefs. Through norms, members are able to evaluate group behavior and compare compliance of the membership, which may lead to inclusion or exclusion from the activities of the group.

2   Define rules and highlight their purpose in the team environment.

Rules are a formalization of regulations guiding conduct of a particular activity. In the team environment, rules proscribe specific behaviors to ensure fairness among participants. Ultimately, rules provide guidelines for behavior and outline the consequences when they are broken.

3   What is the difference between discipline and punishment?

Discipline includes a focusing of the mind in order to control behavior. Key components of discipline are a holistic awareness of self and others and understanding that self-sacrifice is important for the success of all. The promotion of a strong sense of discipline is essential in the maintenance of a productive team environment. Punishment on the other hand, is the imposition of suffering or loss as retribution for an offense. It is a negative form of reinforcement. The exclusive use of punishment may work in the short term but quickly becomes ineffective and is ultimately debilitating to the team environment in the long term.

4   How can positive discipline be utilized by team leaders?

Positive discipline is means to address behavior by rewarding the positive rather than punishing the negative. The use of positive discipline is linked to cooperative leadership. Team leaders utilize firmness, while recognizing the importance of respect and trust in all interactions.

REVIEW QUESTIONS

1   How do norms impact the team environment?

2   What is the difference between social and performance norms?

3   How do norms emerge and change in the team setting?

4   How is self-discipline related to collective discipline?

5   How can the team members reinforce team culture and team rules?

EXERCISES

1   Case Study: At the beginning of the season Coach Clark sat down with his university women's soccer team to discuss the formation of rules. Each athlete had input into the process. The group identified that

being late was disrespectful to other players and the coach and it would not be tolerated. The consequences for being late to practice would involve a warning for the first infraction, running extra sprints for the second infraction and sitting out a game for the third. Being late for a game, on the other hand, was seen as a more serious offense. Players were instructed that they must be at the field one hour prior to kick-off in order to warm-up and receive proper instructions. Moreover, being late for warm-up it would mean sitting out that game.

After travelling to the site of an away game in a large metropolitan center, the team had arrived well enough in advance of the game. Coach Clark decided to allow the players to have some free time prior to the preparation for the game. Sara, a central defender, was a leader on the team and a key member of the defensive back line. She had a friend who was coming to watch the game. She asked Coach Clark if she could venture off site to grab a bite to eat with her friend. Coach Clark agreed but reminded Sara that she had to be back one hour prior to kick-off. Sara agreed and went off with her friend to enjoy the city. Time passed and it grew closer to the hour before the game. All players were accounted for with the exception of Sara. She had lost track of time and could not arrange for transportation back to the field. She arrived 40 minutes before kick-off full of apologies and excuses. Coach Clark was upset that Sara had put him in this predicament. Sara was an important part of the team throughout the season. This was an important game that would decide the team's fate going into the playoffs.

(a) What would happen if Coach Clarke were to sit Sara?

(b) What would happen if Coach Clarke were to let Sara play even though she was late?

(c) Do rules help reinforce the norms of the team? Explain why/why not.

(d) What should Coach Clarke do?

2   Practical Activity: A code of conduct is one method of developing or changing team norms. Using the example below to help guide you, select a sport you are familiar with and develop a code of conduct for that sport. Keep in mind the norms you are trying to achieve, age of the participants, and competitive level. If you have an opportunity to try this in the real world, involve team members in the development of the code and have each team member (coaches included!) sign the code to show their commitment.

Code of Conduct for Club Volleyball Team	

1 Play in practice as you would in a game
    • Use proper technique
    • Put forth effort
2 Stay focused, be in the moment
    • Be ready to go on the court at any time
    • Stay on topic during training
	3 Be positive and supportive
	    • Cheer for your team mates
	4 Communication is key
	    • Listen attentively to team mates and coaches
	    • Be respectful to officials
	    • Clearly state issues when they arise

ADDITIONAL READING

Carron, A.V. & Eys, M.A. (2012). *Group dynamics in sport*. Morgantown, WV: Fitness Information Technology, Inc.

Colman, M.M. & Carron, A.V. (2001). The nature of norms in individual sport teams. *Small Group Research, 32*, 2, 206–222. doi: 10.1177/1046496401032200204

Fink, A. & Smith, D.J. (2012). Norms in sports contests: The Tour de France. *Journal of Sport Management, 26*, 43–52.

Hellison, D.R. (2011). *Teaching personal and social responsibility through physical activity*. Champaign, IL: Human Kinetics.

Papaioannou, A. (1998). Goal perspectives, reasons for being disciplined, and self-reported discipline in physical education lessons. *Journal of Teaching in Physical Education, 17*, 421–441.

Prapavessis, H. & Carron, A.V. (1997). Sacrifice, cohesion, and conformity to norms in team sports. *Group Dynamics: Theory, Research and Practice, 1, 3*, 231–240. doi: 10.1037/1089-2699.1.3.231

Widmeyer, W.N., Brawley, L.R. & Carron. A.V. (1990). The effects of group size in sport. *Journal of Sport and Exercise Psychology, 12*, 2, 177–190.

REFERENCES

Bond, R. (2005). Group size and conformity. *Group Processes & Intergroup Relations, 8, 4*, 331–354. doi: 10.1177/1368430205056464

Carron, A.V. (1980). *Social psychology of sport*. Ithaca, NY: Mouvement Publications.

Carron, A.V. & Eys. M.A. (2012). *Group dynamics in sport*. Morgantown, WV: Fitness Information Technology, Inc.

Colman, M.M. & Carron, A.V. (2001). The nature of norms in individual sport teams. *Small Group Research, 32*, 2, 206–222. doi: 10.1177/1046496401032200204

Deci, E.L. & Ryan, R.M. (2000). Self-determination theory and the facilitation of intrinsic motivation, social development and well-being. *American Psychologist, 55*, 68–78.

Dreikurs, R. (1968). *A new approach to discipline: Logical consequences*. New York, NY: Hawthorne Books.

Dreikurs, R. & Cassel, P. (1972). *Discipline without tears*. Toronto, ON: Alfred Adler Institute of Ontario.

Fink, A. & Smith, D.J. (2012). Norms in sports contests: The Tour de France. *Journal of Sport Management, 26*, 43–52.

Hellison, D.R. (1995). *Teaching responsibility through physical activity*. Champaign, IL: Human Kinetics.

Hellison, D.R. (2011). *Teaching personal and social responsibility through physical activity*. Champaign, IL: Human Kinetics.

Hollander, E.P. (1958). Conformity, status and idiosyncrasy credit. *Psychological Review, 65, 2*, 117–127.

Jones, B.J., Wells, L.J., Peters, R.E. & Johnson, D.J. (1993). *Guide to effective coaching principles and practice*. Dubuque, IA: Brown & Benchmark.

Kasan, S. (2012, April 21) Penguins stay above with complete effort. *NHL.Com Network*. Retrieved from http://penguins.nhl.com/club/news.htm?id=628950

Lynch, J. (2001). *Creative coaching*. Champaign, IL: Human Kinetics.

Martens, R. (2004). *Successful coaching* (3rd ed.). Champaign, IL: Human Kinetics.

Mott, P.E. (1965). *The organization of society*. Englewood Cliffs, NJ: Prentice-Hall.

Nelsen, J. (1981). *Positive discipline*. Fair Oaks, CA: Sunrise Press.

Nelsen, J. (2006). *Positive discipline* (4th ed.). New York, NY: Ballintine Books.

Papaioannou, A. (1998). Goal perspectives, reasons for being disciplined, and self-reported discipline in physical education lessons. *Journal of Teaching in Physical Education, 17*, 421–441.

Penrod, S. (1986). *Social psychology* (2nd ed.). Englewood Cliffs, NJ: Prentice-Hall.

Prapavessis, H. & Carron, A.V. (1997). Sacrifice, cohesion, and conformity to norms in team sports. *Group Dynamics: Theory, Research and Practice, 1, 3*, 231–240. doi: 10.1037/1089-2699.1.3.231

Tozer, J. (1997). *Leading initiatives: Leadership, teamwork and the bottom line.* Port Melbourne, Vic: Butterworth-Heinemann.

Turman, P.D. (2003). Athletic coaching from an instructional communication perspective: The influence of coach experience on high school wrestler's preferences and perceptions of coaching behaviors across a season. *Communication Education, 23,* 73–86.

Shaw, M.E. (1981). *Group dynamics: The psychology of small group behavior* (3rd ed.). New York, NY: McGraw-Hill.

Weinberg, R.S. & Gould, D. (2003). *Foundations of sport & exercise psychology* (3rd ed.). Champaign, IL: Human Kinetics.

Widmeyer, W.N., Brawley, L.R. & Carron, A.V. (1985). *The measurement of cohesion in sport teams: The group environment questionnaire.* London, ON: Sport Dynamics.

Widmeyer, W.N., Brawley, L.R. & Carron, A.V. (1990). The effects of group size in sport. *Journal of Sport and Exercise Psychology, 12, 2,* 177–190.

Chapter 35

Creating adaptive motivational climates in sport and physical education

JOAN L. DUDA, ATHANASIOS G. PAPAIOANNOU, PAUL R. APPLETON, ELEANOR QUESTED AND
CHARALAMPOS KROMMIDAS

SUMMARY

The scientific literature, anecdotal evidence and our personal experience speak to the impact of coaches and teachers on the quality of engagement in sport and educational settings. This chapter pulls from contemporary theories of motivation and identifies key dimensions of the social psychological environment or *motivational climate* operating in sport and physical education (PE) that hold significance for the motivation and cognitive, emotional and behavioural responses of athletes and students. Achievement goal frameworks point to the importance of considering the degree to which the climate is more task- and/or ego-involving. Self-Determination Theory focuses on the relevance of the autonomy and socially supportive aspects of the climate, the controlling behaviours of leaders, and the degree to which the environment is marked by structure. Athlete/PE student outcomes which are associated with such distinctions in the motivational climate are reviewed. The chapter concludes by indicating how this theoretical and empirical work on the 'motivational climate' has led to interventions aiming to enhance athletes' and students' participation in sport and physical education.

INTRODUCTION

Coaches and teachers matter when it comes to the motivation of athletes/students and whether their participation is positive and likely to be sustained or resulting in negative consequences. Consider the following three hypothetical scenarios which reflect very different experiences for the young athletes and PE students depicted. What environments are their coaches/teachers creating? Why and how are the behaviours of these coaches/teachers having such different impacts?

Scenario One: Seán loves participating in football and looks forward to coming back next season. He is not the most gifted player on the team but understands the important role he plays. His coach always talks about giving your best effort and informs Seán about ways he can keep improving his football skills. Following the advice of their coach, all the players on Seán's team help decide what to work on in training. Even when they lose the game, it is clear to Seán and his teammates that the coach is behind them.

Scenario Two: Growing up, John has liked to play active games but is not the most coordinated or physically strong student in his PE class. His current teacher prefers to have the students compete against each other in different sporting activities during PE and it is clear who are the better 'athletes' and who struggles. John worries that the others are better than him, feels worse about his physical capabilities and does not enjoy PE. He no longer has any interest or gives any effort in PE class.

Scenario Three: Kate is a talented young athlete and is on scholarship at an elite tennis academy. Kate has always played the game because she found tennis to be fun and she wanted to be a professional tennis player one day. However, the environment at the academy is starting to erode her intrinsic motivation. Her coach provides feedback in a very intimidating fashion and talks often about all the money that she will earn if she makes it in professional tennis. When she doesn't perform well, the coach lets Kate know that she has let him down. Kate finds herself very stressed when competing and doesn't feel that the goals being set for her tennis development are her own. Kate is considering dropping out of the sport.

Figure 35.1 Young boys and girls with coach.

OBJECTIVES

After reading this chapter you should be able to:

1   Define the concept of 'motivational climate'.

2   Distinguish between the behaviours of a coach/teacher which contribute to the motivational climate being more task- and/or ego-involving.

3   Describe sport and PE environments which are characterised by autonomy and social support in contrast to controlling behaviours.

4   Indicate an understanding of how theory and research on the 'motivational climate' have led to interventions in sport and PE.

5   Discuss the implications of this work for optimising the behaviour of coaches and PE teachers.

THE MOTIVATIONAL CLIMATE IN SPORT AND PHYSICAL EDUCATION: THEORETICAL BASES, RESEARCH FINDINGS AND INTERVENTION STRATEGIES

Introduction to the concept of the motivational climate in sport and physical education from an AGT and SDT perspective

In the scenarios presented above, differential cognitive, emotional and behavioural responses to engagement in sport and PE are presented. In general, athletes and PE students, regardless of their ability level, can work hard, enjoy what they are doing, optimise their skill development and handle setbacks. However, those involved in sport and physical education settings could also be riddled with anxiety, hold back on giving effort, lose interest in the activity, and 'dropout' psychologically if not behaviourally as well. This maladaptive pattern of response can be realised by athletes or students who do *not* have high competence and capacity in the physical domain. Even the talented can end up having negative experiences in and reactions to sport or PE.

The question is, what makes the difference in terms of which 'scenario' we are likely to observe? Theory and related research indicate that variability in motivational processes play an important role in distinguishing between positive engagement (i.e., participation that is sustained, contributes to well-being, promotes personal growth and optimal functioning) or involvement in sport or PE that is compromised. Our understanding of which types of motivation are more likely to lead to positive as well as negative responses in athletes and students is informed by two contemporary theories of motivation, namely Achievement Goal Theory (AGT) drawing in particular from the work of Nicholls (1989) and Dweck (1986), and Self-Determination Theory (SDT) as developed by Deci and Ryan (1985; Ryan and Deci, 2000). From an AGT standpoint, when individuals have a propensity to judge their ability in a self-referenced manner (i.e, are strong in their task orientation) and participate in sport or PE for more autonomous reasons (i.e., out of their own volition, because they enjoy and/or personally value the benefits of the activity), the motivational processes manifested are more adaptive. More controlled reasons for engagement in sport or PE (e.g., for the extrinsic rewards, because one feels compelled to be involved) and the tendency to be concerned with demonstrating superiority and primarily judge one's ability level based on normative comparison reflect less optimal/more dysfunctional motivational practices and perspectives. Important to the focus of this chapter, in both AGT and SDT, the social environment (created by significant others such as coaches and teachers) is assumed to be a key contributor to whether more adaptive or maladaptive motivational processes and associated positive or negative outcomes are likely to occur.

Drawing from both AGT and SDT, we can define the *motivational climate* in sport and PE as the social psychological environment that is created by coaches or teachers via what they typically say or do and captures how they tend to provide feedback, evaluate, and organize matters in training/competitions or classes, respectively. The degree to which athletes/students input into and are considered in decisions made by the coach/teacher also contributes to the motivational atmosphere. The interpersonal aspects of the relationship between the athlete/student and his or her coach/teacher also comprise the motivational climate which is operating; e.g., is the coach cold and distant? Does the student feel the PE teacher respects and cares for him or her?

AGT centres on the *task-involving* and *ego-involving* features of the environments manifested in sport and PE. The theory predicts that a motivational climate which is more task-involving (and/or less ego-involving) corresponds to more adaptive motivational processes and positive outcomes. A large body of research in sport and PE provides support for these predictions (Duda & Balaguer, 2007).

When a motivational climate is more task-involving, the coach or teacher emphasises the importance of giving one's best effort, supports collaboration, and shows he or she values athlete/student learning, personal growth, skill improvement and task mastery. A task-involving coach/teacher tends to provide instruction and encouragement following mistakes. If the sport or PE motivational climate is more ego-involving, then rivalry between athletes/students is encouraged, emphasis is placed on having to be 'the best' and those who are more talented and successful receive preferential treatment by the coach or teacher. In an ego-involving atmosphere, it is made apparent to athletes/students that mistakes are to be avoided as errors are often followed by a punitive response. Within a sport or PE setting that is marked by ego-involving characteristics, the athletes and students know where they stand on the ability ladder (i.e., are they superior or not as good as the others?). They also realise that, in the eyes of the coach or teacher, being at the top of that ladder is what is most valued.

When we look at the motivational climate from the perspective of SDT, other features of the environment are highlighted. A first, central feature of the social environment which is emphasised as being motivationally significant in SDT is *autonomy support*. An autonomy supportive coach or teacher provides meaningful choices, solicits input, and indicates that he or she understands and appreciates the perspective of the athletes/students. SDT also takes into account the degree to which the motivational climate is marked by *social support*. A coach or PE teacher who is socially supportive demonstrates that he or she cares about and respects his/her athletes or students as people, independent of their ability levels or quality of their performance. Finally, based on SDT, we also need to consider the degree to which a coach or teacher is *controlling*. In a highly controlling motivational climate, a coach or teacher tends to intimidate his or her athletes or students, makes the decisions, and doesn't ask for or respect their opinions. A controlling coach or teacher gets the message across that his or her approval is contingent on the athlete/student performing well and doing as requested. Using extrinsic rewards as 'carrots' is another behaviour that would be considered controlling. Consistent with the predictions of SDT, a large number of studies conducted in sport and PE have supported links between autonomy and/or socially supportive environments, adaptive motivational processes, and positive outcomes. Further, previous sport and PE research has provided evidence for the expected relationships between low autonomy supportive/

more controlling environments, more maladaptive motivational characteristics, and heightened negative responses in athletes and students.

An integrative framework has been proposed (Duda, 2013), which pulls together these motivation-related dimensions of the motivational climate from an AGT and SDT perspective. This integrative approach conceptualises the motivational climate as being more *empowering* when that social environment is highly task-involving, autonomy supportive and socially supportive. A coach or teacher who exhibits consistent and prominent ego-involving and controlling behaviours creates a motivational climate that is more *disempowering* for his or her athletes.

In the following sections of this chapter, we summarise the research findings illustrating the benefits of an environment which is marked by more empowering features in the contexts of sport and physical education. We also briefly review literature which points to the apparent costs or negative implications of climates marked by more disempowering characteristics. This work will be reviewed from the lens of AGT as well as SDT. Within sport and PE settings, we then highlight recent intervention efforts to enhance athlete/PE students' engagement and well-being which have been grounded in AGT, SDT and the integrative approach to the motivational climate.

Correlates of perceptions of task- and ego-involving motivational climates

Past studies of the coach- and PE teacher-created motivational climate from an AGT perspective have provided findings that are consistent with theoretical predictions (Duda & Balaguer, 2007). This body of research confirms that perceptions of a task-involving environment are generally associated with positive intrapersonal and interpersonal outcomes. For example, athletes' and PE students' perceptions of a task-involving climate have been related to:

- more enjoyment, satisfaction, and interest whilst participating in sport and in PE;
- reduced levels of anxiety and concerns about performing, and lower fear of failure;
- greater commitment to training and practice, and dedication to learning new skills;
- heightened well-being, including positive affect, subjective vitality, and self-esteem;
- more constructive peer relationships;
- the view that the purpose of sport includes fostering good citizenship, development of prosocial values such as social responsibility, collaboration, and cooperation, and to encourage a physically active lifestyle;
- positive moral functioning and sportspersonship values, such as a greater respect of the game, rules, and officials, and more mature moral reasoning;
- a reduced likelihood to demonstrate antisocial behaviours during competition;
- lower symptoms of burnout;
- greater cohesion within the team;
- the view (by athletes and PE students, respectively) that positive feedback, training and instruction, and social support is provided by the coach and by the PE teacher;
- increases in performance;
- the belief that effort leads to success in sport and in PE; and
- increased likelihood of persisting in sport and active participation in PE.

The findings concerning the ego-involving features of the coach- and teacher-created climate are also aligned with the tenets of AGT. Athletes' and PE students' perceptions of an ego-involving environment have been linked to negative achievement behaviours and undesirable cognitive and emotional responses, including:

- higher levels of anxiety and heightened performance-related worries;
- a tendency to avoid practice and reduce effort in response to failure;

- the belief that comparing favourably with others is an important determinant of sport achievement;
- lower quality of friendships and greater peer conflict;
- contingent self-worth (or the tendency to base one's self-esteem on performances in sport or other such achievement activities);
- lower levels of perceived closeness with the coach, and views that the coach and the PE teacher provide more punishment-oriented feedback;
- maladaptive perfectionistic tendencies and self-handicapping;
- greater reported ill-being, including negative affect, emotional and physical exhaustion (burnout symptoms);
- less mature moral reasoning and greater antisocial behaviour;
- psychological difficulties during competition and the use of avoidance coping strategies; and
- a greater likelihood to drop-out of sport (which tends to be a voluntary activity in which it is possible to cease one's participation).

Although the majority of studies examining the coach- and teacher-created motivational climate have adopted a cross-sectional design, a number of studies employ a more complex research methodology. Longitudinal research is necessary if we are to determine whether the psychological environment created by the coach is associated with changes in athletes' experiences in sport over time (e.g., start to end of the season). One of the first studies to determine the correlates of a perceived task- and ego-involving motivational climate on athletes' emotional responses over time was conducted by Reinboth and Duda (2006). In their study of university-level athletes assessed at the beginning and toward the end of a competitive season, a perceived task-involving climate positively related to athletes' feelings of vitality at both time points.

A longitudinal design was recently adopted by Ntoumanis and colleagues (2012), who examined the relationship between features of the coach-created climate (from an AGT perspective) with moral attitudes, burnout and vitality, and indices of investment in a sample of British youth athletes. This study involved three time points (midseason, end of season, start of next season) over a one year period. Ntoumanis and colleagues reported that a perceived coach-created, task-involving climate positively and consistently predicted athletes' prosocial attitudes and vitality in sport, as well as their intentions to continue representing their current team. Athletes' perceptions of an ego-involving climate were consistently (and negatively) associated with their intentions to continue playing on their team. Finally, an ego-involving climate was not significantly associated with antisocial attitudes (i.e., cheating and sportsmanship) and burnout at the start of the season, but these relationships became significant and stronger over time.

Within the PE setting, a longitudinal study by Papaioannou, Marsh and Theodorakis (2004) involving more than 200 PE classes revealed that increases in the perceived task-involving features of the PE climate positively related to changes in reported effort and enjoyment in the PE class over time. Further, when the class environment created by the PE teacher became more task-involving, students reported increasingly more positive attitudes and intentions to participate in sport and physical activity.

Correlates of perceptions of autonomy- and socially-supportive and controlling motivational climates

In support of SDT, studies (for a recent review of the literature, see Ntoumanis, 2012) examining the correlates of autonomy-support has confirmed this facet of the coach-/teacher-created motivational climate to be associated with athletes' and PE students':

- greater intrinsic motivation and satisfaction in sport and in PE;
- higher levels of subjective vitality and positive emotions, and lower levels of depression;
- reduced burnout symptoms;
- perceptions of team identification and cohesion;
- reporting a quality relationship with their coach and their PE teacher;
- sportsmanship and prosocial behaviours;
- leisure-time physical activity intentions and continued participation in sport.

In contrast to the correlates of the perceived autonomy-supportive behaviours of coaches and teachers, comparatively less is known about the consequences of controlling leader styles for athletes and particularly PE students. Within the context of physical education, Nicaise and colleagues (Nicaise, Bois, Fairclough, Amorose & Cogérino, 2007) found that PE students perceived teacher criticism as controlling and this had negative effect on their effort, enjoyment and performance in physical education.

One reason for the lack of studies on the implications of controlling environments is that researchers did not have a valid and reliable measure of this aspect of coach/teacher behaviours until recently. However, Bartholomew and colleagues (2010) addressed this limitation in the sport context by developing the Controlling Coach Behaviors Scale (CCBS), which is composed of four sub-scales (assessing controlling use of rewards, conditional regard, intimidation, and excessive personal control). Bartholomew, Ntoumanis, Ryan, Bosch, and Thøgersen-Ntoumani (2011) subsequently examined the correlates associated with athletes' ratings on the CCBS. Across three separate samples, coaches' controlling interpersonal style compromised the psychological and emotional functioning of athletes. For example, perceived coach controlling behaviours were positively associated with female athletes' self-reported disordered eating and depression, and

negatively correlated with subjective vitality. Among junior athletes, perceptions of a controlling climate related to lower levels of the experience of positive emotions and higher levels of negative emotions.

In a large sample of Spanish male footballers, Balaguer and associates (Balaguer et al., 2012) employed the CCBS and an assessment of autonomy support to longitudinally examine the relationship of these environmental dimensions to vitality and burnout symptoms. When the motivational climate was deemed to be more autonomy supportive across the season, the players increased their feelings of energy and reported decreased feelings of being burned out. In contrast, when players viewed their coaches as being more controlling over time, they experienced greater burnout at the end of the season.

Within educational studies that are grounded in SDT, attention has been given to the correlates of socially-supportive behaviours of the teacher. However, limited research has determined the implications of this dimension of the motivational climate created by the coach or PE teacher specifically. One exception in terms of existing sport research is the Reinboth, Duda and Ntoumanis (2004) study of adolescent age British football and cricket players. In their work, perceptions of social support provided by the coach was positively correlated with the athletes' feelings of vitality and satisfaction and interest and was negatively associated with reported physical and emotional exhaustion (a symptom of burnout).

An important and interesting issue embedded in the AGT- and SDT-based research summarised above relates to potential mechanisms by which environments which vary in their motivational characteristics may impact the targeted outcomes. In other words, why might task-involving, autonomy- and socially-supportive motivational climates correspond to more positive responses in athletes/students? What processes could account for the observed associations between perceived ego-involving and controlling coach/PE teacher behaviours and indicators of compromised athlete/student functioning?

Research in this area has pulled from SDT in considering what the mediators of the Social Environment-Outcome relationship might be. Particular emphasis has been placed on the role of 'basic psychological needs'; namely, the need for all people in all contexts to feel competent (i.e., they perceive they can meet the demands of the activity), a sense of autonomy (i.e., that they have volition in their participation and see themselves as having choice and input), and relatedness (i.e., that significant others in that setting care for and respect them). Past studies have demonstrated that sport and PE environments which are more autonomy- and socially-supportive and/or task-involving are more likely to lead to a satisfaction of these basic psychological needs. When athletes/students witness a sense of competence, autonomy and relatedness, they are more likely to exhibit positive cognitive, emotional and behavioural responses. Research also has indicated that more ego-involving and controlling environments are linked to maladaptive responses via their implications for diminished satisfaction of the three psychological needs and/or the view that the psychological needs have been actively impeded or thwarted (Balaguer et al., 2012).

Motivation theory-based interventions in PE and sport

Theoretical models help us better synthesise, comprehend and explain how our world operates. As a result, the literature points to the prudence of using theories when we design and test interventions in the real world. When the aim is to intervene in a sport setting or PE classes to create more adaptive motivational climates, conceptual frameworks such as AGT and SDT provide guidance on which aspects of the environment should be targeted, why, and how. These theories, and related research, also inform us about whether the mechanisms lead to any effect of changes in the motivational climate on athlete/student outcomes.

Coach climate interventions and associated findings

Sport psychologists have manipulated the coach-created motivational climate in intervention-based studies to determine its effect of the quantity and quality of athletes' engagement. Most of these intervention studies have been grounded in AGT (see Roberts, 2012, for a review). One illustration of such an approach is Smith and Smoll's Mastery Approach to Coaching (MAC). MAC was designed to develop, deliver, and evaluate a child-centred educational programme that aimed to benefit young athletes. This training programme helps coaches promote healthy achievement in all areas of a child's life, including sports, by giving coaches specific behavioural guidelines on how they could adopt a mastery approach to coaching. MAC emerged from Smith and Smoll's original work concerning the assessment of coaching behaviours (Coaching Behavior Assessment System; Smith, Smoll, & Hunt, 1977) and a coach-based intervention entitled "Coaching Effectiveness Training" (CET) (Smith, Smoll, & Curtis, 1979).

MAC retains the behavioural approach embedded in CET and incorporates elements of AGT, by including some guidelines for creating a task-involving motivational climate in youth sport. Coaches are encouraged to engage in specific behaviours, including positive reinforcement, mistake-contingent encouragement, corrective instruction delivered in a positive and encouraging manner, and sound technical advice. A series of nondesirable behaviours are also idenified in MAC, such as nonreinforcement of positive behaviour and effort, failing to encourage athletes to learn from mistakes, as well as mistake-contingent punishment. An additional theme within MAC is the emphasis placed on success as giving maximum effort, having fun, and developing as an athlete, rather than winning at all costs and outperforming others.

With regards to evaluating the effects of MAC, results have demonstrated that athletes who played for coaches trained in MAC princi-ples report signicantly higher levels of a task-involving climate and lower levels of an ego-involving climate compared to athletes in a control condition. Furthermore, children report significant increases in task-involving goals and decreases in ego-involving goals, as well as lower levels of anxiety when they play for coaches trained in the MAC principles (Smith, Smoll, & Cumming, 2007a, b).

In addition to changing athletes' motiva-tion and related outcomes, sport psychologists have taken guidance from AGT and have manipulated the coach-created motivational climate to foster important life skills in young performers. This was recently demonstrated in a study by Maro and colleagues (2009), who implemented a task-involving intervention within a programme (EMIMA) designed to equip young children in Tanzania with foot-ball skills and HIV/AIDS life skills. Within EMIMA, peers were trained as coaches to deliver information, knowledge, and skills concerning football performance as well as HIV/AIDS prevention. From these coaches, a group received training on creating a task-involving motivational climate that would increase the children's mastery engagement in football and AIDS education activities. Thus, there were two intervention groups in this study; the normal life skills programme and a group with task-involving principles built into the football sessions. There were also two control groups; a group who received HIV/AIDS education through the school system and a group of children who did not attend school or the football programme. When compared to children in the control groups, children in both intervention conditions reported signifi-cantly higher HIV/AIDS life skills at the end of the project. The study also revealed that chil-dren exposed to a more task-involving climate reported greater increases in most of the life skills compared to normal intervention group.

In contrast to AGT-informed interventions, relatively few studies have attempted to modify dimensions of the motivational climate drawing from SDT. However, an inter-vention study by Pelletier and colleagues (1986) confirms the benefits for athletes' motivation when the coach-initiated climate is more autonomy-supportive. In their study, Pelletier et al. developed a workshop for swimming coaches that aimed to foster their understand-ing of how to be more autonomy-supportive. One year later, swimmers working with more autonomy-supportive coaches were more intrinsically motivated than a control group of swimmers. Furthermore, the findings revealed a decrease in dropout rates (compared to the previous year) for the intervention swimmers (from 36% to 5%), while dropout rates for the control group remained at 35%.

Although there have been attempts to use AGT or SDT to inform interventions in sport, intervention studies have generally targeted isolated features of the coach-created motiva-tional climate, such as the degree of autonomy support or task-involving cues. The potential benefits of these interventions can be consid-ered limited, as they have failed to integrate AGT and SDT and train coaches to create a more empowering climate; one that is high in autonomy-support, social support and task-involving (Duda, 2013). With the same reason-ing in mind, it seems prudent to have coaches better understand the likely drawbacks of a disempowering environment; i.e., a motiva-tional climate that is highly ego-involving and controlling (Duda, 2013).

The importance of educating coaches about the advantages of and strategies contributing to an empowering motivational climate were recently recognised in a large European inter-vention study (i.e., the 'PAPA' or Promoting Adolescent Physical Activity Project; www.projectpapa.org). The PAPA project concerns the further development, delivery and evalua-tion of a coach education programme (Empow-ering Coaching™) within the context of grassroots football across five European coun-tries (i.e., England, France, Greece, Norway, and Spain) (Duda, Quested, et al., 2013). Grounded in the integrated model of the motivational climate (Duda, 2013), the Empowering Coaching™ programme aims to help coaches be more task-involving and autonomy- and social-supportive (and de-emphasise ego-involving cues and controlling behaviours) in community-based as well as elite youth sport programmes. Based on the assumptions of AGT and SDT, a more empowering coach-created climate is expected to foster children's autonomous motivation for and quality engagement in sport, sustained participation, as well as promoting their psychological health.

Physical education climate interventions

In most of these studies the main focus was the promotion of mastery goals usually through interventions in task structure and authority structure and less often through direct manipulation of teachers' feedback (e.g., Viciana, Cervello & Ramirez-Lechuga, 2007). For example, in two separate year-long studies in Greece the PE teachers focused particularly on the promotion of positive attitudes towards exercise and the implementation of student-centred teaching styles, such as Mosston's (1996) inclusion and reciprocal teaching styles (Digelidis, Papaioannou, Laparidis & Christodoulidis, 2003; Christodoulidis, Papaioannou & Digelidis, 2001). Personal goal setting programmes for exercise promotion and process goals for sport skill development were emphasised, while the number of competitive activities were reduced. The interventions had positive effects on the task-involving climate, students' task-orientation and positive attitudes towards exercise. At the same time, they were particularly successful in terms of diminishing the ego-involving climate and decreasing students' ego-orientation. The positive effects of student-centred teaching styles on task-involving climate emerged in other interventions too, for example, in a four-week intervention study in PE (Morgan, Sproule & Kingtson, 2005) and in a ten-week interven-

tion in a girls' school (Goudas, Biddle, Fox & Underwood, 1995).

Most of the interventions were based primarily on AGT but the transfer of decision making from teacher to student is an important implication stemming from SDT too. An example of a year-long intervention based both on AGT and SDT was the study of Jaakkola and Liukkonen (2006). They trained four Finnish PE teachers on how to implement these theories in their PE classes through consultation meetings (between researchers and PE students) that occurred two to four times a month. This intervention had positive effects on students' self-determination and task orientation. In general, the involvement of PE teachers in the creation of a positive motivational climate is considered important for the promotion of a task-involving climate in PE.

In addition to these studies in Greece and Finland, interventions in PE have been conducted in several other countries, such as in the UK (e.g., Morgan & Kingston, 2008), USA (e.g., Solmon, 1996), Spain (e.g., Cecchini, Gonzalez, Carmona, et al., 2001) and Brazil (Valentini & Rudisill, 2004). Braithwaite, Spray and Warburton (2011) review several interventions in PE which focused simultaneously on multiple components of the motivational climate, such as task structure, authority, recognition of effort or ability, heterogenous or homogenous ability grouping, evaluation, flexible or inflexible time to practice. The effects of these studies were generally successful in terms of the manipulation of motivational climate but the size of the effects, particularly in studies involving multiple teachers, were usually small or moderate.

Milosis and Papaioannou (2007) suggested that if teachers want a really high task-involving climate in PE, they should make learning and improvement in PE meaningful to their students. In addition to the aforementioned intervention components these authors incorporated life skills development as an important component of a PE programme aiming to help students understand that through PE they can learn how to improve themselves in any part of life. Milosis and Papaioannou (2007) provide several details about their interdisci-plinary programme in PE which had substantial positive effects on motivational climate, students' self-concept and achievement goal adoption and students' satisfaction not only in PE but in other academic subjects too.

CONCLUSION

The concept of adaptive motivational climate became popular in the 1990s but most of the interventions emerged in the last decade. Most of the manipulations of motivational climate in sport and PE were primarily based on AGT while the adoption of the SDT was primarily used for the promotion of athletes' and PE students' autonomy and less for the satisfaction of their needs for relatedness which is particularly important in adolescence. With few exceptions like the PAPA study (Duda et al., in press) most of the existing interventions included a small number of coaches or PE teachers who voluntarily participated in these studies. These were probably highly motivated individuals who wanted to make a change in the way they coach and teach in order to improve the motivation of their athletes and PE students. However, reality is more complex than this and it includes coaches and teachers who have divergent achievement goals and a variety of beliefs about coaching and peda-gogy. It is much easier to create a high task-involving climate when coaches are highly task-oriented themselves but more difficult when grassroot coaches are primarily concerned with their team's win or loss next Sunday or when PE teachers resist changes to their teaching. If we want to create positive motivational climates we should focus on how to increase coaches' and PE teachers' task orientation and how to make them less controlling individuals.

There are further challenges though. The climate in a team or in a PE class is not only determined by coaches or teachers but quite significantly by athletes' and students' goals and behaviours. Athletes and students bring their own belief systems, goals and habits in their teams and classes. These goals, beliefs and habits are largely determined by parents, peers and other socialization factors. Effective interventions in youth sport should focus not only on coaching but also on parental practices and maybe on peer settings. Some even argue that in underdeveloped areas interventions should be made at a local level, in neighbourhoods etc. Certainly, the question is whether a single coach can make such an impact on athletes, parents and peers without the support of other agents. Obviously, interventions involving several agents concurrently seem to have the most promising effects. On the other hand, based on the existing evidence we can also argue that those athletes or students who mostly had high task-involving and very supportive coaches and teachers were very lucky indeed because they acquired positive experiences through their participation in sport that boosted their motivation not only in sport but also possibly in life.

LEARNING AIDS

1   What is broadly understood in the literature by the phrase 'motivational climate'?

The term 'motivational climate' describes the features of the social environment that hold motivational relevance. The motivational climate created in sport and PE has also been described as the social-psychological environment surrounding players during training and performance, as well as during other coach–player (or student–teacher) interactions. Coaches or teachers are critical to the shaping of this climate via what they typically say or do, how they provide instructions, feedback, evaluation, and other aspects associated with organisation of training and performance matters.

2   What are the two prominent features of the motivational climate, according to achievement goal theory (AGT)?

AGT identifies two aspects of the social environment that hold motivational relevance, and these are termed task-involving and ego-involving features of the climate. Task-involving motivational climates are characterised by an emphasis on the value of effort and improvement and the importance of each individual's role. Thus, the importance of doing one's best is recognised as an overriding value. When the climate in sport or PE is more ego-involving, the emphasis tends to be on having to 'be the best'. In such environments, rivalry between athletes or students may be encouraged, the more able receive preferential treatment and praise whereas those who are less successful are ignored or punished for mistakes.

3   What three features of the motivational climate are highlighted by self-determination theory (SDT)?

The extent to which the atmosphere promotes autonomy support is a prominent feature of the motivational climate according to SDT. Autonomy supportive coaching or teaching emphasises the provision of meaningful choices, involving athletes/students in decision making, providing rationale for requests and showing that one takes the perspective of the athletes/students. The degree of social support is also recognised to contribute to the motivational atmosphere. Socially supportive teaching/ coaching involves the demonstration of care and respect for athletes or students regardless of their level of engagement or performance. Controlling aspects of the environment are also considered within the SDT framework. The types of coach/teacher behaviour that contribute to a highly controlling motivational climate include intimidation, restriction of athlete/student input and decision making and the application of contingencies or rewards to coerce behaviour.

4   Drawing on the integrative framework proposed by Duda (2013), what are the features of an *empowering* and a *disempowering* motivational climate?

More empowering motivational climates are likely to be high in task-involving, autonomy-supportive and socially-supportive features. In addition, the prevalence of ego-involving and controlling coach/ teacher behaviours would be minimal or non-existent.

More disempowering motivational climates are likely to be high ego-involving and controlling coach/ teacher behaviours. Such environments would still be considered disempowering, even if empowering features were also present to some degree.

REVIEW QUESTIONS

1   Identify common correlates/motivational outcomes that stem from task-involving and autonomy-supportive climates and common motivational outcomes that stem from ego-involving and controlling motivational climates.

2   Identify the dimensions of the motivational climate in sport which were manipulated in intervention studies in order to create a positive motivational climate. What was the main focus of interventions in these studies?

3   Identify the dimensions of the motivational climate in PE which were manipulated in intervention studies. Based on these, what would you suggest to a PE teacher in order to create a positive motivational climate in PE?

EXERCISES

1   Goal: To conduct a case study of the motivational climate created by a coach of your choice. To identify the characteristics of the motivational climate created by the coach.

Description: Identify a sports coach of your choice. Conduct an informal interview with him/her about the strategies he/she uses to motivate children in sport. Prior to the interview, consider what types of questions to ask in order to be able to explore the different motivational dynamics in the sport setting as a function of the environment he/she creates. Remember, the coach will not be familiar with terms such as 'autonomy-supportive', 'ego-involving' etc. Therefore you will need to create questions that explore the different types of behaviours the coach exhibits or strategies that he or she employs. Make some notes on his/her replies and later consider which dimensions of the multidimensional climate are likely to be more or less prevalent in the setting this coach is likely to create. Next, observe this coach in a training session. As you observe, make notes on the aspects of the motivational climate (pulling from existing theoretical perspectives highlighted in this chapter) that you see him/her exhibit. Drawing from both methods of data collection, write a summary report of the climate created by this coach. Were there any discrepancies between the coach's perceptions of the environment he/she creates and what you observed to be objectively the case? Why do you think this might be? Overall, do you consider this to be an adaptive environment for children to participate in sport?

2   Goal: To produce a guide for PE teachers that explains how and why to create a more empowering environment in PE classes.

Description: Produce a small guide that could be shared with PE teachers that explains (in simple terms) why it is important to create a more empowering climate in PE. Generate a series of examples of what PE teachers can say and do to enhance the degree to which that climate they create is empowering.

ADDITIONAL READING

Duda, J.L. & Balaguer, I. (2007). Coach-Created Motivational Climate. In S. Jowett & D. Lavallee (Eds.), *Social Psychology in Sport* (pp.117–130). Leeds, UK: Human Kinetics.

Jaakkola, T. & Digelidis, N. (2007). Establishing a positive motivational climate in physical education. In J. Liukkonen (Ed.), *Psychology for Physical Educators* (2nd ed.) (pp.3–16). Champaign, IL: Human Kinetics.

Ntoumanis, N. & Biddle, S.J.H. (1999). A review of motivational climate in physical activity. *Journal of Sport Science, 17,* 643–665.

Papaioannou, A. & Goudas, M. (1999). Motivational climate of the physical education class. In Y.V. Auweele, F. Bakker, S.J.H. Biddle, M. Durand & R. Seiler (Eds.), *Psychology for Physical Educators* (pp.51–68). Champaign, IL: Human Kinetics.

REFERENCES

Balaguer, I., González, L., Fabra, P., Castillo, I., Mercé, J. & Duda, J.L. (2012). Coaches' interpersonal style, basic psychological needs and the well- and ill-being of young soccer players: A longitudinal analysis. *Journal of Sports Sciences, 30,* 1619–1629.

Bartholomew, K., Ntoumanis, N., Ryan, R., Bosch, J. & Thøgersen-Ntoumani, C. (2011). Self-Determination theory and diminished functioning: The role of interpersonal control and psychological need thwarting. *Personality and Social Psychology Bulletin, 37,* 1459–1473.

Bartholomew, K., Ntoumanis, N. & Thøgersen-Ntoumani, C. (2010). The controlling interpersonal style in a coaching context: Development and initial validation of a psychometric scale. *Journal of Sport and Exercise Psychology, 32,* 193–216.

Braithwaite, R., Spray, C.M. & Warburton, V.E. (2011). Motivational climate interventions in physical education: A meta-analysis. *Psychology of Sport and Exercise, 12,* 628–638.

Cecchini, J., Gonzalez, C., Carmona, A., Arruza, J., Escarti, A. & Balague, G. (2001). The influence of the physical education teacher on intrinsic motivation, self-confidence, anxiety, and pre- and post-competition mood states. *European Journal of Sport Science, 1,* 1–11.

Christodoulidis, T., Papaioannou, A. & Digelidis, N. (2001). Motivational climate and attitudes towards exercise in Greek senior high school: A year-long intervention. *European Journal of Sport Science, 1,* 1–12.

Deci, E.L. & Ryan, R.M. (1985). *Intrinsic Motivation and Self-Determination in Human Behavior.* New York: Plenum Publishing Co.

Digelidis, N., Papaioannou, A., Christodoulidis, T. & Laparidis, K. (2003). A one-year intervention in 7th grade physical education classes aiming to change motivational climate and attitudes towards exercise. *Psychology of Sport & Exercise, 3,* 195–210.

Duda, J.L. (2013). The conceptual and empirical foundations of Empowering Coaching™: How the stage was set for the PAPA project. *International Journal of Sport and Exercise Psychology* 11(4), 311–318.

Duda, J.L. & Balaguer, I. (2007). Coach-Created Motivational Climate. In S. Jowett & D. Lavallee (Eds.), *Social Psychology in Sport* (pp.117–130). Leeds, UK: Human Kinetics.

Duda, J.L., Quested, E., Haug, E., Samdal, O., Wold, B., Balaguer, I., Castillo, I., Sarrazin, P., Papaioannou, A., Ronglan, L-T., Hall, H.K. & Cruz, J. (2013). Promoting adolescent health through an intervention aimed at improving the quality of their participation in Physical Activity (PAPA): Background to the project and main trial protocol. *International Journal of Sport and Exercise Psychology*, 11(4), 319–327.

Dweck, C.S. (1986). Motivational processes affecting learning. *American Psychologist, 41,* 1040–1048.

Goudas, M., Biddle, S., Fox, K. & Underwood, M. (1995). It ain't what you do, it's the way that you do it. Teaching style affects children's motivation in track and field lessons. *The Sport Psychologist, 9(3),* 254–264.

Jaakkola, T. & Liukkonen, J. (2006). Changes in students' self-determined motivation and goal orientation as a result of motivational climate intervention within high school physical education classes. *International Journal of Sport and Exercise Psychology, 4(3)*, 302–324.

Maro, C., Roberts, G.C. & Sørensen, M. (2009). Using sport to promote HIV/AIDS education for at risk youths: An intervention using peer coaches in football. *Scandinavian Journal of Medicine and Science in Sport, 19*, 129–141.

Milosis, D. & Papaioannou, A. (2007). Interdisciplinary teaching, multiple goals and self-concept. In J. Liukkonen (Ed.), *Psychology for Physical Educators* (Vol. 2) (pp.175–198). Champaign, IL: Human Kinetics.

Morgan, K. & Kingston, K. (2008). Development of a self-observation mastery intervention programme for teacher education. *Physical Education and Sport Pedagogy, 13(2)*, 102–109.

Morgan, K., Sproule, J. & Kingston, K. (2005). Effects of different teaching styles on the teacher behaviours that influence motivational climate and pupils' motivation in physical education. *European Physical Education Review, 11*, 257–285.

Nicaise, V., Bois, J.E., Fairclough, S.J.F., Amorose, A.J. & Cogérino, G. (2007). Girls' and boys' perceptions of physical education teachers' feedback: Effects on performance and psychological responses. *Journal of Sports Sciences, 25(8)*, 2007, 915–926.

Nicholls, J.G. (1989). *The competitive ethos and democratic education*. Cambridge, MA: Harvard University Press.

Ntoumanis, N. (2012). A self-determination theory perspective on motivation in sport and physical education: Current trends and possible future research directions. In G.C. Roberts & D.C. Treasure (Eds.), *Motivation in Sport and Exercise:* (Vol. 3) (pp.91–128). Champaign, IL: Human Kinetics.

Ntoumanis, N., Taylor, I. & Thøgersen-Ntoumani, C. (2012). A longitudinal examination of coach and peer motivational climates in youth sport: Implications for moral attitudes, well-being, and behavioral investment. *Developmental Psychology, 48*, 213–223.

Papaioannou, A., Marsh, H. & Theodorakis, Y. (2004). A multilevel approach to motivational climate in physical education and sport settings: An individual or group level construct? *Journal of Sport & Exercise Psychology, 26*, 90–118.

Pelletier, L.G., Blais, M.R. & Vallerand, R.J. (1986). The integration and maintenance of change with an elite swimming team: An application of a model for sport psychology. Unpublished manuscript, University of Ottawa, Ottawa, Canada.

Reinboth, M. & Duda, J.L. (2006). Perceived motivational climate, need satisfaction and indices of well-being in team sports: A longitudinal perspective. *Psychology of Sport and Exercise, 7*, 269–286.

Reinboth, M., Duda, J.L. & Ntoumanis, N. (2004). Dimensions of coaching behavior, need satisfaction, and the psychological and physical welfare of young athletes. *Motivation and Emotion, 28*, 297–313.

Roberts, G.C. (2012). Motivation in sport and exercise from an achievement goal theory perspective: After 30 years, where are we? In G.C. Roberts & D.C. Treasure (Eds.), *Motivation in Sport and Exercise:* (Vol. 3) (pp.5–58). Champaign, IL: Human Kinetics.

Ryan, R.M. & Deci, E.L. (2000). Self-determination theory and the facilitation of intrinsic motivation, social development, and well-being. *American Psychologist, 55*, 68–78.

Smith, R.E., Smoll, F.L. & Cumming, S.P. (2007a). Effects of a motivational climate intervention for coaches on young athletes' sport performance anxiety. *Journal of Sport & Exercise Psychology, 29*, 38–58.

Smith, R.E., Smoll, F.L. & Curtis, B. (1979). Coach effectiveness training: A cognitive-behavioral approach to enhancing relationship skills in youth sport coaches. *Journal of Sport Psychology, 1*, 59–75.

Smith, R.E., Smoll, F.L. & Hunt, E.B. (1977). A system for the behavioral assessment of athletic coaches. *Research Quarterly, 48*, 401–407.

Smoll, F.L., Smith, R.E. & Cumming, S.P. (2007b). Effects of a motivational climate intervention for coaches on changes in young athletes' achievement goal orientations. *Journal of Clinical Sport Psychology, 1*, 23–46.

Solmon, M.A. (1996). Impact of motivational climate on students' behaviors and perceptions in a physical education setting. *Journal of Educational Psychology, 88*, 731–738.

Valentini, N. & Rudisill, M.E. (2004a). An inclusive mastery climate intervention and the motor skill development of children with and without disabilities. *Adapted Physical Activity Quarterly, 21*, 330–347.

Viciana, J., Cervelló, E.M. & Ramírez-Lechuga, J. (2007). Effect of manipulating positive and negative feedback on goal orientations, perceived motivational climate, satisfaction, task choice, perception of ability, and attitude toward physical education lessons. *Perceptual and Motor Skills, 105*, 67–82.

Chapter 36

Communication in sport teams

PHILIP SULLIVAN, SOPHIA JOWETT AND DANIEL RHIND

SUMMARY

This chapter will deal with communication in sport teams. Communication is a basic and necessary process between individuals in any group or team setting. It refers to the exchange of information between individuals. There are a variety of ways to exchange this information (e.g., talking, body language) and many types of information that can be communicated (e.g., strategy, technique, interpersonal acceptance). We will discuss the mechanics and concepts of communication, and focus particularly on communication between coaches and athletes as well as between athletes. We will conclude with strategies for how to optimize communication within teams.

INTRODUCTION

Mark Messier is a member of the Hockey Hall of Fame. He is the second leading scorer in the history of the National Hockey League, and was the captain of six teams that won the league championship – the Stanley Cup. He is also the only player to captain two different teams to Stanley Cup victories: the Edmonton Oilers and New York Rangers. When he was traded to the Rangers, a team that had not won the championship in 51 years, he was immediately assumed to be responsible for ending that drought. Messier's first action in this role may appear to have been a curious one. He insisted on changing the Rangers' dressing room. At that time, the locker room was set up with a large table in the middle of the room, which would be topped with sport drinks and other contents the players would need before games and between periods. Messier demanded that the table be moved to one of the walls. Veteran players and coaching staff questioned why. As it was set up, it was equal distance for all players to reach what they needed; if it was moved, some players would have to walk across the room while others would not have to move. It seemed fairer the way it was. But Messier insisted, and when pressed for a reason, he said that the table had to be moved because it blocked the line of sight between players, and when he and other players talked to each other, they needed to be able to see each other's face, to look one another in the eyes. The table was moved (Leigh, 1992).

Messier's decision is a good example of intra-team communication for several reasons. It shows how one of the great leaders in team sport viewed communication between teammates as a top priority. And it emphasized a subtle, but powerful aspect of communication – eye contact. After reading this chapter, we hope that you will have a better understanding of the obvious and subtle components of intra-team communication.

OBJECTIVES

After reading this chapter, you should be able to:

1 Recognize the key elements of communication.
2 Understand which factors influence communication in sport teams.
3 Understand how to optimize communication between teammates.
4 Understand strategies to enhance communication between coaches and athletes.

GENERAL COMMUNICATION CONCEPTS

In its simplest sense, communication refers to the sending of messages. As such, it is an essential and ubiquitous human behavior. The sending and receiving of information is necessary for people to interact in any context. Within sport, communication can be seen in such examples as a coach explaining strategy to her team, or a captain yelling at his teammates to hustle. It is also seen in less obvious interactions, such as two players giving each other a high five, or a star athlete tweeting his opinion.

To truly understand communication, we need to have a precise definition. A good working definition is that communication is the dynamic process by which a sender transmits a message through a medium to a receiver. The key elements of this definition are:

- **Sender**: who sends the message
- **Receiver**: to whom the message is sent
- **Message**: the content of the process; what is said (or written, or texted ...)
- **Medium**: the way that the message is sent (e.g., face-to-face, texting, phone, body language)

According to this definition, communication is not a simple act, it is a dynamic process.

People send and receive messages constantly, sometimes overlapping each other. And the sending and receiving of information typically requires more than one act, but rather a continuous process.

Types of media

The most common media through which messages are communicated within sports teams are:

- Verbal/face-to-face
- Telephone or computer
- Nonverbal/body language

Face-to-face communication refers to the sending of messages verbally while in close physical proximity with one another (i.e., talking). When we think of communication in sport teams, this is typically what we envision. Examples would include a coach lecturing a player, or a quarterback calling a play in the huddle during a football game.

The telephone has traditionally been used as a medium of communication in sport teams. From youth sport, where coaches will phone players (or their parents) about schedules to elite sport, where teammates will phone each other to stay in contact during the off season, the telephone is a useful and popular way to send certain messages in sports. Recently, the use of computer media, such as texting and email, has become more popular for sending messages between coaches and teammates. Also, services such as YouTube and Skype allow for the transfer of information to wider audiences than just one-on-one communication.

Nonverbal communication tends to be an overlooked medium in communication, but is particularly relevant to sport. Body language is the use of body positioning and gesture to send messages. Some obvious examples would be players giving each other a pat on the back, a player rolling her eyes when a coach talks to her, or a frustrated player giving fans "the finger". Another aspect of this medium is proxemics. This refers to the use of body space between sender and receiver. This in itself is part of the medium. If a coach tells a player to calm down, or tells a player the same thing while reducing the distance between them (i.e., "getting in his face"), the message has changed because of that aspect of the medium. Finally, paralinguistics, or aspects of the tone of voice, are part of this medium. A goalie yelling at his defencemen about a turnover is a different communication than if the same words are spoken calmly.

Because communication is such a dynamic process, it is possible for different elements to result in a different communication process, even if all the other elements remain unchanged. For example, the same message to different receivers would constitute different communications. A coach yelling at a backup to hustle is not the same communication as if she were to yell the same message at her star player. Medium in particular is an influential element. People tend to assume that as long as you say the same message to the same person, it doesn't matter which medium you use, but this can become quite problematic. It is not uncommon to receive an email and not be sure if the sender's tone is serious or joking. Even

though the other elements of the process would have not changed – same sender, same message, and same receiver – the choice of a different medium (i.e., email as opposed to face-to-face) changes the process and, in this case, makes the communication less efficient.

Finally, one cannot ignore the context within which communication occurs. Context refers to the social climate in which the communicators (i.e., the sender and receiver) act. For example, teammates would most likely communicate in a different manner if their coaches were present than if they were by themselves; a coach may choose to phrase his message differently when his players' parents are present compared to when the team is in the locker room. Because sport is defined by individuals and teams attempting to accomplish a task, the most obvious distinction between contexts in sport is between task-relevant and task-irrelevant contexts. Task-relevant contexts include games and practices. Task-irrelevant contexts include situations such as team socials.

Types of content

At the heart of communication is the message. Having information that one wants someone else to be aware of is why people communicate. There are a wide variety of types of contents in messages. Because this information is valuable, communication can be seen as the transfer of resources, and there are different types of resources that are communicated. A coach instructing an athlete involves different content than two teammates saying that they respect one another. Within sport, there are probably two main contents of discussion – *information* and *closeness*. *Information* includes any communication relative to the task at hand, such as tips on strategy or technique, or motivational discussions. *Closeness* refers to discussion of socially-oriented content such as interpersonal attraction and respect, as well as dislike.

ATHLETE–ATHLETE COMMUNICATION

In game communication

In game communication, communication between athletes during games, tends to be more relevant than out of game communication. It is more related to outcomes such as performance and therefore has been the focus of more research. Typically, in game communication is task-oriented in nature. The amount of tactical talk between teammates during games tends to be related to how successful the team is (LeCouteur & Feo, 2011) and how much teammates like each other (Williams & Widmeyer, 1991). Tactical talk refers to any communication used to direct a teammate to undertake specific tactics, or to inform a teammate of the speaker's own tactical movement. Patterns of talk are typically short (one or two words) with little repetition.

The most obvious characteristic of communication during games is that it tends to be defined by game action. For instance, Hanin (1992) studied communication patterns in volleyball games. He described four types of communication – orientation, stimulation, evaluation, and task-irrelevant. *Orientation* referred to those discussions by teammates regarding planning and coordinating performance. *Stimulation* was defined as messages aimed to motivate teammates to maintain or increase activity levels. *Evaluation* discussions were those that dealt with positive or negative appraisals of prior performance. *Task-irrelevant* communications were those messages that had no bearing on performance. Hanin found that volleyball teams tend to display a relatively stable pattern of communication in their games. Teammates would primarily display orientation prior to performance, stimulation during performance, and evaluation after performance. Overall, teams' communication patterns appeared to be primarily stimulation based.

Similar research has been conducted on pairs of tennis players (Lausic, Tennenbaum, Eccles, Jeong, & Johnston, 2009). Like Hanin's (1992) study, communication patterns were built around performance routines. These messages are typically communicated between points during tennis play and are dominated by emotional and action statements. Half of the messages were emotional in nature, typically messages designed to motivate the partner, and another quarter were action, or instructional messages. Winning teams were found to communicate more frequently and more consistently than losing teams.

Therefore, during games, communication (which is typically verbal) tends to follow a pattern around the flow of play. The content typically is task-focused, either information such as tips about technique, or motivation. And these are discussed quickly and discretely before and after game action.

Out of game communication

Although game action is obviously relevant in sports, teammates spend a substantial amount of their time in social contexts as well. Activities such as team dinners, travel time, or even "down time" before and after competition are contexts in which teammates will continue to communicate. Messages in these situations tend to be less task oriented, and more focused on interpersonal closeness and social inclusion.

Sullivan and Feltz (2003) conducted a series of studies on what teammates discussed and found that the majority of content in teammates' discussion focused on two primary themes. One theme was team identity, which included acceptance of each other and distinctiveness from other teams. The other theme was conflict management – whether teammates managed disagreements in constructive or destructive fashions. Studies have found that these communication patterns are related to how cohesive teams are, and how well they perform.

Strategies for effective team communication

Sullivan (1993) described a communication primer designed for optimal communication between teammates. Effective communication between teammates is characterized by team members listening to one another and building on each other's ideas. These processes create feelings of understanding, respect, and trust, which are essential for team functioning. His program was based on the following principles of communication between teammates:

Effective listening: Communication is a two-way interaction and one of the best ways to encourage effective communication is to be an effective listener. When communicating with teammates, allow them time to talk, as well as time to be silent and collect their thoughts. Don't react in ways that discount their opinions. Ask questions for them to clarify their thoughts and emotions, and avoid questions that are judgmental. And remember body language as a listener – eye contact and a relaxed body posture are excellent ways for teammates to display effective listening during interactions.

Openness: Teammates should communicate in an open and accepting environment. To ensure effective communication between teammates, a norm of group openness should be established. Each individual should be comfortable expressing and listening to a variety of social- and task-oriented topics. Such openness should still be respectful and inclusive. Individuals should speak for themselves – use terms such as "I", instead of "people", or "men".

Support: Just because individuals feel free to be open with respect to their thoughts, opinions, and emotions does not mean that these

Figure 36.1 Group football talk.

expressions will be accepted. There should be a team norm of respecting the thoughts, feelings, and experiences of others. Individuals should be encouraged to try to understand as opposed to argue, to try and see the speaker's point of view.

Self-Disclosure: A key component to establishing a norm of team openness and support is to promote self-disclosure. Individuals need to be willing and prepared to share their own emotions and thoughts. Individuals should be comfortable expressing themselves, and with the reaction this might produce in others. This may be a risk, but it is a risk that should be embraced within teams.

COACH–ATHLETE COMMUNICATION

The coach–athlete relationship is fundamental to athletic success and satisfaction. The communication between the coach and athlete plays a central role in how the quality of the relationship is developed and maintained. Indeed, it can be said that communication is the fuel that will propel the relationship to success or slow them down to a standstill.

Jowett (2007) proposed the 3+1C conceptualization of the quality of the relationship formed between a coach and an athlete. This suggests that the relationship has four key elements: closeness, commitment, complementarity, and co-orientation. *Closeness* relates to the emotional aspect of the coach–athlete relationship and hence concerns the feelings of both individuals. Key elements of closeness therefore include whether the coach and athlete like, respect, trust, and appreciate each other. *Commitment* reflects the cognitive element of the coach–athlete relationship and therefore relates to the thoughts of the coach and athlete towards their relationship. Specifically, commitment concerns the extent to which the coach and athlete want to work with one another now and in the future. *Complementarity* refers to the behavioral element of the coach–athlete relationship. In particular, complementary relationships are those in which the coach and athlete are responsive, relaxed, and ready to do their best.

The '+1C' of Jowett's (2007) 3+1Cs conceptualization focuses on the coach's and athlete's interrelated feelings, thoughts, and behaviors. In other words, the way in which a coach perceives the relationship (direct perspective) and how they believe the athlete perceives the relationship (meta-perspective) are both important considerations. The *direct perspective* therefore focuses on how a coach/athlete feels, thinks, and behaves regarding their sporting relationship (as this is defined by the 3Cs). It therefore consists of direct closeness (e.g., I like my coach/athlete), direct commitment (e.g., I am committed to my coach/athlete), and direct complementarity (e.g., I am responsive to my coach/athlete). The *meta-perspective* focuses on how a coach/athlete believes their athlete/coach feels, thinks, and behaves relative to them within the context of the sporting relationship (as this is defined by the 3Cs). It therefore consists of meta-closeness (e.g., "My coach/athlete likes me"), meta-commitment (e.g., "My coach/athlete is committed to me"), and meta-complementarity (e.g., "My coach/athlete is responsive").

The importance of coach–athlete communication

It has been suggested that no aspect of the coach–athlete relationship is more important than communication (Spink, 1991). Clearly, the critical role played by communication runs throughout Jowett's 3+1C (2007) conceptualization. Communicative acts will have the potential to both convey and influence how the coach and athlete feel, think, and behave in relation to the partnership. Effective communication will help to develop a foundation upon which athletic success can be built. Expert coaches can often be distinguished based on their ability to communicate effectively (Bloom, 1996).

Effective communication can help to foster relationships that are associated with a range of positive outcomes. It can ensure that both the coach and athlete are satisfied and performing to their best whilst sustaining their interest in continuing their engagement with the sport. Interventions that have targeted communication have been found to have a positive impact on key outcomes. For example, Chambers and Vickers (2006) designed an intervention that aimed to develop the effectiveness of swimming coaches' communication with their athletes through the use of questioning strategies. Benefits for the athletes were reported in relation to increased performance as well as improved communication and more positive interactions with the coach. Furthermore, Coach Effectiveness Training (CET) also focuses on enhancing communication skills and on developing a positive environment (Smoll & Smith, 1993). CET has been associated with improvements in relation to enjoyment, participation, and social cohesion (Smoll & Smith, 1993).

Perhaps the importance of communication is best illustrated when it breaks down. Poor communication can lead to conflict, fear of failure, and burnout. Research with Olympic teams highlighted that poor communication between the coach and the athletes was a key contributing factor to under performance (Gould, Guinan, Greenleaf, Medbery, & Peterson, 1999).

Factors influencing the coach–athlete communication process

Jowett and Poczwardowski (2007) proposed an integrated model that emphasizes the importance of communication along with a range of associated antecedent and outcome variables. It is suggested that communication "sandwiches" the quality of the relationship. Specifically, communication affects the relationship developed, and the relationship developed affects communication (e.g., type, frequency, quality, etc). Jowett and Poczwardowski's (2007) integrated model also proposes that communication is affected by individual difference characteristics, relationship characteristics, and socio-cultural characteristics.

The communication process between a coach and an athlete will be influenced by the individual difference characteristics of both individuals. These include a wide range of factors such as age, gender, experience, personality, and cultural background. All of these factors will combine to influence the personal expectations of an individual when approaching any relationship in sport. For example, race has been shown to have a significant influence. Jowett and Frost (2007) conducted semi-structured interviews with elite black professional footballers who had white coaches. Participants revealed that they viewed coach–player communication as being important but that they believed that the level of openness between themselves and their coach was inhibited due to the fact that they perceived there to be a risk that they would be misunderstood.

Beyond intrapersonal factors, the characteristics of a given relationship will also have a key role to play. For example, Lorimer and Jowett (2009) found that female coaches were more accurate than male coaches in inferring the feelings and thoughts of their athletes. In terms of athletes, the highest empathic accuracy was reported for female athletes working with male coaches, with the lowest scores being associated with all female coach–athlete dyads. Discrepancies in age, experience, and power will also shape the communication between the coach and the athlete.

Socio-cultural characteristics also merit consideration. For instance, social norms related to coach–athlete interaction may differ based on factors such as the type of sport, the competitive level, and the culture and policies of the broader sport organization. All of these individual, relational, and socio-cultural factors ensure that communication is a complex process that is specific to each dyad. Despite this, one can highlight general principles that can help to optimize communication within all coach–athlete relationships.

Figure 36.2 Basketball talk.

Strategies to enhance communication

Relationship maintenance can be defined as the strategies used by coaches and athletes to keep their relationship in a specified state (Rhind & Jowett, 2010). A series of strategies have been highlighted based on research with a range of coaches and athletes that can help to maintain relationship quality (Rhind & Jowett, 2010, 2011, 2012). They all fundamentally rely on effective communication:

Conflict management: It is important to identify, discuss, resolve, and monitor potential areas of disagreement. These could relate to any aspect of the relationship and include factors intrinsic (e.g., training schedules, performance goals, tactics, team selection) and extrinsic (e.g., personal life, the media,

fans) to sport. A culture needs to be created and supported in which both the coach and the athlete feel able to disclose when they are experiencing an area of conflict relevant to the relationship. Effective relationships are often not those without conflict but those that effectively manage areas of conflict. Clear processes should be in place to voice, discuss, and develop solutions to this conflict such that it does not escalate and negatively impact the relationship.

Openness: This concerns the ability to encourage open lines of communication. When working with groups of athletes it can be difficult to find the time to communicate with each athlete on an individual basis. However, it is often the quality of any interaction that is important rather than the quantity.

Just a minute at the start or end of a training session can help the coach to keep up to date with the athlete's circumstances on an informal basis. To support this, a coach can consider having more formal processes. These may include having meetings with each athlete at key stages before, during, and at the end of a season. Furthermore, a system of "office hours" can be established such that an athlete can sign up to meet with the coach after a training session. Simply knowing that the opportunity is available could help to develop a climate of openness within the relationship.

Motivation: The importance of motivation as a concept within sport is well established. However, there is a need not only to motivate the coach or athlete but to specifically motivate him/her to maintain his/her relationship with the coach or athlete. This is a subtle yet important distinction. A useful task is to consider "Why am I working with this coach/athlete? Why is s/he working with me?" Through understanding and communicating these reasons effectively, one can help to maintain the commitment within the relationship, and therefore the overall quality.

Preventative: These strategies concern discussing expectations and what should happen if these are not met. A good example of this is the use of a coaching contract or a relational code of conduct. This sets out what is expected of the coach and athlete, what the goals are, and how these are to be achieved. Both parties can sign the agreement and it can then be displayed in the training environment to represent a constant reminder of what is expected. This should be revisited periodically to help to avoid future areas of conflict. Clearly, the content of the contract will differ depending on the specific contexts. A coach working at the recreational level, for example, within the youth sport context may stipulate the athletes are required to turn up on time, be ready to participate, and to help each other during training. In contrast, a coach and athlete working at the highest level may have aspirations of Olympic gold and thus focus more on the specifics of training, diet, and season plans. Despite these variations, a coaching contract can help to set the broader context within which communication in the relationship takes place and ensure that both parties are working within the same parameters.

Assurance: An important element of the coaching process is to assure the athletes that the coach believes in and is committed to working with him/her. This can be communicated to the athlete physically through being positive during training and competitions. It can also be communicated virtually through being available, should the need arise, through alternative methods such as email or mobile phone.

Support: There may well be specific times during the relationship when communication is particularly critical. Coaches and athletes can go through difficult times as a result of experiences both inside sport (e.g., poor performance, injury) as well as outside sport (e.g., family illness, job-related stress). It is at these times that the key skills of listening and empathizing are particularly important.

Social networks: One must avoid viewing the coach–athlete relationship as existing in a bubble. Clearly, it is part of a web of different relationships with key significant others such as teammates, other members of the training squad, parents, friends, family, and other support staff (e.g., managers, sports scientists, agents). Effective communication channels need to be developed with this social network. This helps the coach and athlete to feel part of a bigger picture that will in turn help to enhance their relationship. Creating opportunities to communicate away from the training ground or competitive environment will facilitate this process. Examples of this include pre- or post-season parties or team building activities.

Key outcomes associated with good communication

Rhind and Jowett (2011) administered the Coach–athlete Relationship Maintenance Questionnaire (CARM-Q) to 146 athletes and

105 coaches. Closeness was strongly associated with the use of openness and social network strategies. Thus, the more an individual reported having open lines of communication and regularly socializing with his/her coach/athlete, the higher the level of direct and meta-closeness they associated with the relationship. Commitment was most strongly associated with the use of motivational, assurance, and support strategies. In other words, if an individual worked to sustain clear reasons for both partners to remain in the relationship, showed their partner that they could count on them, and supported them when required, they would be likely to perceive higher levels of direct and meta commitment within the dyad. In terms of complementarity, this was found to be linked with the use of conflict management and preventative strategies. Therefore, coaches and athletes who discussed their expectations and managed areas of disagreement were likely to report higher levels of direct and meta-complementarity within the relationship.

Key considerations when communicating

One should keep in mind that messages are communicated all of the time through both verbal and nonverbal ways. As such, one must consider the following steps:

- What message do you want to communicate to the coach or athlete? This requires an ability to be reflexive and to develop a self-awareness of one's own preferences.
- How can the message best be communicated to the coach or athlete? This may be through a formal face-to-face meeting, a more informal discussion, or in writing.
- Where should the message be communicated? This could be publicly, in front of the training squad, in a private meeting, during training, or within the competitive environment.
- Who is the receiver? A key asset of an effective coach is the ability to adapt one's communicative strategies to best suit the characteristics and preferences of the receiver. A generic communication strategy is unlikely to be effective to all athletes and hence a coach needs to learn about each individual athlete and adapt their approach accordingly.
- Has the message been received? This is a vital consideration. The communication process includes not only the message being sent but also being received in the way in which it was intended. The sender thus needs to check the receiver's interpretation of the message. This can be achieved through asking the receiver to relay the message to the sender in his/her own words. Simply asking whether the message was understood may not highlight any misinterpretation.

LEARNING AIDS

1 Which element of communication was stressed by Mark Messier at the beginning of the chapter?

Messier strongly believed in eye contact as an essential medium of intra-team communication.

2 What are the main topics of conversation between teammates?

Information and closeness. Information includes any communication relative to the task at hand, such as tips on strategy or technique, or motivational discussions. Closeness refers to discussion of socially-oriented content such as interpersonal attraction and respect, as well as dislike.

3   Explain how communication between teammates is related to game performance.

Hanin (1992) found that teammates display orientation (i.e., planning) prior to performance, stimulation (i.e., motivation) during performance, and evaluation (i.e., appraisals) after performance.

4   Explain the difference between the direct perspective and meta-perspective in coach–athlete communication.

The direct perspective focuses on how a coach/athlete feels, thinks, and behaves regarding their sporting relationship. The meta-perspective focuses on how a coach/athlete believes their athlete/coach feels, thinks, and behaves relative to them within the context of the sporting relationship.

5   Explain why conflict management is an important strategy to enhance coach–athlete communication.

It is important to identify, discuss, resolve, and monitor potential areas of disagreement, and a culture needs to be created and supported in which both the coach and the athlete feel able to disclose when they are experiencing an area of conflict relevant to the relationship.

REVIEW QUESTIONS

1   Discuss how media could affect the communication of a message.

2   Describe the two main themes of communication between teammates outside of sport performance.

3   Explain how Jowett's 3+1C model applied to communication between coaches and athletes.

4   Discuss how demographic factors may influence coach–athlete communication.

EXERCISES

1   What suggestions would you have for a team that displays too much social communication during competition?

2   How could you improve a situation where a coach has trouble communicating with her athletes?

ADDITIONAL READING

Carron, A.V. & Eys, M. (2012). Communication in groups. *Group dynamics in sport* (pp.340–354). Morgantown, WV: Fitness Information Technology.

Jowett, S. & Lavallee, D. (2007). *Social psychology in sport*. Champaign, IL: Human Kinetics.

Lausic, D., Tenenbaum, G., Eccles, D., Jeong, A. & Johnston, T. (2009). Intrateam communication and performance in doubles tennis. *Research Quarterly for Exercise and Sport, 80*, 281–290.

Sullivan, P.A. (1993). Communication skills for interactive sports. *The Sport Psychologist, 7*, 19–91.

REFERENCES

Bloom, G.A. (1996). Competition: Preparing for and operating in competition. In J.H. Salmela (Ed.), *Great job coach! Getting the edge from proven winners* (pp.138–179). Ottawa, Canada: Potentium.

Chambers, K.L. & Vickers, J.N. (2006). Effects of bandwidth feedback and questioning on the performance of competitive swimmers. *The Sport Psychologist, 20,* 184–197.

Gould, D., Guinan, D., Greenleaf, C., Medbery, R. & Peterson, K. (1999). Factors affecting Olympic performance: Perceptions of athletes and coaches from more and less successful teams. *The Sport Psychologist, 13,* 371–394.

Hanin, Y. (1992). Social psychology and sport: Communication process in top performance teams. *Sport Science Review, 1,* 13–28.

Jowett, S. (2007). Interdependence analysis and the 3 + 1Cs in the coach–athlete relationship. In S. Jowett & D. Lavallee (Eds.), *Social psychology in sport* (pp.15–27). Champaign, IL: Human Kinetics.

Jowett, S. & Frost, T.C. (2007). Race/Ethnicity in the all male coach–athlete relationship: Black footballers' narratives. *Journal of International Sport and Exercise Psychology, 3,* 255–269.

Jowett, S. & Poczwardowski, A. (2007). Understanding the coach–athlete relationship. In S. Jowett & D. Lavallee (Eds.), *Social psychology in sport* (pp.3–14). Champaign, IL: Human Kinetics.

Lausic, D., Tenenbaum, G., Eccles, D., Jeong, A. & Johnston, T. (2009). Intrateam communication and performance in doubles tennis. *Research Quarterly for Exercise and Sport, 80,* 281–290.

LeCouteur, A. & Feo, R. (2011). Real time communication during play: Analysis of teammates' talk and interaction. *Psychology of Sport and Exercise, 12,* 124–134.

Leigh, M. (1992). Sudden Impact. *Sports Illustrated, 76(10),* 44.

Lorimer, R. & Jowett, S. (2009). Empathic accuracy, meta-perspective, and satisfaction in the coach–athlete relationship. *Journal of Applied Sport Psychology, 21,* 201–212.

Rhind, D.J.A. & Jowett, S. (2010). Initial evidence for the criterion-related and structural validity of the long versions of the Coach–Athlete Relationship Questionnaire. *European Journal of Sport Science, 10 (6),* 359–370.

Rhind, D.J.A. & Jowett, S. (2011). Linking maintenance strategies to the quality of coach–athlete relationships. *International Journal of Sport Psychology, 41,* 55–68.

Rhind, D.J.A. & Jowett, S. (2012). Development of the Coach–Athlete Relationship Maintenance Questionnaire (CARM-Q). *International Journal of Sports Science and Coaching, 7 (1),* 121–137.

Smoll, F.L. & Smith, R.E. (1993). Educating youth sport coaches: An applied sport psychology perspective. In J.M. Williams (Ed.), *Applied sport psychology: Personal growth to peak performance* (2nd ed., pp.36–57). Mountain View, CA: Mayfield.

Spink, K. (1991). The psychology of coaching. *New Studies in Athletics, 6,* 37–41.

Sullivan, P.A. (1993). Communication skills for interactive sports. *The Sport Psychologist, 7,* 19–91.

Sullivan, P.J. & Feltz, D.L. (2003). The preliminary development of the Scale for Effective Communication in Team Sports (SECTS). *Journal of Applied Social Psychology, 33,* 1693–1715.

Williams, J. & Widmeyer, W.N. (1991). The cohesion performance outcome relationship in a co-acting sport. *Journal of Sport and Exercise Psychology, 13,* 364–371.

Chapter 37

Transformational leadership

KATIE L. MORTON, BENJAMIN D. SYLVESTER, A. JUSTINE WILSON, CHRIS LONSDALE AND MARK R. BEAUCHAMP

SUMMARY

The purpose of this chapter is to apply knowledge gained from research on transformational leadership theory to better understand psychological factors and engagement behaviors in sport and exercise contexts. First, we consider the importance of leadership within sport and exercise settings. Following this, the transformational leadership framework is introduced and research from organizational settings is summarized with regard to its implications for understanding leadership behavior and its effects in diverse sport and exercise settings. Research from the sport and exercise psychology literature is then reviewed, with a specific focus on how transformational leadership behaviors utilized by coaches and other influential figures are associated with a variety of adaptive cognitions (e.g., motivation) and behaviors (e.g., performance) amongst those being led. Finally, attention is given to how transformational leadership can be developed through intervention and how theory can be applied to practice in order to foster performance and other salient outcomes.

INTRODUCTION

How do leaders get the very best out of others? Often, it is the smallest things that can have the most profound and powerful effects. Consider the example of Jake White, head coach of the South African team at the 2007 Rugby World Cup. On the day before the final he gave personalized hand-written letters to every player on the team (there were 22 players in the match day squad). In this letter, he revealed how proud he was of his players and how proud their families would be of their accomplishments. White explained to each player what made him special, how his role was essential to the team, and what was

expected of him. He also thanked every player in these personalized accounts for their contributions to the team (Ackford, 2007).

As will become evident from reading this chapter, the account described above represents a prototypical example of *individualized consideration*, which corresponds to one of the four dimensions of transformational leadership. What should also be evident from this account is that the (individually considerate) behaviors exemplified by Jake White reflect 'simple' actions that most (if not all) human beings can display. The same goes for the other dimensions of transformational leadership, namely *idealized influence, inspirational motivation,* and *intellectual stimulation.* In short, transformational leadership involves processes whereby leaders elevate and get the very best out of others. The reason why this framework of leadership is pertinent to the context of sport, exercise, and performance psychology, is that the qualities exemplified through transformational leadership have not only been found to consistently predict improved individual and team functioning, but can also be fostered through intervention.

OBJECTIVES

After reading this chapter you should be able to:

1 Define the terms *laissez-faire*, transactional, and transformational leadership.
2 Explain why transformational leadership is important in sport settings (e.g., coaching).
3 Explain why transformational leadership is important in exercise and health settings (e.g., leadership by physical education teachers, parents).
4 Explain how transformational leadership can be developed through intervention.

THE IMPORTANCE OF LEADERSHIP

Leadership is broadly defined as the behavioral processes of influencing individuals and teams towards the attainment of specific objectives or goals (Northouse, 2001), and is a topic that has received a vast amount of attention in the sport and exercise psychology domain in recent decades. A number of different approaches to the study of leadership in sport and exercise have been proposed and empirically tested. One of the most extensively used leadership frameworks within sport settings corresponds to Chelladurai's (1990) Multidimensional Model of Leadership (MML). The core tenet of the MML includes recognition that the achievement of adaptive athlete outcomes (i.e., athlete satisfaction and performance) is dependent on: (a) the unique contributions of a leader's characteristics (e.g., coaching experience); (b) situational characteristics (e.g., competitive level); and (c) athlete characteristics (e.g., athlete age). Chelladurai operationalized this model through the development of the Leadership Scale for Sports (LSS) that assesses the potential contributions of five dimensions of leadership behavior; training and instruction, social support, positive feedback, as well as democratic and autocratic behaviors.

Despite the contributions of this framework, a growing body of leadership research from outside the field of sport and exercise psychology has accumulated over the past two decades, highlighting the critical value of a range of leadership behaviors that were simply not incorporated within the LSS, or indeed other widely used models of sport/exercise leadership (e.g., Smoll & Smith, 1989). Although leadership behaviors such as the provision of training/instruction and positive feedback (as operationalized within the LSS) provide a *basis* (or foundation) for supporting human development, in order to get the very best out of others, additional leadership behaviors are required that inspire and challenge others to maximize their potential. In this chapter, we turn our attention to these specific leadership behaviors, and in particular, those that are subsumed within the context of transformational leadership theory.

WHAT IS TRANSFORMATIONAL LEADERSHIP THEORY?

The term 'transformational leadership' was first brought to public attention by the early political writings of Burns (1978). However, it was not until Bernard Bass and his colleagues (Bass, 1985; Bass & Riggio, 2006) conceptualized and operationalized this construct that the study of transformational leadership began to proliferate. Bass and colleagues conceptualized transformational leadership within a Full Range model (also referred to as transformational leadership theory) that also includes *transactional* and *laissez-faire* leadership dimensions.

Within the Full Range model, *laissez-faire* leadership reflects the most passive and ineffectual form of leadership that is characterized by an avoidance of responsibilities and a hesitancy to make decisions. Not only is *laissez-faire* leadership ineffective, but it has also been found to be consistently associated with a range of *negative* consequences including follower performance decrements and job dissatisfaction (Judge & Piccolo, 2004).

Beyond *laissez-faire* leadership, Bass (1998) conceptualized a series of *transactional leadership* (or 'stick and carrot') actions that include management-by-exception and contingent reward behaviors. *Management-by-exception* (MBE) includes an active and a passive form, that broadly include 'monitoring' and 'corrective' behaviors/transactions. *Active MBE* involves continuously monitoring followers' performance with the anticipation of catching mistakes before they become a serious problem, whereas *passive MBE* involves waiting for mistakes to be made before taking corrective action. Active MBE is associated with small but positive correlations with follower performance and satisfaction. Conversely, passive MBE is associated with negative follower outcomes, similar to those associated with *laissez-faire* leadership behaviors (e.g., performance decrements; Judge & Piccolo, 2004).

Contingent reward involves clarifying expectations, setting goals, providing feedback, and providing rewards and recognition that are contingent on successful task completion and achievement. This form of transactional leadership is positively associated with job performance, motivation, and (job and leader) satisfaction among those being led (Judge & Piccolo, 2004). In short, contingent reward represents the most adaptive form of transactional leadership.

In contrast to the behaviors exemplified by MBE and contingent reward, transformational leadership behaviors transcend 'stick and carrot' transactions between leader and follower and involve inspiring, motivating, and encouraging those being led to exceed minimal performance expectations and to develop to their fullest potential. According to Bass (1998), transformational leadership is not a substitute for transactional approaches. Instead, transactional leadership provides the foundation for effective leadership, and transformational behaviors build upon this transactional base to bring about extra effort and performance in individuals and teams. This concept is termed an *"augmentation effect"* (Bass, 1998, p. 5) and evidence for this effect has been derived in a number of studies (e.g., Hater & Bass, 1988).

Bass and colleagues (1985; Bass & Riggio, 2006) conceptualized this type of leadership as comprising four behavioral dimensions, namely: *idealized influence, inspirational motivation, intellectual stimulation* and *individualized consideration*. *Idealized influence* takes place when the leader behaves as a role model to followers, engendering a sense of mutual trust and respect, and displaying integrity. In essence, idealized influence involves 'practicing what we preach' and 'doing what's right because it's the right thing to do'. *Inspirational motivation* involves leader behaviors that instill a sense of confidence and optimism in those being led to do more than they originally thought possible. This is achieved by providing a clear vision of what can be accomplished and persistently encouraging and inspiring followers to achieve high standards. *Intellectual stimulation* occurs when leaders challenge those being led to think for themselves and contribute to decision-making processes by questioning commonly-held beliefs and assumptions. They help followers to become confident in their ability to approach problems and issues in innovative ways. Finally, *individualized consideration* takes place when leaders display genuine care and concern for followers' unique needs and abilities. They display empathy and compassion and behave as a mentor for individual achievement and development.

Although the Bass model is perhaps the most common conceptualization of transformational leadership, other models related to this construct have also been developed and utilized. For example, Podsakoff, MacKenzie, Moorman, and Fetter (1990) conceptualized six dimensions of transformational leadership in terms of articulating a vision, providing an appropriate role model, fostering acceptance of group goals, high performance expectations, individualized support, and intellectual stimulation. More recently, Hardy et al. (2010) drew from the Podsakoff model, while also incorporating elements of the Bass model, to describe a framework that included inspirational motivation, role modelling, fostering acceptance of group goals and teamwork, high performance expectations, intellectual stimulation, and individualized consideration. Of direct relevance to this chapter, the approach used by Hardy and colleagues has also been utilized to understand the predictive effects of leadership behaviors in sport (e.g., Arthur, Woodman, Ong, Hardy, & Ntoumanis, 2011; Callow, Smith, Hardy, Arthur, & Hardy, 2009). This research is described in greater detail below.

Figure 37.1 Research on transformational leadership in sports has received increased attention in recent years. Photo by Richard Lam, UBC Athletics. Reprinted courtesy of the University of British Columbia.

Research on transformational leadership has been conducted within a variety of contexts including but not limited to banking, the military, hospitals, education and more recently, sport and exercise. Transformational leadership is theorized to be related to elevated levels of individual follower performance, as well as superior performance accomplishments at the group and organization levels. With regard to individual level outcomes, a multitude of studies have demonstrated that perceptions of transformational leadership are associated with improved motivation-related cognitions among those being led, such as elevated self-efficacy beliefs (e.g., Kark, Shamir, & Chen, 2003) and intrinsic motivation (e.g., Shin & Zhou, 2003). Leaders who exhibit transformational leadership behaviors empower rather than control their followers, and are theorized to increase followers' self-efficacy beliefs by expressing positive evaluations, communicating high performance expectations, and displaying optimism for followers' ability to meet such expectations (Shamir, House, & Arthur, 1993). Similarly, transformational leadership involves encouraging self-expression among those being led (Sheldon, Turban, Brown, Barrick, & Judge, 2003), which enables the development of autonomy-supportive relationships; a key determinant of intrinsic motivation.

Perceptions of transformational leadership by followers have been shown to lead to improved attitudinal constructs such as greater satisfaction with and trust in the leader and a greater sense of commitment (e.g., Podsakoff, MacKenzie, & Bommer, 1996). Furthermore, when followers perceive their leaders to display high levels of transformational leadership, then those same followers tend to respond with improved behavioral patterns such as greater task engagement (e.g., Zhu, Avolio, & Walumbwa, 2009) and improved performance at an individual level (e.g., Walumbwa, Avolio, & Zhu, 2008). Interestingly, these relations between transformational leadership and task performance have been found to be mediated by a range of *intra-personal* (e.g., self-efficacy, intrinsic motivation, improved attitudes) and *inter-personal* (trust in the leader, satisfaction in the leader) factors (e.g., Walumbwa & Hartnell, 2011). Collectively, these findings suggest that the way in which leaders interact with others through displays of transformational leadership, subsequently influences how people think about themselves and their own capabilities, as well as their respective leaders, and these social cognitions directly predict task-engaged behaviors.

In relation to group-level outcomes, it has been suggested that displays of transformational leadership behaviors result in a greater internalization of the values and vision of the leader by group/team members, thus enabling followers to become more committed to the collective interests of the group (Dionne, Yammarino, Atwater, & Spangler, 2004). Studies have highlighted that displays of transformational leadership are related to improved group cohesion (Wang & Huang, 2009), which itself represents an important predictor of subsequent group performance. Similarly, in team settings, when leaders make use of transformational leadership approaches, team members tend to respond with improved team communication and better conflict management actions (Dionne et al., 2004). Taken together, it is clear that transformational leadership enhances team performance by generating synergy among team members.

TRANSFORMATIONAL LEADERSHIP IN SPORT

In many ways, the context of competitive sport directly mirrors organizational settings. For example, common criteria for success in both business and sport relate to individual and team *performance* and the achievement of specific goals and objectives. Therefore, it has been suggested that the relationship between transformational leadership behaviors and follower outcomes, as observed in organizational and occupational contexts, directly applies to sport settings (e.g., Charbonneau, Barling, & Kelloway, 2001). Although the transformational leadership framework is highly relevant to sporting contexts, the application of this leadership model to sport has been somewhat limited. Nevertheless, a growing body of research over the last decade has adopted the transformational leadership framework in order to better understand how leadership behaviors in the sporting domain are related to athletes' cognitive (e.g., motivation to perform well) and behavioral (e.g., effort, performance) responses. In this section we provide an overview of this work.

Charbonneau et al. (2001) conducted one of the first studies of transformational leadership in sport using university-level athletes and coaches from both individual and team sports. This study found that athletes who perceived that their coach utilized transformational leadership behaviors demonstrated greater performance (as rated by their coaches), and this relationship was mediated by athlete intrinsic motivation. In a more recent study in the context of martial arts, Rowold (2006) provided support for the *augmentation effect* of transformational leadership that was described earlier. Specifically, in this study, the effects of transactional coaching behaviors in relation to students' satisfaction with their coach, effort, and their perceptions of coaching effectiveness, were augmented by the effects of transformational leadership. Rowold concluded that martial arts coaches may benefit from utilizing transformational leadership behaviors *in addition to* transactional behaviors such as providing contingent rewards and actively monitoring performance accomplishments.

The studies described above primarily focused on individual-level outcomes in sport, such as individual performance accomplishments, motivation, and perceptions of coaching effectiveness. A growing number of studies in sport have also looked at a range of salient team-level outcomes. For example, a study by Callow et al. (2009) examined ultimate Frisbee players' perceptions of transformational leadership, as displayed by their coaches, and how this was associated with team cohesion. The results demonstrated that specific dimensions of transformational leadership including 'fostering acceptance of group goals and promoting teamwork', 'high performance expectations', and 'individual consideration' significantly predicted team cohesion. Furthermore, the relationships between the aforementioned coaching transformational leadership behaviors and team cohesion were moderated by the performance level of the athletes. That is, some of these relationships (i.e., between 'individual consideration' and task cohesion) were only shown in high performance athletes whereas others (i.e., between 'fostering acceptance of group goals and promoting teamwork' and cohesion) were only shown in low performance athletes. This study highlights the importance of taking into account relevant *contextual* variables when applying theory to practice. Specifically, the authors suggested that leadership behaviors that emphasize teamwork may be particularly important early on in a group's respective development, but less so when teams are at a more advanced stage of team development. Similarly, the authors suggested that leadership behaviors that reflect individualized/ personalized consideration are likely to be particularly pertinent once team members are highly experienced. However, the authors did not provide an explanation for why such individually considerate behaviors would be less pertinent/appropriate for low performance athletes. Further research is required to verify the robustness of these moderation effects.

Nevertheless, the Callow et al. study adds to the growing evidence that suggests follower characteristics are important contextual variables that might buffer the potential transference effects of transformational leadership and ultimately influence leader effectiveness. In addition to the *performance level* of the athletes/ teams, another recent study demonstrated that athletes' *personality traits* may moderate the transformational leadership-follower outcome relationship. Specifically, Arthur et al. (2010) found that athlete narcissism (a personality trait in which individuals high in narcissism exaggerate their talents and accomplishments and believe that they are special and unique) moderated the relationship between perceived transformational coaching behaviors and leader-inspired extra effort in adolescent athletes from a variety of sports (e.g., netball, soccer, track and field, golf). This finding suggests that coaching behaviors that emphasize the importance of teamwork and group goals were not as effective for narcissistic athletes when compared to athletes low in narcissism. As an explanation for this finding, Arthur and colleagues suggested that it is possible that narcissists withhold effort when group goals are promoted as they are more concerned with self-enhancement.

A study by Tucker, Turner, Barling, and McEvoy (2010) examined the role of transformational leadership and children's aggression in youth ice hockey. This study built on initial evidence that transformational leaders model pro-social behaviors and thus followers are less likely to demonstrate aggressive behaviors if led by a transformational leader. This is because transformational leaders 'do the right thing', they set high expectations (for non-aggressive behaviors), they challenge followers to think differently (i.e., raise questions as to whether aggressive behavior is appropriate) and behave as a mentor to others and lead them in the right direction. The study by Tucker et al. (2010) demonstrated that the relationship between coaches' transformational leadership and players' aggression was mediated by team aggression, which suggests that transformational leaders indirectly affect individual

Figure 37.2 Transformational leadership involves going beyond one's own self-interests to get the very best out of others. Photo by Richard Lam, UBC Athletics. Reprinted courtesy of the University of British Columbia.

athletes' propensity to aggress by discouraging aggression at the group-level. This has important implications for sport as it highlights that aggressive behavior can be learned from coaches and that a transformational leadership approach to coaching is not only related to improved performance, but may also lead to the development of pro-social behaviors among athletes.

In conclusion, a growing number of studies have applied the tenets of transformational leadership theory to the context of sport and the evidence to date suggests that transformational leadership behaviors are advantageous for both individual athletes and teams. That is, perceptions of transformational leadership behaviors in sport are associated with improved performance-related cognitions, perceptions of leader effectiveness, and improved group dynamics. Furthermore, there is evidence that coaches' transformational leadership behaviors are associated with improved athletic performance and the development of pro-social behaviors among athletes.

TRANSFORMATIONAL LEADERSHIP IN EXERCISE AND HEALTH CONTEXTS

In recent years, transformational leadership theory has also been applied to the exercise psychology domain with a view to understanding how various social agents (i.e., fitness leaders, physical education teachers, parents) might be able to facilitate adaptive health-related outcomes in others through their use of transformational behaviors, especially in relation to physical education settings (i.e., transformational *teaching* behaviors; Beauchamp et al., 2010) and the context of the family (i.e., transformational *parenting* behaviors; Morton et al., 2010).

Effective exercise instructors utilize leadership styles that enrich participants' enjoyment of classes and foster their intentions to engage in future exercise classes. For example, these instructors might use participants' names, give frequent individual attention, provide positive and encouraging feedback, and recognize participants' efforts (Turner, Rejeski, & Brawley, 1997). In many ways these behaviors directly mirror aspects of the transactional-transformational leadership model. In the first empirical study to apply transformational leadership theory to physical activity settings, Beauchamp, Welch and Hulley (2007) examined the relationships between exercise instructors' use of transactional and transformational behaviors and the self-efficacy beliefs of participants who were enrolled in a ten-week structured exercise class. This study revealed that for new exercisers, contingent reward behaviors were positively associated with elevated self-efficacy beliefs among novice exercisers to overcome barriers and schedule exercise into their daily lives. None of the transformational leadership behaviors in this study, however, were found to augment the effects of transactional leadership in relation to participants' self-efficacy beliefs. As one potential explanation for this finding, Beauchamp et al. suggested that the limited contact that exists between exercise leaders and participants in this type of class setting (aerobics, fitness) limits opportunities for leaders to display transformational leadership behaviors, and thereafter maximize the quality of leader–follower exchanges.

In contrast to the limited opportunities for leader–member interactions that exist within standard exercise class settings, physical education (PE) teachers are in an ideal position to develop effective relationships and make a lasting impression on others (i.e., students). Indeed, research has emphasized that positive experiences in PE can play a substantive role in encouraging young people to adopt physically active lifestyles as they progress into adulthood (Sallis & McKenzie, 1991).

Figure 37.3 Transformational leadership theory has recently been applied to physical education settings. Photo by Mark Beauchamp. Reprinted courtesy of Mark Beauchamp.

It has been suggested that effective leadership is synonymous with effective teaching (Beauchamp et al., 2010). For example, both leadership and teaching are concerned with elevating others to achieve a set of objectives. With this in mind, a recent body of research has applied transformational leadership theory to school-based physical education settings. Initial qualitative evidence suggests that teachers' use of transformational teaching behaviors, as reported by students, is positively associated with students' adaptive responses in physical education, such as positive beliefs and attitudes towards physical education, enjoyment of physical education, and in-class physical activity behaviors (Morton, Keith & Beauchamp, 2010). In a subsequent study, Beauchamp et al. (2010) found that adolescents' perceptions of their teachers' transformational behaviors were associated with greater self-determined motivation and positive enjoyment of physical education. Furthermore,

preliminary experimental evidence has demonstrated that transformational leadership behaviors can be developed by school physical education teachers through intervention (Beauchamp, Barling, & Morton, 2011). The results of this study by Beauchamp et al. revealed that teachers in the intervention condition (which involved a one day workshop) were reported by their students to display higher levels of transformational teaching at follow-up. Furthermore, students reported improved levels of self-determined motivation, self-efficacy, and intentions to be physically active in their leisure time than those in the control group.

From the perspective of adolescent health promotion, although children and adolescents spend substantive time at school, they also spend considerable time at home pursuing leisure-time activities. *Parents* fulfill an important role in supporting the health and psychological well-being of their children. Indeed, the types of behaviors that parents utilize with their children are shown to impact their children's subsequent physical activity (and other health-related) behaviors. The application of transformational leadership theory to the parenting domain was highlighted initially by Zacharatos, Barling, and Kelloway (2000). Specifically, Zacharatos and her colleagues examined the extent to which transformational leadership behaviors used by parents within the home might translate into adolescents demonstrating these same behaviors in the context of their peer-interactions in sport. This study revealed that ratings of adolescents' transformational leadership (as assessed by their coaches and peers) were predicted by parents' displays of transformational leadership behaviors. This suggests that children, in part, learn these types of behaviors from their parents.

Interestingly, transformational leadership processes have been described as analogous to parent–child dynamics in many respects (Popper & Mayseless, 2003). For example, both leaders (within organizational settings) and parents (within families) play an important role in motivating and encouraging others, and helping them to realize their potential. A recent study by Morton and colleagues (2011) demonstrated that adolescents' perceptions of their parents' behaviors (i.e., transformational *parenting*) were positively associated with adolescents' self-regulatory efficacy beliefs (i.e., their confidence in their ability to monitor, set goals, and overcome barriers) to both engage in regular physical activity and sustain a healthy diet. Interestingly, adolescents' perceptions of their parents' transformational parenting behaviors were also able to explain a significant amount of variance (29%) in indices of adolescent life satisfaction. In light of the predictive effects of transformational

Figure 37.4 Preliminary evidence suggests that transformational leadership behaviors used by parents may predict health-enhancing cognitions and behaviors among their children. Photo by Mark Beauchamp. Reprinted courtesy of Mark Beauchamp.

parenting behaviors in relation to adaptive adolescent health-related outcomes, it seems pertinent in future research to examine the potential of parenting interventions, guided by transformational leadership theory to foster adolescent health and well-being.

HOW TO PROMOTE TRANSFORMATIONAL LEADERSHIP IN SPORT AND EXERCISE CONTEXTS

> Leaders are made, they are not born. They are made by hard effort, which is the price which all of us must pay to achieve any goal that is worthwhile. (Vince Lombardi)

There is an important question that is crucial to advancing our understanding of leadership in sport and exercise: Can we develop and train transformational leadership through intervention? In the final section of this chapter, we address this question by providing a review of what is known about developing transformational leadership and also by providing practical examples of how this framework of leadership can be implemented in sport and exercise settings.

There is a lack of experimental studies in sport and exercise psychology that have examined whether transformational leadership behaviors can be enhanced through intervention. However, extensive research has been conducted in other settings that provides support for the premise that transformational leadership can be developed through training. The first published study to demonstrate that transformational behaviors can be developed among individuals in leadership roles was conducted in a large financial organization (the study involved bank managers) and revealed that not only were bank managers rated (by their followers) as displaying greater transformational leadership following the training, the intervention also resulted in improvements in employee commitment to the organization and branch sales performance (Barling, Weber, & Kelloway, 1996).

In terms of how transformational leadership interventions actually work, such initiatives typically have the overall goal of convincing the leaders that they can make a difference and bring about positive changes in their followers' behaviors through their own leadership. This serves to increase leaders' self-efficacy beliefs and ultimately leads to increased effort and perseverance to develop their transformational behaviors. Kelloway and Barling (2000) presented a conceptual framework for delivering transformational leadership interventions that has since been utilized in a number of contexts for leadership development, including business and educational settings. This framework draws primarily from social learning theory (Bandura, 1986) and emphasizes that for the successful development of transformational leadership behaviors, interventions require:

- A clear demonstration of what transformational behaviors look like in practice. This also includes providing specific examples depending on the context of the intervention (e.g., coaching, teaching, parenting).
- The provision of opportunities for leaders to carry out those transformational behaviors (e.g., through role-play activities).
- Feedback on the performance of the transformational behaviors over the course of the intervention. This can include feedback from those being led (e.g., anonymous questionnaires) or feedback from the intervention facilitators/counselors (e.g., one-to-one feedback sessions following an initial training workshop).
- More recently, it has been suggested that a *self-regulation* component should also be considered (Beauchamp et al., 2011) whereby leaders are encouraged to set challenging, yet achievable goals related

to their utilization of transformational behaviors on a day-to-day basis. Specifically, this could involve having leaders build 'action plans' specifying *how* they will achieve their goals, and developing implementation strategies to convert these transformational leadership goals into productive actions.

Despite intervention-based work on transformational leadership across diverse domains of human achievement, research on transformational leadership in sport has relied primarily on cross-sectional and observational designs, thus limiting any inferences of causality. In future, research that tests the efficacy of training initiatives guided by transformational leadership theory, through the use of *experimental* designs, is clearly needed. In relation to exercise and health settings, there is some (albeit preliminary) evidence for the efficacy of transformational *teaching* interventions for use in school-based physical education settings (Beauchamp et al., 2011).

When taken together, a growing body of research has accumulated to suggest that transformational leadership behaviors can be developed through intervention, and result in moderate to large effects in terms of improved attitudinal and behavioral responses among others (Avolio, Reichard, Hannah, Walumbwa, & Chan, 2009). If the same effects are observed in sport and physical activity contexts (and only time will tell), this might have far-reaching implications for enhancing sport performance, physical activity participation, and possibly positive youth development. Drawing on the extant literature on transformational leadership development, coaches might be encouraged (and evaluated through intervention) to do the following:

- Treat players with respect to earn their respect (idealized influence).

- Lead by example – for example, if coaches expect players to be on time, then the coach should model these same behaviors (idealized influence).
- Remain optimistic and enthusiastic about what their athletes can accomplish. A coach's enthusiasm can be contagious and if the players know that the coach believes in them, then they will believe in themselves as well (inspirational motivation).
- Articulate a compelling vision of what is possible – map out what you want athletes to do, not what you don't want them to do (inspirational motivation).
- Encourage athletes to provide input and feedback in developing team strategies. It is much easier for players to support and get behind a strategy if they understand it and are part of the decision-making process (intellectual stimulation).
- Try to understand each player on the team well enough to be able to identify their specific strengths and weaknesses; this will help coaches to support their personal growth and development (individualized consideration).

It can take time for leaders to adopt, learn, and demonstrate newly-acquired leadership behaviors, even after exposure to effective leadership development initiatives. It is important to be aware that changes will not happen overnight and that coaches, teachers, and parents should be encouraged to focus on fostering small yet achievable improvements in their transformational leadership behaviors, that can be incorporated into daily routines and sustained over time. A major next step for research examining transformational leadership in sport and exercise is to determine the efficacy of training programs for the development of transformational leadership in sport and physical activity settings.

CONCLUSIONS

Evidence from qualitative and observational studies suggests that displays of transformational leadership by coaches, teachers, and parents are related to a range of salient achievement outcomes among those being led. If additional empirical research can ascertain whether transformational leadership behaviors can be enhanced among these social agents through intervention, the potential implications for sport-related motivation and performance, as well as lifelong physical activity participation are far-reaching.

LEARNING AIDS

1   From the most passive form of leadership to the most active form, what are the different types of transactional leadership behavior described by Bass (1998) and what do these leadership behaviors involve?

Passive management-by-exception takes place when the leader focuses on mistakes of others, after the mistake has been made, and usually responds with punishment. Active management-by-exception involves leader behaviors that focus on monitoring others' actions in order to prevent mistakes from being made. Finally, contingent reward involves the exchange of good performance/behaviors with feedback and rewards.

2   What are the four dimensions of transformational leadership as conceptualized by Bass and his colleagues (1985; Bass & Riggio, 2006) and what behaviors constitute these dimensions?

Idealized influence: This involves the leader behaving as a role model to others and leading through the demonstration of personally-held values and beliefs. It is about doing what is right, not what is expedient.

Inspirational motivation: This involves being optimistic about what others can achieve and setting high yet achievable goals and instilling a sense of confidence in those being led to achieve these goals.

Intellectual stimulation: This involves getting others to think about old problems in new ways and encouraging them to think for themselves.

Individualized consideration: This involves recognizing individual needs and abilities, taking a genuine interest in those being led and displaying a sense of care, concern and compassion.

3   How does transformational leadership influence salient individual-level outcomes in sport and exercise settings?

When leaders display transformational behaviors, this can affect how individuals think about themselves. For example, perceptions of transformational leadership are associated with improvements in followers' self-efficacy beliefs, intrinsic motivation, and affective responses (e.g., enjoyment). Perceptions of transformational leadership can also affect how individuals perceive their leader (satisfaction with the leader and trust in the leader). Taken together, these intra-individual (self-efficacy, motivation, enjoyment) and inter-individual (satisfaction with the leader, trust in the leader) cognitions are theorized to mediate the effects of transformational leadership behaviors in relation to followers' individual behavioral (e.g., performance) responses.

4   How does transformational leadership impact group-level outcomes?

Transformational leadership behaviors result in enhanced team performance by generating synergy among team members. Specifically, when leaders (e.g., coaches) make consistent use of transformational strategies, this enables a greater internalization of the values and vision of the leader, improved group commitment, and greater group cohesion, which collectively enables the group to function effectively.

REVIEW QUESTIONS

1   Think of the very best leader you have had in any context (e.g., boss, teacher, parent, coach) and also the very worst leader you have had. Try to think of how they behaved and how these behaviors made you feel. Effective leaders *elevate* others, whereas dreadful leaders *demean* others. How do the behaviors (actions) of your exemplary leader (that you highlighted in this exercise) align with the four dimensions conceptualized within transformational leadership (idealized influence, inspirational motivation, intellectual stimulation and individualized consideration)?

2   Identify and describe how individuals in sport or exercise leadership positions (e.g., coaches, physical education teachers, parents) could utilize idealized influence, inspirational motivation, intellectual stimulation, and individualized stimulation in their *daily interactions* with others.

EXERCISE

1   **Putting transformational leadership into practice: setting transformational leadership goals:**
Transformational leadership involves maximizing the quality of relationships with others. Transformational leaders place great importance on *empowering* others and *encouraging* them to go beyond what they thought was originally possible. If you are interested in *taking action* and developing your own leadership skills, try to set (and monitor) specific goals related to your use of transformational leadership in your daily interactions with others. Variations of the SMART goal setting framework have been widely endorsed within both the organizational and sport psychology literatures (e.g., Doran, 1981). With a slight variation on this guiding framework we encourage leaders to set goals for their own behavioral development that are:

- Specific: For example, "I will take the time to learn the names of ALL of my students in the first two weeks of term", rather than "I really should find out more about my students".

- Measurable: How do you know that you have achieved your goal for transformational leadership development? It should be measurable so that you know how you are progressing.

- Action-oriented: You should have a plan of action to ensure your goal becomes a reality.

- Realistic: Changes may take time so keep your goals realistic and work on goals that you can realistically incorporate into your daily interactions with students, athletes, and colleagues.

- Time-based: These goals should be achievable within a specific timeframe (e.g., the next two weeks).

- Important to YOU! You are more likely to pursue those goals that are *genuinely important to you*.

Think of goals for yourself in both the short term (i.e., to remain enthusiastic throughout the coaching session, or to set aside five to ten minutes after training to chat to specific individual players regarding their important role on the team) and the long term (i.e., to develop effective and lasting relationships with all students/athletes).

ADDITIONAL READING

Bass, B.M. & Riggio, R.E. (2006). *Transformational leadership* (2nd ed.). New Jersey: Lawrence Erlbaum Associated, Inc.

Beauchamp, M.R. & Eys, M.A. (2008). *Group dynamics in exercise and sport psychology: Contemporary themes*. New York: Taylor & Francis.

Jackson, P. & Delehanty, H. (1995). *Sacred hoops*. New York: Hyperion.

Singh, A. (2004). Nelson Mandela's Lessons in Leadership. *Financial Mail*. Available at: http://free.financialmail.co.za/report04/mandela04/vmandela.htm.

REFERENCES

Ackford, P. (2007, December 2). Jake White: 'Final will live with me forever'. *The Telegraph*. Available at: http://www.telegraph.co.uk/sport/rugbyunion/international/southafrica/2327309/Jake-White-Final-will-live-with-me-forever.html

Arthur, C.A., Woodman, T., Ong, C.W., Hardy, L. & Ntoumanis, N. (2011). The role of athlete narcissism in moderating the relationship between coaches' transformational leader behaviours and athlete motivation. *Journal of Sport & Exercise Psychology*, 2011, 33, 3–19.

Avolio, B.J., Reichard, R.J., Hannah, S.T., Walumbwa, F.O. & Chan, A. (2009). A meta-analytic review of leadership impact research: Experimental and quasi-experimental studies. *The Leadership Quarterly*, 20, 764–784. http://dx.doi.org/10.1016/j.leaqua.2009.06.006

Bandura, A. (1986). *Social foundations of thought and actions: A social cognitive theory*. Englewood Cliffs, NJ: Prentice-Hall.

Barling, J., Weber, T. & Kelloway, E.K. (1996). Effects of transformational leadership training on attitudinal and financial outcomes: A field experiment. *Journal of Applied Psychology, 81*, 827–832. http://dx.doi.org/10.1037/0021-9010.81.6.827

Bass, B.M. (1985). *Leadership and performance beyond expectations*. New York: Free Press.

Bass, B.M. (1998). *Transformational leadership: Industry, military, and educational impact*. Mahwah, NJ: Erlbaum.

Bass, B.M. & Riggio, R.E. (2006). *Transformational leadership* (2nd ed.). New Jersey: Lawrence Erlbaum Associated, Inc.

Beauchamp, M.R., Barling, J., Zhen, L., Morton, K.L., Keith, S. & Zumbo, B.D. (2010). Development and psychometric properties of the transformational teaching questionnaire. *Journal of Health Psychology, 15*, 1123–1134. http://dx.doi.org/10.1177/1359105310364175

Beauchamp, M.R., Barling, J. & Morton, K.L. (2011). Transformational teaching and adolescent self-determined motivation, self-efficacy, and intentions to engage in leisure time physical activity: A randomized controlled pilot trial.

Applied Psychology: Health and Well-Being, 3, 127–150. http://dx.doi.org/10.1111/j.1758-0854.2011.01048.x

Beauchamp, M.R., Welch, A.S. & Hulley, A.J. (2007). Transformational and transactional leadership and exercise-related self-efficacy: An exploratory study. *Journal of Health Psychology, 12*, 83–88. http://dx.doi.org/10.1177/13591053070 71742

Burns, J.M. (1978). *Leadership.* New York: Harper & Row.

Callow, N., Smith, M.J., Hardy, L., Arthur, C.A. & Hardy, J. (2009). Measurement of transformational leadership and its relationship with team cohesion and performance level. *Journal of Applied Sport Psychology, 21*, 395–412. http://dx.doi.org/10.1080/10413200903204754

Charbonneau, D., Barling, J. & Kelloway, E.K. (2001). Transformational leadership and sports performance: The mediating role of intrinsic motivation. *Journal of Applied Social Psychology, 31*, 1521–1534. http://dx.doi.org/10.1111/j.1559-1816.2001.tb02686.x

Chelladurai, P. (1990). Leadership in sports: A review. *International Journal of Sport Psychology, 21*, 328–354.

Dionne, S.D., Yammarino, F.J., Atwater, L.E. & Spangler, W.D. (2004). Transformational leadership and team performance. *Journal of Organizational Change Management, 17*, 177–193. http://dx.doi.org/10.1108/09534810410530601

Doran, G.T. (1981). There's a S.M.A.R.T. way to write management's goals and objectives. *Management Review, 70*, 35–36.

Hardy, L., Arthur, C.A., Jones, G., Shariff, A., Munnoch, K., Isaacs, I. & Allsopp, A.J. (2010). The relationship between transformational leadership behaviours, psychological, and training outcomes in elite military recruits. *The Leadership Quarterly, 21*, 20–32. http://dx.doi.org/10.1016/j.leaqua.2009.10.002

Hater, J.J. & Bass, B.M. (1988). Superiors' evaluations and subordinates' perceptions of transformational and transactional leadership. *Journal of Applied Psychology, 73*, 695–702. http://psycnet.apa.org/doi/10.1037/0021-9010.73.4.695

Judge, T.A. & Piccolo, R.F. (2004). Transformational and transactional leadership: A meta-analytic test of their relative validity. *Journal of Applied Psychology, 89*, 755–768. http://psycnet.apa.org/doi/10.1037/0021-9010.89.5.755

Kark, R., Shamir, B. & Chen, G. (2003). The two faces of transformational leadership: Empowerment and dependency. *Journal of Applied Psychology, 88*, 246–255. http://psycnet.apa.org/doi/10.1037/0021-9010.88.2.246

Kelloway, E.K. & Barling, J. (2000). What we have learned about developing transformational leaders. *Leadership and Organization Development Journal, 21*, 355–362. http://dx.doi.org/10.1108/01437730010377908

Morton, K.L., Barling, J., Rhodes, R.E., Masse, L.C., Zumbo, B. & Beauchamp, M.R. (2011). The application of transformational leadership theory to parenting: Questionnaire development and implications for adolescent self-regulatory efficacy and life satisfaction. *Journal of Sport & Exercise Psychology, 33*, 688–709.

Morton, K.L., Keith, S.E. & Beauchamp, M.R. (2010). Transformational teaching and physical activity: A new paradigm for adolescent health promotion? *Journal of Health Psychology, 15*, 248–257. http://dx.doi.org/10.1177/1359105309347586

Northouse, P.G. (2001). *Leadership: Theory and practice* (2nd ed.). Thousand Oaks, CA: Sage.

Podsakoff, P.M., MacKenzie, S.B. & Bommer, W.H. (1996). Transformational leader behaviours and substitutes for leadership as determinants of employee satisfaction, commitment, trust, and organisational citizenship behaviours. *Journal of Management, 22*, 259–298. http://dx.doi.org/10.1177/014920639602200204

Podsakoff, P.M., MacKenzie, S.B., Moorman, R.H. & Fetter, R. (1990). Transformational leader behaviors and their effects on followers' trust in leader, satisfaction, and organizational citizenship behaviors. *The Leadership Quarterly, 1*, 107–142. http://dx.doi.org/10.1016/1048-9843(90)90009-7

Popper, M. & Mayseless, O. (2003). Back to basics: Applying a parenting perspective to transformational leadership. *The Leadership Quarterly, 14*, 41–65. http://dx.doi.org/10.1016/S1048-9843(02)00183-2

Rowold, J. (2006). Transformational and transactional leadership in martial arts. *Journal of Applied Sport Psychology, 18*, 312–325. http://dx.doi.org/10.1080/10413200600944082

Sallis, J.F. and McKenzie, T.L. (1991). Physical education's role in public health. *Research Quarterly for Exercise and Sport, 62*, 124–137.

Shamir, B., House, R.J. & Arthur, M.B. (1993). The motivational effects of charismatic leadership: A self-concept based theory. *Organization Science, 4*, 577–594. http://dx.doi.org/10.1287/orsc.4.4.577

Sheldon, K.M., Turban, D.B., Brown, K.G., Barrick, M.R. & Judge, T.A. (2003). Applying self-determination theory to organizational research. *Research in Personnel and Human Resource Management, 22*, 357–393. http://dx.doi.org/10.1016/S0742-7301(03)22008-9

Shin, S.J. & Zhou, J. (2003). Transformational leadership, conservation and creativity: Evidence from Korea. *Academy of Management Journal, 46*, 703–714. http://dx.doi.org/10.2307/30040662

Smoll, F.L. & Smith, R.E. (1989). Leadership behavior in sport: A theoretical model and research paradigm. *Journal of Applied Social Psychology, 19*, 1522–1551. http://dx.doi.org/10.1111/j.1559-1816.1989.tb01462.x

Tucker, S., Turner, N.A., Barling, J. & McEvoy, M. (2010). Transformational leadership and children's aggression in team settings: A short-term longitudinal study. *The Leadership Quarterly, 21*, 389–399. http://dx.doi.org/10.1016/j.leaqua.2010.03.004

Turner, E.E., Rejeski, W.J. & Brawley, L.R. (1997). Psychological benefits of physical activity are influenced by the social environment. *Journal of Sport & Exercise Psychology, 34*, 119–130.

Walumbwa, F.O., Avolio, B.J & Zhu, W. (2008). How transformational leadership weaves its influence on individual job performance: The role of identification and efficacy beliefs. *Personnel Psychology, 64*, 793–825. http://dx.doi.org/10.1111/j.1744-6570.2008.00131.x

Walumbwa, F.O. & Hartnell, C.A. (2001). Understanding transformational leadership-employee performance links: The role of relational identification and self-efficacy. *Journal of Occupational and Organizational Psychology, 84*, 153–172. http://dx.doi.org/10.1348/096317910X485818

Wang, Y.S. & Huang, T.C. (2009). The relationship of transformational leadership with group cohesiveness and emotional intelligence. *Social Behavior and Personality, 37*, 379–392. http://dx.doi.org/10.2224/sbp.2009.37.3.379

Zacharatos, A., Barling, J. & Kelloway, E.K. (2000). Development and effects of transformational leadership in adolescents. *The Leadership Quarterly, 11*, 211–226. http://dx.doi.org/10.1016/S1048-9843(00)00041-2

Zhu, W., Avolio, B.J., Walumbwa, F.O. (2009). Moderating role of follower characteristics with transformational leadership and follower work engagement. *Group and Organization Management, 34*, 590–619. http://dx.doi.org/10.1177/1059601108331242

Chapter 38

Athlete leadership

Theory, research, and practice

TODD M. LOUGHEAD, LAUREN MAWN, JAMES HARDY AND KRISTA J. MUNROE-CHANDLER

SUMMARY

This chapter focuses on the nature of athlete leadership and its development. First, a definition of athlete leadership is introduced along with the various types of athlete leaders. This is followed by a discussion of the theories and conceptual models used to examine athlete leadership. Then, a description of the tools used to measure athlete leadership including the Leadership Scale for Sports, Revised Leadership Scale for Sport, Player Leadership Scale, and the Differentiated Transformational Leadership Inventory is offered. Research conducted on athlete leadership can be grouped into three areas: (a) the characteristics of athlete leaders; (b) the quantity of athlete leaders within teams; and (c) the leadership behaviors exhibited by athlete leaders. Research carried out in each of the three areas is reviewed. Given the importance of athlete leadership, several types of leadership development programs are outlined and their usefulness is discussed.

INTRODUCTION

We feel we have several individuals who bring leadership and we're very comfortable having several individuals with "A's" and other people serving in a leadership group. (Jacques Martin, former coach of the Montreal Canadiens, on the importance of formal and informal leaders; *The Gazette*, October 1, 2009)

We know we need each other to be successful and we know we have a good group of leadership in here that will offer different things. (Mike Cammalleri, NHL player, on the importance of athlete leaders serving various roles; *The Gazette*, October 1, 2009)

The players have reacted extremely well when working in a team, therefore it made sense to create a leadership team who can continue our togetherness. (Michael Maguire, Wigan Warriors rugby league team coach, defying tradition by appointing a leadership team in place of a customary single captain; Skysports.com, January 12, 2012)

It has been suggested that effective leadership is the most important factor in achieving team excellence and success (Zaccaro, Rittman, & Marks, 2001). Leadership in sport has been assigned great importance by both athletes and coaches with the majority of research examining the role of the coach (Chelladurai, 2007). Indeed, the quotations at the beginning of this chapter provide anecdotal evidence concerning the importance of athlete leadership. Coaches and athletes alike value the inclusion of athlete leaders on a team, the impact of having many athlete leaders, and the various roles these leaders fulfill.

OBJECTIVES

After reading this chapter you should be able to:

1   Define what is meant by the term athlete leadership.
2   Discuss key theories useful for studying athlete leadership.
3   Understand the various tools used to evaluate athlete leadership.
4   Summarize the research that has been conducted in the area of athlete leadership.
5   Discuss ways to develop effective leaders in sport.

DEFINITION OF ATHLETE LEADERSHIP

Over the last six decades more than 65 different taxonomies have been advanced in an attempt to define leadership (Northouse, 2001). After surveying these numerous attempts, Northouse identified four common features central to leadership: (1) leadership is a process, it is not a trait nor a characteristic but rather an interactive event between leaders (e.g., athlete leaders) and followers (e.g., teammates); (2) leadership involves influence; (3) leadership occurs within a team context; and (4) leadership involves goal achievement. Based on these four features, Northouse argued that, theoretically, every group member can display leadership and consequently defined it as "a process whereby an individual influences a group of individuals to achieve a common goal" (p. 3).

While the majority of research in sport has traditionally examined the coach as *the* leader, the leadership provided between and amongst teammates, labeled as athlete leadership, has garnered some attention. Historically, the study of athlete leadership has suffered from a lack of clear and consistent definition, leading to difficulty in measuring and comparing research findings against one another. In order to guide research, we drew upon Northouse (2001) to define athlete leadership as an athlete occupying a formal or informal role who influences team members toward a common goal (Loughead, Hardy, & Eys, 2006). Embedded in this definition are two types of athlete leaders based on their role within the team: (1) formal athlete leaders—individuals who are formally designated as leaders by the team, such as a team captain; and (2) informal athlete leaders—individuals who emerge as leaders by interacting with other team members.

THEORIES AND CONCEPTUAL MODELS USED TO STUDY ATHLETE LEADERSHIP

To date, theories and conceptual models used to study athlete leadership have borrowed from either sport coaching research or organizational psychology. The primary theories have included behavioral models of leadership, and transformational and transactional leadership.

Multidimensional Model of Leadership

Chelladurai (1993) advanced a model for the study of coaching leadership in sports, the Multidimensional Model of Leadership (MML), which has also been used to guide the examination of athlete leadership in sport. The MML is a linear model composed of antecedents, leadership behaviors, and outcomes. The antecedents include situational, leader, and member characteristics. Situational characteristics refer to specific demands within the situation, such as group goals and the type of task (e.g., individual versus team sport). Leader characteristics are the leaders' personal features, such as their personality, age, or experience in sport. Finally, member characteristics consist of the team members' personal characteristics, such as age of the athlete, cultural background, and maturity.

The throughput of leadership behavior is categorized into three types of behaviors: required, preferred, and perceived. *Required* behaviors are those behaviors in which the leader should engage. *Preferred* behaviors are those behaviors the group members desire from the leader. Both required and preferred behaviors are influenced by the antecedents of situational and member characteristics. Finally, *perceived* behaviors are those the leader actually does and are influenced by the leader's characteristics, required leader behaviors, and preferred leader behaviors.

In his conceptualization of the model, Chelladurai (1993) outlined two outcomes: team member satisfaction and performance. However, research has identified additional outcomes including commitment and motivation (Todd & Kent, 2004), cohesion (Vincer & Loughead, 2010), skill development (Alfermann, Lee, & Würth, 2005), intention to return (Spink, 1998), and athlete burnout (Vealey, Armstrong, Comar, & Greenleaf, 1998). It is important to note the outcomes provide feedback to the leader that will influence the perceived leader behaviors (Chelladurai, 2007).

Transformational and transactional leadership

While transformational leadership theory has been popular in organizational psychology since the mid-1980s, the field of sport psychology has recently adopted this theoretical approach in examining both coach and athlete leadership. Burns' (1978) seminal work introduced the concepts of transactional and transformational leadership to the area of organizational psychology. He explained that transactional leadership, which focuses on the leader–follower exchange, is the most pervasive form of leadership and is the most typical approach when leading. This leadership style shapes behavior with the leader promising rewards or threats contingent on a follower's performance. In contrast, he described transformational leadership in terms of motivating the people around you, making them more aware of the importance of outcomes and influencing them to transcend their own self-interest for the sake of the team.

While there are several forms of transformational leadership, the version that has garnered the most research was formulated by Bernard Bass (1990) with the development of a new paradigm of transformational leadership—the Full Range of Leadership (FRL) model. According to this paradigm, effective leadership incorporates transformational, transactional, and non-leadership behaviors. In particular, the FRL model suggests that every leader demonstrates a full range or spectrum of leadership behaviors at various points and to varying degrees. As Figure 38.1 indicates, non-leadership is the most ineffective form of leadership behavior and is often viewed as the absence of leadership rather than displaying negative or non-productive leadership behaviors. In essence, this non-leadership style is viewed as a failure to lead. Bass viewed transactional leadership to represent the exchange of contingent reward and/or punishment between the leader and follower. Transactional leadership was conceptualized

Ineffective   Effective

Figure 38.1 Full Range of Leadership model.

as a more effective form of leadership than non-leadership. The final component of the FRL model consists of transformational leadership, which is believed to be the most effective form of leadership. Transformational leadership focuses upon building relationships with followers based on emotional, personal, and inspirational exchanges with the end goal of follower development. Transformational leadership is proposed to elevate followers' levels of maturity, ideals, concern for task achievement, concern for the well-being of the team and others, as well as their self-actualization.

MEASURING ATHLETE LEADERSHIP

To date, there is no gold standard inventory that measures athlete leadership behaviors. Typically, researchers have measured athlete leadership based on their theoretical paradigm. The Leadership Scale for Sports (LSS; Chelladurai & Saleh, 1980) was one of the first measures of athlete leadership. Although originally designed to assess coaching behaviors, the LSS was modified to measure athlete leadership by altering the statement that preceded the survey's items (e.g., Loughead & Hardy, 2005; Vincer & Loughead, 2010). In the original version, the statement reads "My coach" whereas in the athlete leader version the statement reads "The athlete leader(s) on my team." This modified version of the LSS assesses the same five dimensions as the coaching version. *Training and Instruction* examines the athlete leader's behavior aimed at improving teammates' performance by emphasizing strenuous training, teaching the skills, tactics, and techniques of the sport. *Positive Feedback* assesses the athlete leader's behavior that reinforces and rewards good performance. *Social Support* measures the athlete leader's behavior in relation to showing a concern for teammates' welfare and having good interpersonal relations with them. *Democratic Behavior* assesses the extent to which the athlete leader involves their teammates in decision making. *Autocratic Behavior* assesses behavior concerning the athlete leader's independence in decision making and personal authority.

While the LSS measured five athlete leadership behaviors, Kozub and Pease (2001) developed a measurement tool, the Player Leadership Scale (PLS), by combining items from the LSS (Chelladurai & Saleh, 1980) and the Leader Behavior Description Questionnaire (Halpin, 1957). The PLS assesses athlete leadership along two lines—task and social factors. The task factor measures athlete leadership that is concerned with the attainment of the team's goals, while the social factor reflects leadership aimed at developing and maintaining relationships amongst teammates. A criticism of the PLS is that athlete leadership is measured by only task and social leadership indices which limits a researcher's ability to determine the specific behaviors athlete leaders exhibit (Loughead & Hardy, 2005).

The Differentiated Transformational Leadership Inventory (DTLI; Hardy et al., 2010) has been used to study the athlete leadership behaviors from a transformational perspective. The DTLI was developed using two inventories from organizational psychology, the Multifactor Leadership Questionnaire Form 5-X (MLQ 5-X; Bass & Avolio, 1995) and the Transformational Leadership Inventory (TLI; Podsakoff, MacKenzie, Moorman, & Fetter, 1990). Specifically, two behaviors were taken from the MLQ 5-X: *Inspirational Motivation* (Motivate and inspire teammates by stressing goals and viewing the future with optimism), and *Individualized Consideration* (Pays attention to individual teammate's needs for growth and achievement), while five sub-scales were taken from the TLI: *Intellectual Stimulation* (Fosters innovation and creativity by approaching problems with new perspectives), *Appropriate Role Model* (Sets an example for people to follow), *Fostering the Acceptance of Group Goals* (Promotes cooperation and gets teammates to work together towards a common objective), *High Performance Expectations* (Demonstrates expectations of excellence, quality, and performance from teammates), and *Contingent Reward* (Positive reinforcement of appropriate behavior in exchange for rewards).

ATHLETE LEADERSHIP RESEARCH

Research on athlete leadership, while in its infancy, can be grouped into three areas: (1) the characteristics of athlete leaders; (2) the quantity of athlete leaders within teams; and (3) the leadership behaviors exhibited by athlete leaders.

Characteristics of athlete leaders

Research examining the characteristics of athlete leaders has been sporadic over the last three decades. Despite the dearth of information, a profile of an athlete leader can be compiled based on the research findings. It would appear that athlete leaders occupy both formal and informal leadership roles within their teams (e.g., Loughead et al., 2006). Regardless of leadership roles, athlete leaders tend to self-rate and are rated by their teammates and coaches as being skilled performers (e.g., Yukelson, Weinberg, Richardson, & Jackson, 1983). Moreover, research has found that athlete leaders are typically upperclassmen (i.e., 3rd or 4th players; Loughead et al., 2006) and play central positions (Glenn & Horn, 1993). Finally, athlete leaders were liked by their teammates (Tropp & Landers, 1979), felt liked by their teammates and displayed higher levels of intrinsic motivation (Price & Weiss, 2011), and indicated a higher internal locus of control (Yukelson et al., 1983), which distinguished them from non-athlete leaders.

Quantity of athlete leaders

Glenn and Horn (1993) noted that coaches believe that teams require one or two athletes to help direct and motivate teammates. To test this assumption, Loughead and Hardy (2005) sampled intercollegiate athletes engaged in both independent (e.g., track and field) and interactive (e.g., soccer) team sports. Participants were asked to name the athletes on their teams who provided leadership to them. The majority of participants (65.1%) listed both formal and informal athlete leaders as providers of leadership. Furthermore, the authors calculated the percentage of athletes serving in either a formal or informal role, reporting that 27% of athletes on sports teams served as athlete leaders. For instance, on a team with 22 roster spots, roughly six players would provide leadership to their teammates.

Although the number of perceived athlete leaders on a team has been examined, it was not known whether this percentage reflected the ideal number of athlete leaders on a given sport team. Using open-ended questions, Crozier, Loughead, and Munroe-Chandler (2013) asked over 100 intercollegiate athletes to indicate what constitutes the ideal number of formal and informal athlete leaders on a given team. Participants believed that 85.5% of athletes on a team should assume a leadership role. Specifically, the results showed that 19% of athletes on a roster should occupy a formal leadership role, while 66.5% of athletes should have an informal leadership role. For example, a roster with 22 players, the ideal number of formal leaders would be four, while 14 athletes would serve as informal athlete leaders. Therefore, 18 of the 22 players on the roster would be considered athlete leaders. In addition, over half of the participants indicated that all athletes should display some type of leadership behavior. Taken together, the findings suggest that ideally more athletes should be occupying a leadership role than currently reported within teams.

An alternative method of research investigating the number of athlete leaders examined it in relation to various aspects of the team environment such as athlete satisfaction, cohesion, and communication. Eys, Loughead, and Hardy (2007) examined the relationship between the number of athlete leaders across task (leadership aimed at achieving team objectives), social (leadership aimed at ensuring team harmony), and external (leadership that promotes the team within the community) leadership functions and athlete satisfaction. The findings showed that varsity athletes who perceived a relatively equal number of leaders across the three leadership functions were more satisfied with their athletic experience than those who perceived an uneven number of athlete leaders. Further, Hardy, Eys, and Loughead (2008) showed that there is a negative relationship between the number of task leaders and both task cohesion and communication. The authors suggested that having a core of task athlete leaders would contribute to more effective communication and enhanced perceptions of task cohesion.

Athlete leadership behaviors

Another line of research has focused on the leadership behaviors of athlete leaders. What follows is a review of the quantitative studies,

organized by the inventory used to measure athlete leadership. Using the LSS (Chelladurai & Saleh, 1980), Loughead and Hardy (2005) examined whether athlete leaders and coaches differed on their leadership behaviors. On one hand, results indicated that coaches exhibited more *Training and Instruction* and *Autocratic Behavior* than athlete leaders. On the other hand, athlete leaders displayed more *Social Support*, *Positive Feedback*, and *Democratic Behavior* leadership behaviors than coaches. In an examination of cohesion, Vincer and Loughead (2010) found the athlete leader behaviors of *Training and Instruction* and *Social Support* were positively associated with task and social cohesion, while *Democratic Behavior* was positively related to task cohesion. In contrast and as expected, *Autocratic Behavior* was negatively related to both task and social cohesion.

In a study using the PLS, Kozub and Pease (2001) sampled 126 high school basketball players. Each player rated their coach's leadership behaviors using the LSS and rated their teammates' task and social leadership behaviors using the PLS. Players who perceived a higher frequency of *Democratic Behavior* from their coach were viewed by their teammates as displaying greater task leadership. Further, players who perceived higher frequency of *Social Support* and *Democratic Behavior* from their coach received higher social leadership ratings from their teammates.

In regards to the DTLI, Callow, Smith, Hardy, Arthur, and Hardy (2009) examined the relationship between transformational leadership behaviors of team captains and cohesion amongst collegiate ultimate Frisbee players. The results showed a positive relationship between the transformational leadership behaviors of *Fostering the Acceptance of Group Goals and Promoting Team Work*, *High Performance Expectations*, and *Individual Consideration* with task cohesion. Additionally, a positive relationship was also found between team captains' *Fostering the Acceptance of Group Goals and Promoting Team Work*, and *Intellectual Stimulation* with social cohesion.

Using a qualitative methodology, Dupuis, Bloom, and Loughead (2006), and Holmes, McNeil, and Adorna (2010) examined perceptions of athlete leadership. Despite using differing perspectives (captain versus athletes), similar results were found. Both studies found that athlete leaders needed to be effective communicators, serve as a role model for their teammates, show a good work ethic, and display a positive attitude. In addition, Dupuis et al. found that captains should treat teammates as individuals depending on their needs and help enhance a team's cohesiveness.

Based on the research to date, it seems evident that having athlete leaders on sport teams is advantageous. Crozier et al. (2013), using an open-ended questionnaire with inter-collegiate athletes, showed the presence of athlete leaders was critical in helping to clarify a teammate's role and expectations on how to behave (i.e., team norms). Additionally, athlete leaders enhanced cohesiveness and teamwork by fostering an environment whereby teammates could work together and focus on the task more effectively. Further, athlete leaders assisted in establishing and guiding their team towards goals and objectives, helped to motivate teammates, provided social support, and were good role models for their teammates. All of these benefits were seen as a way to enhance individual and team outcomes such as teammates' satisfaction with athletic experience and achievement of better performances.

ATHLETE LEADERSHIP DEVELOPMENT

Considering the relative infancy of research into athlete leadership it is not surprising that few studies have been conducted to ascertain how to develop athlete leaders. Those researchers who have examined the development of athlete leaders have mainly focused on captains (e.g., Dupuis et al., 2006). What follows are suggestions, derived from research in both athlete leadership and global leadership domains, on how to develop athlete leadership.

Before detailing these suggestions it is worth highlighting two issues salient to leader development programs. The first issue pertains to naturally occurring leadership development, while the second issue concerns the selection of potential athlete leaders and their willingness to develop their leadership potential. As for the first issue, Grandzol, Perlis, and Draina (2010) conducted a season-long investigation into the leadership practices of team captains and team members within NCAA sport. It was found that both types of athletes demonstrated increased leadership practices as the season progressed, although this development was most marked for team captains. These findings suggest that leadership qualities can develop naturally and that those who are afforded opportunities (i.e., captains) demonstrate the greatest development. These findings dovetail with the observation that over the years teams have benefited from very effective athlete leaders who have not necessarily received any type of leadership training. However, this does not mean that those provided with such opportunities (e.g., captains) *optimally* enhance their leadership skills. Theory-based leader development programs may play an important role in achieving this.

The second issue relates to formal training programs where it is possible that not all athletes want to develop their leadership potential. Voelker, Gould, and Crawford (2011) noted that some captains believe that leadership cannot be learned but rather people are born good leaders. While we would obviously contend that this is not the case, it does help to illustrate how important it is to promote athlete leader development programs appropriately while simultaneously highlighting the importance of selecting the right athletes for such training. Accordingly it is crucial to consider the key stakeholders in the athlete leadership development process presented in Figure 38.2.

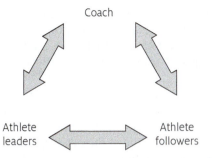

Coach

Athlete leaders

Athlete followers

Figure 38.2 Stakeholders in the athlete leadership development process.

Most of the discussion herein focuses on different aspects of the interrelated triangle illustrated in Figure 38.2 and we believe that all leadership development programs need to consider equally the coordination and feedback from all stakeholders. In addition, the arrows indicate that the interplay between stakeholders (e.g., feedback, communication, coordination) ought to be two-way to maximize effectiveness of the development of athlete leadership. We have outlined below five issues salient to the selection of athlete leaders; for example, which athletes should receive leadership training and who should be involved in this selection process. A glance at these points reveals a plethora of philosophical and logistical factors worthy of consideration, and the factors highlighted likely represent a platform for further thought.

1 **What type of leaders should be developed; task, social or external leaders?**
   • All three types of leader roles should be developed; an emphasis should be placed on fostering *balanced* athlete leadership with an equal number of task, social, and external leaders as this fosters greater follower satisfaction (Eys et al., 2007). It should be noted that athletes could fulfill one, two, or all three leadership roles.
2 **Who is best placed to select the leaders for development; team, coach, or practitioner?**
   • Bucci, Bloom, and Loughead (2012) found coaches reported selecting athletes

with values closely aligned with the team's identity, greater maturity, more playing experience, and who lead by example, worked hard, followed plans, and were always willing to play. Coaches also felt that leadership qualities outside the game were equally important, such as being generous and honest, taking care of teammates, and setting a good example.
   • The neglected stakeholders in the selection of leaders are the athlete followers. It would appear that coaches' and athlete followers' views of athlete leadership are important. Smoll and Smith (1989) stated that "leader effectiveness resides in both the behaviors of the leader and the eyes of the beholder" (p. 1544) reflecting the need to assess athlete followers' perceptions and evaluations of leader behaviors.
   • Coaches should seek out the perspective of athlete followers in selecting leaders as well as consider how well athlete leaders will work alongside coaches and their vision for the team.
3 **Who receives athlete leadership development training? Captains only, team members with leadership qualities, or potential future leaders?**
   • This depends on the coach and team philosophy. Some coaches employ a "flat" approach to leadership (Bucci et al., 2012). All members of a team are developed to ensure that everyone is capable of doing the right thing at the right time.
   • More commonly, a hierarchical approach to leadership is employed where the coach is situated at the top of the hierarchy as the ultimate decision maker, a select few players lead the team from within (e.g., captains making key decisions during competition), and finally, all other athletes are at the bottom of the hierarchy.
4 **Should leaders be selected and developed to substitute for aspects not displayed by coaches or to reinforce the behaviors of their coaches?**
   • Loughead and Hardy (2005) found support for a compensation approach.

Coaches exhibited *Training and Instruction* and *Autocratic Behaviors* to a greater extent than athlete leaders but athlete leaders exhibited more *Social Support*, *Positive Feedback*, and *Democratic Behaviors* than coaches.

• As the two sources of leadership seem to serve different functions it may be beneficial to assess coach leadership behaviors to identify those not performed and then develop athlete leaders to employ these behaviors so that followers benefit from a full range of leadership behaviors.

5 **Should leaders be selected who already demonstrate central components of leadership (e.g., respect of teammates, work ethic, interpersonal skills)?**

• Selecting leaders who possess some of these components might help to minimize the time, effort, and investment required as it would only be necessary to hone these already existent skills.

• An important factor to consider is the goal of leadership. If the goal of athlete leadership development relates strictly to enhance performance, it may be more salient to select athletes who already possess these components. If the goal of athlete leadership development is to develop people and their life skills, encouraging all athletes to enhance their leadership skills to some degree would be more consistent with this philosophy. The former approach is more aligned to the hierarchical approach and the latter more aligned to the "flat" approach previously outlined above.

Captain leadership development

After resolving who might make effective athlete leaders, the issue of how to most effectively develop the leadership skills needs to be addressed. Recent research on the development of captains as leaders has employed a formal educational approach. The development program designed by Gould and Voelker (2010) consists of a one-day workshop focused on captains' leadership training and a self-study guide. Captains are introduced to the key concepts of team cohesion, motivation, peer modeling, and communication. While the authors' approach to leadership development does not seem to be grounded in a particular leadership theory, all of these aspects have been shown to be influenced by leadership (Beauchamp, Barling, & Morton, 2011; Callow et al., 2009; Hardy et al., 2008). For instance, Paradis and Loughead (2012) found that athlete leadership was related to team cohesion, which in turn was related to athlete satisfaction. This type of result highlights the importance of an education-oriented approach to leader development. In these one-day workshops, captains are also encouraged to discuss the assessment and improvement of their own leadership in relation to these mechanisms and consequences to assist them in conducting a brief self-analysis. Captains are then asked to identify common problems they may experience on teams and are subsequently presented with challenging questions and scenarios associated with being a leader to work through. The final part of the workshop focuses on facilitators providing feedback and addressing any questions the captains may have.

Transformational leadership training

As indicated earlier, transformational leadership provides a set of behaviors and involves being aware of how a leader's behaviors relate to the needs of followers. Transformational leadership can be taught to people at all levels within organizations and teams (Bass & Avolio, 1990). Two different approaches have been advocated for developing transformational leadership. Both approaches are based on providing workshops centered on translating the transformational leadership behaviors into domain specific leader behaviors. The first approach deals directly with the leaders themselves (cf. Barling, Weber, & Kelloway, 1996) whereas the second approach develops leadership behaviors indirectly by working through coaches to train the leaders (cf. Hardy et al., 2010). In both approaches, trainee leaders and their followers complete a measure of transformational leadership (e.g., MLQ 5-X or DTLI) to determine the leaders' specific strengths and weaknesses; in particular, which behaviors could be most improved upon. A common component of both approaches is a workshop training session provided to familiarize the athletes with the central components of transformational leadership, which is then followed by specific behavioral training sessions.

Within the workshop sessions, athletes are asked to elicit the strengths and weaknesses of a good athlete leader and outline the best and worst characteristics of that leader. The characteristics identified are then mapped onto the transformational leadership behaviors as proposed by transformation leadership theory. Following this mapping exercise, a few different approaches have been advocated within the literature; all prompting the athletes to think about how they could incorporate the behaviors into their own leadership. For example, Beauchamp et al. (2011) asked participants to watch videos and read short stories on how leadership works. Barling et al. (1996) utilized role playing to get participants to feel what a change in leadership behaviors is like. Hardy et al. (2010) used "a day in the life" exercise, asking participants to examine a normal day in their domain and how that would change if transformational leadership was applied. All of these approaches were designed to encourage participants to focus their efforts on changes to their everyday leader behaviors.

Within the published literature, most leadership interventions have followed up these workshops with individual coaching sessions with participants. The purpose of these sessions are twofold: (1) to provide developmental feedback to participants on the behaviors that were identified as weaker based on responses to the transformational leadership measures; and (2) to encourage participants to

identify and set goals pertaining to changing their leadership behaviors. It is likely that these sessions also represent opportunities for athlete leaders to gain social support (e.g., answers to any questions) as well as foster more internalized forms of motivation to implement changes to their leadership style. In addition, practitioners may consider utilizing an extension of the Butler and Hardy (1992) performance profile technique, something we call leadership profiling, as a tool for identifying skills and qualities required for effective leadership. In doing so, the practitioner is able to gain insight and understanding of an athlete leader's perceived need for areas of leadership improvement. This profiling technique in turn allows for the specific and personally salient areas of weakness to be targeted through leadership development programs or mentoring. As a result, leadership profiling does not represent a form of intervention in itself; rather, it provides a theory-based platform for use in interventions tailored to each individual athlete leader.

Coach mentoring

For athlete leadership development to be effective and sustainable, it is critical to involve the coaches from the outset as they play a pivotal role in helping athlete leaders understand their leadership roles (Bucci et al., 2012). To facilitate the discussion between the coach and athlete leaders on coordinated leadership roles, practitioners could employ Kahn, Wolfe, Quinn, Snoek, and Rosenthal's (1964) conceptualization of role ambiguity (i.e., scope of responsibilities, behavioral responsibilities, evaluation of role performance, and consequences of not fulfilling role responsibilities) as a reference. Indeed, within sport teams the benefits of such coordinated leadership roles have not been capitalized on, often with athlete leaders being an underutilized resource. To this effect, coaches often neglect the specific development of athlete leaders despite being best positioned to do so. Coaches have an important role to play in athlete leadership development because of their influence in choosing formal leaders (such as captains) and also through the close relationship they foster with those chosen leaders. Coaches can cultivate and mentor athlete leaders via a number of methods such as: (1) providing developmental feedback on leadership behaviors and suggestions how to improve; (2) teaching leadership principles to captains; (3) sharing their own past experiences and lessons learned; (4) role modeling best practices; (5) challenging athletes to apply their leadership knowledge; (6) creating meaningful opportunities for leaders to practice leading; and (7) providing a supportive environment for athletes to learn from mistakes.

Coaches are also ideally placed to implement a peer mentoring system whereby athletes currently serving in leadership roles mentor potential future athlete leaders. If such systems were implemented across a number of teams within the same organization (e.g., teams within the same university or club), this would have the added advantages of broadening the experiences discussed and exposing leaders to alternative ideas on effective leadership, better allowing leaders to develop their own approach to leading their team. Further, it would assist in the development of team norms concerning leadership roles within organizations, reinforcing group identity, and enhancing team cohesion. Nonetheless, the real gain from peer-based mentoring programs is enhanced effectiveness due to the fact participants are able to interact with each other within and outside of the sports setting. Additionally, the close similarity in roles of the mentors and mentored (i.e., leadership roles) allow for role modeling, which is likely to enhance efficacy beliefs concerning capability to lead. Finally, a mentoring scheme, whether that be between coaches and athletes or athlete leaders and athlete followers is likely to foster the coordination, communication, and feedback between all stakeholders outlined in Figure 38.2. For instance, to be successful, a mentor needs to be fully aware of both the coach's demands on the athlete leader in addition to the behaviors that athlete followers need and respond to. Being fully aware of these dynamics is also likely to enhance perceptions concerning leadership role clarity.

LEARNING AIDS

1   Identify the characteristics of athlete leaders.

Athlete leaders can occupy either a formal or an informal leadership role within their teams. Athlete leaders are typically well liked by their teammates, tend to be upperclassmen, play in central positions, are intrinsically motivated, and have an internal locus of control.

2   List the athlete leadership behaviors that are measured by the Leadership Scale for Sports and the Differentiated Transformational Leadership Inventory.

The five leadership behaviors measured by the Leadership Scale for Sports are: Training and Instruction, Democratic Behavior, Positive Feedback, Social Support, and Autocratic Behavior. The Differentiated Transformational Leadership Inventory measures the following leadership behaviors: Inspirational Motivation, Individualized Consideration, Intellectual Stimulation, Appropriate Role Model, Fostering the Acceptance of Group Goals, High Performance Expectations, and Contingent Reward.

3   Explain the two goals of follow-up sessions after having completed a leadership workshop.

(1) To provide feedback to workshop participants on the leadership behaviors that requires development, and (2) To identify and set goals in order to change leadership behavior.

4   Explain the benefits of peer mentoring for developing more effective athlete leaders.

There are numerous benefits to having athletes peer mentor one another. Exposing athletes to alternate ideas of what constitutes effective leadership is one benefit. Another benefit of mentoring is that it helps to develop effective team norms, reinforces a team's identity, and enhances team cohesion. Other benefits include increased athlete interaction inside and outside of the sports setting, role modeling, and better communication and coordination amongst stakeholders.

REVIEW QUESTIONS

1   Describe the distinction between transformational and transactional leadership behaviors.

2   Discuss the role of the coach in fostering the development of athlete leadership.

3   Describe the points when considering the selection of athlete leaders.

4   Describe the research results when examining the behaviors exhibited by athlete leaders and how these behaviors impact the team environment.

5   Explain the differences in how athlete leadership behaviors are measured.

EXERCISES

1   Drawing from your personal experience in sport and critical thinking skills, describe up to four instances when ignoring the followers' perspective of leadership on a team would be problematic.

2   Reflection-based activity: Consider the athlete leadership provided on your current or previous sport team. Are you able to recognize any of the behaviors described in the chapter? Which behaviors strike a particular cord with you and why? Are there any behaviors that would benefit from further development and how might doing so be helpful? If you were the coach of this team, how would you optimally develop the leadership from within the team?

3   Observation-based activity: After gaining permission to do so, observe a team match, practice session or both. When doing so apply the Full Range Model of Leadership to the athlete leadership behaviors displayed. Are there any behaviors in need of development? How might you go about developing them?

ADDITIONAL READING

Callow, N., Smith, M.J., Hardy, L., Arthur, C.A. & Hardy, J. (2009). Measurement of transformational leadership and its relationship with team cohesion and performance level. *Journal of Applied Sport Psychology, 21,* 395–412. doi: 10.1080/10413200903204754

Glenn, S.D. & Horn, T.S. (1993). Psychological and personal predictors of leadership behavior in female soccer athletes. *Journal of Applied Sport Psychology, 5,* 17–34. doi: 10.1080/10413209308411302

Loughead, T.M. & Hardy, J. (2005). An examination of coach and peer leader behaviors in sport. *Psychology of Sport and Exercise, 6,* 303–312. doi: 10.1016/j.psychsport.2004.02.001

Price, M.S. & Weiss, M.R. (2011). Peer leadership in sport: Relationships among personal characteristics, leader behaviors, and team outcomes. *Journal of Applied Sport Psychology, 23,* 49–64. doi: 10.1080/10413200.2010.520300

REFERENCES

Alfermann, D., Lee, M.J. & Würth, S. (2005). Perceived leadership behavior and motivational climate as antecedents of adolescent athletes' skill development. *Athletic Insight: The Online Journal of Sport Psychology, 7,* 14–36.

Barling, J., Weber, T. & Kelloway, E.K. (1996). Effects of transformational leadership training on attitudinal and financial outcomes: A field experiment. *Journal of Applied Psychology, 81,* 827–832. doi: 10.1037/0021-9010.81.6.827

Bass, B.M. (1990). From transactional to transformational leadership: Learning to share the vision. *Organizational Dynamics, 18,* 19–31. doi: 10.1016/0090-2616(90)90061-S

Bass, B.M. & Avolio B.J. (1990). The implications of transactional and transformational leadership for individual, team, and organizational development. *Research in Organizational Change and Development, 4,* 231–272.

Bass, B.M. & Avolio, B.J. (1995). *Transformational leadership development: Manual for the Multifactor Leadership Questionnaire.* Palo Alto, CA: Consulting Psychologists Press.

Beauchamp, M.R., Barling, J. & Morton, K.L. (2011). Transformational teaching and adolescent self-determined motivation, self-efficacy, and intentions to engage in leisure time physical activity: A randomised controlled pilot trial. *Applied Psychology: Health and Well-being, 3,* 127–150. doi: 10.1111/j.1758-0854.2011.01048.x

Bucci, J., Bloom, G.A., Loughead, T.M. & Caron, J.G. (2012). Ice hockey coaches' perceptions of athlete leadership. *Journal of Applied Sport Psychology, 24,* 243–259. doi: 10.1080/10413200.2011.636416

Burns, J.M. (1978). *Leadership.* New York: Harper & Row.

Butler, R.J. & Hardy, L. (1992). The performance profile: Theory and application. *The Sport Psychologist, 6,* 253–264.

Callow, N., Smith, M.J., Hardy, L., Arthur, C.A. & Hardy, J. (2009). Measurement of transformational leadership and its relationship with team cohesion and performance level. *Journal of Applied Sport Psychology, 21,* 395–412. doi: 10.1080/10413200903204754

Chelladurai, P. (1993). Leadership. In R.N. Singer, M. Murphey & L.K. Tennant (Eds.), *Handbook of research on sport psychology* (pp.647–671). New York: Macmillan.

Chelladurai, P. (2007). Leadership in sports. In G. Tenenbaum, & R.C. Eklund (Eds.), *The sport psychology handbook* (pp.113–135). Indianapolis, IN: Wiley Publishing Inc. doi: 10.1002/9781118270011

Chelladurai, P. & Saleh, S.D. (1980). Dimensions of leader behavior in sports: Development of a leadership scale. *Journal of Sport Psychology, 2,* 34–45.

Crozier, A.J., Loughead, T.M. & Munroe-Chandler, K.J. (2013). Examining the benefits of athlete leaders in sport. *Journal of Sport Behavior, 36,* 346–364.

Dupuis, M., Bloom, G.A. & Loughead, T.M. (2006). Team captains' perceptions of athlete leadership. *Journal of Sport Behavior, 29,* 60–78.

Eys, M.A., Loughead, T.M. & Hardy, J. (2007). Athlete leadership dispersion and satisfaction in interactive sport teams. *Psychology of Sport and Exercise, 8,* 281–296. doi: 10.1016/j.psychsport.2006.04.005

Glenn, S.D. & Horn, T.S. (1993). Psychological and personal predictors of leadership behavior in female soccer athletes. *Journal of Applied Sport Psychology, 5*, 17–34. doi: 10.1080/1041320930841 1302

Gould, D. & Voelker, D.K. (2010). Youth sport leadership development: Leveraging the sports captaincy experience. *Journal of Sport Psychology in Action, 1*, 1–14. doi: 10.1080/21520704.2010. 497695

Grandzol, C., Perlis, S. & Draina, L. (2010). Leadership development of team captains. *Journal of College Student Development, 51*, 401–418.

Halpin, A.W. (1957). *Manual for the Leadership Behavior Description Questionnaire.* Unpublished manuscript, Fisher College of Business, The Ohio State University, Columbus, Ohio.

Hardy, J., Eys, M.A. & Loughead, T.M. (2008). Does communication mediate the athlete leadership to cohesion relationship? *International Journal of Sport Psychology, 39*, 329–345.

Hardy, L., Arthur, C.A., Jones, G., Shariff, A., Munnoch, K., Isaacs, I. & Allsopp, A.J. (2010). The relationship between transformational leadership behaviors, psychological, and training outcomes in elite military recruits. *Leadership Quarterly, 21*, 20–32. doi: 10.1016/j.leaqua.2009. 10.002

Holmes, R.M., McNeil, M. & Adorna, P. (2010). Student athletes' perceptions of formal and informal team leaders. *Journal of Sport Behavior, 33*, 442–465.

Kahn, R.L., Wolfe, D.M., Quinn, R.P., Snoek, J.D. & Rosenthal, R.A. (1964). *Organizational stress: Studies in role conflict and ambiguity.* New York: Wiley.

Kozub, S.A. & Pease, D.G. (2001). Coach and player leadership in high school basketball. *Journal of Sport Pedagogy: Teaching and Coaching in Sport, 7*, 1–15.

Loughead, T.M. & Hardy, J. (2005). An examination of coach and peer leader behaviors in sport. *Psychology of Sport and Exercise, 6*, 303–312. doi: 10.1016/j.psychsport.2004.02.001

Loughead, T.M., Hardy, J. & Eys, M.A. (2006). The nature of athlete leadership. *Journal of Sport Behavior, 29*, 145–158.

Northouse, P.G. (2001). *Leadership: Theory and practice* (2nd ed.). Thousand Oaks, CA: Sage.

Paradis, K.F. & Loughead, T.M. (2012). Examining the mediating role of cohesion between athlete leadership and athlete satisfaction in youth sport. *International Journal of Sport Psychology, 43*, 117–136.

Podsakoff, P.M., MacKenzie, S.B., Moorman, R.H. & Fetter, R. (1990). Transformational leader behaviors and their effects on followers' trust in leader, satisfaction, and organizational citizenship behaviors. *Leadership Quarterly, 1*, 107–142. doi: 10.1016/1084-9843(90)90009-7

Price, M.S. & Weiss, M.R. (2011). Peer leadership in sport: Relationships among personal characteristics, leader behaviors, and team outcomes. *Journal of Applied Sport Psychology, 23*, 49–64. doi: 10.1080/10413200.2010.520300

Smoll, F.L. & Smith, R.E. (1989). Leadership behaviors in sport: A theoretical model and research paradigm. *Journal of Applied Social Psychology, 19*, 1522–1551. doi: 10.1111/j.1559-1816. 1989.tb01462.x

Spink, K.S. (1998). Mediational effects of social cohesion on the leadership behavior-intention to return in sport. *Group Dynamics: Theory, Research, and Practice, 2*, 92–100. doi: 10.1037/ 1089-2699.2.2.92

Todd, S.Y. & Kent, A. (2004). Perceptions of the role differentiation behaviors of ideal peer leaders: A study of adolescent athletes. *International Sports Journal, 8*, 105–118.

Tropp, K.J. & Landers, D.M. (1979). Team interaction and the emergence of leadership and interpersonal attraction in field hockey. *Journal of Sport Psychology, 1*, 228–240.

Vealey, R.S., Armstrong, L., Comar, W. & Greenleaf, C.A. (1998). Influence of perceived coaching behaviors on burnout and competitive anxiety in female college athletes. *Journal of Applied Sport Psychology, 10*, 297–318. doi: 10.1080/ 10413209808406395

Vincer, D.J.E. & Loughead, T.M. (2010). The relationship between athlete leadership behaviors and cohesion in team sports. *The Sport Psychologist, 24*, 448–467.

Voelker, D.K., Gould, D. & Crawford, M.J. (2011). The experience of high school sport captains. *The Sport Psychologist, 25*, 47–66.

Yukelson, D., Weinberg, R., Richardson, P. & Jackson, A. (1983). Interpersonal attraction and leadership within collegiate sport teams. *Journal of Sport Behavior, 6*, 28–36.

Zaccaro, S.J., Rittman, A.L. & Marks, M.A. (2001). Team leadership. *The Leadership Quarterly, 12*, 451–458. doi: 10.1016/S1048-9843(01)00093-5

Part Six

Career, life skills and character development through sport

EDITED BY BRENDA LIGHT BREDEMEIER AND ATHANASIOS G. PAPAIOANNOU

Chapter 39

Athletes' career development and transitions

NATALIA STAMBULOVA AND PAUL WYLLEMAN

SUMMARY

This chapter has three foci. First, it focuses on the stages that athletes go through during their multi-year *athletic career* and also in their psychological, psychosocial, and academic-vocational development. The second and particular focus of this chapter is on *career transitions* as turning phases in *career development*. Successfully coping with athletic and non-athletic, *normative* (i.e., predictable) and *non-normative* (i.e., less predictable) *transitions* allows greater opportunity for an athlete to live a long and successful life in sport as well as being able to adjust effectively to the post-sports career. Alternatively, failure in coping with a transition leads to a *crisis* that is often followed by negative consequences such as premature dropout from sport, neurosis, alcohol/drug abuse, etc. The third focus of the chapter is on *career assistance*, that is, on a set of interventions that help athletes to optimize their career development and prepare for and/or cope with career transitions.

INTRODUCTION

We start this chapter by acquainting you with the career of Martin B, a Swedish professional football player. Martin was born in 1986 in a medium-sized city in Sweden. In 1992 (i.e., being just six years old) he was introduced to football at pre-school, and he subsequently joined a children's football team in his hometown. In 1994, Martin watched the Football World Championship on TV and was inspired by observing play of the international elite. In

1995 (i.e., when he was nine years old) Martin made his first career plan, that is, to play in the national championship at the age of 14, and to play professionally in Italy by the time he was 16 years old. After making this plan, he started its realization, and during the next three years he practiced every day, independently in addition to regular practices with the team. His parents noticed that Martin was so fanatically focused on football that he almost "forgot" his friends. They tried to persuade him to find a better balance in life, but Martin persisted to stay on his track. In 1999, (i.e., aged 13) he experienced serious problems at school and also with his health (chronic fatigue) that coincided with his name appearing for the first time in the media with an epithet "talent". In 2001 (i.e., 15 years old) Martin experienced a disappointment of not being selected to the Swedish national team, but then signed his first professional contract with FK Örebro for the junior team. From then on his career developed rapidly. In 2002, he played for the Swedish national (junior) team, signed a contract with an agent, had try-outs in Chelsea and Ajax and received very favourable coverage in the media. In 2003, Martin made a successful debut playing in FK Örebro's senior team, he also moved to his own apartment, became interested in developing relationships with girls and met his first love. At the same time, he experienced serious problems in his studies and also in his relationships within the club. The highlight of 2003 was signing a contract with Inter Milan and moving to Italy. Adapting to a new culture and a new club environment was not easy. He found that the life of a professional football player was not as attractive as he imagined. In spring 2004 Martin got injured and spent time in the hospital feeling very alone. He recovered, came back to play, but was injured again. During the summer he spent time in Sweden with his family and girlfriend but when he went back to Italy he became very depressed and attempted to commit suicide. He was resuscitated by doctors and then taken home by his mother. After the rehabilitation period Martin tried to play football again (in Sweden) and was moderately successful. At the end of 2005, he decided to terminate his athletic career. In his post-sport career Martin became a journalist, and he shared his athletic career experiences in a book he published in Sweden (Bengtsson, 2011).

Martin's career story is dramatic and unique but at the same time it contains some typical features that are characteristic of athletes' career development and transitions. For example, in this story we find career stages, transitions, and crises. We also can see that Martin needed assistance to cope with some of the career transitions, especially with his transition to Inter Milan, which he could not manage. Martin's story provides us with a lesson that coaches and sport psychology consultants should focus not only on athletes' performance problems but should also take a broader perspective on their athletic and life careers.

OBJECTIVES

After reading this chapter, you should be able to:

1 Define an athletic career.
2 Understand the holistic lifespan perspective.
3 Describe stages in athletes' athletic, psychological, psychosocial and academic-vocational development.
4 Define a career transition and describe major athletes' transitions.
5 Understand a transition process and outcomes.
6 Define career assistance.
7 Describe major perspectives and types of career transition interventions.

UNDERSTANDING LIFE CAREER AND ATHLETIC CAREER

Life career is the most generic term used in psychology to define "the fate of a man running his/her life cycle in a particular society at a particular time." (Hughes, 1971 cited in Salmela, 1994). Based on this definition, each person has just one career lasting a lifetime, and therefore, an athletic career appears to be just one part or aspect of the life career.

Several definitions of an athletic career proposed in sport psychology emphasize its different aspects. Wylleman, Theeboom, and Lavallee (2004) defined athletic career as "a succession of stages and transitions that includes an athlete's initiation into and continued participation in organized competitive sport and that is terminated with the athlete's (in)voluntary but definitive discontinuation of participation in organized competitive sport" (p. 511). In this definition, the authors adopted a developmental perspective and viewed career as a cycle, with the career stages and transitions unfolding within the structure of organized competitive sport. Alfermann and Stambulova (2007) defined athletic career as "a multi-year sport activity voluntarily chosen by the person and aimed at achieving his/her individual peak in athletic performance in one or several sport events" (p. 713). In this definition other facets of athletic careers such as choice, long-term commitment, striving for upward career movement, and the possibility of having a specialized or generalized career, are highlighted. Specialized careers are characterized by athletes only competing in one sport during their entire career. In a generalized athletic career athletes practice and compete in several sports at the same time or successively, and then narrow their focus to one or two. Careers can also be of different levels, such as local, national, international, and professional, depending on the highest level in competitions achieved by the athlete. International amateur and professional careers are also called elite careers.

UNDERSTANDING CAREER DEVELOPMENT AND DESCRIPTIVE CAREER MODELS

Career development is defined as proceeding through career stages and transitions. Descriptive career models in sport psychology (Salmela, 1994; Stambulova, 1994; Wylleman & Lavallee, 2004) provide a sequence of career stages, describe characteristic features of each stage, and predict normative transitions between adjacent stages. In spite of the fact that these models were created in various sociocultural contexts, it is possible to identify a common pattern in a sequence of stages, including: initiation, development/specialization, mastery/perfection, and discontinuation stages of an athletic career (see also Chapter 2 in this book, Nurturing talent in youth sport).

There are four stages of athletic development. During *the initiation stage* children are engaged in fun, playful sport/exercise activities of different kinds and perceive sport as merely playing a game. Parents, siblings and peers stimulate their interest and support their sport involvement. During *the development stage* athletes narrow their focus to one-two sport disciplines and begin to set sport-related goals, practice in a more structured way, and take part regularly in competitions. Coaches, peers and parents form athletes' major social network supporting them in learning sport specific skills, increasing physical fitness level, and demonstrating learned competencies in competitions. During *the mastery stage* athletes become experts in their sports, and feel responsible for their practices and competition performances. Coaches often turn into mentors/advisers, and parents play a less active role as athletes take more control of major aspects of their careers themselves. This stage can be further divided into three sub-stages, such as progress in amateur senior/elite sport, professional sport involvement, and maintenance of sport involvement/ achievements with parallel preparation for the career termination. During the *discontinuation stage* athletes stop participating in competitions on the level they had achieved but they might continue to exercise or to do sports for recreational purposes. From that point onwards their focus is fully on starting a new professional career in or outside sports.

An influential current trend in the career topic is *a holistic lifespan perspective*, that is, an understanding of athletes' development as multifaceted, and an athlete as a person doing sport and having other life issues (studies, work, family, peers, etc.). The developmental model of transitions faced by athletes (Wylleman & Lavallee, 2004; Wylleman, Alfermann, & Lavallee, 2004) can be seen as an embodiment of the holistic lifespan perspective because it combines the stages in athletes' athletic, psychological, psychosocial, and academic-vocational development, outlines athletes' normative athletic and non-athletic transitions, and "roughly" aligns the stages and transitions with chronological age markers (Figure 39.1).

The developmental model consists of four layers. The top layer represents four stages in *athletic development* (see above in this section) and four normative athletic transitions, where athletes transition into organized competitive sports (at 6–7 years of age), into an intensive level of training and competition (at age 12–13), into the senior level of competition (at 18–19 years of age), and to the post-sport career (at 28–30 years of age). The second layer presents athletes' *psychological development* with childhood (up to 12 years of age), adolescence (13–18 years of age), and adulthood (from 19 years of age) as developmental stages and relevant transitions (i.e., from childhood to adolescence, and from adolescence to adulthood). The third layer is representative of the changes that can occur in the athlete's *psychosocial development* and sport related network including their parents, siblings, peers, coaches, and spouse/partner. The final layer contains the specific stages at academic-vocational level with transitions into primary education/elementary school (at 6–7 years of age), into secondary education/high school (from ages 12–13), into higher education/ college or university (at 18–19 years of age), and to a work place (at about 25 years of age). One of the basic tenets of the developmental model is that all layers of athletes' development are interrelated. This also means that athletic and non-athletic career transitions might coincide

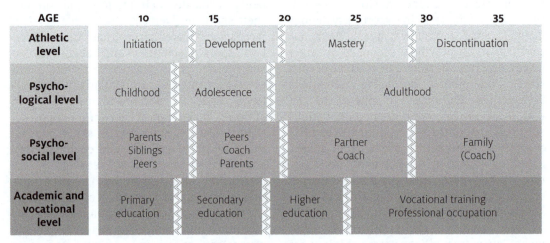

AGE	10	15	20	25	30	35
Athletic level	Initiation	Development		Mastery		Discontinuation
Psycho-logical level	Childhood	Adolescence		Adulthood		
Psycho-social level	Parents Siblings Peers	Peers Coach Parents		Partner Coach		Family (Coach)
Academic and vocational level	Primary education	Secondary education	Higher education	Vocational training Professional occupation		

Note: The dotted zigzag lines indicate that the age at which the transition occurs is an approximation.

Figure 39.1 Developmental model of transitions faced by athletes (Wylleman & Lavallee, 2004).

and influence athletes' success in sport and other spheres of life. This model, which has been used in research on transition experiences of, amongst others, rookie ice-hockey players (Bruner, Munroe-Chandler, & Spink, 2008), adolescent event riders (Pummell, Harwood, & Lavallee, 2008) and Olympic athletes (Wylleman, Reints, & Van Aken, 2012), has recently been developed further as two more layers of athletes' development were added based on empirical data, namely athletes' physical and financial development (Reints, 2011). In this new form the model is also renamed as the holistic athletic career model.

UNDERSTANDING CAREER TRANSITIONS AND EXPLANATORY MODELS

Career transitions are turning phases or shifts in athletes' development associated with a set of specific demands that athletes have to cope with in order to continue successfully in sport and/or other spheres of their life. As mentioned in the previous section, athletes' transitions are classified into athletic and non-athletic, as well as into *normative* and *non-normative*. *Normative transitions* are relatively predictable based on the logic of athletic, psychological, psychosocial and academic-vocational development, for example, the transition to senior sport or athletic retirement, the transition from secondary school to college or university, among others. *Non-normative transitions* are less predictable, such as transitions caused by injury, divorce, moving abroad, changing team or coach. The predictability of normative transitions creates an opportunity to prepare athletes to cope with them in advance. Alternatively, the low predictability of non-normative transitions explains why athletes might find these more difficult to cope with.

The transition process, outcomes, and factors involved are the major foci of the career transition explanatory models (Schlossberg, 1981; Stambulova, 2003; Stambulova et al. 2009; Taylor & Ogilvie, 1994, 2001) that are outlined below.

Human adaptation to the transition model

This model (Schlossberg, 1981, 1984) explains the process of transition in terms of the interaction of four sets of factors including: *situation* (i.e., how the transition is perceived by the individual), *self* (i.e., the individual's

profile), *support* (i.e., availability of different kinds of social support), and *strategies* (e.g., information seeking or direct action). A combination of these factors is recommended to take into account in a transition intervention. While this model is not sport related, it was successfully adopted in sport psychology research and also stimulated development of sport specific career transition models that follow.

Athletic career termination model

This model (Taylor & Ogilvie, 1994, 2001) deals with the last athletic normative transition – from sport to the post-sport career – and focuses on *reasons* for sport career termination, *factors related to adaptation* (developmental experiences, self-identity, perceptions of control, social identity, and tertiary contributors), *available resources* (coping skills, social support, pre-retirement planning), and *quality of the transition* with two alternative outcomes such as *healthy transition*, and *transition distress*. In terms of the transition distress outcome, a need for interventions with both preventive and distress-coping perspectives is outlined.

Athletic career transition model

This model (Stambulova, 2003) is designed to explain not only the final normative athletic transition but also other types of transitions that occur during an athletic career (Figure 39.2). In this model a transition is considered as a process of coping with a set of *transition demands.* In the coping process athletes use various *coping strategies* (e.g., planning, practicing more than opponents, searching for professional support, etc.) to deal with the transition demands. Effectiveness of coping is seen as dependent on a dynamic balance between the coping resources and barriers. *Resources* refer to the various internal and external factors that facilitate the transition (e.g., previous athletic and personal experiences, social and professional support available, etc.), and *barriers*, to the various internal and external factors that interfere with the coping process (e.g., low self-efficacy, lack of financial support). The model entails two primary transition outcomes: a successful transition and a crisis transition. A *successful transition* is the result of effective coping, that is, a good fit between transition demands and the athletes' coping resources and strategies.

Crisis transition is a result of ineffective coping because the athlete is low in resources, and/or high in barriers, and/or using inappropriate coping strategies. Crisis is also conceptualized as a transition that the athlete has to make but is not able to cope with independently, and for which he/she perceives a need for transition intervention. Further, according to the model, the crisis transition can have two possible secondary outcomes: "delayed" successful transition (in the case of effective intervention) or unsuccessful transition (in the case of no or ineffective intervention) associated with *negative consequences* (e.g., premature dropout, neuroses, overtraining, eating disorders, substance abuse, etc.). Career transition interventions outlined by the model include crisis-prevention, crisis-coping, and negative-consequences-coping interventions (these will be explained later).

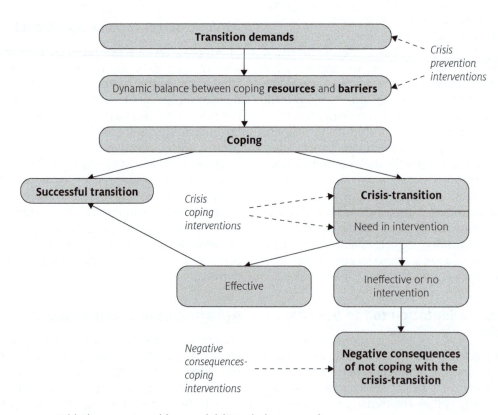

Figure 39.2 Athletic career transition model (Stambulova, 2003).

Relevant to this model is the athletes' crisis-transition study (Stambulova, 2003) that was based on the analysis of athletes' crisis-narratives. The study provided: (a) a set of symptoms of crisis-transitions such as a loss of self-esteem, chronic emotional discomfort, hypersensitivity to mistakes and failures, disorientation in decision-making, and dysfunctional behavior; and (b) an empirical classification with 15 types of athletes' crises based on their major content such as relationship crisis, crisis of re-adaptation after a break, crisis of overtraining, or moral crisis to name a few.

CAREER RESEARCH: AN INTERNATIONAL PERSPECTIVE

Over the last two decades international sport psychology societies have acknowledged the importance of athletic career transitions. For example, the European Federation of Sport Psychology (FEPSAC) published two position statement papers on the subject, namely on the significance of career transitions (FEPSAC, 1997) and on the impact of the termination of the athletic career (FEPSAC, 1999). Recently, Stambulova, Alfermann, Statler, and Côté (2009) presented the International Society of Sport Psychology (ISSP) Position Stand on athletes' career development and transitions. The authors emphasized a diversity of sociocultural contexts athletes belong to and that, in fact, career models reflect common patterns in athletes' careers and transitions. Depending on age, gender, type of sport, level in sport, and individual profile, as well as related sport system and culture, individual athletes' careers and transitions can vary considerably. Various personal characteristics (e.g., innate potential or athletic identity) and features of sociocultural contexts (e.g., public visibility of sport, jobs available in a sport system for retired athletes, etc.) can work as resources and/or barriers in different transitions across athletes' careers.

Analysing career research in sport psychology from an international perspective, it can be concluded that as interest for this theme has grown worldwide, researchers have been internalizing their research foci from relevant sociocultural contexts. For example, key topics for North American researchers include: athletic retirement, athletic identity, transitions of student-athletes, athletes' adaptation in new settings and cultures (e.g., Murphy, Petitpas, & Brewer, 1996; Petitpas, Brewer, & Van Raalte, 2009; Schinke, Michel, Gauthier, Danielson, Peltier, Enosse et al., 2006; Sinclair & Orlick, 1993). The hallmark for European career researchers is the holistic lifespan perspective applied to the athletic retirement, the junior-to-senior transition, dual careers in sport and studies, and to athletes' crises (e.g., Cecić Erpič, Wylleman, & Zupančič, 2004; Pummell et al., 2008; Stambulova, 1994, 2003; Torregrosa, Boixadós, Valiente, & Cruz, 2004; Wylleman & Reints, 2010). Australian career researchers emphasize athletic retirement and identity issues (e.g., Fraser, & Fogarty, 2011; Grove, Lavallee, & Gordon, 1997; Jackson, Dover, & Mayocchi, 1998). Finally, South American, Asian, and African researchers have been found to show a growing interest in studying athletes' transitions, especially the transition into the post-sports career (see in Stambulova & Ryba, 2013).

WHAT WE KNOW ABOUT ATHLETES' WITHIN CAREER TRANSITIONS

In the domain of within-career transitions, researchers are currently most interested in *the transition from-junior-to-senior/elite sports* that can be explained by a particular difficulty and also importance of this transition for athletes who want to achieve an elite or professional level in sports. As shown by Vanden Auweele, De Martelaer, Rzewnicki, De Knop, and Wylleman (2004), only 17 per cent of elite junior athletes had been found to make the successful transition to senior elite sports within a five-year period. The most visible studies on within-career transitions during adolescent years, and specifically, on the transition from junior to senior sports, have been conducted in Russia, the United Kingdom, Canada, and Sweden. In the Russian project (Stambulova, 1994) a mixed sample of individual and team sports athletes in the junior-to-senior transition was examined. Two British projects studied event equestrians in the transition from club to regional level (Pummell et al., 2008), and team sports players in the academy-to-first-team-transition from the perspective of coaches (Finn & McKenna, 2010). The Canadian project focused on ice hockey players' transition to elite level (Bruner et al., 2008), and the Swedish project (Stambulova, Franck, & Weibull, 2012) – on the process and outcomes of the junior-to-senior transition in a sample of individual and team sports athletes. Shared research findings of these studies can be summarized as follows. The junior-to-senior/elite transition is perceived by athletes as a big step associated with much higher standards in practice and performance than they experienced before. Issues outside sports are also very important, with studies and social aspects proving the most demanding. Athletes' ambitions to succeed in this transition and to meet the expectations of significant others, together with uncertainty about success in coping, lead to high stress and increased sensitivity to social influences. Therefore, social support, especially from coaches, plays a pivotal role in the transition process. Coaches believe that coping strategies such as thoughtful problem solving, acceptance of responsibility, self-control, and positive reappraisal are beneficial to the transition success. Research also confirmed that successful coping with the junior-to-senior/elite transition is associated with athletes' identity development and personal maturation.

WHAT WE KNOW ABOUT TRANSITIONS OF STUDENT-ATHLETES

North American studies on transitions of college/university student-athletes, and European dual career research provide more insight into the transitions of student-athletes. Petitpas et al. (2009) summarized North American research on student-athletes. The authors stated that a transition from high school to college puts a set of demands on the incoming students. The students have to meet new academic requirements, face the challenges of living away from home, create new relationships, and manage their time and energy. As they join a sport program, they have to adjust to demanding sport participation at the intercollegiate level and new teammates and coaches, as well as athletic career termination upon graduation from the college. Potential non-normative athletic transitions for student-athletes include injury and de-selection from the team.

Career development and transitions of student-athletes in Europe are considered under "a dual career" umbrella. Dual career is defined as a career with two major foci: sport, and studies or work. Relevant research deals with student-athletes who combine sport and education at regular schools, sport classes, sport boarding schools or universities. Studies in Belgium, France, Germany, Spain, Slovenia, and Sweden (e.g., Elbe & Beckmann, 2006; see more in Stambulova & Ryba, 2013) adopt the holistic lifespan perspective to demonstrate multiple benefits of a dual career (e.g., balanced lifestyle, reduced stress, good conditions for developing life skills, higher employability after sport) and to emphasize related problems and demands, especially when athletes experience transitions to a new level in sport and/or education. For example, results of the Swedish study on student-athletes' transition to the national elite sport school (Stambulova, Engström, Franck, & Linnér, 2012) showed that transitioning athletes experience new demands in sport, studies, and also in their private life (e.g., cooking and cleaning); they adjust easier to the "sport part" of their dual careers than to the "educational part", and their athletic identity is significantly higher than their student identity; they report "giving 100 per cent" to be their main coping strategy in all they are doing, and therefore they can be at risk for chronic fatigue or even burnout.

In 2011, the European Union (EU) Commission created an ad-hoc group of experts on dual careers to analyse the current status of exist-ing dual career programs and develop "European guidelines on dual careers of athletes" (the task was completed in 2012). This document recommends policy actions in support of dual careers in high-performance sport including special arrangements between sport and educational systems that are not only aimed at assisting talented athletes to successfully sustain both athletic and academic-vocational development, but also ensuring their readiness for athletic retirement.

WHAT WE KNOW ABOUT ATHLETES' TRANSITION TO THE POST-SPORT CAREER

Athletes' transition to the post-sport career or athletic retirement has been the most popular topic of career transitions research worldwide. Earlier studies emphasized athletes' difficulties and metaphorically described athletic retirement as "a social death" followed by downward social mobility of retired athletes. Later studies re-conceptualized athletic retirement to "a social rebirth", creating new opportunities for former athletes. Currently, athletic retirement is studied based on the transition frameworks (see above), and researchers focus on reasons for career termination, retirement demands, resources and barriers, coping strategies, and quality of adaptation. It is shown that several factors are "weighted" in the decision-making process and become responsible for an athlete's decision to terminate. Some of these factors relate to sport (e.g., stagnation, injuries, lack of financial support) and others to the future life (e.g., job offer, wish to start a family). The more the athlete retires within the context of future plans, the easier his/her retirement process can be.

International research (for overview see Alfermann & Stambulova, 2007; Lavallee & Wylleman, 2000; Taylor & Ogilvie, 2001) identified retired athletes' major transition demands to include: (a) starting a new professional career in or outside sports; (b) solving an "identity problem" (i.e., reducing their athletic identity and developing new identities relevant to their new careers); (c) reorganizing their lifestyle (with sport/exercise included only for recreational purposes); (d) renewing their social network (i.e., finding friends outside sport); and (e) dealing with family issues (e.g., own family, parenthood, house-holding duties). International data showed that about 80 per cent of athletes experience athletic retirement as a successful transition and about 20 per cent experience retirement as a crisis. Successful adaptation to the post-sport career lasts between 8 and 18 months. Negative consequences of not coping with this transition include alcohol/drug abuse, downward social mobility, and health-related problems (e.g., depression, neurosis). Researchers also agree that resources assisting athletes in the transition to the post-sport career consist of: (a) retirement planning in advance (i.e., when the athlete is still active in sport); (b) voluntary termination; (c) multiple personal identity and positive experiences in roles other than the athlete role; and (d) effective social support from family, coach, peers, and sport organizations. All these facilitate athletes' control over the retirement process and their active coping strategies in dealing with major transition issues. Alternatively, a high and exclusive athletic identity might cause an "identity crisis" (i.e., self-misinterpretation), while a lack of support from coaches, sport peers, and sport organizations might lead to additional difficulties with retirement planning and further adaptation. Recently, researchers emphasized that macro-social context (e.g., culture, sport system) had an impact on the retirement process. This was confirmed in the European Perspectives on Athletic Retirement Project, which involved a series of cross-cultural studies on athletes' adaptation to the post-sport career. The researchers found common and culture-specific patterns in retirement of German, Lithuanian, and Russian (Alfermann, Stambulova, & Zemaityte, 2004) as well as French and Swedish (Stambulova, Stephan, & Jäphag, 2007) athletes. The core of the common patterns consisted of pro-active retirement planning (i.e., when still being an active athlete) associated with voluntary athletic career termination, more positive and less negative emotional reactions to retirement, and using more active (i.e., problem solving) and less

defensive (i.e., emotion-focused) coping strategies. Retired athletes agreed not only upon the strong importance of social support from family and friends, but also about the lack of support from sport organizations. Specific patterns consisted, for example, of prevalence of job-related reasons for retirement (e.g., a job offer) and active coping strategies in the German sample, high athletic identity and more negative than positive reaction to retirement in the Lithuanian sample, the lowest level of retirement planning and much defensive coping in the Russian sample, prevalence of health-related reasons for retirement (e.g., injury) and searching for a new career mainly within the sport system in the French sample, and the highest level of retirement planning and searching for jobs outside sports in the Swedish sample. To briefly sum up, the European Perspectives on Athletic Retirement Project attracted the attention of other researchers to the multilevel sociocultural context that might contain both resources and barriers for athletes' retirement.

CAREER ASSISTANCE

Career assistance is a relatively new trend in sport psychology consulting that focuses on helping athletes with various issues related to their careers in and outside of sport. Stambulova (2010) used an umbrella term "professional culture of career assistance" to summarize a set of related concepts and theoretical frameworks, as well as career consultants' shared values, principles, and professional strategies/tools used in their work with athlete-clients. The core of the career assistance professional culture consists of the following principles:

- A *whole career approach*, to help athletes cope with both normative and non-normative transitions throughout the whole course of an athletic career.
- A *whole person approach*, to help them deal with transitions in various spheres of life.

- A *developmental approach*, to help athletes link their past career experiences, present situation, and perceived future.
- An *activity-specific approach*, to take into account not only common but also type-of-sport-specific demands in each athletic transition.
- A *culture-specific approach*, to help athletes adjust within a particular sport system and culture.
- A *multicultural approach*, to provide services to athletes who are of a different culture.
- An *individual approach*, to accommodate the athletes' perceptions of the transition and their idiosyncratic resources and barriers.
- A *transferable skills approach*, to teach them life skills applicable both in and outside sport.

- *A multilevel approach,* to address both traumatic symptoms and the issues behind the symptoms (e.g., perceptions, decisions, attributions, attitudes, etc.).
- *An empowerment approach,* to help athletes develop coping resources and strategies, allowing them to become autonomous after the intervention.

Career assistance services/interventions are provided by individual consultants (both educational and clinical) and also within career assistance programs. Below we first outline career assistance programs and then describe major perspectives in, and types of, career transition interventions.

Career assistance programs

Since the end of the 1980s, career assistance programs (CAPs) for retiring/retired athletes, active elite junior/senior athletes and student-athletes have been established in different parts of the world. Such programs are defined as "integrated and comprehensive combinations of workshops, seminars, educational modules, individual counseling and/or a referral network providing individualized and/or group-oriented multidisciplinary support services to athletes with regard to their athletic participation, developmental and lifestyle issues, and educational and vocational development" (Wylleman, et al., 2004, p. 511). Recently, 27 CAPs located in Europe, North America, Oceania, Asia, and Africa were investigated (Reints, 2011) in terms of the services they provide to junior, senior, and retired athletes. As shown in this study, service providers prioritize a preventive perspective that is helping athletes to prepare for forthcoming transitions, and especially for athletic retirement. Available in the CAPs are: (a) services related to education (e.g., distance learning, tutors, and flexible schedules); (b) career management (e.g., job placement and application skills); (c) life skills training (e.g., goal setting and media skills); (d) financial

management (e.g., reimbursement of service provision); and (e) health related services (e.g., nutrition training, medical support).

Gordon, Lavallee, & Grove (2005) provided an in-depth review of CAPs. The authors argued that contemporary sport characterized by early specialization, commercialization and globalization, public visibility of sport stars, international migrations and transnationalism, increase athletes' potential vulnerability in career transitions and also a need for CAPs. Four major CAPs, including the International Olympic Job Opportunities Program, the United States' Career Assistance Program for Athletes, the Canadian Olympic Athlete Career Centre, and the Athlete Career and Education Program that operated in Australia and the United Kingdom, were described in terms of their content, target groups, and style of service delivery. From their descriptions, the CAPs can be deemed to be really helpful to athletes, providing a good addition to the athletes' coping resources. But the authors strongly advocated for evidence-based research demonstrating effects of the programs and transition services/interventions involved.

Career transition interventions

Helping athletes to prepare for and cope with athletic and non-athletic, normative and non-normative transitions is a central aspect in career assistance. Two major perspectives in career transition interventions, the preventive/supportive and crisis/negative consequences coping perspectives, have been identified in the literature (Stambulova, 2012). *The preventive/supportive perspective* covers interventions aimed at enhancing athletes' awareness about forthcoming/current transition demands and aiding timely development of all necessary resources for effective coping. These interventions may assist athletes' readiness for a normative career transition and/or support during the transition process. The following are brief definitions of relevant intervention types.

- *Career planning interventions* are counseling interventions aimed at assisting athletes to increase their self-awareness, to set realistic career goals bridging their past, present, and future, and to prepare in advance for the forthcoming transitions.
- *Life development interventions/life skills training* consist of needs assessment, education, and training with regard to sets of transferable life skills (e.g., effective communication, dealing with success and failure, time/energy/stress management) that are skills applicable in both sports and other spheres of life.
- *Lifestyle management interventions* consist of counseling, education and training aimed at helping athletes to combine sport and other activities in life, to prioritize between them, and to manage time and energy in a way that helps athletes to maintain good health and well-being.
- *Identity development interventions* include counseling, education, and training aimed at helping athletes in self-exploration and development of multidimensional personal identities. These interventions work to prevent athletic identity foreclosure in athletes (i.e., their single-minded focus on sport), through counseling and education that stimulate their identity exploration and awareness, as well as through practical exploration of new social/professional roles (e.g., coach, team captain).
- *Cultural adaptation interventions* consist of needs assessment, counseling, education, and training aimed at helping athletes adjust to the new sociocultural environment when moving to another country to play sports or to do both sport and studies. Practitioners help athletes to increase their awareness of the new culture and to find consensus between their previous values, perceptions, habits, etc. and ones required/expected by people in the new culture.

The crisis/negative consequences coping perspective covers interventions assisting athletes to analyse their crisis/traumatic situations and to find the best available ways to cope. This perspective is represented by:

- *Crisis-coping educational interventions* aimed at helping athletes to analyse the crisis-situation, generate alternatives in coping, making an action plan, and increasing their self-efficacy to cope with the crisis. These interventions are useful during the initial phase of the crisis when athletes feel distressed and disoriented, but still do not experience any clinical symptoms.
- *Clinical interventions* are applied when athletes experience clinical symptoms related to overtraining, neuroses, psychosomatic illnesses, substance abuse, negative identities, eating disorders, anger and aggression, grieving, clinical depression, and suicidal thoughts, which often are negative consequences of not coping with previous or current transitions. These interventions are mostly counseling interventions based on various psychotherapeutic approaches, such as psychoanalysis, existential therapy, or cognitive-behavioral therapy.

It is easy to see some obvious overlaps between these various types of career transition interventions. For example, exploring new social roles as a part of identity development interventions contributes also to the athlete's lifestyle management and life skills training. Life development interventions can even be seen as "cementing" different types of transition interventions. Such overlaps are not surprising as all the interventions deal with various aspects of the transition process and adopt a holistic approach. These overlaps also facilitate combining various types of interventions to best meet the particular needs of the athlete.

CONCLUSION

In this chapter we discussed key concepts, theoretical frameworks, research, and applied work related to athletes' career development and transitions. This particular area of research and practice was built up and structured in sport psychology mainly during the last two decades. To briefly sum up, the current status of the career transition topic in sport psychology is characterized by: (a) sport-specific definitions of key concepts (e.g., athletic career, career transition, career assistance); (b) classifications of athletes' transitions, related theoretical frameworks, and interventions; (c) a holistic lifespan perspective and a solid body of knowledge about athletes' transitions and factors involved; (d) professional practice experiences accumulated in CAPs; and (e) principles, values, intervention strategies/tools, etc. integrated into the professional culture of career assistance. Achievements in the area are also visible through an increasing amount of career transition publications and international symposia, elevated inclusion of career assistance into applied sport psychology education programs and certification criteria for sport psychology consultants in many countries.

Meanwhile, we expect that more will be done. Career research is expected to become more ecologically and culturally sensitive as well as more sport-specific, that is, focus on the multilevel sociocultural contexts and sport characteristics (e.g., Stambulova & Ryba, 2013; Wylleman, Reints, & De Knop, 2010) relevant to athletes' career development and transitions. More studies should be conducted on the athletic and non-athletic transitions using the holistic lifespan perspective and various methodologies/designs (e.g., narratives, longitude, cross-cultural, intervention and case studies). In regard to career assistance services it is necessary to further increase its visibility in applied sport psychology, promote career assistance services among athletes and coaches, create international networks of career consultants assisting each other in working with transnational athletes, develop further CAPs, and evaluate their effectiveness using rigorous research approaches. The key issue for career assistance is to provide timely professional help to prevent crisis situations, similar to that described in this chapter's introduction, and facilitate athletes' successful careers in sport and life.

LEARNING AIDS

1 Define an athletic career.

   An athletic career can be defined as a sequence of stages and transitions in an individual's athletic development aimed at achieving his/her peak in athletic performance in one or several sport events.

2 Explain what is meant by a holistic lifespan perspective.

   In the holistic lifespan perspective athletes' development is considered as multifaceted, and an athlete as a person doing sport and having other life issues (studies, work, family, peers, etc.).

3   Describe the stages in athletes' athletic, psychological, psychosocial and academic-vocational development.

In an athletic career, athletes proceed through initiation, development, mastery, and discontinuation stages. The stages in their psychological development are represented by childhood, adolescence, and adulthood. The stages in athletes' psychosocial development are marked by changes in their sport-related network. The stages in their academic-vocational development consist of primary, secondary, and higher education and/or work.

4   Define career transitions and describe the major transitions for athletes.

Career transitions are turning phases or shifts in athletes' development associated with a set of specific demands that athletes have to cope with in order to continue successfully in sport and/or other spheres of their life. Athletes experience transitions in sport and other spheres of life; some of them are normative (e.g., athletic retirement or the transition to secondary school) and others are non-normative (e.g., injury).

5   Define career assistance.

The aim of career assistance is to prepare for and help athletes with various issues related to their careers in and outside of sport (e.g., transitions).

6   Describe major perspectives and types of career assistance interventions.

There are two major perspectives in career transition interventions: preventive/supportive (e.g., career planning, life development interventions) and crisis/negative consequences coping (e.g., crisis-coping educational and clinical interventions).

REVIEW QUESTIONS

1   Reflect on the similarities, differences and complementarity between descriptive and explanatory career models.

2   Reflect on the importance of the holistic lifespan perspective in career transition research.

3   Provide arguments for the importance of career assistance for athletes.

4   Define career assistance programs (CAPs). What are main target groups of the CAPs? What services do CAPs typically provide?

5   Is there a CAP in your country? If so, describe its content (e.g., use its website for information).

EXERCISES

1   Use the models and approaches described in this chapter to reflect on Martin's case as presented in the introduction to this chapter. What support services would you provide for each of the transitions faced by Martin?

2 Analyse your own career based on the developmental model of transitions faced by athletes. What were and what could be the normative and non-normative transitions that influence the development of your career?

ADDITIONAL READING

Stambulova, N. (2012). Working with athletes in career transitions. In S. Hanton & S. Mellalieu (Eds.), *Professional practice in sport psychology: A review* (pp.165–194). London, UK: Routledge.

Stambulova, N. & Ryba, T.V. (Eds.) (2013). *Athletes' careers across cultures*. London, UK: Routledge.

Wylleman, P. & Lavallee, D. (2004). A developmental perspective on transitions faced by athletes. In M. Weiss (Ed.), *Developmental sport and exercise psychology: A lifespan perspective* (pp.507–527). Morgantown, WV: Fitness Information Technology.

Wylleman, P. & Reints, A. (2010). A lifespan perspective on the career development of talented and elite athletes: Perspectives on high-intensity sports. *Scandinavian Journal of Medicine & Science in Sports, 20 (Suppl. 2)*, 101–107.

REFERENCES

Alfermann, D. & Stambulova, N. (2007). Career transitions and career termination. In G. Tenenbaum and R.C. Eklund (Eds.), *Handbook of sport psychology* (3rd edn, pp.712–736). New York: Wiley.

Alfermann, D., Stambulova, N. & Zemaityte, A. (2004). Reactions to sports career termination: A cross-national comparison of German, Lithuanian, and Russian athletes. *Psychology of Sport and Exercise, 5*, 61–75.

Bengtsson, M. (2011). *I skuggan av San Siro: Från proffsdröm till mardröm* [In the shadow of San Siro: From a professional dream to a nightmare]. Stockholm, Sweden: Norstedts.

Bruner, M.W., Munroe-Chandler, K.J. & Spink, K.S. (2008). Entry into elite sport: A preliminary investigation into the transition experiences of rookie athletes. *Journal of Applied Sport Psychology, 20*, 236–252.

Cecić Erpič, S., Wylleman, P. & Zupančič, M. (2004). The effect of athletic and non-athletic factors on the sports career termination process. *Psychology of Sport and Exercise, 5*, 45–60.

Elbe, A-M. & Beckmann, J. (2006). Motivational and self-regulatory factors and sport performance in young elite athletes. In D. Hackfort and G. Tenenbaum (Eds.), *Essential processes for attaining peak performance* (pp.137–157). Oxford: Meyer & Meyer Sport.

FEPSAC (1997). Position statement on sports career transitions. Downloaded from http://www.fepsac.com/activities/position_statements/

FEPSAC (1999). Position statement on sports career termination. Downloaded from http://www.fepsac.com/activities/position_statements/

Finn, J. & McKenna, J. (2010). Coping with academy-to-first-team transitions in elite English male team sports: The coaches' perspective. *International Journal of Sport Science and Coaching, 5*, 257–279.

Fraser, L. & Fogarty, G. (2011). An investigation of athletic identity, career choices and decision-making difficulties of Australian elite athletes. *Journal of Science and Medicine in Sport, 14S*, e84–e85.

Gordon, S., Lavallee, D. & Grove, J.R. (2005). Career assistance program interventions in sport. In D. Hackfort, J. Duda & R. Lidor (Eds.), *Handbook of research in applied sport and exercise psychology: International perspectives* (pp.233–244). Morgantown, WV: Fitness Information Technology.

Grove, J.R., Lavallee, D. & Gordon, S. (1997). Coping with retirement from sport: The influence of athletic identity. *Journal of Applied Sport Psychology, 9*, 191–203.

Jackson, S.A., Dover, J.D. & Mayocchi, L.M. (1998). Life after gold: Experiences of Australian Olympic gold-medalists, *The Sport Psychologist*, 12, 2, 119–136.

Lavallee, D. & Wylleman, P. (Eds.) (2000). *Career transitions in sport: International perspectives*. Morgantown, WV: Fitness Information Technology.

Lavallee, D., Gordon, S. & Grove, R. (1997). Retirement from sport and the loss of athletic identity. *Journal of Personal and Interpersonal Loss, 2*, 129–147.

Murphy, G.M., Petitpas, A.J. & Brewer, B.W. (1996). Identity foreclosure, athletic identity, and career maturity in intercollegiate athletes. *The Sport Psychologist*, 10, 239–246.

Petitpas, A.J., Brewer, B.W. & Van Raalte, J.L. (2009). Transitions of the student-athlete: Theoretical, empirical, and practical perspectives. In E.F. Etzel (Ed.), *Counseling and psychological services for college student-athletes* (pp.283–302). Morgantown, WV: Fitness Information Technology.

Pummel, B., Harwood, C. & Lavallee, D. (2008). Jumping to the next level: A qualitative examination of within career transition in adolescent event riders. *Psychology of Sport and Exercise, 9*, 427–447.

Reints, A. (2011). Validation of the holistic athletic career model and the identification of variables related to athletic retirement. (Doctoral dissertation). Vrije Universiteit Brussel, Belgium.

Salmela, J.H. (1994). Phases and transitions across sports career. In D. Hackfort (Ed.), *Psycho-social issues and interventions in elite sport* (pp.11–28). Frankfurt: Lang.

Schinke, R.J., Michel, G., Gauthier, A., Danielson, R., Peltier, D., Enosse, L., Pickard, P. & Pheasant, C. (2006). The adaptation to elite sport: A Canadian Aboriginal perspective. *The Sport Psychologist, 20*, 435–448.

Schlossberg, N.K. (1981). A model for analyzing human adaptation to transition. *The Counseling Psychologist, 9*(2), 2–18.

Schlossberg, N.K. (1984). *Counseling adults in transitions*. New York: Springer.

Sinclair, D.A. & Orlick, T. (1993). Positive terminations from high-performance sport. *The Sport Psychologist, 7*, 138–150.

Stambulova, N. (1994). Developmental sports career investigations in Russia: A post-perestroika analysis. *The Sport Psychologist, 8*, 221–237.

Stambulova, N. (2003). Symptoms of a crisis-transition: A grounded theory study. In N. Hassmén (Ed.), *SIPF Yearbook 2003* (pp.97–109). Örebro, Sweden: Örebro University Press.

Stambulova, N. (2010). Professional culture of career assistance to athletes: A look through contrasting lenses of career metaphors. In T.V. Ryba, R.J. Schinke & G. Tenenbaum (Eds.), *Cultural turn in sport psychology* (pp.285–314). Morgantown, WV: Fitness Information Technology.

Stambulova, N., Alfermann, D., Statler, T. & Côté, J. (2009). ISSP Position Stand: Career development and transitions of athletes. *International Journal of Sport & Exercise Psychology, 7*(4), 395–412.

Stambulova, N., Engström, C., Franck, A. & Linnér, L. (2012). Swedish athletes' transition and adaptation during the first year at national elite sport schools. In *Proceedings of the 27th Annual Conference of the Association for Applied Sport Psychology* (pp.133–134). Atlanta, GA.

Stambulova, N., Franck, A. & Weibull, F. (2012). Assessment of the transition from junior to senior sports in Swedish athletes. *International Journal of Sport & Exercise Psychology, 10* (2), 1–17.

Stambulova, N., Stephan, Y. & Järphag, U. (2007). Athletic retirement: A cross-national comparison of elite French and Swedish athletes. *Psychology of Sport and Exercise, 8*, 101–118.

Taylor, J. & Ogilvie, B.C. (1994). A conceptual model of adaptation to retirement among athletes. *Journal of Applied Sport Psychology, 6*, 1–20.

Taylor, J. & Ogilvie, B.C. (2001). Career termination among athletes. In R.N. Singer, H.A. Hausenblas & C.M. Janelle (Eds.), *Handbook of sport psychology* (2nd ed., pp.672–691). New York: Wiley.

Torregrosa, M., Boixadós, M., Valiente, L. & Cruz, J. (2004). Elite athletes' image of retirement: The way to relocation in sport. *Psychology of Sport and Exercise, 5*, 35–44.

Vanden Auweele, Y., De Martelaer, K., Rzewnicki, R., De Knop, P. & Wylleman, P. (2004). Parents and coaches: A help or harm? Affective outcomes for children in sport. In Y. Vanden Auweele (Ed.), *Ethics in youth sport* (pp.179–193). Leuven, Belgium: Lannoocampus.

Wylleman, P., Alfermann, D. & Lavallee, D. (2004). Career transitions in perspective. *Psychology of Sport and Exercise, 5*, 7–20.

Wylleman, P., Reints, A. & Van Aken, S. (2012). Athletes' perceptions of multilevel changes related to competing at the 2008 Beijing Olympic Games. *Psychology of Sport and Exercise, 13* (5), 687–692.

Wylleman, P., Theeboom, M. & Lavallee, D. (2004). Successful athletic careers. In C. Spielberger (Ed.), *Encyclopedia of applied psychology. Vol. 3* (pp.511–517). New York: Elsevier.

Chapter 40

Developing social and emotional skills

TARU LINTUNEN AND DANIEL GOULD

SUMMARY

In this chapter, we will introduce the concept of social and emotional competence, which is a product of *social and emotional learning* (SEL), in the context of sport and exercise. Socially and emotionally competent athletes and coaches are skilled in five interrelated sets of cognitive, affective, and behavioral competencies: *self-awareness, self-management, social awareness, relationship skills, and responsible decision making*. These competencies, in turn, should provide a foundation for better adjustment and performance as reflected in more positive social behaviors, less emotional distress, and improved success in sport and life. SEL programs also increase social and emotional development by establishing a safe and caring learning environment in which children and adults are actively engaged in sports. The topic of SEL is critical because most youth sport organizations have social-emotional development as one of their primary goals, and they use such terms as social-emotional growth or life skills training. Examples of SEL related life skills programs will also be introduced.

INTRODUCTION

In sport, emotions are ever present, even though we do not necessarily pay attention to how we express and/or manage them. For example, there are occasions when a coach has to deal with angry or upset parents. Some parents may want their child to play more and others may question the judgment of the coach. Another example is when a new member of a team arrives. How does it feel to come to the training session of a team for the first time and not know anyone there? Or how

does it feel to be "cut" from the team, learn that you cannot continue in your team any more, or that you are being transferred to another team?

We can start dealing with the circumstances that arise in these examples by analysing the feelings that these events evoke. Feelings contain a great deal of information and affect the way we behave. Harnessing the power of feelings promotes both group dynamics and coaching: unprocessed feelings ruminate in one's mind and hinder the functionality of a team or an individual. A great deal of potential is lost in sport due to lack of social and emotional skills in athletes and coaches of all ability levels.

Social and emotional skills need to be taught to coaches, teachers, sport instructors, and athletes through demonstration, modeling, discussions, reflections on one's experiences and practice. Mere sport and physical activity participation does not teach these skills (Danish & Hale, 1981; Gould & Carson, 2008). Even though physical education and most sport organizations set goals related to social and emotional skills, such as personal development, fair play and character education, coaches seldom seek to improve these skills by applying a specific method. They might be uncertain how to facilitate or teach these competencies in practice. For example, they do not always know how to resolve conflicts, how to approach parents or how to behave in a flexible way. Fortunately, several programs have been constructed for advancing social-emotional skills. Later in this chapter, we will introduce a theoretical SEL framework and programs that have been used successfully in sports.

OBJECTIVES

After reading this chapter you should be able to:

1   Define social and emotional learning and social and emotional skills.
2   Explain the relevance and effects of social and emotional learning in sport and exercise.
3   Consider sport and exercise experience as an opportunity to coach, learn and apply social and emotional skills.
4   Start practicing social and emotional skills in sport and exercise contexts.

UNDERSTANDING SOCIAL AND EMOTIONAL LEARNING

In order to improve interaction, performance and well-being in sports, it is essential that effective approaches are developed. One way to do this is to develop the social and emotional competence of coaches, teachers, parents, and athletes. In this chapter, we will introduce the concept of social and emotional competence, which is a product of *social and emotional learning* (SEL), in the context of sport and exercise.

SEL is a comprehensive approach to build competence, reduce risk factors, and foster protective mechanisms for positive youth adjustment and development. It is a process for helping children and adults develop life skills that are fundamental for life effectiveness. SEL teaches the skills we need to handle ourselves, our relationships, and our work effectively and ethically (Durlak, Weissberg, Dymnicki, Taylor, & Schellinger, 2011). These skills include recognizing and managing our emotions, setting and achieving positive goals, developing care and concern for others, establishing positive relationships, making responsible decisions, and handling challenging situations constructively and ethically (Elias et al. 1997). They are the skills that allow children to calm themselves when angry, make friends, resolve conflicts respectfully, work in groups, and make ethical and safe choices.

Social and emotional skills are part of life skills, which is a broader concept in the field of *positive youth development* (see Gould & Carson, 2008). Thus, all social and emotional skills are life skills, but not all life skills are social and emotional skills. Danish, Forneris, Hodge, and Heke (2004) define life skills as those skills that enable individuals to succeed in different environments in which they live, such as school, home, and in their neighborhoods. Life skills can be behavioral (communicating effectively with peers and adults) or cognitive (making effective decisions), social (being assertive) or emotional (being aware of emotions). Gould and Carson (2008) defined life skills as "those internal personal assets, characteristics and skills such as goal setting, emotional control, self-esteem, and hard work ethic that can be facilitated and developed in sport and are transferred for use in non-sport settings". According to these definitions, communication and social-emotional skills are central life skills. In a similar way, athletes defined social skills as the most important life skill (Jones & Lavallee, 2009) and outstanding coaches had well-established philosophies that placed primary importance on developing athletes socially (Collins, Gould, Lauer, & Chung, 2009). They also infused the development of life skills into all aspects of their coaching rather than just reserving a few minutes a day to work on them.

Social-emotional skills are of particular importance for sport leaders, coaches and teachers of physical education. Socially and emotionally competent behavior helps create a supportive learning atmosphere, positive experiences, and enjoyment, which are impor-tant goals – and means – in sport and physical education. It is important that participants have opportunities for positive experiences and enjoyment. This provides them with a good foundation for the practice of life-long exercise activity and good sports performance. In addition, sport and physical education classes are action-oriented and provide numerous opportunities for interaction and real-life situations that the coach can use to facilitate SEL (Lintunen & Kuusela, 2007). Both practical and professional experience supports the usefulness of taking advantage of relevant social-emotional skills in the sport context. The idea is that by facilitating awareness and providing coaches with skills in social-emotional learning, both the well-being of the coaches and their ability to create a safe and positive environment for learning increase. Similarly, modeling the behavior of the coach is also central for the social and emotional learning of athletes so coaches who develop good social-emotional competencies will have athletes who do so. In addition, coaches' own well-being depends on interpersonal dynamics and is constructed in the coach–athlete, coach–coach, and coach–parent interaction (see Soini, Pyhältö, and Pietarinen, 2010).

CORE SEL SKILLS

Social-emotional competence is multivariate, composed of skills and knowledge that are integrated across the emotional, cognitive, and behavioral domains of development (Domitrovich, Cortes and Greenberg, 2007). The proximal goals of SEL programs are to foster the development of five interrelated sets of cognitive, affective and behavioral competencies: *self-awareness*, *self-management, social awareness, relationship skills,* and *responsible decision making* (Collaborative for Academic, Social, and Emotional Learning, 2003, 2012; Zins & Elias, 2006) (Figure 40.1). In addition, Figure 40.1 shows the core skills of Gordon's theory of social interaction (2003), which links the different SEL competences with observable characteristics that can be taught (for example, listening skills, I-messages and conflict resolution and team building skills).

An inspection of Figure 40.1 reveals that SEL is comprised of five competencies (shown in the large inner circle). These include two intrapersonal competencies: self-management and self-awareness, and three interpersonal competencies: social awareness, relationship skills, and responsible decision making. The smaller circles on the outside of the larger circle of competencies represent examples of skills that are necessary for SEL to take place. These include the clear expression

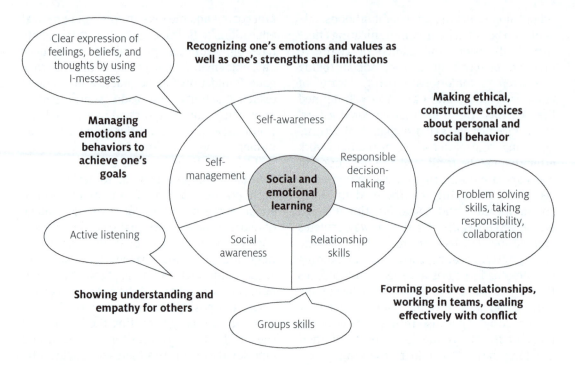

Figure 40.1 Core competences of social and emotional learning (Collaborative for Academic, Social, and Emotional Learning, 2003, 2012) in the center, and corresponding skills in the theory of Gordon (2003) in speech balloons. Adapted from Collaborative for Academic, Social, and Emotional Learning (2003, 2012) with permission.

of feelings, beliefs, and thoughts by using I-messages, active listening, group interaction skills, problem-solving skills, taking responsibility and collaboration. Finally, the end result of SEL includes such things as recognizing one's emotions as well as values, strengths and limitations, managing emotions and behaviors to achieve goals, showing understanding and empathy for others, working in teams and dealing effectively with conflict, and finally, making ethical and constructive choices about personal and social behavior. Keeping this overview in mind, skills for achieving each of the specific SEL competencies will now be discussed in more depth.

Self-awareness and self-management

Socially and emotionally competent athletes and coaches are self-aware. They are able to recognize their emotions, describe their interests and values, and accurately assess their strengths. They know their emotions, how to manage and regulate them (e.g., taking slow deep centering breaths to manage anxiety), and ways to express them constructively (e.g., squeezing a towel when frustrated in golf versus throwing one's club). This enables them to better handle stress, control impulses, and motivate themselves to persevere in overcoming obstacles to goal achievement (Martins, Ramalho, & Morin, 2010; Zeidner, Matthews, & Roberts, 2012). These abilities are thought to be important for social interaction because emotions serve communicative and social functions. Research has demonstrated that emotions drive attention, learning, and memory (LeDoux, 2012).

A somewhat parallel concept to the self-awareness, self-management, and social awareness aspects of SEL is *emotional intelligence*. Emotional intelligence encompasses the processing of emotional information: perceiving emotions, using emotions to facilitate thinking, understanding emotions and regulating and managing one's own emotions and the emotions of others (Mayer & Salovey, 1997; Salovey & Mayer, 1990). Emotional intelligence is a hierarchical concept. According to researchers, the management of emotions is challenging if the person cannot recognize or describe the reason for the emotion (Joseph and Newman, 2010). Emotion regulation is important for social interaction because it influences emotional expression and behavior directly. An inappropriate outburst of anger, for example, can destroy a coach–athlete relationship. Emotion regulation can operate through cognitive (e.g., thinking before acting), expressive (e.g., telling, drawing, dancing, or writing about feelings), behavioral (e.g., going running) and physiological (e.g., relaxation) processes. It is a domain in which, as with sport skills, practicing is essential for expert performance (Lopes, Salovey, Côté & Beers, 2005).

The theory of social interaction of Gordon (2003) and an intervention program based on the theory link the different SEL competences with observable characteristics that can be taught (Figure 40.1). For example, an I-message is a statement that describes the person's feelings, thoughts, values, wants, needs, and wishes. For example, common I-messages would include statements like "Missing these shots really frustrates me", "It is going to feel so good when I make it to the top of this hill", or "When Peter's dad questions my coaching he makes me really angry." Since I-messages only express the inner reality of the sender, they do not contain evaluations, judgments or interpretations of others (Adams, 1989). I-messages are important because it is easier to interact with other people if you are able to tell others how you feel without their having to guess what is going on in your mind. Making one's feelings and thoughts known to others

facilitates team-building (Rovio & al., 2012). At the same time, the person becomes visible to others. Expressing one's feelings in words clarifies and enhances interaction with others. Naming feelings also gives justification to them. For example, an athlete might say "I am afraid that this hard ball will hurt me when it hits my head." or "I really enjoyed being on your team." A coach might say "I am delighted that you collected all the clubs. It gives me more time to move to the next place." Expressing and naming one's feelings then is a good way to better understand your own emotions whether you are a coach or an athlete.

Social awareness

Social awareness means being able to take the perspective of others and empathize with them, recognizing and appreciating individual and group similarities and differences, and recognizing and using family, school, and community resources (Collaborative for Academic, Social, and Emotional Learning, 2003).

For example, active listening is a powerful way of communicating empathy. It is a basic skill in interaction and an essential aspect of orientation courses in counseling. It is a listening method in which the listener reflects back to the speaker his or her understanding of what the person has said (Ivey & Bradford Ivey, 2003, pp. 125–147; Weare, 2004, pp. 116–119). This is meant to confirm that the listener has understood the message and to give the speaker a chance to correct the listener if necessary. More important, however, is that active listening communicates the listener's acceptance of the speaker's thoughts and emotions. It helps the speaker recognize his or her feelings, thoughts, values, wants, and wishes.

Active listening is useful when another person has a problem. Active listening does not involve dispensing advice or making suggestions, and it is nonjudgmental. It requires that the listener makes the speaker believe that he is really listening to him and valuing him, and wants to understand what he has to say. Unfortunately, it is not always included in coach and athlete training programs, even though it might be of value in many of the social interaction occasions that arise in sport.

For instance, you can more effectively deal with an angry or upset parent by observing the following active listening guidelines: If the parent of a young athlete comes to you to complain about poor communication or unfair distribution of play time, focus on what he is saying and the feelings your actions have raised in him instead of defending yourself or making excuses. For example, Mr. Sorenson approaches Coach Frederick after the game and immediately starts shouting, "Why did you not play Caroline? No wonder we lost. All you ever do is play your favorites and I am getting sick of it." Coach Fredrick's first instinct is to scream back at Mr. Sorenson as he can't believe what he is being accused of. However, he catches himself and remembers what he learned about active listening. So Coach Fredrick calmly says "I understand that you are frustrated and upset about Caroline's lack of playing time and the fact we lost today." By having his feelings acknowledged Mr. Sorenson seems to calm down some and stops yelling. By actively listening to the upset parents, like Mr. Sorenson, and calming them down by reflecting and returning back to the issues you have heard and the feelings you have possibly identified in him, you will be able to start a discussion on the matter without emotional turmoil and without laying guilt trips on each other. This is a much better option than engaging in a shouting match with an upset parent.

Active listening is also an essential element of motivational interviewing, which is an evidence-based intervention strategy in the treatment of lifestyle problems like the sedentary lifestyle. Motivational interviewing is a form of collaborative conversation for strengthening a person's own motivation and commitment to change. It is designed to strengthen an individual's motivation for and movement toward a specific goal by eliciting and exploring the person's own reasons for change within an atmosphere of acceptance and compassion. The overall goal of motivational interviewing is to increase the client's intrinsic motivation and autonomy so that change arises from within rather than being imposed from without (Miller & Rollnick, 2002). For example, Ursella, a fitness instructor, might refrain from bluntly telling a sedentary client how to exercise more. Instead, she motivationally interviews him asking a series of questions about the barriers that prevent him from exercising and then what possible solutions he could use to overcome the barriers. They then work together to derive specific plans for a more active lifestyle; plans that the client owns and is more motivated to adhere to because he helped formulate them.

A systematic review and meta-analysis of randomized controlled trial experiments showed that motivational interviewing outperforms traditional advice giving in the treatment of a broad range of behavioral problems and diseases (Rubak, Sandbæk, Lauritzen, & Christensen, 2005). Similar results have been found in interventions promoting physical activity (Harland et al. 1999; Rasinaho, Hirvensalo, Törmäkangas, Leinonen, Lintunen, & Rantanen, 2011). Coaches and physical educators should employ motivational interview if their goal is long-term behavioral change.

Relationship skills

Relationship skills deal with establishing and maintaining healthy and rewarding relationships based on cooperation, resisting inappropriate social pressure, and on preventing, managing, and resolving interpersonal conflict and seeking help when needed (Collaborative for Academic, Social, and Emotional Learning, 2003).

In the theory of Gordon (2003), the tools for *relationship skills* include positive and confrontation I-messages, mediating skills, and avoidance of roadblocks. Positive and confrontation I-messages are used to give effective feedback.

Basically these consist of three parts: (1) a description of the athlete's behavior; (2) the coach's feeling about this behavior; and (3) the tangible effect of the athlete's behavior on the coach. An example of a triple-barreled confrontation I-message is "I am disturbed by your wandering around during the practice, which is why I cannot concentrate on coaching". No advice is given how the person should behave (because they know how they should behave) but the athlete's behavior is explained as well as the coach's feelings and the effects of those behaviors.

What is so interesting about confrontational I-messages, is that when a person (the athlete in this example) hears what problems his behavior has created for his coach, he often has a genuine feeling of guilt, which raises empathy, instills in him a feeling of responsibility for what he has caused to another person and a will to correct the situation. He can then be given the opportunity to realize himself how he can make his behavior more constructive. He is not given instructions on how to change his behavior. He does it himself. While confrontational I-messaging may not always work (e.g., some athletes may not feel guilt in above example) it has been shown to work in many different situations because the recipient takes responsibility for his own behavior. Thus, it is a good noninvasive strategy to use in instructional settings.

Messages that are experienced as damaging fruitful interaction, for example, judging, praising or mockery, are called the roadblocks of communication (Gordon, 2003). Roadblocks are common responses that get in the way of good listening. They tend to label an individual by generalizing his occasional behavior as part of his personality. "You are lazy, because you have not done your assignments" is a typical roadblock. Whenever possible physical educators, coaches and fitness trainers should avoid these types of messages.

Teamwork is a crucial relationship skill. Team climate develops from how participants perceive the relationships among group members (Weinberg & Gould, 2011, p. 167). The relationship skills of groups and teams can be promoted through team building (TB) methods. Development of a well-functioning team has been one of the core interests in sport settings. The purpose of TB is to promote and enhance the effectiveness of a group (Carron, Eys, & Burke, 2007). Such enhancement can be made through task-oriented (e.g., goal-setting, role clarification) or through group or relationship-oriented (e.g., interpersonal-relation schemes, problem solving) approaches (Rovio, Arvinen-Barrow, Weigand, Eskola, & Lintunen, 2010). TB is a longitudinal, planned and structured on-going dynamic process of learning which requires close mutual and continuous participation from all parties involved (Yukelson, 1997).

The most commonly used approaches to team building include setting team goals (i.e. the process of establishing specific, measurable, and time-targeted objectives), role clarification (i.e. specifying the distribution of work by discussing and negotiating roles that are necessary for a team to accomplish a task – who will shoot and pass in basketball), development of interpersonal relations (i.e. exertion of power, communication or cooperation in a team), and problem solving (i.e. defining problems affecting team functioning and finding solutions to them) (for a review of TB methods see Rovio et al., 2010).

With regards to goal setting, there is an abundance of research that investigates goal setting within an individual sport context, but research on team sports is limited (Rovio, Eskola, Gould, & Lintunen, 2009). At group level goal setting has been suggested to enhance collaboration and communication (Weldon & Weingart, 1993). Group norms are a vital part of setting group goals (Rovio et al., 2012). Group goals that are created by the players are similar to norms or rules governing expected player behavior. First, intermediate goals or rules include norms for behavior concerning training and playing, for example, "giving one's best." Second, the goals involve norms of behavior concerning the creation of a supportive environment, for example "equality," "taking others into consideration," and "support". Rules need to be established within the group. Working rules (e.g., "Do not make derogatory remarks towards other children.") guide the behavior of the group members and create an atmosphere of psychological safety, which is a starting point for an individual's active group behavior. Individual goals lose their meaning if there are problems in the group's process, such as in collaboration, interaction, decision making, or in group relationships (for example, power/status or emotional relationships). Establishing group norms as a part of team goal-setting approach has the combined benefits of promoting group harmony and cohesion, as well as supporting the achievement of the team's primary task objectives. In the next example problems of group relationships in an ice hockey team were solved with establishment of team norms:

> We divided the players into four small groups. One of the groups consisted of more dominant players who also played for the national team, and another group consisted of the so-called "quiet" players. The groups were discussing a topic: "Are all players equal." By dividing the groups by player characters, we managed to get the more dominant players to think about how the less dominant and more quiet players interact and behave in a group, as well as allowing the more "quiet" players to have a chance to have a voice and behave in a group in their preferred way. The conversations were very open and facilitated togetherness and belonging.
>
> (Rovio et al., 2012).

The players in the study highlighted the importance of developing positive team norms regarding behavior and work commitment. They helped to achieve the long-term outcome goals set by the team.

Furthermore, research on role clarity is currently in its infancy. Some evidence exists that supports the theory that positive role perceptions have a positive influence on group cohesion, individual satisfaction, and efficacy (Eys, Schinke, & Jeffery, 2007). The intention of the interpersonal relations approach of team building is to develop interpersonal relations within a group or a team, and this is achieved by placing emphasis on the atmosphere and style of functioning of the group/team in question (Salas, Rozell, Mullen, & Driskell, 1999). The issues addressed may include various interpersonal-relation schemes (e.g., team/group role, norm, power, communication, and emotional relations), exertion of power, obstacles to cooperation, interpersonal competition, communication processes (i.e. listening, sending and receiving messages), and possible resistance to the group/team processes. The main focus of the interpersonal relations approach is to emphasize teamwork through effective communication, by providing mutual support, and sharing emotions. This can be achieved by using the SEL skills described above. This approach relies on the assumption that a team with well-developed interpersonal relations is an effective team. Such a team is characterized by open communication, good cooperation skills, and greater readiness to find solutions to possible problems (Rovio et al., 2010).

Cooperative skills are especially important for participants to learn and most likely result when members of a group, class or team share common goals, respect one another, and are rewarded for their joint actions versus individual performance. Research also shows that cooperation is learned and that it is also influenced by the structure of the class or game and the goals and approach emphasized by teachers and coaches (Orlick, 1978; Weinberg & Gould, 2011).

The problem-solving approach of team building aims to identify and define possible crucial problems affecting group functioning, attempting to find solutions to them. After identifying and defining problems and different needs, the group is able to draw plans of action, implement, and evaluate the success of such actions (Gordon, 2003; Tannenbaum, Beard, & Salas, 1992). Acquiring good problem-solving skills can improve group/team effectiveness, and in comparison to other team building methods, teams with good problem-solving skills are more likely to be able to handle its problems more independently as a group without external assistance or influence. In addition, while rehearsing and learning systematic problem-solving methods, the group processes are already directly influenced, and thereby improved during the actual learning process.

Despite the suggestions on applicable team-building approaches to sport usually only one or two TB methods have been used simultaneously. Exploring the effect of one single TB method, instead of adopting a multifaceted approach, is problematic because of the nature of TB process. As TB is a multivariate treatment process, it should therefore be promoted and studied as a multivariate issue (Dunn & Holt, 2003; Rovio et al., 2010).

Responsible decision making

The final part of the SEL model is *responsible decision making*: making decisions based on consideration of ethical standards, safety concerns, appropriate social norms, respect for others, and likely consequences of various actions; applying decision-making skills to sport situations; contributing to the well-being of one's community (Collaborative for Academic, Social, and Emotional Learning, 2003). Sport, physical activity and physical education have long been considered suitable contexts for teaching responsible decision making and the advancement of positive moral development – development of character. However, numerous media accounts also highlight the poor decision making, lack of character formation and bullying behavior that all too often occur in sport. This certainly suggests that mere sport participation does not result in SEL relative to responsible and ethical decision making. Experts in social emotional growth have concluded that athletes and coaches need to be taught values about taking responsibility for themselves and others (Hellison, 2010).

Values are central in responsible decision making. They are learned through modeling and identification in childhood (Gordon, 2003). In youth, values are also learned through reflection where young people talk about and discuss their experience and actions. There are two main approaches to values education (Veugelers, 2000). First, values education can be seen as transmitting values that often come from social rules or cultural norms. So a physical educator tells her class why it is important not to bully other children or a coach tells his athletes about the importance of teamwork. A value education approach seeks to strengthen the transfer of values in education by means of conveying rules and developing a certain moral climate. Second, according to the critical thinking approach values education can be seen as a type of dialogue where people are gradually brought to their own realization of what is good behavior for themselves and their community (Veugelers, 2000). Critical thinking aims to develop a reflection on values and a value development by means of analysing and comparing opinions. For instance, research on moral development (the process by which young people learn how to decide what it right or wrong) in sport has shown that young people better improve their moral reasoning when teachers and coaches engage in discussions with them about moral issues (e.g., ask participants why is it wrong to run up the score on the other team or steal equipment) (Bredemier & Shields, 1995).

According to Gordon (2003), you cannot force others to adopt your values. You can only be a model of your values and arrange opportunities for dialogue and reflection of values. For example, athletes and coaches can discuss how they understand the words: justice, honesty, human dignity, responsibility, care, and concern in sport.

TEACHING SOCIAL AND EMOTIONAL SKILLS

Those involved in sport programming have long been interested in understanding how to maximize the learning of social and emotional skills in sport participants, particularly children and youth. Researchers have also begun to study the area, examining the benefits and detriments of participation (e.g., Dworkin, Larson, & Hansen, 2003; Hansen, Larson, & Dworkin, 2003), the efficacy of interventions designed to teach social and emotional competences (e.g., Weiss, 2006) and the process by which coaches learn and teach life skills (Gould, Collins, Lauer & Chung, 2006).

A meta-analysis of research in the school environment concluded that programs which concentrate on social and emotional competencies can result in gains that are central to the goals of all schools. The gains include improved atmosphere, more effective learning, better behavior, and higher motivation (Durlak, Weissberg, Dymnicki, Taylor, & Schellinger, 2011). These studies suggest that the most effective programs teach both emotional and social competencies explicitly and focus on the whole learning environment. Similar results can also be expected in the sport environment. Providing athletes with social and emotional learning programs that are characterized by safe, caring, and well-managed learning environments and instruction in social and emotional skills addresses many barriers in sport through enhancing attachment and participation, reducing risky behaviors and promoting positive development. Communication skills can be taught but are easily forgotten if not maintained in every-day practice. For example, after participating in the teacher effectiveness training teachers learned to use significantly more active listening, confrontation I-messages and messages supporting autonomy (Talvio et al., 2012).

The studies that have examined the outcomes of using and learning social and emotional skills in sport and physical education contexts have resulted in increases in social responsibility, goal knowledge, and social interests (Brunelle et al., 2007) and enhanced knowledge about life skills (Danish & Nellen, 1997; Goudas & Giannoudis, 2008). In addition, life skills training has resulted in an improvement in sport skills, denoting that when life skills training is appropriately embedded in sport or physical education training, learning does not take place at the expense of learning sport skills (Gould & Carson, 2008).

Three sets of conditions have been associated with *positive youth development* through out-of-school activities. These include: (1) the context – an appropriate psychologically and physically safe environment; (2) external resources surrounding young people with a positive community and caring mentors; and (3) internal assets learning skills that are important for managing life situations (Weiss, 2006). It has also been shown that coaches who were recognized as effective at teaching desirable emotional and social skills are characterized by four areas of competence: (1) having a well-developed coaching philosophy that places primary importance on developing life skills; (2) excellent coach–athlete relationship skills; (3) specific social and emotional skill teaching strategies; and (4) the ability to be aware of context specific conditions that influence life skills development. Specific strategies for teaching desirable social and emotional skills include both direct methods like reinforcement and instruction and indirect methods like creating motivational climate by emphasizing certain goals and exposing young people to peer models. Evidence shows, however, that life skills strategies are not viewed as separate and distinct coaching activities by coaches but are infused into their general coaching strategies (Gould et al., 2006). Most interesting is the recent theorizing on how coaching and mentoring youth involves balancing efforts to structure and lead youth while also allowing youth opportunities to make some meaningful decisions and choices on their own (Larson, 2006).

In summary, physical educators, fitness instructors and coaches can facilitate social emotional learning by employing a number of strategies on a regular basis. These include:

- Making SEL a priority and also making intentional and consistent efforts to create environments that are conducive to SEL. This involves intentional efforts to teach skills that underlie social-emotional competencies.
- Becoming more aware of their own and others' emotions by using and teaching good communication techniques like I-messaging, active listening and motivational interviewing.
- Enhancing relationship skills by using confronting I-messaging to give feedback, avoiding the use of communication roadblocks such as judging and mockery, using team building strategies such as role clarification, establishing group or team goals, group or team norms and problem solving.
- Facilitating responsible decision making through values education and by enhancing critical thinking through discussions.
- Adopting formal SEL programs like SUPER or Teaching Personal and Social Responsibility (see below).

EXAMPLES OF PROGRAMS FOR TEACHING SOCIAL AND EMOTIONAL SKILLS

Reading books is not the most effective way to learn social and emotional skills. Like motor skills, they must be practiced. Learner-centered, dialogical and action-oriented teaching and learning methods are essential. Examples of evidence-based social and emotional learning programs can be found on two publications of CASEL (Collaborative for Academic, Social, and Emotional Learning, 2003, 2012). CASEL (http://www.casel.org) is an organization that works to advance the science and evidence-based practice of social and emotional learning.

In addition, Gordon Training International (http://www.gordontraining.com/) provides useful resources. Gordon's Teacher Effectiveness Training (TET) is a four-day training program that offers teachers and coaches communication and conflict resolution skills. I-messages, active listening, and conflict resolution methods are taught in the course (Gordon, 2003). The course has also been adapted to young participants, is available in several languages, and has been used in physical education (see Lintunen and Kuusela, 2007).

Sports related programs are provided, for example, by Life Skills Center in Virginia Commonwealth University. SUPER (Sports United to Promote Education and Recreation) is a character-building, sports-based life skills program. SUPER is comprised of a series of 18 modules developed to be taught like sports clinics where participants are involved in three sets of activities: learning the physical skills related to a specific sport, learning life skills related to sports in general, and playing sport (http://www.lifeskills.vcu.edu/super.html; Danish, 2002).

Another approach used in sport context is *Teaching Personal and Social Responsibility* model (TPSR) which was developed to help students learn to be responsible by giving them increasing amounts of responsibility and by carefully shifting a significant portion of decision-making responsibilities to them (Hellison, 2010). The model promotes self and social responsibility by empowering students to take more responsibility for their actions and lives and by teaching them to be concerned about the rights, feelings, and needs of others. The TPSR model's levels can be described as moving from irresponsibility to responsibility, moving from respect for oneself to respect and concern for others. These behaviors would be first developed within the physical education class or sports setting and then used outside of the gym, in the home and community settings. The TPSR Alliance is the center for these activities (http://www.tpsr-alliance.org/).

Different SEL-related programs target different social and emotional skills. Accord-ing to our experience coaches, teachers, and parents who participate in one course and learn useful skills often want to get more training and learn more useful tools for social interaction. Then social and emotional learn-ing becomes an assignment for the rest of the individual's life.

CONCLUSION

To sum up, in this chapter we introduced the concept of SEL and discussed how Gordon's social emotional learning core competencies model can be used to help facilitate the devel-opment of young people in sport and physical activity contexts. While this is a relatively new area of research in sport and exercise, where more work is needed to define the field and to develop further sport specific applications, the initial work has much to offer practitioners. Both individual and group level applications can greatly facilitate efforts to enhance social-emotional competencies like responsibility, empathy, and teamwork in young people. It is an area that we cannot ignore.

LEARNING AIDS

1   What are the five key competences of SEL?

   The five key social and emotional competences are self-awareness, self-management, social awareness, relationship skills, and responsible decision making.

2   Identify different sport and exercise-related emotion management processes.

   Emotion regulation or emotion management can operate through cognitive, expressive, behavioral and physiological processes. It is a domain in which practicing is essential for expert performance.

3   Which of the key SEL competences are more individual-level and which are more social level characteristics?

   Self-management and self-awareness belong to the intrapersonal or individual level, and social awareness, relationship skills, and responsible decision making to the interpersonal level of competences.

REVIEW QUESTIONS

1   Why is SEL important in sport and exercise context?

2   Why are roadblocks harmful for communication?

3   How can sport build responsibility?

EXERCISES

1   Practice positive I-messages and active listening:

  a) Send or tell five positive I-messages to your friends, team mates, or coaches.

  b) When someone tells you that he or she has a problem, listen carefully, and return the message (facts and feelings) back to the sender with your own words. Do this with at least two different people. Write a reflective learning log where you describe experiences and feelings of your own and the reactions of the persons with whom you interacted.

2   Go to the website of Teaching Personal and Social Responsibility Alliance (http://www.tpsr-alliance. org/). Identify the five steps of the TPSR model and indicate how you would help a group or a team to develop from irresponsibility to a higher level of responsibility.

ADDITIONAL READING

Lintunen, T. & Kuusela, M. (2007). Social and emotional learning in physical education. In J. Liukkonen, Y. Vanden Auweele, W. Vereijken, D. Alfermann & Y. Theodorakis. (Eds.), *Psychology for physical educators* (pp.75–83). Champaign, IL: Human Kinetics.

REFERENCES

Adams, L. (1989). *Be your best.* New York: The Putnam Publishing Group.

Bredemeier, B. & Shields, D. (1995). Moral development and children's sport. In F. Smoll & R. Smith (Eds.), *Children and youth in sport: A biopsychosocial perspective* (pp.381–401). Indianapolis: Brown & Benchmark.

Brunelle, J., Danish, S. & Forneris, T. (2007). The impact of a sport-based life skill program on adolescent prosocial values. *Journal of Applied Developmental Science, 11* (2), 43–55.

Carron, A.V., Eys, M.A. & Burke, S.M. (2007). Team cohesion. In S. Jowett & D. Lavallee (Eds.), *Social psychology in sport* (pp.91–102). Champaign, IL: Human Kinetics.

Collaborative for Academic, Social, and Emotional Learning. (2003). *Safe and sound: An educational leader's guide to evidence-based social and emotional learning programs.* Chicago, IL: Author.

Collaborative for Academic, Social, and Emotional Learning. (2012). *2013 CASEL GUIDE: Effective social and emotional learning programs preschool and elementary school edition.* Chicago, IL: Author.

Collins, K., Gould, D., Lauer, L. & Chung, Y. (2009). Coaching life skills through football: Philosophical beliefs of outstanding high school football coaches. *International Journal of Coaching Science, 3,* 29–54.

Danish, S.J. (2002). *SUPER (Sports United to Promote Education and Recreation) program: Leader manual and student activity book* (3rd ed.). Richmond: Virginia Commonwealth University, Life Skills Center.

Danish, S.J., Forneris, T., Hodge, K. & Heke, I. (2004). Enhancing youth development through sport. *World Leisure, 46* (3), 38–49.

Danish, S. & Nellen, V. (1997). New roles for sport psychologists: Teaching life skills through sport to at-risk youth. *Quest, 49* (1), 100–113.

Danish, S.J. & Hale, B.D. (1981). Toward an understanding of the practice of sport psychology. *Journal of Sport Psychology, 3,* 90–99.

Domitrovich, C.E., Cortes, R.E. & Greenberg, M.T. (2007). Improving young children's social and emotional competence: A randomized trial of the preschool "PATHS" curriculum. *The Journal of Primary Prevention*, Vol. 28, No. 2, March 2007. DOI: 10.1007/s10935-007-0081-0

Dunn, J.G.H. & Holt, N.L. (2003). Collegiate ice hockey players' perceptions of the delivery of an applied sport psychology program. *The Sport Psychologist, 17,* 351–368.

Durlak, J.A., Weissberg, R.P., Dymnicki, A.B., Taylor, R.D. & Schellinger, K.B. (2011). The impact of enhancing students' social and emotional learning: A Meta-Analysis of School-Based universal interventions. *Child Development, 82*(1), 405–432.

Dworkin, J.B., Larson, R. & Hansen, D. (2003). Adolescents' accounts of growth experiences in youth activities. *Journal of Youth and Adolescents,* 32(1), 17–26.

Elias, M.J., Zins, J.E., Weissberg, T.P., Frey, K.S., Greenberg, M.T., Haynes, N.M., Kessler, R., Schwab-Stone, M.E. & Shriver, T.P. (1997). *Promoting social and emotional learning: Guidelines for educators.* Alexandria, VA: Association for Supervision and Curriculum Development.

Eys, M.A., Schinke, R.J. & Jeffery, S. (2007). Role perceptions in sport groups. In M. Beauchamp & M. Eys (Eds.), *Group dynamics advances in sport and exercise psychology: Contemporary themes* (pp.99–116). Oxford: Routledge.

Gordon, T. (2003). Teacher effectiveness training: The program proven to help teachers bring out the best in students of all ages. New York: Three Rivers Press.

Goudas, M. & Giannoudis, G. (2008). A team-sports-based life-skills program in a physical education context. *Learning and Instruction, 18,* 528–536.

Gould, D. & Carson, S. (2008). Life skills development through sport: Current status and future directions. *Sport and Exercise Psychology Review, 1,* 58–78.

Gould, D., Collins, K., Lauer, L. & Chung, Y. (2006). Coaching life skills: A working model. *Sport and Exercise Psychology Review,* 2(1), 10–18.

Hansen, D.M., Larson, R.W. & Dworkin, J.B. (2003). What adolescents learn in organized youth activities: A survey of self-reported developmental experiences. *Journal of Research on Adolescence, 13*(1), 25–55.

Harland, J., White, M., Drinkwater, C., Chinn, D., Farr, L. & Howel, D. (1999). The Newcastle exercise project: A randomised controlled trial of methods to promote physical activity in primary care. *British Medical Journal, 319,* 828–832.

Hellison, D. (2010). *Teaching personal and social responsibility* (3rd ed.). Champaign, IL: Human Kinetics.

Ivey, A.E., Bradford Ivey, M. & Zalaquett, C.P. (2009). *Intentional interviewing and counselling: Facilitating client development in a multicultural society* (7th ed.). Belmont, CA: Cengage Learning.

Jones, M.I. & Lavallee, D. (2009). Exploring the life skills needs of adolescent athletes. *Psychology of Sport and Exercise, 10,* 159–167.

Joseph, D.L. & Newman, D.A. (2010). Emotional intelligence: An integrative meta-analysis and cascading model. *Journal of Applied Psychology, 95,* 54–78.

Larson, R. (2006). Positive youth development, willful adolescents, and mentoring. *The Journal of Community Psychology, 34,* 677–689.

LeDoux, J. (2012). Rethinking the emotional brain. *Neuron, 73*(4), 653–676. DOI: 10.1016/j.neuron.2012.02.004 .

Lintunen, T. & Kuusela, M. (2007). Social and emotional learning in physical education. In J. Liukkonen, Y. Vanden Auweele, W. Vereijken, D. Alfermann & Y. Theodorakis. (Eds.), *Psychology for Physical Educators* (pp.75–83). Champaign, IL: Human Kinetics.

Lopes, P.N., Salovey, P., Côté, S. & Beers, M. (2005). Emotion regulation abilities and the quality of social interaction. *Emotion, 5,* 113–118.

Martins, A., Ramalho, N. & Morin, E. (2010). A comprehensive meta-analysis of the relationship between emotional intelligence and health. *Personality and Individual Differences, 49,* 554–564.

Mayer, J.D. & Salovey, P. (1997). What is emotional intelligence? In P. Salovey & D.J. Sluyter (Eds.), *Emotional development and emotional intelligence: Implications for educators* (pp.3–31). New York: Basic Books.

Miller, W.R. & Rollnick, S. (2002). *Motivational interviewing: Preparing people for change.* New York: Guilford Press.

Orlick, T. (1978). *The cooperative sports and games book.* New York: Pantheon.

Rasinaho, M., Hirvensalo, M., Törmäkangas, T., Leinonen, R., Lintunen, T. & Rantanen, T. (2011). Effect of physical activity counseling on physical activity of older people in Finland (ISRCTN 07330512). *Health Promotion International* 27, 463–474. doi:10.1093/heapro/dar057.

Rovio, E., Arvinen-Barrow, M., Weigand, D.A., Eskola, J. & Lintunen, T. (2010). Team building in sport: A narrative review of the program effectiveness, current methods, and theoretical underpinnings. *Athletic Insight: The Online Journal of Sport Psychology* 2(2), 147–164. http://www.athleticinsight.com/.

Rovio, E., Arvinen-Barrow, M., Weigand, D.A., Eskola, J. & Lintunen, T. (2012). Using team building methods with an ice hockey team: An action research case study. *The Sport Psychologist*, 26, 4, 584–603.

Rovio, E., Eskola, J., Gould, D. & Lintunen, T. (2009). Linking theory to practice – Lessons learned in setting specific goals in a junior ice hockey team. *Athletic Insight*, 11, 2, 21–38.

Rubak, S., Sandboek, A., Lauritzen, T. & Christensen, B. (2005). Motivational interviewing: A systematic review and meta-analysis. *British Journal of General Practice*, 55, 305–312.

Salas, E., Rozell, D., Mullen, B. & Driskell, J.E. (1999). The effect of team building on performance. *Small Group Research*, 30, 309–329.

Salovey, P. & Mayer, J.D. (1990). Emotional intelligence. *Imagination, Cognition, and Personality*, 9, 185–211.

Soini, T., Pyhältö, K. & Pietarinen, J. (2010). Pedagogical well-being: Reflecting, learning and well-being in teachers' work. *Teachers & Teaching*, 16 (6): 735–751.

Talvio, M., Lonka, K., Komulainen, E., Kuusela, M. & Lintunen, T. (2012). The development of the Dealing with Challenging Interaction (DCI) method to evaluate teachers' social interaction skills. *Procedia – Social and Behavioral Sciences*, 69, 24, 621–630. doi:http://dx.doi.org/10.1016/j.sbspro.2012.11.454.

Tannenbaum, S.I., Beard, R.L. and Salas, E. (1992). Team building and its influence on team effectiveness: An examination of conceptual and empirical developments. In K. Kelley (Ed.), *Issues, theory, and research in industrial/organizational psychology* (pp.117–153). Amsterdam: Elsevier.

Veugelers, W. (2000). Different ways of teaching values. *Educational Review*, 52 (1), 37–46.

Weare, K. (2004). *Developing the emotionally literate school*. London: Sage Publications.

Weinberg, R.S. & Gould, D. (2011). Foundations of sport and exercise psychology (5th ed.). Champaign, IL: Human Kinetics.

Weiss, M.R. (2006). The First Tee 2005 research summary: Longitudinal effects of the First Tee Life Skills Education Program on positive youth development. St. Augustine, FL: The First Tee.

Weldon, E. & Weingart, L.R. (1993). Group goals and group performance. *British Journal of Social Psychology*, 32, 307–334.

Yukelson, D. (1997). Principles of effective team building interventions in sport: A direct services approach at Penn State University. *Journal of Applied Sport Psychology*, 9, 73–96.

Zeidner, M., Matthews, G. & Roberts, R.D. (2012). The emotional intelligence, health, and well-being nexus: What have we learned and what have we missed? *Applied Psychology: Health and Well-Being*, 4, 1–30. doi:10.1111/j.1758-0854.2011.01062.x

Zins, J.E. & Elias, M.J. (2006). Social and emotional learning. In G.G. Bear & K.M. Minke (Eds.), *Children's needs III: Development, prevention, and intervention* (pp.1–13). Bethesda, MD: National Association of School Psychologists.

Chapter 41

Promoting morality and character development

DAVID LIGHT SHIELDS AND BRENDA LIGHT BREDEMEIER

SUMMARY

Sport is a moral activity, and it encourages and displays dimensions of participants' character. In this chapter, we introduce key theory and research on moral reasoning and action in sports, and elaborate on dimensions of personal character as they relate to sport experience. The purpose, however, is not to provide an exhaustive review of the literature. Excellent reviews are available elsewhere (e.g., Kavussanu, 2007, 2008; Shields & Bredemeier, 2007, 2008; Weiss, Smith, & Stuntz, 2008). Our aim is to identify key themes and draw from findings to provide practical guidance for those who want to support the ethical quality of the sport experience. Thus, in this chapter, practical strategies for promoting moral development, moral action, and positive character are identified and elaborated.

INTRODUCTION

Issues of fairness, respect, and responsibility color the fabric of sports as much as dye colors garments. Sports provide participants with opportunities for heroic displays of moral courage, and contemptuous displays of moral corruption. Thirty years ago, there was very little theoretical, empirical, or applied work on morality or character in the context of sport. Today, the situation has changed dramatically. The last decades have seen a burgeoning of work in this area. Our understandings of the influence of sport on character development and the complex processes of moral functioning in sport have grown exponentially.

Amidst that complexity, a few simple ideas stand out. First, there is nothing automatic

about sports building character. There is nothing inherent in the physical performance of sports that facilitates character growth. It is the human element – the relationships with teammates, opponents, officials, coaches, fans – that carries moral significance. In short, it is the character of the interpersonal relationships that influences the character of the participants.

A second idea is that the moral significance of sports is not predetermined. The moral quality of the sport experience is not fixed by the rule-structure of the game; it is not a simple by-product of the competitive context; nor is it controlled by any other externality. All those who participate in sports make choices about which values, which ethical norms, they will put into action. Importantly, these are not often fully conscious, thought-out decisions. But they are choices nonetheless.

A third simple, yet important, idea is that leadership matters. Leaders cannot dictate the moral character of those under their charge, but they do have influence. Coaches, for example, cannot force an athlete to believe in the importance of fairness; nonetheless, they can inspire high ideals. They can nurture a climate of mutual respect. They can model, encourage, and articulate moral norms that become cornerstones of team culture.

In this chapter, these fundamental ideas will be elaborated, the research on which they are based will be briefly summarized, and practical guidance for leaders will be offered.

 ## OBJECTIVES

After reading this chapter, you should be able to:

1   Identify key dimensions of morality and character that relate to sport.
2   Implement strategies for promoting more adequate forms of moral reasoning in sport.
3   Understand how to support moral action in sport.
4   Understand and promote growth in multiple dimensions of character.
5   Distinguish between genuine competition and degenerated forms of contesting.

MORALITY AND CHARACTER IN SPORT

We have organized this section of the chapter into four main headings. In the first, promoting moral development, we identify key theoretical constructs undergirding the concept of moral development. We then share strategies for promoting moral reasoning development. Second, we turn to moral action. The sports literature is rich with empirical data on moral functioning, which includes many processes in addition to moral reasoning. Some processes work to optimize moral functioning, others to disrupt it. In the third section, we focus on character development. Character is a complex construct, and we identify multiple dimensions of character concluding, again, with practical suggestions. Finally, we address the theme of promoting genuine competition. This section serves as both a summary and extension of the preceding sections.

PROMOTING MORAL DEVELOPMENT

What makes an action moral? Is an athlete acting morally when she admits to a referee that she committed a foul? Is helping an injured opponent moral? At first blush, these appear to reflect norms of honesty and altruism which most people consider moral virtues. Yet these actions might arise from less honorable motives. A person might confess an infraction to the referee, for example, to try to curry favor. An athlete might help an opponent in distress simply to enhance his reputation. When it comes to morality, motives matter. Reasons matter. Morality involves doing the right thing for the right reasons (Blasi, 1990).

If morality is tied to reasoning, then it is a developmental process. Babies have very primitive forms of reasoning, toddlers somewhat less so. As the child matures, more adequate forms of reasoning replace less adequate forms. Imagine, for example, that you interview three youths of unspecified age. You ask them, "When you are competing, is it OK to cheat if you won't get caught?" Here are their answers:

- Youth 1: No. If you cheat, others might cheat too. So it doesn't really help you.
- Youth 2: No. Cheating is wrong. Good people don't cheat.
- Youth 3: No. Cheating violates the idea of fairness which is at the very heart of the contest. When you enter the game, you make an implicit promise to abide by the rules.

You may notice that each response is more adequate than the preceding one. Youth 1 only thinks about the situation from a self-interested perspective. Youth 2 expands the range of concerns to include social perceptions based on idealized notions of good people. The third youth extends the range of concerns still further by incorporating ideas of fairness and moral principle. As people mature, their thinking about moral issues becomes more comprehensive, integrated, and complex.

Moral development theory

The central premise of moral development theory is that people gradually become aware of a broader range of moral concerns, and they are able to coordinate them within more sophisticated patterns of thinking. Though theorists differ in their characterizations of this developmental process, the basic idea that moral thinking becomes more adequate with age and experience is widely shared. Within the sport realm, two theorists have been particularly influential.

Lawrence Kohlberg's (1981, 1984) theory of moral development was the most prominent of the stage theory models. According to Kohlberg, children progress through a regular, age-related, and universal sequence of stages in moral reasoning. Growth through the stages follows an invariant sequence, but it is not

automatic. People's development can plateau or stabilize at any point. Growth to each succeeding stage depends on experience. Those who have opportunities for role-taking, who are frequently exposed to higher stage reasoning, who actively participate in a variety of legitimate groups, and who take on social responsibilities are more likely to progress through the stages.

Kohlberg's model focused on the developing sophistication of internal thought-processes. In contrast, Norma Haan (Haan, Aerts, & Cooper, 1985), who was highly influenced by Kohlberg, took a more social psychological approach. Her interest was less in how people thought about moral issues in the abstract; rather, she was interested in how they engaged with others. She studied how people subtly negotiated mutual responsibilities within interpersonal contexts.

Today, moral stage theories are less popular than they were in the 1970s–1990s. Still, it is difficult to overestimate Kohlberg's influence on moral psychology. His revolutionary ideas have had lasting impact. Prime among these enduring ideas is that moral reasoning undergoes development with age and experience, and that adequate reasoning is at the core of what it means to act morally.

Moral reasoning in sport

Research on moral reasoning in sport has found that people's stage of development has important correlates. For example, higher level moral reasoning has been shown to correlate with less aggression (Bredemeier, 1985, 1994), better sportspersonship (Horrocks, 1977), and more prosocial beliefs about fair play (Stephens, Bredemeier, & Shields, 1997).

Does participation in sport promote moral reasoning development? Researchers have used multiple theoretical frameworks and measures to try to answer this question (Bredemeier & Shields, 1998), but results have been inconclusive (see Shields & Bredemeier, 2007, 2008). Overall, the findings from these studies underscore the fact that broad generalizations about "sports" are unlikely to be helpful. The developmental stimuli provided by a rugby match are likely to differ from those of a tennis tournament. Sports vary by degree of contact allowed and numerous other features; each constellation of features will encourage unique interpersonal and sociocultural dynamics. In addition, each sport tends to have its own subculture and implicit moral norms. There are also differences based on age, gender, competitive level, and leadership. Even within a single team, participants' own appraisals of the experience may vary substantially (Vallerand & Losier, 1994; Weiss & Bredemeier, 1991).

Game reasoning

Lawrence Kohlberg maintained that people's stage of moral reasoning remained relatively stable across context or issue. If a person thinks with Stage 3 reasoning in one situation, they are likely to use Stage 3 reasoning in other contexts. One of the intriguing phenomena to come out of the Bredemeier and Shields' studies was a finding that when athletes reasoned about moral issues in sports, their average moral reasoning level was lower than when those same athletes discussed similar moral issues outside of sports (Bredemeier & Shields, 1984, 1986). To account for this reasoning divergence between sport and life, they proposed a theory of "game reasoning" (Bredemeier & Shields, 1986; Shields & Bredemeier, 1995, 2005; cf. Long et al., 2006).

Sports have unique moral features that are not typically present in most life situations. First, while everyday morality often requires subordinating self-interest or balancing it with the interests of others, contests, by design, pit people's game-relevant interests in opposition and everyone is expected to pursue their own interest. Second, to some extent, moral responsibility is concentrated in the roles of officials. Third, the context is artificial in the sense that the "good" to be distributed (winning or plac-

ing) is purely symbolic and the means to seek it (e.g., tossing a ball through a hoop) are arbitrary conventions. Together, these conditions create a "zone of freedom" in which athletes are relatively unencumbered by the normal demands of ethics. As one athlete put it:

> The pressure is different in sports and life. It's harder to make decisions in life because there are so many people to think about, different people to worry about. In sports you're free to think about yourself (quoted in Bredemeier & Shields, 1986, pp. 262–263).

Of course, the moral freedom of sport is far from absolute. While athletes are set free to focus on their own interest and pursue victory with vigor, they need to do so within defined procedures (rules), with deference to those charged with enforcing regulations (officials), and with due respect to all who participate in the contest and to the traditions of the game itself (sportsmanship). Just as in everyday life, moral behavior in sport depends upon adequate moral reasoning. So what can coaches do to promote it?

Promoting moral reasoning development

There is some empirical evidence that coaches can, with appropriate guidance, promote moral reasoning development (Bredemeier et al., 1986; Cecchini et al., 2007; Hassandra et al., 2007). The key educational strategy is to take advantage of opportunities for *dialogue* about moral issues. As simple and straightforward as this suggestion sounds, it is frequently neglected in practice. Coaches often prefer one-directional communication. But moral reasoning is unlikely to advance when athletes are simply passive recipients of the coach's exhortations. Youth need to be provided with abundant opportunities to discuss their views of whether something is right or wrong and why; they need to share their perspective on what values are at the core of sports and the team experience. These dialogues need to occur in two primary settings: peer-to-peer and youth-with-adult.

There are many ways to stimulate such dialogue. For example, sports are a frequent theme in movies and these can be tapped for their dialogue-creation potential. In *The Legend of Bagger Vance,* for example, a one-time golf prodigy is on the comeback trail and the movie reaches its climax when he is able to challenge the world's greatest golfer. During the big match, he leans down to brush twigs away from the ball when the ball moves. No one witnessed what happened except the golfer, his caddy, and a young boy who desperately wants his hero to win. The boy encourages him to ignore the ball's movement since it didn't provide an unfair advantage. A coach could show that scene, and then facilitate a discussion about what the athlete should do. Similarly, coaches could use current news stories, illustrations from the history of their sport, autobiographies of athletes or coaches, and numerous other sources in similar ways.

Some of the most beneficial dialogues will arise naturally from the on-going experience of the team. Regardless of the sport, both teammates and opponents will act in ways that are questionable. While a coach should avoid embarrassing or shaming an athlete, these can become rich sources for reflection on "who are we?" and "what do we stand for?" Of course, coaches need to embrace and model appropriate behavior if they are to be effective facilitators of moral dialogue.

PROMOTING MORAL ACTION

Moral reasoning is one of many influences on actual behavior. For example, sometimes people act out of impulse, unconscious motivations, or intuitions, and then, post hoc, fabricate reasons to justify their choice (Haidt, 2001). In real life, our decisions and behaviors arise from complex interactions of multiple influences, some conscious, some not. Two theorists have provided sport researchers with sophisticated models for elaborating on sources of moral action: James Rest and Albert Bandura.

Rest's four component model of moral functioning

To provide a conceptual framework for synthesizing and organizing the complex processes that are required for moral behavior, James Rest (1984) proposed a model that has been very influential (cf. Shields & Bredemeier, 1995). Rest worked largely within the Kohlbergian tradition, but he placed moral reasoning into a much broader framework of *moral functioning* processes.

Rest began by asking a straightforward question: Psychologically, what must have occurred before a person acts morally? In response, he suggested that the person must have: (1) interpreted the situation to identify its moral dimensions and possible action alternatives, along with their likely consequences; (2) reasoned (consciously or otherwise) about the situation from a moral vantage point and decided on the right course of action; (3) prioritized the moral option over other competing values, such as pragmatic self-interest; and (4) sustained their moral intention into action. In short, to act morally, a person must engage in moral: (1) interpretation; (2) judgment; (3) choice; and (4) implementation. These processes are not linear and interact continuously.

Each of the four components of Rest's model is composed of a number of discrete psychological processes. In other words, "interpretation" is not itself a psychological process; rather, it is the outcome of a number of distinct processes. For example, to interpret a situation, a person may engage in perspective-taking, empathy, categorization, cognitive framing, script retrieval, and numerous other processes.

Moral functioning in sport

The use of Rest's model has been advocated by a number of sport psychologists. Since each component of the model taps into a number of psychological processes, a complete operationalization of it would be a daunting task. Instead, sport researchers have usually sought to investigate "moral functioning" by focusing on the outcome of each component. The most common strategy has been to briefly present a dilemma, followed by questions that ask respondents what they think is right (Component 2), what they would choose to do (Component 3), and how frequently they have exhibited the behavior (Component 4). The interpretation component is usually dropped, since the measures begin with dilemmas that already identify the relevant moral issues. Though there are limitations to the strategy (cf. Bredemeier & Shields, 1998; Kavussanu, 2008), research on moral functioning utilizing these measures has been robust.

Researchers have been particularly interested in the connection between moral functioning and achievement motivation (or goal orientation). The latter concept is usually defined in terms of two contrasting goals (Nicholls, 1989). An athlete is "task-oriented" when their goal is to improve and develop mastery. In contrast, an athlete is "ego-oriented" when their goal is to demonstrate superiority over others. Though the details are complex, the general finding from numerous studies is that task orientation tends to be associated with high moral functioning, including prosocial behavior, while ego orientation tends to correlate with less desirable moral functioning (cf., Kavussanu, 2008; Shields & Bredemeier, 2007).

Moral functioning is also related to environmental factors. The "motivational climate" and "moral atmosphere" have been studied extensively. The metaphors of *climate* and *atmosphere* refer to norms that are encouraged by significant others, such as coaches, parents, and teammates. Norms related to achievement motives are collectively called the "motivational climate," which can function to encourage either a task (a "mastery climate") or an ego (a "performance climate") orientation (Ames, 1992). Norms that reflect behavioral expectations related to moral issues are collectively called the "moral atmosphere" (Shields & Bredemeier, 1995). For example, if teammates expect one another to cheat, that would reflect a moral atmosphere unsupportive of positive moral functioning.

Both the motivational climate (e.g., Ommundsen et al., 2003) and the moral atmosphere (e.g., Romand et al., 2009; Shields et al., 2007; Steinfeldt et al., 2011; Stephens, 2001) have been shown to relate to moral functioning. For example, Miller found that a performance climate predicted low moral functioning, whereas a mastery climate predicted more mature moral reasoning (Miller, Roberts & Ommundsen, 2005). Kavussanu and Spray (2006) found that a moral atmosphere condoning cheating and aggression was associated with a performance motivational climate, and both corresponded to low levels of moral functioning.

Bandura's model of moral action

Albert Bandura (1991, 1999, 2002) proposed a model of moral action that features three sets of processes. The first two, proactive and inhibitive processes, sustain moral standards. Proactive morality occurs when a person manifests positive, humane behavior. Inhibitive morality occurs when a person succeeds in refraining from acting poorly. For example, the ability to empathize with another person is a proactive process. Inhibitive processes are illustrated by an athlete who suppresses a temptation to hit an opponent.

Prosocial and antisocial behavior in sport

Most research in sport has focused on the inhibitive dimensions of morality. Stated differently, it has focused on such antisocial behaviors as cheating, doping, aggression, and disrespectful behavior – action options that are ideally suppressed. Maria Kavussanu and colleagues have emphasized the need to conceptually distinguish between the prosocial and antisocial dimensions of morality, recognizing that they may have distinct developmental pathways and situational antecedents (Sage, Kavussanu, & Duda, 2006). With the development of *The Prosocial and Antisocial Behavior in Sport Scale* (Kavussanu & Boardley, 2009), this line of research will, no doubt, continue to grow.

Moral disengagement

In contrast to both proactive and inhibitive processes, Bandura's third moral action process, *moral disengagement*, functions to impede moral action. Moral disengagement is a collective term referring to eight distinct psychological processes that function to reduce or eliminate the self-reproof that one would otherwise experience from contravening moral standards. When an athlete excuses her aggressive act by saying "she had it coming," for example, she is using a disengagement process (Corrion et al., 2009).

The theme of moral disengagement has received considerable attention from sport researchers (see Boardley & Kavussanu, 2011, for a review), boosted by the availability of a valid and reliable measure of moral disengagement in sport (Boardley & Kavussanu, 2007, 2008). Boardley and Kavussanu (2009), for example, have found that the relationships among motivational climate variables and ethical behaviors were mediated by moral disengagement.

Qualitative studies of moral disengagement in sport have examined the specific disengagement mechanisms that athletes tend to favor. Traclet and colleagues, for example, found that football (soccer) players tended to displace responsibility onto others and use moral rationalizations (Traclet et al., 2011). In a study of basketball and taekwondo athletes, Corrion et al. (2009) found that the processes

of displacement and diffusion of responsibility, attribution of blame, minimizing of consequences, and euphemistic labeling were all prevalent.

Promoting moral action in sport

Despite the divergent theoretical models that underlie the work of Rest and Bandura, similar recommendations can be drawn from their work. The concepts of motivational climate and moral atmosphere provide unifying themes that cut across the approaches. If coaches are successful in promoting a mastery climate and a strong, prosocial moral atmosphere, then athletes are more likely to engage in positive behaviors, and avoid the excuses provided by moral disengagement.

Strategies for building a mastery-oriented motivational climate are discussed elsewhere in this volume (see Chapter 36), so our focus here will be on moral atmosphere. A strong moral atmosphere occurs when everyone shares common expectations for positive, prosocial behavior, along with expectations that such negative behaviors as cheating and aggression will be avoided. The key point to remember about collective norms is that they cannot be dictated from the top down. They can only be built through discussion and participatory decision making. That is not to say that coaches cannot provide inspiration and direction.

To build a strong moral atmosphere, the coach needs to share responsibility so that everyone feels that the team's moral norms are an expression of their own commitments. Everyone needs to feel like they are accountable to one another to uphold those norms. Kohlberg used the term "collective responsibility" to refer to this idea that everyone is responsible for the enforcement of the team's norms (Power, Higgins, & Kohlberg, 1989; Shields & Bredemeier, 1995). The same dialogue processes that we recommended earlier can be used to build this sense of collective responsibility to the team's shared moral norms.

PROMOTING CHARACTER DEVELOPMENT

As we turn to the concept of character, we face a linguistic difficulty. How character has been defined varies by history, location, philosophical and psychological commitments, and political ideology (Berkowitz, 2002). We are not going to seek to resolve those centuries-old controversies. Instead, we simply note that character is often (but not always) defined in terms of a preferred set of virtues. Moral action is often judged against moral principle; a person's character is often judged against a set of virtues.

Dimensions of character

Up to this point, we have focused primarily on moral character. Writing for educators, Shields (2011) expanded the meaning of character to include four distinct dimensions: moral character, intellectual character, civic character, and performance character. What unites the dimensions of character is that they all reflect dispositions toward certain forms of value-laden action. All four are relevant to sport. Since we have already discussed moral character, in this section we reflect on the other three dimensions.

Intellectual character, which highlights such virtues as open-mindedness, curiosity, critical thinking, reflectiveness, and truth-seeking, is evident in sport when athletes reflect on the social and philosophical dimensions of sport. When an athlete thinks critically about the role of elite athletes in culture, for example, they are exhibiting intellectual character. So, too, when they reflect on how sports foster stereotypes about race or gender roles. Athletes with well-developed intellectual character are likely to think about sports in light of issues of social justice, cultural purpose, and deeper dimensions of human experience.

Civic character is also relevant to sport. Sport teams are small communities. As such, every team has distinct roles, power hierarchies, modes of social organization, processes of decision making, and means of participation. Within sports, participants often learn about the rights and responsibilities of belonging to a social organization. Consequently, participation in sports carries implications for civic character (LaVoi et al., 2004). This raises a question seldom addressed: *Should leadership in sports operate differently in democratic countries than in more autocratic societies?* If sports are to nurture a civic character appropriate to a democracy, then the sport team itself, it would seem, needs to reflect democratic processes and procedures (Shields & Bredemeier, 2011a).

What remains is the dimension of *performance character*. Performance character refers to those qualities or virtues that enable a person to translate intention into effective action. It consists of such qualities as dedication, resilience, perseverance, emotional control, and other self-management skills. No doubt, sports provide a rich setting for the development of these personal qualities. Generally, this is beneficial. Still, the reader is reminded that developing performance character is valuable only insofar as it serves ethical goals. "Dedication," for example, can support prosocial behavior, but it can also lead to steroid use or playing through dangerous injury. As Coakley and Donnelly (2009) point out, many problematic behaviors in sport arise from conformity to a sport "ethic" that equates dedication with doing whatever it takes to win.

Empirical research on sports and character

Compared to the morality research, empirical work on sports and character is sparse. In one intriguing investigation, Greenwood and Kanters (2009) utilized a set of character-related measures developed in a large-scale, longitudinal investigation of positive youth development. Interestingly, they found that

643

those athletes who described themselves as having higher ability also scored higher on the character variables. In addition, higher character scores were associated with higher task motivation scores.

The character theme that has received the most investigation by sport researchers is *sportspersonship*. Sportspersonship cuts across multiple dimensions of character and can be thought of both as a set of attitudes/values and as behavior that gives expression to them. It requires maintaining balance between seriousness and play, intrinsic and extrinsic motives, and self-assertion and respectful decorum. Most importantly, it involves sustaining integrity during the intensity and stresses of competition.

Empirically, the most widely used assessment of sportspersonship is the Multidimensional Sportspersonship Orientation Scale (MSOS; Vallerand et al., 1997). The MSOS defines sportspersonship in terms of five dimensions: full commitment, respect for social conventions, respect for rules and officials, respect for the opponent, and lack of a negative approach.

Studies of sportspersonship have found that it (as a whole or in part) is positively related with task orientation (Gano-Overway et al., 2005; Ryska, 2003) and negatively with ego orientation (Ryska, 2003). Not surprisingly, a mastery motivational climate also has been found to relate positively to aspects of sportspersonship, while the reverse is true for a performance climate (Ommundsen et al., 2003). Sportspersonship is also associated with autonomous motivation (Ntoumanis & Standage, 2009) and intrinsic reasons for sports participation (Ryska, 2003; Vallerand & Losier, 1994).

Another topic of interest to researchers has been the personal and social influences on an athlete's sportspersonship. Shields and Bredemeier (2007) found that the best predictors of young athletes poor sport behaviors were the perceived behaviors of coaches and spectators. Similarly, Arthur-Banning et al. (2009) found that spectator and coach behaviors were predictive of player behaviors.

Promoting character development in sport

In an effort to aid practitioners, Bolter and Weiss (2012) developed the Sportsmanship Coaching Behaviors Scale (SCBS). It contains six positive coaching behaviors (setting expectations, reinforcing positive behaviors and sanctioning negative ones, and discussing, teaching and modeling good sportsmanship), along with two behaviors to avoid (modeling poor sportsmanship and prioritizing winning over ethics).

The Bolter and Weiss (2012) measure provides useful guidance for those wanting to promote character. However, we would add a cautionary note. Coaches sometimes mistake behavioral conformity with positive character. Character cannot be dictated or imposed. Rewards and sanctions can shape behavior, but they are much less effective at changing underlying values, beliefs, and thoughts. For this reason, we believe the most important recommendation stemming from Bolter and Weiss (2012) is to *discuss* issues of character and sportspersonship. Genuine, deep dialogue is the coach's best friend when it comes to character education.

PROMOTING COMPETITION

According to Kohn (1992), competition almost invariably leads good people to behave badly. In part, this is because the structure of contests requires people to set aside their usual ethical framework. Normally, a core principle of ethics is this: Do not prioritize your personal interests over the legitimate interests of others. But contestants operate with a different core principle: Put your interests and those of your teammates first. Pursuing victory single-mindedly, with intensity and determination, is what contestants are *supposed to do*. And when the major purpose of contesting is understood as separating winners from losers, it is easy to understand how ethical compromises occur.

We have proposed "contesting theory" as a way to untangle some of the complexities that arise in competitive contexts (Shields & Bredemeier, 2009, 2011b, 2011c). The central premise of contesting theory is that the meaning of a contest is not determined by its outward structure. Rather, to have meaning, contests are necessarily interpreted. And that interpretation is done through use of largely unconscious "conceptual metaphors" (Lakoff & Johnson, 1980). In brief, contests can be understood as either "like wars" or "like partnerships." This process of metaphorical interpretation, which typically occurs outside of conscious awareness, needs to be considered if we are to understand moral dynamics in sports.

The root meaning of competition is "to strive *with*." Genuine competition draws from the partnership metaphor and focuses on how the striving for victory provides mutual benefit. Opponents, through the challenge that they provide each other, enable an upward spiral of intensity and effort that can culminate in optimal achievement. When contests are understood through the metaphor of partnership, the contestants' main goal is to experience an exhilarating quest for excellence. That is what genuine competition is all about and it is an understanding of competition that supports ethical behavior.

But there is an alternative. Drawing from a metaphor of war, contests can be viewed as battles for supremacy. Interpreted this way, the main goal is to conquer the opponent and claim the spoils (tangible or psychological) of victory. To distinguish this alternative process from true competition, we call it *decompetition*. Decompetition is contesting that has devolved into striving *against*, rather than striving *with*. While genuine competition supports moral integrity, decompetition pushes against it.

According to contesting theory, people have many misconceptions about the meaning, purpose, and dynamics of competition, and learning to compete is an essential component of learning to engage in sport. Moreover, it is a learning process that can help shape character and one's approach to contests in all dimensions of life.

CONCLUSION

To conclude the chapter, let us emphasize that to promote morality and character through sports is neither easy nor impossible. It is challenging, yet achievable. We hope this chapter has helped to identify some of the key ideas and practices that will enable leaders to take steps in that direction. More work – theoretical, empirical, and educational – is clearly needed to fill in the gaps in our knowledge and practice. But practitioners need not wait. There is sufficient knowledge on which to move forward. We hope readers will take up the challenge.

LEARNING AIDS

1   Identify the four dimensions of "character."

    Intellectual, moral, civic, and performance character.

2   Explain how moral and motivational variables interrelate.

    Generally, task-orientation and mastery climate support moral functioning, while ego-orientation and performance climate are often linked with poorer moral functioning.

3   Describe a positive moral atmosphere.

    A positive moral atmosphere exists when everyone believes that everyone is committed to acting ethically.

4   Explain the difference between competition and decompetition.

    Both are forms of contesting. Competition is contesting understood through a "contest-is-partnership" metaphor. It is an enjoyable questing for excellence. Decompetition is contesting understood through a "contest-is-war" metaphor. It is focused on demonstrating superiority over others and/or gaining extrinsic benefits through winning.

REVIEW QUESTIONS

1   What makes an action moral?

2   What is the main strategy available to promote development of moral reasoning?

3   Can you describe game reasoning and provide examples?

4   Can you name the four dimensions of character and provide sport examples of each?

5   Discuss your experiences with "moral disengagement."

EXERCISES

1   Describe the steps you would take to build a positive moral atmosphere on a team. What approaches to leadership would you use? How would you address rule violations?

2   How could you use Rest's model of moral functioning to identify where moral problems might occur with an athlete or team?

3   Read an account of a sport "scandal," then use Bandura's model of "moral disengagement" to analyse it.

ADDITIONAL READING

Kavussanu, M. (2008). Moral behavior in sport: A critical review of the literature. *International Review of Sport and Exercise Psychology, 1(2)*, 124–138.

Shields, D. & Bredemeier, B. (1995). *Character development and physical activity*. Champaign, IL: Human Kinetics.

Shields, D. & Bredemeier, B. (2007). Advances in sport morality research. In G. Tenenbaum & R.C. Eklund (Eds.), *Handbook of sport psychology* (3rd ed., pp.662–684). Hoboken, NJ: John Wiley & Sons.

Shields, D. & Bredemeier, B. (2009). *True competition: A guide to pursuing excellence in sport and society*. Champaign, IL: Human Kinetics.

Shields, D. & Bredemeier, B. (2011c). Contest, competition, and metaphor. *Journal of the Philosophy of Sport, 38*, 27–38.

REFERENCES

Arthur-Banning, S., Wells, M.S., Baker, B.L. & Hegreness, R. (2009). Parents behaving badly? The relationship between the sportsmanship behaviors of adults and athletes in youth basketball games. *Journal of Sport Behavior, 32(1)*, 3–18.

Ames, C. (1992). Achievement goals, motivational climate, and motivational processes. In G.C. Roberts (Ed.), *Motivation in sport and exercise* (pp.161–176). Champaign, IL: Human Kinetics.

Bandura, A. (1991). Social cognitive theory of moral thought and action. In W.M. Kurtines & J.L. Gewitz (Eds.), *Moral behavior and development: Advances in theory, research, and application* (Vol. I., pp.45–103). Hillsdale, NJ: Lawrence Erlbaum Associates.

Bandura, A. (1999). Moral disengagement in the perpetration of inhumanities. *Personality and Social Psychology Review, 3*, 193–209.

Bandura, A. (2002). Selective moral disengagement in the exercise of moral agency. *Journal of Moral Education, 31*, 101–119.

Berkowitz, M.W. (2002). The science of character education. In W. Damon (Ed.), *Bringing in a new era in character education* (pp.43–63). Stanford, CA: Hoover Institution.

Blasi, A. (1990). Kohlberg's theory and moral motivation. In D. Schrader (Ed.), *New directions in child development: Vol. 27. The legacy of Lawrence Kohlberg* (pp.51–57). San Francisco: Jossey-Bass.

Boardley, I.D. & Kavussanu, M. (2007). Development and validation of the Moral Disengagement in Sport Scale. *Journal of Sport & Exercise Psychology, 29*, 608–628.

Boardley, I.D. & Kavussanu, M. (2008). The Moral Disengagement in Sport Scale–Short. *Journal of Sports Sciences, 26(14)*, 1507–1517.

Boardley, I.D. & Kavussanu, M. (2009). The influence of social variables and moral disengagement on prosocial and antisocial behaviours in field hockey and netball. *Journal of Sports Sciences, 27(8)*, 843–854.

Boardley, I.D. & Kavussanu, M. (2011). Moral disengagement in sport. *International Review of Sport and Exercise Psychology, 4(2)*, 93–108.

Bolter, N.D., Weiss, M.R. (2012). Top of Form Coaching for character: Development of the Sportsmanship Coaching Behaviors Scale (SCBS). *Sport, Exercise, and Performance Psychology, 1(2)*,73–90.

Bredemeier, B. (1985). Moral reasoning and the perceived legitimacy of intentionally injurious sport acts. *Journal of Sport Psychology, 7*, 110–124.

Bredemeier, B. (1994). Children's moral reasoning and their assertive, aggressive, and submissive tendencies in sport and daily life. *Journal of Sport and Exercise Psychology, 16*, 1–14.

Bredemeier, B. & Shields, D. (1984). Divergence in moral reasoning about sport and life. *Sociology of Sport Journal, 1*, 348–357.

Bredemeier, B. & Shields, D. (1986). Game reasoning and interactional morality. *Journal of Genetic Psychology, 147*, 257–275.

Bredemeier, B. & Shields, D. (1998). Assessing moral constructs in physical activity settings. In J. Duda (Ed.), *Advances in sport and exercise psychology measurement* (pp.257–276). New York: Fitness Information Technology, Inc.

Bredemeier, B., Weiss, M., Shields, D. & Shewchuk, R. (1986). Promoting moral growth in a summer sport camp: The implementation of theoretically grounded instructional strategies. *Journal of Moral Education, 15*, 212–220.

Cecchini, J.A., Montero, J., Alonso, A., Izquierdo, M. & Contreras, O. (2007). Effects of personal and social responsibility on fair play in sports and self-control in school-aged youths. *European Journal of Sport Science, 7(4)*, 203–211.

Coakley, J. & Donnelly, P. (2009). *Sports in Society: Issues and Controversies* (2nd ed.). New York: McGraw-Hill.

Corrion, K., Long, T., Smith, A.L., d'Arripe-Longueville, F. (2009). "It's not my fault; it's not serious": Athlete accounts of moral disengagement in competitive sport. *The Sport Psychologist, 23(3)*, 388–404.

Gano-Overway, L., Guivernau, M., Magyar, T.M., Waldron, J. & Ewing, M. (2005). Achievement goal perspective, perceptions of the motivational climate, and sportspersonship: Individual and team effects. *Psychology of Sport and Exercise, 6,* 215–232.

Greenwood, P.B. & Kanters, M.A. (2009). Talented male athletes: Exemplary character or questionable characters? *Journal of Sport Behavior, 32(3)*, 298–324.

Haan, N., Aerts, E. & Cooper, B. (1985). *On moral grounds: The search for practical morality.* New York: New York University Press.

Haidt, J. (2001). The emotional dog and its rational tail: A social intuitionist approach to moral judgment. *Psychological Review, 108*, 814–834.

Hassandra, M., Goudas, M., Hatzigeorgiadis, A. & Theodorakis, Y. (2007). A fair play intervention program in school Olympic education. *European Journal of Psychology of Education, XXII*, 99–114.

Horrocks, R.N. (1977). Sportsmanship. *Journal of Physical Education and Recreation, 48*, 20–21.

Kavussanu, M. (2007). Morality in sport. In S. Jowett & D. Lavallee (Eds.), *Social psychology in sport* (pp.265–277). Champaign, IL: Human Kinetics.

Kavussanu, M. (2008). Moral behavior in sport: A critical review of the literature. *International Review of Sport and Exercise Psychology, 1(2)*, 124–138.

Kavussanu, M. & Boardley, I.D. (2009). The Prosocial and Antisocial Behavior in Sport Scale. *Journal of Sport & Exercise Psychology, 31(1)*, 97–117.

Kavussanu, M. & Spray, C.M. (2006). Contextual influences on moral functioning of male youth footballers. *The Sport Psychologist, 20(1)*, 1–23.

Kohlberg, L. (1981). *Essays on moral development. Vol. 1: The philosophy of moral development.* San Francisco: Harper & Row.

Kohlberg, L. (1984). *Essays on moral development. Vol. 2: The psychology of moral development.* San Francisco: Harper & Row.

Kohn, A. (1992). *No contest: The case against competition* (Rev. ed.). Boston: Houghton Mifflin.

Lakoff, G. & Johnson, M. (1980). *Metaphors we live by.* Chicago: University of Chicago Press.

LaVoi, N., Power, F.C., Shields, D., Bredemeier, B. & Duda, J. (2004). *Civic engagement and sport: A pilot study of collegiate female athletes.* Paper presented at the Association for the Advancement of Applied Sport Psychology conference, Minneapolis, MN.

Long, T., Pantaléon, N., Bruant, G. & d'Arripe-Longueville, F. (2006). A qualitative study of moral reasoning of young elite athletes. *The Sport Psychologist, 20(3)*, 330–347.

Miller, B.W., Roberts, G.C. & Ommundsen, Y. (2005). Effect of perceived motivational climate on moral functioning, team moral atmosphere perceptions, and the legitimacy of intentionally injurious acts among competitive youth football players. *Psychology of Sport and Exercise, 6(4)*, 461–477.

Nicholls, J.G. (1989). *The competitive ethos and democratic education.* Cambridge, MA: Harvard University Press.

Ntoumanis, N. & Standage, M. (2009). Morality in sport: A self-determination theory perspective. *Journal of Applied Sport Psychology, 21(4)*, 365–380.

Ommundsen, Y., Roberts, G.C., Lemyre, P.N. & Treasure, D. (2003). Perceived motivational climate in male youth soccer: relations to social-moral functioning, sportspersonship and team norm perceptions. *Psychology of Sport and Exercise, 4(4)*, 397–413.

Power, F.C., Higgins, A. & Kohlberg, L. (1989). *Lawrence Kohlberg's approach to moral education.* New York: Columbia University Press.

Rest, J. (1984). The major components of morality. In W. Kurtines & J. Gewirtz (Eds.), *Morality, moral behavior, and moral development* (pp.24–40). New York: Wiley.

Romand, P., Pantaléon, N. & D'Arripe-Longueville, F. (2009). Effects of age, competitive level and perceived moral atmosphere on moral functioning of soccer players. *International Journal of Sport Psychology, 40(2)*, 284–305.

Ryska, T.A. (2003). Sportsmanship in young athletes: The role of competitiveness, motivational orientation, and perceived purposes of sport. *Journal of Psychology: Interdisciplinary and Applied, 137(3)*, 273–293.

Sage, L., Kavussanu, M. & Duda, J. (2006). Goal orientations and moral identity as predictors of prosocial and antisocial functioning in male association football players. *Journal of Sports Sciences, 24(5)*, 455–466.

Shields, D. (2011). Character as the aim of education. *Phi Delta Kappan, 92(8)*, 48–53.

Shields, D. & Bredemeier, B. (1995). *Character development and physical activity.* Champaign, IL: Human Kinetics.

Shields, D. & Bredemeier, B. (2005). Can sports build character? In D. Lapsley & F.C. Power (Eds.), *Character psychology and education* (pp.121–139). Notre Dame, IN: University of Notre Dame Press.

Shields, D. & Bredemeier, B. (2007). Advances in sport morality research. In G. Tenenbaum & R.C. Eklund (Eds.), *Handbook of sport psychology* (3rd ed., pp.662–684). Hoboken, NJ: John Wiley & Sons.

Shields, D. & Bredemeier, B. (2008). Sport and the development of character. In L. Nucci & D. Narvaez, *Handbook of moral and character education* (pp.500–519). New York: Routledge.

Shields, D. & Bredemeier, B. (2009). *True competition: A guide to pursuing excellence in sport and society.* Champaign, IL: Human Kinetics.

Shields, D. & Bredemeier, B. (2011a). Coaching for civic character. *Journal of Research in Character Education, 9(1)*, 25–33.

Shields, D. & Bredemeier, B. (2011b). Why sportsmanship programs fail, and what we can do about it. *JOPERD: Journal of Physical Education, Recreation & Dance, 82(7)*, 24–29.

Shields, D. & Bredemeier, B. (2011c). Contest, competition, and metaphor. *Journal of the Philosophy of Sport, 38*, 27–38.

Shields, D.L., LaVoi, N.M., Bredemeier, B.L. & Power, F.C. (2007). Predictors of poor sportspersonship in youth sports: Personal attitudes and social influences. *Journal of Sport & Exercise Psychology, 29(6)*, 747–762.

Steinfeldt, J.A., Rutkowski, L.A., Vaughan, E.L. & Steinfeldt, M.C. (2011). Masculinity, moral atmosphere, and moral functioning of high school football players. *Journal of Sport & Exercise Psychology, 33(2)*, 215–234.

Stephens, D.E. (2001). Predictors of aggressive tendencies in girls' basketball: An examination of beginning and advanced participants in a summer skills camp. *Research Quarterly for Exercise and Sport, 72*, 257–266.

Stephens, D., Bredemeier, B. & Shields, D. (1997). Construction of a measure designed to assess players' descriptions and prescriptions for moral behavior in youth sport soccer. *International Journal of Sport Psychology, 28*, 370–390.

Traclet, A., Romand, P., Moret, O. & Kavussanu, M. (2011). Antisocial behavior in soccer: A qualitative study of moral disengagement. *International Journal of Sport and Exercise Psychology, 9(2)*, 143–155.

Vallerand, R.J., Briere, N.M., Blanchard, C. & Provencher, P. (1997). Development and validation of the Multidimensional Sportspersonship Orientations Scale. *Journal of Sport and Exercise Psychology, 19*, 197–206.

Vallerand, R.J. & Losier, G.F. (1994). Self-determined motivation and sportsmanship orientations: An assessment of their temporal relationship. *Journal of Sport and Exercise Psychology, 16*, 229–245.

Weiss, M.R. & Bredemeier, B.J. (1991). Moral development in sport. In K.B. Pandolf & J.O. Holloszy (Eds.), *Exercise and sport science reviews* (Vol., 18, pp.331–378). Baltimore: Wilkins & Wilkins.

Weiss, M.R., Smith, A.L. & Stuntz, C.P. (2008). Moral development in sport and physical activity. In T.S. Horn (Ed.), *Advances in sport psychology*, (3rd ed., pp.187–210). Champaign, IL: Human Kinetics.

Chapter 42

Controlling anger and aggression

CHRIS J. GEE AND LUKE R. POTWARKA

SUMMARY

Aggression, anger and violence have become all too familiar stains on the fabric of competitive sport. With injury rates consistently on the rise and youth participation rates consistently on the decline, it appears that "cleaning up" competitive sport is on the verge of becoming a central item on the agenda of many sport governing bodies (CCES, 2011). This chapter will attempt to shed light on some of the larger social and historical links between aggressive behavior and competitive sport, while simultaneously providing current and future sport practitioners with tangible strategies and solutions for addressing the issue. Through this chapter the reader will come to understand the complexity and multidimensionality surrounding the existence of aggression and anger within competitive sport, and will come to realize that its eventual removal will require a great deal of effort, commitment, and change from all competitive levels (youth through to professional) of the sporting world. Nevertheless, this chapter provides a number of grassroots strategies that can be adopted and implemented immediately that have the potential to begin curbing these unwanted behaviors.

INTRODUCTION

Anger and aggression have seemingly been inherent within power/performance sports (e.g., ice hockey, football, rugby, wrestling, boxing) since their inception. In fact, some early theorists posited that competitive sport actually served the broader social agenda by providing a forum through which these innate pent up human emotions could be released in a safe and acceptable manner. For example, Brill (1963) called sport "a salutary purgation of combative instincts which, if dammed up within, would break out in a disastrous way" (p. 97), while Scott (1958) stated that "a considerable amount of aggression is used in hitting, kicking and flinging the ball,...herein lies the principle opportunity for the catharsis of aggression" (p. 241). While the tenets and hypotheses upon which these early theories were based have overwhelmingly been discredited or replaced with more contemporary theoretical explanations, the centrality and pervasiveness of anger and aggression in many power/performance sports remains quite strong to this day. Unfortunately, the idealistic intentions behind the inclusion of physical contact in many sports (e.g., turning boys into men) no longer reflect these historic ideals. No longer are tackles in football and body checks in hockey used as strategic techniques by defensive players; rather each instance appears to have become an opportunity for one player to try to inflict as much pain and suffering on their opponent as physically possible. These acts of physicality appear to have gone from simply being "part of the game" to the focal point of the competitive contest, and in doing so, have led to the perceived rise in the frequency and severity of these transgressions (CCES, 2011). It seems that just when we thought we had seen the worst act of sport violence imaginable, an act that would finally be considered the upper limit of acceptability, inevitably something more heinous follows. Many sport practitioners speculated

that it would be the death of an athlete that would finally cause the social and political appetite to change towards cleaning up sport, but unfortunately there have been several athletes who have lost their lives as the direct result of aggressive physical contact (e.g., Don Sanderson, 2009—ice hockey; Manny Castillo, 2009—high school rugby). Consequently it appears that not even the death of young promising athletes can force the sporting community to critically discuss the relevance and legitimacy of aggressive behavior.

The purpose of this chapter is to help the reader better understand the historical and social origins of aggressive behavior in sport, thus providing context for the situation in which we currently find ourselves. In addition, this chapter intends to highlight the role that sport and exercise psychologists can play in helping athletes, and more importantly sport governing bodies, attempt to control and ultimately reduce the expression of anger and aggression within their respective sports.

Figure 42.1 Hockey.

OBJECTIVES

After reading this chapter you should be able to:

1 Clearly define and differentiate aggressive behavior from other forms of physical contact.
2 Understand how aggressive behaviors are learned and modeled.
3 Explain the existence of aggressive behavior from a historical, social and psychological perspective.
4 Develop a list of strategies for parents, coaches, athletes and sporting administrators aimed at reducing aggressive behavior.

WHAT IS AGGRESSIVE BEHAVIOR?

The term "aggression" is frequently used in a variety of social contexts and has subsequently developed a number of relatively ambiguous meanings (Widmeyer, Dorsch, Bray, & McGuire, 2002). For example, it is common to hear of "aggressive salespeople" who relentlessly attempt to complete the commercial transaction, or "aggressive base runners" in baseball who sacrifice their bodies and take risks in order to help improve their team's chances for success. Within ice hockey, the term aggressive has been used to describe players who compete in an energetic, fast-paced, and physical (i.e., body checking) manner. Using these conceptualizations of the term, especially those with a sport focus, aggression is portrayed as a desirable attribute that is implicitly associated with competitive success.

In contrast, within the sport and exercise psychology literature, aggression is defined as "any overt act (verbal or physical) that has the capacity to cause psychological or physical injury to another. The act must be purposeful (non-accidental) and chosen with the intent of causing harm" (Stephens, 1998, p. 277). In other words, the defining characteristics of the term aggressive behavior (as it is applied to this chapter) are that these behaviors are overt, purposeful, and initiated with the intent to cause physical or psychological harm to another individual.

One of the largest obstacles facing the academic study of aggressive behavior in sport is the ability to distinguish between aggres-

sive behavior and other forms of legitimate physical contact (e.g., body checking in hockey, tackling in football and rugby) that are inherent within many of today's most popular sports (Kerr, 2008; Maxwell & Moores, 2007). As outlined above, the defining characteristic of aggressive behavior is the "intent to cause harm". As intent is a cognitive construct (i.e., something the athlete "thinks"), and therefore not something that a researcher can explicitly observe, inferences must be made about the intent of any given act. Confounding this process even further is that several forms of aggressive behavior are widely legitimized and revered within power/performance sports. For example, fighting in competitive ice hockey has become so commonplace that many people perceive it as part of the game (Bushman & Wells, 1998; Gee & Potwarka, 2007; Smith, 1983). Generally speaking, most acts of violence that transpire within the confines of competitive sport are not perceived as "real violence", which is partially the reason that athletes rarely face criminal responsibility for their within-competition actions, even when they far exceed what would be considered acceptable (Gee & Sullivan, 2004; Gee & Potwarka, 2007). Consequently, as individuals interested in the study of aggressive behavior it is imperative that we attempt to challenge the normative codes governing the social context of competitive sport, and attempt to identify and classify these transgressions in as objective a fashion as possible.

HISTORICAL CONNECTION BETWEEN AGGRESSION AND SPORT

Many early sporting events, especially those with a physical element (e.g., boxing, wrestling), were used as training activities to prepare soldiers for war (e.g., Spartans, Romans, Greeks). Not only did these activities keep the soldiers in good physical condition, the content of the activity mirrored the exact skill sets that these soldiers would need to employ on the battlefield. As physical strength and dominance ultimately became associated with masculinity (as men were the only ones allowed to be soldiers, and thus were given the task of protecting the community) these sports started to become popular in non-war times and among non-soldiers as feats of strength (or a way to test one's manliness). As different sporting contests and activities began to evolve, male dominance remained a common element for some time. Generally speaking, it was men who participated in sport and sporting prowess and physical competence became inherently tied to the dominant masculine ideology.

The next major historical influence over our current sporting model, and the lynchpin that ties aggressive behavior to sport today, was the introduction of rugby schools during the Victorian Era in places like England. During the Industrial Revolution we witnessed the emergence of the middle class. This emerging middle class quickly began to erode the power and prestige previously held by the ruling class. In response, the upper class instituted boarding schools (also known as rugby schools), where young boys were to be turned into "men". The main facilitator and curriculum of this transformation was the sport of rugby. The belief was that rugby would teach young men many of the life skills that they would need in order to be successful, the most important of which was to be tough and physically dominant. Interestingly, these are still the ideals that many people attach to youth sporting programs, and the outcomes that they desire for their children (and thus the reason they enroll them in these sporting activities).

Overall then, sport has historically been a social context in which aggressive and physical behavior have been taught (i.e., reinforced), and ultimately associated with what it means to be a man. Although sports can be sites to resist and challenge dominant gender ideology, the reinforcement of physicality and aggression as central to what it means to be a "man" remains an inherent component of many of our most popular and male-dominated sporting activities.

Due to the historical associations between aggression and masculinity, and because most of the research to-date in the sport sciences has focused on male athletes, the current chapter takes on a very male-oriented perspective. All of the strategies and suggestions aimed at curbing aggressive behavior within sport would apply to athletes irrespective of gender. For readers interested in studying aggression among female athletes, the authors refer you to the work of Nancy Theberge (1997, 2000, 2003).

HOW DO ANGER AND FRUSTRATION RELATE TO AGGRESSIVE BEHAVIOR?

Anger and frustration have received a considerable amount of empirical attention as antecedents of sport-specific aggressive behavior. While their importance to the understanding of aggressive behavior has evolved over time, the general consensus still remains that both anger (a more dispositional construct) and frustration (a negative affective response that is elicited within competition) play a prominent role in increasing the *likelihood* that an athlete will act aggressively.

As was mentioned above, anger is a personality or dispositional construct, whereas frustration is an emotional response to something that transpires within the competitive context (i.e., something that happens that makes you mad). Therefore, the strategies aimed at controlling or reducing aggressive behavior in sport must focus both on the athlete's broader social development (the development of an angry and aggressive personality), as well as the competitive sporting environment itself (situations or factors within sport that cause athletes to become frustrated).

AGGRESSION AND ANGER AS LEARNED BEHAVIORS

Human behavior is learned over time, not something that we are born with. Significant others (i.e., parents, teachers, coaches, siblings), through actions and verbalizations send very direct and indirect messages to children regarding the attitudes, beliefs, traits and behaviors that are ultimately expected of them (Bandura, 1977). In short, human behaviors, attitudes, and beliefs are learned vicariously by imitating and internalizing the dominant dispositions of the important people in our lives. We tend to adopt the characteristics that are consistently associated with positive reinforcement from these significant others, while avoiding those that are routinely punished (Bandura, 1977). The process is far more complex than "monkey see, monkey do", but the analogy does reflect the central tenet of social learning theory which is the concept of modeling and internalizing the behaviors that we see others displaying and being rewarded for.

While the process of socialization is believed to be an ongoing one, "childhood is a particularly malleable period, as it is the period of life when enduring social skills, personality attributes, and social orientations are laid down" (Maccoby, 1992, p. 1006). As such, any discussion pertaining to the etiology of aggressive behavior in sport must first focus on the dominant behaviors and attitudes that are being modeled and reinforced in children within the broader social community. This notion is especially true for young men, as strength, physical dominance and power are all heralded within the dominant masculine ideology. Indeed, many young boys are taught at a very early age that being physically aggressive is not only acceptable behavior, but that it is socially rewarded. Because becoming a "man" or displaying one's "masculinity" is believed to be something that boys must actively work at, competitive sports like ice hockey, football and rugby are believed to provide young boys with a forum through which aggressive behavior can be modeled, learned and ultimately celebrated (Coakley & Donnelly, 2009). This learning process is expedited and significantly reinforced in the eyes of the young observer when acts of aggression receive large scale public applause (e.g., fans cheering at a hockey game when a fight breaks out) and considerable media attention. This degree of social reinforcement associated with aggressive behavior sends a clear and strong message to impressionable young boys about what it means to be a "man" in today's society and the importance that aggression and physical dominance play in its social definition.

HOW DO WE CONTROL AGGRESSION AND ANGER IN SPORT?

The answer to this question is complex and multidimensional; however, all interventions fall into one of two general categories: (1) those aimed at the individual athlete; and (2) those aimed at the competitive sporting environment.

Interventions aimed at athletes

Given the centrality that aggression and physicality play in the dominant masculine ideology, the most impactful interventions aimed at reducing aggressive behavior in sport would actually target the broader social definition of "masculinity". Until there are socially acceptable ways of being "masculine" that place less emphasis on physical strength and dominance, competitive power/performance sports (and their focus on aggression and violence) will continue to play a central role in the process of male gender socialization and the reinforcement of these traits. This type of macro-level social change will likely be measured in decades rather than years, therefore more focused and targeted interventions are required in order to enact more immediate change.

The role of parents and coaches in creating non-aggressive team norms

Coaches and parents can play a very significant role in shaping the attitudes, perceptions and behaviors of young athletes. A great deal of research by sport scientists has demonstrated that coaches' and parents' attitudes towards sport aggression are strong predictors of athletes' actual within-competition behavior. For example, Smith (1979) found that parents' approval of fighting in hockey was significantly correlated with their children's actual on-ice fighting behavior over a competitive season. In fact, Smith (1979) found that the father's perception of fighting was the strongest predictor of the athlete's actual on-ice behavior, and was in fact a stronger predictor than the athlete's own perception of the legitimacy of fighting in hockey.

Athletes' perceptions of the importance that their coaches place on winning was also found to be correlated with athletes' self-reported likelihood of engaging in aggressive behavior, especially if the aggression was perceived as having the capacity to help the team win (Stephens, 2000; Stephens & Bredemeier, 1996). Consequently, similar to athletes' perceptions of their parents, if they believe that their coach legitimizes and reinforces the use of aggressive behavior, especially in instances where it has a performance-related consequence, athletes appear significantly

more willing to engage in these types of within-competition behaviors.

The cumulative effect of the two previously mentioned reference groups (parents and coaches) is the development of team norms pertaining to the use of aggressive behavior. Even though broader social forces promote the use of aggressive behavior among young boys, and these norms are even more widely accepted and legitimized within the sporting context itself, coaches and parents of individual teams still have the ability to create their own codes of conduct for their specific athletes. Parents and coaches define the behaviors that will be deemed acceptable among their athletes, and can directly apply reinforcement or punishment accordingly. In the social context of the team, coaches can apply additional punishment for aggressive behavior, above and beyond what is administered by the league (e.g., the coach can bench or suspend the player). By clearly defining what is acceptable and unacceptable within the team dynamic, and administering reinforcement and punishment consistently and accordingly, coaches and parents can significantly shape the behaviors of their athletes (social learning theory).

For such a strategy to be effective, team norms must be explicitly discussed and understood by all athletes. Previous research on aggression has shown that athletes self-reported use of aggressive behavior is heavily influenced by how they think others in their immediate environment would want them to behave. For example, Matza (1964) found that when he interviewed boys separately regarding their use of aggressive behavior they would frequently report that they would like to be less violent, and that they only acted violently in the presence of the other boys. Therefore, all the boys acted aggressively because they perceived the other members of the group as desiring this behavior, when in fact all the boys wanted to behave less aggressively but feared group ostracism. Matza (1964) termed this phenomena "mutual misunderstanding". Other researchers have supported this "perceptive assumption" hypothesis, by suggesting that athletes who frequently display aggressive behavior may be over-conforming to dominant gender, team and sport normative codes of conduct. A similar explanation has been put forward to explain the presence of misogynistic and homophobic banter in many male locker rooms (Andre & Holland, 1995; Coakley & Donnelly, 2009). Again, the hypothesis is that athletes engage in these behaviors as a way of explicitly and outwardly adhering to what they believe "others" expect of them and the dominant gender ideology, and not necessarily because they want to behave in this manner.

By making team norms more explicit, coaches and parents can take the perceptual guesswork out of the equation. Coaching education programs should also place additional emphasis on providing coaches and parents with tangible strategies for creating these positive team atmospheres and for shaping athletes' behaviors accordingly.

Strategies to help athletes control their emotions

As mentioned previously, anger and frustration oftentimes increase an athlete's probability of engaging in an aggressive act. Consequently, any steps that sport practitioners can take to help athletes control their emotions while competing should have a positive effect on reducing the likelihood of an aggressive episode.

Avoiding retaliation

Most acts of aggression that are precipitated by anger or frustration are acts of retaliation (Sheldon & Aimar, 2001). Therefore, the first step towards reducing aggression is to help athletes identify common triggers (e.g., trash talking, hard hits, personal mistakes), and then to provide them with the cognitive skills and strategies necessary to self-diagnose their current emotional state during the competitive contest. Both of these steps will help increase an athlete's level of conscious competence with respect to avoiding retaliatory aggressive behavior. Once an athlete is able to identify when their frustration and anger levels are increasing the next step is to provide them with the skills and strategies necessary to address these negative emotional states.

Self-talk can be a very powerful psychological strategy in these circumstances. The athlete is trained to say specific cue words (e.g., "forget about it", "relax", "calm", "let it go", "control", "no retaliation") when they feel themselves becoming frustrated. Through practice and repetitive pairing, these cue words eventually allow athletes to focus and control their emotional responses, and to override what would have previously been their natural response to frustration (i.e., aggressive outburst). Several very successful teams have made this type of disciplined playing style a central component of their competitive strategy. In many sports, penalty infractions result from retaliatory behaviors, and thus, the ability to compete in a controlled and disciplined fashion oftentimes represents a significant competitive advantage (especially when the other team is trying to put you off your game, or get your more talented players penalized). By helping athletes identify when they are becoming frustrated, and subsequently providing them with a cognitive strategy for addressing this negative emotional state, they inevitably begin making more productive and strategic behavioral choices in the face of provocation.

Similarly, *rehearsal training* can also help athletes identify common within-competition triggers, and through repetition, learn to play through them. Using this strategy, coaches will simulate game-like conditions during practice (e.g., loud crowd noise, pushing and shoving by players, hooking, holding) to expose their athletes to these anticipated provocative stimuli. The belief is that, over time, athletes will become accustomed to these distractions and acts of provocation, and be able to actively and consciously manage their emotional state more effectively during competitions.

Pre-competitive anxiety and arousal

Anxiety refers to the "cognitive concerns and autonomic responses that accompany a stressful situation, particularly when the perceived situational demand exceeds the individual's ability to meet the demand in personally meaningful situations" (Naylor, Burton, Crocker, 2002, p. 134). Anxiety is something that we have all experienced at one time or another (e.g., nervous feelings and thoughts of "what could go wrong" right before we have had to deliver a speech in front of a large audience). These same thoughts of doubt and elevated levels of arousal (e.g., increased heart rate, sweaty palms) are common among athletes prior to competition (especially prior to really important competitions). Recent research has highlighted a link between athletes' levels of pre-competitive anxiety and the strength and frequency of their expressed anger during competition (Esfahani & Gheze Soflu, 2010). In other words, the more nervous and apprehensive athletes feel before a competition, the higher the likelihood that they will experience and express feelings of anger while competing. As noted, these feelings of anger place athletes at a higher disposition for engaging in aggressive behavior.

Pre-competitive anxiety is one of the most frequently cited psychological issues faced by athletes (Gee, 2010). It manifests itself both cognitively and somatically, and therefore oftentimes requires sport practitioners to apply a multidimensional approach towards treating it. Below are some of the most common techniques employed by sport and exercise psychologists aimed at reducing pre-competitive anxiety.

Relaxation strategies: In order to address the somatic aspects of pre-competitive anxiety (e.g., increased breathing rate, increased heart rate, sweaty palms) sport psychologists often work with athletes on various relaxation strategies. *Progressive relaxation,* where athletes tense and relax specific muscle groups for 10 seconds at a time, is a popular technique.

This approach is intended to help athletes become more conscious of their bodies, especially with respect to how they hold and manifest stress. By helping athletes become more conscious of their emotional and somatic states, they will be in a better position to identify when they are experiencing counterproductive emotional states, thus placing athletes in a better position to proactively address such states before they impair their performance.

Biofeedback is another form of relaxation training aimed at the somatic dimension of pre-competitive anxiety. With biofeedback, athletes are taught through experience what various autonomic responses (e.g., heart rate, breathing rate, pulse) feel like when they are elevated. For example, using a treadmill and a stethoscope, athletes can directly experience what an elevated heart rate feels and sounds like. Athletes are then taught through systematic training sessions how to control and regulate these physiological responses. As a result, not only are athletes more apt to recognize when they are experiencing elevated arousal, but now also possess the skills necessary to regulate these anatomical responses back down into their optimal ranges. Biofeedback, and the general relaxation techniques that are learned as part of it, can be applied by athletes before, during or after a competition.

Finally, *deep breathing* and *meditation* are also relaxation strategies that can directly combat elevated somatic anxiety. Both of these strategies help athletes block out external distractions and focus internally on soothing stimuli such as their breathing or a positive mantra statement. Again, the focus of these strategies is to lower an athlete's elevated autonomic responses to levels that are compatible with optimal performance and emotional control.

Cognitive strategies: A central component of pre-competitive anxiety is the cognitive appraisal process that athletes undertake. Therefore, strategies aimed at addressing pre-competitive anxiety must also include a cognitive intervention component.

Cognitive restructuring is the central tenet of these types of intervention strategies. While such strategies can take on a variety of forms (e.g., thought stopping, self-talk, imagery), the fundamental principal is that psychologists work with athletes to "reframe" the way in which they are appraising the competitive situation. As mentioned earlier, anxiety arises when athletes appraise the situation as exceeding their abilities, while simultaneously placing a high degree of importance on succeeding (i.e., they are about to play the best team in the finals and all of their friends and family have come to watch). With cognitive anxiety, many of the thoughts that athletes have are fundamentally irrational (i.e., not grounded in reality or fact). For example, athletes may believe that there is a 0% chance that they can be successful, which is an obvious and irrational overgeneralization. In competitive sport there is always a chance that you can be successful, no matter who the opponent is. Athletes may also envision their friends and family laughing or judging them, again leading to heightened feelings of nervousness and anxiety. In reality, friends and family are more likely to be supportive and empathetic in the event of a poor performance. Overall, cognitive restructuring is a process whereby sport psychologists help athletes think about and evaluate the situation more rationally and from a more positive and optimistic perspective. By doing so, athletes begin to appraise the situation in less threatening terms (e.g., losing isn't the end of the world), and inevitably lower their pre-competitive anxiety and subsequent somatic arousal.

In both cases, controlling these pre-competitive emotional states is believed to lower the likelihood that an athlete will engage in aggressive behavior, by minimizing the frequency and strength of their anger response.

A number of athlete-focused intervention strategies were presented in the above section. While all of these interventions make intuitive sense, and have demonstrated efficacy in other experimental contexts, no empirical research to-date has examined the impact of an athlete-focused intervention on aggressive behavior. Consequently, this reflects a significant gap in the study of sport-specific aggression, and thus is a ripe area of inquiry for future sport scientists.

Interventions aimed at the competitive sporting context

The previous section focused specifically on the types of interventions that sport and exercise psychologists can employ when working directly with athletes. This section will take a more macro-level perspective and focus on the things that sport governing bodies can consider when attempting to address these same issues.

Strategies aimed at reducing frustration

As was identified earlier in the chapter, frustration is believed to be a strong catalyst in the expression of aggression. Consequently, any steps that sport governing bodies can take to reduce the amount of frustration that athletes' experience, should inevitably have a direct effect on the frequency and severity of these acts.

Previous research in the sport sciences has identified a number of situational factors believed to elicit frustration, all of which have been empirically correlated with higher frequencies of aggressive behavior [losing (Volkamer, 1971; Leith, 1989), losing at home (Neave & Wolfson, 2003); losing by a large margin (Gee, 2011; Gee & Leith, 2007), losing late in the game (Gee & Sullivan, 2006; Kelly & McCarthy, 1979), stalling (Widmeyer, 2002), making mistakes (Brice, 1990), physical provocation from an opponent (Sheldon & Aimar, 2001), poor officiating (Brice, 1990)]. As is evident from this list, losing is a common and strong precursor to the expression of anger and aggression during competition. This is in part because of the importance and broader social labels that we place on winning, especially among young males where sporting and physical competence are central pillars of the dominant masculine ideology (Young, 2000). Consequently, male athletes are highly motivated to avoid appearing physically incompetent or inferior, and as such are susceptible to becoming frustrated and angered when the competitive outcome is not in their favor.

Some recreational and youth leagues have attempted to remove "losing" from the sporting environment by omitting all references to the score (e.g., no scoreboard, score is not kept by the league, every teams gets in the playoffs). However, the reality is that due to the zero-sum nature of most competitive sports, losing is an inevitable part of the game. Nevertheless, there are still a number of ways that sport governing bodies can attempt to limit or

reduce the amount of frustration experienced by athletes.

Mercy rule: Some sports, like baseball, have adopted a "mercy rule" into their youth divisions, in which offensive and defensive teams switch places (offensive team goes back into the field, and the defensive team goes up to bat) after a predetermined number of offensive points have been scored. In so doing, the offensive team cannot remain at bat indefinitely and the overall score differential between the two teams is managed to some degree. These same leagues oftentimes have a total score mercy rule as well, whereby if one team is leading by a certain number of points at a particular juncture in the game (e.g., half way) then the game is ended at that point. Again, the purpose of the mercy rule is to limit

Figure 42.2 Basketball.

the scoring discrepancy between the two teams, and to give the losing team a chance to switch to offence, even if they haven't earned it through their performance.

Rivalries: Research has demonstrated that anger and aggression are elevated between teams who compete against one another more frequently (Widmeyer & McGuire, 1997). With geography and travel costs routinely factored into competitive scheduling, many sports are now inherently creating rivalries between teams. When teams compete this frequently, aggressive tensions and frustration from one game inevitably have the potential to carry over into the next. This leads to a continual escalation of aggressive and anger-based undertones, which significantly elevates the likelihood that an aggressive episode will be witnessed. Rivalry contests, unlike competitive contests between teams that don't know each other or who play each other infrequently, start off at the outset with elevated negative emotions rather than these emotions building up throughout the game. The emotional undertones that are present within a rivalry situation can be further exacerbated by the media, as they try to create additional excitement and spectatorship by focusing on the probability of violence between the two teams. In this case, athletes are almost forced to act aggressively against one another, as that is what everybody has come to see.

Overall, these elevated feelings of anger and hatred can significantly increase the probability that athletes will exhibit aggressive behavior. Consequently, anything that sport governing bodies can do to minimize the number of times that two teams face each other will have a direct effect on minimizing the development of a rivalry and the increased likelihood of anger and aggression which often results.

Instant replay: Perceived poor officiating and missed calls have been linked to athlete frustration and aggressive behavior (Brice, 1990). Officials only have limited attentional resources, and must attempt to focus on a number of external stimuli simultaneously. Thus, it is inevitable that some infractions or important calls will go unnoticed. Unfortunately, when these missed infractions have direct implications over the outcome of the competitive contest they can lead to frustration and anger among athletes and coaches. In an attempt to address the "human" nature of officiating, many sports have adopted the use of instant video replay. By allowing game officials to review particularly important or close plays using videotape, they have the ability to slow down, rewind and pause the competitive action to ensure the validity of their final decision. Some sports allow coaches to "challenge" game officials' decisions, which again provides a channel and a remedy to vent these feelings of frustration that can result from unintentional mistakes on the part of game officials.

Equal distribution of talent: Another common source of frustration among athletes is the unequal distribution of talent that can occur in team sports. In almost all levels of competitive sport certain teams have a distinct advantage (i.e., monetary, geographical, historical) in attracting the best players. In some leagues, this creates such discrepancy in the talent between various teams that one or two teams consistently win the championship every year. Of course, this can create frustration and desperation among the other teams, both of which have the potential to act as catalysts for aggressive behavior. In an attempt to address the unequal distribution of talent, many sport governing bodies have adopted a number of strategies. Many professional leagues have attempted to create parity through the draft process by giving lower ranking teams the first picks. Amateur leagues have introduced geographical boundaries, whereby athletes have to compete for their local teams unless given a written release to play elsewhere. Salary caps in professional sports were also introduced to ensure that small market teams had a relatively equal playing field upon which to build a competitive franchise. Many university and collegiate programs have strict rules around changing schools, most of which include having to sit out at least a year after transferring. All of these strategies have been developed to protect against the unequal distribution of talent, in an attempt to create competitive parity whenever possible. Competitive parity is yet another strategy for reducing anger and frustration, both of which reduce the likelihood of aggression.

Strategies aimed at increasing punishment

As mentioned previously, human beings model and internalize behaviors, attitudes and beliefs that are positively reinforced, while overwhelmingly avoiding those that are consistently punished (Bandura, 1977). Within the context of power/performance sports (e.g., hockey, football, rugby), the use of violent and aggressive behavior is not only rewarded and legitimized, but in many cases it is revered. As such, in many ways the benefits of playing aggressively (e.g., strategic, adhere to normative expectations of masculinity) appear to significantly outweigh the consequences (e.g., minor penalty infraction). With this in mind, one strategy to reduce aggressive behavior is to significantly increase the punishment associated with these transgressions, not only to the individual but also the team. If the consequences of players' actions were more inherently tied to their team's likelihood for success, and we assume that teams and coaches want to be successful, then it follows that this strategy would likely facilitate team norms and social pressures towards a non-aggressive style of play. For example, if certain aggressive infractions (fighting, hitting from behind, spearing) were penalized with a penalty shot, rather than the standard two-minute penalty, it is very likely that such rule violators would not receive such a favorable reaction from either their coach or teammates (Gee & Potwarka, 2007). In this instance, engaging in aggressive behavior would be perceived as selfish and reckless, and thus, running contrary to the team's ultimate goal of winning. Players who continued to display this type of conduct would likely find themselves ostracized by their teammates and subsequently punished by their coach.

Increasing the consequences of aggression at a league level also appears to be an effective strategy for reducing the frequency of these transgressions because it takes the onus of playing less aggressively off the athlete, and forces a behavior change on all players simultaneously. As such, it should not threaten athletes' perceived masculinity or teams' identities, as the league administration becomes the sacrificial scapegoat for both athlete and team compliance. Gee (2010) provided some preliminary empirical support for the efficacy of these league-level punitive differences on the frequency of aggression in youth ice hockey. While holding a number of critical factors constant (i.e., age, gender, sport, achievement orientation, legitimacy perceptions, parents attitudes, moral reasoning level, perceived masculinity) the author demonstrated significant differences in the frequency of aggressive penalties between leagues with contrasting punitive policies. One league adopted the traditional NHL rulebook, where acts like fighting were penalized with a five-minute major penalty, whereas the other league adopted automatic misconduct penalties and subsequent suspensions for the same infraction. This league also adopted a three penalty maximum per game before a player received a game misconduct penalty and single game suspension. While these results are certainly preliminary, they do suggest that increasing the punishment associated with aggressive behavior may reduce the frequency by which athletes display it.

Introducing legal punishment has also been suggested as a strategy for addressing the more serious acts of within-competition aggression (Gee & Potwarka, 2007). Athletes have historically been immune to the criminal laws that govern broader social discourse, under the auspices that aggression in sport is the result of the speed, physicality and emotion inherent in the game, and therefore are simply natural and expected parts of the competitive environment. Currently, athletes who are involved in these serious incidents receive their punishment from league governed tribunals, which primarily utilize monetary fines, suspensions, and expulsions as their methods of punishment (Berry & Smith, 2000). However, researchers have argued that the punishments levied by these sport governing bodies are nothing more than public relations tools used to deflect public criticism, and therefore, do little to actually deter athletes' aggressive behavior (Benedict, 1998; Benedict & Yaeger, 1998; Berry & Smith, 2000). All major sport governing bodies (e.g., FIFA, NHL, NFL) appear to handle within-competition instances of aggression in a similar "in-house" manner, in all cases trying to insulate and separate sporting behaviors from the rules that govern broader social deportment. In fact, Gee and Sullivan (2004) and Gee and Potwarka (2007) suggest that this lax stance on within-competition aggression is at least partially responsible for the escalation in the seriousness of aggression that some sports are witnessing. The fact that these serious acts of within-competition violence continually receive seemingly "slap on the hand" reactions from sport governing bodies, appears to be sending the message to athletes that there is no upper limit on what is deemed unacceptable in the heat of competition. By introducing legal punishment for these extreme cases, a clear line in the sand can finally be drawn.

Removing physical contact

Some youth leagues have opted to remove the use of physical contact in an attempt to curb aggressive behavior. This strategy is not a likely option for all sports (e.g., tackling is a central component of both football and rugby), and something that will not likely be replicated at the higher and more competitive

levels of these sports. Nevertheless, research does appear to suggest that violence begets violence, and that physical contact is one of the most frequently cited antecedents of aggressive behavior (Brice, 1990; Sheldon & Aimar, 2001; Smith, 1983). Not only will removing body contact have a direct effect on reducing aggression, it also allows younger athletes to focus their attention on mastering the fundamental skills (e.g., passing, shooting, dribbling, running) of their sport (Widmeyer, 2002).

Change the professional sporting model

The final strategy for reducing anger and aggression within sport targets the way in which the professional version of these power/performance sports are structured, marketed, and ultimately consumed by younger individuals. It should come as little surprise that professional athletes are role models for younger athletes, and thus have a profound effect on the way that younger athletes play the game. For example, Smith (1979) found that young hockey players routinely witnessed star NHL players committing acts of aggression through the media, and that they adopted these aggressive acts into their competitive behavioral repertoires. One boy remarked "sneaky elbows, little choppy slashes, Bobby Clarke style." Smith subsequently cross-referenced these self-report comments with players' penalty statistics and found a higher frequency of penalties among those athletes that self-reported engaging in these types of behaviors. These findings highlight the fact that young athletes consciously adopt and internalize these behaviors into their own style of play as a result of watching their professional idols.

Similar results were also found among college and high school football players, with these athletes routinely citing media sources (e.g., televised games and media print of the NFL) as strong influences over how they played the game (Mugno & Feltz, 1985). Consequently, rules and messages pertaining to the expression of anger and aggression will have the most profound effect on these sports if they are administered and reinforced at the highest levels. Men's professional ice hockey for example, in an attempt to reduce concussions and other head injuries, has adopted rules specific to "hits to the head". Currently the NHL is taking a close look at the role of fighting in ice hockey and is seriously considering removing it from the game. These rule changes will undoubtedly have direct implications on the way that youth ice hockey is played.

CONCLUSION

There are a number of very practical ways in which anger and aggressive behavior can be addressed within the competitive sporting environment. The larger question, however, is whether or not there is (or ever will be) a "real" appetite for removing these behaviors from these power/performance sports.

As mentioned earlier, competitive sport remains to this day one of the most profound sites for the transmission and reinforcement of gender norms, especially for young boys as it relates to aggressive behavior. Parents routinely report putting young boys into power/performance sports like hockey, football and rugby to "learn to take their lumps" and "to toughen them up" (Smith, 1983; Young, 2000). Consequently, until physical dominance and aggression are no longer central pillars of the dominant masculine archetype, these sports will remain as institutions where these attributes are continuously modeled, reinforced and ultimately celebrated.

Secondly, aggressive behavior is a source of entertainment, and thus something that many professional sporting organizations actively market to consumers. Rivalries are marketed as pending "blood baths" in an attempt to draw in more spectators. Sports news channels frequently fill their highlight reels with clips of fights and other forms of aggressive and violent behavior. Entrepreneurs have even exploited people's fascination with sport-specific violence by producing and selling DVDs that focus exclusively on these acts (i.e., Don Cherry's "Rockem Sockem" series). Therefore, the removal or penalization of violence and aggression could be seen from this perspective as counterproductive to the "business" of sport.

Interestingly however, it appears that many professional sports are currently at a crossroad of sorts. On the one hand, they appear to need violence and aggression to sell tickets and to create marketing buzz around their product. On the other hand, star players are being knocked out and forced to retire at an alarming rate as a result of the violence and lack of respect currently being witnessed in many of these professional sports. As such, more than any other time in recent memory, sport governing bodies appear willing to listen to solutions and strategies aimed at addressing violence and anger within their respective sports. Changes at the professional and elite levels of sport will inevitably have direct "trickle-down" effects on the expression and legitimacy of violence and aggression in amateur and youth sporting leagues. Consequently, for any real change to occur, it appears necessary that it begins at the top.

LEARNING AIDS

1   What are the problems faced by those studying anger and aggression in sports?

Researchers encounter three main challenges when studying anger and aggression in sports. First, it is difficult for researchers to distinguish aggressive behavior from that which might be considered "acceptable" forms of physical contact (e.g., body checking in hockey, tackling in football and rugby). Second, aggression is understood as an "intent" to cause harm to others, which is cognitive construct, and therefore difficult to observe directly. Third, many forms of aggressive behavior are celebrated, encouraged, and believed to be just "part of the game". In other words, what may constitute a criminal offense outside the realm of sport may not be considered "real" violence within the confines of sport. Thus, individuals interested in the study of aggressive behavior should attempt to challenge the normative codes that govern competitive sport environments.

2   Can incidents of anger and aggression in sports be conceptualized as learned behaviors?

Yes. Renowned psychologist Albert Bandura teaches us that human behavior can be learned vicariously by imitating and internalizing the dominant dispositions of the important people in our lives (e.g., parents, teachers, coaches, siblings). We tend to adopt behaviors that are consistently associated with positive reinforcement from these significant others, while avoiding those that are routinely punished (Bandura, 1977). As noted, athletes who engage in aggressive acts of violence and aggression are sometimes applauded in the sports media and revered by their coaches.

3   Discuss reasons why people (and organizations) may resist the implementation of strategies aimed at reducing anger and aggressive behavior in competitive sport.

Although there are several sources of resistance to the practical interventions, which are offered at the end of the chapter, two are worthy of noting here. First, if competitive power and performance sports continue to be sites that reinforce dominant masculine ideologies (e.g., sports "toughen boys up" or "part of being male is being aggressive"), attempts to reduce incidents of violence and aggression (via the deployment of interventions) will be challenged. Second, team owners and league officials may have a vested interested in ensuring aggression and violence remain "part of the game". Sometimes these individuals believe that such acts have entertainment value, and therefore, they attempt to leverage violent images and narratives within their marketing efforts. Targeting violence and aggression at the professional and elite levels may have a "trickle-down" effect on the expression and legitimacy of violence and aggression in amateur and youth sporting leagues.

REVIEW QUESTIONS

1   Define aggressive behavior in your own words, and describe how it differs from other forms of physical contact that are acceptable within certain sports.

2   List three strategies for reducing aggressive behavior in sport that target the athlete specifically.

3   What role do professional sport leagues play in the aggression and anger witnessed within amateur sport? What role could the media play in addressing aggressive behavior?

4   How can coaches have a direct effect on the reduction of aggressive behavior? Write your answer as if it were content in a coaching education seminar.

EXERCISES

1   Attend a sporting event where physical contact is permitted. Create a checklist of all the behaviors and actions that meet the definition of aggression presented in this chapter. Try to also include the following information:

- the time of the incident;
- the score between the two teams when the incident occurs;
- whether the aggressor was a member of the home or away team;
- whether or not the action was penalized by the game official.

Upon the conclusion of the competitive context, revisit this list and assess the degree to which your findings align with previous research.

2   Interview people regarding their views/explanations/perspectives as to why athletes engage in aggressive behavior. Ensure that they are discussing acts that meet our conceptual definition of aggression, and not simply acts that are acceptable components of the game. Try to interview people who have experience with, or are involved in, competitive sport, as well as people who have little or no involvement in sport. Compare their responses and critically examine them against what you have learned through this chapter.

ADDITIONAL READING

Coakley, J. & Donelly, P. (2009). *Sports in society: Issues and controversies.* Toronto: McGraw Hill Ryerson Higher Education.

Gee, C.J. & Potworka, L.R. (2007). The impact of introducing legal punishment on the frequency of aggressive behaviour in professional ice hockey: Using the Todd Bertuzzi incident as an ecological case study. *Athletic Insight, 9* (3). http://www.athleticinsight.com/Vol9Iss3/Legal Punishment.htm

Gee, C.J. & Leith, L.M. (2007). Aggressive behaviour in professional ice hockey: A cross cultural comparison of North American and European born NHL players. *Psychology of Sport and Exercise, 8* (4), 567–583.

Jewell, R.T. (2011). *Violence and aggression in sporting contests: Economics, history and policy.* London: Springer.

REFERENCES

Andre, T. & Holland, A. (1995). Relationship of sport participation to sex role orientation and attitudes towards women among high school males and females. *Journal of Sport Behavior, 18,* 241–248.

Bandura, A. (1977). *Social Learning Theory.* Ohio: Prentice-Hall.

Benedict, J.R. (1998). *Athletes and acquaintance rape.* Thousand Oaks, CA: Sage Publications.

Benedict, J.R. & Yaeger, D. (1998). *Pros and cons: The criminals who play in the NFL.* New York: Warner Books.

Berry, B. & Smith, E. (2000). Race, sport, and crime: The misrepresentation of African Americans in team sports and crime. *Sociology of Sport Journal, 17,* 171–197.

Brice, J.G. (1990). Frustration in ice hockey: Extent, antecedents and consequences. Unpublished master's thesis. University of Waterloo, Waterloo, ON.

Brill, A.A. (1963). Why man seeks sport. *North American Review,* 85–99.

Bushman, B.J. & Wells, G.L. (1998). Trait aggressiveness and hockey penalties: Predicting hot tempers on the ice. *Journal of Applied Psychology, 83,* 969–974.

CCES (2011, May). Violence in sport identified as one of the top 6 threats to sport. *CCES Media Release, 164,* 30.

Coakley, J. & Donnelly, P. (2009). *Sports in society: Issues and controversies.* Toronto: McGraw Hill Ryerson Higher Education.

Esfahani, N. & Gheze Soflu, H. (2010). The comparison of pre-competitive anxiety and state anger between male and female volleyball players. *World Journal of Sport Sciences, 3,* 237–242.

Gee, C.J. (2010) Predicting the use of aggressive behaviour among Canadian amateur hockey players: A psychosocial examination. An unpublished doctoral dissertation. University of Toronto.

Gee, C.J. (2010). How does sport psychology actually improve athletic performance? A framework to facilitate athletes' and coaches' understanding. *Behavior Modification, 34* (5), 386–402.

Gee, C.J. (2011). Aggression in competitive sports: Using direct observation to evaluate incidence and prevention focused intervention. In J. Luiselli & D. Reed (Eds.) (pp.199–210) *Behavioral sport psychology: Evidence-based approaches to performance enhancement.* Springer.

Gee, C.J. & Leith, L.M. (2007). Aggressive behaviour and performance in professional ice hockey: A cross-cultural comparison of North American and European born players. *Psychology of Sport and Exercise, 8,* 567–583.

Gee, C.J. & Sullivan, P.J. (2004). Boys will be boys: The naturalistic explanation still dominates the sporting world. *The Brock Review, 8,* 61–72.

Gee, C.J. & Sullivan, P.J. (2006). Using a direct observation approach to study aggressive behaviour in ice hockey: Some preliminary findings. *Athletic Insight, 8* http://www.athletic insight.com/Vol8Iss1/DirectObservation.htm

Gee, C.J. & Potwarka, L.R. (2007). The impact of introducing legal punishment on the frequency of aggressive behaviour in professional ice hockey: Using the Todd Bertuzzi incident as an ecological case study. *Athletic Insight, 9* (3). http://www.athleticinsight.com/Vol9Iss3/Legal-Punishment.htm

Kelly, B.R. & McCarthy, J.F. (1979). Personality dimensions of aggression: Its relationship to time and place of action in ice hockey. *Human Relations, 32,* 219–225.

Kerr, J.H. (2008). A critque of the development of the Competitive Aggressiveness and Anger Scale. *Psychology of Sport and Exercise, 9,* 721–728.

Leith, L.M. (1989). The effect of various physical activities, outcome, and emotional arousal on subject aggression scores. *International Journal of Sport Psychology, 20,* 57–66.

Maccoby, E.E. (1992). The role of parents in the socialization of children: An historical overview. *Developmental Psychology, 28,* 1006–1017.

Maxwell, J.P. & Moores, E. (2007). The development of a short scale measuring aggressiveness and anger in competitive athletes. *Psychology of Sport and Exercise, 8,* 179–193.

Mugno, D.A. & Feltz, D.L. (1985). The social learning of aggression in youth football in the United States. *Canadian Journal of Applied Sport Sciences, 10,* 26–35.

Naylor, S., Burton, D. & Crocker, P.R.E. (2002). Competitive anxiety and sport performance. In J.M Silva & D.E. Stevens (Eds.), *Psychological foundations of sport* (pp.132–154). Boston, MA: Allyn & Bacon.

Neave, N. & Wolfson, S. (2003). Testosterone, territoriality, and the home advantage. *Physiology and Behaviour, 78,* 269–275.

Scott, J.P. (1958). *Aggression.* Chicago, IL: University of Chicago Press.

Sheldon, J.P. & Aimar, C.M. (2001). The role aggression plays in successful and unsuccessful ice hockey behaviours. *Research Quarterly for Exercise and Sport, 72,* 304–309.

Smith, M.D. (1979). Towards an explanation of hockey violence: A reference other approach. *Canadian Journal of Sociology, 4,* 105–123.

Smith, M.D. (1983). *Violence and sport.* Toronto, ON: Butterworths.

Stephens, D.E. (1998). Aggression. In J.L. Duda (Ed.), *Advances in sport and exercise psychology measurement* (pp. 277–294). Morgantown, WV: Fitness Information Technology.

Stephens, D.E. (2000). Predictors of likelihood to aggress in youth soccer: An examination of coed and all-girls teams. *Journal of Sport Behaviour, 23,* 311–323.

Stephens, D.E. & Bredemeier, B. (1996). Moral atmosphere and judgments about aggression in girl's soccer: Relations among moral and motivational variables. *Journal of Sport and Exercise Psychology, 18,* 158–173.

Theberge, N. (1997). "It's part of the game": Physicality and the production of gender in women's hockey. *Gender and Society, 11,* 69–87.

Theberge, N. (2000). Gender and sport. In J. Coakley & E. Dunning (Eds.), *Handbook of sport studies* (pp. 322–333). New York: NY. Sage.

Theberge, N. (2003). "No fear comes": Adolescent girls, ice hockey, and the embodiment of gender. *Youth and Society, 34,* 497–516.

Volkamer, M. (1971). Investigation into aggressiveness in the competitive social system. *Sportwissenshaft, 1,* 33–64.

Widmeyer, W.N. (2002). Reducing aggression in sport. In J.M Silva & D.E. Stevens (Eds.) *Psychological foundations of sport* (pp.380–395). Boston, MA: Allyn & Bacon.

Widmeyer, W.N. & McGuire, E.J. (1997). Frequency of competition and aggression in professional ice hockey. *International Journal of Sport Psychology, 28,* 57–66.

Widmeyer, W.N., Dorsch, K.D., Bray, S.R. & McGuire, E.J. (2002). The nature, prevalence, and consequence of aggression in sport. In J.M Silva & D.E. Stevens (Eds.) *Psychological foundations of sport* (pp.328–351). Boston, MA: Allyn & Bacon.

Young, K. (2000). Sport and violence. In J. Coakley & E. Dunning (Eds.), *Handbook of sport studies* (pp.382–407). New York: NY. Sage.

Chapter 43

Passion for sport and exercise

ROBERT J. VALLERAND, JÉRÉMIE VERNER-FILION AND YVAN PAQUET

SUMMARY

The purpose of the present chapter is to present the Dualistic Model of Passion (Vallerand et al., 2003) and show its importance for sport and exercise psychology. Passion is defined as a strong inclination toward a self-defining activity that people like (or love), find important, and in which they invest time and energy. Specifically, the model proposes the existence of two types of passion (harmonious and obsessive). Harmonious passion is hypothesized to lead to more adaptive outcomes than obsessive passion. This is because with harmonious passion people autonomously engage in the activity that they love. Conversely, with obsessive passion, people engage in the activity that they love because of an internal pressure. Results of several studies reveal that passion matters with respect to a number of important outcomes for sport and exercise psychology such as emotions, psychological well-being, cognitive processes, physical health, performance, and interpersonal relationships. Also discussed in this chapter are the development of passion and the practical applications in the domain of sport and exercise.

INTRODUCTION

Each day, millions of individuals engage in sport and exercise. For many of them, sport and exercise represent more than just an ordinary activity they engage in routinely. It is something special, something that they are passionate about. They love their favorite sport or exercise, find it meaningful and important, and engage regularly in it. Such a passion for this activity leads them to experience a number of positive outcomes. Yet, at times, less positive outcomes may be experienced.

The purpose of this chapter is to present a recent conceptualization of passion (Vallerand, 2008, 2010; Vallerand et al., 2003), the Dualistic Model of Passion, and show its applicability to the realm of sport and exercise. Through the presentation of the model, it will become clear why passion sometimes leads to positive outcomes, and sometimes it does not. Following a discussion on the concept of passion and the presentation of the model, we review research on the role of passion as it pertains to intrapersonal and interpersonal outcomes. We then discuss the development of passion. Finally, we conclude with suggestions for practical applications.

The stories of Mary and William illustrate briefly how passion may influence athletes and exercisers. Mary has been playing soccer her whole life. On the other hand, William has been running ever since he was able to stand up. Both Mary and William love their respective activity, find it important and spend lots of time and energy on it. Their activity has come to define them, as it is now part of who they are. Mary *is* a soccer player, just as William *is* a runner. This passion for their activity has led them to work hard for several years, enabling them to attain excellence in their respective field, as Mary has recently been offered a scholarship to play soccer in college, while William is in tremendous shape and has recently completed his first marathon. Nevertheless, while both are passionate toward their respective activity, they differ in some ways when it comes to their activity involvement. For instance, Mary takes soccer very seriously and trains really hard. She is focused on the task at hand and remains positive. Her life,

however, isn't only about soccer. She can shift her attention to other important life activities, such as studying or spending time with friends. She manages to achieve balance between the demands of her sport and the other aspects of her life. Like Mary, William trains really hard and takes running very seriously. However, running is all that matters for William. He thinks and talks about it all the time, even at the expense of his enjoyment of other life activities. When training, he is focused solely on his performance. When not training, he feels guilty for wasting precious running time. He doesn't find much interest in other life activities such as work, as he's always thinking about his next running session. Thus, William's passion for running is interfering with other life activities and, as a result, he is not as happy as he should be, both while running and when doing something else.

One reason why these two individuals are both similar and different with respect to the practice of their respective activity has to do with passion. They are undoubtedly both passionate for their activity, but they experience their passion differently and because of this, experience different outcomes.

OBJECTIVES

After reading this chapter, you should have:

1. An understanding of the Dualistic Model of Passion (DMP; Vallerand et al., 2003).
2. A better understanding of its applicability to the realm of sport and exercise.
3. Knowledge of the role of passion in outcomes experienced in sport and exercise.
4. Knowledge of the processes involved in the development of passion.
5. Comprehension of research that provides support for our conceptualization of passion.
6. An understanding of practical implications for developing passion in sport and exercise.

THE DUALISTIC MODEL OF PASSION

Despite much attention from philosophers (see Rony, 1990, for a review), little empirical attention has been given to the concept of passion from a psychological standpoint. The

Dualistic Model of Passion (DMP) was developed in order to address this issue. In line with Self-Determination Theory (Deci & Ryan, 2000), the DMP posits that people engage in various activities throughout life in the hope of satisfying the basic psychological needs of autonomy (a desire to feel a sense of personal initiative), competence (a desire to interact effectively with the environment), and relatedness (a desire to feel connected to significant others). With time and experience, most people eventually start to display preference for some activities, especially those that are enjoyable and allow the satisfaction of the aforementioned basic psychological needs. Of these activities, a select few will be perceived as particularly important and enjoyable and will have some resonance with how we see ourselves. These activities thus become passionate activities.

According to the Dualistic Model of Passion (Vallerand, 2008, 2010; Vallerand et al., 2003), passion is defined as *a strong inclination toward a self-defining activity (person or object) that one likes (or even loves), finds important, and in which one invests time and energy*. Thus, four elements characterize a passion for a given activity: we love the activity, we highly value it as it is important and meaningful for us, we engage in it on a regular basis (i.e., several hours per week), and it is part of our identity as it comes to define us. In fact, passionate activities are so important to people that they become part of our identity. For example, those who are passionate about playing soccer or running refer to themselves as "soccer players" and "runners" rather than individuals who merely enjoy their sport. This process, through which the activity comes to define us, is called internalization. Internalization refers to the process by which what was once "out there" – in the outside world – becomes part of us (Deci, Egharri, Patrick, & Leone, 1994). In other words, what was once external to the self becomes a part of it. Thus, the passionate activity (e.g., playing basketball) becomes internalized into one's identity (see Deci et al., 1994; Vallerand, Fortier, & Guay, 1997) because of its importance to the individual (see Deci et al., 1994).

Of major importance is that the internalization of a passionate activity can take place in two different ways, which leads to two different types of passion. One type of internalization is referred to as an autonomous internalization. An autonomous internalization of a passionate activity occurs when individuals freely accept the activity as important for them (Deci & Ryan, 2000; Sheldon, 2002; Vallerand, 1997). This type of internalization leads to a harmonious passion, as people choose to engage in their passionate activity without any contingencies attached to it. The activity thus remains in harmony with other aspects of the person's life as it occupies a significant, but not overpowering, space in the person's identity. With harmonious passion the authentic integrating self (Deci & Ryan, 2000) is at play, allowing the person to fully partake in the passionate activity with an openness that is conducive to positive experiences (Hodgins & Knee, 2002). In other words, with harmonious passion, our inner self is at play. The passionate activity is under our full control and connects well with other aspects of our self and life. There is a smooth integration between who we are (our identity) and this activity. Consequently, with harmonious passion, people should be able to fully focus on the task at hand and experience positive outcomes both during and after task engagement. Furthermore, when prevented from engaging in their passionate activity, people with a harmonious passion should be able to adapt well to the situation and focus their attention and energy on other tasks that need to be done. Thus, there should be little or no conflict between the person's passionate activity and other life domains. Finally, with harmonious passion, the person is in control of the activity and can decide when and when not to engage in the activity. In our example above, Mary is harmoniously passionate about soccer.

The second type of internalization is referred to as controlled internalization (Deci & Ryan, 2000; Sheldon, 2002; Vallerand, 1997).

A controlled internalization of a passionate activity originates from intra- and/or interpersonal pressure attached to the activity, such as contingencies of self-esteem or social acceptance (e.g., Crocker & Park, 2004; Mageau, Carpentier, & Vallerand, 2011), or because the feeling of excitement derived from activity engagement is uncontrollable. A controlled internalization leads to obsessive passion. In other words, the activity becomes part of us because not only do we love it but also because it brings us other more extrinsic benefits such as being popular or liked by other people or giving us a boost in self-esteem when we do well. Thus, the controlled internalization of the activity is not as "pure" as with the autonomous internalization. As such it is more superficial, includes extrinsic elements, and thus does not fully access the authentic or inner self. One consequence of this less than optimal internalization is that one's passion for the activity is not fully under the control of the self. Consequently, people with an obsessive passion can find themselves in the position of experiencing an uncontrollable urge to partake in the activity they view as important and enjoyable. They cannot help but to engage in the passionate activity, as the passion controls them. Consequently, people with an obsessive passion risk experiencing conflict and other negative affective, cognitive, and behavioral consequences during and after activity engagement. Individuals with an obsessive passion come to display a rigid persistence toward the activity, as they often cannot help but to engage in the passionate activity. While such persistence may lead to some benefits (e.g., improved performance in the activity), it may also come at a high cost for the individual, potentially leading to less than optimal functioning within the confines of the passionate activity because of the lack of flexibility that it entails. In addition, such a rigid persistence may lead the person to experience conflict with other aspects of his/her life (when one should be doing something else, for instance), as well as to frustration and rumination about the activity when prevented from engaging in it. William, in our example, is obsessively passionate about running.

RESEARCH ON PASSION FOR SPORT AND EXERCISE

Over the past 10 years or so, over 100 studies have been conducted on harmonious and obsessive passion, both by our own research group and by other research laboratories around the world. Such research has been conducted in a number of contexts, one of which is sports and exercise. In the present chapter, we focus on research carried out in this life context. For a discussion on the role of passion in other contexts (e.g., work, leisure, video gaming, gambling, etc.), the reader is referred to Vallerand (2008, 2010). In addition, although much research has been conducted in a number of different laboratories around the world, because of space limitation, we focus on our own research. Finally, it should be noted that research in sport has been conducted with most types of sport participants, including athletes (e.g., Vallerand et al., 2006), coaches (e.g., Lafreniere, Jowett, Vallerand, Donahue, & Lorimer, 2008), referees (e.g., Philippe, Vallerand, Andrianarisoa, & Brunel, 2009), and fans (e.g., Vallerand, Ntoumanis et al., 2008). Again, because of space limitations, we focus here on research with athletes and exercisers. Readers interested in research with the other types of sport participants are referred to Vallerand, Donahue, & Lafreniere (2011) and Vallerand (2012a).

We begin our review with a description of the initial research conducted in Vallerand et al. (2003, Study 1), followed by research on the intra- and interpersonal consequences of passion. We then present research on the development of passion. Finally, we conclude the chapter with some practical applications and a summary.

Initial research on the concept of passion

The purpose of the initial validation study (Vallerand et al., 2003, Study 1) was to test some of the basic premises of the conceptualization of passion. To that end, college students were asked to complete a questionnaire containing the Passion Scale with respect to an activity that they liked, that they valued, and in which they invested time and energy on a regular basis (i.e., the passion definition). Interestingly, although this activity could be in any area (e.g., music playing, video gaming, reading, etc.), over 60% of our sample indicated that their passionate activity involved either a sport or a type of physical activity. This finding underscores the fact that the results from this study are highly pertinent for the field of sport and exercise. In addition to the Passion Scale, participants completed other scales allowing us to correlate the Passion Scale with other constructs of theoretical interest. This study yielded several findings of interest, including four discussed here. First, results revealed that 84% of the participants had at least a moderate level of passion toward an activity in their lives. Thus, it would appear that it is a majority of people who have a passion for an activity in their lives, and not simply a privileged minority (this finding has been obtained repeatedly; see Vallerand, 2010). Second, participants reported spending an average of 8.5 hours per week on the activity. It thus appears that passionate activities entail heavy involvement. Third, participants had been engaging in the passionate activity for an average of almost six years. This finding underscores the fact that such activities do not simply reflect a passing interest but are meaningful to people and remain so over a long period of time.

A fourth finding of interest is that the results of exploratory and confirmatory factor analyses provided strong support for the existence of two separate constructs corresponding to harmonious and obsessive passion. Subsequent research has supported the bi-factorial structure of the Passion Scale in a number of life contexts and activities including sports and exercise (see Vallerand, 2010, for a review). For instance, Marsh et al. (2013) have shown that the scale is reliable and valid and is equivalent both in English and French, for both men and women, across various age groups, and for a number of different activities. Thus, the scale can be readily used for most if not all types of sports and forms of exercise.

Finally, results from this initial validation study also revealed that both harmonious and obsessive passion were positively associated with measures of activity valuation, with time involvement, and with the perception that the activity was a passion, thereby providing support for the conceptual definition of passion. In addition, while both types of passion were seen as being part of one's identity, only obsessive passion was positively related to a measure of conflict with other life activities. In sum, initial research has provided preliminary support for some of the basic premises of the Dualistic Model of Passion. Subsequent research focused on the study of outcomes associated with the two types of passion, as well as its development.

Passion and affective consequences

The DMP postulates that the type of passion one holds toward an activity plays a significant role in the affective consequences he or she is likely to experience both during and after activity engagement, as well as when prevented from engaging in the passionate activity. More precisely, harmoniously passionate individuals ought to experience more positive affective consequences and less negative affective consequences than individuals with an obsessive passion. This is because with harmonious passion, people volitionally engage in the passionate activity with an openness (Hodgins & Knee, 2002) and a mindfulness (Brown, Ryan, & Creswell, 2007) that allow them to fully partake in the activity and thus to experience positive affective experiences more fully. This is not the case with obsessive passion where one's engagement is more defensive and is less conducive to full engagement in the activity.

The above hypotheses were tested and supported in the initial validation study by Vallerand and colleagues (2003, Study 1). Results showed that when controlling for obsessive passion, harmonious passion was positively related to positive affect during task engagement, but was negatively related to negative affect, especially shame. Conversely, when controlling for harmonious passion, obsessive passion was positively related to negative affect, such as shame and anxiety and was unrelated to positive affect. These results were replicated in two studies with basketball players (Vallerand et al., 2006, Studies 2 and 3). Specifically, when controlling for obsessive passion, harmonious passion was positively related to vitality and positive affect in basketball, while unrelated to negative affect. In contrast, obsessive passion was only positively related to negative affect. Moreover, when people are prevented from engaging in their passionate activity (playing basketball), obsessive passion is positively related to negative affect (e.g., guilt, anxiety) while harmonious passion is not (Vallerand et al., 2003, Study 1).

Because passionate activities are a central part of one's identity, they also come to influence one's life in general. Results of a longitudinal study involving intercollegiate (American) football players (Vallerand et al., 2003, Study 2) showed that, over the course of an entire season, harmonious passion predicted increases in positive affect in life in general but was unrelated to negative affect, whereas obsessive passion was associated with increases in negative affect but was unrelated to positive affect.

Finally, passion research has also looked at the ability of passionate individuals to predict their future affective states (i.e., affective forecasting) following success and failure events within the purview of the passionate activity. Because it is more closely connected to the self

than obsessive passion, harmonious passion should be able to make more accurate predictions of their future emotional states. This hypothesis was supported in a study with sport fans (Verner-Filion, Lafreniere, & Vallerand, 2012). In this study, it was found that harmonious passion was associated with greater accuracy (or better affective forecasting) when predicting the emotional consequences following a win or a defeat of their favorite team. In contrast, obsessive passion was unrelated to affective forecasting accuracy.

In sum, it would appear that passion for sports and exercise matters with respect to the emotions that people experience both inside and outside the purview of the activity. Harmonious passion is associated with more positive emotions, both in the activity and in life in general. In contrast, obsessive passion is related to the experience of negative emotions in the activity, when prevented from engaging in the activity, and in life in general. Similar results were obtained with coaches (Lafreniere et al., 2008, Study 1; Philippe et al., 2009, Study 1). In addition, harmonious passion seems to lead one to being able to correctly identify the positive and negative emotions likely to be experienced under success and failure more than obsessive passion (Verner-Filion et al., 2012).

Passion and psychological well-being

Psychological well-being entails being satisfied with one's life, perceiving that one's life is worth living, and also that one is living up to his or her potential (i.e., high levels of self-realization). Because it allows one to experience positive affective states on a regular basis, it was hypothesized that harmonious passion for a given activity should be positively associated with psychological well-being, whereas obsessive passion should not. These hypotheses have been confirmed repeatedly as pertains to a variety of passionate activities (see, Vallerand, 2012b). These findings have also been obtained with sport and exercise participants. For instance, harmonious passion has been found to be positively related to subjective well-being, while obsessive passion was unrelated to these indices with water polo players and synchronized swimmers (Vallerand, Mageau et al., 2008, Study 2) and basketball players (Vallerand et al., 2006, Study 2).

Research has also focused on the mediating processes involved in the relationship between passion and psychological well-being. In line with Fredrikson's (2001) Broaden-and-Build theory, it is proposed that positive emotions play a mediating role between harmonious passion and psychological well-being. This is because positive emotions allow one to have access to the self and full set of cognitive repertoire, thereby facilitating the use of adaptive processes. Because obsessive passion is typically unrelated to positive emotions, it should not be related to psychological well-being. Rousseau and Vallerand (2008) tested this hypothesis in a study with older adults who were passionate exercisers over a two-month period. Results from a path analysis revealed that harmonious passion positively predicted positive affect while exercising, which led to increases in psychological well-being over time. In contrast, obsessive passion was unrelated to positive affect but positively predicted negative affect. However, negative affect was unrelated to psychological well-being.

Overall, empirical evidence reveals that harmonious passion may positively contribute to psychological well-being. Furthermore, it appears that the positive effects of harmonious passion on psychological well-being takes place through its impact on positive affect. On the other hand, obsessive passion does not seem to contribute to psychological well-being and may even detract from it through its impact on negative affect and conflict with other life activities (see Vallerand, Paquet, Philippe, & Charest, 2010).

Passion and cognitive processes

Based on the DMP, it would be expected that harmonious passion facilitates adaptive cogni-tive processes (such as concentration, flow, and better decision making), whereas obsessive passion should not, or at least should have less positive effects than harmonious passion. As mentioned previously, this is because harmonious passion entails an open, mindful, task engagement while obsessive passion facilitates a more defensive form of activity engagement. Research supports this hypothesis in a number of contexts and activities (e.g., Vallerand et al., 2003, Study 1). For instance, in sports, in research with soccer referees, harmonious passion correlated more strongly with concentration on the passionate activity than on the obsessive passion (Philippe et al., 2009). Other research with soccer fans also demonstrated that obsessive passion in soccer fans prevented full concentration on other life activities taking place on the same day as the passionate activity, while this was not the case for harmonious passion (i.e., game; Vallerand, Ntoumanis et al., 2008).

Another interesting cognitive concept is flow (Csikszentmihalyi, 1978). Flow refers to a desirable cognitive state that people experience when they become completely immersed in an activity. Much research in a number of areas has shown that harmonious passion positively predicts the experience of flow during task engagement, while obsessive passion does not (e.g., Forest, Mageau, Sarrazin, & Morin, 2011). Results from the Vallerand et al. (2003, Study 1) research as well as that conducted in sports with soccer referees replicated these findings (Philippe et al., 2009). Finally, in the latter study, referees with a harmonious passion displayed better decision-making than those with an obsessive passion.

In sum, the two types of passion lead to different levels of cognitive functioning. Harmonious passion leads to the most adaptive types of cognitive processes, whereas obsessive passion leads to the least adaptive types.

Passion and physical health

Passion may affect physical health in a number of ways. For instance, passion may positively contribute to health by leading people to engage regularly in physical activity, to get in better physical shape, and to experience increase physical well-being over time. However, passion can also put people's health at risk, by leading them to engage in risky sport or exercise behavior or because of ill-advised rigid persistence in the activity. Cycling is a good example. In spring, summer, and fall, this activity can be a lot of fun and promote health. In contrast, it can be very hazardous during the winter if you decide to cycle on the icy and snowy roads of the Province of Quebec. It is not recommended to cycle under such extreme conditions as cyclists may experience falls and injuries. Vallerand and colleagues (2003, Study 3) showed that those cyclists who engage in winter cycling in Quebec display higher levels of obsessive passion than those who do not. No differences were found with respect to harmonious passion.

Other research has looked at the role of passion in susceptibility to injury and found that obsessive passion may constitute a risk factor for injuries in runners (Stephan, Deroche, Brewer, Caudroit, & Le Scanff, 2009). Rip, Fortin, and Vallerand (2006) went one step further and showed that both types of passion protect against acute injuries but that obsessive passion is a risk factor for *chronic* injuries. This is because with obsessive passion, people cannot stop activity engagement and thus run when they should not and risk aggravating an acute injury. Finally, research with yoga exercisers revealed that only those with a harmonious passion were able to derive positive psychological and health benefits from their regular engagement (Carbonneau, Vallerand, & Massicotte, 2010). Those with an obsessive passion even experienced an increase in negative emotions over time!

In sum, the general picture derived from the research described above is that, obsessive passion may lead to some negative effects through rigid persistence and engagement in risky behavior in the activity, while harmonious passion can lead to more positive effects on one's health.

Passion and performance

The Dualistic Model of Passion posits that passion represents a key determinant of high-level performance. This is so because passion leads athletes to engage in a specific form of practice that focuses on improving one's skills, called deliberate practice (Ericsson & Charness, 1994). Indeed, if one is to engage in an activity for long hours for several years (sometimes a lifetime) to get better at one's sport or form of exercise, one must love the activity dearly, and have the desire to keep on practicing even when times are rough. Given what we know about passion, both forms of passion should lead participants to engage in deliberate practice that, over time, should lead to improved performance. This relationship was supported in several studies in a variety of activities ranging from music, dramatic arts, and sports and using objective indicators of performance (see Vallerand, 2010, for a review).

With respect to sport, one study with basketball players (Vallerand, Mageau et al., 2008, Study I) revealed that both types of passion led to engagement in deliberate practice that, in turn, led to higher levels of objective performance. Another study was conducted with water polo players and synchronized swimmers (Vallerand, Mageau et al., 2008, Study 2) in order to examine exactly how passion contributes directly to deliberate practice, and indirectly to sport performance. In line with Elliot (1997), it was proposed that achievement goals should represent important mediators between passion and deliberate practice. Results identified the existence of two roads to high-level athletic performance. The first is triggered by harmonious passion that fuels mastery goals (a focus on the development of personal competence and task mastery) that lead to deliberate practice that, in turn, leads to performance. The second road to performance is more complex and emanates from obsessive passion. This type of passion fuels mastery goals (that lead to performance through deliberate practice) but mostly performance-approach goals (a focus on the attainment of personal competence relative to others) and performance-avoidance goals (a focus on avoiding incompetence relative to others) that negatively and directly influences performance. In addition, only individuals with a harmonious passion experience psychological well-being while attempting to reach high levels of performance in sport. These findings run contrary to the popular adage: "no pain no gain". Rather, it appears that it is possible to reach the highest levels of performance through a painless, even happy, passionate engagement in the sport and exercise to the extent that it is harmonious in nature.

Passion and interpersonal outcomes

The coach–athlete relationship is one of the most important ones in sport (Mageau & Vallerand, 2003). A better understanding of this relationship is important if we are to help athletes and exercisers reach their goals in sport and exercise while feeling good during engagement in sport and exercise. We believe that the type of passion one holds for sport or exercise represents an important factor that should allow both athletes and coaches to experience high quality relationships. Specifically, harmonious passion should be more likely to foster positive relationships with others in the context of their sport because it leads people to fully immerse themselves in the activity and to experience positive emotions that may be shared with others. Initial research conducted on this issue in a field setting revealed that athletes' harmonious passion toward their sport was positively related to various indices of relationship satisfaction with their coach, whereas obsessive passion was mostly unrelated to those relationship indices (Lafreniere et al., 2008, Study 1). This first study, however, did not address the mediating role of emotions in the process. A subsequent research with coaches did so (Lafreniere et al., 2008, Study 2), and confirmed the role of positive affect, generally experienced by coaches while coaching, as a mediator of the relation between harmonious passion toward coaching and perceived relationship quality with their players. Obsessive passion was unrelated to positive affect or relationship with the athletes.

Subsequent research with basketball players replicated these findings with respect to teammates. Specifically, it was found that harmonious passion led the athletes to experience positive emotions during the basketball camp. In turn, positive emotions predicted the quality or relationships that developed among teammates over the course of the week-long basketball camp (Philippe, Vallerand, Houlfort, Lavigne, & Donahue, 2010, Study 3). Furthermore, it was found in this study that obsessive passion led to relationships of lower quality with teammates through its influence on negative affect.

In sum, preliminary evidence reveals that harmonious passion matters with respect to the development and maintenance of positive relationships between coach and athletes, as well as among teammates. Conversely, it appears that obsessive passion leads to more negative relationships. Such effects seem to be mediated by either positive or negative emotions, as pertains to harmonious and obsessive passions, respectively.

ON THE DEVELOPMENT OF PASSION

The above research documents the role of passion in a variety of outcomes. As such, it would thus appear important to have a better understanding as to how passion develops. According to the DMP (Vallerand, 2008, 2010; Vallerand et al., 2003), there are at least three processes through which an interesting activity such as sport and exercise can transform into a passionate activity: 1) activity selection; 2) activity valuation; and 3) the type of internalization process that takes place.

First, activity selection refers to the person's preference for the activity over other activities. To the extent that the person feels that such selection reflects true choice and interests and is consonant with her or his identity, it should promote the development of passion toward that activity. Activity valuation (or the subjective importance given to the activity by the person) is expected to play an important role in the internalization of the identity. Research has indeed shown that when the object of interest is highly valued and meaningful, one is inclined to internalize the valued object, to make it part of him- or herself (Aron, Aron, & Smollan, 1992; Deci et al., 1994). The more important (or valued) the activity is, the more the activity will be internalized in the person's identity and the more passionate the person will be toward the activity.

Furthermore, the DMP proposes that the type of passion that will develop depends on the type of internalization that takes place. To the extent that the internalization process takes place in an autonomous fashion, then a harmonious passion will develop; if the internalization is carried in a controlled fashion, an obsessive passion will develop. The DMP further posits that social environment and personal factors will influence the internalization process. More precisely, social environment (i.e., parents, coaches, peers, etc.) and personal factors (i.e., individual differences and personality processes) that promote a person's autonomy will facilitate the autonomous internalization process and thus lead to the development of a harmonious passion. In contrast, controlling social environment and personal factors will facilitate the controlled internalization process and thus lead to the development of an obsessive passion.

The role of social environment in the development of passion was explored in a recent study with students who had never played a musical instrument (Mageau et al., 2009, Study 3). Results demonstrated that high autonomy support from close adults (parents and teachers) as well as children's activity valuation were conducive to the development of harmonious passion. However, high levels of parental perceived valuation and lack of autonomy support (i.e., controlling behavior) were found to predict the development of obsessive passion. As for personal factors, research conducted with water polo players and synchronized swimmers (Vallerand et al., 2006) demonstrated that valuation of the sport activity coupled with an autonomous personality (as assessed by the Global Motivation Scale; Guay, Mageau, & Vallerand, 2003) predicted harmonious passion. In contrast, valuation of the activity coupled with a controlled personality style predicted obsessive passion. Moreover, harmonious passion was conducive to subjective well-being over time while obsessive passion was unrelated to it.

The DMP further posits that a passion for an activity continues developing in an ongoing process after it has initially developed. It is proposed that variations in activity valuation will lead to subsequent modulation in the intensity of the passion. In addition, the presence or absence of social and personal factors that pertain to the autonomous versus controlled internalization process will influence the ongoing development of passion in a corresponding fashion. Thus, although the predominant type of passion is usually in operation, it is possible to reinforce the predominant passion or to make the other type of passion operative depending on which type of social or personal factors is made salient.

In sum, results presented in this section provide support for the DMP as it pertains to the development of passion. Research is needed to determine more clearly how passion develops, as well as how the newly developed passion varies as a function of prevalent social and personal factors in sport and exercise.

PRACTICAL APPLICATIONS

Research reviewed in this chapter has shown that harmonious passion is generally more positively related to positive consequences than obsessive passion. Therefore, it would seem appropriate to propose ways to facilitate harmonious passion. Promoting harmonious passion can be done at each of the three steps of the development of passion described previously, namely activity selection, activity valuation, and the internalization of the activity in identity. More specifically, the role of the social environment at each of the three stages is crucial, especially with children and adolescents. Adults are in a prime position to promote children's harmonious passion, especially if they nurture their needs for autonomy, competence, and relatedness (Deci & Ryan, 2000; Vallerand, 1997, 2010). With respect to the first step of activity selection, parents and physical educators should encourage children to engage in a variety of sports and exercises. Trying out different sports and forms of exercise should help children (and teenagers) select activities that they enjoy, that make use of their abilities and strengths (see Forest et al., 2012), and that fit with the their sense of identity. Consequently, such activities should be subsequently internalized in identity and eventually become a passion.

Autonomy support is also recommended for the two other stages of passion development. For instance, with respect to the second step in the passion development process, namely valuation of the selected sport activity, noncontrolling and supportive parents, physical educators, and coaches who teach by example and serve as models may provide the necessary impetus to lead young athletes to invest further in the sport activity and value it even more. The role of peers is also important because friends' influence becomes increasingly important as children move toward puberty (Eccles & Wigfield, 2002). Enhanced valuation of the selected activity may then lead to its internalization in identity.

Finally, providing autonomy support to children while engaging in their valued, selected activity should also ensure that the internalization of activity, which takes place in the third step of passion development, is autonomous in nature, thereby leading to harmonious passion for the activity. Thus, promoting children's sense of autonomy (Deci & Ryan, 2000) by providing opportunities for choice, ownership, or "voice" regarding decisions and behaviors should facilitate the development of harmonious passion. For example, athletes who have recently started playing soccer would be more likely to develop a harmonious passion toward this sport if their coaches clearly explain to them why it is important to practice daily and give them opportunities to choose from a variety of practice regimens. Conversely, the chances are that coaches who impose pressure or coerce athletes to practice more are likely to lead to the development of obsessive passion. Later on, once harmonious passion has developed, providing autonomy support and minimizing pressure still remains important to ensure that harmonious passion is maintained.

CONCLUSION

Sport and exercise play a significant role in many people's lives. More often than not, people engaged in sport and exercise are not simply motivated, they are passionate toward their activity. The purpose of the present chapter was to present the DMP (Vallerand, 2008, 2010; Vallerand et al., 2003), a conceptualization on passion that enables us to have a better understanding of the psychological forces that may lead athletes, exercisers, and other sport participants (e.g., coaches, fans and referees) to sustain intense engagement in sport and exercise and to experience different types of outcomes in the process.

Specifically, this chapter has shown that two types of passion, namely harmonious and obsessive passion, matter greatly for athletes and exercisers, because they lead to a host of consequences (affect, cognitions, subjective well-being, performance, physical health, etc.). Harmonious and obsessive passions typically lead to adaptive and maladaptive outcomes, respectively. Furthermore, we have described the nature of processes through which passion develops. Harmonious passion results from an important and valued activity that has been internalized in one's identity in an autonomous fashion. In contrast, obsessive passion results from an important and valued activity internalized in one's identity in a controlled fashion. Moreover, we have proposed practical applications especially as pertains to the development of passion. Autonomy support (i.e., providing choices in activity selection and in decision regarding the activity, developing noncontrolling and supportive relationships with parents and coaches, etc.) is recommended for the development of harmonious passion.

In sum, it would appear that the construct of passion aptly describes the phenomenological experiences, processes, and outcomes that sport participants and exercisers go through in their activity.

LEARNING AIDS

1 Define passion.

Passion is defined as a strong inclination toward a self-defining activity (person or object) that one likes (or even loves), finds important, and in which one invests time and energy.

2 Explain the two types of internalization process.

An autonomous internalization of a passionate activity occurs when individuals freely accept an activity is important for them. This type of internalization leads to a harmonious passion, as people choose to engage in their passionate activity without any contingencies attached to it.

A controlled internalization of a passionate activity originates from intra- and/or interpersonal pressure attached to the activity, such as contingencies of self-esteem or social acceptance, or because the feeling of excitement derived from activity engagement is uncontrollable. A controlled internalization leads to obsessive passion.

3 Describe the two types of passion.

Harmonious passion: Passionate activity in which people engage without any contingencies, which occupies a significant, but not overpowering, space in the person's identity, allowing the person to fully partake in the passionate activity with an openness that is conducive to positive experiences, both during and after task engagement. The activity is thus under full control and connects well with other aspects of the self. There is little or no conflict between the person's passionate activity and other life domains, as people can decide when to and when not to engage in the activity.

Obsessive passion: Passionate activity in which people engage because of both the intrinsic (i.e., pleasure, love for the activity, etc.) and the extrinsic (i.e., self-esteem contingencies, social recognition, etc.) benefits attached to the activity. Thus, the activity is not fully under control of the self and people cannot help but engage in the passionate activity. Therefore, people with an obsessive passion display a rigid persistence toward the activity, leading to conflict with other aspects of the self.

4 Discuss the "two roads to performance".

The harmonious road: Harmonious passion fuels mastery goals and deliberate practice, which in turn lead to performance. Furthermore, individuals with harmonious passion experience psychological well-being while attempting to reach high levels of performance in sport.

The obsessive road: Obsessive passion also fuels mastery goals (that lead to performance through deliberate practice) but mostly performance-approach goals and performance-avoidance goals that negatively and directly influence performance. Furthermore, obsessive passion is not associated with the experience of psychological well-being.

5 Explain how autonomy support contributes to the development of a harmonious passion.

First, autonomy supportive parents, physical educators, and coaches may provide the necessary impetus for young athletes to invest further in the sport activity and value it even more. Peers are also important, especially toward puberty. Enhanced valuation of the selected activity may then lead to its internalization in identity.

Second, providing autonomy support to children when engaging in their valued, selected, activity should also ensure that the internalization of activity is autonomous in nature, thereby leading to harmonious passion for the activity. Providing opportunities for choice, ownership, or "voice" regarding decisions and behaviors should promote children's sense of autonomy, and thus, the development of harmonious passion. Even once harmonious passion has developed, providing autonomy support and minimizing pressure remains important to ensure that harmonious passion is maintained.

REVIEW QUESTIONS

1 What are the criteria that characterize passion?

2 How is harmonious passion defined? How is obsessive passion defined?

3 Which type of passion is more likely to contribute to positive psychological adjustment and why?

4 What are the two roads to excellence?

5 What are the processes involved in the development of passion? Describe each process.

6 How can harmonious passion be best achieved? How can obsessive passion be achieved?

EXERCISES

Jim is a volleyball player. He has been playing since he was little, as both his parents also are volleyball players. Early on, Jim's parents directed him toward this sport. Even though Jim wanted to try other sports, his parents were always reluctant as they both thought volleyball was the best sport for him. However, Jim always felt that he had to continue playing volleyball because he did not want to disappoint his parents, even though he loves this sport and spends a lot of time and energy practicing hard.

On the other hand, Emily has a passion for dancing. This passion developed gradually, however. During her childhood, her parents allowed her to discover and experience various activities. They provided her with choices, alternative and great support in her decisions. With time, Emily chose to invest more time and energy in dancing, which was the activity that satisfied her the most.

1   What is the type of passion that Jim is most likely to have developed toward volleyball? What about Emily? Explain why.

2   Explain the role of Jim and Emily's parents in the development of their respective passion.

3   What kind of emotions is Jim most likely to experience when playing volleyball? Or when he is prevented from playing other sports? Explain.

4   Who is more likely to attain high levels of performance? Jim or Emily? What consequences might be associated with the attainment of such level of performance for Jim? And Emily?

ADDITIONAL READING

Vallerand, R.J. (2008). On the psychology of passion: In search of what makes people's lives most worth living. *Canadian Psychology-Psychologie Canadienne, 49*, 1–13. doi: 10.1037/0708-5591.49.1.1

Vallerand, R.J. (2010). On passion for life activities: The Dualistic Model of Passion. In M.P. Zanna (Ed.), *Advances in experimental social psychology* (Vol. 42, pp. 97–193). New York, NY: Academic Press.

Vallerand, R.J. (2012). Passion for sport and exercise: The Dualistic Model of Passion. In G. Roberts & D. Treasure (Eds.), *Advances in motivation in sport and exercise* (Vol. 3, pp. 160–206). Champaign, IL: Human Kinetics.

Vallerand, R.J., Blanchard, C., Mageau, G.A., Koestner, R., Ratelle, C., Leonard, M. & Marsolais, J. (2003). Les passions de l'Ame: On obsessive and harmonious passion. *Journal of Personality and Social Psychology, 85*, 756–767. doi: 10.1037/0022-3514-85.4.756

REFERENCES

Aron, A., Aron, E.N. & Smollan, D. (1992). Inclusion of other in the Self Scale and the structure of interpersonal closeness. *Journal of Personality and Social Psychology, 63*, 596–612.

Brown, K.W., Ryan, R.M. & Creswell, J.D. (2007). Mindfulness: Theoretical foundations and evidence for its salutary effects. *Psychological Inquiry, 18*, 211–237. doi: 10.1080/1047840070 1598298

Carbonneau, N., Vallerand, R.J. & Massicotte, S. (2010). Is the practice of yoga associated with positive outcomes? The role of passion. *The Journal of Positive Psychology, 5*, 452–465. doi: 10.1080/17439760.2010.534107

Crocker, J. & Park, L.E. (2004). The costly pursuit of self-esteem. *Psychological Bulletin, 130*, 392–414. doi: 10.1037/0033-2909.130.3.392

Csikszentmihalyi, M. (1978). Intrinsic rewards and emergent motivation. In M.R. Lepper & D. Greene (Eds.), *The hidden costs of reward* (pp.205–216). Hillsdale, NJ: Eribaum.

Deci, E.L., Egharri, H., Patrick, B.C. & Leone, D.R. (1994). Facilitating internalization: The self-determination perspective. *Journal of Personality, 62*, 119–142.

Deci, E.L. & Ryan, R.M. (2000). The "what" and "why" of goal pursuits: Human needs and the self-determination of behavior. *Psychological Inquiry, 11*, 227–268. doi: 10.1207/S15327965pli 1104_01

Eccles, J.S. & Wigfield, A. (2002). Motivational beliefs, values, and goals. *Annual Review of Psychology, 53*, 109–132. doi: doi:10.1146/annurev. psych.53.100901.135153

Elliot, A.J. (1997). Integrating the "classic" and "contemporary" approaches to achievement motivation: A hierarchical model of approach and avoidance achievement motivation. In M.L. Maehr & P.R. Pintrich (Eds.), *Advances in motivation and achievement* (Vol. 10, pp.143–179): Greenwich, CT: JAI Press.

Ericsson, K.A. & Charness, N. (1994). Expert performance: Its structure and acquisition. *American Psychologist, 49*, 725–747.

Forest, J., Mageau, G.A., Crevier-Braud, L., Dubreuil, P., Bergeron, E. & Lavigne, G.L. (2012). Harmonious passion as a mediator of the relation between signature strengths' use and optimal functioning at work: Test of an intervention program. *Human Relations, 65(9)*, 1233–1252. doi:10.1177/0018726711433134.

Forest, J., Mageau, G.A., Sarrazin, C. & Morin, E.M. (2011). "Work is my passion": The different affective, behavioural, and cognitive consequences of harmonious and obsessive passion toward work. *Canadian Journal of Administrative Sciences/Revue Canadienne des Sciences de l'Administration, 28*, 27–40. doi: 10.1002/cjas.170

Fredrickson, B.L. (2001). The role of positive emotions in positive psychology: The broaden-and-build theory of positive emotions. *American Psychologist, 56*, 218–226.

Guay, F., Mageau, G.A. & Vallerand, R.J. (2003). On the hierarchical structure of self-determined motivation: A test of top-down, bottom-up, reciprocal, and horizontal effects. *Personality and Social Psychology Bulletin, 29*, 992–1004. doi: 10.1177/0146167203253297

Hodgins, H.S. & Knee, C. (2002). The integrating self and conscious experience. *Handbook of self-determination research* (pp.87–100). Rochester, NY: University of Rochester Press; US.

Lafreniere, M.A.K., Jowett, S., Vallerand, R.J., Donahue, E.G. & Lorimer, R. (2008). Passion in sport: On the quality of the coach–athlete relationship. *Journal of Sport & Exercise Psychology, 30*, 541–560.

Mageau, G.A., Carpentier, J. & Vallerand, R.J. (2011). The role of self-esteem contingencies the distinction between obsessive and harmonious passion. *European Journal of Social Psychology, 41*, 720–729.

Mageau, G.A. & Vallerand, R.J. (2003). The coach–athlete relationship: A motivational model. *Journal of Sports Sciences, 21*, 883–904. doi: 10.1080/0264041031000140374

Mageau, G.A., Vallerand, R.J., Charest, J., Salvy, S.J., Lacaille, N., Bouffard, T. & Koestner, R. (2009). On the development of harmonious and obsessive passion: The role of autonomy support, activity specialization, and identification with the activity. *Journal of Personality, 77*, 601–646. doi: 10.1111/j.1467-6494. 2009.00559.x

Marsh, H.W., Vallerand, R.J., Lafreniere, M.A.K., Parker, P., Morin, A.J.S., Carbonneau, N., Paquet, Y. (2013). Passion: Does one scale fit all? Construct validity of two-factor passion scale and psychometric invariance over different activities and languages. *Psychological Assessment, 25*, 796–809.

Philippe, F.L., Vallerand, R.J., Andrianarisoa, J. & Brunel, P. (2009). Passion in referees: Examining their affective and cognitive experiences in sport situations. *Journal of Sport & Exercise Psychology, 31*, 77–96.

Philippe, F.L., Vallerand, R.J., Houlfort, N., Lavigne, G.L. & Donahue, E.G. (2010). Passion for an activity and quality of interpersonal relationships: The mediating role of emotions. *Journal of Personality and Social Psychology, 98*, 917–932. doi: 10.1037/a0018017

Rip, B., Fortin, S. & Vallerand, R.J. (2006). The relationship between passion and injury in dance students. *Journal of Dance, Medicine & Science, 10*, 14–20.

Rony, J.-A. (1990). *Les passions*. Paris: Presses Universitaires de France.

Rousseau, F.L. & Vallerand, R.J. (2008). An examination of the relationship between passion and subjective well-being in older adults. *International Journal of Aging & Human Development, 66*, 195–211. doi: 10.2190/AG.66.3.b

Sheldon, K.M. (2002). The self-concordance model of healthy goal striving: When personal goals correctly represent the person. *Handbook of self-determination research.* (pp.65–86): Rochester, NY: University of Rochester Press.

Stephan, Y., Deroche, T., Brewer, B.W., Caudroit, J. & Le Scanff, C. (2009). Predictors of perceived susceptibility to sport-related injury among competitive runners: The role of previous experience, neuroticism, and passion for running. *Applied Psychology: An International Review, 58*, 672–687. doi: 10.1111/j.1464-0597.2008.00373.x

Vallerand, R.J. (1997). Toward a hierarchical model of intrinsic and extrinsic motivation. In M.P. Zanna (Ed.), *Advances in experimental social psychology* (Vol. 29, pp.271–360). San Diego, CA: Academic Press.

Vallerand, R.J. (2008). On the psychology of passion: In search of what makes people's lives most worth living. *Canadian Psychology-Psychologie Canadienne, 49*, 1–13. doi: 10.1037/0708-5591.49.1.1

Vallerand, R.J. (2010). On passion for life activities: The Dualistic Model of Passion. In M.P. Zanna (Ed.), *Advances in experimental social psychology* (Vol. 42, pp.97–193). New York, NY: Academic Press.

Vallerand, R.J. (2012a). Passion for sport and exercise: The Dualistic Model of Passion. In G. Roberts & D. Treasure (Eds.), *Advances in motivation in sport and exercise* (Vol. 3, pp.160–206). Champaign, IL: Human Kinetics.

Vallerand, R.J. (2012b). The role of passion in sustainable psychological well-being. *Psychology of Well-Being: Theory, Research and Practice, 2*, 1–21.

Vallerand, R.J., Blanchard, C., Mageau, G.A., Koestner, R., Ratelle, C., Leonard, M., Marsolais, J. (2003). Les passions de l'Ame: On obsessive and harmonious passion. *Journal of Personality and Social Psychology, 85*, 756–767. doi: 10.1037/0022-3514-85.4.756

Vallerand, R.J., Donahue, E.G. & Lafreniere, M.A.K. (2011). Passion for sport. In T. Morris & P. Terry (Eds.), *The new sport and exercise psychology companion* (pp. 583–607). Morgantown, WV: Fitness Information Technology.

Vallerand, R.J., Fortier, M.S. & Guay, F. (1997). Self-determination and persistence in a real-life setting: Toward a motivational model of high school dropout. *Journal of Personality and Social Psychology, 72*, 1161–1176.

Vallerand, R.J., Mageau, G.A., Elliot, A.J., Dumais, A., Demers, M.A. & Rousseau, F. (2008). Passion and performance attainment in sport. *Psychology of Sport and Exercise, 9*, 373–392. doi: 10.1016/j.psychsport.2007.05.003

Vallerand, R.J., Ntoumanis, N., Philippe, F.L., Lavigne, G.L., Carbonneau, N., Bonneville, A. & Maliha, G. (2008). On passion and sports fans: A look at football. *Journal of Sports Sciences, 26*, 1279–1293. doi: 10.1080/02640410802123185

Vallerand, R.J., Paquet, Y., Philippe, F.L. & Charest, J. (2010). On the role of passion for work in burnout: A process model. *Journal of Personality, 78*, 289–312. doi: 10.1111/j.1467-6494.2009.00616.x

Vallerand, R.J., Rousseau, F.L., Grouzet, F.M.E., Dumais, A., Grenier, S. & Blanchard, C.M. (2006). Passion in sport: A look at determinants and affective experiences. *Journal of Sport & Exercise Psychology, 28*, 454–478.

Verner-Filion, J., Lafreniere, M.-A.K. & Vallerand, R.J. (2012). On the accuracy of affective forecasting: The moderating role of passion. *Personality and Individual Differences, 52*, 849–854. doi: 10.1016/j.paid.2012.01.014

Part Seven

Enhancing health and well-being

EDITED BY NIKOS L.D. CHATZISARANTIS AND ATHANASIOS G. PAPAIOANNOU

Chapter 44

Physical activity and feeling good

PANTELEIMON EKKEKAKIS AND SUSAN H. BACKHOUSE

SUMMARY

Physical activity can make participants feel better, an effect that has wide-ranging applications for promoting mental health and increasing motivation for continued physical activity participation. Numerous studies have shown that physical activity can lower anxiety and depression, two mental health problems that impact the quality of life of millions of people. Furthermore, if certain conditions are met, physical activity can increase feelings of energy and calmness, thus offering a healthful alternative to widely consumed but unhealthy chemical agents that are often used as affective-state regulators (e.g., sugar, caffeine, alcohol, nicotine). This chapter summarizes the key findings in this line of research and outlines what exercise professionals can do to increase the likelihood that physical activity will result in positive affective experiences.

INTRODUCTION

Since the dawn of exercise psychology in the late 1960s and early 1970s, understanding the effects of physical activity on how people feel has been a major research focus. What justifies this level of interest? There are at least two important reasons. First, if physical activity, either a single session (what is referred to in the literature as "acute" activity) or a long-term program lasting several weeks or months (what is referred to in the literature as "chronic" activity), can make people feel better, this may have implications for improving people's mental health. Anxiety and mood disorders, such as depression, are among the leading causes of disability worldwide. The standard approaches to treatment, namely drugs and psychotherapy, can be effective for many people but also have considerable cost and, especially in the case of drugs, some very undesirable side-effects. On the other hand, physical activity is not only inexpensive and safe but also offers a multitude of additional benefits for the cardiovascular, metabolic, immune, muscular, and skeletal systems.

The second reason why exercise psychologists are interested in how physical activity makes people feel is because, as was explained in Chapter 6, the positive or negative feelings people associate with physical activity may influence their motivation for future participation and adherence. People generally choose to do what makes them feel better and tend to avoid what makes them feel worse. So, it is reasonable to expect that, if participants feel better during and after physical activity, they may be more inclined to incorporate regular physical activity into their lives. Conversely, if physical activity consistently makes them feel worse, their motivation may be diminished.

For these reasons, how people feel in response to physical activity is of extraordinary importance. In this chapter, we review the main conclusions from this line of research (see Figure 44.1).

OBJECTIVES

After reading this chapter you should be able to:

1 Explain the main challenges in designing studies to establish a cause-and-effect relationship.
2 Define anxiety and depression.
3 Describe the main types of anxiety and mood disorders.
4 Summarize the effects of physical activity on anxiety and depression.
5 Identify conditions that promote the "feel-better" effects of physical activity.

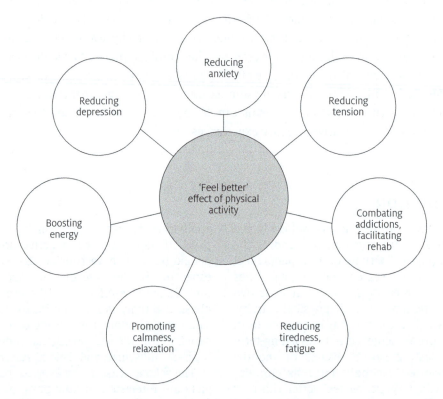

Figure 44.1 Physical activity can make people feel better. This effect has several important applications, from helping individuals control anxiety and depression, to acting as a healthy substitute for many unhealthy substances that people use to lower tension and tiredness and increase energy and calmness (e.g., sugar, caffeine, nicotine, alcohol), to facilitating rehabilitation from addictions.

THE CHALLENGE OF ESTABLISHING CAUSATION

Despite mounting evidence for its effectiveness in ameliorating a range of mental health problems, physical activity is not yet widely recognized as a form of treatment by clinicians. On the other hand, exercise psychologists have been extolling the benefits of physical activity for mental health with great conviction for decades. This striking difference of opinion stems primarily from differing evaluations of the quality of the research evidence (which may, in turn, reflect some degree of bias on both sides). This issue is complex but understanding it is crucial for evaluating this literature in a balanced and scientifically responsible manner.

You have probably heard the expression "correlation does not equal causation." For example, let's say that a researcher administers questionnaires to the 3,000 members of a local community, assessing their amount of regular physical activity and their levels of depression. Let's also imagine that, by analysing these data, the researcher finds a substantial negative correlation (for example, $r = -0.40$) between physical activity and depression, indicating that higher levels of self-reported physical activity are associated with lower levels of depression (and vice versa). Would this finding enable the researcher to conclude that physical activity is an effective method for reducing depression?

As tempting as this might be for anyone who believes in the benefits of physical activity, the answer is no, one would not be justified in drawing this conclusion. The reason is that this finding is merely a correlation. That physical activity reduces depression is just one possibility. However, based only on this correlation, an equally likely interpretation is that high levels of depression reduce one's willingness to be physically active. In other words, the direction of causality might be reversed. Finally, it is also possible that high physical activity and low depression might be due to some third factor, such as socioeconomic status or genetics.

So, how can one prove causation? The most direct way is by conducting well-designed experimental studies. In an experimental study, researchers recruit individuals who are chronically sedentary and have been diagnosed with the condition they are interested in treating (e.g., anxiety, depression). These individuals must be a representative sample of the population to which one wishes to generalize the findings (e.g., British men and women between 40 and 65 years of age, or male patients with cardiovascular disease). Researchers then randomly assign these participants to either an "experimental" group that will follow a program of physical activity or a "control" group.

This seems straightforward but conducting such a study well is far from easy. For example, what should the members of the control group do? Would it be appropriate to measure their anxiety or depression, then send them home for a few months, and then measure their anxiety and depression again to see if they changed? A good control group is one that does everything that the experimental group does except for what is presumed to be the "active ingredient" of the treatment; in this case, physical activity. In other words, the participants assigned to the control group must meet each other with the same frequency and for the same length of time as the participants in the experimental group, they must receive the same amount of attention from the investigators and, ideally, they must be doing something that creates in them the same expectation of benefit as the physical activity presumably creates in the members of the experimental group. This "expectation of benefit" is what is commonly referred to as the "placebo" effect.

It is crucial for this "expectation of benefit" to be controlled for at least two reasons: (a) because most people are aware that physical activity is supposed to benefit health; and (b) because most mental health variables (such as anxiety and depression) are measured by self-reports and reflect subjective thoughts and feelings that cannot be corroborated by other, more objective, evidence. Therefore, it is possible that some of the participants in the experimental group will report that they feel better solely because they are taking part in an activity they know to be good for them. For this reason, in well-designed studies, the members of the control group are not simply sent home but they engage in activities that should make them believe that they are doing something positive and beneficial, such as attending informational seminars, doing very low amounts of physical activity, or even taking a placebo "drug" (e.g., a sugar pill).

The challenge of designing a good experiment does not end here. Besides having a good control group, a well-designed study should also satisfy several other requirements. For example, it is important that the researchers in charge of administering the questionnaires or conducting the interviews for the assessment of the mental health variables be unaware of whether the participants they interact with were members of the experimental or the control group. The reason is that this knowledge could bias their behavior (e.g., they may smile more or provide more thorough explanations to members of the experimental group). A good study should also provide convincing evidence that any positive effects can be attributed specifically to the physical activity, not to other aspects of the treatment. For example, it is well established that social interaction and group support can help reduce depression and improve perceived quality of life. If a physical activity intervention is administered in groups, as is usually done, one cannot be certain whether any positive outcomes can be specifically attributed to the physical activity as opposed to socializing among group members. How the study is advertised and how participants are recruited into the study is also important. For example, if a study is advertised as an investigation of "exercise for treating depression," it would be more likely to attract individuals with a positive view of exercise or individuals who believe in the potential therapeutic effects of exercise. Another crucial consideration is how to handle those study participants who are allocated to the physical activity group but drop out before the end of the intervention. If these individuals are ignored, and only those who persist until the end are included in the statistical analyses, the results would reflect only the "best case scenario," namely, what happens to those individuals who are willing to accept the treatment (possibly because the treatment was effective for them). So, to reduce this potential bias, in well-designed studies, dropouts are included in the analyses, often substituting their missing values by carrying forward their last valid score. This type of analysis is known as "intention to treat" analysis.

Even if all of these precautions are taken, however, physical activity interventions still face some insurmountable challenges. Ideally, a research participant should not be aware of whether she or he was assigned to the experimental group and is, therefore, receiving the "active ingredient," the treatment that is supposed to produce benefits. Likewise, the person administering the treatment should not be aware of whether the treatment contains the active ingredient or is simply a placebo. Such experimental designs, which are standard in drug research, are called "double-blind" since both the participants and the experimenters who come in contact with the participants are unaware of group assignment. Clearly, this type of blinding is impossible in physical activity studies. A person who is exercising knows that she or he was assigned to the exercise group and, conversely, the person who is not exercising knows that she or he was not assigned to the exercise group. Furthermore, the person leading the exercise also knows that all those taking part in the exercise program were assigned to the exercise group. Therefore, there is no way to fully control for the expectation of benefits associated with exercise (since the members of the control group cannot be doing the exact same thing) and no way to be sure that exercise leaders maintain perfect impartiality (i.e., do not exhibit some level of pro-exercise bias through verbal or non-verbal cues). For these reasons, from a strictly methodological standpoint, the quality of physical activity experimental studies will never be as high as that which clinicians have come to expect of drug studies.

Studies investigating the effects of physical activity on mental health have typically addressed some of these methodological issues, but not all. In many studies, for example, recruitment procedures favored individuals with pro-exercise attitudes, outcome assessors were not blinded to group assignment, and dropouts were simply excluded from the analyses. These weaknesses allow alternative explanations for the findings, enabling skeptics to speculate that perhaps any positive changes were not due to physical activity but some source of bias in the experimental design.

Besides strong experimental studies, another source of evidence that can be used to support the establishment of a cause-and-effect relation between physical activity and mental health is the study of neurobiological mechanisms. If studies using modern neuroimaging methods with humans or more invasive neuroscientific methods with experimental animals show changes in the brain that are consistent with a therapeutic effect, this would strengthen the argument for a causal relation. For example, the main approach used in the treatment of depression is to administer drugs that correct deficiencies in serotonin neurotransmission (called selective serotonin reuptake inhibitors or SSRIs). Studies with experimental animals have shown that exercise also raises the levels of serotonin, essentially mimicking the effect of the drugs but doing so naturally and without harmful side effects. Although this type of evidence is very informative, it is also subject to certain limitations. Animals cannot provide self-reports, so one cannot be certain whether observed changes in brain chemistry truly translate to better mental health. Scientists have to infer how the animals feel from their overt behavior. However, drawing analogies between animal behavior and human feelings, such as depression or anxiety, relies on assumptions that may or may not be true.

Overall, providing strong evidence of a causal relation between physical activity and mental health is very challenging. Exercise scientists have been trying to improve the quality of experimental studies for decades but there is still considerable ground to cover. Therefore, exercise practitioners should approach the available evidence cautiously and critically.

PHYSICAL ACTIVITY AND ANXIETY

Anxiety is an unpleasant emotional state characterized by multiple clusters of symptoms: (a) cognitive, including thoughts of failure and negative future consequences; (b) emotional, including fear and distress; (c) behavioral, including nervousness and tension; and (d) physiological, including the activation of the sympathetic branch of the autonomic nervous system (which speeds up the heart and raises blood pressure) and the activation of the major neuroendocrine stress systems (the sympathetic adrenal-medullary system and the hypothalamic pituitary adrenal-cortical system).

What determines whether an anxiety response is induced is the cognitive appraisal of threat (see Figure 44.2). This appraisal is a process in which two subjective quantities are weighed against each other: on one hand is the perception of what the situation demands of the person (e.g., how much skill or preparation is required to succeed) and, on the other hand, is one's perceived preparedness to meet these demands. For example, in the case of academic examination anxiety, an anxiety response is induced when one perceives that the exam will be difficult and that one's level

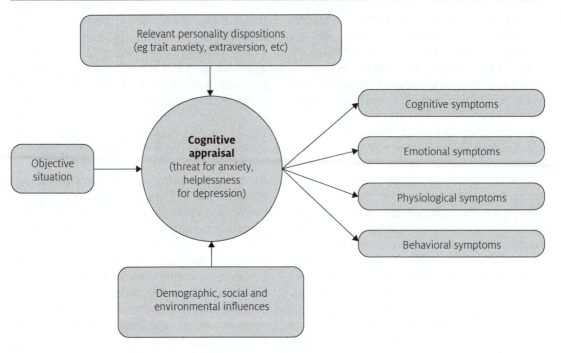

Figure 44.2 The defining element in the process of unpleasant emotions, such as anxiety, and unpleasant moods, such as depression, is the cognitive appraisal. In the case of anxiety, what is appraised is threat, usually against one's goals, self-image, and overall well-being. In the case of depression, what is appraised is helplessness (i.e., that there is no solution or escape). Such appraisals are under the influence of a multitude of factors, including personality dispositions, developmental histories, and environmental conditions. The outcomes of such appraisals are clusters of symptoms that are collectively recognized as the experiences of anxiety or depression.

of preparation is inadequate given the anticipated degree of difficulty. This appraisal process is influenced by such factors as the perceived unpredictability of the situation, the value or importance that is placed on the outcome, one's past history and experience with similar situations and, critically, one's personality. Specifically, some individuals are predisposed to detect threat even in situations that are objectively innocuous or to exaggerate the degree of the threat that the situations pose. This predisposition is called trait anxiety. High trait-anxious individuals tend to experience anxiety more frequently and more intensely than low trait-anxious individuals.

Some degree of anxiety is a common part of daily life. Even a high level of trait anxiety does not necessarily entail a disorder. Anxiety is diagnosed as a disorder if it becomes so frequent, intense, persistent, and uncontrollable that it has a significant debilitating effect across multiple domains, including one's professional career, family life, and social activities. According to the *Diagnostic and Statistical Manual of Mental Disorders*, which is published by the American Psychiatric Association and is the main clinical guide for diagnosing psychological disorders, the category of anxiety disorders includes multiple types of anxiety that differ in important respects. For example, a panic attack is characterized by intense apprehension and is often accompanied by fear of impending doom and very unsettling physiological symptoms (e.g., shortness of breath, chest pains, choking sensations). Agoraphobia is anxiety about being in places or situations (particularly those involving large crowds) from which escape might be difficult. Specific phobias are fears provoked by exposure to various specific objects or situations (e.g., snakes or hot irons). Social phobia is a fear of situations in which other people are present, particularly if those people are perceived as being there to evaluate one's performance or worth. Obsessive-compulsive disorder is characterized by persistent obsessive fear (e.g., of being contaminated) accompanied by compulsions aimed at controlling the cause of the obsession (e.g., constantly washing one's hands). Post-traumatic stress disorder is characterized by episodes during which one relives a past traumatic event, such as war, a mugging, or a rape. Generalized anxiety disorder is characterized by excessive worry and apprehension about the likelihood of undesirable outcomes in one's life; this worry is present more days than not for a period of at least six months and the person, despite efforts, finds it hard or impossible to control it.

Accurate estimates about the prevalence of mental health disorders are extremely difficult to obtain. The main reason is that there can only be a record that someone is suffering if she or he asks for professional help. However, many individuals suffering from mental health problems, including clinical anxiety, do not ask for help. There are several possible explanations for this but perhaps the most likely ones relate to the stigma still attached to receiving a diagnosis for a mental disorder and the high cost of treatment. Consequently, most official figures significantly underestimate the actual extent of the problem. One exception is a study conducted in the United States (called the National Comorbidity Survey Replication), in which trained clinicians traveled the country and conducted in-home diagnostic interviews with over 9,000 people, selected to be a representative sample of the entire population. That study showed that the lifetime prevalence of anxiety disorders was 28.2% in 2001–03, up from 24.9% in 1990–92. The

12-month prevalence was 18.1% in 2001–03, up from 17.2% in 1990–92. As high as these percentages are, one should keep in mind that the frequency of anxiety problems increases in response to such events as economic downturns, natural disasters, acts or terrorism, or large-scale accidents.

Several reviews of the research literature conducted in recent years converge on the same conclusion: exercise is associated with reductions in anxiety (Herring, O'Connor, & Dishman, 2010). These reductions are typically not large (they are closer to what researchers characterize as medium-sized effects) but they are clinically meaningful (i.e., they are considered large enough to have an appreciable beneficial effect on people's quality of life). By all indications, men and women experience reductions in anxiety of equal magnitude. Contrary to some initial assumptions that only aerobic exercise is effective, it appears that both aerobic and resistance training may be equally effective, but the number of studies examining the effects of resistance training remains low. The degree of improvement in aerobic capacity (i.e., maximal oxygen uptake) and, therefore, the adaptation of the cardiovascular system to exercise training, is not correlated with the degree of anxiety reduction. This means that experiencing gains in fitness is not a prerequisite for experiencing reduced levels of anxiety. However, how different levels of activity frequency, duration, and intensity influence the degree of anxiety reduction remains unknown. There are some indications that shorter activity interventions (e.g., 8–10 weeks) may result in larger reductions in anxiety than longer interventions. However, this finding may be confounded by different levels of adherence; adherence is known to progressively decline as activity interventions get longer, but not all published reports have provided information on program adherence. So, it is possible that shorter interventions appear to be more effective only because the participants were still exhibiting high levels of adherence to the program.

The mechanism by which physical activity can lower anxiety is not fully understood. A reasonable hypothesis is that physical activity may influence the pattern of cognitive appraisal that is at the core of anxiety. As discussed earlier, an anxiety response is induced when the individual perceives that what is expected in a particular situation exceeds his or her perceived ability. Physical activity has been shown to raise people's level of self-confidence. This effect starts with what people believe that they can do physically and, in most cases, it expands to cover more domains of human function. In a word, people who exercise begin to develop a sense of empowerment, a belief that they are in control of their lives. As plausible as this hypothesis is, it is unlikely to fully explain why physical activity reduces anxiety levels. It is interesting to note, for example, that after programs of exercise training, experimental animals, such as mice, also show significant reductions in behaviors considered indicative of anxiety. Because these results are unlikely to be caused by changes in cognitive appraisals similar to those made by humans, the animal studies suggest that biological mechanisms (such as positive changes in brain neurotransmitters) may also account for the anxiety reductions.

As noted in the previous section, the challenge of improving the methodological quality of studies investigating the effects of exercise on anxiety remains. Therefore, although the research results that have been obtained so far are clearly promising, they should not be considered definitive. Many important questions remain unanswered and should be investigated through well-designed studies in the future.

PHYSICAL ACTIVITY AND DEPRESSION

Depression is a mental health disorder characterized by disturbed mood. Depression typically occurs in recurring episodes. What clinicians call a major depressive episode is a period of at least two weeks, during which an individual experiences deep sadness and a loss of interest in or an inability to derive pleasure from almost all activities, including those that the individual used to find interesting and pleasurable. Furthermore, during a major depressive episode, the individual exhibits significant changes in appetite and eating behaviors (and, therefore, visible changes in body weight), disturbed sleep (either too much or too little), noticeable changes in activity patterns (either significant reductions in activity or restlessness and agitation), feelings of decreased energy, perceptions of worthlessness or guilt, disruptions of cognitive patterns (difficulty maintaining concentration or making decisions), and thoughts of suicide.

Like anxiety, a core characteristic of depression is a problematic pattern of cognitive appraisal. Unlike anxiety, however, the type of appraisal that is the hallmark of depression is not just that more is expected of the individual in a particular situation than what the individual can offer. In depression, an individual believes that there is no solution, no recourse, no escape, nothing that can be done and no one that can help. This pattern of appraisal is termed "learned helplessness" (see Figure 44.2). The individual who perceives a problem (e.g., foresees layoffs) may initially respond with anxiety and try to react (e.g., by preparing a résumé and submitting it to many potential new employers). However, after multiple failures despite what one perceives to be decent effort, one starts to develop a more passive outlook, being led to believe that there will never be a way out of the impasse. In other words, many individuals whose mental health is initially affected by anxiety, later transition to depression. This accounts for the high comorbidity between anxiety and depression (at rates of 50% or higher).

Individuals suffering from depression often tend to develop some "irrational beliefs"; that is, thoughts that represent exaggerations or over-generalizations, with no basis in fact. For example, one may believe that she or he is the "unluckiest person on the planet" or that "everything will always go wrong for me." Perceived failures in one domain (such as employment) or at one point in time are generalized to one's life overall (e.g., "I am a failure, I have always been a failure, I will always be a failure"). Such dysfunctional cognitions lead to the conclusion that there is no point in even trying, which ultimately results in passivity. Consequently, depression can have a devastating effect on quality of life.

In the most severe cases, depression may lead to suicide, making depression a potentially lethal disorder. In fact, up to 15% of individuals with severe depressive episodes die by suicide. Among individuals with major depression over the age of 55 years, suicide death rates quadruple. Among elderly individuals with major depression who are admitted to nursing homes, the risk of death by suicide increases substantially during the first year.

If an individual experiences one or more major depressive episodes (based on the diagnostic criteria mentioned earlier), a clinical diagnosis of major depressive disorder can be issued. If the depressed mood lasts for a long time (at least two years) but other symptoms are below the threshold required for a diagnosis of major depressive disorder, the condition is diagnosed as dysthymic disorder. If major depressive episodes alternate with manic or milder (so-called "hypomanic") episodes, then the individual is diagnosed with bipolar disorder (I or II, respectively). Manic episodes are characterized by unusually and inappropriately elevated mood and, occasionally, high levels of irritability, or even violence and abuse, lasting for at least one week. Furthermore, during manic episodes, individuals may show disproportionately inflated self-esteem (even reaching delusional levels, such as believing that one is an expert on issues that one knows nothing about), decreased need for sleep, accelerated but incoherent speech (with multiple, disconnected but intermingling, lines of thought), distractibility, excessive involvement in goal-directed activities (e.g.,

starting multiple projects simultaneously, without regard about their feasibility), general agitation, and increased susceptibility to pleasurable activities without considering costs or consequences (e.g., gambling one's life savings or purchasing unnecessary goods on credit).

In the United States, the lifetime prevalence of mood disorders is 20.8% (major depressive disorder, 16.6%; dysthymia, 2.5%; bipolar disorder I and II, 3.9%). Within a 12-month period, the prevalence is 9.5% (major depressive disorder, 6.7%; dysthymia, 1.5%; bipolar disorder I and II, 2.6%). Of those individuals with major depressive disorder, the severity of the disease is characterized as mild in 10.4%, moderate in 38.6%, severe in 38.0%, and very severe in 12.9% of the cases. On average, major depressive episodes last for 16 weeks. In 59.3% of cases, patients reported severe or very severe impairment in important life roles (e.g., as professionals, parents, or spouses). Importantly, fewer than half (41.9%) of individuals with major depressive disorder receive adequate treatment.

Numerous epidemiological studies, involving thousands of participants, have shown that there is a significant inverse correlation between the amount of physical activity and the severity of depressive symptoms that people report. Furthermore, as explained in more detail in Chapter 51, experimental studies of increasingly improving methodological quality show that activity interventions can significantly lower depression among individuals with mood disorders (primarily major depressive disorder and, more recently, bipolar disorder). These reductions are typically large and clinically meaningful (Greer & Trivedi, 2009). They also appear regardless of whether the depressive symptomatology was assessed via self-report questionnaires or via clinical interviews by expert assessors. Two additional observations appear consistently across studies. First, levels of depression become progressively lower, so longer programs typically lead to larger reductions. Second, the magnitude of the reductions is larger for those participants who report higher levels of depression at baseline, which is not surprising since these individuals have more room for improvement. Neither the minimum dose of activity that is necessary for lowering depression nor the dose that maximizes this effect is presently known. Preliminary studies, however, show that the frequency, duration, and intensity of exercise that is presently recommended for general health benefits (i.e., 5–7 days per week, at least 30 minutes per day, moderate intensity) suffice to lower depression. Recent studies have also provided evidence that the effects of exercise are considerably larger than those associated with a placebo drug. Furthermore, the benefit cannot be attributed to social interaction since even exercising alone (in a room with no one else present) is still effective for lowering depression. In addition, the argument that exercise is causally related to reductions in depression is strongly supported by animal research, which shows that exercise induces specific measurable changes in brain function that can account for its antidepressant effects.

Three main criticisms have been leveled against this research. First, there are persistent questions about the methodological quality of the available studies. These questions focus on such issues as whether the outcome assessors were blinded to group allocation or whether the results were biased by the exclusion of those participants who were initially allocated to the exercise group but later withdrew. Second, researchers have raised the possibility that the willingness to be physically active and the tendency to respond positively to an activity intervention (e.g., by experiencing an antidepressant effect) reflect a common genetic predisposition rather than the postulated causal effect of activity. Third, practitioners often raise questions about the practical meaningfulness of these results given that most depressed individuals tend to avoid physical activity. These are all substantive criticisms that warrant close scrutiny in future studies.

These lingering questions notwithstanding, the evidence supporting an antidepressant effect of physical activity is now strong enough to substantiate a case for using physical activity in clinical practice. This is especially important in light of growing indications that antidepressant medications, despite high cost and considerable risk of adverse side-effects (including increased risk of suicidal thoughts), are no more effective than placebo for cases of mild to moderate depression. However, cases of mild to moderate depression currently account for the majority of prescriptions for antidepressant medications. Thus, recent clinical guidelines issued by the National Institute for Health and Clinical Excellence in the United Kingdom recommend that for "people with persistent subthreshold depressive symptoms or mild to moderate depression" clinicians should consider offering options that do not involve medications, including "a structured group physical activity programme."

Figure 44.3 Anxiety and depression are prevalent mental health problems in industrialized countries. Standard treatment approaches, namely psychiatric drugs and psychotherapy, incur a high economic cost and are associated with wide-ranging side-effects. Physical activity is an effective alternative that is free, safe, and associated with numerous collateral health benefits.

PHYSICAL ACTIVITY AND "FEELING BETTER"

Anxiety and depression are mental health problems that can escalate to severe levels and have a devastating effect on quality of life. Besides those, however, daily function and satisfaction with life are also affected by a variety of feelings that humans find unpleasant and wish to change. For example, people smoke cigarettes and drink alcohol to relieve tension and relax, or consume caffeinated beverages and eat sugary snacks to get a boost of energy. These methods rely on external chemical agents (nicotine, alcohol, caffeine, sugar) to alter one's affective state. Unfortunately, all of these methods are costly and none can be considered healthful. Especially when overused, all of them have long-term negative consequences.

A growing evidence base demonstrates that physical activity is a very potent alternative regulator of affect, which is made even more appealing if one considers that physical activity produces numerous additional benefits for the body and mind, is free, and has virtually no negative side-effects (Puetz, O'Connor, & Dishman, 2006; Reed & Buck, 2009; Reed & Ones, 2006). Numerous studies have shown that bouts of physical activity, particularly if the intensity is self-selected (as in a self-paced walk), cause individuals to experience a pleasant high-activation state (energy and invigoration). If the intensity is somewhat vigorous (as in a brisk walk or a jog), the pleasant high activation that is experienced during the activity is typically followed by a pleasant low-activation state (calmness and serenity) that may last for some time thereafter.

Because of these powerful effects, researchers have begun exploring the potential of using physical activity for alleviating urges to consume the aforementioned potentially harmful substances typically used as mood regulators. This may be especially significant for individuals seeking to disentangle themselves from those substances, such as nicotine or ethanol, which can be addictive. These studies are based on a "hedonic competition" or "hedonic substitution" hypothesis, according to which the reason why people feel the urge to consume these substances, and the reason they may even become addicted, is because they desire the pleasant changes in their affective states that these substances produce. If, however, physical activity can successfully compete with these substances in inducing these desirable affective changes, then it may eventually replace them as an equally effective substitute. While the evidence base supporting this hypothesis is still growing, the results are promising. For example, bouts of physical activity can attenuate urges for cigarettes, alcoholic drinks, or sugary snacks, substantially extend the time between irrepressible urges, and effectively reduce the daily consumption of these products. In animal research, it has been found that animals that were made to be dependent on alcohol and illicit drugs, such as cocaine, amphetamine, and "ecstasy," lowered their dependence as they gained access to a running wheel. Studies on humans who are recovering from alcoholism, smoking, or drug addiction similarly show that the incorporation of physical activity in their treatment program facilitates the recovery process.

LIMITS OF THE FEEL-BETTER EFFECT

Skeptics of the physical activity-induced "feel-better" phenomenon often pose this challenging question: if physical activity is as pleasant as its supporters claim, then why are the rates of physical activity participation so low? After all, it is clear that humans enthusiastically pursue all sorts of endeavors that make them feel better, from eating and drinking (often to excess) to engaging in intimate relationships.

This is a reasonable and intriguing question, so it has forced researchers to consider whether there are limits to the "feel-better" effects described earlier in this chapter. Indeed, studies have shown that several factors may contribute to experiencing reduced levels of pleasure during physical activity. These factors pertain to the attributes of the physical activity itself, the characteristics of the individuals, the physical properties of the environment, and the perceived features of the social context. For example, reductions in pleasure have been observed when the intensity of physical activity exceeded the ventilatory threshold (the level at which one starts to breathe more heavily and describes the effort as "somewhat hard" or "hard"). If, however, an individual is overweight or obese, has been sedentary for a long period of time, lacks confidence in her or his physical ability, or is self-conscious about negative evaluations that others may make about her or his physical appearance, then reductions in pleasure during physical activity may occur even with lower levels of intensity. Likewise, reductions in pleasure may occur if the environmental conditions are adverse (e.g., high heat or humidity). The social environment is also crucially important. Participants feel better when the exercise leader provides positive feedback and supports a sense of autonomy (i.e., that one does what one wants, not what one is instructed to do) or when other members of the group show enthusiasm and willingness for social interaction. On the other hand, if the leader emphasizes appearance-related rather than health-related benefits or the social setting exacerbates concerns about physical appearance (e.g., if one is surrounded by wall-to-wall mirrors and super-fit individuals in tight clothing), the possibility of negative affective changes is increased.

Unfortunately, conditions that may make physical activity an unpleasant experience occur often in practice. In other words, the "feel-better" effect associated with physical activity should not be considered automatic but rather conditional. The factors that can reduce the pleasure associated with physical activity may collectively explain the currently low levels of physical activity participation and the high rates of dropout. As noted in the introduction of this chapter, in the long run, human beings tend to gravitate toward pursuits that make them feel better and tend to avoid those that make them feel worse.

GUIDELINES FOR OPTIMIZING THE AFFECTIVE RESPONSES TO PHYSICAL ACTIVITY

Researchers are only now beginning to explore the conditions that make it more likely to experience increased pleasure during and following physical activity. Much remains to be discovered. Nevertheless, some preliminary recommendations can be issued based on what is known up to this point.

First, the importance of monitoring the affective responses of participants during and after physical activity cannot be overemphasized. Oftentimes, what the exercise professional believes that the participant is feeling and what the participant is actually feeling might not agree. So, the systematic use of standardized rating scales that allow the participants to describe their feelings can promote communication and provide a basis for adjustments before it is too late. The simple rating scales presented in Chapter 6 (i.e., the Feeling Scale and the Felt Arousal Scale) can be used for this purpose. These measures are short enough (they consist of one question each) that they can be used repeatedly without becoming intrusive. Maintaining records of affective responses for each participant, and comparing the effects of different activity programs on those responses, provides the exercise professional with an invaluable

Figure 44.4 Physical activity can make people feel better. However, this feel-better effect is not experienced by everyone in every situation. Exercise professionals should ensure that the conditions are conducive to a pleasurable response by following the guidelines for optimizing the affective responses to physical activity.

evidence base for offering individualized recommendations (e.g., designing tailor-made physical activity programs that promote pleasant experiences and, therefore, motivation for continued participation).

Second, it is important for participants to feel in control of their physical activity and confident that they can do it. Therefore, it is crucial that professionals allow participants as much autonomy as possible in selecting the types and amounts of physical activity they wish to do. Evidence, for example, demonstrates that individuals may feel pleasant at higher levels of intensity if they control the intensity. On the other hand, if they perceive that the intensity is controlled by the exercise professional, the same level of intensity may lead to reduced pleasure. Considerable evidence also demonstrates that the intensity

most individuals select on their own is not only experienced as pleasant but it also suffices to produce gains in cardiorespiratory fitness. Similarly, studies have shown that, when individuals are instructed to select an intensity that makes them feel "good," the intensity they select is sufficient to elicit fitness gains. When individuals are "pushed" to exceed the intensity that they would have self-selected, even by a small amount (e.g., walk 10% faster), they reach intensities that are not only experienced as significantly less pleasant but are also unnecessarily high and potentially risky. Therefore, exercise professionals should reconsider their role: they should refrain from dictating what participants should be doing and, instead, enable participants to do what they prefer. Exceptions should be made only in cases in which factors such as unreasonable fear or misinformation cause individuals to select either activities that are unlikely to produce any benefits or activities that may be unsafe given their capabilities or health condition. To foster confidence, professionals should also ensure that, whatever participants choose to do would not cause them to perceive their performance as a failure (e.g., if the participant expresses the wish to do something that the professional knows to be grossly unrealistic). To meet this goal, participants should be encouraged to progress in small increments, preferably by increasing duration and frequency (which are less likely to have a negative impact on pleasure) before increasing intensity (which is more likely to have a negative impact on pleasure).

Third, exercise professionals must be aware of the limitations of cognitive techniques that are often used as means of "manipulating" how participants, especially novice ones, feel during physical activity. Due to some of the aforementioned factors (i.e., high body weight, low cardiorespiratory fitness), many individuals may experience displeasure and discomfort during the early stages of their participation. The recommendations that are typically offered to participants for dealing with these negative affective experiences include: (a) using music or television to turn their attention away from bodily symptoms of strain and fatigue (called "attentional dissociation"); (b) convincing themselves that they "can do it" (i.e., boosting their self-efficacy); and (c) viewing these unpleasant feelings as "a good thing," a sign that their body is getting stronger (i.e., using what is known in psychotherapy as "cognitive reframing" or "reappraisal"). Although there is at least some evidence that these techniques can be effective in improving how one feels during a bout of strenuous activity, their effectiveness is limited. When the intensity is high enough that participants cannot keep their heart rate steady (i.e., they are close to "maxing out" physiologically), these techniques are very unlikely to help participants feel better. Both the participants themselves and the professionals supervising them should be realistic in this regard. If the negative affective responses cannot be controlled, the best solution is to lower intensity (see previous point).

Fourth, although research on how personality influences affective responses to physical activity is still at an early stage, there is compelling evidence that different individuals may exhibit different affective responses to the same physical activity stimulus. These individual differences may reflect a variety of factors, from different genetic makeups to different prior experiences with physical activity. Regardless of the source of these differences, exercise professionals should be aware that participants, even of the same gender, age, health status, and level of physical conditioning, will likely differ in what types and amounts of physical activity they prefer or they can tolerate without experiencing adverse affective changes. For example, although all individuals will find certain intensity levels "too low" and others "too high," the percentages of their maximal physiological capacity to which these labels apply will likely differ considerably between different individuals.

For exercise professionals, this means that they should not operate under the assumption that what one participant finds pleasant will also be found pleasant by another participant.

Fifth, extra care must be taken if the physical activity is to take place in the presence of others who might be perceived as critical observers (e.g., individuals of vastly superior levels of physical ability). Especially for individuals who have the tendency to appraise situations as posing an evaluative threat (e.g., individuals with a high degree of social anxiety, including anxiety about their physique), it is important to eliminate from the environment elements that might trigger such appraisals. Therefore, exercise professionals should be careful to avoid making interindividual comparisons, placing emphasis on appearance-related motives for participation, or drawing attention to individuals. Instead, an effort should be made to define success as progressing in comparison to self-referenced baselines, emphasizing health over appearance as the prime motive for participation, and cultivating a cooperative team atmosphere by encouraging group cohesion (e.g., by building social support dyads or networks and promoting the idea of shared goals).

Sixth, exercise professionals should be aware that certain categories of participants face special challenges and should be considered "high risk" for experiencing negative affective responses and dropping out. These include individuals who are obese or severely deconditioned after long periods of sedentary living and individuals with mental health problems, such as anxiety and depression. Individuals in these categories may approach physical activity with negative preconceptions, possibly stemming from negative previous experiences (e.g., memories of exhaustion, pain, or public embarrassment). Obesity, extreme deconditioning, and negative affectivity have all been shown to be associated with exaggerated perceptions of exertion during physical activity and with increased risk of dropout. Conducting an initial interview aimed at uncovering fears associated with physical activity can provide the exercise professional with information that can be used to prevent the inadvertent reinforcement or exacerbation of these fears.

In closing, it is important for exercise professionals to remember that pleasure and displeasure are powerful motives in human behavior (see Figure 44.5). Physical activity can make participants feel better, an effect that can have wide-ranging and life-changing applications, from promoting mental health to aiding individuals deal with harmful addic-

tions. However, this "feel-better" effect is neither automatic nor guaranteed. Unless the physical activity is properly implemented and calibrated for each individual participant, it may result in a range of unpleasant experiences, from exhaustion to shame, which may, in turn, lead to long-term avoidance of activity. For this reason, the systematic monitoring of the pleasure and displeasure that participants experience in response to physical activity should become an integral component of daily practice for all responsible exercise professionals.

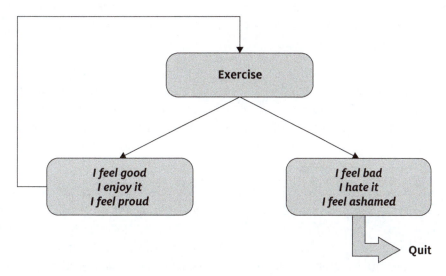

Figure 44.5 Humans generally tend to do what makes them feel better and avoid what makes them feel worse. This is also the case in the domain of physical activity. Therefore, if participants consistently experience reduced pleasure from physical activity, the likely outcome is non-adherence and dropout. If, on the other hand, participants feel better during and after physical activity, there is a strong possibility that they will make physical activity a regular part of their daily lives.

LEARNING AIDS

1   Summarize the key characteristics of a well-designed experimental study.

The most crucial feature of a well-designed experiment is the random allocation of participants to the experimental and control groups. A successful control condition is one that matches the experimental condition in everything but the "active ingredient" whose effectiveness is investigated (e.g., the physical activity). This includes the characteristics of the participants, the extent of the interactions the participants have with the investigators, and, crucially, the expectation of benefit. Furthermore, in well-designed experimental studies, the group to which a participant has been allocated should be concealed from those investigators responsible for assessing the outcome(s) and, ideally, from all investigators that come in contact with participants and even from the participants themselves ("double-blind"). Finally, statistical analyses should not be limited only to those participants who completed the study but should include all participants initially randomized to conditions ("intention to treat" analysis).

2   Explain what the "placebo" effect is.

The placebo effect is a phenomenon in which perceived and even actual improvement occurs in a certain outcome (e.g., anxiety or depression symptoms) even in the absence of an active treatment, merely as a result of an expectation of benefit. Placebo (i.e., physiologically inert) treatments are commonly used as controls in experimental research (e.g., to control for the fact that participants who exercise are expecting to benefit because they believe exercise to be beneficial).

3   Define "anxiety" and "depression".

Anxiety is an unpleasant emotional state characterized by cognitive, emotional, behavioral, and physiological symptoms. It is elicited following a cognitive appraisal of threat (that more is expected of the individual in a given situation than what the individual can do). Depression is a mood disturbance characterized by deep sadness, loss of interest, and inability to derive pleasure from almost all activities. The cognitive appraisal that typically underlies depression is "learned helplessness," the belief that there is nothing one can do to improve one's current condition.

4   Identify the criteria for the diagnosis of a major depressive episode.

During a major depressive episode, an individual may experience depressed mood, loss of interest or pleasure in nearly all activities, changes in appetite and eating behaviors, disturbed sleep, noticeable changes in activity patterns, feelings of decreased energy, perceptions of worthlessness or guilt, disruptions of concentration or making decisions, and thoughts of suicide.

5   Summarize what the exercise professional can do to make it more likely that physical activity will be experienced as pleasant.

Exercise professionals should: (a) consistently monitor the participants' affective responses and maintain a record of how these change in response to modifications in the exercise program; (b) promote a sense of autonomy (the belief that the exerciser is in control); (c) minimize the chances of early failure experiences, to build confidence; (d) respect the limits of cognitive regulation techniques (e.g., attentional dissociation, cognitive reframing, boosting self-efficacy) by ensuring that exercisers do not reach unnecessarily high levels of intensity; (e) exhibit sensitivity to individual differences by avoiding one-size-fits-all exercise prescriptions; (f) emphasize self-improvement and health-and-wellness-related motives for participation; and (g) maintain a safe social environment, without elements that could be perceived as posing an evaluative threat (e.g., mirrors, other individuals of vastly superior fitness, interindividual comparisons, emphasis on physical appearance or skill).

REVIEW QUESTIONS

1   What is a "double blind" experimental design and what advantages does it have?

2   How is an anxiety response induced?

3   How is the cognitive appraisal associated with depression different from that associated with anxiety?

4   What is the "hedonic competition" or "hedonic substitution" hypothesis?

EXERCISE

1   During the week, choose two different physical activity sessions (we assume that you are physically active at least twice per week). These sessions should be as different as possible but you can choose in what way they differ (e.g., in terms of mode, duration, or intensity). For example, one activity might be going for a walk in the park with your dog and the other might be a basketball game. When you do each activity take three copies of the Feeling Scale and the Felt Arousal Scale with you (see Chapter 6). Rate how you feel before, once during (preferably near the middle of the session), and after these sessions. Then, use graphing software to plot your results. Discuss which session made you feel more pleasant high activation during the activity and more pleasant low activation afterwards, as well as possible reasons for the differences.

ADDITIONAL READING

Blumenthal, J.A. & Ong, L. (2009). A commentary on 'Exercise and depression' (Mead et al., 2009): And the verdict is... *Mental Health and Physical Activity, 2,* 97–99.

De Moor, M.H., Boomsma, D.I., Stubbe, J.H., Willemsen, G. & de Geus, E.J. (2008). Testing causality in the association between regular exercise and symptoms of anxiety and depression. *Archives of General Psychiatry, 65,* 897–905.

Ekkekakis, P. & Backhouse, S.H. (2009). Exercise and psychological well-being. In R. Maughan (Ed.), *Olympic textbook of science in sport* (pp.251-271). Hoboken, NJ: Wiley-Blackwell.

Mead, G.E., Morley, W., Campbell, P., Greig, C.A., McMurdo, M.E.T. & Lawlor, D.A. (2010). Exercise for depression. *Mental Health and Physical Activity, 2,* 95–96.

Wolff, E. & Ströhle, A. (2009). Causal associations of physical activity/exercise and symptoms of depression and anxiety. *Archives of General Psychiatry, 67,* 540–541.

REFERENCES

Greer, T.L. & Trivedi, M.H. (2009). Exercise in the treatment of depression. *Current Psychiatry Reports, 11*, 466–472.

Herring, M.P., O'Connor, P.J. & Dishman, R.K. (2010). The effect of exercise training on anxiety symptoms among patients: A systematic review. *Archives of Internal Medicine, 170*, 321–331.

Puetz, T.W., O'Connor, P.J. & Dishman, R.K. (2006). Effects of chronic exercise on feelings of energy and fatigue: A quantitative synthesis. *Psychological Bulletin, 132*, 866–876.

Reed, J. & Buck, S. (2009). The effect of regular aerobic exercise on positive-activated affect: A meta-analysis. *Psychology of Sport and Exercise, 10*, 581–594.

Reed, J. & Ones, D.S. (2006). The effect of acute aerobic exercise on positive activated affect: A meta-analysis. *Psychology of Sport and Exercise, 7*, 477–514.

Chapter 45

Physical activity and cognitive functioning

YU-KAI CHANG AND JENNIFER L. ETNIER

SUMMARY

Physical activity is a healthy lifestyle factor that has been shown to benefit cognitive performance. Over the past four decades, numerous studies have examined the relationship between physical activity and cognition using a variety of approaches. This chapter provides a review of contemporary evidence from a variety of research perspectives including studies using epidemiological, experimental, and meta-analytic approaches, studies with chronic exercise and acute exercise paradigms, studies focused on older adults with or without cognitive impairment, and studies examining children's academic performance. Although more research is encouraged to further clarify the relationship between physical activity and cognitive performance, the current evidence generally supports that both chronic exercise and acute exercise benefit cognitive performance in these populations. Practical implications of the extant literature are considered as well as directions for future research.

STORY

Elizabeth is a housewife who participates in exercise regularly in the gym. One day, she had a talk with Kevin, her exercise instructor, about recent life changes in her family. Her father, Rex, had been diagnosed with mild cognitive impairment (MCI) and is distraught about his inability to remember things. Rex's doctor explained to the family that although MCI is not as serious as dementia, MCI is a risk factor for dementia. Elizabeth is also anxious about her daughter Joanna's academic performance, and is considering telling Joanna that she has to quit participating in an after-school exercise program to devote more time to her studies. After hearing about Elizabeth's concerns, Kevin advised Elizabeth to get her father involved in an exercise program and explained that exercise is effective in preventing cognitive decline in adults in general and also in those who have MCI. Kevin also encouraged Elizabeth to allow Joanna to maintain her exercise participation because research suggests that children who are more physically active actually perform better academically. There is also some research showing that when you add exercise to a child's day it benefits their cognitive performance. Elizabeth took Kevin's advice and became more observant of the role of physical activity in her family. Rex was pleased that he was becoming stronger and after a few months felt that his memory was better. Elizabeth also recognized that Joanna seemed to complete her homework assign-

ments faster and with fewer errors on days when she had exercised. Elizabeth is excited about these observations and asked Kevin for more information about how and why exercise might contribute to cognitive benefits for both her father and her daughter who were at very different points in terms of their own cognitive challenges.

INTRODUCTION

Cognition, cognitive function, and cognitive performance are general terms describing a wide variety of activities that require thoughtful behavior. These activities can be categorized as falling into cognitive domains including memory, problem solving, decision making, attention, perception, and communication (Herrmann, Yoder, Gruneberg, & Payne, 2006). Effective performance in these cognitive domains is necessary for functioning well in daily life and is one of the major components of people's judgments of their health-related quality of life. For example, being able to remember items on a grocery list or to problem-solve how to use a universal remote control to turn on a television and a cable box are cognitive functions that many people rely on regularly.

The relationship between exercise and cognition has been investigated in several different populations (e.g. older adults, younger adults, and children), in a variety of settings (e.g. using laboratory-based cognitive tasks, measuring academic achievement in school), and using different exercise paradigms (e.g. chronic exercise, acute exercise). This chapter is organized by discussing the effects of long-term regular participation in exercise (also referred to as chronic exercise), by exploring the effects of a single session of exercise (also called acute exercise), and by describing the implications of this research with regards to physical activity recommendations to improve cognition.

 OBJECTIVES

After reading this chapter, you should be able to:

1 Understand what cognition and age-related cognitive decline are.
2 Be aware of how physical activity influences cognition across the lifespan.
3 Describe studies testing the relationship between physical activity and cognition using various research designs.
4 Discuss key factors that might influence the exercise–cognition relationship.
5 Understand the current recommendations of exercise to benefit cognitive performance.

CHRONIC EXERCISE

Many researchers have been interested in understanding the potential of chronic exercise to benefit cognitive performance. The

majority of studies conducted in this area have focused on older adults. This is likely because older adults tend to experience declines in cognitive performance and, hence, they might benefit the most from physical activity participation. However, more recent research has also begun to explore the potential benefits of chronic exercise for children. Given that their cognitive abilities are just developing, it is logical that they might also benefit from physical activity participation. An additional direction of current research is focused on understanding more about whether the particular mode of the exercise is important for determining the cognitive benefits.

Older adults

Cognitive decline and aging: As previously explained, cognitive performance is important for everyday functioning and for quality of life. Unfortunately, cognitive function tends to decline with advancing age. In particular, many aspects of cognition (e.g., memory, speed of processing) reach their peak ability at approximately 20 years of age and then linearly decrease with increased age (Salthouse, 2009). This decline in cognitive abilities is termed age-related cognitive decline and represents normal changes that are expected with aging. An example of this would be a 70-year old woman who has difficulty using a universal remote to control both a television and a cable box or who walks into a room to do something, but then cannot remember what that something was. Although age-related cognitive decline is evident when we examine large groups of people at a variety of ages (which would be described as cross-sectional research), there are individuals who do not experience this age-related cognitive decline and healthy lifestyle factors, including physical activity, have been shown to be predictive of resistance to cognitive decline with advancing age. In fact, a variety of studies have examined the relationship between physical activity and cognition and the evidence is promising.

There are other more severe forms of cognitive decline that are also evidenced in advancing age. Mild cognitive impairment (MCI) describes a decline in cognitive performance that is greater than the average decline for a particular age and education level, but is not severe enough to be considered dementia. Although MCI is not severe enough to affect a person's ability to function in daily life, people with MCI are at greater risk of converting to dementia. This type of mild impairment might be exemplified by a 70-year old woman who asks the same question repeatedly without remembering the answer and who has a decrease in her ability to remember names.

Lastly, dementia is a more severe form of clinical decline that includes a decrease in memory abilities and a decrease in at least one other area of cognition which together negatively affect the person's ability to function in daily life. An example of this could be a 70-year old woman who is having difficulty remembering what she did yesterday and who is not able to problem-solve to find where she put the gallon of milk she just brought home from the grocery store. There are several different types of dementia with Alzheimer's disease perhaps being the most well-known.

In examining the relationship between physical activity and cognition, it is important to consider the effects on each of these various types of cognitive decline. Promising evidence from epidemiological research (see "Designs in epidemiological research" below) supports the hypothesis that chronic exercise benefits cognitive function with advancing age and can even delay MCI and dementia. This is important for the quality of life of older adults (and their families) and because of the large percentage of individuals with MCI (e.g., in U.S. adults over 71 years of age, approximately 22% have MCI and approximately 14% have dementia, Brookmeyer et al., 2011). Further, with the growing population of older adults, these numbers are expected to increase dramatically in the future.

Designs in epidemiological research

Epidemiological research describes studies that test large numbers of individuals to investigate the causes of particular health outcomes (e.g. stroke, diabetes, dementia, and physical inactivity). In epidemiological studies that are described as using cross-sectional designs, participants' current cognitive functioning is examined relative to their current physical activity levels. This allows for conclusions to be drawn regarding the relationship between current activity and current cognitive performance. In case-control studies, participants are asked to recall their physical activity behavior at an earlier time in their life and this is related to the participants' current level of cognitive function. Conclusions from these studies describe how past physical activity relates to current cognitive performance.

In prospective longitudinal studies, physical activity is measured at one point in time and is used to predict cognitive performance at a later time. Conclusions from these studies are similar to those drawn from case-control studies because they describe how past physical activity predicts current cognitive performance. However, prospective longitudinal studies are stronger than case-control studies for two reasons. First, because measures of current physical activity tend to be more accurate than asking people to recollect how active they were. Second, because in prospective longitudinal studies, researchers can assure that participants are the same in terms of cognitive performance and other relevant variables (like education level) at baseline and hence can have more confidence in attributing differences or changes in cognitive performance to the baseline differences in physical activity.

Findings from epidemiological research: Researchers who have used epidemiological approaches have typically used cross-sectional designs or prospective longitudinal approaches. In particular, researchers measure physical activity using self-report measures (questionnaires) and then measure cognitive performance at the same time or at some time in the future (typically one or more years later). When measuring cognitive performance, some researchers have used laboratory-based measures of cognitive performance. An example of an often-used laboratory-based measure of cognitive performance is the Stroop Test. In the word condition of this test, participants are asked to read as quickly as possible a list of names of colors (e.g., red, blue, green). This is considered a measure of information-processing. They are next asked to perform the color-word condition of the test, which requires that they identify the color of ink that color names are written in. In this case, each color name is written in a different color of ink (e.g., the word "red" might be printed in blue ink). The participant has to suppress the more innate response of reading what the letters spell to instead identify the color of ink. Hence, this is considered to include both information-processing and inhibition skills. Other researchers have used clinical diagnostic measures of cognitive performance that allow them to make judgments about MCI and dementia. These diagnostic measures focus on memory and include questions like what day of the year it is and who is the current President. In all of the studies reviewed here, participants have been "older" when the measures of cognitive performance have been taken; hence this research has focused on physical activity and cognitive performance in advancing age.

In the studies that have focused on laboratory-based measures of cognitive performance, results typically show that participants who are physically active perform better on cognitive measures and experience less decline in cognitive performance over time as compared to participants who are sedentary. Of particular note amongst these studies is a prospective study in which the sample was large enough to allow researchers to compare varying levels of physical activity. Weuve et al. (2004) found that when compared to those who did very little physical activity, some activity was better, but more activity was the best. These results support the idea that there is a dose-response relationship between physical activity and cognitive performance which means that increasingly greater cognitive benefits result from increasingly more physical activity.

In studies that have tested the relationship between physical activity and a subsequent diagnosis with clinical cognitive impairment, the results of several studies show that physical activity is predictive of less risk of clinical impairment and many also support that of a dose-response relationship. Of interest in this group of studies is a prospective study conducted by Abbott et al. (2004) in which dose-response relationships were examined. Abbott et al. found that participants who walked less than 0.25 miles per day were more likely to be diagnosed with dementia as compared to those who walked more. Importantly, the amount of protection increased with increasing distances walked daily. As compared to those who walked less than 0.25 miles daily, those who walked one–two miles daily were 25% less likely and those who walked more than two miles daily were 50% less likely to be diagnosed with dementia seven years later. Thus, these results suggest that increasingly more physical activity participation results in increasingly less risk of dementia.

Another study of particular interest was one in which the effects of physical activity on dementia risk were examined in twin pairs to help us understand how the environmental variable of exercise impacts people with similar inherited (genetic) risk for dementia. Using case-control analysis, Andel et al. (2008) compared the effects of physical activity

between twin pairs when one of the twins had dementia or Alzheimer's disease and the other did not and when there were differences in their physical activity levels in younger age. In twin pairs, they found that an individual who was more physically active in younger age was approximately 34% less likely to have dementia at follow-up than was his/her twin who was less physically active in younger age. This finding suggests that the positive relationship between exercise in younger age and a decreased risk of dementia exists even after controlling for genetic and familial factors.

In summary, results from large-scale epidemiological studies suggest a protective effect of physical activity for cognitive impairment and dementia. Further, the results indicate that the relationship is dose-response in nature such that higher doses of physical activity have greater protective benefits than smaller doses of physical activity. Additionally, results from one study provide evidence that the protective effects of physical activity on dementia are evident above and beyond inherited risk factors.

Although the results of this epidemiological evidence are intriguing, there are two important limitations of this research that should be noted. First, because researchers have relied upon self-report measures to assess physical activity, information regarding the specifics of the exercise bout such as the mode of exercise (e.g., running, strength training, dance), the intensity of exercise (e.g., how hard they were exercising), the number of days of exercise per week, the length of each exercise session, and the overall length of time of participation in exercise is often lacking. This is important because this lack of specific information makes it difficult to *prescribe* exercise to older adults in a way that would be most likely to benefit their cognitive performance. Second, epidemiological studies only allow us to draw conclusions about associations or relationships between variables. In other words, because we cannot control everything about the participants who were more physically active (e.g., perhaps those who were more physically active also had a better diet, got more and better quality sleep, or were more engaged in other types of cognitive activities) and because it is plausible that persons with better cognitive performance are *more able to* remain physically active (e.g., because they can think better, they can also be more physically active), we cannot fully tease apart the direction of the causal relationship between physical activity and cognitive performance. That is, epidemiological studies can only tell us that the two variables are related, they cannot tell us that differences in one variable (e.g., physical activity) are *responsible* for differences in the other (e.g., cognitive performance).

Randomized controlled trials: To make inferences about causation requires the use of randomized controlled trial (RCT) designs. In RCTs, participants are randomly assigned to an exercise intervention or a control condition and cognitive performance is assessed following the intervention. By using random assignment (and when the sample is large enough), the researcher assures that there are no differences between the groups in the exercise intervention and in the control condition at the beginning of the study. Thus, one can assume that participants start out the same with regards to cognitive performance and other variables that might affect cognitive performance. By conducting an actual exercise intervention, the researcher also controls the specifics of the exercise and insures that participants receive the intended dose of exercise. Several RCTs have been conducted to test a causal relationship between chronic exercise and cognition. In these studies, the expectation is that sedentary individuals who participate in an aerobic exercise program that is of sufficient intensity and duration will experience physiological benefits (these benefits are actually assessed in some studies) and that these will result in an improvement in cognitive performance.

Colcombe et al. (2004) conducted a study that provides an example of RCTs examining the effects of chronic exercise on cognition in cognitively-normal individuals. Older cognitively-normal, sedentary adults were randomly assigned to an aerobic exercise group or a toning and stretching control group. Participants in the aerobic exercise group exercised at moderate-to-vigorous intensity for 40–45 minutes, three times per week for six months (this is the dose of the exercise). Participants in this group improved their aerobic fitness (a physiological benefit) as compared to those in the control group. In addition, aerobic exercisers also improved their cognitive performance from pre-test to post-test while the control group showed no significant change over this same time period. Given the use of the RCT design and the findings of the study, the authors were able to conclude that participation in this dose of exercise *results* in cognitive benefits.

Baker et al. (2010) conducted a study that provides an illustration of the use of an RCT design to test the effects with cognitively impaired individuals. Thirty-three sedentary adults aged from 55 to 85 years with MCI were randomly assigned to either an aerobic exercise group or a stretching control group. The aerobic exercise group exercised at vigorous intensity for 45–60 minutes per day, four days per week for six months. The control group participated in stretching and balance exercises. Results indicated that those in the exercise group improved cardiovascular fitness and cognitive performance compared to the control group.

These studies provide evidence that physical activity participation is linked to cognitive performance in a *causal* fashion. That is, by increasing one's physical activity in the manner described in these studies, older sedentary adults who are cognitively normal or who have MCI can expect to perform better cognitively than their peers who remain sedentary. Importantly, in both of the studies, the researchers measured aerobic fitness to confirm that there was a physiological change in response to the exercise intervention.

Meta-analytic reviews: One way to present evidence regarding the effects of chronic exercise on cognition is to examine the findings of meta-analytic reviews (see "Reviews of scientific evidence" below). Several meta-analytic reviews have been conducted to summarize the research exploring the effects of physical activity on cognitive performance. Etnier et al. (1997) conducted a review including 134 studies. Overall, results indicated that exercise has an effect on cognitive performance, but that the effect is small when examined across all age groups and all cognitive tasks. Because of the aforementioned expectation that larger effects might be evident for older adults, several meta-analytic reviews have been conducted to summarize the findings of studies focused exclusively on older adults. These meta-analytic reviews indicate that when RCTs are conducted with older adults, effects are larger than seen with the general population and that the particular size of the effect depends upon the specific cognitive task being assessed (Angevaren, Aufdemkampe, Verhaar, Aleman, & Vanhees, 2008; Colcombe & Kramer, 2003; Smith et al., 2010). Of particular interest is the finding reported by Colcombe and Kramer (2003) that the largest exercise effect was found for the cognitive domain of executive function. This is important because executive function is considered a "higher-order" cognitive ability that is critical for activities of daily living (see "Exercise function" below).

Reviews of scientific evidence

Numerous studies have been conducted to explore the effects of physical activity on cognitive performance. To integrate these findings, researchers typically use one of two methods. One method is to provide a narrative review of the literature. In a narrative review, studies addressing a particular research question are read and synthesized by the researchers. Narrative reviewers then typically offer their opinion as to what the evidence shows by discussing strengths and weaknesses of the evidence and provide suggested directions for future research.

A second method is a meta-analytic review. A meta-analytic review (which is also referred to as a meta-analysis) is a review in which the researcher uses statistical techniques to mathematically summarize the findings from studies examining the same research question. The advantage of the meta-analytic review over a narrative review is that by using statistical techniques, researchers can quantify the overall findings from the research and can base their conclusions on objective evidence. In addition, meta-analytic reviewers are able to categorize the studies based upon particular variables (also known as moderators) and can then use statistical techniques to find out if the effects of physical activity are different based upon these variables. For example, they could use age group as a moderator to look at studies testing the effects with older adults separately from those testing the effects with children. This would allow them to determine if the effects of physical activity on cognitive performance were different between these two age groups.

Generally, the conclusions from meta-analytic reviews are judged as providing a high scientific level of evidence (LOE) and meta-analytic reviews that only include studies using RCT designs are viewed as providing the highest LOE.

Physical activity and children's academic achievement

In addition to the literature on older adults, a growing body of research has also investigated the association between school-based physical activity and academic performance for children. Typically, in this area of research, relationships between physical activity (or fitness) and cognitive performance are tested; however, it should be noted that the body of research is limited by the fact that most of the studies have not used RCTs.

In a recent narrative review, Rasberry et al. (2011) identified 50 studies testing the relationship between physical activity and cognitive performance in children. The authors classified studies based upon whether they were focused on school-based physical education, recess, classroom activity studies, or extracurricular physical activity. Results of the review generally revealed a positive relationship between physical activity (including physical education) and academic achievement. In addition, in the studies in which researchers increased time in physical education (PE) at the expense of time in other classes, the increased time in PE was not found to adversely influence academic performance. This finding could be interpreted as providing evidence that school systems can increase PE time to achieve the physical and mental health benefits, and this will not have a negative effect on cognitive performance. Specifically, Raspberry et al. presented evidence that increasing PE participation from twice per week to five times per week was positively associated with measures of math, reading, writing, attention, self-esteem, and planning behavior. With regards to recess, the authors found that structured or unstructured free play during recess was positively associated with attention, concentration, and a child's ability to stay focused on a task. In classroom activity studies, results showed that classes that involved short physical activity or movement in the beginning of the period benefited children's math, reading, language, memory, and concentration.

Lastly, participation in school sport inside or outside of regular school PE programs had a positive relationship with math, reading, language, and grade point averages.

Thus, this review is strongly supportive of a positive relationship between physical activity and cognitive performance when examined in the schools. However, it is important to realize that none of the studies reviewed were RCTs; hence conclusions that physical activity *causes* improvements in cognitive performance cannot be made.

Exercise mode

Most studies examining the effect of chronic exercise on cognition have tested the effects of aerobic exercise as opposed to other types of exercise such as resistance exercise (e.g., strength training). In fact, some of the research in this area has used resistance exercise as a control condition which suggests that the researchers view the benefits to cognition as being unique to aerobic exercise. However, other researchers have tested the effects of resistance exercise in isolation and in combination with aerobic exercise. In their meta-analysis, Colcombe and Kramer (2003) reported a larger effect for studies using a combination of aerobic exercise and strength exercise than for aerobic exercise alone. This suggests that resistance exercise might provide additional benefits for cognitive performance.

A recent narrative review focused specifically on resistance exercise and cognition supported the potential of resistance exercise as a strategy to facilitate cognition in older adults. Chang, Pan, Chen, Tsai, and Huang (2012) indicated that only a few studies have examined resistance exercise effects with results from these studies suggesting that to achieve benefits, the load should be from 60 to 80% of one Repetition Maximum (RM), exercises should be performed with approximately seven movements executed in two sets and separated by two minutes of rest, and training should be conducted at least twice per week for two to 12 months. When performed in this way, benefits were observed for a variety of cognitive outcomes.

Other investigators have shifted their attention to lower intensity forms of exercise that might be considered meditative movement (Larkey, Jahnke, Etnier, & Gonzalez, 2009). This type of physical activity might be particularly attractive for older adults because it is low impact and, hence, has a lower risk of injury or of exacerbating chronic conditions. One form of meditative movement that has been studied relative to cognitive performance is Tai Chi Chuan. Tai Chi Chuan is a mind–body exercise derived from Chinese martial arts. Although there are only a few studies that have examined the effects of Tai Chi Chuan on cognition, current evidence supports the potential beneficial effects of Tai Chi Chuan for the cognitive performance of older adults (Chang, Nien, Tasi, & Etnier, 2010). Given that beneficial effects of exercise on cognition have been observed for aerobic exercise, resistance exercise, and meditative movements, further research is warranted to improve our understanding of the particular exercise components that are critical for cognitive benefits.

Summary of chronic exercise and cognition

Numerous studies have been conducted to test the effects of chronic exercise on cognitive outcomes. When examined in older adults using epidemiological designs, research generally supports that physical activity participation is protective against age-related cognitive declines and clinical cognitive declines. Reviews of the studies with older adults that have used RCTs allow for conclusions related to cause and effect. That is, chronic exercise has been shown to *cause* improvements in cognitive performance.

Additionally, there is evidence which suggests that benefits to cognitive performance are evident with aerobic exercise, resistance exercise, and lower intensity activities like Tai Chi Chuan; however future research is needed to further our understanding of the potential of these various forms of exercise and to provide guidance with regards to the prescription of physical activity to enhance cognitive performance. Studies testing the association between physical activity and cognitive performance specifically in children also tend to support beneficial relationships, but the effects of physical activity on cognitive performance have not been satisfactorily examined using RCTs. Thus, although evidence supports that physical activity performed by children is *associated* with better cognitive performance, at this time we cannot confidently say that physical activity participation *causes* cognitive benefits for children.

ACUTE EXERCISE

Another line of research has focused on the impact of a single bout of exercise on cognitive performance. This research has been reviewed using meta-analytic techniques and results indicate that the effects are consistently observed, but tend to be small in size (Chang, Labban, Gapin, & Etnier, 2012; Lambourne & Tomporowski, 2010). However, the results also indicate that larger effects are possible when the acute exercise is administered in a particular way. In other words, the size of the effect that is observed is dependent upon factors such as type of cognition, level of exercise intensity, and a combination of these factors.

Type of cognition

One interesting finding in the acute exercise literature is that the type of cognitive task being assessed might determine the size of the effect of acute exercise on cognitive performance. In their meta-analytic review, Chang, Labban, et al. (2012) reported that the effects of acute exercise on cognitive performance are influenced by the particular cognitive domain being assessed. Generally, acute exercise facilitates cognitive performance in the domains of information-processing (e.g., the word condition of the Stroop Test), attention, crystallized intelligence (e.g., vocabulary tasks), and executive function (e.g., the color-word condition of the Stroop Test). It should be noted that although the most commonly used measures to test the effects of acute exercise on cognitive performance are relatively simple cognitive tasks, many recent studies have begun to examine more complex higher order cognitive tasks such as measures of executive function. In fact, executive function is the only cognitive domain that was shown to improve both during exercise and following cessation of exercise (Chang, Labban et al., 2012). Results of another recent meta-analysis further support that moderate intensity exercise significantly improves executive function (McMorris, Sproule, Turner, & Hale, 2011).

Executive function

Executive function, also known as executive control, is an umbrella term used to describe a group of cognitive functions that are viewed as "higher-order" or "metacognition". The executive control processes are necessary to accomplish purposeful and goal-directed behaviors, and in the exercise science literature have typically been described as planning, scheduling, inhibition, and working memory (Colcombe & Kramer, 2003). An example of an executive function task that emphasizes planning would be figuring out the steps necessary to enter someone's phone number into your cell phone's address book. An example of an executive function task that requires working memory would be figuring out the change you are owed when you purchase an item with cash at the store.

Exercise intensity

Another variable of interest in this literature is exercise intensity. Tomporowski (2003) observed that following very high intensity aerobic exercise, most studies reported either no change or an impairment in cognitive performance. In contrast, numerous studies have found positive effects on cognition following exercise at sub-maximal intensity. In a recent meta-analytic review of this literature, Chang, Labban et al. (2012) reported that exercise performed at moderate or lower intensity facilitated cognitive performance when assessed immediately following exercise, while exercise above moderate intensity failed to affect performance immediately post-exercise. In contrast, when cognitive performance was assessed after a delay following exercise, exercise above light intensity benefited cognitive performance, but cognitive performance was most positively influenced by acute exercise at more vigorous intensities (but not maximal intensity).

Although the results of meta-analytic reviews can provide indirect evidence in support of the relationship between exercise intensity and cognitive performance, individual studies designed specifically to test dose-response relationships provide more direct evidence. Studies that test dose-response relationships not only provide a test of the theoretical basis for a link between exercise intensity and cognitive performance, but also provide foundational knowledge to establish exercise prescription (see "Exercise prescription" below). Typically, studies designed to test dose-response relationships have examined cognitive performance at multiple exercise intensity conditions. Generally, these studies have shown that moderate exercise intensity leads to the best cognitive performance as compared to light and vigorous intensity exercise (Arent & Landers, 2003; McMorris, Collard, Corbett, Dicks, & Swain, 2008).

Exercise prescription

When using a pharmacological treatment to obtain a desired outcome, patients are given a prescription that tells them the dose to use (e.g., 500 mg), how much to take (e.g., two pills), how often to take the medicine (e.g., every four hours), and for how long they should take the medicine (e.g., for 24 hours). Ideally, researchers will one day be able to prescribe exercise in a similar way to achieve a desired outcome such as a moderate improvement in cognitive performance. If exercise prescription becomes possible, then the exercise prescription would define the parameters of the exercise program designed for a specific health purpose (e.g., to reduce all-cause mortality, cancer, stress) and a particular population (e.g., normal population, people with disability). The exercise prescription would be designed by trained professionals in order to make the program safe and effective. Generally, exercise prescription would involve components including exercise mode, intensity, duration, frequency, and progression. Studies examining dose-response relationships could be used to establish the specifics of an exercise prescription.

Combining exercise intensity and cognitive task type

An intriguing direction for future research is to begin to understand how variables that influence the relationship between physical activity and cognitive performance might act together. For instance, it may be possible that the dose-response relationship between exercise intensity and cognitive performance differs depending upon the particular type of cognitive performance that is assessed. This possibility was supported in a study by Chang and Etnier (2009) in which they investigated the dose-response effects of resistance exercise performed at four intensities (i.e. control, 40%, 70%, and 100% of 10 RM) on cognitive performance. There was a linear positive relationship between intensity and information-processing, such that increasing exercise intensities resulted in increasingly faster performance. However, there was an inverted-U relationship between intensity and executive function, indicating that performance improved from low intensity to moderate intensity but then got worse when the participant performed high intensity resistance exercise. This is an intriguing finding because it suggests that moderate intensity exercise benefits both types of cognitive performance,

but that high intensity exercise is beneficial when performing information-processing tasks and is detrimental when performing executive function tasks. This finding illustrates the challenges of being able to prescribe exercise to benefit cognition because it shows that with an acute session of resistance exercise, the relationship between intensity and cognitive performance is influenced by the particular type of cognitive performance you are interested in.

Summary of acute exercise and cognition

The literature on the effects of acute exercise on cognitive performance demonstrates that there is a benefit, but that the benefit tends to be fairly small. Variables that can influence the size of the effect include the type of cognition assessed, exercise intensity, and the timing of the performance of the cognitive task relative to the exercise session. There is evidence that larger effects may be observed for measures of executive function than are seen with more simple cognitive measures. Intensity of the exercise and timing of the administration of the cognitive measure relative to the exercise also influence the effect. When the cognitive task is performed during exercise, lower intensities are better.

When the cognitive task is performed after a delay following the exercise, higher intensities have a bigger effect. Lastly, it is possible that these variables cannot be considered in isolation because they may work together to determine the effects on cognitive performance.

PRACTICAL IMPLICATIONS

One of the ultimate goals of research is to establish practical implications. In the field of exercise psychology, practical application is reliant upon an understanding of dose-response relationships that can guide exercise prescription. When thinking of physical outcomes that result from chronic physical activity, fairly precise exercise prescriptions have been made with regards to exercise mode, intensity, duration, frequency, and length of participation (American College of Sports Medicine, 2010). However, when considering cognitive outcomes that result from chronic physical activity, Etnier (2009) indicated that our current state of the evidence does not allow for exercise recommendations that are as precise as with physical outcomes. Thus, further research is needed to allow us to fine-tune our recommendations; nonetheless,

Etnier (2009) indicated that evidence supports the recommendation that individuals should exercise using a combination of aerobic and resistance exercise, for 20 to 60 minutes, almost daily, for six months or longer.

Similarly to chronic exercise, the acute exercise literature does not clearly support a specific exercise prescription for acute exercise to benefit cognition. However, we tentatively propose recommendations for acute exercise based upon the relatively recent comprehensive review of this literature conducted by Chang, Labban et al. (2012). Thus, we expect that the largest cognitive effects will be observed following a combined session of aerobic and resistance exercise performed at very light (< 50% HR maximal) to moderate (64% to 76% HR maximal) intensity for more than 11 minutes (ES from 0.12 to 37).

CONCLUSION

In summary, the following conclusions can be drawn from the extensive literature reviewed above. Epidemiological, experimental, and meta-analytic results support the conclusion that chronic exercise is predictive of lesser risk of cognitive impairment and of better cognitive performance for both cognitively-impaired and cognitively-normal adults. In addition, research supports the theory that children who participate in a variety of physical activities (e.g. physical education, recess, classroom activities, extracurricular physical activity) experience benefits that are observed in their academic performance. Lastly, empirical research and meta-analytic reviews support that cognitive performance is improved following acute bouts of exercise. It has been emphasized that we need more research to examine the dose-response relationship between specific exercise components and cognition to allow us to establish clear exercise prescription/recommendations for application in the real world.

In order for man to succeed in life, god provided him with two means, education and physical activity. Not separately, one for the soul and the other for the body, but for the two together. With these two means, men can attain perfection.

Plato, fourth century, BC

LEARNING AIDS

1 Describe the different experimental designs that have been used in epidemiological research.

Epidemiological research generally describes studies with large numbers of subjects that are used to investigate the causes of health outcomes.

2 Explain what is meant by "chronic exercise" and "acute exercise".

Chronic exercise describes long-term regular participation in exercise, while acute exercise represents a single session of exercise.

3 Identify aspects of cognition and executive function and describe how they are measured.

Cognition is a general term describing a wide variety of activities that require thoughtful behavior and that can be categorized as memory, problem solving, decision making, attention, perception, and communication. Executive function is "higher-order" or "meta-cognition" that is a necessary to accomplish purposeful and goal-directed behaviors. In the exercise science literature, executive function tasks have typically included tasks that measure planning, scheduling, inhibition, and working memory.

4 Discuss the general findings of exercise across different populations (older adults with or without cognitive impairment and children's academic performance).

Generally, research has shown that chronic exercise is related to better cognitive performance and to a reduction in the risk of clinical cognitive decline and evidence also indicates that this is a causal effect that can be observed in older adults with or without cognitive impairment; however, whether physical activity participation causes cognitive benefits for children and younger adults needs more investigation. In regard to acute exercise, a small beneficial effect on cognitive performance is generally demonstrated.

5 Describe the concept and components of exercise prescription.

The concept of exercise prescription comes from the perspective of pharmacological treatments. Relative to exercise, the prescription components would consist of exercise mode (the type of exercise), intensity (how hard the exercise is), duration (how long the exercise session lasts), frequency (how many times per week), and progression (how the exercise changes with fitness gains). Generally, the identification of the specific exercise prescription that would most benefit a particular health outcome should be obtained through dose-response studies.

REVIEW QUESTIONS

1 Discuss the evidence supporting the statement that different populations (e.g. older adults who are cognitively intact and older adults with cognitive impairment) could experience cognitive benefits through exercise.

2 Is it reasonable to cut physical education or related programs in order to improve children's academic performance?

3   What is the best research design that can be used to infer causation? Explain what we know about the effects of exercise on cognition when studies have used this type of research design.

4   What do the meta-analytic results show in the reviews that focused on the effects of chronic exercise and acute exercise on cognition?

5   What factors might influence the relationship between exercise and cognition considering both chronic exercise and acute exercise paradigms?

6   Are we ready to prescribe exercise for cognition? What is the recommended exercise prescription for cognition based upon the current evidence?

EXERCISES

1   Using the research presented in the chapter, prepare a presentation for older adults with mild cognitive impairment and for healthy older adults. In your presentation, discuss the current research evidence relative to the relationship between exercise and cognition. Also, discuss the practical implications.

2   Find a computerized measure of cognitive performance online and use it to measure performance in one of the following conditions: a) to evaluate cognitive performance prior to and after a single bout of aerobic exercise; and b) to measure the differences in performance between a single bout of aerobic exercise and a single bout of resistance exercise.

ADDITIONAL READING

Hillman, C.H., Erickson, K.I. & Kramer, A.F. (2008). Be smart, exercise your heart: exercise effects on brain and cognition. *Nature Reviews Neuroscience, 9*, 58–65.

Ratey, J.J. & Loehr, J.E. (2010). The positive impact of physical activity on cognition during adulthood: A review of underlying mechanisms, evidence, and recommendations. *Reviews in the Neurosciences, 22*, 171–185.

REFERENCES

Abbott, R.D., White, L.R., Ross, G.W., Masaki, K.H., Curb, J.D. & Petrovitch, H. (2004). Walking and dementia in physically capable elderly men. *Journal of the American Medical Association, 292,* 1447–1453.

American College of Sports Medicine (2010). *ACSM's guidelines for exercise testing and prescription* (8th ed.). New York: Lippincott Williams and Wilkins.

Andel, R., Crowe, M., Pedersen, N.L., Fratiglioni, L., Johansson, B. & Gatz, M. (2008). Physical exercise at midlife and risk of dementia three decades later: A population-based study of Swedish twins. *The Journals of Gerontology Series A: Biological Sciences and Medical Sciences, 63,* 62–66.

Angevaren, M., Aufdemkampe, G., Verhaar, H.J., Aleman, A. & Vanhees, L. (2008). Physical activity and enhanced fitness to improve cognitive function in older people without known cognitive impairment. *Cochrane Database of Systematic Reviews* CD005381. doi: 10.1002/14651858.CD005381.pub3

Arent, S.M. & Landers, D.M. (2003). Arousal, anxiety, and performance: A reexamination of the inverted-U hypothesis. *Research Quarterly for Exercise and Sport, 74*, 436–444.

Baker, L.D., Frank, L.L., Foster-Schubert, K., Green, P.S., Wilkinson, C.W., McTiernan, A., Cholerton, B.A. (2010). Effects of aerobic exercise on mild cognitive impairment: A controlled trial. *Archives of Neurology, 67*, 71–79.

Chang, Y.K. & Etnier, J.L. (2009). Exploring the dose-response relationship between resistance exercise intensity and cognitive function. *Journal of Sport and Exercise Psychology, 31*, 640–656.

Chang, Y.K., Labban, J.D., Gapin, J.I. & Etnier, J.L. (2012). The effects of acute exercise on cognitive performance: A meta-analysis. *Brain Research, 1453*, 87–101. doi: 10.1016/j.brainres.2012.02.068

Chang, Y.K., Nien, Y.H., Tasi, C.L. & Etnier, J.L. (2010). Physical activity and cognition in older adults: The potential of Tai Chi Chuan. *Journal of Aging and Physical Activity, 18*, 451–472.

Chang, Y.K., Pan, C.Y., Chen, F.T., Tsai, C.L. & Huang, C.C. (2012). Effect of resistance exercise training on cognitive function in healthy older adults: A review. *Journal of Aging and Physical Activity, 20*, 497–516.

Colcombe, S.J. & Kramer, A.F. (2003). Fitness effects on the cognitive function of older adults: A meta-analytic study. *Psychological Science, 14*, 125–130.

Colcombe, S.J., Kramer, A.F., Erickson, K.I., Scalf, P., McAuley, E., Cohen, N. & Elavsky, S. (2004). Cardiovascular fitness, cortical plasticity, and aging. *Proceedings of the National Academy of Sciences of the United States of America, 101*, 3316–3321.

Etnier, J.L. (2009). Physical activity programming to promote cognitive function: Are we ready for prescription? In W.J. Chodzko-Zajko, A.F. Kramer & L.W. Poon (Eds.), *Enhancing cognitive functioning and brain plasticity* (Vol. 3). Champaign, IL: Human Kinetics.

Etnier, J.L., Salazar, W., Landers, D.M., Petruzzello, S.J., Han, M. & Nowell, P. (1997). The influence of physical fitness and exercise upon cognitive functioning: A meta-analysis. *Journal of Sport and Exercise Psychology, 19*, 249–277.

Herrmann, D.J., Yoder, C., Gruneberg, M. & Payne, D. (2006). *Applied cognitive psychology: A textbook* (1st ed.). Philadelphia: Lawrence Erlbaum Associates.

Lambourne, K. & Tomporowski, P.D. (2010). The effect of exercise-induced arousal on cognitive task performance: A meta-regression analysis. *Brain Research, 1341*, 12–24. doi: 10.1016/j.brain res.2010.03.091

Larkey, L., Jahnke, R., Etnier, J. & Gonzalez, J. (2009). Meditative movement as a category of exercise: Implications for research. *Journal of Physical Activity and Health, 6*, 230–238.

McMorris, T., Collard, K., Corbett, J., Dicks, M. & Swain, J.P. (2008). A test of the catecholamines hypothesis for an acute exercise-cognition interaction. *Pharmacology, Biochemistry and Behavior, 89*, 106–115. doi: 10.1016/j.pbb.2007. 11.007

McMorris, T., Sproule, J., Turner, A. & Hale, B.J. (2011). Acute, intermediate intensity exercise, and speed and accuracy in working memory tasks: A meta-analytical comparison of effects. *Physiology and Behavior, 102*, 421–428.

Rasberry, C.N., Lee, S.M., Robin, L., Laris, B.A., Russell, L.A., Coyle, K.K. & Nihiser, A.J. (2011). The association between school-based physical activity, including physical education, and academic performance: A systematic review of the literature. *Preventive Medicine, 52*, Supplement, S10-S20. doi: 10.1016/j.ypmed.2011. 01.027

Salthouse, T.A. (2009). When does age-related cognitive decline begin? *Neurobiology of Aging, 30*, 507–514. doi: 10.1016/j.neurobiolaging.2008. 09.023.

Smith, P.J., Blumenthal, J.A., Hoffman, B.M., Cooper, H., Strauman, T.A., Welsh-Bohmer, K. & Sherwood, A. (2010). Aerobic exercise and neurocognitive performance: A meta-analytic review of randomized controlled trials. *Psychosomatic Medicine, 72*, 239–252. doi: 10.1097/ PSY.0b013e3181d14633

Tomporowski, P.D. (2003). Effects of acute bouts of exercise on cognition. *Acta Psychologica, 112*, 297–324.

Weuve, J., Kang, J.H., Manson, J.A.E., Breteler, M., Ware, J.H. & Grodstein, F. (2004). Physical activity, including walking, and cognitive function in older women. *Journal of the American Medical Association, 292*, 1454–1461.

Chapter 46

Sitting psychology

Towards a psychology of sedentary behaviour

STUART J.H. BIDDLE AND TRISH GORELY

SUMMARY

Exercise psychology has typically investigated moderate-to-vigorous physical activity (MVPA). Recent evidence shows that high levels of sedentary behaviour (sitting time) can also be detrimental to health, often independent of MVPA. Therefore, we need to better understand the behavioural epidemiology of sedentary behaviour as well as physical activity. This chapter defines sedentary behaviour and how to measure it, summarises evidence on the health outcomes of sedentary behaviour, outlines factors associated with high levels of sitting, and discusses possible ways to reduce sedentary behaviour. The focus is on psychology while making reference to wider social and environmental influences.

INTRODUCTION

Is this your typical day?

- Get up; sit having breakfast
- Sit in the car to work
- Sit at work for most of the day
- Sit in the car to go home
- Go for a 30 minute run
- Sit and watch TV with dinner
- Go to bed.

If you are thinking that the 30-minute run 'saves the day', think again! Almost the whole day is 'sedentary' (sitting). Read on to see why this is harmful, and what we might be able to do about it. Our conclusion is to 'move more and *sit less*'.

Sport and exercise psychology has seen many developments over the years, including the burgeoning of health-related issues through 'exercise psychology'. Typically, this has involved the study and application of psychological factors associated with participation in moderate-to-vigorous physical activity (MVPA) for health, including behaviour change, as well as psychological outcomes of physical activity. Behavioural and biological health scientists are now showing great interest in 'sedentary behaviour' (sitting time) mainly due to technology-driven behaviours that are largely sedentary and possible links to adverse health outcomes. However, little is known about the psychological factors associated with sedentary behaviour and whether theories and approaches adopted in exercise psychology can be transferred to this different set of behaviours.

OBJECTIVES

After reading this chapter, you should be able to:

1 Define sedentary behaviour and specify the main forms of sedentary behaviour.
2 Summarise the main correlates of sedentary behaviour.
3 Understand the main evidence summarising the links between high levels of sitting and deleterious health outcomes.
4 Outline the evidence concerning the effectiveness of interventions to reduce sedentary behaviour.
5 Describe the key psychological frameworks and models that might be helpful in understanding sedentary behaviour.
6 Consider the appropriateness of strategies for reducing sedentary behaviour.

BEHAVIOURAL EPIDEMIOLOGY FRAMEWORK APPLIED TO SEDENTARY BEHAVIOUR

A 'Behavioural Epidemiology Framework' has been adopted as a heuristic guide for many health behaviours, including physical activity (Sallis & Owen, 1999). Behavioural epidemiology itself is concerned with the distribution and aetiology of behaviours that are thought to be associated with disease outcomes as well as how these behaviours are associated with disease outcomes in the population. In relation to sedentary behaviour, this framework leads to five key questions:

1 What is the association between sedentary behaviour and health outcomes?
2 How do we measure sedentary behaviour?
3 What factors are associated with different levels of sedentary behaviour (correlates)?
4 What interventions are successful for changing sedentary behaviours?
5 How can we translate findings from research into practice?

WHAT IS SEDENTARY BEHAVIOUR?

Sedentary behaviour is, essentially, 'sitting time'. It refers to "any waking behaviour characterized by an energy expenditure ≤1.5 METs while in a sitting or reclining posture" (Sedentary Behaviour Research Network, 2012). Typical examples include TV viewing, computer use, sitting at work or school, and car travel. Conversely, any standing behaviour can be thought of as non-sedentary. It is therefore possible to meet recommended levels of physical activity (e.g., 30 minutes per day for adults), and be classified as 'active', but at the same time take part in high levels of sedentary behaviour. That is, the two behaviours can co-exist. This means that it is important not to refer to those with low levels of physical activity as 'sedentary', as is often the case in the literature. Instead, we should use the term 'inactive'.

These issues are very important from the point of view of psychology and behaviour change. Understanding and changing behaviours can only be effective if we properly define and target the appropriate behaviours. For this reason, it is essential that we separate physical activity (or inactivity) from sedentary behaviours. They are different clusters of behaviours that may have different behavioural antecedents and thereby require different behaviour change theories, frameworks and approaches.

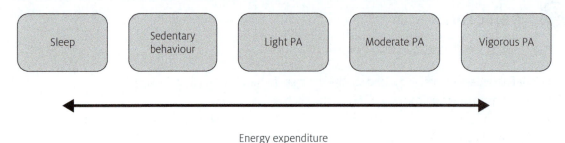

Energy expenditure

Figure 46.1 A depiction of an energy expenditure continuum whereby 'light physical activity' (e.g., light ambulation, but not moderate physical activity) falls between sedentary behaviour and MVPA. This helps us to see how sedentary behaviour and light PA are likely to easily substitute for each other (i.e., when not sitting there is a good chance you are in light PA, such as standing), but less likely to be in moderate or vigorous PA.

HOW DO WE ASSESS DIFFERENT SEDENTARY BEHAVIOURS?

The measurement of sedentary behaviour is challenging because of the variety of behaviours involved and the often intermittent and incidental nature of these behaviours. Currently, there is a lack of consensus on the most appropriate methods of assessing sedentary behaviour (Atkin et al., 2012).

Self-reports have been widely used but often lack validity (Atkin et al., 2012; Bryant, Lucove, Evenson, & Marshall, 2007; Clark et al., 2009) and few existing instruments have been assessed for their capacity to identify change in behaviour over time. In addition, self-report methods have predominantly focused on TV viewing or other screen-based behaviours. This may be problematic as people find many ways to be sedentary and TV viewing time does not appear to be a good marker of overall sedentary behaviour (Biddle, Gorely, & Marshall, 2009; Sugiyama, Healy, Dunstan, Salmon, & Owen, 2008). Recent work has attempted to develop more refined self-report measures that assess multiple sedentary behaviours (e.g., TV viewing, reading, socialising) and/or domain-specific behaviours, (e.g., sitting at work or at home, motorised travel) (Clark et al., 2009; Hardy, Booth, & Okely, 2007; Marshall, Miller, Burton, & Brown, 2010). These show promise, but further development

and validation work is required. An advantage of self-report over other methods is that self-report allows for the assessment of behaviour type (e.g., watching TV vs. sitting reading) and context (e.g., alone, with family members etc) which may be particularly useful for intervention design.

Accelerometry is increasingly being used for assessment of sedentary time. This approach overcomes the recall limitations of self-report methods and can provide an objective assessment of overall levels of sedentary behaviour, and also patterns of sedentary behaviour across a day. However, accelerometry is not without limitations, for example, the detection of specific behaviours is not currently possible and there is a lack of consensus as to the most appropriate way to process accelerometer data which limits comparability between studies. Nonetheless, accelerometers are now being used to assess sedentary time in large-scale surveillance studies (Colley et al., 2011; Matthews et al., 2008).

Other objective instruments have been developed to specifically assess body posture (e.g., ActivPAL – PAL Technologies Ltd, Glasgow, UK). These have demonstrated good reliability and validity in the limited research conducted to date (Atkin et al., 2012). However, similar to other objective methods, posture monitors do not currently provide information on the type of behaviour being undertaken or the social or environmental context in which it occurs.

The best choice of measurement approach will be determined by the specific question to be addressed. However, given the limitations in all existing sedentary measurement technologies it is possible that multiple measurement approaches will be needed.

WHAT ARE THE KEY HEALTH OUTCOMES OF SEDENTARY BEHAVIOUR?

Young people

A recent systematic review provided a comprehensive examination of the relationship between sedentary behaviour and six health indicators in young people aged 5–17 years (Tremblay et al., 2011). The authors reported that sedentary behaviour (primarily assessed through TV viewing) was associated with unfavourable body composition, decreased fitness, lowered scores for self-esteem and pro-social behaviour and decreased academic achievement. In addition, the findings suggested that increased sedentary time was associated with increased metabolic and cardio-vascular disease risk factors, although the evidence was not as strong for these factors. The authors concluded that the findings showed consistent evidence for an inverse relationship between sedentary behaviour and health outcomes in young people.

Tremblay et al. (2011) included all eligible studies regardless of design. In contrast, the systematic review of Chinapaw et al. (2011) only included prospective studies examining the relationship between childhood sedentary behaviour and health indicators. Using these stricter inclusion criteria the authors found insufficient evidence for a longitudinal relationship between 'sedentary time' (usually TV time) and body mass index (BMI), blood pressure, blood lipids or bone mass. However, moderate evidence was found for an inverse longitudinal relationship between 'sedentary time' and aerobic fitness. These authors concluded that the possible detrimental health effects of prolonged or excessive sitting on health indicators in young people needs further study, with stronger designs.

Sedentary behaviour has also been associated with other health outcomes not included in these reviews. For example, high levels of television viewing have been associated with negative effects on sleep, attention, and interpersonal relationships (Jolin & Weller, 2010), aggression, sexual behaviour, and substance use (Strasburger, Jordan, & Donnerstein, 2010) and unhealthy eating (Pearson & Biddle, 2011). Furthermore, children who are high television viewers tend to remain high television viewers, relative to others over time (Biddle, Pearson, Ross, & Braithwaite, 2010), and therefore may be at greater risk of negative health outcomes.

Adults

In a review of prospective studies, Proper et al. (2011) concluded that there was moderate evidence for a positive relationship between sitting time and the risk for type 2 diabetes and strong evidence for associations with all-cause and cardiovascular disease (CVD) mortality (Wilmot et al., 2012). Similarly, Edwardson et al.'s (2012) meta-analysis showed that those in the highest sedentary group had a 73% increased risk of metabolic syndrome compared with those in the lowest sedentary group. This remained unchanged when accounting for physical activity, thus suggesting that sedentary behaviour is an independent risk factor. However, sedentary behaviour, mainly in the form of TV viewing, has also been shown to cluster with other deleterious lifestyle practices, such as a poor diet (Pearson & Biddle, 2011), which could act to overestimate the independent effect of sedentary behaviour.

The majority of the evidence has focused on the link between total sedentary time, or individual sedentary behaviours (e.g., TV viewing) and health. However, emerging evidence is suggestive that the nature of sedentary behaviour may also be important. For example, it might be informative to know if periods of sitting are prolonged or whether they take place in a more sporadic form. Healy et al. (2008) found that objectively assessed breaks in sedentary time were beneficially associated with waist circumference, BMI, triglycerides, and 2-h plasma glucose, and these associations were independent of total sedentary time and MVPA. Increasing the number of breaks from sitting may therefore be important for health.

MENTAL HEALTH OUTCOMES OF SEDENTARY BEHAVIOUR

For many years, psychologists have been interested in the relationship between physical activity and mental health. More recently, associations have been tested between sedentary behaviour and markers of mental well-being. There are several large cross-sectional studies showing an inverse association between sedentary behaviour (usually screen time) and mental health in young people (Biddle & Asare, 2011). In addition, one longitudinal cohort study showed higher levels of depression in young adulthood being associated with higher levels of TV viewing, and total media exposure, but not computer games, in youth (Primack, Swanier, Georgiopoulos, Land, & Fine, 2009).

Similar cross-sectional trends have been found in adults. Hamer et al. (2010) reported data from the 2003 Scottish Health Survey and found that higher levels of TV and screen-based entertainment were associated with lower levels of mental well-being when controlling for confounders, including physical activity. Atkin et al. (2011) found similar trends when assessing a wider variety of non-occupational sedentary behaviours, but only for women. However, future research requires confirmation of such findings using intervention and prospective designs to test for 'reverse causality' effects (i.e., those with poorer mental health choosing to be more sedentary).

CORRELATES: WHAT FACTORS ARE ASSOCIATED WITH SEDENTARY BEHAVIOUR?

Correlates are factors associated with behaviours. They may not necessarily be causally related. They allow for the identification of possible mediators and moderators in interventions. Typically, correlates can be grouped under the categories of socio-demographic, biological, psychological, behavioural, social/cultural, and environmental.

Young people

Research examining the correlates of sedentary behaviour in young people has focused predominantly on the correlates of screen-viewing. Several systematic reviews of the correlates of sedentary behaviour covering different age groups of young people have been published (Cillero & Jago, 2010; Gorely, Marshall, & Biddle, 2004; Hinkley, Salmon, Okely, & Trost, 2010; Uijtdewilligen et al., 2011; van der Horst, Chin A Paw, Twisk, & Van Mechelen, 2007).

The first published review of correlates of sedentary behaviour in young people found that only TV viewing had been studied often enough to warrant review (Gorely et al., 2004). The review included papers for 2–18 year olds but did not differentiate results by age. Body weight, snacking, parent viewing habits, day of the week, and having a TV in the bedroom were all positively associated with TV viewing time. Higher TV viewing levels were also associated with low socio-economic status (SES), single parent households, ethnic minorities, and 9–13 year olds. Van der Horst et al., (2007) updated this review and also differentiated between children (4–12 years old) and adolescents (13–18 years old). These authors concluded that there was insufficient evidence to draw conclusions about correlates of sedentary behaviour in children. However, for adolescents they reported a positive relationship between watching TV/video and sex (male), ethnicity (non-White European), BMI and depression, and a negative relationship for watching TV/video with SES and parental education.

Cillerio and Jago (2010) examined the correlates of screen-viewing in children younger than eight years of age and found that age, ethnicity (non-White European), family TV viewing, maternal depressive symptoms, parental body mass and media access were positively associated with TV viewing. In addition those from lower socio-demographic groups watched more television. However, there were no clear gender differences in TV viewing patterns. Higher levels of parental TV viewing were associated with higher levels of child TV viewing. There were inconsistent associations for TV viewing with the presence of a TV in the child's bedroom, number of TVs in the house and general TV access of TV viewing in this age group. These authors also examined computer use and found that boys and older children had higher levels of computer use.

Hinkley et al. (2010) focused on the correlates of sedentary behaviour in preschool children (3–5 years old). In this young age group sex was not associated with TV viewing, and had an unclear association with overall sedentary levels measured by accelerometry. Outdoor playtime had no association with TV viewing. Age, body mass index, parental education and ethnicity had an unclear relationship with TV viewing within this narrow age group.

The majority of work examining the correlates of sedentary behaviour in young people has employed cross-sectional designs limiting opportunities to identify causality. Partially to address this, Uitdewilligen et al. (2011) limited their systematic review to only prospective studies, finding very few studies meeting this inclusion criteria, and concluding that there is insufficient evidence on the correlates of sedentary behaviour.

Collectively, these findings suggest that although a number of correlates of young people's TV viewing have been identified, most of these are unmodifiable correlates (moderators) and more work with better designs is required to identify the modifiable correlates (mediators) of sedentary behaviour. In addition, the correlates of sedentary behaviours, other than screen-viewing behaviours, have received little attention and this gap needs to be addressed to facilitate the development of effective interventions to reduce the time children and adolescents spend on sedentary behaviours.

Adults

The data on correlates of sedentary behaviour in adults is rather patchy, relying largely on self-reported estimates of sedentary time and often only a few sedentary behaviours, such as TV viewing. This is particularly limiting given that single behaviours may not be good markers of overall sedentary time and that there are likely to be different correlates for different behaviours.

A review by Owen et al. (2011) suggested that TV viewing is associated with lower socio-economic status, and the nature of the built environment. There is a negative association between TV viewing and having a more 'walkable' neighbourhood. In addition, some occupations will involve long periods of sitting. Psychological correlates have not been identified with any consistency (Rhodes, Mark, & Temmel, 2012).

INTERVENTIONS: CAN WE REDUCE SEDENTARY BEHAVIOUR?

Young people

With the increasing awareness of the potential negative effects of high levels of sedentary behaviour there has been increasing interest in interventions that attempt to reduce sedentary behaviour in young people. The majority of these interventions focus on reducing television viewing or screen media use in 8–11 year old children with few interventions in the early years or adolescence (Maniccia, Davison, Marshall, Manganello, & Dennison, 2011). The interventions have taken place in schools, homes, community settings and clinics. Regardless of the primary setting of the intervention almost all studies include a home component (Schmidt et al., 2012) and the majority of interventions are delivered to both the child and the parents (Steeves, Thompson, Bassett, Fitzhugh, & Raynor, 2011).

In a meta-analysis including only studies that specifically targeted a reduction in sedentary behaviour, Biddle et al. (2011) found a small, significant and robust effect in favour of the intervention group (Hedges' g= −0.192, p=.001) indicating that it is possible to change sedentary behaviour in young people. Similar sized effects have been reported in other meta-analyses that focused only on sedentary behaviour interventions for weight management and/or have also included studies that were designed to increase physical activity but have had an assessment of sedentary behaviour as a secondary outcome (e.g., Kamath et al., 2008; Maniccia et al., 2011). Few moderators have been identified although there is some evidence that effects may be greater in children rather than adolescents, or when treatment duration is longer than six months, or when studies measure in-treatment outcomes rather than post-treatment outcomes (Kamath et al., 2008). Biddle et al. argue that the small effect observed may reflect real difficulties in changing a behaviour that has a strong habitual element and strong environmental cues. While the effects of sedentary behaviour interventions appear modest, these small changes across a population could have large public health implications given the prevalence or screen media use among young people (Biddle et al., 2011; Maniccia et al., 2011).

Interventions to reduce sedentary behaviours have been underpinned by a number of theoretical perspectives, most commonly social cognitive theory and behavioural choice theory (Steeves et al., 2011). However, given the likely strong habitual element of many sedentary behaviours, theoretical perspectives that directly address the automatic nature of habit may be required. This is addressed later in the chapter.

The reviews of Schmidt et al. (2012) and Steeves et al. (2011) focused on the strategies employed within interventions to reduce screen time among children. Effective interventions employed multiple behaviour modification strategies with the most common being goal setting and self-monitoring, followed by pre-planning, problem solving and positive reinforcement (Steeves et al., 2011). However, interventions that also included electronic monitoring devices or contingent TV devices to assist behaviour change were the most effective (Schmidt et al., 2012; Steeves et al., 2011). Electronic monitoring devices allow participants to set a time goal or budget for viewing after which point the television will not be turned on. Contingent TV devices may be open loop or closed loop. In a closed loop system TV viewing is made contingent on a concurrent behaviour such as stationary cycling. In open loop systems, TV viewing is made contingent on physical activity accumulated at other times, allowing participants to choose when they use the TV time they have earned. While the inclusion of these devices has considerable effects on reducing TV viewing (estimated reductions of between 30 and 90%; (Steeves, et al., 2011) little is known about the long-term effectiveness and sustainability of device use (Schmidt et al., 2012; Steeves et al., 2011). In addition, there are questions over acceptability within families (Schmidt et al., 2012) and there is little information on how long the reduction in TV viewing would remain once the devices are removed (Steeves, et al., 2011). Furthermore, using screen viewing as a reward for completing physical activity appears counterintuitive if a reduction in screen viewing is the goal and may be problematic as there is a risk that using TV as a reward may actually lead to an increased liking for TV (Steeves et al., 2011).

In summary, interventions to reduce sedentary screen use have been shown to be successful, particularly among pre-adolescent children. The most effective interventions include both behaviour modification techniques and electronic TV control devices or making TV contingent on other behaviours. Future interventions need to build on this work to identify effective strategies in younger children and adolescents and to examine the long-term sustainability of behaviour change.

Adults

Interventions with adults are currently scarce but likely to grow rapidly over the next few years. Currently, outcome data do exist but these are often measures of sedentary behaviour as secondary outcomes of interventions designed to increase physical activity. It is not known whether similar effects are possible when sedentary behaviour is targeted more directly.

In a review of adult studies purporting to analyse interventions for reducing sitting in the workplace, Chau and colleagues (2010) located six studies; all were designed to increase physical activity. This may have accounted for the lack of intervention effectiveness as far as sitting was concerned.

A recent feasibility trial with Australian adults aged 60 years and over used a 45 minute face-to-face meeting to assist participants to reduce sitting time and to increase breaks in sitting (Gardiner, Eakin, Healy, & Owen, 2011). Various strategies were offered, including goal setting and self-monitoring. The intervention was successful with a small reduction in sedentary time of 3.2% and an increase in the number of breaks from sedentary time. Participants reduced their sedentary time mainly in the day, and increased their breaks in sedentary time in the evening. This raises two important issues for consideration in the future: a) intervention strategies can be used to both reduce total sedentary time and increase the number of breaks; and b) the likelihood that strategies may be differentially effective at certain times of the day. Other trials are ongoing to test whether sedentary behaviour reduction is possible in younger adults at risk of type 2 diabetes (Wilmot et al., 2011). This involves a structured education approach and self-monitoring.

Until further intervention evidence is available, possible strategies may need to involve a mixture of individual (goal-setting, self-monitoring, prompts), social (targeted social support) and environmental actions (e.g., modified office design such as standing desks and waste bins away from desks; standing or walking meetings; public prompts and signs).

Initial intervention evidence on the use of standing desks in the workplace is promising. For example, Pronk et al. (2012) reported reductions in sitting using this approach by over 1 hour per day while also reporting less back and neck pain and enhanced mood states.

WHAT IS THE ROLE OF PSYCHOLOGY IN UNDERSTANDING AND CHANGING SEDENTARY BEHAVIOUR?

Theories used in physical activity research: do they apply to sedentary behaviour?

Exercise psychology has typically relied on a few social cognitive theories either to help explain participation in physical activity or to inform intervention design. The most common approaches have been Social Cognitive Theory, including extensive study of self-efficacy, the Theory of Planned Behaviour (TPB), and the Transtheoretical Model (TTM) (Biddle, Hagger, Chatzisarantis, & Lippke, 2007). However, it is not known to what extent models applied to one health behaviour (i.e., physical activity) will transfer optimally to explain other behaviours (i.e., sedentary behaviour). It is also likely that different sedentary behaviours, such as recreational TV viewing and office-based sedentary desk work, will have different antecedents and thereby require different approaches for behaviour change. This has yet to be tested. Moreover, different theoretical approaches may be required. For example, Epstein and colleagues have used Behavioural Choice Theory (see below) in sedentary behaviour interventions with young people (Epstein & Roemmich, 2001). In addition, psychologists may need to consider theories allied to notions of 'habit' and less conscious processing when investigating ubiquitous sedentary behaviours. For example, the TPB is based on notions of conscious decision making (attitudes, subjective norms and perceived behavioural control) to arrive at behavioural intentions. It is not likely that people 'intend' to sit or not to sit at their work desk, or at their TV set, at least in the sense of deliberate conscious processing. They just 'do', they are driven towards the behaviour by relatively automatic processing based on habit, social norms and environmental cues. Table 46.1 illustrates that physical activity and example sedentary behaviours may be affected by different factors and influences, including different levels of conscious processing.

OTHER PERSPECTIVES FOR A SEDENTARY BEHAVIOUR RESEARCH AGENDA

Behavioural choice theory

Epstein and colleagues have used 'behavioural choice theory' (BCT) as a framework for the study of sedentary behavior and physical activity in children (Epstein & Roemmich, 2001). Based on 'behavioural economics' (Zimmerman, 2009), BCT proposes that choosing a specific behaviour, such as playing a sedentary computer game, will be a function of: a) the accessibility; and b) the reinforcement value of the behaviour. In using this approach to explain and modify young people's propensity for sedentary technology pursuits, Epstein and colleagues have shown that by making alternative active behaviours more accessible, and sedentary pursuits less reinforcing, reductions in sedentary behaviour and increases in physical activity are possible (Epstein & Roemmich, 2001; Epstein, Saelens, & O'Brien, 1995). The challenge for interventions is to find ways of making physical activity more appealing (reinforcement value) and easy to do (accessible) relative to competing behaviours, such as sedentary behaviours. The latter are unlikely to become less appealing as manufacturers strive to find ways of making computer technology interesting, appealing, and easy to use (e.g., games, ipads, etc). This suggests that researchers should avoid trying

Table 46.1 *Possible differentiating qualities between moderate-to-vigorous structured physical activity (MVPA) and two example sedentary behaviours*

Quality	MVPA	Sedentary Behaviour: TV viewing	Sedentary Behaviour: office desk work
Frequency across the day/week	Low; likely to be no more than once per day	High; regular, prolonged bouts of sedentary behaviour likely on a daily basis, particularly in evenings and at weekends	High; regular, sustained, and prolonged bouts of sedentary behaviour during office hours
Daily duration	Short (e.g., 30–60 mins); <7% of waking day	Long, such as 2–3 hours per day	Very long, such as 6–7 hours a day, with only periodic breaks
Effort	Moderate-to-high	Low	Low
Conscious processing	Moderate-to-high; requires planning	Low and habitual	Low (none?) and habitual
Primary behavioural 'drivers'	Mix of individual motivation and goals, and supportive social and physical environment	Habit; social norms; physical environment	Habit; social norms/ job expectations; physical environment

to make sedentary technology less appealing (possibly a losing battle), but rather utilise technology to self-monitor and motivate sedentary behaviour change.

Habit and nudging

Health behaviour change can be brought about through deliberative (reflective) processing or more automatic processes. The latter is associated with notions of 'habit' and, more recently with the popular concept of 'nudging' (Marteau, Ogilvie, Roland, Suhrcke, & Kelly, 2011). Nudging is when behaviours are encouraged through little or no incentives rather than so-called 'nannying' approaches, such as through government policies and legislation. Examples of nudging would be environmental changes that encourage walking stairs by placing attractive looking staircases in the most accessible positions. Nudging less sedentary

behaviour might involve some of the environmental changes proposed elsewhere in this chapter, such as removing chairs from some meeting rooms, thus encouraging standing meetings, or providing standing desks in the workplace.

Habit involves behavioural patterns learned through context-dependent repetition, hence when a particular context is encountered, such as sitting down in the lounge at home, it is sufficient to automatically cue the habitual response of, say, switching on the TV. In novel contexts, behaviour is more likely to be regulated by conscious decisions through intentions, but in familiar contexts behaviour will be much more affected by habit. Given the high frequency of many sedentary behaviours, such as sitting at a desk at work, or sitting in front of the TV at home, it is easy to see how habitual such behaviours become.

SOME THOUGHTS ON TRANSLATION

The final stage of the behavioural epidemiology framework is to translate findings into practice. For sedentary behaviour, we still know rather little about what strategies are most effective for recuing sitting time, particularly for adults. That said, we do know that sedentary behaviour comes in multiple forms and therefore a multi-pronged attack is required. Table 46.2 gives some examples of possible sedentary behaviour reduction strategies. These are based on a mix of research evidence and expert opinion.

Table 46.2 *Example sedentary behaviour reduction strategies*

Behaviour	Strategy	Target population	Target location or context
TV viewing	Agree family goals for viewing time; select favourite programmes only. No meals in front of TV. No TV in bedrooms.	All; possible focus on families	Home; leisure time (evenings and weekend)
Computer use: recreational	Set goal of specific tasks, then finish. Switch off when not in use. Stand for some tasks on tablet computers.	All; possible focus on families	Home; leisure time (evenings and weekend)
Computer use: work	Break it up with other work tasks (e.g., filing; stand while reading on paper); use standing desk or similar arrangement for computer.	Those who work tasks involve extensive use of computers	Work
Sitting at work	Break up work tasks with walking and standing (while still working). Stand during breaks. Walking breaks. Standing meetings. Make-shift or purpose-built standing desks.	All in largely sedentary work occupations	Work
Car travel	Reduce car travel and replace with public or active transport; increase standing while using public transport (e.g. at stations).	Drivers and passengers	Commuting and leisure time
Overall sitting	Break each 30 minute period of sitting with at least 5 minutes of standing or light physical activity. Modify environment to allow tasks to be done while standing.	All	All

CONCLUSION

Sedentary behaviour is becoming a widely researched field of study alongside physical activity. Psychologists have a role to play in helping us understand the correlates of sedentary behaviour and strategies for sedentary behaviour change. Given the current challenging environment we face – one that encourages and facilitates sedentary behaviour – bold and imaginative solutions are required.

LEARNING AIDS

1   What is sedentary behaviour and how does it differ from 'physical inactivity'?

Sedentary behaviour is time spent sitting. It is waking behaviour with low energy expenditure. Examples include TV viewing, computer use, sitting at work, and car travel. This means that any standing behaviour or light activity (such as strolling or 'pottering' around the house) can be thought of as non-sedentary. It is possible to meet recommended levels of physical activity (e.g., 30 minutes per day of moderate-to-vigorous physical activity for adults), and therefore be classified as 'active', but at the same time take part in high levels of sedentary behaviour. If someone does not meet guidelines for physical activity, they might be labelled 'inactive', but not necessarily 'sedentary'.

2   Why might sedentary behaviour not be highly associated with moderate-to-vigorous physical activity?

Displacement of sitting behaviours into 'non-sitting' might involve time undertaking light as well as moderate-to-vigorous physical activity (MVPA). This means that the association between sedentary behaviour time will be highly correlated with light physical activity (typically r >0.8) but not necessarily with MVPA (r ~0.3).

3   Why might sedentary behaviour be more regulated by automatic rather than conscious processing?

Sedentary behaviour is often prompted and regulated by social norms and environmental cues (e.g., provision of chairs). Therefore, rather than view humans as being consciously motivated to sit, or believe that processes of conscious decision making and 'reasoned action' take place in deciding whether to sit, it is more likely that unconscious processes are at work. This will be through cueing of habitual responses that have been learned over many years and prompted by environments. One conclusion, therefore, is that behaviour change for the reduction of sedentary behaviour may require environmental change, such as provision of standing desks or removal of chairs from some locations.

REVIEW QUESTIONS

1   What are the key advantages and disadvantages of using self-report instruments for assessing sedentary behaviour?

2   What do you consider to be a key correlate of sedentary behaviour in young people and how might you use this information to design a behaviour change intervention?

3   If you conduct an intervention to reduce TV viewing in children, what key questions might you ask to ascertain the acceptability of such an intervention being used again in the future?

4   What would you advise a company to do to reduce sitting time at work while also keeping productivity high?

EXERCISES

1   Write 500 words on why you think we should prioritise sedentary behaviour reduction in public health policy.

2   Monitor the behaviours of one adolescent in your family (or in a friend's family) through one school day using the one-day diary provided below. Follow the instructions carefully. Once the diary has been filled in, create behaviour categories from the behaviours written into the diary. You should be able to create 6–10 categories, such as recreational screen use, physical activity, sedentary hobbies, homework, etc. Assume that all behaviours are carried for the full 15 minutes. Then:

    a   Calculate daily minutes in each category.

    b   Plot when these behaviours are more likely to occur over the course of the day.

    c   Write a short report on the behaviours of this person and speculate how and where sedentary time could be reduced.

    d   What are some of the advantages and limitations of this approach if we assessed several hundred adolescents in this way?

3   Interview an elderly relative in your family about their typical day. Take about 30 minutes to do this. Record the conversation. Interview questions should focus on the following issues:

    a   How they spend their day (types of tasks, times, etc.).

    b   How they would feel if they were advised to sit for less time. What do they think about this? How might they do it?

Write a short report on the interview and illustrate your key points with quotes from the interview. Draw three conclusions.

ONE-DAY DIARY

Instructions

- This diary is for you to keep a record of things you normally do outside of school.
- To help, the diary asks you to record what you are doing every 15 minutes when you are not in school. We know this is quite difficult because you have to remember to fill the diary in AND have a pen or pencil handy.
- Please fill the diary in EVERY 15 minutes. Try not to rely on your memory! Do it at the time. The longer your leave it, the more you might forget!
- Remember, during the four days that you keep the diary it is important that you do the things you would normally.

Example

Every 15 minutes, we would like you to answer three quick questions. All questions refer ONLY to what is happening at that EXACT time. The first question asks about the MAIN thing you are doing at that exact time. The other questions ask about where you are and who you are with at that exact time.

Here is an example of what a page in your diary might look like:

BEFORE SCHOOL			SCHOOL DAY 1
Time	**What are you doing? (Write activity)** e.g., sleeping, eating, doing homework, talking with friends, watching TV, listening to music, on telephone, walking to school, etc.	**Where are you? (Circle one number)** 1 = My bedroom, 2 = Living room, 3 = Kitchen, 4 = Bathroom, 5 = Other room in own house, 6 = Friend's house, 7 = In town (inside), 8 = In town (outside), 9 = At school, 10 = In car, bus, train, taxi, etc., 11 = Other inside area (please describe), 12 = Other outside area (please describe)	**Who's with you? (Circle one number)** 1 = I'm alone, 2 = Friends, 3 = Family, 4 = Friends & Family, 5 = Other (e.g., teacher, coach, doctor, dentist, etc).
7:00 am 1	THE MAIN THING I AM DOING IS: Having breakfast	1 2 **(3)** 4 5 6 7 8 9 10 11 12	1 2 **(3)** 4 5
7:15 am 2	THE MAIN THING I AM DOING IS: Having breakfast	1 2 **(3)** 4 5 6 7 8 9 10 11 12	1 2 **(3)** 4 5
7:30 am 3	THE MAIN THING I AM DOING IS: Brushing teeth	1 2 3 **(4)** 5 6 7 8 9 10 11 12	**(1)** 2 3 4 5
7:45 am 4	THE MAIN THING I AM DOING IS: Making sandwiches	1 2 **(3)** 4 5 6 7 8 9 10 11 12	1 2 **(3)** 4 5
8:00 am 5	THE MAIN THING I AM DOING IS: Being driven to school	1 2 3 4 5 6 7 8 9 **(10)** 11 12	1 2 **(3)** 4 5
8:15 am 6	THE MAIN THING I AM DOING IS: Being driven to school	1 2 3 4 5 6 7 8 9 **(10)** 11 12	1 2 **(3)** 4 5
8:30 am 7	THE MAIN THING I AM DOING IS: Talking	1 2 3 4 5 6 7 8 9 10 11 **(12)** at newsagents next to school	1 **(2)** 3 4 5
8:45 am 8	THE MAIN THING I AM DOING IS: Talking	1 2 3 4 5 6 7 8 **(9)** 10 11 12	1 **(2)** 3 4 5

BEFORE SCHOOL			SCHOOL DAY 1
Time	**What are you doing? (Write activity)** e.g., sleeping, eating, doing homework, talking with friends, watching TV, listening to music, on telephone, walking to school, etc.	**Where are you? (Circle one number)** 1 = My bedroom 2 = Living room 3 = Kitchen 4 = Bathroom 5 = Other room in own house 6 = Friend's house 7 = In town (inside) 8 = In town (outside) 9 = At school 10 = In car, bus, train, taxi, etc. 11 = Other inside area (please describe) 12 = Other outside area (please describe)	**Who's with you? (Circle one number)** 1 = I'm alone 2 = Friends 3 = Family 4 = Friends & Family 5 = Other (e.g., teacher, coach, doctor, dentist, etc.).
7:00 am 1	THE MAIN THING I AM DOING IS:	1 2 3 4 5 6 7 8 9 10 11 12	1 2 3 4 5
7:15 am 2	THE MAIN THING I AM DOING IS:	1 2 3 4 5 6 7 8 9 10 11 12	1 2 3 4 5
7:30 am 3	THE MAIN THING I AM DOING IS:	1 2 3 4 5 6 7 8 9 10 11 12	1 2 3 4 5
7:45 am 4	THE MAIN THING I AM DOING IS:	1 2 3 4 5 6 7 8 9 10 11 12	1 2 3 4 5
8:00 am 5	THE MAIN THING I AM DOING IS:	1 2 3 4 5 6 7 8 9 10 11 12	1 2 3 4 5
8:15 am 6	THE MAIN THING I AM DOING IS:	1 2 3 4 5 6 7 8 9 10 11 12	1 2 3 4 5
8:30 am 7	THE MAIN THING I AM DOING IS:	1 2 3 4 5 6 7 8 9 10 11 12	1 2 3 4 5
8:45 am 8	THE MAIN THING I AM DOING IS:	1 2 3 4 5 6 7 8 9 10 11 12	1 2 3 4 5

You do not need to record during school time, please continue after school has finished – thank you.

AFTER SCHOOL			SCHOOL DAY 1
Time	**What are you doing?** **(Write activity)** e.g., sleeping, eating, doing homework, talking with friends, watching TV, listening to music, on telephone, walking to school, etc.	**Where are you?** **(Circle one number)** 1 = My bedroom 2 = Living room 3 = Kitchen 4 = Bathroom 5 = Other room in own house 6 = Friend's house 7 = In town (inside) 8 = In town (outside) 9 = At school 10 = In car, bus, train, taxi, etc. 11 = Other inside area (please describe) 12 = Other outside area (please describe)	**Who's with you?** **(Circle one number)** 1 = I'm alone 2 = Friends 3 = Family 4 = Friends & Family 5 = Other (e.g., teacher, coach, doctor, dentist, etc).
3:00 pm 9	THE MAIN THING I AM DOING IS:	1 2 3 4 5 6 7 8 9 10 11 12	1 2 3 4 5
3:15 pm 10	THE MAIN THING I AM DOING IS:	1 2 3 4 5 6 7 8 9 10 11 12	1 2 3 4 5
3:30 pm 11	THE MAIN THING I AM DOING IS:	1 2 3 4 5 6 7 8 9 10 11 12	1 2 3 4 5
3:45 pm 12	THE MAIN THING I AM DOING IS:	1 2 3 4 5 6 7 8 9 10 11 12	1 2 3 4 5
4:00 pm 13	THE MAIN THING I AM DOING IS:	1 2 3 4 5 6 7 8 9 10 11 12	1 2 3 4 5
4:15 pm 14	THE MAIN THING I AM DOING IS:	1 2 3 4 5 6 7 8 9 10 11 12	1 2 3 4 5
4:30 pm 15	THE MAIN THING I AM DOING IS:	1 2 3 4 5 6 7 8 9 10 11 12	1 2 3 4 5
4:45 pm 16	THE MAIN THING I AM DOING IS:	1 2 3 4 5 6 7 8 9 10 11 12	1 2 3 4 5
5:00 pm 17	THE MAIN THING I AM DOING IS:	1 2 3 4 5 6 7 8 9 10 11 12	1 2 3 4 5
5:15 pm 18	THE MAIN THING I AM DOING IS:	1 2 3 4 5 6 7 8 9 10 11 12	1 2 3 4 5
5:30 pm 19	THE MAIN THING I AM DOING IS:	1 2 3 4 5 6 7 8 9 10 11 12	1 2 3 4 5
5:45 pm 20	THE MAIN THING I AM DOING IS:	1 2 3 4 5 6 7 8 9 10 11 12	1 2 3 4 5

AFTER SCHOOL			SCHOOL DAY 1
Time	**What are you doing?** **(Write activity)** e.g., sleeping, eating, doing homework, talking with friends, watching TV, listening to music, on telephone, walking to school, etc.	**Where are you?** **(Circle one number)** 1 = My bedroom 2 = Living room 3 = Kitchen 4 = Bathroom 5 = Other room in own house 6 = Friend's house 7 = In town (inside) 8 = In town (outside) 9 = At school 10 = In car, bus, train, taxi, etc. 11 = Other inside area (please describe) 12 = Other outside area (please describe)	**Who's with you?** **(Circle one number)** 1 = I'm alone 2 = Friends 3 = Family 4 = Friends & Family 5 = Other (e.g., teacher, coach, doctor, dentist, etc.).
6:00 pm 21	THE MAIN THING I AM DOING IS:	1 2 3 4 5 6 7 8 9 10 11 12	1 2 3 4 5
6:15 pm 22	THE MAIN THING I AM DOING IS:	1 2 3 4 5 6 7 8 9 10 11 12	1 2 3 4 5
6:30 pm 23	THE MAIN THING I AM DOING IS:	1 2 3 4 5 6 7 8 9 10 11 12	1 2 3 4 5
6:45 pm 24	THE MAIN THING I AM DOING IS:	1 2 3 4 5 6 7 8 9 10 11 12	1 2 3 4 5
7:00 pm 25	THE MAIN THING I AM DOING IS:	1 2 3 4 5 6 7 8 9 10 11 12	1 2 3 4 5
7:15 pm 26	THE MAIN THING I AM DOING IS:	1 2 3 4 5 6 7 8 9 10 11 12	1 2 3 4 5
7:30 pm 27	THE MAIN THING I AM DOING IS:	1 2 3 4 5 6 7 8 9 10 11 12	1 2 3 4 5
7:45 pm 28	THE MAIN THING I AM DOING IS:	1 2 3 4 5 6 7 8 9 10 11 12	1 2 3 4 5
8:00 pm 29	THE MAIN THING I AM DOING IS:	1 2 3 4 5 6 7 8 9 10 11 12	1 2 3 4 5
8:15 pm 30	THE MAIN THING I AM DOING IS:	1 2 3 4 5 6 7 8 9 10 11 12	1 2 3 4 5
8:30 pm 31	THE MAIN THING I AM DOING IS:	1 2 3 4 5 6 7 8 9 10 11 12	1 2 3 4 5
8:45 pm 32	THE MAIN THING I AM DOING IS:	1 2 3 4 5 6 7 8 9 10 11 12	1 2 3 4 5

AFTER SCHOOL			SCHOOL DAY 1
Time	**What are you doing? (Write activity)** e.g., sleeping, eating, doing homework, talking with friends, watching TV, listening to music, on telephone, walking to school, etc.	**Where are you? (Circle one number)** 1 = My bedroom 2 = Living room 3 = Kitchen 4 = Bathroom 5 = Other room in own house 6 = Friend's house 7 = In town (inside) 8 = In town (outside) 9 = At school 10 = In car, bus, train, taxi, etc. 11 = Other inside area (please describe) 12 = Other outside area (please describe)	**Who's with you? (Circle one number)** 1 = I'm alone 2 = Friends 3 = Family 4 = Friends & Family 5 = Other (e.g., teacher, coach, doctor, dentist, etc).
9:00 pm 33	THE MAIN THING I AM DOING IS:	1 2 3 4 5 6 7 8 9 10 11 12	1 2 3 4 5
9:15 pm 34	THE MAIN THING I AM DOING IS:	1 2 3 4 5 6 7 8 9 10 11 12	1 2 3 4 5
9:30 pm 35	THE MAIN THING I AM DOING IS:	1 2 3 4 5 6 7 8 9 10 11 12	1 2 3 4 5
9:45 pm 36	THE MAIN THING I AM DOING IS:	1 2 3 4 5 6 7 8 9 10 11 12	1 2 3 4 5
10:00 pm 37	THE MAIN THING I AM DOING IS:	1 2 3 4 5 6 7 8 9 10 11 12	1 2 3 4 5
10:15 pm 38	THE MAIN THING I AM DOING IS:	1 2 3 4 5 6 7 8 9 10 11 12	1 2 3 4 5
10:30 pm 39	THE MAIN THING I AM DOING IS:	1 2 3 4 5 6 7 8 9 10 11 12	1 2 3 4 5
10:45 pm 40	THE MAIN THING I AM DOING IS:	1 2 3 4 5 6 7 8 9 10 11 12	1 2 3 4 5
11:00 pm 41	THE MAIN THING I AM DOING IS:	1 2 3 4 5 6 7 8 9 10 11 12	1 2 3 4 5
11:15 pm 42	THE MAIN THING I AM DOING IS:	1 2 3 4 5 6 7 8 9 10 11 12	1 2 3 4 5
11:30 pm 43	THE MAIN THING I AM DOING IS:	1 2 3 4 5 6 7 8 9 10 11 12	1 2 3 4 5
11:45 pm 44	THE MAIN THING I AM DOING IS:	1 2 3 4 5 6 7 8 9 10 11 12	1 2 3 4 5

ADDITIONAL READING

Biddle, S.J.H. (2011). Fit or sit? Is there a psychology of sedentary behaviour? *Sport & Exercise Psychology Review, 7*(2), 5–10.

Marshall, S.J. & Ramirez, E. (2011). Reducing sedentary behavior: A new paradigm in physical activity promotion. *American Journal of Lifestyle Medicine*, DOI: 10.1177/1559827610395487.

Owen, N., Healy, G.N., Matthews, C.E. & Dunstan, D.W. (2010). Too much sitting: The population health science of sedentary behavior. *Exercise and Sport Sciences Reviews, 38*(3), 105–113.

Salmon, J. (2010). Novel strategies to promote children's physical activities and reduce sedentary behaviour. *Journal of Physical Activity & Health, 7*(Suppl. 3), S299–S306.

REFERENCES

Atkin, A.J., Adams, E., Bull, F.C. & Biddle, S.J.H. (2011). Non-occupational sitting and mental well-being in employed adults. *Annals of Behavioral Medicine, 43*, 181–188.

Atkin, A.J., Gorely, T., Clemes, S.A., Yates, T., Edwardson, C., Brage, S., Salmon, J., Marshall, S.J. & Biddle, S.J.H. (2012). Methods of measurement in epidemiology: sedentary behaviour. *International Journal of Epidemiology, 41*, 1460–1471.

Biddle, S.J.H. & Asare, M. (2011). Physical activity and mental health in children and adolescents: A review of reviews. *British Journal of Sports Medicine, 45*, 886–895. doi:810.1136/bjsports-2011-090185.

Biddle, S.J.H., Gorely, T. & Marshall, S. (2009). Is television viewing a suitable marker of sedentary behaviour in young people. *Annals of Behavioral Medicine, 38*, 147–153.

Biddle, S.J.H., Hagger, M.S., Chatzisarantis, N.L.D. & Lippke, S. (2007). Theoretical frameworks in exercise psychology. In G. Tenenbaum & R.C. Eklund (Eds.), *Handbook of sport psychology* (3rd ed., pp.537–559). Hoboken: NJ: John Wiley.

Biddle, S.J.H., O'Connell, S. & Braithwaite, R.E. (2011). Sedentary behaviour interventions in young people: A meta-analysis. *British Journal of Sports Medicine, 45*, 937–942. doi:910.1136/bjsports-2011-090205.

Biddle, S.J.H., Pearson, N., Ross, G.M. & Braithwaite, R. (2010). Tracking of sedentary behaviours of young people: A systematic review. *Preventive Medicine, 51*, 345–351.

Bryant, M.J., Lucove, J.C., Evenson, K.R. & Marshall, S. (2007). Measurement of television viewing in children and adolescents: A systematic review. *Obesity Reviews, 8*(3), 197–209.

Chau, J.Y., van der Ploeg, H.P., van Uffelen, J.G.Z., Wong, J., Riphagen, I., Healy, G.N., Gilson, N.D., Dunstan, D.W., Bauman, A.E., Owen, N. & Brown, W.J. (2010). Are workplace interventions to reduce sitting effective? A systematic review. *Preventive Medicine, 51*, 352–356.

Chinapaw, M., Proper, K., Brug, J., van Mechelen, W. & Singh, A. (2011). Relationship between young people's sedentary behaviour and biomedical health indicators: A systematic review of prospective studies. *Obesity Reviews,* doi: 10.1111/j.1467-789X.2011.00865.x.

Cillero, I.H. & Jago, R. (2010). Systematic review of correlates of screen-viewing among young children. *Preventive Medicine, 51*, 3–10.

Clark, B.K., Sugiyama, T., Healy, G.N., Salmon, J., Dunstan, D.W. & Owen, N. (2009). Validity and reliability of measures of television viewing time and other non-occupational sedentary behaviour of adults: A review. *Obesity Reviews: An Official Journal Of The International Association For The Study Of Obesity, 10*(1), 7–16.

Colley, R.C., Garriguet, D., Janssen, I., Craig, C.L., Clarke, J. & Tremblay, M.S. (2011). Physical activity of Canadian children and youth: Accelerometer results from the 2007 to 2009 Canadian Health Measures Survey. *Health Reports, 22*, 15–23.

Edwardson, C.L., Gorely, T., Davies, M.J., Gray, L.J., Khunti, K., Wilmot, E.G., Yates, T. & Biddle, S.J. (2012). Association of sedentary behaviour with metabolic syndrome: A meta-analysis. *PLoS ONE, 7*(4), e34916.

Epstein, L.H. & Roemmich, J.N. (2001). Reducing sedentary behaviour: Role in modifying physical activity. *Exercise and Sport Sciences Reviews, 29*(3), 103–108.

Epstein, L.H., Saelens, B.E. & O'Brien, J.G. (1995). Effects of reinforcing increases in active behavior versus decreases in sedentary behavior for obese children. *International Journal of Behavioral Medicine, 2,* 41–50.

Gardiner, P.A., Eakin, E.G., Healy, G.N. & Owen, N. (2011). Feasibility of reducing older adults' sedentary time. *American Journal of Preventive Medicine, 41*(2), 174–177.

Gorely, T., Marshall, S.J. & Biddle, S.J.H. (2004). Couch kids: Correlates of television viewing among youth. *International Journal of Behavioural Medicine, 11,* 152–163.

Hamer, M., Stamatakis, E. & Mishra, G. (2010). Television- and screen-based activity and mental well-being in adults. *American Journal of Preventive Medicine, 38*(4), 375–380.

Hardy, L.L., Booth, M.L. & Okely, A.D. (2007). The reliability of the Adolescent Sedentary Activity Questionnaire (ASAQ). *Preventive Medicine, 45*(1), 71–74.

Healy, G.N., Dunstan, D.W., Salmon, J., Cerin, E., Shaw, J.E., Zimmet, P.Z. & Owen, M. (2008). Breaks in sedentary time: Beneficial associations with metabolic risk. *Diabetes Care, 31,* 661–666.

Hinkley, T., Salmon, J., Okely, A. & Trost, S. (2010). Correlates of sedentary behaviours in preschool children: A review. *International Journal of Behavioral Nutrition and Physical Activity, 7*(1), 66.

Jolin, E.M. & Weller, R.A. (2010). Television viewing and its impact on childhood behaviors. *Current Psychiatry Reports, Online First.*

Kamath, C.C., Vickers, K.S., Ehrlich, A., McGovern, L., Johnson, J., Singhal, V., Paulo, R., Hettinger, A., Erwin, P.J. & Montori, V.M. (2008). Behavioral interventions to prevent childhood obesity: A systematic review and meta-analyses of randomized trials. *Journal of Clinical Endocrinology & Metabolism, 93*(12), 4606–4615.

Maniccia, D.M., Davison, K.K., Marshall, S.J., Manganello, J.A. & Dennison, B.A. (2011). A meta-analysis of interventions that target children's screen time for reduction. *Pediatrics, 128*(1), e193–e210.

Marshall, A.L., Miller, Y.D., Burton, N.W. & Brown, W.J. (2010). Measuring total and domain-specific sitting: A study of reliability and validity. *Medicine & Science in Sports & Exercise, 42*(6), 1094–1102.

Marteau, T.M., Ogilvie, D., Roland, M., Suhrcke, M. & Kelly, M.P. (2011). Judging nudging: Can nudging improve population health? *British Medical Journal, 342,* d228.

Matthews, C.E., Chen, K.Y., Freedson, P.S., Buchowski, M.S., Beech, B.M., Pate, R. & Troiano, R.P. (2008). Amount of time spent in sedentary behaviors in the United States, 2003–2004. *American Journal of Epidemiology, 167,* 875–881.

Owen, N., Sugiyama, T., Eakin, E.E., Gardiner, P.A., Tremblay, M.S. & Sallis, J.F. (2011). Adults' sedentary behavior: Determinants and interventions. *American Journal of Preventive Medicine, 41*(2), 189–196.

Pearson, N. & Biddle, S.J.H. (2011). Sedentary behaviour and dietary intake in children, adolescents and adults: A systematic review. *American Journal of Preventive Medicine, 41*(2), 178–188.

Primack, B.A., Swanier, B., Georgiopoulos, A.M., Land, S.R. & Fine, M.J. (2009). Association between media use in adolescence and depression in young adulthood: A longitudinal study. *Archives of General Psychiatry, 66*(2), 181–188.

Pronk, N.P., Katz, A.S., Lowry, M. & Payfer, J.R. (2012) Reducing occupational sitting time and improvind worker health: The Take-a-Stand Project, 2011. *Preventing Chronic Disease, 9,* 110323. DOI: http://dx.doi.org/110310.115888.pcd110329.110323.

Proper, K.I., Singh, A.S., van Mechelen, W. & Chinapaw, M.J.M. (2011). Sedentary behaviors and health outcomes among adults: A systematic review of prospective studies. *American Journal of Preventive Medicine, 40*(2), 174–182.

Rhodes, R.E., Mark, R.S. & Temmel, C.P. (2012). Adult sedentary behavior: A systematic review. *American Journal of Preventive Medicine, 42*(3), e3–e28.

Sallis, J.F. & Owen, N. (1999). *Physical activity and behavioral medicine.* Thousand Oaks, CA: Sage.

Schmidt, M.E., Haines, J., O'Brien, A., McDonald, J., Price, S., Sherry, B. & Taveras, E.M. (2012). Systematic review of effective strategies for reducing screen time among young children. *Obesity,* doi:10.1038/oby.2011.1348.

Sedentary Behaviour Research Network (2012). Letter to the Editor: Standardized use of the terms "sedentary" and "sedentary behaviours". *Applied Physiology, Nutrition & Metabolism, 37,* 540–542.

Steeves, J.A., Thompson, D.L., Bassett, D.R., Fitzhugh, E.C. & Raynor, H.A. (2011). A review of different behavior modification strategies designed to reduce sedentary screen behaviors in children. *Journal of Obesity*, Article ID 379215, 379216 pages, doi:379210.371155/372012/379215.

Strasburger, V., Jordan, A. & Donnerstein, E. (2010). Health effects of media on children and adolescents. *Pediatrics, 125*, 756–767.

Sugiyama, T., Healy, G., Dunstan, D., Salmon, J. & Owen, N. (2008). Is television viewing time a marker of a broader pattern of sedentary behavior? *Annals of Behavioral Medicine, 35*, 245–250.

Tremblay, M., LeBlanc, A., Kho, M., Saunders, T., larouche, R., Colley, R., Goldfield, G., Connor Gorber, S. (2011). Systematic review of sedentary behaviour and health indicators in school-aged children and youth. *International Journal of Behavioral Nutrition and Physical Activity, 8*, 98.

Uijtdewilligen, L., Nauta, J., Singh, A., Van Mechelen, W., Twisk, J., Van der Horst, K. & Chinapaw, M.J. (2011). Determinants of physical activity and sedentary behaviour in young people: A review

and quality synthesis of prospective studies. *British Journal of Sports Medicine, 45*, 896–905.

van der Horst, K., Chin A Paw, M., Twisk, J. & Van Mechelen, W. (2007). A brief review on correlates of physical activity and sedentariness in youth. *Medicine and Science in Sports and Exercise, 39*(8), 1241–1250.

Wilmot, E.G., Davies, M., Edwardson, C., Gorely, T., Khunti, K., Nimmo, M., Yates, T. & Biddle, S.J.H. (2011). Rationale and study design for a randomised controlled trial to reduce sedentary time in adults at risk of type 2 diabetes mellitus: project stand (Sedentary Time and diabetes). *BMC Public Health, 11*(1), 908.

Wilmot, E.G., Edwardson, C.L., Achana, F.A., Davies, M.J., Gorely, T., Gray, L.J., Khunti, K., Yates, T. & Biddle, S.J.H. (2012). Sedentary time in adults and the association with diabetes, cardiovascular disease and death: Systematic review and meta-analysis. *Diabetologia, 55*(11), 2895–2905.

Zimmerman, F.J. (2009). Using behavioral economics to promote physical activity. *Preventive Medicine, 49*(4), 289–291.

Chapter 47

Exercise prescription

SWARUP MUKHERJEE

SUMMARY

A regular and appropriately prescribed exercise program is safe for most individuals and has beneficial effects of health, fitness and quality of life. An exercise-training program works best when individually tailored and it should integrate the science of exercise physiology with behavior change principles to promote positive changes in the individual physical activity habits and lifestyle behavior. A regular exercise program should include aerobic, strength, flexibility and neuromotor exercises that should be done over and above the routine daily activities. For optimal gains in health and fitness, the exercise program should be adapted according to the goals, physical attributes, exercise response and lifestyle of the individual. The present chapter provides a practical approach to understanding the concepts and principles of exercise prescription and its application in developing customized exercise programs for apparently healthy adults with the goal of improving overall health and fitness.

INTRODUCTION

Regular participation in physical activity and exercise is associated with several physiological, psychological, metabolic health and fitness benefits and improved quality of life in men and women of all ages. Although physical activity, exercise and physical fitness are closely related and apparently overlapping constructs, they are distinct terms signifying specific physical and physiological attributes based on scientific evidence supporting exercise recommendations (ACSM, 2011). Physical activity represents any muscular activity in the form of bodily movements that raises the energy expenditure proportional to the work done. Exercise is a planned, structured and repetitive form of physical activity with the primary objective of improving health and fitness and subsequently their maintenance over a period of time. Physical fitness encompasses a set of measurable health and skill-related attributes that enables an individual to carry out daily tasks with vigor and alertness, without undue fatigue and with ample energy for leisure-time pursuits (Caspersen, Powell & Christenson, 1985).

Every individual pursuing an exercise program has a predetermined set of goals intended to be achieved as an outcome of the program. Moreover, there are wide variations in people's health and fitness status, motivation, age, occupation, lifestyle constraints, social influences, educational status, perspectives and understanding (ACSM, 2006b). Therefore, an ideal exercise-training program is the one that caters to individual health and fitness goals and is further customized to accommodate the variations in individual characteristics. The American College of Sports Medicine (ACSM) defines exercise prescription as the process of designing a regimen of physical activity in a systematic and individualized manner (ACSM, 2010, 2011). The principles of exercise prescription are based on application of scientific evidence on the physiological, psychological and health benefits of exercise training. Therefore, the process of exercise prescription is an art that integrates the science of exercise physiology with behavior change principles that promote positive changes in individual physical activity habits and lifestyle behavior (ACSM, 2010, 2011; Blair, LaMonte, & Nichaman, 2004).

While there is a substantial body of evidence on benefits of regular exercise on physical fitness and metabolic health parameters, regular exercise can also positively impact the mental health and psychological well-being of an individual. Mental health has been established as fundamental to overall health (U.S. Department of Health and Human Services, 1999). Mental disorders are major public health problems that can significantly compromise the overall well-being and quality of life of affected persons. Regular physical activity can have positive effects of mood and anxiety (Scully, Kremer, Meade, Graham, & Dudgeon, 1998), promote sleep (Youngstedt, 2005) and enhance general well-being in healthy individuals. Exercise also has an effect on self-esteem and can influence people's perceptions of their physical self and identity in a positive manner (Fox, 1999). Moreover, a physically inactive lifestyle may be related to the development of mental disorders like depression and anxiety (Dunn, Trivedi, & O'Neal, 2001; Goodwin, 2003).

Amongst the mental health problems, depression and anxiety disorders are the most common (Kessler et al., 1994) and are frequently accompanied by tendencies to passivity and withdrawal and the affected individuals often have low levels of physical fitness compared to the general population (Martinsen et al., 1989). Depression by itself has a greater disease burden globally than coronary heart disease and cerebrovascular disease (Murray & Lopez, 1997). Several epidemiological studies have reported associations between sedentary lifestyles and depression with the strongest correlation for women and adults above 40 years of age (Buckworth & Dishman, 2002). Physical activity can reduce the risk of depression and has been associated with lower prevalence of major depression and certain phobias (Goodwin, 2003). Regular exercise has been found to improve emotional, cognitive and bodily symptoms leading to better mental health and to be more effective in depressed patients who were non-responsive to antidepressant medication (Trivedi, Geer, Grannemann, Chambliss & Jordan, 2006). The existing body of evidence is also suggestive that physical activity is as effective as psychotherapy and more effective than behavioral interventions especially for the management of mild to moderate depression (Craft & Landers, 1998). Furthermore, the introduction of exercise programs in early treatment of depression could reduce the duration of therapeutic latency (Knubben et al., 2007). Generally, aerobic, strength and flexibility exercises have been reported to have similar effects on depressive scores (Sexton, Mære & Dahl, 1989).

Anxiety disorders constitute a significant group of related mental health conditions and exercise has been reported to significantly reduce the state of anxiety both for subjects with normal or elevated levels of anxiety (Raglin, 1997). Aerobic exercise has anxiolytic effects on healthy people and has been reported to be more effective than strength and mobility exercise in patients with high trait or generalized anxiety disorder (Long & Stavel, 1995). Acute bouts of exercise have been found to have antipanic effects in healthy subjects (Strohle et al., 2005). In addition, exercise might also be beneficial for post-traumatic stress disorders

(Manger & Motta, 2005). This chapter is intended to help both exercise sciences students and health and fitness professionals to understand the concepts and principles of exercise prescription and its application to develop customized exercise programs for apparently healthy adults with the goal of improving overall health and fitness.

OBJECTIVES

After reading this chapter you will be able to:

1. Understand the physiological and psychological aspects and benefits of exercise.
2. Understand the concept of dose-response relationship in exercise prescription.
3. Provide pre-participation screening recommendations.
4. Apply the recommendations and guidelines for different forms of exercise to develop individually tailored exercise programs.
5. Identify the sequence, type and intensity of activities for maximal safety and optimal health and fitness benefit of an exercise program.

THE DOSE-RESPONSE RELATIONSHIP IN EXERCISE PRESCRIPTION

Epidemiological studies have provided evidence that a dose-response relationship exists between physical activity and fitness with the health-related benefits (Blair et al., 2004; Hakkinen, Pakarinen, Alen, Kauhanen, & Komi, 1988; Kahn et al., 2002; U.S. Department of Health and Human Services, 2008). This relationship is also reflected in the 1996 U.S. Surgeon General's report which concluded that significant health benefits can be obtained with moderate amounts of physical activity and additional benefits can be gained through greater amounts of physical activity (U.S. Department of Health and Human Services, 1996). In terms of exercise prescription, the dose of physical activity required to achieve higher gains in performance is different from that needed for improvements in health-related outcomes (e.g. lowered blood pressure, decrease in body fat, increase in lean body mass or change in blood lipids) or fitness gains (e.g. increase in lactate threshold, changes in heart rate reserve or VO_{2max}).

While exercise has an effect on numerous health and fitness parameters, some variables like heart rate, sympathetic nervous response, and blood lactate are rather quick to adapt to exercise. In contrast, adaptations in other physiological variables like the VO_{2max}, blood lipids and capillary density take a relatively longer time (Saltin & Golnick, 1983). The differences in the response of various physiological variables to a dose of exercise makes it clear that it is improbable that prescribing a single dose of exercise can address all aspects of health and/or fitness. However, based on comprehensive research evidence, in 1995 the ACSM and CDC issued general recommendations to improve health status in adults (Pate et al., 1995), which can be summarized by the dose-response curve in Figure 47.1.

The dose-response curve reflects that the lower the baseline physical activity status, the greater the health benefit associated with a given increase in physical activity. The recommendation stated that "every adult should accumulate 30 minutes or more of moderate-intensity (3–6 METs) physical activity on most, preferably all days of the week." To meet the 30-minute goal, intermittent bouts of shorter duration (10 minutes) were also suggested to be a suitable option (Pate et al., 1995; U.S.

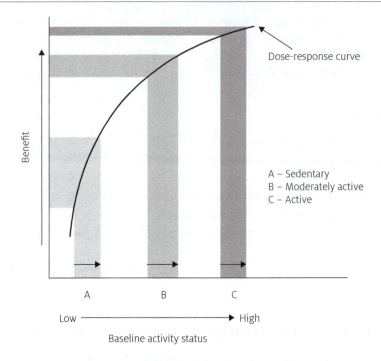

Figure 47.1 The dose-response curve representing the best estimate of the relationship between physical activity (dose) and health benefit (response). From Pate et al., 1995, "Physical activity and public health" in *Journal of the American Medical Association*, 273: 402–407. Chicago, IL: American Medical Association.

Department of Health and Human Services, 1996). The 2007 update of the physical activity recommendation (Haskell et al., 2007) was consistent with the 1995 version but further elaborated the approaches to meet the goals using moderate and/or vigorous exercise:

> To promote and maintain health, all healthy adults aged 18–65 years need moderate-intensity aerobic physical activity for a minimum 30 minutes a day on five days a week or vigorous-intensity aerobic physical activity for a minimum of 20 minutes on three days a week.

These recommendations are to do physical activity over and above the routine daily activities. Eventually, resistance training was also added (8–10 exercises, 8–12 repetitions, two or more non-consecutive days per week) to the recommendations. Subsequently, the 2009

and 2011 ACSM position stands provided further guidelines to optimize the efficacy of resistance training and to tailor the program variables to individual goals for maximum health benefits.

Exercise prescription generally has five essential components:

1 Duration of exercise bout
2 Intensity of exercise bout
3 Frequency of exercise participation
4 Mode or type of exercise
5 Progression.

In addition to these five components, there are a number of terms used in exercise prescription. Nieman (2007) has provided a useful glossary of these terms as applies to exercise prescription. These five components should be used and customized to individual needs in the exercise prescriptions for individuals of all ages, fitness and health levels. However, the emphasis of this chapter is on the application of exercise principles in apparently healthy populations. Amongst the abovementioned five components, the exercise duration, intensity, frequency and type are used to calculate the 'dose' of exercise that is expected to generate the desired response as health or fitness gain.

In calculation of the dose of exercise, the duration of exercise for each exercise session can be as:

- Number of minutes of the exercise session
- Total energy expended in the exercise session (kcal)
- Energy expended per kilogram body weight

The exercise intensity can be based on:

- % maximal heart rate (%HRmax)
- % VO_{2max}
- Maximal heart rate reserve (HRmax – HRrest)
- Rating of perceived exertion (RPE)
- The lactate threshold (LT)

The exercise frequency could be:

- Number of times per day
- Number of days per week

In addition to these, the type or the mode of exercise relates to whether cardiovascular (aerobic), resistance (muscular strength and endurance), flexibility or neuromotor exercises are used in the training program. It has been recommended that all adults should do a variety of exercises to improve the components of physical fitness (ACSM, 1998a, 2011). Moreover, a variety of exercise types has been recommended to prevent overuse injuries especially in middle-aged and older adults (ACSM, 1998b). The adherence to the exercise program may also be improved by including a range of exercise activities although the evidence is limited in this context. When considering the modalities for an exercise program, individual characteristics and available equipment and facilities should be taken into account. These constraints may limit the scope of the exercise prescription to a few selected exercise modes that might not address all aspects of physical fitness. Based on a combination of frequency and intensity of exercise, general recommendations have been provided (see Table 47.1) for the types of exercise to be included in a health and/or fitness training program for apparently healthy adults (ACSM, 2010).

Table 47.1 *General exercise recommendations for healthy adults*

Weekly frequency (d·wk⁻¹) devoted to an exercise program)	Do these types of exercises
At least 5 d·wk⁻¹	Moderate intensity (40% to < 60% of VO2R) aerobic activities (cardiovascular endurance), weight-bearing exercise, flexibility exercise
At least 3 d·wk⁻¹	Vigorous intensity (≥ 60% VO2R) aerobic activities, weight-bearing exercise, flexibility exercise
3–5 d·wk⁻¹	A combination of moderate and vigorous intensity aerobic activities, weight-bearing exercise, flexibility exercise
2–3 d·wk⁻¹	Muscular strength and endurance, resistance exercise, calisthenics, balance and agility

A specific dose of exercise could generate a response like changes in resting blood pressure, body weight change, reduction in % body fat, increased insulin sensitivity, VO_{2max}, and mood elevation. Physical activity can bring about favorable changes in health and physical fitness by:

- Improved fitness (especially aerobic fitness) leading to improved health.
- Improve both fitness and health simultaneously.
- Improve fitness without effect on a specific health outcome.

- Improve a specific health outcome but not fitness.

With the available data supporting the dose-response relationship between physical activity and health outcomes, it would be reasonable to state with respect to exercise, "some is good; more is better" (ACSM, 2011). However, the shape of the dose-response curve may depend upon the intended health outcome and the baseline level of physical activity of the individual (Haskell et al., 2007).

PRE-PARTICIPATION SCREENING

Whilst participation in physical activity is associated with numerous health and fitness benefits, it also involves risks. Although the most common risk is related to musculoskeletal injuries (Almeida, Williams, Shaffer, & Brodine, 1999; Hootman et al., 2001), the risks of greater concern are transient increase in the chances of occurrence of myocardial ischemia and sudden cardiac death associated with strenuous exercise (Thompson et al., 2007). Therefore, it is vital that the health objective of increasing moderate-to-vigorous physical activity should include the practice of screening the individuals at risk of the adverse effects of exercise participation. To enhance the safety of exercise participation and to develop safe and effective exercise programs, the likely participants should be screened for the suggestive signs and symptoms and the presence of risk factors of cardiovascular, pulmonary and metabolic diseases and other conditions that may need special considerations (Gordon, 1993; Maron et al., 2001). The purposes of pre-participation health screening are to:

- Identify individuals with medical contra-indications for exclusion from exercise programs until those conditions have been abated or are under control.

- Identify persons with clinically significant conditions that might require a medically supervised exercise program.
- Identify individuals at increased risk for diseases due to age, symptoms and risk factors who should undergo a medical evaluation and exercise testing before starting an exercise program or increasing the intensity, frequency or duration of the current program.
- Recognition of special needs of individuals that may affect exercise testing and programming.

The pre-participation screening can be either self-guided or professionally guided. For maximizing the participation safety, it is crucial to ensure that the screening procedures and tools are of established validity and accuracy with respect to the individual's health history, present medical conditions, signs and symptoms, exercise habits, dietary habits and other relevant lifestyle factors.

As the self-guided screening is initiated and dealt with by the individual with minimal or no professional supervision, it is of consequence that an easy-to-use screening tool be used for the purpose. It has been recommended that at the basic level, previously inactive men over age 40 and women over 50, and those at high-risk for cardiovascular (CVD) disease should consult a physician prior to starting an exercise program of unaccustomed and vigorous physical activity (U.S. Department of Health and Human Services, 1996). Apparently, the commonest instrument for self-guided screening is the Physical Activity Readiness Questionnaire (PAR-Q; Figure 47.2) that can alert individuals at risk to seek medical opinion before participation (Canadian Physical Activity Guidelines, 2011).

Other screening tools may include the AHA/ACSM Health/Fitness facility pre-participation Screening Questionnaire (ACSM, 2003, 2007), self-administration surveys required as a registration procedure of health/fitness facilities and public promotional materials of physical activity safety.

Physical Activity Readiness Questionnaire - PAR-Q (revised 2002)

PAR-Q & YOU

(A Questionnaire for People Aged 15 to 69)

Regular physical activity is fun and healthy, and increasingly more people are starting to become more active every day. Being more active is very safe for most people. However, some people should check with their doctor before they start becoming much more physically active.

If you are planning to become much more physically active than you are now, start by answering the seven questions in the box below. If you are between the ages of 15 and 69, the PAR-Q will tell you if you should check with your doctor before you start. If you are over 69 years of age, and you are not used to being very active, check with your doctor.

Common sense is your best guide when you answer these questions. Please read the questions carefully and answer each one honestly: check YES or NO.

YES	NO	
☐	☐	**1. Has your doctor ever said that you have a heart condition and that you should only do physical activity recommended by a doctor?**
☐	☐	**2. Do you feel pain in your chest when you do physical activity?**
☐	☐	**3. In the past month, have you had chest pain when you were not doing physical activity?**
☐	☐	**4. Do you lose your balance because of dizziness or do you ever lose consciousness?**
☐	☐	**5. Do you have a bone or joint problem (for example, back, knee or hip) that could be made worse by a change in your physical activity?**
☐	☐	**6. Is your doctor currently prescribing drugs (for example, water pills) for your blood pressure or heart condition?**
☐	☐	**7. Do you know of any other reason why you should not do physical activity?**

If you answered

YES to one or more questions

Talk with your doctor by phone or in person BEFORE you start becoming much more physically active or BEFORE you have a fitness appraisal. Tell your doctor about the PAR-Q and which questions you answered YES.

- You may be able to do any activity you want — as long as you start slowly and build up gradually. Or, you may need to restrict your activities to those which are safe for you. Talk with your doctor about the kinds of activities you wish to participate in and follow his/her advice.
- Find out which community programs are safe and helpful for you.

NO to all questions

If you answered NO honestly to all PAR-Q questions, you can be reasonably sure that you can:

- start becoming much more physically active – begin slowly and build up gradually. This is the safest and easiest way to go.
- take part in a fitness appraisal – this is an excellent way to determine your basic fitness so that you can plan the best way for you to live actively. It is also highly recommended that you have your blood pressure evaluated. If your reading is over 144/94, talk with your doctor before you start becoming much more physically active.

DELAY BECOMING MUCH MORE ACTIVE:

- if you are not feeling well because of a temporary illness such as a cold or a fever – wait until you feel better; or
- if you are or may be pregnant – talk to your doctor before you start becoming more active.

PLEASE NOTE: If your health changes so that you then answer YES to any of the above questions, tell your fitness or health professional. Ask whether you should change your physical activity plan.

Informed Use of the PAR-Q: The Canadian Society for Exercise Physiology, Health Canada, and their agents assume no liability for persons who undertake physical activity, and if in doubt after completing this questionnaire, consult your doctor prior to physical activity.

No changes permitted. You are encouraged to photocopy the PAR-Q but only if you use the entire form.

NOTE: If the PAR-Q is being given to a person before he or she participates in a physical activity program or a fitness appraisal, this section may be used for legal or administrative purposes.

"I have read, understood and completed this questionnaire. Any questions I had were answered to my full satisfaction."

NAME ____________________

SIGNATURE ____________________ DATE ____________________

SIGNATURE OF PARENT or GUARDIAN (for participants under the age of majority) ____________________ WITNESS ____________________

Note: This physical activity clearance is valid for a maximum of 12 months from the date it is completed and becomes invalid if your condition changes so that you would answer YES to any of the seven questions.

CSEP SCPE © Canadian Society for Exercise Physiology   Supported by: Health Canada Santé Canada

continued on other side...

Figure 47.2 Physical Activity Readiness (PAR-Q) Form. (Source: Physical Activity Readiness Questionnaire, Canadian Society of Exercise Physiology).

GENERAL COMPONENTS OF EXERCISE TRAINING

Each exercise session should comprise of the following components:

- Warm-up and stretching
- Conditioning
  - Aerobic, resistance, flexibility or neuro-motor exercise
  - Sports-related activity
- Cool down and stretching

A warm-up is defined as a group of exercises done prior to an activity. It involves low-to-moderate intensity exercises and stretches to facilitate the transition of physiological, biomechanical and bioenergetic mechanisms from rest to exercise state (Alter, 2004; ACSM, 2010). Depending upon the intended exercise, the sport, level of participation, age and environmental conditions, the warm-up phase should consist of 5–20 minutes of aerobic or muscular endurance activity. This leads to an increase in the body temperature and reduces the incidence and severity of post-exercise muscle soreness. It also stimulates sweating that prevents excessive rise in the body temperature during the actual exercise or sports activity. Warm-up activities may include jogging, stationary cycling, rowing on the rowing ergometer or activities similar to that involved in the sport to be played. However, as a note of caution, the intensity of warm-up should never be high enough to cause muscle glycogen depletion and fatigue (Katch, McArdle, & Katch, 2011).

Flexibility exercises are meant to increase the joint range of motion. However, their inclusion in routine warm-up is an issue of debate. While some researchers suggest stretching prior to aerobic warm-up activities, others recommend performing them only after the body temperature has been elevated (Alter, 2004; Katch et al., 2011). Muscle, tendon and ligament elasticity depend upon blood saturation, and connective tissues with low blood saturation have poor stretching ability and are more susceptible to damage. Moreover, warming up shifts the tension from the muscle attachment to the muscle belly and increases the ease of muscle fiber recruitment (Peterson, 1999) and hence it might be safer to do stretching exercises following active warm-up.

Following the exercise session or the sports activity, a cool-down or warm-down phase is recommended. This should involve 5–10 minutes of low-to-moderate intensity aerobic and/or muscular endurance activity that causes gradual return of heart rate and blood pressure to normal and facilitates the removal of metabolic waste products from the muscles accumulated during the higher intensity exercise period. The cool-down phase is also important as it minimizes the chance of hypotensive bouts after an exercise session (Howley & Franks, 2007).

EXERCISE PRESCRIPTION FOR CARDIORESPIRATORY FITNESS

Low levels of aerobic fitness are consistently associated with significantly increased risk of premature death from all causes but especially cardiovascular diseases. Moreover, a reduced risk of cardiovascular morbidity and mortality has been reported with improved cardiorespiratory fitness especially in middle-aged and older adults (Blair et al., 1995; Lee et al., 2011; Sui, LaMonte, & Blair, 2007). Aerobic exercise programs also cause substantial improve-ments in the symptoms in cases of moderate to severe depression and can also be an effective complementary treatment for patients with affective disorders (Knubben et al., 2007). Furthermore, aerobic exercise has been found to be more effective in treatment of anxiety states than other forms of training. Hence, high aerobic fitness is considered to be the most important health-related fitness component of an exercise program. Cardiorespiratory fitness is the capability to continue strenuous tasks involving large muscle groups for extended periods of time. Functionally, aerobic fitness represents the ability of the circulatory and the respiratory system to supply oxygen to the working muscles during moderate-to-vigorous activity (ACSM, 2002a, 2006b).

For obtaining the intended health/fitness benefits from an aerobic exercise program, a minimum level of cardiorespiratory fitness should be achieved. According to the overload principle, exercise below a minimum threshold will fail to challenge the body sufficiently to increase the $\dot{V}O_{2max}$ and changes in other physiological variables (ACSM, 1998a, 2010). However, owing to the differences in individual responses to a particular training load, differences in the existing levels of cardiorespiratory fitness in healthy men and women and a non-linear decline in cardiorespiratory fitness with advancing age when not accompanied by a program of regular exercise (Fleg et al., 2005), the minimum threshold differs from person to person. The ACSM 2010 guidelines can be referred to for the sex and age-specific norms for cardiorespiratory fitness ($\dot{V}O_{2max}$ in ml·kg^{-1}·min^{-1}) in apparently healthy adults.

Frequency of cardiorespiratory exercise

When calculating the exercise dose, the duration and intensity are the primary factors taken into consideration. However, the exercise frequency (number of days per week in the program) has its own significance. Overall, the research evidence suggests that for beneficial effects on cardiorespiratory endurance and body composition, at least thrice a week exercise is required with no more than two days between subsequent bouts of exercise (ACSM, 1998a, 2006b). Although health and fitness gains can occur in some people with even one or two exercise sessions per week at moderate to vigorous intensity ($\geq$ 60% $\dot{V}O_{2max}$) (Lee & Skerrett, 2001), such intensity may not be safe or comfortably tolerated by all adults. The

ACSM 2010 guidelines recommend moderate-intensity aerobic exercise at least five days a week or vigorous intensity exercise at least three days a week, or a combination of moderate-to-vigorous intensity exercise 3–5 days a week for the majority of adults to achieve and maintain health/fitness benefits. This is not to imply that exercise > 5 days a week will not bring about additional benefits but for health-related outcomes, optimal gains are apparently achieved with a frequency of 3–5 days per week (ACSM, 2006a). Vigorous intensity exercise > 5 days a week may benefit in terms of additional gains like weight loss and increase in $\dot{V}O_{2max}$ but at the same time increases the risk of musculoskeletal injuries. Hence, such an exercise dose is generally not advisable for most adults. However, vigorous exercise > 5 days a week may be better tolerated if a variety of exercise modes (running, cycling, rowing, swimming, basketball, racquet sports) that avoids overload of a particular body part or a muscle group are used in the exercise program.

Quantity and duration of cardiorespiratory exercise

The exercise duration is the amount of time for which the physical activity or exercise is performed at the desired intensity. It may be measured in terms of duration per session, day or week or by the total energy expenditure. A dose-response relationship exists between the calories expended per week through physical activity and exercise and the health/fitness benefits (Haskell et al., 2007). While several studies have provided evidence on the dose-response relationship between physical activity levels and health outcomes, data is sparse on the specific quantity and quality of physical activity for the health benefits. Prospective cohort studies involving diverse populations have showed that an energy expenditure of about 1000 kcal·wk^{-1} of moderate-intensity physical activity or approximately 150 min·wk^{-1} or 30 min·d^{-1} is associated with lower rates of cardiovascular disease and premature mortality (Haskell et al.,

2007; Lee & Skerrett, 2001). Although, a greater quantity of exercise with caloric expenditure of ≥ 2000 kcal·wk^{-1}, or 250–300 min·wk^{-1} or 50–60 min·d^{-1} results in greater health/fitness benefits especially in terms of weight loss (ACSM, 2001). With respect to mental health, 3–5 days of exercise a week with a weekly energy expenditure of 17.5 Kcal/kg/week has been found to have significantly larger reductions in depression compared to those who exercised less with energy expenditure of 7 Kcal/kg/wk (Dunn, Trivedi, Kampert, Clark, & Chambliss, 2005). For worthwhile reductions in anxiety scores, moderate intensity exercise programs of more than 21 minutes per session for a minimum of 10 weeks has been suggested (Petruzello et al., 1991). In terms of time, the ACSM 2010 and 2011 guidelines recommend moderate-intensity exercise for a minimum 30 min·d^{-1} on five or more days a week to a total of 150 minutes, or vigorous intensity cardiorespiratory exercise for at least 20–25 minutes a day on ≥ 3 d·wk^{-1} to a total of 75 minutes, or at least 20–30 minutes of moderate and vigorous intensity exercise on 3–5 d·wk^{-1} for most adults.

Evidence on the effect of continuous versus intermittent exercise has been provided by many studies (Donnelly, Jacobsen, Heelan, Seip, & Smith, 2000; Murphy, Nevill, Nevill, Biddle, & Hardman, 2002). Multiple bouts of shorter duration exercise seem to be of greater appeal to most people and can lead to health/fitness benefits provided the exercise is performed at a moderate-to-vigorous intensity. Therefore, as an effective alternative to continuous exercise, multiple bouts of at least 10 minutes of intermittent exercise can also be accumulated to meet the minimum duration recommendations (ACSM, 2010). However, continuous moderate intensity exercise has been found to be more effective in improving mood symptoms than intermittent exercise (Osei-Tutu & Campagna, 1998).

Intensity of cardiorespiratory exercise

The intensity of exercise is apparently the most important component of the exercise prescription and the health/fitness benefits are directly related to the exercise intensity. Intensity is the extent of overload required to bring about a training effect. For most people, a minimum intensity threshold exists for health/fitness benefits below which the intensity will not challenge the physiological systems sufficiently for gains in the cardiorespiratory fitness (ACSM, 1998a; 2010). The evidence related to minimum intensity threshold is seemingly related to the initial state of fitness of the subjects (ACSM, 1998a; Swain & Franklin, 2002). The lower is the fitness level of a person, the lesser is the exercise intensity threshold for training effect and vice versa. Clinical trials showed that while the minimum intensity threshold of $\leq 30\%$ of oxygen uptake reserve (VO$_2$R) was found for subjects with a VO$_{2max}$ of < 40 ml·kg^{-1}·min^{-1}, a minimum threshold of 45% of VO$_2$R was required in subjects with baseline VO$_{2max}$ values of 40–51 ml·kg^{-1}·min^{-1} (Swain & Franklin, 2002). Furthermore, other studies have showed that while a training intensity of 70–80% of VO$_{2max}$ was required in moderately trained athletes, near maximal (95–100% VO$_{2max}$) training intensities were essential for improvements in VO$_{2max}$ in elite athletes (Midgley, McNaughton, & Wilkinson, 2006). Therefore, owing to the variations in fitness levels, it may be rather challenging to precisely prescribe a general exercise intensity threshold for cardiorespiratory fitness.

Generally, a moderate intensity exercise at 40–60% of VO$_2$R or 60–80% of VO$_{2max}$ has been recommended as the minimum to achieve cardiorespiratory fitness goals in most adults (Haskell et al., 2007). Moderate intensity exercise has also been reported to cause greater improvements in psychological responses compared to vigorous intensity exercise (Moses et al., 1989). In terms of metabolic equivalent (METs), for people weighing 68–91 kg, moderate and vigorous intensity is equivalent to 3–5.9 METs and ≥ 6 METs respectively. The ACSM guidelines recommend that a combination of moderate- (40 to $< 60\%$ of VO$_2$R) and vigorous-intensity ($> 60\%$ of VO$_2$R) exercise seems to be ideal for health/fitness improvements in most adults (ACSM, 2010, 2011). If improvement in health and lowering the disease risk are the primary objectives, the exercise intensity can be lower (< 40% of VO_2R) with frequency and duration becoming the more significant aspects of exercise prescription (ACSM, 2006b). Evidence suggests that low-moderate intensity exercise can lower the risk of cardiovascular diseases and other chronic conditions despite not causing any significant changes in $\dot{V}O_{2max}$. Moderate intensity exercises like walking have also been more effective in improving depression and anxiety scores than vigorous intensity programs (Dishman & Buckwort, 1996). Moreover, a rise in exercise intensity above moderate levels may adversely affect the long-term adherence to exercise. However, greatest gains in health and fitness are experienced by individuals who are capable of regular, sustained, higher-intensity exercise (Donnelly et al., 2000; Dunn et al., 1999; Murphy et al., 2002; Pate et al., 1995). The exercise intensity can be estimated by the following methods:

- Peak heart rate method:
  Target HR = HR_{max} × % Intensity desired
- HR reserve method:
  Target HR = [(HR_{max} – HR_{rest}) × % intensity desired] + HR_{rest}
- Peak VO_2 method:
  Target VO_2 = $\dot{V}O_{2max}$ × % Intensity desired
- VO_2 reserve method:
  Target VO_2R = [($\dot{V}O_{2max}$ – VO_{2rest}) × % intensity desired] + VO_{2rest}
- % MET_{max} method:
  Target MET = [($\dot{V}O_{2max}$)/ 3.5 ml·kg^{-1}·min^{-1}] × % intensity desired
- Rating of perceived exertion: use Borg's scale or OMNI scale

All the above methods, when used for exercise prescription, have been shown to cause improvements in the cardiorespiratory fitness. However, apparently no study has compared all the methods simultaneously. Hence, it may not to be reasonable to assume that one method

might be superior or at least equally effective to the other. Moreover, the relationship between the methods of intensity estimation and the actual energy expenditure can vary depending upon factors like the age, fitness level, body composition, resting HR, exercise mode, exercise intensity and the exercise test protocol (Byrne & Hills, 2002; Johnson et al., 2000; Strath et al., 2000). While all the above-mentioned methods are useful, the HRR and VO_2R methods have been found to reflect energy expenditure more accurately. The HR_{max} and the $\dot{V}O_{2max}$ methods seem to have a higher probability of underestimation or overestimation of exercise intensity. For examples of calculation of the exercise intensity using the above methods, the reader is referred to the ACSM 2010 resource manual for guidelines for exercise testing and prescription. Classification of aerobic exercise intensity comparing the more commonly used methods is provided in the table overleaf (Table 47.2).

A direct method of exercise prescription may be used where the HR and VO_2 are measured during an exercise test. This method is based on the relationship between the HR and oxygen uptake (Figure 47.3) that is used to estimate the target HR range as the appropriate intensity for cardiorespiratory fitness training effect.

Although the direct measurements of HR and VO_2 are recommended for precise exercise prescription, it may not always be feasible to accurately measure the HR_{max} and $\dot{V}O_{2max}$ by exercise testing. In these situations, the use of age-predicted HR_{max} using the classic '220 – age' equation or other equations and estimation of exercise intensity using the indirect methods is practical and acceptable (Gellish et al., 2007; Tanaka, Monahan, & Seals, 2001). However, it is to be emphasized that although these equations provide fairly accurate estimations of HR_{max}, for a given individual, there might be a standard deviation of 10–12 beats·min^{-1}. Therefore, the target HR prescribed using indirect methods should be considered as guideline exercise intensity and should be preferably used with additional measures of intensity.

Table 47.2 *Classification of exercise intensity for cardiorespiratory fitness*

Intensity	% HRR or % VO_2R	$\%HR_{max}$	$\%VO_{2max}$	RPE (6–20 scale)
Very light	< 30	< 57	< 37	<9 (< very light)
Light	30–39	57–63	37–45	9-11 (very light-fairly light)
Moderate	40–59	64–76	46–63	12-13 (fairly light – somewhat hard)
Vigorous	60–89	77–95	64–90	14-17 (somewhat hard – very hard)
Near-maximal to maximal	≥ 90	≥ 96	≥ 91	≥ 18 (≥ very hard)

Table adapted from: ACSM Guidelines, 2010, Swain and Leuholtz, 1997, U.S. department of Health and Human Services, 2008.

HRR – heart rate reserve; VO_2R – oxygen uptake reserve; $\%HR_{max}$ – percent of maximum heart rate; $\%\dot{V}O_{2max}$ – percent of maximum oxygen uptake; RPE – rating of perceived exertion.

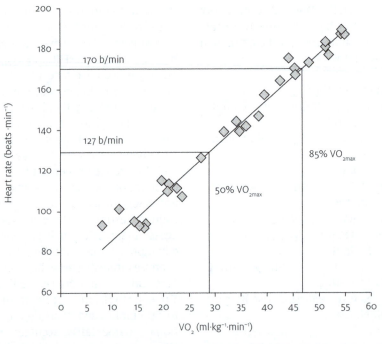

Figure 47.3 Exercise prescription using the HR method based on the relationship between HR and VO_2. A 'best fit' line has been drawn through the data points on the HR-VO_2 plot. This exercise test for $\dot{V}O_{2max}$ was done on a physical education student (male, age, 24.6 years, body mass, 66 kg, height, 1.73 m) during the exercise physiology laboratory session. The $\dot{V}O_{2max}$ was 54.34 ml·kg^{-1}·min^{-1} and the HR_{max} was 189 beats·min^{-1}. The 50% $\dot{V}O_{2max}$ was 27.15 ml·kg^{-1}·min^{-1} and the 85% $\dot{V}O_{2max}$ was 46.18 ml·kg^{-1}·min^{-1}. The corresponding target HR was 127 and 170 beats·min^{-1} respectively.

The rating of perceived exertion (RPE) can be used as either a primary or an adjunct measure of exercise intensity in apparently healthy adults. The perception of effort during cardiorespiratory exercise is an outcome of a combination of sensory inputs from local factors (exercising muscles and joints) and central factors (increase in HR and respiratory rate). Therefore, RPE can be used both independently as well as in combination with HR or pulse rate to prescribe exercise intensity (Noble, Borg, Jacobs, Ceci, & Kaiser, 1983; Whaley, Woodall, Kaminsky, & Emmett, 1997). With the RPE method, the person gets gradually habituated to correlate the THR range with a particular effort sensation. This eventually reduces the need for frequent pulse rate measurements. Over a period of time, the perception of effort might become a more effective measure of exercise intensity than the HR-VO_2 method for a desired training effect. Borg's RPE scale (Borg, 1974; Noble et al., 1983) (Figure 47.4) and the OMNI scale (Robertson et al., 2003, 2004 ; Utter et al., 2004) are more commonly used instruments to estimate RPE for prescribing exercise intensity.

The RPE range of 12–17 on Borg's scale equates to moderate-to-vigorous exercise intensity range. While the RPE method is reliable, simple to use, cost-effective, individualized and has good correlation with VO_{2max} and lactate threshold (Hetzler et al., 1991; Robertson et al., 1990), the RPE scale may be less accurate in children, obese and elderly subjects. Furthermore, different modes of exercise may elicit different RPE despite the intensity being at the same % VO_{2max} level (Borg, 1985; Garcin, Whaley et al., 1997).

Mode or type of cardiorespiratory exercise

Exercise mode or type is perceived to be an important factor for long-term adherence and hence sustaining the health/fitness benefits of physical activity. The activities should be selected based upon individual interests, time,

6	No exertion at all
7	Extremely light
8	
9	Very light
10	
11	Light
12	
13	Somewhat hard
14	
15	Hard (heavy)
16	
17	Very hard
18	
19	Extremely hard
20	Maximal exertion

Figure 47.4 Borg's Rating of perceived exertion scale. From G. Borg 1998. (Borg RPC scale © 1970, 1985, 1994, 1998.)

work and lifestyle constraints, available facilities, individual functional capacities and personal goals. For improving cardiovascular fitness, rhythmic and aerobic type exercises using large muscle groups and that require minimum skill are recommended (ACSM, 2010). Common exercises of such a nature include walking, jogging, running, cycling, swimming, hiking, rowing, slow dancing, elliptical exercise, stepping etc. In addition, skill-requiring activities in the form of recreational sports participation like racquet sports, soccer and basketball can also be pursued to improve aerobic fitness. Ideally, the individual should be encouraged to participate in a variety of activities as it avoids overloading a particular body part or muscle group, prevents monotony of exercise, accommodates factors like weather, travel and time constraints, increases chances of long-term exercise adherence and improves overall fitness, motor abilities and skills.

Progression of cardiorespiratory exercise program

Progression in an exercise program primarily depends upon exercise tolerance, health and fitness status, age and individual goals. In the initial stage of the exercise program, an increase in duration by 5–10 minutes every 1–2 weeks over 4–6 weeks is recommended for an average adult (ACSM, 1998a, 2011). To avoid muscle soreness, risk of injury and adverse effect on exercise adherence, the intensity at this stage should be 40–60% of VO_{2max} and the frequency 3–4 times per week (ACSM, 2006b). Following 4–6 weeks of exercise adherence, the exercise intensity, frequency and/or duration can be gradually increased over the next 4–8 months depending upon the exercise tolerance and training adaptations. This period can be longer for older and deconditioned persons. Following any change in the exercise dose, it is important to carefully monitor the individual for possible adverse effects and exercise tolerance and if necessary, adjustments should be made in the exercise prescription. Once the intended fitness goals have been achieved the maintenance phase starts, lasting for 5–6 months during which the exercise participation continues on a regular and sustained basis.

EXERCISE PRESCRIPTION FOR MUSCULAR FITNESS

Improved muscle strength is associated with lower cardiovascular risk (Jurca et al., 2004; 2005), lowered risk of all-cause mortality (Fitzgerald, Kampert, Morrow, Jackson, & Blair, 2004), and improved functional capacities (Brill, Macera, Davis, Blair, & Gordon, 2000). In addition to gains in strength, resistance training adaptations include positive changes in the body composition (Hunter, McCarthy, & Bamman, 2004; Hunter et al., 2010), improved blood glucose levels (Castaneda et al., 2002; Sigal et al., 2007) and higher insulin sensitivity (Brooks et al., 2007; Klimcakova et al., 2006). Strength-increasing exercises also increase the bone mineral density and content and bone strength (Kohrt, Bloomfield, Little, Nelson, & Yingling, 2004; Maimoun & Sultan, 2011). These adaptations may be significant in preventing and/or reversing osteoporosis. Furthermore, resistance training may also reduce the chance of developing musculoskeletal disorders like osteoarthritis and reduce the extent of disability in these conditions (Slemenda et al., 1998). There is also some suggestive evidence that resistance training may be effective in conditions like anxiety disorders and depression (Cassilhas, Antunes, Tufik, & de Mello, 2010; Oeland, Laessoe, Olesen, & Munk-Jorgensen, 2010). Therefore, muscular fitness is an essential and important component of exercise training programs for health and wellness.

Muscular fitness comprises gains in strength, endurance and power. A specifically designed resistance training program is required for improvements in each of these parameters. For maximum training effect, individualization of the program variables (volume, intensity, frequency and rest intervals) is important to meet the intended goals (ACSM, 2009). However, the dose-response relationship between muscular fitness and health benefits is currently not strongly supported by research evidence. Moreover, there is insufficient supportive evidence on the existence of a minimum threshold of resistance-training stimulus for health-related muscular fitness (Bemben & Bemben, 2011). The focus of this chapter is to provide an understanding of the basic principles of resistance training to develop programs for muscular fitness and health benefits in adults.

Types of resistance training exercises

Muscular fitness can be improved using different types of resistance training equipment like free weights, stack weights, pneumatic resistance machines and resistance bands. Different systems of resistance training are available that can be opted for a resistance training program (Table 47.3). If performed with the right technique, resistance training can improve all the components of muscular fitness, including strength, endurance and power.

Resistance training for healthy adults should include dynamic exercises involving concentric and eccentric muscle actions recruiting multiple muscle groups (ACSM, 2009). The exercises should focus on major muscle groups of shoulders, arms, chest, trunk, back, hips and legs. Functionally important muscle groups like quadriceps, hamstrings, calf muscles, abdominals and biceps should also be worked upon using single joint exercises. Moreover, both the agonists and the antagonists of a muscle group should be trained to prevent muscle imbalances.

Table 47.3 *Systems of resistance training*

System	Load
Single-set system	One set per exercise, 8–12 RM
Multiple set system	Minimum 3 sets per exercise, 4–6 RM
Light-to-heavy system	Start with set of 3–5 reps with light weight Add 5 lbs and repeat set of 3–5 reps Keep adding 5 lbs until only one rep can be performed
Heavy-to-light system	Opposite of light-to-heavy regimen
The triangle program	Start with light-to-heavy system Immediately followed by heavy-to-light system
Super-set system	First type: multiple sets two exercises same body part but opposing muscle groups 8–10 reps; No rest in-between Second type: one set of several exercises same muscle group or body part rapid succession
Circuit program	Series of exercises, 10–15 reps, 40%–60% RM Performed one after another Minimal rest in-between
Split-routine system	Different types and multiple sets of exercises for each body part Only a few body parts exercised per session e.g. arms and chest on Monday and Thursday Shoulders and abdomen on Wednesday and Saturday

Source: Adapted from Fleck & Kraemer (2003).

Resistance training technique

Resistance training exercises should be done using the correct form and technique irrespective of training status or age. The repetitions should be performed in a controlled manner through full range of motion of a joint. Breathing technique of inhalation during the eccentric phase and exhalation during the concentric phase should be followed and breath holding should be discouraged during the repetitions (ACSM, 2009). Excessive eccentric loading should be avoided as it may lead to muscle damage and injuries. Improper technique would compromise the health/fitness gains and also increase the risk of post-exercise muscle soreness and musculoskeletal injuries. Moreover, factors like posture, grip, handwidth and foot stance can change the muscle activation affecting the exercise outcomes. Therefore, it might be beneficial, especially for beginners, to seek professional instructions on resistance training techniques, exercises and programs.

Components of resistance training

Resistance training or weight training includes the following variables that can be adjusted according to the intended goals and as the fitness gains occur with training (Baechle & Earle, 2000; Fleck & Kremer, 2003).

- Repetitions to fatigue: Generally, low repetitions (3–8) lead to strength gains and high repetitions (15–30) lead to muscular endurance.
- Sets: A particular number of repetitions constitute a set. One set might be fine to begin with but as the strength gains occur, it should be increased to three or more sets for continued benefits.
- Rest between sets: This depends upon whether the intention is to increase strength or the muscle mass. Shorter rest interval ($\leq$ 1 min) is used for building up the muscle mass while relatively longer

rest intervals ($\geq$ 2 minutes) are used for strength gains. For a general fitness program, rest intervals of 2–3 minutes seem to be ideal for gains in strength and muscle mass (ACSM, 2009).
- Sequence of exercises: Generally, the large muscle groups are exercised first followed by smaller muscle groups. However, there is a lot of variability between exercisers of different categories (weightlifters, bodybuilders, powerlifters) in the choice of the order of exercises.

Frequency of resistance exercise

An optimum resistance training frequency (number of training sessions per week) for any individual is influenced by multiple factors like age, level of training, recovery capability, lifestyle, dietary habits, other kinds of exercise (cardiorespiratory, sports) performed during the week, volume and intensity of training, the type of exercise selected and the number of muscle groups trained per session. For apparently healthy adults, training each major muscle group 2–3 days a week with 48 hours of recovery between sessions for the same muscle group has been recommended for general muscular fitness (ACSM, 2010). Although three days per week has been found to be superior to two days per week (Graves, Pollock, Jones, Colvin, & Leggett, 1989), three days produced similar increase in strength when volume was equated (Candow & Burke, 2007). Multiple muscle groups may be trained in the same session or they may be split into selected muscle groups per session. For untrained individuals, a frequency of three days per week seems to be optimum for strength gains (Rhea, Alvar, Burkett, & Ball, 2003).

Type of resistance training exercises

Resistance training exercise can be single joint (isolated) or multiple joint (compound resistance) types. Both the modalities have been found to be effective for strength gains in the targeted muscle groups (Kraemer & Ratamess, 2004). Multiple-joint exercises like bench press, squats, chest press and shoulder press require complex neural responses and are more effective in increasing overall strength (Stone et al., 1998). Single-joint exercises like biceps curls, triceps extension, knee curls and knee extension target specific muscle groups without the need for high skill levels and much technical involvement. For health/fitness improvements in most adults, unilateral and bilateral single and multiple joint resistance exercises with greater emphasis on multiple joint exercises targeting both agonist and antagonist muscle groups should be included in the resistance training program (ACSM, 2009, 2010).

Volume of resistance exercise

The volume of resistance exercise is determined by the total number of repetitions performed in a session multiplied by the resistance used and is reflective of the duration the muscles are being stressed (Tran, Docherty, & Behm, 2006). The resistance training volume affects the neural (Hakkinen et al., 1988), hypertrophic (Tesch, Komi, & Hakkinen, 1987), metabolic (Ratamess et al., 2007) and hormonal (Gotshalk et al., 1997; Kraemer et al., 1991) responses leading to subsequent adaptations to resistance training. The load or volume of resistance training can be based on the percentage of 1 RM, or a targeted number of repetitions, or within a loading zone (5–8 RM). The training volume can be altered by changing the number of repetitions per set, changing the number of sets or changing the number of exercises done per session.

Most adults show improved muscular fitness (increased muscle mass and strength) with two to four sets per muscle group using a combination of resistance exercises for the same muscle group with a 2–3 minutes of between-sets rest interval (ACSM, 2002b, 2009). Although > 2 sets are more effective, even a single set of resis-

tance exercise can lead to significant improvements in muscle strength, particularly for beginner level exercisers (ACSM, 1998a, 2009). The higher the resistance, the fewer the number of repetitions required. For improvements in the muscle strength, mass as well as endurance to some extent, a resistance exercise that allows 8–12 reps per set is recommended. This is equivalent to a resistance of 60–80% of 1 RM of an individual (ACSM, 2010). For example, if the 1 RM for bench press is 100 kg for a person, a resistance of 60–80 kg should be selected for the resistance exercise. For multiple sets per exercise, the first set should be close or equal to 12 reps and gradually decline to about 8 reps by the last set. It is important to note that the reps in a set should be to the point of fatigue and not failure as this might increase the possibility of muscle soreness and injuries (ACSM, 2002b). If the objective is improvement in muscle endurance, higher number of reps (15–30) with lower intensity ($\leq$ 50% of 1 RM) with shorter rest intervals should be performed. Previously sedentary and older individuals have a higher risk of musculoskeletal injuries as they begin a resistance exercise program. Therefore, these individuals should start with more reps with low-moderate resistance type exercises. Subsequent to adaptations and improved muscular conditioning, the intensity of resistance can be increased with 8–12 reps per set (ACSM, 1998b, 2002b, 2010, 2011).

Progression of resistance exercise program

Resistance exercise programs should start with a minimum threshold load for health/fitness benefits. With appropriately followed resistance training programs, on an average about 20–30% of the strength improvements occur in the first six months. The early strength gains are in the form of neural adaptations followed by an increase in the muscle mass (Baechle & Earle, 2000; Fleck & Kraemer, 2003). As adaptations occur, the muscles should be subjected to greater stimuli in the form of overload for continued gains in muscular fitness. It must be understood that the effect of resistance training is specific to the training methods, the type of contraction, training intensity and the body part, and depends on the overloading of the muscle groups (Baechle & Earle, 2000; Feigenbaum & Pollock, 1999; Kraemer & Ratamess, 2004; Morrissey, Harman, & Johnson, 1995; Rhea et al., 2003; Sale, 1988; Starkey et al., 1996).

There are many ways of applying the progressive overload concept in resistance training programs. The most common approach is to increase the resistance once the number of reps with the present resistance can be performed with ease. The increase in the resistance should be such that the same number of reps can be performed in a set without severe difficulty and fatigue in the last rep of the set. Additional ways of progression are to increase the number of sets per muscle group or the number of days per week in the program. Once the desired level of muscular fitness is achieved, it can be maintained by training one day a week, and keeping the resistance constant (ACSM, 2002b, 2009).

EXERCISE PRESCRIPTION FOR FLEXIBILITY

Flexibility exercises have been long practiced for increased joint movement range, enhanced functional ability, athletic performance and overall relaxation and well-being. Millions of people across the world practice stretching-based postures incorporated into many different forms of exercise and activities like yoga, tai-chi, gymnastics, dance forms like ballet and combat sports like wushu and tae kwon do. Flexibility is defined as the capability of joint movement through full range of motion (ROM). In addition to improved range of joint movements, flexibility has also been found to beneficially affect postural stability and balance (Costa, Graves, Whitehurst, & Jacobs, 2009). Moreover, despite the gradually reducing joint ROM with age, all age groups can benefit from flexibility training (ACSM, 1998a, 2010, 2011; American Geriatric Society Panel, 2001; Decoster, Cleland, Altieri, & Russel, 2005). Therefore, flexibility training is a valuable component of an exercise program for health, fitness and wellness.

A flexibility program is a planned, deliberate and regular program of exercises that leads to progressive increase in the ROM of a joint or a set of joints over a period of time (Alter, 2004). The majority of benefits of stretching are due to the improved ROM. As the muscles are extended beyond their normal length, they adapt by increasing the ROM across a joint. There are basically three types of flexibility:

- Static flexibility: involves slow stretching of a muscle/tendon group and holding the stretch for a period of time. A static stretch should be held in position for 10–60 seconds for optimum benefit (Roberts & Wilson, 1999).
- Dynamic flexibility: involves gradual movements from one body position to another with a progressive increase in reach and the ROM as movements are repeated several times (McMillan, Moore, Halter, & Taylor, 2006).
- Ballistic flexibility: involves bobbing, bouncing and rebounding stretches in a rhythmic manner using the momentum of the moving body segment to produce the stretch (Woolstenhulme, Griffiths, Woolstenhulme, & Parcell, 2006).

A fourth type of flexibility is called proprioceptive neuromuscular facilitation (PNF). It involves an isometric contraction of a muscle-tendon group followed by a static stretching (relaxation) of the same group (Sharman, Cresswell, & Riek, 2006). For optimum gains, the PNF technique should include a 6 second contraction followed by a 10–30 second assisted stretch (ACSM, 1998a). PNF and static stretching have been found to cause greater improvements in the joint ROM than dynamic stretching (Decoster et al., 2005; Kokkonen, Nelson, Eldredge, & Winchester, 2007). PNF can lead to greater improvements in flexibility in some joints compared to the other stretching techniques. However, the need for a partner limits its practical usefulness. Ballistic stretching, if performed with the correct technique and rhythm can increase flexibility to the same extent as static stretching (Covert, Alexander, Petronis, & Davis, 2010; Witvrouw, Mahieu, Roosen, & McNair, 2007). However, this type of stretching movements may have higher injury potential and should be recommended only to those regularly participating in sports (e.g. basketball, volleyball, handball) requiring such movements.

Evidence is suggestive of multiple health, fitness and performance benefits of improved flexibility (Alter, 2004; Malliaropoulos, Papalexandris, Papalada, & Papacostas, 2004; Pope, Herbert, Kirwan, & Graham, 2000):

- Improved physical fitness, posture, balance
- Improved self-image
- Enhanced coordination between body parts and better movements
- Better sports skills performance
- Muscular relaxations and reduced muscle soreness
- Mental relaxation
- Reduced risk and severity of low back ache
- Injury prevention

With the growing evidence of the fitness-related and functional benefits of improved flexibility, the ACSM included flexibility training in their 1998 position stand (ACSM, 1998a).

The current guidelines recommend for most adults a stretching exercise program of at least 10 minutes duration involving major muscle-tendon groups (shoulder girdle, chest, neck, trunk, lower back, hip, legs and ankles) with four or more repetitions per muscle group performed for a minimum of 2–3 days per week (ACSM, 2010). However, greater improvements in joint ROM are achieved with daily flexibility training (Feland, Myrer, Schulthies, Fellingham & Measom, 2001; Guissard & Duchateau; 2006). As tolerated, all four types of stretching can be included in the exercise program. While stretching, it is safer and effective to restrict the stretch to the limit of discomfort or mild tightness within the ROM and not venture into the zone of pain. A few additional stretching guidelines are provided below:

- Stretching exercise is most effective when the muscle temperature is elevated through light-moderate intensity cardiorespiratory or muscular endurance exercises
- Stretching should be performed both before and after the conditioning phase
- Stretching following exercise may be preferable for sports for which muscle strength, power and endurance are important for performance

Although currently the research findings on certain aspects of improved flexibility is inconclusive, the overall body of evidence seems sufficiently convincing to include flexibility training as part of a general fitness program, either as an independent component or as a supplement to cardiorespiratory and resistance exercise.

EXERCISE PRESCRIPTION FOR NEUROMOTOR TRAINING

Neuromotor training, also known as functional training, includes exercises that attempt to mimic the specific physiological and movement demands of real-life activities. Training for functional fitness involves a range of activities that condition the body using integrated movements. These exercises include perceptual skills training and movement skill training like balance, coordination, gait and agility. The activities are multi-directional and multiplanar with feedback from posture, body position sense and motion. Examples of activities that are widely used for functional fitness include tai-chi, yoga and qigong, which are all minimal-impact activities that involve low-velocity muscle contractions and include combinations of neuromotor, resistance and flexibility exercises. Essentially, functional training activities involve speeding up (force production), slowing down (force reduction) and stabilization. Therefore, the outcomes of functional training would be improved muscle balance, better joint stability and enhanced movement control. These attributes lead to improved fitness, better techniques and skills and reduced risk of injuries. Such outcomes of an exercise program are of immense benefit especially to older individuals (Bird, Hill, Ball, Hetherington, & Williams, 2011; Karinkanta et al., 2007; Li, Devault, & Van Oteghen, 2007).

However, the outcomes of neuromotor training can be reasonably conceived to improve functional performance and quality of life in all adults of different age groups.

There is limited research on the minimum threshold or the frequency and duration of neuromotor training for health/fitness benefits. The studies differ in the type, duration and the frequency of exercise used. Moreover, the studies have used varying lengths of training programs and there has been a lack of a standardized measure quantifying the outcome of training (Wu, 2002). Studies that showed improvements in functional fitness used exercise sessions of $\geq$ 20–30 minutes with a training frequency of $\geq$ 2–3 days a week. The ACSM 2010 guidelines recommend neuromuscular exercises such as yoga and tai-chi at least 2–3 days a week for older adults who are at a greater risk of falls or have mobility impairment.

EXERCISE ADOPTION AND ADHERENCE

Exercise can lead to positive health outcomes only if a person adopts a physically active lifestyle, engages in regular exercise and adheres to the exercise program. Despite the huge body of evidence on the health/fitness benefits of exercise, there are significantly greater numbers of adults who fail to meet the activity recommendations compared to the number who achieve the criteria for daily physical activity (Center for Disease Control and Prevention, 2008; Guthold, Ono, Strong, Chatterji, & Morabia, 2008). It has been reported that less than 7% of individuals who primarily walk for exercise actually do so with the appropriate intensity, frequency and duration to meet the activity recommendations (Rafferty, Reeves, McGee, & Pivarnik, 2002). Despite colossal efforts initiated by governments, issuance of public health and activity guidelines by health governing bodies like ACSM and CDC and greater degree of flexibility offered in exercise types and patterns, the prevalence of physically inactive behavior and sedentary life-

styles continue to be high in all age groups among various populations. Behavioral interventions to increase physical activity have shown limited and inconsistent success on exercise adherence with dropout rates for structured exercise programs being close to 90% (Marcus et al., 2006).

Meta-analysis studies have reported that the factors related to exercise prescription like the duration, intensity and frequency have little effect on exercise adherence (Rhodes, Warburton, & Murray, 2009). However, evidence is more convincing on moderate intensity exercise leading to greater chances of exercise continuation than vigorous intensity exercise (Cyarto, Brown, & Marshall, 2006; Kahn et al., 2002; Rhodes et al., 2009). The mode of exercise, although widely perceived to be a useful tool for exercise motivation, has been found to be of limited effect in exercise adherence (Rhodes et al., 2009). However, some evidence exists on supervised structured programs and home-based exercise programs being effective in exercise adherence (Cox, Burke, Gorely, Beilin, & Puddey, 2003; Rhodes et al., 2009).

Paucity of studies on adoption and adherence of resistance, flexibility and neuromotor exercise programs make it challenging to recommend strategies to encourage physically active behavior and exercise continuation. Exercise programs tailored to individual characteristics and lifestyles have been shown to improve adherence to physically active behavior (Marcus et al., 2006). These interventions have included increasing social support, reducing barriers to exercise and making social and environmental changes to exercise programs. The ACSM 2010 guidelines provide some useful recommendations to improve exercise adherence:

- Obtain healthcare provider support for the exercise program
- Clarify individual needs to establish the motive for exercise

- Identify individualized, attainable goals and objectives for exercise
- Identify safe, convenient, and well-maintained facilities for exercise
- Identify social support for exercise
- Identify environmental support and reminders for exercise
- Identify motivational exercise outcomes for self-monitoring of exercise progress and achievement (e.g. exercise logs and step counters)
- Emphasize and monitor the acute or immediate effects of exercise (e.g. reduced blood pressure, blood sugar, need for medications)
- Emphasize variety and enjoyment in exercise programs
- Establish a regular schedule for exercise
- Provide qualified, personable, and enthusiastic exercise professionals
- Minimize muscle soreness and injury by participation in exercise of moderate intensity, particularly in the early phase of exercise adoption.

CONCLUSION

The health benefits of regular exercise and physically active lifestyle are indisputable. Although exercise participation involves some risks, the benefits of regular exercise far outweigh these risks and lead to significant health and fitness gains, reduced cardiovascular and all-cause mortality and improved quality of life in the majority of adult population. Adults of all age groups should make committed efforts to reduce the sedentary time and engage in physically active behavior involving both frequent short bouts of active minutes as well as the structured exercise session during the day. For optimum health/fitness benefits and enhanced quality of life, a comprehensive exercise program involving cardiorespiratory, resistance, flexibility and neuromotor training in adequate dose and quality should be prescribed. The prescription, progression and maintenance of an exercise program should be based upon individual characteristics like age, health status, lifestyle, intended goals, baseline fitness and response to training. While professional consultation may not be necessary for all, novice exercisers, elderly persons, at-risk individuals and those with health-related conditions might benefit from such expert support. Lastly, since long-term adherence to physical activity is a major challenge to exercise programs, individual preferences, enjoyable activities, variations in exercise types, behavior change strategies and social and environmental support systems should be incorporated in the prescribed exercise regimen.

LEARNING AIDS

1   What are the general principles of physical activity?

Overload: the most fundamental principle of physical activity. It signifies that physical activity should be performed in greater than normal amounts for fitness and/or health benefits.

Progression: as an individual starts responding to exercise, the overload should be gradually increased for sustained improvements in health and fitness.

Specificity: a specific type of exercise is needed for improvements in specific fitness component.

Reversibility: lack of activity results in loss of fitness and health benefits.

Individuality: benefits of exercise varies between individuals.

2   What is aerobic exercise?

Aerobic exercise involves activities during which the body is able to supply sufficient oxygen to sustain the activity at the desired intensity for a prolonged period of time. Examples include jogging, dancing, swimming, cycling.

3   What is VO_{2max}?

VO_{2max} or maximum aerobic capacity is a person's maximum capability to take in and transport oxygen to the working muscles during maximal intensity exercise. This test is a good indicator of one's cardiovascular fitness. A number of laboratory as well as field-based protocols are available for the determination of VO_{2max} in an individual.

4   What is the criterion for moderate intensity exercise?

Moderate intensity exercise is physical activity that is within an individual's capacity that can be comfortably sustained for a prolong duration. It is about 40–60% of individual VO_{2max} or 60–75% of HRmax respectively.

5   What is anaerobic exercise?

Anaerobic exercise involves activities that are performed at a higher intensity at which the body's need for oxygen is greater than the capability to supply it. Examples include sprinting, sprint swimming, sprint cycling, weightlifting.

6   What is 1RM?

1RM or one repetition maximum is the maximum amount of load or resistance an individual can lift or move. For example, 1RM is the maximum load lifted once; 3RM is the maximum load lifted thrice. It should be remembered that 3RM is not 1/3rd of 1RM.

7   What are the different types of muscle contractions?

There are several types of muscle contractions.

a) Isotonic contractions are made up of two types:

1. Concentric contractions: the muscle length shortens as the muscle contracts, e.g., flexion of a joint.

2. Eccentric contractions: the muscle length increases as it contracts, e.g., extension of a joint.

b) Isometric contractions: the muscle length remains unchanged as force is generated against a load.

c) Isokinetic contractions: this involves isotonic-concentric movements using a machine that controls the velocity and resistance.

8 What are the agonist and antagonist muscles in the context of flexibility?

The agonist muscles are the muscle group being stretched, while the antagonist muscles are the muscle group on the opposite side of the limb, e.g., Biceps-Triceps; Quadriceps-Hamstrings. To prevent muscle imbalance, it is important to perform flexibility exercises in a manner that provides sufficient stretch to both agonist and antagonist muscles.

REVIEW QUESTIONS

1 What are the physiological and psychological benefits of a regular exercise program?

2 Explain the dose-response relationship in exercise prescription.

3 What are the objectives of pre-participation health screening?

4 What are the different methods of prescribing the exercise intensity for a cardiorespiratory exercise program?

5 What are the resistance training variables that can be adjusted as the fitness improves with training?

6 What are the different types of flexibility? Provide the fundamental guidelines for safe and effective stretching.

EXERCISES

1 An individual has a maximum heart rate of 176 b·min⁻¹ and a resting heart rate of 74 b·min⁻¹. Calculate the target heart rate range using the peak heart rate method and the heart rate reserve method.

2 Prescribe an exercise program for a 38-year-old overweight male. He has been trying to lose weight, improve his aerobic fitness and also to improve his muscle strength for the past two years. However, he has not achieved the desirable results. He has now come to your health and fitness center, hopeful that you are the one who can help him achieve his health and fitness goals.

Medical/injury history: Nil

Preferences: Running, cycling and tennis

Avoidances: Swimming

Availability: 4–5 days a week including either Saturday or Sunday with maximum one hour **per session per day.**

Goals

- Lose weight (body fat: 5–6 kg)
- Improve aerobic fitness
- Improve muscle strength, especially in lower limbs
- Wants to firm up his upper body without gaining too much bulk

Being the fitness instructor for the above client, you will see him about once every month. He has a heart rate monitor.

ADDITIONAL READING

ACSM (2010). *ACSM's Guidelines for Exercise Testing and Prescription* (8th ed.), PA: Lippincott Williams & Wilkins.

Nieman, D.C (2010). Exercise testing and prescription. A health-related approach. (7th ed). NY: McGraw-Hill.

Biddle, S.J.H., & Mutrie, N. (2008). Psychology of physical activity. Determinants, well-being & interventions. (2nd ed) London: Routledge.

REFERENCES

ACSM. Position Stand. (1998a). The recommended quantity and quality of exercise for developing and maintaining cardiorespiratory and muscular fitness, and flexibility in healthy adults. *Medicine and Science in Sports and Exercise*, 30(6), 975–991.

ACSM. Position Stand. (1998b). Exercise and physical activity for older adults. *Medicine and Science in Sports and Exercise*, 30(6), 992–1008.

ACSM. Position Stand. (2001). Appropriate intervention strategies for weight loss and prevention of weight regain for adults. *Medicine and Science in Sports and Exercise*, 33, 2145–2156.

ACSM. (2002a). *ACSM's exercise management for persons with chronic diseases and disabilities.* Champaign, IL: Human Kinetics.

ACSM. Position Stand. (2002b). Progression models in resistance training for healthy adults. *Medicine and Science in Sports and Exercise*, 34, 364–380.

ACSM. (2003). *ACSM fitness book* (3rd ed.). Champaign (IL): Human Kinetics.

ACSM. (2006a). *ACSM's metabolic calculations handbook.* PA: Lippincott Williams & Wilkins.

ACSM. (2006b). *ACSM's guidelines for graded exercise testing and prescription* (7th ed.). PA: Lippincott Williams & Wilkins.

ACSM. (2007). *ACSM's health/fitness facility standards and guidelines* (3rd ed.). Champaign, IL: Human Kinetics.

ACSM. Position Stand (2009). Progression models in resistance training for healthy adults. *Medicine and Science in Sports and Exercise*, 41(3), 687–708.

ACSM. (2010). *ACSM's guidelines for exercise testing and prescription* (8th ed.). PA: Lippincott Williams & Wilkins.

ACSM. Position stand. (2011). The recommended quantity and quality of exercise for developing and maintaining cardiorespiratory, muscular, and neuromotor fitness in apparently in healthy adults: Guidance for prescribing exercise. *Medicine and Science in Sports and Exercise*, 43 (7), 1334–1359.

Almeida, S.A., Williams, K.M., Shaffer, R.A. & Brodine, S.K. (1999). Epidemiological patterns of musculoskeletal injuries and physical training. *Medicine and Science in Sports and Exercise*, 31(8), 1176–1182.

Alter, M.J. (2004). *Science of flexibility* (3rd ed.). Champaign, IL: Human Kinetics.

American Geriatric Society Panel on Exercise and Osteoarthritis. (2001). Exercise prescription for older adults with osteoarthritis pain: consensus practice recommendations. A supplement to the AGS Clinical Practice Guidelines on the management of chronic pain in older adults. *Journal of the American Geriatric Society*, 49(6), 808–823.

Baechle, T.R. & Earle, R.W. (2000). *Essentials of strength training and conditioning* (2nd ed.). Champaign, IL: Human Kinetics.

Bemben, D.A., Bemben, M.G. (2011). Dose-response effect of 40 weeks of resistance training on bone mineral density in older adults. *Osteoporosis International*, 22(1), 179–186.

Bird, M., Hill, K.D., Ball, M., Hetherington, S. & Williams, A.D. (2011). The long-term benefits of a multi-component exercise intervention to balance and mobility in healthy older adults. *Archives of Gerontology and Geriatrics*, 52(2), 211–216.

Blair, S.N., Kohl, H.W. 3rd., Barlow, C.E., Paffenbarger, R.S. Jr., Gibbons, L.W. & Macera, C.A. (1995). Changes in physical fitness and all-cause mortality. A prospective study of healthy and unhealthy men. *The Journal of the American Medical Association*, 273(14), 1093–1098.

Blair, S.N., LaMonte, M.J. & Nichaman, M.Z. (2004). The evolution of physical activity recommendations: How much is enough? *American Journal of Clinical Nutrition*, 79(suppl), 913S–920S.

Borg, G.A. (1974). Perceived exertion. *Exercise and Sport Science Reviews*, 2, 131–153.

Borg, G. (1985). *An Introduction to Borg's RPE-Scale*. Ithaca, NY: Movement Publications.

Borg, G. (1998). *Borg's perceived exertion and pain scales*. Champaign, IL: Human Kinetics.

Brill, P.A., Macera, C.A., Davis, D.R., Blair, S.N. & Gordon, N. (2000). Muscular strength and physical function. *Medicine and Science in Sports and Exercise*, 32(2), 412–416.

Brooks, N., Layne, J.E., Gordon, P.L., Roubenoff, R., Nelson, M.E. & Castaneda-Sceppa, C. (2007). Strength training improves muscle quality and insulin sensitivity in Hispanic older adults with type 2 diabetes. *International Journal of Medical Sciences*, 4(1), 19–27.

Buckworth, J. & Dishman, R.K. (2002). *A guide to treatments that work*. Champaign, IL: Human Kinetics.

Byrne, N.M., Hills, A.P. (2002). Relationships between HR and VO_2 in the obese. *Medicine and Science in Sports and Exercise*, 34(9), 1419–1427.

Canadian Physical Activity Guidelines (2011). Canadian Society for Exercise Physiology. Retrieved from http://www.csep.ca/cmfiles/publications/parq/par-q.pdf

Candow, D.G. & Burke, D.G. (2007). Effect of short-term equal-volume resistance training with different workout frequency on muscle mass and strength in untrained men and women. *Journal of Strength and Conditioning Research*, 21(1), 204–207.

Caspersen, C.J., Powell, K.E. & Christenson, G.M. (1985). Physical activity, exercise, and physical fitness: Definitions and distinctions for health-related research. *Public Health Reports*, 100, 126–131.

Cassilhas, R.C., Antunes, H.K., Tufik, S. & de Mello, M.T. (2010). Mood, anxiety, and serum IGF-1 in elderly men given 24 weeks of high resistance exercise. *Perceptual and Motor Skills*, 110(1), 265–276.

Castaneda, C., Layne, J.E., Munoz-Orians, L., Gordon, P.L., Walsmith, J., Foldvari, M. & Nelson, M.E. (2002). A randomized controlled trial of resistance exercise training to improve glycemic control in older adults with type 2 diabetes. *Diabetes Care*, 25(12), 2335–2341.

Center for Disease Control and Prevention (2008). Prevalence of self-reported physically active adults—United States, 2007. *Morbidity and mortality Weekly Report*, 57(48), 1297–1300.

Costa, P.B., Graves, B.S., Whitehurst, M. & Jacobs, P.L. (2009). The acute effects of different durations of static stretching on dynamic balance performance. *Journal of Strength and Conditioning Research*, 23(1), 141–147.

Covert, C.A., Alexander, M.P., Petronis, J.J. & Davis, D.S. (2010). Comparison of ballistic and static stretching on hamstring muscle length using an equal stretching dose. *Journal of Strength and Conditioning Research*, 24(11), 3008–3014.

Cox, K.L., Burke, V., Gorely, T.J., Beilin, L.J. & Puddey, I.B. (2003). Controlled comparison of retention and adherence in home- vs center-initiated exercise interventions in women ages 40–65 years: the S.W.E.A.T. study (Sedentary Women Exercise Adherence Trial). *Preventive Medicine*, 36(1), 17–29.

Craft, L.L. & Landers, D.M. (1998). The effects of exercise on clinical depression resulting from mental illness: a meta-analysis. *Journal of Sport & Exercise Psychology*, 20, 339–357.

Cyarto, E.V., Brown, W.J. & Marshall, A.L. (2006). Retention, adherence and compliance: important considerations for home- and group-based resistance training programs for older adults. *Journal of Science and Medicine in Sport*, 9(5), 402–412.

Decoster, L.C., Cleland, J., Altieri, C. & Russell, P. (2005). The effects of hamstring stretching on range of motion: a systematic literature review. *The Journal of Orthopaedic and Sports Physical Therapy*, 35(6), 377–387.

Dishman, R.K. & Buckwort, J. (1996). Increasing physical activity: a quantitative synthesis. *Medicine and Science in Sports and Exercise*, 28, 706–719.

Donnelly, J.E., Jacobsen, D.J., Heelan, K.S., Seip, R. & Smith, S. (2000). The effects of 18 months of intermittent vs. continuous exercise on aerobic capacity, body weight and composition, and metabolic fitness in previously sedentary, moderately obese females. *International Journal of Obesity Related Metabolic Disorders*, 24, 566–572.

Dunn, A.L., Marcus, B.H., Kampert, J.B., Garcia, M.E., Kohl, H.W. & Blair, S.N. (1999). Comparison of lifestyle and structured interventions to increase physical activity and cardiorespiratory fitness. *The Journal of the American Medical Association*, 281, 327–334.

Dunn, A.L., Trivedi, M.H., Kampert, J.B., Clark, C.G. & Chambliss, H.O. (2005). Exercise treatment for depression. Efficacy and dose response. *American Journal of Preventive Medicine*, 28, 1–8.

Dunn, A.L., Trivedi, M.H. & O'Neal, H.A. (2001). Physical activity dose-response effects on outcome of depression and anxiety. *Medicine and Science in Sports and Exercise*, 33, S587–S597.

Feigenbaum, M.S. & Pollock, M.L. (1999). Prescription of resistance training for health and disease. *Medicine and Science in Sports and Exercise*, 31, 38–45.

Feland, J.B., Myrer, J.W., Schulthies, S.S., Fellingham, G.W. & Measom, G.W. (2001). The effect of duration of stretching of the hamstring muscle group for increasing range of motion in people aged 65 years or older. *Physical Therapy*, 81(5), 1110–1117.

Fitzgerald, S.J.B.C., Kampert, J.B., Morrow, J.R. Jr., Jackson, A.W. & Blair, S.N. (2004). Muscular fitness and all-cause mortality: a prospective study. *Journal of Physical Activity and Health*, 1, 7–18.

Fleck, S.J. & Kraemer, W.J. (2003). *Designing Resistance Training Programs*. Champaign, IL: Human Kinetics.

Fleg, J.L., Morrell, C.H., Bos, A.G., Brant, L.J., Talbot, L.A., Wright, J.G. & Lakatta, E.G. (2005). Accelerated longitudinal decline of aerobic capacity in healthy older adults. *Circulation*, 112(5), 674–682.

Fox, K.R. (1999). The influence of physical activity on mental well-being. *Public Health Nutrition*, 2 (3a), 411–418.

Garcin, M., Vandewalle, H. & Monod, H. (1999). A new rating scale of perceived exertion based on subjective estimation of exhaustion time: A preliminary study. *International Journal of Sports Medicine*, 20, 40–43.

Gellish, R.L., Goslin, B.R., Olson, R.E., McDonald, A., Russi, G.D. & Moudgil, V.K. (2007). Longitudinal modeling of the relationship between age and maximal heart rate. *Medicine and Science in Sports and Exercise*, 39 (5), 822–829.

Goodwin, R.D. (2003). Association between physical activity and mental disorders among adults in the United States. *Preventive Medicine*, 36, 698–703.

Gordon, S.M.B.S. (1993). Health appraisal in the non-medical setting. In J.L. Durstine, A.C. King & P.L. Painter (Eds.), *ACSM's resource manual for guidelines for exercise testing and prescription* (pp.219–228). PA: Lea & Febiger.

Gotshalk, L.A., Loebel, C.C., Nindl, B.C., Putukian, M., Sebastianelli, W.J., Newton, R.U. & Kraemer W.J. (1997). Hormonal responses to multiset versus single-set heavy-resistance exercise protocols. *Canadian Journal of Applied Physiology*, 22 (3), 244–255.

Graves, J.E., Pollock, M.L., Jones, A.E., Colvin, A.B. & Leggett, S.H. (1989). Specificity of limited range of motion variable resistance training. *Medicine and Science in Sports and Exercise*, 21(1), 84–89.

Guissard, N. & Duchateau, J. (2006). Neural aspects of muscle stretching. *Exercise and Sport Sciences Reviews*, 34(4), 154–158.

Guthold, R., Ono, T., Strong, K.L., Chatterji, S. & Morabia, A. (2008). Worldwide variability in physical inactivity a 51-country survey. *American Journal of Preventive Medicine*, 34(6), 486–494.

Hakkinen, K., Pakarinen, A., Alen, M., Kauhanen, H. & Komi, P.V. (1988). Neuromuscular and hormonal responses in elite athletes to two successive strength training sessions in one day. *European Journal of Applied Physiology*, 57(2), 133–139.

Haskell, W.L., Lee, I.M., Pate, R.R., Powell, K.E., Blair, S.N., Franklin, B.A. & Bauman, A. (2007). Physical activity and public health: Updated recommendation for adults from the American College of Sports Medicine and the American Heart Association. *Medicine and Science in Sports and Exercise*, 39 (8), 1423–1434.

Hetzler, R.K., Seip, R.L., Boutcher, S.H., Pierce, E., Snead, D. & Weltman, A. (1991). Effects of exercise modality on ratings of perceived exertion at various lactate concentrations. *Medicine and Science in Sports and Exercise*, 23, 88–92.

Hootman, J.M., Macera, C.A., Ainsworth, B.E., Martin, M., Addy, C.L. & Blair, S.N. (2001). Association among physical activity level, cardiorespiratory fitness, and risk of musculoskeletal injury. *American Journal of Epidemiology*, 154(3), 251–258.

Howley, E.T. & Franks, B.D. (2007). *Fitness professional's handbook* (5th ed.). Champaign, IL: Human Kinetics.

Hunter, G.R., McCarthy, J.P. & Bamman, M.M. (2004). Effects of resistance training on older adults. *Sports Medicine*, 34(5), 329–348.

Hunter, G.R., Brock, D.W., Byrne, N.M., Chandler-Laney, P.C., Del Corral, P. & Gower, B.A. (2010). Exercise training prevents regain of visceral fat for 1 year following weight loss. *Obesity (Silver Spring)*, 18(4), 690–695.

Johnson, P.J., Winter, E.M., Paterson, D.H., Koval, J.J., Nevill, A.M. & Cunningham, D.A. (2000). Modelling the influence of age, body size and sex on maximum oxygen uptake in older humans. *Experimental Physiology*, 85(2), 219–225.

Jurca, R., LaMonte, M.J., Church, T.S., Earnest, C.P., Fitzgerald, S.J., Barlow, C.E. & Blair, S.N. (2004). Associations of muscle strength and fitness with metabolic syndrome in men. *Medicine and Science in Sports and Exercise*, 36(8), 1301–1307.

Jurca, R., LaMonte, M.J., Barlow, C.E., Kampert, J.B., Church, T.S. & Blair, S.N. (2005). Association of muscular strength with incidence of metabolic syndrome in men. *Medicine and Science in Sports and Exercise*, 37(11), 1849–1855.

Kahn, E.B., Ramsey, L.T., Brownson, R.C., Heath, G.W., Howze, E.H., Powell, K.E. & Corso, P. (2002). The effectiveness of interventions to increase physical activity. A systematic review. *American Journal of Preventive Medicine*, 22 (Suppl 4), 73–107.

Karinkanta, S., Heinonen, A., Sievanen, H., Uusi-Rasi, K., Pasanen, M., Ojala, K. & Kanus, P. (2007). A multi-component exercise regimen to prevent functional decline and bone fragility in home-dwelling elderly women: randomized, controlled trial. *Osteoporosis International*, 18(4), 453–462.

Katch, V.L., McArdle, W.D. & Katch, F.I. (2011). *Essentials of exercise physiology* (4th ed.) PA: Lippincott Williams & Wilkins.

Kessler, R.C., McGongale, K.A., Zhao, S., Nelson, C.B., Hughes, M. & Eschleman, S. (1994). Lifetime and 12 months prevalence of DSM-III-R psychiatric disorder in United States. *Archives of General Psychiatry*, 51, 8–19.

Klimcakova, E., Polak, J., Moro, C., Hejnova, J., Majercik, M., Viguerie, N. & Stich, V. (2006). Dynamic strength training improves insulin sensitivity without altering plasma levels and gene expression of adipokines in subcutaneous adipose tissue in obese men. *The Journal of Clinical Endocrinology and Metabolism*, 91(12), 5107–5112.

Knubben, K., Reischies, F.M., Adli, M., Schlattmann, P., Bauer, M. & Dimeo, F. (2007). A randomized, controlled study on the effects of a short-term endurance training program in patients with major depression. *British Journal of Sports Medicine*, 41, 29–33.

Kohrt, W.M., Bloomfield, S.A., Little, K.D., Nelson, M.E. & Yingling, V.R. (2004). American College of Sports Medicine. Position Stand: physical activity and bone health. *Medicine and Science in Sports and Exercise*, 36(11), 1985–1996.

Kokkonen, J., Nelson, A.G., Eldredge, C. & Winchester, J.B. (2007). Chronic static stretching improves exercise performance. *Medicine and Science in Sports and Exercise*, 39(10), 1825–1831.

Kraemer, W.J., Gordon, S.E., Fleck, S.J., Marchitelli, L.J., Mello, R., Dziados, J.E. & Fry, A.C. (1991). Endogenous anabolic hormonal and growth factor responses to heavy resistance exercise in males and females. *International Journal of Sports Medicine*, 12(2), 228–235.

Kraemer, W.J. & Ratamess, N.A. (2004). Fundamentals of resistance training: Progression and exercise prescription. *Medicine and Science in Sports and Exercise*, 36, 674–688.

Lee, D.C., Sui, X., Ortega, F.B., Kim, Y.S., Church, T.S., Winett, R.A. & Blair, S.N. (2011). Comparisons of leisure-time physical activity and cardiorespiratory fitness as predictors of all-cause mortality in men and women. *British Journal of Sports Medicine*, 45 (6), 504–510.

Lee, I.M. & Skerrett, P.J. (2001). Physical activity and all-cause mortality: what is the dose-response relation? *Medicine and Science in Sports and Exercise*, 33 (6), S459–S471; discussion S493–S494.

Li, Y., Devault, C.N. & Van Oteghen, S. (2007). Effects of extended tai chi intervention on balance and selected motor functions of the elderly. *The American Journal of Chinese Medicine*, 35(3), 383–391.

Long, B.C. & van Stavel, R. (1995). Effects of exercise training on anxiety: a meta-analysis. *Journal of Applied Sport Psychology*, 7, 167–189.

Maimoun, L. & Sultan, C. (2011). Effects of physical activity on bone remodeling. *Metabolism*, 60 (3), 373–388.

Malliaropoulos, N., Papalexandris, S., Papalada, A. & Papacostas, E. (2004). The role of stretching in rehabilitation of hamstring injuries: 80 athletes follow-up. *Medicine and Science in Sports and Exercise*, 36, 756–759.

Manger, T.A. & Motta, R.W. (2005). The impact of an exercise program on posttraumatic stress disorder, anxiety and depression. *International Journal of Emergency Mental Health*, 7, 49–57.

Marcus, B.H., Williams, D.M., Dubbert, P.M., Sallis, J.F., King, A.C., Yancey, A.K. & Claytor, R.P. (2006). Physical activity intervention studies: what we know and what we need to know: a scientific statement from the American Heart Association Council on Nutrition, Physical Activity, and Metabolism (Subcommittee on Physical Activity); Council on Cardiovascular Disease in the Young and the Interdisciplinary Working Group on Quality of Care and Outcomes Research. *Circulation*, 114 (24), 2739–2752.

Maron, B.J., Araújo, C.G., Thompson, P.D., Fletcher, G.F., de Luna, A.B., Fleg, J.L. & Bazzarre, T.L. (2001). Recommendations for preparticipation screening and the assessment of cardiovascular disease in masters athletes: an advisory for healthcare professionals from the working groups of the World Heart Federation, the International Federation of Sports Medicine,

and the American Health Association Committee on Exercise, Cardiac Rehabilitation, and Prevention. *Circulation*, 103(2), 327–334.

Martinsen, E.W., Strand, J., Paulsson, G. & Kaagestad, J. (1989). Physical fitness level in patients with anxiety and depressive disorders. *International Journal of Sports Medicine*, 10, 58–62.

McMillian, D.J., Moore, J.H., Hatler, B.S. & Taylor, D.C. (2006). Dynamic vs. static-stretching warm up: the effect on power and agility performance. *Journal of Strength and Conditioning Research*, 20(3), 492–499.

Midgley, A.W., McNaughton, L.R. & Wilkinson, M. (2006). Is there an optimal training intensity for enhancing the maximal oxygen uptake of distance runners?: empirical research findings, current opinions, physiological rationale and practical recommendations. *Sports Medicine*, 36(2), 117–132.

Morrissey, M.C., Harman, E.A. & Johnson, M.J. (1995). Resistance training modes: Specificity and effectiveness. *Medicine and Science in Sports and Exercise*, 27, 648–660.

Moses, J., Steptoe, A., Matthews, A. & Edwards, S. (1989). The effects of exercise training on mental well-being in the normal population: a controlled trial. *Journal of Psychosomatic Research*, 33, 47–61.

Murphy, M., Nevill, A., Nevill, C., Biddle, S. & Hardman, A. (2002). Accumulating brisk walking for fitness, cardiovascular risk, and psychological health. *Medicine and Science in Sports and Exercise*, 9, 1468–1474.

Murray, C.J.L. & Lopez, A.D. (1997). Global mortality, disability and the contribution of risk factors: Global burden of disease survey. *Lancet*, 349, 1436–1442.

Nieman, D.C. (2007). Exercise testing and prescription. A health-related approach. (6th ed). NY: McGraw-Hill.

Noble, B.J., Borg, G.A.V., Jacobs, I., Ceci, R. & Kaiser, P. (1983). A category-ratio perceived exertion scale: Relationship to blood and muscle lactates and heart rate. *Medicine and Science in Sports and Exercise*, 15, 523–528.

Oeland, A.M., Laessoe, U., Olesen, A.V. & Munk-Jorgensen, P. (2010). Impact of exercise on patients with depression and anxiety. *Nordic Journal of Psychiatry*, 64(3), 210–217.

Osei-Tutu, K.E.K. & Campagna, P.D. (1998). Psychological benefits of continuous vs.

intermittent moderate intensity exercise. [abstract]. *Medicine and Science in Sports and Exercise*, 30 Suppl, 5: S117.

Pate, R.R., Pratt, M., Blair, S.N., Haskell, W.L., Macera, C.A., Bouchard, C. & Wilmore, J.H. (1995). Physical activity and public health: A recommendation from the Centers for Disease Control and Prevention and the American College of Sports Medicine. *The Journal of the American Medical Association*, 273(5), 402–407.

Peterson, J. (1999). Ten reasons why warming up is important. *ACSM's Health & Fitness Journal*. 3 (1), 52.

Petruzello, S.J., Landers, A.C., Hatfield, B.D., Kubitz, K.A. & Salazar, W. (1991). A meta-analysis on the anxiety-reducing effect of acute and chronic exercise: outcomes and mechanisms. *Sports Medicine*, 11, 143–182.

Pope, R.P., Herbert, R.D., Kirwan, J.D. & Graham, B.J. (2000). A randomized trial of preexercise stretching for prevention of lower-limb injury. *Medicine and Science in Sports and Exercise*, 32, 271–277.

Rafferty, A.P., Reeves, M.J., McGee, H.B. & Pivarnik, J.M. (2002). Physical activity patterns among walkers and compliance with public health recommendations. *Medicine and Science in Sports and Exercise*, 34(8), 1255–1261.

Raglin, J.S. (1997). Anxiolytic effects of physical activity. In W.P. Morgan (Ed.), *Physical activity and mental health* (pp.107–126). Washington, DC: Taylor & Francis.

Ratamess, N.A., Falvo, M.J., Mangine, G.T., Hoffman, J.R., Faigenbaum, A.D. & Kang, J. (2007). The effect of rest interval length on metabolic responses to the bench press exercise. *European Journal of Applied Physiology*, 100 (1), 1–17.

Rhea, M.R., Alvar, B.A., Burkett, L.N. & Ball, S.D. (2003). A meta-analysis to determine the dose response for strength development. *Medicine and Science in Sports and Exercise*, 35 (3), 456–464.

Rhodes, R.E., Warburton, D.E. & Murray, H. (2009). Characteristics of physical activity guidelines and their effect on adherence: a review of randomized trials. *Sports Medicine*, 39(5), 355–375.

Roberts, J.M. & Wilson, K. (1999). Effect of stretching duration on active and passive range of motion in the lower extremity. *British Journal of Sports Medicine*, 33, 259–263.

Robertson, R.J., Goss, F.L., Auble, T.E., Cassinelli, D.A., Spina, R.J., Glickman, E.L. & Metz, K.F. (1990). Cross-modal exercise prescription at absolute and relative oxygen uptake using perceived exertion. *Medicine and Science in Sports and Exercise*, 22, 653–659.

Robertson, R.J., Goss, F.L., Dube, J., Rutkowski, J., Dupain, M., Brennan, C. & Andreacci, J. (2004). Validation of the adult OMNI scale of perceived exertion for cycle ergometer exercise. *Medicine and Science in Sports and Exercise*, 36, 102–108.

Robertson, R.J., Goss, F.L., Rutkowski, J., Lenz, B., Dixon, C., Timmer, J. & Andreacci, J. (2003). Concurrent validation of the OMNI perceived exertion scale for resistance exercise. *Medicine and Science in Sports and Exercise*, 35, 333–341.

Sale, D.G. (1988). Neural adaptation to resistance training. *Medicine and Science in Sports and Exercise*, 20 (suppl), S135–S145.

Saltin, B. & Gollnick, P.D. (1983). Skeletal muscle adaptability: Significance for metabolism and performance. In L.D. Peachey, R.H. Adrian & S.R. Geiger (Eds.), *Handbook of physiology*, (pp.555–632). Baltimore: Lippincott Williams & Wilkins.

Scully, D., Kremer, J., Meade, M.M., Graham, R. & Dudgeon, K. (1998). Physical exercise and psychological well-being: a critical review. *British Journal of Sports Medicine*, 32, 111–120.

Sexton, M., Mære, A. & Dahl, N.H. (1989). Exercise intensity and reduction in neurotic symptoms. *Acta Psychiatrica Scandinavia*, 80, 231–235.

Sharman, M.J., Cresswell, A.G. & Riek, S. (2006). Proprioceptive neuromuscular facilitation stretching: mechanisms and clinical implications. *Sports Medicine*, 36(11), 929–939.

Sigal, R.J., Kenny, G.P., Boule, N.G., Wells, G.A., Prud'homme, D., Fortier, M. & Jaffey, J. (2007). Effects of aerobic training, resistance training, or both on glycemic control in type 2 diabetes: a randomized trial. *Annals of Internal Medicine*, 147(6), 357–369.

Slemenda, C., Heilman, D.K., Brandt, K.D., Katz, B.P., Mazzuca, S.A., Braunstein, E.M. & Byrd, D. (1998). Reduced quadriceps strength relative to body weight: a risk factor for knee osteoarthritis in women? *Arthritis and Rheumatism*, 41(11), 1951–1959.

Starkey, D.B., Pollock, M.L., Ishida, Y., Welsch, M.A., Brechue, W.F., Graves, J.E. & Feigenbaum, M.S. (1996). Effect of resistance training volume on strength and muscle thickness. *Medicine and Science in Sports and Exercise*, 28, 1311–1320.

Stone, M.H., Plisk, S.S., Stone, M.E., Schilling, B.K., O'Bryant, H.S. & Pierce, K.C. (1998). Athletic performance development: volume load—I set vs. multiple sets, training velocity and training variation. *NSCA Journal*, 20, 22–31.

Strath, S.J., Swartz, A.M., Bassett, D.R. Jr., O'Brien, W.L., King, G.A. & Ainsworth, B.E. (2000). Evaluation of heart rate as a method for assessing moderate intensity physical activity. *Medicine and Science in Sports and Exercise*, 32 (Suppl 9), S465–S470.

Strohle, A., Feller, C., Onken, M., Godeman, F., Heinz, A. & Dimeo, F. (2005). The acute antipanic activity of aerobic exercise. *American Journal of Psychiatry*, 162, 2376–2378.

Sui, X., LaMonte, M.J. & Blair, S.N. (2007). Cardiorespiratory fitness as a predictor of nonfatal cardiovascular events in asymptomatic women and men. *American Journal of Epidemiology*, 165(12), 1413–1423.

Swain, D.P. & Franklin, B.A. (2002). VO$_2$ reserve and the minimal intensity for improving cardiorespiratory fitness. *Medicine and Science in Sports and Exercise*, 34(1), 152–157.

Tanaka, H., Monahan, K.D. & Seals, D.R. (2001). Age-predicted maximal heart rate revisited. *Journal of the American College of Cardiology*, 37, 153–356.

Tesch, P.A., Komi, P.V. & Hakkinen, K. (1987). Enzymatic adaptations consequent to long-term strength training. *International Journal of Sports Medicine*, 8(Suppl), 66–69.

Thompson, P.D., Franklin, B.A., Balady, G.J., Blair, S.N., Corrado, D., Mark estes III, N.A. & Costa, F. (2007). Exercise and acute cardiovascular events placing the risks into perspective: a scientific statement from the American Heart Association Council on Nutrition, Physical Activity, and Metabolism and the Council on Clinical Cardiology. *Circulation*, 115(17), 2358–2368.

Tran, Q.T., Docherty, D. & Behm, D. (2006). The effects of varying time under tension and volume load on acute neuromuscular responses. *European Journal of Applied Physiology*, 98 (4), 402–410.

Trivedi, M.H., Geer, T.L., Grannemann, B.D., Chambliss, H.O. & Jordan, A.N. (2006). Exercise as an augmentation strategy for treatment of major depression. *Journal of Psychiatric Pratice*, 12, 205–213.

U.S. Department of Health and Human Services. (1996). *Physical Activity and Health: A Report of the Surgeon General*. Atlanta, GA: U.S. Department of Health and Human Services, Centers for Disease Control and Prevention, National Center for Chronic Disease Prevention and Health Promotion.

U.S. Department of Health and Human Services. (1999). *Mental Health: A Report of the Surgeon General*. Rockville, MD: U.S. Department of Health and Human Services, Substance Abuse and Mental Health Services Administration, Center for Mental Health Services, National Institutes of Health, National Institute of Mental Health.

U.S. Department of Health and Human Services. (2008). *Physical Activity Guidelines Advisory Committee Report*. Retrieved from http://www.health.gov/paguidelines/Report/pdf/CommitteeReport.pdf

Utter, A.C., Robertson, R.J., Green, J.M., Suminski, R., McAnulty, S.R. & Nieman, D.C. (2004). Validation of the adult OMNI scale of perceived exertion for walking/running exercise. *Medicine and Science in Sports and Exercise*, 36, 1776–1780.

Whaley, M.H., Woodall, T., Kaminsky, L.A. & Emmett, J.D. (1997). Reliability of perceived exertion during graded exercises testing in apparently healthy adults. *Journal of Cardiopulmonary Rehabilitation*, 17, 37–42.

Witvrouw, E., Mahieu, N., Roosen, P. & McNair, P. (2007). The role of stretching in tendon injuries. *British Journal of Sports Medicine*, 41(4), 224–226.

Woolstenhulme, M.T., Griffiths, C.M., Woolstenhulme, E.M. & Parcell, A.C. (2006). Ballistic stretching increases flexibility and acute vertical jump height when combined with basketball activity. *Journal of Strength Conditioning Research*, 20(4), 799–803.

Wu, G. (2002). Evaluation of the effectiveness of tai chi for improving balance and preventing falls in the older population—a review. *Journal of the American Geriatrics Society*, 50(4), 746–754.

Youngstedt, S.D. (2005). Effects of exercise on sleep. *Clinics in Sports Medicine*, 24, 355–365.

Chapter 48

Adherence to physical activity

NIKOS L.D. CHATZISARANTIS, MARTIN S. HAGGER, MASATO KAWABATA
AND SVIATLANA KAMAROVA

SUMMARY

Regular participation in physical activities has become an important concern in recent years for governments and organizations worldwide. However, a finding is that physical activity interventions are not very effective. Such a trend may be due to the fact that content of physical activity interventions is not always informed by psychological theories despite that these theories have been shown to predict and explain physical activity participation. Therefore, theory-based interventions may be the first important step toward developing effective physical activity interventions. The present chapter describes theories of motivation, their limitations, and points out how theories can be used to inform physical activity interventions.

INTRODUCTION

Despite the health risks associated with physical inactivity, the general population is insufficiently active (Biddle, 1997). In addition, little is known about how to promote physical activity participation (Hagger, Chatzisarantis, & Biddle, 2002a). Indeed, a number of studies have demonstrated that interventions are not very successful in promoting physical activity participation (Chatzisarantis & Hagger, 2005; Haynes, McKibbon, & Kanani, 1996). One reason for this is that content of interventions has not been always informed by rigorous theories of human motivation (Hardeman, Johnston, Johnston, Bonetti, Wareham, & Kinmonth, 2002). The present chapter reviews some major theories of human motivation and provides some insights into how theory can inform practice.

OBJECTIVES

After reading this chapter you will be able to:

1 Describe theories of health behavior and their effects on physical activity participation.
2 Point out similarities and differences between theories.
3 Critically evaluate theories of health behavior and point out strengths and limitations of these theories.
4 Use theory to develop physical activity interventions.

THEORIES OF EXERCISE ADHERENCE

Motivational versus volitional theories of human motivation

One of the aims of theories of human motivation is to identify: (i) important psychological antecedents of physical activity participation; and (ii) psychological processes through which those antecedents affect physical activity participation. A psychological antecedent is a psychological event (i.e., attitude) that 'causes' physical activity participation. Psychological theories have aims and as a consequence they should be evaluated according to their aims and objectives. For example, psychologists generally agree that there are motivational theories that explain intentions, that is, why some individuals intend to exercise whereas some others do not. These theories are important because they provide information as to how we can help non-intenders to intend to exercise. However, a limitation of these theories is that they do not explain very well why individuals do not accomplish their intentions. For example, a number of researchers have documented that 57% of those who intend to exercise fail to do so within a one-year period (Orbell & Sheeran, 1998; Webb & Sheeran, 2006). Because of this 'gap' between intention and behavior, a number of researchers have developed volitional theories that explain the processes underpinning translation of intentions into action (Gollwitzer, 1990). In the next section, we introduce motivational and volitional theories of human motivation such as the theory of planned behavior, self-determination theory, transtheoretical model and implementation intentions and explain how these theories can be used to motivate adherence to physical activities or sport.

The theories of reasoned action and planned behavior

The theories of reasoned action and planned behavior have been influential in explaining physical activity participation. These theories posit that the construct of *intention* is an important antecedent of physical activity participation. These theories also propose that people are rationale decision-makers who choose to engage in physical activity or sport by processing information relating to the benefits and costs associated with physical activity (Fazio, 1990). Importantly, these theories explain intention formation and do not offer any explanation for the processes that underpin the translation of intentions into actual participation in physical activities (Ajzen, 2002b).

Theory of reasoned action

According to the theory of reasoned action, the performance of physical activity is function of a person's physical activity intentions. According to Ajzen (1991), intention indicates how hard people are willing to try and how much effort they expect to exert toward engaging in physical activities. Intention is function of attitudes and subjective norms. Attitudes refer to positive or negative evaluations toward physical activity. Subjective norms indicate the extent to which individuals believe that significant others (e.g., teachers, parents) approve or disapprove participation in physical activities. Overall, the theory of reasoned action predicts that individuals report strong physical activity intentions when they evaluate physical activity positively and believe that significant others approve participation in physical activities.

The theory of reasoned action also addresses antecedents of attitudes and subjective norms. The theory proposes that attitudes are function of benefits and costs (*behavioral beliefs*) and their evaluation of these benefits and costs (*outcome evaluations*) (Ajzen & Fishbein, 1980). Similarly, subjective norms are function of normative beliefs which describe expectations that important referent individuals approve or disapprove of physical activity participation (Ajzen, 1991; Ajzen & Fishbein, 1980). Motivation to comply describes tendencies to endorse the wishes of the salient referents. The theory of reasoned action is shown in Figure 48.1.

To date, a number of studies have supported the basic tenets of the theory of reasoned action (Hagger, Chatzisarantis, & Biddle, 2002b). Specifically, in the exercise domain, tests of the theory of reasoned action have demonstrated that intentions predict physical activity participation. In addition, it has been shown that attitudes exert strong influences on intentions with a lesser role for subjective norms (Hagger, Chatzisarantis, & Biddle, 2002b). However, some studies have documented that age influences the effect of subjective norms and attitudes on intentions. For example, Wankel, Mummery, Stephens, and Craig (1994) pointed out that while the effect of subjective norms on intentions increases with age the converse is true for attitudes (see also Hagger et al., 2002b).

In addition to confirming basic tenets of the theory of reasoned action, there are studies that reveal behavioral and normative beliefs related to physical activity. Behavioral beliefs observed in the literature include: 'friendships,' 'weight control,' 'health,' 'time,' 'fun,' 'get fit,' 'stay in shape,' 'improve skills,' 'get an injury' (Hagger, Chatzisarantis, Biddle, & Orbell, 2001). Important referents include parents, grandparents, siblings, friends and schoolteachers (Hagger et al., 2001).

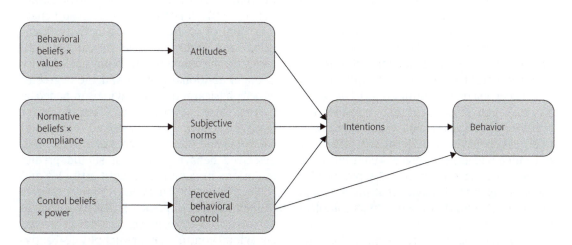

Figure 48.1 The theories of reasoned action and planned behavior.

Theory of planned behavior

Although the theory of reasoned action has been successful in predicting and explaining participation in physical activities, this theory was designed to explain behaviors that are under complete volitional control. This means that the theory was designed to explain behaviors that individuals could perform at a satisfactory level if they were exerting a significant amount of effort. To illustrate this through an example, consider that one of my life aspirations is to become the next US president. The achievement of this life aspiration is impossible for the first author of this chapter because he is not a US citizen. No matter how hard he tries, he almost guarantees that he will never become the next US president. Consider now another of his life aspirations, that is, to become the next Greek president. This can be a more realistic aspiration because he is a Greek citizen. If he tries hard enough, he may become the next Greek president. Hence, his aspiration to become the next Greek president is 'to some extent' under his volitional control. However, even this aspiration is not under his 'complete' volitional control because there are obvious circumstances and barriers that may prevent his efforts to become the next Greek president.

Ajzen (1985) suggested that the boundary condition of *complete* volitional control was a limitation of the theory because it is difficult to meet in real life. As Ajzen (1985) acknowledged: "Even very mundane activities, which can usually be performed (or not performed) at will, are sometimes subject to the influence of factors beyond one's control" (p. 24). For example, although most of us may consider the behavior of 'eating an apple every day' a relatively easy behavior to perform, still forgetting or limited budgets may prevent us from doing so. For this reason, Ajzen (1985) proposed a theory of planned behavior that predicts and explains behaviors that are not under complete volitional control.

As in the theory of reasoned action, the theory of planned behavior proposes that intention is an antecedent of physical activity behavior and that intention is function of attitudes and subjective norms with corresponding behavioral beliefs and normative beliefs, respectively. However, the theory of planned behavior also proposes that when perceived control over behavior is incomplete then perceived behavioral control can influence physical activity participation (Ajzen, 1985).

According to Ajzen (1991), the construct of perceived behavioral control is similar to Bandura's (1977) construct of self-efficacy that indicates ability to engage in physical activities. The construct of perceived behavioral control is also function of *control beliefs* and *perceived power* of these beliefs (Ajzen, 1985). Control beliefs refer to the perceived presence of factors that may facilitate or impede physical activity participation. Perceived power describes perceived impact facilitative or inhibiting factors may have on physical activity participation (Ajzen, 1985). According to the theory of planned behavior, it is possible to calculate an indirect measure of perceived behavioral control by multiplying each control belief by its corresponding perceived power ratings (Ajzen, 1991).

The inclusion of perceived behavioral control in the theory of reasoned action is important because it reveals barriers that influence physical activity participation (Ajzen, 1985). In addition, if perceived behavioral control predicts physical activity intentions and behavior, the researcher can ascertain the extent to which physical activity is under volitional control and the degree to which physical activity behavior is impeded by barriers (Ajzen, 1985). Further, Ajzen and Driver (1991) suggested that perceived behavioral control would exert two types of effects. First, perceived behavioral control should predict intentions in conjunction with attitudes and subjective norms. This additive effect reflects the *motivational* influence of perceived control on intentions to exercise. Second, perceived behavioral control may predict physical activity behavior directly when perceptions of behavioral control are realistic. This direct effect reflects the effect of actual, real constraints or barriers to doing the behavior. These relationships are shown in Figure 48.1.

In the exercise domain, studies have supported the effects of perceived behavioral control in a variety of exercise contexts such as school settings, workplace and in different populations including young people (Hagger et al., 2001), clinical populations (Courneya, Blanchard, & Laing, 2001; Courneya, Keats, & Turner, 2000), and the general population (Wankel et al., 1994). In addition, studies have documented that perceived behavioral control predicts both physical activity intentions and behavior (Hagger et al., 2002b). Further, some studies pointed out that the effect of perceived behavioral control on physical activity intentions is stronger for women and older populations (Wankel et al., 1994).

A large number of studies have also identified barriers and facilitating factors related to exercise such as 'weather,' 'age,' 'heart pain,' 'budget,' 'fatigue,' 'time' (Godin, Valois, Jobin, & Ross, 1991; Hagger et al., 2001; Wankel et al., 1994). Studies have demonstrated that control beliefs vary across different populations and activities. For example, barriers related to 'weather' and 'equipment' characterize control beliefs for outdoor activities (Ajzen, 1991). Age and 'fear of having a heart attack' are control beliefs that are endorsed by older and clinical populations (Godin et al., 1991). However, these beliefs are not endorsed by younger populations (Wankel et al., 1994).

Designing interventions based on the theories of reasoned action and planned behavior

One reason for which tests of the theories of reasoned action and planned behavior are useful is that they can inform the development of physical activity interventions (Chatzisarantis & Hagger, 2005; Hardeman et al., 2002). Given that research has shown that attitudes and perceptions of control are the most impor-

tant antecedents of physical activity intentions, it can be suggested that interventions should target attitudes and perceived behavioral control.

The theories of reasoned action and planned behavior propose that attitudes and perceived behavioral control can change by changing their underlying beliefs. According to Ajzen (2002a) changes in beliefs are most likely to be effective when modal salient beliefs are targeted. Modal beliefs are the most popular beliefs that are endorsed by majority of individuals. Modal salient beliefs can be identified by using open-ended questionnaires that ask individuals to list beliefs about physical activity participation (Ajzen & Fishbein, 1980).

Some studies have already used open-ended questionnaires to identify modal salient beliefs in the exercise domain. For example, Hagger et al. (2002) found that young people endorsed 'fitness,' 'fun,' 'skills,' 'injuries,' and 'body temperature' as their salient behavioral beliefs. This means that exercise interventions should try to change these particular behavioral beliefs. That said, the large variation in modal beliefs across populations and behaviors suggests that interventions should be tailored toward the modal beliefs of the target population. For example, interventions that aim to promote exercise among adults should target behavioral beliefs of adults and not beliefs of other populations.

After identifying beliefs, the theories of reasoned action and planned behavior propose that persuasive communications in the form of advertisements, face-to-face discussion or any other method can be applied in designing interventions (Ajzen & Fishbein, 1980). Persuasive communications involve arguments endorsing the benefits of physical activity while at the same time downplaying the costs. For example, a persuasive appeal that aims to change the attitudes of adolescents toward exercise may take the form of the following text:

Participating in regular exercise is fun. You will learn how to play a new game or sport.

Physical activity also improves your general level of fitness while at the same time it makes you feel good.

This persuasive appeal should change young people's attitudes because it targets the accessible behavioral beliefs of young people. Unfortunately, there are not many studies that examined effectiveness of the theory of planned behavior in promoting participation in physical activities and some of the studies have produced inconsistent results and have had significant limitations. Specifically, Rodgers and Brawley (1993) reported that a physical activity intervention produced changes in attitudes, self-efficacy and participation in an exercise program. However, Smith and Biddle (1999) found that a physical activity intervention did not change attitudes, subjective norms, perception of control, and intentions. These inconsistent results may be owed to targeting non-accessible behavioral beliefs. Indeed, Chatzisarantis and Hagger (2005) pointed out that interventions targeting accessible beliefs changed attitudes and intentions but not physical activity participation. Therefore, an important avenue for future research is to examine effectiveness of intervention programs that target accessible versus non-accessible beliefs.

Limitations of the theories of reasoned action and planned behavior

One limitation of the theories of reasoned action and planned behavior is that they do not indicate how persuasive messages should be structured. As a consequence, practitioners need to consult other theories of persuasion in developing interventions. The elaboration-likelihood model is a model of persuasion that shows how persuasive messages can be structured so that practitioners obtain maximal effects (Petty & Cacioppo, 1986). According to this model, there are two routes to attitude change. A central route induces attitude change through thoughtful elaboration processes. Elaboration describes the extent to which individuals are motivated to think carefully about the arguments that are contained in a persuasive communication. Elaboration is measured by counting the number of thoughts that a person generates during information processing and/or by evaluating the quality of arguments presented in the persuasive communication (Petty & Cacioppo, 1986). There is also a peripheral route to attitude change which occurs as a result of automatic/associative processes. The elaboration likelihood model predicts that attitude change through the central route induces greater temporal persistence and resistance to counter persuasion than attitude change that arises from peripheral route.

The elaboration-likelihood model has been used in studies of attitude change but there is a relative dearth of research examining this model in conjunction with the theory of planned behavior. Quine, Rutter, and Arnold (2001) documented that a series of persuasive messages that motivated young cyclists to elaborate accessible beliefs was successful in changing behavioral beliefs and normative beliefs but not perceived barriers related to wearing a helmet. Therefore, an interesting avenue for future research is to design and evaluate exercise interventions that take into consideration assumptions underlying the elaboration-likelihood model and assumptions underlying the theory of planned behavior.

Another limitation of interventions that are founded on the theories of reasoned action and planned behavior is that they can induce positive intentions among non-intenders by changing behavioral beliefs, normative beliefs, and/or control beliefs. However, these interventions cannot help people convert intention into actual participation in physical activities. This is because the theories are *motivational theories* that can only facilitate strong intentions. In contrast, *volitional theories* of intention are most appropriate in facilitating the enactment of behavioral intentions and can be implemented alongside interventions based on the theories of reasoned action and planned behavior.

Self-determination theory

Self-determination theory is a theory of human motivation which assumes that individuals possess three basic and universal psychological needs for autonomy (need to experience oneself as initiator and regulator of one's action), competence (need to produce outcomes and understand the instrumentalities leading to these outcomes), and relatedness (need to experience satisfactory relationships with others and with the social order more in general). The theory proposes that satisfaction of universal psychological needs facilitates optimal motivation and experienced psychological well-being. The theory also proposes that, if psychological needs are thwarted, individuals are more likely to experience ill-being and exhibit less optimal forms of motivation (Deci & Ryan, 1985).

Based on assumptions related to psychological needs, self-determination theory differentiates interpersonal contexts into autonomy supportive contexts that facilitate satisfaction of the psychological need for autonomy and controlling contexts that frustrate the psychological need for autonomy. Deci and Ryan (1985) also identified three critical contextual factors that influence satisfaction of the psychological need for autonomy and behavioral persistence. The first contextual factor is *provision of meaningful rationale* and it describes the extent to which practitioners explain to individuals, in a meaningful way, why attempts to engage in physical activities are important (Deci, Eghari, Patrick, & Leone, 1994; Deci & Ryan, 1985). *Perspective taking* is a second characteristic of autonomous contexts and it describes the extent to which practitioners encourage expression of personal opinions (Deci & Ryan, 1985). In contrast, absence of perspective taking is a characteristic of

controlling contexts and it is present when practitioners disregard expression of personal opinions about physical activity programs (Deci et al., 1994). Provision of choice is a feature of autonomous contexts and it is present in those contexts when practitioners provide individuals with freedom to choose whether or not to engage in physical activities (Deci et al., 1994). The opposite of free choice is forced choice, a characteristic of controlling environments, and it is present in those environments when practitioners force or coerce individuals into a decision (Moller, Deci, & Ryan, 2006).

Thus far research has documented that perceptions related to autonomy support predict physical activity intentions and behavior (Chatzisarantis, Hagger, Biddle, Smith, & Wang, 2003; Hagger & Chatzisarantis, 2012). Evidence also points out that the effects of perceptions of autonomy support on physical activity behavior are mediated by perceptions related to satisfaction of basic psychological needs (Edmunds, Ntoumanis, & Duda, 2008). Overall, research has revealed that self-determination theory provides a useful framework that helps practitioners and researchers predict and explain physical activity participation.

Designing interventions based on self-determination theory

An intervention based on self-determination theory requires practitioners to provide rationale about benefits of physical activity. This practice (i.e., *provision of rationale*; Deci et al., 1994) is similar to interventions and practices that stem from the theory of planned behavior (Ajzen, 1991). However, interventions that are based on self-determination theory place also emphasis on interpersonal context in which rationale is communicated. Interpersonal context refers to the ways that practitioners communicate rationale to individuals. If the practitioner obliges individuals to engage in physical activities, then the communication climate is controlling. On the other hand, if the practitioner creates rapport with people by being empathetic and by providing choice, then the communication climate is autonomy supportive.

There are many different ways through which a practitioner can facilitate rapport. One way to achieve this is to acknowledge difficulties associated with completing an intervention program (i.e., *perspective taking*; Deci et al., 1994). Another way is to inform individuals that their opinion about the intervention program is valued highly and encourage them to express their opinion about how the program can be modified so that it serves their needs and desires. Sense of choice can be enhanced by using modal operators such as 'may' and 'could' during communication and avoid using pressuring modal operators such as 'should' and 'must.'

To date, studies have shown that behavioral change is more lasting when practitioners are autonomy supportive. In a meta-analysis of empirical evidence, Ng, Ntoumanis and Thorgensen et al. (2012) demonstrated that changes in perceptions of autonomy support were effective in promoting health-related behaviors including physical activity. In addition, Chatzisarantis and Hagger (2009) demonstrated that interventions that facilitate autonomy supportive climates were more effective in promoting physical activity than interventions that communicated benefits of physical activity only. Interestingly, in a recent field experiment, Chatzisarantis, Hagger, Kamarova, and Kawabata, (2012) documented that autonomy supportive intervention programs promoted participation in physical activities for a larger proportion of individuals relative to interventions that provided a rationale only. These findings are important as they suggest that physical activity interventions that are founded on self-determination theory produce a larger effect for a greater proportion of individuals. In addition, evidence suggests that effectiveness of physical activity interventions can be considerably increased by communicating rationale and benefits of physical activity in autonomy supportive ways.

Implementation intentions and the translation of intentions into action

One limitation of motivational theories is that they do not explain how intentions are translated into physical activity participation. People often forget to carry out their intentions or implementation of intentions may be interrupted by other competing goal-directed behaviors (Gollwitzer & Brandstatter, 1997; Verplanken & Faes, 1999). One approach that has been put forward to resolve the intention-behavior gap is implementation intentions. Implementation intentions are self-regulatory strategies that ask people to plan in advance *when*, *where*, and *how* to exercise. According to Gollwitzer (1990), implementation intentions assist people convert their intentions into actual participation in physical activities by helping them remember when they are supposed to exercise or by assisting people to recognize opportunities for action (Gollwitzer & Brandstatter, 1997; Orbell, Hodgkins, & Sheeran, 1997).

Recent research has evaluated the effectiveness of interventions that *combine* motivational techniques with volitional techniques such as implementation intentions in influencing physical activity (Koestner, Lekes, Powers, & Chicoine, 2002; Milne, Orbell, & Sheeran, 2002; Prestwich, Lawton, & Conner, 2003; Sheeran & Silverman, 2003). Research has corroborated the utility of these combined techniques in increasing physical activity participation. For example, in a study conducted by Milne et al. (2002) it was documented that implementation exercises strengthened the utility of attitudes in influencing physical activity participation. Similarly, Sheeran and Silverman (2003) found that an intervention that combined an application of the theory of planned behavior and implementation intentions was more effective in promoting attendance at health and training courses than an intervention that was based on the theory of planned behavior only (see also Prestwich et al., 2003). In a series of experimental and field studies Chatzisarantis and colleagues have also documented that implementation exercises were more beneficial for individuals who were forced to exercise and less so for individuals whose psychological need for autonomy was satisfied (Chatzisarantis, Hagger, & Wang, 2010).

Transtheoretical model

The transtheoretical model is a stage-model of behavioral change that incorporates behavior change along with social cognitive constructs to identify the progression that people undergo when changing behaviors (Prochaska & DiClemente, 1982). Central to this model is the premise that people pass through stages towards making a behavior change and each stage is characterized by a particular pattern of psycho-social and behavioral variables. The stages of change are precontemplation, contemplation, preparation, action, and maintenance. At the *precontemplation* stage people do not intend to exercise and they do not experience a need to change behaviors. *Contemplators* have realised the need for change and are thinking about doing so. However, at contemplation stage individuals have no clear idea about how to make the change. People who are in the *preparation* stage want to change and are making the necessary personal and social adjustments and commitment towards changing behavior. In the *action* stage, people actually engage in physical activities and they are beginning to make successful and unsuccessful attempts to change their behavior. During this stage people may relapse to a previous behavioral pattern more akin to their former unhealthy lifestyle. Finally, the *maintenance* stage is characterized by a continuity of successful and consistent engagement in physical activities.

These *stages of change* are the most widely adopted aspects of the model, although there are also levels of change and *processes of change* (see Table 1). Processes of change refer to sets of psychological factors that motivate people to move from one stage to another. The transtheoretical model proposes a number of key factors such as *self-efficacy* (Bandura, 1977) and *decisional balance*. Self-efficacy refers to an individual's beliefs in their ability to make desired behavioral changes to gain desirable outcomes. Research adopting the transtheoretical model has supported differences in the level of self-efficacy across the stages of change, with the highest coinciding with people in the maintenance stage and the lowest for those in the precontemplation stage (Armitage, Povey, & Arden, 2003).

Decisional balance reflects people's beliefs about the advantages and disadvantages of engaging in physical activities. When the advantages outweigh the disadvantages, the person will be in the preparation stage (Prochaska et al., 1994). In summary, the research supported effectiveness of self-efficacy and decisional balance in explaining changes across states of change (Marshall & Biddle, 2001). The transtheoretical model has also been investigated within the framework of theory of planned behavior. There are some similarities between antecedents of intention in the theory of planned behavior and the decisional balance and self-efficacy constructs in the transtheoretical model. For example, the belief-based measures of attitude reflect the advantages and disadvantages (behavioral beliefs). In addition, the perceived behavioral control variable is similar to a self-efficacy construct.

Table 48.1 *Stages and processes of change*

Pre-contemplation	Contemplation	Preparation	Action	Maintenance
Consciousness raising: public education using mass media, small groups	Self-revaluation: re-evaluation of self-image through group activities. Values clarification exercises	Self and social liberation: belief that one can change and commit to change and create social conditions that facilitate change	Using and fostering social support through peer groups	Continuing positive reinforcement and social support through continuance of support groups
Dramatic relief: taking action to reduce anxiety and negative emotions through role playing, grieving, testimonies			Contingency management: reinforcing positive steps towards desired behaviors	Stimulus control: remove triggers for unhealthy behavior
Environmental re-evaluation: learning how one's actions affect self-others through discussions with family members			Counter-conditioning: learning to substitute healthy behaviors for problem behaviors	Maintain self-efficacy: maintain confidence to resist temptation through regular discussions

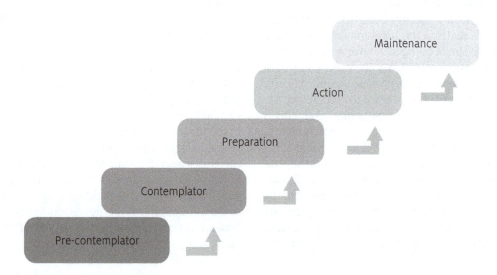

Figure 48.2 The theories of reasoned action and planned behavior.

CONCLUSION

Overall, there has been considerable progress in research that aims to identify psychological determinants of participation in physical activities or sport. Thus far evidence suggests that attitudes and perceived behavioral control and autonomy supportive interpersonal contexts constitute three important determinants of physical activity participation. However, it is also important to note that although interventions that target these variables are effective in changing physical activity intentions, their effectiveness in altering participation levels in physical activities or sport is relatively low. To that end, interventions combining strategies that aim to change intentions and implementation exercises that help individuals enact their previously formed intentions may be a good way to motivate adherence to physical activities and sport.

LEARNING AIDS

1 What is a persuasive communication?

It is an intervention technique that is endorsed by theory of planned behavior. A persuasive communication involves a message that endorses benefits of physical activity and downplays disadvantages of physical activity.

2 What is interpersonal context?

Interpersonal context refers to the communication climate: it describes ways through which an intervener communicates the health message to recipients of these messages. In self-determination theory the communication climate can be autonomy supportive or controlling.

3 What is the benefit associated with intervention programs that involve implementation intention exercises?

Implementation exercises help individuals fulfill their plans. Motivational techniques stemming from self-determination theory and theory of planned behavior do not address issues related to effective translation of intentions into actions.

4 What is the difference between the transtheoretical model and the theory of planned behavior?

The theory of planned behavior addresses antecedents of physical activity. This theory does not indicate how these antecedents change as individuals move from one stage to another. The transtheoretical model describes how different antecedents influence physical activity across different stages.

REVIEW QUESTIONS

1 Describe the theory of planned behavior and self-determination theory.

2 Design interventions that are based on tenets of self-determination theory or theory of planned behavior.

3   What is the difference in the content of interventions that are based on the theory of planned behavior and self-determination theory?

4   What is the benefit of an intervention that is based on implementation intentions?

5   Describe the transtheoretical model.

EXERCISES

1   This exercise will help you identify beliefs about physical activity participation. Following Ajzen's theory of planned behavior, develop and conduct interviews that identify behavioral, normative and control beliefs for (i) young individuals (15 to 17 years old) and (ii) pensioners. Then on the basis of these interviews develop persuasive messages that target physical activity behavior for young individuals and pensioners. After completing this exercise (i) you will realize that beliefs about physical activity vary greatly across different groups of individuals and as a consequence (ii) understand that physical activity interventions should be tailored around beliefs of your target population.

2   Develop implementation intention exercises for physically inactive individuals. Then ask a group of physically inactive individuals do your implementation exercises and evaluate whether these exercises have been beneficial in terms of changing physical activity habits.

ADDITIONAL READING

A useful resource for understanding theory based intervention can be found at Ajzen's website at: http://people.umass.edu/aizen/tpb.html.

Ajzen, I., Albarracín, D. & Hornik, R. (Eds.) (2007). *Prediction and change of health behavior: Applying the reasoned action approach.* Mahwah, NJ: Lawrence Erlbaum Associates.

Deci, E. & Ryan, R. (1985). *Intrinsic motivation and self-determination in human behavior.* Springer.

REFERENCES

Ajzen, I. (1985). From intentions to actions: A theory of planned behavior. In J. Kuhl & J. Beckmann (Eds.), *Action-control: From cognition to behavior* (pp.11–39). Heidelberg: Springer.

Ajzen, I. (1991). The theory of planned behavior. *Organizational Behavior and Human Decision Processes, 50,* 179–211.

Ajzen, I. (2002a). Perceived behavioral control, self-efficacy, locus of control, and the theory of planned behavior. *Journal of Applied Social Psychology, 32,* 1–20.

Ajzen, I. (2002b). Residual effects of past on later behavior: Habituation and reasoned action perspectives. *Personality and Social Psychology Review, 6,* 107–122.

Ajzen, I. & Driver, B.L. (1991). Prediction of leisure participation from behavioral, normative, and control beliefs: An application of the theory of planned behavior. *Leisure Sciences, 13,* 185–204.

Ajzen, I. & Fishbein, M. (1980). *Understanding attitudes and predicting social behavior.* New Jersey: Prentice Hall.

Armitage, C.J. & Conner, M. (2001). Efficacy of the theory of planned behaviour: A meta-analytic review. *British Journal of Social Psychology, 40,* 471–499.

Armitage, C.J., Povey, R. & Arden, M.A. (2003). Evidence for discontinuity patterns across the stages of change: A role for attitudinal ambivalence. *Psychology and Health, 18,* 373–386.

Bandura, A. (1997). *Self-efficacy: The exercise of control.* New York: Freeman.

Biddle, S.J.H. (1997). Cognitive theories of motivation and the physical self. In K.R. Fox (Ed.), The physical self (pp.59–82). Champaign, IL: Human Kinetics.

Chatzisarantis, N.L.D. & Hagger, M.S. (2005). Effects of a brief intervention based on the theory of planned behavior on leisure time physical activity participation. *Journal of Sport and Exercise Psychology, 27,* 470–487.

Chatzisarantis, N.L.D. & Hagger, M. (2009). Effects of an intervention based on Self-Determination Theory on self-reported leisure-time physical activity participation. *Psychology and Health, 24,* 29–48.

Chatzisarantis, N.L.D., Hagger, M. & Wang, J. (2010). Evaluating the effects of implementation intention and self concordance on behaviour. *British Journal of Psychology, 101,* 705–718.

Chatzisarantis, N.L.D., Hagger, M.S., Biddle, S.J.H., Smith, B. & Wang, J.C.K. (2003). A meta-analysis of perceived locus of causality in exercise, sport, and physical education contexts. *Journal of Sport and Exercise Psychology, 25,* 284–306.

Chatzisarantis, N.L.D., Hagger, M.S., Kamarova, S. & Kawabata, M. (2012). When effects of the universal psychological need for autonomy on health behaviour extend to a large proportion of individuals: A field experiment. *British Journal of Health Psychology, 17,* 785–797.

Courneya, K.S. (1995). Understanding readiness for regular physical activity in older individuals: An application of the theory of planned behavior. *Health Psychology, 14,* 80–87.

Courneya, K.S., Blanchard, C.M. & Laing, D.M. (2001). Exercise adherence in breast cancer survivors training for a dragon boat competition: A preliminary investigation. *Psycho-Oncology, 10,* 444–452.

Courneya, K.S., Keats, M.R. & Turner, A.R. (2000). Social cognitive determinants of hospital-based exercise in cancer patients following high-dose chemotherapy and bone marrow transplantation. *International Journal of Behavioral Medicine, 7,* 189–203.

Deci, E.L. & Ryan, R.M. (1985). *Intrinsic motivation and self-determination in human behavior.* New York: Plenum Press.

Deci, E.L., Eghrari, H., Patrick, B.C. & Leone, D.R. (1994). Facilitating internalization: The self-determination theory perspective. *Journal of Personality, 62,* 119–142.

Edmunds, J., Ntoumanis, N. & Duda, J.L.D. (2008). Testing a self-determination theory based teaching style in the exercise domain. *European Journal of Social Psychology, 38,* 375–388.

Fazio, R.H. (1990). Multiple processes by which attitudes guide behavior: The MODE model as an integrative framework. In M.P. Zanna (Ed.), *Advances in Experimental Social Psychology* (Vol. 23, pp.75–109). San Diego, CA: Academic Press.

Feather, N.T. (1982). Expectancy-value approaches: Present status and future directions. In N.T. Feather (Ed.), *Expectations and actions: Expectancy-value models in psychology* (pp.395–420). Hillsdale, NJ: Erlbaum.

Godin, G., Valois, R., Jobin, J. & Ross, A. (1991). Prediction of intention to exercise of individuals who have suffered from coronary heart disease. *Journal of Clinical Psychology, 47,* 762–772.

Gollwitzer, P.M. (1990). Action phases and mindsets. In E.T. Higgins & R.M. Sorrentino (Eds.), *The handbook of motivation and cognition: Foundations of social behavior* (Vol. 2, pp.53–92). New York: Guilford Press.

Gollwitzer, P.M. & Brandstatter, V. (1997). Implementation intentions and effective goal pursuit. *Journal of Personality and Social Psychology, 73,* 186–199.

Hagger, M.S. & Chatzisarantis, N.L.D. (2012). Transferring motivation from educational to extramural contexts: A review of the trans-contextual model. *European Journal of Psychology of Education, 27,* 195–212.

Hagger, M.S., Chatzisarantis, N.L.D & Biddle, S.J.H. (2002a). The influence of autonomous and controlling motives on physical activity intentions within the theory of planned behaviour. *British Journal of Health Psychology, 7,* 283–297.

Hagger, M.S., Chatzisarantis, N.L.D & Biddle, S.J.H. (2002b). A meta-analytic review of the theories of reasoned action and planned behavior in physical activity: Predictive validity and the contribution of additional variables. *Journal of Sport and Exercise Psychology, 24,* 3–32.

Hagger, M.S., Chatzisarantis, N., Biddle, S.J.H. & Orbell, S. (2001). Antecedents of children's physical activity intentions and behaviour: Predictive validity and longitudinal effects. *Psychology and Health, 16*, 391–407.

Hardeman, W., Johnston, M., Johnston, D.W., Bonetti, D., Wareham, N.J. & Kinmonth, A.L. (2002). Application of the theory of planned behaviour change interventions: A systematic review. *Psychology and Health, 17*, 123–158.

Haynes R., McKibbon, K. & Kanani, R. (1996). Systematic review of randomised trials of interventions to assist patients to follow prescriptions for medications. *Lancet, 348*, 383–386.

Koestner, R., Lekes, N., Powers, T.A. & Chicoine, E. (2002). Attaining personal goals: Self-concordance plus implementation intentions equals success. *Journal of Personality and Social Psychology, 83*, 231–244.

Marshall, S.J. & Biddle, S.J.H. (2001). The transtheoretical model of behavior change: A meta-analysis of applications to physical activity and exercise. *Annals of Behavioral Medicine, 23*, 229–246.

Milne, S.E., Orbell, S. & Sheeran, P. (2002). Combining motivational and volitional interventions to promote exercise participation: Protection motivation theory and implementation intentions. *British Journal of Health Psychology, 7*, 163–184.

Moller, A.C., Deci, E.L. & Ryan, R.M. (2006). Choice and ego-depletion: The moderating role of autonomy. *Personality and Social Psychology Bulletin, 32*, 1024–1036.

Ng, J., Ntoumanis, N., Thogersen-Ntoumani, E.C., Deci, E.L., Ryan, R.M., Duda, J.L. & Williams, G.C. (2012). Self-Determination Theory applied to health contexts: A meta-analysis. *Perspectives on Psychological Science, 7*, 325–340.

Orbell, S., Hodgkins, S. & Sheeran, P. (1997). Implementation intentions and the theory of planned behavior. *Personality and Social Psychology Bulletin, 23*, 945–954.

Orbell, S. & Sheeran, P. (1998). 'Inclined abstainers': A problem for predicting health related behaviour. *British Journal of Social Psychology, 37*, 151–165.

Petty, R.E. & Cacioppo, J. (1986). *Communication and persuasion: Central and peripheral routes to attitude change.* New York: Springer-Verlag.

Prestwich, A., Lawton, R. & Conner, M. (2003). The use of implementation intentions and the decision balance sheet in promoting exercise behaviour. *Psychology and Health, 10*, 707–721.

Prochaska, J.O. & DiClemente, C.C. (1982). Transtheoretical theory: Towards a more integrated model of change. *Journal of Consultative Clinical Psychology, 19*, 276–288.

Prochaska, J.O., Velicer, W.F., Rossie, J.S., Goldstein, M.G., Marcus, B.H., Rakowski, W., Fiore, C., Harlow, L.L., Redding, C.A., Rosenbloom, D.A. & Rossi, S.R. (1994). Stages of change and decisional balance for 12 problem behaviors. *Health Psychology, 13*, 39–46.

Quine, L., Rutter, D. & Arnold, L. (2001). Persuading school-age cyclists to use safety helmets: Effectiveness of an intervention based on the theory of planned behaviour. *British Journal of Health Psychology, 6*, 327–345.

Rodgers, W.M. & Brawley, L.R. (1993). Using both self-efficacy theory and the theory of planned behavior to discriminate adherers and dropouts from structured programs. *Journal of Applied Sport Psychology, 5*, 195–206.

Sheeran, P., Norman, P. & Orbell, S. (1999). Evidence that intentions based on attitudes better predict behaviour than intentions based on subjective norms. *European Journal of Social Psychology, 29*, 403–406.

Sheeran, P. & Silverman, M. (2003). Evaluation of three interventions to promote workplace health and safety: Evidence for the utility of implementation intentions. *Social Science and Medicine, 56*, 2153–2163.

Smith, R.A. & Biddle, S.J.H. (1999). Attitudes and exercise adherence: Test of the theories of reasoned action and planned behaviour. *Journal of Sports Sciences, 17*, 269–281.

Verplanken, B. & Faes, S. (1999). Good intentions, bad habits, and effects of forming implementation intentions on healthy eating. *European Journal of Social Psychology, 29*, 591–604.

Wankel, L.M., Mummery, W.K., Stephens, T. & Craig, C.L. (1994). Prediction of physical activity intention from social psychological variables: Results from the Campbell's survey of well-being. *Journal of Sport & Exercise Psychology, 16*, 56–69.

Webb, T.L. & Sheeran, P. (2006). Does changing behavioural intentions engender behavior change? A meta-analysis of the experimental evidence. *Psychological Bulletin, 132*, 249–268.

Chapter 49

Counselling to promote physical activity

SARAH J. HARDCASTLE AND ADRIAN H. TAYLOR

SUMMARY

Despite the compelling evidence of the health benefits of being physically active, few people are sufficiently active to benefit their health and there is a need to focus on effective interventions to increase motivation for continued physical activity participation. Counselling interventions, such as motivational interviewing show promise in facilitating lifestyle behavioural changes through the promotion of autonomous motives for change. This chapter summarises the key principles and strategies used in motivational interviewing and outlines what exercise professionals can do to increase the likelihood that counselling will promote behaviour change. Based on the underlying principles of motivational interviewing and the strategies employed, there is real promise that motivational interviewing interventions are likely to promote long-lasting, sustained behaviour change. This is because of its central emphasis on eliciting personal motives for change, working through ambivalence, building confidence and promoting more autonomous forms of motivation.

INTRODUCTION

The links between physical activity and physical and mental health are widely acknowledged in global policy documents (e.g., WHO, US Surgeon General's Report, UK's CMO's Report) and systematic reviews are regularly updated and published. Despite the evidence of the health benefits of physical activity, few people are sufficiently active to benefit their health and there is a need to focus on effective interventions to increase PA. Ecological models have been proposed for understanding the correlates and factors influencing physical activity, and a focus on different settings has helped to build an evidence base for how to increase physical activity in the natural environment, in the workplace and in educational settings, by active commuting, in various social and domestic settings (e.g., childcare groups, elderly care homes, gardening), and in leisure settings (e.g., through sport and leisure facilities), and in primary (i.e., initial places of access to general practitioners, nurses and other health professionals for prevention and treatment) and secondary health care for inpatient and outpatients (e.g., treatment and rehabilitation services for heart disease, cancer, mental illness).

In this wide range of settings, health professionals and exercise and sports practitioners may have the opportunity to facilitate increases in physical activity explicitly for the prevention and treatment of health problems, or simply for enjoyment, pleasure and social benefits. This chapter identifies contrasting psychological approaches that are being used to help promote behaviour change. The effec-

tiveness of traditional approaches will be discussed, linked to other chapters in this book about various theories of behaviour change. The chapter will then focus on less directive and more client-centred approaches that fall under the umbrella of motivational interviewing (MI). The focus throughout will be mainly on individual counselling approaches, simply because much less is known about the effectiveness of group-based counselling for promoting physical activity.

OBJECTIVES

After reading this chapter you should be able to:

1   Explain why motivational interviewing is a promising behaviour change intervention.
2   Define the 'spirit' underpinning motivational interviewing.
3   Describe the four guiding principles of motivational interviewing.
4   Identify the four micro-skills necessary for effective counselling.
5   Summarise strategies used in an MI session to explore motivation and ambivalence.

THE IMPORTANCE OF COUNSELLING

In the UK and other countries, a popular way of promoting physical activity has been via something called a primary care exercise referral or exercise on prescription scheme (ERS) (http://www.bhfactive.org.uk/sites/Exercise-Referral-Toolkit/). Typically, doctors identify a patient who is overweight or with low mood and given them a prescription to take to a local exercise facility (gym), perhaps involving a free or subsidised entrance fee to attend twice a week for 10 weeks. The patient will arrive at the gym, various bits of information about lifestyle and health will be collected and they will be given an introduction to the equipment or exercise options will be made available to them by an exercise practitioner. A progressive programme will be set with periodic reviews of progress and limited supervision. The practitioner may work with the client to encourage the person to remain a gym member after the prescription but may have had little or no formal training in

health behaviour change techniques for sustaining an increase in physical activity more generally. A recent review (Pavey et al., 2011) highlighted the not surprising consequential effects. Compared with control participants, in randomised controlled trials those referred to ERS were no more physically active after 9–12 months.

We can speculate why this is, but across the 20 studies reviewed only 72% of those referred actually started the exercise programme and there was then only 48% adherence. Few studies attempted to identify the determinants of uptake and adherence. It seemed that women were more likely to begin an ERS but were less likely to adhere to it than men, and older people were more likely to begin and adhere to an ERS. It is also clear from other literature that a range of psychosocial factors do appear to predict who will adhere to exercise programmes. This book provides the background and application for a range of theories, so there is no need to refer to this extensive literature. But theories have little utility unless they can be applied and change in both cognitions and behaviour can result.

A temptation in counselling is to simply give information about the likely health benefits of becoming more physically active, and the risks attached to not changing. A number of theories such as the Health Belief Model, and Protection Motivation Theory, at least in part, focus on elevating fear and perceived risk as an approach to motivating clients to become more physically active. Social cognitive theory includes a construct called outcome expectancy, and the theories of reasoned action and planned behaviour are founded on the notion that beliefs about exercise influence whether attitudes about an action are favourable or not, which in turn influences intentions to change behaviour. By attempting to increase a client's belief that exercise will have a health benefit, more favourable attitudes emerge and there is a greater likelihood that the client becomes more physically active.

In general, a focus on eliciting fear has limited effect (Plotnikoff & Trinh, 2010) without also helping to develop a client's confidence to change their behaviour and overcome the barriers that may have contributed to doing less physical activity, and *perceived competence* to do physical activity. Also, one reason why eliciting fear may have limited effect is that the link between doing physical activity and any outcomes (other than immediate changes in affect) such as weight, heart disease, Type 2 diabetes and depression are rather intangible and distal, especially in younger and healthy population groups.

Constructs related to perceived confidence, competence and self-perceptions also feature across a number of theories. Indeed self-efficacy (from social cognitive theory) is one of the strongest predictors of future behaviour.

To help someone increase physical activity a focus on increasing self-efficacy is well justified in the literature. Counselling can seek to build confidence in several ways:

1 Highlighting *performance accomplishments* by engaging the client in successful memories of past physical activities or by breaking down the behaviour into amounts that have been achieved (e.g., confidence to walk 3×10 minutes a day v 30 minutes per day).
2 Identifying and highlighting how others, similar to the client, may have been able to achieve the desired behaviour.
3 By understanding and resolving the client's perceived barriers to achieving the desired behaviour.
4 By encouraging the client to re-appraise the perceived emotional and physiological states associated with the behaviour. If exercise is regarded as hard and unpleasant then elicit confidence to achieve more moderate intensity physical activity.
5 Encouraging clients to monitoring their own behaviour and set SMART goals (that are progressive) also helps build self-efficacy.

When clients express low self-efficacy, the goals may be unrealistic and there may be doubts about overcoming barriers. Barrier self-efficacy, linked to perceived behavioural control (see theory of planned behaviour), has an important influence on future behaviour. So even when an individual is ready to implement a plan to do more physical activity there may be emotional, social, and environmental factors that interrupt those plans. Helping clients to plan how to overcome those barriers and increase self-regulatory efficacy is also a useful approach.

MAKING SENSE OF ALL THIS THEORY

The above paragraphs may have left the reader who is less familiar with exercise psychology rather bewildered by the overlap between theories and which theoretical constructs to select and focus on to help clients to increase physical activity. Michie and colleagues (2005) went through a carefully planned process to help simplify things. At the end of the process they identified twelve domains to explain behaviour change as follows: (1) knowledge; (2) skills; (3) social/professional role and identity; (4) beliefs about capabilities; (5) beliefs about consequences; (6) motivation and goals; (7) memory, attention and decision processes; (8) environmental context and resources; (9) social influences; (10) emotion regulation; (11) behavioural regulation; and (12) nature of the behaviour. Space does not permit further elaboration of all of these but it should be fairly evident how much of the discussion above focuses on 1, 4, 5, 6, 8, 9, 11, and to some extent 12.

Michie, Abraham and colleagues have continued to unpick what does actually go on when behaviour change counsellors operate by devising a related taxonomy of behaviour change techniques. They first demonstrated that they could reliably identify 26 techniques that had been used in different interventions described in the literature (Abraham & Michie, 2008) specifically for changing diet and physical activity. Michie and colleagues (2009) then identified the overall effects of diet and physical activity interventions on changing behaviour and which techniques specifically influenced effectiveness. Combining the results from 122 evaluations reviewed ($N = 44,747$) (with on average six techniques being used in each intervention compared with 0.8 in the control comparison group) there was an overall moderately large effect size of 0.31 (95% confidence interval [CI] _ 0.26 to 0.36) (when comparing intervention with control group), with no difference in effectiveness between diet and physical activity interventions. Further analysis identified that of the 26 techniques shown in Table 49.1 when 'prompt

Table 49.1 *Taxonomy of behaviour change techniques considered for their effectiveness in promoting a healthy diet and physical activity*

T1	provide information on behaviour-health link	T14	provide contingent rewards
T2	provide information on consequences	T15	teach to use prompts/cues
T3	provide information about others' approval	T16	agree a behavioural contract
T4	prompt intention formation	T17	prompt practice
T5	prompt barrier identification	T18	use of follow-up prompts
T6	provide general encouragement	T19	provide opportunities for social comparison
T7	set graded tasks	T20	plan social support/social change
T8	provide instruction	T21	prompt identification as role model/position advocate
T9	model/demonstrate the behaviour	T22	prompt self talk
T10	prompt specific goal setting	T23	relapse prevention
T11	prompt review of behavioral goals	T24	stress management
T12	prompt self-monitoring of behaviour	T25	motivational interviewing
T13	provide feedback on performance	T26	time management

self-monitoring of behaviour' and one other self-regulation technique were considered, the intervention appeared to be even more effective. Of the five self-regulation techniques, 60% of the evaluations prompted intention formation (T4), 50% provided feedback on performance (T13), 38% prompted self-monitoring of behaviour (T12), 22% prompted specific goal setting (T10), and 16% prompted review of behavioural goals (T11).

In summary, these behaviour change techniques are derived from a variety of theories and are used with varying degrees of effectiveness by counsellors attempting to promote physical activity. In the above review, whether or not the technique was used was the only consideration. It does not tell us if specific techniques could be more or less effective when matched with whether the participants were ready to change.

Motivational readiness to change is a central construct within the transtheoretical model (TTM) and highlights the need to match interventions to 'stage of change'. Stages are defined as: (1) pre-contemplation; (2) contemplation; (3) preparation; (4) action; and (5) maintenance. The stages were derived from interviews to assess the cognitive and behavioural processes that smokers go through when giving up smoking. The model has since been applied to help understand how people also change other behaviours. Practitioners are then guided towards using specific cognitive or behavioural strategies matched to which stage a client is in. Space does not permit a full exploration of the TTM and evidence for its effectiveness but the TTM does provide a fairly pragmatic model for facilitating behaviour change, which has been very widely considered in the behavioural sciences.

In Table 49.1 above, T25 is labelled as 'motivational interviewing'. This may seem a rather vague term but captures much more, to the extent that the rest of the chapter is devoted to this. Much of what has been discussed so far is probably irrelevant if there isn't a positive relationship between client and counsellor. We don't mean that the two generally 'get on' with each other. Consider the potential consequences of the following beliefs that a counsellor may have:

- The client ought to change
- The client is ready to change
- The client's health is a prime motivating factor for them
- Clients are either motivated to change or not
- A tough approach is always best
- I'm the expert – the client should follow my advice

Advocates of motivational interviewing (MI) believe that these beliefs can lead to a rather one-sided interaction with a less than positive relationship, which may do little to engage a client in the process of behaviour change.

MOTIVATIONAL INTERVIEWING: A DIFFERENT APPROACH TO COUNSELLING

MI has become a popular counselling method for promoting lifestyle behavioural changes including increased physical activity, weight loss and smoking cessation amongst individuals who are ambivalent about behaviour change (i.e., most people!).

MI is essentially a humanistic approach in contrast to other cognitive-behavioural approaches (i.e., according to MI, behaviour change is not about insufficient knowledge or skills). In contrast, other dominant theories within exercise psychology are underpinned by the need to foster positive attitudes, develop control (e.g., theory of planned behaviour) or develop self-regulation techniques, planning and coping skills (e.g., social cognitive theory and the health action process approach model). Miller and Rollnick (2009) nicely summarise the collaborative, autonomy supportive essence of MI in the phrase: *"You have what you need*, (for behaviour change), *and together we'll find it"* (p. 134). MI is distinctive therefore in placing the client at the centre of and as the expert in their own behaviour change and departs from other cognitive-behavioural approaches discussed previously that seek to challenge attitudes, beliefs or impart knowledge or develop self-regulation skills.

The spirit of motivational interviewing: digging for treasure together

At the heart of MI is its *'spirit'* which refers to the style of interaction between the practitioner and client (a particular way of being with people). According to MI, the style of interaction should be one of *collaboration*, evocation and *autonomy*. Adherence to the spirit is crucial and is a strong predictor of behaviour change. An essential component of the spirit is a collaborative environment where the practitioner and client function as a partnership, where the client's perspectives are respected. The practitioner is a supportive partner rather than a persuasive expert and MI's collaborative spirit stands in contrast to more prescriptive, expert-driven interventions commonly implemented within the physical activity domain. In synergy with collaboration, evocation involves the practitioner drawing out the client's personal motivations (and hence arguments) for behaviour change. In this way, the role of the practitioner is to elicit rather than impart wisdom and knowledge, drawing on the perceptions, values and emotions from the client (Miller & Rollnick, 2002). The final component that makes up the spirit is the emphasis on autonomy and personal choice. The responsibility, ability and the decision to bring about behaviour change are entirely under the client's control. The provision of autonomy support is not unique to MI and features strongly in self-determination theory, whereby the provision of autonomy has been shown to improve exercise adherence and

promote more autonomous forms of behavioural regulation for exercise.

Key principles of motivational interviewing

Beyond the spirit of MI, and fundamental to its approach and communication style, are four guiding principles that are taught to practitioners to improve the therapeutic alliance and increase the likelihood of behaviour change. These four principles are: (1) express empathy; (2) develop discrepancy; (3) roll with resistance; and (4) support self-efficacy. These will each be discussed in turn.

Express empathy

The ability to express *empathy*, show understanding and display a genuine desire to understand the client's perspective is at the crux of the communication style employed in MI. The expression of empathy can be seen through the effective use of reflective listening (explained below under the heading 'Microskills') and the expression of empathy has been shown to be a strong predictor of behaviour change outcomes.

Development of discrepancy

According to Miller and Rollnick (2002) behaviour change is motivated in part by a perceived discrepancy between present behaviour and the client's broader goals and values. When current behaviour is seen to be in disharmony with important personal goals (such as improving health, losing weight, controlling blood pressure), there is thought to be an increased likelihood of behaviour change. In essence, helping the client to foresee such discrepancy is likely to enhance their decision for change. Strategies and skills aimed at developing discrepancy will be discussed in later sections but include 'looking over the hypothetical fence' (strategy) and using particular forms of reflective listening such as amplified reflection (micro-skills).

Roll with resistance

Rolling with resistance is the recognition and acceptance that the client feels ambivalent about behaviour change. When resistance is evoked, clients tend not to change. Therefore, resistance should be kept to a minimum and as such, the practitioner avoids confrontation and argumentation or direct persuasion, but instead 'rolls' with the resistance. The micro-skill of 'amplified reflection' can be used effectively when rolling with resistance. Here is an example of using amplified reflection: "So you're saying you have absolutely NO time at all to exercise?" When a client is resistant, it is also useful to emphasise personal choice and control: "Do you have any ideas as to how we may resolve this dilemma?" or "I don't want to push you into making a decision. You will be the best judge if this is the right time to consider making this change".

Support self-efficacy

The final guiding principle of MI is to support the belief that the client has the ability and resources to change. MI seeks to enhance a client's self-efficacy, increasing their belief in their capacity for change. The enhancement of self-efficacy is proposed to be one of the mechanisms by which motivational interviewing changes physical activity behaviour.

Micro-skills in motivational interviewing (OARS)

The practice of MI involves skilful use of particular techniques (micro-skills and strategies) that are consistent with the overarching 'spirit' and principles of MI. Together, the spirit, principles, micro-skills and strategies aim to increase 'change talk' and reduce 'sustain talk' (maintenance of the status quo). Here, we turn from the 'relational' component of MI to the more 'technical' components of MI. The latter is not MI in the absence of the former. The OARS micro-skills acronym stands for open questions, affirming, reflective listening and summarising and is used to explore ambivalence and elicit personal motives for change.

Ask open-ended questions

The first skill is to ask open-ended questions (e.g., what brought you here today?). This is an important skill since client talk time is a reasonable indicator of likely effectiveness. Foster et al. (2005) point out that: "The more a clinician speaks during a session, the less effective the session will be for the patient" (p. 233). Open-ended questions are vital to get the client to do the talking, and hence thinking, about behaviour change.

Affirmations

Affirmations are statements or gestures of appreciation for the client's strengths and are useful in supporting self-efficacy. Some examples of affirmations include: "I appreciate you coming in today" and "Thank you for sharing your concerns about your diabetes with me".

Reflective listening

Reflective listening is thought to be one of the most important yet difficult skills necessary for effective MI. Reflective listening helps the client to feel understood and allows the client to continue talking and elaborating, without interference from the practitioner. In essence, what people really need in MI is 'a good listening to' and effective reflective listening achieves this without the practitioner directing or leading the consultation. Here is an example of reflective listening:

Client: "I have started to exercise, but I'm a little upset that I don't seem to be losing any weight".

Practitioner: "It sounds as though you are trying, but you are frustrated that you haven't seen any results yet".

Research has demonstrated that a reflective listening style actively promotes change talk, while an instructive and commanding style increases resistance, and when resistance is evoked, clients tend not to change.

Summarising

The final micro-skill is the provision of summary statements offered periodically to summarise a topic that has been discussed within a session. Such a summary strengthens what has been previously mentioned, shows the client that you have been actively listening and opens the door for further elaboration. The client is also able to hear their personal change talk (regarding a lack of exercise for example) for a third time and thereby strengthen motivation to change.

Strategies in motivational interviewing

Typical strategies adopted in MI include *agenda setting/setting the scene; assessing importance and confidence; exploration of the pros and cons,* and, the *'two possible futures' strategy* (looking over the hypothetical fence). Such strategies have been found to help elicit change talk, develop discrepancy and enhance readiness, and commitment for change. The aforementioned strategies belong to what has been called phase one of MI, where the focus is on building motivation for change, eliciting change talk, and, resolving ambivalence about behaviour change. Once a client is sufficiently motivated to change (i.e., ready, willing and confident), we move to phase two of MI where the strategies focus on strengthening commitment to change and arriving at a change plan. Strategies within the second phase include 'helping with decision making', 'strengthening commitment to change' and 'arriving at a change plan'.

Agenda setting and setting the scene

The goal of agenda setting is to provide clients with an opportunity to discuss that which they are most ready and willing to change or talk about. Good examples to start a MI session include: "I usually talk to people in a situation like yours about diet, exercise, that sort of thing. How do you feel? Which of these do you feel you would like to talk about, or is there something else you would like to discuss?" Another could be: "I understand the doctor is concerned about your weight. I wonder how you feel about your current diet?"

Assessing readiness, importance and confidence

This strategy can be achieved by either asking open-ended questions such as "How do you feel at the moment about (change)?" Or "people differ quite a lot in how ready they are to change their (behaviour). How about you?" or by using importance and confidence rulers that begins with two questions. The first question is "How important is it for you, personally, to increase your physical activity? If 0 was not at all important and 10 were very important, what number would you give yourself?" The second question is "If you decided right now that you wanted to increase your physical activity level, how confident do you feel about succeeding with this? Again if 0 stands for not at all confident and 10 stands for very confident, what number would you give yourself?" Following the client's response, a MI facilitator would follow with two probing questions: (1) "You gave yourself a score of X. Why are you an X and not a lower number?" to elicit change talk; and (2) "What would have to happen for you to be X (a higher number)?" and/or "What stops you from moving up from an X (lower number) to a Y (higher number)?" to elicit the barriers that the patient typically experienced. The MI practitioner could then summarise the client's responses and, if barriers were cited by the client, prompt the client to identify potential solutions, whilst seeking permission to list additional resolutions.

Exploration of the pros and cons

At the heart of MI is the acceptance of ambivalence about change. The goal of MI is to understand and facilitate resolution of client ambivalence in the direction of a healthier lifestyle. A decisional matrix can be used (see Figure 49.1). Decisional-balance is explored through the use of open-questions such as: "What are the good things about staying as you are (inactive)?"; "What are the not-so-good things about staying inactive?"; "What are the not-so-good things about increasing your physical activity (changing your diet)?"; "What would be the good things about (change) increasing your physical activity level?". The discussion should be summarised, acknowledging all sides of the ambivalence but with the emphasis on the disadvantages of staying the same and the benefits of behaviour change (hence, the directive element to MI).

Phase one: two possible futures strategy

This strategy, also known as 'looking over the hypothetical fence' appears to be particularly useful in developing discrepancy and resolving dissonance. Figure 49.2 demonstrates an example of this strategy applied to physical activity. The purpose of the strategy is to get clients talking about how their lives may be different if they do, or do not change. "If you were to change (i.e., exercise regularly), what would it be like? How would you feel? How would things be different?" On the other hand, "If you decide that now is not the right time for you to change and we meet up in a couple of years and your physical activity level has stayed the same, what would things be like for you? What about that concerns you the most?"

The aforementioned strategies belong to phase one of MI, where the focus is on building motivation for change and resolving ambivalence. Figure 49.3 demonstrates how such strategies can be usefully employed in sequence during a motivational interviewing intervention.

Phase two: strengthening commitment to change

At phase two, the client has sufficient motivation and confidence to change. Therefore, the focus moves away from building motivation and resolving ambivalence to strengthening commitment to change and arriving at a change plan. The two main hazards in phase two are over-prescription ("Now that you're ready, here's what you should do") or insufficient direction (i.e., it will not be helpful at this point to respond with a reflection to the statement "I'm not sure what kind of physical activity would be best for me to try"!!).

Helping with decision making

The key questions to ask the client at the beginning of phase two include: "Where do we go from here?" or "What's the next step?", "What are your options?" and "How can I help you succeed?" In this phase, there may be less use of reflections by the practitioner but information exchange is a critical skill. There are only two circumstances in which practitioner 'expertise' or 'knowledge' is offered in MI; when a person requests it or by asking for permission to share. For example, "Would it help you if I tell you what has worked for other people or what they have found helpful?" Other examples include: "I have an idea that may be relevant. Do you want to hear it?" or "Let me describe some possibilities and you tell me which of them (if any) make the most sense to you".

Arriving at a change plan

Ideally, this strategy involves: (1) setting goals (What is the first step? What is it that you want to change?; (2) considering options; and (3) arriving at a specific change plan. At this point, it is important to allow some time to brainstorm ideas and possible solutions and alternatives without premature focus on one particular course of action. Searching questions may

	Pros	Cons
Change (Increase physical activity)		
No change		

Figure 49.1 Decisional matrix for physical activity.

Exercise

Two Possible Futures

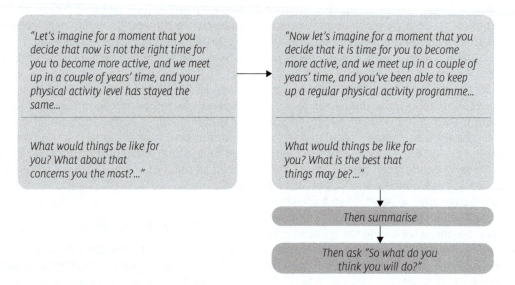

"Let's imagine for a moment that you decide that now is not the right time for you to become more active, and we meet up in a couple of years' time, and your physical activity level has stayed the same...

What would things be like for you? What about that concerns you the most?..."

"Now let's imagine for a moment that you decide that it is time for you to become more active, and we meet up in a couple of years' time, and you've been able to keep up a regular physical activity programme...

What would things be like for you? What is the best that things may be?..."

Then summarise

Then ask "So what do you think you will do?"

Figure 49.2 Looking over the hypothetical fence.

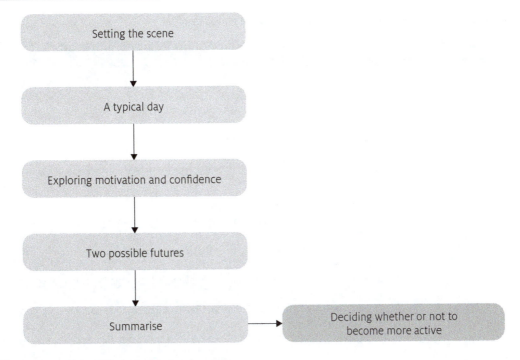

Figure 49.3 Using MI strategies in sequence.

include: "What might work for you?", "How might that work out?" and getting the client to think about obstacles to achieving change, such as: "What might stand in your way?". A change plan could be undertaken verbally or, if helpful to the client, with a 'change plan worksheet'. Table 49.2 is a summary of MI principles and an overview of micro-skills and strategies that target/develop the principle in practice.

In summary, the strategies outlined here are not to be applied on clients but may be used as a way of structuring the conversation so that clients do most of the talking (and hence thinking) about behaviour change. The spirit of MI is fundamental. It's possible to do MI without the use of these strategies, although they can be fruitfully used in MI. However, it's impossible to do MI outside of the underpinning spirit and principles that are crucial to its approach. You cannot or should not attempt to the 'technical' part of MI (the strategies) without the 'relational' part.

Effectiveness of motivational interviewing

Interventions adopting MI have shown promise in promoting physical activity in comparison to standard treatments or controls. Reviews and syntheses of research using MI have revealed that both number and duration of MI sessions are related to behaviour change. For example, a meta-analytic synthesis of 72 RCTs using MI in health-related contexts revealed that the technique was more effective in improving behavioural (e.g., number of cigarettes, alcohol consumption) and health related (e.g., body mass index, cholesterol) outcomes relative to usual care control groups (e.g., advice giving) in 80% of studies (Rubak, Sandbaek, Lauritzen & Christensen, 2005). The size of the MI effect was large for direct indexes of behaviour (e.g., number of cigarettes, $d = 1.32$; alcohol consumption, $d = 14.64$) and small-to-medium for outcomes associated with behaviour change (e.g., body mass index, $d = 0.72$; cholesterol, $d = 0.27$) relative to usual

Table 49.2 *Matching the micro-skills and strategies to the principles of MI*

Key principles	How?
Express empathy	Agenda setting Reflective listening
Develop discrepancy	Pros and cons Two possible futures strategy Importance ruler Amplified reflection

Roll with resistance	Avoid argumentation or direct persuasion
	  Double sided reflection: "So on one hand you're saying...but on the other you're saying..."
	  Amplified reflection: "So you're saying that you have got absolutely NO time at all to exercise?"
	  Shifting focus: "I understand what you're saying, what would be useful for you to talk about?"
	  Emphasise personal choice and control: "Do you have any ideas as to how we may resolve this dilemma? I do not want to push you into making any decision. You will be the best judge of what is the right time to consider making this change."

Support self-efficacy	Offer Affirmations Confidence ruler/confidence building Helping with decision making

care. Of MI encounters lasting 60 minutes, 81% of studies demonstrated an effect compared to only 64% of studies with an encounter equal to or less than 20 minutes. Furthermore, an effect was found in only 40% of studies with only one counselling session, but in 87% of studies with more than five.

However despite such research, several authors (e.g., Bennett et al., 2007; Greaves et al., 2008) have been unable to replicate this relationship. For example, although Hardcastle et al. (2008) found high attendees (three to five sessions) to increase their vigorous physical activity, walking, and overall physical activity compared to low attendees (two or less MI sessions), no significant dose response relationship was identified. To our knowledge, the study by Hardcastle, Blake & Hagger (2012) is the first to demonstrate a clear dose-response effect within physical activity research using

multiple MI sessions. The optimum number of sessions would appear to be four or five hours/ sessions of MI.

How does MI work? The mechanisms for behaviour change

A lack of research on the active ingredients of MI has made it difficult to draw firm conclusions regarding how MI facilitates behaviour change. MI was originally hypothesised to promote behaviour change through the elicitation of and reinforcement of 'change talk' (the technical component) and through a relational component in that empathic understanding and positive regard are therapeutic skills that create an autonomy supportive environment whereby clients can explore change. According to Apodaca & Longabaugh (2009), client change talk and experience of discrepancy were both related to more favourable outcomes whilst practitioner MI-inconsistent behaviour was related to less favourable outcomes in comparison to both standard care (Carroll et al., 2006) and other active treatments (Karno & Longabaugh, 2005). There is increasing evidence that the 'relational' aspects (adherence to MI spirit) are as important or perhaps more important than the technical aspects in facilitating behaviour change.

The notion that adherence to MI spirit is essential and perhaps more important than the technical/mechanical strategies adopted is evidenced in the fact that studies employing didactic manuals on the strategies/techniques of MI have shown to be less effective (e.g., Hettema et al., 2005; Lundahl et al., 2009). In studies where there wasn't a specific manual used to guide MI, the effect size found was double that of studies that used a structured MI practitioner manual (Hettema et al., 2005).

Adopting such a mechanical approach may cause some practitioners to force change talk prematurely, which could increase client resistance and subsequently lead to poorer outcomes. Further evidence pointing to the importance of the relational aspects in MI effectiveness is that group-delivered MI appears to be less effective than individually delivered MI (Lundahl et al., 2009). Adherence to the spirit and principles of MI is essential and further research is needed to explore how MI works and the particular mechanisms of change. In relation to the specific strategies, there is some evidence that the decisional balance activity is related to improved outcomes.

Despite the dearth of evidence as to how and why MI interventions work, research has demonstrated that MI interventions lead to increases in self-efficacy, although, to date, there is limited data to demonstrate its role as a mechanism despite researchers acknowledging its potential role. Hardcastle, Blake & Hagger (2012) provide evidence that an increase in stage of change predicted physical activity change (both for total physical activity and

walking) following MI, and is consistent with a central purpose of MI; that is, to increase client readiness to change. In the study by Hardcastle, Blake and Hagger (2012), increases in stage of change, social support and self-efficacy were the key psychological variables that significantly increased as a result of the intervention. This is consistent with the theoretical underpinnings of MI and the common strategies adopted within MI. Specifically, we would expect readiness to change (and hence motivation) to increase given the emphasis placed on strategies to build motivation including agenda setting, decisional balance, assessing importance and eliciting change talk. The two possible futures strategy was also used as a tool to build motivation for change by evoking and strengthening patients' personal reasons for change. Increasing client confidence is an explicit aim of MI and self-efficacy has been implicated as a key mediator of change in behavioural outcomes.

Development of motivational interviewing skills

Learning MI and developing skill in delivery of MI has been likened to learning to play a musical instrument. MI is not easy to learn or master and research suggests that competency is not quickly developed through independent study or merely by attending workshops, but requires sustained practice with feedback and supervision over time. The typical approach to training is a two-day workshop that would be a mix of didactic delivery of material and experiential exercise such as role-plays. A comprehensive list of training events worldwide can be found on motivationalinterviewing.org. It may be more effective to offer more sessions (four sessions) over a longer period (i.e., four months) to provide opportunities for personal performance feedback (e.g., from audiotapes) and individual supervision to increase the effectiveness of training and improve practitioner competency.

LEARNING AIDS

1   Summarise the 'spirit' of motivational interviewing.

The 'spirit' of MI refers to the style of interaction between the practitioner and client. Three words are used to explain this style of interaction: collaboration, evocation and autonomy. Collaboration refers to the partnership between the practitioner and client, where the client's perspectives are respected. In this manner, the practitioner is a supportive partner rather than a persuasive expert. Evocation involves the practitioner drawing out the client's personal motivations for behaviour change. Finally, autonomy refers to the emphasis on personal choice. The responsibility, ability and the decision to bring about behaviour change rests with the client.

2   Identify the four guiding principles of motivational interviewing.

The four guiding principles of motivational interviewing are: (1) express empathy; (2) develop discrepancy; (3) roll with resistance; and (4) support self-efficacy.

3   Summarise the OARS micro-skills in motivational interviewing.

The OARS acronym refers to the essential micro-skills necessary for effective motivational interviewing and stands for open questions, affirming, reflective listening and summarising.

4   Describe specific strategies the exercise professional may use in a MI session to explore motivation and ambivalence.

There are several strategies that could be used in a MI session in order to explore motivation and ambivalence. These include an exploration of the pros and cons/use of a decisional matrix; assessing importance of PA and confidence to participate; and two possible futures (looking over the hypothetical fence).

REVIEW QUESTIONS

1   What is the optimal 'dose' of motivational interviewing to increase PA participation?

2   How is phase one in motivational interviewing different from phase two?

3   How could you develop discrepancy?

4   What does it mean to 'roll with resistance'?

5   Why might it be important to actively ask a client about the good things about staying physically inactive?

EXERCISE

During the week, choose two different individuals who are currently sedentary or insufficiently active. With the first participant, by giving advice, try to promote physical activity (i.e., tell them the guidelines, the links between physical activity and health, describe ways they could integrate physical activity into their lifestyle). With the second participant, try using motivational interviewing strategies (i.e., agenda setting, exploring motivation and confidence) and aim to follow the principles and 'spirit' of motivational interviewing. Immediately after each session, make some notes and reflect on how the sessions went. Which style was more effective? Discuss which session appeared to be more effective and speculate on the reasons why.

ADDITIONAL READING

Mason, P. & Butler, C.C. (2010). *Health behaviour change*. 2nd edition. Elsevier Limited.

Rollnick, S., Miller, W.R. & Butler, C.C. (2008). *Motivational interviewing in health care: Helping patients change behaviour*. Guilford Press.

Rosengren, D.B. (2009). *Building motivational interviewing skills: A practitioner workbook*. Guilford Press.

REFERENCES

Abraham, C. & Michie, S. (2008). A taxonomy of behavior change techniques used in interventions. *Health Psychology, 27*, 379–387.

Apodaca, T.R. & Longabaugh, R. (2009). Mechanisms of change in motivational interviewing: A review and preliminary evaluation of the evidence. *Addiction, 104*, 705–715.

Bennett, J.A., Lyons, K.S., Winters-Stone, K., Nail, L.M. & Scherer, J. (2007). Motivational interviewing to increase physical activity in long-term cancer survivors: a randomised controlled trial. *Nursing Research, 56*, 18–27.

Carroll, K.M., Ball, S.A., Nich, C., Martino, S., Frankforter, T.L., Farentinos, C., Kunkel, L.E., Mikulich-Gilbertson, S.K., Morgenstern, J., Obert, J.L., Polein, D., Snead, N. & Woody, G.E. (2006). Motivational interviewing to improve treatment engagement and outcome in individuals seeking treatment for substance abuse: A multisite effectiveness study. *Drug and Alcohol Dependence, 81*, 301–312.

Foster, G.D., Makris, A.P. & Bailor, B. (2005). Behavioral treatment of obesity. *American Journal of Clinical Nutrition, 82*, 230S–235S.

Greaves, C.J., Middlebrooke, D., O'Loughlin, L., Holland, S., Piper, J., Steele, A., Gale, T., Hammerton, F. & Daly, M. (2008). Motivational interviewing for modifying diabetes risk: a randomised controlled trial. *British Journal of General Practice, 58*, 535–540.

Hardcastle, S., Blake, N. & Hagger, M.S. (2012). The effectiveness of a motivational interviewing Primary-Care based intervention on physical activity and predictors of change in a disadvantaged community. *Journal of Behavioral Medicine, 35*, 318–333.

Hardcastle, S., Taylor, A.H., Bailey, M. & Castle, R. (2008). A randomised controlled trial on the effectiveness of a primary health care based counselling intervention on physical activity, diet & CHD risk factors. *Patient Education and Counselling, 70*, 31–39.

Hettema, J., Steele, J. & Miller, W.R. (2005). Motivational interviewing. *Annual Review of Clinical Psychology, 1*, 91–111.

Karno, M.P. & Longabaugh, R. (2005). An examination of how therapist directiveness interacts with patient anger and reactance to predict alcohol use. *Journal of Studies on Alcohol, 66*, 825–832.

Lundahl, B. & Burke, B. (2009). The effectiveness and applicability of motivational interviewing: A practice-friendly review of four meta-analyses. *Journal of Clinical Psychology, 65*, 11, 1232–1245.

Michie S., Abraham, C., Wittington, C., McAteer, J. & Gupta, S. (2009). Effective techniques in healthy eating and physical activity interventions: A meta-regression. *Health Psychology, 28*, 690–701.

Michie, S., Johnston, M., Abraham, C., Lawton, R., Parker, D. & Walker, A. on behalf of the

"Psychological Theory" Group (2005). Making psychological theory useful for implementing evidence based practice: a consensus approach. *Quality & Safety in Health Care, 14*, 26–33.

Miller, W.R. & Rollnick, S. (2002). *Motivational interviewing: preparing people to change.* New York: Guilford Press.

Miller, W.R. & Rollnick, S. (2009). Ten things that motivational interviewing is not. *Behavioural and Cognitive Psychotherapy, 37*, 129–140.

Pavey, T.G., Taylor, A.H., Fox, K.R., Hillsdon, M., Anokye, N., Campbell, J.L., Foster, C., Green, C., Moxham, T., Mutrie, N., Searle, J., Trueman, P. & Taylor R.S. (2011). Exercise referral schemes in primary care: An effective approach to enhancing physical activity and improving health outcomes? *British Medical Journal.* Nov 4; 343: d6462.

Plotnikoff, R.C. & Trinh, L. (2010). Protection motivation theory: is this a worthwhile theory for physical activity promotion? *Exercise & Sport Science Review, 38*, 91–98.

Rubak, S., Sandbaek, A., Lauritzen, T. & Christensen, B. (2005). Motivational interviewing: A systematic review and meta-analysis. *British Journal of General Practice, 55*, 305–312.

Chapter 50

Organizational and community physical activity programs

KOJI TAKENAKA AND LEONARD D. ZAICHKOWSKY

SUMMARY

In this chapter, we introduce organizational and community intervention programs for enhancing physical activity, and present some examples. Rather than simply reviewing basic theoretical principles, we first discuss how behavior change theories and techniques should be applied to real-world situations. It is shown that the success of intervention depends on successfully bridging theory and practice. We begin by presenting two case studies (1 and 2) of specific organizational and community intervention programs undertaken in Japan. We discuss the recruitment strategies adopted and the behavior change targeted for program participants, as well as typical outcomes of the interventions that aimed to enhance physical activity in both settings. Additionally, as a different perspective from behavior change, we present a further two case studies (3 and 4) on how regional and climate-related community-based sport or physical activity can promote lifelong physical and social activity. We present examples of how the winter sports of hockey and curling serve to provide Canadians with an outlet to develop and maintain lifelong health and fitness, by tapping into their passion for national and local sport.

INTRODUCTION

Despite evidence supporting the positive physical, psychological, and social effects of engaging in exercise, this does not necessarily lead people to adopt or maintain a physically active lifestyle. Although people understand the positive effects of exercise, they often find excuses for not adopting a healthy lifestyle.

The excuses for leading a sedentary lifestyle and barriers to adopting a healthy one are varied and include job commitments, family obligations, injuries, bad weather, and preferring to use the Internet or watch TV to name but a few (Stetson et al., 2005; Takenaka et al., 2010, 2011).

Changing physical activity behaviors by eliminating excuses and barriers can be attempted through a behavior change approach called self-management, or self-regulation. This approach starts from individuals' readiness for change and their current behavior in order to help them adopt and maintain a physically active lifestyle. The approach educates them about health problems that can occur if they fail to adopt a healthy lifestyle that includes physical activity. Accordingly, strategies from recruitment to maintenance must be carefully designed in physical activity behavior interventions.

OBJECTIVES

1   Understand how to translate a particular theoretical model into practice with regard to the development of physical activity programs for organizations and communities.

2   Learn specific steps in each type of intervention: defining the target group and its needs, selecting recruitment strategies, specifying the intervention method, assessing the outcomes, and revising the program.

3   Acquire practical knowledge from examples of interventions based on behavior change theories applied according to population characteristics and understand how to select the best recruitment strategies for a particular purpose.

4   Learn self-management techniques to enhance physical activity adherence in practical situations.

5   Understand how passion for a particular traditional sport allows for the promotion of health and fitness in Canadian youth and adults.

CASE STUDIES FOR ORGANIZATIONAL AND COMMUNITY INTERVENTIONS

While we can see the actual candidates for program participants in the case of organizational situations such as worksites, this is not possible in the general case of community situations, making recruitment more difficult. Thus, the recruitment method should be differentiated from the program contents in any intervention. In this section we first present two case studies of organizational and community intervention programs in Japan. Second, as there is more community-based dissemination of traditional or climate-specific sports than specific intervention programs, we introduce two case studies of sports-based programs running in Canada.

CASE STUDY 1: ORGANIZATIONAL INTERVENTION IN A JAPANESE INDUSTRY

A sample population of 474 workers in the manufacturing industry was selected as the target for an organizational intervention program to enhance physical activity in small-town communities in Japan. As one of our recruitment strategies, we first examined the health needs of the employees and then sent need-matched messages inviting them to join the program. After participants were selected, each participant was provided with a pedometer and weekly self-assessment sheet and was encouraged to increase their number of daily steps. Participants also received stage-matched information via newsletter articles on the basis of the transtheoretical model for behavior change (Tables 50.1, 50.2: Prochaska and DiClemente, 1983; Prochaska et al., 1992; Burbank and Riebe, 2002), as well as health-related information corresponding to their individual needs.

Recruitment procedure

The following strategies were adopted to recruit program participants: 1) distribution of recruiting posters and leaflets; 2) persuasion of working team leaders to encourage the participation of other workers; 3) implementation of a needs survey concerning each worker's desire for weight loss, physical fitness, and stress management; and 4) analysis of the needs survey data.

The data analysis for a total of 224 employees revealed the largest proportion of workers wanted to lose weight (42.0%), followed by wanting better physical fitness (41.5%). Corre-sponding to individual needs determined by the survey (i.e. weight loss, physical fitness, and stress management), a different recruiting message was sent to each worker via an invitation letter urging them to apply for the program. Also, to encourage their participation in each of the three segments of the program, the information in the invitation letter was adjusted to each worker's individual need.

As a result, significantly more program participants could be recruited through the needs-adjusted recruitment strategy (total: 33.5%; weight loss: 15.6%; physical fitness: 13.4%; and stress management: 4.5%) was able to acquire than through standard recruitment strategies (8.0%). The needs-matched approach may therefore recruit more participants than conventional approaches.

Table 50.1 *The four dimensions of the transtheoretical model of behavior change (adapted from Prochaska et al., 1992)*

Dimension	Description
Stage of change	The stages of change represent ordered categories along a continuum of motivational readiness. The five stages are: • Precontemplation • Contemplation • Preparation • Action • Maintenance
Processes of change	The processes of change explain how individuals move through the stages of change. They are 10 strategies that describe the techniques that individuals use to modify their thoughts, feelings and behavior. Five of the processes are labeled as experiential and five are labeled behavioral. Experiential processes have been shown to be used primarily during earlier stages of and behavioral during later stage transitions.
Self-efficacy	Self-efficacy represents the situation specific self-confidence that people have that they can cope with behavior change without relapsing. Self-efficacy is an intermediate/outcome measure that is hypothesized to vary depending on stage of change.
Decisional balance	The decisional balance construct refers to the relative weighting of the pros and cons of change. The decisional balance is an intermediate/outcome measure that is hypothesized to vary across the stages of change and with the type of behavior being considered.

Table 50.2 *Experiential and behavioral processes (adapted from Burbank and Riebe, 2002). Experiential processes are used primarily during earlier stages of and behavioral during later stage transitions*

Experiential processes	Contents
Consciousness raising	Efforts by the individual to seek new information and to gain understanding and feedback about the problem behavior. Obtaining information about the current behavior in order to better understand the impact the behavior has on self and others. Increase awareness of the consequences of the problem behavior.
Dramatic relief	Affective aspects of change, often involving intense emotional experiences related to the problem behavior. A type of catharsis in which the individual moves closer to change through direct emotional response to the behavior he or she is trying to change.
Self-reevaluation	Emotional and cognitive reappraisal of values by the individual regarding the problem behavior. Seeks change through cognitive or emotional appraisal of the impact of the behavior on him- or herself.
Environmental reevaluation	Consideration and assessment by the individual of how the problem affects the physical and social environments. The individual begins to assess his or her impact on the surrounding environment.
Social liberation	Awareness, availability, and acceptance by the individual of alternative, problem-free lifestyles in society. Recognition that societal norms are moving to promote a healthier lifestyle that is free of the effects of the problem behavior.
Behavioral processes	**Contents**
Counter-conditioning	Substitution of alternative behaviors for problem behavior. Seek ways to substitute healthier behaviors for the current problem behavior.
Helping relationships	Trusting, accepting, and using the support of caring others during attempts to change the problem behavior. The support of friends or loved ones during the process of change.
Reinforcement management	Changing the contingencies that control or maintain the problem behavior. Seek ways to continually reinforce positive behaviors and decrease problem behaviors. Some kind of rewarded system.
Self-liberation	The individual's choice and commitment to change the problem behavior, including the belief that one can change. Process benefits from the extent to which the commitment is made to others.
Stimulus control	Control of situations and other causes that trigger the problem behavior. Be altered to provide cues for positive, healthier behaviors.

Intervention program

Participants (78 men, 15 women; mean age 39.4 years, age range 30–60 years) started the intervention program designed to increase their number of daily steps through the use of a pedometer and self-assessment sheet (Figure 50.1). Each week they also received a health promotion newsletter based on the stages of behavior change (Figure 50.2). First, on the reverse side of the newsletter, stage-matched information for behavior change was presented in the upper section and corresponded to either low motivation (pre-action stages: precontemplation, contemplation, and preparation) or high motivation (post-action stage: action and maintenance). In the bottom section, information was provided on health behavior in relation to each health need (losing weight, better physical fitness, or stress relief) identified by the survey during recruitment. Hence, six combination articles—2 (stage-matched behavior information) × 3 (weight loss, physical fitness, and stress management)—were presented in each typed newsletter for each participant. Topics were presented in the form of the six articles (2 stages × 3 health needs) and in the form of tips for behavior change in each weekly newsletter over a 10-week intervention period (Table 50.3).

Results

As shown in Figure 50.3, the mean number of steps per week increased rapidly from the first week to the second week and remained at an increased level until the end of the program. The mean number of steps was 7,665 (7,833 men, 6,795 women) over the 10 weeks, and no difference was evident between the high- and low-motivation groups.

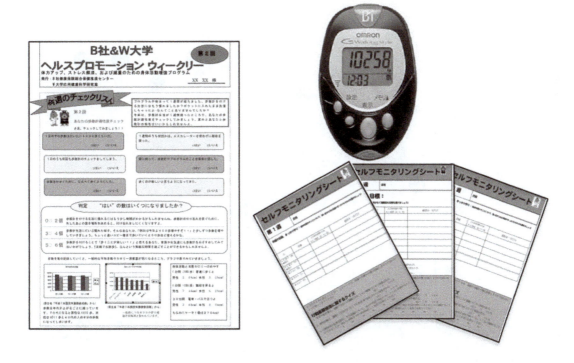

Figure 50.1 The program materials: Health Promotion Weekly, pedometer and self-monitoring sheet.

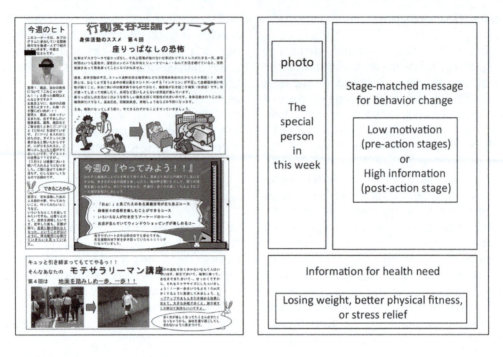

Figure 50.2 The reverse-side articles of Health Promotion Weekly: stage-matched information for behavior change (upper right) and health need information (bottom).

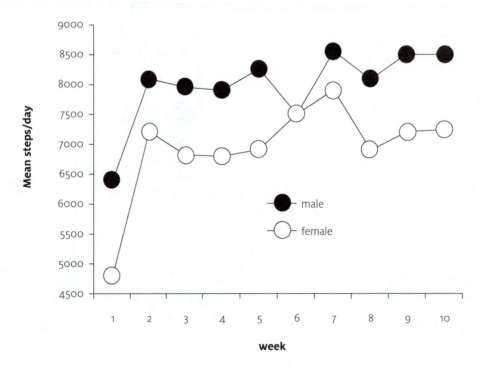

Figure 50.3 The mean number of steps per week for 10 weeks.

Table 50.3 *Topics of newsletter for each participant—2 (stage-matched behavior information) x 3 (weight loss, physical fitness, and stress management). Topics were presented as fix-typed articles—2 (stage) x 3 (health needs) – and as tips for behavior change each week over 10 weeks*

	Stages × Health needs				
Week	pre-action stages	Post-action stages	weight loss	physical fitness	stress management
Week 1	What is physical activity?	What is physical activity?	Eating three times per day	Raising heel up during waiting time	Deep breathing when irritating and being nervous
Week 2	Emphasizing pros	Committing yourself	Not substitute sweat for meal	Giving out no remote	stretching before going to bed
Week 3	Increasing knowledge	Reminding yourself	Chewing lots when eating	Isometric stopping between sitting and standing	Stress relief in Japanese bath
Week 4	Warning of risk	Substituting alternatives 1	Cooking for being on a diet	Strengthening during walking	Good sleeping methods
Week 5	Comprehending benefits	Enlisting social support	Choosing healthy Japanese food for dining out	Squat exercise as routine activity	How to smile in daily life
Week 6	Weighting pros against cons	Rewarding yourself	Taking water or tea instead of carbonated drink	Exercise using towel after morning face-wash	"Sukiyaki" to encourage people to stay strong
Week 7	Caring about consequences to others	Substituting alternatives 2	Watch out, ice cream after eating broiled meat	Stretching in front of desk	Telling someone your troubles
Week 8	Increasing healthy opportunities	Stimulus control	Hook of convenient foods	Small exercise during commuting	Effect by changing outward appearance
Week 9	Self-efficacy	reappraisal of effect	Courage of leaving portion of food	How and when to do sit-ups in worksite	Stress relief effect by physical activity
Week 10	Relapse prevention	Relapse prevention	Attention, lunch in high calorie	Isometrics for back muscles at home	Recommendation of various diversion

Figure 50.4 shows the percentage of pre-action and post-action activity at pre-intervention, post-intervention, and follow-up. Although there was no difference between the high- and low-motivation groups, the percentage of post-action stage activity was significantly higher than that of the pre-action stage at post-intervention and follow-up. In addition, as seen in Figure 50.5, intervention reduced the number of physical complaints for each participant. In particular, the percentage of physical complaints such as shoulder discomfort, back pain, and headache gradually decreased over the course of the intervention program.

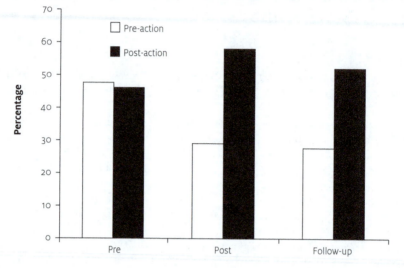

Figure 50.4 The percentage of pre-action and post-action activity at pre-intervention, post-intervention, and follow-up.

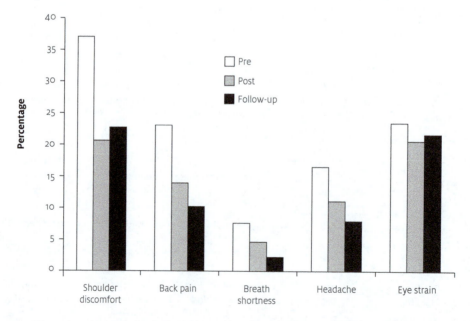

Figure 50.5 The percentage of physical complaints at pre-intervention, post-intervention, and follow-up.

CASE STUDY 2: COMMUNITY INTERVENTION IN JAPAN

Metabolic syndrome is a combination of health risks caused by accumulated fat around the main organs and these risks include obesity, elevated blood pressure, and diabetes. According to a recent survey (Japanese Ministry of Health, Labour and Welfare, 2010), around 20 million Japanese in their 40s to 70s are already suffering from or are likely to suffer from the condition, a number that has increased considerably over the past two decades. Citizens aged between 40 and 74 are obliged by the Japanese Ministry of Health, Labour and Welfare to take an annual health examination in order to detect persons at high risk for metabolic syndrome (although not enough numbers of persons have taken it) and then, as a high-risk approach, to offer continuous health guidance to those deemed at high risk in order to improve the tendency. In order to prevent or improve the condition, it is essential to maintain a balanced lifestyle and to exercise regularly. However, as the number of habitual exercisers has not been shown to increase, a more effective prevention approach is needed to ensure positive behavior change.

Community intervention involved approaching urban citizens in the Tokyo metropolitan area and developing an intervention program to increase their number of steps through the use of a pedometer. We also mailed newsletters containing articles on behavior change. Targets were citizens under 65 years of age who were aware of their lack of physical activity in daily life and who felt anxious about future health problems, but who were not patients of a medical facility. Most participants were middle-aged men who had no time to exercise because of work commitments. The purpose of the program was to: 1) motivate participant adoption of behavior change by reducing psychological burden; 2) use various recruitment strategies to enroll the target population; and 3) enhance physical activity as an habitual activity through the use of effective behavior change education sent by mail.

Recruitment procedure

It is usually more difficult to collect information on the health needs of a larger community population directly from citizens for recruitment purposes than it is from workers in an organization. Therefore, we tried to increase the target population's exposure to and contact points with the program content and recruitment information through the following steps.

1 Introducing basic knowledge on metabolic syndrome and announcing the program in a special-feature article of the city report before starting the official recruitment process.
2 Conducting a seminar on the prevention of metabolic syndrome and announcing the forthcoming program to the attendees.
3 Distributing recruitment posters and leaflets to city facilities and companies (Figure 50.6).
4 Introducing and announcing the program at events in the city and introducing and announcing the activities of lay health advisors in the city.
5 Recruiting participants via the city's public health department website.
6 Distributing program content and application forms in a mass media communication undertaken by the city's public relations office.
7 Introducing the program on our own department website in a public agency.

As a result, 170 persons (69 men, 101 women; mean age, men 49.42 years, women 48.89 years; age range 20–65 years) joined the program. Mean body mass index was 25.6 for men and 23.6 for women. We asked participants at the start of the program from which informational resource they first learned

Figure 50.6 Recruitment poster (left) and leaflet (right) for the community intervention.

about the program: response to city reports accounted for 34% of participants, recruiting leaflets for 19%, recruiting posters for 12%, public health department website 10%, and introduction from friends 10%. We also examined the reasons for joining the program (Table 50.4 and the keywords from the program information that the applicants used in their application to the program (Table 50.5).

Intervention program

At the start of the program, participants were divided into two groups corresponding to their usual activity level as they reported in the survey. We first recommended an increase in walking frequency for the low-level physical activity group and a longer walking time for the high-level activity group. The number of participants in the high-level activity group was limited because they were not the audience targeted by the recruitment strategies.

Information and handouts provided

Information and handouts were traded for self-monitoring postcards after we had confirmed receipt of the postcards. Handouts consisted of four newsletters, we sent out one every three weeks, that presented a series of articles on behavior change education (self-management techniques) such as minimum change strategy, overcoming obstacles, making cues and rewards, and relapse prevention (Figure 50.7), as well as motivational information such as encouraging messages, behavior contracting, stage-matched messages, and goal-setting principles.

Self-management techniques

Participants learned self-management techniques such as prompts (stimulus control), self-monitoring, goal-setting, problem-solving, and reinforcement by assimilating

Table 50.4 *Reasons for application to the program*

Order	Reason	Frequency
1	chronic disease prevention	112
2	health promotion	93
3	losing weight	89
4	lack of exercise	84
5	better physical fitness	51
6	anxiousness of health problem	49
7	high possibility to continue	34
8	cooperation with university	30
9	no charge	29
10	lower burden	24
10	convenience	24
12	curiosity	23
13	walking	22
14	stress management	20
14	support for continuity	20
16	pedometer	18
14	city project	15
18	solution for time deficit	14
19	rehabilitation	6
20	academism	5
20	life satisfaction	5

Table 50.5 *Keywords of program information in the recipe for application to the program*

Order	Keyword	Frequency
1	beginning from the activity I can do	57
2	government-academia research	53
3	walking	42
4	recruitment for non-exercisers	41
5	small change	40
5	increasing daily life's steps	40
5	metabolic syndrome prevention	40
8	duration: 3 months	25
9	support for continuity	24
9	offering by family members and friends	24
11	brochure and pedometer presentation	21
11	correspondence education by mail	21
13	individualized advice	20
13	university academism	20
15	participation with family member or friend	15
16	feedback of blood testing result	14
17	individual-paced beginning	13
18	sense of season	6
18	activity recording	6
20	utilization of home page	4

Figure 50.7 A series of articles of behavior change education sent using the four newsletters.

newsletter content and they recorded their daily steps and, through self-monitoring, set goals for the 12-week intervention period. A verbal, physical, or symbolic prompt can be a cue that initiates a behavior, so the goal was to increase cues for the desired behavior, physical activity, or number of steps while at the same time decreasing cues for competing behaviors, such as using a car, elevator, or escalator. Examples of such cues include slogans, Post-it notes, placement of exercise equipment in visible places, and performing exercises at the same time and place every day.

Self-monitoring of physical activity with a pedometer has been frequently employed in behavioral management techniques, and goal-setting can be an effective motivational technique and strategy for improving physical activity behavior and adherence. In this program, participants learned how to set realistic goals through self-monitoring the

number of steps and improving their management ability. Problem-solving is a technique for identifying physical, psychological, and social barriers and for solving them. Participants learned from the newsletter articles how to overcome individual barriers to physical activity as well as common barriers such as the Japanese rainy season. Reinforcement is a powerful determinant of future behavior, and therefore incentives or rewards can be useful for increasing physical activity adherence. We introduced a variety of rewards via the newsletter articles to reinforce behavior, and the number of steps served as feedback during the intervention period. Relapse prevention was also introduced, whereby participants were made aware of high-risk situations—such as bad weather, job fatigue and family obligations that often lead to slacking off or relapse—and they were given some tips to prevent relapse.

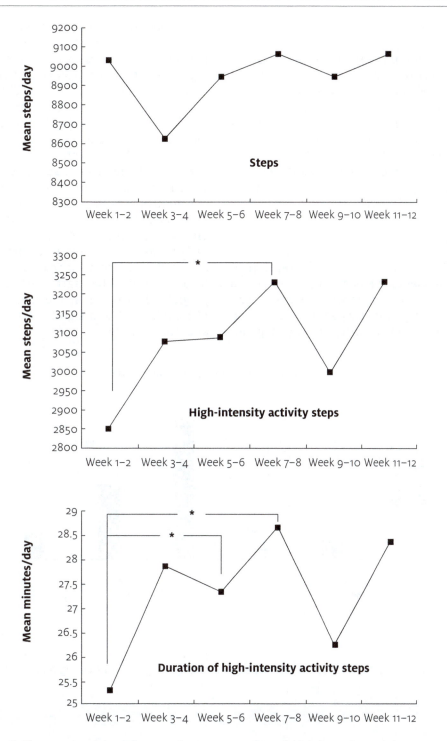

Figure 50.8 The mean number of steps, the mean number of high-intensity activity steps, and the duration of high-intensity activity steps with respect to each two-week period for 12 weeks.

Assessments

A pedometer (Omron HJ-111-K) that measured the number of steps, level of high-intensity activity, and duration of high-intensity activity was provided to each participant at the start of the program. In addition, participants received self-assessment postcards to record the three types of pedometer data and their awareness of mental and physical improvements, and returned a postcard after 2, 6, 10, and 12 weeks of activity.

Results

Most of the 170 participants (85.9%) returned the self-assessment postcards. Figure 50.8 shows the mean number of steps, mean number of high-intensity activity steps, and duration of high-intensity activity steps for each two-week period over the 12 weeks. Although no difference was found in the mean number of steps, the mean number of high-intensity activity steps and the duration of high-intensity activity did show a significant difference between periods. Specifically, participants showed improvement in the intensity of walking (walking faster with higher intensity) despite no change in the number of steps. Stage distribution also changed throughout the program. The number of participants at the contemplation stage became much smaller as the program continued and some moved to higher stages, as shown in Figure 50.9. We also compared some index parameters of blood between the start and end of the program. In particular, the mean value of LDL cholesterol was significantly improved after the program.

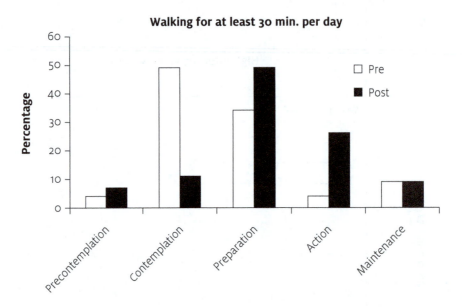

Figure 50.9 The change in distribution of behavior change stages from the beginning to the end of program.

CASE STUDIES 1 AND 2: LIMITATIONS AND FUTURE RESEARCH

We have described two behavior change programs targeted to organizational and community settings. These intervention programs could be adjusted to the characteristics of each environment. For example, some Japanese employees spend long hours in their work environment and have close relationships with colleagues. In this case, we used certain elements such as social support as an ingredient in the intervention to enhance cohesion within the organization. The same does not apply to people in the community, who are not familiar with each other because of social separation. Therefore, taking a commercial approach to recruitment might be a suitable means of prompting participation: the use of various forms of media, such as newsletters and magazines to be delivered by mail or via the Internet, would be a powerful way to distribute information on behavior change techniques for both organizational and community interventions. Although such strategies were successful in the two cases presented, further study of the approach is necessary because neither intervention included a control group. The inclusion of a control group in both organizational and community interventions would enhance evidence-based practice. Moreover, other elements such as work type, age, and sex of the participants should be considered in the future.

Another limitation is related to setting the target audience in concrete terms. In case study 1, although the participants were classified into six types—2 (stage-matched behavior information) × 3 (weight loss, physical fitness, and stress management)—the main purpose was to increase the number of steps recorded by the pedometer. Thus, it is unclear whether this purpose fitted all participants well. Also, in the case of community intervention, the participants included some regular exercisers who were not at high risk for metabolic syndrome although they were included in the target population. A more sophisticated recruitment strategy is needed to better focus on the target population in the future.

The case studies presented are just two examples from a wide variety of programs available which are based on different theories not covered in this chapter (but may be covered elsewhere in this book, such as self-determination theory in Chapter 5) and various intervention methods reflecting different traditions and community models (e.g., social marketing, media studies, and communication technology ecological models). Further reading on these models is recommended (e.g., Glanz, Lewis, & Rimer, 2008).

CASE STUDY 3: COMMUNITY INTERVENTION IN VANCOUVER, CANADA

Sometimes we do not appreciate that traditional sports, games, or dances might have a tremendous impact on the promotion of physical activity and public health. One of the authors, having been born and raised in Canada, never appreciated Canadians' passion for the sport of hockey until he moved to the United States and lived there for 40 years. After retiring from a professorship at Boston University, he returned to Canada and took on the position of Director of Sport Science for the Vancouver Canucks professional hockey club.

He saw this as an opportunity not only to bring science to professional sport but also to use professional sport as a tool to promote sport and physical activity within the city (the community). Of particular interest was the opportunity to help design a training facility that would serve not just as a training venue for the Vancouver Canucks hockey club, but also as a facility that would be used by the city of Vancouver for promoting sport, health, and wellbeing for all its residents, from youth to seniors. The City Council and the privately owned Vancouver Canucks agreed on a location for the facility and are currently in the process of finalizing the architectural plans. The training facility will be a three-story, "state of the art" training facility and community sport center. Approximately 45% of the area will be earmarked for exclusive use by the professional hockey club (e.g., the locker room area, training area, and management offices) and the remainder will be shared with the community of Vancouver. Included in the over 100,000 square feet facility will be a full-sized hockey ice surface, sport science high performance center, sports medicine area, restaurant, day care center, and hotel. The ice hockey arena will be available to the community when not in use by the Canucks. Likewise, parts of the sport science area and sports medicine area will be made available to the community.

Although there are arguments against using professional sports clubs as models for training and developing physical fitness and cognitive, emotional, and moral attributes in our youth, the reality is that young and old alike develop an extraordinary identity with their community professional sports team(s). Designed appropriately, using the best research from youth sport development, a professional sports organization-community partnership makes a lot of sense (Figure 50.10). This unique partnership in Vancouver is designed to promote sport as well as health and wellbeing for city residents and, unlike many professional sports venues worldwide, the facilities will be available for public use. To highlight just how unique and important this project is, for example, it would be unheard of for the residents of Milan to have open access to the AC Milan soccer training facility or for young baseball players in Tokyo to use the training facilities of the Tokyo Giants baseball club.

Figure 50.10 Hockey.

Why a professional sports club-community partnership?

In most communities throughout the world, residents have a strong identity with the top sports organization in their area. Where there is a professional sports team, residents of all ages are strong supporters. If a professional sports team does not exist in a particular community then the followers tend to identify with their amateur club, or in the United States, with a university sports team. Ice hockey in Canada has a passionate nationwide following. Indeed, hockey is Canada's national pastime, although lacrosse is considered its national sport. International Ice Hockey Federation (IIHF) statistics show that Canada has more ice rinks and registered players than any other country in the world. The United States has the second highest number of facilities and participants, followed by Russia. Most young Canadian boys dream of being a player

in the National Hockey League, a league that consists of seven clubs in Canadian cities and 23 American cities. Now that women's hockey is an Olympic sport, young Canadian girls also aspire to play at the highest level in this sport. However, it is important that Canadian youth be active participants in the sport and not just passive observers watching on television. The most recent data from Statistics Canada (2005) indicate that youth sport participation (for children aged 5–14 years) in Canada has declined significantly over the past decade. This is true for both boys and girls. The 2005 data showed a participation rate of 51% in all youth sports. Surprisingly, hockey had a participation rate of 11%, making it third behind swimming (12%) and soccer (20%). It appears then that, unfortunately, the Canadian passion for hockey is more as a supporter than as an active participant.

One of the positive and unique features of hockey in Canada is that communities

Figure 50.11 Curling.

encourage adults to continue playing the sport long after their youth programs, college, Olympic, and professional careers have finished. Referred to as "adult", "recreational", or "old timer" hockey, Canada has over 50,000 old timer hockey clubs and an estimated one million participants. The old timer clubs have hockey teams that include not only adults in their 30s, but also those in their 40s and upwards, sometimes even those in their 80s. The city of Vancouver has a very active old timers hockey program at all ages and ability levels and is expected to benefit greatly from the venue being built by the Vancouver Canucks and city of Vancouver.

Partnerships between elite sport clubs and a community can be a desirable model to promote sport and physical activity, not only for the youth of a nation, but also for young and older adults. All segments of the population enjoy having an identity with an elite sports club, and being able to participate in the same venue can provide extra motivation to stay physically active. The Vancouver model is one that other cities throughout the world should consider adopting.

CASE STUDY 4: CURLING AS A LIFETIME SPORT FOR MAINTAINING HEALTH AND WELLNESS IN CANADA

Another appreciation that struck the author upon his return to Canada was how the sport of curling has impacted the mind-body development of Canadian citizens. Although relatively unheard of in most parts of the world, curling is part of the Canadian way of life.

Curling is another sport played on an ice rink where four participants slide eight granite stones (also called rocks) across a 46-meter-long by 5-meter-wide sheet of ice towards a target area. Although quite different, it resembles to some extent the sports of bowling and shuffleboard. The objective of the game is to score points by placing the stones closest to the "bulls-eye" in the target. When releasing the stone, the player can turn the stone clockwise or counter clockwise and thus make the stone "curl" around other stones. Two team members with brooms sweep the ice as the stone slides towards the target, affecting the spin and speed of the stone. A great deal of strategy goes into choosing the ideal path for stone placement and superb eye-hand coordination is required to be an excellent curler. In some circles, curling is referred to as "chess on ice".

During youth, one of the authors made fun of the sport, believing it was a sport for "old" people that did not provide much physical exercise. However, after returning to Canada, and observing the continued popularity of the sport, as well as now being "older", he has a new found appreciation for curling.

The historical evolution of the sport is quite interesting. It is thought to have originated in Scotland in the early 16th century and was brought to Canada by Scottish settlers. The Royal Montreal Curling Club established in 1807 is thought to be the oldest sporting club in North America (http://www.royalmontreal-curling.ca/node/1). According to the World Curling Federation, curling is one of the fastest growing international sports, with approximately 40 nations participating in the sport. Curling became an official Olympic sport at the 1998 Nagano Olympics. Although Canada has the highest number of participants in the sport, curling is also relatively popular in the U.K. (especially Scotland), the United States, Sweden, Norway, Switzerland, Denmark, Finland, and Japan. Canada has over 1000 curling clubs, and the sport is particularly popular in small rural communities. The reason for its popularity is that it provides many Canadians the opportunity to be physically active during the long, cold winter months and enables them to engage socially with other members of the community. According to the Canadian Curling Association, over one million Canadians, nearly 3% of the Canadian population, play the sport each year. Other interesting statistics include: the majority of curlers fall into the 35–49 year age bracket, followed by those aged 50–64: 10.4% live in small prairie town communities; most are active volunteers in the community; and 49% of Canadian curlers consider themselves to be "health enthusiasts", or strong believers in the benefits of regular exercise for personal wellness. In Canada, curlers range in age from seven years old to "masters", those more than 60 years of age.

In general, curling is an amateur sport, although most recreational curlers compete in club tournaments (called bonspiels), to win modest prizes. There are, however, professional curlers that compete at national and international level and earn a significant income through sponsorships. In addition to Olympic competition in curling, world championships are also held for men, women, mixed (both men and women), juniors, and seniors.

The sport of curling in Canada was used as a case example in this chapter to illustrate how a particular winter sport can be such a positive social force for a community, and indeed a country. The sport has excellent participation statistics throughout Canada and relies on history and tradition to maintain participation across generations and within families. Compared to other sports, the cost of belonging to clubs and participating, as well as equipment costs, are relatively small. Programs for youngsters begin as early as age seven and continue through old age. The Canadian government has recently allowed for a Child Tax Credit so that parents can encourage their children to be more active physically. The sport is unique in that it allows for male and female participation as well as "mixed" curling (men and women playing together). Curling has also been adapted so that wheelchair users and others unable to get into a curling posture can participate in the sport. Another attraction for the sport is that unlike many other team sports, curling does not require excessive physical speed and strength from the players. Rather it relies more on the development of cognitive strategy, balance, and perceptual-motor coordination. Curling also has a strong emphasis on "good sportsmanship". Even at the highest level of competition, players are expected to "call their own fouls". A match traditionally begins with players shaking hands with each member of the opposing team, and it is also traditional for the winning team to buy the losing team a drink after the match. In addition, when being far behind in score, conceding a match is considered an honorable act, rather than being viewed negatively as quitting, as happens in many other sports.

This case example illustrates well how a love of sport can engage people of all ages in the community in sports with physical and social benefits that can last a lifetime.

LEARNING AIDS

1   Define physical activity.

Caspersen et al. (1985) define physical activity as any bodily movement produced by the skeletal muscles that results in energy expenditure. Physical activity in daily life can be categorized into occupational, sports, conditioning, household, or other activities.

2   What is behavior change?

This refers to any transformation or modification of human behavior such as physical activity or exercise. In public health, behavior change refers to a broad range of activities and approaches focusing on individuals, communities, and environmental influences on behavior.

3 Explain the transtheoretical model.

The transtheoretical model of behavior change assesses an individual's readiness to engage in healthier behavior, and provides strategies, or processes of change, to guide the individual through the stages of change to Action and Maintenance.

4 What is meant by "self-management"?

In the field of medicine and health care, this term has been applied to mean the interventions, training, and skills by which patients with a chronic condition, disability, or disease can effectively take care of themselves. In the area of health behavior change, it indicates cognitive-behavioral techniques to maintain or improve individual health behavior.

REVIEW QUESTIONS

1 Explain how recruitment techniques should differ between organizational and community populations.

2 Explain several self-management techniques designed to change physical activity behavior.

3 Think about how to apply the transtheoretical model to your target organizational or community population.

4 Think about how behavior change approaches combined with the nature of delivery would affect physical activity or exercise intervention.

EXERCISES

1 Develop the messages to persuade persons on each stage to increase physical activity by applying the transtheoretical model.

2 Develop your own recruitment procedure for adapting conditions to your target audience.

ADDITIONAL READING

Biddle, J.H. & Mutrie, N. (2008). Psychology of physical activity: determinants, well-being and interventions, 2nd edition, London: Taylor & Francis Group.

Glanz, K., Rimer, B.K. & Viswanath, K. (2008). *Health behavior and health education: Theory, research, and practice*, 4th edition. San Francisco: A Wiley Company.

Kreuter, M., Farrell, D., Olevitch, L. & Brennan, L. (2000). *Tailoring health messages: customizing communication with computer technology.* London: Lawrence Erlbaum Associates, Publishers.

Prochaska, J.O., Norcross, J.C. & DiClemente, C.C. (1994). *Changing for good: the revolutionary program that explains the six stages of change and teaches you how to free yourself from bad habits.* New York: W. Morrow.

Sallis, J. F. & Owen, N. (1999). *Physical activity & behavioral medicine.* SAGE Publications, Inc: CA.

Takenaka, K. (2012). *Psychology for exercise and health* (in Japanese). Tokyo: Asakura Shyobo.

Wieting, S.G. & Lamoureux, D. (2001). Curling in Canada. In Stephen G. Wieting (Ed.), *Sport and* *memory in North America* (pp.140–153), London: Frank Cass. www.curling.ca

 ## REFERENCES

Burbank, P.M. & Riebe, D. (2002). *Promoting exercise and behavior change in older adults: Intervention with the transtheoretical model.* New York: Springer Publishing Company.

Caspersen, C.J., Powell, K.E. & Christenson, G.M. (1985). Physical activity, exercise, and physical fitness: Definitions and distinctions for health-related research. *Public Health Reports*, 100, 126–131.

Glanz, K., Rimer, B.K. & Viswanath, K. (2008). *Health behavior and health education: Theory, research, and practice*, 4th edition. San Francisco: A Wiley Company.

Prochaska, J.O. & DiClemente, C.C. (1983). Stages and processes of self-change in smoking: Toward an integrative model of change. *Journal of Consulting and Clinical Psychology*, 5, 390–395.

Prochaska, J.O., DiClemente, C.C. & Norcross, J.C. (1992). In search of how people change: Applications to addictive behaviors. American Psychologist, 47, 1102–1114.

Statistics Canada, General Social Survey, 1992 and 2005. Top 10 organized sports of 5- to 14-year-olds in 2005. http://www.statcan.gc.ca/pub/11-008-x/2008001/t/10573/5214759-eng.htm

Stetson, B.A., Beacham, A.O., Frommelt, S.J., Boutelle, K.N., Cole, J.D., Ziegler, C.H. & Looney, S.W. (2005). Exercise slips in high-risk situations and activity patterns in long-term exercisers: An application of the relapse prevention model. *Annuals of Behavioral Medicine*, 30, 25–30.

Takenaka, K., Ohba, Y. & Mitsuishi, H. (2010). Assessment of coping with high-risk situations for exercise slip and lapse among regular exercisers. *Japanese Journal of Physical Education, Health and Sport Sciences*, 55, 157–168.

Takenaka, K., Fijisawa, Y. & Mitsuishi, H. (2011). Assessment of psychological burden to high-risk situations to induce exercise slip and lapse and practical coping strategies. *Japanese Journal of Health Psychology*, 23, 61–74.

Chapter 51

Physical exercise and major depressive disorder in adult patients

IOANNIS MORRES, AFRODITI STATHI, EGIL W. MARTINSEN AND MARIT SØRENSEN

SUMMARY

This chapter provides an understanding of physical exercise as a treatment modality for adult patients diagnosed with major depression as a primary disorder. The profile of major depressive disorder is defined, and evidence derived from clinical trials for the antidepressant effect of physical exercise is presented. Also, the most effective exercise protocols are identified. Finally, recommendations are provided as to how exercise consultancy in depressed patients could be applied in order to increase motivation and participation rates in exercise on referral programs endorsed by general practitioners (GPs) and realized in the pragmatic setting of routine practice in the community.

INTRODUCTION

Louis (pseudonym) is a 32-year-old male patient with major depressive disorder, repeatedly admitted to hospital within a 3-year period. At the latest admission (lasted 164 days), Louis' severity of depression was mild-moderate (score of 17 on the Beck Depression Inventory [BDI] [Beck, Rush, Shaw, & Emery, 1979]). At day 20, fitness training was added to medication and cognitive-behavioral therapies, and consisted of stationary cycling, treadmill walking/running, and resistance exercises delivered in small groups for 45 minutes, 3 days per week for a period of 20 weeks. Fitness training was associated with more positive emotional and behavioral responses compared to medica-

tion; Louis felt fit, enjoyed himself, and received enough support with regards to fitness training. Fitness training was also associated with positive changes in various aspects of Louis' functioning including enhanced coping strategies, sustained efforts to continue activities, and improved awareness of physical well-being. This experience was combined with a reduction of .75 standard deviation in depression, measured daily during the fitness-training program on a 7-item scale. At discharge, Louis' depression had improved from mild-moderate to mild (BDI score of 13). (Van de Vliet, VandeAuweele, Knapen, Rzewnicki, Onghena, & Van Coppenolle, 2004).

OBJECTIVES

After reading this chapter you should be able to:

1 Conceptualize major depressive disorder.
2 Explain how major depressive disorder is diagnosed, and classified in terms of severity.
3 Describe the most effective exercise protocols for patients with major depressive disorder.
4 Provide evidence-based consultancy to depressed patients in order to increase motivation and adopt and maintain a physically active lifestyle.
5 Prescribe an effective exercise program.

MAJOR DEPRESSIVE DISORDER

Depression is a serious mental health disorder that causes severe human suffering and in the worst case ends with suicide. Apart from being a lethal disorder, depression is also an independent risk factor to other disorders, like cardiovascular disorders, and it is associated with substantial reduction in lifetime expectancy. Moreover, depression is a psychosocially disabling disorder. In the United Kingdom, the London School of Economics (2006) reports that depression explains a significant portion of the unemployment variance as 40 per cent of all incapacity benefits are given to people with mental illness. To this extent, it is unsurprising that depression has been identified since the mid 1990s as the leading cause of disability worldwide and the second top contributor to the global health burden of disease by the year of 2020 (Murray & Lopez, 1996, 1997). As a consequence, the World Health Organization has ranked depression as a top treatment target (Üstün, 2001).

Together with anxiety and substance misuse disorders, depressive disorders are the most common mental disorders, and major depressive disorder (MDD) is the most common. According to the *Diagnostic and Statistical Manual of Mental Disorders*, Fourth Edition, DSM-IV, (American Psychiatric Association, 1994), major depressive disorder (MDD) has the following diagnostic criteria. One of the two symptoms, low mood or anhedonia (lack of interest or pleasure) is necessary, in addition to no less than four of the following symptoms: lack of concentration, disturbed sleep, disturbed appetite or weight, fatigue, psychomotor retardation or agitation, feelings of worthlessness, and persistent thoughts of death or suicide. The symptoms should be present for at least two weeks, and cause impaired functioning. Epidemiological studies indicate that 16 per cent of the population in the United States will meet criteria for MDD across the lifespan, with women being almost two times more vulnerable than men (Kessler et al., 2003). Given that MDD is the most common type of depression, the term depression and MDD will be used interchangeably in the current chapter.

The severity of depression is psychometrically assessed by means of self- as well as clinician-rated measures. The Beck Depression Inventory (BDI; Beck, Steer, & Brown, 1996 and BDI-II; Beck, Ward, Mendelsohn, Mock, & Erbaugh, 1961), and the Hamilton Rating Scale for Depression (HAMD-17; Hamilton, 1960) are the most common self- and clinician-rated measures, respectively.

The classical treatment forms of depression are medication and various modes of psychotherapy. These forms of treatment, however, are often seen as costly, not easily accessible, not always effective, time-consuming, and are associated with social stigma. Medication may have unpleasant side effects, and dropout rates may be high. Moreover, almost 50 per cent of depressed people do not take medication as prescribed, and thus cannot benefit accordingly. Furthermore, the classical treatment forms cannot meet the increased physical health needs of depressed patients. In general, depressed patients show a sedentary unhealthy lifestyle, including cigarette smoking, unhealthy nutrition and physical inactivity, leading to low levels of physical fitness. To this extent, depression is associated with increased levels of mortality and premature death rates. The physical health aspect of depression is an important therapeutic consideration due to the fact that prolonged psychiatric hospitalization is inversely related to the poor physical health of the depressed patients (Schubert, Yokley, Sloan, & Gottesman, 1995).

As a consequence, inexpensive, easily accessible, and cost-effective antidepressant interventions that ensure physical health benefits are essential to support the classical treatment forms of depression. Physical exercise is a valuable adjunct on account of the aforementioned qualities.

THE ANTIDEPRESSANT EFFECT OF PHYSICAL EXERCISE

The Greek philosopher and physician Hippocrates (460–377 BC), widely recognized as the father of medicine in the Western civilization, recommended physical exercise for the treatment of melancholy (depression). In the modern era, Franz and Hamilton (1905) and Vaux (1926) were pioneer researchers in the field of physical exercise and depression, and were the first to report on the positive effects of physical exercise on depression.

Ever since, a limited number of trials, randomized controlled clinical trials (RCTs) and controlled clinical trials (CTs) have been conducted on adult patients diagnosed with major depressive disorder as a primary disorder, and referred by health services. However, all of the trials have repeatedly indicated the association of physical exercise with antidepressant effect. Specifically, eight RCTs have compared aerobic exercise favorably or equally to other exercise modalities or traditional psychiatric interventions. Aerobic exercise was more effective than stretching (Knubben, Reischies, Adli, Schalttman, Bauer, & Dimeo, 2007), low intensity and relaxation (Bosscher, 1993), and similarly effective to relaxation, yoga and stretching (Veale, Le Fevre, Pantelis, de Souza, Mann, & Sargeant, 1992b). Compared to traditional treatments, aerobic exercise was equally effective to time limited or unlimited psychotherapies (Greist, Klein, Eischens, Faris, Gurman, & Morgan, 1979), and more effective than occupational therapy (Martinsen, Medhus, & Sandvik, 1985), psychotherapy and antidepressants (Veale, Le Fevre, Pantelis, de Souza, Mann, & Sargeant, 1992a), antidepressants (Pilu et al., 2007), antidepressants and electroconvulsive therapy (ECT) (Schuch, Vasconcelos-Moreno, Borowsky, & Fleck, 2011). In two CTs, aerobic exercise compared favorably to psychotherapy and antidepressants (Bosscher, Van Tilburg, & Mellenberg, 1997) and antidepressants (De la Cerda, Cervello, Cocca, & Viciana, 2011).

The antidepressant effect of aerobic exercise was recorded in both self- and clinician-rated outcome measures. Seven trials (Knubben et al., 2007; Veale et al., 1992a, 1992b; Schuch et al., 2011; Pilu et al., 2007; Bosscher et al., 1997; Greist et al., 1979) used clinician-rated, and three (Bosscher, 1993; Martinsen et al., 1985; De la Cerda et al., 2011) used self-rated primary outcomes of depression. As a consequence, the alleviation of depression through aerobic exercise is confirmed by the patients as well as the clinicians.

Patients showed a wide range of severity classifications; treatment-resistant (Pilu et al., 2007), normal-mild (Bosscher, 1993), moderate (Knubben et al., 2007; De la Cerda et al., 2011; Bosscher et al., 1997), moderate-severe (Veale et al., 1992a, 1992b; Martinsen et al., 1985; Greist et al., 1979), severe (Schuch et al., 2011; Pilu et al., 2007) and non-medicated (Bosscher, 1993;

Greist et al., 1979) depressed patients. Noteworthy, non-medicated (Bosscher, 1993; Greist et al., 1979), and treatment-resistant depressed patients (Pilu et al., 2007) challenge health professional practice (Beesley, & Mutrie, 1997; Shelton, & Papakostas, 2008). It seems therefore, that aerobic exercise could be an effective strategy in depression management at different levels of depression severity.

Both indoor and outdoor aerobic exercise protocols were found, and were mainly delivered in supervised group sessions. Indoor (clinic gym); aerobic exercise in equipment-based supervised conditions delivered either in groups (Pilu et al., 2007) or individual (Knubben et al., 2007; Schuch et al., 2011). Outdoor (park); group-based and supervised aerobic exercise (Veale et al., 1992a, 1992b; De la Cerda et al., 2011; Martinsen et al., 1985). Outdoor (park); aerobic exercise (Bosscher, 1993; Bosscher et al., 1997) on the basis of individual induction and group supervision (Bosscher, 1993), and individual supervision (Bosscher et al., 1997). It is not clear as to whether fitness gains are associated with higher depression relief because of the limited number of studies taking relevant measures. However, when fitness measures were taken, aerobic exercise resulted in fitness gains (increases in the maximum work capacity [Vo_{2max}]) and higher antidepressant effect than both antidepressant medication and psychotherapy (Bosscher et al., 1997; Veale et al., 1992a), or occupational therapy (Martinsen et al., 1985).

Two of the reviewed RCTs examined if the degree of adherence to the exercise program influenced the antidepressant effect of aerobic exercise. Aerobic exercise showed equal antidepressant effect to yoga, relaxation and stretching (Veale et al., 1992b), and higher effect to psychotherapy and antidepressants (Veale et al., 1992a) in patients with 100 per cent as well as >50 per cent adherence rates to the exercise program.

Most studies have addressed the effect of adding exercise to other forms of treatment, as both the exercise and control group patients in the majority of trials were on concurrent treatments including antidepressants and psychotherapy (Veale et al., 1992a, 1992b), antidepressants and sleep-deprivation (Knubben et al., 2007), non-medicated care (Bosscher, 1993; Greist et al., 1979), antidepressants and ECT (Schuch et al., 2011), antidepressants (De la Cerda et al., 2011; Pilu et al., 2007), and occupational therapy (Martinsen et al., 1985).

A direct comparison between aerobic exercise and a placebo was not controlled by any of the reviewed trials. Indirect evidence, however, provides optimistic findings in favor of aerobic exercise. First, the higher antidepressant effect of aerobic exercise compared to psychotherapy was seen in groups with similar outcome expectations (Bosscher et al., 1997). Second, the effect of aerobic exercise against equal or less effective types of exercise was seen in two (Knubben et al., 2007; Veale et al., 1992b) of five RCTs. The latter finding decreases further placebo speculations for aerobic exercise. These speculations were derived from the disappointment of the unimproved, in terms of depression, control group that was not assigned to the aerobic exercise intervention (Bosscher, 1993). Finally, the higher effect of aerobic exercise compared to stretching remained significant after controlling for the influence of parallel treatments (antidepressants/sleep-deprivation) (Knubben et al., 2007).

METHODOLOGICAL QUALITIES AND CLINICAL TAXONOMY

The reviewed trials, although demonstrating a positive effect to aerobic exercise on depression, have methodological deficits in the design, conduct, analysis, and reporting. These deficits include lack of intention-to-treat analyses, blinded assessor, random allocation, concealed allocation, and/or baseline imbalance in outcome measures between the intervention and control group. In addition, few studies have adequate follow-up assessments.

Given that higher risks of bias are associated with larger treatment effects (Schulz, 2001; Schulz, Chalmers, Hayes, & Altman, 1995), the reviewed trials were classified on the basis of top methodological qualities. To this extent, trials fulfilling most of the aforementioned methodological quality criteria were analysed in terms of the exercise protocols and the involved dose-response relationship.

In this manner, conclusions are drawn from trials with more robust designs. Examples are presented below.

In addition, to provide students or practitioners of routine practice with clarified findings on how to apply physical exercise in practice, we carried out a clinical taxonomy on the reviewed trials by separately grouping those with either inpatients or outpatients.

EXERCISE IN PRACTICE

In this section we will give examples of how exercise may be delivered to depressed patients. In the first RCT (Knubben et al., 2007), the exercise dose included daily supervised and individual interval training for 30 minutes. Inpatients exercised for ten days, in a hospital gym. In each session, inpatients walked five times for a period of three minutes at an intensity corresponding to a lactate concentration of three mmol/l in capillary blood and a heart rate of 80 per cent of the maximum. After each workload, inpatients walked at half speed for three minutes to rest. In the second RCT (Pilu et al., 2007) the exercise dose included supervised group-based interval training that consisted of two sessions of 50 minute-aerobic training per week for eight months on their preferred choice of 20 cardio-fitness machines. Patients selected a different cardio-fitness machine every four minutes. The exercise sessions took place in a hospital. In the third RCT (Schuch et al., 2011) the exercise dose included aerobic exercise three times per week for three weeks at a preferred intensity (provided that 16kcal/kg/week was completed). Inpatients exercised on an individual and supervised mode in a hospital gymnasium on equipment-based, preferred exercises of stationary bicycle, treadmill or elliptic. In the last RCT with depressed inpatients (Martinsen et al., 1985), the exercise dose included a 60-minute aerobic session at the intensity of 50–70 per cent of the Vo_{2max}, three times per week for nine weeks. Inpatients exercised under supervision in a park and in small groups using walking and jogging. This was supplemented, to a limited extent, with cycling or swimming at their preference. Finally, only one reviewed trial (CT) recruited depressed outpatients (De la Cerda et al., 2011). The exercise dose included aerobic exercise three times per week for eight weeks at low intensity. Outpatients were women, exercised in one group under supervision in a hospital gymnasium, using fun dance, low impact aerobic gymnastics, and walking. The use of three types of exercise suggests that a number of depressed patients participated in a preferred type/s of exercise, especially since the latter type (walking) is preferred by the majority of mental health patients.

Collectively, the exercise dose included three sessions per week for eight (De la Cerda et al., 2011), nine (Martinsen et al., 1985), or three (Schuch et al., 2011) weeks at the low-moderate intensity of 50–70 per cent of the maximum work capacity (Vo_{2max}), aligning with the national and international physical activity recommendations. The corresponding exercise protocols of these trials reflected on preferred type or intensity of exercise. In addition, both short-term aerobic exercise protocols (ten days) and long-term exercise protocols (eight months) (Knubben et al., 2007; Pilu et al., 2007) provided antidepressant effects. The latter exercise protocol also reflected the patients' preferences regarding the type of exercise.

Examples of exercise programs in depressed outpatients

1. Intervention: 3 x 45 minutes per week for eight weeks, supervised cardiovascular exercises in a group that aimed at increasing heart rate and lung function. Duration was gradually increased to 60 minutes. Protocol consisted of warm-up, low impact aerobic gymnastics, fun dance and walking oriented exercises to cardiovascular, and cool down work. The location was a hospital gymnasium. No dropouts were seen. All patients were prescribed antidepressants. Depression (BDI-II) improved from moderate into minimal-mild (De la Cerda et al., 2011).

Examples of exercise programs in depressed inpatients

1. Intervention: Three times per week for three weeks on self-selected exercise modality (stationary bicycle, treadmill, or elliptic) as well as on self-selected intensity exercise provided that 16Kcal/kg/week would be completed. Location was at university hospital. No dropouts were seen. All patients were prescribed antidepressants, and a limited number (six per cent) were prescribed electroconvulsive therapy. Depression (HAMD-17) was improved from severe to normal (Schuch et al., 2011).

2. Intervention: 3 x 60 minutes per week for nine weeks, supervised jogging and walking in groups. The location was a park. Exercises were supplemented by cycling and swimming according to the patient's preference. Intensity was set at 50–70 per cent of the maximum work capacity (Vo_{2max}), measured at baseline. Duration was gradually increased to 60 minutes. Dropouts were 14 per cent. All patients were prescribed to psychotherapy and occupational therapy. A third of the patients were prescribed antidepressants. Depression (BDI) improved from moderate-severe to mild-moderate (Martinsen et al., 1985).

3. Intervention: Three minutes interval-aerobic individual walking, five times a day for ten days at a mean intensity corresponding to a lactate concentration of three mmol/l in capillary blood and to 80 per cent of the maximum heart rate. Three-minute bouts were undertaken at half-speed between workloads. Gradual increases in treadmill elevation to maintain intensity. Supervisor provided feedback on walking techniques, muscle complaints, amount of exertion. Location was in university hospital. No dropouts were seen. The majority of the patients were prescribed antidepressants, and a third of the patients sleep-deprivation. Depression (Bech-Rafaelsen Melancholy Scale-BRMS) was improved from moderate to mild (Knubben et al., 2007).

4. Intervention: Sixty minutes/two times week/32 weeks, five minute warm up, 50 minutes training on a self-selected cardiofitness machine, switching every four minutes (20 machine options). Five minute cooling down/stretching. Inpatients exercised in groups and supervised. The location was a hospital gym. No dropouts were seen. All patients were prescribed antidepressants. Depression (HAMD-17) was improved from severe to mild (Pilu et al., 2007).

PHYSICAL EXERCISE AND DEPRESSED PATIENTS IN PRIMARY CARE

In the reviewed trials, depressed inpatients showed encouraging low dropout rates ranging from 0 to 27 per cent. In one study of outpatients, no dropout was seen (De la Cerda et al., 2011); this is an encouraging result because depressed outpatients often show disappointing dropout rates when they are referred by GPs to exercise on referral scheme programs (these programs last 12–14 weeks, and are realized in public or private leisure facilities). In particular, mental health referrals (consisting mainly of depressed outpatients) show the lowest adherence rates in the uptake (adoption-first actual exercise session) and completion (maintenance) stages amongst all referral groups. In detail, they show the lowest uptake rates of all health referral groups (D'Silva, 2006; Stathi, Milton, & Riddoch, 2006), lower uptake than physical health referrals (60% vs. 69%, p<0.001) (Crone, Johnston, Gidlow, Hensley, James, 2008), lower completion rates than physical health referrals (>80% attendance; 22% vs. 34%) (Crone et al., 2008), and the lowest completion rates of all health referrals (Dugdill, Graham, & McNair, 2005; D'Silva, 2006; Stathi et al., 2006). Also, the evaluation of an exercise referral scheme in Wales, in the UK, reports that mental health referrals were less likely to adhere to and complete the program than physical health referrals (Murphy et al., 2010).

A typical explanation to this problem indicates that a-motivation is the predominant symptom of the depressed patients. However, some studies have shown that mental health patients, including depressed patients, valued exercise, and evaluated it as more appealing than other therapies (Fleischmann, 2003; Sigurdsson, Olafsdóttir, & Gottfredsson, 2008; Ussher, Stanbury, Cheesman, & Faulkner, 2007). These positive findings are supported by studies on the preceding referral stages to the uptake and completion stages. Specifically, in the stages between the referral endorsement by the GP and the attendance of the first exercise referral scheme appointment with the exercise consultant, the mental health referrals appear to be highly motivated; in comparison to physical health referrals, mental health referrals represented the top predictor to exercise attendance uninfluenced by GP related factors (e.g., distance from the surgery, etc), and scored the top attendance rate at the first exercise referral scheme appointment (Harrison, McNair, & Dugdill, 2005). Also, fewer mental health than physical health referrals (six per cent vs. 10 per cent) dropped-out between the referral endorsement and the first appointment (Crone et al., 2008) despite the four to six week delay between services (Stathi et al., 2006). Hence, the stage of the first exercise referral scheme appointment with the exercise consultant appears to be the crucial cross-point that signifies: 1) the decrease of the initial motivation of

the depressed patients in the preceding stage of the referral endorsement; and 2) the increase of the dropout rates of the depressed patients in the subsequent stages of the uptake and completion of the exercise program.

Consultancy aims to motivate the patient to uptake, and complete the exercise on referral program. The motivation is described by the way it is regulated on a continuum from lack of motivation (a-motivation) through externally controlled regulation (external, introjected and identified) to internally controlled motivation (integrated and intrinsic). Consultancy is often medically oriented, aiming to enforce the patients' motivation to take up and complete the exercise program on the basis of extrinsically controlled regulation. Extrinsically regulated motivation includes motives of external ("I exercise because I was told by my doctor or others"), introjected ("I ought to exercise for my health") and identified ("I exercise to obtain health benefits") orientation.

According to the Self-Determination Theory (SDT) (Deci & Ryan, 1985) the regulation of the patient's motivation will be affected by the degree of satisfaction of three basic psychological needs through the activity. The psychological needs are the needs for competence, autonomy, and relatedness. They are defined as follows: 1) competence is a sense of mastery and the perception of being effective in executing the behavior; 2) autonomy refers to an internal locus of control and the perception that the behavior is self-selected; and 3) relatedness is the satisfied involvement with others and a sense of belonging. The more these needs are satisfied, the more likely the motivation is to be internally regulated. The more internally regulated, the stronger the motivation, and the more likely is engagement in the behavior in question. This has been documented to be the case also with psychiatric patients (with mixed diagnoses) (Sørensen, 2006). Internally regulated physical activity motives gave higher odds ratios for being physically active. There was also a relationship between intrinsically regulated motivation and the experience of symptom reduction during exercise (Sørensen, 2006). Thus, recommendations will be given as to how exercise consultancy could be structured to address intrinsically motivated exercise participation.

RECOMMENDATIONS ON EXERCISE CONSULTANCY

Intrinsic motivation is generated through a self-determined behavior on the basis of interest, pleasure, and fun, implemented for the sake of the activity itself rather than an external reason such as commitments or rewards. Intrinsic motivation is realized within a secure environment, belonging and responsive to initiations social milieu to ensure relatedness. Intrinsic motivation is catalysed with competence enforcement via optimal challenges, and effectance promoting feedback (approval and agreement with an appropriate action) to subjects responsible enough for the competent performance to feel autonomy; while competence is necessary for any type of motivation, perceived autonomy is required for the motivation to be intrinsic (Ryan & Deci, 2000a, 2000b). Noteworthy interventions that provide synergetic and not individual support for the needs of autonomy, relatedness, and competence go hand in hand with greater engagement in the behavior (Deci, Eghari, Oatrick, & Leone, 1994).

The practical applications of this knowledge for exercise consultants are thus:

In order to make the motivation more intrinsically regulated it is important to try to satisfy the three basic needs (for autonomy, competence and relatedness) through the engagement in physical activity. To achieve this, the following techniques are suggested:

1   Give autonomy support: provide options, support own initiatives, provide positive feedback, enforce self-selection, participants take part in decisions, create internal locus of control.
2   Support experience of competence: optimal challenges, approval when appropriate, stimulate self-efficacy, avoid providing rewards or mentioning external benefits, avoid judgmental approaches, utilize instructions for safety reasons only.
3   Support relatedness; promote noncompetitive types of activities, enforce positive and mastery oriented climate, work on social support and relationships, create feelings of belonging to group.

Further readings on self-determination theory and related applications can be found in the present volume in Chapter 5 Promoting motivational coaching environments by Ntoumanis and Mallett and in Chapter 48 Adherence to physical activities and sport by Chatzisarantis, Hagger, Kawabata and Kamarova.

LEARNING AIDS

1   Describe the concept and the diagnostic criteria of major depressive disorder.

Major depressive disorder is a serious mental illness that includes low mood or anhedonia, in addition to no less than four of the following symptoms: lack of concentration, disturbed sleep, disturbed appetite or weight, fatigue, psychomotor retardation or agitation, feeling of worthlessness, and persistent thoughts of death or suicide. The symptoms should be present for at least two weeks, and cause impaired functioning.

2   Present the methodological deficits of the reviewed trials, and explain why these deficits influence conclusions on the most effective exercise program.

Various methodological deficits have been recorded in the reviewed trials including lack of random allocation, concealed allocation, intention-to-treat analysis, blinding of assessor/s and/or baseline imbalance in outcome measures between the intervention and control group. Given that increased risk of bias is related with larger treatment effects, methodological deficits might contribute to an overestimation of treatment effects.

3   Define how physical exercise protocols may be optimally delivered in practice in major depressive disorder including the exercise modality, and the frequency, duration, and intensity of exercise.

Indoor as well as outdoor supervised aerobic exercise delivered for three times per week over a period of three, eight or nine weeks appear to have antidepressant effects. The corresponding exercise protocols included three or more exercise modalities, reflecting in large on the patients' preferences. The corresponding intensity exercise was low-moderate.

4   Describe the different types of regulation of motives for exercise.

Extrinsically regulated motives lead to exercise participation on the basis of external reasons including rewards, awards, and desired outcomes. Intrinsically regulated motives lead to exercise participation on the basis of internal reasons (interest, pleasure and fun) including for the sake of the exercise itself.

5   Discuss how the exercise consultancy should address motivation to exercise in order to increase the uptake (adoption) and maintenance (completion) of the exercise on referral programs.

In contrast to extrinsically regulated motives, intrinsically regulated motives are associated with higher odds ratios for being physically active and with decreased illness symptoms during exercise. Consultancy is suggested to ensure that the patient could be self-determined in terms of the type/s of exercise on the basis of pleasure, fun, and interest. In addition, consultancy is suggested to provide the appropriate feedback toward the satisfaction of autonomy, relatedness, and competence.

REVIEW QUESTIONS

1   Present the psychological, social and physical aspects of major depressive disorder.

2   Present the methodological deficits of trials that examined the antidepressant effect of physical exercise.

3   Identify the most effective exercise protocols and the involved dose-response relationship between physical exercise and depression.

4   Describe the three SDT psychological needs of autonomy, competence and relatedness, and explain as to how these needs could be enforced.

EXERCISES

Please consider the following steps toward the prescription of an exercise program to an adult patient with major depressive disorder:

1   Familiarize yourself with the administration of a self-reported inventory that measures the severity of depression.

2   Familiarize yourself with the three SDT psychological needs of autonomy, competence and relatedness.

3   Practice techniques as to how the three SDT psychological needs can be supported.

4   Evaluate your progress.

5   Design an exercise consultancy session in order to enforce the intrinsic motivation of a patient with major depressive disorder.

6   Collaborate with a health professional (e.g., GP) and an exercise scientist regarding: a) the referral of a patient with major depressive disorder to an exercise program; and b) the measure of the self-reported severity of depression.

   ● Discuss with the exercise scientist how a consultancy session on the basis of intrinsic motivation could be provided to a patient who is about to adopt the health behavioral pattern of physical exercise.

   ● Discuss with the exercise scientist the practical perspectives toward the facilitation of the patient to select the preferred type/s of exercise.

   ● Discuss with the exercise scientist examples of exercise programs, in particular of the exercise programs that included three times of aerobic exercise per week for three, eight, or nine weeks at low to moderate intensity exercise.

   ● Throughout the exercise program, participate in the follow-up assessment/support of the patient, and discuss with the exercise scientist the enforcement of the patient's three psychological needs by means of the relevant techniques.

7   At the end of the program, record the attendance rates of the patient to the prescribed exercise program. Participate in the measurement of the severity of depression. Compare the baseline with the discharge score of depression.

8   In the scenario of an early dropout, try to record the reasons that caused it.

ADDITIONAL READING

Martinsen E.W. (2008). Physical activity in the prevention and treatment of anxiety and depression. *Nordic Journal of Psychiatry*, 62 suppl. 47: 25–29.

Rethorst, C.D., Wipfli, B.M. & Landers, D.M. (2009). The antidepressant effects of exercise: a meta-analysis of randomized trials. *Sports Medicine*, 39(6): 491–511.

REFERENCES

American Psychiatric Association (1994). *Diagnostic and statistical manual of mental disorders*. 4th Edition, Washington, DC: American Psychiatric Association.

Beck, A.T., Ward, C.H., Mendelsohn, M., Mock, J. & Erbaugh, H. (1961). An inventory for measuring depression. *Archives of General Psychiatry, 4*, 561–571.

Beck, A.T., Rush, A.J., Shaw, B.F. & Emery, G. (1979). *Cognitive therapy of depression*. New York: The Guilford Press.

Beck, A.T., Steer, R.A. & Brown, K. (1996). *Beck Depression Inventory* (2nd ed.). San Antonio, TX: Harcourt Brace.

Beesley, S. & Mutrie, N. (1997). Exercise is beneficial adjunctive treatment in depression. *British Medical Journal, 315*, 1542–1543.

Bosscher, R.J. (1993). Running and mixed physical exercises with depressed psychiatric patients. *International Journal of Sport Psychology, 24*, 170–184.

Bosscher, R.J., Van Tilburg, W. & Mellenberg, G.J. (1997). Running and depression. In Vermeer, A., Bosscher, R.J. & Broadhead, G.D. (Eds.). *Movement across lifespan* (pp.131–146). VU University Press, Amsterdam.

Crone, D., Johnston, L.H., Gidlow, C., Hensley, C. & James, D.V.B. (2008). Uptake and participation in physical activity referral schemes in the UK: An investigation of patients referred with mental health problems. *Issues in Mental Health Nursing, 29*, 1088–1097.

D'Silva, C. (2006). Evaluation of uptake and effectiveness of exercise referral schemes in Angus, Scotland. University of Dundee.

De la Cerda, P., Cervello, E., Cocca, A. & Viciana, J. (2011). Effect of an aerobic training program as complementary therapy in patients with moderate depression. *Perceptual and Motor Skills, 112*, 3, 1–9.

Deci, E.L. & Ryan, R.M. (1985). *Intrinsic motivation and self-determination in human behavior*. New York: Plenum Press.

Deci, E.L., Eghari, H., Patrick, B.C. & Leone, D.R. (1994). Facilitating internalization: The self-determination theory perspective. *Journal of Personality, 61*, 119–142.

Dugdill, L., Graham, R.C. & McNair, F. (2005). Exercise referral: the public health panacea for physical activity promotion? A critical perspective of exercise referral schemes; their development and evaluation. *Ergonomics, 48*, 11–14, 1390–1410.

Fleischmann, H. (2003). What do psychiatric patients expect of inpatient psychiatric hospital treatment? *Psychiatric Praxis*, May; 30, Supp 2:S 136–139.

Franz, S.I. & Hamilton, G.V. (1905). The effects of exercise upon the retardation in conditions of depression. *American Journal of Insanity, 62*, 239–256.

Greist, J.H., Klein, M.H., Eischens, R.R., Faris, J., Gurman, A.S. & Morgan, W.P. (1979). Running as treatment of depression. *Comprehensive Psychiatry, 20*, 41–54.

Hamilton, M.A. (1960). A rating scale for depression. *Journal of Neurological Neurosurgery, 23*, 56–62.

Harrison, R.A., McNair, F. & Dugdill, L. (2005). Access to exercise referral schemes – a population based analysis. *Journal of Public Health, 27*, 4, 326–330.

Kessler, R.C., Berglund, P., Dempler, O., Jin, R., Koretz, D., Merikangas, K.R., Rush, A., Walters, E.E. & Wang, P.S. (2003). The epidemiology of major depressive disorder; results from the national comorbidity survey replication (NCS-R). *Journal of The American Medical Association 289*, 3095–3105.

Knubben, K., Reischies, F.M., Adli, M., Schlattmann, P., Bauer, M. & Dimeo, F. (2007). A randomized, controlled study on the effects of a short-term endurance training programme in patients with major depression. *British Journal of Sports Medicine, 41*, 29–33.

London School of Economics and Political Science. Centre for Economic Performance, Mental Health Policy Group (2006). *The depression report: a new deal for depression and anxiety disorders*. Centre for Economic Performance, London School of Economics and Political Science, London, UK.

Martinsen, E.W., Medhus, A. & Sandvik, L. (1985). Effects of aerobic exercise on depression: a controlled study. *British Medical Journal, 291*, 109.

Murphy, S., Raisanen, L., Moore, G., Edwards, R.T., Linck, P., Hounsome, N., Williams, N., Din, N.U. & Moore, L. (2010). *The evaluation of the National Exercise referral Scheme in Wales. Welsh Assembly Government Social Research*.

Murray, C.J.L. & Lopez, A.D. (1996). *The global burden of disease: A comprehensive assessment of mortality, inquiries, and risk factors in 1990 and projected in 2020.* Harvard School of Public Health and the World Health Organization.

Murray, C.J.L. & Lopez, A.D. (1997). Alternative projections of mortality and disability by cause, 1990–2020: Global Burden of Disease Study. *Lancet, 349,* 1498–1504.

Pilu, A., Sorba, M., Hardoy, M.C., Floris, A.L., Mannu, F., Seruis, M.L., Velluti, C., Carpiniello, B., Salvi, M. & Carta, M.G. (2007). Efficacy of physical activity in the adjunctive treatment of major depressive disorders: preliminary results. *Clinical Practice & Epidemiology in Mental Health, 3,* 8.

Ryan, R.M. & Deci, E.L. (2000a). Self-determination theory and the facilitation of intrinsic motivation, social development, and well-being. *American Psychologist, 55,* 68–78.

Ryan, R.M. & Deci, E.L. (2000b). Intrinsic and extrinsic motivations: Classic definitions and new directions. *Contemporary Educational Psychology, 25,* 54–67.

Schubert, D.S.P., Yokley, J., Sloan, D. & Gottesman, H. (1995). Impact of the interaction of depression and physical illness on a psychiatric unit's length of stay. *General Hospital Psychiatry, 17,* 326–334.

Schuch, F.B., Vasconcelos-Moreno, M.P., Borowsky, C. & Fleck, M.P. (2011). Exercise and severe depression: Preliminary results of an add-on study. *Journal of Affective Disorders, 133(3),* 615–618.

Schulz, K.F. (2001). Assessing allocation concealment and blinding in randomised controlled trials: why bother? *Evidence Based Nursing, 4,* 4–6.

Schulz, K.F., Chalmers, I., Hayes, R.J. & Altman, D.G. (1995). Empirical evidence of bias. Dimensions of methodological quality associated with estimates of treatment effects in controlled trials. *Journal of The American Medical Association, 273,* 408–412.

Shelton, R.C. & Papakostas, G.I. (2008). Aygmentation of antidepressants with a typical antipsychotics for treatment-resistant major depressive disorder. *Acta Psychiatrica Scandinavica, 117:* 253–259.

Sigurdsson, E., Olafsdóttir, T. & Gottfredsson, M. (2008). Public views on antidepressant treatment: Lessons from a national survey. *Nordic Journal of Psychiatry, 62:* 374–378.

Sørensen, M. (2006). Motivation for physical activity of psychiatric patients when physical activity was offered as part of treatment. *Scandinavian Journal of Medicine and Science in Sports, 16:* 391–398.

Stathi, A., Milton, K. & Riddoch, C. (2006). Evaluation of the London Borough of Camden exercise referral scheme. London Sport Institute at Middlesex University.

Ussher, M., Stanbury, L., Cheesman, V. & Faulkner, G. (2007). Physical Activity preferences and perceived barriers to activity among persons with severe mental illness in the United Kingdom. *Psychiatric Services, 58,* 3, 405–408.

Üstün, T.B. (2001). The world-wide burden of depression in the 21st century. In M. Weisseman (Eds.), *Treatment of depression: Bridging the 21st century* (pp.35–45). Geneva, Switzerland: World Health Organization.

Van de Vliet, P., Vanden Auweele, Y., Knapen, J., Rzewnicki, R. Onghena, P. &Van Coppenolle, H. (2004). The effect of fitness training on depressed patients: An intra-individual approach. *Psychology of Sport and Exercise, 5:* 153–167.

Vaux, C.L. (1926). A discussion of physical exercise and recreation. *Occupation Therapy and Rehabilitation, 6,* 30–33.

Veale, D., Le Fevre, K., Pantelis, C., de Souza, V., Mann, A. & Sargeant, A. (1992a). Aerobic exercise in the adjunctive treatment of depression. A randomized controlled trial. *Journal of the Royal Society of Medicine, 85,* 541–544.

Veale, D., Le Fevre, K., Pantelis, C., de Souza, V., Mann, A. & Sargeant, A. (1992b). Aerobic exercise in the adjunctive treatment of depression. A randomized controlled trial. *Journal of the Royal Society of Medicine, 85,* 541–544.

Part Eight

Clinical issues in sport psychology

EDITED BY TRISHA LEAHY

Chapter 52

Eating disorders

TRENT A. PETRIE AND CHRISTY GREENLEAF

SUMMARY

Athletes (and their bodies) are often idealized, yet many face weight- and body-related pressures that may contribute to problematic and unhealthy eating and weight control behaviors, as well as psychological distress. The physical nature of sport and the competitive sport environment place male and female athletes' bodies in the spotlight, where not only are their performances evaluated, but often their physiques as well. Eating disorders can be difficult to detect within athletes because some pathogenic behaviors, such as strict caloric intake and monitoring and excessive training, are assumed to be characteristics of serious athletes. However, such behaviors can lead to serious health consequences and can be detrimental to performance. Thus, sport and exercise psychology consultants should be knowledgeable about a) prevalence of eating disorders, b) sport environment factors associated with disturbed body and eating behaviors, c) discrepancies between social and sport body ideals, d) identification of pathogenic weight-control and eating behaviors, and e) strategies for creating body healthy sport environments for athletes.

INTRODUCTION

Case study 1: John, diver

From when he first started diving, John's goal was to compete at the national level and ultimately make it to the Olympics. Although he had moved up from the junior level, he had not yet broken through to be able to represent the U.S. team internationally. His dives had a high degree of difficulty, but he was not receiving the scores he needed to be competitive. In his mind, his body did not have the lines, leanness, or muscular definition that he felt the judges preferred and he thought that this contributed to his lack of success. Over the years, he also became increasingly self-

conscious about his body size and shape (he felt he was not measuring up to his teammates or competitors), which only contributed to his self-doubt and lack of confidence.

After a recent meet in which he had not performed well and had overheard a judge comment to his coach that he looked "fat," John committed to losing weight to gain a leaner body that he thought would be viewed more positively by judges. Initially, he lost some weight by adopting a strict low-calorie, low-fat diet, and by exercising aerobically in addition to his scheduled workouts, and his coach commented that John's dives seemed "better." However, in time the weight loss stopped and he began to react to his hunger and low self-esteem by binge eating every few days. As this cycle of bingeing and restriction continued, John became frustrated and disgusted with himself for not being able to follow his diet and lose the weight he wanted. One day, after a binge, he made himself throw up. Although vomiting provided temporary relief, he soon felt guilty and embarrassed about what he had done. All John had wanted to do was lose some weight to be leaner, but now he felt depressed and out of control; his self-esteem was at its lowest point ever and his diving was beginning to suffer as well.

Case study 2: Sarah, runner

Sarah had achieved success earlier in her distance running career and expectations were high concerning how far she could go. To help her reach her performance goals, she moved across the country, far away from her family and support system, to train with a new coach and group of runners. Although she was excited about the opportunity to work with such an elite group, she also was nervous to leave her family and friends and felt unsure about how she would do. The first few months of training went well and she made considerable progress, improving her technique, physical conditioning, and performances. As a result, her coach wanted her to begin training for a national meet that was six months away and would be her "introduction" in the running world.

Sarah threw herself into training at such a high level of intensity that none of her teammates could match her effort. She started doing extra mileage, without her coach's knowledge, and began to obsess about what she ate and how "fat" she was. Within two months of beginning this intensive training, she had stopped menstruating and her body started to breakdown. She was experiencing muscle pulls and strains that did not seem to respond to treatment. Although the athletic trainers, in consultation with her coach, restricted her formal training and focused on healing her body, she continued to run without their knowledge

because she was worried she would not be ready for the meet if she did not train. As time passed, it became clear to her coach and athletic trainers that she was not recovering; in fact, she was getting worse. She had lost even more weight, continued to be amenorrheic, and now had bad shin splints. Although everyone around her knew she was struggling and not healthy, Sarah denied that she was having any real problems.

These case studies show that although athletes often are viewed as paragons of physical health and psychological wellness, they experience many general and sport-specific pressures and demands that can contribute to the development of body image concerns (e.g., self-consciousness, dissatisfaction), psychological distress (e.g., negative mood states), and eating disorders (e.g., restriction, binge–purge). As illustrated by the cases of John and Sarah, eating disorders and body image concerns are not limited to just women; both male and female athletes may become dissatisfied with their bodies and engage in a range of pathogenic weight control behaviors (Greenleaf, Petrie, Carter, & Reel, 2009, 2010; Petrie, Greenleaf, Reel, & Carter, 2008). In this chapter, we define eating disorders and provide an overview of their prevalence, describe how the sport environment may increase athletes' risk, discuss the body-image paradox that exists for athletes, and provide information about how eating disorders may be identified and prevented within sport environments.

Figure 52.1 An unhealthy focus on weight can be problematic for athletes.

OBJECTIVES

After reading this chapter, you should be able to:

1   Delineate eating disorder diagnoses.
2   Identify signs, symptoms and related problems associated with the disorders.
3   Describe the prevalence of the disorders among non-athletes and athletes.
4   Discuss the factors within the sport environment that may increase athletes' risk of developing an eating disorder.
5   Describe the competing body images that exist for many athletes.
6   Understand how professionals identify athletes with eating disorders and what coaches, athletic trainers, athletic administrators, and sport governing bodies can do to prevent their development.

WHAT ARE EATING DISORDERS AND WHAT IS THEIR PREVALENCE?

Clinical disorders

Clinical eating disorders (EDs) are psychiatric disorders that involve pathogenic eating and weight control behaviors and disturbed weight-related cognitions and perceptions (APA, 2000), and include anorexia nervosa (AN), bulimia nervosa (BN), and eating disorders not otherwise specified (EDNOS).

Anorexia nervosa: AN involves maintaining low body weight for age and height (generally through caloric restriction), having a distorted body image and inaccurate perceptions of body weight, being extremely fearful of gaining weight, and over-valuing body weight for self-evaluation. Although the prevalence of AN is low among non-athletes, adult women (0.5% to 0.9%) have slightly higher rates than men (0.05% to 0.3%; Hudson, Hiripi, Pope, & Kessler, 2007).

Bulimia nervosa: BN involves episodic binge eating, where the individual often feels out of control, and subsequent compensatory behavior (e.g., vomiting, dieting, excessive exercise), as well as an extreme influence of body weight and shape on self-evaluation. Among adult non-athletes, the lifetime prevalence of BN is 1% to 3% for women and 0.1% to 0.5% for men (APA, 1994; Hudson et al., 2007).

EDNOS: Individuals with EDNOS have some of the symptoms of AN or BN, but either not all symptoms are present or are not at the needed level of severity. A lifetime prevalence rate of 9.0% for 18-year-old female Finns (Isomaa et al., 2009), and point prevalence rates from 2.5% to 3.3% for female undergraduates in the United States (Crowther et al., 2008) have been reported.

Binge eating disorder (BED) is a form of EDNOS that involves episodic binge eating without compensation and often follows weight loss and restrictive eating. Lifetime prevalence rates of BED are estimated between 0.7% and 4% (APA, 2000); higher rates have been found for women (3.5%) than men (2%; Hudson et al., 2007).

Subclinical disorders

Subclinical EDs include disturbed eating behaviors and attitudes that are problematic and unhealthy, and that may develop into clinical EDs over time (Stice, Marti, Shaw, & Jaconis, 2009). Like clinical EDs, subclinical EDs involve psychological and physical symptoms, such as distorted body image, negative self-beliefs, and the use of pathogenic eating and weight control behaviors, such as restricting caloric intake, binge eating, excessive exercising, and/or self-induced vomiting. Generally, prevalence rates are higher than clinical, for both men and women (Crowther et al., 2008; Isomaa et al., 2009; Tylka & Subich, 2002); among male and female U.S. undergraduates, subclinical rates range from 37% to 39%, respectively (Cohen & Petrie, 2005; Tylka & Subich, 2002).

PREVALENCE AMONG ATHLETES AND OTHER PERFORMERS

Prevalence rates of clinical EDs among older adolescent and adult athletes appear to be slightly higher than in the general population. Among U.S. female collegiate and international elite athletes, AN rates are estimated between 0% and 6.7%, BN between 0% and 12.1%, and EDNOS between 2% and 13.4% (Greenleaf, Petrie, Carter, & Reel, 2009; Johnson, Powers, & Dick, 1999; Sundgot-Borgen & Torsveit, 2004). Among U.S. male collegiate and international elite athletes, AN rates are low (0%), whereas BN (0% to 7.5%) and EDNOS (0% to 9.7%) are somewhat higher (Petrie, Greenleaf, Reel, & Carter, 2008; Johnson et al., 1999; Sundgot-Borgen & Torsveit, 2004). Rates appear slightly higher among elite than college-level athletes.

Subclinical EDs, as well as individual pathogenic weight control behaviors, are more prevalent than clinical EDs (e.g., Greenleaf et al., 2009; Johnson et al., 1999; Petrie et al., 2008; Torstveit et al., 2008). Among U.S. collegiate athletes, 25.5% of women and 19.2% of men may be subclinical. These athletes also engage in a wide range of eating and weight control behaviors, including: binge eating (two or more times/week – 7.8% females & 9.3% males), exercising to burn calories (two or more hours/day – 25.2% females & 37% males), and dieting or fasting (two or more times/year – 15.6% females & 14.2% males). Very few athletes (< 5%) use more extreme behaviors, such as self-induced vomiting, diuretics, or laxatives.

Athletes also experience a range of related conditions, in part because of the centrality of the body within sport. Like the previously described disorders, these conditions can be quite serious and negatively affect physical and psychological functioning.

Female Athlete Triad: The Female Athlete Triad ("triad") involves three interrelated conditions: disordered eating, amenorrhea, and osteoporosis. The "triad" is associated with increased risk of injury (e.g., stress fractures), medical complications (e.g., infertility), and psychological problems (e.g., anxiety, depression) (ACSM, 2007). There appears to be a relatively low co-occurrence of all three conditions of the "triad," ranging from 1.2% in high school athletes (Hoch et al., 2009; Nichols, Rauh, Lawson, Ji, & Barkai, 2006) to 2.7% at the college level (Beals & Hill, 2006; Reel, SooHoo, Doetsch, Carter, & Petrie, 2007) to 4.3% among elite Norwegian athletes (Torstveit & Sundgot-Borgen, 2005); for only two conditions, rates have ranged from 5.4% to 27%. Across all competitive levels, rates appear to be highest among athletes from lean-build, endurance, and/or aesthetics sports.

Muscle dysmorphia: Muscle dysmorphia (MD) involves an extreme preoccupation with a perceived lack of muscularity and distorted body image (Olivardia, 2001). Individuals with MD may view their bodies as small and weak (even when not), engage in excessive exercise and weight training, hide or cover up their physique, take nutritional supplements, including, in some cases, anabolic steroids, and experience a range of psychological disturbances, such as depression, anxiety, poor self-concept, and increased suicide risk. MD is more prevalent among men, although some women do experience it, and is thought to develop primarily during late adolescence (Murray et al., 2010) when boys may experience a great deal of social pressure to attain a muscular and powerful body. MD may be most prevalent in sports where strength and muscularity are prominent, such as weight lifting and body building.

SPORT ENVIRONMENT AS A RISK FACTOR

Athletes not only are exposed to the general sociocultural messages about appearance, body, and weight that are ubiquitous in Western society and reinforced by families, friends, and through the media, but also experience sport-specific pressures that may increase their focus on their bodies and negatively influence how they feel about themselves and how they look. Sport environments, particularly at the collegiate, national, and elite levels, are closed and tightly regulated and athletes generally are told how to behave in the areas of their lives having to do with their bodies, exercise, and eating. As a result, the pressures they feel to conform can be powerful.

Coaches, who spend the most time with athletes and have the most influence on them, do contribute to these pressures, but there are other sources within the sport environment to consider as well. In the sections that follow, we identify five different sources of pressure, though acknowledge that they may overlap and several may be present at once for an athlete. Singly or in combination, these pressures may contribute to athletes experiencing psychological distress (e.g., low self-esteem, depression), body dissatisfaction, and disordered eating behaviors (e.g., restricting caloric intake, taking muscle gain supplements).

Weigh-ins: Some coaches weigh their athletes on a regular basis and may set "weight goals" for them, even though these goals may be unhealthy and below the athlete's ideal for performance. Such a focus on weight may lead some athletes, such as gymnasts or divers like John, to weigh themselves regularly.

Although weight loss may be the focus within many sports, particularly for girls and women, in other sports (e.g., American football), the goal may be to gain weight, which can be a source of pressure as well. Whether the goal is weight loss or gain, when weigh-ins are conducted in public (e.g., among teammates), weights are posted where others can see (e.g., locker rooms), or if playing time is based on reaching weight goals, athletes can become hyper-sensitive about their body size and shape and self-conscious about how they look and may spend considerable psychological energy monitoring their appearance and attending to even the slightest imperfection.

Focus on diet and weight loss: Because low body fat is often mistakenly viewed as a primary reason for performance success, there can be a strong focus on weight loss within the sport environment. As such, athletes, like John and Sarah, may try to lose weight through dieting and, perhaps, excessive exercise. Female athletes often are encouraged by their coaches to engage in these behaviors, and both male and female collegiate athletes report that exercising and dieting/fasting are the two primary mechanisms they use to lose weight. Unfortunately, as illustrated in the second case study, a focus on dieting and weight loss does not necessarily translate into healthier eating and adequate intake of nutrients. Athletes like Sarah may consume fewer calories than is necessary for their energy needs, and may eat substandard levels of protein and carbohydrates, which may have a negative effect on their health and performance.

Sport body stereotypes: There are certain body types that coaches, fans, judges, and even athletes themselves, associate with different sports. We expect rugby players to be large and strong, and distance runners lanky and lean. Female gymnasts' bodies are supposed to be tiny, compact and powerful (but look "light and graceful"), whereas basketball players should be tall. These "sport body stereotypes" can influence coaches', athletes' and other sport personnel's perspectives and lead them to have unrealistic ideas about what body sizes and shapes are acceptable within a given sport. For example, John, the diver in the first case study, believed that his body fell short of the ideal physique for someone in his sport. Athletes who do not conform to these expectations may experience internal and external pressures to modify their bodies to fit the stereotype and may begin to evaluate themselves and their bodies solely through the lens of body size/shape as opposed to functionality.

Revealing uniforms: In some sports, uniforms leave little to the imagination as to athletes' bodies and may become a primary source of appearance and weight pressure within the sport environment. Wearing such uniforms may lead athletes, such as John in the first case study, to become more self-conscious about their physique; when that happens, they may begin to view their bodies as objects to be evaluated and judged. Taking such a perspective on one's body may cause athletes, particularly females, to become ashamed of and dissatisfied with how they look.

Although some men's sports have revealing attire (e.g., swimming and wrestling), these types of uniforms are more common in female sports. Interestingly, in certain sports, female athletes are required to wear uniforms that appear to provide no functional performance benefit and may, indeed, cause feelings of psychological and physical discomfort (Thompson & Sherman, 2010). For example, consider the differences in the uniforms of male and female beach volleyball players – skintight two-piece bathing suits for women and loose, baggy shorts and t-shirts for men. So, if wearing skintight uniforms provided a performance advantage, why don't male beach volleyball players wear nothing but form-fitting, brief, Lycra swimming suits? The fact that male athletes do not wear such uniforms suggests that there are other reasons for their choice of uniform. Requiring athletes, male or female, to wear uniforms that highlight (and reveal) their bodies when there is no functional or performance advantage gained by doing so may simply become another and unneeded source of pressure that can detract from the athletes' ability to compete at their best.

Coaches, teammates, and judges: General messages about weight, appearance, diet, and body size are communicated daily by family, friends and the media. Athletes, though, also may receive such messages from coaches, teammates, and judges, and what these individuals communicate can have a negative influence on athletes' perceptions of themselves and their bodies. These communications may be direct, such as when a coach tells an athlete he needs to get stronger or when an athlete comments on what her teammate is about to eat ("You're not going to eat that, are you?"), or indirect, such as when it is "known" that certain judges give higher scores to athletes with specific body types or when a coach gives more playing time to athletes who maintain restrictive diets and are very lean. John, for example, overhears a judge's comment about his physique, which reinforces John's belief that his body does not conform to what judges expect and reward. Over time, such expectations about body type, eating behaviors, and weight can become woven into the team's social fabric and then act as a powerful set of norms that athletes follow, even when it's to their detriment (physically and psychologically).

THE BODY IMAGE PARADOX

Although athletes generally report positive feelings about their appearance and physique, to understand their experiences with their bodies we must consider the social context, which is the sport environment. For women, the Western societal ideal is thin, lean and toned, yet with ample breasts and slightly curvaceous hips: *Sports Illustrated* and Victoria's Secret models illustrate this ideal. For men, leanness and muscularity, with considerable definition, represents the ideal and is the body type of the men seen in the pages of popular health and fitness magazines and the actors who portrayed the strippers in the movie, *Magic Mike*. For both women and men, these socially prescribed body ideals are fairly unrealistic particularly as weight trends amongst adults in Western cultures are toward overweight or obesity. Thus, for many men and women, there will be a discrepancy between what they are told they "should" look like and the reality of what their bodies actually are. The greater this discrepancy, the more they may become dissatisfied with the size and shape of their bodies and experience a range of negative emotions (e.g., shame, frustration, sadness).

Athletes who compete in "gender appropriate" sports often have bodies that are consistent with social standards of appearance and beauty. For example, figure skating is typically viewed as a feminine sport in which athletes demonstrate grace, flexibility, coordination, and emotional expression (all "feminine" characteristics). Female figure skaters also are expected to be small, petite, and thin, which parallels the body ideal for women. On the other hand, American football is considered "gender appropriate" for boys and men because football players embody the masculine characteristics of toughness, domination, and competitiveness; their bodies also closely approximate societal ideals in that they are big, strong, and powerful. For some athletes, particularly males in certain sports (e.g., wrestling, volleyball, swimming), their physical training results leads to physiques that are muscular, lean, and powerful – a close approximation of the societal ideal. It is not surprising, then, that these athletes generally are satisfied with their body size and shape and feel positively toward themselves in terms of "being a man".

Not all athletic bodies conform to prescribed societal body ideals. In fact, the athletic body ideal for some sports may be quite different from the societally-prescribed body ideal, which may lead to internal conflict. Within sport performance environments, female athletes appreciate, value, and feel proud of their muscles and the physical functionality of their bodies; their strength gives them confidence to compete at their best in their chosen sport. For example, female swimmers may develop muscular shoulders and upper bodies that are advantageous for their sport performance and are associated with positive feelings about their body within the athletic context because of its ability to perform. Yet, in social situations outside of sport, these same athletes may feel self-conscious about and uncomfortable with their bodies because of how disparate they are from the societal ideal. This perceived conflict between social and athletic body images likely occurs because of the incongruence between the physical performance advantages of strength and power that go along with having a muscular body and the societal expectation that attractive women are lean and toned, but not "too" toned and definitely not "too" muscular. Thus resides the paradox – female athletes may compartmentalize their body images to survive. They may have an athletic/sport body image that is strong, muscular, and powerful; they take pride in the functionality of their body in the sport environment. They also may have a societal body image where they downplay their strength and power as they attempt to more closely approximate society's expectations of how a woman should look.

Although male athletes often report fairly high levels of body satisfaction, how they evaluate their physique also may be affected by the sport context. Boys and men participating in sports that require body types that are inconsistent with societal norms and may be thought of as "gender inappropriate," such as figure skating or distance running, may be dissatisfied or uncomfortable with their bodies in social situations. For example, male cross country runners' lean, thin bodies are good for distance running, yet socially, they may be more dissatisfied with their physiques than those athletes who are bigger and more muscular. For other athletes, such as American football players, the body required for their sport may actually be larger (i.e., fatter) than the societal ideal. For instance, offensive linemen are expected to have large, heavy, and powerful bodies, which may lead to them to feel uncomfortable with or self-conscious of how they look when in nonathletic social situations.

INTERVENING WITH ATHLETES: CREATING A "BODY-HEALTHY" SPORT ENVIRONMENT

Because of the connection that exists between sport-specific pressures, those that originate from the behaviors, attitudes, values, and messages of important social agents in the sport environment (e.g., coaches and teammates), and disordered eating behaviors and body image concerns (e.g., Anderson et al., 2011; Galli et al., 2011), we begin this section by discussing how changing the sport environment may reduce athletes' risk. By "body-healthy" sport environment we mean that athletes' physical and psychological well-being is the central focus of coaches, administrators, medical personnel and anyone else assisting with their training. Taking such an approach means changing the view that maximizing performance trumps all other considerations or potential physical or psychological cost to the athlete. Healthy athletes – in terms of weight, physical status, physiological functioning, nutrition, and psychological well-being – will perform better than those who are compromised in any of these areas.

To bring about such environmental change (and how coaches, parents, and administrators, to name a few, think about weight and performance), we offer several suggestions and also refer the reader to Bonci et al. (2008), who provided detailed information regarding the identification, prevention, and management of eating disorders in U.S. collegiate athletic departments.

Disconnecting weight and performance: Superior athletic performances cannot be determined based on some ideal body weight or body fat percentage (Bonci et al., 2008); in fact, across all sports, there is considerable variability in the body sizes, shapes, and weights of high-level performers (Thompson & Sherman, 2010). Despite this reality, many coaches will monitor their athletes' eating patterns, track their weight, and assess their body fat at different times throughout a competitive season. These behaviors put an unhealthy focus on weight and body size/shape and may, subtly or directly, pressure athletes to exercise excessively, take muscle-gain supplements, restrict caloric intake, and/or vomit, which can lead to physical problems, such as menstrual irregularities and/or the loss of lean body mass. When athletes adopt these behaviors to change their weight, performances may be compromised because of inadequate energy supplies, insufficient strength and coordination, fatigue, and/or lack of physical confidence. John and Sarah, the athletes in our case studies, illustrate this point. Thus, to create a healthier environment, coaches and other sport personnel can disconnect weight and performance, deemphasize weight change, and encourage healthier avenues for improving performance (e.g., skill development, proper nutrition, mental toughness).

Eliminating weigh-ins and weight requirements: Generally, these requirements are unnecessary and in almost all instances should be eliminated. Instead, we suggest that a) athletes only be weighed for medical reasons (e.g., monitoring hydration), b) weigh-ins, if done, be conducted by medical personnel (e.g., athletic trainers) and *never* by coaches, c) athletes know why they are being weighed and asked whether they want to be told their weight, d) weigh-ins, if done, be conducted in private, and e) athlete's weight be kept private/confidential and *never* posted publicly (e.g., in the locker room). Further, direct or indirect comments about an athlete's weight or body shape should not be made.

If weight change (gain or loss) could be beneficial for the athlete's health, well-being, and potentially, performance, decisions to proceed should be made by a sport management team (SMT) that comprises various professionals, such as strength and conditioning staff, medical personnel, a nutritionist, an exercise physiologist, a mental health practitioner, etc. Before recommending weight change strategies, the SMT should evaluate all aspects of the athlete's current physical condition and training to determine if other behavioral changes are warranted instead (or in addition to). Throughout, the athlete should be involved in the program's implementation and monitoring, and the focus should always be on the athlete's health.

Changing weight/body-focused norms: Within an entire sport (e.g., wrestling) or just specific to one team (e.g., a soccer coach expecting players to look "feminine"), there may be expectations about weight, eating, body size/shape, and appearance. Coaches and teammates may communicate these expectations, both directly and indirectly, leading to the development of norms that can reinforce existing unhealthy beliefs as well as influence the adoption of new pathogenic behaviors. John, the diver described in the case study, may have been influenced to engage in disordered weight control and eating behaviors by other divers and the behaviors considered "normal" within his training environment. With such norms in place, athletes will experience pressure to conform, and may end up engaging in unnecessary and potentially unhealthy behaviors, such as exercising in addition to normal workouts, not eating after training, vomiting after a large meal, and/or taking muscle-enhancing supplements, such as steroids. Although adopting policies regarding not weighing athletes or using a nutritionist for meal planning may help address unhealthy norms, coaches and athletes must modify their attitudes and beliefs about weight, body, and appearance as well as the behaviors (unhealthy) that they believe are acceptable. Change may take time and considerable effort.

Educating coaches: Although many coaches at both the collegiate and elite levels have received some training regarding eating disorders (e.g., attended a workshop), additional education regarding how to identify, refer, and assist athletes with eating disorders is needed. First, if coaches' knowledge is limited, then programs, workshops and educational materials can be made available to them, emphasizing how to create a health-focused sport environment that does not compromise performance. Second, coaches can learn about the body image paradox, the fact that athletes may hold dual body images, one related to their sport (and likely based on their bodies' functionality) and one related to social ideals (and likely based on appearance), and these body images may be in conflict – what is good for their sport may not be good for them socially. Third, coaches can understand how influential they are in their athletes' lives and how their comments about body and weight may affect their athletes' self-esteem, confidence, body image, and ultimately, performance. If coaches are connecting weight and performance, they can learn to disconnect the two and consider other avenues for their athletes to improve performances. Finally, coaches can learn how to speak about health, nutrition, and performance in a manner that does not emphasize body and weight, and can solicit the assistance of dieticians to help their athletes maximize the effects of good nutrition on performance. In the case of Sarah, although her coach and trainers were focused on her physical health related to her injuries, they did not fully grasp the seriousness of her situation and may have benefited from education and programs designed to improve knowledge regarding signs and symptoms of pathogenic and disordered eating.

PREVENTION PROGRAMS

Unfortunately, coaches and other sport personnel may be resistant to making changes in their sport. Thus, prevention efforts may need to be offered directly to athletes, particularly those who are experiencing body image concerns, have internalized societal messages about body and self, and/or are in a sport environment where body and appearance pressures are high. Primary prevention programs are designed to prevent new cases of a disorder or condition, such as disordered eating, from emerging in a targeted population. Such programs have been shown to be effective amongst female non-athletes (Stice, Shaw, & Marti, 2007), though few studies have been done with athletes (e.g., Becker, McDaniel, Bull, Powell, & McIntyre, 2012; Smith & Petrie, 2008). The effectiveness of these studies appears to be based on their targeting at-risk individuals (e.g., women who have body image concerns), their use of interactive and experiential formats, and their incorporating content that focused on body-acceptance or reduction of the thin-ideal through the creation of cognitive-dissonance, such as when women argue against (or behave in a manner contrary to) societal ideals regarding weight, body, and appearance.

IDENTIFICATION AND TREATMENT

Even with such environmentally and individually-based prevention efforts, there still is a need for screening, identification and, unfortunately, treatment. There are two time frames when screening and identification might occur. First, during pre-participation physical examinations, athletes can provide information regarding their eating and nutritional status, body- and weight-related attitudes, and psychological well-being and, for girls and women, their menstrual functioning (Bonci et al., 2008). Such information may be obtained through interviews, paper and pencil questionnaires, or a combination of the two, and care must be taken to maintain its confidentiality (e.g., not sharing responses with coaches). Second, athletes' behaviors, attitudes, mood states, and physical and psychological functioning can be monitored by coaches and medical staff throughout the year.

When athletes are identified as experiencing disordered eating attitudes and/or behaviors, a meeting should be scheduled with a member of the SMT to gather more information. Although we cannot provide detailed information about this initial meeting (see Thompson & Sherman, 2010), we do want to highlight a few important points. First, confidentiality must be maintained at all times and any limits to confidentiality communicated directly with the athlete. For example, will information be shared with parents and/or coaches? Second, the meeting should be set up by someone who has a good relationship with the athlete (e.g., athletic trainer). Third, the focus of the meeting should be on the athlete's health and well-being (as opposed to weight and/or performance). If the SMT member who has this initial meeting is not trained in eating disorder assessment, then this person's goal becomes helping the athlete feel comfortable talking about his/her situation. Ideally, this meeting would result in a determination of whether the observed symptoms indicate an eating disorder or related psychological problem and if a referral for treatment is needed.

By identifying athletes early in the development of an eating disorder, we can minimize the negative effects of the suspected disorder by helping them get treatment. If the athlete is subclinical or engaging in pathogenic weight control behaviors, the development of more severe problems, such as the "triad" or a clinical ED, may be avoided. The health and well-being of athletes is an ethical and legal obligation of sport institutes, sport organizations, and coaches/trainers and creating a body-healthy training environment, having a screening process in place, and developing explicit policies regarding identification and treatment are three ways that demonstrate how to meet this obligation.

Regarding treatment, there are a few issues that exist when working with an athlete with an ED, which may not arise when treating non-athletes. First, in most instances, the mental health or health care providers (e.g., psychologist, psychiatrist, nutritionist) who provide treatment are likely not going to be part of the sport environment (or team/organization). Thus, confidentiality and how information will be shared (or not) with the coaches, athletic trainers, and other sport personnel must be considered and addressed at the outset. Sharing information may be needed so decisions can be made about continued physical training and/or participation in competitions. If an adult, the athlete must provide explicit consent for such communication to occur, unless the consent has been made previously as part of a medical care agreement with the sport/performance organization. After consenting, the athlete always should be made aware of what is being communicated to anyone in the sport environment.

Second, because physical health may be compromised, decisions must be made about whether or not the athlete should be allowed to continue to train and compete while in treatment. If the athlete's overall physical health and nutritional status is not put at risk and if the treatment itself is not compromised by training/competing, then remaining involved

is a viable option. Such decisions should involve input from all the professionals who are involved in the athlete's treatment, including physician, psychologist, and nutritionist. At all times the athlete's health status and progress in treatment should be monitored; training should be limited immediately if health or treatment are affected.

Finally, because athletes are part of a larger system (e.g., teams, organizations), absences from training or competition cannot be hidden easily. In fact, such absences are likely to be noticed and commented upon by teammates, other personnel, and potentially even the press. Thus, athletes (and perhaps their parents) who are undergoing treatment should be proactive and think through how (and what) they will communicate to others about their treatment or potential absence. Developing a plan of action that is comfortable for the athlete will help minimize fallout from the absence. It can be useful to view an ED as an injury and the treatment as rehabilitation. Such an approach normalizes the process and can destigmatize the disorder.

CONCLUSION

Despite their high level of physical activity, fitness, and seemingly ideal physiques, male and female athletes do experience body image concerns and engage in pathogenic eating and weight control behaviors, sometimes to the point of being at the clinical or subclinical levels. Athletes' risk of developing such problems may be increased by unique pressures within the sport environment and by the fact that, for some, their athletic physiques, which may be ideal for sport performance, are incongruent with general societal ideals for men

and women about body size, shape, and appearance.

However, creating a body-healthy sport environment can help to counteract these potentially negative messages. When coaches emphasize health over performance, nutrition over dieting, and physical fitness over weight loss, and accept athletes' natural body size and shape (as opposed to demanding that they meet some stereotypical ideal), they communicate an acceptance of athletes' bodies and an understanding of the need to eat nutritiously to perform at one's best.

LEARNING AIDS

1   What are the key symptoms of anorexia nervosa and bulimia nervosa?

Anorexia nervosa includes a low body weight for age and height, disturbances in body image and inaccurate perceptions of body weight, fear of gaining weight, and undue influence of body weight on self-evaluation. In post-menarcheal women, it causes the loss of menses.

Binge eating, with feelings of being out of control, and subsequent compensatory behavior (e.g., vomiting, dieting, excessive exercise), and a negative influence of body weight and shape on self-evaluation describe bulimia nervosa.

2   What are the Female Athlete Triad and muscle dysmorphia?

The "triad" includes the interrelated conditions of disordered eating (or extreme caloric restriction), amenorrhea, and osteoporosis. MD involves an extreme preoccupation with a perceived lack of muscularity and distorted body image.

3   How is the sport environment a risk factor for the development of eating disorders among athletes?

Within the sport environment, there are unique pressures that may be communicated, directly and indirectly, by coaches, judges, other sport personnel, and even teammates about how athletes should look and behave. Having to participate in team weigh-ins, having coaches/teammates focus on diet and weight, playing in a sport that has uniforms that highlight or reveal the athletes' body, and having a body size/shape that does not correspond to the physique expected for athletes in that sport are just some of the pressures that may heighten athletes' focus on their physiques, weight, and appearance, and increase their risk of developing an eating disorder.

4   What are three key issues that might arise in the treatment of athletes with eating disorders?

Confidentiality. Individuals within the sport environment, such as coaches and athletic trainers, may want to be informed about athletes' progress in treatment so decisions about communicating information must be made in consultation with the athletes and only made with their permission (or that of their parents if the athlete is a minor).

Decisions about whether or not athletes are allowed to continue to train and compete (and at what level) during treatment need to be made with the athletes' health and well-being in mind. If athletes' care and health are not compromised as a result, participating in training may be allowed.

Athletes are part of larger systems (e.g., teams, organizations) so their absence for treatment may be noticed and commented upon by others. Decisions should be made in advance on what information, if any, will be released regarding the athletes' absence. Viewing the eating disorder as an injury can help destigmatize the process of obtaining treatment.

REVIEW QUESTIONS

1   What are the relative prevalence rates of clinical and subclinical eating disorders among male and female athletes?

2   What are three ways to create a "body-healthy" sport environment?

3   Explain the "body image" paradox that exists for athletes.

4   What times in a sport season are ideal for gathering information that might help identify athletes who are experiencing body image concerns or disordered eating behaviors?

5   What specific factors within the sport environment can increase the risk of unhealthy eating or weight control behaviors among athletes?

EXERCISES

1   Review the case examples at the beginning of the chapter. In considering each case, discuss how you would approach each athlete to discuss your concerns about their health and well-being. What potential difficulties might you encounter in broaching your concerns and referring them for treatment?

2   Find someone who has participated in sport at a competitive level (e.g., high school, select/club, college, elite) and talk with them about any pressures they have experienced from coaches, teammates, and other sport personnel regarding their body size/shape, their weight, their eating, or anything else related to their physique/appearance. How do their experiences compare to the issues raised in this chapter?

ADDITIONAL READING

Anderson, C., Petrie, T. & Neumann, C. (2012). Effects of sport pressures on female collegiate athletes: A preliminary longitudinal investigation. *Sport, Exercise, and Performance Psychology, 1,* 120–134.

de Bruin, A., Oudejans, R., Bakker, F. & Woertman, L. (2011). Contextual body image and athletes' disordered eating: The contribution of athletic body image to disorder eating in high performance women athletes. *European Eating Disorders Review, 19,* 201–215.

Petrie, T. & Greenleaf, C. (2012). Eating disorders in sport. In S. Murphy (Ed.), *Handbook of Sport and Performance Psychology* (pp.635–659). Oxford University Press: New York.

REFERENCES

American College of Sports Medicine. (2007). The female athlete triad. *Medicine and Science in Sports and Exercise, 39,* 1867–1882.

Anderson, C., Petrie, T.A. & Neumann, C. (2011). Psychosocial Correlates of Bulimic Symptomatology Among NCAA Division I Female Collegiate Gymnasts and Swimmers/Divers. *Journal of Sport & Exercise Psychology, 33,* 483–505.

Beals, K.A. & Hill, A.K. (2006). The prevalence of disordered eating, menstrual dysfunction, and low bone mineral density among US collegiate athletes. *International Journal of Sport Nutrition and Exercise Metabolism, 16*, 1–23.

Becker, C.B., McDaniel, L., Bull, S., Powell, M. & McIntyre, K.P. (2012). Can we reduce eating disorder risk factors in female college athletes? A randomized exploratory investigation of two peer-led interventions. *Body Image, 9*, 31–42.

Bonci, C., Bonci, L., Granger, L., Johnson, C., Malina, R., Milne, Ryan, R. and Vanderbunt, E.M. (2008). National Athletic Trainers' Association position statement: Preventing, detecting, and managing disordered eating in athletes. *Journal of Athletic Training, 43*, 80–108.

Cohen, D.L. & Petrie, T.A. (2005). An examination of psychosocial correlates of disordered eating among undergraduate women. *Sex Roles, 52*, 29–42.

Crowther, J., Armey, M., Luce, K., Dalton, G. & Leahey, T. (2008). The point prevalence of bulimic disorders from 1990 to 2004. *International Journal of Eating Disorders, 41*, 491–497.

Galli, N., Reel, J., Petrie, T., Greenleaf, C. & Carter, J. (2011). Preliminary development of the weight pressures in sport scale for male athletes. *Journal of Sport Behavior, 34*, 47–68.

Greenleaf, C., Petrie, T.A., Carter, R. & Reel, J.J. (2009). Female collegiate athletes: Prevalence of eating disorders and disordered eating behaviors. *Journal of American College Health, 57*, 489–495.

Greenleaf, C., Petrie, T.A., Carter, R. & Reel, J.J. (2010). Psychosocial risk factors of bulimic symptomatology among female athletes. *Journal of Clinical Sport Psychology, 4*, 177–190.

Hoch, A.Z, Pajewski, N.M., Moraski, L., Carrera, G.F., Wilson, C., Hoffman, R.G., Schimke, J.E. & Gutterman, D.D. (2009). Prevalence of the female athlete triad in high school athletes and sedentary students. *Clinical Journal of Sports Medicine, 19*, 421–428.

Hudson, J.I., Hiripi, E., Pope, H.G. & Kessler, R.C. (2007). The prevalence and correlates of eating disorders in the National Comorbidity Survey replication. *Biological Psychiatry, 61*, 348–358.

Isomaa, R., Tsomaa, A., Marttunen, M., Kaltiala-Heino, R. & Bjorkqvist, K. (2009). The prevalence, incidence and development of eating disorders in Finnish adolescents – A two-step 3-year follow-up study. *European Eating Disorders in Review, 17*, 199–207.

Johnson, C., Powers, P.S. & Dick, R. (1999). Athletes and eating disorders: The National Collegiate Athletic Association study. *International Journal of Eating Disorders, 26*, 179–188.

Murray, S.B., Rieger, E., Touyz, S.W. & de la Garza García, Y. (2010). Muscle dysmorphia and the DSM-V conundrum: Where does it belong? A review paper. *International Journal of Eating Disorders, 43*, 483–491.

Nichols, J.F., Rauh, M.J., Lawson, M.J., Ji, M. & Barkai, H.S. (2006). Prevalence of the female athlete triad syndrome among high school athletes. *Archives of Pediatric and Adolescent Medicine, 160*, 137–142.

Olivardia, R. (2001). Mirror, mirror on the wall, who's the largest of them all? The features and phenomenology of muscle dysmorphia. *Harvard Review of Psychiatry, 9*, 254–259.

Petrie, T.A., Greenleaf, C., Reel, J. & Carter, J. (2008). Prevalence of eating disorders and disordered eating behaviors among male collegiate athletes. *Psychology of Men & Masculinity, 9*, 267–277.

Reel, J., SooHoo, S., Doetsch, H., Carter, J.E. & Petrie, T.A. (2007). The female athlete triad: Is the triad a problem among Division I female athletes? *Journal of Clinical Sport Psychology, 1*, 358–370.

Smith, A. & Petrie, T. (2008). Reducing the risk of disordered eating among female athletes: A test of alternative interventions. *Journal of Applied Sport Psychology, 20*, 392–407.

Stice, E., Shaw, H. & Marti, C. (2007). A meta-analytic review of eating disorder prevention programs: Encouraging findings. *Annual Review of Clinical Psychology, 3*, 207–231.

Stice, E., Marti, C.N., Shaw, H. & Jaconis, M. (2009). An 8-year longitudinal study of the natural history of threshold, subthreshold, and partial eating disorders from a community sample of adolescents. *Journal of Abnormal Psychology, 118*, 587–597.

Sundgot-Borgen, J. & Torstveit, M.K. (2004). Prevalence of eating disorders in elite athletes is higher than in the general population. *Clinical Journal of Sports Medicine, 14*, 25–32.

Thompson, R. & Sherman, R. (2010). *Eating disorders in sport*. New York: Routledge.

Torstveit, M. & Sundgot-Borgen, J. (2005). The Female Athlete Triad exists in both elite athletes and controls. *Medicine & Science in Sports & Exercise, 37*, 1449–1459.

Torstveit, M., Rosenvinge, J. & Sundgot-Borgen, J. (2008). Prevalence of eating disorders and the predictive power of risk models in female elite athletes: A controlled study. *Scandinavian Journal of Medicine & Science in Sports, 18*, 108–118.

Tylka, T. & Subich, L. (2002). A preliminary investigation of the eating disorder continuum with men. *Journal of Counseling Psychology, 49*, 273–279.

Chapter 53

Sexual abuse in elite sport

TRISHA LEAHY

SUMMARY

Organized competitive sport is a fundamental social institution, a microcosm of the larger society. Thus, not surprisingly, social problems that occur in society also emerge in sport. Sexual abuse is one of the problems that has been documented across all levels of the sporting structure, including the elite level. The empirical documentation of the prevalence, and impact of sexual abuse in sport has emerged slowly compared with other community sectors. Consequently, sport psychology training programs have historically not included this topic in their curricula. Yet recent research consistently indicates that athletes who have been sexually abused, either within sport or outside of sport, constitute a proportion of the sport psychologist's client group. Sport psychologists need to have the specific skill sets and competencies to be able to integrate interventions for healing and recovery into the athlete's life with minimum disruption to the athlete's ability to continue to develop in their sport and compete at the highest level. This brief chapter provides readers with an introductory overview of sexual abuse, its impact on athletes, and on current intervention knowledge applied within the elite sport context.

INTRODUCTION

I remember, just pretty much if he said jump, I'd jump. I never questioned whatever he said, then one night we were overseas, and he gave me a massage. He said, I had to have a massage before competing, and I'd never even question it. Now I remember one of the other athletes, she was a lot older than me, said, "Why are you going to his room for a massage?" And I sort of went, "Uhm, isn't that what every athlete does before they compete, they go to the coach's room for a massage...?" I had no idea...and of course it wasn't just a massage... (Leahy, 2001, p. 355).

We were such an elite squad, we were so much better than all the other squads that we were training with, and we were kept very much to ourselves. No-one ever interfered with us cause we were so elite, no one ever questioned what we were doing...he played us off together as well so (pause) it never entered my mind at all that others could possibly be experiencing the same thing (pause), I didn't even think about it. This was something that was happening to me and it was between me and him and nobody else knew... (Leahy, 2001, p. 360).

The above experiences reported by elite athletes who had been sexually abused by their coaches are unfortunately not unique. Sport is a social institution and participants in sport will inevitably experience some of the problems existing in society. The occurrence of sexual abuse in sport has been systematically documented (e.g., Brackenridge et al., 2008; Fasting et al., 2008; Kirby et al., 2008; Leahy et al., 2002, 2008; Vanden Auweele et al., 2008) with remarkably similar experiences being reported by athletes in different countries. In this chapter I will provide an overview of the prevalence of sexual abuse in sport, describe a trauma-based understanding of the psychological impact of sexual abuse on athletes, and discuss therapeutic intervention principles.

 ## OBJECTIVES

After reading this chapter, you should be able to:

1 Define sexual abuse.
2 Describe the prevalence of sexual abuse in sport and the impact of different definitions on reported prevalence rates.
3 Understand the psychological impact of sexual abuse from a trauma perspective.
4 Understand the key principles and phasing of therapeutic interventions for traumatized survivors of sexual abuse.

DEFINITIONS

In most legal jurisdictions in general, sexual abuse is considered to be any sexual activity with a child or an adult where informed consent is not, or cannot be given. Sexual abuse may include non-contact, contact, and invasive sexual acts. Non-contact sexual abuse refers to abusive acts which do not involve sexually touching a victim (e.g., exposure to sexual acts and exhibitionism). In relation to children, non-contact acts that legally constitute a criminal offence include engaging a child in pornographic photography, exposing a child to pornographic materials, and involving a child in sexually explicit conversation. For adults, sexually explicit conversation, jokes, innuendo and similar acts may not constitute a breach of criminal law but do apply to civil sex discrimination legislation in many jurisdictions. Depending on the context, such behaviors are generally considered to constitute sexual harassment. Contact sexual abuse refers abusive acts which involve physical contact with the victim (e.g., sexual touching, fondling, and masturbation). Invasive sexual abuse refers to abusive acts involving oral, vaginal, and anal penetration of the victim by objects, or body parts. Both contact and invasive sexual abuse may involve the victim being forced to perform the acts described above, either on the perpetrator or on another victim.

PREVALENCE OF SEXUAL ABUSE IN SPORT

Reported prevalence rates of sexual abuse in sport vary according to the definitions used, the methodologies employed, and the different groups sampled. Rates ranging from 2% (Tomlinson & Yorganci, 1997) to 17% (Leahy, Pretty & Tenenbaum, 2002) to 22% (Kirby et al., 2000) have been reported and such figures are broadly comparable to those reported internationally in community samples (Krug, Dahlberg, Mercy, Zwi, & Lozano, 2002). In Leahy et al.'s study, of 370 international and club level athletes surveyed, approximately 30% of the female athletes and 21% of the male athletes reported that they had experienced some form of sexual abuse (not necessarily in sport) prior to the age of eighteen. When further questioned as to whether or not this had occurred within their sports environment, almost half (46%) of the international level, and 25% of the club level athletes reporting sexual abuse, indicated that the abuse had been perpetrated by someone associated with their sport. In other words, for athletes who reported being sexually abused, and who were involved in competitive sport at the elite level, the perpetrator was as likely to be someone from within the sport environment as not. Studies indicate that perpetrators within sports systems are primarily male, and in positions of authority, trust or guardianship. These individuals have included officials, coaches, other athletes, and support staff, such as sports massage therapists, sport psychologists, and athletic trainers (e.g., Brackenridge et al., 2008; Kirby et al., 2000; Leahy et al., 2002).

THE PSYCHOLOGICAL IMPACT OF SEXUAL ABUSE ON ATHLETES

A trauma framework is commonly used to understand the psychological impact of sexual abuse. This framework includes the concepts of post-traumatic stress disorder (PTSD) and dissociation as primary responses to trauma (American Psychiatric Association [APA], 2000). Core post-traumatic symptoms include re-experiencing, avoidance, and hyperarousal (APA, 2000). Symptoms related to re-experiencing and hyperarousal can include intrusive thoughts, physiological arousal, reactivity to trauma cues, and hypervigilance. Avoidant symptoms can include avoidance of thoughts, feelings, places, or people associated with the trauma (APA). For example, a female athlete abused by her coach during her junior-level career describes this re-experiencing and intrusion when she was with her boyfriend,

> I would have bad dreams at night, lots of nightmares about it, and just a horrible time. I'd wake up in the middle of the night and I'd, you know, be next to my boyfriend and I'd just start hitting him and saying, "Get away" (Leahy, 2001, p. 377).

Dissociation is "a disruption in the usually integrated functions of consciousness" (APA, 2000, p. 477), and the symptomatology (e.g., amnesia, derealization, depersonalization) involves a splitting between the "observing self" and the "experiencing self." During a traumatic experience, peritraumatic (immediately during the event) dissociation provides protective detachment from overwhelming affect and pain. For example, an athlete sexually abused by his coach poignantly tries to describe his experience as a junior-level athlete, but ultimately lapses into a dissociatively influenced silence,

> Uhm, I don't know, I don't remember thinking about it. I don't, [pause] I don't. So possibly it was yeah, uhm [pause] your standard definition of someone just shutting it out while it happened. I don't know, I [pause], I, [pause], yeah [sighs into silence] (Leahy, 2001, p. 387).

However if dissociation continues, it can result in severe disruption within the usually integrated functions of consciousness, memory, identity, or perception of the environment. For example, one athlete sexually abused by a coach for many years during his junior-level career, described his sense of being disconnected from himself:

> I never consciously thought about it. I can't ever remember having any thoughts at all

about it happening. So there were two sides to me, the quiet part that I didn't even acknowledge or never really [long pause], and then the part that seemed to be pretty mainstream development (Leahy, 2001, p. 387).

Where the abuse is prolonged and repeated and perpetrated by those in positions of trust, guardianship or authority, as is typically the case in sport contexts (Brackenridge et al., 2008; Courtois, 2004; Kirby et al., 2000; Leahy, et al., 2002), an additional set of interrelated, or secondary trauma-based symptoms, can develop. Some of the athletes this author has worked with have struggled with sexual abuse trauma-related issues of not only dissociation and post-traumatic stress symptomatology but also the recognized secondary and associated responses to sexual abuse trauma such as impaired self-reference, depression, substance abuse, eating disorders, and other emotional, relational and behavioral difficulties. The term "complex trauma" has been developed to explain these post-traumatic, dissociative and related secondary symptoms (Courtois, 2004).

In general, the secondary trauma symptomatology can be understood as impacting seven areas of functioning (Courtois, 2004). The first area is affect dysregulation (inability to regulate the intensity of affective responses), and this is illustrated by an athlete recalling the emotional impact of a violent sexual assault at a sports event:

> Everything that was happening was extraordinarily intense, uhm...on some days I was fantastic,...but, uhm, [pause], on other days I was, uhm, just shit [long pause, weeping]. You know I just couldn't go out and I'm like, a really outgoing person (Leahy et al., 2003, p. 663).

The second area of functioning affected by the trauma of sexual abuse includes alterations in attention and consciousness leading to dissociative symptoms, as previously described above. This dissociation is illustrated by an

athlete sexually abused by his coach throughout his years as a junior-level athlete:

> I can't really remember my junior career, its like a big blank, like even though we achieved so much, and we were the best team and we trained, and we used to joke around with each other, but I don't know, I just felt like I wasn't there a lot of the time (Leahy, 2001, p. 386).

A self-perception embedded in a sense of guilt, shame, and responsibility for the abuse is the third area of functioning likely to be affected. One athlete sexually abused by her coach as a junior-level athlete said, ten years after the abuse had stopped, "I couldn't say no. I wasn't strong enough to do something about it, and I've been trying not to blame myself, but I still do (Leahy, 2001, p. 402).

Traumatized attachment to the perpetrator is the fourth recognized element of the traumatic impact of prolonged sexual abuse. It refers to the situation where, the perceived powerful perpetrator, and his worldview, becomes the centre of the athlete's universe. Traumatized attachment is illustrated in the following statement by a female athlete sexually abused by her coach throughout her junior-level career,

> ... eventually, I wasn't aware of any other male. Like, I just wasn't aware [long pause] like, I was just in this little dream world and he was the only male, but, uhm, [pause] and nothing mattered except for my coach. I used to think that, uhm, the most important thing was that I was training and listening to him, and if we were all training the way he wanted us to train, then I was happy and that's, that's about the only way I can explain it (Leahy, 2001, p. 389).

The fifth area of functioning disrupted by the trauma of sexual abuse is in the realm of relationship. Difficulties with trust and intimacy are commonly reported by survivors and are evident in a comment by an athlete who, as a junior-level athlete had been sexually abused by her coach for many years:

> ... I've had a lot of trouble with boyfriends. It's only in the last few months that I can actually feel comfortable with a boyfriend, like that he's not threatening. It's been years where I just haven't been able to be close to a boy. I just don't trust them. So I'd, for someone that I'd care about, you know, I'd throw it away because, you know, I just don't trust them (Leahy, 2001, p. 394).

Summarization and medical conditions frequently reported in the sexual abuse trauma literature have also been observed in athlete survivors and represent the sixth area of disruption of fundamental processes. For example, a female athlete survivor said of the impact of her abuse:

> I was tired. Sick...I was coming off my most successful competition ever in my career, and at a training competition, I just passed out, and that was it. From that competition on, it was, uhm [pause], like I had problems with my sinuses, infections, and I don't know if it was psychosomatic or not, but I

had to really cut down my training because I'd break down (Leahy, 2001, p. 396).

The seventh area of disrupted functioning within the complex trauma conceptualization concerns attributions of hopelessness and despair as poignantly expressed by a female athlete abused for many years by her coach:

> It was hard because I felt like I was just this disease. I really felt like I had no control over what was going on with the coach... I didn't realize there was another way out [pause] or there was another option for me" (Leahy, 2001, p. 283).

From the above descriptions, it is clear that sexual abuse can have a profound impact on athletes' lives. Effective treatment provision depends on the sport psychologist's ability to be able to effectively negotiate the complex dynamics of recovery and engage the athlete in collaborative decision making about the recovery pathway. This requires an in-depth understanding of the complex presentation of traumatic symptomatology, including the core post-traumatic and dissociative symptoms and the additional secondary symptoms which impact on seven broad areas of functioning.

THERAPEUTIC INTERVENTION

In the following section I briefly overview the key treatment principles and phases of treatment according to current standards of care. However, in order to be able to effectively engage in a healing, therapeutic relationship with traumatized athlete survivors of sexual abuse, specific training, ongoing professional development, peer supervision and personal therapy should be undertaken. When working with traumatized athlete survivors of sexual abuse, the basic principles of good therapeutic practice apply. These include communicating with the athlete about informed consent and confidentiality, and clarifying professional roles and boundaries. Within an overall ethos of main-

taining an environment of athlete empowerment and normalizing complex trauma responses, the psychologist should address issues of safety, including agreeing on emergency procedures, and exploring the nature of adjunctive treatment options, as necessary. Therapeutic interventions should be aimed at developing the necessary self-, and symptom-management competencies (such as emotional regulation) to maintain a level of functioning that allows the athlete to successfully maintain his or her lifestyle. For high performance athletes this will include consideration of the athlete's ability to maintain ongoing training requirements and performance levels.

Athletes' (and psychologists') expectations for treatment for complex post-traumatic conditions need to be managed as a longer overall timeframe, with more frequent sessions, and a longer duration for each session may be required. Dissociation, avoidance and motivated forgetting are likely to be extensively used as defense and coping mechanisms to keep painful material, or even the psychologist at a distance. Additionally the traumatized athlete's difficulties with establishing trust require patience and understanding in order for the psychologist to be able to maintain an authentic emotional engagement and a strong therapeutic alliance with the athlete. There may be recurrent testing of therapeutic boundaries and the psychologist's trustworthiness. It is essential that the psychologist demonstrates and provides a stable, reliable, well-bounded treatment relationship framework, which is the foundation upon which therapeutic work will proceed.

The prevailing consensus model of treatment follows a three-phased macro-cycle. However, this process is not linear because the issues addressed in each phase may emerge repeatedly as treatment progresses.

The first phase: The first phase focuses on symptom management, self-care and skill-building. The establishment of the therapeutic alliance, the development of personal safety strategies, and education to clarify the psychotherapy process and normalize the traumatic impact of the sexual abuse are some of the key tasks to be achieved in the first phase. Self-management competencies, including emotional regulation and life stabilization skills, and identifying social support systems are important elements of skill building.

Cognitive-behavioral interventions, commonly used in sport psychology are very applicable in this phase to build healthy coping strategies. As mentioned previously, trauma related somatization and medical conditions may pose a challenge to the athlete's ability to train and maintain the level of confidence necessary for elite performance. Therefore, for high performance athletes, self-care will involve the maintenance of proper nutrition, training recovery and injury prevention discipline.

With the focus of the first phase being on skill building and self-management, athletes often report improvements in quality of life at this time. It is not unusual for the athlete to request that therapy be terminated or for a break to be taken at this point, as there may be significant amelioration of distress and a greater sense of well-being and the athlete may feel enough in control of his or her life to proceed without further therapy. If considered, it is important to ensure that an option to return to therapy at a later date is discussed with the athlete. For high performance athletes, who are familiar with periodized training regimes, structuring therapy into "micro-cycles" can help to normalize recovery and integrate it into the athlete's high performance lifestyle. To facilitate the athlete's competition goals, priority tasks in each micro-cycle can be targeted at ensuring sufficient self-regulatory skills are in place to allow the athlete to continue to compete at key events. Being able to maintain achievement of sports performance goals is important as it can combat the sense of hopelessness the athletes feel about themselves and their lives that traumatized survivors of sexual abuse may feel.

The second phase: In this phase the trauma experience or experiences are directly processed in a gradual, sequenced manner. The key task of this phase is to resolve post-traumatic symptoms and to allow the development and integration of an understanding of the abuse experience into the athlete's life in such a way as to allow ongoing self-development that is not confined by past trauma. For example, an athlete illustrates how she has recovered from the trauma of the multi-year sexual abuse perpetrated by her coach and has come to an empowered meaning attribution of her survival that provides a positive self-enhancing narrative:

Now I see that he was in a position of power, and he shouldn't have [done that]...I mean I totally see the kind of person he was, how he manipulated us. I don't have any of those demons at all. I think surviving that and surviving the training has made me really strong (Leahy, 2001, p. 399).

At the start of this phase a return to the basic issues of informed consent, clarification of expectations and demystifying the process must be again discussed. Self-management, stabilization, and emotional modulation skills must be solidly in place. Pacing and intensity have to be carefully managed to prevent overwhelming the athlete's healthy coping resources.

For high performance athletes, guided imagery techniques in trauma processing work can be very useful as athletes who have had exposure to sport psychology are generally familiar with them. However, written or oral recounting, art and other expressive media are also useful in recounting experiences. During this process, the psychologist must be able to be fully and genuinely present with the athlete. It is important to acknowledge and normalize emotional responses, and provide a containing environment for this often-painful work. One of the treatment goals is to facilitate the recovery of healthy affect regulation. This requires a therapeutic environment in which a vulnerable athlete can freely express, accurately label, and consequently learn to trust his or her emotions. Therefore, during this phase, the psychologist must be able to facilitate the safe expression and management of very intense emotions, such as rage, shame, grief and mourning. If a sport psychologist is uncomfortable with, for example, anger or views it as an undesirable, or negative emotion, then this will encourage continued suppression and block the recovery of healthy affect regulation.

The third phase: The third phase occurs when the trauma has been processed and the athlete is ready to begin reconnecting with social relationships that may have been fractured, or difficult to maintain due to the trauma dynamic. One of the therapeutic goals in this phase is to facilitate the development of present day relationships that are free from trauma-based responses. During this phase it is important to continue to facilitate the development of relational skills by consistently modeling good communication, and demonstrating consistent emotional processing skills during the negotiation of the inevitable misunderstandings that may arise within the therapeutic relationship.

During the third phase, the termination process will need to be effectively managed. Effective management can be a challenge when working with traumatized survivors because it may trigger feelings of abandonment, loss and grief. Sport Psychologists working in an institutional environment with residential athletes have the opportunity to be able to work through termination in a slow and gradual manner with maximum supportive monitoring. Sport Psychologists should always refrain from dual relationships with athletes, but additionally, should be particularly careful with this vulnerable group of athletes to not engage in post-termination relationships outside the therapy structure. The possibility of a future return to therapy with the sport psychologist needs to remain open as future challenges may trigger new crises in the athlete's life. A return to therapy cannot happen if the sport psychologist has developed a post-termination relationship (e.g. friend, etc) with the athlete.

CONCLUSION

Athletes who have been sexually abused will inevitably constitute a proportion of the population with whom sport psychologists work and come into contact. There is evidence that the impact of sexual abuse on athletes, and their recovery needs can be understood from a trauma-based framework. Sport psychologists need to have the specific skill sets and competencies to be able to integrate interventions for healing and recovery into the athlete's life with minimum disruption to the athlete's ability to continue to develop their skills in sport and train and compete at the highest level.

LEARNING AIDS

1   What are the core post-traumatic symptoms?

Core post-traumatic symptoms include re-experiencing, avoidance, and hyperarousal. Symptoms related to re-experiencing and hyperarousal can include intrusive thoughts, physiological arousal, reactivity to trauma cues, and hypervigilance. Avoidant symptoms can include avoidance of thoughts, feelings, places, or people associated with the trauma.

2   What is dissociation?

Dissociation is understood as a disruption in the usually integrated functions of consciousness. Dissociative symptomatology (e.g, amnesia, derealization, depersonalization) involves a splitting between the "observing self" and the "experiencing self."

During a traumatic experience, peritraumatic (immediately during the event) dissociation provides protective detachment from overwhelming affect and pain. However, if dissociation continues, it can result in severe disruption within the usually integrated functions of consciousness, memory, identity, or perception of the environment.

3   What is meant by complex trauma?

As well as core post-traumatic and dissociative symptomatology, a further set of other interrelated, or secondary symptoms, has been observed in traumatized survivors of sexual abuse. The term "complex trauma" has been developed to explain the full range of post-traumatic, dissociative and related secondary symptom clusters.

4   Summarise the key treatment principles of the helping process.

- *The basic principles of any good therapeutic intervention apply, including communicating with the athlete about informed consent and confidentiality, and clarifying professional roles and boundaries. Within an overall ethos of maintaining an environment of athlete empowerment and normalizing complex trauma responses, the psychologist should address issues of safety, including agreeing on emergency procedures, and exploring the nature of adjunctive treatment options, as necessary.*

- *Therapeutic interventions should be aimed at developing the necessary self-, and symptom-management competencies to maintain a level of functioning that allows the athlete to successfully maintain his or her lifestyle, including maximizing the ability to maintain training and performance levels.*

- *It is essential that the psychologist demonstrates and provides a stable, reliable, well-bounded treatment relationship framework, which is the foundation upon which therapeutic work will proceed.*

- *Specific training, ongoing professional development and peer supervision are required.*

REVIEW QUESTIONS

1 Define the various forms of sexual abuse.

2 Describe the impact of sexual abuse using a trauma framework.

3 What are the seven areas of functioning that may be impacted by the secondary trauma symptom clusters?

4 Why might therapy take longer with traumatized survivors of sexual abuse?

5 What are the key therapeutic tasks in each of the three phases of treatment?

EXERCISES

1 According to current standards of care, how would you plan a therapeutic intervention for an athlete who has been sexually abused by a coach? What are the challenges you would expect to meet in this process and how would you prepare yourself to deal with them?

2 Locate a trauma counselor in your area and interview him/her on how he/she works with survivors of sexual abuse. How does that data compare with and further inform what you had previously answered in review question 1?

ADDITIONAL READING

Brackenridge, C.H. (2001). *Spoilsports: Understanding and preventing sexual exploitation in sport.* London: Routledge.

Herman, J.L. (1997). *Trauma and recovery. From domestic abuse to political terror* (2nd ed.). New York: Basic Books.

Leahy, T. (2010a). Sexual abuse in sport. Implications for the sport psychology profession. In T.V. Ryba, R.J. Shinke & G. Tenenbaum (Eds.), *The cultural turn in sport psychology* (pp.315–334). Morgantown. WV: Fitness Information Technology.

Leahy, T. (2010b). Working with adult athlete survivors of sexual abuse. In S.J. Hanrahan &

M.B. Andersen (Eds.), *Routledge handbook of applied sport psychology* (pp.303–312). Oxford: Routledge.

IOC Medical Commission (2007). *Consensus statement on sexual harassment and abuse in sport.* Available at http://multimedia.olympic.org/pdf/en_report_1125.pdf, retrieved August 17 2008.

UNICEF (2005). *UN human rights standards and mechanisms to combat violence against children.* Florence: UNICEF Innocenti Research Centre.

REFERENCES

American Psychiatric Association. (2000). *Diagnostic and statistical manual of mental disorders* (4th ed.). Text revision. Washington DC: Author.

Brackenridge, C.H., Bishopp, D., Moussalli, S. & Tapp, J. (2008). The characteristics of sexual abuse in sport: A multidimensional scaling analysis of events described in media reports.

International Journal of Sport and Exercise Psychology, 4, 385–406.

Courtois, C.A. (2004). Complex trauma, complex reactions: Assessment and treatment. *Psychotherapy: Theory, research, practice, training. 41*, 412–425.

Fasting, K., Brackenridge, C.H., Miller, K.E. & Sabo, D. (2008). Participation in college sports and protection from sexual victimization. *International Journal of Sport and Exercise Psychology, 4*, 427–441.

Kirby, S., Greaves, L. & Hankivsky, O. (2000). *The dome of silence: Sexual harassment and abuse in sport*. Halifax, NS: Fernwood Publishing.

Kirby, S.L., Demers, G. & Parent, S. (2008). Vulnerability/prevention: Considering the needs of disabled and gay athletes in the context of sexual harassment and abuse. *International Journal of Sport and Exercise Psychology, 4*, 407–426.

Krug, E.G., Dahlberg, L.L., Mercy, J.A., Zwi, A.B. & Loranzo, R. (2002). *World report on violence and health*. World Health Organization: Geneva.

Leahy, T. (2001). [Sexual abuse and long-term traumatic outcomes in a non-psychiatric sample of adult Australian athletes]. Unpublished raw data.

Leahy, T., Pretty, G. & Tenenbaum, G. (2002). Prevalence of sexual abuse in organised competitive sport in Australia. *Journal of Sexual Aggression, 8*, 16–35.

Leahy, T., Pretty, G. & Tenenbaum, G. (2003). Childhood sexual abuse narratives in clinically and non-clinically distressed adult survivors. *Professional Psychology: Research and Practice, 34*, 657–665.

Leahy, T., Pretty, G. & Tenenbaum, G. (2008). A contextualised investigation of traumatic correlates of childhood sexual abuse in Australian athletes. *International Journal of Sport and Exercise Psychology, 4*, 366–384.

Tomilson, A. & Yorganci, I. (1997). Male coach/ female athlete relations: gender and power relations in competitive sport. *Journal of Sport and Social Issues, 2*, 134–155.

Vanden Auweele, Y., Opdenacker, J., Vertommen, T., Boen, F., Van Niekerk, L., De Martelar, K. & De Cuyper, B. (2008). Unwanted sexual experiences in sport: Perceptions and reported prevalence among Flemish female student athletes. *International Journal of Sport and Exercise Psychology, 4*, 354–365.

Chapter 54

Substance abuse

MATTHEW P. MARTENS AND JESSICA L. MARTIN

SUMMARY

The purpose of this chapter is to discuss effective intervention strategies for athletes experiencing substance use problems. The chapter begins with a review of prevalence rates of alcohol, recreational, and performance enhancing drug use among athletes. Next, the chapter discusses ways to assess for the presence of substance use problems among athletes, including structured diagnostic interviews designed to assess for the presence of an alcohol use disorder and self-report questionnaires that can be used as more informal screening tools. Several empirically supported interventions, namely Motivational Interviewing, Relapse Prevention, Contingency Management, and 12-Step Programs are then addressed. This section includes considerations for implementing these interventions specifically among athletes. Finally, issues associated with implementing substance abuse services within athletic organizations are discussed.

INTRODUCTION

"James" is in his second year of college at a US university. He has an athletic scholarship that he is in danger of losing due to poor performance. James did not use drugs in high school and only drank alcohol sporadically. However, since beginning college his alcohol use has increased, and he now often socializes with heavy drinking teammates. James initially confined his drinking to Saturday nights, but later found himself drinking on both Friday and Saturday nights, and then sometimes during the week. His grades were adequate during his first semester, but declined the second semester and resulted in academic probation. His athletic performance also declined over the course of his first year. During the summer following his first year James continued to drink heavily on the weekends, and also tried marijuana with high school friends who did not participate in athletics. During James' second year, his athletic performance continued to decline, and his coaches began to wonder if he had an injury he was hiding. During a meeting with the team's athletic trainer James confided that he had been drinking heavily lately, and also occasionally using marijuana. The sports medicine staff is now attempting to determine the most appropriate course of action for James.

OBJECTIVES

After reading this chapter, you should be able to:

1 Summarize prevalence rates of alcohol and drug use among athletes.
2 Identify symptoms of a substance use disorder.
3 Describe the distinctions among various intervention strategies for substance abuse.
4 Identify ways that existing interventions can be used among athletes.

PREVALENCE OF SUBSTANCE ABUSE AMONG ATHLETES

Substance abuse is a major public health problem. For example, in the United States approximately 8% of the adult population met past-year diagnostic criteria for an alcohol use disorder and 2% met past-year diagnostic criteria for a drug use disorder (Grant et al., 2004a; 2004b). In many nations, the prevalence of substance use disorders is higher among subgroups like college students and other young adults (Dantzer, Wardle, Fuller, Pampalone, & Steptoe, 2006). Research has also shown that substance abuse disorders co-occur with a variety of other mental health problems (Grant et al., 2004b). Additionally, the economic costs of substance abuse are considerable. For example, one review of alcohol-related direct and indirect economic effects across 12 countries found that in 2007 such costs ranged from 0.60% to 5.44% of the country's Gross Domestic Product (Thavorncharoensap, Teerawattananon, Yothasamut, Lertpitakpong, & Chaikledkaew, 2009). Fortunately, there are a number of effective interventions for individuals struggling with substance abuse disorders. The primary purpose of this chapter is to review these interventions and discuss how they can be used among athletes.

Alcohol

The most commonly-studied comparison of substance use rates between athletes and non-athletes is in the area of alcohol use. Studies among adolescents have shown either similar rates of alcohol use between athletes and non-athletes or greater use among athletes (Lisha & Sussman, 2010; Lorente, Peretti-Watel, Griffet, & Grélot, 2003). Other research has shown that the relationship between sports participation and alcohol use is related to other factors. For example, one study of adolescents found that sports participation was associated with accelerated problem alcohol use, but only among those who did not participate in other academic extracurricular activities like foreign language clubs and debate team (Mays, DePadilla, Thompson, Kushner, & Windle, 2010). Other studies among adolescents have shown that male athletes were more likely to report problem alcohol use than male non-athletes, but female athletes were at less risk for problem alcohol use than female non-athletes (Mays & Thompson, 2009). A study of high school students in France found that among males, playing a team sport or competitive sport represented a risk factor for heavy alcohol use (Martha, Grelot, & Peretti-Watel, 2009).

Studies have compared rates of heavy alcohol use between college athletes and non-athletes in the United States, UK, and France with results consistently indicating that both male and female athletes were more likely than male and female non-athletes, respectively, to report excessive levels of alcohol consumption (e.g., Lorente, Souville, Griffet, & Grélot, 2004; Nelson & Wechsler, 2001; Partington et al., 2012). In these studies, the binge drinking rates of female athletes were similar to that of male non-athletes. These studies also reported that athletes were more likely than non-athletes to experience a variety of alcohol-related problems (e.g., academic difficulties, trouble with authorities).

Few studies have compared alcohol use rates between adult athletes and non-athletes, but some evidence indicates that elite (e.g., professional) adult athletes are more likely to report higher levels of problem drinking than non-athletes (e.g., Dietze, Fitzgerald, & Jenkinson, 2008; O'Brien, Blackie, & Hunter, 2005). The research on elite athletes has not been as extensive as those that sampled adolescents and college students (e.g., smaller, less representative samples). Additionally, no published studies among individuals in any age group have examined differences in alcohol disorders between athletes and non-athletes. Nonetheless, the preponderance of the literature suggests that participating in athletics can be a risk factor for problematic alcohol use.

Recreational drugs

Most studies have shown that those participants at all levels of athletics are less likely than their peers to report illicit recreational drug use (Lisah & Sussman, 2010). Studies among adolescents have shown that those participating in athletics were less likely than other students to report using substances such as smoking marijuana, cocaine, and psychedelics (e.g., Diehl et al., 2012; Papaioannou, Karastogiannidou & Theodorakis, 2004; Peretti-Watel et al., 2003). Similarly, national studies of college athletes have reported less lifetime and past-30 day prevalence of recreational drug use than national studies of the general college student population (National Collegiate Athletic Association, 2012). It may be that factors such as random drug testing and concern about drugs' impact on sport performance are unique deterrents of recreational drug use among athletes.

Despite the relatively low rates of recreational drug use among athletes, it is nonetheless important to examine effective intervention strategies for preventing and reducing such use among this group for at least two reasons. First, recreational drug use may be problematic among certain groups of athletes (e.g., approximately one-fourth of United States college athletes reported using marijuana in the past year). Undoubtedly, many athletes who do use recreational drugs will experience negative social, academic, health, and/or legal consequences as a result. Additionally, for athletes who are subject to penalties from drug testing, there are unique, negative consequences of substance use in the form of lost educational opportunities, being barred from playing one's competitive sport, and significant economic punishments such as fines, suspensions, and loss of endorsement opportunities.

Performance enhancing drugs

Preventing performance enhancing drug use is not only important due to the potential negative health-related effects on athletes (see van Amsterdam, Opperhuizen, & Hartgens, 2010), but also because its use has an impact on the overall structure governing organized sport itself. Virtually all organized competitive sports have clear rules governing both the games themselves and allowable behaviors among those who participate in the sport. In most instances the use of certain substances that can provide a competitive advantage is not allowed. Thus, athletes using such banned substances are committing an ethical/legal violation based on the accepted standards for their particular sport.

In general, studies among athletes at all competitive levels have found relatively low rates of performance enhancing drug use. For example, past year prevalence rates of steroid use in a national sample of United States college athletes was only 0.4% (National Collegiate Athletic Association, 2012), whereas prevalence rates in a national sample of college students in general was 0.3% (Johnston, O'Malley, Bachman, & Schulenberg, 2010). In

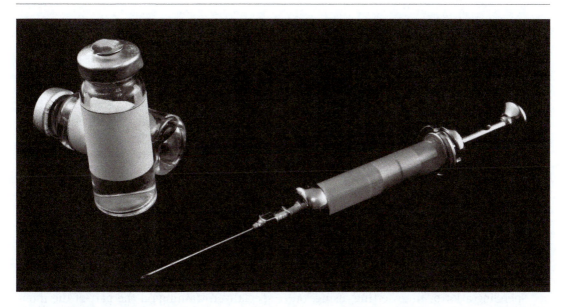

Figure 54.1 Performance-enhancing drugs can result in many negative consequences for athletes who choose to use them.

both samples males were more likely than females to report steroid use. Performance enhancing drug use does seem to vary by sport. For example, the most recent data among college athletes in the United States reported past year prevalence rates of 2.3% for baseball and football players, compared to less than 1% for track and field athletes and tennis players. Studies among high school and college students from Sweden, Norway and other developed countries have shown that use of performance enhancing drugs is more common among those student athletes who report heavy alcohol consumption and illicit drug use (e.g., Kindlundh, Isacson, Berglund, & Nyberg, 1999; Papadopoulos, Skalkidis, Parkkar, & Petridou, 2006; Wichstrøm, 2006). The rate of performance enhancing drug

use among professional or other elite athletes is largely unknown, due to a lack of studies on the topic. Evidence in the form of failed drug tests indicate that some professional and other elite athletes are using performance enhancing drugs, and their use may be more common in sports where high levels of strength and/or endurance are deemed necessary. Even if rates of performance enhancing drug use among athletes are generally low, the potential health-related risks associated with excessive use of some performance enhancing drugs, such as negative cardiovascular effects, liver toxicity, and mental health problems among heavy anabolic steroid users (van Amsterdam et al., 2010), warrants the development of effective intervention strategies.

ASSESSING SUBSTANCE ABUSE PROBLEMS

The next section of the chapter is focused on how to determine if an individual is engaging in hazardous substance use. Accurate assessment is a precursor to identifying and effectively intervening with those experiencing problems with alcohol and other drugs, and

there are a number of measures and other tools that clinicians and researchers use to do so. The two most commonly-used categories of measures are diagnostic or other structured interviews and self-report questionnaires.

Diagnostic/structured interviews

A structured, diagnostic interview, where the clinician asks a specified set of questions designed to assess for the presence of a mental health disorder, is considered the most reliable and valid way to assess for the presence of a substance use disorder. A substance use disorder (American Psychiatric Association, 2013) has a set of specific criteria that are defined in terms of the substance in question (e.g., alcohol dependence, cocaine abuse):

1 Taking the substance in larger amounts or for longer than you meant to;
2 Wanting to cut down or stop using the substance but not managing to;
3 Spending a lot of time getting, using, or recovering from use of the substance;
4 Cravings and urges to use the substance;
5 Not managing to do what you should at work, home or school, because of substance use;
6 Continuing to use, even when it causes problems in relationships;
7 Giving up important social, occupational or recreational activities because of substance use;
8 Using substances again and again, even when it puts you in danger;
9 Continuing to use, even when you know you have a physical or psychological problem that could have been caused or made worse by the substance;
10 Needing more of the substance to get the effect you want (tolerance);
11 Development of withdrawal symptoms, which can be relieved by taking more of the substance.

An individual with two–three symptoms is considered to have a "mild" substance use disorder; four–five symptoms is considered a "moderate" substance use disorder, and the presence of six or more symptoms is considered a "severe" substance use disorder.

Structured diagnostic interviews are designed to assess for the presence or absence of a specific disorder. Interviewers use a standardized protocol to determine if an individual has experienced each symptom of the disorder, which is then used to make a decision regarding whether or not the individual meets diagnostic criteria. Because in a structured interview one can assess for the presence of each diagnostic symptom, clarify questions if the interviewee is confused or does not understand a question, and follow-up if an interviewee provides an ambiguous response, such interviews are considered the most reliable and valid means of assessing for the presence of a specific disorder. However, diagnostic interviews can be time consuming and require specialized training on the part of the interviewer, which makes them challenging to use in many clinical and research situations.

Self-report questionnaires

An alternative strategy for assessing problems associated with substance use is to use self-report questionnaires. The measures are typically very brief (<10 items) and can be completed by an individual without the presence of a clinician. Questions on these measures typically assess quantity of, frequency of, and problems associated with substance use. There are a number of brief questionnaires used as screens for potential alcohol and/or drug problems, which typically include items assessing quantity of, frequency of, and/or problems associated with substance use. These measures generally include some type of threshold that is used to assess for the presence of problematic substance use. In a clinical setting, those who exceed the cut-off score would be referred for further assessment and/or treatment. These types of brief questionnaires have the advantage of being inexpensive and easy for the individual to complete. However, they are not designed to formally assess for the presence of a clinical disorder.

INTERVENTIONS FOR SUBSTANCE ABUSE PROBLEMS

Motivational interviewing

Over the past 20 years Motivational Interviewing (MI: Miller & Rollnick, 2002) has become a popular framework for intervening with those experiencing problems with alcohol and other drugs. The purpose of MI is to help individuals resolve ambivalence about changing their own behaviors. In this framework, resistance to change is considered a normal state of affairs, and clinicians are trained to assess an individual's readiness to change behaviors and work accordingly with the person. MI is conceptualized as client-centered, in that clinicians work with a client rather than telling or directing the person, empower individuals receiving the interventions by eliciting their own reasons for changing behavior, and stress personal responsibility for changing behaviors. Much of a MI session is focused on attempting to increase "change talk" in a client, which are statements in favor of changing behavior that are associated with actual behavior change.

MI interventions are guided by several core principles, including expressing empathy, developing discrepancy, "rolling" with resistance, and supporting self-efficacy. Expressing empathy refers to attempting to understand the client's beliefs, values, and perspectives regarding the behavior in question. For example, rather than making an initial judgment based on previous clinical experience about why it is that an athlete is having difficulty reducing her drug use, an empathic response would involve trying to understand her perspective on decisions to use drugs and why she believes she is having difficulty reducing the behavior. Developing discrepancy involves working with the individual to identify inconsistencies between current behavior (e.g., getting drunk on a daily basis) and larger goals, values, aspirations, etc. (e.g., becoming an elite athlete). Rolling with resistance refers to the process of not directly confronting resistance

when it emerges, but instead addressing it with the individual using a variety of non-confrontational strategies. Finally, supporting self-efficacy is important when an individual expresses the desire to actually change his or her behavior. In such instances the clinician can both reinforce the client's commitment to change and help him/her develop specific strategies to facilitate change.

Within the context of a MI intervention there are a number of specific techniques that are used to help facilitate change talk and subsequent behavior change. The acronym OARS (Open-ended questions, Affirmations, Reflective listening, Summarizing) identifies four of the most basic: asking open-ended rather than closed-ended questions, using affirmation when the individual expresses an interest in or intent to change, engaging in reflective listening, and periodically summarizing what has been discussed in a session or appointment.

Of these techniques, reflective listening often forms the core of the interaction between the clinician and client. Reflections involve the clinician providing the individual with his or her understanding of the client's words and/or message in an effort to facilitate change. Three common types of reflections are simple, double-sided, and amplified. Simple reflections involve acknowledging the thoughts, feelings, and intent of what an individual is saying, and can be used to illustrate empathy on the part of the clinician. For example, if an athlete says "It's just so hard to not go out drinking with my teammates because it's so ingrained in our team culture," an example of a simple reflection would be: "It sounds like you're concerned that if you change your drinking habits, it could impact your relationship with your teammates." The tone of the reflection is not definitive and does not simply involve repeating what the athlete said; instead, it reflects an attempt to understand the underlying concern expressed by the athlete. A double-sided reflection acknowledges an individual's reasons for and against change, and can be useful at directly addressing ambivalence on the part of the client. For example, assume that an athlete early in a session discussed reasons for wanting to cease marijuana use, but later in the session noted how difficult that might be. An example of a double-sided reflection would be "On the one hand you're saying that you would find it hard to stop smoking marijuana, but on the other hand earlier you expressed concerns that marijuana use is hurting your development as an athlete." A double-sided reflection can thus be effective at helping the individual re-focus on changing behavior when resistance to or doubts about change occur. Finally, an amplified reflection involves providing an exaggerated response to an individual's statement in an effort to elicit a less extreme response. For example, if an athlete said "you know, all athletes like to go out and drink," an example of an amplified reflection would be "What you're saying is that every single athlete at this university regularly goes out and gets drunk." Ideally, this reflection would result in a less extreme response from the athlete, like "Well, I suppose not all athletes here get drunk all the time, just some of the ones I know."

Other techniques that are used in MI-based interventions include decisional balance exercises and personalized feedback. In a decisional balance exercise the facilitator asks the individual to discuss the pros and cons of engaging in the behavior in question. Doing so can help establish rapport, lower resistance by acknowledging that there may be desirable outcomes associated with the behavior in question, and provide the clinician with information that can be used later in the meeting. Personalized feedback involves providing the individual with specific information tailored to his or her behaviors that is designed to increase discrepancy and thereby enhance motivation to change. One commonly used piece of feedback is personalized normative information, where the individual receives feedback on how his or her behaviors compare to the actual behaviors of a relevant reference group. For example, an athlete might receive personalized information indicating that he consumes approximately 14 drinks per week, thinks the typical college athlete consumes approximately 20 drinks per week, but that in reality the typical athlete only consumes approximately 8 drinks per week. Theoretically, such feedback would cause the athlete to reconsider his current drinking habits.

One appealing aspect of using MI-based interventions among athletes is that they can be easily targeted toward issues that are particularly relevant to them. For example, asking an athlete to discuss the pros and cons of substance use in terms of its prior impact on his or her athletic performance might be an initial strategy for facilitating a larger discussion about reducing alcohol and/or other drug use. Similarly, personalized feedback could be tailored to be specifically relevant to athletes. In one study the researchers developed personalized feedback that included unique sport-related content, such as negative sport-related consequences experienced as a result of alcohol use, the potential negative impact of one's drinking habits on subsequent sport performance, and injury risk associated with use of alcohol (Martens, Kilmer, Beck, & Zamboanga, 2010).

MI-based interventions have strong empirical support in the research literature (e.g., Cronce & Larimer, 2011), and can be effectively delivered in a very brief amount of time. In-person MI-based interventions have not yet been tested specifically among athletes, but studies have shown that personalized feedback-only interventions were effective in reducing alcohol use among college athletes (e.g., Martens et al., 2010). Therefore, considering their empirical support, ability to be tailored towards the unique needs of athletes, and relatively brief format, MI-based interventions should be considered as a primary option for those attempting to reduce substance use among athletes.

Relapse Prevention

Relapse Prevention (RP) refers to an intervention or treatment approach designed to avoid situations that are associated with increased likelihood of substance use or abuse (Witkiewitz & Marlatt, 2004). The approach is rooted in cognitive-behavioral theories of treatment, in that the person with the substance use problem is first taught to identify maladaptive thoughts and/or behaviors that are likely to result in using or abusing the substance in question. After identifying such "triggers," the clinician works with the individual to develop strategies to avoid or cope with situations that previously resulted in problematic substance use. For example, a college athlete might realize that she is more likely to drink alcohol in an unsafe manner when she is socializing with certain teammates or at a specific bar or pub. RP might then focus on strategies for socializing with different teammates, engaging in different behaviors when socializing with "high-risk" teammates, and/or avoiding the environment that triggers binge drinking episodes.

RP can focus on either abstaining from a substance or using it in less harmful manner. RP strategies often center on increasing alternative coping strategies, which subsequently enhance an individual's self-efficacy to avoid using or abusing the substance in question. For example, alcohol skills training programs that have focused on strategies such as increasing drink refusal skills, limiting the quantity/rate of consumption when drinking, developing alternative coping mechanisms, and blood alcohol level discrimination have been shown to be effective at reducing alcohol use among college students (Larimer & Cronce, 2002). Similarly, alcohol and drug reduction skills programs targeted to specific personality types have been shown to be effective among adolescents (Conrod, Castellanos-Ryan, & Mackie, 2011). It is important to stress that these effective RP programs go beyond simply providing general educational information to the individual, which has been shown to be ineffective at reducing drug and alcohol use (Larimer & Cronce, 2002).

Another component of some RP programs involves challenging an individual's expectations of the perceived positive effects of using a substance. Research has consistently shown that some of the effects of a substance can be attributed to the individual's expectancies regarding using the substance (e.g., enhanced mood, increased sexual prowess) rather than the physiological effects of the substance itself. Some studies have shown that programs focused on challenging these expectancies and correcting individual misperceptions results in reductions in substance use (e.g., Wood et al., 2007). Other common aspects of RP involve learning how to manage emotional states associated with substance use (e.g., recognizing that feeling nervous about a new social situation results in increased alcohol use), managing cravings for a substance, and increasing social support for avoiding substance use (e.g., spending more time with friends who do not use alcohol or are moderate drinkers).

RP strategies can be applied with athletes experiencing a wide array of substance use problems. Among those experiencing significant substance-related problems, topics such as avoiding triggers for relapse, managing cravings for a substance, and coping with affective states that lead to substance abuse can form the core of individual psychotherapy or other intensive treatments. RP can also be used as a preventive intervention among those who may just be beginning to experience problems associated with their substance use, or who are currently experiencing relatively mild problems. Such individuals would be good candidates for cognitive behavioral skills training programs addressing behaviors such as healthy coping strategies, drink or drug refusal skills, and ways to limit intake of a substance. These types of programs could easily incorporate athlete-specific content in order to make them more appealing, and perhaps efficacious, among athletes. For example, a clinician working with a distance runner who uses marijuana and regularly binge drinks could provide targeted information about the effects of these substances on cardiovascular capacity and their association with increased injury risk, and work with the individual to access sources of social support on his or her team that promote less drinking and drug use. Such targeted RP interventions have not been studied among athletes, but the strong support for RP among the population in general (Witkiewitz & Marlatt, 2004) makes it a viable intervention strategy for athletes experiencing problems associated with substance use.

Contingency Management

Contingency Management (CM) is based on basic operant principals, in that behavior increases when its consequences are reinforcing to the individual. In CM interventions, individuals are usually provided tangible external incentives as a consequence for engaging in the target behavior. For example, those participating in a CM intervention might receive vouchers that can be redeemed for specific goods and services for providing a negative drug test (e.g., Budney, Moore, Rocha, & Higgins, 2006). Theoretically, after the individual repeatedly engages in the target behavior in order to obtain the external incentives, other "natural" reinforcers emerge that subsequently motivate the behavior. For example, a high school athlete receiving a CM intervention who initially stopped smoking marijuana in order to receive vouchers for sporting goods might see her performance improve, begin to do better in school, and have fewer arguments with her parents. If such outcomes are reinforcing to the student, she will be likely to continue abstaining from marijuana use even after the CM incentives have been removed. A recent meta-analysis showed that CM had stronger treatment effects than other types of substance abuse interventions (Dutra et al., 2008).

One major challenge with CM interventions involves verifying the target behavior, which is arguably the most essential aspect of a CM program. It is crucial that those managing a CM intervention for substance use accurately determine if the behavior in question has in fact occurred (i.e., not using the substance). If this does not occur, then the external incentives lose their reinforcing properties because they can be provided incorrectly (i.e., provided when an individual actually used the substance or not provided when in fact no substance use occurred). Thus, CM interventions have been more commonly used for substances where a urine test can reliably assess substance use over a relatively long preceding period of time. It is more difficult to use CM for substances like alcohol that are metabolized relatively quickly.

It is important to note that a form of CM already exists in many sporting leagues and organizations, namely drug testing, although the focus is typically on punishment for undesirable behavior rather than incentives for desirable behavior. The most frequently employed model of drug testing is one where an athlete receives some type of sanction for using a banned performance enhancing and/or recreational substance. This sanction can be relatively mild (e.g., a warning or recommendation for treatment for testing positive for marijuana) to very severe (e.g., losing an Olympic medal or a professional athlete being suspended without pay for testing positive for a performance enhancing substance).

Although drug testing programs utilize principles consistent with CM, they are probably not best classified as CM interventions. This is because they are usually not specifically targeted toward individuals with substance use problems (although some organizations do additional testing for athletes who have had prior positive tests) and are not focused on providing external incentives beyond continued athletic participation for refraining from substance use. However, many sporting organizations have access to the necessary facilities to implement CM interventions (e.g., drug testing capabilities), so there is potential for the intervention to be applied in a more extensive manner within a sporting context. One challenge would be to develop effective incentives for athletes participating in a CM program. In general, substance use treatment settings offer small cash or voucher based incentives, which may be enough of an incentive for an individual to initially not use a certain drug, but it is unclear if such incentives would motivate various populations of athletes. Certainly, professional teams could choose to provide meaningful incentives for negative drug tests (e.g., contract bonuses), but would have to consider the economic impact of doing so. Smaller incentives may be viable among amateur athletes, but in some cases organizational restrictions would have to be considered (e.g., NCAA rules for college athletes in the United States). Nonetheless, given the powerful effects CM interventions have shown in the research literature (Dutra et al., 2008), researchers and clinicians working with athletes experiencing relatively severe substance use problems should consider strategies for implementing CM programs within their organizations.

12-Step programs

The final type of intervention for substance use problems that will be discussed is the oldest and one that is most commonly associated with substance abuse treatment: 12-step programs. Many people equate 12-step programs with Alcoholics or Narcotics Anonymous (AA/NA), and these programs are certainly the most common mechanism for entry into a 12-step program. However, 12-step programs can also be integrated into treatments delivered by mental health professionals (Project MATCH Research Group, 1997).

Twelve-step programs conceptualize substance abuse as a disease that is characterized by craving and loss of control. This "disease model" of addiction considers substance abuse a result of an underlying psychological or biological susceptibility. Abstinence is the only acceptable goal of 12-step programs, and one of the core requirements of a 12-step program is to turn oneself over to a "higher power." In most instances the higher power will be God or some type of spiritual being. Twelve-step treatment involves "working the program," meaning that the individual successfully completes a series of 12 steps in a defined order. For example, the first step involves admitting that one is powerless over his/her addiction, the sixth step involves being ready for God to remove defects of character, and the twelfth step involves carrying the message from one's spiritual awakening to other addicts and practicing the 12-step principles in all of one's affairs. Twelve-step treatment generally occurs via regular attendance at AA or NA meetings that are facilitated by peers who are also in recovery, obtaining and working with a sponsor who is in recovery him or herself, and becoming actively involved in activities associated with AA or NA. When integrated in the context of a formalized treatment setting, activities in a 12-step based program will be focused on working the steps (e.g., treatment groups focusing on specific steps, individual therapy focusing on embracing the identity of being an addict).

Evaluating the efficacy of 12-step programs is challenging, because many of them are anonymous by nature. However, the research that has been conducted suggests that they can be as effective as other approaches (Project MATCH Research Group, 1997). It is also important to note that even though all 12-step programs will presumably be focused on the same overall process, there will be considerable inconsistency across programs due to the manner in which they are structured (e.g., membership changes in meeting attendance, differences in activities from one sponsor to another).

In most instances it is unlikely that an athletic team or organization would be in a position to establish its own 12-step services, and many athletes may be reluctant to attend a 12-step program for fear of being stigmatized. One of the core tenets of 12-step programs is that sponsors or other providers must be in recovery and have successfully worked the 12 steps themselves, and by definition AA/NA meetings are peer driven. Thus, many profes-sionals who provide substance abuse services do not directly follow a 12-step based program. However, among athletes experiencing consid-erable substance use problems, for whom abstinence is a desirable treatment goal, and who are amenable to the tenets of 12-step programs, participation in such programs should be encouraged.

IMPLEMENTING SUBSTANCE USE SERVICES IN ATHLETIC ORGANIZATIONS

The final section of the chapter will focus on unique considerations for attempting to imple-ment substance use interventions within the context of an athletic organization. Athletic teams and other organizations have a reputa-tion for being insular and wary of those not affiliated with the organization, particularly in regards to potentially controversial issues like substance use (Martens, Kilmer, & Beck, 2009). However, in many cases athletes in need of substance use interventions will be most likely to receive the necessary services if they are integrated with or supported by the sporting organization to which they belong. For example, a college athlete in the United States would be more likely to access substance abuse treatment if there were a provider located within his or her athletic department than if he or she had to go out into the commu-nity and find appropriate services. Thus, it is important to consider ways in which athletic organizations can be encouraged to provide substance use treatment services.

One important strategy for convincing athletic organizations to provide substance use services is to highlight the relationship between substance use and poor athletic performance. Substance use can negatively impact performance via the debilitating effects of the substance itself (Schwenk, 1997) or through suspensions or other sanctions asso-ciated with positive drug tests. Continued employment for many coaches and other athletic administrators is due largely to the success they have in terms of wins and losses, so convincing them that substance use services have the potential to improve athletic performance may increase the likelihood of its support.

Another potential strategy involves provid-ing empirically supported services in the context of organizational mandates. For exam-ple, in the United States the National Colle-giate Athletic Association mandates that college athletes at member institutions be provided with drug and alcohol education, so clinicians at such institutions could work with the athletic department to provide brief inter-ventions that also have strong empirical support. Similarly, professional organizations like the National Football League hold annual seminars for rookies prior to entering the league that address a wide array of issues. Brief substance use preventive interventions could be incorporated into these seminars.

Finally, implementing substance use services within an athletic organization would likely require the support or endorsement of other health professionals already working with the athletes in the organization. Team physicians, physical therapists, and athletic trainers are generally well-ingrained and well-respected within athletic departments, and can provide political support should adminis-trators within a sporting organization be resistant to providing substance use services. Additionally, these health care professionals will often be the first to recognize when an athlete may be experiencing a substance use problem, and can be trained to either deliver brief interventions themselves or refer the athlete to more intensive services. Finally, departments with an appropriately licensed applied sport psychologist with training in substance abuse issues would have an internal resource to help those athletes with potentially more severe problems.

CONCLUSION

Substance abuse is a considerable worldwide public health problem, and athletes are by no means exempt from its influence. In fact, for some substances like alcohol, athletes may be a particularly at-risk group. Fortunately, a number of effective intervention and treatment strategies exist for substance use problems, many of which are relatively brief and can be delivered for little cost. It is important that health care providers, coaches, and other athletic administrators responsible for athletes' well-being are aware of the existence of these interventions, and athletes in need of such services be provided appropriate opportunities to receive them.

LEARNING AIDS

1   Are athletes particularly at risk for substance abuse problems?

Substance abuse is an important public health problem, and athletes are not immune from its negative effects. Some groups of athletes (e.g., US college athletes) are more at-risk than the general population for heavy alcohol use.

2   How are substance use problems/disorders identified?

Formal substance use disorders are assessed via a defined set of diagnostic criteria, usually in the form of a structured interview. Briefer self-report assessments can also be used as screening tools for the possibility of substance-related problems.

3   What are effective treatments for substance abuse problems?

Motivational Interviewing, Relapse Prevention, Contingency Management, and 12-Step programs are distinct interventions that have been shown to be effective at reducing substance use. Each intervention encompasses unique techniques that are designed to help the individual address his or her problems with alcohol and other drugs.

4   How might substance abuse programming be implemented into athletic organizations?

There are several important considerations for integrating substance abuse services within an athletic organization, such as convincing administrators and coaches of the relationship between substance abuse and poor athletic performance, and obtaining buy-in from medical staff (e.g., team physicians, athletic trainers).

REVIEW QUESTIONS

1 What are the prevalence rates of alcohol and other drug use among different groups of athletes, and how do they compare to prevalence rates among the general population?

2 How does one determine if an individual meets diagnostic criteria for a formal substance use disorder?

3 What are effective strategies for intervening with individuals with substance use problems, and how are these strategies similar and different from each other?

4 What are the unique challenges associated with implementing substance use interventions among athletes?

EXERCISES

1 You have been asked by an athletic department to design a program to help athletes struggling with substance use issues. This program needs to have resources for those experiencing both relatively minor and more severe problems. Design the content of this program and describe how it will be implemented, including the professionals that will provide the services.

2 Imagine that you are a counselor at the university where "James" (the athlete from the introduction) attends school. Assume the sports medicine staff has contacted you for advice on how to handle James' case. Identify the questions that you would ask of the sports medicine staff in order to obtain more information about the situation and a preliminary plan for helping James receive the services that he needs.

ADDITIONAL READING

Dunn, M., Thomas, J.O., Swift, W. & Burns, L. (2011). Recreational substance use among elite Australian athletes. *Drug and Alcohol Review, 30,* 63–68.

Lisha, N.E. & Sussman, S. (2010). Relationship of high school and college sports participation with alcohol, tobacco, and illicit drug use: A review. *Addictive Behaviors, 35,* 399–407.

McDuff, D.R. & Baron, D. (2005). Substance use in athletics: A sports psychiatry perspective. *Clinics in Sports Medicine, 24,* 885–897.

REFERENCES

American Psychiatric Association. (2013). *Diagnostic and statistical manual of mental disorders* (5th edition). Arlington, VA: American Psychiatric Publishing.

Budney, A.J., Moore, B.A., Rocha, H.L. & Higgins, S.T. (2006). Clinical trial of abstinence-based vouchers and cognitive-behavioral therapy for cannabis dependence. *Journal of Consulting and Clinical Psychology, 74,* 307–316.

Conrod, P.J., Castellanos-Ryan, N. & Mackie, C. (2011). Long-term effects of a personality-targeted intervention to reduce alcohol use in adolescents. *Journal of Consulting and Clinical Psychology, 79,* 296–306.

Cronce, J.M. & Larimer, M.E. (2011). Individual-focused approaches to the prevention of college student drinking. *Alcohol Research and Health, 34*, 210–221.

Dantzer, C., Wardle, J., Fuller, R., Pampalone, S.Z. & Steptoe, A. (2006). International study of heavy drinking: Attitudes and sociodemographic factors in university students. *Journal of American College Health, 55*, 83–89.

Diehl, K., Thiel, A., Zipfel, S., Mayer, J., Litaker, D.J. & Schneider, S. (2012). How healthy is the behavior of young athletes? A systematic literature review and meta-analyses. *Journal of Sport Science & Medicine, 11*, 201–220.

Dietze, P., Fitzgerald, J. & Jenkinson, R.A. (2008). Drinking by professional Australian Football League (AFL) players: Prevalence and correlates of risk. *Medical Journal of Australia, 189*, 479–483.

Dutra, L., Stathopoulou, G., Basen, S.L., Leyro, T.M., Powers, M.B. & Otto, M.W. (2008). A meta-analytic review for psychosocial interventions for substance use disorders. *American Journal of Psychiatry, 165*, 179–187.

Grant, B.F., Dawson, D.A., Stinson, F.S., Chou, S.P., Dufour, M.C. & Pickering, R.P. (2004a). The 12-month prevalence and trends in DSM-IV alcohol abuse and dependence: United States, 1991–1992 and 2001–2002. *Drug and Alcohol Dependence, 74*, 223–234.

Grant, B.F., Stinson, F.S., Dawson, D.A., Chou, S.P., Dufour, M.C., Compton, W., Pickering, R.P. & Kaplan, K. (2004b). Prevalence and co-occurrence of substance use disorders and independent mood and anxiety disorders. *Archives of General Psychiatry, 61*, 807–816.

Johnston, L.D., O'Malley, P.M., Bachman, J.G. & Schulenberg, J.E. (2010). *Monitoring the Future national survey results on drug use, 1975–2009: Volume II, college students and adults ages 19–45*. (NIH Publication No. 10–7585). Bethesda, MD: National Institute on Drug Abuse.

Kindlundh, A.M., Isacson, D.G., Berglund, L. & Nyberg, F. (1999). Factors associated with adolescent use of doping agents: Anabolic-androgenic steroids. *Addiction, 94*, 543–553.

Larimer, M.E. & Cronce, J.M. (2002). Identification, prevention and treatment: A review of individual-focused strategies to reduce problematic alcohol consumption by college students. *Journal of Studies on Alcohol, 63* (Suppl. 14): 148–163.

Lisha, N.E. & Sussman, S. (2010). Relationship of high school and college sports participation with alcohol, tobacco, and illicit drug use: A review. *Addictive Behaviors, 35*, 399–407.

Lorente, F.O., Peretti-Watel, P., Griffet, J. & Grélot, L. (2003). Alcohol use and intoxication in sport university students. *Alcohol and Alcoholism, 38(5)*, 427–430.

Lorente, F.O., Souville, M., Griffet, J. & Grélot, L. (2004). Participation in sports and alcohol consumption among French adolescents. *Addictive Behaviors, 29*, 941–946.

Martens, M.P., Kilmer, J.R. & Beck, N.C. (2009). Alcohol and drug use among college athletes. In E. Etzel (ed.) *Counseling and Psychological Services for College Student Athletes* (pp.451–475). Morgantown, WV: Fitness Information Technology.

Martens, M.P., Kilmer, J.R., Beck, N.C. & Zamboanga, B.L. (2010). The efficacy of a targeted personalized drinking feedback intervention among intercollegiate athletes: A randomized controlled trial. *Psychology of Addictive Behaviors, 24*, 660–669.

Martha, C., Grelot, L. & Peretti-Watel, P. (2009). Participants' sports characteristics related to heavy episodic drinking among French students. *International Journal of Drug Policy, 20*, 152–160.

Mays, D., DePadilla, L., Thompson, N.J., Kushner, H.I. & Windle, M. (2010). Sports participation and problem alcohol use: A multi-wave national sample of adolescents. *American Journal of Preventive Medicine, 38*, 491–498.

Mays, D. & Thompson, N.J. (2009). Alcohol-related risk behaviors and sports participation among adolescents: An analysis of 2005 Youth Risk Behavior Survey data. *Journal of Adolescent Health, 44*, 87–89.

Miller, W.R. & Rollnick, S. (2002). *Motivational interviewing: Preparing people to change addictive behavior* (2nd ed.). New York: The Guilford Press.

National Collegiate Athletic Association (2012). *National Study of Substance Use Trends Among NCAA College Student-Athletes*. Indianapolis, IN: Author. Retrieved from http://www.ncaa publications.com/p-4266-research- substance-use-national-study-of-substance-use-trends-among-ncaa-college-student-athletes.aspx.

Nelson, T.F. & Wechsler, H. (2001). Alcohol and college athletes. *Medicine and Science in Sports and Exercise, 33*, 43–47.

O'Brien, K.S., Blackie, J.M. & Hunter, J.A. (2005). Hazardous drinking in elite New Zealand sportspeople. *Alcohol and Alcoholism, 40,* 239–241.

Papadopoulos, F.C., Skalkidis, I., Parkkar, J. & Petridou, E. (2006). Doping use among tertiary education students in six developed countries. *European Journal of Epidemiology, 21,* 307–313.

Papaioannou, A., Karastogiannidou, C. & Theodorakis, Y. (2004). Sport involvement, sport violence and health behaviours of Greek adolescents. *The European Journal of Public Health, 14,* 168–172.

Partington, S., Partington, E., Heather, N., Longstaff, F., Allsop, S., Jankowski, M., Stephens, R. & St. Clair Gibson, A. (2012). The relationship between membership of a university sports group and drinking behaviour among students at English Universities. *Addiction Research and Theory, 10,* 1–9.

Peretti-Watel, P., Guagliardo, V., Verger, P., Pruvost, J., Mignon, P. & Obadia, Y. (2003). Sporting activity and drug use: Alcohol, cigarette and cannabis use among elite student athletes. *Addiction, 98,* 1249–1256.

Project MATCH Research Group (1997). Matching alcoholism treatments to client heterogeneity: Project MATCH posttreatment drinking outcomes. *Journal of Studies on Alcohol, 58,* 7–29.

Schwenk, T. (1997). Psychoactive drugs and athletic performance. *The Physician and Sportsmedicine, 25,* 32–37.

Thavorncharoensap, M., Teerawattananon, Y., Yothasamut, J., Lertpitakpong, C. & Chaikledkaew, U. (2009). The economic impact of alcohol consumption: A systematic review. *Substance Abuse Treatment, Prevention, & Policy, 4,* 20.

van Amsterdam, J., Opperhuizen, A. & Hartgens, F. (2010). Adverse health effects of anabolic-androgenic steroids. *Regulatory Toxicology and Pharmacology, 57,* 117–123.

Wichstrøm, L. (2006). Predictors of future anabolic androgenic steroid use. *Medicine and Science in Sports and Exercise, 38,* 1578–1583.

Witkiewitz, K. & Marlatt, G.A. (2004). Relapse prevention for alcohol and drug problems: That was Zen, this is Tao. *American Psychologist, 59,* 224–235.

Wood, M.D., Capone, C., Laforge, R., Erickson, D.J. & Brand, N.H. (2007). Brief motivational intervention and alcohol expectancy challenge with heavy drinking college students: A randomized factorial study. *Addictive Behaviors, 33,* 2509–2528.

Chapter 55

Sport injuries

URBAN JOHNSON AND LESLIE PODLOG*

SUMMARY

The focus of this chapter is on the psychological aspects of injury occurrence, recovery, and return to sport. The chapter begins with a description of the most commonly tested model – Williams and Andersen Stress-Injury Model – used to examine injury risk factors. We then examine research that has tested the various factors posited to influence injury occurrence and discuss different psychological interventions aimed at injury reduction. Following our discussion of pre-injury risk factors, the focus turns to an examination of models used to describe athlete responses to injury as well as the personal and situational factors influencing injury responses. Finally, we conclude with a review of issues facing athletes returning to sport following injury and strategies to address return-to-sport concerns.

INTRODUCTION

David, a talented 23-year-old volleyball player is a member of one of the best teams in the country, and is aspiring to play at an international level. Over the past couple of weeks he has experienced a generalized low mood, tiredness, and a lack of motivation to train and compete. His negative mindset is partly due to the fact that his team has endured a high physical training load over the past few weeks in preparation for a prestigious regional competition. Ultimately, however, the foremost reason for David's fatigue and negative mood is because of social problems at home. A close relative of David's has become very sick and

was recently hospitalized for a life-threatening illness. At the day of competition, David is unable to fully focus on the game, and unlike usual, does not want to play in the important match. He just does not feel 'in balance' at the moment. However, as David is the star player on the team, everybody expects him to play at his best and to lead the team to victory. Needless to say, David feels both internal pressures to avoid disappointing his teammates, and external pressures to play at his best from the coach, teammates, and the media. In a moment of poor concentration, David badly twists his ankle, at the start of the match. The sports

*   The first author would like to acknowledge PhD students Andreas Ivarsson and Ulrika Tranaeus for valuable comments on this chapter. The second author would like to thank Morgan Hall for his review of the manuscript.

medicine specialist indicates he has a third-degree ankle sprain and ruptured ligaments. After visiting the doctor, David is informed that he will be out of play for several months. He is devastated by the news. After several weeks of feeling angry, frustrated, and depressed, David realizes he will only resume his competitive activities if he takes a more positive and proactive approach to his rehabilitation. His rehabilitation presents numerous challenges including the need to manage the physical pain of regaining ankle function, rehabilitation setbacks, isolation from teammates, and worries that he will not return to pre-injury levels. After five long months, David begins sport-specific exercises and functional agility tests. Several strength and balance tests reveal that David's ankle functioning appears quite high. Nonetheless, he remains concerned that his ankle will be able to withstand the rigors of competitive play and that he will perform as he did pre-injury. He is also worried about his ability to execute skills with a high level of proficiency. Despite these concerns, he experiences a sense of excitement and anticipation as he prepares for his first match in a week's time.

OBJECTIVES

After reading this chapter, you should be able to:

1   Describe Williams and Andersen stress-injury model.
2   Describe different psychosocial antecedents to sport injury.
3   Discuss different psychological intervention studies aimed at preventing injury.
4   Describe different models of response to injury.
5   Discuss the personal and situational factors influencing athletes' post-injury response.
6   Describe the psychosocial factors influencing athletes' return to sport following injury.

PREVALENCE OF SPORT INJURIES

Risk of injury in sport

Over the past two decades conceptual, empirical and applied knowledge regarding the psychology of injury has grown substantially. Still, given the magnitude and severity of injuries each year, the search for continued knowledge about the causes of injury occurrence continues. For example, soccer, the most internationally popular sport, has relatively high injury rates. Ristolainen, Heinonen, Waller, Kujala, and Kettunen (2009) found that 92% of elite Finnish male and 79% of Finnish female soccer players reported at least one injury per year. High injury rates have also been found in Swedish elite athletes with 65–95% reporting at least one injury during a single season. In other popular sports, such as swimming and tennis (juniors), injury rates of 2.65 and 1.70 per 1000 practicing hours have been reported (Ristolainen et al., 2009 and Hjelm, Werner & Renstrom, 2010).

In addition to an epidemiologic interest in sport injury, high injury rates are of concern to those involved in assisting athletes with the psychosocial consequences of injury. A wealth of evidence indicates that sport injury can be an extremely stressful and emotionally disruptive event for elite athletes, particularly in cases where the injury is severe and the athlete is heavily invested in sport (Brewer, 2007). In addition to having to cope with the physical stresses of injury (e.g., pain, discomfort, the rigors of rehabilitation), athletes must contend with the psychosocial stresses of injury such as threats to self-esteem, threats to athletic career involvement, and isolation from peers.

Given the profound physical and psychosocial burden of injury, efforts aimed at minimizing injury risk are of importance. As highlighted below, the purpose of this section is to: 1) present the most commonly examined injury risk model – Williams and Andersen's (1998) Stress-Injury Model; 2) examine different psychosocial antecedents (i.e., precursors) of sport injury; and 3) describe psychological interventions aimed at injury prevention.

Williams and Andersen Stress-Injury Model

In an attempt to identify psychological risk factors for sport injury, several conceptual models have been developed. The most influential and well tested of these models is Williams and Andersen's Stress-Injury Model (1998). Williams and Andersen posit that a potentially stressful situation will generate a stress response varying in intensity along a continuum (see Figure 55.1). The strength of the stress response is influenced by how threatening the

athlete perceives the situation to be (i.e., the extent to which the demands of the situation outweigh the perceived ability to meet such demands, and the negative consequences of an inability to meet situational demands). Three broad categories of variables – personality traits (e.g., trait anxiety, perfectionism, Type A behavior), history of stressors (e.g., major life event stress, daily hassles, previous injury history), and coping strategies/resources (e.g., psychological skill use, social support) – are also suggested to influence the strength of the stress response and the subsequent likelihood of injury. Personality traits, history of stressors and coping resources are thought to operate in isolation or interactively to influence athletes' appraisal or assessment of potentially stressful situations (e.g., a demanding practice, an important competition). The mechanism by which the stress response is believed to increase injury occurrence is through attentional and somatic changes, such as increased distractibility and peripheral narrowing, muscle tension, fatigue, and reduced timing/coordination.

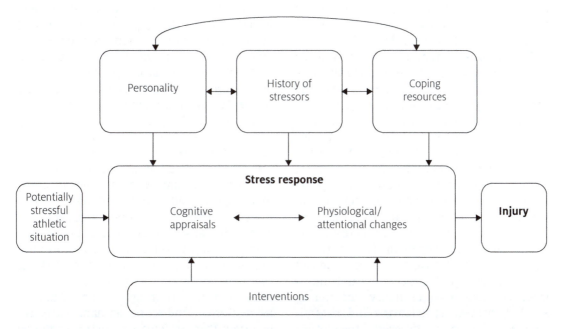

Figure 55.1 The stress and injury model. (From Psychosocial antecedents of sport injury: Review and critique of the stress and injury model by J.M. Williams and M.B. Andersen, 1998. Copyright 1998 Reproduced by permission of Taylor & Francis, Inc., http://www.routledge-ny-com).

Psychosocial factors influencing the stress–injury relationship

Researchers have examined many of the psychosocial risk factors articulated in Williams and Andersen's (1998) model.

Personality: Several personality characteristics have been found to influence the strength of the stress–injury relationship. Personality characteristics may predispose individuals to perceive fewer situations and events as stressful, or they may dispose individuals to be more susceptible to the effects of stressors such as major life events and daily hassles. Relationships have been found between injury outcome and risk factors such as passion for sport (Steffen, Pensgaard, & Bahr, 2009), state anxiety (Sibold, Howard & Zizzi, 2011), and stress susceptibility (Johnson & Ivarsson, 2011). Most of this research was conducted on male, elite, or competitive athletes. Importantly, there are some inconsistent findings regarding the influence of personality factors on injury risk. For instance, researchers using nonspecific sport measures have found inconclusive results regarding trait anxiety and incidence of athletic injury.

History of stressors: Since Holmes' study in 1970, many others have examined the relationship of life stress to athletic injury. The vast majority of these studies have found a positive relationship between injury and high life stress (Steffen et al., 2009), daily hassles (Ivarsson, Johnson, & Podlog, 2013), and life changes (Sibold & Howard, 2011). For example, Rogers and Landers (2005) found that negative life event stress increased the likelihood that athletes experienced a narrowing of their peripheral vision, which in turn increased the likelihood of injury. Rogers and Landers (2005) also found that effective coping skills helped buffer the negative effects of stress and diminished the likelihood of injury occurrence. Similarly, Ivarsson et al. (2013) found that trait anxiety and negative life event stress influenced athletes' tendency to experience daily hassles. The cumulative influence of daily hassle subsequently increased athletes' susceptibility to injury. These findings suggest that preoccupation with life change and chronic daily hassles may negatively impact concentration on training and competition, and increase the likelihood of injury. However, researchers have also found contrasting results showing no relation between other history of stress variables, namely previous injury history, and frequency or severity of injury (Hanson, McCullagh, & Tonymon, 1992). Furthermore, the finding that even positive life events can be related to injury outcome suggests that further research is needed to untangle the complex influence that history of stressors have on athletes' injury susceptibility (Petrie, 1993).

Coping resources: Coping resources include a wide variety of behaviors and social networks that help the individual deal with the problems, joys, setbacks, and stresses of life. Coping resources may come from the environment (e.g., friends, family) or from personal resources (e.g., social competence, healthy diet). The presence of good coping resources may directly protect the individual against injury, or may attenuate the negative effects of stressors or the effects of personality.

Several studies have supported the link between general coping resources and athletic injury. Williams, Tonymon, and Wadsworth (1986) found that athletes low in coping resources were more likely to get injured. Hanson et al. (1992) found that coping resources were the best discriminator for both severity and number of injuries: those who sustained more injuries had significantly fewer coping resources than their non-injured counterparts. Similarly, Maddison and Prapavessis (2005) found it possible to prevent sport injuries by improving the athletes' coping skills, especially through stress management and self-confidence training. Perna, Antonio, Baum, Gordon, and Schneiderman, (2003) also reported that athletes practicing cognitive behavioral stress management reported fewer injury days than athletes in the control group.

Moreover, Johnson and Ivarsson (2011) found that junior soccer players with ineffective coping skills (e.g., high levels of worry) incurred an increased number of injuries.

Other ineffective coping skills identified in the literature are self-blame, behavioral disengagement, and denial.

PSYCHOLOGICAL INTERVENTION STUDIES AIMED AT INJURY PREVENTION

Although empirical support exists for the relationship between psychosocial antecedents and injury outcome, far fewer studies have examined the impact of controlled intervention studies that might lessen the stress response and reduce injury vulnerability. This section surveys a number of studies testing the efficacy of various psychological skill interventions in reducing injury occurrence. In one of the first accounts, DeWitt (1980) found that basketball and football players detected a noticeable decrease in minor injuries after participation in a cognitive and physiological (biofeedback) training program. At the 1987 Olympic Sports Festival, Murphy (1988) conducted relaxation sessions with members of a team, five of whom had minor injuries and two serious injuries. Practicing relaxation training after every workout until competition resulted in all 12 athletes being able to compete. Additionally, nine intervention studies have been conducted in an effort to examine the efficacy of particular injury risk reduction strategies. May and Brown (1989) used attention control, imagery, mental skills training, team building, communication, relationship orientations, and crisis interventions for individuals, pairs, and groups of U.S. alpine skiers in the 1988 Olympics in Calgary. The authors reported that their interventions led to reduced injuries, increased self-confidence, and enhanced self-control. Schomer (1990) examined the effects of associative versus dissociative thought patterns with ten marathon runners. According to Schomer, consistent body monitoring (associative thinking) was responsible for the elimination or minimization of overuse injuries. In a different line of research, Davis (1991) focused on prevention treatment (stress management) using imagery with collegiate swimmers and football players to reduce injuries. The program involved progressive relaxation combined with imagined rehearsal of swimming and football skills and related content during the competitive season. Davis reported a remarkable 52% reduction in swimming injuries and a 33% reduction in football injuries. In a well-controlled study, Kerr and Goss (1996) used a stress-management intervention with 24 elite gymnasts over an eight-month period. The gymnasts were matched in pairs according to sex, age, and performance level. Results showed that there were considerably fewer injuries in the intervention group than in the control group (not statistically significant). Furthermore, stress levels were significantly lower for the intervention group than for members of the control group. Perna, Perna, Antonio, and Schneiderman (1998) found that a four-week cognitive behavioral stress management (CBSM) intervention was effective in reducing injury and illness in collegiate rowers. In another intervention study, Maddison and Prapavessis (2005) identified 48 competitive rugby players with an at-risk psychological profile for injury (i.e., trait anxiety, history of stressors, poor coping resources) and randomly assigned them to either a CBSM intervention or a control condition. Results showed that those in the intervention condition reported missing less time due to injury compared to their non-intervention counterparts. The intervention group also had an increase in coping resources and a decrease in worry following the program. In a study by Johnson, Ekengren, and Andersen (2005), 32 at-risk soccer players were identified on the basis of the Williams and Anderson Stress-Injury Model (Williams & Anderson, 1998). The researchers were interested in studying whether a psychologically-based intervention program, organized in a pre-post test treatment-control group design, would result in a lower incidence of injuries for competitive soccer players, than for a matched control group. Four intervention techniques were used six to eight times over a five-month period. The techniques were somatic and cognitive relaxation, stress management, goal-setting training, attribution, and self-confidence training. A critical incident diary was used to monitor progress. While the experimental group only experienced three injuries, 21 injuries were incurred in the control group, highlighting the effectiveness of the intervention program. In still another study, Noh, Morris & Andersen (2007) examined the effects of two psychological interventions designed to reduce injury among ballet dancers by developing coping skills during a 12-week intervention period. The dancers were assigned to three conditions: control; autogenic training; and a broad-based coping skills condition (such as imagery and self-talk). It was found that the ballet dancers who took part in the broad-based coping skills condition developed enhanced coping skills and spent less time injured than the control group. Finally, in a cognitive-behavioral biofeedback intervention study (Edvardsson, Ivarsson & Johnson, 2012) participants from four elite football high schools (16–19 years old) were divided into one experiment and one control group. The experimental group participated in a nine-week intervention period consisting of seven sessions, including: somatic relaxation, thought stopping, emotion/problem-focused coping, goal setting, biofeedback training as well as keeping a critical incident diary. Results showed that there were noticeably fewer injuries in the intervention group (0.38 injury/person) than in the control group (1.0 injury/person), however the difference was not statistically significant. Collectively, the aforementioned studies suggest the promise of cognitive-based stress-management training and relaxation techniques in reducing injury susceptibility. Most studies to date, however, have been limited by small sample sizes, a lack of control conditions, and relatively short follow-up assessment periods. Such limitations indicate the need for further research using true experimental designs, larger sample sizes, and longer follow-up periods.

THE REHABILITATION PHASE

Once injury has occurred, athletes must contend with a range of rehabilitation challenges and hurdles. How an athlete responds to such demands will largely dictate the success of recovery efforts and the likelihood of an effective return to sport. In an effort to better understand athletes' cognitive, emotional and behavioral responses to injury as well as the multitude of factors influencing such responses, several conceptual models have been proposed. The purpose of this section is to: 1) examine the basic assumptions of the two most researched models – grief-loss and stage models and cognitive appraisal models; and 2) to examine the personal and situational factors influencing athletes' injury responses. From a practical standpoint, understanding athletes' injury responses is important for facilitating positive coping to rehabilitation demands and for ensuring optimal rehabilitation adherence. Moreover, research on the mind-body connection suggests that thoughts and emotions such as anxiety and frustration can have a significant impact on physiological healing processes, for example, blood flow to an injured limb, swelling or muscle tension (Christian, Graham, Padgett, Glaser, Kielcolt-Glaser, 2006). Additionally, examination of the personal and environmental factors influencing athletes' rehabilitation can help identify factors to be targeted for intervention purposes. Understanding athletes' injury responses, and the personal and situational factors associated with such responses, therefore has clear practical implications.

Grief-loss stage models

Although a number of stage models have been offered in the sport injury literature, common to all stage models is the assumption that injury represents a loss of some aspect of the self; while the stage element suggests that psychological responses to injury follow a predictable pattern. Several variations of stage models have been applied to sport injury, all of which have evolved from the influential work *On Death and Dying* by Elizabeth Kubler-Ross (1969). Her interviews with terminally ill patients revealed that individuals moved through a series of stages as they came to terms with their own mortality: disbelief, denial and isolation; anger; bargaining; depression; and finally, acceptance and resignation. Sport psychologist Bob Rotella (1982) was among the first to suggest that athletes may experience a similar emotional response to injury. In support of the model, athletes have reported a sense of loss over an inability to participate in the sport that defines them, a feeling of alienation from teammates, coaches and training partners, and a sense of isolation from training partners and competition environments (e.g., Tracey, 2003). Additionally, it is apparent that many athletes may experience some, many, or even all of the emotions proposed in Kubler-Ross' model. For example, denial, anger, and depression following injury have been reported across various studies (Brewer, 2007). Despite some support for the model, it is evident that each athlete does not necessarily experience all of the proposed emotions or in the suggested order, a criticism which can be leveled against virtually all stage

models. In particular, researchers have found that the model fails to reflect the diversity of athlete responses to injury, does not capture the individualized nature of injury responses, nor does it explain fluctuations occurring in relation to rehabilitation progress and setbacks (Brewer, 2007; Tracey, 2003; Wiese-Bjornstal, 2010). Finally, a failure to identify what prompts an athlete to move from one stage to the next suggests the value of examining other injury response models.

Cognitive appraisal injury models

In an effort to account for the individualized nature of injury response, several cognitive appraisal models of injury have been proposed. An implicit assumption of cognitive appraisal models is that injury represents a stressor that leads to a continuous cycle of thoughts (i.e., cognitions), feelings (i.e., emotions), and actions (i.e., behaviors). The most well-tested cognitive appraisal model is Wiese-Bjornstal, Smith, Shaffer, and Morrey's (1998) Integrated Model of Psychological Response to Sport Injury and Rehabilitation. Wiese-Bjornstal and colleagues incorporate the Williams and Andersen (1988) Stress-Injury Model into their post-injury cognitive appraisal model. As initially proposed in the stress-injury model, personality characteristics, a history of stressors, coping resources, and interventions interact with or work in isolation to influence athletes' stress response and the subsequent likelihood of injury occurrence. The researchers propose that the same factors that determine injury risk also influence athletes' psychological response to injury. The key premise of this model is that each individual may respond differently to an injury depending upon one's assessment of the meaning of the injury, its perceived consequences, and one's ability to cope with the consequences. Cognitive appraisals are hypothesized to influence athletes' emotional and subsequent behavioral responses in a cyclical fashion. In other words, athletes' thoughts about their injury influence their emotions, which in turn influence actions and behaviors (e.g., rehabilitation adherence). Last, Wiese-Bjornstal et al., (1998) suggest that a host of personal and situational factors influence the manner in which athletes appraise or assess their injury. In support of the integrated model, researchers have found that injury cognitions (e.g., causal attributions, injury and rehabilitation concerns, comparisons to others) are associated with emotional (e.g., depression, anxiety, frustration; Tracey, 2003) and behavioral responses (e.g., adherence; Brewer et al., 2000). Moreover, a number of personal and situational factors highlighted below have been linked with athletes' cognitive, affective and behavioral responses to injury (Brewer, 2007). It is to some of these personal and situational factors that we now turn our attention.

Personal factors: A number of personal and personality factors have been found to influence athletes' injury appraisals as well as their emotional and behavioral response to injury. These individual difference variables include age, previous injury history, motivation to return to sport, pain tolerance, and confidence in one's ability to effectively overcome rehabilitation demands (Brewer, 2007). In general, older athletes, those with previous injury experience, greater self-motivation, pain tolerance and rehabilitation efficacy exhibit more positive cognitive appraisals and less negative emotional responses in relation to injury occurrence. Moreover, personality factors such as optimism, hardiness, and tough-mindedness have all been found to positively impact athlete cognitive and emotional responses to injury. For example, pessimism has been positively associated with negative mood (e.g., tension, depression, anger), while hardiness and optimism have been positively associated with positive emotions (vigor, and higher esteem). Finally, personal factors, mostly related to perception of treatment, may exert significant influence on athletes' injury responses and the effectiveness of their rehabilitation efforts. Some of these factors include a belief that rehabilitation exercises are effective, the perceived value of rehabilitation to the athlete, and hours a week of sport involvement (Brewer, 2007).

Situational factors: In addition to individual (i.e., within-person) factors influencing athlete responses to injury, it is important to recognize that injury recovery takes place within a particular context or environment. This environment can have important ramifications for athletes' injury responses and the quality and nature of their rehabilitation ex-periences. One of the most important environmental factors influencing athletes' rehabilitation is the relationship between the sports medicine practitioner (e.g., physiotherapist) and athlete (Wiese-Bjornstal, 2010). Given the close proximity and regularity of contact, sport medicine practitioners may be ideally positioned to influence athletes' rehabilitation behavior, provide needed social support, and facilitate referral when necessary. Rehabilitation specialists who effectively match the type of support provided with that needed by athletes, who build empathetic and genuine relationships, and who demonstrate effective listening and communication skills, increase the likelihood of successful rehabilitation and return-to-sport outcomes. With regard to social support, a fairly substantial body of literature highlights its impact on athlete responses to rehabilitation, one important behavioral response being adherence to rehabilitation (i.e., the extent to which athletes follow practitioner recommended guidelines and rehabilitation protocols). Findings suggest that athletes want, need, and benefit from various types of social support including emotional support, tangible assistance, information about effective recovery, and active listening (Bianco, 2001). Conversely, when athletes fail to receive appropriate support (i.e., the right type of support, at the right time, and in the appropriate amount), and when poor practitioner–athlete relations exist, rehabilitation adherence and outcomes tend to suffer (Granquist, Podlog, Engel & Newland, under review). In short, in order to maximize physical recovery it is imperative to pay attention to the interpersonal qualities demonstrated by the rehabilitation team.

In addition to patient–practitioner interactions, other situational factors, such as athletes' level of sport participation, the timing of injury in the season, and the athletes' playing or scholarship status may all impact responses to injury and the rehabilitative process (Wiese-Bjornstal, 2010). In general, the higher the level of participation, the higher the athlete's playing status, and the closer the injury to an important competition, the greater the negativity of athletes' injury responses. Finally, other situational factors implicated in athletes' injury rehabilitation relate to the provision and use of psychological skill interventions. In particular, use of goal-setting, imagery, and reviewing case studies of other athletes who have successfully recovered from injury (i.e., role models) have all been found to facilitate injury reha-

bilitation. For example, Cupal and Brewer (2001) found that relaxation and imagery were able to reduce pain and increase strength in the injured area. Similarly, the use of self-directed cognitive coping strategies can predict favorable outcomes (accepting injury, focusing on getting better, thinking positive and using imagery; e.g., Gould, Udry, Bridges & Beck, 1997). It is believed that the main mechanism underpinning the psychological skill use/recovery relationship is that psychological skills influence adherence to treatment protocols. Studies typically indicate that adherence to rehabilitation is important in ensuring optimal clinical and functional rehabilitation outcomes (Brewer, 2007). The aforementioned findings highlight the impact of personal and situational factors on athletes' injury responses and their injury rehabilitation effectiveness. An awareness of these factors may facilitate intervention efforts and increase the likelihood of enhanced clinical and return-to-sport outcomes.

THE RETURN-TO-SPORT TRANSITION

For many athletes the culmination of their injury rehabilitation is the return to full competitive play. With recent advances in sport medicine and rehabilitation techniques it is apparent that athletes may regain clinical and functional measures of rehabilitation (e.g., proprioception, range of motion, strength, muscular endurance) in a hastened fashion. Despite high rates of physical recovery from injury, it is apparent that a range of psychological and social factors may play a significant role in athletes' readiness to resume competitive activities. This section focuses on: 1) the psychosocial challenges experienced among returning athletes; and 2) strategies for addressing return-to-sport concerns.

Return-to-sport challenges

Among the most commonly reported challenges in the return to sport relates to athletes'

sense of competence. Competence refers to the perception that one is capable or effective in one's pursuits or endeavors. For many athletes, an injury and the associated time away from sport may raise questions about their physical competencies or the ability to attain desired levels of future athletic proficiency. Competence-based concerns typically include worries about the impact of injury on the ability to execute sport-specific skills, to attain or surpass pre-injury performance levels, or to avoid re-injury (Podlog, Dimmock, Miller, 2011). Physical fitness concerns, uncertainties about meeting the expectations of others, and impression management concerns about appearing incompetent in front of coaches, teammates, or fans may also be prevalent.

In addition to competence-based concerns, autonomy issues may represent a significant psychological hurdle to the returning athlete.

Autonomy refers to the idea that an individual has the ability to exert influence or control over one's circumstances, to self-endorse one's actions, and to make personal choices that reflect an individual's interests and goals. The extent to which an athlete is free from external pressures or perceives that she is returning to sport for personally endorsed motives such as a love of the game is an indication of an athlete's autonomy in the return to competition. Certainly, some athletes are encouraged by coaches and others to return at a time and pace of their own choosing and experience feelings of autonomy regarding return-to-competition decisions (Podlog et al., 2011).

In contrast, ample evidence highlights the pressures put on athletes to return to sport, even when clinical/functional indicators suggest the prematurity of such actions. For example, Murphy and Waddington (2007) reported that English Premier soccer league players felt pressures from coaches and sport medicine practitioners to play through pain and injury. Bianco (2001) reported similar pressures among Canadian national team skiers, the latter of whom indicated that they returned to competition prematurely to avoid negative judgments from coaches and to meet specific return deadlines.

Pressures to return not only emanate from external sources but from athletes themselves. Athletes often internalize beliefs that they must push their physical limits relying on the principle of "no pain, no gain". Moreover, those who exclusively identify with the athlete role, who display strong perfectionist tendencies, and who experience regular anxiety may be at greatest risk for self-induced pressures to return (Podlog et al., 2011). It is also common for athletes to shorten their recovery due to competence concerns mentioned previously, for example, an increasing lack of confidence in the ability to perform their skills, concerns over losing too much fitness, or a desire to compete in an upcoming competition.

Finally, athletes, coaches and sport medicine practitioners have highlighted issues pertaining to athletes' sense of connection to relevant others and to their sport. In particular, identity concerns, isolation from team camaraderie, and inadequate social support have all been recognized as salient challenges among returning athletes (Podlog et al., 2011). For many athletes, identity issues arise given the belief that they are not a "true athlete" unless they are competing or fully involved on the field of play. Closely tied to identity concerns are feelings of isolation from coaches, teammates, and training partners. Perceptions of isolation typically occur as a by-product of athletes' removal from their usual training and competition venues and the increased time spent in rehabilitation settings. Finally, inadequate levels of social support have been documented. Athletes in various studies have suggested their coaches were unsympathetic towards injury, that coaches failed to demonstrate a belief in their ability to make a successful return, and did not provide sufficient advice, guidance and information about how to train or build up muscles during the re-entry period. It is readily apparent that a number of relational issues may have significant bearing on the extent to which athletes feel prepared to resume competitive activities.

Strategies for addressing return-to-sport concerns

The above findings suggest the need for sport psychology and sport medicine practitioners to remain vigilant in their attempts to reduce competence, autonomy and relatedness-based concerns. The satisfaction of competence needs may be met through the provision of functional progressions and the use of psychological interventions such as goal-setting, relaxation, healing/performance imagery, and modeling techniques. One key method to enhance athlete confidence in the return to competition is through the use of functional progressions. This technique, commonly employed in rehabilitation settings, involves a series of incremental steps that enable athletes to safely and gradually resume greater sport-specific function. Additionally, a focus on process goals (e.g., strength and fitness measures, technical skills) may reduce return-to-sport anxieties by focusing athletes' attention on factors under their control. Relaxation techniques such as deep breathing and progressive muscular relaxation may be useful in reducing stress and promoting blood flow to the injured limb, thus promoting healing and reducing the likelihood of re-injury. Relaxation paired with imagery exercises can also be used to enable injured athletes to see themselves' performing without hesitation or re-injury anxiety (Cupal & Brewer, 2001). Finally, modeling techniques may be useful in building perceptions of competence for the return to competition. For example, athletes can be encouraged to meet with other formerly injured athletes to discuss how the latter successfully overcame their re-injury anxieties. Similarly, athletes can be paired with another athlete who is proficient in certain rehabilitation exercises so the less experienced athlete can learn and model how to execute the rehabilitation exercises correctly. Such models may enhance motivation and reinforce the belief that 'If others can successfully return, so can I.' Providing models may have the additional benefit of fostering athletes' sense of relatedness and diminish feelings of isolation.

A number of strategies may be effective in enhancing athlete autonomy in the return to competition. First, soliciting athlete motivations for a return to sport may promote the belief that the return to competition is self-endorsed rather than instigated by feelings of guilt, or the perception that one must return to meet external deadlines or demands (Podlog & Eklund, 2010). Moreover, providing athletes with options and choices regarding sport-specific exercises will likely foster the belief that the return to sport is self-initiated (Podlog & Eklund, 2007). Finally, encouraging input into decisions regarding the return will likely foster perceptions of involvement in, ownership of, and control over return-to-competition circumstances (Podlog & Dionigi, 2010).

CONCLUSION

It is also important to ensure that athletes feel related to and connected with their coach, teammates and their sport (Podlog et al., 2011). To this end, coaches and sports medicine specialists can hold one-on-one meetings with athletes to set goals, engage in active listening, show empathy and support, and indicate to the athlete that they believe in their ability to make a full recovery. With regard to social support, sport psychologists and others can provide a range of support types including some of those previously mentioned. Moreover, ensuring that athletes remain involved in team functions or training to whatever extent possible may help offset feelings of distance from one's sport and from relevant others. Coaches may give athletes specific roles or functions on the team so they feel valued and included. Ensuring that athletes remain involved in their sport in some capacity will help diminish identity concerns and feelings of alienation often encountered throughout the injury recovery and return processes. For more information on each of these strategies the interested reader is encouraged to examine David Pargman's third edition of the *Psychological Bases of Sport Injury* and Jean Williams' textbook, *Applied Sport Psychology: Personal Growth to Peak Performance* (2009, sixth edition).

LEARNING AIDS

1   Williams and Andersen's Stress-Injury Model suggests that there are three categories of psychological factors that will influence an athlete's appraisal of the situation. These categories are personality (e.g., competitive state anxiety), history of stressful events (e.g., negative life event stress), and coping (e.g., social support). These categories are also suggested to influence the strength of the stress response and the subsequent likelihood of injury.

2   In the literature, several psychosocial factors are linked to sport injury occurrence. Cited factors include low self-esteem, state anxiety, life event stress and daily hassles, worry and denial. Many of these factors can be addressed through systematic intervention in order to reduce or minimize injury occurrence.

3   Several intervention studies have been used to effectively reduce or prevent injury. Among the most commonly used psychological strategies are stress-management training, goal-setting, self-confidence training, imagery and self-talk. However, some studies have failed to demonstrate significant reductions in injury between intervention and control groups.

4   Understanding athlete responses to injury is important for facilitating positive coping to rehabilitation demands, ensuring optimal rehabilitation adherence, and promoting physiological healing processes. Additionally, examination of the personal and environmental factors influencing athletes' rehabilitation can help identify factors to be targeted for intervention purposes.

5   Numerous personal factors including age, previous injury history, motivation to return to sport, pain tolerance, and confidence in one's ability to effectively overcome rehabilitation demands have been found to influence athlete responses to injury. Moreover, situational factors such as social support, athletes' level of sport participation, the timing of injury in the season, and athletes' playing status may all impact responses to injury.

6   Issues pertaining to athletes' sense of competence, autonomy, and relatedness have been found to influence the return to sport following injury. Competence concerns such as worries over attaining pre-injury levels, autonomy issues in the form of internal and external pressures to return to sport, and relational concerns such as isolation from team members and inadequate social support, all suggest the need for psychosocial intervention.

REVIEW QUESTIONS

1   Identify and describe three different psychosocial antecedents to injury occurrence.

2   If you were to design an intervention program for competitive athletes, what psychological strategies would you employ? Why did you select these particular strategies?

3   It is often said that an athlete's ability to employ a variety of proactive coping strategies is associated with effective adaptation and positive rehabilitation outcomes. What is your standpoint about this statement?

4   Discuss the key assumptions of Kubler-Ross' Grief-Loss Stage Model and Wiese-Bjornstal et al. (1998) Integrated Model of Psychological Response to Sport Injury and Rehabilitation.

5   Describe the competence, autonomy, and relational concerns common among athletes returning to sport following injury.

6   Discuss practical strategies for addressing competence, autonomy, and relational issues among returning athletes.

EXERCISES

1   After reading this chapter you should now be aware that an athlete's personality factors (e.g., trait anxiety), history of stressors (e.g., daily hassles, major life events, previous injury), and coping skills may increase or decrease the risk of injury. Your task is to develop a list of nine interview questions – three for each risk factor – that you could use to assess athletes' susceptibility for sport injury. After you have developed your list of interview questions, find three competitive athletes to interview. Summarize any consistent or opposing messages/themes across the interviews in a four-page report. Your report should include subheadings describing the major themes that emerge from your interviews.

2   Design a psychological skills intervention program that will help competitive athletes (team or individual sport) with a long-term injury return to competitive sport. In completing the exercise, you will need to identify five to six key strategies that you would implement in your program and provide a rationale for including each strategy. Be sure to describe the content of each strategy (e.g., develop an imagery script, outline a set of injury-specific goals and recovery timelines), indicate when the specific strategy will be employed during the rehabilitation process, and discuss who will implement each strategy (e.g., the coach, sport physiotherapist, sport psychologist).

ADDITIONAL READING

Heil, J. & Podlog, L. (2012). Injury and performance. In S.M. Murphy (Ed.), *The Oxford handbook of sport and performance psychology* (pp.593–617). New York, NY: Oxford University Press.

Podlog, L., Dimmock, J. & Miller, J. (2011). A review of return to sport concerns following injury rehabilitation: Practitioner strategies for enhancing recovery outcomes. *Physical Therapy in Sport, 12*, 43–48.

Williams, J.M. & Andersen, M.B. (2007) Psychosocial antecedents of sport injury and interventions for risk reduction. In G. Tenenbaum & R. Eklund (Eds.), *Handbook of sport psychology.* (3rd ed., pp.379–403). New York: John Wiley and Sons.

REFERENCES

Bianco, T. (2001). Social support and recovery from sport injury: Elite skiers share their experiences. *Research Quarterly for Exercise and Sport, 72,* 376–388.

Brewer, B.W. (2007). Psychology of sport injury rehabilitation. In G. Tenenbaum & R.C. Eklund (Eds.), *Handbook of sport psychology,* (3rd ed., pp.404–424). Hoboken, NJ: John Wiley & Sons, Inc.

Brewer, B.W., Cornelius, A.E., Van Raalte, J.L., Petitpas, A.J., Sklar, J.H., Pohlman, M.H., Krushel, R.J. & Ditmar, T.D. (2000). Attributions for recovery and adherence to rehabilitation following anterior cruciate ligament reconstruction: A prospective analysis. *Psychology and Health, 15,* 283–291.

Christian, L.M., Graham, J.E., Padgett, D.A., Glaser, R. & Kiecolt-Glaser, J.K. (2006). Stress and wound healing. *Neuroimmodulation, 13,* 337–346.

Cupal, D.D. & Brewer, B.W. (2001). Effects of relaxation and guided imagery on knee strength, reinjury anxiety, and pain following anterior cruciate ligament reconstruction. *Rehabilitation Psychology, 46,* 28–43.

Davis, J.O. (1991). Sport injuries and stress management: An opportunity for research. *The Sport Psychologist 5,* 175–182.

DeWitt, D.J. (1980). Cognitive and biofeedback training for stress reduction with university athletes. *Journal of Sport Psychology, 2,* 288–294.

Edvardsson, A., Ivarsson, A. & Johnson, U. (2012). Is a cognitive-behavioural biofeedback intervention useful to reduce injury risk in junior football players? *Journal of Sports Science and Medicine, 11,* 331–338.

Gould, D., Udry, E., Bridges, D. & Beck, L. (1997). Coping with season-ending injuries. *The Sport Psychologist, 11,* 379–399.

Granquist, M., Podlog, L., Engel, J. & Newland, A. (in press). Certified athletic trainers' perspectives on rehabilitation adherence within collegiate athletic training settings. *Journal of Sport Rehabilitation.*

Hanson, S.J., McCullagh, P. & Tonymon, P. (1992). The relationship of personality characteristics, life stress, and coping resources to athletic injury. *Journal of Sport & Exercise Psychology, 14,* 262–272.

Hjelm, N., Werner, S. & Renstrom, P. (2010). Injury profile in junior tennis players: a prospective two-year study. *Knee Surgery, Sports Traumatology, Arthroscopy, 18,* 845–850.

Holmes, T.H. (1970). Psychological screening. In *Football injuries* (pp.211–214). Paper presented at a workshop sponsored by Subcommittee on Athletic Injuries, Committee on the Skeletal System, Division of Medical Science, National Research Council, February 1969. Washington, DC: National Academy of Science.

Ivarsson, A., Johnson, U. & Podlog, L. (2013) Psychological predictors of injury occurrence: A prospective investigation of professional Swedish soccer players. *Journal of Sport Rehabilitation, 22,* 19–26.

Johnson, U. & Ivarsson, A. (2011). Psychological predictors of sport injuries among junior soccer players. *Scandinavian Journal of Medicine & Science in Sports, 1,* 129–136.

Johnson, U., Ekengren, J. & Andersen, M.B. (2005). Injury prevention in Sweden: Helping soccer players at risk. *Journal of Sport & Exercise Psychology, 1,* 32–38.

Kerr, G. & Goss, J. (1996). The effects of a stress management program on injuries and stress levels. *Journal of Applied Sport Psychology, 8,* 109–117.

Kolt, G. & Roberts, P.D.T. (1998). Self-esteem and injury in competitive field hockey players. *Perceptual and Motor Skills, 87,* 353–354.

Kubler-Ross, E. (1969). *On death and dying: What the dying have to teach doctors, nurses, clergy, and their own families.* New York, NY: Macmillan.

Maddison, R. & Prapavessis, H. (2005). A psychological approach to the prediction and prevention of athletic injury. *Journal of Sport & Exercise Psychology, 27,* 289–310.

May, J.R. & Brown, L. (1989). Delivery of psychological service to the U.S. Alpine ski team prior to and during the Olympics in Calgary. *The Sport Psychologist, 3,* 320–329.

Murphy, P. & Waddington, I. (2007). Are elite athletes exploited? *Sport in Society, 10,* 239–255.

Murphy, S.M. (1988). The on-site provision of sport psychology service at the U.S. Olympic Festival. *The Sport Psychologist, 2,* 337–350.

Noh, Y-E., Morris, T. & Andersen, M.B. (2007). Psychological intervention programs for reduction of injury in ballet dancers. *Research in Sports Medicine, 15,* 13–32.

Pargman, D. (Ed.). (2007). *Psychological bases of sport injuries* (3rd ed.). Morgantown, WV: Fitness Information Technology.

Perna, F.M., Antonio, M. & Schneiderman, N. (1998). Psychological intervention prevents injury/illness among athletes [Abstract]. *Journal of Applied Sport Psychology, 10* (Suppl.), 53–54.

Perna, F.M., Antonio, H.M., Baum, A., Gordon, P. & Schneiderman, N. (2003). Cognitive behavioral stress management effects on injury and illness among competitive athletes: A randomized clinical trial. *Annals of Behavior Medicine, 25,* 66–73.

Petrie, T.A. (1993). Coping skills, competitive trait anxiety, and playing status: Moderation effects of the life stress-injury relationships. *Journal of Sport & Exercise Psychology, 5,* 1–16.

Podlog, L., Dimmock, J. & Miller, J. (2011). A review of return to sport concerns following injury rehabilitation: Practitioner strategies for enhancing recovery outcomes. *Physical Therapy in Sport, 12,* 43–48.

Podlog, L. & Dionigi, R. (2010). Coach strategies for addressing psychosocial challenges during the return to sport from injury. *Journal of Sports Sciences, 28,*1197–1208.

Podlog, L. & Eklund, R.C. (2007). Professional coaches perspectives on the return to sport following serious injury. *Journal of Applied Sport Psychology, 1,* 44–68.

Podlog, L. & Eklund, R.C. (2010). Returning to competition following a serious injury: The role of self-determination. *Journal of Sports Sciences, 28,* 819–831.

Ristolainen, L., Heinonen, A., Waller, B., Kujala, U.M. & Kettunen, J.A. (2009). Gender differences in sport injury risk and types of injuries: a retrospective twelve-month study on cross country skiers, swimmers, long distance runners and soccer players. *Journal of Sport Science and Medicine, 8,* 443–451.

Rogers, T.M. & Landers, D.M. (2005). Mediating Effects of Peripheral Vision in the life event Stress/Athletic Injury Relationship. *Journal of Sport Exercise Psychology, 27,* 271–288.

Rotella, R.J. (1982). Psychological care of the injured athlete. In D.N. Kulund (Ed.), *The injured athlete* (pp.213–224). Philadelphia, PA: Lippincott.

Schomer, H.H. (1990). A cognitive strategy training program for marathon runners: Ten case studies. *South African Journal of Research in Sport, Physical Education, and Recreation, 13,* 47–78.

Sibold, J., Howard, A. & Zizzi, S. (2011). A comparison of psychosocial and orthopedic data in injured college athletes: novel application of hurdle regression. *Athletic Insight, 13,* 1–12.

Steffen, K.S., Pensgaard, A.M. & Bahr, R. (2009). Self-reported psychological characteristics as risk factors for injuries in female youth football. *Scandinavian Journal of Medicine and Science in Sports, 19,* 442–451.

Tracey, J. (2003). The emotional response to the injury and rehabilitation process. *Journal of Applied Sport Psychology, 15,* 279–293.

Wiese-Bjornstal, D.M. (2010). Psychology and socioculture affect injury risk, response, and recovery in high-intensity athletes: a consensus statement. *Scandinavian Journal of Medicine and Science in Sports, 20,* 103–111.

Wiese-Bjornstal, D.M., Smith, A.M., Shaffer, S.M. & Morrey, M.A. (1998). An integrated model of response to sport injury: Psychological and sociological dynamics. *Journal of Applied Sport Psychology, 10,* 46–69.

Williams, J.M. (Ed.). (2009). *Applied sport psychology: Personal growth to peak performance* (6th ed.). Mayfield, CA: McGraw-Hill Higher Education.

Williams, J.M., Tonymon, P. & Wadsworth, W.A. (1986). Relationship of stress to injury in intercollegiate volleyball. *Journal of Human Stress, 12,* 38–43.

Williams, J.M. & Andersen, M.B. (1998). Psychosocial antecedents of sport injury: Review and critique of the stress and injury model. *Journal of Applied Sport Psychology, 10,* 5–25.

Part Nine

Professional development and practice

EDITED BY JUDY L. VAN RAALTE AND ANTOINETTE M. MINNITI

Chapter 56

Developing professional philosophy for sport psychology consulting practice

ARTUR POCZWARDOWSKI, MARK W. AOYAGI, JAMIE L. SHAPIRO AND JUDY L. VAN RAALTE

SUMMARY

Professional philosophy is one of the fundamental elements of effective sport psychology consulting practice. In this chapter, we review sport and performance psychology concepts and present empirical and practical information relevant for understanding the multifaceted and interrelated issues comprising professional philosophy. We describe connections between various elements of professional philosophy and sport psychology consultation. We close the chapter with recommendations for developing professional philosophy for sport psychology consultancy that highlight the importance of self-reflection and supervision. Review questions and exercises are provided to consolidate learning and nurture the reader's interest in enhancing consulting excellence.

INTRODUCTION

Learning about sport psychology theory, mental training guidelines, and other principles in *applied sport psychology* provides a foundation for applied sport psychologists. Development of a professional philosophy is another important component that contributes to effective sport psychology consultation. Why is a professional philosophy important? Consider the case of Svetlana, a 17 year-old tennis player who struggles during competition and does not seem to be playing up to her potential. How will Svetlana's sport psychology consultant decide which sport psychology

theories and principles to rely upon? What mental training approaches will the consultant decide to use, if any? Where will the sport psychology consultant and Svetlana plan to meet, in an office or at the courts in her training and competition environment? What information about the consultation will be shared with Svetlana's parents who are paying for sport psychology consultation? Knowledge of sport psychology theories and principles alone does not supply a ready solution to a particular consulting situation such as Svetlana's case. Indeed, knowledge of interventions can lead the practitioner to be caught in "intervention-based" thinking (Aoyagi & Poczwardowski, 2012, p. xiv), which is the tendency to find a particular intervention and to use it in many circumstances, rather than approach each situation from a broader perspective to try and understand what is happening with the athlete. A professional philosophy can be an effective first step and foundation upon which to base work with clients in applied sport psychology.

OBJECTIVES

After reading this chapter, you should be able to:

1   Appreciate professional philosophy as an important element guiding successful sport psychology practice.
2   Articulate several dimensions of a professional philosophy and support these dimensions with theoretical and empirical insights.
3   Outline implications of a well-delineated professional philosophy for applied work.
4   Initiate and guide your own exploration in an effort to identify the major attributes of your professional philosophy.
5   Formulate educational goals and self-reflective activities that can help you use and refine your professional philosophy.

UNDERSTANDING AND DEVELOPING PROFESSIONAL PHILOSOPHY

Experienced consultants emphasize the importance of professional philosophy in successful and satisfying sport psychology practice. For example, Burt Giges (former-president of the Association for Applied Sport Psychology [AASP]) stated, "It [professional philosophy] is absolutely the most important aspect. Compared to my philosophy and how I understand this person in their life, it pales by comparison and almost doesn't matter what technique I use" (Poczwardowski & Sherman, 2011, p. 516). Also, according to Keegan (2010), qualitative research indicates that developing one's professional philosophy is not a one-time task (e.g., modifications need to be expected), and his reflection on the role of professional philosophy in his career was summarized as follows: "I wish someone had told me about this" (p. 48). Keegan adds that this process of articulating or re-articulating one's philosophy is very complex, especially when attempted by newcomers to the field. Clear understanding of one's professional philosophy seems to be essential to professional growth and increased self-awareness because the practitioner is the tool of intervention (Poczwardowski, Sherman, & Henschen, 1998).

PROFESSIONAL PHILOSOPHY IN SPORT PSYCHOLOGY SERVICE DELIVERY

Corlett (1996) demonstrated how professional philosophy impacts a consultant's approach to work with their clients through examining *sophist* and *Socratic* approaches. A sophist philosophy is concerned with the shortest path to success in practical matters of life and emphasizes immediate needs of the individual. Consequently, a sophist approach results in providing recipes and skills. In sport psychology practice, practitioners who espouse sophist approaches, whether knowingly or unknowingly (an important distinction when attempting to delineate your own professional philosophy), focus on skill development and concrete, instruction-based interactions with their clients. A practitioner who works from a sophist perspective with Svetlana, the tennis player, might suggest imagery as an effective part of Svetlana's between-points routine during competition, leading her through a series of steps over several weeks to learn this skill, encouraging her to practice it in her personal time, during tennis training, and finally apply it during tournament matches.

On the other hand, a professional philosophy built on a Socratic approach involves developing a broader knowledge base and insight in navigating life affairs. A person's knowledge of himself or herself becomes of particular importance to being successful (or virtuous). A practitioner working from a Socratic approach (again, knowingly or unknowingly) might aim to enhance Svetlana's self-knowledge by asking open-ended questions that promote self-examination and reflection. Practicing from this perspective, Svetlana might be asked about her best matches and to reflect on the characteristics of her thoughts and actions. Contrasting her best matches with weaker performances might be a next step in Svetlana's self-exploration. Although conceptually distinct, a blend of sophist and Socratic approaches can be effectively used by sport psychology consultants

(see Friesen & Orlick, 2010; Orlick, 1989; Poczwardowski & Sherman, 2011; Ravizza, 2002).

Keegan (2010) differentiated between "practitioner-led" and "client-led" approaches to conducting consulting sessions "with practitioner-led being the label taken to represent CBT [cognitive-behavioral therapy], cognitive, behavioral, sophist and more paternalistic approaches; whilst client-led has been used as a label to represent humanistic, counseling and Socratic approaches" (p. 43). Development of a professional philosophy may include deciding upon practitioner-led or client-led approaches but also includes assumptions, beliefs, and practice preferences regarding behavior changes that facilitate enhanced performance, enjoyment, and personal fulfillment.

Poczwardowski, Sherman, and Ravizza (2004) defined *professional philosophy* as "the consultant's beliefs and values concerning the nature of reality (sport reality in particular), the place of sport in human life, the basic nature of a human being, the nature of human behavior change, and also the consultant's beliefs and values concerning his or her potential role in, and the theoretical and practical means of, influencing their clients toward mutually set intervention goals" (p. 449). Further, they identified five interrelated aspects of professional philosophy: (a) personal core beliefs and values; (b) theoretical paradigms in psychology; (c) model of practice and the consultant role; (d) intervention goals; and (e) intervention techniques and methods (see Figure 56.1).

PERSONAL CORE BELIEFS AND VALUES

The foundation of a professional philosophy is *core beliefs* and *values*. Core beliefs are the explanations you have learned from important others (such as parents, coaches, professors, and mentors) that you have developed to help understand why people are the way that they are. Values consist of your sense for how things 'should' be and your preferences for certain outcomes or courses of action. When

considering core values and beliefs, you are urged to consider the question, "Who shall I be?" rather than "What shall I do?" (Aoyagi & Portenga, 2010).

For many, an important step in the process of identifying core values and beliefs is a curiosity and openness to considering alternative explanations. For example, Poczwardowski et al. (2004) noted that free will and determinism

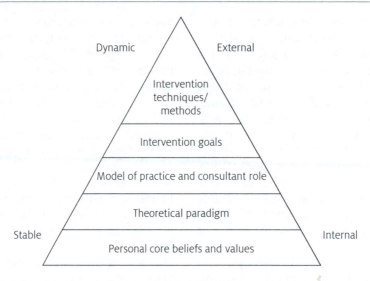

Figure 56.1 Hierarchical structure of professional philosophy. Reprinted from A. Poczwardowski, C.P. Sherman, and K. Ravizza, 2004, "Professional philosophy in the sport psychology service delivery: Building on theory and practice," *The Sport Psychologist* 18(4): 445–463 © Human Kinetics Publishers, Inc.

are core beliefs. That is, some people believe that they are in control of their own lives and that their choices (free will) determine their outcomes. Other people believe that their lives are largely pre-destined (determinism). Poczwardowski et al. also noted a distinction between rationality (using logical reasoning to guide behavior) and irrationality (illogical decision making, subject to emotionality) and a distinction between fundamental goodness/badness (do people generally seek to treat themselves and others well or are they predisposed toward harmful choices and actions?).

Core beliefs and values vary among cultures, professions, and individuals, and may change over time. It is useful to be aware of your core beliefs and values and how they interact with service delivery and interactions with clients. When Poczwardowski and Sherman (2011) interviewed 10 eminent sport psychology consultants, they found that their values were person-focused including: "[client's] freedom, autonomy, and rationality in decisions and actions; respect for truth, privacy, and commitments; and concern for human dignity and equality" (p. 524). Adding

to your evolving consulting practice of assigning mental training to your clients, you might ask Svetlana if she is willing to practice vividness and controllability of imagery on her own, or if she would prefer to incorporate it into the first 15 minutes of each of her upcoming sessions with you. Here, you clearly keep Svetlana's best interests in mind and emphasize autonomy in her decision-making, as well as invite collaborative decision-making about the course of your consultation (i.e., the value of human dignity and equality).

Many consultants look to the ethics codes of their profession to further their understanding of professional beliefs and values (see Chapter 62, this volume). The American Psychological Association's Ethical Principles and Code of Conduct (APA, 2010) includes five General Principles: Principle A: Beneficence (provide benefit) and Nonmaleficence (do no harm); Principle B: Fidelity (form trusting relationships) and Responsibility; Principle C: Integrity; Principle D: Justice; and Principle E: Respect for People's Rights and Dignity. These aspirational principles underline core values and beliefs about the practice of sport psychology.

THEORETICAL PARADIGM

Theoretical paradigms (often called theoretical orientations) derive from the parent discipline of psychology which may include, "a consistent perspective on human behavior, psychopathology, and the mechanisms of therapeutic change" (Prochaska & Norcross, 2010, p. 4). Many theories serve to provide generalized explanations of human personality and behaviors, how problems develop, and how to address, change, or remedy these problems. Counseling psychology theories more strongly focus on enhancement, development, growth, and enjoyment (e.g., Danish, Petitpas, & Hale, 1992).

The theoretical paradigm to which you subscribe is most effectively employed if it is derived from your core beliefs and values. For example, if you believe that people are fundamentally good and they want to grow, learn, and develop their full potential, then the *Humanistic* paradigm will suit your belief. Conversely, the *Psychoanalytic* paradigm reflects the belief that people are fundamentally flawed and are caught in inner conflicts further manifested in anxiety; while *Behaviorism* portrays humans as neutral (neither good nor bad) and focuses on rewards and contingencies to shape behavior. A complete explanation of these theories is beyond the scope of this chapter, but it should be noted that in addition to these three theories there are several other prominent theories among which *Cognitive-Behavioral Theory* (CBT; based on the notion that thoughts impact emotions which both then influence actions) from which many sport psychology interventions are derived. *Existentialism*, *Gestalt*, *Interpersonal*, and *Acceptance* and *Mindfulness-Based Theories* are other prominent theories that add to practitioners' thinking about human behavior: how it came about and how it can be changed. It should also be noted that the most frequently identified theoretical orientation amongst practitioners is known as *Integrative*. An integrative approach is an intentional and scientifically-derived combination of two or more theoretical paradigms (Prochaska & Norcross, 2010). Aspiring sport psychology practitioners must also familiarize themselves with theories of performance excellence (Aoyagi & Poczwardowski, 2012). These theories are derived from the naturalistic observations and implicit understandings identified by preeminent sport psychology practitioners. While these theories are just being introduced into the professional literature and still require empirical explorations, they are an essential aspect for all developing professional philosophies in sport psychology.

For example, if your theoretical orientation is essentially cognitive-behavioral, you might decide to collaborate with Svetlana on identifying her thoughts behind the "mental blocks" (e.g., "I must be perfect or I will fail my parents") and explore ways of neutralizing them (they lose their power to have a negative effect on her thinking prior to and during the matches and tournaments) or change them into more productive ones (e.g., "Even if I double-fault once in a while, I can still have a good match. Anyway, I love tennis and I play for myself. Plus, my parents were always on my side. I'm going to nail this next serve."). The ultimate goal in your work from a cognitive-behavioral, growth-centered perspective might be to create a consistent set of cognitions (e.g., thoughts, images, attitudes, expectations) that have a potential to facilitate positive pre-competitive and competitive mental states. Clearly, identifying a theoretical paradigm with which you identify is an essential component of your professional philosophy. Your theoretical orientation is related in many important ways to your model of practice.

MODEL OF PRACTICE AND CONSULTANT ROLE

The *model of practice* employed by a sport psychology practitioner is usually related to core beliefs and values, theoretical paradigm endorsed, level and type of education, practice, and supervision. Additionally, client factors (e.g., presenting issues, requests) and the context in which the consultation takes place (e.g., individual setting, athletic club) can influence practice models and consulting roles. Aoyagi and Poczwardowski (2011) reviewed models of sport psychology practice and delivery including: (a) *psychological skills training* (PST) *models*; (b) *counseling models*; and (c) *the interdisciplinary sport science model*.

PST models include directions for work with the clients that are based on the relevant ingredients of athletic excellence. For example, a practitioner using a PST model to work with Svetlana might implement imagery training, concentration skill-building, and activation management techniques (both relaxing and energizing). A practitioner using a counseling model might promote the client's learned resourcefulness, in which new skills are learned and attitudes are modified to successfully cope with the stressful events of the tennis training process, tournament play, and athletic career development. For example, based on the Littlefoot approach (Petitpas, 2000), the consultant would attempt to understand the problem before trying to fix it, be inquisitive about Svetlana's stories, put doubts in her self-doubts, plan for plateaus and setbacks, and help her to generalize the newly-acquired skills and attitudes to other, non-sport areas of life. Finally, the interdisciplinary sport science model grounds its intervention on the interplay between the status in the training process (e.g., preseason versus season goals and training volumes and intensities as well as recovery), biomechanical demands of the skill (e.g., recent changes to one's technique), nutrition, and other sport training issues. Consequently, practitioners within this model specifically emphasize the integration of sport preparation (very often periodized to achieve high levels of athletic performance) with mental training, which can also be periodized. Periodization of mental training builds on a number of components of physical training interacting with mental training goals and methods (Holliday, Burton, Sun, Hammermeister, Naylor, & Freigang, 2008). If your professional philosophy includes an interdisciplinary sport science model, you might invite Svetlana's coach (after obtaining her permission and observing other measures to ensure confidentiality) to collaborate on the best possible mental training that will integrate the demands of her physical training. Alternatively, Svetlana herself (depending on her knowledge of tennis training) might be an excellent source of this information. Nevertheless, you might find out from the coach or from Svetlana that she (and the rest of her team) is going through the most demanding part of the preparatory phase, so rightly she reported feelings of – what she referred to as – burnout (and potentially [a hypothesis in your case conceptualization] misplaced the attribution of it to the pressure felt from her parents). Consequently, Svetlana, the coach, and you might agree on more frequent relaxation sessions for the next two weeks and the development of energizing imagery scripts.

Poczwardowski and colleagues' (Poczwardowski & Sherman, 2011; Poczwardowski et al., 1998) *sport psychology service delivery* (SPSD) model includes a number of factors that are essential for effective sport psychology consulting: professional boundaries, professional philosophy, making contact, assessment, conceptualizing athletes' concerns and potential interventions, range, types, and organization of service, program implementation, managing the self as an intervention instrument, program and consultant evaluation, conclusions and implications, and leaving the setting. A revised model (SPSD-R, 2011) provided a new organization to the existing elements and added elements to this re-organized structure. The new elements were as follows: the working interpersonal alliance (comprising the consultant–client relationship, the consultant variables, and the client variables), immersion, the 'goodness of fit', and person-focused values (e.g., freedom, autonomy, respect for truth, privacy, and commitments; and concern for human dignity and equality).

Working with Svetlana within the SPSD framework, you would need to reflect on your professional boundaries, your competence achieved through education, training, and supervision (e.g., "Am I qualified to include parents as the consultees in the consultation?"), ethical considerations presented in the request (e.g., how much of what takes place in the sessions with Svetlana will you reveal to her parents [confidentiality]?), and legal issues i.e., working with a child). The SPSD model holds the promise of being a valuable tool in approaching one's individual consulting prac-

tice (e.g., Van Raalte, 2003) and can also be successfully used in guiding organizational solutions to strategic and systematic delivery of sport psychology services (Henriksen & Diment, 2010), including a clearly identified professional philosophy.

Aligned with these choices from among the practice models is your definition of the *role* that you might choose given the consultation context. An *educational* (versus *clinical*) role is a natural alternative in working with Svetlana (i.e., she could view you as her mental coach). Beyond this formal role of the educator about the inner game of tennis, with time (and given your qualifications and competencies), you might evolve as an advisor to both Svetlana and her coach on her decision-making for prioritizing athletic goals and personal issues (informal role). A direct relationship between these roles and models will be seen in how you and Svetlana (and perhaps her coach) will co-decide the intervention goals.

INTERVENTION GOALS

Intervention goals often include performance enhancement, personal growth, career transition, health and healthy lifestyle (e.g., substance abuse, eating habits), daily living, romantic and family relationships, coach–athlete relationships, and team effectiveness (e.g., cohesion, effective leadership and communication, organizational citizenship). Setting goals in any or all of these areas is important because they help focus one's energy and time on what is most vital in achieving both short-term (current tennis season) and long-term (being invited to the national team) objectives. If Svetlana is interested in developing intervention goals, you

might work collaboratively to identify her priorities. Perhaps Svetlana tells you that she would like to work on being more mentally effective when playing tournament matches, to have a better relationship with her parents, and to introduce more balance in her life. Consequently, you and Svetlana might develop consistent ways of relaxing and recharging on a daily basis, opening lines of communication with her parents, investing in non-sport hobbies, and re-vitalizing social interactions with a group of her closest friends. Once goals are decided upon, then intervention techniques and methods can be used to achieve the goals.

INTERVENTION TECHNIQUES/METHODS

Vealey (1988, 2007) presented a model in which she clearly differentiated between methods (tools to develop psychological skills

[intervention techniques and methods]) and psychological skills for individual and team performance enhancement and well-being.

Examples of psychological skills are self-confidence, concentration, and motivation. On the other hand, intervention techniques and methods may include goal setting, self-talk, imagery, arousal regulation, cognitive restructuring, exploring current experiences and performance/life issues to attach new meanings to them, and addressing life dreams and career goals. These interventions may be delivered individually, as part of a standardized training program, in person, or via video or the Internet.

An interesting approach to expanding the plethora of intervention techniques and methods was proposed by Hammermeister (2000; as cited by Holiday et al., 2008, p. 210) and was termed the "mental training drill menu." Building on the above differentiation, the intervention techniques and methods involved energizing/relaxing, imagery, self-talk, and goal setting, and the psychological skills included motivation, attention control, energy management, stress management, and self-confidence. Thus, a sport psychology consultant would develop a whole array (a menu) of techniques (tools) to help the client develop a targeted mental skill. For example, Svetlana might be presented with a choice of drills (e.g., imaging a successful past tournament performance [serves and returns], imaging a successful future tournament performance [serves and returns], imaging an effective pre-point routine, imaging effective post-point routines after a poor shot), clearly utilizing imagery as a tool to raise consistency in her serves and returns through improved concentration. The intervention techniques chosen are strongly related to intervention goals, models of practice, theoretical paradigms, personal core beliefs and values, and athlete interests and talents.

In sum, all aspects of professional philosophy significantly shape the consultant's choices while approaching a given client in a given consultation context. This dynamic process starts at the core personal values and involves theoretical paradigms (those established in traditional psychology and those recently emerging from practice in applied sport psychology). Professional choices include various models of practice and different formal and informal roles that the consultant can take on depending on the situation. Finally, intervention goals and intervention techniques and methods are most commonly equated with what sport psychology practitioners 'do' and, again, will depend on the more fundamental aspects of the consultant's professional philosophy as well as the dynamically changing context involving both the client-related and situational factors.

RECOMMENDATIONS FOR DEVELOPING PROFESSIONAL PHILOSOPHY FOR CONSULTANCY

As noted in the chapter and in the reviewed literature (e.g., Corlett, 1996; Friesen & Orlick, 2010; Orlick, 1989; Ravizza, 2002), pursuing clarity in your philosophical approach protects and serves the interests of your future clients (e.g., individuals, teams, organizations). Questions to consider when developing a professional philosophy for consultancy include: What are the values that guide your life and professional goals? What is your theoretical orientation concerning behavior change? What is the population with whom you could work most effectively? What is your preferred model of practice? Consideration of these questions may lead to additional questions that will enrich your self-awareness and professional philosophy. Careful consideration of your professional philosophy is a form of *reflective practice* (i.e., self-reflection on real life challenges and issues encountered in day-to-day consultation), which is an important part of professional development (e.g., Anderson,

Knowles, & Gilbourne, 2004). The areas for sport psychology consultants' self-explorations include their values, prejudices, consulting experiences, different sources of professional knowledge (e.g., empirical, personal, ethical), and social norms. Structured and systematic self-reflective activities can enhance professional growth and development across different stages in one's consulting career. Thus, self-reflection is a long-term professional commitment and also results in an ongoing refining of one's professional philosophy.

Self-reflection, however, may not be sufficient to fully develop a professional philosophy. *Supervision*, which involves an interpersonal relationship between a supervisee and supervisor can be especially useful in developing competent, knowledgeable, and ethical practitioners while keeping the welfare of clients in the sharpest focus (Van Raalte & Andersen, 2000). Supervisors are advised to develop a supervision model (see Silva, Metzler, & Lerner, 2011 for a review), such as one where supervisees move from dependence on the supervisor (and more structure and guidance in developing a professional philosophy) to autonomy from the supervisor (consistent implementation and refinement of the supervisee's professional philosophy on their own). Knowles, Gilbourne, Tomlinson, and Anderson (2007) described how supervision helped a supervisee's professional philosophy development. Over the course of three years, the practitioner-in-training (under supervision) developed a self-reflective cycle as part of the processing of consulting sessions. The cycle included description, thoughts and feelings, evaluation, analysis, conclusion, and action plan and yielded gains in understanding and refining of the practitioner-in-training's professional philosophy. In addition to supervision, ongoing scrutiny of the professional literature and attendance to conferences and professional meetings enhance the development and evolution of a professional philosophy.

CONCLUSION

Sport psychology consultancy is multifaceted and involves a number of interrelated components (e.g., professional boundaries, professional philosophy, person-focused values, making contact, the working interpersonal alliance, assessment, conceptualizing athletes' concerns and potential interventions, program implementation, managing the self as an intervention instrument, program and consultant evaluation, and conclusions and implications). A practitioner must consider these components while engaging in work with a client to adequately account for the challenges involved in behavior change that is aimed at performance enhancement and well-being. Critical to this success is the practitioner's professional philosophy. Professional philosophy is complex and its structure includes personal core beliefs and values, using theoretical paradigms in psychology, choosing a model of practice and the consultant role, deciding on intervention goals, and intervention techniques and methods. All these elements dynamically add to consulting strategies and interactions with a client in both sport and non-sport settings. A clearly delineated professional philosophy has the potential to guide the students as well as both young and seasoned practitioners in navigating the complexities of consulting work. Self-reflection, supervision, and ongoing learning in the field are essential in acquiring and refining sport psychology competencies and are extremely valuable tools in developing one's professional philosophy.

LEARNING AIDS

1   Discuss the importance of developing a professional philosophy – why is this essential for one's consulting practice?

Professional philosophy is an important component that contributes to effective sport psychology consultation. Specifically, having knowledge of sport psychology theories and principles alone will not supply a ready solution to a particular consulting situation. In navigating the variety of real-life scenarios, professional philosophy guides a consultant's decision-making whenever guidelines are not available. Further, well-delineated professional philosophy allows consultants to overcome the problem of "intervention-based" thinking, and in general helps them to become knowledgeable, competent, and ethical practitioners.

2   Identify and describe the five elements of a professional philosophy.

(1) Personal core beliefs and values (beliefs: explanations to help understand why people are the way that they are; values: sense for how things 'should' be and one's preferences for certain outcomes or courses of action); (2) theoretical paradigms in psychology (or theoretical orientations: humanistic, psychoanalytic, behaviorism, cognitive-behavioral, other [e.g., integrative]); (3) model of practice (psychological skills training [PST] models; counseling models, and the interdisciplinary sport science model) and the consultant role (educational versus clinical); (4) intervention goals; and (5) intervention techniques (e.g., performance enhancement, personal growth, career transition, health and healthy lifestyle, daily living, romantic and family relationships, coach–athlete relationships, and team effectiveness) and methods (goal setting, self-talk, imagery, arousal regulation, cognitive restructuring, exploring current experiences and performance/life issues to attach new meanings to them, and addressing life dreams and career goals).

3   What might you do to ensure ongoing development and refinement of your professional philosophy?

(a) Guiding questions (e.g., What are the values that guide your life and professional goals? What is your theoretical orientation concerning behavior change? What is the population with whom you could work most effectively? What is your preferred model of practice?). (b) Reflective practice (long-term self-explorations and self-evaluative [self-reflective] activities). See below for 'Exercises 1 and 2.' And (c) Supervision (growing and developing under the guidance of an established professional who is qualified to provide supervision [mentorship]).

REVIEW QUESTIONS

1   Given the interrelated nature of the five elements of professional philosophy, how do personal core beliefs and values impact the choice of intervention goals?

2   Describe the relationships between professional knowledge, professional philosophy, and professional ethics.

3   How do supervision and self-reflective approach to consulting add to professional development?

EXERCISES

1   Develop your professional philosophy. Consider the following in your formulation of this philosophy:

   a   What are your most important values in terms of helping others?

   b   What is your theory of human behavior? Why do you think people behave the way they do?

   c   How do people change?

   d   Describe some of your values and prejudices and explain how these might affect your consulting.

   e   What role will you play in consulting with athletes or performers in helping them achieve their goals?

2   Reflect on your most recent sport or performance psychology consultation.

   a   Describe the consultation situation in some detail (what occurred?).

      i   Discuss your subjective impressions of the consultation.

      ii   Discuss your objective information (e.g., client's feedback, your observation of the client in practice and competitive settings) about the consultation.

   b   Discuss your professional philosophy in relation to the consultation.

   c   Summarize your experiences with this consultation.

      i   What went well?

      ii   What did not go well? What could have been better?

      iii   What can you do next time to improve the session or consultation?

3   A professional philosophy is something that develops and evolves over time.

   a   Interview two sport psychology professionals to learn about their current professional philosophies and how their professional philosophies evolved over time.

   b   Compare and contrast their professional philosophies.

   c   What experiences, resources, and processes affected the development of their professional philosophies?

   d   How will what you learned from the professionals that you interviewed affect your own professional philosophy?

ADDITIONAL READING

Andersen, M.B., Van Raalte, J.L. & Harris, G. (2000). Supervision II: A case study. In M. Andersen (Ed.), *Doing sport psychology* (pp.167–179). Champaign, IL: Human Kinetics.

Brown, D., Pryzwansky, W.B. & Schulte, A.C. (2011). *Psychological consultation and collaboration. Introduction to Theory and Practice* (7th ed.). Boston: Pearson Education.

Hamilton, L.H. & Robson, B. (2006). Performing arts consultation: Developing expertise in this domain. *Professional Psychology: Research and Practice, 37,* 254–259.

Hill, K.E. (2001). *Frameworks for sport psychologists: Enhancing sport performance.* Champaign, IL: Human Kinetics.

Holt, N.L. & Strean, W.B. (2001). Reflecting on initiating sport psychology consultation: A self-narrative of neophyte practice. *The Sport Psychologist, 15,* 188–204.

Tonn, E. & Harmison, R.J. (2004). Thrown to the wolves: A student account of her practicum experience. *The Sport Psychologist, 18,* 324–340.

REFERENCES

Anderson, A.G., Knowles, Z. & Gilbourne, D. (2004). Reflective practice for sport psychologists: Concepts, models, practical implications, and thoughts on dissemination. *The Sport Psychologist, 18,* 188–203.

Aoyagi, M.W. & Poczwardowski, A. (2011). Models of sport psychology practice and delivery: A review. In S.D. Mellalieu & S. Hanton (Eds.), *Professional practice issues in sport psychology: Critical reviews* (pp.5–30). London and New York: Routledge.

Aoyagi, M. & Poczwardowski, A. (Eds.) (2012). *Expert approaches to sport psychology: Applied theories of performance excellence.* Morgantown, WV: Fitness Information Technology.

Aoyagi, M. & Poczwardowski, A. (2012). Preface. In M. Aoyagi and A. Poczwardowski (Eds.), *Expert approaches to sport psychology: Applied theories of performance excellence* (pp.xiii–xviii). Morgantown, WV: Fitness Information Technology.

Aoyagi, M. & Portenga, S. (2010). The role of positive ethics and virtues in the context of sport and performance psychology service delivery. *Professional Psychology: Research and Practice, 41,* 253–259.

Corlett, J. (1996). Sophistry, Socrates, and sport psychology. *The Sport Psychologist, 10,* 84–94.

Danish, S.J., Petitpas, A.J. & Hale, B.D. (1992). A developmental-educational intervention model of sport psychology. *The Sport Psychologist, 6,* 403–415.

Friesen, A. & Orlick, T. (2010). A qualitative analysis of holistic sport psychology consultants' professional philosophies. *The Sport Psychologist, 24,* 227–244.

Henriksen, K. & Diment, G. (2011). Professional philosophy: Inside the delivery of sports psychology service at Team Denmark. *Sport Science Review, 20,* 5–21.

Holliday, B., Burton, D., Sun, G., Hammermeister, J., Naylor, S. & Freigang, D. (2008). Building the better mental training mousetrap: Is periodization a more systematic approach to promoting performance excellence? *Journal of Applied Sport Psychology, 20,* 199–219.

Keegan, R.J. (2010). Teaching consulting philosophies to neophyte sport psychologists: Does it help, and how can we do it? *Journal of Sport Psychology in Action, 1,* 42–52.

Knowles, Z., Gilbourne, D., Tomlinson, V. & Anderson, A.G. (2007). Reflections on the application of reflective practice for supervision in applied sport psychology. *The Sport Psychologist, 21,* 109–122.

Orlick, T. (1989). Reflections on sportpsych consulting with individual and team sport athletes at Summer and Winter Olympic Games. *The Sport Psychologist, 3,* 358–365.

Petitpas, A.J. (2002). Managing stress on and off the field: The Littlefoot approach to learned resourcefulness. In M. Andersen (Ed.), *Doing sport psychology.* (pp.33–43). Champaign, IL: Human Kinetics.

Poczwardowski, A. & Sherman, C.P. (2011). Revisions to the Sport Psychology Service Delivery (SPSD) heuristic: Explorations with experienced consultants. *The Sport Psychologist, 25,* 511–531.

Poczwardowski, A., Sherman, C. & Henschen, K.P. (1998). A sport psychology service delivery heuristic: Building on theory and practice. *The Sport Psychologist, 12,* 191–207.

Poczwardowski, A., Sherman, C. & Ravizza, K. (2004). Professional philosophy in the sport psychology service delivery: Building on theory and practice. *The Sport Psychologist, 18,* 415–429.

Prochaska, J.O. & Norcross, J.C. (2010). *Systems of psychotherapy: A transtheoretical analysis* (7th ed.). Belmont, CA: Brooks/Cole.

Ravizza, K. (2002). A philosophical construct: A framework for performance enhancement. *International Journal of Sport Psychology, 33,* 4–18.

Silva, J.M., Metzler, J.N. & Lerner, B. (2011). *Training professionals in the practice of sport psychology* (2nd ed.). Morgantown, WV: Fitness Information Technology.

Van Raalte, J.L. (2003). Provision of sport psychology services at an international competition: The XVI Maccabiah Games. *The Sport Psychologist, 17,* 461–470.

Van Raalte, J.L. & Andersen, M.B. (2000). Supervision I: From models to doing. In M. Andersen (Ed.), *Doing sport psychology* (pp.153–165). Champaign, IL: Human Kinetics.

Vealey, R.S. (1988). Future directions in psychological skills training. *The Sport Psychologist, 2,* 318–336.

Vealey, R.S. (2007). Mental skills training in sport. In G. Tenenbaum & R. Eklund (Eds.), *Handbook of sport psychology* (3rd ed., pp.287–309). Hoboken, NJ: John Wiley and Sons, Inc.

Chapter 57

Understanding athletes' psychological needs

BURT GIGES AND PAUL McCARTHY

SUMMARY

Psychological needs are fundamental requirements of personal growth, health, and well-being, for athletes and the wider population alike. They are long-range, broad, and enduring. At any stage of development and in any type of activity, these elements exist and influence our functioning (Deci, 2002; Erikson, 1950). Among the more common ones are the need for security, autonomy, identity, self-worth, mastery, intimacy, belonging, and a sense of meaning or purpose in life (Erikson, 1950; Frankl, 1992; Maslow, 1987). Although needs appear frequently in our daily language, they are not usually part of our everyday awareness. Therefore, it is important to understand how needs are satisfied, what happens when they are not, and how they influence individuals' wants, feelings, and behaviors. This chapter will discuss how sport psychology practitioners can identify and understand athletes' psychological needs, and help them with needs that have not been fulfilled.

INTRODUCTION

Psychological needs are as important to growth as physical needs, and this is arguably more evident in sport and exercise contexts than in most others. Unless both are satisfied, growth may be impaired (Deci, 2002; Maslow 1987). Deci pointed out that innate psychological needs are necessary conditions for psychological growth, integrity, and well-being; and that satisfaction of these basic needs facilitates autonomous motivation. It is therefore important to be able to recognize when a particular need is not being met. For example, when an athlete does not have a sense of security, anxiety may result and interfere with performance and relationships. If athletes do not view themselves as independent and in charge of themselves (need for autonomy), when faced with difficult challenges they may experience a sense of powerlessness and feel like victims who lack adequate resources. When athletes have no self-worth or a sense of meaning or purpose in their lives, they may be vulnerable to depression.

In contrast to those whose needs are not met, athletes who feel secure tend to have the following: an appreciation of their ability to cope with challenges (mastery); a sense of their own value (self-worth); an awareness of their independence and ability to make meaningful choices (autonomy); a capability for close relationships (intimacy) and integration within a group (belonging); and, a sense of purpose in their lives. Such individuals can function without being distracted by their own unmet needs, and they are better equipped to function effectively and respond more openly to others.

OBJECTIVES

After reading this chapter, you should be able to:

1 Identify and describe basic psychological needs of athletes.
2 Recognize how athletes' basic psychological needs are satisfied.
3 Understand the relationship between athletes' needs and wants.
4 Describe the consequences of athletes' unmet needs.
5 Understand the concept of acquired needs for athletes.
6 Recognize the importance of self-awareness.

UNDERSTANDING BASIC CONCEPTS

Understanding athletes' basic psychological needs begins with identifying them and defining what they mean. A brief description of the key needs that this chapter will focus on is as follows: (a) *security*: the importance of feeling safe and not preoccupied with imminent danger; (b) *identity*: a clear sense of yourself and who you are; (c) *autonomy*: being in charge of yourself, independent, and able to make choices; (d) *self-worth*: recognition of your own value and importance; (e) *self-acceptance*: ability to acknowledge your shortcomings without self-criticism; (f) *mastery*: a sense of your competence and ability to successfully meet challenges; (g) *intimacy*: a longing to have relationships with closeness, trust, and mutual acceptance; (h) *belonging*: being an integral part of a group and connected to others; and (i) *meaning/purpose*: being aware and dedicated to something worthwhile beyond yourself.

THE CONCEPT OF BASIC AND ACQUIRED NEEDS

When basic psychological needs are not met, and direct satisfaction is blocked or not available, people might depend on dysfunctional solutions to satisfy these deficits. Basic needs may then change into 'acquired needs', or attempts to compensate for unmet basic needs, which can sometimes create their own set of problems. The following table illustrates what may happen when these attempts are themselves the source of problems. The ideas underlying this perspective derive from the strategic, interactional approaches from family systems research centers (Watzlawick, Weakland, & Fisch, 1974).

These basic and acquired needs are expanded on in the paragraphs below. Importantly, they should be distinguished from the place in which they are often seen (or achieved) in a sporting context – i.e., competitive arenas. Particularly in sport, *competitiveness* may be deemed a basic need by some individuals. Thus, it is mentioned in this chapter to clarify and highlight that competitiveness is not a basic need, but instead it should be recognized as an opportunity for athletes to meet their actual basic needs, such as autonomy, mastery, and belonging.

Table 57.1 *Basic needs and their (potential) corresponding acquired needs*

Basic needs (modified from Maslow)	Acquired needs (solution becomes problem)
Safety and security	Control/dominate (*or the opposite*)
Self-worth	Placate/seek approval (*or the opposite*)
Self-acceptance	Criticize/judge/disapprove (self or others)
Autonomy	Dependency/defiance/rebellion
Mastery	Avoidance/pessimism
Relationship/intimacy	Objectification of others/partners
Belonging (group or cause)	Withdraw/join faction
Meaning/purpose	Addiction/hedonism

When the need for safety and security has not been met during psychological development, an uncertainty clouds all areas of functioning, including work, play, and relationships. This can lead to a persistent undercurrent of anxiety, with an internal turmoil that seeks an external solution, and may result in attempts to control other athletes, situations, or events. This pattern of behavior may be called a 'need to control', but – like competitiveness – is not actually a true need. Rather, it is behavior that has an urgency driven by the unmet need for security. An alternative coping mechanism might be for an individual to manipulate others to assume responsibility for what is the individual's own behavior. For athletes, both approaches would cause problems, resulting in either conflict with team members, or lack of confidence about their own decisions and performance.

Similarly, a lack of self-worth and self-esteem might lead to placating behavior and a constant 'need' to seek the coach's approval; or the opposite might occur, such as inflating oneself by boasting or putting others down. The absence of self-acceptance can lead to being self-critical and judgmental about one's skill, effort, or performance. The damage done by self-criticism includes lack of self-confidence, diminished self-worth, and self-punitive behavior. These feelings and actions can lead to overtraining and burnout in athletes. Alternatively, a lack of self-acceptance can manifest itself as repeated disapproval of

others' behavior, which can create conflict within a team and/or with coaches.

Athletes who do not have a sense of their own independence or their ability to make choices (autonomy) may also become too dependent on coaches or teammates. And those who believe they cannot cope with difficult challenges (mastery) might avoid them by not exerting sufficient effort and not practicing conscientiously. For those who have difficulty developing and maintaining intimate relationships, the result might be abuse of partners or treating partners as objects. This sort of behavior may spill over into athletes' training and competition arenas (e.g., with training partners or other competitors).

Although many athletes are members of teams, some do not have a real sense of belonging or connection to others. As a result, they may withdraw from full participation and feel isolated. Their withdrawal is an attempt to cope with the feelings of not belonging, but unfortunately this contributes to the very isolation the athlete is trying to avoid.

Somewhat related to the feeling of belonging is the importance of having a sense of meaning and purpose in life – something that is larger than oneself and goes beyond personal issues. Athletes whose lives have meaning only in sport, whose whole identity is about being an athlete, and whose main purpose in life is sport participation, may experience an inner emptiness even when involved in sport. In seeking to avoid or fill this emptiness, they may turn to alcohol, drugs, or a hedonistic way of life. For these athletes, when they are faced with the ending of their sport experience, the transition to other careers or activities may be quite difficult (Pearson & Petitpas, 1990).

NEEDS AND WANTS

Needs are essential elements of psychological well-being. Wants are the main channel for fulfillment of needs. Therefore, a thorough discussion of wants is included in this chapter as they apply to the athletic domain. If we consistently don't get what we want, our needs may not be satisfied. And if we don't get what we need, we may *want* (lack) a lot. Eric Hoffer (1952), a philosopher and writer, believed that you can never get enough of what you don't really want; i.e., substitute gratification does not satisfy our needs. For example, if an athlete needs to feel a sense of mastery in their sport, then no amount of food or drink will satisfy their actual need instead.

The sporting environment provides several opportunities for athletes to be reminded that what they want (a personal best or an Olympic medal) can often be what they don't have. For successful athletes, most of what they have achieved is the result of their wanting something and being able to get it (often through hard work and years of training). But sometimes when individuals achieve their wants or goals, they frequently lose touch with wanting the very things that they spent years focused on obtaining. When they no longer want the same things, athletes can usually discard the respective want or goal and move on to another, as some other want will usually present itself (e.g., from initially just 'making the team', to 'being the highest goal-scorer').

In sport and other domains, the word 'need' is often used to exert more influence on others to give us what we want. Everything we do is connected to something we want. That does not necessarily mean we will enjoy the activity we choose; but if an important result is sought, we may choose the less pleasant behavior. For example, if an athlete is invited to a party the night before an important game, he or she may prefer to party rather than to stay at home to rest. However, the athlete may choose to stay at home because being ready for the big game is more important than the party. This has been called a 'priority of wants' (Giges, 1996).

This principle also leads to the understanding that there are no 'have to' behaviors. Our decisions about what we do comes from whatever wants are most important to us. If athletes lose sight of this, their decisions and actions will seem like things they *have to* do. For example, the following dialogue represents a discussion between an athlete and a sport psychologist regarding the athlete's perceived 'have to' dilemma.

Athlete: I 'have to' go to practice.
Sport psychologist: No, you don't.
Athlete: What do you mean, "No, I don't"? If I don't go to practice, then I won't know the plays.
Sport psychologist: So, you won't know the plays...
Athlete: Right. If I don't know the plays, then I'll be benched.
Sport psychologist: OK, so, you'll be benched...
Athlete: Again, "So"? If I'm benched, then I won't get to play.
Sport psychologist: OK...
Athlete: I don't want to be benched. I want to play!
Sport psychologist: Oh, now I understand. You want to play, and a way to do that and not be benched is to know the plays, and a great way to do that is to go to practice. So you don't "have to" go to practice, but going to practice is a great way to help you get what you want.

The point is slightly overstated here in order to highlight that this perspective is not just a difference in semantics. It actually affects the quality of peoples' lives because it reflects their approach to tasks as well as their perceptions of them. Individuals are ultimately able to decide what they do (autonomy); i.e., they are in charge of themselves, rather than being the victim of outside pressure. Even when someone is strongly influenced by 'shoulds', there are underlying wants, such as avoiding guilt, criticism, disapproval, reprimand, or rejection. Everything that individuals do is indeed connected to something they want.

In the context of sport, it is important to recognize that there may be several possible reasons for athletes being unclear about what they want. The more that sport psychology consultants understand about the reasons why athletes lack clarity about what is wanted, the better the support that can be provided to that individual. Some reasons for lack of clarity include that athletes may have:

- given up their first choice (e.g., if they can't achieve the gold medal that they really want, they don't want anything else);
- conflicting wants (e.g., two opposite wants – such as *performing well in the next-day's competition* and *partying with friends the night before* – which are so close to being equal, that athletes may not know which they want more). In these instances, what they choose to do indicates their preference in the moment, even if they are not aware of what they want.
- discounted the importance of what they want (e.g., if their coach made them feel that their wants don't matter, they may lose touch with what they want).
- feared criticism or judgment for being 'selfish' if they say what they want, and so in time they learn not to say it directly (e.g., a runner may not want to tell the coach that they would prefer to focus on their individual event rather than that *plus* a team relay event, and so instead tells the coach they don't get on with members of the relay team in order to avoid running the relay).
- thought they didn't deserve what they wanted, hence were reluctant to ask for it. This may (un-/consciously) lead to attempts to justify getting what they want without asking for it. For example, if a married athlete wants a night out with friends instead of staying at home, an argument may be provoked that leads to, "That's it, I'm going out!" This feeling of being justified avoids feeling guilty.
- uncertainty about what to do next. For instance, after a change in sporting status (such as career transition or termination), there may be a period where athletes struggle to find new interests or excitement.

Some athletes are clear about what they want to achieve, but for a variety of reasons they may not succeed. When that happens, the emotional experience will depend on the meaning the individual has attached to that performance or outcome. If the intended want was not deemed to be very important by the athlete, then it may only cause minor disappointment. But if it was considered highly important, then not getting it may trigger hurt, anger, or fear. For example, athletes may feel hurt if they interpret that they are not valued by their coach; anger if they judge the opponent as selfish or cruel; or fear if they think they might never achieve the level of performance that they want.

NEEDS AND EMOTIONS

When needs are satisfied, positive emotions will most likely be present. We can be more fully present, peaceful and relaxed, interested in and more responsive to others, curious about our environment, ready to take on new challenges, and able to enjoy our activities and relationships. When needs are not met, we are likely to feel unhappy, anxious, discouraged, depressed, and chronically angry. If the latter is true, there are three choices that individuals can make: (1) do nothing; (2) get involved in a dysfunctional solution; or (3) pursue satisfaction in a healthy way. If athletes choose to do nothing, it may lead to increased feelings of restlessness, uneasiness, frustration, and dissatisfaction – with themselves and others, and with their personal and sporting lives. The consequences of dysfunctional solutions were discussed in the section above on acquired needs (e.g., dependency, withdrawal, avoidance). The third option is likely to yield the best overall outcome – including the presence of positive emotions – but pursuing satisfaction of needs requires self-awareness, openness to change, and new behavior, and can be quite a challenging road for many athletes/individuals to follow.

POSITIVE EMOTIONS

Sport psychology consultants and researchers are often concerned with the role of emotions in sport. Knowing about emotions and the unique influence they have on thoughts and behavior provides practitioners and researchers with valuable insights to help athletes perform better in sport settings, as well as enjoy the processes and outcomes of this involvement. In this section, the way that positive emotions function within sport psychology consultations will be explained. It is important to note that emotions should not be solely categorized as either positive or negative. Also, it is useful to understand that emotions serve particular functions, and although these functions may have changed over time, they have retained their usefulness from our ancestral past to present day circumstances.

To appreciate the value of emotions in sport, consider how sport would be without them; for example, no smiling, no crying, no laughing, no hope, no expectation, and no disappointment. This portrayal of sport is not how we typically think of it, as sporting environments are typically associated with quite contrasting emotions such as sadness and happiness, pride and shame, hope and despair. When consulting with athletes in professional practice, practitioners need to balance their own emotional experiences in that respective context, whilst retaining a healthy perspective for the athlete's behavior, sensation, cognitions, relationships, and environment. For instance, some athletes endeavor to feel hopeful and inspired because their current (poor) condition has drained the energy they once had to train and compete.

The experience of other athletes presents explicit examples of what is possible despite the perceived impossibility of the current situation. Here is an example: In 1954, the Australian runner, John Landy, ran the mile event on three occasions. For each run his time was 4 minutes and 2 seconds, and he reflected, "Two little seconds are not much, but when you're on the track those fifteen yards seem solid and impenetrable, like a cement wall" (Bannister, 2004, p. vii). Through his medical studies, Roger Bannister knew that this could not be true. And on a wet and windy day in May 1954, helped by his friends Chris Chataway and Chris Brasher, he ran the first sub-four minute mile.

Such sensational anecdotes are great examples of situations in sport where there are diverse emotions, and they offer at least three functions when working with athletes. First, they serve as examples to dispute an athlete's thoughts and feelings about the present situation and probabilities about the future. Second, they present a constructive discussion for the client and sport psychology consultant to explore how emotions debilitate but also facilitate performance and well-being. In this instance, we might explore how an athlete's psychological needs are satisfied or frustrated within sport. Finally, we examine the traits of emotional thinking (e.g., jumping to an opinion, thinking in 'black and white', catastrophic impressions, and irrational judgments) and logical thinking (e.g., rational, evidence-based, maintaining context and perspective), in particular, their roles for our survival and self-fulfillment (Peters, 2012).

Sport scientists seek to unravel the mystery of performance excellence with objective explanations. Emotions, whether positively-valenced or negatively-valenced, filter through our mental lives and by knowing and accepting their worth, we appreciate their functions more obviously (McNulty & Fincham, 2012). This perspective emphasizes that the balance of emotions suitable for performance excellence is different to those for psychological well-being. The emotional mix necessary for performance excellence might contrast with the emotional mix needed to make new friends. For example, higher levels of anger might profit a performer in combative sport but such a high level of anger in a social setting is unnecessary (and not appropriate).

Consultations with athletes, coaches, and parents and, thus, the psychological interventions that are developed will all contain references to emotion. Often, though not always, negatively-valenced emotions can be heard in the client's narrative, and so efforts by the sport psychology consultant are aimed at understanding this experience and dealing with the effects of such emotions. Rather than just labeling emotions (and psychological traits and processes) as positive or negative, it seems more sensible to adopt a contextual view of emotions (and psychological traits and processes). In other words, we can understand why we feel as we do in particular surroundings but recognize that the circumstances might change over time. Knowing why we feel happy, sad, or anxious in different contexts can present opportunities for us to choose how we (prefer to) think and feel in that context in future. For instance, research has demonstrated that interpreting somatic sensations of unwanted anxiety in functional terms aids

performance in exams (Jamieson, Mendes, Blackstock, & Schmader, 2010). In sport, early research has similarly shown that athletes can be taught to view their anxiety as facilitative (Hanton & Jones, 1999).

Following this line of thinking, the pursuit of positively-valenced emotions seems obvious if these emotions (e.g., happiness, excitement, enjoyment) serve an advantage in performance settings or psychological well-being. Consultants should be aware of the athlete's personality, sport, gender, and competitive setting to maintain a contextual grip on the information they gather. The ultimate objective is to recognize the emotional needs of each individual within their environment, without trying to apply a predetermined emotional formula for success. For instance, if a golfer smiles after missing a three-foot putt for birdie, we might presume he does not care about his putting; however, we can only speculate about what he is thinking and feeling about that missed birdie putt. He might be smiling because he knows he cannot undo what he has done or he trusted the line of his putt, but the ball did not drop into the hole. To provide the best service to athletes, consultants must accept that there may be several possibilities for athletes' emotional experiences, so it is important to be open-minded when interpreting them.

As suggested above, emotions have survived human evolution because they have retained purpose in our lives and are functional in different settings (e.g., sport, social, family, organizational). However, emotions can be dysfunctional when they prevent us from reaching constructive goals. When we acknowledge, accept, and learn from our emotional experiences, the probability of functioning productively within and outside sport grows. This enlightenment means that consultants can apply the most suitable resources to help athletes cope when their emotions are harmful to them. The mechanics of this process might involve the sport psychology consultant inspecting what triggered a particular emotion (e.g., excitement, anger), and establishing how the athlete reacted to and/or dealt with it. This assessment allows the athlete to understand how they are currently thinking and behaving, and so increases the chance that they will make constructive adjustments in future. The ultimate aim is to increase the athlete's self-awareness and ability to reflect on past experiences in order to promote positive emotions and behaviors.

NEEDS AND BEHAVIORS

Self-awareness paves the way to a fuller knowledge of ourselves, a better ability to observe what we need and don't need, and an opportunity for change. We usually become aware of a problem behavior after it occurs. With repetition of this experience, awareness begins to occur earlier and may even occur during the behavior. Eventually, the awareness may occur before the actual behavior, and when this happens, a choice can be made to behave differently. This becomes an opportunity for change (Giges, 1996).

Consider athletes who have low self-esteem because of a strong internal critic. To help them build a sense of their own worth may require decreasing the impact of the self-criticism. Trying to contradict the self-criticism and convince them that they are worthwhile rarely has much impact. What sometimes is helpful is allowing some uncertainty to enter the equation, e.g., "Maybe I'm not worthless." Behaviors that encourage this process and build self-worth include treating themselves as if they are already worthwhile, using behaviors such as self-nurturing, self-encouragement, self-support, and self-appreciation. Learning these behaviors might require the support of a clinical or educational sport psychologist.

Figure 57.1 Pictured above is a consultation with an elite runner who had anxiety about returning to competition after injury.

NEEDS AND SPORT PSYCHOLOGY CONSULTATION

In sport psychology consultation, the relationship between the consultant and the athlete is an important element for understanding the consultative process (Petitpas, Giges, & Danish, 1999). Therefore, it is useful to know something about the origins of a consultant's professional training, to help appreciate what he or she brings to the session. A description of the background and approach of the first author's work is included here to assist readers in understanding its different elements.

The beginning of the above specified work was in medical research, where the emphasis was placed on the importance of careful observation and evaluation, with the aim of inquiring about how something worked and what happened to make a difference. What followed, and formed the theoretical foundations of the consultative work, were the study and practice of four major psychological systems: psychodynamic theory, gestalt therapy, transactional analysis, and cognitive therapy. A brief description of each framework is provided below to help understand the range of approaches that can be used when working with clients to address their needs.

The first model, psychodynamic theory, is considered the oldest (the 'grandfather') of theoretical approaches, and its roots can be traced to Freudian psychoanalysis, with which it is most commonly associated (Hill, 2001). Aspects of this approach have also been developed and adopted into more recent models used by practitioners. This model emphasizes the following principles: (a) all behavior has meaning; (b) past events and unconscious processes influence present functioning; and (c) the relationship between the practitioner and the client is a key element in the work of the consultation process.

In contrast, gestalt therapy (Perls, Hefferline, & Goodman, 1951) highlights the significance of awareness and present experience – or, how the athlete functions in the 'here and now' and the existence of polarities in the same individual (opposite wants, opposite feelings, and opposite thoughts).

In gestalt therapy, the term 'organismic self-regulation' refers to an internal psychological process consisting of a continuing flow of needs and satisfactions. Specifically, when a need emerges into the foreground of our experience, it can either be satisfied or interrupted. If it is satisfied, it then recedes into the background, allowing another need to emerge. This process continues unless it is interrupted by a troubling thought, an uncomfortable feeling, conflicting desires, or external influences. When this happens, the need remains unsatisfied and interferes with the flow and with optimal functioning until the interruption is removed (Giges, Petitpas, & Vernacchia, 2004, p. 438).

The third approach, transactional analysis (Berne, 1961), describes the 'child' and 'parent' within, and their influence on internal dialogue, communication, and relationships. There are two types of child according to this approach: (1) the 'natural child' who is the spontaneous, intuitive, creative, playful part; and (2) the 'adapted child' who is the compliant/defiant, placating, submissive/rebellious part, who grows in response to parental and societal demands. Similarly, there are two categories of 'parent': (1) the 'nurturing parent' who supports, nourishes, and protects the child; and (2) the 'critical parent' who reprimands, judges, criticizes the child, and imposes all the 'shoulds'.

The final approach (Beck, 1961), cognitive therapy, highlights thinking or cognition as the major determinant of feelings and behavior. Thus, faulty thinking or irrational beliefs, become the source of significant problems in communication and relationships (Ellis, 1993). Practitioners who apply this approach operate on the premise that the individual's (internal) interpretation of an event or situation is more powerful than the (external) stimulus itself.

Philosophical perspective

The culmination and synthesis of the above views represents several years of training, research, and professional practice. These relevant experiences will be unique for each sport psychology consultant, and it would be difficult to overstate the value of reflecting on those experiences as part of the process for helping practitioners to understand the needs of their clients and athletes. The quote below reflects a summarizing of the approaches, training, research, and experiences referred to above:

> Although originally trained as a clinician, with a background in medical research, I've come to see myself more as an educator. This change involved a shift from the medical model of illness and disease to a growth and development model (Danish, Petitpas, & Hale, 1992), in which problems are seen as the result of learned thinking patterns. The focus of my work with athletes and others is to help them change those patterns that contribute to distressed feelings or troublesome behavior, and to remove the barriers to their optimal functioning. This focus is primarily on present experience, based on the hypothesis that past negative experiences might recede into the background, were it not for the fact that present patterns of thinking and feeling keep them in the foreground. The language used by the person is followed very closely, because it not only expresses present thoughts and feelings, but also contributes to their development. I believe that what we learned in the past can be changed by what we learn in the present. (Giges, 2010)

A fundamental principle in helping others is that sport psychology consultants must be able to recognize their own needs well enough to assure that the work they do primarily addresses the needs and goals of athletes rather than their own. Mark Young (1998) expressed the idea that the journey of learning the art of helping others is a personal one that requires practitioners to know themselves as they learn to help others. Although our needs are not usually in our everyday awareness, there are many questions we can ask ourselves to increase our awareness of what we feel, want, and do. Answers to such questions will give important information about what our needs are and whether they are being met.

Needs assessment

With this self-awareness, what can we, as sport psychology practitioners, do to help athletes satisfy their needs? This process begins by conducting a comprehensive needs assessment. The consultant's tools to accomplish this assessment are observation, inquiry, intuition, and experience. We can use these tools to explore several areas of an athlete's function, including work, recreation, relationships, patterns of thinking and behaving, how wants and feelings are handled, and whether needs are being met. Important questions to consider include: (1) What needs are not being sufficiently attended to?; (2) What attempts are being made to satisfy those needs?; and (3) What is in the way of the attempts being successful? When we have some information about these areas and answers to these questions, we will have some ideas about where to focus the work, and begin to address the deficiency.

One of the basic assumptions of this approach is that healing would take place naturally if it wasn't the case that *something is interfering*. Therefore, the direction of the work is to remove the barrier or diminish its impact on the athlete's performance or well-being. Although beyond the scope of this chapter, a detailed discussion of this approach can be found in Giges' chapter, "Removing psychological barriers: Clearing the way" (Giges, 2000). The main elements of the process involve identifying the barriers, exploring their meaning and impact, and initiating change. The barriers may be grouped according to whether they are cognitive, affective, behavioral, or conative (pertaining to wants or desires). They can be identified by carefully listening to the language of the athlete, observing the tone of voice, rate of speech, facial expressions, gestures, or posture. The following are some examples of barriers to athletes' needs being met according to each category: (a) *cognitive*: self-criticism, self-doubt, and unrealistic expectations; (b) *affective*: anxiety, shame, and hurt feelings; (c) *behavioral*: overtraining, impulsiveness, and giving up; and (d) *conative*: low motivation, loss of interest, and conflicting wants.

Once the needs assessment is conducted, athletes are generally unclear about how to begin the process of removing barriers and meeting their needs. Thus, a key role of the sport psychol-ogy consultant is to help athletes with this process, which starts with assisting them to initi-ate change (Giges, 1995). Two important princi-ples in helping people initiate change are: (1) a change in awareness is often the first step in changing, even before behavior change occurs, and this can be accomplished at the beginning of the work; and (2) beginning change demonstrates the ability to change, and serves as a confidence builder for further change. When athletes engage with this process with the guidance of the sport psychologist, it means they can progress past their barriers, with the objective of ensuring their needs (and perhaps wants) are fulfilled.

CONCLUSION

Athletes' needs and wants form an integral part of their existence, and so meeting these needs is paramount to their growth as individ-uals and competitors. Working with sport psychology consultants, athletes can learn to recognize what their needs are, and to under-stand the influence of needs on performance. In order to help athletes to fulfill their poten-tial, it is important to ensure that their identi-fied needs are met, that they can achieve their goals in the context of positive emotion, and ultimately that they learn to self-regulate by maintaining awareness of current needs.

LEARNING AIDS

1 Explain the importance of psychological needs.

   Psychological needs are fundamental requirements of personal growth, health, and well-being. At any stage of development and in any type of activity, these elements exist and influence our functioning.

2 Summarize the differences between basic needs and acquired needs.

   Basic needs consist of the need for security, autonomy, identity, self-worth, mastery, intimacy, belonging, and a sense of meaning or purpose in life. Acquired needs are not really needs, but rather dysfunctional attempts to compensate for the deficiency when basic needs are not met.

3 Discuss how you might help an athlete with a 'have to' dilemma.

   Everything we do is connected to something we want. When athletes are not aware of their wants, they may think they 'have to' do something. Helping them become more aware of their underlying wants allows them to realize they have a choice, and thus to feel less pressured or victimized.

4 Identify some reasons that athletes might not know what they want.

   They may have given up their first choice, have conflicting wants, discount the importance of what they want, fear criticism for focusing on their want, or do not feel deserving of saying what they want.

REVIEW QUESTIONS

1 What are some basic psychological needs?

2 What are some consequences of unmet needs?

3 How are needs satisfied in everyday life?

4 What is meant by acquired needs?

5 What is the relationship between wants and needs?

EXERCISES

These exercises can be used by sport psychology students, beginning consultants, and experienced practitioners to increase their self-awareness.

1 Awareness of needs: In answering the following questions, spend at least five minutes contemplating each answer. Go well beyond your first response. If nothing comes to mind after your first response, allow time for something to come up that you might not have thought about before. Sometimes, repeating the question is useful if no answer comes to mind.

   a Which basic psychological needs are you aware of? Review this list and select all that apply.

   Security   Autonomy   Identity   Self-worth

   Mastery   Intimacy   Belonging   Meaning or purpose in life

   For needs that you are aware of, answer the following questions:

   b Which needs are you comfortable with?

   c Which needs are you uncomfortable with?

   d What is the nature of that discomfort?

   e What, if anything, will you do about that discomfort?

   f Which needs are not currently being satisfied?

   g What are you reactions (thoughts, feelings, wants, behavior) to that awareness?

   h What, if anything, do you plan to do about satisfying that need?

   i Describe what barriers you anticipate in doing that?

   j What might you do to remove or avoid those barriers?

   k Read the instructions for Part I(a) above. Review the list of basic psychological needs. Which needs are you *not* aware of? Select all that apply. For needs that you are not aware of, answer the following questions.

      i What are your reactions (thoughts, feelings, wants, and behaviors) to not being aware?

      ii What might account for you not being aware?

      iii Is not being aware something you want to change?

iv   If yes, what might be a beginning to making that change? (This might take more time.)

v   Is that something you think you will do? If not, what might be in the way of doing it?

vi   If you don't want to change not being aware, what might account for that choice?

vii What is your reaction to making the choice to remain unaware?

viii Think of three people who are important to you. For each of them, which needs do you think are not being satisfied?

ix   For each of them, what do you see or hear that accounts for your opinions?

2   Self-reflection: For each question, look for more than one answer.

   a   What are your main sources of enjoyment or satisfaction?

   b   What gives you good feelings about yourself?

   c   What do you want that you are not currently getting?

   d   What need would be served if you got what you want?

   e   What are your reactions (thoughts, feelings, wants, behaviors) to not getting what you want?

   f   What might give you bad feelings about yourself?

   g   What leads to your feeling guilty?

   h   What leads to your feeling hurt? What do you believe is the explanation of your feeling?

   i   What leads to your feeling embarrassed?

   j   What leads to your feeling ashamed?

   k   What do you fear?

   l   What do you pretend?

   m   Which questions were uncomfortable to answer? What might account for the discomfort?

3   Needs and activities

   a   Make a detailed list of your activities for a typical day in your life. Arrange the activities in time segments of 1–2 hours each.

   b   For each time segment, identify one or more basic needs that are being addressed.

   c   Repeat step 1 for what would be an 'ideal' day in your life.

   d   For each time segment, identify one or more basic needs that are being addressed.

   e   Compare the typical day with the ideal day.

   f   Identify changes you want to make in the typical day to bring it closer to an ideal day.

   g   Describe what barriers you anticipate to initiating those changes.

   h   Consider what you might do to remove or avoid the barriers.

ADDITIONAL READING

Andersen, M.B. (Ed.). (2005). *Sport psychology in practice.* Champaign, IL: Human Kinetics.

Van Raalte, J.L. & Brewer, B.W. (Eds.). (in press). *Exploring sport and exercise psychology* (3rd ed.), Washington, DC: American Psychological Association.

REFERENCES

Bannister, R. (2004). *The first four minutes.* Gloucestershire, UK: The History Press.

Beck, A.T. (1967). *Depression: Clinical, experimental, and theoretical aspects.* New York: Hoeber.

Berne, E. (1961). *Transactional analysis in psychotherapy.* New York: Grove Press.

Danish, S.J., Petitpas, A.J. & Hale, B.D. (1992). A developmental-educational intervention model in sport psychology. *The Sport Psychologist, 6,* 403–415.

Deci, E.L. (2002). Facilitating autonomous self-regulation through support of basic psychological needs. *Journal of Sport & Exercise Psychology, 24* (Suppl.), S50.

Ellis, A. (1993). Fundamentals of rational-emotive therapy for the 1990s. In W. Dryden & L. Hill (Eds.), *Innovations in rational-emotive therapy.* Newbury Park, CA: Sage Publications.

Erikson, E. (1950). *Childhood and society.* New York: W. W. Norton.

Frankl, V. (1992). *Man's search for meaning: An introduction to logotherapy.* Boston: Beacon Press.

Giges, B. (1995). *How People Change.* Keynote address presented at the annual meeting of the Association for Applied Sport Psychology, New Orleans, LA.

Giges, B. (1996). *Self-awareness for sport psychology practitioners.* Workshop presented as part of a Workshop Series on Contemporary Issues in Sport Psychology, Department of Psychology, Springfield College, Springfield, MA.

Giges, B. (2000). Removing psychological barriers: Clearing the way. In M.B. Andersen (Ed.) *Doing sport psychology* (pp.17–31), Champaign, IL: Human Kinetics.

Giges, B. (2010). Retrieved from http://www.burtgiges.com/Home_Page.php

Giges, B., Petitpas, A.J. & Vernacchia, R.A. (2004). Helping coaches meet their own needs: Challenges for the sport psychology consultant. *The Sport Psychologist,* December, *18, 4,* 430–444.

Hanton, S. & Jones, G. (1999). The effects of a multi-modal intervention program on performers. II. Training the butterflies to fly in formation. *The Sport Psychologist, 13,* 22–41.

Hill, K.L. (2001). *Frameworks for sport psychologists: Enhancing sport performance.* Champaign, IL: Human Kinetics.

Hoffer, E. (1952). *The ordeal of change.* New York: Harper & Row.

Jamieson, J.P., Mendes, W.B., Blackstock, E. & Schmader, T. (2010). Turning the knots in your stomach into bows: Reappraising arousal improves performance on the GRE. *Journal of Experimental Social Psychology, 46,* 208–212.

Maslow, A. (1987). *Motivation and personality* (3rd ed.). New York: Harper & Row.

McNulty, J.K. & Fincham, F.D. (2012). Beyond positive psychology? Toward a contextual view of psychological processes and well-being. *American Psychologist, 67,* 101–110.

Pearson, R. & Petitpas, A. (1990). Transition of athletes: Pitfalls and prevention. *Journal of Counseling and Development, 69,* 7–10.

Perls, F., Hefferline, R.F. & Goodman, P. (1951). *Gestalt therapy: Excitement and growth in the human personality.* New York: Dell.

Peters, S. (2012). *The chimp paradox: The mind management programme to help you achieve success, confidence and happiness.* London: Vermilion.

Petitpas, A.J., Giges, B. & Danish, S.J. (1999). The sport psychologist-athlete relationship: Implications for training. *The Sport Psychologist,* September, *13, 3,* 344–357.

Watzlawick, P., Weakland, J.H. & Fisch, R. (1974). *Change: Principles of problem formation and problem resolution.* New York: W. W. Norton.

Young, M.E. (1998). *Learning the art of helping: Building blocks and techniques.* Columbus, OH: Merrill Publishing.

Chapter 58

Using quantitative psychological assessment to optimize athletes' and exercise participants' physical performance

MARIA PSYCHOUNTAKI, NEKTARIOS A. STAVROU, SYMEON P. VLACHOPOULOS, JUDY L. VAN RAALTE AND ANTOINETTE M. MINNITI

SUMMARY

Psychological assessment is an essential part of an applied sport and exercise psychologist's work. To be effective, applied sport and exercise psychologists should become knowledgeable about assessment tools so that they can ensure optimal service delivery and evaluation. Feedback from appropriate assessments is useful for informing athletes' psychological programs and/or participants' integration to exercise programs. The selection of tests, questionnaires and the overall range of measures and instruments will depend on the goal of the evaluation and/or diagnosis. However, as a starting point, sport and exercise psychologists may want to consider assessing individual characteristics (trait measures), sport-specific traits and psychomotor skills (for athletes), and other psychological factors related to team or exercise group perceptions and sport or exercise-related states.

INTRODUCTION

Case study: Anna's swimming coach asked her to seek advice from a sport psychologist when he recognized that she was experiencing intense stress prior to and during competitions, and thus because her performance was not matching her usual training standards.

The sport psychologist began the consultation process with Anna by conducting a comprehensive psychological assessment that included questionnaires and interviews. In line with best practice, the sport psychologist ensured the measures used were valid, reliable, and relevant (e.g., whenever possible, scales should be domain- and/or sport-specific). Based on the symptoms that Anna presented with, the consultant believed she would benefit from both general and sport-specific tests to fully understand the extent of her stress and to examine her self-confidence levels. By administering appropriate quantitative assessment tools, the sport psychologist was able to identify, classify, and assess Anna's current situation. After interpreting the findings of both the assessment tools and the interview information, the sport psychologist was able to work with Anna to better understand her stress and to develop a suitable, tailored program for her.

The consultant's assessment indicated that Anna's high competitive anxiety stemmed from deeper causes, such as poor self-esteem (low ratings on a self-esteem questionnaire), lack of sport self-confidence (low ratings on a sport-specific self-confidence inventory), and

trait competitive anxiety (high ratings on a competitive anxiety test).

Anna received feedback from the sport psychologist in the form of a bespoke assessment report in which an outline of the results was presented both graphically (e.g., using pie charts and line graphs) and in writing. The meaning of the graphs and her individual scores was explained to her (e.g., how they compared to the possible range of scores and normative values). These quantitative findings – in conjunction with relevant qualitative data – provided valuable information for establishing Anna's psychological program. That is, the sport psychologist, the athlete, and the coach were able to work together to prioritize and set goals in order to ensure a strong foundation for the athlete's psychological development – the aim of which was to improve self-esteem, self-confidence, and stress management. Three years later, Anna qualified for the Beijing Olympic Games where she set two national records.

OBJECTIVES

After reading this chapter, you should be able to:

1   Recognize the importance of quantitative psychological assessment for athletes and exercise participants.
2   Understand relevant criteria for the selection of appropriate psychological tests.
3   Appreciate the contribution of both social and physical environments for athletes/exercisers so that assessments are fit for purpose.
4   Identify an appropriate range of assessment measures for evaluation of athletes/exercisers.

THE PURPOSE AND PROCESS OF PSYCHOLOGICAL ASSESSMENT

Psychological assessment constitutes a key aspect of any sport psychologist's role. Assessments are conducted to obtain useful information for the development of programs for athletes, sport teams, exercise participants, and professionals.

The main purpose of the evaluation and/or diagnosis process is to gather information about athletes' or exercise participants'

strengths and to look for areas to improve. Typically, assessment should involve both quantitative and qualitative methods. The focus of this chapter will be on quantitative assessment so, when the term "assessment" or "evaluation" is used, it will refer to quantitative aspects unless otherwise stated.

The quantitative approach is characterized by several advantages. Quantitative assessment results are easily interpreted by exercisers, athletes, coaches and parents. These measures can be used to describe the psychological profile of the athlete or exerciser and detect changes across different training and competitive situations. Relevant tools can help to identify areas for improvement as well as the benefits gained following interventions. When an evaluation is properly conducted, it provides fruitful information regarding the design of a psychological program which can in turn be effectively applied toward the improvement of, e.g., athletes' or exercisers' performance engagement and emotional state.

In the sport and exercise psychology literature, there are three major directories of psychological tests: *Advances in Sport and Exercise Psychology Measurement* (Duda, 1998), *Directory of Psychological Tests in the Sport and Exercise Sciences* (Ostrow, 2002), and *Measurement in Sport and Exercise Psychology* (Tenenbaum, Eklund, & Kamata, 2012). Before administering questionnaires or other formal assessment instruments or tests, a number of parameters need to be considered: (a) the purpose and theoretical background of the assessment test; (b) the psychometric indices and extent of the measure's adaptation for the intended population; (c) the age group to which it will be administered for the ideal selection of a questionnaire/instrument/test. Other important parameters that should be considered include: (a) the commitment of exercisers, athletes, and coaches to the assessment process; and (b) the establishment of a distinctive link among sport psychologists, exercisers, coaches, and athletes so that questionnaires/tests are honestly and accurately completed. The appropriate assessment tool varies depending upon the purpose of the assessment, the needs of the individuals being assessed and the quality of the tools.

Psychological assessment is often conducted in two or three stages: (a) initial assessment; (b) optional midway assessment; and (c) final assessment. Evaluations can be administered on an individual or group basis. In this chapter, we will focus mainly on the initial assessment as an integral part of the applied sport psychologist's work with athletes and exercise participants.

ATHLETE PSYCHOLOGICAL ASSESSMENT

In the context of athlete psychological assessment, it is possible to assess a wide range of factors. To create a psychological profile, practitioners may want to consider assessing: (a) general trait characteristics and cognitive functioning ability; (b) sport trait characteristics; (c) psychomotor capability; (d) sport team characteristics; and (e) sport state characteristics. Data generated from such profiles can be used to assist with the development and structure of sport psychology interventions.

General trait characteristics and cognitive function

Efforts to identify the ideal sport personality have proven fruitless, as a global sport personality is only minimally or not even at all related to participation or performance in sports (Schurr, Ashley, & Joy, 1977). That is, those who have the most promising psychological profiles are not necessarily the best athletes or exercisers. Conversely, those with less optimal profiles may perform at high levels. Therefore, applied sport psychologists may find that assessment tools are most useful in gathering information about strengths and weaknesses, setting goals, and organizing interventions in a beneficial way. Acquiring a comprehensive understanding of exercisers and athletes can allow sport and exercise consultants to establish solid foundations for intervention programs aiming for personal development and improvement. For those assessment tools focused on clinical concerns, proper training is required for test administration and interpretation.

In the case study presented above, Anna's assessment provides evidence that she may be vulnerable in the context of her sport. Detecting these issues can be the basis for setting goals which may eventually resolve the reasons of her vulnerability. Furthermore, changes on these measures over time can be used to document Anna's progress. Some of the widely-assessed trait characteristics are presented below.

Trait anxiety is an individual's inclination to negatively interpret his/her everyday life situations, and is considered an aspect of their personality (Spielberger, 1966). It is important to understand how athletes typically perceive threatening circumstances, for example, in a sporting environment, as this may affect their preparation and training leading up to competition. Previous measures designed to assess general trait anxiety include: Taylor's (1953) Manifest Anxiety Scale; the IPAT Anxiety Scale (Scheier & Cattell, 1960); and, more recently, the State-Trait Anxiety Inventory trait form (Spielberger, Gorsuch, Lushene, Vagg, & Jacobs, 1983).

Self-esteem relates to the way a person assesses their abilities and personality. The extent to which an athlete has high or low self-esteem may influence their willingness to engage and/or persevere in sport. Fostering athletes' self-esteem can improve both performance and their personal growth and development (Zinsser, Bunker, & Williams, 2010). The Self-Esteem Scale (Rosenberg, 1965) is a brief (10-item) one-dimensional assessment tool that measures global self-esteem and, thus, provides general (rather than sport-specific) information about this concept.

Aggression refers to a person's tendency to display aggressive behavior (physical aggressiveness, verbal aggressiveness, anger and hostility). Sport may be an environment where athletes learn to control or curb aggression and this is important because, as some sport psychologists have indicated, aggressive acts can negatively relate to athletic performance (Gill, 2000); however, others have noted that aggression may enhance performance

outcome (Widmeyer, 1984). This trait can be measured using Buss and Perry's (1992) Aggression Questionnaire, which assesses the four domains noted above.

Cognitive functioning refers to the ability to process information immediately and effectively and is based on the general cognitive ability of a person, rather than their knowledge, education, or social status. It is important to assess athletes' cognitive functioning because competitive sports requires swift and successful decision making. Cognitive functioning has a temporal component whereby it matures in childhood, peaks during young adulthood, and then declines after middle age (Dishman & Chambliss, 2010). A widely-used, nonverbal test to assess cognitive functioning is the Standard Progressive Matrices (Raven, Court, & Raven, 1992). It is a test suitable to assess people with respect to their immediate capacity for observation and clear thinking as well as their ability to understand meaningless figures presented in an observation. The scale is designed to cover the whole range of intellectual development an individual can display, such as their ability to find a missing piece to complete a pattern.

Social desirability is the tendency of an individual to describe themselves in favorable, socially desirable terms to attain the approval of others. It is important that when interpreting individual responses, sport psychologists can trust they are an accurate reflection of the athlete's behavior, rather than how they would like the consultant to think of them. Therefore, it is crucial that the Social Desirability Scale (Crowne & Marlowe, 1960) be administered in conjunction with the above scales to account for this potential conflict.

Sport trait characteristics

In addition to assessing general traits, it can be valuable to measure traits specifically related to sports. Sometimes, general traits are reflected in sport, but there may also be sport-specific traits that are worth considering. With regard to Anna's case, we noted her low self-esteem and high trait anxiety in her personal life. The same was true in her sport life: low sport-confidence and high trait competitive anxiety. These findings were the primary reason that the applied sport psychologist supported Anna on both a personal and sport-oriented basis.

When sport trait questionnaires are used in the context of the initial psychological assessment, athletes respond based on how they feel "generally" or "usually" when they compete. Weinberg and Gould (2006) stated that: "Sport-specific measures of personality predict behavior in sport settings better than general personality tests do" (p. 34). Some sport psychology consultants avoid the use of global personality measures or general psychological characteristics and focus instead on sport-specific ones. Below are some widely used sport-specific traits and their respective tests.

Competition anxiety refers to an athlete's tendency to display high levels of stress before a competition. The Sport Competition Anxiety Test (Martens, 1977) consists of 15 items which record physical and emotional symptoms of anxiety. Another competition anxiety test is the Sport Anxiety Scale (Smith, Smoll, & Schutz, 1990). It is a multi-dimensional measure that assesses athletes' somatic trait anxiety (e.g., perceived anxiety related to stomach tension), worry trait anxiety (e.g., the extent to which one typically experiences self-doubts), and concentration disruption (e.g., the degree to which an athlete tends to experience disruptive thoughts during competition).

Sport-confidence is the belief or degree of certainty that athletes usually possess with regard to their ability to be successful in sport. The Sport-Confidence Inventory (Vealey, 1986) (trait version) is a 13-item questionnaire that is commonly used to assess individuals' perceptions about their capability in the sporting domain.

Coping is a conscious process of constantly changing cognitive and behavioral efforts to manage specific external and/or internal demands based on an individual's resources (Lazarus, 2000). Athletes tend to use similar coping strategies in all situations that they encounter (Giacobbi & Weinberg, 2000). The Athletic Coping Skills Inventory-28 (Smith, Schultz, Smoll, & Ptacek, 1995) was developed to assess seven psychological skills deemed to constitute the athlete's overall personal coping resources (coping with adversity, peaking under pressure, goal setting and mental preparation, concentration, freedom from worry, confidence and achievement motivation, and coach-ability). It is a widely accepted instrument with good psychometric properties.

Sport motivation refers to the reasons for which athletes participate in their sports. There are various questionnaires that assess athletes' participation motives, and instrument selection largely depends on age and/or competitive level. Relevant measures generally focus on assessment of both internal and external motives. The Behavioral Regulation in Sport Questionnaire (Lonsdale, Hodge, & Rose, 2008) is one such measure of competitive sport participants' intrinsic and extrinsic motivation as well as a-motivation in relation to their sport participation.

Task and ego goals refer to the way in which athletes define success and the meanings they attribute to it. Understanding these enables applied sport psychologists to understand how athletes define success and failure. The Task and Ego Orientation in Sport Questionnaire (Duda & Nicholls, 1992) assesses achievement goals in sport by means of measuring task and ego goal orientations. Athletes who are characterized by high task orientation define success as personal improvement, learning, and task mastery. Athletes typified by high ego orientation feel successful when they perform better than other athletes.

Psychomotor assessment

A series of computer-assisted applications have been used to measure psychomotor abilities. These applications can provide important information to athletes, their coaches, and researchers about a range of athletes' abilities such as reaction time, anticipation time, attention-concentration, dynamic stability, kinesthesia, movement coordination, hand-eye coordination, and learning process/capability. The above-mentioned features constitute some of the basic psychomotor skills that can be measured to provide information regarding specific characteristics for athlete performance. However, it should be noted that, like sport personality, psychomotor performance cannot independently predict elite sport performance.

Reaction time is one of the most widely measured characteristics of athletes. In some sports, there is a need for a simple auditory reaction time (e.g., track-and-field, swimming) or a simple visual reaction time (e.g., shooting). In other sports, the athlete's capacity to react appropriately and quickly to composite stimuli is necessary. Thus, an estimation of the athlete's reaction time can be based on auditory, visual, or composite stimuli. There are a number of computer-based programs to measure reaction time. The Vienna Test System (VTS) is typical of these assessment tools. The VTS consists of various tests, e.g., reaction time tests. The Movement Detection Test (MDT) by Hackfort is one of the tests run on the basis of the VTS (Hackfort, Kilgallen, & Hao, 2009).

Tests measuring *concentration and attention* are widely used in psychological assessment because these factors are closely related to athlete performance. However, they are difficult to measure in the sport domain (Vallerand, 1983). For the assessment of concentration, self-report questionnaires and computerized tests are available. The Cognitrone test is based on Reulecke's (1991) theoretical model. According to this model, concentration is a focused attention characterized by three elements: energy, function, and precision. The computerized test program provides information regarding the number of correct and incorrect answers as well as the response time for these reactions. An additional test used for the examination of concentration is the *continuous* or *sustained attention test*. It examines the level of an individual's concentration when faced with a rather low information load. Athletes' performances on concentration tests can be compared across time (e.g., to show improvement) and they can be correlated to emotional state (e.g., anxiety, self-confidence), which can be useful information for sport psychology practitioners.

Psychomotor tests can be used to assess motor learning, balancing ability, kinesthesia, sensorimotor coordination, and anticipation time. *Motor learning* refers to the way in which athletes can facilitate the acquisition of skills by understanding or manipulating aspects of the learning process. A *stability platform* is a tool within motor learning that can be employed to provide important information about athlete stability, which is particularly important for sports such as sailing, shooting, or gymnastics. *Kinesthesia* constitutes a crucial factor that is related to several characteristics such as athletes' technical execution. Moreover, kinesthesia is typical of expert performers whereas it is deficient in novice athletes. It is measured in athletes' hands or legs through active movement and/or passive movement. During the test, subjects wear a blindfold mask and are asked to move their arm or foot as closely as they can to a target position within a 90°-range. *Sensorimotor coordination* also provides helpful information regarding athletes' movement reaction and capability and is a significant factor in team (i.e., volleyball, football) and individual sports (i.e., tennis, fencing, wrestling). The tests of sensorimotor coordination that have been developed, assess the eye-hand, hand-hand, and eye-hand-foot athletes' coordination. During a coordination test athletes maneuver in a three-dimensional room by using their hands and/or feet (Prieler, 2011). In other tests, athletes move a metal pointer with both hands around an anodized star pattern or watch through a mirror to follow the pattern without leaving it. Based on the above, it is clear that the usefulness of evaluation of psychomotor characteristics relies on a combination of competition demands and the specific elements that characterize each sport.

Sport team variables

Individual athletes often function within the context of a team. Therefore, assessment of team-related variables such as cohesion and leadership can be informative. Data collected from such assessments may be used by sport psychology consultants for the benefit of coaches and athletes working at individual and group levels.

The Group Environment Questionnaire (GEQ; Widmeyer, Brawley, & Carron, 1985) is a widely used instrument for measuring *cohesiveness* in sport teams. The GEQ focuses on how attractive the team is to individual athletes and how they perceive the team as a whole with regard to sport tasks and social relationships. Research has indicated that both task and social cohesion are associated with performance improvements (Carron, Colman, Wheeler, & Stevens, 2002).

A *sociogram* is a tool that involves the entire team in order to measure social cohesion in team sports. It discloses affiliation and attraction among team members including: the presence of cliques, friendship choices within the team, and social isolation of team members. To collect information for the sociogram, team members are asked specific questions, such as "name the three teammates in the team you would most like to room with" or "name the three teammates you would most like to practice with". Collecting this sort of data can bring up sensitive issues within a team so it is particularly important that athletes' confidentiality is ensured. An important benefit of this approach is that the contribution and perceptions of all team members are included in the results.

When it comes to assessing *leadership*, there are measures of athletes' leadership abilities and measures of athletes' preferences and perceptions of coach leadership behavior. The Sport Leadership Behavior Inventory (SLBI; Glenn & Horn, 1993) is a context-specific measure of peer leadership that was developed for use with team sport athletes. It is based on the approach which regards leadership as an interaction between individual characteristics and the environment or particular situation. The measure consists of 25 items, and there is also a shortened 11-item version that Glenn and Horn validated to provide a user-friendly scale for peer and coach assessments.

The Leadership Scale for Sports (LSS; Chelladurai & Saleh, 1980) is used to assess coach leadership behavior. It includes three versions, that is, the athletes' preferences for specific leadership behavior, the athletes' perceptions of their coaches' behavior, and the coaches' perceptions of their own behavior. The LSS comprises 40 items which constitute five dimensions: training and instruction, autocratic behavior, democratic behavior, social support, and positive feedback. Athletes tend to prefer coaches who allow athlete participation in decision making, provide positive feedback, and who give a lot of tactical and technical instruction (Martin, Jackson, Richardson, & Weiller, 1999).

Sport state characteristics

In addition to the trait psychological and psychomotor assessment, the athletes' psychological state is also evaluated. For some athletes, their normal levels of anxiety, mood, and flow differ from their experiences before, during, or after competition or in certain training situations. Therefore, it can be useful for sport psychology consultants to assess particular states experienced by athletes. The Competitive State Anxiety Inventory-2 (CSAI-2; Martens, Burton, Vealey, Bump, & Smith, 1990) is widely used in the sport domain. The CSAI-2 is a 27-item self-report instrument measuring the intensity of somatic anxiety, cognitive anxiety, and self-confidence that an athlete feels prior to, during or just after his/her competition. A "direction" scale was later included in the CSAI-2 to measure the facilitating or debilitating nature of the experienced intensity of each factor to subsequent performance (Jones & Swain, 1992).

Flow has been described by Csikszentmihalyi (1990) as a holistic sensation where people consider themselves to be totally absorbed or on automatic pilot. The Flow State Scale-2 (FSS-2; Jackson & Eklund, 2002) is a 36-item self-report scale developed by Jackson and Marsh (1996) to assess the magnitude of flow characteristics experienced during a specific event. The FSS-2 assesses the challenge-skill balance, action-awareness merging, clear goals, unambiguous feedback, concentration on task at hand, sense of control, loss of self-consciousness, transformation of time, and the autotelic experience. Moreover, a global flow score is included in the measure to understand better the concept of flow experience through a more holistic perspective. Flow has been found to relate to both the performance and

psychological skills that athletes tend to use, such as keeping control of emotions and thoughts and maintaining appropriate levels of activation and relaxation (Jackson, Thomas, Marsh, & Smethurst, 2001).

Mood refers to the emotional condition of individuals in their everyday lives. Mood has been found to be related to sport performance. The Profile of Mood States (POMS-short form; Shacham, 1983) is an appropriate tool for the assessment of an individual's emotional condition. Although not designed as a sport-specific measure, the POMS has been used extensively with athletes and is therefore included in this section. The POMS-short form consists of 37 items and describes six different aspects of emotional life; that is, tension, depression, vigor, hostility, fatigue, and confusion. The total score of the POMS derives from the equation: Total Mood = Tension + Depression + Hostility + Fatigue + Confusion – Vigor + 100 (the number 100 is added so that we can always have a positive rate). The lower the total score, the better the examinee's profile.

EXERCISE PARTICIPANT PSYCHOLOGICAL ASSESSMENT

Exercisers are similar to competitive athletes in that both are involved in physical activity. However, the goals and motivation of exercisers differ from competitive athletes. To create a psychological profile of exercisers, sport and exercise psychologists may want to consider assessing: (a) exercise-specific trait characteristics; (b) exercise-specific state characteristics; and (c) exercise-specific psychological environment characteristics.

Psychological testing that uses instruments based on quantitative methods may prove useful in the exercise domain to improve the quality of the exercise participants' experiences, and – for most structured settings – the effectiveness of the teaching approach employed by the exercise instructor to enhance exercise adherence. Psychological instruments may be used to quantify various psychological characteristics that are related to

positive and negative experiences of exercise participants during a program, and their subsequent behavior. Such characteristics may include motivation for exercise participation and self-perceptions related to exercise. Instruments of this type assess participants' exercise-specific traits, states, and perceptions of the psychological environment.

The rationale for measuring psychological characteristics both at trait and state levels is based on the bottom-up hypothesis (see Vallerand, 2007). According to this hypothesis, repeated exposure of an exercise participant to a specific exercise program and a particular instructional style may lead to more generalized changes in a particular psychological characteristic. For instance, received support from the instructor in every single exercise class may result in a more generalized change of one's attitude towards exercise in a positive direction. Repeated exposure to an environment providing choice can contribute to higher levels of relatively enduring autonomous motivation (Moustaka, Vlachopoulos, Kabitsis, & Theodorakis, 2012). Hence, both an exercise state assessment used in each single exercise class and an exercise trait assessment would be important to evaluate the extent to which repeated exposure to a particular instructional style might influence changes at a more general level.

Exercise-specific trait characteristics

A number of exercise-specific traits such as types of regulation of exercise behavior, exercise enjoyment, physical self-evaluations, social physique anxiety, and strength of exercise identity are related to exercise behavior. This list is not exhaustive but serves to provide examples of key exercise-specific traits, guidelines for selecting traits, the instruments to measure them, and discussion about the ways they can be used to set goals for the development of intervention programs. The criteria that may be used for the selection of particular instruments to measure exercise-specific traits should take into account both theoretical and psychometric considerations.

An example trait is the construct of behavioral regulations in exercise, which can be measured by the Behavioral Regulation in Exercise Questionnaire-2 (BREQ-2; Markland & Tobin, 2004). The BREQ-2 assesses individuals' reasons for exercising so as to determine why people differ on the frequency and persistence of their exercise behavior. These reasons are outlined in four categories that reflect both a sense of pressure to exercise – either externally-imposed (external regulation) or self-imposed (introjected regulation) – and a sense of choice and willingness to do so, because it is important (identified regulation) or because it is fun to exercise (intrinsic motivation). The exercise-specific trait of behavioral regulations might be an important trait to consider

for a number of reasons: (a) it is part of a larger theory (self-determination theory: SDT; Ryan & Deci, 2007) that explains why identified regulation and intrinsic motivation are considered to be more important motives to be enhanced, if enjoyable, regular, and long-term exercise behavior is promoted; (b) research evidence exists showing that identified regulation and intrinsic motivation have been linked to more frequent and long-term exercise behavior; (c) the theory provides principles that may be applied in practice by the exercise instructor to enhance these two self-determined motives for exercise; and (d) research evidence exists showing that the BREQ-2 produces reliable and valid scores in relation to the assessment of these motives to exercise.

Other examples of psychological instruments that fulfill these criteria include the Physical Self-Perception Profile (PSPP; Fox & Corbin, 1989) that assesses how individuals perceive and evaluate various aspects of their physical self such as sport competence, physical condition, body attractiveness, and physical strength, and the Social Physique Anxiety Scale (SPAS; Hart, Leary, & Rejeski, 1989) that quantifies the anxiety people experience when worried about how others evaluate their bodies.

Exercise-specific state characteristics

Exercise-specific state assessments are useful in quantifying the characteristics measured in the context of a single bout of exercise class rather than in exercise in general. Such state assessments are important in that they capture the "here and now" of the psychological characteristic of interest, allowing for the comparison of scores across exercise sessions. Furthermore, this enables sport psychology consultants to examine whether, for instance, a change in the exercise setting (e.g., new class instructor, new walking route) may correspond to a change in the level of the characteristic for an exercise participant across exercise sessions. The reasons that individuals participate in the particular exercise class may be identified using the Situational Motivation Scale (Guay, Vallerand, & Blanchard, 2000) where participants are asked why they have taken up today's exercise. Also, levels of state social physique anxiety may be measured using the State Social Physique Anxiety Scale (S-SPAS; Martin Ginis, Murru, Conlin, & Strong, 2011) rather than the Social Physique Anxiety Scale (SPAS) which is the respective trait measure.

Exercise-specific psychological environment

A number of psychological instruments exist that may quantify the exercise environment. Examples of positive psychological environments include "autonomy-supportive environments" in which, according to Self-Determination Theory, participants feel that their psychological needs for autonomy (feeling in charge of their exercise), competence (feeling effective when accomplishing tasks), and relatedness (feeling a sense of belonging to the exercise group) are fulfilled, and a "mastery-oriented environment" where participants feel that personal improvement and their efforts to execute correctly intended exercises are emphasized and rewarded. Similarly, the aforementioned criteria for the selection of instruments appropriate to measure the exercise-specific traits and states apply to the selection of instruments to measure characteristics of psychological environments. For instance, the Exercise Climate Questionnaire (Edmunds, Ntoumanis, & Duda, 2006) is appropriate to measure how much an autonomy-supportive environment is promoted and includes items that assess the extent to which the exercise instructor provides participants with choices and options, conveys confidence in participants' ability to do well in the program, and encourages questions.

CONCLUSION

This chapter has highlighted the importance of quantitative psychological assessment in both sport and exercise contexts. Practitioners must be mindful of the purpose of the evaluation for the athlete/exercise participant and, equally, ensure that both the social and physical environment is considered when designing a psychological program. Consultants are able to choose from a range of valid and reliable tests, and in so doing must be mindful that the measures are fit-for-purpose (i.e., for the situation and the individual). To be effective, when working with clients, it is imperative that applied sport and exercise psychologists conduct a range of assessments to serve as a foundation for the development of interventions and psychological programs. Ideally, a combination of quantitative and qualitative methods will be implemented to provide a comprehensive psychological profile for athletes and/or exercise participants. Finally, it is essential that practitioners develop programs that include continuous and consistent feedback from athletes and exercise participants, as the process of improvement will inevitably be a dynamic one.

LEARNING AIDS

1 Discuss the rationale and usefulness of measuring psychological characteristics at trait, state, or team level in the sport context.

Assessments are conducted to obtain useful information for the development of psychological preparation programs for individual and team sports. Thorough evaluations of psychological characteristics allow sport psychologists to gather information about athletes' strengths and weaknesses, and this can be done by way of examining how the athlete behaves "typically" (trait) or in particular situations (state), as well as how s/he may operate independently and/or within a team or group setting.

2 Explain why it is important to assess psychomotor skills in a sport context.

Evaluation of psychomotor skills can provide important information about an athlete's performance, improvement, and learning process. The extent to which assessment of psychomotor characteristics can be useful relies on a combination of competition demands and the specific elements that characterize each sport. In conjunction with sport psychological assessment, the information obtained about athletes' psychomotor skills can be helpful for athletes, coaches, and sport psychologists for development of physical and mental training programs.

3 Discuss the rationale for measuring psychological characteristics both at trait and state level in the context of exercise.

The rationale for measuring psychological characteristics both at a trait and a state level in exercise is based on the bottom-up hypothesis, which indicates that repeated exposure of an exercise participant to a specific exercise program and a particular instructional style (assessment in a single exercise class; i.e., state assessment), may lead to more generalized changes (assessment in exercise in general; i.e., trait assessment) in a particular psychological characteristic. Thus, both types of assessment would be important for evaluating the extent to which repeated exposure to a particular instructional style might influence changes at a more general level.

4 Explain why it is important to measure the psychological environment in an exercise class from a practical standpoint.

According to theory, enhancement of specific psychological environments (e.g., an autonomy-supportive environment) leads to greater levels of exercise enjoyment and increased adherence to exercise. Therefore, quantifying the extent to which a psychological environment is created, as perceived by the exercise participant, may function as an index of the quality of the exercise program offered by the exercise instructor.

REVIEW QUESTIONS

1   Why are psychological measurements important to an applied sport and exercise psychologist's work?

2   What is the difference between general trait, and sport trait and state measurements in the sport context?

3   Why might an applied sport and exercise psychologist measure team cohesion in team sports?

4   Describe the criteria used to reach a decision with regard to the selected measures for a psychological assessment in the context of exercise.

5   What is the benefit for the sport and exercise psychologist practitioner of selecting appropriate measures of psychological traits, states, and the perceived psychological environment in exercise?

EXERCISES

1   Create your own psychological assessment bulletin for an athlete by selecting parameters you believe will assist you in obtaining a complete picture of his/her profile. Justify your decisions by giving reasons and then apply them within a case study.

2   Evaluate the frequency with which the exercise instructor enacts specific autonomy-supportive behaviors during exercise in general as perceived by the participants. Assess the extent to which the participants' psychological needs for autonomy, competence, and relatedness are satisfied in exercise in general, both at the beginning of an exercise period and one month afterwards, in the context of a group exercise setting. Examine the link between levels of perceived autonomy support by the exercise instructor and the changes in psychological need satisfaction scores.

ADDITIONAL READING

Beckmann, J. & Kellmann, M. (2003). Procedures and principles of sport psychological assessment. *The Sport Psychologist, 17*(3), 338–350.

Gill, L.D. (2000). *Psychological dynamics of sport and exercise*. Champaign, IL: Human Kinetics.

Nideffer, R.M. & Sagal, M.S. (2001). *Assessment in sport psychology*. Morgantown, WV: Fitness Information Technology.

REFERENCES

Buss, H.A. & Perry, M. (1992). The aggression questionnaire. *Journal of Personality and Social Psychology, 63*(3), 452–459.

Carron, A.V., Colman, M., Wheeler, J. & Stevens, D. (2002). Cohesion and performance in sport: A meta-analysis. *Journal of Sport and Exercise Psychology, 24*, 168–188.

Chelladurai, P. & Saleh, S.D. (1980). Dimensions of leader behaviors in sports: Development of a leadership scale. *Journal of Sport Psychology, 2*, 34–45.

Crowne, D.P. & Marlowe, D. (1960). A new scale of social desirability independent of psychopathology. *Journal of Consulting Psychology, 24*, 349–354.

Csikszentmihalyi, M. (1990). *Flow: The psychology of optimal experience.* New York: Harper & Row.

Dishman, R.K. & Chambliss, H.O. (2010). Exercise psychology. In J.M. Williams (Ed.), *Applied sport psychology: Personal growth to peak performance* (pp.563–595). Boston, MA: McGraw-Hill.

Duda, J. (1998). *Advances in sport and exercise psychology measurement.* Morgantown, WV: Fitness Information Technology, Inc.

Duda, J. & Nicholls, J.G. (1992). Dimensions of achievement motivation in schoolwork and sport. *Journal of Educational Psychology, 84,* 290–299.

Edmunds, J., Ntoumanis, N. & Duda, J.L. (2006). A test of self-determination theory in the exercise domain. *Journal of Applied Social Psychology, 36,* 2240–2265.

Fox, K.R. & Corbin, C.B. (1989). The Physical Self-Perception Profile: Development and preliminary validation. *Journal of Sport and Exercise Psychology, 11,* 408–430.

Giacobbi, P. & Weinberg, R. (2000). An examination of coping in sport: Individual trait anxiety differences and situational consistency. *Sport Psychologist, 14,* 42–62.

Gill, D. (2000). *Psychological dynamics of sport and exercise* (pp.314–327). New York: Macmillan.

Glenn, S.D. & Horn, T.S. (1993). Psychological and personal predictors of leadership behavior in female soccer athletes. *Journal of Applied Sport Psychology, 5,* 17–34.

Guay, F., Vallerand, R.J. & Blanchard, C. (2000). On the assessment of state intrinsic and extrinsic motivation: The Situational Motivation Scale (SIMS). *Motivation and Emotion, 24,* 175–213.

Hackfort, D., Kilgallen, C. & Hao, L. (2009). The Action Theory-Based Mental Test and Training System (MTTS). In E. Tsung-Min Hung, R. Lidor & D. Hackfort (Eds.), *Psychology of sport excellence* (pp.9–14). Morgantown, WV: Fitness Information Technology.

Hart, E.A., Leary, M.R. & Rejeski, W.J. (1989). The measurement of social physique anxiety. *Journal of Sport and Exercise Psychology, 11,* 94–104.

Jackson, S.A. & Eklund, R.C. (2002). Assessing flow in physical activity: The Flow State Scale-2 and Dispositional Flow Scale-2. *Journal of Sport and Exercise Psychology, 24,* 133–150.

Jackson, S.A. & Marsh, H.W. (1996). Development and validation of a scale to measure optimal experience: The Flow State Scale. *Journal of Sport and Exercise Psychology, 18,* 17–35.

Jackson, S.A., Thomas, P.R., Marsh, H.W. & Smethurst, C.J. (2001). Relationships between flow, self-concept, psychological skills, and performance. *Journal of Applied Sport Psychology, 13(1),* 129–153.

Jones, G. & Swain, A. (1992). Intensity and direction as dimensions of competitive state anxiety and relationships with competitiveness. *Perceptual and Motor Skills, 74,* 467–472.

Lazarus, R.S. (2000). How emotions influence performance in competitive sports. *The Sport Psychologist, 14,* 229–252.

Lonsdale, C., Hodge, K. & Rose, E.A. (2008). The Behavioral Regulation in Sport Questionnaire: Instrument development and initial validity evidence. *Journal of Sport and Exercise Psychology, 30,* 323–355.

Markland, D. & Tobin, V. (2004). A modification to the Behavioral Regulation in Exercise Questionnaire to include an assessment of amotivation. *Journal of Sport and Exercise Psychology, 26,* 191–196.

Martens, R. (1977). *Sport Competition Anxiety Test.* Champaign, IL: Human Kinetics.

Martens, R., Burton, D., Vealey, R.S., Bump, L.A. & Smith, D. (1990). Development and validation of the Competitive State Anxiety Inventory-2. In R. Martens, R.S. Vealey & D. Burton (Eds.), *Competitive anxiety in sport* (pp.117–190). Champaign, IL: Human Kinetics.

Martin, S., Jackson, A., Richardson, P. & Weiller, K. (1999). Coaching preferences of adolescent youths and their parents. *Journal of Applied Sport Psychology, 11,* 247–262.

Martin Ginis, K.A., Murru, E., Conlin, C. & Strong, H.A. (2011). Construct validation of a state version of the social physique anxiety scale among young women. *Body Image, 8,* 52–57.

Moustaka, F.C., Vlachopoulos, S.P., Kabitsis, C. & Theodorakis, Y. (2012). Effects of an autonomy-supportive exercise instructing style on exercise motivation, psychological well-being and exercise attendance in middle age women. *Journal of Physical Activity and Health, 9,* 138–150.

Ostrow, A.C. (Ed.). (2002). *Directory of psychological tests in the sport and exercise sciences.* Morgantown, WV: Fitness Information Technology, Inc.

Prieler, J. (2011). *Manual sensomotor coordination*. Austria: Schuhfried GmbH.

Raven, J.C., Court, J.H. & Raven, J. (1992). *Standard progressive matrices*. Oxford: Oxford Psychologists Press.

Reulecke, W. (1991). Konzentration als trivalente Performanzvaiable – theoretische Praemissen, Rastermodell und empirisches Umsetzungsbeispiel [Concentration as trivalent performance variable – theoretical premises, raster model and empirical examples for realization]. In J. Janssen, E. Hahn, H. Strang & M. Wegner (Eds.), *Konzentration und Leistung* (pp.63–73). Goettingen: Hogrefe.

Rosenberg, M. (1965). *Society and the adolescent self-image*. Princeton: Princeton University Press.

Ryan, R.M. & Deci, E.L. (2007). Active human nature: Self-determination theory and the promotion and maintenance of sport, exercise, and health. In M.S. Hagger & N.L.D. Chatzisarantis (Eds.), *Intrinsic motivation and self-determination in exercise and sport* (pp.1–19). Champaign, IL: Human Kinetics.

Scheier, I.H. & Cattell, R.B. (1960). *Handbook and test kit for the IPAT 8-parallel-form anxiety battery: Repeated measurement of changes in anxiety level over time in adults and young adults*. Institute for Personality and Ability Testing.

Schurr, K.T., Ashley, M.A. & Joy, K.L. (1977). A multivariate analysis of male athlete characteristics: Sport type and success. *Multivariate Experimental Clinical Research, 3,* 53–68.

Shacham, S. (1983). A shortened version of the Profile of Mood States. *Journal of Personality Assessment, 47,* 305–306.

Smith, R.E., Schultz, R.W., Smoll, F.L. & Ptacek, J.T. (1995). Development and validation of multidimensional measure of sport-specific psychological skills: The Athletic Coping Skills Inventory-28. *Journal of Sport and Exercise Psychology, 17,* 379–398.

Smith, R.E., Smoll, F.L. & Schutz, R.W. (1990). Measurement and correlates of sport-specific cognitive and somatic trait anxiety: The Sport Anxiety Scale. *Anxiety Research, 2,* 263–280.

Spielberger, C.D. (1966). Theory and research on anxiety. In C.D. Spielberger (Ed.), *Anxiety and behaviour* (pp.3–22). New York: Academic Press.

Spielberger, C.D., Gorsuch, R.L., Lushene, R.E., Vagg, P.R. & Jacobs, G.A. (1983). *Manual for the State-Trait Anxiety Inventory – Form Y*. Palo Alto, CA: Consulting Psychologists Press.

Taylor, J.A. (1953). A personality scale of manifest anxiety. *Journal of Abnormal Social Psychology, 48,* 285–290.

Tenenbaum, G., Eklund, R.C. & Kamata, A. (2012). *Measurement in sport and exercise psychology*. Champaign, IL: Human Kinetics.

Vallerand, R.J. (2007). A hierarchical model of intrinsic and extrinsic motivation for sport and physical activity. In M.S. Hagger & N.L.D. Chatzisarantis (Eds.), *Intrinsic motivation and self-determination in exercise and sport* (pp.255–279). Champaign, IL: Human Kinetics.

Vallerand, R.J. (1983). Attention and decision-making: A test of the predictive validity of the Test of Attentional and Interpersonal Style in a sport setting. *Journal of Sport Psychology, 5,* 449–459.

Vealey, R. (1986). Conceptualization of sport-confidence and competitive orientation: Preliminary investigation and instrument development. *Journal of Sport Psychology, 8,* 221–246.

Weinberg, R.S. & Gould, D. (2006). *Foundations of sport and exercise psychology*. Champaign, IL: Human Kinetics.

Widmeyer, W.N. (1984). Aggression-performance relationships in sport. In J.M. Silva & R.S. Weinberg (Eds.), *Psychological foundations of sport* (pp.274–286). Champaign, IL: Human Kinetics.

Widmeyer, W.N., Brawley, L.R. & Carron, A.V. (1985). *The measurement of cohesion in sport teams: The group environment questionnaire*. London, UK: Sports Dynamics.

Zinsser, N., Bunker, L. & Williams, J.M. (2010). Cognitive techniques for building confidence and enhancing performance. In J.M. Williams (Ed.), *Applied sport psychology: Personal growth to peak performance* (pp.305–335). Boston, MA: McGraw-Hill.

Chapter 59

Issues in the diagnosis of psychopathological disorders

HENRY (HAP) DAVIS IV, JOHN P. SULLIVAN, CHRIS CARR, DAVID B. COPPEL, ADAM SHUNK,
JENNIFER CARTER, SCOTT GOLDMAN, THOMAS HAMMOND AND PATRICK H.F. BAILLIE

SUMMARY

With so many individuals engaged in sports competition, and with an estimated 20% of the general population likely to personally experience a mental illness in their lifetime (Public Health Agency of Canada, Canada, 2006), it should not be surprising that some elite athletes may experience psychopathological disorders. The pressures of the sport environment, for some, may become too great, and result in decompensation and distress.

In this chapter, we discuss some of the more likely mental health diagnoses that may arise in the context of sport performance. While almost any coach, trainer, or athlete will have a range of strategies for managing pre-performance anxiety or post-loss disappointment, the skilled sport psychologist must be able to distinguish between what falls within this "normal" range and what may represent a mental health concern, crossing over into the realm of significant pathology. The dividing line rests in being able to apply formal diagnostic criteria, thereby avoiding either downplaying major problems (e.g., normalizing eating disorders as being "part of the sport") or exaggerating situational stressors (e.g., an athlete's anxiety about "making the team").

INTRODUCTION

The chapter addresses depressive, anxiety, sleep, impulse control, substance-related, eating, attention-deficit/hyperactivity, post-concussion syndrome, and personality disorders and provides a broad overview of legal issues in psychological diagnosis.

OBJECTIVES

After reading this chapter, you should be able to:

1   Identify the main disorders found among student and elite athletes.
2   Explain the key issues associated with specified disorders.
3   Understand the incidence and possible risk of athletes developing a psychological problem.
4   Appreciate that working on performance issues with athletes may also involve working on an identified disorder.

DEPRESSIVE DISORDERS

The majority of athletes will experience some form of negative affect or low mood following an unfavorable event in competitive sport or in daily life. However, this is not depression. Major Depressive Disorder (MDD), as defined with the Diagnostic and Statistical Manual of Mental Disorders (DSM-5), features a profound shift in mood and motivation that is more likely to occur accompanying a major setback (American Psychiatric Association, 2013; Craighead, Cheets, Brosse, & Ilardi, 2007; Davis et al., 2008).

While the prevalence of MDD among athletes varies in the literature, studies have shown that the risk of depression for athletes is no greater than those facing the general population, at approximately 21% (Yang et al., 2007). In our own research, the risk for high performance athletes who compete internationally may be twice as high as that found among age-matched peers at approximately 50% (Baillie, Davis IV, & Ogilvie, 2014; Hammond, Gialloretto, Kubas, & Davis, 2013). Female athletes appear to be at greater risk for developing depression consistently across studies.

A variety of clinician-administered and self-rated scales can be used to identify depressive symptoms and assess their severity (Soleimani, Lapidus, & Iosifescu, 2011). However – as it is critical to the objective and accurate diagnosis of MDD – a clinician will need to evaluate the athlete's symptoms through a conversational interview which is used to establish the presence of a depressive experi-ence for at least a two-week duration, featuring symptoms that include low mood, loss of desire and interests and, in addition, these are accompanied by clinically significant changes in appetite, sleep, agitation or motor slowing, fatigue or low energy, negative self-reference or guilt, concentration deficit, and suicidal risk or suicidal thinking (see DSM-5).

Diagnostic and case conceptualization not only rely on the interpretation of symptoms, medical conditions, and comorbidities, but also an understanding of issues specific to the context of sport that may contribute to the development of a mood disorder. A comprehensive evaluation will also involve gaining a history of challenges to mood (Beedie, Terry, & Lane, 2000), appraisals of negative cognitions and emotion regulation abilities in response to stress (Carter & Garber, 2011), self-esteem (Orth, Robins, & Roberts, 2008), general self-regulation history (Davis, Botterill, & MacNeill, 2002), training recovery practices (Kellmann, 2010), neurobiological responses to adversity (Panksepp, 2004), and family history of mood disorder (Joormann, Cooney, Henry, & Gotlib, 2012).

As part of the athlete's case formulation, the clinical sport psychologist may be required to recommend treatment and evaluate its effects. Among psychologically-based treatments, cognitive behavioral therapy is one approach that has received considerable empirical support and demonstrated efficacy (Craighead et al., 2007). Following the intervention, the clinical sport psychologist must evaluate if the athlete has responded to the treatment protocol and, if not, discuss medical care. Antidepressants – specifically, Selective Serotonin Reuptake Inhibitors (SSRIs) – have become first-line treatments for most individuals with depression (Nemeroff & Schatzberg, 2007). SSRIs have been shown to be effective in treating symptoms of depression with overall effects estimated at 50% (Li, Kuk, & Rush, 2012) with the onset of efficacy requiring four to six weeks (Soleimani, Lapidus, & Iosifescu, 2011). Side effects commonly associated with SSRIs include nausea, gastrointestinal disturbance, insomnia, nervousness, and sexual dysfunction (Nemeroff & Schatzberg, 2007). With an established athlete–sport psychologist relationship, the psychologist is optimally positioned to evaluate this cluster of possible adverse side effects.

ANXIETY DISORDERS

Whether discussing "performance" anxiety or anxiety disorder (e.g., phobia or generalized anxiety), the construct of this emotion remains relatively similar. Specifically, anxiety has a unique set of properties that differentiates it from other emotions. For athletes and non-athletes, the cognitions that induce anxiety tend to be about the future. Second, the future element that the individual is anxious about is always a perceived threat or danger. It should be noted two types of threats exist: 1) threat to safety (i.e., "that guy is going to injure me"); and 2) threat to ego integrity (i.e., "if I lose, then I am a loser"). Third, anxiety has cognitive *and* physiological elements. Physiological symptoms may include but are not limited to muscle tension, headaches, gastrointestinal issues, increased heart rate, and difficulty breathing.

Key to diagnosing anxiety in athletes is understanding that fear and avoidance are two different, but not independent, learning processes (Bugelski, 1938; Konorski, 1950). In Mowrer's well-established *Two-Factor Theory*, fear was a product of sign learning (Mowrer, 1956, 1960a, 1960b). Specifically, a signal was paired to a noxious event, such as a shock, which lead to the organism eventually experiencing fear to the signal. In contrast, avoidance was a product of solution learning, trial and error learning, or response substitution. The organism was rewarded, relieved, reinforced by engaging in a behavior that effectively reduced the intensity of the fear. Mowrer (1956) suggested, "Hence we are led to speak of *two types* of 'fear conditioning': conditioned *arousal* of fear and conditioned *relaxation*, or relief, thereof" (p. 117). To the extent that avoidance is successful, fear is stronger because the bond between the signal and the noxious event is never extinguished, even if they are no longer paired (Levis & Brewer, 2001). If an elicited fear for an athlete is never extinguished, then avoidance will continue to be reinforced because it provides relief. Thus, an elicited fear impacts avoidance and avoidance impacts an elicited fear.

Because the demands on athletes are somewhat unique, fear and avoidance problems may require unique assessment. Thus, the functioning of an athlete with an anxiety problem may present differently to that of a non-athlete. For example, an athlete may be functioning well below their personal norm, but may not meet the DSM-5 criteria for an anxiety disorder. Specific examples are found in the differences between post-traumatic stress disorder (PTSD) and the experience of a traumatic championship loss. For example, post-traumatic stress disorder may occur after a bobsleigh accident, which critically injures one teammate and leaves two others in hospital. The surviving, non-injured athlete may experience the noxious event (the crash) with fear of ever competing again with sufficient speed to win or with avoidance of their teammates who have been hospitalized. Personal failure deemed to account for the loss of a major championship, however difficult, may not meet the DSM-5 criteria for anxiety disorder. Sport psychologists are called on to distinguish this important difference noting the degree and full scope of symptom expression.

Psychological intervention to reduce the impact of the noxious stimulus – to teach effective coping – flows from intelligent diagnosis. Because many treatments for anxiety disorders are empirically validated, one course of action is to adapt these treatments to the athlete. Goldman (2003) applied Ellis's theory within the context of the athletic experience. Another course of action may be to alter treatments specific to the athletic mind. An example of augmenting validated treatment for athletes would be Goldman's (2004) compe-

tence induction technique, which, in turn, is based on Suinn's (1990) anxiety management training.

Even if the anxiety rises to the threshold of *disorder* it may still be grounded in the sport experience and treated within the framework of sport performance. Anxiolytic treatments to consider for athletes include: Wolpe's (1981) reciprocal inhibition; Jacobson's (1938) progressive muscle relaxation; Beck's (1976) cognitive behavior therapy; Ellis's rational emotive behavior therapy (Ellis & Ellis, 2011; Ellis & Harper, 1961); Hayes's acceptance and commitment therapy (Hayes & Smith, 2005); and Linehan's (1995) dialectical behavior therapy. Further, many of these treatments can be enhanced with biofeedback technology.

SLEEP DISORDERS

Sleep insufficiency has measurable negative effects on the central nervous system (CNS; e.g., on reaction time, recovery, and functioning). In sport, inadequate sleep can lead to poor performance during practice and on game days, and can also contribute to increased injury risk. Thus, the sport psychologist will evaluate sleep quality, quantity, and consistency as significant influences on player health and performance.

Disorders of sleep are often overlooked even though this class of maladjustment is both classified within both the ICD-10 (International Classification of Mental and Behavioral Disorders) and the DSM-5 (Stores, 2007; World Health Organization, 1992). The sport psychologist should be familiar with both diagnostic methods as well as with the work of the European Sleep Research Society (ESRS), founded in 1971, and the American Academy of Sleep Medicine (originally the American Sleep Disorders Association).

Clinical issues of sleep are putatively more prevalent among athletes due to travel, changing sleep environments, time zone changes, and disruption in schedules. Derman and colleagues identified sleep difficulties as part

of a cycle of under-recovery and *chronic fatigue* in athletes (Derman et al., 1997). The assessing sport psychologist will track these factors together with others such as unpredictable work flow, changing scope of responsibility, irregular work/rest cycle/hours, reduced social connections, and large amount of travel, as these may become a storm of increased stressors that can impact the overall health and performance of athletes.

Rest impacts the CNS with general musculoskeletal effects (e.g., on sharpness, reaction times, skill execution). The sport psychologist, therefore, notes players who show increased fatigue (Mah, Mah, Kezirian, & Dement, 2011) and knows that reduced sleep is not only a risk factor for injury and concussion but for chronic diseases states (i.e., hypertension, diabetes, obesity) and mood disorders and anxiety (Centers for Disease Control and Prevention (CDC), 2011; Chapman, McKnight-Eily, Perry, & Anda, 2008).

Difficulty falling and staying asleep, daytime sleepiness, movement during sleep which reduces its quantity, and breathing issues during sleep are all problems that are attended to by the assessing psychologist, who will also be aware that there are currently 78 recognized sleep disorders described by the ICD-10 and DSM-5. These may be grouped into four main categories: 1) problems falling and staying asleep (insomnia); 2) problems staying awake (excessive daytime sleepiness); 3) problems sticking to a regular sleep schedule (sleep rhythm problem); and 4) unusual behaviors during sleep (sleep-disruptive behaviors). The first three categories are known as dyssomnias (e.g., insomnia, narcolepsy, sleep apnea, and restless leg syndrome) and these may be further divided into intrinsic and extrinsic sleep disorders, in conjunction with informa-

tion provided by the psychologist. The clinician notes environmental and behavioral factors relevant to dyssomnias such as inadequate sleep hygiene, altitude insomnia, adjustment sleep disorder, and alcohol-dependent sleep disorder.

The fourth category, unusual behaviors during sleep, relates especially to parasomnias for which the psychologist assesses partial arousal or disorders that may interfere with sleep stage transitions, such as sleepwalking, night terrors, sleep talking, nightmares, sleep paralysis, and REM sleep behavior disorder (see material provided by the Institute of Medicine).

IMPULSE CONTROL DISORDERS

Sport psychologists frequently evaluate inappropriate, explosive anger, late-night online gambling, and self-mutilation. These three concerns are examples of impulse control disorders (ICDs) and are classified by the inability to manage/resist impulses and related behaviors that may be maladaptive or cause personal distress to self or others. They are characterized by symptoms such as feeling tension, strong emotions, and/or anxiety. This "tension" is relieved with the performance of an impulsive behavior or series of behaviors that temporarily relieve the unwanted tension, but with potential long-term consequences (see ICD-10 and DSM-5).

The psychologist will not confuse ICDs with anxiety/obsessive compulsive disorders (OCD) or substance use-related disorders, which share the neurological underpinnings and behavioral components of ICDs. In particular, the orbital cortex, basal ganglia, and thalamus, and the neurotransmitters dopamine and serotonin are thought to be involved in this broad range of disorders (Grant, Brewer, & Potenza, 2006; Temcheff, Derevensky, & Paskus, 2011). Still, there are key clinical and biological differences (Potenza, Koran, & Pallanti, 2009). All ICDs involve the loss or lack of control in certain situations, especially under times of stress or tension. The aberrant

behavior is not premeditated and is outside of the individual's control. The impulsive behavior often has significant legal, monetary, or societal consequences. For example, the legal ramifications of kleptomania are often criminal shoplifting charges.

The key issue for the sport psychologist is to be aware that the problem exists and to encourage open discussion among athletes. Pathological gambling has received much recent attention regarding research and prevention, and it is relevant to sport psychology (Holden, 2010). The NCAA gambling survey (2008) found that approximately 30% of male and 7% of female student-athletes acknowledged gambling on sporting events (Huang, Jacobs, Derevensky, Gupta, & Paskus, 2007). Pathological gambling is often overlooked as gambling is imbedded in many sporting cultures and environments, but its impact on overall health is significant. Huang et al. (2007) found direct associations between gambling and multiple risk behaviors (i.e., increased prevalence of substance use, disordered eating, and high risk sexual behavior) that are similar to those with substance use-related disorders. Untreated and undiagnosed ICDs often lead to exacerbation of comorbid emotional disorders including anxiety, mood, and sleep disorders. Although most mental health issues are diffusely spread throughout the population, ICDs seem to be concentrated/clustered with other mental health disorders (Kessler et al., 2005; Kessler, Chiu, Demler, Merikangas, & Walters, 2005).

Secondary to the primary diagnosis is the assessment of comorbid clinical issues such as depression and anxiety. The sport psychologist will evaluate both, knowing that there is a range of comorbidity in pathological gambling; for example, some occur with suicidal implications, and each with life status and performance implications for athletes (Lorains, Cowlishaw, & Thomas, 2011). For the athlete with intermittent explosive rage, the sport psychologist will evaluate other possibilities such as comorbid post-traumatic stress disorder or substance abuse.

SUBSTANCE-RELATED DISORDERS

The clinical sport psychologist may be confronted with an athlete who presents with behavioral, cognitive, and affective symptoms associated with a Substance-Related Disorder. Unique to this disorder is the sociological concept of positive and negative deviance related to behavioral patterns of use (Hughes & Coakley, 2001). Athletes tend to use substances for two primary purposes: 1) recreational use (mostly drugs of abuse such as alcohol, marijuana, opiates); and 2) performance enhancement (e.g., anabolic steroids, HGH). It is important that the sport psychologist understands and explores the athlete's motivation for use of substances, and obtains a clear and accurate history (from the athlete and other resources such as the coach, family, and medical staff) related to their substance use patterns, to determine if the use is maladaptive or unhealthy – leading to clinically significant impairment in general functioning or resulting in a substance-specific syndrome or constituting a contravention of codes for fairness in sport.

Although there is limited data concerning the use of substances amongst elite professional/Olympic athletes, the collegiate student-athlete population has been well-examined. In their most recent survey, the National Collegiate Athletics Association (NCAA) found that over 83% of the survey participants (NCAA Division I-II-III student-athletes) reported use of alcohol over the past year, which increased by 5% from 2005 to 2009. In addition, findings indicated that survey participants reported that over 22% used marijuana within the past 12 months (up 1.4% from 2005 to 2009); 3.3% of participants reported use of narcotics; and 6.4% of participants reported the non-prescribed use of Adderall or Ritalin, with 4.3% reporting use with a prescription (Bracken, 2012). This data included over 20,000 participants with a breadth of age and diversity demographics and represents a large population of collegiate student-athletes from 18–22 years.

One role for the assessing psychologist will be to determine if the athlete demonstrates clinical symptomology of a substance-related abuse or dependence diagnosis (see DSM-5), whether treatment is required and, if so, what approach will be most effective. Often, the athlete's use of substances has already negatively impacted his/her family, social group, academics, and relationships before negatively impacting their athletic performance. Interventions can range from outpatient counseling to intensive outpatient therapy (2–3 days/week for 3–5 hours each day) to inpatient treatment (typically 28–42 days for most inpatient care). Traditional cognitive-behavioral therapies have been shown to be effective in the outpatient care of substance-related disorders, and motivational interviewing (Miller & Rollnick, 2013) has most recently been encouraged as a therapeutic model of intervention for athletes with abuse issues. Regardless, a competent clinical sport psychologist will assess how best to utilize professional resources in the substance abuse treatment domain.

EATING DISORDERS

In the area of eating disorders – beyond DSM-5 and the ICD-10 criteria – a key part of the diagnosis is evaluating an athlete's denial of problems and the athlete's failure to discern when behaviors are unhealthy. Denial may be shadowed by the following elements: 1) problems inherent within the calculation of body mass index (BMI); 2) eating disorder symptoms masquerading as "dedication"; 3) difficulty discriminating between an extreme behavior and an eating disorder symptom; and 4) the high prevalence of eating disorder symptoms fostering misperceptions about what should be "normal".

The current diagnosis for anorexia nervosa includes an extremely low weight – below a BMI of 17.5. The index is a standard measure using height and weight (World Health Organization, 1992). It does not account for increased muscle mass in athletes that permits grossly undernourished athletes to meet each criterion for anorexia nervosa, except the BMI criterion. The sport psychologist must know that application of the standard criteria is a flawed approach, and thus make allowances for any known increases in muscle weight. If possible, anthropometric data should be obtained to guide in this analysis.

Most athletes are driven by at least some level of perfectionism. Elite athletes train until they get it just right. So it is important to ask: "Do they abstain from 'unhealthy' food? Do they comply exactly with their coach's instructions?" High-achieving athletes share symptoms with persons in the general population – their behavior, on the other hand, may be unique to sport. When an athlete runs extra miles between practices, her coach praises her dedication. What the coach doesn't know is that for many athletes with eating disorders the extra running is an equivalent to purging. Likewise, athletes strive to eat "healthy" as a means to improve performance. The sport psychologist notes, however, whenever careful, "healthy" eating and extra workouts are combined with other risk factors, such as eliminating certain foods altogether. Saying, "I have learned to watch that my diet does not load up on the glycemic index" may reflect an insidious pattern of denial of nutritional needs under the mask of dedication.

Athletics is a culture of extremes. How does one define exercise abuse in an individual who trains for his sport 4–5 hours a day? If he's using exercise to maintain a negative energy balance and is exhibiting other signs of compulsion and lack of control, then he indeed may be abusing exercise. And what if the athlete has to eat 5,000 calories to maintain his weight – is that binge-eating?

When diagnosing eating disorders in athletes, the clinical sport psychologist remembers the criteria for binge eating disorder – the consumption of a significantly large amount of food *and* the feeling of being out of control. If the athlete's consumption is roughly the same as his/her teammates and he/she doesn't feel out of control in this consumption, then very likely the diagnosis is not binge eating.

Finally, eating disorder symptoms (occasional food restriction, binge-eating, purging through exercise abuse, diet pills, self-induced vomiting) plague high performance sport, and particularly affect those athletes in "lean" sports. Quite a few suffer eating disorder symptoms that are subclinical but problematic; these athletes may go undiagnosed because their circumstance and behavior is common among their peers and because the diagnostic criteria for eating disorders are not met (Greenleaf, Petrie, Carter, & Reel, 2009). Revised criteria, potentially in DSM-5, which have elevated new clusters of disordered eating to clinical significance, do not fully ameliorate this diagnostic issue. For instance, the diagnosis of Avoidant/Restrictive Food Intake Disorder now appears in the DSM-5 but some student athletes who meet several criteria (i.e., in showing a significant weight loss and relying on nutritional supplements as their preference to available team meals) may be subclinical for this disorder if the disorder is significantly overshadowed by and better explained by a depressive or anxiety disorder. Therapy must still address the eating. And, therapy recommendations, coaching, medical, and sport science consultations, travel considerations, workout planning, and competition strategies must each factor in this composite of four highlighted issues. Without doing so, the athlete's health is placed at risk, and health issues are of far greater priority to the sport psychologist than performance will ever be.

ATTENTION-DEFICIT/HYPERACTIVITY DISORDER

Attention-Deficit/Hyperactivity Disorder (ADHD) – characterized by inattention, impulsivity, and hyperactivity – is one of the most common psychological disorders among children and adolescents. Athletes are no exception. In this section, four key diagnostic issues underlying the development of rational clinical intervention are highlighted.

An estimated 2–5% of school-aged children are diagnosed with ADHD, with boys experiencing the disorder more than girls (see DSM-5). The prevalence rate of ADHD is not well documented in athletes, but some theorists have proposed that it may be more prevalent in athletes due to a tendency for individuals with ADHD to be drawn to physical activity (Burton, 2000). In one study by Heil and colleagues (Heil, 2000; Heil, Hartman, Robinson, & Teegarden, 2002), a prevalence rate of 7.3% was identified in a population of athletes and this rate varied between sports.

The assessing sport psychologist notes how ADHD – composed of two major symptom clusters: inattention and hyperactivity (disinhibition) – manifests and affects sport performance as well as social and academic functioning. Inattention is characterized by persistent difficulty in directing and sustaining attention toward a task, while disinhibition is often manifested by an inability to suppress impulsive behaviors or employ thinking abilities. Some of the most successful athletes have been diagnosed with ADHD including Olympic gold medal winner Michael Phelps and Olympic 100-meter champion Justin Gatlin, who made it publicly known they have ADHD.

Individuals with ADHD also experience a variety of other difficulties such as developmental, cognitive, behavioral, emotional, academic, and even medical difficulties and comorbidities (Barkley & Murphy, 2006). Individuals with ADHD are also at an increased risk for: substance abuse, academic underachievement, impaired peer relationships, dangerous driving, and delinquent and impulsive risky behaviors.

A key aspect of the diagnosis of ADHD is that the clinical sport psychologist may be engaged to provide documentation of ADHD in support of an application for medical treatment. Amphetamine-derived psychostimulant medications, such as Adderall and Ritalin, are effective and proven treatments for ADHD (Jensen et al., 2001). However, these medications are not well understood in the context of athletics and they appear to pose some potential benefits and risks toward performance and health of an athlete. Stimulant medications may impair thermoregulation, mask symptoms of fatigue and elevate heart rate that could pose cardiac and general health risks. There are also concerns with a growing trend of nonmedical misuse of stimulants being abused as a party drug or taken without a prescription for its academic effects.

Stimulants may also result in performance-enhancing effects through both physiological functions (decreased time to exhaustion, increased acceleration, prolonged peak performance, and improved balance), as well as improved cognitive abilities (improved attention to task, positive affect, aggression, and decreased pain sensation). A common side effect of stimulants is appetite suppression, which could have either a positive or negative impact based on the sporting event.

As a result, the undocumented use of stimulants is banned by most governing bodies including the International Olympic Committee (IOC) and the NCAA. The NCAA and the IOC, through the World Anti-Doping Agency, each have therapeutic use exemption policies for determining when ADHD treatment is necessary. Exemptions may be obtained with very thorough medical and psychological evaluation, inclusive of neuropsychological testing. A diagnosis *must* be granted with written approval by the regulatory body before the medication use is considered sanctioned. The clinician(s) who makes the diagnosis must always remember to verify that written approval has been obtained. Dialogue and advocacy for the diagnostic position may be required before approval is granted.

Unfortunately, the criteria by which an athlete with ADHD may obtain a therapeutic use exemption (TUE) for his or her use of prescribed stimulants are neither readily available to clinicians nor understood. Drug testing policies amongst professional sports are even more poorly defined; moreover, they lack consensus and they do not provide clear guidelines for the responsible or therapeutic use of stimulants.

Given the potential risks and drug testing sanctions, it is important for both athletes with ADHD and the psychologists providing care to them to be knowledgeable about these factors. In light of the above, psychosocial treatment efforts to deal with the behavioral, emotional, and cognitive issues are a critical piece of comprehensive treatment (Barkley & Murphy, 2006).

POST-CONCUSSION SYNDROME/DISORDER

Concussion, or mild traumatic brain injury (mTBI), is a complex pathophysiologic process affecting the brain, induced by traumatic (direct or indirect) biomechanical forces, which typically results in the rapid onset and spontaneous recovery of short-lived impairment of neurologic function; a range of symptoms may or may not involve a loss of consciousness (Herring et al., 2011; McCrory et al., 2009). The clinical sport psychologist must be competent to know the signs and symptoms of mTBI. In addition, the psychologist will frequently be called on to document the pattern of recovery, noting clearance of symptoms, functional recovery, and residual symptoms.

Acute signs and symptoms following a concussive event can include physically-based or somatic signs such as headache, dizziness, balance problems, nausea, visual disturbance, fatigue/drowsiness, and light or noise sensitivity; cognitive symptoms can include confusion, fogginess, slowed processing, poor concentration/poor focus, verbal expressive problems, and poor memory (anterograde or retrograde amnesia); emotional symptoms can include emotional lability, irritability, anxiety, and sadness; and sleep disturbances can also emerge (onset insomnia, discontinuity, or hypersomnia). These temporary post-concussion symptoms are thought to resolve themselves in the vast majority of cases, with a gradual, stepwise timeframe of recovery being most common.

Information regarding clinical management and research regarding concussed athletes has substantially grown over the last 10 years, and the field of "sports neuropsychology" (Lovell et al., 2003; Webbe, 2011) has emerged. Data from sports-related concussions (SRC) suggests recovery for most athletes occurs within one to three weeks (Iverson, 2011), with professional athletes recovering faster than collegiate athletes, who recover faster than high school athletes. While the vast majority of individuals recover completely from concussions, there is a group of individuals with persisting or lingering symptoms/deficits beyond the expected timeframes of recovery, who are described as having post-concussion syndrome (PCS) or post-concussion disorder. The syndrome is described, according to the ICD-10, as the occurrence of head trauma with loss of consciousness that precedes symptom onset by a maximum of four weeks, with three or more symptom categories (physical/somatic, emotional, subjective cognitive symptoms without neuropsychological evidence of marked impairment, insomnia, reduced alcohol tolerance), and "preoccupation with above symptoms and fear of brain damage with hypochondriacal concern and adoption of sick role" (World Health Organization, 1992).

In contrast to the ICD-10, the DSM-5 requires a history of head trauma that has caused significant cerebral concussion, neuropsychological evidence of difficulty in attention and memory, and three or more symptoms that last at least three months and have onset shortly after head trauma or represent substantial worsening of previous symptoms (fatigue, disordered sleep, headache, dizziness, irritability, anxiety/depression/affect lability, changes in personality, apathy, or lack of spontaneity); these symptoms result in significant impairment in daily function that reflects decline from previous level.

The subset of concussed individuals who have persistent symptoms in the physical, cognitive, or affective modalities, has been estimated to be between 10–15% of those who have had a mild head injury (Wood, 2004) and, given the significant and enduring impact of these varied symptoms, have been described as the "miserable minority" (Ruff, Camenzuli, & Mueller, 1996). A similar percentage of people with a history of mTBI still report persistent symptoms and deficits one year post-injury (Pagulayan, Hoffman, Temkin, Machamer, & Dikmen, 2008).

When symptoms persist over three months post-injury, the impact on the athlete can often be seen in their reduced general level of function. The persistence of symptoms that produce PCS is thought to be influenced by a variety of factors. In general, physiologic factors are seen as largely contributory to the origin of acute post-concussive symptoms, with psychological factors more contributory to the persistence of symptoms beyond the expected recovery timeframe. Wood's (2004) discussion of a diathesis-stress paradigm for PCS reviews the interaction between physiological and psychological factors, including motivational factors, different coping styles, the role of attribution, and iatrogenic factors. Athletes with persistent symptoms or PCS are typically faced with restriction of activities (both physical and cognitive) as part of their treatment; these restrictions or changes in activity level can be helpful in lowering symptoms caused by physical or cognitive exertion, but may also trigger significant emotional symptoms (frustration, sadness, anxiety) and social consequences (social withdrawal, social or interpersonal stress). For student-athletes who miss school as a result of concussion symptoms, the academic stress of having to make up schoolwork and, at some point, also keep up with schoolwork, is substantial and produces secondary stress symptoms. For some athletes, the loss of training and social interaction with their teammates for a prolonged timeframe can produce a loss of identity and depressed mood. These emotional consequences can be seen as secondary to the concussion, but appear to play a primary role in the maintenance of persistent symptoms, and can ultimately influence cognitive functioning.

PERSONALITY DISORDERS

Without a doubt, the world of sport has seen its share of famous characters, including Babe Ruth, Muhammad Ali, Joe Namath, Don Cherry, and Florence Griffith-Joyner, athletes whose personalities and presence outside of competition made them seem larger than life. Strong personality features, though, can negatively impact on team dynamics and on the individual's ability to focus on his or her sport performance. When personality features begin to cause distress in social, occupational or other areas of functioning, the diagnosis of a personality disorder must be considered.

Personality disorders can also be described as learned behavior strategies that, for the individual, afford coping in one environment, but cause difficulty in other environments due to a lack of flexibility or adaptability by the individual (Turner, 1984). For example, displaying a massively large ego in the sport context may intimidate other competitors, garner increased media attention, and enhance endorsement contract potential. However, in the athlete's private life, such a self-absorbed, emotionally exuberant manner may create marital disharmony, distance and conflict, and generally superficial relationships.

Individuals with narcissistic personality disorder have a pervasive pattern of grandiosity and marked needs for admiration from others (see DSM-5). They also lack empathy for others. In a team context, athletes with these features may be quite demanding (e.g., seeking more time with coaches, asking for special travel arrangements, missing curfew as a result of following their own rules) and, hence, highly disruptive. Even when formal diagnostic criteria are not satisfied, narcissistic personality traits of a team leader can negatively affect team morale and cohesion. Along with their suggestion that sports builds characters, not character, Ogilvie, Tutko, and Thomas (1971) bluntly wrote, "If you want to build character, try something else."

Individuals with histrionic personality disorder (HPD, DSM-5) have a pervasive pattern of excessive emotionality and attention-seeking behavior. When not the center of attention, athletes with HPD may engage in behaviors that sabotage both themselves and the team, as drawing focus back to themselves may be more important than any achievement in sport competition.

We cannot explore here each of the eleven personality disorders identified in DSM-5, but the prudent sport psychologist will have to be aware of the signs of a personality disorder in the athletic environment, often looking to the effects on team dynamics of one or two particularly disruptive athletes. The criterion of impaired functioning may not be a feature of the individual as much as of the team, facing the fallout from a problematic athlete. Interventions may range from behavior therapies to cognitive therapies but, given the challenges inherent in treating any personality disorder (Bateman & Fonagy, 2000), over time, the sport psychologist may be put in the position of supporting the team (and coaches) in determining their responses to the athlete with a personality disorder.

LEGAL ISSUES IN DIAGNOSIS

As noted earlier in this chapter, the diagnosis of ADHD and the likely use of pharmacological interventions must be approved by a sport regulatory body – with full documentation retained by the diagnosing professional – in order for the involved athlete to avoid prosecution for unauthorized use of restricted substances. Any psychologist practicing in the realm of sport must be aware of various other regulatory and legal issues that arise with respect to diagnosis.

The most obvious issue with respect to regulation of diagnostic capacity relates to the area of mental health that the professional is authorized to make a formal diagnosis. In some jurisdictions, that right belongs exclusively to physicians (including but not limited to psychiatrists) and no other medical service provider may make a diagnosis. In other jurisdictions, the type of training obtained by the service provider is more important than his or her job designation or profession (e.g., Varela, 2008). Put simply, to avoid potential liability for making an erroneous diagnosis or one not authorized in law, the skilled and cautious sport psychologist will ensure adequate training both in terms of formal diagnostic assessment and in terms of local regulatory conditions. For sport psychologists traveling with teams, those regulations may change several times in the course of a single road trip.

CONCLUSION

Among the diagnoses having greatest prevalence in an athlete population, this chapter has outlined what are deemed the more salient diagnostic issues. In a perfect scenario every practitioner who makes a diagnosis is competent to practice in both sport and clinical psychology. Alternatively, sport performance professionals – who are not licensed – will still appreciate the importance of knowing the DSM-5 criteria for the disorders we have reviewed and will, therefore, be in the optimal position to expeditiously assist an athlete by referral. It is not sufficient to know simply when an athlete has psychological concerns; every psychologist and sport professional, alike, must know what to do about these concerns. Positioning appropriate psychological counseling and intervention for an athlete starts with the practitioner appreciating how the sometimes unique dynamics of sport impact mental health diagnostics, understanding limits to the scope of practice, and – again, in a manner that is unique to sport – communicating effectively among an athlete's sport science and coaching support team.

LEARNING AIDS

1   Explore how the features of a DSM-5 diagnosed Major Depression in athletes may be expected to be similar to and distinct from those seen in a clinical setting.

The depressed athlete may describe a discrete performance-related onset with a period of acute fatigue following major competition. In this instance, the depression may evolve with discouragement, self-criticism, and a loss of interest that extends beyond sport to include additional features. Depression among other athletes may not have an acute onset and may stem from a performance or sport context. In this case, it will appear similar to that which is seen in a clinical population. The duration and severity of functional impairment may also differ between populations depending on factors related to performance expectations, performance outcomes, socialization pressures, coach–athlete dynamics, academic stress, injury, family of origin stress, under-recovery and other factors.

2   Discuss how attention deficits may be identified in athletes, who may be first to bring it to the attention of the sport psychologist, and what should be done if deficits are suspected.

Coaches may be best suited to notice that the athlete does not sustain focus in training and competition. As a result, the sport psychologist will work with coaches so that they know what to look for in an athlete's listening and processing of coaching information, in their focus during training and competition runs, and when undertaking precompetition mental preparation. Athletes may, however, also state explicitly that they have difficulty keeping their focus at these same key periods. When a deficit is suspected, a review of DSM-5 criteria should precede the referral to a sport neuropsychologist.

3   Discuss challenges in diagnosing problems such as substance or alcohol abuse or eating disorder among athletes when there is a high level of denial of observed behaviors underpinning the diagnosis.

The denial of symptoms may stem from concerns about competition eligibility, from ignorance, from fears of social disapproval, and from the need to preserve self-esteem. Research pertaining to each indicates that the clinician must develop an athlete's trust in order to open an honest dialogue about not only the symptoms for the full diagnosis but also what symptoms need exploration and attention in treatment. Rumor, hearsay, fan sightings, journalists, and even YouTube or Twitter postings may also contribute to the challenge in identifying what symptoms require inclusion in the diagnostic workup. Athletes may offer denials of general reports about them on a valid basis, with external reports being invalid altogether or outdated.

REVIEW QUESTIONS

1   Compare the presentation of depression and anxiety symptoms in athletes, giving attention to overlap (common comorbidity) and distinction.

2   Neuropsychological challenges of Attention Deficit Disorder may be exaggerated during recovery from mild traumatic brain injury. Discuss.

3   If a parent, coach, or athletic director asks you how you are qualified to diagnose one of the problems discussed in this chapter, how would you respond with sufficient detail to inspire confidence in your competency and sufficient generality to protect the athlete's right to privacy?

4   Discuss how you would work with external physician and psychiatric support to supplement your treatment of a psychological disorder.

5   If you are competent to diagnose a mental disorder in an athlete when would you and when would you not undertake to diagnose and treat the athlete in a team context?

6   Discuss a) how you would go about determining if an athlete's interest in online gambling has reached a level of clinical significance, and b) how you would engage the athlete into a consideration of how this may be unhealthy and how it may undermine athlete effectiveness.

7   Evaluate whether there could be a liability for the practitioner as well as for the team if the sport behavior professional is unable, due to licensure or training, to diagnose a mental condition.

EXERCISES

1   You are working with a team and you usually talk to athletes on the field after practice or in the locker room. Would you make an exception to this practice if you wanted to address a clinical issue? How would you go about explaining why you are making a shift in your usual manner? Discuss this with your classmates in a small group.

2   Interview several coaches to see how they would want you to report to them on the diagnosis of a psychological diagnosis. Note that some would want you to divulge information that would be privileged and discuss with the coaches why this is not possible.

3   You decide that your diagnosis of an eating, drinking, or anxiety problem required more information. Consider what observational questionnaires can be used to assist you? Discuss with coaches how they would feel about assisting you with this.

4   Interview 2–3 athletes with the starting question of "what was the most psychologically challenging time you have had in the past 18 months?" Ask the athletes next, "What would have helped you at that time?" And, "would you have wanted to see a team psychologist or someone qualified within your team, someone who understood your schedule and pressures?"

5   Interview 2–3 coaches with the same focus as above.

ADDITIONAL READING

Clark, L.A. (2007). Assessment and diagnosis of personality disorder: Perennial issues and an emerging reconceptualization. *Annual Review of Psychology 58*, 227–257.

Grant, J.E., Brewer, J.A., Potenza, M.N. (2006). The neurobiology of substance and behavioral addictions. *CNS Spectrums, 11*(12), 924–930.

Kellmann, M. (Ed.) (2002). *Enhancing Recovery: Preventing Underperformance in Athletes.* Champaign, IL: Human Kinetics.

Kessler, R.C., Berglund, P., Demler, O., Jin, R., Meri-kangas, K.R., Walters, E.E. (2005). Lifetime prevalence and age-of-onset distributions of DSM-IV disorders in the National Comorbidity Survey Replication, *Archives of General Psychiatry, 62*(6), 593–602.

Ogilvie, B. & Tutko, T.A. (1966). *Problem Athletes and How To Handle Them.* London: Pelham Books Ltd.

Robinson, T.E. & Berridge, K.C. (2003). Addiction. *Annual Review of Psychology, 54*, 25–53.

Uliaszek, A.A., Zinbarg, R.E., Mineka, S., Craske, M.G., Griffith, J.W., Sutton, J.M., Epstein, A. & Hammen, C. (2012). A longitudinal examination of stress generation in depressive and anxiety disorders. *Journal of Abnormal Psychology, 121*(1), 4–15.

Van Raalte, J.L. & Brewer, B.W. (Eds.) (2013). *Exploring Sport and Exercise Psychology*, 3rd Edition. Washington, D.C.: American Psychological Association.

REFERENCES

American Psychiatric Association. (2013). *American Psychiatric Association: Diagnostic and Statistical Manual of Mental Disorders*, Fifth Edition. Arlington, VA: American Psychiatric Association.

Baillie, P.H.F., Davis IV, H. & Ogilvie, B.C. (2014). Working with elite athletes. In J.L. Van Raalte & B.W. Brewer (Ed.), *Exploring sport and exercise psychology* (pp.401–425). Washington, DC, US: American Psychological Association.

Barkley, R.A. & Murphy, K.R. (2006). *Attention-deficit hyperactivity disorder, A clinical workbook* (3rd ed.). New York, NY, US: Guilford Press.

Bateman, A.W. & Fonagy, P. (2000). Effectiveness of psychotherapeutic treatment of personality disorder. *The British Journal of Psychiatry, 177*, 138–143. doi:10.1192/bjp.177.2.138.

Beedie, C.J., Terry, P.C. & Lane, A.M. (2000). The profile of mood states and athletic performance: Two meta-analyses. *Journal of Applied Sport Psychology, 12*(1), 49–68.

Bracken, N.M. (2012). 2012–2013 National Study of Substance Use Trends Among NCAA College Student-Athletes. Available at: http://www.ncaa.org/wps/wcm/connect/public/NCAA/Resources/Research/NCAA+Studies+of+Substance+Use+Habits+of+College+Student-Athletes

Bugelski, R. (1938). Extinction with and without sub-goal reinforcement. *Journal of Comparative Psychology, 26*(1), 121–134. doi:10.1037/h0057091.

Burton, R.W. (2000). Mental illness in athletes. In D. Begel & R.W. Burton (Eds.), *Sport psychiatry: Theory and Practice* (pp.61–81). New York: W.W. Norton.

Canada, G.O. (2006). *The human face of mental health and mental illness in Canada 2006*. Ottawa, Canada: Public Health Agency of Canada; The Government of Canada.

Carter, J.S. & Garber, J. (2011). Predictors of the first onset of a major depressive episode and changes in depressive symptoms across adolescence: Stress and negative cognitions. *Journal of Abnormal Psychology, 120*(4).

Centers for Disease Control and Prevention (CDC). (2011). Unhealthy sleep-related behaviors—12 States, 2009. *MMWR. Morbidity and mortality weekly report, 60*(8), 233–238.

Chapman, D.P., McKnight-Eily, L., Perry, G.S. & Anda, R.F. (2008). Short communication: The relationship between depression and sleep apnea and insomnia: A brief review. In A.B. Turley & G.C. Hofmann (Eds.), *Life style and health research progress* (pp.9–15). Hauppauge, NY: Nova Biomedical Books.

Craighead, W.E., Cheets, E.S., Brosse, A.L. & Ilardi, S.S. (2007). Psychosocial treatments for major depressive disorder. In P.E. Nathan, J.M. Gorman (Eds.), *A guide to treatments that work* (pp.271–287). New York: Oxford University Press.

Davis, H., Botterill, C. & MacNeill, K. (2002). Mood and self-regulation changes in underrecovery; An intervention model. In M. Kellmann (Ed.), *Enhancing recovery: Preventing underperformance in athletes* (pp.161–179). Champaign, IL: Human Kinetics.

Davis, H., Liotti, M., Ngan, E.T., Woodward, T.S., Van Snellenberg, J.X., van Anders, S.M., Smith, A. & Mayberg, H.S. (2008). fMRI BOLD signal changes in elite swimmers while viewing videos of personal failure. *Brain Imaging and Behavior, 2*(1), 84–93.

Derman, W., Schwellnus, M.P., Lambert, M.I., Emms, M., Sinclair-Smith, C., Kirby, P. & Noakes, T.D. (1997). The 'worn-out athlete': A clinical approach to chronic fatigue in athletes. *Journal of Sports Sciences, 15*(3), 341–351.

Ellis, A. & Ellis, D.J. (2011). History. In A. Ellis & D.J. Ellis (Eds.), *Rational Emotive Therapy* (pp.7–15). Washington, DC: American Psychological Association.

Ellis, A. & Harper, R.A. (1961). *A guide to rational living*. Oxford, England: Prentice-Hall.

Grant, J.E., Brewer, J.A. & Potenza, M.N. (2006). The neurobiology of substance and behavioral addictions. *CNS spectrums, 11*(12), 924–930.

Greenleaf, C., Petrie, T.A., Carter, J. & Reel, J.J. (2009). Female collegiate athletes: prevalence of eating disorders and disordered eating behaviors. *Journal of American college health: J of ACH, 57*(5), 489–495.

Hammond, T., Gialloretto, C., Kubas, H. & Davis, H., 4th. (2013). The prevalence of failure-based depression among elite athletes. *Clinical Journal of Sports Medicine,* (Epub ahead of print).

Hayes, K. & Smith, S. (2005). *Get out of your mind and into your life: The new acceptance and commitment therapy*. New York: New Harbinger Publications.

Heil, J., Hartman, D., Robinson, G. & Teegarden, L. (2002). Attention Hyper-Activity Disorder in Athletes. Hidden Disabilities in Sport. Available at: http://hidden-disabilities-in-sport.org/node/9

Heil, J. (2000). The injured athlete. In Y.L. Hanin (Ed.), *Emotions in sport*. (pp.245–265). Human Kinetics: Champaign.

Herring, S.A., Cantu, R.C., Guskiewicz, K.M., Putukian, M., Kibler, W.B., Bergfeld, J.A., Boyajian-O'Neill, L.A., Robert Franks, R., Indelicato, P.A., Lowe, W., O'Connor, F.G. & Thorson, D.C. (2011). Concussion (mild traumatic brain injury) and the team physician: a consensus statement—2011 update. *Medicine and Science in Sports and Exercise, 43*(12), 2412–2422.

Holden, C. (2010). Psychiatry. Behavioral addictions debut in proposed DSM-V. *Science, 327*(5968), 935.

Huang, J., Jacobs, D.F., Derevensky, J.L., Gupta, R. & Paskus, T.S. (2007). A national study on gambling among US college student-athletes. *Journal of American College Health, 56*(2), 93–99.

Hughes, R. & Coakley, J. (2001). Positive deviance among athletes: The implications of overconformity to the sport ethic. In A.

Yiannakis & M.J. Melnick (Eds.), *Contemporary Issues in Sociology of Sport* (pp.361–374). Champaign, IL: Human Kinetics.

Iverson, G.L. (2011). Evidence-based neuropsychological assessment in sport-related concussion. In F.M. Webbe (Ed.), *Handbook of Sport Neuropsychology* (pp.131–153). New York, NY, US: Springer Publishing Co.

Jensen, P.S., Hinshaw, S.P., Swanson, J.M., Greenhill, L.L., Conners, C.K., Arnold, L.E., Abikoff, H.B., Elliott, G., Hechtman, L., Hoza, B., March, J.S., Newcoin, J.H., Severe, J.B., Vitiello, B., Wells, K. & Wigal, T. (2001). Findings from the NIMH Multimodal Treatment Study of ADHD (MTA): Implications and applications for primary care providers. *Journal of Developmental and Behavioral Pediatrics, 22*(1), 60–73.

Joormann, J., Cooney, R.E., Henry, M.L. & Gotlib, I.H. (2012). Neural correlates of automatic mood regulation in girls at high risk for depression. *Journal of Abnormal Psychology, 121*(1), 61–71.

Kellmann, M. (2010). Preventing overtraining in athletes in high-intensity sports and stress/recovery monitoring. *Scandinavian Journal of Medicine & Science in Sports, 20 Suppl 2*, 95–102.

Kessler, R.C., Berglund, P., Demler, O., Jin, R., Merikangas, K.R. & Walters, E.E. (2005). Lifetime prevalence and age-of-onset distributions of DSM-IV disorders in the National Comorbidity Survey Replication. *Archives of General Psychiatry, 62*(6), 593–602.

Kessler, R.C., Chiu, W.T., Demler, O., Merikangas, K.R. & Walters, E.E. (2005). Prevalence, severity, and comorbidity of 12-month DSM-IV disorders in the National Comorbidity Survey Replication. *Archives of General Psychiatry, 62*(6), 617–627.

Konorski, J. (1950). Mechanisms of learning. In *Symposia Society for Experimental Biology* (pp.409–431). Cambridge, England: Cambridge University Press.

Levis, D.J. & Brewer, K.E. (2001). The neurotic paradox: Attempts by two-factor fear theory and alternative avoidance models to resolve the issues associated with sustained avoidance responding in extinction. In R.R. Mowrer & S.B. Klein (Eds.), *Handbook of contemporary learning theories* (pp.561–597). Mahwah, NJ: Lawrence Erlbaum Associates Publishers.

Li, J., Kuk, A.Y.C. & Rush, A.J. (2012). A practical approach to the early identification of antidepressant medication non-responders.

Psychological Medicine: A Journal of Research in Psychiatry and the Allied Sciences, 42(2), 309–316. doi:10.1017/S0033291711001280.

Lorains, F.K., Cowlishaw, S. & Thomas, S.A. (2011). Prevalence of comorbid disorders in problem and pathological gambling: Systematic review and meta-analysis of population surveys. *Addiction, 106*(3), 490–498. doi:10.1111/j.1360-0443.2010.03300.x.

Lovell, M.R., Collins, M.W., Iverson, G.L., Field, M., Maroon, J.C., Cantu, R., Podell, K., Powell, J.W., Belza, M. & Fu, F.H. (2003). Recovery from mild concussion in high school athletes. *Journal of Neurosurgery, 98*(2), 296–301.

Mah, C.D., Mah, K.E., Kezirian, E.J. & Dement, W.C. (2011). The effects of sleep extension on the athletic performance of collegiate basketball players. *Sleep, 34*(7), 943–950.

McCrory, P., Meeuwisse, W., Johnston, K., Dvorak, J., Aubry, M., Molloy, M. et al. (2009). Consensus Statement on Concussion in Sport: the 3rd International Conference on Concussion in Sport held in Zurich, November 2008. *British Journal of Sports Medicine, 43 Suppl 1*, i76–i90. doi:10.1136/bjsm.2009.058248.

Miller, W.R. & Rollnick, S. (2013). *Motivational interviewing: Helping people change (3rd edition)*. New York, NY: Guilford Press.

Mowrer, O.H. (1960a). Revised Two-Factor Theory and the Concept of Habit. In Mowrer, O.H. *Learning theory and behavior* (pp.212–252). Hoboken, NJ: John Wiley & Sons Inc.

Mowrer, O.H. (1960b). Two-Factor Learning Theory: Versions One and Two. In Mowrer, O.H., *Learning theory and behavior* (pp. 63–91). Hoboken, NJ: John Wiley & Sons Inc.

Mowrer, O.H. (1956). Two-factor learning theory reconsidered, with special reference to secondary reinforcement and the concept of habit. *Psychological Review, 63*(2), 114–128. doi:10.1037/h0040613.

Nemeroff, C.B. & Schatzberg, A.F. (2007). Pharmacological treatment for unipolar depression. In P.E. Nathan, D.G. Gorman (Eds.), *A guide to treatments that work* (pp.271–287). New York: Oxford University Press.

Ogilvie, B., Tutko, T. & Thomas, A. (1971). Sport: If you want to build character, try something else. *Psychology Today, 5*(5), 61–63.

Orth, U., Robins, R.W. & Roberts, B.W. (2008). Low self-esteem prospectively predicts depression in adolescence and young adulthood. *Journal of Personality and Social Psychology, 95*(3), 695–708.

Pagulayan, K.F., Hoffman, J.M., Temkin, N.R., Machamer, J.E. & Dikmen, S.S. (2008). Functional limitations and depression after traumatic brain injury: examination of the temporal relationship. *Archives of Physical Medicine and Rehabilitation, 89*(10), 1887–1892.

Panksepp, J. (2004). *Textbook of biological psychiatry.* New Jersey: Wiley-Liss.

Potenza, M.N., Koran, L.M. & Pallanti, S. (2009). The relationship between impulse-control disorders and obsessive-compulsive disorder: a current understanding and future research directions. *Psychiatry research, 170*(1), 22–31.

Ruff, R.M., Camenzuli, L. & Mueller, J. (1996). Miserable minority: emotional risk factors that influence the outcome of a mild traumatic brain injury. *Brain injury, 10*(8), 551–565.

Soleimani, L., Lapidus, K.A. & Iosifescu, D.V. (2011). Diagnosis and treatment of major depressive disorder. *Neurologic clinics, 29*(1), 177–193, ixCI: Copyright © 2011.

Stores, G. (2007). Clinical diagnosis and misdiagnosis of sleep disorders. *Journal of neurology, neurosurgery, and Psychiatry, 78*(12), 1293–1297.

Temcheff, C., Derevensky, J. & Paskus, T. (2011). Pathological and disordered gambling: A comparison of DSM-IV and DSM-V criteria.

International Gambling Studies, 11*(2), 213–220. doi :10.1080/14459795.2011.581677.

Turner, R.M. (1984). Assessment and treatment of borderline personality disorder. Paper presented at the 18th meeting of the Association for the Advancement of Behavior Therapy, Philadelphia, PA.

Varela, J. (2008). Mental health treatment and treatment providers. *The Prosecutor, 38*(3). Available at: http://www.tdcaa.com/node/2497

Webbe, F.M. (2011). *The handbook of sport neuropsychology.* New York, NY: Springer Publishing Co.

Wood, R.L. (2004). Understanding the 'miserable minority': a diasthesis-stress paradigm for post-concussional syndrome. *Brain injury, 18*(11), 1135–1153.

World Health Organization. (1992). *International Statistical Classification of Diseases and Related Health Problems, Tenth Revision (ICD-10).* Geneva: World Health Organization.

Yang, J., Peek-Asa, C., Corlette, J.D., Cheng, G., Foster, D.T. & Albright, J. (2007). Prevalence of and risk factors associated with symptoms of depression in competitive collegiate student athletes. *Clinical Journal of Sport Medicine: Official Journal of the Canadian Academy of Sport Medicine, 17*(6), 481–487.

Chapter 60

Technological advancements in sport psychology

THOMAS SCHACK, MAURIZIO BERTOLLO, DIRK KOESTER, JONATHAN MAYCOCK AND KAI ESSIG

SUMMARY

The advent of new technologies has significantly altered the progression of sporting achievements. Sport technology has become increasingly important for recording, analyzing, and optimizing athletic performances. This chapter provides an overview of technological advancements in sport psychology, and highlights their key characteristics and useful applications. We describe techniques that enrich the physical environment of athletes, such as virtual, augmented, and mixed realities. Then we explain attentional, auditory, and brain-related technologies such as eye tracking, sonification, and EEG that can help to improve the cognitive processes of athletes, and serve as diagnostic and training tools. The chapter concludes with a discussion of the ethical and practical implications of technological advancements for sport and sport psychologists.

INTRODUCTION

Athletes can profit from advances in engineering, material science, biomechanics, neuroscience, communication, and information technologies to maximize their training and sport performances. Scientists and engineers are developing technologies that are changing the way sport is practiced, played, analyzed, scored, and watched (Fuss, Subic, Strangwood, & Metha, 2013). Examples of this include ingestible computers (e.g., using a thermometer pill to wirelessly transmit core body temperature to an outside computer), intelligent clothes (e.g., embedding materials with electronics to measure biometric data), biomimicry (e.g., imitating nature for inspira-

tion, such as mimicking a gecko's toes to increase adhesive strength while moving), neurotechnology for monitoring and improving mental skills (e.g., employing neurofeedback and transcranial direct current stimulation), carbon nanotechnology (i.e., the engineering of functional systems at the molecular scale), computational fluid dynamics (e.g., optimizing flow for swimsuits), digital imaging and video (e.g., giving viewers the feeling that they are close to the action), reactive materials (e.g., using light, breathable, and washable shin guards to protect athletes from injuries), robotics (e.g., facilitating the testing of equipment and surfaces), and 3D body scanners that analyze body geometry and kinematics. These advances mean that more and more sport-related factors can be tracked, monitored, optimized, refined, and disseminated in creative and practical ways that improve athlete performance.

OBJECTIVES

After reading this chapter, you should be able to:

1 Understand technological advancements and their application for sports.
2 Select appropriate neurotechnology for diagnostics, monitoring, and improvement of mental skills.
3 Define a multimodal and multidimensional system for monitoring one or more sports.
4 Illustrate the differences between augmented and virtual realities, and consider how these techniques can be applied to various sports.

TECHNOLOGICAL TOOLS AND THEIR APPLICATIONS IN SPORT PSYCHOLOGY

Computer-based procedures for visual feedback (e.g., Schack & Hackfort, 2007) such as virtual reality (VR), augmented reality (AR), and neurotechnology have been developed for use in the military, medicine, sport, and neuropsychology. Sport psychologists use, test, and modify these technologies to make empirical and applied aspects of sport psychology more visible and attractive for athletes, other disciplines (e.g., business), and institutional investors. The application of these technological tools in applied sport psychology should be embedded in a conceptual understanding of action and mental coaching in sports (see Schack & Bar-Eli, 2007; Schack & Hackfort, 2007). A fundamental action situation in applied sport settings consists of the following components: person, task, and environment (Schack & Hackfort, 2007); and these factors are related to each other and the action taking place (Figure 60.1).

Sport performance depends on the current physical and mental condition of the athlete (person), the situational demand or the type of sport (task), and the conditions under which the task is carried out (e.g., competition vs. training environment). From an action situation perspective, actions are organized intentionally in line with a person's subjective interpretation of a given person–environment–task constellation.

Virtual and augmented realities can be used to provide various perceptual (e.g., visual, auditory and/or tactile) information as additional sources of feedback in the learning process. For example, if an application is focused on the person (athlete), then eye tracking systems or neurotechnology may prove beneficial for improving performance by influencing or reproducing task conditions. This process should provide functional and performance-based links to competition tasks. The condition of tasks can also be reproduced with the help of virtual reality (e.g., a virtual golf course), whereby environmental conditions are effectively controlled, thus providing training opportunities when the weather is poor.

The assumption of intentionality in action theory has important implications. First, it implies an internal representation of the person–environment–task constellation. Second, it requires a functional understanding of how intentions (ideas) find their path from the center to the periphery. In the action regulation system, the brain/cognitive processes

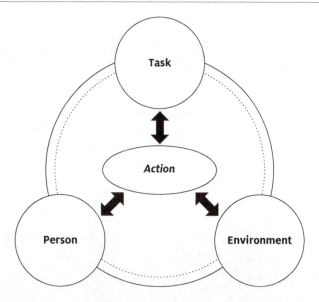

Figure 60.1 Action situation as a person–environment–task constellation (adapted from Schack & Hackfort, 2007).

are regarded as the center, and the muscles/body movements are the periphery. Cognitive tools such as self-instruction and imagery forge an important link between intentions and external behavior. Use of technology can support the development and modification of such links.

CREATING AND ENRICHING THE PHYSICAL ENVIRONMENT OF ATHLETES

In the following sections we describe how technology can be used to provide athletes with internal and external information, and how this information can be used for training and to improve performance. We describe technologies that can enrich the physical environment of athletes, and also improve attention, auditory facilities, and neurocognitive components of personal performance.

Virtual reality (VR): Athletes can interact with computer-simulated environments by way of *virtual reality* technology (e.g., VR golf courses). The environment can be a simulation of the real world or an imaginary world (see Figure 60.2) providing an interactive and immersive experience in a simulated autonomous world (Burdea & Coiffet, 2003; Zeltzer, 1992). This is achieved via computer genera-

tion of sensory impressions that are delivered to the human senses. The type and quality of these impressions determine the level of immersion and the extent to which the participant feels 'present' in the virtual setting. Additionally, the environment itself must provide realistic responses to the user's actions so that users can act in the same way as they would in a real environment, and without the need to adjust behavior significantly to interface effectively.

Virtual reality systems are complex and require additional input/output (IO)-hardware devices, special drivers, and software. In general, *input devices* (e.g., body tracking systems, eye tracking systems, data gloves, dexterous manipulators, 3D mice and bats, space balls) are responsible for interaction,

Figure 60.2 Virtual reality in karate.

whilst *output devices* (e.g., 3D glasses, surround displays, head-mounted displays, HMDs) are responsible for the feeling of immersion. Software is responsible for control and synchronization of the whole environment.

There are different degrees of immersion attainable in virtual environments. In *full immersion* conditions, a user wears a HMD or a shutter glass that provides 3D visual and audio information. Inputs are possible through the use of handheld input devices. In *partial level of immersion* conditions, the scene is projected into the environment using large monitors and 'head up' displays. Simulations may include additional sensory information, such as sound, proprioceptive, or tactile feedback. Virtual reality is used across a range of sports including rugby, handball, soccer, and table tennis (Bideau et al., 2010).

When VR is applied to sports, the motor learning or behavior of the subject plays a major role. It has been suggested that people who use highly detailed VR setups become better players and learn more quickly than the average player, even if they have never played the game before (e.g., Burdea & Coiffet, 2003).

Virtual reality can overcome many of the limitations of video presentations and has several advantages over this latter medium, such as:

1 The added benefit of subjects and simulated opponents being able to interact with one another while displayed information is carefully controlled and modified;
2 The allowance for complete control and fine-tuning of factors that affect a player's judgment, ensuring reproducibility and ecological validity;
3 An enhanced sense of presence for players by way of tracking head movements and updating viewpoints in real time;
4 Greater depth of information than videos can provide;
5 Intuitive ways of human–computer interaction, whereby users can watch and manipulate simulated environments similarly to how they would normally act in the real world;
6 The ability to test different designs or models without the need to build expensive prototypes.

Because of these advantages, a player's perspective and behavior within a VR environment can correspond closely to their perspective and behavior in real-life environments. For example, Craig, Berton, Rao, Fernandez, and Bootsma (2006) used VR to study curved free kicks in soccer. The researchers asked professional soccer players to judge whether a range of (simulated) free kicks would end up in the goal or not, and found that participants could imagine realistic free kicks while keeping all other variables (e.g., ball speed) constant. This allowed them to draw conclusions regarding players' abilities to incorporate information about spin, and then use this information to accurately predict where the ball would end up.

Brunett, Rusdorf, and Lorenz (2006) developed V-Pong, an immersive table tennis simulation, where they used an integrated physics engine to manage three major features of the simulation – i.e., ball movement, collision modeling, and game strategy – to let players interact with the ball in real time. Two possible ways of ball movement – flying and rolling – improved the sensation of immersion and the extent to which players enjoyed the game. The collision model considered all six objects involved in the game: the ball, two bats, the table, the net, and the ground. Finally, the game strategy modeled opponents' virtual behaviors. The authors found that users with no VR environment experience could use their system without any training because of how closely the simulation was to a real table tennis environment.

The above studies demonstrate the advantages of VR to facilitate better understanding of the perception-action loop, which may allow for better sport analysis. Furthermore, these studies demonstrate that athletes and coaches can benefit from VR settings. VR technologies have been used to improve coach–athlete interaction to support technical preparation and to realize competition-like training settings (for examples cf. CITEC, Bielefeld University, Germany at https://www.cit-ec.de/research/SEMORE).

Augmented reality (AR): Over the last few years, advances have been made in *augmented reality* (Milgram, Takemura, Utsumi, & Kishino, 1994) for application in domains such as robotics, telemanipulation, and the military. The most common definition of augmented reality is that of Azuma (1997), who stated that AR systems have the following three characteristics: (1) they combine real and virtual environments; (2) they are interactive in real time; and (3) they are registered in 3D. Augmented reality systems overlay digital computer-generated data, such as audio, visual and tactile information on top of a live, direct or indirect view of a physical, real-world environment (Duh & Billinghurst, 2008). In AR sport environments, the data from multi-sensory components, audio/visual systems, actuators (types of motors used for moving or controlling mechanisms or systems), and virtual actors are all recorded at different rates, and so have to be synchronized to achieve realistic adaptations to athletes' movements and, thus, an enhanced experience (see Figure 60.3).

With the help of advanced AR technology, information about the surrounding real world becomes interactive and digitally manipulable. Thus, AR makes the environment richer in terms of feedback and creates a mixed reality between our environment and movement-related, computer-generated feedback. In contrast to VR, in which the user is often completely embedded in an artificial world, AR is on a continuum between reality and virtuality (Milgram et al., 1994). Augmented reality techniques hold potential when training for game situations, when practicing techniques, and for the provision of real time performance feedback. In many fields of sport, a central goal is to bring different kinds of movement patterns to the attention of the athlete. This can be accomplished through the use of AR, and research suggests that AR use improves athletes' performance (Bideau et al., 2010).

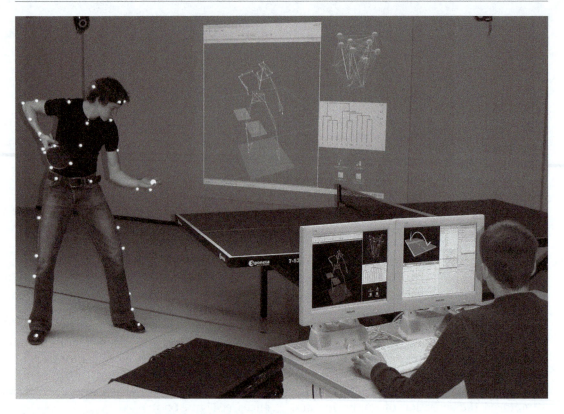

Figure 60.3 Augmented reality for table tennis training.

TECHNOLOGIES TO IMPROVE ATTENTION, AUDITORY SENSIBILITY, AND PSYCHO-PHYSICAL STATE

In the following sections we describe how perceptual-cognitive skills can be investigated using eye tracking technologies (Holmqvist et al., 2011). Additionally, we explain how sonification (i.e., the transformation of data relations into perceived relations in an acoustic signal for the purposes of facilitating communication or interpretation; Hermann, 2008), relaxation egg chairs, heart rate, and EEG feedback/neurofeedback can be used to improve personal performance in sport.

Eye tracking: The term *eye tracking* denotes the process of monitoring and recording participants' gaze positions when they look at 2D or 3D stimuli. Researchers are interested in exact gaze positions measured in 2D or 3D coordinates and therefore measure spatial-temporal scan paths (Holmqvist et al., 2011). Fully mobile, head-mounted eye-tracking systems allow participants to move in an unlimited working range and to grasp, touch, and manipulate objects of interest. This is especially important for dynamic environments, such as sports. Mobile systems consist of a head and an eye camera either attached to a bicycle helmet, or by way of a headset that uses glasses with integrated cameras. The computer that controls the eye tracker and stores the data is contained in a backpack and is connected by a cable to the cameras.

There is a spatial and functional relationship between eye movements and whole body movements or movements of body segments. For example, to achieve good hand-eye coordination, both parts must work together in smooth and efficient patterns. In goal-directed movements, the selection of task-relevant objects and locations is determined by the goals of the moving person. Hollands, Patla, and Vickers (2002) found that prior to changing the direction of walking, participants aligned their gaze with the endpoint of the required travel path, thus suggesting that eye movements are related to movement goals. Similarly, Heinen, Jeraj, Vinken, and Velentzas (2012) found a relationship between gaze behavior and movement in a complex gymnastic skill, namely the backward salto performed as a dismount on the uneven bars. Thirteen expert gymnasts were instructed to fixate a light spot on the landing mat, which varied systematically with regard to each gymnast's landing distance during the downswing phase when performing a salto dismount. They found variations in the hip angle at the top of the backswing, the duration of the downswing phase, the hip-angle prior to kick-through, and the landing distance as a function of different gaze locations on the landing mat.

Essig, Prinzhorn, Maycock, Ritter, and Schack (2012) implemented an interface between a monocular mobile eye tracking system and a motion tracking system to further investigate the spatial and functional relationship between eye movements and whole body movements or movements of body segments. This sort of interface may prove useful for investigating the amount of information required for successful motion execution, or the way that athletes react in unusual playing situations.

Sonification: A method that involves sound signals and supplies humans with information about their surroundings is *sonification*. For example, Geiger counters, particle detectors that measure ionizing radiation use auditory feedback for radiation levels. Sonification has also been applied in sport science to represent kinematic data, such as joint angles

(Effenberg, 2011; Schaffert, Mattes, & Effenberg, 2010). Hermann, Ungerechts, Toussaint, and Grote (2012) used sonification to make audible the hydrodynamic pressure field induced by the hand action of a female freestyle swimmer. Swimmers and experts of self-induced flow physics can now make use of this highly relevant information. The benefits of sonification in swimming research that the authors highlight are that: (1) sound can be accessible without requiring visual attention (which is difficult underwater); (2) human auditory perception has a high temporal resolution, allowing tightly-closed interaction loops in online applications (e.g., to create sonified videos that allow the swimming researchers to better interrelate action, data and sound for a real-time pressure sonification while swimming); and (3) humans are highly sensitive to rhythms and changes of rhythms, and these patterns occur frequently in repetitive, coordinated body movements.

Other researchers have also indicated that auditory information is a useful feedback tool for improving sport performance. Murgia, Hohmann, Galmonte, Raab, and Agostini (2012) found second-order biofeedback techniques to be effective in various sports, particularly those where rhythm is crucial. Researchers recorded natural sounds produced by athletes during actions, such as those created from the physical impact of limbs/equipment with air/water, and then had athletes listen to the recordings before and during the reproduction of the same gestures. They found that athletes were more accurate and effective in carrying out sport movements when listening to their own sounds.

Further technologies that are widely used by athletes include: (1) relaxation egg chairs (Warrior, 2012) with built-in speakers and a large screen video monitor can be used to practice relaxation and stress management techniques; (2) heart rate variability biofeedback helps to learn to change the heart rate when it is displayed on the monitor in order to enhance health, performance and well-being for personal feedback and stress reduction; and (3) EEG biofeedback/neurofeedback as a technology-based learning technique to train the person to modify his or her own brainwaves by displaying them on a computer screen (Schwartz & Andasik, 2003). EEG biofeedback can be a powerful tool to help reduce or eliminate attention problems, anxiety, or anger in high performing athletes by improving concentration, decision making during competition, and regulation of emotions.

TECHNOLOGIES TO IMPROVE NEUROCOGNITIVE COMPONENTS OF PERSONAL PERFORMANCE

Neurotechnologies (NT) are used to monitor and improve performance based on information about the individual neurocognitive status of the subjects assessed via cognitive or neurophysiological measurements. Neurotechnology is a set of procedures, methods, tools, and devices that affect human understanding of the brain and various aspects of consciousness, thought, and higher order activities in the brain and motor memory. It includes technologies that are designed to monitor, improve, and treat brain function, and it allows researchers and clinicians to visualize and stimulate brain and memory structures and functions.

Neuroscience methods: Information on the structure and function of the human brain can be obtained in a variety of ways. *Positron emission tomography* (PET) and *functional magnetic resonance imaging* (fMRI) are particularly interesting for the evaluation of brain structures, but they can also be used for recording brain functions. To function properly, the brain requires sufficient amounts of glucose and oxygen, which are supplied through blood vessels. Both PET and fMRI methods measure changes in local blood flow. Since these changes can be localized within a few millimeters, the neural activity underlying cognitive processes can be estimated. Another advantage of PET and fMRI is their capability to measure brain activity in deeper areas (subcortical structures) such as the basal ganglia that play an important role in movement execution and control. With these techniques it is also possible to measure activity in the whole brain.

In contrast, *near-infrared spectroscopy* (NIRS), which can also measure brain functions with high spatial resolution, is largely limited to regional measurements, i.e., the whole brain cannot normally be investigated in one session and subcortical structures can also not be measured with NIRS. However, for sport scientists NIRS can be beneficial because it is a mobile method. That is, NIRS can be applied in field settings. Also, it is less susceptible to movement artifacts. Since participants wear the sensors in a cap, they do not have to perform the experimental task in a specific position and can move more freely. A general disadvantage of all three methods, however, is the low temporal resolution when investigating cognitive processes. Other methods such as *electroencephalography* (EEG) and *magnetoencephalography* (MEG) are better suited for measuring rapid (cognitive) processes, particularly during training (see Hatfield & Kerick, 2007).

Electroencephalography and MEG both externally monitor brain activity via electrodes placed on the scalp. Electroencephalography records changes in electrical fields due to neuronal activity (slow post-synaptic potentials), whilst MEG captures changes in the magnetic field that are associated with electric activity. Brain activity that can be captured by either technique is largely limited to the cortex, the outer part of the brain. The most prominent advantage of these two methods is their high temporal resolution. That is, brain functions that support cognitive functions can be recorded in real time. Also, these measures do not require overt responses from participants. Another advantage of EEG is that it is less expensive than PET or fMRI scans and is essentially a mobile technique (Thompson, Steffert, Ros, Leach, & Gruzelier, 2008). It is possible to bring the equipment into field settings, although participants' movements can still pose a challenge as they can evoke muscle artifacts.

Multidimensional approaches: Multidimensional approaches combine neurotechnology measures and VR scenarios and have been successfully applied in competitive sports (Schack & Hackfort, 2007) such as dance (Bläsing, Puttke, & Schack, 2010), judo (Weigelt, Ahlmeyer, Lex, & Schack, 2011), and tennis (Schack & Mechsner, 2006). The first part of the approach involves assessing the mental representation structure of the participant via the structural dimensional analysis of mental representation (SDA-M). These results are used to design an appropriate intervention. These interventions are derived from databases that include information about the connection between mental representation structure and performance at different skill levels. The intervention routines are conducted using AR and include verbal items and gestures to explain these parts of the movement, which are identified as movement problems (Schack, Bockemuehl, Schütz, & Ritter, 2008). Moreover, particular exercise instructions are given to improve the performance of identified problem areas. In sport, this method adds value to the learning process because it means coaches can provide focused, informed feedback by taking into account the athlete's mental representation structure of movements. A virtual agent can support the coach–athlete interaction and provide a useful medium for improving sport importance.

HOW TO CHOOSE THE APPROPRIATE NEUROTECHNIQUES IN SPORT PSYCHOLOGY

Several neuroimaging techniques have been applied to sport science and coaching domains for the purposes of monitoring activity and improving performance (Yarrow, Brown, & Krakauer, 2009; Hillmann, Erickson, & Kramer, 2008). Determining the best method depends on the setting, the research question, and the intended purpose. For instance, PET and fMRI are useful in laboratory or clinical settings where the body posture is not of critical relevance, because subjects must lie still in the recording device (Tashiro, Itoh, Fujimoto, Masud, Watanuki, & Yanai, 2008). Positron emission tomography and fMRI are particularly suitable for investigating the neural correlates of imagery skills in athletes (Holmes & Calmels, 2008), for exploring subcortical structures, such as basal ganglia during coordination task (De Luca, Jantzen, Comani, Bertollo, & Kelso, 2010), and for aiding rehabilitation after concussion or injuries (Pulsipher, Campbell, Thoma, & King, 2011). Electroencephalography and MEG are particularly suited for investigating rapid processes such as visuo-spatial attention required for aiming and shooting (Del Percio et al., 2009). Electroencephalography has successfully been used to monitor motor learning and enhance performance in golf putting (Pitto, Novakovic, Basteris, & Sanguineti, 2011).

IMPLICATIONS OF TECHNOLOGY FOR SPORT AND SPORT PSYCHOLOGISTS

According to the *Technology Acceptance Model* (TAM; Davis, Bagozzi, & Warshaw, 1989), an information systems theory that models how users come to accept and use technology, there are at least two primary factors that influence the acceptance of new technologies: (1) the degree to which people believe that using particular systems enhance their performance (perceived usefulness); and (2) the degree to which people believe that the use of particular systems is free of effort (perceived ease-of-use). A reliable and simple use is a prerequisite for a broad acceptance of new technologies in sports. Techniques that do not work properly or that restrict athletes during movement are unlikely to be accepted. Therefore, aesthetics, 'joy-of-use', and positive sensations athletes and researchers get when using products are important design considerations.

In addition to acceptability, another factor to consider is user experience, the way sport psychologists and athletes feel about using a product, system or service, and their confidence in the product. *Usability* describes the extent to which a product can be used by sport psychologists and athletes to achieve specified goals with effectiveness, efficiency, and satisfaction in a specified context. Only when all factors are considered in the relevant sporting context, will new technologies be accepted and widely used. Ongoing considerations include ensuring that technologies in sport are useful and easier to interact with than those of the past, whereby future technologies need to progress alongside our evolving human needs.

LEARNING AIDS

1   Identify key concepts related to technological advancements in sport psychology.

Athletes can profit from advances in engineering, material science, biomechanics, neuroscience, communication and information technologies to maximize their training and sport performances. Aside from this, technical systems are helping athletes to analyze their performance over weeks, months or even over the course of a season in order to create profiles that can then be used for diagnostics and training purposes. Examples of technologies that can help athletes are, among others, intelligent clothes, biomimicry, neurotechnology for monitoring and improvement of mental skills, and 3D body scanners.

2   Describe the main differences between AR and VR.

VR is a technology which allows a user to interact with a specific computer-simulated environment (for instance a golf course), regardless of whether that environment is a simulation of the real world or an imaginary world. VR is an interactive and immersive (with the feeling of presence) experience in a simulated (autonomous) world. AR systems have the following three characteristics: (1) they combine real and virtual environments; (2) they are interactive in real time; (3) they are registered in 3D. Thus, AR makes the environment richer in terms of feedback and creates a mixed reality between the environment and movement-related, computer-generated feedback. AR is on a continuum between reality and virtuality. With VR, in contrast, the user is completely embedded in an artificial world.

3   Summarize various brain-related technologies and their sport psychology applications.

An important constraint for the selection of a method from cognitive neuroscience is the requirement of the experimental task. PET (positron emission tomography) and fMRI (functional magnetic resonance imaging) can be applied to estimate the neural activity underlying cognitive processes in the whole brain, incl. subcortical structures. They are useful in laboratory and clinical settings where body posture is not of critical relevance. They are particularly useful for investigating the neural correlates of imagery skills or to help in rehabilitation and intervention after concussion or injuries. In contrast, NIRS (near-infrared spectroscopy), measures brain functions with a high spatial resolution, but is limited to regional measurements and is less susceptible to movement artifacts. Because it is mobile and poses fewer constraints on the participants, it can be applied in different field settings. Electroencephalography (EEG) and magnetoencephalography (MEG) monitor the brain activity from the outside, i.e., at the scalp. They have a high temporal resolution and therefore they are better suited for measuring fast (cognitive) processes (in real time). EEG and MEG are particularly useful for investigating the specific brain rhythms in visuo-spatial attention tasks (such as aiming), motor learning processes (such as the systematic associations between EEG synchronization effects and better performances in a [virtual] ball putting task), or to enhance knowledge about the central mechanisms generating our behavior.

4   Discuss advantages of VR/AR techniques compared to traditional techniques such as video presentations.

VR and AR have many advantages over traditional presentation techniques. Athletes and simulated opponents can interact with one another while the experimenter can carefully control and modify the displayed information, i.e., tune all factors affecting the players' judgement, ensuring reproducibility and ecological validity. A player's feeling of presence can be enhanced by tracking head movements and by updating their viewpoint in real time, providing crucial depth information. VR and AR provide an intuitive way of human–computer interaction: the users can watch and manipulate the simulated environment in a similar way to how they interact in the real world. Both techniques allow the testing of different designs or models without the need to build expensive prototypes. The disadvantages of VR and AR are, among others, the experimental setting is much more complicated, expensive hardware is needed, the different modalities have to be synchronized, technical knowledge is necessary and the data analysis is complex.

5   Explain the implications of using technological advancements in applied work.

New technologies are only accepted and used in sports if athletes believe that using particular systems can enhance their performance (perceived usefulness) and are easy to use (perceived ease-of-use). Techniques that cannot be used efficiently and satisfactorily in a specified context (usability), without positive sensations (aesthetics and 'joy-of-use'), or restrict athletes during movement are unlikely to be accepted. Future technologies need to progress alongside our evolving human needs.

REVIEW QUESTIONS

1   What are the different degrees of immersion in virtual environments?

2   What is the relationship between gaze behavior and movement for complex skills?

3   Why is AR useful for improving athlete performance?

4   What are the advantages and disadvantages of using modern technologies in sport?

EXERCISES

1   Describe the application of new technologies in a particular defensive sport situation (e.g., for a handball goalkeeper).

2   Consider ways that sonification can be applied to non-water sports, such as badminton.

3   Identify several ways that you can use to investigate the importance of key information, which must be considered by players during game play, using eye tracking and VR.

4   Identify a sporting scenario and explain how new multimodal approaches could outperform traditional unimodal training methods to improve athlete performance.

5   Outline an argument you would use in order to persuade a coach to use modern technologies (e.g., eye tracking, mental training based on mental representation, or neurotechnologies) to improve team performance.

REFERENCES

Azuma, R.T. (1997). Survey of augmented reality. *Journal Presence: Teleoperators and Virtual Environments, 6,* 355–385.

Bideau, B., Kulpa, R., Vignais, N., Brault, S., Multon, F. & Craig, C. (2010). Using virtual reality to analyse sports performance. *IEEE Computer Graphics and Applications, 30,* 14–21.

Bläsing, B., Puttke, M. & Schack, T. (2010). *Neurocognition of dance.* London: Psychology Press.

Brunett, G., Rusdorf, S. & Lorenz, M. (2006). V-Pong: An immersive table tennis simulation. *IEEE Computer Graphics and Applications, 26,* 10–13.

Burdea, G. & Coiffet, P. (2003). *Virtual reality technology.* Hoboken, NJ: Wiley.

Craig, C.M., Berton, E., Rao, G., Fernandez, L. & Bootsma, R.J. (2006). Judging where a ball will go: The case of curved free kicks in football. *Naturwissenschaften, 93*(2), 97–101.

Davis, F., Bagozzi, P. & Warshaw, P. (1989). User acceptance of computer technology – a comparison of two theoretical models. *Management Science, 35,* 982–1003.

De Luca, C., Jantzen, K.J., Comani, S., Bertollo, M. & Kelso, J. (2010). Striatal activity during intentional switching depends on pattern stability. *The Journal of Neuroscience, 30,* 3167–3174.

Del Percio, C., Babiloni, C., Bertollo, M., Marzano, N., Iacoboni, M., Infarinato, F., Lizio, R., Stocchi, M., Robazza, C., Cibelli, G., Comani, S. & Eusebi, F. (2009). Visuo-attentional and sensorimotor alpha rhythms are related to visuo-motor performance in athletes. *Human Brain Mapping, 30,* 3527–3540.

Duh, H.B.-L. & Billinghurst, M. (2008). Trends in augmented reality tracking, interaction and display: A review of ten years of ISMAR. In *7th IEEE/ACM International Symposium on Mixed and Augmented Reality (Sept. 2008),* 193–202.

Effenberg, A.O. (2011). Enhancing motor control and learning by additional movement sonification. In T. Hermann, A. Hunt & J. Neuhoff (Eds.), *The Sonification Handbook* (pp.549–552). Berlin: Logos Verlag.

Essig, K., Prinzhorn, D., Maycock, J., Ritter, H. & Schack, T. (2012). Automatic analysis of 3D gaze coordinates on scene objects using data from eye-tracking and motion-tracking systems. In

Eye Tracking Research & Applications (ETRA 2012), Santa Barbara, California, USA.

Fuss, F., Subic, A., Strangwood, M. & Mehta, R. (2013). *Routledge handbook of sports technology and engineering*. New York, NY: Taylor & Francis.

Hatfield, B.D. & Kerick, S.E. (2007). The psychology of superior sport performance: A cognitive and affective neuroscience perspective. In G. Tenenbaum & R.C. Eklund (Eds.), *Handbook of sport psychology* (3rd ed, pp.84–109). Hoboken, NJ: Wiley.

Heinen, T., Jeraj, D., Vinken, P.M. & Valentzas, K. (2012). Land where you look? Functional relationships between the gaze and movement behaviour in a backward salto. *Biology of Sports, 29*, 177–183.

Hermann, T. (2008). Taxonomy and definitions for sonification and auditory display. In P. Susini & O. Warusfel (Eds), *Proceedings of the 14th International Conference on Auditory Display (ICAD)*, Paris, France: IRCAM.

Hermann, T., Ungerechts, B., Toussaint, H. & Grote, M. (2012). Sonification of pressure changes in swimming for analysis and optimization. *Program of the International Conference on Auditory Display (ICAD 2012)*, Atlanta, GA, USA, June 18–22.

Hillmann, C.H., Erickson, K.I. & Kramer, A.F. (2008). Be smart, exercise your heart: Exercise effects on brain and cognition. *Nature Reviews Neuroscience, 9*, 58–65.

Hollands, M.A., Patla, A.E. & Vickers, J.N. (2002). Look where you are going: Gaze behaviour associated with maintaining and changing the direction of locomotion. *Experimental Brain Research, 143*, 221–230.

Holmes, P. & Calmels, C. (2008). A neuroscientific review of imagery and observation use in sport. *Journal of Motor Behavior, 40*, 433–445.

Holmqvist, K., Nyström, M., Andersson, R., Dewhurst, R., Jarodzka, H. & van de Weijer, J. (2011). *Eye tracking: A comprehensive guide to methods and measures*. New York, NY: Oxford University Press.

Milgram, P., Takemura, H., Utsumi, A. & Kishino, F. (1994). Augmented reality: A class of displays on the reality-virtuality continuum. In *SPIE Vol. 2351-34 (Proceedings of telemanipulator and telepresence technologies)*, 282–292.

Murgia, M., Hohmann, T., Galmonte, A., Raab, M. & Agostini, T. (2012). Recognizing one's own motor actions through sound: The role of temporal factors. *Perception, 41*, 976–987.

Pitto, L., Novakovic, V., Basteris, A. & Sanguineti, V. (2011). Neural correlates of motor learning and performance in a virtual ball putting task. *IEEE International Conference of Rehabilitation Robot*, Zurich, Switzerland, June 29 – July 1, 2011.

Pulsipher, D.T., Campbell, R.A., Thoma, R.J. & King, J.H. (2011). A critical review of neuroimaging applications in sports concussion. *Current Sports Medicine Reports, 10*, 14–20.

Schack, T. & Bar-Eli, M. (2007). Psychological factors in technical preparation. In B. Blumenstein, R. Lidor & G. Tenenbaum (Eds.), *Psychology of sport training* (pp.62–103). Oxford: Meyer & Meyer Sport.

Schack, T. & Hackfort, D. (2007). An action theory approach to applied sport psychology. In G. Tenenbaum & R.C. Eklund (Eds.), *Handbook of Sport Psychology* (3rd ed, pp.332–351). Hoboken, NJ: Wiley.

Schack, T. & Mechsner, F. (2006). Representation of motor skills in human long-term memory. *Neuroscience Letters, 391*, 77–81.

Schack, T., Bockemuehl, T., Schütz, C. & Ritter, H. (2008). Augmented Reality im Techniktraining. *BISp-Jahrbuch 2007/8*. (S. 235–240) Bonn: BGoMedia GmbH & Co. KG.

Schaffert, M., Mattes, K. & Effenberg, A.O. (2010). A sound design for acoustic feedback in elite sports. *Lecture Notes in Computer Science (including subseries Lecture Notes in Artificial Intelligence and Lecture Notes in Bioinformatics), 5954*, 143–165.

Schwartz, M.S. & Andasik, F. (2003). *Biofeedback: A Practitioner's Guide*. New York: Guilford Press.

Tashiro, M., Itoh, M., Fujimoto, T., Masud, M.M., Watanuki, S. & Yanai, K. (2008). Application of positron emission tomography to neuroimaging in sports sciences. *Methods, 45*, 300–306.

Thompson, T., Steffert, T., Ros, T., Leach, J. & Gruzelier, J.H. (2008). EEG applications for sport and performance. *Neuroimaging in the Sports Sciences Methods, 45*, 279–288.

Warrior, F. (2012). Egg chairs – a modern classic. Retrieved December 15, 2012, from http://nationalfurnituresupply.com/blog/2012/09/egg-chair-a-modern-classic/.

Weigelt, M., Ahlmeyer, T., Lex, H. & Schack, T. (2011). The cognitive representation of a throwing technique in judo experts: Technological ways for individual skill diagnostics in high performance sports. *Psychology of Sport and Exercise, 12*, 231–235.

Yarrow, K., Brown, P. & Krakauer, W. (2009). Inside the brain of an elite athlete: The neural processes that support high achievement in sports. *Nature Reviews Neuroscience, 10*, 585–596.

Zeltzer, D. (1992). Autonomy, interaction, presence. *Journal Presence: Teleoperators and Virtual Environments, 1*, 127–132.

Chapter 61

Professional training, supervision, and continuing education

ANTOINETTE M. MINNITI AND JUDY L. VAN RAALTE

SUMMARY

Effective sport psychology consultants and researchers engage with robust professional training, supervision, and continuing education practices. Training should include a balance of education and practical experiences that allow individuals to become established experts, whilst ongoing supervision and professional development form an important extension of this process. There are varied training systems across and within nations. The following chapter presents an overview of essential features related to professional training, supervision, and continuing education (CE).

INTRODUCTION

Case study: Guinevere is a final-year undergraduate student from the United Kingdom (UK), who is currently completing her degree in psychology. She is considering a career in sport psychology, but is unsure how to proceed. Guinevere is concerned that pursuing a sport psychology career will mean several more years of education and cost, but after speaking with someone in her psychology department, she discovered that her current degree means she is well-placed to apply for and earn a master's degree (MSc) in sport and exercise psychology. Guinevere was referred to the list of British Psychological Society (BPS)-accredited MSc Sport and Exercise Psychology courses in the UK and advised of the impor-

tance of attending an accredited course if she wanted to eventually become a qualified sport psychologist. She was also told that it would be helpful for her to read sport and exercise psychology texts, to get involved with research on campus, and to consider attending sport and exercise psychology conferences.

The above scenario reflects the *initial* stages of Guinevere's career journey toward becoming a qualified sport psychologist in the UK. Subsequent stages include enrolling in a graduate program, completing coursework, doing applied work with teams and athletes, being supervised, and ongoing professional development. The precise path that can be taken to become appropriately qualified varies across disciplines (i.e., psychology, exercise science, kinesiology) and nations. It is essential for those interested in sport psychology to learn about the national and/or federal systems relevant to them, particularly if intra- or inter-national moves are planned, as local regulations and procedures affect opportunities to work as a sport psychology practitioner and/or researcher.

OBJECTIVES

After reading this chapter you should be able to:

1   Understand why sport psychology professionals should be appropriately trained.
2   Describe key aspects of an effective supervisor–supervisee relationship.
3   Identify a range of potential opportunities that reflect continuing education (CE), such as books, video, conferences, formal CE or continuing professional development (CPD) programs; and
4   Have an awareness of professional training, supervision, and CE practices that can be applied to both academic and applied positions.

PROFESSIONAL TRAINING AND EXPERTISE

Practitioners who work with people in a sport psychology context need to have expert and specialized knowledge in the field and a range of interpersonal (e.g., communication, empathy) and technical (e.g., applying theory to practice, interview) skills. The overarching objective of the extensive training required to become a recognized sport psychology professional is to ensure proficiency, that duty of care is met, and that clients receive the best possible services (Silva, Metzler, & Lerner, 2011). Although there are numerous approaches to effective sport psychology service delivery, all good practitioners take the following approaches: develop and maintain professional boundaries; establish a *professional philosophy*; use appropriate strategies for making contact with clients; understand assessment tools and their use; employ strategies used for conceptualization of athletes' concerns and potential interventions; clarify the range, types, and organization of sport psychology services; develop strategies for effective program implementation; manage themselves as intervention instruments; conduct program and consultant evaluation;

and leave the setting upon completion of sport psychology services (Poczwardowski, Sherman, & Ravizza, 2004).

Poczwardowski et al. (2004) note that development of a professional philosophy is an important tool that helps ensure effective delivery of sport psychology services. They describe professional philosophy as being based upon a hierarchical structure that includes elements that are both explicitly referred to and implicit within sport psychology literature. Components of a professional philosophy can be placed on a continuum from the most stable and internal to most dynamic and external, including: (a) personal core beliefs and values; (b) theoretical paradigm concerning behavior change; (c) models of practice and the consultant's role; (d) intervention goals; and (e) intervention techniques and methods. Sport psychologists who understand and communicate their professional philosophy clearly are likely to be effective in developing rapport with their clients and meeting their own and their clients' goals. A practitioner's professional philosophy can serve as the basis and guiding principle for sport psychology service delivery.

Other key components required to 'do' sport psychology include: preparation, education, personal development as a counselor, designing mental training programs, supervision, and ongoing professional and personal development, including reflective practice (Silva et al., 2011). It takes a combination of classroom experiences (theoretical knowledge) and practical skills development (listening, empathy, interviewing) to become proficient. Well-trained sport psychologists are most able to be effective and provide services competently to athletes, teams, and coaches. Poorly-trained or ineffective sport psychologists can do harm to individuals, teams, and the reputation of the field of sport psychology.

The terms professional training and development of expertise principally refer to the extensive body of opportunities that can be accessed through educational and professional or accrediting organizations. Within higher education institutions/universities there are undergraduate (e.g., Bachelor of Arts in Psychology in the US; Bachelor of Science (Hons) in Psychology in the UK), postgraduate (PG; e.g., Master of Science in Psychology in the US; MSc in Sport and Exercise Psychology in the UK), and ultimately research- (primarily in the UK and Australia) or professional training-focused (primarily in the US) doctoral (Ph.D. or Psy.D.) degrees that provide increasing levels of expertise, respectively. The emphasis of theoretical and applied content alongside the overall structure or design of different courses varies across countries.

Regardless of where a student is trained, it is expected that certain learning outcomes are to be accomplished. These might include: (1) knowledge base (expertise); (2) research and evaluation (understanding of ethical codes and ability to evaluate, interpret, and design basic research studies); (3) information and technological literacy (e.g., appropriate and ethical implementation of technology related to client records); (4) critical thinking skills (use of creative thinking and scientific approaches when solving problems related to athletes,

teams, coaches, and sports organizations); (5) application of counseling skills (identify, evaluate, and ethically apply psychological theories, models, and techniques in counseling and consultation work); (6) values (e.g., integrity, confidentiality); (7) communication skills (oral, written, interpersonal); (8) sociocultural and international awareness (e.g., understanding of how differences influence beliefs); (9) personal development (self- and client-reflective practices); and (10) career planning and development (application of psychological knowledge for lifelong learning).

Students in Australia or the UK, like Guinevere, would normally complete an undergraduate (UG) degree in general psychology (another possibility is that some students undertake sport science UG degrees that include a prominent psychology pathway), and then go on to complete a taught master's degree in sport and exercise psychology. In the US, however, students may embark on kinesiology or exercise science UG degrees, or general psychology UG degrees, or may major in both areas. Subsequent progression to master's and doctoral degrees are most likely to be in the psychology field for those who want to become chartered or licensed practitioners, and in the kinesiology or exercise science field for those who want to be researchers or university professors. McCullagh, Noble, and Portenga (2013) describe the different education pathways that have developed with regard to the growth of sport and exercise psychology in different countries, noting that one reason for this variation is that some nations have multiple professional associations for the discipline.

Although it is beyond the scope of this chapter to detail the certification and licensure routes across all countries (please see Zizzi, Zaichkowsky, & Perna, 2013, for a review of certification practices in various countries), it is worth noting some key overarching features related to this aspect of professional training and expertise. In particular, for the countries where educational systems or curricula are strongly interlinked to the professional bodies (which is the case in Australia and the UK, for example), the pathway to becoming a sport psychologist is restricted, but clear, in that students are required to complete their UG and PG degrees at recognized higher education institutions based in their country (e.g., successfully undertaking programs that are Australian Psychological Society-accredited or BPS-accredited, respectively).

In contrast, in countries where there may be more than one primary professional association connected to sport and exercise psychology research and/or practice, such as in the United States, there are more opportunities and pathways to enter the field, but the process of licensure and accreditation is less definite. Currently in the US, for example, the American Psychological Association (APA) has identified sport and exercise psychology as a 'proficiency area' (professional specialty), but there is no licensure credential that practitioners can obtain via APA's professional body (see www. apa47.org). The Association of Applied Sport Psychology (AASP) in the US has a certification process for individuals to become Certified Consultants, AASP (CC, AASP), but there is currently no exam and AASP cannot provide nationally-recognized licensure qualifications (see www.appliedsportpsych.org).

Regardless of the professional training that future sport psychologists are required to complete, it is standard practice for professional trainees of the discipline to successfully engage with supervision practices, which will be discussed in the next section of this chapter.

SUPERVISION

Van Raalte and Andersen (2014) describe supervision as an ongoing process that is iterative in nature. To be an effective sport psychologist, the scientist-practitioner should be prepared to embark on a journey that has no specified end point, and can frequently benefit from self- and peer-reflection (e.g., trusted professional colleagues) along the way. The main objective of supervision is the same as for professional training and development of expertise. That is, to ensure that clients' interests are the focus of the counseling process, and that clients are receiving the best possible care from the sport psychologist.

Given the importance of the primary purpose of supervision, this feature is prominent across all programs and countries, and its inclusion in various sport psychology degrees and training programs is typically distinguished by the specified number of hours that are required (e.g., a minimum of 300 to 500 hours), areas of focus, which are generally associated with the intended area of practice that the consultant wants to branch into (e.g., clinical versus educational sport psychology), and relative staging or progression that is required according to the relevant professional organization. For example, the BPS operates a two-stage supervision process which includes: (1) obtaining Graduate Membership of the Society with the Graduate Basis for Chartered Membership (GBC), and completing either a Society-accredited MSc in Sport and Exercise Psychology, or having completed the Qualification in Sport and Exercise Psychology (Stage 1) Examinations; followed by (2) a period of supervised practice as a Trainee Sport and Exercise Psychologist; whereby (3) the total period of training, including time spent on the MSc and supervised practice must be a minimum of three-years full time or the part-time equivalent. Once both stages of the process are fully completed, individuals may achieve the Society's Chartered Status (see http://www. bps.org.uk). Completing both qualifications gives individuals the necessary PG training to achieve the Society's Chartered Status and be eligible to apply for registration with the Health Care and Professions Council (HCPC), which is required in the UK if sport and exercise psychologists want to offer their services to the public (see http://www.hcpc-uk.org/).

Supervision typically begins with the establishment of the *supervisor–supervisee relationship*. The potential supervisor and supervisee meet and determine if they are going to work together. Then, if they decide to proceed, a particular *model of supervision* is generally discussed and then employed. Sport psychology supervision often involves behavioral, cognitive-behavioral, phenomenological, psychodynamic, and developmental approaches (for a discussion of supervision models see Van Raalte & Andersen, 2000). Further, supervision generally progresses as the supervisee gains skill. As Stoltenberg, McNeill, and Delworth (1998) describe in their Integrated Developmental Model, supervisees typically move through three progressive levels, gradually representing less to more autonomous states. They begin with a high self-focus and limited self- and other-awareness, and then the focus on the client increases but supervisees may still be unclear about the therapeutic relationship (because it is generally complex and indefinite), and finally, supervisees become more able and confident and are appropriately discriminating as to when they need to seek counsel from their supervisor.

Andersen et al. (2000) provide a sport psychology specific example of supervisor–supervisee communications that span a year of supervision for an Australian apprentice sport psychologist. This chapter includes excerpts and discussions associated with the initial telephone contact between parties, the supervision intake, and additional meetings between the supervisor and supervisee. The content is insightful with respect to the supervisee's development and gradual *establishment of autonomy*, and may provide reassurance to other supervisees that their queries and concerns are 'normal' and part of the natural development of any practitioner.

The main characteristics that define effective supervisor–supervisee relationship include: open communication lines; positive and constructive two-way feedback; consistent and frequent self- and supervisor-based reflection; evidence-based and, thus informed decision-making for both supervisors and supervisees; flexibility (e.g., in how one operates/behaves); discussion about ethics and any arising ethical dilemmas; and willingness to receive feedback (Andersen, Van Raalte, & Harris, 2000; Silva et al., 2011; Van Raalte & Andersen, 2000). Another important feature of effective supervision and supervisory relationships is clear documentation of work with clients, which is also essential for application for licensure and required for maintenance of credentials (e.g., for auditing purposes conducted by professional organizations). To ensure clarity for all involved, supervisors and supervisees may want to consider completing a supervisory skills inventory such as the one presented by Van Raalte and Andersen (2000) that assesses perceptions related to: (1) information and technical support; (2) the extent to which supervisory responsibilities are fulfilled; (3) interpersonal communication; (4) supervisee autonomy; and (5) degree of professionalism (of either/both parties).

Supervisors should regularly provide supervisees with evaluations of supervisee progress and *competence* (Silva et al., 2011). Honest and consistent feedback can help ensure constructive and productive support with regard to both parties. In addition, it may be valuable to administer instruments such as that developed by Harmison (2004) to enable clients to identify strengths and weaknesses of the supervisee.

The importance of ensuring an effective supervisory process can be understood most clearly when we consider the value of getting the best care to the client, and the benefits associated with developing confident and caring sport psychology consultants. For practitioners, the process is only beginning when they undertake an appropriate professional training program and supervisory relationship. Ongoing professional development is paramount to ensuring that sport psychologists are providing the most current evidence-based practice, whilst exhibiting a clear willingness to continuously develop themselves; thus, the next section of this chapter addresses this aspect.

CONTINUING EDUCATION/CONTINUING PROFESSIONAL DEVELOPMENT

Continuing education (CE) and continuing professional development (CPD) are interchangeable terms that reflect methods of *counselor self-enhancement* following the achievement of credentials, licensure, and/or accreditation. The purpose of CE and CPD is to provide sport psychologists with up-to-date research and practical knowledge relevant to the discipline. This information can, in turn, be used to continuously inform scientist-practitioners' empirical and applied practices. Ongoing education and development can consist of a wide range of opportunities such as short- and/or long-term seminar attendance, videos, reading of texts and research papers, completion of formal CE/CPD workshops, research engagement and dissemination (e.g., conference attendance and presentations, membership with professional organizations, publication in peer-reviewed journals), and consistent peer feedback and supervision involvement.

Similar to professional training and supervision, examples of continuing education are internationally pervasive since this process is central to ensuring the integrity of the profession and optimal care for clients. For example, most countries have professional organizations that provide one or more of the above-mentioned opportunities to their members (and, in many cases, non-members), which are often available at conferences as well as being coordinated throughout the year at varied locations. Continuing education workshops, in particular, are generally available prior to the commencement of main conference proceedings, and so they afford scientists and/or practitioners with the opportunity to bene-fit from both the workshop content, and also from peer networking that is facilitated by the pre-conference workshop. Thus, an added benefit is that CE workshops may provide advantages that are reserved for such unique forums or occurrences, whereby national and/or international colleagues are able to connect and share international practices.

Silva et al. (2011) discuss counselor self-enhancement, highlighting the importance of sport psychology consultants frequently returning to the point at which they started, that is, to return to learning about the field and continuing to expand their knowledge and experience even after they have become established in their careers. An important part of the ongoing educational process can involve 'giving back' to the profession and becoming a supervisor or continuing education provider in one's own right, once the practitioner has attained his or her credentials. In addition, the authors highlight the value of engaging in sport and/or physical activity, as this may allow the consultant to have greater and/or genuine appreciation for the subject matter that they are working on with their clients.

Regardless of the extent to which scientist-practitioners engage in ongoing education, what is clear is the value of this practice for the consultant and the client. At the time of writing, the current state of professional training, supervision, and continuing education is highly robust and exciting, including continual developments that we can identify and highlight in all of these areas within the discipline. These future trends are discussed in the final section below.

FUTURE TRENDS

Developments associated with professional training for sport and exercise psychologists, first and foremost, mirror the evolving systems within the discipline which are set by various countries and their professional organizations (e.g., in the UK, education and accredited programs have recently become linked to chartered status). Trends in the discipline also reflect the growing demand from professionals within the field to ensure best practice, and that well-trained consultants represent the discipline. In Hays' (2012) chapter on performance psychology, she refers to future directions related to education, such as ensuring that comprehensive graduate-level training exists for future practitioners, rather than students having siloed or fragmented opportunities (e.g., as sometimes occurs across/between psychology and kinesiology departments). In addition, she highlights the importance of assuring that professional programs clearly define competency standards, that these standards are met, and that appropriate benchmarks related to practice and ethics are established.

More recently, there has been growing interest for sport and exercise psychology consultants to share their knowledge outside of their respective discipline (e.g., with businesses, the military, musicians). This expansion of sport psychology into the more general area of performance psychology may continue in the years ahead. This interest has already created a rise in continuing education and professional development workshops in performance psychology.

In summary, professional training and expertise, supervision, and continuing education are fundamental components for the development of effective sport and exercise psychologists. This chapter has explored the purpose and benefits of these elements, provided examples of each of the three key components, and considered how they might share similarities and also be different across programs and countries. The future of sport and exercise psychology training holds considerable promise in that there is demand for effective service delivery and quality assurance, both within and outside of the field, and as the discipline has matured, so have the professional bodies and organizations that maintain and develop its standards.

LEARNING AIDS

1   Explain why sport psychology professionals should be appropriately trained.

The primary objective of appropriate professional training for sport and exercise psychologists is to ensure that clients receive the best possible care, and that the individuals delivering the service are up-to-date on current research and applied techniques or practices.

2   Describe key aspects of effective supervisor–supervisee relationships.

Effective supervisor–supervisee relationships will include a number of similar features including: good communication; positive and constructive two-way feedback; consistent and frequent self- and supervisor-based reflection; evidence-based and informed decision-making for both parties; flexibility; discussion of ethics and any arising ethical dilemmas; and willingness to receive feedback.

3   What types of continuing education programming are available for sport psychologists?

Sport psychologists can benefit from a range of CE and CPD opportunities including informal seminars and formal CE/CPD workshops (e.g., 'how to work with elite youth athletes'), conferences, videos, texts, and research papers.

4   What professional training, supervision, and CE practices can be applied to both academic and applied positions?

In addition to opportunities cited above, both academic and applied positions can benefit from membership with various professional organizations, publication in peer-reviewed journals, and consistent peer feedback and supervision involvement.

REVIEW QUESTIONS

1   Imagine you are an undergraduate interested in becoming a sport psychologist. What questions should you ask and what steps should you take to prepare yourself for this career?

2   In your own words, describe the importance of a professional philosophy. Use an example to illustrate how a professional philosophy affects sport psychology consulting.

3   Explain how supervision enhances the delivery of sport psychology services.

4   What forms of counselor self-enhancement do you think are most effective and why?

EXERCISES

1   Interview a sport psychologist. What aspects of their training did they think were most important? What types of supervision are they involved with? How much and what type of continuing education do they get each year?

2   Develop an informational brochure for students interested in sport psychology. Describe the training needed to become a sport psychologist in your area and the benefits of studying sport psychology.

3   Consider your education and training. What have you done that has prepared you to become a sport psychologist? If you wanted to pursue a career in sport psychology, what additional steps would you need to take to reach your goal?

4   Outline and create a Performance Psychology presentation to introduce a key aspect of the field. Identify a focus (e.g., building team dynamics) and consider both theoretical and practical elements that you would want to incorporate. Discuss aspects of your professional philosophy that guided the development of your presentation.

ADDITIONAL READING

Andersen, M.B., Van Raalte, J.L. & Brewer, B.W. (2001). Sport psychology service delivery: Staying ethical while keeping loose. *Professional Psychology: Research and Practice, 32,* 12-18.

Aoyagi, M.W., Portenga, S., Poczwardowski, A., Cohen, A.B. & Statler, T. (2012). Reflections and directions: The profession of sport psychology past, present, and future. *Professional Psychology: Research and Practice, 43,* 32–38.

IN THE HUDDLE. (2012). *Journal of Sport Psychology in Action, 3,* 208–212. doi:10.1080/21520704.2012.720539

REFERENCES

Andersen, M.B., Van Raalte, J.L. & Harris, G. (2000). Supervision II: A case study. In M.B. Andersen (Ed.), *Doing sport psychology* (pp.167–180). Champaign, IL: Human Kinetics.

Harmison, R.J. (2004, October). *The pursuit of professional training via a master's degree in sport psychology.* Paper presented at the 19th annual meeting of the Association for the Advancement of Applied Sport Psychology, Minneapolis, MN.

Hays, K.F. (2012). The psychology of performance in sport and other domains. In S. Murphy & P. Nathan (Eds.), *The Oxford handbook of sport and performance psychology,* (pp.24–45). New York: Oxford University Press.

McCullagh, P., Noble, J.M. & Portenga, S. (2013). Education for sport and exercise psychology. In J.L. Van Raalte & B.W. Brewer (Eds.), *Exploring sport and exercise psychology (3rd ed.).* Washington, DC: American Psychological Association.

Poczwardowski, A., Sherman, C.P. & Ravizza, K. (2004). Professional philosophy in the sport psychology service delivery: Building on theory and practice. *The Sport Psychologist, 18,* 445–463.

Silva III, J.M., Metzler, J.N. & Lerner, B. (2011). *Training professionals in the practice of sport psychology (2nd ed.).* Morgantown, WV: Fitness Information Technology.

Stoltenberg, C.D., McNeill, B.W. & Delworth, U. (1998). *IDM supervision: An integrated developmental model for supervising counselors and therapists.* San Francisco, CA: Jossey-Bass.

Van Raalte, J.L. & Andersen, M.B. (2000). Supervision I: From models to doing. In M.B. Andersen (Ed.), *Doing sport psychology* (pp.153–166). Champaign, IL: Human Kinetics.

Van Raalte, J.V. & Andersen, M.B. (2014). Supervision. In J.L. Van Raalte & B.W. Brewer (Eds.), *Exploring sport and exercise psychology (3rd ed.).* Washington, DC: American Psychological Association.

Zizzi, S., Zaichkowsky, L. & Perna, F. (2013). Certification in sport and exercise psychology. In J.L. Van Raalte & B.W. Brewer (Eds.), *Exploring sport and exercise psychology (3rd ed.).* Washington, DC: American Psychological Association.

Chapter 62

Ethical issues in sport and exercise psychology

DIETER HACKFORT AND GERSHON TENENBAUM

SUMMARY

In sport and exercise psychology, practitioners and researchers are often required to assess and manage ethical issues. The purpose of this chapter is to provide guidance and resources related to ethical considerations in applied and empirical work in this field. Key terms and relevant concepts are outlined as they relate to ethics in sport and exercise psychology. Differences between morals and ethics are described, since the terms are interrelated but professionals should understand they have distinct properties. This chapter addresses the ways in which ethics are specifically situated in the sport and exercise psychology profession. Finally, consequences in terms of risk assessment for ethical decision making are briefly discussed.

INTRODUCTION

The following represents an example scenario involving a sport psychology consultant and his client. The challenges posed by this scenario highlight important differences between what is considered appropriate for the relationship between a client and consultant compared to, say, that for an athlete and their longtime coach.

Over the past year a male sport psychology consultant has conducted several performance enhancement support sessions with a female athlete, of which the primary focus was on the development of mental strategies for competition. After numerous sessions, the athlete began to noticeably shift the focus from sport performance to her private life, and she also invited the consultant to meet her family and visit her private home. While on the one hand, the practitioner thought it would be a good opportunity to learn more about the athlete and her social support system; on the other hand, he had doubts about the kind of relationship the athlete was interested in developing.

In this situation, the consultant was faced with a difficult situation where he wanted to maintain a good working relationship with his client, but he needed to ensure his professional behavior was not compromised by way of a shift in his relationship with her. In light of his professional ethical guidelines, he made the appropriate decision to discuss and provide clear boundaries with his client. He felt that it was not only a question about right or wrong behavior in this case, but also that he was at risk of violating ethical standards and could otherwise run into a conflict.

The above thumb sketch describes an ethical dilemma that can be experienced by sport psychology consultants. As in a variety of professions, compromising situations may be experienced by sport and exercise psychology practitioners and researchers. Thus, national and international organizations in both psychology and sport and exercise psychology have developed and they have published standards and guidelines to which their members must adhere. These standards are designed to both support their members in establishing appropriate working relationships with their clients, and also to ensure clients receive the most appropriate care (Koocher & Keith-Spiegel, 2008).

 ## OBJECTIVES

After reading this chapter, you should be able to:

1 Understand the background and key concepts related to ethical principles and moral guidelines.
2 Understand the relevance and potential complexity of ethical issues in sport and exercise psychology.
3 Recognize how ethical standards can be applied to a range of scenarios in sport and exercise psychology.
4 Access relevant resources for national and international ethical codes in the profession.

BACKGROUND AND KEY CONCEPTS

Historically, ethics have been considered important across a range of domains (e.g., sport, social, political, business), and they are widely regarded as essential to human conduct and life. In 1785, the well-known German philosopher, Immanuel Kant, stated that there are three central questions to be answered in human life: (1) what can I know?; (2) what shall I do?; and (3) what may I hope? (cf., 1965 reference). The second question, about knowing what to do, relates to ethical issues. The three questions are interrelated, but in this chapter the focus is on ethics and, thus, an emphasis is given to behaviors and conduct to be practiced within the sport and exercise psychology domain.

Ethical issues – i.e., the discussion and application of ethical standards, norms, and principles in everyday life, as well as in professional practice – have become increasingly significant in recent years (Kitchener, 2000). Given that sport, exercise, and psychology are three unique bodies of knowledge from which the profession has emerged, this area therefore necessitates unique consideration when deriving ethical guidelines. In general terms, ethical principles are needed to provide guidance for acceptable social living, and to organize and manage appropriate professional relations. Such principles are generated by social debates and are based on human experiences; they rely on professional values and monitoring of professional behavior.

Increasingly, ethical issues have received attention in the sport and exercise psychology domain (Etzel & Watson, 2011). For purposes of developing theory and practice in this area, it is necessary to reflect on ethics in sport to meet the new challenges in the field; particularly issues related to high performance sport, professional sport, and sport business. In sport and exercise psychology, ethical orientation and guidelines for scientists, researchers, consultants, mental coaches, and clients must refer to both ethical standards in psychology, and ethical guidelines for professional activities and business in sports.

When considering ethical issues in any arena it is important to reflect on the association between reason (e.g., 'why does my client want me to visit their home?') and consequence (e.g., 'what might happen if I visit my client at home?'). It is useful for professionals to be aware of and respond accordingly to the norms within cultures and/or sub-cultures that they may operate. For example, sport and exercise psychology professionals need to be particularly mindful of the normative ethics related to the various teams and sports within which they work. Normative ethics is a discipline that looks for consistency and justification of moral requirements, where the aim is to identify the moral values people *should* hold. Thus, responding to ethical dilemmas requires sport and exercise psychology professionals to make judgments based on values and virtues, which essentially represent acceptable ethical standards within that particular sport context.

As well as normative ethical considerations, sport and exercise psychology professionals need to understand the applied ethics associated with moral dilemmas. Applied ethics refer to contemporary problems in a specific field (Shields & Bredemeier, 2007), and respective professional bodies have been tasked with providing the necessary guidelines needed to manage them in practical (e.g., how to work with clients who take performance-enhancing drugs) and empirical (e.g., how to conduct research with special populations in sport) contexts. Thus, continuous discussion and updated codes of ethics are required to satisfy the ongoing developments related to the respective morals and virtues of the domain. As a final point here, it should also be noted that there are some general values or principles, such as duty of care to all human beings for their physical and mental well-being, that will normally supersede domain-specific ethics.

Ethics and morals

Although the terms are sometimes used interchangeably, an important distinction should be made between *morals* and *ethics*. Specifically, morals pertain to everyday life conventions, especially for social living (e.g., athletes should abide by 'fair play'); whereas ethics are largely based on reflections and take a critical position with regard to morals (e.g., coaches are required to maintain professional relationships with their athletes). According to Shields and Bredemeier (2007), "morality is concerned with people's rights and duties. It involves thinking and dialoguing about needs and interests; what is fair, and what is compassionate. It is about respect and responsibility. In our daily life morality is experienced as an *ought* about what should be done. People behave morally when they do the right thing for the right reason" (p. 663). In sport and exercise psychology, practitioners and researchers are called upon to consider not only the right and good thing to do in a given situation (guided by the normative ethics), but also what is necessary in order to maintain the integrity of the professional client–consultant relationship.

THE MEANING OF ETHICAL ISSUES IN A PROFESSION

In 1957, Huntington identified three important characteristics that distinguish professions from other endeavors, vocations, or jobs. These features were expertise, responsibility, and 'corporateness'. In the context of ethical considerations for professionals in sport and exercise psychology, responsibility is a central issue. Huntington went on to explain:

> The professional man is a practicing expert, working in a social context, and performing a service, such as the promotion of health, education, or justice, which is essential to

the functioning of society...the essential and general character of his service and his monopoly of his skill impose upon the professional man the responsibility to perform the service when required by society...the profession thus becomes a moral unit positing certain values and ideals, which guide its members in their dealing with laymen. This guide may be a set of unwritten norms transmitted through the professional educational system or it may be codified into written canons of professional ethics (p. 9).

Accordingly, professional ethics and moral principles serve to provide three key functions for the scientific and professional community: (1) orientation; (2) protection, and (3) control. Specifically, moral principles play a key role in the *orientation*, the development of intentions, planning, and the organization of actions. And these principles *protect* against misleading calculations and provide a certain kind of *control* in the decision-making process when controversial motives might be activated; e.g., when a financial profit is associated with socially questionable behavior. In sport and exercise psychology research and practice, such principles serve to regulate the expectations and actions of the psychologist and the client.

Actions can be perceived as purposive behaviors, which are always, implicitly or explicitly, associated with and organized to meet individual or social values. Values are defined by Schwartz (1994) as "desirable trans-situational goals, varying in importance, that serve as guiding principles in the life of a person or a social entity" (p. 21). According to Knoppers, Ten Boom, Buisman, Elling, and De Knop (2001) values are "seen as meanings or interpretations of the human existence; that is, social constructions that are viewed as guidelines for actions" (p. 22). Simply put, it is important to understand the values of both the client and sport and exercise psychology professional, as they inform the ethical guidelines by which both parties operate.

In summary, moral principles are guidelines for the conduct of acceptable professional behavior, and prevent critical or protect against unacceptable demands and behavior. Ultimately, ethical principles provide standards to control and evaluate the expectations and demands of a profession; moreover, they clearly define what kind of attitude, approach, and behavior is acceptable or unacceptable within the organization and profession. In the next section, we refer specifically to professional and ethical behaviors in sport and exercise psychology, and summarize orientations of acting responsibly and ethically in research, teaching, and provision of services to ensure the dignity and welfare of individuals, athletes, volunteers, administrators, teams, colleagues, students, and the general public.

ETHICAL REQUIREMENTS AND PRINCIPLES IN SPORT AND EXERCISE PSYCHOLOGY

Ethical requirements in sport and exercise psychology broadly correspond to two main areas: (1) the application of knowledge and skills, which include the appropriate teaching, education, and training for practitioners and researchers; and (2) aspects that are bespoke to research, which include factors associated with data collection and publication. We refer to each of these briefly.

Ethics in the application of knowledge

Codes of ethics for practitioners are aimed at providing guidelines and standards for the professional orientation to those who practice and conduct research in sport and exercise psychology. Professional codes of ethics have been established by national societies for several countries, including the United States of America, Australia, Britain, Canada, and Germany, and also the International Society of Sport Psychology (ISSP). A code of ethics represents a set of principles or standards that a group agrees to follow, and also refers to guidelines for moral behavior. The structure of such codes is similar and typically encompasses the articulation of fundamental values, principles for ethical decision-making, and guidelines for application and the handling of conflicts or violations. The main ethical issues which require ethical codes are described below.

Competence: A practitioner can only offer and conduct services for which he or she has acquired the sufficient level of competency. Competency requires a sound knowledge base of theory and practice, and consists of ongoing professional activities whereby individuals are informed about current research and practical techniques through reading, continuous education, peer consultation, and supervision. Certified or officially recognized practitioners are required to successfully complete approved tests and supervised practical experience and training in order to be formally authorized or licensed to practice. Thus, individuals who have not earned the requisite qualifications from their relevant professional body(ies) would be deemed to misrepresent themselves and the field, and ultimately to be conducting themselves in an illegal manner. Although this process will somewhat vary across countries – and even within some countries, such as the United States – the rigor of the process means that only those individuals who have undergone the appropriate training and tests can be deemed legally competent.

Respect: Respect refers to the experience, insight, and knowledge of other people. Respect is fundamental for all professional contact with clients, students, research participants, and colleagues. Respect of individual differences includes: culture, ethnicity, nationality, religion, education, gender, socioeconomic status, and physical or mental abilities/disabilities. In this context it is essential to avoid any form of harassment including sexual harassment and discrimination, and to ensure fair treatment of all clients without exception.

Integrity: Integrity is a key characteristic for developing relationships with clients, research participants, and students. It is founded on openness, accuracy, honesty, and straightforwardness. Specifically, for a psychologist integrity involves accuracy in reporting test results, openness and candor in clarifying possible intervention consequences, and honesty in financial matters. In this context, it is essential to avoid misrepresentation of professional capacities and conflicts of interest, and to maintain individual and social trust and confidence.

Responsibility: Responsibility refers to the profession, science, and society. Practitioners and scientists in sport and exercise psychology conduct their affairs in such a way that it will contribute to beneficial purposes and the welfare of human beings, avoid harm, and prevent misuse. That means also being mindful of any potential risk to clients, research participants, colleagues, and oneself. In this context, it is essential to be aware of and establish proper professional boundaries and to accept personal responsibility for professional decisions.

Confidentiality: Confidentiality encompasses the collection, recording, accessing, storage, dissemination, and disposal of data and information, and it is associated closely with privacy and consent. Privacy is the legal right not to reveal personal information; e.g., thoughts, feelings, habits, likes, and dislikes. In the event that such privacy is compromised, it is necessary to first attain consent. In order to receive consent and establish confidentiality, clients, research participants, and further potential subjects must be informed about intended aims and the selected methods and means to be used. Audio, video, and photographic recordings should be taken only with explicit permission of the subjects. Furthermore, clients must provide their consent prior to being referred to by the researcher or practitioner (e.g., 'X has given me permission to discuss his/her case...'). In this context, it is essential that all disclosures are appropriately communicated and exclusively undertaken with awareness of the responsibility for the individuals concerned and society. In case of any conflict, it is advisable to seek advice from a professional colleague and to maintain appropriate documentation.

Further details about ethical norms and moral guidelines that have been established by leading national and international societies in psychology and sport and exercise psychology are easily accessible online for most professional bodies. A brief description of some of these organizations is below, followed by their respective websites.

Psychology organizations:

(a) *American Psychological Association* (APA). The American Psychological Association is the largest scientific and professional organization representing psychology in the United States. It includes 137,000 members comprised of researchers, educators, clinicians, consultants, and students, and it is the world's largest association of psychologists. (See: http://www.apa.org/ethics/code.html)

(b) *Australian Psychological Society* (APS). The Australian Psychological Society is the largest professional association for psychologists in Australia, representing over 20,000 members. Its members represent a wide range of disciplines and experience and the organization advocates for psychologists at all levels of government. The APS continuously promotes the contributions that psychology makes to people's health and well-being, to ensure there is a wide understanding about the important social issues facing Australian society. (See: http://www.psychology.org.au/about/ethics/#s1)

(c) *Canadian Psychological Society* (CPS). The Canadian Psychological Association is the national association for the science, practice and education of psychology in Canada. With over 6,600 members and affiliates, the CPS is the largest professional association for psychology in Canada. (See: http://www.cpa.ca/aboutcpa/committees/ethics/codeofethics/)

Sport and exercise psychology organizations:

(a) *Association for Applied Sport Psychology* (AASP). This organization is an international, multidisciplinary, professional society that offers certification to qualified professionals in the field of sport, exercise, and health psychology. (See: http://appliedsportpsych.org/about/ethics/code)

(b) *International Society of Sport Psychology* (ISSP). The International Society of Sport Psychology is an organization devoted to promoting research, practice, and development in the discipline of sport psychology throughout the world. The ISSP is the only worldwide organization of scholars explicitly concerned with sport psychology. (See: http://www.issponline.org/p_codeofethics.asp?ms=3)

Other organizations that provide useful information and outline ethical guidelines include: American College of Sports Medicine; British Psychological Society; European Federation of Sport Psychology; German Association of Sport Psychology; Spanish Federation of Sport Psychology; and Japanese Society of Sport Psychology. This list is by no means exhaustive, and the reader is encouraged to review a range of organizations' ethical policies and guidelines.

Additionally, it is worth noting that psychology organizations often have specified divisions to represent the sub-disciplines in the area (e.g., within APA is 'Division 47: Exercise and Sport Psychology'), and these are worth referring to in regard to domain-specific aspects for sport and exercise psychology. Also, there are useful texts that address ethics and ethical issues which have been authored by sport and exercise psychologists. For example, Nideffer (1981) presented the first book on ethics in sport psychology, and more recently texts have included chapters on ethics in applied sport psychology (Gordin & Balague, 2005), and sport and exercise psychology (Etzel & Watson, 2011; Van Raalte & Brewer, in press).

Ethics in research

As well as the abovementioned ethical issues associated with the application of knowledge, there are ethical considerations unique to conducting research in sport and exercise psychology. Research is the act of applying methods of inquiry aimed at testing hypotheses, or the act of exploration and describing the phenomenon we observe (Tenenbaum & Driscoll, 2005). When planning and conducting responsible research, sport and exercise psychology professionals must understand research ethics and the ethical dilemmas that are commonly associated with empirical work.

Appropriate ethical guidelines for experimentation were thoroughly considered in The Belmont Report (1979) in the United States, The Nuremberg Code (1949), and The Helsinki Declaration (1974). These guidelines have formed the ethical cornerstones for many organizations that employ researchers in the biomedical and behavioral-social domains. Although it is widely acknowledged that an acceptable code of ethics is needed to undertake empirical work, it is clear that a universality of ethics is likely impossible (Jago & Bailey, 2001; Pojman, 1995). Research necessitates domain-specific ethical guidelines to safeguard the emotional, mental, and physical safety needs that are relative to its participants; and, thus, sport and exercise psychology requires its own tailored guidelines. To develop relevant ethical standards for the area, it is important to first decide upon the research paradigm, and then consider its requirements; e.g., population sample, type of data, instrumentation, interventions, and publication. Once these factors are clear, appropriate ethical codes can be determined to protect the emotional, mental, and physical safety of the participants engaged with the specified research.

According to our conceptualization, there are two dominant research paradigms: (1) qualitative (or impressionistic or descriptive); and (2) quantitative (or positivistic). The former is explorative and usually does not require prior assumptions about the world, while the other is inductive and consists of set rules the researcher must follow. Qualitative methods for research and exploration are performed in natural environments, and the researcher uses techniques such as non-obtrusive observation, complete participation (action methodologies), interviews, archives, stories, and published materials to generate the 'know-how' about the people or phenomenon he/she seeks to understand. Thus, the main ethical concerns in implementing methods classified in this paradigm relate to permissions to conduct the study (i.e., communication with the observed and/or their authority), use of authentic materials and observations, verification of interpretation with the observed, and permission for publication. Thus, the main ethical concerns are related to the integrity of the individuals in the studied cultural setting; that is, one must not harm the people and society that are being studied.

The quantitative paradigm refers to the testing of hypotheses that are derived from theory, and it utilizes two types of methods: (1) correlation methods, where no interventions or manipulations take place; and (2) experimental methods where causality is inferred by manipulating conditions, environments, and individuals. The main ethical concerns here relate to the people, instrumentation, and interventions. The researcher must ethically select the sample for the study, inform the selected participants about their rights, risks, and expected behaviors, and also ensure they are willingly taking part in the research. The instruments must be valid and reliable, the interventions must be humane and non-invasive/safe, data must be accurate (e.g., not be unethically altered), and, finally, results and conclusions must be truthfully presented and published. The APA, ISSP, and AASP ethical guidelines and principles cover these aspects of ethical conduct in more detail. Once the researcher decides to carry out a research plan, he/she must consider the ethical requirements and consequences at each phase of implementation.

At the outset of the research endeavor, importance and value of the imposed scientific questions must be considered. Questions about the innovative contribution and scientific merit of the research are considered. For the quantitative-positivistic paradigm, the method entails sampling, instrumentation, intervention, procedure, data analysis and handling, and publication. Each of these segments has ethical considerations associated with participant safety. When the research is completed, a set of ethical rules applies to debriefing the participants, managing files (storage and distinction), and accuracy of the results for publication or dissemination.

A prominent issue in considering ethics is the risk-benefit ratio – especially in cases where risk may cause physical, mental, emotional, behavioral, or any other form of harm to the participant. Although researchers may consider there is a 'greater good' for their investigation, it is critical that participants are not exposed to unacceptable risks. Ethics committees are tasked with assessing projected costs and benefits, and they must ensure they protect participants by carefully and responsibly considering research proposals. Possible benefits of the research must be considered from both personal and societal perspectives. Protection of participants and awareness of the risk-benefit ratio necessitates: (a) voluntary informed consent to participate; (b) the overarching goal to bring beneficial outcomes to society; (c) historical knowledge of the domain; (d) avoidance of undue suffering; (e) prevention of research with possible incidence of death; (f)

risks that do not exceed humanitarian benefits; (g) proper protection, resources, and facilities to avoid injury or disability; (h) guidance by highly-skilled researchers; (i) free will to withdraw from the research at any time; and (j) readiness to terminate the experiment in case of serious risk of injury, disability or death (McNamee, Olivier, & Wainwright, 2007, p. 24–25).

Within the ethical review process, there are several important steps to take and considerations about the project that need to be addressed, including:

(a) *Ethics and research review:* Prior to conducting the study, an approved ethics committee must review and approve the proposed research in view of its benefits, scientific merit, and all ethical considerations listed herein.

(b) *Sampling:* Studies should ensure fair and appropriate representation (e.g., randomization, stratified randomization by gender/minority, socio-economic status).

(c) *Safety, including age and health status:* There must be a secure research environment and practical work should utilize trained assistants and ensure that harm is avoided at all costs (e.g., by conducting a risk assessment). Assure each participant is healthy and able to take part in the experiment. Avoid using under-aged participants in studies where this is unnecessary. Children should not be included in research that presents more than minimal risk (e.g., data collection should be non-invasive).

(d) *Confidentiality:* All possible precautions should be undertaken to prevent identification of participants' personal details or results (e.g., researchers should use participant ID and coding systems).

(e) *Rewards, compensation, and benefits:* Where appropriate, equal benefits should be provided to all participants (e.g., compensation for travel).

(f) *Willingness to participate:* Individuals should understand their involvement and be willing participants; ensuring this is the case will also help to limit social desirability responses (i.e., participants replying or acting in such a way as to appear socially desirable and, thus, providing inaccurate responses).

(g) *Informed consent form:* Risks, benefits, experimental conditions, and safety regulations must all be included in the consent form, which must be given to participants prior to conducting the experiment and then signed by them once they have had the opportunity to ask questions. Participants must have the option to withdraw from the study at any time without consequences.

(h) *Methods:* The instrumentation and measures must be valid, reliable, and safe. Clear, unbiased language must be used in questionnaires and instructions. Wherever possible, the most current equipment should be used. Also, the protocol should be efficient and calibrated prior to testing, questionnaires should be prepared in advance, and the intervention must be designed to avoid risks to physical or psychological well-being. Deception must be avoided as much as possible, and control group participants should receive appropriate attention. It is often a good idea to conduct pilot ('dry-run') tests to work out any potential issues, gauge timing, and make minor adjustments where needed.

(i) *Data handling:* Make every effort to triangulate data sources (assess the same phenomenon multiple ways) to ensure reliable conclusions about the variables of interest; use appropriate data analyses; report truthful data – not only ones that confirm prior expectations; avoid falsification of data; and secure data by using locked filing cabinets and/or passwords.

(j) *Published data:* Assure data and analyses are appropriate before publication, refrain from plagiarism, and give appropriate credit to sources used for developing rationale as well as providing explanations, discussions, and conclusions.

ETHICAL DECISION MAKING AND RISK MANAGEMENT

In sport and exercise psychology, there are several checks and balances to ensure practitioners and researchers follow best practices and adhere to ethical codes of conduct. Even still, ethical decision making is difficult in some cases, and particularly so when ethical principles conflict; e.g., if a client admits to violating rules, then their confidentiality or the consultant's duty of secrecy to them comes into conflict with social responsibility. In such cases, a reasonable decision-making process is needed to bear public scrutiny and to ensure that professionals are making balanced and appropriate decisions.

The Canadian Psychological Association (2000) has suggested and described 10 steps for ethical decision making. The following approach summarizes key components for appropriate risk management: (1) identify norms and people potentially affected by the decision; (2) reflect on options and alternative courses of actions to be taken; and (3) calculate risks and consequences, as well as accountability and responsibility. Importantly, it is advisable for a psychologist experiencing an ethical dilemma to seek consultation or assistance from colleagues or an advisory body (e.g., ethics committee) to appropriately manage the situation (cf., Pope & Vasquez, 2011).

CONCLUSION

In summary, the role of sport and exercise psychology practitioners and/or researchers can be both highly rewarding and also complex, as the field ultimately involves human interaction and all this entails – i.e., challenges *as well as* opportunities for further development. With any such role, professionals must not only be mindful of the potential for ethical dilemmas to arise, but also be able to manage those issues, preferably by way of proactively putting systems into place such as those highlighted above. The example scenario at the start of this chapter highlights one of several possible ethical dilemmas and potential conflicts associated with this field. Thus, this chapter has been designed to introduce readers to relevant concepts, knowledge, and resources in order to address and prepare for such problems.

LEARNING AIDS

1   Explain the difference and relation between the terms 'ethics' and 'morals'.

Morals pertain to everyday life conventions, especially for social living (e.g., athletes should abide by 'fair play'); whereas ethics are largely based on reflections and take a critical position with regard to morals (e.g., coaches are required to maintain professional relationships with their athletes).

2   Describe an ethical dilemma and a violation of moral standards in sport and exercise psychology.

A coach of a basketball team asks the team's psychologist to comment on a list of room sharing plans by athletes during a training camp. One of the athletes is a new member and is also his private client. He once approached the psychologist to help him with his sexuality concern and asked him for full confidentiality (ethical dilemma). The psychologist explained the situation to the coach and asked him to keep it confidential, and assign a single room for the athlete by arguing that he suffers sleep apnea (violation of moral standards).

3   Describe the meaning of the ethical guideline 'respect'.

Respect refers to an attitude and a behavior of appreciation toward others. Respect refers to the acceptance of individual differences such as socio-economic status, and physical or mental abilities/disabilities. For example, an athlete who has a lower socio-economic status or an athlete who is less intelligent than others should not earn less respect from the sport psychologist in his work with the athlete or the team.

4   Identify the role of an ethics committee for a research project.

The role of an ethics committee for a research project is to ensure that the participants in the study are not running the risk of being mentally or socially harmed by the experiment, and to ensure that the researchers are knowledgeable about risks associated with the interventions, instrumentations, analysis of data, confidentiality, publications, and data storing.

5   Describe the essential steps to ensure ethical decision making in a conflict situation.

(1) Identify norms and people potentially affected by the decision; (2) reflect on options and alternative courses of actions to be taken; and (3) consider risks and consequences, as well as accountability and responsibility.

REVIEW QUESTIONS

1   Why are ethical standards needed in the sport and exercise psychology domain?

2   What is the key idea of ethical principles?

3   Which ethical principles are fundamental for professional behavior in sport and exercise psychology?

4   How can a researcher protect himself/herself against a violation of ethical standards?

5   How can someone cope with ethical conflicts?

EXERCISES

1   Analyze the scenario described in the introduction to this chapter, and explain the kind of ethical problem that needs to be addressed, and which moral principle might be at risk. Generate a strategy as to how to handle it with respect to a code of ethics.

2   A colleague asks for your support when he feels that he has a potential conflict of interest – i.e., he was recently approached by an athlete who is a rival competitor of one of his previous clients. Describe the advice you might give to your colleague, and relate your insights and perceived (potential) consequences based on what you have learned from this chapter.

ADDITIONAL READING

Hackfort, D. (2006). A conceptual framework and fundamental issues for investigating the development of peak performance in sports. In D. Hackfort & G. Tenenbaum (Eds.), *Essential processes for attaining peak performance* (pp.10–23). Aachen: Meyer & Meyer.

Nitsch, J.R. (1989). Die Verantwortung des Sportwissenschaftlers – Gedanken zur Berufsethik (The responsibility of the sport scientist – reflections for professional ethics). *Brennpunkte der Sportwissenschaft, 3* (1), 54–71.

Rosenthal, R. (1994). Science and ethics in conducting research, analysing, and reporting psychological research. *Psychological Science, 5,* 127–133.

Silva III, J.M., Metzler, J.N. & Lerner, B. (2011). *Training professionals in the practice of sport psychology* (2nd ed.). Morgantown, WV: Fitness Information Technology.

REFERENCES

American Psychological Association (APA, 2002). http://www.apa.org/ethics/code.html

Association for Applied Sport Psychology (AASP, 2008). http://appliedsportpsych.org/about/ethics/code

Australian Psychological Society (APS, 2007). http://www.psychology.org.au/about/ethics/#s1

Belmont Report (1979). *The National Commission for the Protection of Human Subjects of Biomedical and Behavioral Research,* April 18, 1979.

British Pediatric Association (1992). *Guidelines for the ethical conduct of medical research involving children.* London: BPA.

British Psychological Society (BPS, 2009). Code of ethics and conduct. http://www.bps.org.uk/

sites/default/files/documents/code_of_ethics_and_conduct.pdf.

Canadian Psychological Association (CPA, 2000, 3rd ed.). Canadian code of ethics for psychologists. http://www.cpa.ca/aboutcpa/committees/ethics/codeofethics/

Etzel, E.E. & Watson, J.C. (2011). Ethics. In T. Morris & P. Terry (Eds.), *The new sport and exercise psychology companion* (pp.425–440). Morgantown, WV: FIT.

Gordin, R.D. & Balague, G. (2005). Ethical aspects in applied sport psychology. In D. Hackfort, J.L. Duda & R. Lidor (Eds.), *Handbook of research in applied sport and exercise psychology: International Perspectives* (pp. 419–430). Morgantown, WV: FIT.

Helsinki Declaration (1974). *Regulations and Ethical Guidelines: Ethical Principles for Medical Research Involving Human Subjects.* World Medical Association declaration of Helsinki, National Institute of Health, USA.

Huntington, S. (1957). *The soldier and the state.* Cambridge, Mass.: The Belnap Press of Harvard University Press.

International Society of Sport Psychology (ISSP). http://www.issponline.org/p_codeofethics.asp?ms=3

Jago, R. & Bailey, R. (2001). Ethics and pediatric exercise science: Issues and making a submission to a local ethics and research committee. *Journal of Sport Sciences. 19*, 527–535.

Kant, I. (1965). Grundlagen der Metaphysik der Sitten (Fundamentals of a metaphysics of morals) (1785). Hamburg.

Kitchener, K.S. (2000). *Foundations of ethical practice, research, and teaching in psychology.* Mahwah, NJ: Erlbaum.

Knoppers, A., Ten Boom, A., Buisman, A., Elling, A. & De Knop, P. (2001). Values and norms in sport. In J. Steenbergen, P. De Knop & A. Elling (Eds.), *Values and norms in sport* (pp. 17–32). Aachen: Meyer & Meyer.

Koocher, G.P. & Keith-Spiegel, P. (2008). *Ethics in psychology and the mental health professions: Standards and cases* (3rd ed.). New York: Oxford University Press.

McNamee, M., Olivier, S. & Wainwright, P. (2007). *Research ethics in exercise, health, and sport sciences.* New York, NY: Routledge.

Medical Research Council (1991). *The ethical conduct of research on children.* London, UK: MRC.

Medical Research Council (1992). New MRC guidelines on research ethics. *Bulletin of Medical Ethics, 84* (December), 18–23.

Nideffer, R.M. (1981). *Ethics and practice of applied sport psychology.* Ithaca, NY: Mouvement Publications.

Nuremberg Code (1949). *Trials of War Criminals before the Nuremberg Military Tribunals under Control Council Law No. 10, Vol. 2* (pp. 181–182). Washington, D.C.: U.S. Government Printing Office.

Pojman, L.J. (1995). *Ethics, discovering right and wrong.* Belmont, CA: Wadsworth.

Pope, K.S. & Vasquez, M.J.T. (2011). *Ethics in psychotherapy and counseling: A practical guide* (4th ed.). Hoboken, NJ: John Wiley & Sons.

Schwartz, S.H. (1994). Are there universal aspects in the structure and contents of human values? *Journal of Social Issues, 50 (4)*, 19–45.

Shields, D-L. & Bredemeier, B.L. (2007). Advances in sport morality research. In G. Tenenbaum & R.C. Eklund (Eds.), *Handbook of sport psychology* (3rd ed., pp. 662–684). Hoboken: John Wiley & Sons.

Tenenbaum, G. & Driscoll, M. (2005). Methods of research in sport sciences: Quantitative and qualitative approaches. Oxford, UK: Meyer & Meyer.

Van Raalte, J.L. & Brewer, B.W. (Eds.) (in press). *Exploring sport and exercise psychology* (3rd ed.). Washington, DC: American Psychological Association.

Index

The numbers in **bold** indicate terms of special significance.